FOR REFERENCE
ONLY

About the Editor

Nicolás Kanellos has been professor at the University of Houston since 1980. He is founding publisher of the noted Hispanic literary journal, *The Americas Review* (formerly *Revista Chicano-Riqueña*) and the nation's oldest and esteemed Hispanic publishing house, Arte Público Press.

Recognized for his scholarly achievements, Dr. Kanellos is the recipient of a 1990 American Book Award, a 1989 award from the Texas Association of Chicanos in Higher Education, the 1988 Hispanic Heritage Award for Literature presented by the White House, as well as various fellowships and other recognitions. His monograph, *A History of Hispanic Theater in the United States: Origins to 1940* (1990), received three book awards, including that of the Southwest Council on Latin American Studies.

Among his other books are the *Biographical Dictionary of Hispanic Literature of the United States* (1989), *Mexican American Theater Legacy and Reality* (1987), and *Chronology of Hispanic-American History from Pre-Columbian Times to the Present* (1995).

Dr. Kanellos is the director of a major national research program, Recovering the Hispanic Literary Heritage of the United States, whose objective is to identify, preserve, study, and make accessible tens of thousands of literary documents of those regions that have become the United States from the colonial period to 1960. In 1994, President Bill Clinton appointed Dr. Kanellos to the National Council for the Humanities.

THE
HISPANIC
AMERICAN
ALMANAC

Advisors

Dr. Edna Acosta-Belén, *Director, Center for Caribbean and Latin American Studies, University of Albany*

Dr. Rodolfo Cortina, *Director, Bibliographic Database, Recovering the U.S. Hispanic Literary Heritage Project, and Professor of Spanish, Florida International University*

Dr. Rodolfo de la Garza, *Professor of Political Science, University of Texas at Austin*

Dr. Ricardo Fernández, *President, Lehman College, City University of New York*

Dr. Arturo Madrid, *Director, Tomás Rivera Center, Claremont, California*

Dr. Michael Olivas, *Associate Dean of Law and Director of the Institute for Higher Education Law and Governance, University of Houston*

Contributors

Robert R. Alvarez, *Department of Anthropology, Arizona State University*

Ramiro Burr, *Music Critic, Houston Chronicle*

Gilbert Paul Carrasco, *School of Law, Villanova University*

Lynn E. Cortina, *Coordinator, Recovering the U.S. Hispanic Literary Heritage Project*

José Fernández, *Department of Foreign Language, University of Central Florida*

Gary D. Keller, *Bilingual Review Press, Arizona State University*

Thomas Leonard, *Department of History, Philosophy, and Religious Studies, University of North Florida*

John M. Lipski, *Department of Modern Languages, University of Florida*

Tatcho Mindiola, *Mexican American Studies Program, University of Houston*

Silvia Novo Pena, *Department of English and Foreign Languages, Texas Southern University*

Manuel Peña, *Foreign Languages, California State University, Fresno*

Jacinto Quirarte, *College of Fine and Applied Arts, University of Texas, San Antonio*

F. Arturo Rosales, *Department of History, Arizona State University*

Guadalupe San Miguel, *History Department, University of Houston*

Federico Subervi, *Department of Radio-Television-Film, University of Texas, Austin*

Dennis Valdez, *Chicano Studies Program, University of Minnesota*

Jude Valdez, *College of Business, University of Texas, San Antonio*

THE
HISPANIC
AMERICAN
ALMANAC

A Reference

Work on

Hispanics in

the United

States

Second Edition

Nicolás Kanellos,

editor

GALE

DETROIT • NEW YORK • TORONTO • LONDON

Nicolás Kanellos, *Editor*

Gale Research Staff

Sharon Malinowski, *Editor*

Linda Hubbard, *Managing Editor, Multicultural Team*
L. Mpho Mabunda, Melissa Walsh Doig, *Contributing Editors*
Dawn Barry, Ned Burels, Jeffrey Lehman, David Oblender, *Associate Editors*

Victoria B. Cariappa, *Research Manager*
Barbara McNeil, Gary J. Oudersluys, *Research Specialists*
Norma Sawaya, Cheryl L. Warnock, *Research Associates*
Laura C. Bissey and Sean R. Smith, *Research Assistant*

Jeffrey Muhr, *Technical Support Specialist*

Marlene S. Hurst, *Permissions Manager*
Margaret A. Chamberlain, Maria Franklin, Kimberly F. Smilay, *Permissions Specialists*
Diane Cooper, Edna Hedblad, Michele Lonoconus, Maureen Puhl, Susan Salas, Shalice Shah,
Barbara A. Wallace, *Permissions Associates*
Sarah Chesney and Tyra Phillips, *Permissions Assistants*

Mary Beth Trimper, *Production Director*
Evi Seoud, *Assistant Production Manager*
Shanna Heilveil, *Production Assistant*

Cynthia Baldwin, *Product Design Manager*

C.J. Jonik, *Desktop Publisher*
Randy Bassett, *Image Database Supervisor*
Robert Duncan, Mikal Ansari, *Imaging Specialists*
Pamela Hayes, *Photography Coordinator*

☉™ This book is printed on acid-free paper that meets the minimum requirements
of American National Standard for Information Sciences-
Permanence Paper for Printed Library Materials, ANSI Z39.48-1984.

Library of Congress Catalog Card Number 94-36202
A CIP record is available from the British Library

ISBN 0-8103-8595-3

Printed in the United States of America.

Library of Congress Cataloging-in-Publication Data

Hispanic American almanac : a reference work on Hispanics in the United States / Nicholás Kanellos [editor]. -- 2nd ed.
　　　p. cm.
Includes bibliographical references and index.
ISBN 0-8103-8595-3 (acid-free paper)
　　1. Hispanic Americans.　　　I. Kanellos, Nicollás.
E184.S75H557　1997　　　　　　　　　　　　　96-30189
973'.0468--dc20　　　　　　　　　　　　　　CIP

10　9　8　7　6　5　4　3　2　1

Ofrezco esta labor a mi hijo adorado, Miguel José Pérez Kanellos, con la esperanza de que él, su generación y las que siguen puedan tener plena consciencia de su historia, sus artes, sus tradiciones y acceso a información básica acerca de su gente. Que el pueblo hispano y, particularmente los estudiantes, jamás vuelvan a carecer de básicos recursos informativos en sus bibliotecas y en sus escuelas. Que el pueblo americano en general tenga también acceso y plena consciencia de una parte importante—la contribución hispana—de la identidad nacional estadounidense y la abrace como suya.

I offer this labor of love to my adored son, Miguel José Pérez Kanellos, in hope that he, his generation, and those that follow will be able to possess a complete awareness of their history, arts, and traditions, and have access to basic information about their people. May Hispanic Americans of the United States, and especially Hispanic students, never again be impoverished of basic informational resources in their libraries and schools. May the American people in general have access to and a full awareness of an important part—the Hispanic contribution—of the national identity of the United States and embrace it as theirs.

N.K.

Contents

Acknowledgements xiii
Preface xv
Introduction xvii
Chronology xix

1 • A Historical Overview 1
Spanish Legacy 1
The Indigenous Caribbean
    Populations 4
The Indigenous Mexican Population 7
The Spaniards in the Valley
    of Mexico 11
Movement to the North 12
Anglo Encroachment into the
    Mexican North 19
Mexicans Under U.S. Rule 23
Africa and the Making of Society in Cuba
    and Puerto Rico 25
Independence of Cuba and
    Puerto Rico 28
Early Mexican Immigration to the
    United States 30
The Mexican Revolution and Immigration
    to the United States 34
The "Mexico Lindo" Generation 36
Depression, Repatriation, and
    Acculturation 38
World War II and the Mexican American
    Generation 39
From Chicanos to Hispanics 39
Migration to the United States from
    Puerto Rico 40
Early Settlement of Puerto Ricans in the
    United States 42
The Great Migration 43
Early Cuban Immigration to the United
    States 45
The Revolution of Fidel Castro and Cuban
    Immigration 46
Hispanic Identity in the United States 51

2 • Spanish Explorers and Colonizers 53
Native American Cultures 53
The Age of Exploration: The Caribbean,
    Mexico, and Florida 57
Spanish Expeditions to Florida 59
Spanish Exploration and Colonization of the
    Southwest 69
Spanish Explorations to California 73

3 • Significant Documents 77
Cessation of Louisiana 77
Cessation of Louisiana: Financial
    Arrangement 79
The Monroe Doctrine 80
Peace, Friendship, Limits, and Settlement:
    Treaty of Guadalupe Hidalgo 1848 86
Boundaries: Gadsen Treaty 1853 94
Our America by José Marti 96
Treaty of Peace (Treaty of Paris} 1898 100
Relations with Cuba 103
The "Hay-Herran" Treaty, January 1903 . . 105
The "Hay-Bunau-Varilla Convention,"
    November 1903 111
Treaty of Relations between the
    United States and Cuba, 1934 116
Constitutional Convention of Puerto Rico . 117
Resolutions Approved by the Constitutional
    Convention Relating to the Constitution
    of the Commonwealth of Puerto Rico . . . 130
The North American Free Trade Agreement
    (NAFTA) 131

4 • Historic Landmarks 133
Alabama 133
Arizona 133
California 134
Florida 140
Georgia 140
Louisiana 140
New Mexico 141
Panama Canal Zone 143
Puerto Rico 143

Texas 143
Virgin Islands 147

5 • Relations with Spain and Spanish America **149**
Policy Foundations 149
Developing a Relationship:
  The Nineteenth Century 153
A Period of U.S. Dominance: 1903–1954 . 159
Suppressing Communism: U.S.-Latin
  American Relations Since 1954 165

6 • Hispanics and Race **176**
Racial Ideas among the Spaniards 176
European Americans and the
  Racialization of Hispanics 179
The Hispanic "Race" Today: Self-Perceptions
  and Anglo Impressions 183

7 • Population Growth and Distribution . **185**
Census Bureau Statistics and the Hispanic
  Population 185
Demographics 187
Hispanic Diversity 191

8 • Language **195**
Variations of Spanish Spoken 195
English Usage Among Hispanics 202
Spanish in Business, the Media, and in
  Other Social Environments 203
Bilingualism and Code-Switching 206

9 • The Family **213**
The Institutions of the Hispanic Family ... 215
Puerto Ricans: Born in the United States .. 219
Dominicans 222
Cubans 225
Mexican Americans 228

10 • Women **235**
Hispanic Women in Society 235
Women Making History 238
Women Inscribe Their Identity 240
Selected Outstanding Hispanic Women ... 245

11 • Religion **253**
The Beginnings 253
Instruments of Religious Conversion 254
Our Lady of Guadalupe and the Saints 256
Florida 258
New Mexico 259
Texas 260
Arizona 261
California 262
The Anglo Conquest 262

Developing a Pastoral Approach 263
A Search for Parity 264
Protestantism and Hispanics 264
Popular Religiosity 266
Beyond Orthodoxy 270

12 • Military **273**
U.S. Revolutionary War 273
Mexican War for Independence
  from Spain 274
Mexican-American War 274
U.S. Civil War 274
World War I 275
World War II 275
Conflicts in Korea and Vietnam 276
Outstanding Hispanics in the Military 277

13 • Law and Politics **285**
Origins of Hispanics in the United States .. 285
The Development of U.S.
  Immigration Law 287
The Current Debate Over
  U.S. Immigration Law 289
The Legalization Program 290
Employment Discrimination 291
Police Brutality 291
Federal Legislation Affecting Hispanic
  Americans 292
Important Cases Affecting Hispanic
  Americans 293
Hispanics in the Legal Profession 294
Hispanics in the U.S. Judiciary 301
Presidential Appointment of Hispanics
  to the Courts 304
Hispanics in the Political Process 312
Hispanic Voting and the
  Voting Rights Act of 1965 312
Congressional Hispanic Caucus 314
Hispanics in Congress 314
Selected Prominent Hispanic
  Federal Officials 326
Prominent Hispanic Politicians in
  State Government 333
Prominent Hispanic Metropolitan Leaders . 335
Legal and Political Organizations 337

14 • Business **343**
The Cattle and Livestock Industry 344
Early Merchants and Entrepreneurs 346
Twentieth-Century Immigration and
  Hispanic Business 348
Hispanic-Owned Businesses Today 349
Hispanics in the Corporate World 357
Prominent Hispanics in Business 359

15 • Labor and Employment **365**
Hispanics in Organized Labor 369

Immigration and Migration 372
Hispanic Employment in Industry 377
Federal Employment Programs and Laws . 379
Youth Employment 386
Women's Employment 386
Government Programs 387
Income, Poverty, and Unemployment 388

16 • Education 391
Education of Hispanics in the
    Spanish Period, 1540–1821 392
Education of Hispanics in the
    Mexican Period, 1821–1848 394
Education of Hispanics: The
    American Period in the Nineteenth
    Century, 1850–1900 396
Education of Hispanics in the Twentieth
    Century 402

17 • Scholarship 413

18 • Science 431
A General Overview 431
Prominent Hispanic Scientists 434

19 • Literature 455
The Colonial Period 455
The Nineteenth Century 455
The Early Twentieth Century 458
World War II to the Present 465
Outstanding Hispanic Literary Figures 484

20 • Art 507
The Sources of Hispanic Art 507
Exploration, Settlement, and History of
    Hispanics in the United States 508
New Spaniards and Mexicans:
    1599 to 1848 508
Hispanics and Mexican Americans:
    1848 to the Present 515
Hispanic American Artists:
    1920s through the 1950s 520
Hispanic American Artists:
    1960s and 1970s 524
Hispanic American Artists:
    1970s to the Present 527
Chicano Murals 537

21 • Theater 549
Hispanic Theater in the United States:
    Origins to 1940 549
Post World War II to the Present 564
Outstanding Figures in Hispanic Theater . . 573

22 • Film 587
Depiction of Minority Groups in

Early American Film 587
Conglomeration of the Film Industry
    and the Production Code 591
First Decades: The Bandido, Buffoon,
    Dark Lady, Caballero, and Gangster 593
Hispanics in Film during the 1930s and
    the Era of Social Consciousness 596
Decline of the Production Code,
    Emergence of the Civil Rights Movement,
    and New Developments in Film:
    1960s and 1970s 601
Hollywood Films Since 1980 608
The Emergence of U.S. Hispanic Films . . . 612
Hispanics in Film: Future Directions 623
Outstanding Hispanics in the Film Industry 624

23 • Music 643
The Corrido and Canción-Corrido 646
Música Norteña
    (The Mexican-Texan Conjunto) 651
The Mexican American Orquesta 654
Salsa 660
Latin Jazz/Rock 665
Musica Tropical 665
The Contemporary Music Scene 666
Selected Discography 669

24 • Media 671
Treatment of Hispanics in
    Mainstream Media 671
Newspapers 671
Film 674
Television 676
Advertising 680
Hispanic-Oriented Print Media 681
Hispanic-Oriented Electronic Media 691

25 • Sports 721
Baseball 722
Rodeo 725
Other Sports 726
Prominent Hispanic Athletes 726

26 • Organizations 747

27 • Prominent Hispanics 757

Appendix: Illustrations 775
Glossary 783
General Bibliography 787
Index 791

Acknowledgments

My most sincere thanks to all the scholars who have contributed to this volume, for indulging me in my obsession and for producing such wonderfully researched and written chapters, despite the pressure I exerted on you for making deadlines and supplying illustrations and other materials. My thanks as well to my editors at Gale Research, especially Christine Nasso, Christine Hammes, and Rebecca Nelson, whose guiding hand was always characterized by a gentle touch, whose advice was always offered with compassion and understanding. I feel very fortunate to have become part of the Gale family.

Thanks also to my scholarly advisors, especially Dr. Michael Olivas, who assisted me greatly in contact contributors for this volume. My deepest appreciation and thanks to my assistant, Hilda Hinojosa, who helped organize, type, and maintain oral and written communications with the contributing scholars and with my editors. This, the largest project of my career as a scholar, was brought to press with her able, efficient, and enthusiastic support.

And from my wife, Cristelia Pérez, and my son Miguel, I beg their forgiveness for the months that I spent communicating more with my computer screen than with them. Without Crissy's love, support, and understanding, this project would never have gotten off the ground, much less seen the light of day. Thank you; I love you.

Nicolás Kanellos

Preface

This new, second edition of *The Hispanic American Almanac* is an expanded and revised edition of the enormously successful first edition, which upon its publication was named Outstanding Reference Work by the Reference and Adult Services Division of the American Library Association. The first history-making edition immediately found an audience among reference sections of public and school libraries, and was uniformly praised by librarians, teachers, families, and students who relied on the *Almanac* for their homework assignments. This new second edition greatly expands *The Hispanic American Almanac* with entirely new chapters on Hispanics and Race and Hispanics in the Military. In addition, the chapter on Women and the one on Business have been completely rewritten and expanded in focus and coverage. Information has been updated and additional material has been added to almost all of the chapters. Also, several more photos and illustrations have been added to this new second edition of *The Hispanic American Almanac.*

The Hispanic American Almanac is the research product of a national team of outstanding scholars who unanimously have invested their time, energy, and genius to create the first, one-stop source for information about a broad range of important aspects of Hispanic life and culture in the United States. In their labors for the *Almanac,* as well as in their day-to-day academic work, these scholars have actively engaged in the difficult task of working with original documentary sources, oral interviews, and field work to create a written record of Hispanic life where none existed before. These scholars are among the first in U.S. academic history to research, analyze, and preserve much of the information offered here. The scholars, and this *Almanac,* are dedicated to filling an informational

void relating to the history and culture of Hispanics of the United States—a void that has existed for too long in libraries and classrooms.

Prior to this publication, the scant information that has been available has quite often resulted from prejudice, propaganda, and folklore (quite often created to support the political and economic exploitation of Hispanics) covering a people conquered through war or imported for their labor, but who were never fully incorporated into the national psyche, the national identity, or the national storehouse of educational, economic, and political opportunities.

The vast majority of Hispanics in the United States are working-class citizens. Even those Hispanics in the professional class often share working-class backgrounds. The majority of Hispanics in the United States are *mestizos*—the product of mixed races and cultures, for the American Indian and African heritages have blended in every aspect of everyday life to produce today's Hispanic peoples of the Americas. The Spanish language, which introduced and reinforced a common culture and religion for these peoples for centuries, serves as a unifying factor for Hispanics, regardless of whether or not the individual speaks Spanish in daily life. These central factors—social class, ethnicity, linguistic-cultural background—unify the people and the information presented in *The Hispanic American Almanac,* while also representing the tremendous diversity in racial, ethnic, geographic, and historical backgrounds that exist among Hispanics today.

The final result of this endeavor, we hope, is an easy-to-use compendium that presents an up-to-date overview of each subject, summarizing the known data and presenting new, original research. Moreover, the *Almanac* has been written in a language and style that make it accessible to students and lay people. Illustrations—photographs, drawings, maps, and tables—bring the data to life. For further reading, subject-specific bibliographies as well as a general bibliography provide ready reference to other important sources. A complete index assists the reader in locating specific information. A glossary of Spanish terms has also been included to facilitate the reading of the *Almanac.*

Nicolás Kanellos
University of Houston

Introduction

The Hispanic Population

With a Hispanic population of more than 22 million, the United States is among the largest Spanish-speaking countries in the world. According to the U.S. Census Bureau, the number of Hispanics in this country grew by 53 percent from 1980 to 1990. It is projected that by the year 2000, there will be almost 33 million Hispanics living in the United States.

The Hispanic American Almanac is a one-stop source for information on people of the United States whose ancestors, or they themselves, originated in Spain, the Spanish-speaking countries of South and Central America, Mexico, Puerto Rico, or Cuba.

While the Spanish language is a unifying factor among Hispanics, the diversity that exists within the Hispanic community continues to profoundly influence the collective American experience.

Scope and Contents

The Hispanic American Almanac covers the range of Hispanic civilization and culture in the United States—providing a Chronology and Historical Overview, presenting the facts and figures in such chapters as Law and Politics, and Population Growth and Distribution, and discussing the arts, including Theater, Music, and Film.

Twenty-seven subject chapters were written by scholars in the field of Hispanic studies. These experts have drawn upon the body of their works and new research to compile their chapters, ending each with a list of references that can be used for further research into any of the subjects covered in *The Hispanic American Almanac.* A bibliography at the back of the *Almanac* provides sources for general information on Hispanics.

Concise biographical profiles in many chapters highlight Hispanics who have excelled in their fields of endeavor.

More than 450 illustrations, including photographs, drawings, tables, and figures, punctuate the discussion in each chapter.

The keyword index provides quick access to the contents of the *Almanac.*

A glossary of Spanish terms facilitates the reading of the material.

Suggestions Are Welcome

The managing editor and publisher of *The Hispanic American Almanac* appreciate all suggestions for additions and changes that will make future editions of this book as useful as possible. Please send comments to:

The Hispanic American Almanac
Gale Research
835 Penobscot Building
Detroit, MI 48226

Chronology

50,00–10,000 B.C. Asian peoples migrate to North and South America and continue through 14,000 B.C.

c. 1000 B.C. Celts move into the Iberian Peninsula.

c. 500 B.C. Carthagenians establish themselves on the south coast of Spain.

200 B.C. The Iberian Peninsula becomes part of the Roman Empire.

350–850 A.D. Teotihuacan civilization flourishes in the central plateau of Mexico.

500 A.D. Vandals and Goths invade and conquer the peoples of the Iberian Peninsula.

700–900 A.D. Nahua peoples gain ascendancy in Mexico's central plateau.

711 A.D. The Moors invade and conquer the Visigothic kingdoms of the Iberian peninsula.

718–1492. The Reconquest of the Iberian peninsula takes place. Queen Isabella and King Ferdinand unify Spain through their marriage in 1469, and culminate the reconquest by defeating the last Moorish stronghold—Granada.

1000. Mayan civilization flourishes in the Yucatán peninsula and Guatemala.

1492. The Native American population of the Western Hemisphere may have reached between 35 to 45 million.

August 3, 1492. Christopher Columbus sails from the Spanish port of Palos de Moguer with three ships: the *Pinta,* the *Niña,* and the *Santa María,* his flagship.

October 12, 1492. The Spaniards land on an island called San Salvador—either present-day Watling Island or Samana Cay in the eastern Bahamas.

October 27, 1492. Columbus and his crews land on the northeastern shore of Cuba. Convinced that it is either Cipango or Cathay (in Asia), Columbus sends representatives to the Great Khan and his gold-domed cities, only to find impoverished Arawak living in bohíos.

November 1493. On his second voyage, Columbus discovers the Virgin Islands and Puerto Rico.

1494. After establishing Isabela on La Española (Hispaniola), the first permanent European settlement in the New World, Columbus sets sail and encounters Jamaica in the summer of 1494.

1508. Juan Ponce de León sails in a small caravel for Puerto Rico, where he establishes friendly relations with the native chieftain, Agueibana, who presents him with gold.

1509. Ponce de León is appointed governor of Puerto Rico.

1510. Diego Velázquez de Cuéllar departs with more than 300 men to conquer Cuba, and lands at Puerto Escondido. He is successful in defeating Arawak chieftain Hatuey's guerrilla raids.

1511. Velázquez is commissioned governor of Cuba. That same year the Cuban Indians are subjected to the *encomienda.*

1512. The Jeronymite Fathers in La Española decide to save the decimated Arawak population by gathering them into missions. Soon, missions spread like wildfire throughout the Spanish Empire.

1512. The Laws of Burgos. Promulgated by the Crown, the regulations are in response to the extremely harsh treatment that desperate colonists in the Caribbean imposed on natives through the deplorable *encomienda* system.

1513. Juan Ponce de León lands on the shores of Florida, exploring most of the coastal regions and some of the interior. At the time, there were an estimated 100,000 Native Americans living there.

September 27, 1514. Ponce de León is granted a patent, empowering him to colonize the island of Bimini and the island of Florida.

1515. Diego Velázquez becomes a virtual feudal lord of Cuba, and establishes what are to become Cuba's two largest cities, Santiago and Havana. He also directs the explorations of the Mexican Gulf Coast by Francisco Hernández de Córdoba and his nephew Juan de Grijalva. These expeditions betray the existence of civilizations in the interior of Mexico.

1518. Hernán Cortés sets out from Cuba to explore the mainland of Mexico in order to confirm reports of the existence of large, native civilizations in the interior.

1519. Alonso Alvarez de Pineda claims Texas for Spain.

1519. Hernán Cortés lands on the coast of Veracruz, Mexico.

1520. Explorer Alvarez de Pineda settles the question of Florida's geography: He proves it is not an island, but part of a vast continent.

1520s. Continuing their maritime adventures, the Spanish explorers cruise along the northern shore of the Gulf of Mexico, seeing Alabama, Mississippi, and Texas, and also sailing up the Atlantic coast to the Carolinas.

July 1, 1520. Under the leadership of Cuitlahuac, Moctezuma's brother, the Aztecs force the Spaniards out of Veracruz, just a year after the Spaniards had come into the city. The Spaniards called this *La noche triste* (The Sad Night). Moctezuma was stoned to death by his own people during this debacle.

1521. Cortés and his fellow Spaniards level the Aztec empire's city of Tenochtitlán, and begin building Mexico City on the same site.

1524. King Charles establishes the Council of the Indies, designed to oversee the administration of the colonies of the New World.

1536. Álvar Núñez Cabeza de Vaca returns to Mexico, indirectly involving Spain in exploring and colonizing what becomes the American Southwest: In Mexico City rumors were that Cabeza de Vaca and his companions had discovered cities laden with gold and silver, reviving the legend of the Seven Cities, which dated from the Moorish invasion of the Iberian Peninsula.

1537. Álvar Núñez Cabeza de Vaca returns to Spain and spends some three years writing *La relación,* an account of his wanderings in the North American continent. Published in 1542, *La relación* is a document of inestimable value because of the many first descriptions about the flora, fauna, and inhabitants of what was to become part of the United States.

May 18, 1539. From Havana, Cuba, Hernando de Soto sets sail for Florida; he eventually reaches as far north as present-day Georgia and South Carolina. His expedition later crosses the Great Smoky Mountains into Tennessee. From the mountains, the expedition heads southwest through present-day Georgia and Alabama.

1540. There are an estimated 66 Pueblo villages in the area of New Mexico, growing such crops as corn, beans, squash, and cotton.

April 23, 1541. Coronado sets out to reach Quivira—thought to be the legendary Cities of Gold—near present-day Great Bend, Kansas.

1542. The New Laws are proclaimed. They are designed to end Spain's feudal *encomienda.*

July 1542. Francisco Vásquez de Coronado returns to Mexico City with fewer than 100 of the 300 Spaniards that once formed part of his company.

September 28, 1542. Juan Rodríguez de Cabrillo, a Portuguese sailor commissioned by the viceroy to sail north of Mexico's west coast in search of treasures, enters what he describes as an excellent port—present-day San Diego, California.

1563. Saint Augustine, Florida, the earliest settlement in North America, is founded. It remains a possession of Spain until 1819.

1573. The Franciscan order arrives in Florida to establish missions, which a century later would extend along the east coast of North America, from Saint Augustine, Florida, to North Carolina. The Franciscans also establish a string of missions from Saint Augustine westward to present-day Tallahassee.

1580s. Diseases have all but wiped out the Indians of Puerto Rico. The flourishing of sugar production would now have to await the importation of large numbers of African slaves.

1598. Portuguese sailor Juan de Oñate begins the colonization of New Mexico.

1610. Santa Fe, New Mexico is founded.

1680. A Pueblo Indian named Popé leads a rebellion that forces the Spaniards and Christianized Indians out of northern New Mexico southward toward El Paso, Texas; they found Ysleta just north of El Paso.

1689. In part due to the need to provide foodstuffs and livestock to the rich mining regions in southern Mexico, the first royal *mercedes* (land grants) are granted to Spaniards in the fertile valleys of Monclova, in northern Mexico, just south of the present border.

May 1690. The first permanent Spanish settlement in Texas, San Francisco de los Tejas, near the Neches River, is established.

1691. Father Eusebio Kino, an untiring Jesuit missionary, makes the first inroads into Arizona. By 1700, Kino establishes a mission at San Xavier del Bac, near present-day Tucson; he later establishes other missions in Arizona: Nuestra Señora de los Dolores, Santa Gertrudis de Saric, San José de Imuris, Nuestra Señora de los Remedios, and San Cayetano de Tumacácori.

1693. Despite the fact that Texas is made a separate Spanish province with Don Domingo de Terán as its governor, the Spanish Crown orders its abandonment. Fear of Indian uprisings is the reason given by the Spanish authorities.

1716. Concerns about possible French encroachment prompt the Spaniards to reoccupy Texas in 1716 by establishing a series of missions, serving to both ward off the French and convert the natives to Catholicism. Of these missions, San Antonio, founded in 1718, is the most important and most prosperous.

1718. The San Antonio de Béjar and de Valero churches are built where the city of San Antonio is located today.

1760. After the Seven Years' War, which united France and Spain against Britain, France cedes claims to all lands west of the Mississippi in order not to give them to the victorious British. Overnight, New Spain's territory expands dramatically.

September 17, 1766. The presidio of San Francisco is founded, becoming Spain's northernmost frontier outpost.

1767. King Charles III expels the Jesuits from the Spanish Empire. This event opens the door for the Franciscan conquest of California. This conquest would never have been accomplished without Fray Junípero de Serra.

July 3, 1769. Fray Junípero de Serra establishes the first mission of Alta California in what would become San Diego. Serra eventually founded ten missions, traveled more than 10,000 miles, and converted close to 6,800 natives.

1770–1790. At least 50,000 African slaves are brought to Cuba to work in sugar production.

1774. Pedro de Garcés, a Spanish Franciscan missionary, founds the first overland route to California.

1776. In the American Revolution, because of their alliance with France, the Spaniards are able to obtain lands all the way to Florida.

1776. Anglo-Americans declare their independence from England, and 34 years later Hispanics proclaim their independence from Spain. The thirteen former British colonies come to be known as the United States of America in 1781, and the newly independent people of New Spain name their nation the Republic of Mexico.

1783. Spain regains Florida. In July 1821, the sun finally sets on Spanish Florida when the peninsula is purchased by the United States for $5 million.

1790s–1820s. The Apache threat subsides because of successful military tactics and negotiations on the part of local Spanish leaders, and Hispanic settlements begin to thrive in Pimería Alta (California). At one point as many as 1,000 Hispanics live in the Santa Cruz Valley.

1798. The Alien Act of 1798 grants the U.S. president the authority to expel any alien deemed dangerous. Opposed by President Thomas Jefferson, the Alien Act expires under its own terms in 1800.

1798. The Naturalization Act of 1798 raises the number of years, from 5 to 14, an immigrant has to live in the United States before becoming eligible for citizenship.

1800. Large, sprawling haciendas with huge herds of cattle and sheep characterize the economy and society of northeast New Spain.

1803. A powerful France under Napoleon Bonaparte acquires from Spain the Louisiana Territory, which was ceded during the Seven Years' War in the previous century. Napoleon, vying for dominance in Europe and in need of quick revenue, sells the vast territory to the United States, thus expanding the borders of the infant nation to connect directly with New Spain.

1804. To the consternation of Spain, President Thomas Jefferson funds the historical expedition of Lewis and Clark. Spain is obviously worried that the exploration is a prelude to the settlement of the territory by Anglos.

1810. In Mexico, Father Miguel Hidalgo y Castilla leads the revolt against Spain.

September 16, 1810. With the insurrection of Father Miguel Hidalgo y Castilla, the Spaniards withdraw their troops from the frontier presidios.

1819. When Andrew Jackson leads a U.S. military force into Florida, capturing two Spanish forts, Spain sells Florida to the United States for $5 million under the Onís Treaty.

1820. James Long leads a revolt, ostensibly as part of the Texas independence movement against the Spanish, but obviously he is acting as a filibuster for his countrymen. Spain finally enters into deliberations with Moses Austin, a Catholic from Missouri, to settle Anglo-Catholic families in Texas.

1821. Mexico acquires its independence from Spain. By this time permanent colonies exist in coastal California, southern Arizona, south Texas, and in most of New Mexico and southern Colorado. The imprint of evolving Mexican culture is stamped on today's Southwest. Soon after Mexico gains independence, Anglo-American settlers begin to move into the Mexican territories of the present-day U.S. Southwest, especially Texas.

1823. Erasmo Seguín, a delegate to the national congress from Texas, persuades a willing U.S. Congress to pass a colonization act designed to bring even more Anglo settlers to Texas. Between 1824 and 1830, thousands of Anglo families enter east Texas, acquiring hundreds of thousands of free acres and buying land much cheaper than they could have in the United States. By 1830, Texas has 18,000 Anglo inhabitants and their African slaves, who number more than 2,000.

1823. Fray Junípero de Serra's death does not stop missionary activity in California. His fellow Franciscans establish another 12 missions. The famous mission trail of California includes the missions San Diego de Alcalá (1769), San Carlos de Monterey (1770), San Antonio de Padua (1771), San Gabriel Arcángel (1771), San Luis Obispo de Tolosa (1772), San Francisco de Asís (1776), San Juan Capistrano (1776), Santa Clara de Asís (1777), San Buenaventura (1782), Santa Bárbara (1786), La Purísima Concepción (1787), Santa Cruz (1791), San José de Guadalupe (1797), San Juan Bautista (1797), San Miguel Arcángel (1797), San Fernando Rey (1797), San Luis Rey (1798), Santa Inés (1804), San Rafael Arcángel (1817), and San Francisco Solano (1823).

1829. Slavery in Mexico is abolished by the new republican government that emerges after independence.

1836. The Anglo settlers declare the Republic of Texas independent of Mexico.

1836. The Texas constitution stipulates that all residents living in Texas at the time of the rebellion will acquire all the rights of citizens of the new republic, but if they had been disloyal, these rights are forfeited. Numerically superior Anglos force Mexicans off their property, and many cross the border to Mexico.

1840. To meet the wage-labor demands, 125,000 Chinese are brought to Cuba between 1840 and 1870 to work as cane cutters, build railroads in rural areas, and serve as domestics in the cities. Also, the influx of European immigrants, primarily from Spain, increases during that period. Newly arrived Spaniards become concentrated in the retail trades and operate small general stores called *bodegas.*

1845. Texas is officially annexed to the United States.

1846. The United States invades Mexico under the banner of Manifest Destiny. The Treaty of Guadalupe Hidalgo ends the Mexican War that same year. Under the treaty, half the land area of Mexico, including Texas, California, most of Arizona and New Mexico, and parts of Colorado, Utah, and Nevada, is ceded to the United States. The treaty gives Mexican nationals one year to choose U.S. or Mexican citizenship. Approximately 75,000 Hispanic people choose to remain in the United States and become citizens by conquest.

1848. The gold rush lures a flood of Anglo settlers to California, which becomes a state in 1850. Settlement in Arizona and New Mexico occurs at a slower pace, and they both become states in 1912.

1850. The Foreign Miners Tax, which levies a charge for anyone who is not a U.S. citizen, is enacted.

1851. Congress passes the California Land Act of 1851 to facilitate legalization of land belonging to Californios prior to the U.S. takeover.

1853. General Santa Anna returns to power as president of Mexico and, through the Gadsden Treaty, sells to the United States the region from Yuma (Arizona) along the Gila River to the Mesilla Valley (New Mexico).

1855. Vagrancy laws and so-called "greaser laws" prohibiting bear-baiting, bullfights, and cockfights are passed, clearly aimed at prohibiting the presence and customs of Californios.

1855. The Supreme Court rules that the Treaty of Guadalupe Hidalgo did not apply to Texas.

1857. Anglo businessmen attempt to run off Mexican teamsters in south Texas, violating the guarantees offered by the Treaty of Guadalupe Hidalgo.

1862. Homestead Act is passed in Congress, allowing squatters in the West to settle and claim vacant lands, often those owned by Mexicans.

April 27, 1867. Spanish troops stationed in Puerto Rico mutiny, and are executed by the colonial governor.

1868. Cubans leave for Europe and the United States in sizable numbers during Cuba's first major attempt at independence.

1868. Fourteenth Amendment to the U.S. Constitution is adopted, declaring all people of Hispanic origin born in the United States U.S. citizens.

September 17, 1868. A decree in Puerto Rico frees all children born of slaves after this date. In 1870, all slaves who are state property are freed, as are various other classes of slaves.

September 23, 1868. El Grito de Lares, the shout for Puerto Rican independence, takes place, with its disorganized insurrectionists easily defeated by the Spanish.

October 1868. Cuban rebels led by Carlos Manuel de Céspedes declare independence at Yara, in the eastern portion of the island.

1872. Puerto Rican representatives in Spain win equal civil rights for the colony.

1873. Slavery is finally abolished in Puerto Rico.

1875. The U.S. Supreme Court in *Henderson v. Mayor of New York* rules that power to regulate immigration is held solely by the federal government.

1878. The Ten Years' War, in which Spanish attempts to evict rebels from the eastern half of Cuba were unsuccessful, comes to an end with the signing of the Pact of El Zajón. The document promises amnesty for the insurgents and home rule, and provides freedom for the slaves that fought on the side of the rebels.

1880s. In Cuba, slavery is abolished by Spain in a gradual program that takes eight years. The influx of new European immigrants has made Cuba more heterogeneous, leading to the social diversity that is still apparent today.

1880s. Mexican immigration to the United States is stimulated by the advent of the railroad.

1892. The Partido Revolucionario Cubano is created to organize the Cuban and Puerto Rican independence movement.

1894. The Alianza Hispano Americana is founded in Tucson, Arizona, and quickly spreads throughout the Southwest.

1895. José Martí and his Cuban Revolutionary Party (PRC) open the final battle for independence.

1896. A Revolutionary Junta is formed in New York to lead the Puerto Rican independence movement.

1897. Spain grants Cuba and Puerto Rico autonomy and home rule.

April 1898. The USS *Maine* mysteriously explodes in Havana Harbor. And on April 28, President William McKinley declares war against Spain.

May 1888. The U.S. military invades San Juan in pursuit of Spaniards, and is welcomed by the cheering crowds, longing for independence.

December 10, 1898. Spain signs the Treaty of Paris, transferring Cuba, Puerto Rico, and the Philippines to the United States.

1900s. Brutality against Mexican Americans in the Southwest territories is commonplace. Lynching s and murders of Mexican Americans become so common in California and Texas that, in 1912, the Mexican ambassador formally protests the mistreatment and cites several brutal incidents that had recently taken place.

1900. The Foraker Act establishes a civilian government in Puerto Rico under U.S. dominance. The law allows for islanders to elect their own House of Representatives, but does not allow Puerto Rico a vote in Washington.

1901. The Federación Libre de los Trabajadores (Workers Labor Federation)—or FLT— becomes affiliated with the American Federation of Labor, which breaks from its policy of excluding non-whites.

1902. The Reclamation Act is passed, dispossessing many Hispanic Americans of their land.

1902. Cuba declares its independence from the United States.

1910. The Mexican Revolution begins, with hundreds of thousands of people fleeing north from Mexico and settling in the Southwest.

1911. In Mexico, the long dictatorship of Porfirio Díaz comes to an end when he is forced to resign in a revolt led by Francisco Madero.

1913. Victoriano Huerta deposes Francisco Madero, becoming provisional president of Mexico.

1914. President Woodrow Wilson orders the invasion of Veracruz in an effort to depose Victoriano Huerta, who soon resigns.

1917. During World War I, "temporary" Mexican farm workers, railroad laborers, and miners are permitted to enter the United States to work.

1917. The Jones Act is passed, extending U.S. citizenship to all Puerto Ricans and creating two Puerto Rican houses of legislature whose representatives are elected by the people. English is decreed the official language of Puerto Rico.

February 1917. Congress passes the Immigration Act of 1917, imposing a literacy requirement on all immigrants, aimed at curbing the influx from southern and eastern Europe, but ultimately inhibiting immigration from Mexico.

May 1917. The Selective Service Act becomes law, obligating non-citizen Mexicans in the United States to register with their local draft boards, even though they are not eligible for the draft.

1921. Limits on the number of immigrants allowed to enter the United States during a single year are imposed for the first time in the country's history.

1921. As the first of two national origin quota acts designed to curtail immigration from eastern and southern Europe and Asia is passed, Mexico and Puerto Rico become major sources of workers.

1921. A depression in Mexico causes severe destitution among Mexicans who suddenly find themselves unemployed.

1925. The Border Patrol is created by Congress.

July 1926. Rioting Puerto Ricans in Harlem are attacked by non-Hispanics as the number of Puerto Ricans becomes larger in Manhattan neighborhoods (by 1930 they number 53,000).

1929. With the onset of the Great Depression, Mexican immigration to the United States virtually ceases and return migration increases sharply.

1929. The League of United Latin American Citizens is founded in Texas by frustrated Mexican Americans who find that opportunities for them in the United States are limited.

1930s–1940s. With the onset of the Great Depression, many Mexican workers are displaced by the dominant southern whites and blacks of the migrant agricultural labor force.

1930. The United States controls 44 percent of the cultivated land in Puerto Rico; U.S. capitalists control 60 percent of the banks and public services, and all of the maritime lines.

1930. Within the next four years, approximately 20 percent of the Puerto Ricans living in the United States will return to the island.

1933. The Roosevelt Administration reverses the policy of English as the official language in Puerto Rico.

1933. Mexican farm workers strike the Central Valley, California, cotton industry, supported by several groups of independent Mexican union organizers and radicals.

1933. Cuban dictator Gerardo Machado is overthrown.

September 1933. Fulgencio Batista leads a barracks revolt to overthrow Cuban provisional President Carlos Manuel de Céspedes y Quesada, becoming the dictator of the Cuban provisional government.

1934. The Platt Amendment is annulled.

1938. Young Mexican and Mexican American pecan shellers strike in San Antonio.

1940s–1950s. Unionization among Hispanic workers increases rapidly, as Hispanic workers and union sympathizers struggle for reform.

1940. The independent union Confederación de Trabajadores Generales is formed and soon replaces the Federación Libre de los Trabajadores (FLT) as the major labor organization in Puerto Rico.

1940. Fulgencio Batista is elected president of Cuba.

1941. The Fair Employment Practices Act is passed, eliminating discrimination in employment.

1941. With the U.S. declaration of war in 1941, Hispanics throughout the country enthusiastically respond to the war effort.

1943. Prompted by the labor shortage of World War II, the U.S. government makes an agreement with the Mexican government to supply temporary workers, known as *braceros,* for American agricultural work.

1943. The so-called "Zoot Suit" riots take place in southern California.

1944. Fulgencio Batista retires as president of Cuba.

1944. Operation Bootstrap, a program initiated by the Puerto Rican government to meet U.S. labor demands of World War II and encourage industrialization on the island, stimulates a major wave of migration of workers to the United States.

1946. The first Puerto Rican governor, Jesús T. Piñero, is appointed by President Harry Truman.

1947. More than 20 airlines provide service between San Juan and Miami, and San Juan and New York.

1947. The American G.I. Forum is organized by Mexican American veterans in response to a Three Rivers, Texas, funeral home's denial to bury a Mexican American killed in the Pacific during World War II.

1950s. Throughout the early 1960s, segregation is abolished in Texas, Arizona, and other regions, largely through the efforts of the League of United Latin American Citizens (LULAC) and the Alianza Hispano Americana.

1950s. Immigration from Mexico doubles from 5.9 percent to 11.9 percent, and in the 1960s rises to 13.3 percent of the total number of immigrants to the United States.

1950s–1960s. Black workers continue to be the most numerous migrants along the eastern seaboard states, while Mexican and Mexican-American workers soon dominate the migrant paths between Texas and the Great Lakes, the Rocky Mountain region, and the area from California to the Pacific Northwest.

1950s–1960s. As more and more Puerto Ricans commit to remaining on the U.S. mainland, they encounter a great deal of rejection, but at the same time demonstrate a growing concern for social and economic mobility. Their early employment pattern consists of menial jobs in the service sector and in light factory work—in essence low-paying jobs.

1950. Despite the resurgence of Mexican immigration and the persistence of Mexican cultural modes, Mexican Americans cannot help but become Americanized in the milieu of the 1950s and 1960s, when more and more acquire educations in Anglo systems, live in integrated suburbs, and are subjected to Anglo-American mass media—especially television.

July 3, 1950. The U.S. Congress upgrades Puerto Rico's political status from protectorate to commonwealth.

1951. The Bracero Program is formalized as the Mexican Farm Labor Supply Program and the Mexican Labor Agreement, and will bring an annual average of 350,000 Mexican workers to the United States until its end in 1964.

1952. Congress passes the Immigration and Nationality Act of 1952, also known as the McCarran-Walter Act, reaffirming the basic features of the 1924 quota law by maintaining a restrictive limit on immigration from particular countries. Immigration from the Western Hemisphere remains exempt, except that applicants must clear a long list of barriers devised to exclude homosexuals, communists, and others.

1952. Fulgencio Batista seizes power of Cuba again, this time as dictator, taking Cuba to new lows of repression and corruption.

1954. In the landmark case of *Hernandez v. Texas* the nation's highest court acknowledges that Hispanic Americans are not being treated as "whites." The Supreme Court recognizes Hispanics as a separate class of people suffering profound discrimination, paving the way for Hispanic Americans to use legal means to attack all types of discrimination throughout the United States. It is also the first U.S. Supreme Court case to be argued and briefed by Mexican American attorneys.

1958–1958. Operation Wetback deports 3.8 million persons of Mexican descent. Only a small fraction of that amount are allowed deportation hearings. Thousands of more legitimate U.S. citizens of Mexican descent are also arrested and detained.

1959. The Cuban Revolution succeeds in overthrowing the repressive regime of Batista; Fidel Castro takes power. The vast majority of Cuban Americans immigrate to the United States after this date: between 1959 and 1962, 25,000 Cubans are "paroled" to the United States using a special immigration rule. Large-scale Cuban immigration to the United States occurs much more quickly than that from either Puerto Rico or Mexico, with more than one million Cubans entering the country since 1959.

1959. Most of the two million Puerto Ricans who have trekked to the U.S. mainland in this century are World War II or postwar-era entries. Unlike the immigrant experience of Mexicans, or Cubans before 1959, the majority of Puerto Rican immigrants entered the United States with little or no red tape.

1960s. A third phase of labor migration to the United States begins when the established patterns of movement from Mexico and Puerto Rico to the United States are modified, and migration from other countries increases. The Bracero Program ends in 1964, and, after a brief decline in immigration, workers from Mexico increasingly arrive to work under the auspices of the H-2 Program of the Immigration and Nationality Act of 1952, as well as for family unification purposes, or as undocumented workers.

1960s–1970s. The migrant agricultural work force is changing rapidly. With the rise of the black power and Chicano movements, the appearance of modest protective legislation, and the increasingly successful unionization efforts of farm workers, employers seek to recruit and hire foreign workers to replace the citizens.

1961. Aspira (Aspire) is founded to promote the education of Hispanic youth by raising public and private sector funds. Aspira acquires a national following, serving Puerto Ricans wherever they live in large numbers.

April 1961. Anti-Communist Cuban exiles who are trained and armed by the United States, attempt a foray into Cuba that is doomed from the beginning. The failure of the infamous Bay of Pigs invasion embitters thousands of exiled Cubans, while strengthening Castro's position at home. Many observers throughout the world criticize the Kennedy administration for the attempt to overthrow a legitimately based government.

1962. The United Farm Workers Organizing Committee in California, begun as an independent organization, is led by César Chávez. In 1965 it organizes its successful Delano grape strike and first national boycott. It becomes part of the AFL-CIO in 1966. Today the union is known as the United Farmworkers of America.

October 1962. President Kennedy redeems himself from the Bay of Pigs disgrace by blocking a Soviet plan to establish missile bases in Cuba. Soviet Premier Khrushchev agrees to withdraw the missiles with the proviso that the United States declare publicly that it will not invade Cuba.

1964. Congress enacts the first comprehensive civil rights law since the Reconstruction period when it passes the Civil Rights Act of 1964. One result of the act is the establishment of affirmative action programs. Title VII of the Act prohibits discrimination on the basis of gender, creed, race, or ethnic background, "to achieve equality of employment opportunities and remove barriers that have operated in the past." Discrimination is prohibited in advertising, recruitment, hiring, job classification, promotion, discharge, wages and salaries, and other terms and conditions of employment. Title VII also establishes the Equal Employment Opportunity Commission (EEOC) as a monitoring device to prevent job discrimination.

1964. The Economic Opportunity Act (EOA) is the centerpiece of President Lyndon B. Johnson's War on Poverty. The EOA also creates the Office of Economic Opportunity (OEO) to administer a number of programs on behalf of the nation's poor. These include the Job Corps, the Community Action Program (CAP), and the Volunteers in Service to America (VISTA).

1965. The experienced *braceros* (manual laborers) inspire other Mexicans to immigrate to the United States. Many of these contract laborers work primarily in agricultural communities and in railroad camps until the program ends in 1965.

1965. A border industrialization program, the *maquiladora* (assembly plant), is initiated. Mexico hopes to raise the standard of living in its northern border region, while the United States hopes to avoid the possible negative political and economic consequences of leaving hundreds of thousands of Mexican workers stranded without employment as the Bracero Program is ended.

1965. Although the single aim of the Voting Rights Act of 1965 is African American enfranchisement in the South, obstacles to registration and voting are faced by all minorities. The act's potential as a tool for Hispanic Americans, however, is not fully realized for nearly a decade.

1965. For the first time, the United States enacts a law placing a cap on immigration from the Western Hemisphere, becoming effective in 1968.

1965. Fidel Castro announces that Cubans can leave the island nation if they have relatives in the United

States. He stipulates, however, that Cubans already in Florida have to come and get their relatives. Nautical crafts of all types systematically leave Miami, returning laden with anxious Cubans eager to rejoin their families on the mainland.

1965. A major revision of immigration law results when Congress amends the Immigration and Nationality Act of 1952. The national origin quota system is abolished.

Late 1960s–early 1970s. Intellectual foment and rebellion reign in the United States. Caught up in the mood, young Mexican Americans throughout the country seek a new identity while struggling for the same civil rights objectives of previous generations. This struggle becomes known as the Chicano Movement. The word "Chicano" is elevated from its pejorative usage in the 1920s when it denoted lower-class Mexican immigrants, and from its slang usage of the 1940s and 1950s, to substitute for "Mexicano."

1966. Hundreds of Chicago Puerto Rican youths go on a rampage, breaking windows and burning down many of the businesses in their neighborhoods. Ostensibly, the riots are in response to an incident of police brutality, but the underlying causes are broader, linked to the urban blight that characterizes their life in Chicago.

1966. A program is initiated to airlift Cubans to the United States. More than 250,000 Cubans are airlifted to the United States before the program is halted by Castro in 1973. About 10 percent of the island's population immigrates to the United States between 1966 and 1973.

1968. Chicano student organizations spring up throughout the nation, as do barrio groups such as the Brown Berets. Thousands of young Chicanos pledge their loyalty and time to such groups as the United Farmworkers Organizing Committee, which, under César Chávez, has been a great inspiration for Chicanos throughout the nation. An offshoot of both the farm worker and the student movements, is La Raza Unida party in Texas, an organization formed in 1968 to obtain control of community governments where Chicanos are the majority.

1969. After the establishment of the Central American Common Market in the 1960s leads to economic growth and improved conditions in the region, the border war between Honduras and El Salvador brings its collapse and a rapid decline of economic conditions in Central America.

1970s. Immigration and Naturalization Service (INS) Commissioner Leonard Chapman seeks to increase funding and expand the power of his organization, claiming that there are as many as 12 million undocumented workers in the country. Other observers most commonly place the number in the range of 3.5 million to 5 million people.

1970s–early 1980s. The rise in politically motivated violence in Central America spurs a massive increase in undocumented immigration to the United States.

1970. At this time 82 percent of the Hispanic population of the nation lives in nine states, with the proportion rising to 86 percent in 1990. The major recipients of Hispanic immigrants are California, Texas, and New York, and to a lesser degree Florida, Illinois, and New Jersey.

1970. A Chicano Moratorium to the Vietnam War is organized in Los Angeles. Journalist Rubén Salazar is accidentally killed by police.

1970. The struggle over affirmative action continues when opponents coin the term "reverse discrimination," suggesting that white males are victims of discrimination as a result of affirmative action on behalf of women, blacks, Hispanics, and other under-represented groups.

1970. Brutality against Mexican Americans continues. In *López v. Harlow,* a case filed in an attempt to bring the violence under control, a police officer shoots and kills López, a Mexican American, allegedly in self-defense, because he thought López was about to throw a dish at him.

1970. The amendments constituting the landmark Voting Rights Act of 1970 add a provision that is designed to guard against inventive new barriers to political participation. It requires federal approval of all changes in voting procedures in certain jurisdictions, primarily southern states. This act prevents minority votes from being diluted in gerrymandered districts or through at-large elections.

1971. La Raza Unida Party wins the city elections in Crystal City, Texas.

1972. Ramona Acosta Bañuelos becomes the first Hispanic treasurer of the United States.

1973. The right of the Puerto Rican people to decide their own future as a nation is approved by the United Nations. In 1978, the United Nations recognizes Puerto Rico as a colony of the United States.

1973. An employment discrimination case, *Espinoza v. Farah Manufacturing Company,* argues discrimination toward an employee, Espinoza, on the basis of his citizenship status under the Civil Rights Act. However, the Supreme Court holds that there is nothing in Title VII, the equal employment opportunities provisions of the Civil Rights Act of 1964, that makes it illegal to discriminate on the basis of citizenship or alienage.

1973. The Labor Council of Latin American Advancement (LCLAA) forms to promote the interests of Hispanics within organized labor.

1974. Congress passes the Equal Educational Opportunity Act to create equality in public schools by making bilingual education available to Hispanic youth. According to the framers of the act, equal education means more than equal facilities and equal access to teachers. Students who have trouble with the English language must be given programs to help them learn English.

1975. The Voting Rights Act Amendments of 1975 extend the provisions of the original Voting Rights Act of 1965 and makes permanent the national ban on literacy tests. Critical for Hispanic Americans, the amendments make bilingual ballots a requirement in certain areas.

1977. The Immigration and Naturalization Service (INS) apprehends more than one million undocumented workers each year.

1977. A group of young Cuban exiles called the Antonio Maceo Brigade travels to Cuba to participate in service work and to achieve a degree of rapprochement with the Cuban government.

1978. The median income of Hispanic families below the poverty level falls from $7,238 in 1978 to $6,557 in 1987, controlling for inflation.

1978–1988. Hispanic female participation in the work force more than doubles, from 1.7 million to 3.6 million. In 1988, 56.6 percent of Hispanic women are in the work force, compared with 66.2 percent of white women and 63.8 percent of blacks.

1978–1988. The proportion of Hispanic children living in poverty rises more than 45 percent, and by 1989, 38 percent of Hispanic children are living in poverty.

1979. Political upheaval and civil wars in Nicaragua, El Salvador, and Guatemala contribute to large migrations of refugees to the United States.

1980s. Japanese industrialists take advantage of the maquiladoras by sending greater amounts of raw materials to Mexico where they are finished and shipped duty-free to the United States.

1980s. The rates of immigration approach the levels of the early 1900s: legal immigration during the first decade of the century reached 8.8 million, while during the 1980s, 6.3 million immigrants are granted permanent residence. The immigrants are overwhelmingly young and in search of employment, and Hispanic immigrants continue to account for more than 40 percent of the total.

1980s. Programs to apprehend undocumented immigrants are implemented, and reports of violations of civil rights are reported.

1980. A flotilla converges at Cuba's Mariel Harbor to pick up refugees. By year end, more than 125,000 "Marielitos" migrate to the United States. Castro charges that the exiles he allowed to return on visits had contaminated Cubans with the glitter of consumerism.

1980. The Refugee Act of 1980 removes the ideological definition of refugee as one who flees from a Communist regime, thus allowing thousands to enter the United States as refugees.

April 1980. A bus carrying a load of discontented Cubans crashes through the gates of the Peruvian embassy in Havana and the passengers receive political asylum from Peru. Castro begins to revise his policy of gradually allowing Cubans to leave.

1980–1988. The Reagan administration maintains that affirmative action programs entail quotas, constituting a form of reverse discrimination.

1980–1988. The number of Hispanics in the work force increases by 48 percent, representing 20 percent of U.S. employment growth.

1986. After more than a decade of debate, Congress enacts The Immigration Reform and Control Act (IRCA), creating an alien legalization program: legal status is given to applicants who held illegal status in the United States from before January 1, 1982, until the time of application. The program brings legal status to a large number of undocumented Hispanics.

1987. At this time, 70.1 percent of Hispanic female-headed households with children are living in poverty.

1988. President Ronald Reagan appoints the first Hispanic Secretary of Education: Dr. Lauro F. Cavazos.

1989. Median family income for white families is $35,210; for blacks, $20,210; and for Hispanics,

$23,450. Per capita income is $14,060 for whites, $8,750 for blacks, and $8,390 for Hispanics.

1989. Immigration from the Americas rises from 44.3 percent in 1964 to 61.4 percent. Of the major countries, Mexico accounts for 37.1 percent of total documented immigration to the United States, the next highest number of immigrants being from El Salvador, 5.3 percent.

1990. President George Bush appoints the first woman and first Hispanic surgeon general of the United States: Antonia C. Novello.

1990. The erosion of past civil rights legislation by the Supreme Court during the Reagan and Bush administrations results in efforts by representatives of civil rights, black, and Hispanic organizations to initiate a push for a new Civil Rights Act. A series of compromises produces a watered-down Civil Rights Act in 1991.

1991. The proposed North American Free Trade Agreement between Mexico, the United States, and Canada expands even further the maquiladora concept, offering potentially greater tax abatements for U.S. businesses.

1991. Erosion of past civil rights legislation by the Supreme Court during the Reagan and Bush administrations results in efforts by representatives of civil rights, black, and Hispanic organizations to initiate a push for a new Civil Rights Act in 1990 to return to previous standards. A series of compromises produces a watered-down Civil Rights Act in 1991.

1991. Despite the U.S. Congress' refusal to consider the statehood of Puerto Rico, a referendum is held on the island, clearly showing that the population is in favor of statehood.

March 1991. Unemployment among Hispanics in the United States reaches 10.3 percent, roughly double the rate for whites.

March 1991. A jury exonerates Los Angeles police of the brutal beating of African American Rodney King, which was captured on videotape. African Americans in central Los Angeles are joined by many Latinos in protesting the verdict by rioting for a number of days. The volatile reaction of the minority community leads the country to reassess social and economic policy, as well as police training as it affects minorities.

February 1992. The Farabundo Martí National Liberation Front (FMLN) ends its guerrilla movement by signing a peace treaty with the government of El Salvador. One of the bloodiest civil wars, one that had killed some 75,000 people, finally comes to an end. In exchange for the FMLN laying down its weapons and becoming a legal political party, the government agrees to sweeping changes in the military, including the retirement of more than a hundred officers believed responsible for widespread human rights abuses. El Salvador was a key battleground for the Cold War during the 1980s, with the United States pouring in more than $6 billion in economic and military aid to defeat the FMLN. With the fall of Communist states in Europe, the end of the Cold War brings considerable peace benefits to Central America.

October 23, 1992. President George Bush signs the Cuban Democracy Act, also known as the Torricelli Bill, which bans trade with Cuba by U.S. subsidiary companies in third countries and prohibits ships docking in U.S. ports if they have visited Cuba. The Torricelli Bill is heaving backed by Cuban Americans, and Bush makes a point of signing it in Miami. The passage and signing of the bill illustrate the power of U.S. ethnic groups in creating legislation and affecting foreign policy. Upon passage of the Cuban Democracy Act, the United States is condemned by the United Nations General Assembly for maintaining is 30-year embargo of Cuba; the vote is 59 to 3, with 71 countries abstaining. Even most of the United States' allies either vote to end the embargo or they abstain.

1993. President Bill Clinton names Federico Peña to the position of Secretary of Transportation; he is the first Hispanic to hold that post.

1993. President Bill Clinton names Henry Cisneros to the cabinet position of Secretary of Housing and Urban Development (HUD); he is the first Hispanic to hold that post.

1993. President Bill Clinton appoints Norma Contú, the former director of the Mexican American Legal Defense and Education Fund, to the position of Assistant Secretary for Civil Rights, Department of Education. The president also appoints 25 Hispanics to positions that need confirmation by the Senate, including Nicolás Kanellos to the National Council for the Humanities.

January 1, 1994. The North American Free Trade Agreement (NAFTA) takes effect to eliminate all tariffs between trading partners Canada, Mexico, and the United States within fifteen years from this date. The measure is a first step toward integrating the economies of the three countries and possibly toward the creation in the future of an American common market that will include the whole hemisphere. Regarding Mexico and the United States, on this date 53.8 percent of U.S. imports from Mexico became duty free, while 31 percent of imports from the United States, excluding those imported by maquiladoras, became duty free. The most immediately affected industries are energy, automobiles, textiles, agriculture, electricity, banks and insurance, bus and trucking services, ports, railroads, and telecommunications. NAFTA passage is opposed in the United States by labor unions, which fear the continuing loss of jobs to Mexico, and domestic industries artificially protected by tariffs, such as textiles. In Mexico, revolutionary outbreaks by Mayan peasant farmers in Chiapas are timed to coincide with the beginning of NAFTA, and, in fact, they start shortly after 12:00 a.m. New Year's Day. As many as one thousand Mayan guerrillas, baptizing themselves the Zapatista National Liberation Army (in honor of the revolutionary general Emiliano Zapata), with some of them uniformed and well armed, take over the important southern city of San Cristobal de las Casas, as well as the towns of Ocosingo, Las Margaritas, and others. This leads to bloody confrontations with and repression by the Mexican Army until a cease-fire is accepted by both sides on January 12, with an agreement to dialogue on the problems of the Mayas in Chiapas. The Mayas of southern Mexico, who have suffered poverty and dispossession of their communal lands for years, are now faced with the prospect of imported corn displacing their main farm product and dietary staple. All of this crystallizes in an environment of increasing indigenous overpopulation, poverty, and exploitation as Mexico bows to the demands of foreign debtors, the constraints of the International Monetary Fund to control inflation, and recent devaluations of the peso.

With the economic policy of President Carlos Salinas de Gortari straining to bring Mexico into the "first world," the gap between the select few who are rich, and getting richer under new economic programs, and the poor in Mexico is accentuated. After a cease-fire is established, the government and Mayan rebels sign a tentative 32-point accord on March 2, calling for a new local government designed to serve Indian communities and a redrawn Chiapas state legislature to increase Indian representation; it also calls for the government to build roads, improve schools, upgrade health services, and extend electricity and water to remote areas in Chiapas, the poorest state in the Mexican republic. The government agrees to grant rebels amnesty, to outlaw discrimination against Indians, and to enact laws that would allow officials to confiscate large landholdings in Chiapas and divide them among the peasants. The government also promises to help retrain farmers harmed by NAFTA. In the months following the cease-fire, Mayan farmers proceed t seize some 75,000 acres of ranch lands, claiming that the lands had been stolen from them as far back as 1819. An agrarian court in 1989 had ruled in favor of the Mayas, but the government has done nothing to enforce the ruling.

President Carlos Salinas de Gortari announces, however, that redistribution of farmland is no longer an option in Mexico. Thus, the issue of land remains on the table in the continuing negotiations with the Mayas.

March 23, 1994. Luis Donaldo Colosio, presidential candidate for Mexico's Institutional Revolutionary Party (PRI), is assassinated in Tijuana, Mexico, while campaigning. The conspiracy to assassinate the candidate handpicked by President Carlos Salinas de Gortari is assumed to be political in nature and provokes insecurity in Mexico's trading partners through the North American Free Trade Agreement. On March 24, acting unilaterally, the United States extends a $6 billion line of credit to Mexico. This is followed later by both NAFTA partners, the United States and Canada, moving rapidly to create a multibillion-dollar fund to stabilize Mexico's currency and protect it from onslaughts from global speculation. The centerpiece of the fund is a $6.7 billion line of credit for the Central Bank of Mexico. All three parties to the treaty see their economies as interdependent. Critics charge that the United States has repeatedly shored up and supported the PRI with loans and lines of credit during elections and political transitions to ensure stability. Had it not been for the loans in 1988, they charge, the Party of the Democratic Revolution candidate, Cuauhtémoc Cárdenas, would have defeated Carlos Salinas de Gortari in what was a close election.

November 8, 1994. Californians pass Proposition 187 with 59 percent of the vote. The initiative bans undocumented immigrants from receiving public education and public benefits such as welfare and subsidized health care, except in emergency circumstances; makes it a felony to manufacture, distribute, sell, or use false citizenship or residence documents; and requires teachers, doctors, and other city, county, and state officials to report suspected and apparent illegal aliens to the California attorney general and the Immigration and Naturalization Service (INS). Governor Pete Wilson issues an executive order for state officials to begin following the initiative by cutting off government services to undocumented pregnant women and nursing home patients. On November 9, 1994, eight lawsuits are filed in state and federal courts protesting the measure. On November 16, 1994, Judge William Matthew Byrne, Jr., of the Federal Court in Los Angeles, temporarily blocks California state officials from enforcing the proposition. Mark Slavkin, president of the Los Angeles Unified School District Board, and other officials are threatened with recall efforts for proposing Proposition 187. Similar proposals are being considered on the federal level to severely limit or ban undocumented immigrants from receiving public benefits and attending public schools. Hispanics and other minorities perceive the initiate as an anti-immigrant sentiment stemming from a weak economy.

November 16, 1994.   In Los Angeles, California, Federal District Court Judge William Matthew Byrne, Jr., temporarily blocks the enforcement of Proposition 187, stating that it raises serious constitutional questions. Judge Byrne exempts the provisions that increase penalties for manufacturing or using false immigration documents.

January 1995.   Signatures are collected to put an initiative on the 1996 ballot that states: "Neither the State of California nor any of its political subdivision or agents shall use race, sex, color, ethnicity or national origin as a criterion for either discriminating against or granting preferential treatment to any individual or group in the operation of the State's system of public employment, public education or public contracting." The initiative is labeled Son of 187—a reference to Proposition 187, the immigration-control measure passed by Californians on November 8, 1994.

February 21, 1995.   President Bill Clinton is successful in arranging for an international loan-guarantee package of $53 billion, with $20 million from the United States, to prop up the devalued peso and restore confidence in the Mexican economy. On December 20, 1994, after the PRI ruling party's victory at the polls, outgoing President Carlos Salinas de Gortari allows the peso to float against the dollar, thus revealing the extent of weakness in the economy that has been covered up during negotiations and implementation of the North American Free Trade Agreement (NAFTA). With additional stress to the economy and international investor confidence in Mexico brought on by the assassination of a presidential candidate during the elections and the armed insurrection by Maya Indians in Chiapas, the peso plunges, losing one-third of its value. During January and February, a monetary and investment crisis takes hold of the economy, and the Mexican stock market, *Bolsa,* loses 40 percent of its value. After Clinton is unsuccessful in moving Congress to help abate Mexico's monetary crisis, which also affects the U.S. economy, Clinton taps sources not needing congressional approval to put together the $20 billion package. Clinton goes on to appeal to the International Monetary Fund, Canada, and various European and South American countries to come to the aid of Mexico. As soon as the loan package is announced, both the peso and Mexican stocks stabilize, and the Mexican nation prepares for some of the strictest austerity policies in its history, including placing oil revenues as collateral for the U.S. loans. In the wake of much higher prices for even the most basic of staples, and rising unemployment in Mexico, the United States is bracing for another large wave of immigrant Mexican labor.

1

A Historical Overview

✻ Spanish Legacy ✻ The Indigenous Caribbean Populations ✻ The Indigenous Mexican Population
✻ The Spaniards in the Valley of Mexico ✻ Movement to the North
✻ Anglo Encroachment into the Mexican North ✻ Mexicans Under U.S. Rule
✻ Africa and the Making of Society in Cuba and Puerto Rico ✻ Independence of Cuba and Puerto Rico
✻ Early Mexican Immigration to the United States
✻ The Mexican Revolution and Immigration to the United States ✻ The "Mexico Lindo" Generation
✻ Depression, Repatriation, and Acculturation ✻ World War II and the Mexican American Generation
✻ From Chicanos to Hispanics ✻ Migration to the United States from Puerto Rico
✻ Early Settlement of Puerto Ricans in the United States ✻ The Great Migration
✻ Early Cuban Immigration to the United States
✻ The Revolution of Fidel Castro and Cuban Immigration ✻ Hispanic Identity in the United States

This chapter presents a history of the three major Hispanic groups that have made their home in the United States: Mexicans, Puerto Ricans, and Cubans. Their historical evolution has made each group unique unto itself, but several factors deeply rooted in the formation of their national and cultural identity bind them together. Foremost among these are their link to the mother country Spain and the geographical proximity the three nations share within the Caribbean and the Gulf of Mexico.

✻ SPANISH LEGACY

The first task in understanding Hispanic society in the United States is to view the long gestation period that went into the formation of each of the three main cultures: Mexican, Cuban, and Puerto Rican. All three share many things in common. The main language spoken by the groups is Spanish, most of the inhabitants are Roman Catholics, and much of the folklore is similar.

The Spanish spoken in the two Caribbean islands and in Mexico has its roots in Spain, because it is from there that the main thrust of colonization took place. The Castilian language spoken in Spain can be traced to a long evolution that began with the earliest human inhabitants of the Iberian Peninsula more than 50,000 years ago.

The presence of Paleolithic man (game hunters and cave dwellers) in Iberia has been proved through archaeological evidence left by the culture, the most famous being cave drawings of the animals on which the dwellers depended for food. More advanced cultures are known as Iberian but not much is known about these early agricultural and village people except that they migrated to the peninsula from Africa several thousand years before the birth of Christ.

In about 1000 B.C., a wave of Celtic warriors, hunters, and part-time keepers of livestock converged on the peninsula from somewhere in present-day Hungary near the Danube River. They mixed with the Iberians and established a unique Iberian-Celtic culture. These Gaelic-speaking nomads eventually settled in almost every part of Europe. The strongest cultural vestiges with which most Americans are familiar are those of Scotland, Wales, and Ireland. In Spain and France, cultural manifestations from the Celtic period are also evident, although not as salient as in the British Isles. There is, for example, in northwest Spain a province known as Galicia, where Gaelic characteristics have lingered to the present time. There, such Gaelic modes as the bagpipe and the kilt are used in ceremonies.

Gaelic culture in the rest of Spain, however, was overwhelmed by a series of invasions and colonization efforts which, shortly before the birth of Christ, greatly transformed the linguistic, racial, and economic systems of the peninsula. The first interlopers having significant influence in the evolution of the peninsula were the Greeks and the Phoenicians, who arrived about the same time as the Celts. Both groups went to Iberia to mine tin and establish a series of trading outposts. They were not prodigious colonizers, and Iberian-Celtic culture remained strong, although over time, the more advanced cultural expression of the Greeks and Phoenicians became diffused among the earlier settlers. The Iberian-Celts developed sculpture and other artistic motifs that significantly took on the characteristics of Greek classical realism, and they borrowed technological innovations, such as transportation vehicles and mining techniques.

In the second century B.C., Carthage, a civilization greatly influenced by Greek achievements and centered along a large portion of the North African coast, challenged the expansion of the Roman Empire in Europe and Africa. The Carthaginians were not successful in the Iberian Peninsula, however. They were able to wrest away from the Greeks authority over the region, but in 133 B.C., the Romans defeated the Carthaginian army at Numantia. This was just one of the many Roman victories, that ensured the expansion of Rome into most of Europe, including the Iberian Peninsula.

The Roman colonization of Iberia was classic in every sense of the word. Unlike previous invaders, such as the Greeks, Phoenicians, and Carthaginians, they settled in, families and all, subordinated and enslaved the natives, and set up a plantation system based on slave labor. They remained in the peninsula until their empire began to crumble about A.D. 400. From the Latin-speaking Romans, Iberia acquired some of its most significant linguistic, cultural, political, and economic institutions, in turn giving Spain and Latin America many of their present-day characteristics.

For example, Portuguese and Spanish, which are spoken in Latin America, are only two of four main languages that evolved from the vulgarization of Latin in Iberia. Portuguese was taken to Brazil by the Portuguese, who were never completely under Spanish dominion. Castilian, the language we now call Spanish, became the dominant language everywhere in the Iberian Peninsula except Portugal. The kingdom of Castile managed to conquer and dominate every other region of Iberia except Portugal. It

was the Romans who distinguished between the western and eastern parts of the peninsula, giving the name "Hispania" to the east and "Lusitania" to the west. The word "Spain" came from "Hispania," and although Portugal did not retain "Lusitania" as a place-name, any term associated with that country or its language is still prefixed by "Luso-," just as "Hispanic" refers to Spain or its heritage.

The political system introduced by the Romans had a profound effect on the evolution of government structures at all levels in Spain, and by extension, in its colonies in Spanish America. Perhaps the most enduring feature of this legacy is the careful attention given to the formation of city political culture. The Romans called this process *civitas*. Anyone who travels in almost any town in Latin America can see a faithful replication of the town square, or *plaza*, with its main Catholic church engulfed in a carefully drawn complex of government buildings dominated by the municipal or state center. The Romans also thought that it was the responsibility of government to build a bathhouse, an amphitheater, and a coliseum near the town center, regardless of the size of the town. This tradition, of course, was followed in Latin America, where one can find similar institutions, even in small villages, if only in modest proportions. In the United States, such a civic impulse is certainly present, but not to the same degree as in Latin America. Many U.S. towns and cities took their shape in response to purely economic exigencies, and then some planning, or none at all, followed.

The legal and judicial system in Latin America is quite different from the common law tradition familiar to people living in England and its former colonies. The Latin American judicial system, drawn from the Napoleonic Code, does not have juries. Rather, judges make the final decisions on all cases brought before the courts. Apart from their language and governmental legacies, the Romans were influential in other areas as well. For example, the large farms and ranches found in Latin America, typical of the landholding system in Spain and Portugal, came from the Roman plantation system known as *latifundia*. Finally, Christianity, especially its ensuing branch of Catholicism, was one of Rome's most enduring legacies. In Iberia, religion became Rome's greatest cultural and historical hallmark, to be spread even further 1,000 years later when Spain embarked on its own powerful empire.

Other ethnic groups followed the Romans into Spain, leaving a continuing heritage that also is part of the Hispanic tradition throughout Latin America and in the United States. The most aggressive of these were Germanic tribes that had been migrating from Asia Minor, slowly penetrating every region where Rome held sway. Some Germanic tribes had been within the empire long enough to serve in Roman legions as mercenaries, and many others were romanized by them. When the Roman Empire fell, some of these Germanic tribes began to carve out their own fiefdoms along with other groups in the empire. But outside tribes, more barbaric and less inclined to Roman ways, poured into the former Roman realms, pillaging and carving out their own regional baronies. Vandals, Berbers, and Visigoths moved into the Iberian Peninsula but were eventually romanized. As Roman political influence declined, the Germanic barbarians, already having relinquished many aspects of their language, began to speak one of the variations of Latin evolving in the peninsula, and they embraced Christianity. The latter process was of such intensity that, as the Germanic tribes mixed with the inhabitants of Spain, who by then were an admixture of all the groups that had previously lived in Iberia, they all came to call themselves Christians as a means of identifying themselves ethnically.

During the Dark Ages, the brilliance of Rome in Iberia and all the achievements associated with the empire faded. This was the beginning of feudalism, an era in which hundreds of small baronies, carved out of the vastness of the Roman Empire, resorted to raiding each other for territorial aggrandizement. The economic system that had held the empire together evaporated, leaving in its place a factional economic and political system. Technologically, the Germanic tribes were backward, and they depended a great deal on raising livestock. From the empire of Rome they managed to salvage some rudimentary metallurgical and other techniques of production. Because a great part of their lives was spent raiding and pillaging, the tribes introduced to Iberia a warrior cult, which was perhaps the most important cultural ingredient of their society. Along with this came a rigid code of conduct that usually accompanied such societies. Adherence to Christianity, once they entered into former Roman realms, added a religious fervor to the military code. This impulse found its expression throughout Christian Europe in the Crusades against the Muslim infidels and in Iberia in a phenomenon known as the Reconquest.

Perhaps Iberia would have remained under the solid sway of feudalism, as did the rest of Europe, if it had not been for the invasion of Arabic-speaking Muslims from North Africa in the beginning of the eighth century. More commonly known as the Moors, these latest newcomers to the peninsula remained for 800 years and, next to the Romans, had the greatest influence on the culture of the Iberians. The invasion was spurred by the rise of an Islamic expan-

sion impulse in North Africa, which quickly engulfed the Persian Gulf all the way to India and north into southern Europe. This expansion was inspired by a religious fervor left after the birth of Mohammed, the founder of Islam, who was born in Mecca in the seventh century A.D.

The first Moors crossed the Strait of Gilbraltar into present-day Spain in A.D. 713, and they brought to the peninsula such an advanced culture that its merits could not help but influence the failing feudal structure left in the wake of Rome's decline. The Muslims left few stones unturned in their quest for technological and philosophical knowledge, borrowing and improving on much of what was known to the world at the time. From the Far East they acquired advanced metallurgical skills, including the making of steel, and medicinal knowledge. In the moribund civilizations of the West, Muslims stemmed the decline of Greek and Roman philosophical, agricultural, and architectural systems.

Years of survival in the desert engendered among the Arabs thorough knowledge of how to preserve and manage water resources. This ability, which they put to good use in much of the semiarid peninsula, was a useful inheritance for the Spaniards who settled in similar terrain in the Americas. The Moors pushed the Christians all the way to the northern reaches of Iberia, but many Christians remained behind Moorish lines, where they were tolerated and allowed to maintain and evolve their Christian and Castilian cultures. Along with the Moors came thousands of Jews, who were also tolerated in Islamic domains, and many of whom served as merchants, teachers, and medical practitioners in such great Muslim cities as Sevilla, Granada, and Cordoba.

The surge that pushed the Christians north lasted until the eleventh century, when the Moorish caliphate of Cordoba began to disintegrate into smaller, less-effective kingdoms. The Christian Castilians then embarked on a protracted effort to regain the lands they had lost to the Moors in the previous 300 years. This Reconquest was attempted piecemeal fashion, since Castilians could not mount unified efforts, because both their economic and political systems were feudal.

The Reconquest, in which the Christian Castilians of northern Spain reclaimed lands in southern Spain from the Moors, lasted until 1492, when King Boabdil was ousted from Granada, the last Moorish stronghold, by the forces of the Castilian queen Isabella and her Aragonese husband, Ferdinand. The marriage of these two monarchs from neighboring Iberian kingdoms in 1469 unified the two largest kingdoms on the peninsula and eventually led to the entire unification of Spain. However, the whole

Isabella of Castile.

peninsula was not to be consolidated in this fashion because the Portuguese, in the western portion of Iberia, managed by themselves to defeat and eject the Arab caliphs at the beginning of the fifteenth century, before Castile did.

Before the Catholic Kings, as Ferdinand and Isabella came to be known, could effectively accomplish this unity, however, the power of the feudal lords acquired by partition of former Moorish caliphates had to be curbed. Ferdinand and Isabella accomplished this by several means. First, they embarked on establishing political institutions that challenged the local rule of the nobility. Then, they linked the long struggle of the Reconquest to their own process of consolidation, thus appropriating the nascent nationalism evoked by that struggle to unify the disparate baronies of the peninsula.

In 1492, the Catholic Kings expelled the Moors and the Jews from Spain. In 1493, they acquired from Pope Alexander VI, who himself had been born in Spain, the papal patronage. This was a concession of major proportions, because it gave the Spanish monarchs complete dominion over the operations of the Catholic church in Spain. As one can imagine,

this was a vehicle of great advantage for the consolidation efforts envisioned by the two monarchs.

The long initial struggle to fend off and finally push out the Moors engendered in the Germanic Castilians an even more resilient warrior culture that by 1492 was, no doubt, the most salient expression of their society. Values such as valor, honor, audacity, and tenacity were highly prized. But the Castilians inherited other positive characteristics from the many groups that had invaded and inhabited Iberia. Little was lost from such exposure, so when Columbus sailed and encountered the New World in 1492, Spain was truly a compendium of its multiethnic past. This complexity of cultures became the Hispanic stamp imprinted on its colonies in the New World.

Columbus' fateful voyage certainly changed the course of history. It opened a vast new region for exploration and exploitation for the Europeans.

✳ THE INDIGENOUS CARIBBEAN POPULATIONS

In Mexico, some 25 million Indians lived in the confines of what are now the central regions of the country. Their civilization was quite advanced and, despite major efforts by the Spaniards to eradicate indigenous culture, much has remained to this day. But in the Caribbean, the Indians were fewer, to begin with, and they were not as developed as those on the Mexican and South American mainland. Tragically, cultural and racial genocide took a greater toll in the Caribbean. The indigenous populations there were greatly reduced almost from the outset of the colonization process because of diseases, brought over by Spaniards, to which the Indians were not immune. Nonetheless, the inhabitants of Cuba and Puerto Rico have retained many vestiges of indigenous society. The largest non-Hispanic influence in the Caribbean came from Africa. Thousands of slaves were brought over, first to work the mines, then to work the large sugar plantations that served the Spaniards as the mainstay of the island economies. Today the vestiges of this important heritage are seen in much of Caribbean culture and, of course, in the racial makeup of the Caribbean peoples.

The indigenous groups in the Caribbean were composed mainly of Carib and Arawak, who lived in seminomadic villages throughout the Greater and Lesser Antilles which make up the bulk of the Caribbean islands, and as far south as the coasts of what are today Venezuela and the Guineas. The Carib were considered by the Spaniards to be fiercer than the Arawak, but both groups hunted, fished, and gathered wild plants, such as the manioc root, for food.

Their way of life had evolved very little in thousands of years. Since the traditional methods of obtaining food had always yielded results, few incentives existed for innovation. Their lives revolved around villages that they were prone to abandon when economic need dictated. Politically, they depended on a council of elders for guidance. Religious beliefs were linked to the hunting-gathering economy, and they relied primarily on shamans for observance of rituals. Village homes required very little to build. Those using palm leaves and wood ribbing were among the most sophisticated. Some lived in dugouts that were called *barbacoas*. When the Spaniards moved on to the Central American mainland, they remembered this word and applied it to the cooking of meat in pits, a common form of preparation in central Mexico. Hence, the word "barbecue" has stuck to this day.

Before the Spanish Conquest, the Taino Indians, an Arawakan group that dominated the islands of Cuba and Puerto Rico, had a highly developed social and political system. In the twelfth century, they had displaced, throughout the Antilles, the less developed Ciboney, who lived in cave-like dwellings and who foraged and fished to survive. Taino-Arawak settlement was based on fishing and extensive planting of corn, squash, and chile, the same foodstuffs cultivated on the Mexican mainland. Because of extensive dependence on fishing, the Taino had an extraordinary maritime ability and moved from island to island setting up villages whose populations numbered in the hundreds. But shortly before the Spanish occupation of the Greater Antilles, warlike Carib Indians swept into the Caribbean and drove many of the Arawak out and captured their women. As a result, to the Spaniards, Arawak became known as a language of females. Like the Arawak, the Carib were excellent sailors who crossed much of the Caribbean in huge canoes that were fitted with woven cloth sails and carried as many as 50 people.

The simple lifestyle of the Caribbean's native people were drastically altered after the arrival of Columbus and the Spaniards. The first island settled by the Europeans was Hispaniola, which is the present-day Dominican Republic. Columbus naively ordered his translator to enter into negotiations with the Great Mogul of India, insisting, as he did until

Major paths of early European penetration of the United States.

his death in 1506, that he had found a direct route to India by sailing west from Spain. As quickly deduced by everyone, except Columbus it seems, what the great discoverer had encountered was a gigantic landmass that blocked direct passage to the real India; even so, the name "Indies" stuck. The name "America" was adopted in northern Europe because of the writings of Amerigo Vespucci, the Italian cartographer who explored the newly found lands. The Spaniards, however, always referred to the New World as Las Indias.

The fate of these "Indians," so called because of the colossal miscalculation made by Columbus, was tragic beyond almost any other experience of indigenous peoples in the Americas. From their rude conquest Columbus and his settlers envisioned rewards that the natives were ill prepared to deliver. Columbus, a Genoese from a seafaring merchant tradition, insisting that he was in Asia, expected to trade with the simple Carib and Arawak. The trouble was that the Caribbean natives had no surplus after they took care of their needs, and even if they had, their fare was of little use to Columbus in setting up trading posts.

Most of the Spanish settlers accompanying Columbus were steeped in the tradition of the Reconquest, and they counted on a subjugated population to do their bidding. They expected to establish feudal baronies. Columbus opposed such a tradition, but he capitulated nonetheless and gave his men *encomiendas*. Developed in feudal Spain, the encomienda was booty given to a Spanish conqueror of a Moorish caliphate. The award was usually the land that had belonged to the caliph, and according to Christian standards of the time, the prize was befitting a hero who had defeated the despised "infidels," as the Moorish Muslims were known. But just as the natives were unable to fit into Columbus' trade scheme, they were just as unsuited to provide labor or tribute, for that would have required them to have lived in a more sophisticated society.

The Spanish attempt to establish feudal baronies resulted in a debacle for all parties involved. But it was worse for the Indians, who were either worked to death in gold mines that yielded little gold or were forced to feed the demanding Spaniards. The result was mass starvation. The final blow in this endless chain of mistreatment was the introduction of European diseases, such as smallpox and measles, to which the natives were not immune. This inadvertent intrusion was the most tragic of the European offerings. Numbering over one million in the Caribbean islands before Columbus' voyage, the Indians were eventually ravaged. Indian lineage however, was not extinguished altogether. There were numerous offspring of Spanish-Indian sexual liaisons, resulting in a small but formidable mestizo population, which continued the Indian genes in the islands.

The Conquest of Cuba

When Columbus and his Spanish sailors first arrived on the island that was named Cuba on October 27, 1492, they disregarded the Indian tribes that lived by subsistence agriculture and fishing. Columbus' attention was fixed on Hispaniola, where the first permanent Spanish colony had been established. It was not until 1508 that the island was systematically charted by Sebastián de Ocampo, who circumnavigated the island gathering information about the coastlines and harbors that would prove useful for the eventual occupation.

The first Spanish political system was not established in Cuba, however, until many years after Columbus' encounter with the natives of the Caribbean. Diego Velásquez de Cuéllar was commissioned governor of Cuba in 1511 after he had led an expedition that defeated the Arawak-Taino Indians. Velásquez, who first arrived in the New World at Hispaniola with Columbus' second voyage in 1493, was by then a veteran colonist with many years of experience in dealing with Caribbean natives. In the conquest, which was conducted in typical Spanish fashion, hundreds of men, women, and children were slaughtered. Many fled to the mountains or to other islands, such as Puerto Rico, only to be caught up with again in later expeditions.

Spared the encomienda for some 19 years after the first arrival of Europeans in the Caribbean, Cuban Indians were finally subjected to the abhorrent institution after 1511. Columbus, who had expected trade, not feudal conquest, gave this prerogative to his men in Hispaniola, setting the precedent for the next 60 years of Spanish conquest. Giving this grant was against Columbus' better judgment, but he found that he had no choice because it seemed like the only way to reward the Spaniards who demanded some kind of prize for their participation in the momentous expedition.

Velásquez had no such scruples, and the parceling out of human beings proceeded in hasty fashion. Velásquez himself became a virtual feudal lord of Cuba, and by 1515 he founded what became Cuba's two largest cities, Santiago and Havana. His power was such that he directed the explorations of the Mexican Gulf Coast by Francisco Hernández de Córdoba and his nephew Juan de Grijalva. These expeditions betrayed the existence of civilizations in the interior of Mexico, prodding Velásquez to put his brother-in-law, Hernán Cortés, in charge of the expedition that resulted in the conquest of Mexico.

Velásquez remained governor of Cuba until the 1520s, and, like that of other Spanish conquerors, his rule left an indelible stamp on the formation of Cuban society.

The initial Cuban economy, based on raising livestock and placer-mining of gold, was propped up with labor provided by the ubiquitous encomienda. Because of the demand for pork, cattle hides, and gold in the other Spanish colonies, especially after the conquest of Mexico, Cuba provided tremendous opportunity for the first settlers. Cuba's first governor Diego Velásquez de Cuéllar, who had gotten rich in Hispaniola by engaging in similar activity, repeated his endeavor in Cuba and prospered there as well.

Unfortunately, European disease and the forced labor in the mines took a grim toll and many Indians became ill and died, or were virtually worked to death. The amount of gold on the island was limited. Soon the supply was exhausted, frustrating the Spaniards to such a point that they made the Indians work harder so that decreasing sources could yield the same previous results. Indiscriminate livestock raising was also destructive to the Indian way of life. Huge, untended herds trampled the fragile crops, reducing the harvest on which the Indians depended as their main source of food. Ironically, the Spanish-based economy in Cuba declined very quickly because of competition from livestock raisers in Mexico and in other new colonies.

When silver was discovered in the Zacatecas province of Mexico and Potosí in Peru, a rush to these areas depopulated Cuba when many fickle Spaniards left to find riches elsewhere. They clamored to leave for newly conquered Mexico and Peru, even though the Crown futilely imposed harsh sanctions to those that deserted their encomiendas. The near-abandonment of the initial economy was so disastrous for the Indians that it makes their unwilling sacrifice even more tragic. The surviving indigenous groups must have wished that more of the exploitative Spaniards had left and never returned. But the Cuban economy revived. Because of the ideal position of the island, it became an entrepôt for silver coming from New Spain (roughly the area of present-day Mexico) and Peru and for European goods destined for the rich colonial markets.

Havana's fine harbor allowed the city to achieve dominance by the mid-sixteenth century, even though it did not become the capital of Cuba until 1607. The British and French, anxious to capture the booty offered by incoming ships, subjected the city to numerous attacks. Fortifications made the city safer, and it soon became the most important naval and commercial center for the Spanish colonies in the Caribbean. Ships with gold and silver from Mexico and South America were formed into fleets at Havana in the 1550s so that the Spanish navy could protect them from pirates during the journey back to Spain. By the eighteenth century, Havana was the New World's greatest port.

The Conquest of Puerto Rico

Unlike Cuba, the island of Puerto Rico was not seen by Europeans until Columbus' second voyage to the New World in 1493. The Taino Indians living on the island called it Borinquen, but Columbus renamed it San Juan Bautista, even though he did not attempt to settle the island, concentrating instead on Hispaniola. As in Cuba, the Taino also received a few years of respite from Spanish mistreatment. But 16 years later, Ponce de León and a crew of 50 followers subdued the 30,000 or so inhabitants of the island, and it was renamed Puerto Rico, or "rich port." The Spaniards overwhelmed the large population of Taino Indians by using terror tactics as they approached each village. Reducing the Indians' ability to resist Spanish incursions throughout the Caribbean was lack of cohesion and poor communication among the scattered villages. If they had offered organized resistance, even in the face of superior weapons, horses, and other advantages held by the Spaniards, it would have been impossible for the Spaniards to succeed.

Following the pattern established in the Caribbean, in Puerto Rico the Spaniards immediately set out to raise livestock and other foodstuffs for the expanding colonial market. But sugarcane was also planted after the conquest, and the natives were pressed into the encomienda to tend to these crops. Harsh treatment and lack of experience with systematic labor rendered the Indians almost useless for work on sugar plantations, however. Besides, by the 1580s, diseases had all but wiped out the Indians of Puerto Rico. The flourishing of sugar production would have to await the coming of large numbers of African slaves.

✳ THE INDIGENOUS MEXICAN POPULATION

In Mexico the greatest cultural influence, along with the Spanish language, was its momentous indigenous history. In 1518, Hernán Cortés set out from Cuba to explore the mainland of Mexico in order to confirm reports of the existence of large, native civilizations in the interior. He was originally commissioned by Diego Velásquez, the governor of Cuba, who had received reports of highly developed societies from previous explorers on reconnaissance trips along the Yucatecan and Mexican coasts.

As the Spaniards were to discover, the reports were indeed true beyond their wildest dreams. Civilization in southern Mexico, or Mesoamerica, as the area is known archaeologically, had its beginning in the vast migrations across the Bering Strait over 50,000 years ago. The first humans to cross into the North American continent entered in waves before the strait was inundated by the melting polar caps in 10,000 B.C. Their livelihood depended on hunting the giant mastodons and other big game and gathering wild plants.

Social organization was limited, since they were mobile and traveled in small bands following the trail of animals. At best, they had a leader who ruled by consent of the other hunters and who had proved his worth in both hunting and defending his group from marauders. They lived in caves and rude shelters as they traversed the countryside in their pursuits. Their religious beliefs were simple. Like other Paleolithic big-game hunters from Europe, Africa, and Asia, they worshiped the very game on which they depended for food. Hence, drawings of mastodons and tapirs have been found on the bone artifacts they used as tools, leaving archaeologists to surmise that this was a form of worship.

In Mesoamerica, or southern Mexico, early natives depended upon hunting and gathering, which provided a healthy, plentiful diet (Paleolithic man was bigger than present descendants). They might have continued in this fashion, but a significant climatic change about 7200 B.C. forever altered the course of human history in Mesoamerica. The area became more arid, creating the desert conditions we know today. The lush green land on which large animals depended for food disappeared. Humans had to turn to other sources of food and entered a stage designated the Archaic period. The former hunters became scroungers, depending on wild plants for their sustenance and to a lesser degree on smaller animals for protein. During this long period, which lasted until 2500 B.C., the gatherers became more and more adept at food acquisition and storage, but they also discovered that they could cultivate some of the plants for which they previously scrounged.

This discovery was the first major step toward civilization. Slowly, the inhabitants of Mesoamerica began to plant and irrigate the seeds of wild plants, such as maize, squash, beans, and amaranth. In the process, they also domesticated some of the wild animals they hunted. Unlike in the rest of the world, wild cattle and horses had not survived the decline of big game. Only the bison in the northern part of the continent lived on. Domestic animals included only turkeys and small dogs. Not surprisingly, the course of development for the Indians of the Americas did not include beasts of burden except for the Indians themselves.

In an era called the Formative period, 2500 B.C. to A.D. 250, material progress in Mesoamerica proceeded at an astonishing rate. First, villages appeared throughout the region as new techniques of cultivation resulted in flourishing plots of crops. Terracing, the plowing of platforms on hills, and *chinampas,* (man-made islands on bodies of water,) greatly increased the ability to produce. The resulting surpluses released many workers from agricultural work and made possible the emergence of specialists, such as potters, toolmakers, and even entertainers, such as musicians, acrobats, and dancers.

In addition the simple metaphysical exigencies related to hunting and gathering gave way to a dramatic sophistication in religious practices, a process hastened by the ability to specialize. Farmers increasingly needed more precise prediction of the weather so that planting and harvesting could be planned accordingly. Shaman priests provided this valuable knowledge as they studied the heavens and acquired the astronomical skills necessary to forecast weather changes. Farmers looked to their religious leaders more and more for guidance, leading to a dependence that put the priests with their metaphysical teachings in leadership roles. Such control gave priests political power, which they exercised to their advantage. They demanded tribute and labor from the commoners and leaders alike, until the priesthood and the leadership converged into a theocracy.

At the end of the Formative period, religious leaders demanded the construction of huge temples and other religious institutions. It was at this point that religion started to assume such dominance that the Mesoamerican world revolved entirely around metaphysical arrangements. A pantheon of deities was inspired by the need to pay homage to the elements essential to agriculture. Thus, the most important gods were those that symbolized the sun, the mother earth, and, of course, water.

About A.D. 250, the Americas pre-Columbian civilization reached its apogee and human development entered into the era known as the Classical period. Large urban centers with specialized production techniques entered into trade arrangements with other cities. During the Formative period, between 1200 B.C. and 400 B.C., a high civilization (which in most of Mesoamerica did not appear until the Classical period) had emerged in selected regions of Mesoamerica. A society known today as the Olmec built large cities with ceremonial centers and advanced architecture, pottery, and art. But most important, the Olmec developed a knowledge of astronomy and math that allowed them to invent a calendar system almost as accurate as ours today. Such development was limited to La Venta and San Lorenzo on the Gulf of Mexico, while the rest of Mesoamerica continued in the village mode even after the decline of these great centers.

In the classical era, many communities, especially those of the Maya and Zapotec, whose centers were close to the old Olmec centers, probably were influenced by the older, declined civilization. The Zapotec, in fact, occupied Monte Albán, a city with marked Olmecan characteristics, while the Maya built centers like Chichén Itza in Yucatán and El Tajín in Vera Cruz. The Maya excelled in math and astronomy, a definite inheritance from the Olmec, and they produced the most delicate pieces of art in all the Americas.

The newer methods (terracing and chinampas) of cultivation were more beneficial to the societies of the hilly and lake-filled Valley of Mexico. There Teotihuacán, the most impressive center in the Classical period, was built 25 miles northeast of the what is now Mexico City. The city had over 200,000 inhabitants, huge pyramids, and a large market where the most advanced pottery and obsidian wares were traded.

Throughout Mesoamerica, thriving agricultural communities existed, dedicated to cultivating maize, the ears of which were about ten times larger than during its initial planting in the Archaic period. Maize was king, but an array of other crops were also important in the diet of Mesoamericans. Unfortunately, in the tenth century A.D., one by one the Classical centers in both the highlands and the tropical lowlands declined. Archaeological evidence points to several causes. In the Mayan lowlands, reliance on slash-and-burn agriculture probably led to the exhaustion of the soil. The method works as long as there is plentiful new land to be brought under cultivation. Also, another climate change (bringing even drier weather) prompted nomadic barbarians from the north, known as Chichimecas, to migrate to Mesoamerica looking for water. It is believed that these newcomers pillaged and sacked the cities of Mesoamerica one by one. The Classical period thus came to an end, and although the barbaric newcomers replaced and imitated the old civilizations, they never surpassed them in philosophical or technical achievement. Because of the warlike orientation of the new cities, the era has been called the Militaristic period. This was the state of society when the Spaniards arrived in the early fifteenth century.

After Mesoamerica's Classical period had ended,

the Toltec were the first of the former Chichimeca group of tribes to have approached the degree of development of their predecessors. Their most impressive city was Tula, about 60 miles northwest of the present-day Mexican capital. The center, known for its giant monoliths, which resemble sentries on guard, remained the most important city in the Valley of Mexico until it too fell to other marauding Chichimeca. The Toltec also occupied the city of Monte Albán, which had served the Zapotec before them. According to myth, it is to there that Quetzalcoatl, the god known as the plumed serpent, was banished and expected to return in the future. As with Tula, the Toltec also abandoned Monte Albán, probably for the same reasons.

One of the last Chichimeca tribes to enter the central valley was the Aztec, who just a few years prior had left their mythical homeland of Aztlán in search of a new home, as Huitzilopochtli, their god of the sun, had mandated. According to legend, they would know where to settle once they encountered an eagle devouring a serpent on top of *nopal* (prickly pear cactus) in the middle of a lake. They wandered south looking for the sign and finally saw it in the middle of Lake Texcoco, where they built Tenochtitlán.

This legend has a basis in truth. The Aztec arrived in the Valley of Mexico about the thirteenth century and were such a nuisance, since they continued the Chichimeca life-style of pillaging, that they were banished by Atzcapotzalco leaders to an island in the center of the lake, which they fortified and used as a base of operation. From there they imitated other city-states and built their own magnificent city, which surpassed all the others in size and beauty, while they defeated and dominated the other communities in the lake region. They went through several stages and emperors until the Spaniards conquered them in 1521.

The city was laid out in squares. Perfectly straight causeways allowed merchants to supply Tenochtitlán in the middle of the lake, while they took the city's products to the countryside and other communities. Bernal Díaz del Castillo, one of Hernán Cortés' soldiers, wrote his first impressions of the city some years later: "Gazing on such wonderful sights, we did not know what to say, or what appeared before us was real, for on one side were great cities, and the lake itself was crowded with canoes, and in the Causeway were many bridges at intervals, and in front of us stood the great City of Mexico."

The society, a theocracy, was made of distinct classes known as the *pilli* (aristocracy); the various knighthoods, such as the *jaguar*; the *pochteca* (merchants); and the *macehuales* (commoners). At the bottom were the *mayeques* (serfs), who tilled the land of the nobles, and the *tamines*, who were full-time bearers. When the Spaniards arrived, Moctezuma II was the most powerful and most famous of emperors. He was deified and given equal status with the Aztec sun-god, Huitzilopochtli. They were both demanding, but the sun-god was voracious in his appetite for human sacrifice. The bloody reputation that the Aztec acquired is due to the thirst of this deity.

The Conquest of Mexico

If there were any doubts among the Spaniards about the existence of an advanced civilization in the interior of Mexico, they were put to rest almost as soon as Cortés landed on the Gulf Coast at a bay he named Veracruz. The reports received from the natives first encountered on the Mexican mainland were too compelling for any misgivings. After scuttling some of his ships so that the 400 Spaniards that accompanied him could not return, Cortés set out to find the source of this civilization. Cortés, an audacious conquistador from Estremaduera in southern Spain, had inherited that warrior mentality so deeply ingrained in that part of the Iberian Peninsula. In fact, the intrepid explorer was not interested in doing the bidding of his ostensible benefactor, a fact that Diego Velásquez had discovered too late. Cortés had left Cuba just before the governor gave orders to have him arrested. With the few hundred men he had recruited and organized into a conquest team, Cortés had sailed just in time. In the time-honored tradition of the Reconquest, Cortés wanted to subjugate the civilization of Mexico and establish himself as its feudal lord.

After declaring the landing site a town (Veracruz), the conquistadors set out for the city of Tenochtitlán, which was considered a populous center of great wealth and power. Along the way he and his men encountered resistance in Cholula, but through the intelligence and language-interpreting services offered him by an Indian maiden given to him by Indians in Tabasco, he was able to defeat the Cholulans and continue on to Tenochtitlán. On the way he picked up Indian allies from the city of Tlaxcala. This Indian group became a ready ally because the Aztec were their hated enemy. Various Aztec leaders had attempted to dominate them and force them to pay tribute, as they had done with other cities in the valley for years. But the Tlaxcalans resisted fiercely. Moctezuma, the Aztec emperor who ruled the great city of Tenochtitlán, had spies who had kept him informed of the progress of the approaching Spaniards ever since they had landed on the coast. But he did not know what to make of them. Paradoxically, he was at a loss as to how to deal with the intruders. The Aztec emperor actually thought that Cortés was the long-lost god Quetzalcoatl, and that the rest of the Spaniards were immortal.

By the time the Europeans arrived at the city, Moctezuma was paralyzed with indecision and Cortés seized the opportunity to sequester the vacilating king in his palace. The Spaniards set up house inside the walls of the city, as did the thousands of Tlaxcalan allies. In the meantime, Diego Velásquez, chafing because Cortés undertook his venture without authorization, sent Pánfilo de Nárvaez to arrest him and bring him back to Cuba in irons. Cortés, through his own system of spies, learned of Narváez's arrival at Veracruz and left Tenochtitlán to deal with him. And in another incredible feat, Cortés persuaded the soldiers of his would-be captor to desert and join him.

Upon his return to Tenochtitlán, Cortés found the city in an uproar. In his absence, Pedro de Alvarado, the conquistador lieutenant, mistook an Aztec ritual for a planned uprising and gave orders to slaughter the Indians who were observing the ritual. This was the last straw for the countless Indians who could not understand why Moctezuma had been so passive. Under the leadership of Cuitlahuac, Moctezuma's brother, the Spaniards were forced out on July 1, 1520, just a year after the Spaniards had come into the city. The Spaniards called this *La noche triste* (The Sad Night). Moctezuma was stoned to death by his own people during this debacle.

Cortés was not a man to give up very easily and so he retreated to the town of Coyoacán, where he set up headquarters to plan the defeat of the city. He quickly built brigantines and armed them with cannons. With his own original soldiers, supplemented by the defectors from Narváez and the thousands of Tlaxcalans, Cortés laid siege to the city, not allowing supplies to go in. In time he attacked the starving Aztec and the neighboring Tlatelolcans, who were also devastated by the European diseases to which the Mesoamericans were not immune. Cuitlahuac himself was a victim of the ravages.

Cuauhtemoc, from neighboring Tlatelolco, then took command. The siege finally forced a surrender, and Cuauhtemoc was captured with the defenders of the city and executed. He went on to become a hero in the eyes of Mexicans, while Cortés is vilified. Cortés had the city of Tenochtitlán razed, and the beginning of Spanish Mexico commenced with the building of a European city on top of the old Aztec capital. However, the old conqueror was eventually stripped of his power, banished back to Spain, and replaced by professional viceroys who ostensibly represented the needs of the Crown. The Spaniards then ruled Mexico until 1821, a full 300 years after the conquest, indelibly stamping their Hispanic mark on Mexican society. Still, what is considered Indian remained in many ways.

✳ THE SPANIARDS IN THE VALLEY OF MEXICO

After Cortés razed Tenochtitlán, he set out to build a Spanish city, ironically rescuing from the rubble the very same building materials used by the Aztec. His conquistadors then continued to explore and bring under Spanish rule other indigenous communities. Pedro de Alvarado ventured south to the Yucatán Peninsula and Guatemala, while Cortés' enemy and rival, Nuño de Guzmán, brutally subjugated the vast realm of the Tarascans to the west. Cortés dispensed encomienda s left and right as a way of rewarding his men, but he reserved for himself the largest encomienda of all, practically all of Oaxaca. In 1529, he was authorized to use the title El Marqués del Valle de Oaxaca.

In the initial years of the conquest, the encomienda (a commission of land) remained, as in the Caribbean, the main prize sought by conquistadors. Many of the onerous aspects of the institution had been somewhat mitigated with the Laws of Burgos. Promulgated by the Crown in 1512, the regulations were in response to the extremely harsh treatment that desperate colonists in the Caribbean imposed on natives through the deplorable encomienda. Now Spaniards had to abide by regulations that forbade overworking the Indians and that required the *encomendero* (the recipient of an encomienda) to provide for the spiritual welfare of the Indians. This usually consisted of supporting a prelate and building a church within the jurisdiction of the encomienda grant. In New Spain, as the vast territory claimed by Spain on the North American continent came to be called, the encomienda became for the Indians an acculturation vehicle to Spanish ways.

The most important Spanish acquisition for the Indians, usually through the encomienda, was Catholicism. Spanish friars in the beginning of the colonization process exhibited a great amount of zeal, imbued as they were with an inordinate amount of idealism, which characterized the Catholic church during this period of internal reform. They traveled far and wide, proselytizing and winning over hundreds of thousands to the Christian faith. The converts were so numerous, however, that they could not really assimilate Catholicism completely and the tendency was to combine, syncretically, pre-Columbian beliefs with the new teachings.

Indians in the Valley of Mexico adjusted better to the encomienda than those in the Caribbean. Prior to the European conquest, Aztec and other dominant tribes had forced tribute from countless subordinated Indian groups, a process that anticipated the demands of the encomienda. Nonetheless, scant comfort can be taken in this, because it is only in relation to the extreme cruelty in the Caribbean that the measure is made. In reality, treatment of the natives by their new masters was as harsh, if not harsher, than under the Aztec. For one, the Spanish tribute demands differed drastically from what the natives were accustomed to providing. The Europeans had no use for the items considered to be the necessary tribute by the Aztec, such as feather cloaks, leopard skins, obsidian relics, earthen pottery, and foodstuffs, such as maize. They wanted pure gold to use as specie, wheat, European beasts of burden, and European domestic animals, such as sheep, cattle, and pigs. The natives were not really able to provide precious metals in any significant amounts, but the Indians had to alter their agricultural tradition in order to provide the food to which Spaniards were accustomed. In time the natives also began to consume new foodstuffs, and in the process modify their traditional food ways. For example, pork, beef, and mutton were combined with chile, maize, and other vegetables native to the Americas to form the basis for the Mexican food that we know today.

By 1540, another major phenomenon began to drastically change the social and racial character of central Mexico. The prodigious sexual appetite of the Spaniards led to numerous liaisons with the native women. From the moment they set foot on Mexican soil, the conquistadors violated the women of the conquered tribes and took them as concubines, with only a few marrying among the Indians. The consequence was a large progeny of children who were half Spaniard and half Indian. This new racial ensemble came to be known as mestizo, and after a few generations, the possible variations of mixture became so profuse that over 100 categories existed by the end of colonial rule in 1821.

In 1504, Queen Isabella died, and 12 years later King Ferdinand succumbed as well. Succeeding them was their heir, Charles V, who was born to Juana la Loca, daughter of the Catholic Kings, and her Hapsburg husband Prince Phillip of Austria. Neither Isabella nor Ferdinand lived to see the conquest of the great Aztec Empire by conquistadors who were intent on making their prize a personal and feudal domain. It fell to the young king to wrest that realm away from Cortés and his encomenderos, a process begun almost as soon as the value of the conquest was realized. In

1524, Charles established the Council of the Indies, designed to oversee the administration of the colonies of the New World. An *audiencia,* a court of judges and administrators, was appointed in 1527 as a major step in asserting royal control. It was presided over by Nuño de Guzmán, who set out to destroy the power of Cortés, his old rival. But the rapacious Guzmán seemed to be a worse threat than the feudalistic Cortés, and the whole audiencia slate was replaced a year later by a president and judges more loyal to the Crown. To supervise and establish the Catholic faith, Juan de Zumárraga was named archbishop of New Spain in 1527.

The most ambitious move in the effort to consolidate royal power in New Spain was the appointment of Antonio de Mendoza, an extremely capable administrator who served the Crown well as viceroy for many years. In 1542, the New Laws were promulgated, a stroke designed to end the feudal encomienda, ensuring the predominance of Hapsburg control over the area. Mendoza found that he could not effectively implement the restrictive measures without provoking insurrection from the armed encomenderos, and so he opted for allowing the controversial institution to die out on its own. Encomiendas were only good as long as there were Indians to parcel out, but because of the horrible epidemics caused by European diseases, the indigenous population was devastated within a century.

In the meantime, the Spanish zeal for exploration and conquest led to incursions north of the Caribbean islands and Mexico into many regions of what is today the United States. Juan Ponce de León had sailed and landed on the shores of Florida in 1513, exploring most of the coastal regions and some of the interior. Continuing their maritime adventures, the Spanish explorers in the 1520s cruised along the northern shore of the Gulf of Mexico, seeing Alabama, Mississippi, and Texas and also sailing up the Atlantic coast to the Carolinas. Between 1539 and 1541, a large, well-equipped group of explorers led by Hernando de Soto journeyed into the interior of North America looking for mineral wealth, through present-day Florida, Georgia, South Carolina, Alabama, Mississippi, Arkansas, Louisiana, and Texas.

At the same time that De Soto was in the midst of his exploration, Francisco Vásquez de Coronado prepared for a momentous trek that took him and another large group of Spaniards north to present-day Arizona, New Mexico, Texas, and Oklahoma. In 1541, he set out from Mexico City in search of the Seven Cities of Cíbola, a mythical region rumored to rival Tenochtitlán in wealth and splendor. To supply Coronado's party, Hernando de Alarcón sailed up the Gulf of California and took his three ships against the current of the Colorado River, reaching present-day Yuma, Arizona.

✷ MOVEMENT TO THE NORTH

In transcendental terms, Francisco Vásquez de Coronado's trek throughout North America has great historical significance. But at the time, his explorations were considered a disappointment because of the failure to find the fabled cities of Cíbola and Quivera. Dispelling the myths of greater glory and riches in the far north dampened enthusiasm for any further forays so far from the viceroyalty of Mexico City. In addition, the discovery of silver in the immediate north, soon after Coronado returned empty-handed, ensured that the Spaniards would concentrate all their efforts closer to their home base, and the expansion and real settlement northward commenced in earnest.

In 1546, Captain Juan de Tolosa, leading a small expedition of soldiers and missionaries into El Gran Chichimeca, as the wild region north of Querétaro was known, discovered a rich vein of silver in a mountain known as La Bufa. The strike was located in what is now the city of Zacatecas, some 300 miles north of Mexico City. It was the first of a series of finds in a fan-like pattern spreading from Zacatecas into Guanajuato, Querétaro, and San Luis Potosí. The area is known as the Central Corridor because it is located on a plateau escarpment between two large mountain ranges, the Sierra Madre Occidental to the west and the Sierra Madre Oriental to the east. In the last half of the sixteenth century, Spanish officials in Madrid concentrated all their efforts on spurring mining activity both in New Spain and in Peru, where even greater silver deposits were uncovered.

But before the rich minerals could be adequately exploited, the Central Corridor had to be made safe from hostile Indian tribes. Although sparsely settled by the nomadic Chichimecas, the natives resisted the unwelcome intrusion of large numbers of Spaniards and mestizo workers, precipitating 50 years of Indian warfare. By the end of the sixteenth century, the nomads were brought under control through a combination of extensive military and religious proselytizing campaigns. As the mining regions were carved out from Chichimeca territory, thousands of mestizos, sedentary Indians from the former Aztec Empire, and Spaniards migrated to the *reales* (mining camps), settling permanently. The mining economy and the arid desert environment of El Gran Chichimeca engendered unique social conditions where a new Mexican ethnic identity was forged. Here the population was not as linked to either the large, sedentary Indian civilization and culture of the central highlands or the cities that were large centers of administration, commerce, and Spanish culture, such as Mexico City and Puebla.

While the inhabitants of the mining frontier drew on Spain and the more settled Indian areas for cultural continuity, the exigencies of the new environment generated an even more vibrant source of identity and culture. The process was carried north as the mining frontier moved in that direction in the seventeenth and eighteenth centuries. By 1800, the Spaniards had reaped $2.25 billion worth of silver from the vast array of rich mines. In the Spanish system, all wealth belonged to the Crown and the miner was granted a *real* (a royal concession giving him or her the right to exploit the mine). The Crown received one-fifth of all the take, or the royal fifth, however, these concessions would remain in the miner's family, ensuring a continuation of *patria potestad* (the original authorization) usually under a patriarch.

Life for miners was grim. The initial method used for mining was the rathole, in which a lode was followed by digging twisted narrow shafts with hand labor. Indian forced labor was first used through a system called *repartimiento,* but mining required staying power and skill, which Indian workers, forced to travel hundreds of miles on foot from their homes and sedentary life-styles in the highlands, would not muster. Within a few years the grantees of the reales turned to wage labor, and hundreds of thousands of mestizos, who were born in the decades immediately after the conquest in the highlands, poor whites, and acculturated Indians poured into the Central Corridor to work not only in mining but also on the haciendas, which specialized in raising livestock and agriculture for consumption in the reales. Thus, the hacienda became an indispensable corollary to mining, and within a few decades both of these activities determined the social arrangements of the region. The economy, based on wage labor, created a proletariat that was able to work in a more diverse opportunity structure than in the central highlands. For example, the *patio* amalgamation process, used to free the silver from its ore base, was rather complicated. After the ore was excavated from the large shafts, it was carefully sifted and gauged by women and young boys, pulverized with huge ox-drawn millstones, and then spread out into pancakes called *tortas*. It was here that the most important step took place. The *azoguero* (mercury man) applied mercury to the pile until the only portion of the torta that was not mush was the pure silver. Each step required thousands of workers, technicians, machines, and

beasts of burden and vast amounts of resources, such as rope, leather, and iron.

This activity was carried farther north as smaller mining operators followed the missionaries to the frontier. In essence, a persistent pattern emerged in which the missionaries tamed the Indians so that the Hispanic miner could follow, once they were "softened" to European ways. The missionaries provided the service unwittingly, but they served that purpose nonetheless. Parral, at the northern end of the corridor in Chihuahua, and Alamos, in Sonora, were thus settled by Spanish Mexicans. By the mid-1600s, the mines had played out, so then miners in the frontier were forced to settle down and turn to agriculture and the operation of smaller-scale mining known as *gambusino*.

For today's Mexican Americans, the social and cultural transformation of the Central Corridor is particularly important, because the Hispanic culture that emerged in northern New Spain (today's American Southwest) during the colonial period is an extension and reflection of the mining society in this region. In addition, Mexican immigrants who in the early twentieth century swelled existing Hispanic communities throughout the United States came from this region as well, reinforcing the unique Mexicanness that had already been established in the Southwest.

The reasons for settling the extreme northern frontier of New Spain were not as related to mining as they were in the case of the Central Corridor. Nonetheless, the process of colonization was a slow but sustained extension of the northward movement that started with the founding of the Zacatecas mines. By the time Mexico acquired its independence from Spain in 1821, permanent colonies existed in coastal California, southern Arizona, south Texas, and in most of New Mexico and southern Colorado. The imprint of evolving Mexican culture so evident in the Central Corridor was also stamped on today's Southwest. It contained a mestizo-*criollo* (pure-blooded Spanish descendant) racial mixture with a strong reliance on raising livestock, subsistence agriculture, and mining. Leaders of most colonizing expeditions were persons born in Spain, but the rank-and-file soldiers, artisans, and workers in general were of mixed blood (mestizos) or criollos born in New Spain.

The first foray out of the Mexico's Central Corridor, after Francisco Vásquez de Coronado's unsuccessful trek in North America, was in the 1590s into Pueblo Indian territory in northern New Mexico. Fifty years earlier, Coronado had written of these sedentary Indians who lived in large agricultural settlements containing multistory houses with well-

A *vaquero* in early California.

ordered political and religious systems. His attempts to buffet them into encomiendas provoked fierce resistance and, as a result, he and his party were forced to abandon New Mexico. This failure contributed to the overall disillusionment with exploration. Nonetheless, the possibility of exploiting the labor of the Pueblos and saving their souls, modest as this potential might have been, remained a lure after Coronado. The attraction glowed even more 40 years later when Antonio de Espejo reported in 1583 the possibility of silver deposits in New Mexico.

Spurred by Espejo's report, Juan de Oñate, the grandson of a Zacatecas mining pioneer from Spain, was granted a charter to explore into present-day New Mexico as early as 1595. In 1598 he and his group set out along the Central Corridor from the more civilized Zacatecas to the uncertainty of the north. Oñate's party, made up of Spaniards, criollos and mestizos, also contained Tlaxcalan Indians, who had remained loyal to the Spaniards, after helping Hernán Cortés defeat the Aztec in 1521. They served in menial positions as carriers, servants, and laborers. After reaching the Rio Grande, the explorers and missionaries then traveled along the river valley, established a minor post in present-day El Paso,

and continued on up through upper Rio Grande valley into Pueblo Indian territory.

Oñate was ordered to return in 1608, but Franciscan missionaries and settlers remained attracted to the communities of sedentary Indians. Santa Fe was founded in 1610, followed by other settlements. The clerics wanted to convert the Indians, and the civilians hoped to put them into encomiendas and demand gold as tribute. The efforts to enslave the Indians backfired, however. In 1680, a Pueblo Indian named Popé led a rebellion that forced the Spaniards and Christianized Indians out of northern New Mexico southward toward El Paso, and they founded Ysleta just north of El Paso. The latter community is said to have housed the *genízaros* (acculturated Indians made up of Comanche captive-slaves), Christianized Pueblos, and the faithful Tlaxcalans. Sixteen years later, many of those settlers who had fled returned to northern New Mexico and reestablished a Hispanic presence, but with a new respect for the Pueblos.

The Pueblo uprising turned the interest of Spaniards toward Texas. But the story of the exploration of Texas has to be told within the context of the colonization of the large province of Coahuila, of which Texas was an extension. The first newcomers were prospectors searching for precious metals, and indeed some silver mines were opened in Monclova, Coahuila, such as the Santa Rosa. But the diggings were sparse and most of the attention was soon turned to agriculture and livestock. Motivated by the need to provide foodstuffs and livestock to the rich mining regions to the south, in 1689 the first royal *mercedes* (land grants) were granted to Spaniards in the fertile valleys of Monclova, just south of the present border.

The Spaniards in the northeast brought Tlaxcalan Indians to provide labor for their haciendas. Many of these enterprising natives established themselves as artisans in Saltillo and acquired a reputation as excellent weavers and silversmiths. Many of the modern inhabitants of Coahuila and immigrants to Texas from this area are descendants of the Tlaxcalans. Saltillo acquired great importance because it served as an entrepôt between the livestock-raising areas to the north and the silver and mercantile communities to the south. In the eighteenth century, a new dynasty of Spanish kings, the Bourbons, initiated reforms that led to a revitalization of the silver industry. As a consequence, by 1767 Saltillo had become a prosperous commercial hub with a population of over 2,000, and as new settlers arrived to colonize the northeast, they filtered through this beautiful colonial city.

Large, sprawling haciendas with huge herds of

Viceroy Francisco Fernández de la Cueva Enríques, Duke of Albuquerque.

fort in the western extreme of Louisiana, precipitously close to Spanish Texas. The news traveled fast and in 1686 Alonso de León set out to look for the fort and found it destroyed by Indians. Still, the French threat remained, and a Spanish *presidio* (fort) was established near Nacogdoches, Texas. By the early eighteenth century, French Biloxi (established in 1699) and New Orleans (1718) served as junctions for the burgeoning Mississippi trade. The main trading activity of the French with the Indians was in fur pelts. If the Indians did not know how to trap, the French would teach them, provoking the natives to abandon other ways of life and become ever more dependent on trapping. A mission was also established in Nacogdoches in tandem with the fort, a policy that the Spaniards emulated in other parts of their frontier. The Indians, however, did not take to the Christian religion, and in 1700 the mission was abandoned. In the beginning, the Spaniards found little desirable in Texas territory.

At the turn of the century, a persistent priest named Francisco Hidalgo, from his base of San Juan Bautista, a settlement on the Rio Grande about 150 miles west of Laredo, zealously set out to work

cattle and sheep characterized the economy and societal life of the northeast by 1800. The biggest landholding belonged to the Sánchez-Navarro family. It was 16 million acres in size. This latifundia was so immense that it took in almost half of the province, and its mainstay was sheep raising. Peonage was the lot of many of the lower classes, as that was the only method by which *hacendados* (landowners) could deter their workers from going off to work in mines. But hindering the effectiveness of the haciendas were constant depredations by the Comanche, who had learned that raiding the livestock regions was more prosperous than hunting the buffalo. This provoked the Spanish government to establish buffer zones across the Rio Grande, or the Rio Bravo, as it is known in Mexico.

Besides the adversity posed by the Comanche, Spanish officials recognized another threat. While explorations north of the Rio Grande were motivated by the time-honored traditions of prospecting for precious metals and converting the Indians, now defense of the frontier began to acquire more importance. In the 1680s, the French sailed down the Mississippi from the Great Lakes and established a

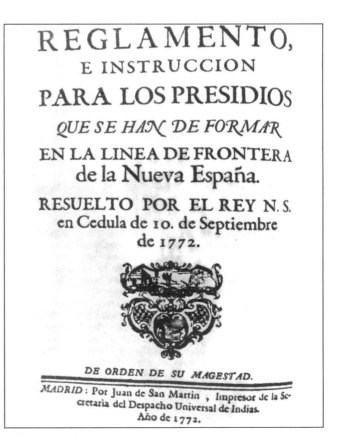

REGLAMENTO,
E INSTRUCCION
PARA LOS PRESIDIOS
QUE SE HAN DE FORMAR
EN LA LINEA DE FRONTERA
de la Nueva España.
RESUELTO POR EL REY N. S.
en Cedula de 10. de Septiembre
de 1772.

DE ORDEN DE SU MAGESTAD.

MADRID: Por Juan de San Martin , Impresor de la Secretaria del Despacho Universal de Indias.
Año de 1772.

Rules that were issued by the King of Spain regarding the founding and governance of presidios on the frontier.

among the Indians north of the river. Initially his requests for support were ignored by Spanish officials, so he sought help from the French, which prompted the Spaniards to act, because they recognized the threat France would pose if her colonists made inroads with the natives. Domingo Ramón in 1717 was sent to colonize along the Nueces River and to build missions. In 1718, the San Antonio de Béjar and de Valero churches were built where the city of San Antonio is located today. The chapel in the de Béjar mission was called El Alamo. The efforts to colonize Texas remained very difficult because of the nomadic, warlike character of the tribes. Therefore, instead of spreading the gospel, the Spaniards spent most of their time pacifying the resistant natives.

The French remained a threat, however. To thwart Spanish efforts to colonize and settle Texas, the French supplied the Indians with firearms and gunpowder. Nonetheless, colonization remained a priority on the Spanish colonial agenda. In 1760, after the Seven Years' War, which united France and Spain against Britain, France ceded claims to all lands west of the Mississippi in order not to give them to the victorious British. Overnight, New Spain's territory expanded dramatically. Then, in the American Revolution of 1776, the Spaniards, because of their alliance with France, were able to obtain lands all the way to Florida. Basically all of that territory had few Hispanic settlers, however. In Texas, most of the Hispanic settlers lived in clusters of villages along the lower Rio Grande Valley. By 1749, 8,993 Hispanics and 3,413 Indians lived in what came to be known as Nuevo Santander. Laredo was on the north bank of the river and Meier, Camargo, and Reynosa were on the south bank. Some Anglo settlers came in the last few decades of the eighteenth century; thus, some south Texas Mexicans have English and Scottish names that can be traced to this era.

Also during this same period, colonists were pushing north and establishing ranches in the Nueces River Valley. The Crown encouraged the settlement of this region in order to create a buffer zone against all intruders, such as the Comanche and the French. By 1835, three million head of livestock, cattle, and sheep roamed the region between the Nueces River and the Rio Grande, and about 5,000 persons inhabited the region. The biggest town in the vast Nuevo Santander province, Reynosa, was larger than Philadelphia in 1776. Most border people did not inhabit the towns, however. Instead, they lived on ranches as tight-knit family groups and clans on land granted by the Spanish Crown. Having to withstand the depredations of the Comanche promoted even tighter cohesion and class cooperation than was true

on the larger haciendas farther south to the interior of Mexico.

Arizona was part of the province of Sonora (a vast desert province in Spain's northern territory), but it acquired a distinct geographical name, Pimería Alta, because of the numerous Pima Indians that inhabited southern Arizona and northern Sonora. Its settlement, then, was simply an extension of the colonization of Sonora. The first Europeans in Sonora were Jesuit missionaries who in 1591 introduced a new religion, European crops, and livestock to Yaqui and Mayo in southern Sonora. The natives were more receptive to the latter offerings than to the former, but they were receptive, nonetheless. When the first Hispanic colonists arrived some 50 years later, they found wheat and other European crops abundantly planted by Indians on mission lands.

Pedro de Perea, a miner from Zacatecas, was allowed the first *entrada* (Spanish Crown colonization sanction) into Sonora in 1640 and he arrived with 40 soldiers in 1641. Because of problems with local leaders in Sinaloa and Jesuit missionaries in Sonora, he went to New Mexico, where he recruited 12 families and five Franciscan priests. The local Jesuits objected to the viceroy in Mexico City, and eventually the Franciscans went back, but the families stayed. Then a series of silver discoveries led to more settlement along the Sonoran River valleys by colonists who came directly from Zacatecas, Durango, and Sinaloa.

By the 1680s, most settlers dedicated their efforts to mining, but many others raised crops and livestock to supply the mines. Farmers and miners lived in the same towns, which usually contained a store for goods not available locally. The Hispanics introduced tools, livestock, and crops never before seen in Sonora. These communities became the focus for the Hispanicization of the Indians, and the Mexicans here evolved a unique cultural system known today in Mexico as *sonorense* (sonoran). It is characterized by an intrepid that was shaped by the necessity of learning to survive in the most challenging environment of the Spanish Empire. As a consequence of Europeanization, basically the same food was eaten by the Hispanics and the mission Indians, a food way relationship that existed between natives and Hispanic colonists throughout Mexico. Meat sustenance consisted of mutton, chicken, pork, and beef. The latter was the mainstay of the poorer people. But weddings, baptisms, funerals, and the Christian holidays were occasion for celebrations, and meat other than beef was consumed by everyone on these special days. The missions and the colonists grew corn, wheat, and, to a lesser degree, barley, beans, chile, sweet potatoes, squash, and some fruits, such as figs, peaches, watermelons, cantaloupes, and citrus fruits.

The influence of the Indian culture on the Mexicans, especially the lower classes, most of whom were mestizos, was inordinate, however. The Hispanic colonists had already acquired a tradition of supplementing their diet with wild plants in the interior of New Spain. These included such staples as *quelites* (wild amaranth) and cactus fruits from the *nopales* (prickly pear) and *pitayas* (organ pipe), but in Sonora they added some of the wild plants gathered by the local Indians, such as the fruit of the saguaro cactus, which grows only in the northern part of the desert.

But it was in the struggle to find water that the native knowledge was the most advantageous. Indians could survey the lay of the land and pinpoint water sources a mile or more away by using vegetation as reference points. The Mexicans would then gratefully name their settlements after the water: Agua Prieta (Dark Water), Agua Linda (Pretty Water), Agua Fría (Cold Water), and so forth. There is no other area in the United States where place-names in honor of water are as numerous.

Mining was of course the focal point of life in New

Spain and engaged both Indian and Hispanic labor. Many Indians entered into the Hispanic economy as workers, drawn by material inducement. Thus, acculturation, which occurred whenever there was any kind of contact between the two groups, intensified in the mining towns. Life for the majority of the miners was wretched because of poor working conditions. Pulmonary ailments, shaft cave-ins, and agonizing work-related aches and pains were common. Faced with such an array of ailments and a lack of doctors, Hispanics continued to use Spanish folk-healing traditions and herbal medicine acquired from Indian Mexico before they moved north to Sonora. Inevitably, the Sonoran indigenous traditions, such as the use of jojoba and aloe vera plants enriched the repertoire of healing techniques and increased medicinal options.

Intense dependence on mining made the Sonoran communities very unstable, because when production of the local mine played out, the community dispersed. Also, mercury, which was indispensable to the amalgamation of silver, was a monopoly of the Spanish Crown. In the seventeenth century, prices were hiked up so high that it was impossible to operate the mines profitably. As happened elsewhere

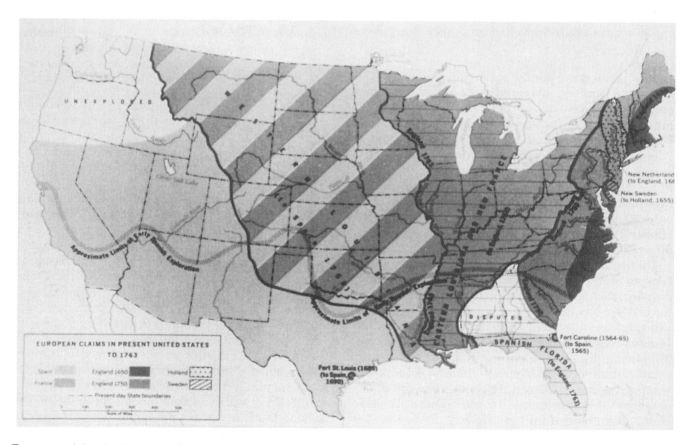

European claims in the United States to 1763.

Presidio and pueblo of Santa Barbara in 1829. (From a lithograph by G. & W. Endicott.)

in New Spain when mining opportunity waned at the end of the century, more and more Mexican settlers engaged in subsistence agriculture rather than mining. But also, as elsewhere in New Spain, the eighteenth-century Bourbon reforms precipitated in Sonora a growing and booming economy. More Hispanics came in from the other provinces of New Spain and from Spain itself. Consequently, the indigenous population declined in proportion. In 1765, only 30 percent of the population was considered Hispanic, while by 1800 that figure had changed to 66 percent.

In the Santa Cruz Valley, Pimas and Tohono O'odom (known as Pápagos by Spaniards) predominated in the northern half near Tucson, and Hispanic settlers occupied the southern part. The missionaries, however, preceded the settlers, pacifying the Indians and making the area safer for colonization. This impetus surged the line of Hispanic settlement even farther north in Sonora to Pimería Alta (northern Sonora and southern Arizona), theretofore the domain of Jesuit missions. In 1691, Father Eusebio Kino, an untiring Jesuit missionary, made the first inroads into Arizona and established a mission in 1700 at San Xavier del Bac, near present-day Tuc-

son, and in 1702 founded another mission some 30 miles south in Tumacácori. In 1706, a presidio was established next to that complex, in Tubac, complementing the mission in much the same way as the haciendas did the reales.

By the 1730s, Hispanic settlers were in what is now the Santa Cruz Valley of the Sonoran Desert, mining silver at Arizonac just south of the present-day border. The name "Arizonac" was Pima for "land of few springs" and is how the state of Arizona derived its name. To deal with disturbances like the uprisings instigated by the Pima in the 1750s or the incursion by the Apache in the 1730s, the Hispanics built presidios and Mexican settlers manned these military garrisons, extending their influence even farther north. Basically, the same pattern of missions and presidio life as in the earlier settlements was established along the Altar and Santa Cruz valley of Pimería Alta in the eighteenth century. Ironically, the farther north Hispanics moved, the more they relied on wheat rather than maize as a staple. This was even true among the Indians. The Tohono O'odom, for example, had taken to making what we know today as "Indian fried bread" and wheat flour tortillas.

Because Jesuit influence in the Spanish Empire had become so pervasive, in 1767 the Bourbons expelled them from the realm, and the Hispanic communities throughout Sonora were forced to undergo significant alterations. After the expulsion, the mission system declined despite the Franciscans' replacing the Jesuit order. Former mission farms were put to livestock raising, and because foodstuffs from the missions were scarce, the Hispanics had to engage in more extended agricultural activity. As a result, Mexican settlements proliferated in the river valleys of the Sonoran Desert. Small villages existed everywhere, and the new arrivals assumed the way of life forged by the earlier settlers. Between the 1790s and 1820s, the Apache threat subsided because of successful military tactics and negotiations on the part of local leaders, and Hispanic settlements began to thrive in Pimería Alta. At one point as many as 1,000 Hispanics lived in the Santa Cruz Valley. But with the independence of Mexico, the Spanish Crown abandoned its fortifications and the Apache lost no time in taking advantage of the opportunity. Overrunning Pimería Alta, they forced Hispanic settlers to the southern part of the desert.

As in Arizona, the establishment of colonies in California was an extension of the Spanish drive into northwestern New Spain. In addition, defense was the utmost consideration in the decision to go farther into the frontier. Like other world powers, the Russians were drawn to the prosperity of eighteenth-century New Spain. They threatened from their outposts in Alaska, compelling the Spaniards to try to halt their southward advance. In 1769, José de Gálvez, an aggressive representative of the Bourbons in New Spain, gave orders to settle Alta California from Baja California, and the same year a tired expedition led by the Franciscan Fray Junípero Serra founded the San Diego mission. A year later another mission was built in Monterey. During this period of flux, Juan Bautista de Anza, the Sonoran-born son of a Spanish official, who himself became an officer, and Pedro de Garcés, a Spanish Franciscan missionary, founded the first overland route to California in 1774.

For the Franciscans, converting numerous California Indians became the main incentive in the drive northward. The first exploration of Juan Bautista de Anza resulted in the reinforcement of a mission along the beautiful Pacific coast in Monterey and the additional building of a presidio. Two years later, de Anza lead another expedition and founded San Francisco, where the presidio is still a landmark.

In a few years, familiar religious and military institutions, the mission and the presidio, dotted the California coastline all the way from San Diego to San Francisco. Soldiers of various racial mixtures, missionaries, and Indians made up the demographic profile of the coast. The soldiers were encouraged to go as settlers and to take their families, as was the tradition in other frontier regions of New Spain. Those who did not have mates found suitable partners among the Indian women, to the chagrin of the missionaries, who considered the mestizo soldiers a bad influence on the Indian communities. As time went by, many of the soldiers became landowners, especially after 1831, when mission property was confiscated by the now independent Mexican government. Some of these former soldiers acquired thousands of acres, laying the foundation for some of the old California families.

✳ ANGLO ENCROACHMENT INTO THE MEXICAN NORTH

While Spain attempted to hold off encroachment into the northern regions of New Spain by other European imperialists, a series of events took place that changed the relationship between the Hispanic and Anglo areas of North America. In 1776, Anglo-Americans declared their independence from En-

Soldier at the Monterey presidio in 1786.

Wife of a presidio soldier in Monterey, 1786.

which greatly weakened the economy and made the new nation vulnerable to outside powers.

The area of greatest weakness was in the far northern frontier. Spain had difficulty in peopling its vast territory in New Spain. This condition made the area vulnerable to outside powers. To augment its forces in the interior of New Spain, which were busy squelching the independence movement that had started on September 16, 1810, with the insurrection of Father Miguel Hidalgo y Costilla, the Spaniards withdrew their troops from the frontier presidios. This further weakened the lines of defense in the north, inviting incursions from the newly independent but aggressive North Americans.

The danger of Yankee encroachment was apparent to the Spaniards much earlier. In 1803, a powerful France under Napoleon Bonaparte acquired from Spain the Louisiana Territory, which she had ceded during the Seven Years' War in the previous century. Napoleon, who was vying for dominance in Europe and needed revenue quickly, sold the vast territory to the United States, and then the borders of the expanding infant nation connected directly with New Spain.

gland, and 34 years later Hispanics proclaimed their independence from Spain. In both areas new nations were formed. The 13 former British colonies came to be known as the United States of America in 1781, and the newly independent people of New Spain named their nation the Republic of Mexico.

Both areas had immense problems as they experimented with new forms of government and attempted to get their economies afloat. Mexico, however, had the most difficult time. Anglo-Americans had a preexisting political structure and economy, which allowed them to make a relatively smoother transition into independent status. While the 13 colonies had been under the colonial tutelage of England, they had enjoyed more freedom than the colonists in the Spanish realms. Spain ruled and controlled the domains with an iron hand and had imposed a rigid economic and social caste system on its colonial subjects, which allowed the Catholic church to have inordinate influence on their everyday lives. As a consequence, the Mexicans were not as well prepared for the democratic ideals to which they aspired in the 1824 constitution. The result was years of confusion and interminable internal strife,

A *patrón* in early California.

Anglo-Americans lost no time in determining what the new acquisition meant for the fledgling country. To the consternation of Spain, President Thomas Jefferson funded the historical expedition of Lewis and Clark in 1804. Spain was obviously worried that the exploration was a prelude to the settlement of the territory by Anglos. Then in 1806, Zebulon Pike, an army officer searching for the headwaters of the Red River in Arkansas, entered Spanish territory in Colorado, built a fort, and raised the colors of the United States. Spanish officials found and destroyed the fortification and arrested Pike and his men. Taken to Santa Fe and then to Chihuahua City farther south, Pike saw more of New Spain than most anybody else who was not a Spanish subject. In the memoirs of his adventure, Pike recognized the potential for trade with Mexico. This peaked the interest of many of his fellow Anglo-Americans.

A series of events in the first half of the nineteenth century demonstrated that Anglo-Americans were anxious to fulfill what they considered their Manifest Destiny—to settle areas beyond their sovereign realm. In 1820, James Long led a revolt, ostensibly as part of the independence movement against the Spanish, but obviously he was acting as a filibusterer for his countrymen. Spain finally entered into deliberations with Moses Austin, a Catholic from Missouri, to settle Anglo-Catholic families in Texas. The rationale for this seemingly paradoxical policy was to people the region between the more populated portions of New Spain and the United States with persons who owed a loyalty to Spain, even if they were not Hispanic. Initially, the Austin colony was made up of 300 families in east Texas who were given generous impresario land grants. The stipulation was that they had to be Catholic, become subjects of the Crown, and abide by Spanish law. Moses died during the process and so the contract was concluded with Stephen, his son. These negotiations were concluded in 1821, right before Mexico acquired its independence under the leadership of Augustine Iturbide, a former Spanish officer who wanted to lead the newly independent nation down the path of monarchy. But Mexico honored the agreements that were established by Spain.

Iturbide was overthrown in 1823 and a more liberal constitutional government was established in 1824. The new constitution called for a president, a congress, 19 states with their own legislatures, and four territories. That same year, Erasmo Seguín, a delegate to the national congress from Texas, persuaded a willing congress to pass a colonization act designed to bring even more Anglo settlers to Texas. Between 1824 and 1830, thousands of Anglo families

General Manuel Mier y Terán, Laredo.

entered east Texas, acquiring hundreds of thousands of free acres and also buying land much cheaper than they could have in the United States. By 1830, Texas had 18,000 Anglo inhabitants and their African slaves, who numbered over 2,000.

Anglo-Americans who had settled in Texas found it difficult to live under Mexican rule from the outset. They had an aversion to the Spanish language and the Mexican laws and legal system (in particular, the nonexistence of juries). In 1824, Texas was joined with Coahuila into a gigantic state, with most of the population residing in the Coahuila portion of the entity. Anglo-Texans rankled at the remoteness of the seat of government in faraway Saltillo in Coahuila, and exacerbating this sentiment was the inability of the Mexican government to provide adequate protection from the marauding Comanche. Anglos also feared the threat to the institution of slavery on which they were so dependent. Indeed, in 1829 the Mexican government abolished slavery during the liberal administration of Vicente Guerrero, the second president under the constitution. The uproar in Texas was so intense that Guerrero decided not to enforce the law. Nonetheless, slaveholders in Texas knew that their days were numbered.

Perhaps the most vexing development for Texans was the Immigration Law of 1830. In 1827, Manuel Mier y Terán, a military officer charged with assessing the general conditions in Texas, concluded that Anglos posed a threat to the sovereignty of Mexico. Then in 1830, a coup d'état by Guerrero's vice president, Anastasio Bustamante, installed a conservative government that was intent on closing off the borders of Mexico to outsiders. The result was the law that forbade any new immigration into Texas, an act that greatly concerned Anglos, who wanted to expand the economy and their culture by emigration from the United States.

All in all, the sentiment for independence from Mexico was on the increase in Texas. In 1832, General Antonio López de Santa Anna ousted Bustamante and was elected president the following year. But he allowed his liberal vice president, Valentín Gómez Farías, to institute some anticlerical reforms against the Catholic church. This provoked powerful Mexican conservatives to act decisively. Somehow, General Santa Anna was persuaded in 1835 to oust his own vice president and to dissolve congress and institute a more closed system than even Bustamante had attempted a few years earlier. One of the first steps taken by Santa Anna under his centralized conservative constitution of *Las Siete Leyes* (The Seven Laws) was to dismantle the state legislatures and dismiss the governors and replace them with military officials. In Texas, Mexican troops were sent to enforce restrictive customs along the Gulf Coast, leading to a skirmish with Anglos, who did not want their trade with the United States disrupted.

To the disgruntled Texans, all seemed lost. The rumblings for independence increased. Late in 1835, Santa Anna sent General Martín Perfecto de Cos to San Antonio to administer the new federal laws, but he was repelled by Anglo-Texans and Mexican Texans who were determined to resist. The Anglos fortified themselves in the mission of El Alamo and awaited the inevitable retribution. Santa Anna decided then to take matters into his own hands and, mustering a large force, descended on San Antonio. Mexican-Texan scouts warned of the impending attack, but Anglo defenders under Colonel Travis did not believe the first messages. When it was obvious that the threat was real, the Anglos prepared for battle. Instead of attacking immediately, the Mexican army laid siege to the fortified mission, which lasted two weeks. The long Kentucky rifles of the defenders had a much longer range than Santa Anna's artillery and muskets and the Texans were able to pick off some of the Mexicans. Travis and his men, who included such legendary heroes as Davey Crockett and Jim Bowie, with their superior weaponry took many Mexican lives in the process. Santa Anna ordered a *degüello* attack, which means taking no prisoners, and all the vastly outnumbered defenders were killed, even after they surrendered.

After the massive defeat at the Alamo, the Texas army, led by General Sam Houston, fled eastward with Santa Anna's troops in hot pursuit. At Goliad, a town east of San Antonio, the Mexicans decisively defeated the Texans, and, as at the Alamo, they took no prisoners. These defeats served to galvanize Texan resistance, and eventually Santa Anna committed a military blunder that led to the defeat of his army and his capture at San Jacinto, located near present-day Houston. The Texans declared their independence and wrested from a reluctant Santa Anna terms of surrender that included Texas' independence. Mexican officials never accepted the agreement reached with Santa Anna, but Texas remained independent, nonetheless, until 1845, when it was annexed to the United States.

The Texas rebellion caused hard feelings between Mexico and the United States, and the rift eventually grew to proportions of war in 1846. In 1836 Mexico had charged the United States with backing the rebels, an allegation denied vehemently by U.S. officials. That the United States immediately recognized the Texas republic was proof enough for the Mexicans, however, and they warned that annexation of Texas by the United States would mean war. Another cause of discord between the two uneasy neighbors was $2 million in damage done to Anglo-American properties in Mexico as a consequence of revolutionary violence in Mexico.

Then in February 1845, the United States voted for the annexation of Texas, and Mexico broke off relations but stopped short of declaring war. Apparently, Mexico at this point was about to recognize Texas' independence and did not want any border problems. Still, the issue that eventually brought the two nations into warfare was the matter of the boundary. When Texans declared their independence in 1836, they claimed the lower Rio Grande as their southern border. The Mexicans insisted that the Nueces River, a few hundred miles to the north, was the border. With the annexation, the United States accepted the Texas version of the boundary dispute.

It was no secret that many Anglo-Americans wanted to fulfill their Manifest Destiny of expanding their country all the way to the Pacific coast. At the very moment of annexation, U.S. officials under President James K. Polk continued trying to buy vast areas of Mexico's northernmost territories, including

Pío Pico (1801–1894) was the last governor of California under Mexican rule.

California. In the fall of 1845, the American president sent John Slidell to Mexico with an offer of $25 million for California, but Mexican officials refused to even see him. General Zachary Taylor was then sent across the Nueces River to set up a blockade of the Rio Grande at its mouth on Port Isabel, and Mexicans retaliated by attacking the U.S. troops on April 25, 1845. Casualties ensued. President Polk immediately went to Congress and obtained a declaration of war against Mexico. There was some opposition, however. Abraham Lincoln, then a congressman from Illinois, and some other colleagues opposed the declaration, but they were in the minority.

Two years of war followed. That it took so long was somewhat surprising, considering Mexico's weak political situation. From the time that Texas was annexed until the war ended in 1847, six different presidents attempted to make foreign policy, quite often at odds with each other. Nonetheless, the Mexican will to resist was underestimated, and it was difficult for an inexperienced U.S. Army to fight on foreign soil. The U.S. invasion took place from four different directions. Troops under General Taylor crossed north across the Rio Grande, while General

Stephen Watts Kearny took an army overland to New Mexico and then to California. There he encountered considerable resistance from the Californios (Mexican Californians) at the Battle of San Pascual before reaching Los Angeles. California was also assaulted by sea by Commodore John C. Fremont. But the most decisive drive was by General Winfield Scott, who bombarded Vera Cruz and then proceeded with the most sizable force all the way to Mexico City, with the Mexicans offering the greatest resistance at Churubusco (part of present-day Mexico City).

Not all Americans supported the war. Newspapers carried reports that General Scott had admitted that his men had committed horrible atrocities. By September, his troops occupied Mexico City. General Santa Anna had been president since December of 1846, but his attempts to fend off the American invasion were hopeless and in November he resigned in disgrace. The Mexicans refused to come to the bargaining table until they were thoroughly routed. Finally, in February 1848, they signed the Treaty of Guadalupe Hidalgo, which brought the war officially to an end.

The treaty provided $15 million for the vast territories of New Mexico, Arizona, and California and parts of Nevada, Utah, and Colorado. The most important provisions of the treaty as far as understanding the history of Mexican Americans had to do with the Mexicans who remained in the territory acquired by the United States. They had a year to retreat into Mexico's shrunken border or they automatically would become citizens of the United States. They would then acquire all the rights of citizens. In addition, the treaty assured southwest Mexicans that their property would be protected and they would have the right to maintain religious and cultural integrity. These provisions, which the Mexican negotiators at the town of Guadalupe Hidalgo had insisted on, seemed protective of the former Mexican citizens, but these stipulations were only as good as the ability and desire to uphold the promises.

✴ MEXICANS UNDER U.S. RULE

The Supreme Court ruled in 1855 that the Treaty of Guadalupe Hidalgo did not apply to Texas, but Mexicans in Texas were supposedly protected under the 1836 constitution of the Republic of Texas, which was modified to become a state constitution in 1845. The territorial acquisition delineated in the Treaty of Guadalupe Hidalgo did not include southern Arizona and southern New Mexico. That region, which included the area from present-day Yuma along the Gila River (25 miles south of Phoenix) all the way to the Mesilla Valley, where Las Cruces, New Mexico, is located, was sold to the United States by General Santa Anna the year that he returned to power in 1853. Ironically, hundreds of Mexicans who in 1848 had moved south into the Mesilla Valley or the Santa Cruz Valley in southern Arizona found themselves in the United States again. The provisions in the Gadsden Treaty regarding Mexicans in the newly annexed territory were similar to those in the Treaty of Guadalupe Hidalgo. Few Mexicans had any faith that any of the provisions protecting Mexicans would be honored, and many were embittered because they felt betrayed by Mexico. But the Mexican government did attempt to attract Mexicans from the southwestern United States into what became the most northernmost Mexican region in the present-day border states. Of the 80,000 or so Mexicans living in the ceded territories, only a few thousand took up the offer.

The promise that the remaining Mexicans would receive all the rights accrued to U.S. citizens did not really materialize. New Mexico, with the largest number of Hispanics, perhaps 60,000, was able to achieve some political self-determination for its citizens. But there and everywhere else in what was now the southwestern United States, the newly minted U.S. citizens were systematically discriminated against. Except in New Mexico, Anglo immigration overwhelmed Mexicans in the newly acquired territories almost from the beginning. In Texas, for example, the population increased from 30,000 in 1836 to 140,000 in 1846. While there was migration from Mexico, this rapid increase in population was mainly due to the influx of Anglos from the United States. Mexicans were outnumbered six to one.

The 1836 Texas constitution stipulated that all residents living in Texas at the time of the rebellion would acquire all the rights of citizens of the new republic, but if they had been disloyal, these rights were forfeited. Numerically superior Anglos, embittered with Mexicans during the rebellion, retaliated by mistreating or forcing Mexicans off their property. Many Mexicans simply crossed the border and went to Mexico. In 1857, Anglo businessmen attempted to run off Mexican teamsters, who had dominated the transport of goods in south Texas since the colonial period, by hiring thugs to strong-arm the carters off the trails. The attempt was not wholly successful, but it demonstrated the increasing antipathy toward Mexicans and a continuing violation of the guarantees offered by the Treaty of Guadalupe Hidalgo.

When Texas joined the union in 1845, only one Mexican Texan was a delegate to the convention that framed the new state constitution. And in the convention itself, there were many who felt that Mexicans should not be allowed to vote. But in the end, they were not denied suffrage. Despite this victory, Mexican Texans were intimidated into not voting, and the result was that few politicians were Mexicans. During the era of the republic, 1836–1845, only a few rich Mexicans living in the San Antonio area acquired political power. Juan Seguín, for example, became mayor of the city only to be forced out after Anglos arrived in larger numbers. After Texas became a state, even fewer Mexicans participated in politics. In 1850, of the 64 members in the state legislature, none were born in Texas or Mexico. Whenever Mexicans did vote, their power was diminished because they were dominated by political bosses who were able to buy in mass the votes of Mexicans. In addition, there were white-only primaries from which Mexicans were barred, and since the Democratic Party dominated in Texas, the elections were really decided in these primaries. Poll taxes, that is, taxes levied for voting, also served to deter from voting those with few economic resources; this included most Mexicans.

In California, while Mexican and Anglos did not have the same legacy of conflict that characterized racial relations in Texas, many of the newcomers were from the U.S. South, where prejudice against racial minorities was the rule. Political participation of Californios was also minimal in the state, although in the beginning their integration was more evident than in Texas. For example, out of 48 delegates, eight Mexican Californians were selected to participate in the state constitutional convention of 1849 when California joined the Union.

The constitutional convention was the last major political event in which Mexicans participated. The gold rush of 1849 attracted thousands of Anglos, which resulted in an even more imbalanced ratio of Mexicans to Anglos. In 1850, Mexicans were 15 percent of the population, but 20 years later that figure dropped to only 4 percent. Political and economic influence declined first in the north, the area that attracted the majority of Anglos, because of the gold fields. The lack of political influence led to legislation contrary to Californio interests. For example, in 1851 the six southern counties where most Mexicans resided were taxed five times the rate of other local entities. In 1855, so-called greaser laws were passed that prohibited bear-baiting, bullfights and cockfights, clearly aimed at prohibiting the customs of the Californios. Vagrancy laws were passed, also aimed at Mexicans, because when a community wanted to force Mexicans out, these laws were applied selectively. One of the most onerous laws was the Foreign Miners tax of 1850, which levied a charge for anyone who was not a U.S. citizen. While some miners were French, Australian, or Irish, most "foreigners" were Mexicans or South Americans, who possessed superior mining skills. There can be no doubt that the tax was designed to eliminate this competition from the gold diggings.

In New Mexico, Mexicans participated more fully in both the economy and in politics than in any other region. A major reason for this was that Hispanic New Mexicans remained a numerical majority until the turn of the century. Anglos came to quickly dominate the southeastern part of the state, but New Mexican Hispanics maintained control in the north around Santa Fe and Albuquerque. From 1850 to 1911, Hispanics dominated most key political slots and controlled the territorial legislature until the 1890s. Ironically, one reason it took so long for the New Mexican territory to become a state was a reluctance among Anglo politicians in Washington, D.C., to allow a new state dominated by Mexicans.

In Arizona, which was part of the New Mexican territory until 1863, Mexicans maintained some political power in the area that was purchased under the Gadsden Treaty in 1853. This was especially true in and around Tucson, which became the territorial capital after Arizona separated from New Mexico. Political and economic cooperation was more evident between Anglos and Mexicans in this area because economic activity depended greatly on trade through the state of Sonora. With the coming of the railroads in the 1880s, however, the relationship between both groups became more strained as a new influx of Anglos who did not need to cooperate with Mexicans overwhelmed the older Anglo population. Politically, this demographic shift translated into lack of political power. The territorial seat was removed to Prescott, away from Mexicans, and eventually to Phoenix when Arizona became a state. Mexicans in southern Arizona retained a modicum of political power, and the few Hispanic legislators in Arizona until the 1950s all came from that section.

Lack of protection for Mexicans in the Southwest was most obvious in the violation of property rights. While the Treaty of Guadalupe Hidalgo was vague regarding property, it did constitute the most definite commitment in the document. As more Anglos entered the Southwest and the area became more economically developed, land values rose and the thirst for land became more apparent. The system of keeping records of property claims differed between Mexico and the United States. As a consequence, proof of title became an immediate burden for Mexicans throughout the newly acquired territories.

To address the issue of property ownership, Congress passed the California Land Act of 1851 to facilitate legalization of land belonging to Californios prior to the takeover. Instead of helping the Californios resolve their property problems quickly, however, official procedures sometimes took years, forcing the ranchers to turn over huge tracts of land to the very lawyers who were adjudicating their cases. Then in 1862, the Homestead Act was passed in Congress, allowing squatters in the West to settle and claim vacant lands. In California, thousands converged on lands claimed by Mexicans, creating legal entanglements that were many times settled in favor of the squatters. Many of the homesteaders were front men for speculators who took these free lands and held them for future use or sale.

In the New Mexico territory, an even slower system, the surveyor of general claims office, was established in 1854. It took that office 50 years to settle just a few claims, and in the meantime many Mexicans in New Mexico were also defrauded of their land in grabs similar to those in California. During the 1890s, for example, as the Santa Fe Railroad was built from Kansas through the northern part of the territory, land speculators known as the Santa Fe Ring concocted ruses that divested hundreds of Hispanic landowners of their farms and ranches. In response, the Mexicans organized into Las Gorras Blancas (The White Caps), bands of hooded night riders who tore down fences and tried to derail trains in the hope of intimidating Anglo land developers and railroad companies into abandoning New Mexico. Then, the establishment of state parks during the early twentieth century contributed to even further erosion of Mexican landholdings in New Mexico.

All in all, New Mexicans did not suffer the same degree of land usurpation as in other parts of the Southwest, but the acreage held by Hispanics prior to the Mexican-American War declined considerably. In the final analysis, while the Treaty of Guadalupe Hidalgo did not precisely define the rights of Mexicans, it is clear that most of the guarantees were not upheld and Mexicans in the Southwest declined considerably, economically and politically, during their experience with Anglo domination. But by the 1890s, considerable immigration from Mexico resulted in the swelling of Mexican communities throughout the Southwest, changing the character of Mexican life in the United States.

✳ AFRICA AND THE MAKING OF SOCIETY IN CUBA AND PUERTO RICO

While New Spain evolved a society made up primarily of an Indian-Spanish race mixture, Africans and Europeans commingled with the few Indian survivors to form the Spanish Caribbean community. Sugarcane transformed the Caribbean region into a lucrative source of wealth for the Spaniards. But because the natives were too few, another adequate source of labor was found in Africa. The slave trade had been started by the Portuguese in the fifteenth century, but it did not become profitable until the great plantation system developed in such American regions as Brazil, the British colonies in North America, and, of course, the Caribbean islands.

The source of slaves in Africa was the western coast between the Senegal River to the north and Angola to the south. They were captured and sold to European traders, usually Portuguese, by slave hunters who many times were also Africans. Varying forms of slavery already existed among these ethnic groups where workers toiled in large-scale agricultural systems. Slaves were sought in this area, rather than in other African areas, because the people there already had some experience with systematic work demands.

The slaving expeditions in West Africa brought untold anguish to the black Africans who were affected by the raids. Families were broken up as the young males (the most sought after) were torn from their roots. That was only the beginning of the suffering, however. In preparation for the odious voyage, captured Africans were first housed in overcrowded slave castles called *barranconas,* where thousands perished. In the trip across the Atlantic, thousands more died in the crowded hulls of the slave ships making their way either to the Caribbean islands or Brazil, where these human beings were auctioned off and sold like cattle in huge markets.

In the Caribbean islands, this human chattel was sent to work the hundreds of plantations developed by colonists from the major European imperial powers. Not all slaves wound up on the plantation fields, however, as they were also sold to artisans as helpers or to the huge households of rich merchants within the plantations themselves. Although males were preferred as slaves, hundreds of thousands of females also entered the market. Women worked just as hard, and it was not lost on slave owners that by coupling slaves of the opposite sex, even by promoting a family structure based on the new conditions encountered in the Caribbean, they could ensure that the offspring of the slaves would be born into slavery. This perpetuated a valuable commodity within their own domain.

Many black slaves found their way to Mexico, especially to the coastal areas of Vera Cruz and Guerrero, where they were concentrated around the port of Acapulco. Their labor was required for sugar plantations as well, although these enterprises were not as extensive as in the Caribbean. Slavery in Mexico was abolished in 1829 by the new republican government that emerged after independence. In Cuba and Puerto Rico, under Spanish rule until the end of the nineteenth century, slavery was legal until late into the nineteenth century. But the growth of slavery everywhere in the Caribbean New World was intimately linked to the fortunes of sugarcane production. However, a large-scale sugar plantation system did not emerge in either Cuba or Puerto Rico until the end of the eighteenth century. Up to that point, independent peasant farmers, squatters that relied little on African slaves, and peons on large haciendas predominated. The development of slavery was slow as a consequence. Between 1550 and 1650, the slave population only increased from 1,000 to 5,000. Nonetheless, in Cuba before the nineteenth century, free Africans were more proportionally numerous than anywhere else in the Western Hemisphere, because the sugar economy was never as ensconced there as in other colonies, such as those of the British. These freedmen engaged in all kinds of trades and activities, creating a class of African-Cubans that enjoyed a status of independence not as attainable to blacks in the British colonies. The ramifications of this more relaxed relationship, at least as it existed before the nineteenth century, is crucial to the persistence of African culture in Cuba.

But that does not mean that life was in any way promising for slaves. Whenever they could, *cimarrones* (runaway slaves) ran away to Orient province, creating scores of fortified communities called *palenques*. Indicative of the discontent of the Africans in Cuba was the persistence of the feared slave rebellions. For example, 300 rebelled on one plantation in 1727, killing practically all of the whites, and one year later all the copper mines were closed off in Santiago because of uprisings in that province.

In the late eighteenth century, the African population began to rise rapidly. Following 30 years of warfare between the European imperial powers, the British occupied Cuba in 1763, ushering in an intensive period of economic development; thus, sugarcane production expanded dramatically. From the time the first African slave stepped foot on Cuba to 1770, 60,000 were introduced to the island. Then between 1770 and 1790 there was a striking increase in slave traffic. At least 50,000 Africans arrived in those years alone. At the end of the century, a unique opportunity arose for investors in Cuban sugar production—the collapse of the Haitian sugar industry after rebels had ravaged that country in the 1790s—leading to an even larger number of slaves on the island. During this time, 30,000 French émigrés and their slaves entered Cuba from Santo Domingo during a time of rising prosperity in sugar and coffee.

The slave population continued to grow into the early nineteenth century, and by 1827, African slaves accounted for about 40 percent of the Cuban population, which was over 700,000. By mid-century, the percentage of African-born slaves expanded to about 70 percent of the slave population and, for the first time, blacks outnumbered whites. In the 1850s, the combination of free Afro-Cubans and slaves made the black population over 56 percent. According to one study, 550,000 slaves were imported into Cuba between 1812 and 1865 despite the worldwide ban on the slave trade that was instituted by the British in the 1820s.

A remarkable expansion in Cuban sugar production accounted for the growth of slave traffic in the nineteenth century. While many slaves toiled on coffee *fincas* or haciendas or tobacco *vegas*, most worked on sugar. The percentage of blacks, which throughout the colonial period had been among the smallest in the Caribbean, was now larger than anywhere else. Quite predictably, during the nineteenth century, slave rebellions became more common. In these, whites were often killed, and retribution was quick and brutal. Suppression of the uprisings was often consummated by the indiscriminate execution of slaves, regardless of their involvement. Rebellions increased because of the larger number of newly arrived slaves from Africa with immediate memories of their lost freedom; they were resentful and less accepting of their lot.

Independence sentiment was retarded in Cuba because of this reliance on slavery by whites. Lacking was the diversity of dissatisfied classes that characterized other colonies in New Spain whose independence struggles started early in the nineteenth century. Island society reflected the dichotomy of the black and white races more than ever. The Haitian example, where the independence movement was unleashed by the pent-up emotions of slaves, struck a familiar chord of fear among the white planter class.

But the world was changing as industrialization and technological innovation required new markets and the use of more diverse amounts of raw materials. Cuba could not remain out of step for long in its use of outmoded methods in the production of sugar. In the second half of the nineteenth century, some Cuban and Spanish capitalists realized that Cuba's success in the impending order required diversified production and the use of wage labor that was cheaper and more efficient than slavery. As a consequence, the sugar industry was modernized, made more competitive, and expanded. Foreign capital from the United States was largely responsible for

the innovations, and the colonial economy passed increasingly into the hands of North Americans.

To meet the wage-labor demands, 125,000 Chinese were brought to Cuba between 1840 and 1870 to work as cane cutters, to build railroads in rural areas, and to serve as domestics in the cities. Also, the influx of European immigrants, primarily from Spain, increased during that period. Newly arrived Spaniards became concentrated in the retail trades and operated small general stores called *bodegas*. In the 1880s, slavery was abolished by Spain in a gradual program that took eight years. The influx of new people in this period made Cuba more heterogeneous, leading to the social diversity that is so apparent today. Immigration to the United States before the revolution of 1959 was more reflective of this racial variety. But as Cubans fled communism in recent years, the outflow came more from the descendants of European emigrants.

In Puerto Rico, although African slaves were brought over almost immediately after the settlement of the island by Spaniards, they never quite acquired the numerical importance that they had in Cuba. In fact, the proportion of slaves in Puerto Rico never exceeded 14 percent. In 1775, for example, out of a total Puerto Rican population of 70,250, only 6,467 were slaves. As a result, 100 years later when slavery was abolished, the transition to wage labor was easier than in Cuba.

In the nineteenth century the slave traffic did increase, but it was not as important in establishing a rural culture as was the case in Cuba. In many regions of Puerto Rico, a large class of rural poor whites and persons with a mixed European, African, and Indian heritage dominated. Their way of life was strictly preindustrial. Country folk eked out a living as peasants, tenants on subsistence farms, or craftsmen in the towns and villages. This group came to be known as *jíbaros* (a South American word for "highlander" or "rustic") and remain to this day an identifiable group in both Puerto Rico and on the U.S. mainland.

As happened in Cuba in the first half of the 1800s, the importation of slaves increased because of an expansion in sugar plantations. At the same time, however, foreign investment and immigration grew, and the mixed classes who comprised the rural peasants and working people were marginalized by an empowered planter class and a large-scale export agricultural system. But the influx of slaves during the nineteenth century was larger than ever and African culture achieved a greater voice at the folk level, albeit mixing with a still strong jíbaro expression.

In Puerto Rico there has not been an upheaval

such as the Mexican Revolution of 1910 or the Cuban Revolution of 1959 that would have provoked large-scale immigration of the middle and upper classes to the United States. As a consequence, the character of Puerto Rican society in the United States is more reflective of Puerto Rico's diversity. Unlike the case of Cubans in Florida, in New York and other cities where Puerto Ricans have gone in large numbers, the fine blend of jíbaro/ mestizo, African, and European cultures is evenly dispersed. In Mexican American society, on the other hand, the impact of the upper classes has been greatly mitigated by their wholesale return to Mexico after the revolution in the 1920s and during the Great Depression. Moreover, since the 1940s, the amplified immigrant stream that continues to arrive to this day is largely working class.

Regardless of the makeup of the Hispanic society in the United States, there is no doubt that African culture brought from both the Spanish Caribbean islands and Mexico has greatly influenced American culture. This phenomenon is especially evident in music. The so-called tropical sound that permeates all of this region with such colorful appellations as *salsa, merengue, mambo, rhumba,* and *jarocho,* has deep roots in the percussion-rich expression of Africa. To see this, all one has to do is observe a (band) playing a variation of this music. The percussion requirements alone mean that individual players are needed for congas, bongos, timbales, and maracas. The religions of Africa have also greatly influenced, in a syncretic fashion, the Catholicism brought over from Spain, producing an array of observances known popularly as *santerismo.* And, of course, the food owes much to Africa, as does the Spanish language.

The most evident African vestige, however, is genetic. Everywhere in the Caribbean and Mexico where slavery was prominent, the Negro features of Africa are evident. A racial consciousness in Hispanic culture is also part of this heritage and has manifested itself in racism and self-hate. Fortunately, in recent years the Caribbean and Mexican people of African descent have undergone a cathartic effort to combat the debilitating effects of racism coming from their own Hispanic compatriots.

✳ INDEPENDENCE OF CUBA AND PUERTO RICO

As is the case with Mexico, independence from Spain and the eventual subordination of the island economies to U.S. interests provide the foundation for understanding migration from Cuba and Puerto Rico. Along with the Philippines, Cuba and Puerto Rico remained the only major Spanish colonies that did not secede during the massive struggles that wracked the entire Spanish Empire in the early nineteenth century. In the second half of the century, both these Caribbean holdings experienced conspiracies and rebellions, although efforts to finally obtain independence were not successful until 1898. In Cuba, a nationalist movement was vitalized in the latter part of the century as Spain's treatment of the colony became increasingly arbitrary. A crosscut of the Cuban classes became more and more resentful as the inept and corrupt colonial government imposed heavier taxes and, through censorship, restricted their freedom.

But much of the sentiment for liberty came from the sizable class of middle-class farmers and merchants who opposed slavery and desired to be free of the Spanish colonial tie. On the first issue, Madrid waffled, and although total freedom was eventually granted to the slaves, it came very slowly. In October 1868, a group of Cuban rebels led by Carlos Manuel de Céspedes, a black general, took advantage of revolutionary fomentation in Spain itself and declared independence at Yara in the eastern portion of the island. This region had few slaves and was a hotbed of emancipation activity.

A provincial government headed by de Céspedes was established in Orient province, where Yara is located, and from there the movement obtained widespread support. A bloody war known as the Ten Years' War, ensued, in which Spanish attempts to evict the rebels from the eastern half of Cuba were unsuccessful. Guerrilla tactics used by the rebels stymied the efforts of Spanish troops, but neither side could really win a clear victory. The war came to an end when both rebels and Spaniards signed the Pact of El Zajón in 1878. The document promised amnesty for the insurgents and home rule; it also provided freedom for the slaves that fought on the side of the rebels.

Eventually, slavery was abolished, but Spain's failure to provide political reform provoked the Cubans to reconsider independence. In 1895, the poet and patriot José Martí opened the final battle for independence. Much of the planning for this insurrection was done in New York, where Martí had obtained Yankee support. But looming darkly behind the whole liberation cause were North American economic and political interests. Because of its proximity, Cuba had strategic value for the United States, but as long as it was under Spain, many Americans thought that it would not fall into the wrong hands. Before the Civil War, Southerners wanted to annex Cuba in order to expand the territory under slavery, but antislavery interests in the

(Confederate officers from Laredo, Texas: Refugio Benavides, Atanacio Vidaurri, Cristóbal Benavides, and John Z. Leyendecker.)

United States thwarted any such plans. In the nineteenth century, Americans tried to buy the island from Spain on several occasions. In 1869, taking advantage of the chaos of the Ten Years War, the United States offered $100 million for the island but was rejected. So it was not surprising, when independence seemed more likely at the end of the nineteenth century, that U.S. officials pressed to influence the unfolding process.

The trajectory toward independence in Puerto Rico was not as conspicuous as in Cuba, but a strong sentiment for freedom emerged, nonetheless. Puerto Rican nationalism was influenced by the same conditions that provoked the feeling in Cuba. While the planter classes expressed a wish for political autonomy from the mother country, they also wanted to maintain an economy based on slavery and peonage. Equivocal and confused about their desires, the criollo elites vacillated and were reluctant to assume the lead toward acquiring independence.

The nationalist movement was directed more by activists from the urban middle class and small farmers. This was especially true after 1850, when the Madrid government assumed a more mercantilistic stance. But despite high-tariff barriers that were designed to force Puerto Ricans to pay more for American-made goods, so that Spanish merchandise would be cheaper, Spain's hold over the Spanish Caribbean steadily declined as it lost control over the sugar trade to the Americans. By 1870, 68 percent of Puerto Rican sugar products were marketed in the United States and only 1 percent were sent to Spain. Exerting its imperial power, Madrid, by the time of independence, managed to regain 35 percent of the market and continued to provide the Caribbean colonies with some finished products. Still, U.S. merchants were buying 61 percent of all Puerto Rican

exports, while providing the lion's share of all industrial machinery necessary for processing sugar cane. Eventually, it became evident to the Puerto Ricans, as it did to the Cubans, that the link to the mother country was both intrusive and unnecessary.

The earliest indication of a strong united Puerto Rican nationalism goes back to 1867. On April 27, a mutiny among Spanish troops stationed on the island provoked the colonial governor, who was uneasy over the possibility of freedom movements, to not only execute the mutineers but also round up and exile known sympathizers of independence. Among these was Ramón Emeterio Betances, who fled to New York, where he joined other like-minded Puerto Ricans and Cubans. On September 23, 1868, this group declared an abortive insurrection known as El Grito de Lares. Members of the *criollo* middle class and free Afro-Cubans who lived in the coffee-growing region of Lares were the main supporters of the effort. The poorly planned attempt was doomed from the outset, and Spain easily defeated the insurrectionists.

But the movement did not die with the failure of the Lares revolt. As in Cuba, Puerto Ricans re-

Albizu Campos, leader of the Puerto Rican independence movement, at a press conference on December 16, 1947.

Luis Muños-Rivera, patriot of Puerto Rican independence.

mained dissatisfied with the mother country's feeble attempts to redress their accumulating grievances. Later in the century, such patriots as the intellectual José Julián Acosta and the young and untiring newspaper editor Luis Muñoz-Rivera were responsible for forcing major concessions from Spain. A covenant was signed in 1897 that granted to both Cuba and Puerto Rico autonomy and home rule.

But much of the movement for complete independence was already set in motion, and these gestures from Spain were too little, too late. Increasingly, a vital core of Puerto Rican conspirators joined their Cuban co-colonialists in a movement for freedom. But every leap toward freedom from Spain threw the revolutionaries into the American sphere of influence. When José Martí initiated the final battles for independence in 1895 in Cuba, much of his preparation was done in the United States. Martí had started his proindependence party, the Cuban Revolutionary party (PRC) in Tampa, Florida. Many of the patriots, such as Tomás Estrada Palma, the first president of independent Cuba, acquired U.S. citizenship while in exile and then returned to the island to join the insurgency. Tragically, the valiant efforts of these patriots involved them with the

United States to such a degree that the final price was costly. In the end, Cuba and Puerto Rico traded one master for another.

Spain's retaliation to Cuban and Puerto Rican rebellion was characteristically harsh. José Martí, who had planned the Cuban insurrection, was killed four months after the struggle began. One year after the insurrection started, Madrid sent General Valeriano Weyler, a hardened veteran who launched the brutal "war with war" campaign to wipe out the rebel movement. In a highly successful campaign, Cuban propagandists in the United States worked hand in hand with the English-language press to evoke sympathy for the Cuban cause against Spain. General Weyler was then pulled out of Cuba to quell the intensity of world public opinion, which had turned against Spain, especially among Americans.

But American support quickly turned into outright confiscation of the Cuban and Puerto Rican rebel cause. When the American battleship the USS *Maine* blew up mysteriously in Havana Harbor in April 1898, "yellow press" newspapers in the United States clamored for war against Spain. President William McKinley, reflecting an American longing for a maritime empire, seized the opportunity and declared war against Spain on April 28. Five months later, Spain capitulated and signed the Treaty of Paris, transferring Cuba, Puerto Rico, and the Philippines to the United States. President McKinley quickly achieved the overseas realm that he wanted.

Cuba, unlike Puerto Rico, was allowed to become independent and promulgate a constitution, but hopes for true Cuban sovereignty were quickly dashed when Cuban politicians were pressured into including the Platt Amendment in their founding document. The provision allowed the United States to intervene militarily in Cuban affairs. The two neighboring Caribbean islands had much in common but had evolved separate cultural and ethnic identities. Overnight, both began an intimate, albeit antagonistic, relationship with the United States. Out of such closeness, migration to the mainland ensued.

❊ EARLY MEXICAN IMMIGRATION TO THE UNITED STATES

Mexican immigration to the United States can roughly be placed in three categories. The first is migrants who were left outside the borders of a shrinking Mexico after 1836, 1848, and 1853 and the natives who, although not really migrants, were considered foreigners in their native land. The second category consists of migrants who continued entering and leaving the U.S. Southwest in a preestablished pattern that preceded the takeover. The third and most important group, in terms of the bigger picture of immigration, are Mexicans who arrived in response to the dramatically expanding need for laborers after the 1880s.

Three significant events occurred in Anglo-Mexican relations that set the stage for this immigration pattern. The Texas Rebellion (1836), the Mexican War (1848), and the Gadsden Purchase (1853) severed immense territorial lands from Mexico and the 80,000 or so Mexicans that were living on them. These Spanish-speaking settlers were dispersed in sparsely settled areas throughout the lost territories. In less than 40 years, they had been subjects of Spain and citizens of Mexico and were now entering a new phase. The inhabitants were descendants of the Spanish Mexican settlers who had migrated from the interior of Mexico and in many areas had pushed aside or conquered the indigenous groups that occupied the land before them.

Now they found themselves conquered and colonized, separated from their political and cultural roots by an invisible and, for a time, unpatrolled boundary line. Initially, they resisted the North American invasion and occupation as best they could. Some chose to retreat within the shrunken borders of Mexico rather than remain under U.S. domination. Many of the Spanish-speaking inhabitants living in the conquered territories had been born on the southern side of what was now the border, in villages like Camargo in Tamaulipas, Ojinaga in Chihuahua, or Tubutama in Sonora. Their present circumstances, brought on by the drama of war and conquest, had originally been dictated by a less dramatic decision to move north within what they considered their home areas. Moving from Tubutama to Tubac, Arizona, for example, was a matter of some 60 miles. The migrant might have had property interests and family kinships in Tubac, so close were relationships between the Altar Valley in northern Sonora and the Santa Cruz Valley of southern Arizona.

To a lesser degree, Mexican areas in northern New Mexico and California shared similar characteristics with the Mexican territories that the new boundary lines now designated as the northernmost outpost. Still, a century of relatively close economic and social relationships between Chihuahua and New Mexico, for example, dictated that the two provinces evolve along similar lines. Until Yankee traders penetrated Santa Fe in the late eighteenth century, Chihuahua was the only link that New Mexican settlements had to civilization, probably being the only source of cultural progression within the realm of larger Spanish society.

In California, a society also evolved that was sepa-rated from the areas that make up the present border regions. A fanciful myth regarding the pure Spanish origins of these Californios and their link to Spain has been perpetuated by romantic writers and Hollywood lore. In reality, the closest ties this society had to Spain were Acapulco, San Blas, and Guaymas, the main sources of supply and trade for this region until Yankee traders rounded the Strait of Magellan in their ships. Like the other frontier outposts, California was sparsely settled and devoid of the comforts and cultural attributes found in such colonial centers as Guanajuato and San Luis Potosí. Moreover, California was populated by colonists whose earlier roots were established in Sonora, and for a long time California was considered an appendage of this northern province.

When the United States took over Mexico's northern territories, it acquired a Mexican population that was for all intents and purposes a continuation of Mexico's frontier north. The inhabitants during the Mexican period had migrated freely back and forth across what was later to become a border. Movement made by parents, grandparents, brothers, uncles, and kin of all types meant that an extensive network of family ties existed in the region that was now politically divided. In southern Arizona, for example, thousands of Mexicans had abandoned their lands for Sonora during the independence period in the early nineteenth century, mostly because of a menacing increase in Indian depredations.

Despite the changed political status, migration within the border region continued during the early occupation period, and immigrants were, for the most part, oblivious to the geopolitical distinctions that national governments made so carefully. Various factors stimulated this migration. In some cases economic inducements, such as the discovery of gold in California, provoked a massive outpouring of miners from Sonora and other parts of Mexico. They arrived before the influx of the Anglo forty-niners, and mining techniques introduced by these northern Mexican miners prevailed in the numerous mining centers of California during the heyday of the gold rush. After 1836, thousands of peons fled the large haciendas of northeast Mexico, seeking their freedom in south Texas; the border was much closer now.

In general, before 1870 there were only minimal economic inducements to Mexican immigration to the United States. Anglos who came after 1836 and 1848 interacted within the native Mexican economy through raising stock and some mining. Markets for southwestern products did expand during the early years of the Anglo takeover, as population growth throughout the territories demanded more foodstuffs. Mexicans in Texas, New Mexico, and California, however, had been trading with American interests in the East before the Texas rebellion and the Mexican border campaign. With the changeover to American rule, trade patterns were little changed, except that markets in the East for cattle hides, tallow, wool, and other stock-raising products widened and diversified. Furthermore, in New Mexico and Arizona a flourishing trade developed as the U.S. Army increased its efforts to subdue and destroy the nomadic Indian tribes. Provisions for troops and Indian reservations were channeled through private merchant houses in Santa Fe, Albuquerque, and Tucson.

Trade with Mexico, which before the nineteenth century had been the main source of external activity in all of the Southwest, continued after 1848, and many Mexicans entered the Southwest as transport workers or to act as agents for merchant houses in Monterrey. During the American Civil War, when southern ports were blocked off by the Union Navy, cotton was transported through Texas to such Mexican ports as Tampico in order to ship the product to European markets. Moreover, Arizona ports of entry to Mexico served California exporters and importers as a gateway to the Mexican ports of Guaymas and Mazatlan for shipping to the United States east around the Cape of Good Hope and over the Isthmus of Panama.

Initially, the labor needs of this slowly expanding economy were met by the resident population. Some immigration from Mexico, Europe, and the eastern United States provided the rest. Except for some cotton in Texas and gold and silver mining in other southwestern areas, there was little requirement for intensive labor use. After 1880, because of the railroad, dramatic changes in the southwestern economy stimulated Mexican immigration tremendously. During the two decades before 1900, 127,000 Mexicans entered the United States from Mexico, one and one-third times as many as the native Mexican population in 1848. Radical economic transformations that occurred not only in the Southwest but in Mexico as well dictated this later trend. By 1900, a railroad network integrated Texas, New Mexico, Arizona, and California with northern Mexico and parts of central and southern Mexico. The economic impact of the railroads soon drew Mexicans into the United States in a movement that dwarfed the influx of previous years. After the 1880s, then, the strong ties that previous *norteño* (northern) immigrants had to the Southwest and its native peoples diminished as railroads induced the migration of Mexicans whose roots were farther and farther from the border.

In northern Mexico, similar railroad building took place during the same years. The new railroads were financed by American interests, and, as in the American Southwest, the northern Mexican economy became linked to the crucial markets of the U.S. industrial basin in the Midwest and the Northeast. In northern Mexico, an economic transformation resulted, and adjacent areas along both sides of the U.S.-Mexican border supported similar agriculture and mining interests that depended completely on the same railroad network to market their products.

The Southwest was still sparsely populated during this period of rapid economic growth. Thousands of Anglos and Europeans had come in before the railroad era, and even more came after trains revolutionized transportation. Initially, many were induced by the discovery of gold and silver, but more consistently they came as farmers, small-scale merchants, and clerks and to work in other middle-sector positions. Many of them were squatters who slowly drew away the lands of the old Mexican elites. But a great many were middle-class entrepreneurs and agents of eastern companies who, during the railroad era, forcibly acquired millions of acres that had once belonged to wealthy Mexicans. It was these entrepreneurs who were responsible for the huge agribusiness and mining development in the Southwest. In the process it was discovered that the resident Mexican population was not sufficient to meet the growing labor needs. The poorer classes of Anglos did not compete with Mexicans because of the low wages offered in agriculture or because of the menial type of labor involved. Besides, many of the poorer Anglos were involved in their own endeavors on small farms and ranches.

In California, Chinese labor continued to be used after the building of the transcontinental railways from northern California during the 1860s and the development of southern California after the 1870s. In the 1880s, the first Chinese exclusion acts were passed by Congress in response to nativist pressures, but surreptitious entry continued into the twentieth century. In other parts of the Southwest, a dependence on Mexican labor remained the only alternative. Since railroad building in most of Mexico had resulted from the same thrust that built the lines in the Southwest, workers from Mexico were used in the construction, and the same reserves were utilized within both political zones. European laborers were also used in the West, but only a small number filtered southwest of industrialized cities like Chicago and Kansas City.

In Mexico, railroad building in the 1880s tapped labor resources according to a geographic pattern. American companies built extensions of the southwest network south from Nogales, El Paso, and Laredo. The southward penetration of these lines provided access to the United States from the interior of the northern states, and the movement back and forth was no longer restricted to the immediate border area. But as railroads spurred other areas of the economy, the competition for Mexican labor became greater, and populations in the Southwest and northern Mexico did not suffice. Late in the 1880s, railway construction reached into the more populated but landlocked areas of Mexico, south of Zacatecas. Now, many of the men from such states as Aguascalientes, Guanajuato, San Luis Potosí, Jalisco, and Michoacán served as seasonal laborers in construction and maintenance of way.

Population pressures in central Mexico were creating a clear surplus of workers by this time. Seasonal workers on large haciendas and small farmers whose inherited plot was too small to support a family were attracted to the railroads nearby, leaving home during the growing seasons and returning for planting and harvesting. Eventually these agricultural workers from central Mexico were induced, with the aid of the government of President Porfirio Díaz, to travel farther north to the sparsely populated regions of Chihuahua and other northern areas where labor was scarce. Becoming accustomed to a money economy, many severed their attachment to agricultural pursuits. Although they maintained their ties to their farms, villages, and haciendas, by the end of the nineteenth century many west-central Mexicans were depending almost exclusively on work in northern Mexico and the U.S. Southwest. By the early 1900s, railroads had penetrated deep into the very populous Bajío and west to the region surrounding Lake Chapala (west-central Mexico), reaching many small towns and ensuring that Mexican labor to the north was plentiful.

Mexican immigrants living in the United States could, in many ways, identify with the Southwest, which at the turn of the century was still very Mexican. Nevertheless, the Mexican was an immigrant in every sense of the word. Unable to speak or understand English, the dominant language, they were subject to immigration laws and regulations and forced to adapt to a foreign pattern of racism and discrimination. The native Mexican American, while faced with similar problems, was able after lengthy exposure to the gringo to make the adaptations necessary for survival and to participate more within the system. In New Mexico, for example, which contained the largest native population of Mexicans after the 1848 takeover, many of the old elites made the transition into the new economic and political structure, which was increasingly dominated by Anglos. In essence, the native was more equipped for survival than the immigrant.

Among the immigrants themselves, adaptation and the difficulty of life in the United States varied. Much depended on their economic conditions when crossing the border, the ability to transport families, the type of labor they performed, the distance between origins in Mexico and ultimate destination in the United States, and the type of community they lived in once in the United States. Before the Mexican Revolution of 1910, because practically all immigrants came from the lower classes, poverty was an endemic problem. The only commodity that such immigrants could trade was their labor.

Proximity to their homes in Mexico, once in the United States, made a difference in their ability to adapt. Northern Mexicans by 1900, like their cousins across the border, had been influenced by Anglo society. Anglo-Americans of all types farmed, operated mines, and ran communications systems and the railroads in northern Mexico, just as they did in the Southwest. Northern Mexico was integrated into the greater U.S. economy in much the same way as the Southwest. The northern Mexicans were immigrants almost before they crossed the border. Besides, they were close to their homes once they crossed, and most took their families with them.

U.S. influence was not as pervasive in central and southern Mexico as it was in the north during the early twentieth century. This was especially true in west-central Mexico (Jalisco, Guanajuato, and Michoacán), where the economy was more independently Mexican, being based on subsistence agricultural and artisan activity. Thus, workers and their families from this part of Mexico, who by 1900 began to comprise a significant proportion of all immigration to the United States, can be considered somewhat distinct from the northern Mexicans and Southwest natives who shared similar characteristics.

The food, Spanish usage, wearing apparel, and music of the central Mexican immigrants all combined to make a contribution to Mexican culture in the United States. These newer immigrants tended to cluster around existing Mexican communities, and their cultures competed with and then mingled with the older norteño-Southwest societies. Distinctions were made among the Mexicans themselves, whenever the three groups were thrown together, and often a social order existed, with the central Mexican at the bottom.

Rapid economic expansion in the Southwest also contributed to the shifting of Mexicans beyond their original native Hispanic centers. Anglos and Mexicans were attracted to the numerous new communities that sprang up along the length of the railway lines in new agricultural sections and in the emerging mining districts. Here the Mexican *colonias*

(Mexican colonies) were all new, made up of displaced Southwest natives and Mexican immigrants. Such communities were formed in cotton-based towns in Texas during the early 1900s, and the same was true of the countless communities in the sugarbeet-growing regions of Colorado and California and in the mines of Arizona and New Mexico.

While the west-central Mexican male lived and worked side by side with his compatriots in all the areas requiring Mexican labor, in the long run he was more mobile. The exigencies of distance and meager resources forced him to travel without his wife and children, and once he was in the United States, hundreds of miles separated him from his home and family. As the railroads required temporary section gangs farther and farther north in the United States, the central Mexican immigrant responded more readily than his coworkers from the American Southwest and northern Mexico. The other immigrants were more reluctant; they preferred to work closer to home within the agricultural sectors where they were initially recruited. Thus, northeastern Mexicans traveled by wagon to the cotton fields of Texas and Oklahoma in the early 1900s, but no farther. Then they returned to their homes in south Texas or northeast Mexico as soon as possible.

By 1915, Mexicans could be found as far north as Chicago and Kansas City. Most were from west-central Mexico. Thus, when the United States demanded a greater amount of labor during World War I, it was the inhabitants of the cities and villages along the railroad lines in Mexico, who already had exposure to the American North, particularly those from the Bajío region of Mexico, who were recruited. During the fifteen years or so following the start of the Mexican Revolution in 1910, a massive outpouring from Mexico greatly changed the demographic profile of Mexicans in the United States.

✳ THE MEXICAN REVOLUTION AND IMMIGRATION TO THE UNITED STATES

The Mexican Revolution entailed a tremendous exodus of human beings fleeing political persecution, military impressment, depressed economic conditions, and simply the cross fire of violent events. The hard-fought struggles and their aftermath bred new social and economic conditions that drastically altered and disrupted Mexican society to the point that many, who would not have emigrated under their previous circumstances, flocked to the United States in large numbers.

Nonetheless, immigration to the United States was curtailed during the early years of the struggles when many Mexicans, from the same classes pro-

viding the bulk of emigration during this period, remained in Mexico and fought for the revolutionary cause. The appeal of the revolution was mixed in different parts of Mexico. In the north, thousands of urban workers, miners, middle-class professionals, small-scale landowners, cowboys, and even *hacendados* (hacienda owners) who supplied their peons as soldiers responded to the composite ideological appeals of the early phases of the revolution. In the south, around the state of Mexico, followers of Emiliano Zapata responded to the appeal to regain land usurped by speculators and hacendados during the reign of Porfirio Díaz. West-central Mexico was not as affected by the destabilizing events of the Díaz regime, but as the revolutionary tide swept to the south, most of the battles were fought in that region.

It is not surprising, then, that the revolution had distinct regional origins when Francisco I. Madero issued the Plan de San Luis Potosí in 1910. The soldiers in the rebel armies reflected these origins. Eventually, hardly any region of Mexico was left untouched by the struggle; almost every citizen and foreigner in the republic was affected. All in all, Mexicans endured 20 years of bloodshed. Many were caught up in the struggle because they believed the revolution was for the best. Others did not want the revolution, because it was not in their interest. The majority simply did not understand it or could not relate to its limited goals. Many of the disaffected, finding their Mexico torn asunder, left. For the first time, large numbers of middle-class Mexicans joined the emigrant streams. They composed a group that was critical to the formation of Mexican expatriate culture in the United States.

Initially, the exodus to the United States was a northern phenomenon, where much of the revolutionary activity originated after 1910. Indeed, in the southern areas that were not accessible to the United States, those uprooted by the peasant struggles sought safety in Mexico City or nearby areas not as affected by the revolution. In general, however, the displacement of people from their homes, in the city and in the countryside, followed the revolutionary tide southward. Many of those fortunate enough to be near the border or near a railroad station attempted to get to the United States.

Most refugees who fled Mexico during the Mexican War were from the lower and middle classes, but families like the Creels and the Terrazas of Chihuahua, and other wealthy *norteños,* lived comfortably while in the United States, accompanied by their liquid assets, which were deposited in American banks along the border. It was not until 1915 that the flight of large numbers of refugees assumed massive proportions in the Bajío and its environs, during a time when not only the direct destruction of the battles, but also the economic side effects of war, served to expel people from Mexico. During the struggles in Mexico, World War I spurred growth in every sector of the U.S. economy, owing primarily to the nation's position as a supplier to warring factions in Europe. Labor requirements had never been so great, yet disruption in trans-Atlantic transportation during the war and utilization of potential European emigrants in opposing armies were beginning to hinder the influx of workers from traditional European sources. When the United States became directly involved, American laborers were drafted, and a vacuum was created in industry, agriculture, mining, and transportation. These sectors looked south of the border to meet demands for expanding labor requirements during a time when Mexico was experiencing one of its worst economic crises.

Obtaining easy access to Mexican labor during this time of duress in Mexico and labor scarcity in the Southwest proved to be more difficult than had been the case in previous years, however. In February, Congress, in response to nativist pressures, enacted the Immigration Act of 1917, imposing a literacy requirement and an eight-dollar head tax on all individual immigrants. The act was passed before the United States entered the war, apparently without considering the manpower shortages that the wartime economy could create. The bill was designed to curb an "undesirable" influx from southern and eastern Europe, an immigrant group characterized by immigration officials as being two-thirds illiterate. Nevertheless, the act ultimately inhibited immigration to the United States from Mexico. Some of the Mexican states, such as Michoacán, a source of large numbers of emigrants, had illiteracy rates as high as 85 percent. In addition, the eight-dollar head tax was prohibitive for most migrants, many of whom arrived at the border destitute. Legal immigration of Mexicans suffered a temporary setback that year.

Surreptitious entry continued, but initially the interests that needed Mexican labor wanted legal, free, and easy access to this valuable reserve to the south. As the summer harvests approached, agriculturists and related interest groups became desperate for legal Mexican labor, and they pressured Congress to waiver implementation of the newly established immigration laws in the case of Mexicans. During June, Congress complied, but the waiver was applicable only to agricultural workers, and there was so much red tape involved in meeting waiver requirements that eventually both the employers and Mexican workers preferred illegal entry. In essence, the general requirement of the Immigration Act of 1917 stimulated clandestine entry into the country. Un-

authorized immigration intensified in later years after the Immigration Act of 1924 required that Mexicans add a ten-dollar visa fee to the already existing head tax, thus increasing the total that every immigrant paid to $18. A lucrative trade emerged after 1917 in smuggling illegal aliens across the Rio Grande. It consisted mainly of ferrying large groups of Mexican laborers on rafts to the U.S. side.

If the 1917 act proved to be an obstacle to legal entry, agriculturalists and other interest groups were more frustrated by what seemed a worse threat to their steady supply of labor. In May 1917, the Selective Service Act became law. While Mexican citizens were not eligible for the draft in the United States, unless they applied for their first naturalization papers, they were obliged to register with the local draft board, a requirement that Mexicans were loathe to comply with for fear of being drafted. Besides, during this era, first-generation Mexican Americans were indistinguishable from many Mexican-born citizens. Consequently, nationals from Mexico were mistakenly drafted anyway.

The conscription problem was eventually resolved and Mexican immigration resumed a normal flow. By 1915 Mexicans were also beginning to enter California in larger numbers. Oriental labor had been heavily relied on in the past, but the southern California agricultural sector had expanded tremendously since 1915, and Chinese workers no longer sufficed. Secretary of Labor William Wilson suggested in June 1917 that the waiver be extended to nonagricultural sectors, such as transportation. The years of rapid economic expansion brought about by U.S. involvement in World War I resulted in Mexican migration to geographic regions that they previously never worked in, in such sectors as oil fields, munitions factories, meat-packing plants, and steel mills. Hundreds of colonias expanded or were established anew in cities such as Los Angeles, Kansas City, Chicago, Phoenix, and Houston. Ironically, few Mexican immigrants settled where traditional southwestern Hispanic culture was strong, such as in northern New Mexico and southern Colorado. Mexicans migrated to work, and work was more plentiful in areas where there were fewer Hispanics, in new agricultural towns, or in industrial cities that were built by Anglos, such as Chicago or Houston.

A lamentable side effect of the struggle was an increase in anti-Mexican prejudice. Americans resented and feared the revolution, which many times was brought to their doorstep at the border. The revolutionary Pancho Villa and his followers, for example, raided into American territory to obtain supplies, and on some occasions Americans were killed in these incursions. In 1914, President Woodrow Wilson ordered the invasion of Vera Cruz in an effort to depose Victoriano Huerta, a general who assassinated President Francisco Madero, the founder of the revolutionary movement, and took over Mexico. To get support from the American people for the invasion, however, Mexicans were cast as undisciplined and violent. By the 1920s, Anglo-American opinion of Mexicans was lower than before the revolution, and these emotions were taken out on Mexicans living in the United States. Americans failed to see that brutality is part of any war, not just a trait manifested by Mexicans during this era. Indeed, strong parallels exist between the behavior of soldiers, both Union and Confederate, during the American Civil War.

✳ THE "MEXICO LINDO" GENERATION

In the 1920s, economic expansion continued, owing to commercial agriculture and large-scale mining activity. But in addition, the United States was experiencing an all-time-high economic expansion in manufacturing. Increasingly, Mexican labor was used in cities. At the same time, immigration increased to floodtide proportions, coming from farther south in central Mexico, including Jalisco, Guanajuato, Michoacán, and San Luis Potosí. With the new infusion of immigrants from areas so remote from the Southwest, Mexicans found few familiar surroundings in agricultural or mining towns and in cities like Houston, Dallas, and Chicago. Also in this period, the vast majority of persons living in the United States who were considered of Mexican origin were either born in Mexico or the children of immigrants; the original Mexican residents of the United States were considered "Americans."

Like many other newcomers to the United States in the late nineteenth and early twentieth centuries, Mexicans came from a peasant or an agricultural village background and were from a country that was only then acquiring a sense of nationhood. An extensive *patria chica* (homeland region) identity existed among the majority of the immigrants as they arrived in the United States. For example, some people identified themselves as Tapatíos, people of northeastern Jalisco and western Guanajuato, while others were Huastecos from southern Tamaulipas, eastern San Luis Potosí, or northern Veracruz. The state of Sonora, cut off in the south by the vastness of the Yaqui and Mayo settlements, to the east by the Sierra Madres, and to the north by U.S. expansion, acquired a strong sense of identity known as *Sonorense*. The bond of each area was forged by common economic activity, distinctive food ways, music, and even phenotypology (physical features).

Mexicans had this provincialism in common with other "new immigrants," such as Italians and eastern Europeans, who tended to have weak national allegiances and strong regional identities. In the initial immigrant settlements, friends and relatives from the same village or province in the old country lived and socialized together, forming parochial clusters within the larger enclave. Often, the immigrants physically segregated themselves in sections with names such as El Michoacanito (Little Michoacán) or Chihuahita (Little Chihuahua). The mining town near Ray, Arizona, was called Sonora, possibly because of the great number of Sonorenses that worked there. In addition, some of the ethnic organizations had a preponderance of members who originated in the same province in Mexico. Divisions based on regional origins were further complicated by significant class differences. Although the vast majority of the Mexicans in the United States were from the lower classes, many upper- and middle-class refugees escaping the violence of the revolution joined them in the immigrant colonias.

The majority of the Mexicans entering the United States between 1910 and 1930 were seeking work and intended to return home. Indeed, many did. But even those who remained harbored a dream of someday going back. Another characteristic of this emerging identity was an exaggerated loyalty to Mexico, coupled with a dutiful celebration of the Mexican patriotic holidays (*fiestas patrias*). Scholar Paul Schuster Taylor, in studying the colonias in the late 1920s noted in *Mexican Labor in the United States: Chicago and the Calumet Region* (1932), "First there is a strong emotional attachment to Mexico and patriotism is heightened, as the Mexicans themselves sometimes note, by their expatriation." The formation of this "México Lindo" (Pretty Mexico) identity became a full-fledged phenomenon in the nation's immigrant colonias.

During the Mexican Revolution, a sizable portion of the Mexican urban middle classes and elites, who were the critical core in Mexico imbued with nationalistic feelings, immigrated to the United States. They were the most important source of nationalism, in addition to being the carriers of *indigenismo* (pride in the Indian heritage of Mexico) and other forms of patriotism.

Obviously, the maintenance of Mexican culture and the Spanish language was seen as the most necessary nationalist statement. The names given to their mutual aid societies, such as La Sociedad Benito Juárez, México Bello, Sociedad Cuauhtemoc, to name a few, demonstrate the close allegiance to Mexico. During this time the self-identifier was Mexicano/a in Spanish and Mexican in English. Even the names given to their barrios had a strong nostalgic ring. In Phoenix, one neighborhood was known as Cuatro Milpas. Its name was derived from a famous musical lament that was immensely popular among Mexicans throughout the United States. Called simply "Las cuatro milpas," the song relates the story of a peasant who returns to his farm after a long absence only to find it in ruin; obviously the farmer's sojourn was interpreted by the immigrants as their stay in the United States.

The musical consumption of Mexican immigrants, in its various forms, is an incisive vehicle for understanding the Mexican colonias in this country. In tandem with other kinds of live entertainment, such as Mexican vaudeville and drama, the musical production of Mexicans was just as important as their religious, political, and economic institutions. All these combined to give the immigrant community the cohesion necessary to be able to defend its interests. Many of the immigrants were successful in their new surroundings, but most were probably disenchanted by discrimination, poverty, inadequate housing, segregation, and the prospect of menial labor. Music had a greater ability to promote cultural reaffirmation in this harsh immigrant milieu, invoking a nostalgia for what they considered a simpler and happier past. The invention of the wax record increased the power of music to reach Mexican farm workers and miners living in tents, far from centers of live entertainment. As a consequence, the phonograph was indispensable, and for vendors selling both items, it became another lucrative opportunity.

Theater productions and other forms of live entertainment, like their musical counterparts, also ranked in importance with the church and other immigrant institutions, and because the troupes were mobile, the medium was taken into the most remote areas where Mexicans lived and worked. Companies like those owned by the renowned actress Virginia Fábregas preferred the large houses of Los Angeles, San Antonio, and Chicago. In agricultural communities and mining towns, smaller tent-show ensembles, called *carpas*, were more common. These entertainment groups were made up of family members who put on skits or performed simple circus-type acts, such as tightrope walking. Larger circuses, such as Circo Escalante, with a full array of acts, often went to larger towns and cities and became the joy of the whole population, not just Mexicans.

Not singing and dancing, but finding work, setting up homes, building churches, and coping with a hostile reception from Anglos dominated the lives of Mexicans in the colonias. Segregation, police brutality, and general rejection drove home the need to coalesce and embrace unity. The badge of inferiority imposed by the Anglo provoked the immigrants to dispel negative stigma by forcefully demonstrating that Mexicans engaged in positive cultural activities. They believed that Mexican artistic and cultural contributions were as good or better than those in Anglo America.

Another strong component of immigrant identity was a form of indigenismo, or the proud recognition of Mexico's pre-Columbian Indian ancestry. This ideology was deeply rooted in Mexican history and given profound expression by Mexican intellectuals and writers in the colonial period and throughout most of the nineteenth century. Understandably, the sentiment was carried to the colonias in the United States by immigrant leaders who deliberately maintained and projected this image. In this respect, reverence to Our Lady of Guadalupe, the Virgin Mother, who is considered to be an Indian, and the homage paid to Benito Juárez, also an Indian, is part of this tradition. Every major colonia in the United States had an organization named after Juárez and a Catholic church named Our Lady of Guadalupe. Religion served to provide more than a spiritual focus. It served to give a sense of purpose to the community, because it was the immigrants themselves who built and maintained the churches.

But in this early era, Mexican immigrants had to contend with intense police brutality, segregation, abuse in the workplace, and general rejection from the mainstream community. El Congreso Mexicanista (The Mexican Congress) was founded in Texas in order to implement a strategic plan to stem the tide of legal abuses and violence against Mexicans. The meeting was attended by representatives from Mexican communities across Texas, and although the lack of political power limited its success, the effort demonstrated that Mexicans were willing to defend themselves. It also served as model for later political mobilization. In later years, many other organizations also strived to end abuses against Mexicans in the justice system, such as the Asamblea Mexicana, organized in Houston in 1925. Perhaps the most distressing abuse was the disproportionate execution of Mexicans in prisons throughout the United States; Mexicans spent much of their collective energy attempting to save condemned men. In many parts of the United States, Mexicans formed organizations, usually called La Liga Protectora Mexicana (The Mexican Protective League), that served to protect the legal rights of Mexicans. On several occasions, Mexican consuls met with the state governor or the board of pardons and paroles, usually accompanied by members of Mexican organizations that had collected petitions with thousands of signatures pressing for clemency.

In 1921, a depression caused severe destitution among Mexicans who suddenly found themselves unemployed. The Mexican government, working through its consulate service, formed *comisiones honoríficas* (honorary commissions) to protect the rights of hundreds of thousands Mexicans who found themselves stranded in many communities and unable to return home after prices for mining and agricultural products had collapsed. Thousands were repatriated with money provided by the Mexican government, but those that remained found themselves destitute until the economy recovered.

Recovery from the 1921 crisis was quick, and economic expansion throughout the 1920s went beyond the boom conditions precipitated by World War I. Mexicans were again in demand, and during this decade their influx dwarfed previous entries. Resistance to Mexican immigration was intense, however. The larger their numbers became in the United States, the more nativists thought Mexicans were a threat to cultural and racial integrity. But employers would not countenance any restriction of a valuable labor supply. Indeed, when the National Origins Quota Act was passed in 1924 to curtail immigration, lobbyists representing agricultural and mining interests managed to persuade Congress not to include the Western Hemisphere. This ensured that the Mexican labor source would be protected. Nativists, such as Representative John C. Box of Texas, wanted to stop immigration from Mexico completely, but in the spirit of the prosperous decade, the desires of the powerful employers who needed Mexican labor were not overcome.

During this period, a product of the heavy inflow was the appearance of many new colonias with familiar México Lindo institutions. The leadership promoted cohesion and unity more successfully when practically everyone was newly arrived, was segregated from the rest of the society, and was working and bringing in some money. They expected their stay in the United States to be temporary, although most stayed until their death. As the American-born children of those who remained grew older, slowly the elders' influence waned as younger family members began to adopt American ways and identify with the United States as their permanent home.

✳ DEPRESSION, REPATRIATION, AND ACCULTURATION

The Great Depression altered the lives of everyone, and it also dramatically changed the evolution of the Mexican colonias. Mexicans who had been so desir-

able as workers in the previous decade became unwanted throughout the United States in the 1930s. From throughout, thousands of Mexicans left, many times pressured by community authorities. But those that resisted repatriation were more rooted and, in most cases, had families with growing children. Indeed, during the decade, a generation grew up that had no memories of Mexico. Their only home had been the barrios in their immigrant communities.

A cultural shift became apparent in the early 1930s. The dominant immigrant posture of the 1920s gave way to "Mexican American" adaptation, which was characterized by assimilation of U.S. values and a less faithful adherence to Mexican culture. By the mid-1930s it was apparent that a fusion of cultures was evolving. Cultural expression of Mexican Americans in this period was obviously influenced by Anglo society. Immigrant symbolism did not disappear in the 1930s, but the reinforcing influence from Mexico declined with the depression-related hiatus in immigration. Ostensibly pure Mexican traditions were barely kept alive by the aging immigrants, who also were losing their influence over younger Mexican Americans born in the United States.

The México Lindo source of identity, then, however virulent it seemed in the initial colonia-building stage, did not survive the massive repatriation of Mexicans that had been provoked by the Great Depression. Repatriation, especially from the large cities, was massive and highly organized. This was especially true in Los Angeles and industrial cities in the Midwest, but thousands left from more rural communities as well. For those remaining in the United States, Americanization was seized upon by the new leadership through organizations such as the Latin American Club in cities like Phoenix and Houston and the Mexican American Political Club in East Chicago. These groups, of course, were intent on achieving political clout. Even the word "Mexican" seemed to be abandoned in this period, as the term "Latin American" attests.

The League of United Latin American Citizens (LULAC), initially very strong in Texas, eventually spread to other parts of the United States. Besides, the leaders of these organizations were no longer immigrants who intended to return to Mexico. They consisted of a new and younger generation that was either born in the United States or very young upon arriving. Overall in the decade, significant alterations took place for the second-generation Mexican Americans that had been born or raised in the United States. Increasingly more graduated from high school, and their expectations from the larger society were more extensive. The depression of the 1930s subsided because of wartime spending, and by the end of the decade, thousands of young Mexican Americans had grown up in this country exposed to the greater Anglo society through such New Deal agencies as the Civilian Conservation Corps and National Youth Administration, both designed to enroll young people and keep them off the streets during this era of massive unemployment.

✳ WORLD WAR II AND THE MEXICAN AMERICAN GENERATION

When the United States declared war in 1941, Mexican Americans responded to the war effort enthusiastically. Despite continuing discrimination, patriotism among Mexican Americans was intense, as they felt like part of the United States. Unlike their parents, they had no direct ties to Mexico. Thousands joined their white and black counterparts in all branches of the armed forces. Most Mexican women stayed behind, but many moved to California and other industrial areas in the boom years of the war and worked in places where Mexicans had never been allowed. The League of United Latin American Citizens (LULAC) spread throughout the United States in the 1940s, and thousands of Mexicans not serving in the military engaged in many "home front" efforts, such as bond drives. After the war, Mexican Americans strove to achieve political power by making good use of their war record. Many Mexican American war veterans were motivated by the continued discrimination that greeted them after the war. In 1947, the American G.I. Forum was organized by Mexican American veterans in response to the denial of a funeral home in Three Rivers, Texas, to bury a Mexican American killed in the Pacific. The organization went on to become a leading advocate for civil rights. In addition, many American Legion posts for Mexican Americans were founded by these same veterans.

Immigration to the United States greatly decreased during the Great Depression, during which time a generation of Mexican Americans was greatly influenced by Anglo culture. Because few new immigrants came, much cultural reinforcement from Mexico was lost. When the war ended, Mexican American GIs came back by the thousands to their barrios in cities and small towns alike. Many young people who had postponed wedding plans during the years of strife now married and had babies. These Mexican American soldiers came back more assertive, ready to take their place in a society that, by any reckoning, they had fought to preserve. After the war, hundreds of young married Mexican American couples moved to the growing suburbs and were further acculturated.

Mexican culture in the United States did not subside despite acculturation, however. The Bracero Program was instrumental in reviving immigration to the United States during the war years, reinstating the crucial link to Mexico. The program, in which U.S. labor agents actually went to Mexico and recruited thousands of workers, was prompted by the wartime need for labor. The experienced *braceros* (manual laborers) inspired many others to immigrate on their own. Many of these contract laborers worked primarily in agricultural communities and in railroad camps until the program ended in 1965; however, some of them stayed, or returned after they were delivered back to Mexico. Ever since then, the renewal of immigration has continued unabated. The Mexican movie industry, which came into its own in the 1940s, by the 1950s dominated the Spanish-speaking market on a worldwide basis and also ensured that Mexican culture entered with a new vigor into Mexican-American communities. It was logical that Mexican movies found a large market in the United States, where so many of Mexico's people were living and where no other medium equaled it as a vibrant exponent of Mexican culture. Only the record industry had as pervasive a Mexicanizing impact on Mexican American culture.

But despite the resurgence of Mexican immigration and the persistence of Mexican cultural modes, Mexican Americans could not help but become Americanized in the milieu of the 1950s and 1960s, when more and more acquired educations in Anglo systems, lived in integrated suburbs, and were subjected to Anglo-American mass media, especially when television came into its own. It is difficult to measure just how pervasive Americanization was at that time, however. Certainly, the culture of Mexican Americans, fused as it was with mainstream society in the United States, was more acceptable. But prejudice and rejection persisted. Nonetheless, Mexican Americans, more integrated into society, were more effective than ever in their efforts to break down obstacles to economic and social mobility. For example, in the 1950s and early 1960s segregation was abolished in Texas, Arizona, and many other communities, largely through the efforts of LULAC and the Alianza Hispano Americana (Hispanic American Alliance), another civil rights organization in the Southwest.

✳ FROM CHICANOS TO HISPANICS

The late 1960s and early 1970s was a time of intellectual foment and rebellion in the United States. Caught up in the mood, young Mexican Americans throughout the country sought a new identity while struggling for the same civil rights objectives of previous generations. This struggle became known as the Chicano movement. The word "Chicano" was elevated from its pejorative usage in the 1920s to denote lower-class Mexican immigrants and from its slang usage of the 1940s and 1950s to substitute for Mexicano. It now symbolized the realization of a newfound and unique identity. Proudly, Chicanos proclaimed an Indo-Hispanic heritage, and accused older Mexican Americans of pathologically denying their racial and ethnic reality because of an inferiority complex.

In the movement, an attempt was made to use some of the same symbols of their immigrant grandfathers, but with a few added touches. Tapping several intellectual traditions, movement leaders attempted to define true ethnic character. Allusions were made to factual and mythical pasts used so often by *indigenistas* (indigenists). For example, the concept of Aztlán, the mythical place of origin of the Aztec, became the Chicano movement name for the Southwest. In addition, participants in the movement differed from the previous Mexican-American generation in that they did not care whether they were accepted and they rejected assimilation. Many of the images they construed reflected their alienation as they blended pachuco cultural modes, *pinto* (ex-convict) savvy, pre-Columbian motifs, and myth with a burning conviction that Chicanos were deliberately subordinated by a racist American society. Chicano student organizations sprang up throughout the nation, as did barrio groups such as the Brown Berets. Thousands of young Chicanos pledged their loyalty and time to such groups as the United Farm Workers Organizing Committee, which, under Cesar Chávez, had been a great inspiration for Chicanos throughout the nation. An offshoot of both impulses, the farm worker and the student movement, was La Raza Unida party in Texas, an organization formed in 1968 to obtain control of community governments where Chicanos were in the majority.

In the 1980s, the term "Hispanic," which has considerable longevity, took a special generic meaning referring to any person living in the United States who is of Spanish ancestry. In the Mexican American community, the term has been eagerly accepted, and only vestiges remain of the virulent nationalism of Chicano movement days evoked to forge an identity. The United Farm Workers Organization and La Raza Unida party, the latter still existing in various communities, are direct heirs of the movement, but they do not seem to have prospered in recent years. Use of "Hispanic" represents a rejection by the Mexi-

can American leadership of both cultural nationalism and radical postures.

In essence, the "Hispanic Generation" is the latest synthesis of radicalism and nationalism. Those Chicanos that identify with "Hispanic" are more nationalistic than the G.I. generation, while rivaling Chicano movement activists in their fervor for civil rights. They also accept a nonwhite racial identity, paying lip service to the concept of Aztlán. But the new upbeat, sophisticated, "professional" image that the term conjures is alluring to the new generation.

The fiestas patrias celebrations have continued down to this date. Unlike those in the 1920s organized by the México Lindo leaders, the historical reasons for celebration do not figure in a very precise fashion. For example, during the Cinco de Mayo celebration, very little is said about the 1862 Battle of Puebla. Instead, the day seems to have been converted into a celebration of the Hispanic presence in the United States.

Today, immigration from Mexico and Latin America continues unabated, a condition that has to be taken into account as we trace the continuing development of Mexican communities throughout the United States. Since the 1960s, a massive influx of Hispanic immigrants has reinforced Hispanic culture in the United States. All in all, the culture and identity of Mexican Americans will continue to change, reflecting both inevitable generational fusion with Anglo society and the continuing influence of immigrants, not only from Mexico, but from throughout Latin America.

✳ MIGRATION TO THE UNITED STATES FROM PUERTO RICO

Most of the two million Puerto Ricans who have trekked to the U.S. mainland in this century are World War II or postwar-era entries. And unlike the immigrant experience of Mexicans, or Cubans before 1959, the vast majority of Puerto Ricans entered with little or no red tape. After 1920, the passage of the Jones Act granted Puerto Ricans citizenship, even if they were born on the island. Migration out of Puerto Rico was a defined trend quite a few years before the Spanish-American War, however, establishing a pattern that would be repeated and accelerated in the twentieth century.

The first migrant wave was stimulated by escalating economic relations between Puerto Rico and the United States. Exchange between both areas actually began in the eighteenth century but did not achieve large proportions until the second half of the nineteenth century. Still a colony of Spain, however, the island was subjected to the mother country's mercantilistic hold, thus trade was clandestine. For Puerto Rican planters and Yankee merchants, the exchange of sugar and molasses produced on the island for American goods that were cheaper than those from Spain was mutually satisfying. The chain of smuggling activity that led to the first Anglo incursions into Texas and California was, significantly, part of this very same process. The economic contact with North Americans eventually resulted in the divestment of Texas, New Mexico, and California from Mexico. A similar fate was in store for Puerto Rico and Cuba.

In the early nineteenth century the economic relationship was sufficiently mature for Cuban and Puerto Rican traders to found a benevolent society in New York to serve merchants and their families from both island colonies. But economic ties were not the only attraction in the United States for Puerto Ricans and Cubans. Many also found in the northern colossus a haven for plotting against Spain. From the time of El Grito de Lares, an insurrection in 1868, to the time Puerto Rican exiles formed part of the Cuban Revolutionary party's governing board at the end of the century, hundreds traveled to the mainland. Staying for years, some sent for families and found employment to sustain themselves. While most of the first exiles were from the criollo middle classes, eventually skilled artisans and laborers, all dissatisfied with Spain's rule, joined their compatriots in New York.

Large-scale immigration, however, is linked more to structural changes in the Puerto Rican economy during the course of the latter nineteenth century than any other condition. The freeing of slaves in the 1870s and the rise of coffee as a significant competitor of sugar created new land-tenure systems and more fluid labor conditions. As in Mexico during the regime of Porfirio Díaz, such radical changes disrupted the fabric of rural life, forcing Puerto Ricans into day agricultural labor or into the urban centers like San Juan. The population also increased dramatically in the course of the nineteenth century, from 583,000 in 1860, to one million in 1900. Meanwhile the labor market was not developing at the same rate. As a consequence, many of the unemployed decided to cast their lot with contractors who sought agricultural workers in other regions of the Caribbean. Eventually others found their way to the United States.

Hastening the process of migration to the United States was the acquisition of Puerto Rico after the Spanish-American War. In May 1898, Spanish fortifications in San Juan were bombarded by the U.S. Navy while U.S. Army troops invaded the rest of the island to ferret out the Spaniards. Cheering crowds,

longing for their independence, enthusiastically welcomed the U.S. forces entering Ponce under General Nelson Miles. Little did they know that soon they would trade the sovereignty of Spain for the tutelage of the United States. Quickly, a military government was established for Puerto Rico under General Guy V. Henry. But the transition was negotiated not with Spain, but with Puerto Ricans led by Luis Muñoz-Rivera. Muñoz had assumed the leadership of the home-rule government granted by the Spanish Crown just before the occupation by the United States, and now he had to deal with another foreign interloper.

A quasi republic under U.S. dominance was established by the Foraker Act in 1900. It created a lower house with 35 members, but the highest-ranking officials had to be appointed by the president of the United States. In essence, there would have been more self-direction under the autonomy agreement reached with Spain right before the American takeover. Muñoz-Rivera continued to serve his people as a politician, however, as an organizer of the Federalist party and as commissioner to the U.S. Congress from the protectorate. To the dismay of Puerto Ricans, this position did not carry very much power.

Then in 1917, the Jones Act, a proviso more to the liking of Puerto Ricans, was enacted. Skillful diplomacy by island politicians resulted in the passage of this congressional bill that created two Puerto Rican houses of legislature whose representatives were more properly elected by the people. More important, in terms of how it would affect future immigration, the act conceded U.S. citizenship to Puerto Ricans.

Despite this victory, Puerto Rico was quickly deluged by American economic interests. Absentee landlords built large, modern sugar plantations that wiped out even more preindustrial subsistence farming than was the case during the last years of the Spanish period. Even coffee production, in which thousands of workers had been employed, declined as the capital-intensive sugar plantations and refineries covered much of the island. In the towns and cities, artisans such as independent shoemakers, carpenters, and other craftsmen found their livelihoods abolished by manufactured commodities produced in the United States.

As a result of the American intervention in Puerto Rico, schools, hospitals, and public projects were built. This development, designed to improve life on the island, also paved the way for the new American investors and hastened the end of a way of life on which most Puerto Ricans depended for survival. Additionally, jobs that employed many women in tobacco factories and domestic service all declined. As the twentieth century progressed, island workers were marginalized and reduced to part-time miscellaneous work, which in Puerto Rico is known as *chiripeo*. Unemployment and underemployment created even greater pressure to leave Puerto Rico.

In the early part of the century, Hawaii's sugar industry was in need of experienced workers, and a few thousand Puerto Ricans were recruited. First they were shipped to New Orleans by ship, then by train to San Francisco, and then by water again for the last leg of the journey. Small colonias emerged in both San Francisco and New Orleans because some workers decided not to make the full trip and remained at these debarkation points. Most of the island people migrated to the eastern seaboard of the United States, however. In 1910, according to census figures, 1,513 Puerto Ricans were living on the mainland, two thirds in New York. Like Mexicans, their fellow Hispanics in the Southwest, Puerto Ricans continued to arrive during World War I and the prosperous 1920s when jobs were plentiful.

U.S. immigration policy also influenced the pattern of migration from Puerto Rico. Two national origin quota acts designed to curtail immigration from eastern and southern Europe and Asia were passed in 1921 and 1924. With fewer workers coming in from these areas, a labor shortage ensued. The Western Hemisphere was not included in the quota policy, however, and so employers turned there for labor. Mexico became a major of source of workers, as did Puerto Rico. It was easier for recruiters to target Puerto Ricans because they could travel freely to the mainland as citizens. By 1930, there were approximately 53,000 living in various North American communities, although most were in New York City. There, they concentrated in Brooklyn, the Bronx, and East Harlem. As their numbers increased in later years, these barrios remained the core areas of first arrival.

✳ EARLY SETTLEMENT OF PUERTO RICANS IN THE UNITED STATES

The establishment of Puerto Rican colonias was similar to that of the Mexican immigrant colonias, characterized earlier as the México Lindo phase of the Mexican American experience. As Puerto Ricans first arrived on the mainland, they looked back to their island origins for identity. Although Puerto Rico, unlike Mexico, was not an independent nation, the vital nationalism pervading the island during the rise of independent sentiment was tapped by newcomers to the United States looking for a source of ethnic consciousness. In the quest for roots during the Puerto Rican struggle for independence from Spain, the pre-Hispanic name of the island, Borin-

quen, was revived. Immigrants, in their new environment, used Borinquen *querido* (beloved Borinquen) to refer to a homeland to which they felt closer once they had left it. When the United States took over the island, love and identification with their roots increased even more, and many Puerto Ricans felt the U.S. occupation was as a continuation of the colonial experience.

This feeling was exacerbated even more when they encountered rejection in this country. In the so-called Harlem Riots, in July 1926, Puerto Ricans were attacked by non-Hispanics as their numbers were becoming larger in Manhattan neighborhoods. As the Puerto Ricans united to defend themselves, symbols of the homeland common to all, regardless of regional origin, became a powerful bond. The Spanish language, perpetuated through a barrage of newspapers, music, and theater, also solidified Borinquen kindredness and allowed Puerto Ricans to identify with other Hispanics in New York, such as Cubans and Spaniards.

The Catholic religion also served as a cohesive ingredient. As it did for Mexicans in Mexico, Catholicism in Puerto Rico took a unique shape according to the exigencies of local island society. On the mainland, the particular features of Puerto Rican worship served as an additional focus, bringing the islanders together in a common ceremony. Still, it was mainly in New York where Catholic churches existed that catered primarily to Puerto Ricans, albeit other Spanish-speakers also attended. Significantly, language affinity was perpetuated in these religious institutions as well.

Formal multipurpose organizations and clubs were probably the most important vehicle for cohesion, and they also served to make Puerto Rican settlement more visible in the city. The most common associations were the *hermandades* (brotherhoods). These societies, which could be traced to emancipation groups in the nineteenth century, provided mutual aid and intensified ethnic nationalism. Attending to primordial needs of the community, the brotherhoods appeared very quickly after the arrival of Puerto Ricans on the mainland. Additionally, merchant organizations and groups associated with labor unions also proliferated.

Political activity was also apparent during the initial building stages of the colonias. Associated with the desire for independence back home, such groups as the Club Borinquen had as their main agenda through such periodical organs as *El Porvenir* (The Future) and *La Revolución* (The Revolution), freedom from colonial rule. But because throughout most of this century Puerto Ricans were citizens before they set out from their homeland, they were able to participate much more than Mexican immigrants in American electoral politics. Usually associating with the Democratic Party, but not always, they organized political groups and joined the ethnic machines prevalent in eastern cities as early as 1918. This of course was one year after the Jones Act granted Puerto Ricans citizenship. In the 1920s, La Liga Puertorriquena (The Puerto Rican League), an organization made up primarily of community associations, became an unabashed supporter of the Democratic Party.

As was the case in the Mexican colonias in the United States, Puerto Rican businessmen perpetuated ethnic bonds by providing Caribbean food, barbershops, religious relics, and, very important, Latin records, and the phonographs to play them. Music and theater were two of the most important exponents of Puerto Rican solidarity, and by the 1930s such theaters as El Teatro Hispano in New York featured not only Spanish-language drama but also musical groups. Puerto Ricans pursued their penchant for music at the family level, as well. Practically every gathering, whether it was a baptism, wedding, or coming-out party, had the obligatory singing trio of two guitar players and a maraca player. The music itself intensified the link with the homeland and defined Puerto Ricans' experience as immigrants. Rafael Hernández, a trained composer and owner of a music store in New York, wrote numerous songs that embodied the spirit of this genre. Hernández's most famous piece is "Lamento Borincano" (Borinquen Lament). The song, like the Mexican "Canción Mixteca" (Mixteca Song), was a poignant but romantic reminder of the beauty and rural simplicity of the homeland.

As happened with Mexican immigrants during the Great Depression, there was a reverse migration. Between 1930 and 1934, probably 20 percent of the Puerto Ricans living in the United States went back to the island, although they were not coerced to the same degree as Mexicans to return home. Those who could hang on to their jobs, primarily in service sectors of New York and other eastern cities, became acculturated more to life in the United States. Moreover, the U.S. cities in which Puerto Ricans lived had a vital urban life that exerted a strong influence on growing families.

✳ THE GREAT MIGRATION

Post World War II Puerto Ricans in the United States

The most massive migration of Puerto Ricans, almost two million, occurred after World War II.

While the wartime Bracero Program brought over 100,000 Mexicans to work in the labor-scarce economy of the war period, Puerto Ricans did not start immigrating in large numbers until the postwar boom era. They came in response to a classical push-pull phenomenon. Simply put, wages were higher and employment was more plentiful than on the island.

Operation Boot Strap, a strategy designed to develop Puerto Rico economically, resulted in altering the employment structure, as had the modernization of the sugar industry earlier in the century. The project was the brainchild of the popular governor Luis Muñoz Marín, the son of nationalist patriot Luis Muñoz-Rivera. The plan emphasized investment, primarily American, in light industry and manufacturing. To a large degree, the process did provide more technical employment for some Puerto Ricans. But as investors turned away from sugar production, agricultural employment declined, and Operation Boot Strap did not adequately provide replacement jobs. Then in the 1960s, petrochemical plants and refineries, activities that required even less labor than light industry, pervaded much of the

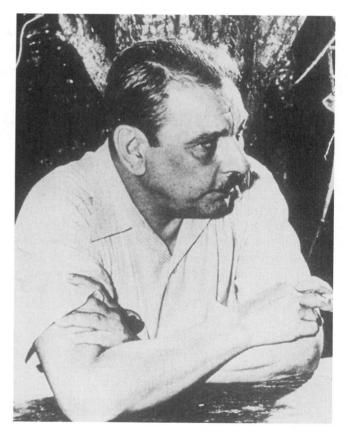

Luis Muñoz Marín, architect of the present commonwealth status of Puerto Rico.

economy. The net result was as inevitable: more migration.

As their numbers increased on the mainland, Puerto Ricans transcended their New York home, moving to textile mill towns in Rhode Island and Connecticut, factories in Chicago, and the steel mills of Pennsylvania, Ohio, and Indiana. The most remarkable feature of the new immigration was that it was airborne. The large volume of passengers leaving Puerto Rico soon drove the price of fares down and gave opportunity to new airlines, which pressed surplus World War II cargo planes into service. By 1947, over 20 airlines provided service between San Juan and Miami and San Juan and New York. In the 1950s, Puerto Ricans were also landing in New Jersey cities and paid, on average, $40 for a one-way ticket.

The newer arrivals, like their Mexican counterparts in Los Angeles and Chicago, crowded into large barrios in New York and other eastern cities. The cold weather in the Northeast was inhospitable and almost unbearable for the hundreds of thousands who had left their warm tropical island. Adaptation in this environment was very difficult, indeed. What is abundantly clear, and here there are some very close parallels to the Mexican American experience during the postwar period, is that early Puerto Rican immigrants built a foundation of organizations and institutions that made life more bearable for later arrivals.

Many second-generation Puerto Ricans acquired some social mobility within the society to which their parents had migrated before the war, and in some cases these first-generation parents were already professionals upon arriving. Basically, however, prewar communities that cushioned the shock for the immigrants were strongly working-class in structure, very much like Mexican Americans. Unlike Mexican Americans, second-generation Puerto Ricans in the 1930s did not coalesce into organizations like the League of United Latin American Citizens, which was started in Texas in 1929 by frustrated Mexican Americans who found practically every avenue to opportunity in the United States blocked. Perhaps for Puerto Ricans in the United States before the 1950s, segregation was not as intense as it was for Mexicans in the Southwest, a problem that was particularly acute in Texas.

Interethnic hostility, however, especially when Puerto Ricans arrived in very large numbers in Italian American or Irish American neighborhoods, peaked into severe hostile rivalries in many northern cities. Much of this hostility was fought out in the streets by gangs of youth who called themselves by colorful names. These rivalries, for better or worse, inspired the famous *West Side Story* by Leonard Bernstein. But the reality of these clashes was not as romantic as those portrayed in the musical between the Sharks and the Jets.

The second-largest concentration of Puerto Ricans outside the New York City area sprang up in the Chicago area. The birth of the Chicago colonias dates to World War II. Today, approximately 200,000 live in the city proper, and many thousands more in Gary and East Chicago, Indiana, and Milwaukee. One of the most important organizations in the early formation of the colonias was the Caballeros de San Juan (Knights of St. John). Its main function was to provide leadership and religious values in the Puerto Rican community. Other groups known as hermandades emerged in the 1950s and 1960s and were similar to the ones formed in New York in the early 1900s. Religion continued to serve as a focal point of the community, and Puerto Ricans identified strongly with the folk level of worship, as did Mexican immigrants. In fact, they shared, in an amicable arrangement, Our Lady of Guadalupe churches in both South Chicago and in East Chicago with Mexicans.

As more and more Puerto Ricans committed to remaining on the mainland during the 1950s and 1960s, they encountered a great amount of rejection, but at the same time they demonstrated a growing concern for social and economic mobility. Their early employment pattern consisted of menial jobs in the service sector of the Chicago economy and in light factory work—in essence low-paying work. And because of housing discrimination, Puerto Ricans were relegated to low-rent but overcrowded housing. Exacerbating these grievances were inequities in the courts and a persistent pattern of police brutality in the barrio.

To face that challenge they resorted, as did Mexican Americans during this same period, to self-help and civil rights organizations. Like Mexican Americans, thousands of Puerto Ricans served in World War II and the Korean conflict. Because many of these soldiers left directly from the island, before they could speak English, the military became an educational experience. Upon being discharged, many opted to remain on the mainland, where economic opportunity seemed to beckon. But even for former soldiers, there were still many obstacles that had to be overcome to achieve any kind of equality.

The emergence of the Puerto Rican Forum in New York in the mid-1950s demonstrated a clear departure from the Borinquen querido organizations of the 1930s and 1940s that defined their identity in terms of political and cultural links to the island. The forum proposed an agenda to eliminate problems associated with urban poverty. In 1961, Aspira (Aspire) was founded to promote the education of youth by raising public and private sector funds. Clearly, both of these organizations were similar to the Mexican American organizations in the Southwest during the same period. Aspira, more than the Puerto Rican Forum, acquired a national following, serving Puerto Ricans wherever they lived in large numbers.

But when these organizations did not seem to alleviate the frustrations and despair that was common in many barrios, the politics of passion broke out. In 1966, hundreds of Chicago Puerto Rican youths went on a rampage, breaking windows and burning down many of the businesses in their neighborhoods. Ostensibly, the riots were in response to an incident of police brutality, but the underlying causes were broader, linked to the urban blight that characterized their life in Chicago. During this time, the rise of militant organizations that rejected the orientation of earlier groups emerged. As the Chicano and black pride movements pervaded the consciousness of their respective communities, a similar voice was heard in the Puerto Rican barrios throughout the country. Foremost among the new militants were the Young Lords, a grass roots youth group that was similar to the Black Panthers in the black community and the Brown Berets in the Chicano. They promoted Borinquen pride and put forth an agenda to change poverty-stricken neighborhoods. In both New York and Chicago, the Young Lords promoted neighborhood improvements using tactics such as sit-ins in service agencies and churches.

Today, Puerto Rican immigration is not as intensive as in past years, nor does it compare to the continuing and massive immigration from Mexico. But Puerto Ricans continue the movement back and forth, and such proximity keeps the fervor of their identity alive. Puerto Rico's status vis-á-vis the United States is still uncertain. In 1953, the island's capacity was upgraded from its protectorate status to commonwealth, a change that had the support of many Puerto Ricans. Today the island is divided, however, over the issue of what the island's relationship should be with the United States. Some would like to see Puerto Rico become a state, while others want independence. Independence, however unlikely, would eliminate the ability of Puerto Ricans to enter and leave the mainland freely. Probably for that reason alone, many who have families scattered on both the island and the mainland oppose such a status.

Puerto Ricans are, next to Mexican Americans, the largest Hispanic group in the United States and will continue to play an important role in the evolution of the rubric Hispanic ethnicity that emerged in the 1980s and is pervading the United States at the present time. Whatever the future brings in terms of the mainland-island political link, the millions of Puerto Ricans who came in the course of the last two centuries have already left their mark.

But the third largest group, influential beyond their numbers in the formation of "Hispanidad," as the poet Octavio Paz termed the identity of Hispanics in the United States, are Cuban Americans.

✳ EARLY CUBAN IMMIGRATION TO THE UNITED STATES

Large-scale Cuban immigration to the United States occurred much more recently than that from either Puerto Rico or Mexico. In fact, over one million Cubans have entered the country since the Cuban Revolution of 1959. But like those of Puerto Ricans, Cuban communities in the United States can be traced back to the nineteenth century. From the outset, Florida, because of its proximity to the island and its Hispanic past, has been the destination of practically all Cubans. Each wave, starting with the first one in the 1860s, has many similar characteristics. A feature that distinguishes Cuban immigration from Mexican and Puerto Rican immigration is that Cubans have come in similar proportions from the middle class and the working class. As has been indicated, most immigrants from Mexico and Puerto Rico have been from the working class.

As early as the first major independence attempt, in 1868, Cubans left for Europe and the United States in sizable numbers. At least 100,000 had left by 1869, both as political refugees and in quest of better economic conditions. The wealthier émigrés fled to Europe to live in relative luxury, but middle-class merchants and professionals went to cities on the U.S. East Coast, such as New York. But the majority were workers who crossed the 90 miles or so to Florida. Cuban cigar manufacturers in Florida that had been operating in Key West since the 1830s eagerly welcomed the new arrivals for their factories. Key West was ideal for cigar-making because of its access to the tobacco plantations of Cuba. But more important, Cuban cigar-makers, such as the Spaniard Vicente Martínez Ybor, abandoned their Cuban operations and relocated to Florida, where they would not be as affected by Spanish mercantilistic policies. By the 1870s, Key West had become practically a Cuban town.

The Cuban community in the Florida town soon manifested strong ethnic solidarity, made even stronger by the affinity they felt for the Cubans fighting for independence back in their island home. Revolutionary clubs were formed to raise funds for the cause and to help such exiles as Carlos Manuel de Céspedes, who were organizing support in New York in the 1860s. A few years before he launched the 1895 independence bid, Jose Martí visited Key West often and considered the Florida town's Cuban community a key source of support for the cause of independence.

Once they established a base, Cubans became involved in local American politics. By 1875, there were more than 1,000 Cubans registered to vote in Monroe County, where Key West is located. The city's first mayor, who had the same given name as his father, was the son of Carlos Manuel de Céspedes, the hero of the Ten Years' War. In 1885, following labor problems in Key West, the manufacturer Martínez Ybor moved his operations to an area east of Tampa. The new development was named Ybor City, and soon other cigar manufactures located in the new complex. Countless cigar workers followed, and Tampa became the center of cigar-making in Florida. As in Key West, ethnic solidarity was bonded by the commitment to Cuban independence. Consequently, class differences were blurred as both wealthy owners and workers saw themselves supporting the same sacred cause. Other Cuban communities in Florida, smaller than the Key West and Tampa enclaves, also supported the independence movement, providing the exile aggregation with strong intraethnic links throughout the state. Racial differences between the white and black Cubans tested the ability to bond, however. The tension became worse in Florida when Jim Crow laws separated the races and Cuban blacks were forced to form their own institutions.

When Cuba was free of Spain, many exiles went back, but for many who had set roots in their respective émigré communities and who had children growing up in the United States, returning was difficult. Significantly, the Cuban presence in Florida during the last half of the nineteenth century was marked by many accomplishments. The first labor movements were Cuban, many businesses were operated and owned by Cubans, bilingual education received an impetus in the state, and, in cities like Key West and Tampa, Cubans were responsible for many improvements in city services and civic culture.

As Cuban political and economic influence increased in the nineteenth century, the Cubans played an increasingly more important role in U.S. policy toward the Spanish colonies in the Caribbean. But while helping the cause of independence, U.S. politicians also wanted to control a Cuba that one day would be free of Spanish dominance. Just as the struggle for Cuban independence had resulted in chaotic conditions leading to emigration, domination by Americans in the twentieth century fostered economic and political tensions that also provoked exile and emigration.

The Florida enclaves, established by earlier immigrants, served the Cubans who continued to arrive in Florida during the first 50 years of this century. Many left Cuba because of continued political turmoil on the island. In the 1920s, for example, a small number of young intellectuals moved to Miami to escape the repressive policies of Gerardo Machado and to plot against him. A dictator who ruled Cuba with the blessing of the United States, Machado was finally overthrown by a worker and student coalition in 1933. His demise was precipitated by the collapse of the U.S. economy, on which Cuba was completely dependent. He and his cronies, then, like countless others before them, also sought asylum in Florida. Since Cuba did not really achieve political peace after Machado's ouster, Miami, as well as other Florida communities, continued to be a refuge for Cubans who were not welcome in Cuba by the politicians in power.

✳ THE REVOLUTION OF FIDEL CASTRO AND CUBAN IMMIGRATION

It was for political reasons that the most dramatic exodus out of Cuba began after 1959. That year, Fidel Castro made his triumphant entry into Havana after he and his revolutionaries had defeated the brutal and repressive regime of Fulgencio Batista, a dictator who had been deeply involved in Cuban politics since the 1930s. Batista was only an army sergeant when in 1935 he led a barracks revolt that overthrew a president installed by the military to replace the banished dictator Antonio Machado. Then the next year, Batista overthrew the government that he himself had helped come to power, and in 1940, after a series of machinations, he was elected the first president under a new constitution promulgated that same year.

Batista had become perhaps the most astute opportunist in the history of Cuba, and he returned Cuba to levels of corruption not seen since the Machado years. But at least in this period, he seemed content to allow democracy to take its course by allowing elections. Two irresolute and corrupt administrations followed Batista's in 1944 and 1948, dashing any hopes that these new leaders would bring political stability and honesty to the troubled island republic. Consequently, many Cubans became disillusioned with the promises of democracy. Then in 1952, Batista seized power again, this time as an arrogant dictator. Batista then took Cuba to new heights of repression and corruption.

For much of this time, Batista had the support of

the United States. Ever since Cuba's independence, Americans had remained ever-vigilant about political events on the island. While policy toward Cuba followed the distinct requirements of the various U.S. administrations, both Republican and Democrat, the main course of foreign policy was to protect the extensive investments held by Americans in Cuba. The Platt Amendment allowed for intervention in Cuba whenever it seemed necessary to an American president. Indeed, before the 1920s, U.S. troops were sent three times to Cuba to intervene in internal affairs.

In the opinion of many Cubans, the United States had blatantly held Cuba as an economic and political colony. Even though the hated Platt Amendment was abrogated in 1934, it was apparent that Americans, during Batista's last rule in the 1950s, controlled most of the economy and much of the political process. By the time a young lawyer named Fidel Castro initiated guerrilla warfare against Batista, the former sergeant's feral methods of running his country began to alienate even the most cynical of American supporters. Thus, when Castro came to power in February 1959, his 26th of July Movement did not meet too much resistance from the United

Fidel Castro.

States, and at home he acquired a wide and popular following.

To Washington officials during the presidency of Dwight D. Eisenhower, Castro turned out to be more than what they bargained for, however. The young revolutionary exhibited an eclectic ideology, but it was clear that the new government was no longer going to permit American dominance, a stance which quickly alienated the Eisenhower administration. Another position, soon embraced by Castro, involved extensive land reform and radical restructuring of the economy. Very quickly, many of those affected, such as landowners and other members of the upper classes, turned against the revolution. Castro, to protect his fledgling movement, repressed those who resisted, and soon thousands of the disaffected left for the United States in a time-honored tradition established during the many previous shake-ups.

Shortly after Fidel Castro's rise to power, he began adopting socialistic ideas and turned to the Cuban Communist party for support, but not before the Eisenhower administration broke off relations with his revolutionary government. Eventually, the Soviet Union pledged its support to Castro, while the American government initiated a plan to welcome refugees. Eisenhower's motives to allow disaffected Cubans to enter the United States unencumbered were largely political. The 1950s were characterized by a cold-war mentality in which the Soviet Union and the United States waged an intense propaganda campaign for world prominence and acceptance. The flight of refugees was correctly anticipated by American officials to be middle class and essential to Cuba's economic well-being. Thus, their escape would deprive Cuba of technical and professional skills, serve as a propaganda victory against communism, and, by extension, deliver a blow to the Soviet Union's world prestige. But the Eisenhower administration projected another role for the exiles. Considering the history of discontented Cubans using the United States as a mustering point for insurgency against governments on the island, American officials foresaw the potential for a repetition with the latest wave of arrivals.

A curious element of the refugee project was a children's program designed to bring over thousands of young Cubans, supposedly to escape forced indoctrination by Castro's government. Wild rumors, abetted by American officials, circulated in Cuba and the refugee community in the United States that children were forcibly taken from their homes and sent to the Soviet Union to receive a Communist education. Within three years, 14,048 mostly male children left Cuba and were fostered in this country by various groups, including the Catholic church.

The first flight of American citizens repatriated from Cuba on December 19, 1966.

Most of these youngsters were scions of the middle and upper classes, and because many were nurtured further in this country, they became fairly well educated. As a consequence, today there are countless middle-aged Cuban professionals who were not rejoined with parents and other family members until their adult years, if at all.

With the election of John F. Kennedy to the presidency, relations between the United States and Cuba did not improve. President Eisenhower had encouraged Cuban refugees to prepare an invasion of Cuba to topple Castro, and in the cold-war atmosphere of the early 1960s, Kennedy subsumed this policy. In April 1961, Cuban exiles who were trained and armed by the United States, but who did not receive direct military support in their invasion, attempted a foray into Cuba that was doomed from the beginning. The failure of the infamous Bay of Pigs invasion embittered the thousands of Cubans who were in exile, but Castro's position at home was strengthened. To many observers throughout the world, especially in the Third World, the United States was clearly taking the side of the usurpers,

who attempted to overthrow a legitimately based government.

With the Bay of Pigs fiasco behind him, Kennedy continued to welcome Cuban refugees and to provide more structured military training for Cubans, most of whom still desired another attempt at overthrowing Cuba's Communist government. But in 1962, Kennedy redeemed himself from the Bay of Pigs disgrace by backing down the Soviet Union on a Russian plan to establish missile bases in Cuba. After this, the more viable of the two courses inherited from the Eisenhower years was to expand the refugee program.

Increasingly, welcoming refugees became more important to the U.S. policy of destabilizing the Cuban revolutionary government than armed insurrection or outright invasion. Such a course deprived Cuba of the merchants, technicians, and professionals so necessary to the island's struggling economy. In the ten years after the disastrous Bay of Pigs invasion, almost 500,000 Cubans left the island. Because of the heavy influx, a special program was initiated to settle the refugees outside of Florida. Although the majority of the fleeing Cubans stayed in Florida, thousands more went to other regions of the United States, especially to California, New York, and Chicago, areas that already had large populations of Hispanics. An elaborate project ensued that included numerous prerogatives for incoming Cubans. Refugee emergency housing, English-language training, federal educational funds for Cuban children, and medical care became part of a package that facilitated the immigration process.

When Lyndon B. Johnson became president after Kennedy's assassination, he vowed to embrace Cubans who wished to leave the island. Cubans then qualified for immigration status under special immigration provisions for refugees fleeing repressive governments. But Fidel Castro himself announced as early as 1965 that Cubans could leave Cuba if they had relatives in the United States. Castro stipulated, however, that Cubans already in Florida had to come and get them at Camarioca Bay. Nautical crafts of all types systematically left Miami to Camioraca, returning laden with anxious Cubans eager to rejoin their families on the mainland. The spectacle of the motley fleet of boats converging on Miami docks was dramatic, but the trip was also dangerous for the thousands of fleeing Cubans. Many of the boats were not seaworthy and capsized. An airlift was then organized with a great deal of publicity and fanfare. Thousands more arrived in the United States before the flights ended in 1973.

Castro also tapped the refugee issue so that he could gain moral backing from the rest of Latin

America and from the millions of Cubans living on the island who still supported him. He charged those who wanted to leave the island with betrayal, branding the emigrants with the epithet *gusano* (worm), which rhymes with *cubano* and is a derogatory name. In addition, he constantly reminded the world that, while Americans welcomed Cubans as displaced persons fleeing political persecution, they would not allow the same considerations to Chileans, Haitians, and other Latin Americans escaping repressive governments.

The final and most dramatic influx of Cubans came in the early 1980s. By that time much of the hard antipathy that Cubans felt toward Castro had become as much ritualistic as real. A generation had grown up in the United States that did not have the same sentiments as their parents. In addition, President Jimmy Carter, determined to depart from the cold-war policies of his predecessors, made advances toward Castro, urging reconciliation with the Cubans in the United States. Remarkably, moderate elements within that community responded and advocated harmonizing relations with the aging Castro. In 1977, a group of young Cuban exiles called the Antonio Maceo Brigade traveled to Cuba to participate in service work and to achieve a degree of rapprochement with the Cuban government. Back in Florida, many of the exiles branded these young envoys as traitors, and a clear message was sent out to rest of the Cuban community that any sympathizers would have to face their wrath.

Nonetheless, Castro's overtures to the exiled Cubans escalated and they were met with some positive response. His offer was the more attractive because he promised to release political prisoners as well, most whom had relatives in the United States. Cuban American adherence to reconciliation with Castro and his government continued to provoke intense opposition from conservative members of the exile community, however. Indeed, some of the advocates of a dialogue with the Communist leader were assassinated by armed paramilitary Cubans, but despite the opposition, relations between the exile community and Castro improved during the Carter years. They improved so much, in fact, that the earlier tact of using the refugee issue for propaganda purposes was lost as the tension abated between Castro and Cubans in the United States.

In April 1980 a dramatic incident received worldwide attention: a bus carrying a load of discontented Cubans crashed through the gates of the Peruvian embassy in Havana and the passengers received political asylum from Peru. When it became apparent that what the gate-crashers really wanted was to leave Cuba, Castro began to revise his policy of grad-

ually allowing Cubans to leave. In a calculated move, the Castro government announced that whoever wanted to leave Cuba should go to the Peruvian embassy. Immediately, 10,000 people crowded in. The Cuban government then processed and gave exit documents to those who came forth. Cuban exiles who happened to be on the island at the time of the embassy gate-crashing, upon their return to Miami, organized a flotilla of 42 boats. With Castro's blessing, they began the round-the-clock evacuation of the "Havana Ten Thousand," and Carter, as did presidents before him, decided to welcome the new influx of Cuban exiles.

Since the flotilla converged at Mariel Harbor to pick up passengers, which totaled over 125,000 by the time the boat-lift ended at the end of 1980, the refugees became known as the Marielito s. The explanation given by Castro for this whole phenomenon was rather simplistic. He charged that his policy of allowing exiles to visit the island had contaminated many erstwhile revolutionaries with the glitter of consumerism. It is probably true that travelers from the United States to the island did tempt Cubans with their abundance of consumer products, convincing many that life in a capitalist society was easier than life in Cuba. Nonetheless, Castro had to accept that socialism was at this point experiencing many difficulties and not delivering on many of the promises made some 20 years earlier.

The new refugees differed significantly from the earlier waves of displaced Cubans. Few were from the middle and upper classes of pre-Castro Cuba, as were most exiles then living in the United States, and there were also some racial differences. The new arrivals were more reflective of the general racial composition of Cuba; many blacks and mulattoes were in the Marielito ranks. Furthermore, in a crafty move, Castro deliberately cast out many political and social misfits during the boat-lift, an act that unfairly stigmatized the majority of 1980 émigrés, who were in the main normal, hardworking Cubans.

During the Marielito exit, Fidel Castro and President Carter became entangled in a now familiar struggle over which country would get more political capital from the refugee issue. Thousands of new arrivals crowded into processing centers, living in tent cities and even a football stadium in Miami. Many of the refugees became frustrated over the delay in being able to leave the camps. For many the stay in these "temporary camps" stretched out into months, even years. The Castro government was quick to imply that the United States was not really that anxious to provide refuge to Cubans who were poor, uneducated, and racially not as white as the previous influx.

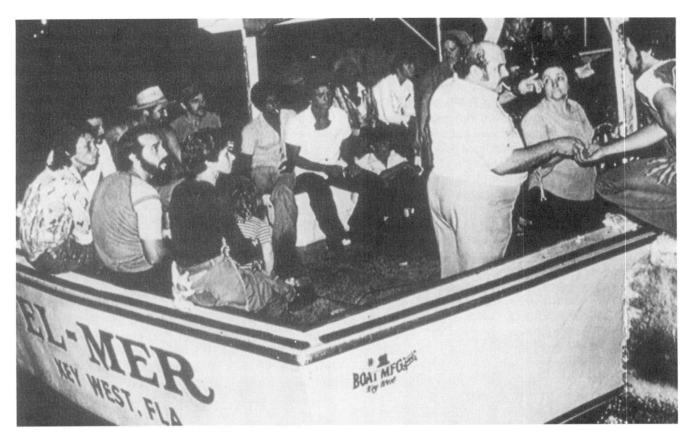

Cubans arriving in Miami during the Mariel boat-lift.

While these charges probably had some validity, the truth was more complex. Unlike previous émigrés, most of the Marielitos did not have families in Florida or elsewhere in the United States, and receiving a discharge from a camp required having an American sponsor. At first Cuban Americans and other Americans were anxious to provide this service, but as the excitement and newness of the boat-lift wore off, sponsors became harder to come by. The stigma suffered by Marielitos also led to difficulties once they were released. To be sure, a hard-core criminal element was dispersed among the new arrivals, but Marielitos were no different than the millions of immigrants who had preceded them to American shores in previous years. They sought to work and to find opportunities in their new environment. After all, that was the reason they had come.

The Cuban community has now acquired such deep roots in the United States that the term "exile" for many is no longer applicable. The post-Castro refugees and their children, along with descendants of Cubans who came to the United States earlier in the century, are now just another ethnic group in this country. They are part of the larger aggregate of Hispanics in the United States, which, of course, includes the Mexican Americans and Puerto Ricans.

As did Mexicans and Puerto Ricans, Cubans before the Castro era immigrated to the United States to work, to flee violence and repression, and, in general, to make a new life for themselves. Consequently, to survive, they forged fraternal organizations and looked to their homeland and culture to provide them with the necessary identity to build strong ethnic solidarity. In this respect Cuban Americans differ little from Mexican Americans and Puerto Ricans.

The vast, overwhelming majority, however, arrived in this country during the past 30 years. To be sure, fewer Cubans than Mexicans have immigrated to the United States in this same period, but the influx of the latter is part of a very long history of massive working-class immigration across the border. Cubans, because of the political conditions that provoked them to leave, were primarily from the more privileged classes. As a consequence, advantages of education, wealth, and racial acceptance allowed them to succeed in the United States at a faster pace than Mexicans and Puerto Ricans. In addition, because it was politically convenient,

Cubans received an inordinate amount of assistance from U.S. administrations, from Eisenhower to Reagan, which helped their effort to settle and adapt. This has provoked invidious comparisons and charges that the cards were stacked in their favor. Much of this sentiment has some foundation in fact, but it also has to be recognized that Cuban Americans have demonstrated a great amount of their own native initiative and drive, a fact that accounts for a large part of their success.

✴ HISPANIC IDENTITY IN THE UNITED STATES

Today an uneasy ethnic solidarity exists among Hispanics in the United States. At the political level there is much rhetoric that attempts to bring them all under one rubric, and, indeed, the term "Hispanic" has been fostered as an agent of this process. While Cubans are conservative on issues dealing with Cuba and communism, they share the same ideology with Mexican Americans and Puerto Ricans when it comes to cultural maintenance and resistance to what many consider debasing American val-

A legally immigrating Cuban woman is reunited with her granddaughter in Miami in 1980.

ues. Another bond is language, an issue that has been forced into the political arena by the "English only" movement. All Hispanics resent the onus placed on them because they speak Spanish, a language that is despised in many quarters of the Anglo-American community.

The development of a rubric *hispanidad* has been facilitated by three Spanish-language television networks and hundreds of radio stations that indirectly pound the message of ethnic bonding into millions of Hispanic homes. Variety entertainment programs, soap operas, and talk shows that air nationally are many times crafted to bring a balanced appeal to the variegated Spanish-speaking peoples taking their turn at the American opportunity structure. A plethora of slick-cover magazines have appeared in the last ten years aimed at all the Hispanic groups. Some use English, others Spanish, or they contain bilingual renditions. This process alone, perhaps unwittingly, is bound to evolve a pan-Hispanicism unique to the United States.

In large cities such as Los Angeles, Chicago, Houston, and Miami, Hispanics of all kinds are thrown together and many times common ties result in an affinity and some mingling. Where they have been together for a longer time, as in Chicago, Mexicans and Puerto Ricans, who have lived together since the 1940s, have merged into political coalitions, and interethnic marriages have produced thousands of Mexican-Puerto Rican offspring. The melding of Salvadorans, Puerto Ricans, Mexicans, and Spaniards in San Francisco has also been transpiring for a long time, and there, during the heady sixties movements, a strong Latino consciousness emerged in such barrios as the Mission District. In Los Angeles and Houston, entrepreneurs have tapped the Hispanic market, creating chains of enormous food stores called El Tíanguis and Fiesta, respectively. These outlets cater to the food tastes of every imaginable Hispanic group.

Another possible scenario is that differences will make for a separate evolution in the respective communities. As each Hispanic group evolves in the United States, with separate identities, they may become ensconced and comfortable in their own elaborated ethnicity. Indeed, this is true of the older and larger Hispanic groupings, who see themselves as Mexican Americans, Cuban Americans, and mainland Puerto Ricans. Hispanics in northern New Mexico, who are for all intents and purposes Mexican Americans, at times even remain insular from this group. So what can be expected from them when it comes to identifying with a larger national denomination?

Furthermore, interethnic prejudices still persist

at the community level between Hispanics. For example, at times Latin Americans or Spaniards living in the United States distance themselves from Mexican Americans or Puerto Ricans so that they will not be mistaken for them by non-Hispanics who hold prejudices against those groups. They may buy into Anglo-American prejudices and unwarranted stereotypes against certain groups in an unconscious effort to ingratiate themselves with the mainstream population. This is true even if back home they might have never dreamed of having these misgivings toward fellow Latins.

Another common source of inter-Hispanic antipathy is based on class origin. If the majority of one group is working class, as is the case with Mexicans, Puerto Ricans, and Central Americans, middle-class immigrants who come from South America often find it difficult to relate to what they consider a lower-class culture. They also demonstrate this orientation, of course, toward the working class back in their homelands. That phenomenon is also borne out among some upper-class Mexicans in the United States who look with disdain at compatriots who come from the *clases populares*.

There is even opposition to amalgamation among some Hispanic intellectuals who see the whole trend toward Hispanicization as a tool of consumerism. Obviously, it would be easier to aim at a large market rather than at disparate groups. There is also a residue of resentment within some in the Hispanic community toward Cuban exiles because of that group's persistent support of a conservative foreign policy toward Latin America. But the ultimate fear is that a bland, malleable ethnic group will emerge.

Regardless, the process is going to find its own level. Despite the destructive prejudices that exist between Hispanic groups or the well-intended admonitions of intellectuals, common roots exist between Hispanics regardless of national or class origin. These will eventually make crucial links that no one can foresee. Rather than resist, Hispanics would be better off trying to shape this irresistible force into a positive ideal of brotherhood and humanity so that they can take their rightful place in the American mosaic, and even become a remarkably potent political power.

References

Acuña, Rudolfo. *Occupied America: A History of Chicanos*. New York: Harper and Row, 1981.

Bannon, John Francis. *The Journey of Alvar Nuñez Cabeza de Vaca*. Chicago: Río Grande Press, 1964.

Bolton, Herbert. *Spanish Exploration in the Southwest 1542–1706*. New York: Barnes and Noble, 1946.

Cabral del Hoyo, Humberto. *The Thumbnail History of Mexico*. Ciudad Mexíco. Comité Norteamericano Pro-Mexíco, 1960.

Claypole, William, and John Robottom. *Caribbean Story*. White Plains, New York: Longman, 1986.

De Leon, Arnoldo. *The Tejano Community*. Albuquerque: University of New Mexico Press, 1982.

García, Mario T. *Mexican Americans*. New Haven: Yale University Press, 1989.

Morales, Julio. *Puerto Rican Poverty and Migration: We Just Had to Try Elsewhere*. New York: Praeger, 1986.

Taylor, Paul Schuster, *Mexican Labor in the United States: Chicago and the Calumet Region*. Berkeley: University of California Press, 1932.

Suchlicki, Jaime. *Cuba: From Columbus to Castro*. Washington: Pergammon, 1986.

Weber, David J. *The Mexican Frontier, 1821–1846: The American Southwest under Mexico*. Albuquerque: University of New Mexico Press, 1982.

F. Arturo Rosales

②

Spanish Explorers and Colonizers

✳ Native American Cultures ✳ The Age of Exploration: The Caribbean, Mexico, and Florida
✳ Spanish Expeditions to Florida ✳ Spanish Exploration and Colonization of the Southwest
✳ Spanish Explorations to California

No one is sure when pre-Columbian inhabitants of the Western Hemisphere first appeared, although scholars generally agree that they originated in Asia. Presumably, they crossed the land bridge that existed between what is now the Soviet Union and Alaska and moved southward. Traveling a few miles per generation, some settled around Canada and the Mississippi Valley, while others migrated to what is today the Southwest, Mexico, Central America, the Caribbean, and all the way down to Cape Horn. By 1492, the Native American population of the Western Hemisphere may have reached between 35 to 45 million.

Over the vast area that is now Canada and the United States—with a few exceptions—the pre-Columbian inhabitants never advanced much beyond hunting, fishing, and subsistence farming. By contrast, those who lived on the Mexican plateau, as well as those who lived in Central America and in the Andean sierras, had demonstrated a high degree of cultural achievement. The great discoveries that they made in science, as well as the great works of art that they created, still affect our lives.

✳ NATIVE AMERICAN CULTURES

The Mayan Civilization

Agriculture had its beginnings around 7000 B.C. when a Native American group known as the Otomí discovered a plant they called *teozintle* that produced edible grain. The Otomí of the southern Mexican plateau apparently perfected the cultivation of teozintle over the years until it produced corn. The development of corn allowed these Native Americans to abandon their nomadic ways, and they began to build permanent dwellings. By 5000 B.C. the Otomíes were cultivating a variety of crops, such as

corn, squash, beans, and chile, as well as weaving garments from vegetable fibers. Eventually, they acquired skills in the making of pottery and utensils. Perhaps from the Otomí sprang the Mayan civilization of Central America and southern Mexico.

Mayan civilization can be divided into three periods: the Preclassic, from about 800 B.C. to about A.D. 300; the Classic, from about A.D. 300 to 1000; and the Postclassic, from about A.D. 1000 to A.D. 1500. Of these three periods, the Classic and the Postclassic were the most important.

The Classic period was centered in the southern jungles of the Yucatán Peninsula, the present-day Mexican states of Chiapas and Tabasco, and the present-day nations of Guatemala, Belize, and Honduras. Among the great Mayan cultural centers of the Classic period were Tikal in Guatemala, Copán in Honduras, and Palenque in Mexico. The Classic period ended shortly before A.D. 1000. No one is sure what caused the Maya to abandon the sites. Some think that it was soil exhaustion, while others believe that it was a civil war.

The Postclassic period began around A.D. 1000. Apparently, ruling nobles toward the end of the Classic period moved to Mayan outposts in northern Yucatán and began to transform them into city-states. Among the great city-states of the Postclassic period were Mayapan, Chichén Itzá, and Uxmal, all of them located on the Yucatán Peninsula.

Thanks to the work of archaeologists and the accuracy of Mayan records, we know more about the Maya than any other Native Americans. Unlike the Aztec or Inca, the Maya never built a centralized empire. At the peak of their civilization, the Maya occupied an area of approximately 200,000 square miles. In that vast area were sovereign city-states sharing in language, culture, and religion. While the

Mayan governmental structure could be characterized as a simple one—a hereditary ruler aided by priests and nobles presided over each city-state—Mayan cultural achievement could not. During both the Classic and the Postclassic periods, the Maya reached a very high state of cultural development, which was reflected in their dress, customs, buildings, and arts.

Mayan intellectual achievements included carved hieroglyphics and watercolor pictographs on fiber paper. Still preserved is the *Popol-Vuh*, the sacred book of the Maya, which traces the creation of man prior to 3151 B.C., and the book of Chilam Balam, known as the masterpiece of Mayan literature. The Maya excelled in chronology; their year was composed of 20 months of 18 days each, to which they added five extra days. The Maya were also accomplished mathematicians. As the late Mayanist Sylvanus Morley wrote in *A History of Latin America* (1967), "For the first time in the history of the human race, they had devised a system of numeration by position involving the concept and use of the mathematical quantity of zero."

Mayan architecture was both original and outstanding. The material used by the Maya in building their cities and pyramids consisted of burnt limestone. Their cities were a collection of temples and monuments embellished with carvings and wall paintings. Mayan architecture was characterized by use of the corbeled roof or false arch as well as the vault.

When the Spaniards first arrived in Yucatán in 1511, the Mayan civilization was in a decadent state as a result of civil wars. Soon the conquerors began the process of destroying the few Mayan cities that were left standing and began building Catholic churches on top of Mayan temples. Ironically, the descendants of the once proud Maya live today in misery and exploitation.

The Aztec Civilization

Undoubtedly, the most famous Native Americans, who inhabited Mexico when Hernán Cortés landed on the coast of Veracruz in 1519, were the Aztec. Around A.D. 1200, when the city of Atzcapotzalco ruled the Central Valley of Mexico, there arrived a tribe of nomads who called themselves Aztec and who said they came from Aztlán (Place of the Herons). Legend has it that the Aztec were moving southward from northern Mexico because one of their gods, Huitzilopochtli, had ordered them to settle where they saw an eagle poised on a cactus and with a snake in its mouth. After wandering from one place to the other, the Aztec supposedly saw the sign on the shores of Lake Texcoco, east of present-day Mexico City. Atzcapotzalco's rulers allowed the Aztec to settle on the lake's shores in exchange for a tribute, and in 1325 the Aztec began to build their capital, Tenochtitlán, in honor of Tenoch.

In 1428, the Aztec launched a surprise attack on Atzcapotzalco, and Aztec armies began to conquer the Central Valley. By the early sixteenth century, Aztec dominance extended from the Central Valley of Mexico to parts of Guatemala. An estimated 20 million people lived in that empire.

The Aztec governmental structure was theoretically a democratic one, with each tribe practicing a certain degree of autonomy. In addition, each tribe appointed a delegate to the Supreme Council, which elected the emperor. In practice, as the Aztec nobility acquired more power, the Aztec Empire became a theocratic oligarchy.

Aztec religion was less spiritual than Mayan religion, and it was certainly a bloodthirsty one. Because their ferocious war-god, Huitzilopochtli, demanded human sacrifices, Aztec warriors were educated from childhood to seek prisoners of war to be offered as sacrifices. In 1487, for example, the Aztec inaugurated the temple of Huitzilopochtli by sacrificing more than 25,000 captives. In short, the Aztec waged war just to placate their war-god.

The Aztec capital of Tenochtitlán was a magnificent city. It had an estimated population of 200,000. Connected by a system of causeways and canals, the city had its own aqueduct. The giant market of Tlatelolco exhibited fresh produce from *chinampas* (floating gardens). In the center of the city there was the magnificent temple of Tenochtitlán, attended by 5,000 priests. Tenochtitlán, in sum, was a city of beauty and pageantry.

Like their predecessors, the Aztec had outstanding knowledge of the medicinal properties of plants, and they were able potters and weavers. Intellectually, however, the Aztec were not original. Their pyramids were merely copies of Toltec architecture, and their sculptures never quite matched those of the Maya. Their writing never went beyond simple pictographs painted on cloth, skin, and magéuy paper. They made no contribution to mathematics or astronomy, and their calendar was a copy of the Toltec calendar. Despite its lack of originality, the Aztec civilization was a splendid one.

The Aztec Empire might have been a prosperous one, but it had a very serious weakness. This flaw was the hostility of the conquered tribes who supplied the victims for the bloodthirsty Huitzilopochtli. Any powerful savior who would curb or destroy the power of the hated Aztec would certainly find allies among these conquered tribes. In 1519, the subjugated tribes were expecting the scheduled visit of the blond Toltec deity Quetzalcoatl, who was going to bring justice and punish the evil ones. Instead of Quetzalcoatl, a blond-haired, blue-eyed Spaniard named Hernán Cortés landed in Veracruz and quickly moved northward to conquer the Aztec Empire. Cortés and his fellow Spaniards leveled Tenochtitlán in 1521 and built Mexico City on the same site. Ironically, the "liberators" would become masters for three centuries.

The Pueblo Culture of the Southwest

The most magnificent archaeological sites and the best-preserved pre-Columbian cultures in the United States are found in the Southwest. There were many Native American cultures in the Southwest, some nomadic, some sedentary. Perhaps the most important was the Pueblo culture.

Descendants of the prehistoric Anasazi people, the Pueblos lived in western New Mexico and the upper Rio Grande area of that state. In addition, there were Pueblo villages in northeastern Arizona. Among the Pueblo peoples at the time of the Spanish arrival were the Zuni, Hopi, Keres, and Tano.

It is speculated that the Pueblos were sedentary people whose life primarily depended on agriculture. At the time of Coronado's expedition to the Southwest in the 1540s, there were an estimated 66 Pueblo villages in the area of New Mexico, growing such crops as corn, beans, squash, and cotton. Chile pepper, a trademark of the Southwest, was apparently not known to the Pueblos. Since water was essential to the arid region where the Pueblos lived, they had a system of irrigation, which consisted of using the runoff from rains. Each Pueblo village also had a cistern. Although the Pueblos lacked the plow, they nevertheless made good use of the digging stick.

Because the Pueblos were extremely concerned with their security, most of their dwellings were built on barren hilltops away from their fertile patches of land. Their houses were made out of stone or adobe and were strong enough to withstand an enemy attack. In pre-Columbian times, Pueblo houses had neither doors nor windows—a security measure—and the only entrance was by means of portable ladders through hatches in the roofs. Essential to the Pueblo village was the *kiva*, a secret underground ceremonial chamber that served both as a ceremonial center and a meeting place. Only males were allowed in the kiva.

Pueblo governmental organization was simple. The Pueblos never achieved any unity beyond the village, for each village was politically autonomous. Land belonged to the community, and each village was ruled by a council of elders varying from ten to 30 members.

The Pueblos were religious people who worshiped the sun and the elements. It is estimated that they devoted half their time to religious activities. Foremost among their ceremonies were the communal dances combining drama, dance, music, and poetry.

Being a sedentary people, the Pueblos had time to create works of art. Pueblo artistic expression showed itself in basketry, weaving, and pottery. Pueblo basketry was known for its geometric design and symmetry. Although the Pueblos did not learn weaving until A.D. 700, they perfected this art through the use of transverse colored patterns and a technique called tie-dyeing. The Pueblos lacked the potter's wheel, but their pottery was carefully crafted by hand and showed gradual changes in design, color, and symbols.

Despite more than 450 years of contact with the white man, the remnants of the pre-Columbian Pueblo of the Southwest have survived to the present.

The Natives of Florida

When Ponce de León landed on the shores of Florida in 1513, there were an estimated 100,000 Native Americans living there. They were divided among six major groups: the Timucua, the Tocobaga, the Apalachee, the Ais and Jeagas, the Tequesta, and the Calusa.

The Timucua, who occupied a diagonal region from northeast Florida to the Tampa Bay area, were mostly hunters but also practiced subsistence farming. About 40,000 strong, they were the most numerous of the Florida natives. The Tocobaga, who lived around the Tampa Bay area, numbered around 7,000. They were mostly fishermen but also cultivated corn, beans, and squash. The Apalachee population of Florida, which existed in the panhandle area, numbered about 25,000. The Apalachee depended on corn and vegetables for their living, but when these ran out they would turn to hunting and fishing. The Ais and Jeagas, who numbered only around 3,000, were the most primitive. Living on the eastern coast of Florida, they never learned agriculture and were principally fishermen and gatherers. South of the Ais and Jeagas, there were some 5,000 Tequesta, who knew no agriculture but were excellent fishermen. Finally, there were the 25,000 fierce Calusa living in an area that extended from Cape Sable to the Tampa Bay area. Nonagricultural, the Calusa lived on shellfish.

Although the Florida natives had no system of writing and made no contribution to the advancement of knowledge, they nevertheless developed organized governments with real authority and were skilled at making pottery. To label all of them primitive would be erroneous.

The Pre-Columbian Inhabitants of the Caribbean

Although anthropologists have found evidence of people who inhabited the Caribbean islands, there is no reliable estimate as to their numbers. Figures have ranged from as low as 60,000 people to as high as seven million. Knowledge regarding their origins is also rather sketchy. The most plausible theory indicates that they originated on the Venezuelan mainland and migrated to the islands more than 1,000 years before the arrival of Columbus. When Columbus discovered the New World, there were four major cultures in the Caribbean: the Guanahatabey, the Ciboney, the Arawak, and the Carib.

The Guanahatabey were the oldest culture group. They were concentrated in the Guanahacabibes Peninsula of western Cuba. The Guanahatabey were extremely primitive and seemed to depend on shellfish for their existence. They had no dwellings and possessed no organizational skills.

The Ciboney was a Stone Age culture. Although remains of the Ciboney have been found in some of the Bahama islands and in areas of Jamaica, they primarily inhabited western Cuba and the southwestern peninsula of the island of Hispaniola. Characterized by their kindness and gentle manners, the Ciboneyes developed a crude form of subsistence agriculture, but fishing was more important to them.

While some of the Ciboney lived in caves, the majority lived in *bajareques* (primitive thatched huts). Ciboney governmental organization was very simple, and its symbol of authority was the *cacique* (village chieftain). Although the Ciboney lacked artistic ability, they had knowledge of the medicinal property of various herbs and plants. Because of their lack of military skills, some of the Ciboney had been subjugated by the Arawak when Columbus first arrived in Cuba.

The Arawak probably originated in Venezuela and spread across the Greater Antilles and the Bahamas. There were two major groups: the Lucayo, who occupied the Bahamas, and the Taino, who inhabited central and eastern Cuba, as well as Hispaniola, Jamaica, and Puerto Rico.

Arawakan settlements ranged from a few *bohíos* to villages of more than 5,000 people. Although matrilineal inheritance characterized Arawakan society, political organization was male-dominated. Each Arawak village was headed by a cacique. Although the cacique was not an all-powerful ruler, he nevertheless was the final authority in all village matters. Cacique leadership was hereditary. When the cacique died, he was replaced by his son. If there was no male heir, the eldest son of the cacique's sister became the new cacique. The cacique was aided by his *nitaínos* (principal advisers). The nitaínos were usually in charge of the labor force, and they were mostly the oldest males in the village. Since Arawak religion was highly organized, the *behique* (priest) occupied an important part in Arawak society. The behique interpreted the signs of the *zemíes* (gods) and was also a medicine man. Each village had a zemí house, where *areítos* (ceremonies) were performed. Finally, there were the *naboríes* (commoners).

Research on Arawak villages seems to indicate that they were located in areas that were conducive to agriculture. Although the Arawak harvested corn, yams, beans, and peanuts, their principal staple was *yuca* (manioc root). From the yucca plant they made a type of unleavened bread called *cassava*. Tobacco was also grown by the Arawak and used by the behique in religious ceremonies in order to attract the spirits. The Arawak supplemented their diet with fish, mollusks, turtle eggs, snakes, bats, and iguanas.

The Arawak had few metallurgical skills. Arawak pottery, on the other hand, showed a degree of sophistication. The Arawak were excellent basket weavers; they made basket fish traps and there is evidence they used a type of basket for carrying water. Another area in which they excelled was wood carving. The Arawak constructed canoes without the help of metal tools, making it possible for them to conduct an intensive island trade. In addition, the Arawak carved out wooden zemí figures and were known for the *macana* (a wooden club used as a weapon). Since cotton was grown on the islands, the Arawak weaved it into hammocks, nets, and bags.

A few years before Columbus' arrival in the New World, Arawak hegemony in the Caribbean was being challenged by the Carib. Little is known about this group, for they were merely island raiders. The Carib were the last of the Native Americans that entered the Caribbean. By 1492, they occupied most of the Lesser Antilles, and Carib warriors had already terrorized the Arawak population of Cuba, Puerto Rico, and Hispaniola.

Knowledge of Carib social and political organization, economic development, and way of life is sketchy at best. They practiced subsistence farming. Unlike the Arawak, they grew crops for dietary purposes only and not for trade. Their religion lacked the zemíes of the Arawak, as well as the ceremonial rituals. Carib political organization was even simpler than that of the Arawak. The Carib cacique busied himself planning raids rather than solving village problems. The Carib raided islands for the dual purpose of finding female slaves and male prisoners. The male Arawak they captured were ritualistically cooked and eaten. (The word *Carib* means cannibal in Arawak.)

According to William Claypole and John Robottom in their *Caribbean Story* (1986), the Carib were decorative people. They applied flower petals and gold dust to their body paint before it dried. They also wore chains of stone and coral around their arms, wrists, and legs. They pierced their nose, lips, and ears to hold ornaments made from fish spines and plates of turtle shells.

As one might expect, the Carib excelled in the area of weaponry. Their arsenal included bows, spears, and *macanas* (wooden clubs). The Carib *piragua* (a narrow, high-prowed canoe) was the fastest and swiftest canoe in the Caribbean, and it was capable of traveling great distances. Carib expansion in the Caribbean was checked only by the arrival of the Spaniards, and later, the British, French, and Dutch.

The year 1492 marked the beginning of the end for the Native Americans of the Caribbean. The Ciboney and Arawak, whom Columbus described as gentle people of great simplicity, disappeared from the cultural scene as a result of diseases and exploitation. A little over a century after Columbus' arrival, the Carib succumbed to British, French, and Dutch firepower.

✳ THE AGE OF EXPLORATION: THE CARIBBEAN, MEXICO, AND FLORIDA

It was near the end of the fifteenth century when the nations of Europe set in motion the discovery and exploration of the New World. The glory of the discovery, exploration, and colonization of this vast mass of land for more than a century and a half fell to practically one nation—Spain.

Spain's discovery and conquest of the New World came at a fortuitous time, for it was after the union of the Crowns of Aragón and Castile and the expulsion of the Moors from their bastion in Granada that Spain could supply manpower. Thus, with men trained in the profession of arms and eager to seek glory under one monarch, one religion, one empire, and one sword, Spain was able to make her greatest contribution to the Renaissance—discovery and colonization of the New World.

The Voyages of Christopher Columbus

Christopher Columbus was not the first European to step foot on the New World. Research has shown that the Scandinavian Leif Eriksson had earned that honor some 500 years before Columbus. Yet, if Columbus was not the first European to step onto American soil, he certainly had the good fortune of being the first one to keep a record of his voyage and

thus establish a permanent presence in the New World.

Christopher Columbus was probably born in Genoa in 1451 and became a sailor at an early age. An intuitive man, Columbus collected and studied maps. From his studies, he gathered that the world was round and that the East could be reached by sailing west. Although he was persistent, Columbus failed to persuade several European monarchs to finance his proposed voyage to the rich island of Cipango (Japan) and the mainland of Cathay (China), where the Great Khan lived. Finally, after a series of pleas, Columbus convinced Queen Isabella of Castile to support his quest. He not only obtained financial backing but also managed to get Isabella to appoint him admiral in the Spanish navy and governor of any land he should discover.

On August 3, 1492, Columbus sailed from the Spanish port of Palos de Moguer with three ships: the *Pinta*, the *Niña*, and the *Santa María*, his flagship. On October 12, 1492, the Spaniards landed on an island called San Salvador—either present-day Watling Island or Samana Cay in the eastern Bahamas. On October 27, they landed on northeastern Cuba. Convinced that it was either Cipango or Cathay, Columbus sent representatives to the Great Khan and his gold-domed cities, only to find impoverished Arawak living in bohíos.

Columbus then sailed eastward to an island he named La Española—Hispaniola—which today is shared by Haiti and the Dominican Republic. On the treacherous coast of La Española, Columbus lost his flagship. With what remained of the *Santa María*, he made a makeshift fort, which he called La Navidad, and set sail for Spain. He reached Palos de Moguer on March 15, 1493.

Columbus was convinced that he had reached the Far East, and the queen responded by granting him a fleet of 17 ships and 1,200 men for a second voyage. Choosing a southerly course, Columbus discovered the Virgin Islands and Puerto Rico before reaching La Española in November 1493. There, he found La Navidad destroyed and no trace of his men. Apparently, the gentle Arawak of La Española could no longer tolerate the abuses of the Spanish garrison and had killed them.

After establishing Isabella, the first permanent European settlement in the New World, Columbus set sail from La Española and discovered Jamaica in the summer of 1494. Obsessed with finding the Great Khan, he sailed for Cuba and back to La Española. Finally, he returned to Spain in 1496.

Although he had little but complaints to show for his efforts, Columbus still remained in the good graces of the Spanish queen and had a positive re-

Frontispiece from the original 1493 edition of Cristóbal Colón's letter to the Catholic Kings describing his discoveries.

sponse from her to his request for a third voyage. On this voyage, in 1498, he sailed south of La Española and on July 31 discovered the island of Trinidad. He then sighted the Venezuelan coast and discovered the mouth of the Orinoco River. He concluded that the Venezuelan coast was Cathay and the Orinoco one of the four rivers of Paradise. But Columbus found no paradise when he returned to La Española. A settlers' revolt had taken place against his brother Bartholomew, whom he had left in charge after his second voyage. The flow of complaints against the Columbus brothers reached Isabella, and she dispatched her chief justice and royal inspector, Francisco de Bobadilla, to investigate. In 1500, a year after his arrival in La Española, Bobadilla ordered Columbus' arrest and sent him in chains to Spain.

Isabella stripped Columbus of his titles, but was willing to give him one more chance—a fourth voyage. With four ships and 150 men, he sailed from Spain in May 1502. After discovering the island of Martinique, he made a few brief stops in the Lesser Antilles and Puerto Rico. He then headed for La Española, where he was denied permission to land by the Spanish authorities on the island. After being rebuffed, he sailed west and cruised the coast of Central America.

After an eight-month search for the Great Khan, Columbus headed for La Española, only to be shipwrecked off Jamaica. Finally, in 1503, rescuers from La Española arrived. In November 1504, returned to Spain. Two years later he died in the Spanish city of Valladolid.

Shortly after Columbus' death, Spain was firmly entrenched in the New World, thanks to his efforts and to those of the Spanish conquistadors who followed.

The Conquest of Puerto Rico

After the expulsion of the Moors from Granada, a great number of men trained in the profession of arms found themselves idle. Since it was difficult for them to adapt to this new way of life, they swarmed to the New World, prepared to conquer land for their king and garner glory for themselves. One such man was Juan Ponce de León, a native of the village of Santervás de Campos, kingdom of León.

Ponce de León was born in 1460. He was a member of one of the oldest families of Spain, the Ponces, and a relative of Rodrigo Ponce, also called the "second Cid Campeador" for his actions against the Moors. The surname León had been acquired by the marriage of one of the Ponces to doña Aldonza de León, sister of Fernando III, conqueror of Seville and father of Alfonso el Sabio.

Ponce de León spent his boyhood serving as page to Pedro Núñez de Guzmán, a powerful nobleman who later became tutor to Prince Ferdinand, brother of Charles V. During his adolescence, Ponce de León entered the profession of arms. He served faithfully and bravely in the struggle to capture Granada from the Moors, and in 1493 he qualified to go with Columbus on his second voyage to the New World.

After his voyage with Columbus, Ponce de León returned to Spain. In 1502, however, he was recalled by the governor of La Española, Nicolás de Ovando, to crush a revolt in Higuey (now Haiti), on the eastern part of the island. He was so successful in extinguishing the revolt that he was appointed second in command by Ovando in 1504. While performing his military duties in the village of Salvaleón, Ponce de León had news that there was gold on the nearby island of Borinquen (Puerto Rico) and obtained a license from Ovando to explore the island and search for it. In 1508, he sailed in a small caravel for Puerto Rico, where he established friendly relations with the native chieftain, Agueibana, who presented him with gold, which was later sent to Ovando.

When Ponce de León returned to La Española from Puerto Rico, he learned that Ovando had been replaced as governor by Diego Columbus, who in turn had appointed Juan Cerón governor of Puerto Rico. Instead of revolting, Ponce de León accepted the situation philosophically. When Ovando reached Spain in 1509, the situation changed drastically, for he persuaded the king to appoint Ponce de León governor of Puerto Rico. So great was the success of Ovando's talk with the king that Ponce de León's appointment as governor of Puerto Rico disregarded the rights of Diego Columbus.

Ponce de León proceeded immediately to establish his supremacy as governor of Puerto Rico by arresting Cerón and enslaving the natives who refused to submit. Perhaps his closest ally in pacifying the natives was Becerrillo, his greyhound. According to the colonial chronicler Gonzalo Fernández de Oviedo, Becerrillo's fierceness proved of such great value to the Spaniards that it led to the coining of a new word in the language—*aperrear*—(to cast to dogs).

While Ponce de León was busy pacifying the natives, the king, perceiving the injustice done to Diego Columbus, deposed Ponce de León as governor and appointed Juan Cerón to the post in 1511. Ponce de León's dismissal did not change the overall picture; the Spanish conquest of Puerto Rico had been completed.

Juan Ponce de León.

The Conquest of Cuba

Two years after Columbus' death, the Spanish Crown became interested in colonizing Cuba. In 1508, Sebastián de Ocampo sailed around the island and began to spread tales that there was gold and silver in Cuba. The governor of La Española, Nicolás de Ovando, chose his most trusted lieutenant, Diego Velázquez, to carry out the task of colonization. A native of Cuéllar, Spain, Velázquez had accompanied Columbus during his second voyage to the New World and later had served in La Española. Velázquez had gained both fame and fortune on that island, and in late 1510 he departed with over 300 men to conquer Cuba.

Velázquez landed at Puerto Escondido, close to where the present-day American naval base of Guantánamo is located. There he met the resistance of Hatuey, an expatriate Arawak from La Española who conducted deadly guerrilla raids against the Spaniards. Hatuey's fighters, however, succumbed to Spanish firepower. Hatuey was captured by Velázquez and condemned to be burned at the stake. He is remembered in Cuban history as the first island hero and a symbol of Cuba's resistance against the foreigners.

After subjugating the Arawak population of the area, Velázquez proceeded to establish the town of Nuestra Señora de la Asunción de Baracoa in 1512. Thus, Baracoa became Cuba's first permanent settlement. By 1517, Velázquez had conquered the entire island.

While there was little gold in Cuba, La Española, and Puerto Rico, the islands nevertheless became the laboratories of the Spanish Empire. It was there where the *repartimiento* (the practice of parceling Native Americans) was carried out by the Spaniards. Eventually, the repartimiento was replaced by the *encomienda* system, which granted a predetermined number of Native Americans and a predetermined amount of land to a deserving Spaniard, known as the encomendero. He, in turn, was entitled to free labor from the Native Americans in exchange for protecting them. The system, however, failed, for the encomenderos exploited the Native Americans mercilessly. It was in the Antilles where the mixing of the races first occurred and where the missions to convert the native population were first established. The islands also served as havens to launch expeditions to other parts of the New World.

✳ SPANISH EXPEDITIONS TO FLORIDA

After the discovery of the New World by Columbus, the nations of Western Europe extended their radius of exploration. In May 1497 the British sent a

Venetian sailor, Sebastian Cabot, to explore the coast of North America. Sailing from Bristol, Cabot supposedly ran down the Atlantic coast from Cape Breton as far south as 38 degrees north latitude. Scarcity of provisions compelled him to abandon his project and return to England.

It is difficult to calculate how far Cabot might have sailed in his southward trek along the eastern coast of North America before he was forced to direct his course toward England. It is equally difficult to determine how much of the southern portion of North America at that time bore the name Florida. We learn from Brinton's *Notes on the Floridian Peninsula* that Florida then included an indefinite extent of territory north and west of present Florida; and in Williams' *The Territory of Florida* (1837), it is said that "the name of Florida was at one period applied to all the tract of country which extends from Canada to the Rio del Norte" along the U.S.-Mexican border. Whatever might have been the southernmost point reached by Cabot in coasting America, it is certain that he did not land in present-day Florida.

During the same month of the same year as Cabot's voyage (May 1497), Amerigo Vespucci, who had been occupied in providing naval equipment for the Spanish monarchs, sailed from the Spanish port of Cádiz on a voyage of exploration to the New World. The possibility that Vespucci had explored the Florida coast was accepted until the 1930s, when discrepancies in the Vespucci documents were discovered by scholars.

Obviously, unidentified mariners had visited the coasts of Florida, but probably not until after 1493. It was in May of that year that Pope Alexander VI issued a Bull of Demarcation for the purpose of dividing the newly discovered lands between Portugal and Spain. Some historians are of the opinion that this Bull of Demarcation is the reason unknown mariners who had explored the Atlantic coast as far down as Florida had judged it expedient to leave their discoveries and exploration unrecorded. As proof of their point, they often offer the fact that Ponce de León and those who followed him found the Florida Indians suspicious and hostile. Although this is evidence of prior discovery, the official credit for discovering Florida goes to Ponce de León, because his voyage in 1513 was made under official Spanish auspices, recorded, and recognized.

Legend tells us that while Ponce de León was in Puerto Rico, he heard of an island lying north of La Española called Bimini, reputedly famous for a spring that restored youth to all who drank its waters. This legend has been used often by some as a reason for Ponce de León's expedition. Historians agree, however, that this was not the prime reason for Ponce de León's voyage. It seems ridiculous that Ponce de León, a robust adventurer who had spent many years fighting the Indians in Puerto Rico and La Española, would have been influenced by such a tale to the extent of expending most of his fortune in outfitting an expedition in order to verify it.

Using the influence he had at court, Ponce de León obtained from Ferdinand a patent in February 1512 allowing him to discover and settle the island of Bimini and granting him the title *adelantado* (advance representative of the king). The patent specified that he was to equip the expedition at his own cost and prohibited him from trespassing on any lands belonging to the Portuguese sovereign. It also provided that the natives found on the island were to be divided among the members of the expeditionary force as slaves. The king also reserved the right to keep one-tenth of all riches that were found. Finally, it provided that a report on the conditions found on the island was to be sent to the king. There is no mention in this patent of the Fountain of Youth, and furthermore there is a complete absence of any provision for Christianizing the Native Americans; it is therefore also surprising that this document was countersigned by the bishop of Palencia.

Armed with this royal grant, the veteran man of arms purchased a vessel in order to go to Spain and make preparations for the conquest of Bimini. Meanwhile, the king, finding Ponce de León's services necessary in Puerto Rico, sent orders to the Council of the Indies to postpone the expedition to Bimini and placed Ponce de León in command of a fort in Puerto Rico.

Thus delayed in the royal service, Ponce de León was unable to obtain supplies until the following year. On March 3, 1513, he set sail from the Puerto Rican port of San Germán with three caravels (the Santiago, the Santa María de la Consolación, and the San Cristóbal), taking along as pilot a native of Palos de Moguer named Antón de Alaminos, who had as a boy accompanied Columbus and whose name would long be associated with explorations around the Gulf of Mexico. Sailing northwest by north, they landed on March 14 in San Salvador, the island where Columbus probably had first landed on his first voyage to the New World. After refitting at San Salvador, Ponce de León navigated on a northwesterly course, and on Easter Sunday, March 27, he sighted the Florida mainland, along which he sailed until the second of April, when he anchored. On some day between the second and eighth of April, Ponce de León went ashore to take possession of this newly discovered land. Some historians believe that Ponce de León was so impressed with the beauty of this land that he named it *La Florida*. Others are of the opinion that he named the land *La Florida* because it was discovered on

Easter Sunday, which in Spanish is called *Pascua Florida*. Although there is no record of the landing place, many historians believe that it was the coastal area between the Saint Johns River and Saint Augustine; others affirm that it was Cape Sable.

Of the landing ceremony there is no record. There could have been no celebration of mass, for there were no priests in the expedition. There was probably no proclamation to the natives to convert to Christianity, for the patent under which Ponce de León was sailing did not require it.

Leaving his first anchorage, Ponce de León started up the coast, but for an unknown reason he turned back and headed in a south-southeasterly course parallel to the coastline. In thus maneuvering, he missed a most important discovery, for had he sailed a little to the north, he would have seen the Saint Johns River; and judging from its size, he would have recognized that what he had discovered was a mainland and not an island, as he imagined Florida to be throughout the voyage. The vessels continued southward until the twentieth of the month when they ran into the Gulf Stream and were forced to anchor.

The following day Ponce de León went ashore and found the natives so hostile that he was obliged to repel the attack by force. In the skirmish with the Indians, two of his men were wounded, and he was forced to retreat to a river that he named Río de la Cruz. Here, 70 natives attacked them, and one was taken prisoner by the Spaniards to give information about the coast and country. On Sunday, May 8, they rounded a cape which Ponce de León named Cabo de las Corrientes, and anchored near a village called Abayoa. After this, they cruised along various islands, which he named Los Mártires.

The Spaniards continued to follow the coast southward, rounding the southern end of the peninsula and following up the western shores. On May 23, they returned southward, and the following day discovered several islands off the coast, on one of which they repaired the San Cristóbal. They remained there until the third of June when the natives descended upon them with a shower of arrows. The Spaniards retaliated by going ashore, capturing four Indian women and breaking two canoes.

On Friday, June 4, while they were preparing to go in search of the cacique (chieftain) Carlos, there came to the ship a canoe with a native who understood Spanish. Some historians cite this incident as proof that the natives had come in contact with Spaniards prior to the voyage of Ponce de León. Others do not consider this incident as sufficient proof, for it is possible that this native was from Cuba or La Española and had been living with the Spaniards for some time.

The native informed the Spaniards that the cacique was to send gold as a gift to them. Because of their greed, the Spaniards fell into the trap and waited. Suddenly, there were 20 canoes surrounding them. A sloop was lowered from one of the vessels, which put the natives on the run. The Spaniards captured four of them; two of these were released and sent to the cacique with a message for peace.

The following day, a sloop was sent out to explore the harbor. The crew were met by some natives who informed them that the cacique would come the next day to trade. As it turned out, the message was nothing more than a plan on the part of Carlos to gain time in order to attack, for at 11 o'clock, 80 canoes attacked one of the ships. The fight lasted until sunset, with no harm to the Spaniards, for the natives were kept at a distance by the Spaniards' artillery. When the natives retreated, Ponce de León decided to leave that hostile land and return to La Española and Puerto Rico.

On June 14, they lifted anchor and retraced part of their former course through the Florida Keys. On June 21, they came upon some small islands, which Ponce de León named Tortugas (turtles), for he had captured 170 turtles there. They sailed back and forth until the September 23, when Ponce de León sent Antón de Alaminos as pilot of one of his vessels in search of the island of Bimini, while he returned to Puerto Rico, arriving on October 10, 1513. He was joined there four months later by Alaminos, who had discovered the island but not the famous fountain reported to be there.

Thus ended the first of a series of unsuccessful ventures by the Spaniards to control the coast of North America. Ponce de León had obtained neither gold nor youth, only hard blows. Yet these blows were not enough to destroy the high spirits of the old soldier, for like a true Spanish hidalgo, he was to come back again, roaring like a lion.

Diego Miruelo

In 1516, three years after Ponce de León's first expedition to Florida, a small brigantine under the command of pilot Diego Miruelo sailed from Cuba and reached the coast of Florida. After trading mirrors and other small objects with the natives, Miruelo returned to Cuba. Upon his return, he enlarged the report of the wealth of Florida, and many Spaniards were lured by the desire to enjoy these riches. The irony of his voyage is that Miruelo, although a pilot, failed to note the latitude of the places he visited. Miruelo's reason for not giving the latitude of the places visited in Florida was probably that he wanted to organize a larger expedition to Florida under royal auspices and was fearful that someone would anticipate this and disclose the location of the places to the governors of Cuba and La Española.

Francisco Hernández de Córdova

In 1517, a year after the voyage of Diego Miruelo, Francisco Hernández de Córdova, a wealthy nobleman who resided in Cuba, sailed with three ships and 110 seasoned men with the object of capturing Bahamian natives and selling them as slaves. Among the men in this expedition was Bernal Díaz del Castillo, who became the chronicler of Hernán Cortes' conquest of the Aztec Empire. Hernández de Córdova sailed westward, but his purpose was frustrated by storms, and he landed on the peninsula of Yucatán. The natives of Yucatán must have been as hostile as the weather he had encountered, for Henández de Córdova, after several battles with the Indians, in which he lost nearly 50 of his men, decided to sail back to Cuba.

Again misfortune pursued him, and on his return trip he encountered such a stout north wind that it drove his vessels from their course. The chief pilot, Antón de Alaminos, who had been the pilot of Ponce de León in his first expedition to Florida, persuaded Hernández de Córdova to cross over to Florida to take refuge from the weather and chart a shorter, safer passage to Cuba. Alaminos drove the ships to the bay previously visited by Ponce de León (Charlotte Harbor), where they anchored to make repairs.

Twenty soldiers, including Bernal Díaz del Castillo and Antón de Alaminos, went ashore. While digging for water, a cascade of arrows descended on the unfortunate Spaniards, wounding six of them, including Bernal Díaz. Simultaneously, the Indians attacked the vessels, inflicting several casualties among the Spaniards. Ashore, the Spanish, fighting in water up to their belts, repelled the natives and captured three of the attackers. In this engagement, all of the Spaniards, including Alaminos, Bernal Díaz, and Hernández de Córdova were wounded. There was also a Spaniard missing in action, a soldier named Berrio, who was acting as sentry on shore; he presumably fell into the hands of the natives.

After this incident, the battered Spaniards sailed for Havana. Upon arrival, Hernández de Córdova sent word of their expedition to Diego Velázquez, governor of Cuba, who welcomed them and rewarded their captain with a feast. Hernández de Córdova died ten days later of the wounds received in his encounter with the Indians of Florida.

Alonzo Alvarez de Pineda

In 1519, two years after the ill-fated expedition of Hernández de Córdova, Antón de Alaminos gave a detailed account of the coast of Florida to the governor of Jamaica, Francisco de Garay, a powerful and ambitious man. Impressed by the report, and determined to conquer a province for himself, Garay outfitted four vessels under the command of his most trusted lieutenant, Alonzo Alvarez de Pineda, to search for a passage dividing the mainland.

Alvarez de Pineda sailed around the northern boundary of the Gulf of Mexico and coasted the western shore of Florida. Unable because of the currents to round the Cape of Florida, he retraced his course, made notes of rivers and bays, and landed at several places where he took possession in the name of Charles V. Then, after coasting nearly 300 leagues, he reached the province of Pánuco (Tampico), where he encountered none other than Hernán Cortés.

Sailing eastward again, Alvarez de Pineda reached the mouth of a great river, the Mississippi. There he found a sizable town and remained 40 days, trading with the natives and repairing his vessels. Pineda reported the land to be rich in gold, since the natives wore gold ornaments in their nose and ears. He also told of tribes of giants and pygmies, but declared these natives to be friendly.

Pineda continued to follow the coast for nine months and returned to Garay in 1520 with the news of this newly discovered province of Amichel. Although he failed to find a strait, the voyage of Alvarez de Pineda settled the question of Florida's geography. He proved that Florida was no longer to be regarded as an island, but part of a vast continent.

Fired by Alvarez de Pineda's account, Garay applied for a patent authorizing him to conquer and settle this new province, which extended from some point near Pensacola Bay to Cabo Rojo in Mexico. A royal patent was indeed issued to Garay in 1521, but in his haste to occupy his new territory, he ignored the final approval and sent four vessels under Diego de Camargo to occupy some posts near Pánuco. The expedition was doomed from the start, for one of the vessels ran into a settlement already established by Cortés and was captured. Cortés, in turn, learned of Camargo's plan.

Alarmed by the news of Camargo's failure, Garay equipped a powerful force to settle Amichel in 1523. Instead of reaching Amichel, Garay landed in the town of San Esteban, Mexico, which Cortés had already founded. He surrendered to Cortés, and with his surrender his dream of conquering Amichel expired.

The Slave Raider Gordillo

In December 1520, Lucas Vázquez de Ayllón, a wealthy judge of the audiencia of Santo Domingo, eager for the glory of discovering a new land, secured the necessary permission and dispatched a vessel to "La Florida" under Francisco Gordillo.

While Gordillo was sailing through the Bahamas, he recognized another vessel commanded by Pedro de Quexos. This vessel was returning from a slave-raiding expedition through the islands. Quexos and Gordillo agreed to sail together, and after nine days they reached the coast near the mouth of a large river, which they named the San Juan Bautista, because they had arrived on June 24, the feast day of the man who had baptized Christ.

Although Ayllón had instructed Gordillo to explore and establish friendly relations with the natives of any new land he might discover, Quexos influenced Gordillo to aid in capturing some 70 natives, with whom they sailed away without exploring the coast.

Upon Gordillo's arrival in Santo Domingo, Ayllón punished him and brought the matter to Diego Columbus. The governor declared the Indians to be free, but many of the group had already died from the treatment received by Quexos and Gordillo.

A Lion Returns to Colonize Florida

After his discovery of Florida in 1513, Ponce de León sailed to Spain to ask the king for a patent to colonize Florida and Bimini. The patent, which was granted on September 27, 1514, empowered him to colonize the island of Bimini and the "island" of Florida, which he had discovered. It also had the provision that the natives submit to the Catholic faith and the authority of Spain; they were not to be captured nor enslaved if they submitted. Provision was also made as to the revenues from the lands, and orders were sent to Diego Columbus to aid with the expedition.

The grant also specified that prior to launching the expedition, Ponce de León was required to wage war against the Carib. Juan Ponce de León sailed to pacify the Carib; after he reached the island of Guadalupe, they ambushed his soldiers and dealt them a severe blow. Forced to retreat to Puerto Rico, Ponce de León remained on the island and apparently abandoned the idea of colonizing Florida. But since the discoverer of Florida was a typical conquistador, the idea of giving up Florida never took root in his mind. So when he heard that the fame of Cortés in Mexico was rivaling his own, he decided to return and settle the land he had discovered.

Although the patent issued in 1514 was good for three years, Ponce de León used his influence at court so that his term was to date from the day he set sail for his new province, since he had been employed in the king's service fighting the Carib. Thus, in 1521, Ponce de León sent a letter to Charles V, dated February 10, asking him for permission to settle Florida. He outfitted two vessels with 200 men, 50 horses, and many domestic animals. There were also several priests to spread the Catholic faith among the natives and render service to the needs of the Spaniards. The expedition departed from the port of San Germán, Puerto Rico, in February 1521.

The exact landing place of his second voyage to the Florida coast is not precisely known, but historians believe it was in the vicinity of Charlotte Harbor, where on his first voyage he had heard of gold. Immediately after they landed, Ponce de León and his men were attacked by the natives. Although wounded by an arrow, Ponce de León bravely led his men against the natives. When the natives attacked again, the "old lion," who by this time lacked the strength of his glory days, ordered his men on board and sailed for Cuba. Within a few days of his return, the fierce conquistador yielded to death. His body was shipped to his beloved island of Puerto Rico.

The old warrior died with his ambition thwarted and without really knowing Florida was part of a continent. But the voyage produced a number of "firsts" for the history of the United States: the first attempt to plant a self-sustaining colony, the first attempt to implant the Catholic religion among the natives, and the first assigned residence for priests.

Lucas Vázquez de Ayllón

Although el Inca Garcilaso de la Vega states in *La Florida del Inca* (1956) that Lucas Vázquez de Ayllón was the leader of the 1521 slave-raiding expedition to Florida, historians believe that el Inca Garcilaso probably confused the role of Vázquez de Ayllón, who sponsored an expedition of exploration of Florida, with that of Francisco Gordillo, the man who actually commanded the expedition and was later reprimanded for disobeying Ayllón's orders. Ayllón was never in Florida prior to his 1526 expedition.

After settling the matter of the surviving native slaves brought back by the Gordillo expedition, Lucas Vázquez de Ayllón sailed to Spain to request a patent for discovery. Charles V not only accepted Vázquez de Ayllón's request but also bestowed upon him the habit of Santiago, making him a member of a prestigious lay order. On June 12, 1513, a patent was conferred on Ayllón. By it, Vázquez de Ayllón was given the title of *Adelantado* (commander) and was empowered to discover and navigate the coast for a distance of 800 leagues. The patent also granted Vázquez de Ayllón rights to fisheries and prisoners of war held by the natives. It also provided for the conversion of natives to the Catholic faith and subsidy for the Dominican missionaries who were to accompany this expedition.

After years of preparation, Vázquez de Ayllón was able to sail from the port of La Plata on the northern coast of Santo Domingo in 1526. His expedition consisted of 500 men and women and 89 horses. There were also three Dominican missionaries and several black slaves. Thus, this was the first attempt in the history of the United States to introduce black slaves to the country.

Vázquez de Ayllón landed not at the mouth of the Saint Johns, but at the mouth of a river he named the Jordán (near Cape Fear, North Carolina). Dissatisfied with the locality, Vázquez de Ayllón sent scouts into the country. Upon their reports, he sailed northward and founded the settlement of San Miguel de Guadalupe (Jamestown). The colony was fated not to prosper, for winter came on; sickness broke out among the Spaniards and many died. Vázquez de Ayllón succumbed to death in October 1526. The Spaniards decided to sail back to Santo Domingo, and of the 500 who sailed with Vázquez de Ayllón, only 150 returned.

The Expedition of Pánfilo de Narváez

Although the expedition of Panfilo de Narváez was one of the most disastrous in the annals of Spanish history, it was one of the expeditions that contributed the most to the history of the southern section of the United States, for one of its members, a stout Spaniard named Álvar Núñez Cabeza de Vaca, made a major contribution to the world's knowledge in his own time by writing *La relación* (*The Account*), an eyewitness account of the ill-fated expedition.

Pánfilo de Narváez was born in Valladolid, Spain, in 1470. When, in 1511, Diego Velázquez was named governor of Cuba, he appointed Narváez, who had a reputation as a tough Indian fighter in Jamaica, as his lieutenant in charge of "pacifying" the natives of Cuba. Narváez distinguished himself from the beginning, and Velázquez entrusted to him the conquest of the rest of the island. In a few years, the faithful servant of Velázquez won the island for his governor. His most famous deed during this contest was the massacre of 500 defenseless natives in the town of Caonao, which brought a strong protest from Fray Bartolomé de las Casas; thus, Narváez was probably the one who initiated the feud between the conquistadors and the missionaries.

Narváez retired to his encomienda but was called by his friend Velázquez to command an expedition to discipline Hernán Cortés, who with a small group of men had conquered the Aztec Empire. With an impressive force of some 900 soldiers, Narváez landed in San Juan de Ulúa, Mexico, in 1520. His first decision after he landed was to arrest Lucas Vázquez de Ayllón, who had been sent by the audiencia in Santo Domingo to prevent a clash between Cortés and Narváez. This decision proved costly for Narváez,

Title page of Cabeza de Vaca's account of his trip, *La relación,* 1542.

because when Ayllón was released, he informed the audiencia of Narváez's conduct.

Narváez then sent three envoys to Cortés and asked for his surrender. Cortés, in turn, showered the men with gifts and gold, and they later returned to the headquarters of Narváez unharmed. By this maneuver, the skillful conqueror of Mexico gained information about the strength of Narváez and also created a "fifth column" (secret sympathizers) in the latter's camp, for many men lured by the tales of gold deserted Narváez.

On May 27, 1520, a force of 250 men commanded by Hernán Cortés launched an attack on Narváez's headquarters in Cempoala. Narváez not only was humiliated but also lost an eye in the battle and was sent to Veracruz, where he was imprisoned until Cortés released him in 1522. Narváez stayed in Cuba, and since he was so impressed with all the gold and jewelry that he had seen in Mexico, sailed to Spain with the illusion that Charles V would reward his services with an appointment as ruler of rich domains.

Narváez must have had strong connections at court, for he was awarded the governorship of Florida, which had been vacant since the death of Juan Ponce de León. On November 17, 1526, Charles V issued a patent to Narváez that granted him the right to discover, conquer, and settle the territory from the Río de las Palmas to the "island" of Florida. The grant also stipulated that Narváez was to build three forts and two settlements. It also granted him the titles of governor and captain-general for life, along with a private estate of ten square leagues and an annual salary of 250,000 *maravedíes*. In addition, he was given 4 percent of the tax levies and had the authority to make slaves of rebellious natives.

The most significant aspect of this document was that for the first time, guidelines were set for the treatment of the natives of "La Florida." Any act of brutality on the part of an officer was to be investigated by the Council of the Indies. The natives were to be treated as free men, and priests were to accompany the expedition in order to protect the natives from mistreatment at the hands of civil or military authorities. The natives were not to be forced to work in mines and were to be paid for their labor. Only with the consent of the priests could a native be assigned to an encomienda.

The 600-man expedition left the Spanish port of San Lúcar de Barrameda on June 27, 1527. The expedition seemed to have been doomed from the start. Upon arriving at La Española, 140 men deserted, and two ships were wrecked by a hurricane near Trinidad, Cuba. After spending the winter in Cuba, the expedition sailed from the Cuban port of Cienfuegos on February 20, 1528. It carried only 400 men.

After hitting a number of sandbars off the Cuban coast, the expedition anchored in the neighborhood of Tampa Bay on April 12, 1528. A few days later, Narváez landed and took possession in the name of the king. Immediately after the landing, Narváez approached a nearby village and asked the natives if there was gold. They indicated by signs that there were great quantities of that precious metal in a province that they called Apalachee—present-day Tallahassee. The natives, of course, wanted the Spaniards to leave their village and, undoubtedly, invented the story.

Lured by the tales of gold and riches, Narváez decided to march inland with the bulk of his expedition. On May 1, 1528, 300 men with meager rations, which amounted to one-half pound of bacon and two pounds of bread per man, marched northward in the direction of the reputedly gold-laden Apalachee. On the June 25, after a 56-day march, the tired Spaniards arrived in Apalachee. Narváez and his men soon realized that Apalachee contained neither palaces nor gold, but fierce natives. Since there was very little food in the area, the Spaniards began to franti-

cally search for it. An Apalachee captive informed Narváez that to the south there was a village called Aute—present-day Saint Marks or Apalachicola—where there was an abundance of food. It was located near the sea.

The Spaniards arrived in Aute nine days after their departure from Apalachee, only to find that the natives had turned to a scorched-earth policy. Tired, hungry, and constantly harassed by the natives, the Spaniards decided to build barges and leave by sea to Mexico, which they estimated to be nearby. It was an incredible task, for they lacked tools and proper knowledge of shipbuilding. The Spaniards sawed down trees with their swords and pikes and made them into planks, transformed their horseshoes into nails, ripped their shirts and made them into sails, and converted the hides of their horses into water skins. Finally, on September 22, 1528, the five barges carrying 242 men set sail.

The makeshift armada sailed close to the Gulf Coast of present-day Florida, Alabama, Mississippi, and Louisiana for more than a month. Narváez's barge abandoned the rest of the barges and was never seen again. As they were approaching the Texas coast, the remaining barges were caught in a hurricane, and 80 men managed to survive by reaching present-day Galveston Island. They named the island Isla de Malhado (Badluck Island).

The natives of Malhado took the Spaniards captive once they landed. A bitter winter descended upon the Spaniards and natives alike, bringing cold, hunger, and disease. The Spaniards even resorted to cannibalism in order to survive. Of the 80 men who reached Malhado, only 15 survived the winter. While in Malhado, some of the Spaniards were forced by the natives to act as medicine men. Álvar Núñez Cabeza de Vaca built a reputation as a medicine man among the natives by simply making the sign of the cross and reciting a Hail Mary and the Lord's Prayer.

In April 1529 Álvar Núñez Cabeza de Vaca, author of *La relación* (*The Account*), found himself among the 15 survivors of Pánfilo de Narváez's failed attempt to colonize Florida. The survivors were captured by natives off the coast of Texas and transported to the Texas mainland by their captors. While on the mainland, 12 of them managed to escape. Cabeza de Vaca and two companions, Jerónimo de Aláñiz and Lope de Oviedo, were left behind because they were too sick. Aláñiz died, but Lope de Oviedo and Cabeza de Vaca were later transferred to Malhado. After some 22 months of traveling back and forth, Cabeza de Vaca and Lope de Oviedo began their journey to freedom. They crossed a number of inlets and arrived at a large bay—present-day Matagorda Bay—where, on the shore, they met several natives. The natives informed them that there were three other men like themselves in the possession of their tribe farther inland. These three were the only survivors of the original 12 escapees (the other nine had died from cold and hunger).

Frightened by the rough treatment he had received at the hands of the natives, Lope de Oviedo deserted Cabeza de Vaca and departed for the island of Malhado. He was never seen again. Two days after Lope de Oviedo's departure, the rest of the tribe arrived near Matagorda Bay with their three other prisoners. Álvar Núñez Cabeza de Vaca, Andrés Dorantes, Alonso del Castillo, and the black slave Estevanico were reunited for the first time in more than three years. The four of them spent the winter of 1532–33 together, and in August 1533 they moved with the natives to the tuna (prickly pear) thickets south of the present-day region of San Antonio. The natives separated the four, but before they were separated they agreed on an escape plan.

Cabeza de Vaca lived with a native tribal group until September 13, 1534. A day later he was met by Castillo, Dorantes, and Estevanico. On September 15, 1534, two days after all of them had been reunited, they began the most daring, difficult, and remarkable escape in the history of the New World.

Wandering from tribe to tribe as medicine men, Cabeza de Vaca, Castillo, Dorantes, and Estevanico traveled thousands of miles through present-day Texas, New Mexico, and Arizona. Traveling naked and barefooted over the treacherous terrain of the Southwest, the three Spaniards and Estevanico learned to conquer the freezing winds of winter and the blistering sun of summer. They had stoically adapted themselves to eat spiders, salamanders, lizards, worms, and prickly pears.

Finally, in February 1536, they found a company of Spanish soldiers 30 leagues from the Spanish settlement of San Miguel in northern Mexico. A few days later, they arrived in San Miguel. Their ordeal was now over. They had survived because they had worked as a unit and had kept their faith. On May 15, 1536, the four of them departed San Miguel. They arrived in Mexico City on June 24, 1536.

Of the four survivors, Alonso del Castillo returned to Spain and was later given an encomienda in Tehuacán, Mexico. Andrés Dorantes joined Viceroy Antonio de Mendoza's conquest of Jalisco, Mexico, and spent the rest of his life in Mexico. Estevanico joined the expedition of Fray Marcos de Niza to New Mexico as a guide and was killed by the natives in 1539 at Hawikuh. As to Álvar Núñez Cabeza de Vaca, he returned to Spain in 1537 and spent some three years writing *La relación,* an account of his wanderings in the North American continent. Pub-

lished in 1542, *La relación* is a document of inestimable value because of the many first descriptions about the flora, fauna, and inhabitants of what later was to become part of the United States.

In 1540, Álvar Núñez Cabeza de Vaca was appointed governor of the Río de la Plata. He arrived in Asunción, Paraguay, in March 1542. Cabeza de Vaca's tenure as governor was characterized by his good treatment of the native population and his reform program. Because of his reforms on behalf of the natives, Cabeza de Vaca became the victim of a coup carried out by other conquistadors on April 25, 1544. He arrived in Seville in chains and was condemned to serve a prison sentence.

After seven years of trials and tribulations, Álvar Núñez Cabeza de Vaca emerged from prison. Disheartened and ill, he busied himself writing the second edition of *La relación,* which was published in 1555 and which also contains the narrative of his days as governor of the Río de la Plata. In 1556, Álvar Núñez Cabeza de Vaca, the most humane and farsighted of the conquistadors and America's first chronicler, died in Spain.

The Expedition of Hernando de Soto

Hernando de Soto was born in 1500 in the Spanish town of Jerez de Badajoz. When he was in his teens he went to Central America and later joined Francisco Pizarro in his conquest of Peru. After remaining in Peru for a few years, de Soto returned to Spain in 1536. Shortly after his return to Spain, the wealthy hidalgo sought out Álvar Núñez Cabeza de Vaca, who had recently returned from his eight-year odyssey across the North American continent. Cabeza de Vaca's reticence during this meeting did nothing more than fire de Soto's imagination and greed, for he was convinced that Florida was covered with gold.

On April 20, 1537, King Charles V granted de Soto a patent naming him governor of Cuba and captain-general of Florida. On April 7, 1538, Hernando de Soto sailed for Cuba. After making provisions for governing the island, he left Havana for Florida on May 18, 1539. De Soto's expedition consisted of 650 men and a large herd of pigs and other livestock.

On May 30, 1539, they arrived at Tampa Bay. Shortly after their landing, they met Juan Ortiz, a member of the Narváez expedition who had been saved by the daughter of the cacique Hirrihigua. Thus, Spanish Florida had its romance story some 68 years prior to that of John Smith and Pocahontas. Unable to find gold in the neighborhood of Tampa Bay, de Soto, accompanied by more than 550 men, marched north along the coast to Apalachee, where they wintered.

Harassed by the natives, de Soto and his expeditionaries departed Apalachee on March 3, 1540, in

A portrayal of Hernando de Soto by an unknown eighteenth-century artist.

search of gold. They took a northeasterly route and reached present-day Georgia.

According to the most recent research, De Soto's route is as follows. In April his troupe crossed the Savannah River and entered South Carolina. After a fruitless search for gold, they headed north and arrived at Xuala—present-day Marion, North Carolina. They then crossed the Great Smoky Mountains into Tennessee. From the mountains, they headed southwest through Georgia and Alabama.

On October 18, 1540, they reached the village of Mauvilla, near Mobile Bay. At Mauvilla, de Soto and his men were attacked by the native chief, Tascaluza, and his allies. Although the Spaniards managed to kill about 3,000 natives, they lost 22 men and 148 were wounded. De Soto was to meet Diego de Maldonado, whom he had sent to Havana to gather supplies, in present-day Pensacola, Florida, sometime in 1540. But he never went to see Maldonado because he did not want to reveal to him that he had failed to find gold. In addition, he had already lost 102 men since his landing at Tampa Bay. The Spaniards were in Mauvilla for about a month and then moved northwest to present-day Mississippi. They spent the 1540–41 winter at Chicasa in northern Mississippi.

On March 4, 1541, as de Soto was about to depart Chicasa, he was attacked by natives. Twelve Spaniards, 59 horses, and 300 pigs were killed in the attack as the Indians managed to set the Spanish camp on fire. The Spaniards retreated to a nearby village and proceeded in a northwesterly direction. On May 9, they saw a great river, the Mississippi. They spent more than a month building barges for the river crossing.

After crossing the mighty river on June 19, 1541, de Soto and his men found themselves in the neighborhood of present-day Horseshoe Lake, Arkansas. Lured by tales of gold and silver from the natives, de Soto moved into the Plains Indians' territory, only to find buffalo skins. On September 13, they saw the Arkansas River. The Spaniards continued to march west but decided to turn back to the southeast as winter was approaching. They spent the winter of 1541–42 at Autiamque—present-day Redfield, Arkansas. It was a harsh winter and by then the expedition had lost 250 men. On March 6, 1542, the expedition set out toward the south, trying to find a way out of their misery. After hearing negative reports concerning the countryside, de Soto became depressed and fell ill. On May 21, 1542, he died in Guachoya—present-day McArthur, Arkansas.

After the death of Hernando de Soto, Luis de Moscoso took command of de Soto's North American expedition. The Spaniards buried de Soto outside Guachoya, but since de Soto had pointed out to the natives that he was immortal, Moscoso ordered that the body be dug up. The Spaniards exhumed de Soto's body, wrapped it in a mantle weighted with sand, and then proceeded to carry it in a canoe out into the Mississippi River. Somewhere in the Mississippi, they cast the body of the golden conquistador. When the natives asked where de Soto was, Moscoso replied that the governor had gone to heaven, from where he would shortly return.

Moscoso thought that the best way to reach Mexico was to go overland, so they proceeded on a southwesterly course as far as present-day Texas. Lack of food and constant Indian attacks forced them to turn back to the Mississippi River, where they knew there was food. The Spaniards wintered near the Mississippi. Early in 1543, they began to build seven boats. They also killed their horses and pigs and dried the meat. On July 2, 1543, they sailed down the river. Two weeks later, they reached its mouth. Finally, on September 10, 1543, they arrived at Tampico, Mexico. Of the 650 men who had walked and sailed more than 3,500 miles, 311 survived an incredible journey.

Although the de Soto expedition was a failure for Spain, it nevertheless was one of the most remarkable in the history of North America. Furthermore, it provided valuable insights into the lifestyles of the natives of the Southeast and their interaction with the Spaniards. As the anthropologist Charles Hudson stated in *De Soto Trail* (1990), "The de Soto expedition was the historical context in which these two cultures met. It was the historical moment in which our forgotten European forebears came into conflict with the likewise forgotten native lords of the Southeast. It constitutes one of the great episodes in the age of European exploration."

The De Luna Fiasco

The disastrous results of Hernando de Soto's expedition put a temporary halt to Spain's interest in colonizing Florida. In 1558, however, King Philip II ordered Viceroy Luis de Velasco to settle Florida. The peninsula's strategic location and the possibility of rival European encroachments in the area prompted the Spanish monarch to take this action.

On June 11, 1559, 1,500 would-be colonists sailed from Veracruz under the command of Tristán de Luna. They arrived in Pensacola on August 18, 1554. The expedition was a disaster from the start. Reconnaissance proved that the area was not conducive to agriculture. On September 19, a hurricane sank 12 of the 13 ships in the harbor, causing great loss of men and cargo. A cold winter followed and lack of provisions forced the settlers to eat nothing but acorns boiled in salt water.

In the spring of 1560, de Luna decided to move his settlers inland, hoping to find food in the neighborhood of present-day Coosa County, Alabama. The hardships, continued, however, and de Luna had no alternative but to retreat to Pensacola. Dissension against de Luna broke out among the settlers during the winter of 1560–61. Many of them refused to carry out his orders. Worried about the colony's fate, the authorities in Havana decided to replace de Luna.

In April 1561, Angel de Villafañe arrived at Pensacola with orders to replace de Luna, evacuate the colonists to Cuba, and settle Santa Elena—present-day Port Royal, South Carolina. Villafañe arrived at Santa Elena in May 1561 and continued to explore the coast as far north as Cape Hatteras. Finding the area unsuitable for colonization, Villafañe left for La Española. Thus, another attempt to settle La Florida had ended in disappointment.

The Conquest of Florida by Pedro Menéndez de Avilés

In 1564, Philip II's fears of a possible rival occupation of Florida materialized when a group of French Huguenots, led by Rene de Laudonniére, settled Fort Caroline on the mouth of Florida's Saint Johns River. Laudonniére, however, would shortly be replaced by Jean Ribault. Exasperated by the news of the French settlement, the Spanish monarch instructed Pedro Menéndez de Avilés to drive the French out of Florida.

Menéndez, considered to be one of the ablest commanders in the Spanish army, carefully laid out his strategy. On June 29, 1565, he set sail from the Spanish port of Cádiz for Puerto Rico. On August 15, he sailed from San Juan carrying 800 soldiers and colonists. The expedition arrived in Florida on August 28. Menéndez named the area Saint Augustine in honor of the saint's feast day.

After scouting the area, Menéndez learned from the natives that the French were some 20 leagues to the north. On September 4, 1565, Menéndez set sail to the north and sighted four French vessels. The French exchanged gunfire with the Spanish vessels and then fled. Menéndez abandoned the attempt to capture them and sailed south toward Saint Augustine.

On September 6, 1565, a Spanish contingent arrived at Saint Augustine and in two days built a crude fort. Two days later Menéndez himself landed

Pedro Menéndez de Avilés.

Drawing of the type of free black militia that were stationed in Spanish colonies in Florida and elsewhere (1795).

and took possession in the name of King Philip II. Thus, Saint Augustine became the first permanent European settlement in what was to become the United States.

Concerned over the possible invasion of Saint Augustine by the French Huguenots, Menéndez decided to attack Fort Caroline by land. Menéndez was right, for Ribault had already sailed with 600 men on September 10, 1565, to attack Saint Augustine. A storm, struck the vessels, however, and the French became shipwrecked on the Florida coast. Unaware of the French calamity, Menéndez marched inland on September 16. After a rough four-day march through the Florida marshes, Menéndez caught the French garrison at Fort Caroline by surprise and inflicted over 130 casualties. After sparing the lives of women and children, Menéndez set out for Saint Augustine.

On September 24, Menéndez arrived at Saint Augustine and learned of the French disaster. A few days later, he and 50 men marched in search of the shipwrecked French. The search netted 208 of Ribault's men. With the exception of 10 of them, who proved to be Catholics, the French were put to death by Menéndez.

On October 10, 1565, Menéndez received news that Ribault and 150 of his men were in the neighborhood of the site where he had previously executed their countrymen. Menéndez quickly set out to capture them. After extensive negotiations, the French surrendered. Once they surrendered, Menéndez executed Ribault and 134 of his men. The site where the massacre took place still bears the name Matanzas (Place of Slaughter). The week after the slaughter, the natives informed Menéndez that there were still some 170 Frenchmen south of Saint Augustine in the neighborhood of present-day Cape Canaveral. On November 26, 1565, Menéndez captured them. This time, however, he spared their lives and gave orders to return them to France.

When news of Menéndez's actions reached France, Charles IX, the French monarch, not only protested but also demanded reparations. Philip II, on the other hand, turned a deaf ear to the French protests and even commended Menéndez for driving the French out of La Florida.

Menéndez was a dreamer who wanted to create a large Spanish colony from Florida all the way north to Canada. The dream, however, would never become a reality. On February 20, 1574, Menéndez was recalled to Spain and given command of Philip II's Spanish Armada, whose purpose was to invade England. But Menéndez, fell ill and died on September 17, 1574.

Menéndez's death halted operations until 1588. The disaster of the Spanish Armada in that year put an end to Spanish supremacy. No one knows if the outcome would have been different had Menéndez lived. Despite the armada's disaster, Florida was firmly in Spanish hands. It remained a Spanish colony until 1763, when Spain was forced to cede Florida to the British. Twenty years later, in 1783, Spain regained Florida. The sun finally set on Spanish Florida in July 1821, when Florida was purchased by the United States for $5 million.

✳ SPANISH EXPLORATION AND COLONIZATION OF THE SOUTHWEST

Fray Marcos de Niza and the Seven Cities of Cibola

Cabeza de Vaca's return to Mexico in 1536 indirectly involved Spain in exploring and colonizing what became the American Southwest. Rumors were started in Mexico City that Cabeza de Vaca and his companions had discovered cities laden with gold and silver, and suddenly the legend of the Seven Cities was revived. The legend started sometime during the Muslim invasion of the Iberian Peninsula. While the Muslims were conquering Portugal, seven Portuguese bishops purportedly crossed the Atlantic and founded the Seven Cities of Antilla, rich in gold and silver.

Convinced that Cabeza de Vaca and his companions had sighted the Seven Cities, Spanish Viceroy Antonio de Mendoza entrusted Fray Marcos de Niza to explore the mysterious land to the north. Mendoza chose Fray Marcos because he was an experienced traveler. The friar had been part of Pedro de Alvarado's conquest of Guatemala and had also participated in the Spanish conquest of Peru.

On March 7, 1539, Fray Marcos left the northern Mexican village of Culiacán with an expedition. He took with him Estevanico, the black slave who had been one of the survivors of the ill-fated Narváez expedition. On March 21, they crossed the Río Mayo. Fray Marcos decided to send Estevanico and a few of his Indian guides as scouts. Estevanico was to mark each "city" that he found with a cross. The larger the cross, the bigger the settlement.

For two months, the friar and his party followed a route marked with crosses. The crosses kept getting larger and the friar thought that he was getting nearer the Seven Cities. Messengers sent by Estevanico informed Fray Marcos that he had seen seven great cities, which the natives called Cíbola. Convinced that they were the Seven Cities, Fray Marcos pushed northward up the Sonora valley and into southeastern Arizona.

In late May, however, Fray Marcos received the stunning news that Estevanico had been killed by the natives as he was approaching the first city—present-day Hawikuh, New Mexico. Undeterred, Fray Marcos pressed on toward the first city of Cíbola. As he approached the city, the friar wrote: "I proceeded on my journey until coming within sight of Cíbola, which is situated in a plain at the base of a round hill. . . . The city is larger than that of Mexico. . . . The chieftains told me that it was the smallest of the seven cities."

Fray Marcos, however, did not want to risk his life and did not enter the city. After taking possession in the name of the king and erecting a cross, Fray Marcos and his expedition started their return to Mexico. They arrived in Mexico City in September 1539. While in Mexico City, Fray Marcos wrote the following report to Viceroy Mendoza: "I was told that there is much gold there and the natives make it into vessels and jewels for their ears, and into little blades with which they wipe away their sweat." If Fray Marcos was not a liar, he certainly wrote what Mendoza wanted to hear.

The Expedition of Francisco Vázquez de Coronado

Lured by Fray Marcos' report of the Seven Cities of Cíbola, Viceroy Mendoza commissioned the governor of the northern Mexican province of Nueva Galicia, Don Francisco Vásquez de Coronado to undertake an expedition to the Seven Cities. Born in Salamanca, Spain, in 1510, Francisco Vásquez de Coronado was a loyal supporter of Mendoza and had helped him put down a native revolt in Mexico in 1537.

The expedition, composed of 300 Spaniards and 800 natives, left Compostela, Nueva Galicia, on February 23, 1540. Fray Marcos was also part of the expedition. By April 1, 1540, the expedition had covered 350 miles from Compostela to Sinaloa. Disgusted with the slow progress of the expedition, Coronado decided to push ahead with 100 men and left Tristán de Arellano in charge of the main force.

With Fray Marcos serving as guide, Coronado and his men marched through the Sonora valley and into southwestern Arizona. Then they veered eastward. On July 7, 1540, after a 1,000-mile journey, they arrived at the first of the Seven Cities—Hawikuh. The Zuñi town did not have the gold that Fray Marcos had described in his report. Instead, hostile natives awaited the Spaniards.

After several scouting forays, Coronado wrote to Mendoza on August 3, 1540: "It now remains for me to tell about the city and kingdom and province of which Fray Marcos gave your Lordship an account. In brief, I can assure you that he has not told the truth in a single thing that he said, except the name of the city and the large stone house. . . . The Seven Cities are seven little villages, all having the kind of houses I have described." Coronado may have saved Fray Marcos from being hacked to pieces by his angered men when he ordered him to carry his report to Viceroy Mendoza.

While waiting for the bulk of his expedition to arrive in Cíbola, Coronado sent scouting parties in hopes of finding gold. One of these parties went into the Hopi villages of northeastern Arizona, but reported that there was no gold in the area. Another one, led by Captain López de Cárdenas, discovered the Grand Canyon, but no precious metals. A third group, led by Hernando de Alvarado, went off to explore a province that the natives called Tiguex—present-day Albuquerque. They then traveled to Cicuye on the upper Rio Grande and then swung eastward along the Pecos River. A Pawnee guide whom the Spaniards called El Turco (the Turk) informed the conquistadors of a rich land called Quivira, but de Alvarado decided to return to Tiguex to await Coronado.

When the bulk of his army reached Cíbola, Coronado decided to follow Alvarado's recommendation and encamped at Tiguex to spend the winter of 1540–41. The Spaniards angered the once friendly Pueblo natives of Tiguex as a result of their outrageous requisitions. The Pueblos revolted and Coronado spent the winter battling them. In one instance, Coronado ordered 200 Pueblo prisoners to be burned at the stake.

On April 23, 1541, Coronado set out to reach Quivira. With "the Turk" leading the way, the Spaniards reached the border of present-day Oklahoma. Informed by the natives that Quivira lay far to the north, Coronado decided to leave the army in the panhandle and set out for Quivira with 30 men on June 1, 1531. After a five-week march, Coronado reached Quivira on July 6. There was no great city, but only a settlement of seminomadic natives. Coronado and his men explored the area for more than a month. The soil was fertile, but there was no gold. While in the area of present-day Wichita, Kansas, the Spaniards discovered that "the Turk" was urging the local natives not to help them. After torturing him, they found out that he had been lying all along about the riches of Quivira. Once he confessed, "the Turk" was condemned to die by garrote.

The disgruntled Spaniards left Quivira in late August and spent the 1541–42 winter in Tiguex. In the spring of 1542, Coronado decided to return to Mexico City. Several Franciscan friars who had accompanied Coronado decided to stay to preach the gospel to the natives. As soon as the soldiers left, they were killed by the natives.

In July 1542, Coronado returned to Mexico City with fewer than 100 of the 300 Spaniards that once formed, according to George Daniels in *The Spanish West* (1976), part of "the most brilliant company ever assembled in search of new lands." Brokenhearted and with his fortune diminished in his quest for Cíbola and Quivira, Coronado died in Mexico City in 1544.

The Rodriguez-Chamuscado Expedition

Coronado's failure only put a temporary halt to Spain's interest in the Southwest. In June 1581, Fray Agustín Rodríguez and Captain Francisco Sánchez Chamuscado left the northern Mexican town of Santa Bárbara in hopes of finding another Mexico. The expedition went into the Conchos-Rio Grande area and continued upstream to the Rio Grande. On August 25, 1581, they reached the first Pueblo villages of New Mexico—the present-day Bernalillo area. The expedition explored the Pueblo country of New Mexico as far north as Queres and as far west as Acoma and Zuñi. Fray Agustín Rodríguez and another Franciscan, Fray Francisco López, decided to stay at Puaray—opposite Bernalillo—to

convert the natives. Sánchez Chamuscado, on the other hand, decided to return to Santa Bárbara. He never made it to his destination, for he fell ill and died. The rest of his party, however, arrived at Santa Bárbara on April 15, 1582.

The Espejo-Beltrán Expedition

Concern over the fate of the two friars in the Rodríguez-Chamuscado expedition prompted the Franciscan community to send a rescue expedition led by the hidalgo Antonio de Espejo and Fray Bernardino Beltrán.

The expedition set out from Santa Bárbara in November of 1582, basically following the Rodríguez-Chamuscado route. Once the Spaniards arrived in Pueblo country, they were told by the natives that the friars had been killed. Probably because he was the main financial backer of the expedition, Espejo decided to continue exploring the area. In May 1583, Beltrán and a few of the men left for Mexico, but Espejo continued exploring the area. He, along with nine other men, marched west in search of La Laguna del Oro (the Lake of Gold). After traveling nearly 50 leagues, he entered western Arizona. In view of the natives' hostility, Espejo decided to return to Mexico.

Espejo and his men arrived in to Mexico on September 10, 1583, claiming that they had discovered La Laguna del Oro. Once again, another tale of riches would lure the Spanish to the Southwest.

Castaño de Sosa and Juan Moriete

The prospect of finding gold mines in Pueblo country prompted Gaspar Castaño de Sosa to organize an unauthorized expedition in 1589. Castaño de Sosa went as far north as Santo Domingo, New Mexico. While Castaño de Sosa was in the Santo Domingo area, the Spanish viceroy of Mexico, Don Luis de Velasco, ordered Captain Juan Morlete to arrest Castaño de Sosa. Following the route of previous expeditions, Morlete reached Santo Domingo in April 1591. He promptly arrested Castaño de Sosa and dispatched him to Mexico City. Morlete kept on exploring the area, but, finding no riches, he returned to Mexico in November 1591.

Francisco Leyva de Bonilla and Antonio Gutiérrez de Humaña

Castano de Sosa's fiasco did not deter two Spaniards, Francisco Leyva de Bonilla and Antonio Gutiérrez de Humaña, from trying their luck. In 1593, they departed Santa Barbara on an unauthorized expedition to Quivira. They traveled to the Santa Fe area and then eastward into Kansas. When they reached a place called the Great Settlement—present-day Wichita, Kansas—an argument ensued between the two leaders. Humaña butchered Leyva de Bonilla, and the Plains Indians later killed Humaña and the rest of the Spaniards on their way back. Only one member of the expedition, Jusepe Gutiérrez, survived to tell the story.

Juan de Oñate Settles New Mexico

Despite the failures of previous authorized and unauthorized expeditions to the Southwest, Mexican Viceroy Luis de Velasco had a keen interest in settling the area. In 1595, he granted a patent in the name of the king to Juan de Oñate to colonize New Mexico.

The choice of Juan de Oñate as adelantado seemed like a good one. A wealthy man, Juan de Oñate was the son of Cristóbal de Oñate, one of the conquerors of Nueva Galicia. He was also married to the great-granddaughter of Aztec emperor Moctezuma. Despite these connections, Oñate was delayed for three years by the monstrous Spanish bureaucracy and the new viceroy, Don Gaspar de Zúñiga.

Finally, on February 7, 1598, the Oñate expedition left Santa Bárbara with 400 men, of whom 130 brought their families. As the expedition approached the San Pedro River, a group of ten Franciscans joined it. On April 19, the expedition reached the sand dunes south of El Paso, and on the fourth of May they arrived at El Paso. They moved upstream along the Rio Grande into the Pueblo country of New Mexico. On the eleventh of July, they arrived at Caypa. Oñate renamed it San Juan de los Caballeros and established a settlement there.

Oñate and his men began to establish contact with the natives of the area, and the Franciscan missionaries began to preach the gospel. After building a church in San Juan de los Caballeros, Oñate sent his nephew, Captain Vicente de Zaldívar, to explore the plains to the northeast and bring herds of buffalo. Zaldívar failed to bring the herds, but brought back plenty of hides and beef.

While awaiting Zaldívar, Oñate sent scouting parties to the Jumano Pueblos and the Zuni. In November 1598, Vicente Zaldívar's brother, Juan, was ambushed by the Acoma Pueblos while on a scouting mission. Saddened by the loss of his nephew, Oñate sent Vicente on a punitive expedition against the Acoma on January 15, 1599. Despite the natives' fierce resistance, the Spaniards laid waste to Acoma, taking with them more than 600 prisoners.

Attempts by Oñate's men to reach the South Sea—the Gulf of California—had failed, so in June 1601, Oñate led an expedition in the opposite direction toward Quivira. The five-month journey to Quivira failed to bring riches.

When Oñate returned to San Juan de los Caballeros, he found the settlement in a chaotic state. Dissatisfied with the lack of economic progress, a group of colonists returned to Santa Bárbara and started a campaign to discredit Oñate and New Mexico. The rumors reached the Spanish Crown, and the king was even contemplating the withdrawal of the Spaniards from New Mexico. Luckily for Oñate, the Spanish viceroy supported him.

Despite his troubles, Oñate was persistent in reaching the South Sea. In October 1604, he left San Juan de los Caballeros with 35 men. They went through the Zuñi and Hopi country, down to the Colorado River. They then moved downstream past the Gila River and reached the Gulf of California. They returned to New Mexico on April 25, 1605. Once more, the Spaniards had failed to find riches.

After two years of trials and tribulations, Oñate resigned from his enterprise. He had spent his entire fortune in colonizing New Mexico and was now in debt. Luis de Velasco, who was once again the Spanish viceroy of New Spain, appealed directly to the king to hold New Mexico. In 1608, the Royal and Supreme Council of the Indies made New Mexico an official province of the viceroyalty of New Spain and appointed Pedro de Peralta governor of New Mexico.

Despite the vicissitudes, including several native uprisings, New Mexico was in Spanish hands until 1680. That year, the native Pueblo leader Popé led a revolt of the Pueblos and pushed the Spanish settlers all the way down to El Paso. It took a dozen years for Spanish forces to reconquer New Mexico. After 1692, however, New Mexico was to be in Spanish control until 1821, when Mexico gained its independence, and with it, New Mexico.

Antonio de León's Settlement of Texas

The land we now call Texas was not unknown to the Spaniards. In 1519, Alonso Alvarez de Pineda claimed it for Spain. A few years later, Alvar Núñez Cabeza de Vaca started his remarkable adventure in Texas. Spanish conquistadors also used Texas as a way-station in their many expeditions. Yet, Spain paid little attention to Texas because it simply lacked the logistical capabilities to settle it.

Fear of French intrusion into Texas prompted the Spanish authorities in Mexico to send five expeditions commanded by Antonio de León. In 1686, de León left Monterrey and reached the Rio Grande. He then followed the river to the gulf and explored the coast. The following year, in his next expedition, he crossed the Rio Grande but had to return to Mexico. In 1688, while on yet another expedition, he crossed the Rio Grande and took a Frenchman named Jean Jarri prisoner.

Spanish fears were confirmed when in 1689 de León discovered the ruins of a French settlement near Garcitas Creek during his fourth expedition. Apparently, the natives had killed the French intruders. During this expedition, de León entered into friendly relations with the Caddo natives. He observed that the Caddo constantly used the word *tayshas* (friends) to refer to the Spaniards. From then on, the Spaniards referred to the territory as "Tejasl."

In May 1690, de León set out on a fifth expedition and established the first permanent Spanish settlement in Texas, San Francisco de los Tejas, near the Neches River.

Despite the fact that Texas was made a separate Spanish province in 1691, with Don Domingo de Terán as its governor, the Spanish Crown ordered its abandonment in 1693. Fear of Indian uprisings was the reason given by the Spanish authorities. The Spanish withdrawal from Texas was not a permanent one. Continued concerns over possible French encroachment into Texas prompted the Spaniards to reoccupy Texas in 1716 by establishing a series of missions to serve two purposes: convert the natives to Catholicism and ward off the French. Of these missions, San Antonio, founded in 1718, was the most important and most prosperous.

On January 9, 1717, war broke out between Spain and France. Reports of a French invasion from Louisiana panicked the Spanish settlers of East Texas, who sought refuge in San Antonio. The invasion force, however, consisted of only seven men who attacked the Spanish settlement of San Miguel, which consisted of one Franciscan brother and one soldier! The invasion, nevertheless, prompted the governor of Coahuila, the Marquis of Aguayo, to march into Texas with a rescue expedition. On April 10, 1721, the Marquis of Aguayo arrived in San Antonio. After resupplying San Antonio, he marched through the interior, looking for French soldiers but found none. His job done, the Marquis returned to Coahuila in 1722, leaving behind a string of missions and presidios.

After the Marquis of Aguayo's departure, the viceroy of New Spain appointed Don Fernando Pérez de Almazán governor of Texas. Pérez de Almazán consolidated Spanish rule over the province. Despite the lack of settlers and the frequency of Comanche raids, Spain was able to maintain its presence in Texas until 1821.

✳ SPANISH EXPLORATIONS TO CALIFORNIA

California owes its name to a mythical island that appeared in the Spanish chivalric novel *Las sergas de Esplandián* (*The Deeds of Esplandian*).

Hernán Cortés, the conqueror of the Aztec Empire, became interested in finding a northwest passage and sent several expeditions to what today is the Mexican state of Baja California.

In 1542, Viceroy Antonio de Mendoza commissioned Juan Rodríguez de Cabrillo, a Portuguese sailor, to sail north of the west coast of Mexico in search of treasures. On September 28, 1542, Cabrillo entered what he described to be an excellent port—San Diego. He then sailed northward. As the ships went along the coast, they found no treasures. Cabrillo died on January 3, 1545. After the death of Cabrillo, Bartholomé Ferrelo took over the expedition and sailed all the way north to the Oregon coast. Disease broke out among the crew, and Ferrelo was forced to return to Mexico. The expedition arrived at the Mexican port of La Navidad on April 14, 1543.

The Expeditions of De Gali, Rodrigues Cermenho, and Vizcaíno

Interest in exploring California waned after the Cabrillo-Ferrelo expedition, but when the Spanish developed a profitable trade between their Philippine colony and Mexico, interest rekindled. Spanish authorities not only saw the need to secure ports in California as possible repair ports for their fleet, but also feared the presence of British pirates in the area. In 1579, Sir Francis Drake had even claimed the California coast for the British.

In 1584, Francisco de Gali was instructed to scout the Alta California coast. In 1595, the Portuguese sailor Sebastiao Rodrigues Cermenho was ordered by Viceroy Luis de Velasco to explore the California coast on his return from the Philippines. Following Gali's course, Rodrigues Cermenho ventured closer to the coast and discovered Monterey Bay in December 1595. He arrived at the Mexican port of La Navidad in January 1596.

The new Spanish viceroy, Monterey, continued Luis de Velasco's policy of finding possible repair ports in California and in May 1602 sent the experienced sailor Sebastián Vizcaíno to scout the area.

Although Vizcaíno's detailed exploration, which lasted 11 months, succeeded in finding the entrance to Monterey Bay, the expedition returned to Acapulco, Mexico, with only one-quarter of its original members. The rest had died of malnutrition. Exploration of Alta California was proving to be costly.

California: The Last Frontier

Russia's announced intentions, rather than the quest for treasures and riches, was largely responsible for Spain's colonization of California. As a reply to the Russian menace, Inspector General Don José de Gálvez decided that the settling of Alta California was essential. He commissioned the governor of Baja California, Don Gaspar de Portolá, to lead an expedition to Alta California. Father Junípero de Serra, the recently arrived Franciscan superior of Baja California, was also part of this expedition.

In January and February 1769, two ships carrying supplies left for San Diego. They were to rendezvous with Portolá's land expedition, which was divided into two parties. One party, commanded by Fernando Rivera Moncada, left Velicatá in Baja California on March 22, 1769. The other party, commanded by Portolá and with Serra as its chaplain, left Loreto in Baja California on May 15, 1769.

After traveling hundreds of miles through treacherous terrain, the two groups joined with the ships in San Diego on July 1, 1769. Two days later Father Serra planted a cross on a San Diego hill, and the construction of the first mission of Alta California followed. San Diego was the first of 21 missions that the Franciscans built in California.

An impatient man, Portolá departed by land to find Monterey. He arrived in Monterey in October, but unconvinced that the harbor he had seen was Monterey, he pushed northward. Days later, he arrived at a large bay. Portolá knew it was not Monterey Bay, so he called it San Francisco. Portolá wanted to continue the search for Monterey, but his tired men refused and he had no option but to return to San Diego. They arrived at San Diego on January 24, 1770.

The restless Portolá was obsessed with finding Monterey, and on May 31, 1770, he and Father Serra boarded the *San Antonio* in search of Monterey. Three days later, they finally reached the elusive harbor. A few days after that, they landed in Monterey, and Father Serra had his second Alta California mission. Portolá returned to Mexico. Spain now had two presidios to guard its empire in Alta California: Monterey to the north and San Diego to the south.

The new Spanish viceroy in Mexico, Don Antonio María Bucareli, wanted to establish another presidio in California. In 1773, he summoned Captain Juan Bautista de Anza, commander of the Tubac presidio in northern Mexico, to establish a route between Monterey and Sonora. In January 1774, de Anza set out on a probing expedition. At the junction of the Gila and Colorado rivers, de Anza established good relations with the cacique Palma and his Yuma natives. He then forded the river and wandered through the desert. On March 22, 1774, he reached Mission San Gabriel near present-day Los Angeles and then continued to Monterey. Anza returned to Tubac and then proceeded to Mexico City to report to

the viceroy. Both of them concluded that a presidio should be established in San Francisco.

In October 1775, de Anza's expedition, consisting of 240 settlers and enough provisions to make San Francisco self-sustaining, departed Tubac. As the expedition reached Yuma country, they were welcomed by chief Palma. On January 2, 1776, they reached San Gabriel. In March, they arrived at Monterey. Finally, on September 17, 1766, the presidio of San Francisco was founded. Spain's northernmost frontier outpost was now a reality. His mission accomplished, de Anza returned to Mexico City. He was later appointed governor of New Mexico.

The California provinces, however, showed little progress. The Yuma became impatient with the Spaniards, and in 1781 they revolted. The Spaniards were able to suppress the uprising, but California remained an isolated province of the Spanish Empire, lacking in colonists and resources. In 1821, Spain's northernmost frontier became part of independent Mexico.

The Missionary Trails

Ferdinand and Isabella, as well as the other Spanish monarchs that succeeded them, thought it was their duty to convert the natives of the New World to the Catholic faith. Although priests were sent to convert the natives, the missions did not begin until 1512. That year, the Jeronymite Fathers in La Española decided to save the devastated Arawak population by gathering them into missions. Soon, missions spread like wildfire throughout the Spanish Empire.

Spain's purpose in adopting the mission system was not only to save the souls of the natives but also to assimilate them. The natives were persuaded to join the mission in order to be taught the Catholic faith, the Spanish language, the Spanish way of life, and various skills. Missions were staffed by members of a religious order and were financially supported by the Spanish Crown. The mission system was really a system of paternalistic theocracy working for Spain and the salvation of souls.

Missions in "La Florida"

In 1573, the Franciscan order arrived in Florida to establish missions. A century after their arrival, they had established a trail of missions along the east coast of North America from Saint Augustine to North Carolina. The Franciscans also established a string of missions from Saint Augustine westward to present-day Tallahassee. Franciscan missions were even founded in the interior of Georgia and Alabama.

Florida and the Southeast were not the only places where missions were established. Missions went side by side with the Spanish colonization of Texas, the Southwest, and California. In many instances, missions assumed the character of political and military outposts against Spain's rivals. In short, they became the most important Spanish colonial institution in what was to become the United States.

Eusebio Kino: The Padre on Horseback

Among the many missionaries that came to the Spanish Empire in North America was Eusebio Kino. A Tyrolean by birth, Eusebio Kino was born in 1644 and studied at the Universities of Freiburg and Ingolstadt. While at Ingolstadt, Kino contracted a serious disease and commended himself to Saint Francis Xavier, the patron saint of the Indies. He then joined the Jesuit order and became a missionary.

Father Kino wanted to go as a missionary to the Philippines, but in 1678 his superiors ordered him to go to Mexico. He arrived in Mexico in 1680. From 1683 until 1686, Kino participated as a missionary in an unsuccessful attempt at settling Baja California.

The enterprise's failure did not deter Father Kino from pursuing his goal as a missionary. In 1687, he got his wish when his superior entrusted him with the missionary effort in the Pimería Alta. It was not an easy task, for the Pimería Alta encompassed a large area—present-day Upper Sonora, Mexico, and southwestern Arizona. The "padre on horseback," as Kino was called, ventured into the arid and hostile country of the Pimería Alta with only his faith and zeal. In less than a year, he founded his first mission, Nuestra Señora de los Dolores, in Sonora, about 100 miles from present-day Tucson.

By the early 1700s Father Kino had established several missions in Sonora and five missions in Arizona. Among his Arizona missions were Nuestra Señora de los Dolores, Santa Gertrudis de Saric, San José de Imuris, Nuestra Señora de los Remedios, San Cayetano de Tumacácori, and San Javier del Bac.

An accomplished farmer and stockman, Father Kino taught the natives new techniques and even encouraged them to plant wheat. In addition to his agricultural endeavors, Father Kino was an excellent cosmographer, astronomer, and mathematician. It was Father Kino who proved that Baja California was not an island but a peninsula.

Father Eusebio Kino died in 1711, at age 66. In his 24 years as a missionary, he had built a trail of 24 missions stretching from Sonora to southern Arizona. It can be stated that Arizona was practically settled by one man, Father Eusebio Kino, "the padre on horseback."

Fray Junipero de Serra and the California Mission Trail

In 1767, King Charles III expelled the Jesuits from the Spanish Empire. This event opened the door for the Franciscan conquest of California. This conquest would never have been accomplished without Fray Junípero de Serra. Miguel José de Serra was born on November 24, 1713, in Petra, Majorca. He entered the Franciscan friary when he was 16. After completing his vows, he took the name Junípero in honor of Brother Junípero, one of Saint Francis of Assisi's companions who was known for his compassion and humility.

Father Serra first arrived in the New World in 1749 with a group of Franciscan missionaries. He began preaching in Mexico City and later served as a missionary with the natives of eastern Mexico. Known for his energy and zeal, Father Serra was sent over to supervise the missionary efforts in Baja California in 1768.

Even though Father Serra was called to supervise the establishments of Franciscan missions in Baja California, he had another goal—to establish other missions in Alta California. This he did, for his order eventually established 21 missions in Alta California. Father Serra's missions in turn became the foundation of the Spanish colonization of California.

Father Serra founded his first mission, San Diego de Alcalá, on July 3, 1769. When he died on August 28, 1784, Father Serra had founded nine missions, traveled more than 10,000 miles, and converted close to 6,800 natives.

Father Serra's death did not stop missionary activity in California. His fellow Franciscans established another 12 missions. Thus, by 1823, the famous mission trail of California included the following missions: San Diego de Alcalá (1769), San Carlos de Monterey (1770), San Antonio de Padua (1771), San Gabriel Arcángel (1771), San Luis Obispo de Tolosa (1772), San Francisco de Asís (1776), San Juan Capistrano (1776), Santa Clara de Asís (1777), San Buenaventura (1782), Santa Bárbara (1786), La Purísima Concepción (1787), Santa Cruz (1791), San José de Guadalupe (1797), San Juan Bautista (1797), San Miguel Arcángel (1797), San Fernando Rey (1797), San Luis Rey (1798), Santa Inés (1804), San Rafael Arcángel (1817), and San Francisco Solano (1823).

Father Serra remains a controversial figure today. His admirers consider him a holy man worthy of canonization. They often refer to his missions as havens of peace and tranquility, where the padres taught the natives to be useful Spanish citizens. Detractors, on the other hand, classify Serra as a ruthless man who never respected the rights of the natives to be free and to live as they wanted. They often have compared the missions to penal institutions and claim their purpose was to enslave and exploit the natives. Despite the controversy, Serra's name still remains an integral part of California's history, and the mission system is essential to an understanding of the Spanish Empire in the New World.

References

Bailey, Helen Miller, and Abraham P. Nasatir. *Latin America: The Development of Its Civilization.* Englewood Cliffs, New Jersey: Prentice Hall, 1973.

Bandelier, Fanny. *The Journey of Álvar Nuñez Cabeza de Vaca.* Chicago: Río Grande Press, 1964.

Bannon, John Francis. *The Spanish Borderlands Frontier 1513–1821.* New York: Holt, Rinehart and Winston, 1970.

Blacker, Irwin R. *The Golden Conquistadors.* Indianapolis: Bobbs-Merrill, 1960.

Bolton, Herbert. *Spanish Exploration in the Southwest 1542–1706.* New York: Barnes and Noble, 1946.

——. *The Spanish Borderlands: A Chronicle of Old Florida and the Southwest.* New Haven: Yale University Press, 1921.

Claypole, William, and John Robottom. *Caribbean Story.* White Plains, New York: Longman, 1986.

Clissold, Stephen. *The Seven Cities of Cibola.* New York: Clarkson N. Potter, 1962.

Daniels, George. *The Spanish West.* New York: Time-Life Books, 1976.

Davis, Frederick. "History of Juan Ponce de Leon's Voyages to Florida." *Florida Historical Quarterly,* 14, July 1935: 7–66.

De Grazia, Ettore. *De Grazia and Padre Kino.* Tucson: De Grazia Gallery in the Sun, 1979.

De Nevi, Don, and Francis Moholy. *Junipero Serra.* New York: Harper and Row, 1985.

Driver, Harold E. *Indians of North America.* Chicago: University of Chicago Press, 1961.

Favata, Martin, and José B. Fernández. *La relación o naufraugios de Álvar Núñez Cabeza de Vaca.* Potomac, Maryland.: Scripta Humanis-tica, 1986.

Fernández, José B. *Álvar Núñez Cabeza de Vaca.* Miami: Ediciones Universal, 1975.

Fernández-Flores, Darío. *Drama y aventura de los españoles en Florida.* Madrid: Ediciones Cultura Hispánica, 1963.

Fernández de Navarrete, Martín. *Colección de los viajes y descu brimientos que hicieron por mar los españoles desde fines del siglo XV.* Buenos Aires: Editorial Guarania, 1945.

Fernández de Oviedo, Gonzalo. *Historia general y natural de las Indias.* Madrid: Ediciones Atlas, 1959.

García Mercadal, José. *Lo que España llevó a América.* Madrid: Taurus, 1959.

Garcilaso de la Vega, el Inca. *La Florida del Inca.* México: Fondo de Cultura Económica, 1956.

Gónzalez de Barcia, Andrés. *Ensayo cronológico para la historia de la Florida.* Gainesville: University of Florida Press, 1951.

Grove Day, A. *Coronado's Quest.* Berkeley: University of California Press, 1964.

Hallenbeck, Cleve. *Journey and Route of Álvar Nuñez Cabeza de Vaca.* Glendale: Arthur H. Clark Company, 1940.

Herring, Hubert. *A History of Latin America.* New York: Alfred A. Knopf, 1967.

Hudson, Charles. "A Synopsis of the Hernando de Soto Expedition, 1539–1543." In *De Soto Trail.* Washington, D.C.: National Park Service, 1990.

James, George W. *The Old Franciscan Missions of California.* Boston: Longwood Press, 1978.

Keen, Benjamin, and Mark Wasserman. *A History of Latin America.* Boston: Houghton Mifflin, 1988.

Knight, Franklin W. *The Caribbean.* New York: Oxford University Press, 1990.

Lowery, Woodbury. *The Spanish Settlements Within the Present Limits of the United States, 1531–1561.* New York: Russell and Russell, 1959.

Masó, Calixto. *Historia de Cuba.* Miami: Ediciones Universal, 1976.

McGann, Thomas F. "The Ordeal of Cabeza de Vaca." *American Heritage,* December 1960: 78–82.

Murga Sanz, Vicente. *Juan Ponce de León.* San Juan: Ediciones de la Universidad de Puerto Rico, 1959.

Rolle, Andrew. *California: A History.* New York: Thomas Y. Crowell, 1969.

Spencer, Robert, ed. *The Native Americans.* New York: Harper and Row, 1965.

Suchlicki, Jaime. *Cuba: From Columbus to Castro.* Washington, D.C.: Pergammon, 1986.

Tebeau, Charlton W. *A History of Florida.* Coral Gables: University of Miami Press, 1971.

——, and Ruby L. Carson. *Florida from Indian Trail to Space Age.* Delray Beach, Florida: Southern Publishing Company, 1965.

Te Paske, John. "Funerals and Fiestas in Early Eighteenth Century St. Augustine." *Florida Historical Quarterly,* January 1973: 97–104.

Terrell, John Upton. *Journey into Darkness.* New York: William Morrow, 1962.

Thomas, David Hurst, ed. *Columbian Consequences.* Washington, D.C.: Smithsonian Institution Press, 1989.

Williams, John L. *The Territory of Florida.* New York: A. T. Goodrich, 1837

José Fernández

3

Significant Documents

✻ Cessation of Louisiana ✻ Cessation of Louisiana: Financial Arrangement ✻ The Monroe Doctrine
✻ Peace, Friendship, Limits, and Settlement: Treaty of Guadalupe Hidalgo 1848
✻ Boundaries: Gadsen Treaty 1853 ✻ *Our America* by José Marti
✻ Treaty of Peace (Treaty of Paris) 1898 ✻ Relations with Cuba
✻ The "Hay-Herran" Treaty, January 1903 ✻ The "Hay-Bunau-Varilla Convention," November 1903
✻ Treaty of Relations between the United States and Cuba
✻ Constitutional Convention of Puerto Rico
✻ Resolutions Approved by the Constitutional Convention Relating to the Constitution of the
Commonwealth of Puerto Rico ✻ The North American Free Trade Agreement (NAFTA)

✻ CESSATION OF LOUISIANA

Treaty Between the United States of America and the French Republic

The President of the United States of America and the First Consul of the French Republic in the name of the French People desiring to remove all source of misunderstanding relative to objects of discussion mentioned in the second and fifth articles of the Convention of the 8th Vendemiaire and 9/30 September 1800 relative to the rights claimed by the United States in virtue of the Treaty concluded at Madrid the 27 of October 1795, between His Catholic Majesty, and the said United States, and willing to strengthen the union and friendship which at the time of the said Convention was happily reestablished between the two nations have respectively named their Plenipotentiaries to wit The President of the United States, by and with the advice and consent of the Senate of said states; Robert P. Livingston Minister Plenipotentiary of the United States and James Monroe Minister Plenipotentiary and Envoy extraordinary of the said states near the Government of the French Republic; And the First Consul in the name of the French people, Citizen Francis Barbe Marbois Minister of the public treasury who after having respectively exchanged their full powers have agreed to the following Articles.

Article I

Whereas by the Article the third of the Treaty concluded at St. Idelfonso the 9th Vendemiaire an 9/1 October 1800 between the First Consul of the French Republic and his Catholic Majesty it was agreed as follows.

His Catholic Majesty promises and engages on his part to cede to the French Republic six months after the full and entire execution of the conditions and Stipulations herein relative to his Royal Highness the Duke of Parma, the Colony or Province of Louisiana with the Same extent that it now has in the hands of Spain, and that it had when France possessed it; and Such as it Should be after the Treaties subsequently entered into between Spain and other States.

And whereas in pursuance of the Treaty and particularly of the third article the French Republic has an incontestible title to the domain and to the possession of the said Territory The First Consul of the French Republic desiring to give to the United States a strong proof of his friendship doth hereby cede to the said United States in the name of the French Republic for ever and in full Sovereignty the said territory with all its rights and appurtenances as fully and in the Same manner as they have been acquired by the French Republic in virtue of the above mentioned Treaty concluded with his Catholic Majesty.

77

Article II

In the cession made by the preceding article are included the adjacent Islands belonging to Louisiana, all public lots and Squares, vacant lands and all public buildings, fortifications, barracks and other edifices which are not private property. The Archives, papers and documents relative to the domain and Sovereignty of Louisiana and it dependencies will be left in the possession of the Commissaries of the United States, and copies will be afterwards given in due form to the Magistrates and Municipal officers of Such of the said papers and documents as may be necessary to them.

Article III

The inhabitants of the ceded territory shall be incorporated in the Union of the United States and admitted as soon as possible according to the principles of the federal Constitution to the enjoyment of all the rights, advantages and immunities of citizens of the United States, and in the mean time they shall be maintained and protected in the free enjoyment of their liberty, property and the Religion which they profess.

Article IV

There Shall be Sent by the Government of France a Commissary to Louisiana to the end that he do every act necessary as well to receive from the Officers of his Catholic Majesty the Said country and its dependencies in the name of the French Republic if it has not been already done as to transmit it in the name of the French Republic to the Commissary or agent of the United States.

Article V

Immediately after the ratification of the present Treaty by the President of the United States and in case that of the first Consul's shall have been previously obtained, the Commissary of the French Republic shall remit all military posts of New Orleans and other parts of the ceded territory to the Commissary or Commissaries named by the President to take possession—the troops whether of France or Spain who may be there shall cease to occupy any military post from the time of taking possession and shall be embarked as soon as possible in the course of three months after the ratification of this treaty.

Article VI

The United States promise to execute such treaties and articles as may have been agreed between Spain and the tribes and nations of Indians until by mutual consent of the United States and the said tribes or nations other suitable articles shall have been agreed upon.

Article VII

As it is reciprocally advantageous to the commerce of France and the United States to encourage the communication of both nations for a limited time in the country ceded by the present treaty until general arrangements relative to the commerce of both nations may be agreed on, it has been agreed between the contracting parties that the French ships coming directly from France or any of her colonies loaded only with the produce and manufactures of France or her said colonies; and the ships of Spain coming directly from Spain or any of her colonies loaded only with the produce or manufactures of Spain or her colonies shall be admitted during the space of twelve years in the Port of New Orleans and in all other legal ports-of-entry within the ceded territory in the same manner as the ships of the United States coming directly from France or Spain or any of their colonies without being subject to any other or greater duty on merchandise or other or greater tonnage than that paid by the citizens of the United States. During the space of time above mentioned no other nation shall have a right to the same privileges in the ports of the ceded territory—the twelve years shall commence three months after the exchange of ratifications if it shall take place in France or three months after it shall have been notified at Paris to the French Government if it shall take place in the United States; It is however well understood that the object of the above article is to favor the manufactures, Commerce, freight and navigation of France and of Spain so far as relates to the importations that the French and Spanish shall make into the said ports of the United States without in any sort affecting the regulations that the United States may make concerning the exportation of produce and merchandize of the United States, or any right they may have to make such regulations.

Article VIII

In future and for ever after the expiration of the twelve years, the ships of France shall be treated upon the footing of the most favored nations in the ports above mentioned.

Article IX

The particular Convention signed this day by the respective Ministers having for its object to provide for the payment of debts due to the Citizens of the United States by the French Republic prior to the

30th Sept. 1800 (8 Vendemiaire an 9) is approved and to have its execution in the same manner as if it had been inserted in this present treaty and it shall be ratified in the same form and in the same time so that the one shall not be ratified distinct from the other.

Another particular Convention signed at the same date as the present treaty relative to a definitive rule between the contracting parties is in the like manner approved and will be ratified in the same form, and in the same time and jointly.

Article X

The present treaty shall be ratified in good and due form and the ratifications shall be exchanged in the space of six months after the date of the signature by the Ministers Plenipotentiary or sooner if possible.

In faith whereof the respective Plenipotentiaries have signed these articles in the French and English languages; declaring nevertheless that the present Treaty was originally agreed to in the French language; and have thereunto affixed their seals. Done at Paris the tenth day of Floreal in the eleventh year of the French Republic; and the 30th of April 1803.

ROB. R. LIVINGSTON
J. A. MONROE
BARBE MARBOIS

Source: "Cession of Louisiana," 30 April 1803, *Treaties and Other International Agreements of the United States of America, 1776–1949*, Vol. 7, pp. 812–815.

✳ CESSATION OF LOUISIANA: FINANCIAL ARRANGEMENT

A Convention Between the United States of America and French Republic

The President of the United States of America and the First Consul of the French Republic in the name of the French people, in consequence of the treaty of cession of Louisiana which has been Signed this day; wishing to regulate definitively every thing which has relation to the Said cession have authorized to this effect the Plenipotentiaries that is to say: the President of the United States has, by and with the advice and consent of the Senate of the Said States nominated for their Plenipotentiaries, Robert R. Livingston Minister Plenipotentiary of the United States and James Monroe Minister Plenipotentiary and Envoy Extraordinary of the Said United States near the Government of the French Republic; and the First Consul of the French Republic in the name

of the French People has named as Plenipotentiary of the Said Republic the citizen Francis Barb Marbois: who in virtue of their full powers, which have been exchanged this day have agreed to the following articles:

Article 1

The Government of the United States engages to pay to the French Government in the manner Specified in the following article the Sum of Sixty millions of francs independent of the Sum which Shall be fixed by another Convention for the payment of the debts due by France to citizens of the United States.

Article 2

For the payment of the Sum of Sixty millions of francs mentioned in the preceding article the United States Shall create a Stock of eleven millions, two hundred and fifty thousand Dollars bearing an interest of Six per cent: per annum payable half yearly in London, Amsterdam or Paris amounting by the half year to three hundred and thirty Seven thousand five hundred Dollars according to the proportions which Shall be determined by the French Government to be paid at either place: The principal of the Said Stock to be reimbursed at the treasury of the United States in annual payments of not less than three millions of Dollars each; of which the first payment Shall commence fifteen years after the date of the exchange of ratifications—this Stock Shall be transferred to the Government of France or to Such person or persons as Shall be authorized to receive it in three months at most after the exchange of the ratifications of this treaty and after Louisiana Shall be taken possession of in the name of the Government of the United States.

It is further agreed that if the French Government Should be desirous of disposing of the Said Stock to receive the capital in Europe at Shorter terms that its measures for that purpose Shall be taken So as to favor in the greatest degree possible the credit of the United States and to raise to the highest price the Said Stock.

Article 3

It is agreed that the Dollar of the United States Specified in the present Convention Shall be fixed at five francs 3333/10000 or five livres eight Sous tournois.

The present Convention Shall be ratified in good and due form, and the ratifications Shall be exchanged in the Space of Six months to date from this day or Sooner if possible.

In faith of which the respective Plenipotentiaries

have Signed the above articles both in the French and English languages, declaring nevertheless that the present treaty has been originally agreed on and written in the French language; to which they have hereunto affixed their Seals.

Done at Paris the tenth of Floreal eleventh year of the French Republic (30th April 1803.)

ROB. R. LIVINGSTON
J. A. MONROE
BARBE MARBOIS

Source: "Cession of Louisiana: Financial Arrangement," 30 April 1803, *Treaties and Other International Agreements of the United States of America, 1776–1949*, Vol. 7, pp. 816, 817.

✹ THE MONROE DOCTRINE

ANNUAL MESSAGE from President James Monroe to the United States Congress, Containing the "Monroe Doctrine," December 2, 1823:

AT THE PROPOSAL of the Russian Imperial Government, made through the minister of the Emperor residing here, a full power and instructions have been transmitted to the minister of the United States at St. Petersburg, to arrange, by amicable negotiation, the respective rights and interests of the two nations on the northwest coast of this continent. A similar proposal has been made by his Imperial Majesty to the Government of Great Britain, which has likewise been acceded to. The Government of the United States has been desirous, by the friendly proceeding, of manifesting the great value which they have invariably attached to the friendship of the Emperor, and their solicitude to cultivate the best understanding with his Government. In the discussions to which this interest has given rise, and in the arrangements by which they may terminate, the occasion has been judged proper for asserting as a principle in which the rights and interests of the United States are involved, that the American continents, by the free and independent condition which they have assumed and maintain, are henceforth not to be considered as subjects for future colonization by any European powers.

It was stated at the commencement of the last session that a great effort was then making in Spain and Portugal to improve the condition of the people of those countries, and that it appeared to be conducted with extraordinary moderation. It need scarcely be remarked that the result has been, so far, very different from what was then anticipated. Of events in that quarter of the globe with which we have so much intercourse, and from which we derive our origin, we have always been anxious and interested spectators. The citizens of the United States cherish sentiments the most friendly in favor of the liberty and happiness of their fellow-men on that side of the Atlantic. In the wars of the European powers in matters relating to themselves we have never taken any part, nor does it comport with our policy so to do. It is only when our rights are invaded or seriously menaced that we resent injuries or make preparation for our defense. With the movements in this hemisphere we are, of necessity, more immediately connected, and by causes which must be obvious to all enlightened and impartial observers. The political system of the allied powers is essentially different in this respect from that of America. This difference proceeds from that which exists in their respective Governments. And to the defense of our own, which has been achieved by the loss of so much blood and treasure, and matured by the wisdom of their most enlightened citizens, and under which we have enjoyed unexampled felicity, this whole nation is devoted. We owe it, therefore, to candor, and to the amicable relations existing between the United States and those powers, to declare that we should consider any attempt on their part to extend their system to any portion of this hemisphere as dangerous to our peace and safety. With the existing colonies or dependencies of any European power we have not interfered and shall not interfere. But with the governments who have declared their independence and maintained it, and whose independence we have, on great consideration and on just principles, acknowledged, we could not view any interposition for the purpose of oppressing them, or controlling in any other manner their destiny, by any European power, in any other light than as the manifestation of an unfriendly disposition toward the United States. In the war between these new governments and Spain we declared our neutrality at the time of their recognition, and to this we have adhered and shall continue to adhere, provided no change shall occur which, in the judgment of the competent authorities of this Government, shall make a corresponding change on the part of the United States indispensable to their security.

The late events in Spain and Portugal show that Europe is still unsettled. Of this important fact no stronger proof can be adduced than that the allied powers should have thought it proper, on any principle satisfactory to themselves, to have interposed by force, in the internal concerns of Spain. To what extent such interposition may be carried, on the same principle, is a question in which all independent powers whose governments differ from theirs are interested, even those most remote, and surely none more so than the United States. Our policy in regard to Europe, which was adopted at an early stage of the wars which have so long agitated that quarter of the globe, nevertheless remains the same, which is, not to interfere in the internal concerns of government for us; to cultivate friendly relations with it, and to any of its powers; to consider the government de facto as the legitimate preserve those relations by a frank, firm, and manly policy, meeting, in all instances, the just claims of every power, submitting to injuries from none. But in regard to these continents, circumstances are eminently and conspicuously different. It is impossible that the allied powers should extend their political system to any portion of either continent without endangering our peace and happiness; nor can anyone believe that our southern brethren, if left to themselves, would adopt it of their own accord. It is equally impossible, therefore, that we should behold such interposition, in any form, with indifference. If we look to the comparative strength and resources of Spain and those new governments, and their distance from each other, it must be obvious that she can never subdue them. It is still the true policy of the United States to leave the parties to themselves, in the hope that other powers will pursue the same course.

The Monroe doctrine finds its recognition in those principles of international law which are based upon the theory that every nation shall have its rights protected and its just claims enforced.

Of course this Government is entirely confident that under the sanction of this doctrine we have clear rights and undoubted claims. Nor is this ignored in the British reply. The prime minister, while not admitting that the Monroe doctrine is applicable to present conditions, states: "In declaring that the United States would resist any such enterprise if it was contemplated, President Monroe adopted a policy which received the entire sympathy of the English Government of that date." He further declares: "Though the language of President Monroe is directed to the attainment of objects which most Englishmen would agree to be salutary, it is impossible to admit that they have been inscribed by any adequate authority in the code of international law." Again he says: "They (Her Majesty's Government) fully concur with the view which President Monroe apparently entertained, that any disturbance of the existing territorial distribution in the hemisphere by any fresh acquisitions on the part of any European state, would be a highly inexpedient change."

In the belief that the doctrine for which we contend was clear and definite, that it was founded upon substantial considerations and involved our safety and welfare, that it was fully applicable to our present conditions and to the state of the world's progress and that it was directly related to the pending controversy and without any conviction as to the final merits of the dispute, but anxious to learn in a satisfactory and conclusive manner whether Great Britain sought, under a claim of boundary, to extend her possessions on this continent without right, or whether she merely sought possession of territory fairly included within her lines of ownership, this Government proposed to the Government of Great Britain a resort to arbitration as the proper means of settling the question to the end that a vexatious boundary dispute between the two contestants might be determined and our exact standing and relation in respect to the controversy might be made clear.

It will be seen from the correspondence herewith submitted that this proposition has been declined by the British Government, upon grounds which in the circumstances seem to me to be far from satisfactory. It is deeply disappointing that such an appeal actuated by the most friendly feelings towards both nations directly concerned, addressed to the sense of justice and to the magnanimity of one of the great powers of the world and touching its relations to one comparatively weak and small, should have produced no better results.

The course to be pursued by this Government in view of the present condition does not appear to admit of serious doubt. Having labored faithfully for many years to induce Great Britain to submit this dispute to impartial arbitration, and having been now finally apprized of her refusal to do so, nothing remains but to accept the situation, to recognize its plain requirements and deal with it accordingly. Great Britain's present proposition has never thus far been regarded as admissible by Venezuela, though any adjustment of the boundary which that country may deem for her advantage and may enter into of her own free will can not of course be objected to by the United States.

Assuming, however, that the attitude of Venezuela will remain unchanged, the dispute has reached such a stage as to make it now incumbent upon the United States to take measures to determine with sufficient certainty for its justification what is the true divisional line between the Republic of Venezuela and British Guiana. The inquiry to that end should of course be conducted carefully and judicially and due weight should be given to all available evidence records and facts in support of the claims of both parties.

In order that such an examination should be prosecuted in a thorough and satisfactory manner I suggest that the Congress make an adequate appropriation for the expenses of a commission, to be appointed by the Executive, who shall make the necessary investigation and report upon the matter with the least possible delay. When such report is made and accepted it will in my opinion be the duty of the United States to resist by every means in its power as a willful aggression upon its rights and interests the appropriation by Great Britain of any lands or the exercise of governmental jurisdiction over any territory which after investigation we have determined of right belongs to Venezuela.

In making these recommendations I am fully alive to the responsibility incurred, and keenly realize all the consequences that may follow.

I am nevertheless firm in my conviction that while it is a grievous thing to contemplate the two great English-speaking peoples of the world as being otherwise than friendly competitors in the onward march of civilization, and strenuous and worthy rivals in all the arts of peace, there is no calamity which a great nation can invite which equals that which follows a supine submission to wrong and injustice and the consequent loss of national self-respect and honor beneath which are shielded and defended a people's safety and greatness.

Source: James Monroe, "Monroe Doctrine" (December 2, 1823), *A Compilation of the Messages and Papers of the Presidents*, edited by James D. Richardson, Vol. II (New York: Bureau of National Literature), p. 207; and John Bassett Moore, *A Digest of International Law,* VI, 401.

Period of the "Roosevelt Corollary"

ANNUAL MESSAGE from President Theodore Roosevelt to the United States Congress, December 3, 1901:

. . . MORE AND MORE the civilized peoples are realizing the wicked folly of war and are attaining that condition of just and intelligent regard for the rights of others which will in the end, as we hope and believe, make world-wide peace possible. The peace conference at The Hague gave definite expression to this hope and belief and marked a stride toward their attainment.

This same peace conference acquiesced in our statement of the Monroe doctrine as compatible with the purposes and aims of the conference.

The Monroe doctrine should be the cardinal feature of the foreign policy of all the nations of the two Americas, as it is of the United States. Just seventy-eight years have passed since President Monroe in his Annual Message announced that "The American continents are henceforth not to be considered as subjects for future colonization by any European power." In other words, the Monroe doctrine is a declaration that there must be no territorial aggrandizement by any non-American power at the expense of any American power or American soil. It is in no wise intended as hostile to any nation in the Old World. Still less is it intended to give cover to any aggression by one New World power at the expense of any other. It is simply a step, and a long step, toward assuring the universal peace of the world by securing the possibility of permanent peace on this hemisphere.

During the past century other influences have established the permanence and independence of the smaller states of Europe. Through the Monroe doctrine we hope to be able to safeguard like independence and secure like permanence for the lesser among the New World nations.

This doctrine has nothing to do with the commercial relations of any American power, save that it in truth allows each of them to form such as it desires. In other words, it is really a guaranty of the commercial independence of the Americas. We do not ask under this doctrine for any exclusive commercial dealings with any other American state. We do not guarantee any state against punishment if it misconducts itself, provided that punishment does not take the form of the acquisition of territory by any non-American power.

Our attitude in Cuba is a sufficient guaranty of our own good faith. We have not the slightest desire to secure any territory at the expense of any of our neighbors. We wish to work with them hand in hand, so that all of us may be uplifted together, and we rejoice over the good fortune of any of them, we gladly hail their material prosperity and political stability, and are concerned and alarmed if any of them fall into industrial or political chaos. We do not wish to see any Old World military power grow up on this continent, or to be compelled to become a military power ourselves. The peoples of the Americas can prosper best if left to work out their own salvation in their own way.

Our people intend to abide by the Monroe doctrine and to insist upon it as the one sure means of securing peace of the Western Hemisphere. The Navy offers us the only means of making our insistence upon the Monroe doctrine anything but a subject of derision to whatever nation chooses to disregard it. We desire the peace which comes as of right to the just man armed; not the peace granted-on terms of ignominy to the craven and the weakling.

Source: Theodore Roosevelt, "1901 Message to the United States Congress" (December 3, 1901), *A Compilation of the Messages and Papers of the Presidents,* edited by James D. Richardson, Vol. XIV (New York: Bureau of National Literature), pp. 6641–6680.

ANNUAL MESSAGE from President Theodore Roosevelt to the United States Congress, December 2, 1902:

. . . THE CANAL Will be of great benefit to America, and of importance to all the world. It will be of advantage to us industrially and also as improving our military position. It will be of advantage to the countries of tropical America. It is earnestly to be hoped that all of these countries will do as some of them have already done with signal success, and will invite to their shores commerce and improve their material condition by recognizing that stability and order are the prerequisites of our successful development. No independent nation in America need have the slightest fear of aggression from the United States. It behooves each one to maintain order within its own borders and to discharge its just obligations to foreigners. When this is done, they can rest assured that, be they strong or weak, they have nothing to dread from outside interference. More and more the increasing interdependence and complexity of international political and economic relations render it incumbent on all civilized and orderly powers to insist on the proper policing of the world.

Source: Theodore Roosevelt, "1902 Message to the United States Congress" (December 2, 1902), *A Compilation of the Messages and Papers of the Presidents*, edited by James D. Richardson, Vol. XIV (New York: Bureau of National Literature), pp. 6709–6724.

ANNUAL MESSAGE from President Theodore Roosevelt at Chicago, April 2, 1903:

I BELIEVE in the Monroe Doctrine with all my heart and soul; I am convinced that the immense majority of our fellow-countrymen so believe in it; but I would infinitely prefer to see us abandon it than to see us put it forward and bluster about it, and yet fail to build up the efficient fighting strength which in the last resort can alone make it respected by any strong foreign power whose interest it may ever happen to be to violate it.

There is a homely old adage which runs: "Speak softly and carry a big stick; you will go far." If the American nation will speak softly and yet build and keep at a pitch of the highest training a thoroughly efficient navy the Monroe Doctrine will go far.

Source: Theodore Roosevelt, in a speech made at Chicago, Illinois on April 2, 1903, *Presidential Addresses and State Papers of Theodore Roosevelt*, Part

One (New York: P. F. Collier and Son; reprint, New York: Kraus Reprint Co., 1970), pp. 257–268.

ANNUAL MESSAGE from President Theodore Roosevelt to the United States Congress, December 6, 1904:

IT IS NOT TRUE that the United States feels any land hunger or entertains any projects as regards the other nations of the Western Hemisphere save such as are for their welfare. All that this country desires is to see the neighboring countries stable, orderly, and prosperous. Any country whose people conduct themselves well can count upon our hearty friendship. If a nation shows that it knows how to act with reasonable efficiency and decency in social and political matters, if it keeps order and pays its obligations, it need fear no interference from the United States. Chronic wrongdoing, or an impotence which results in a general loosening of the ties of civilized society, may in America, as elsewhere, ultimately require intervention by some civilized nation, and in the Western Hemisphere the adherence of the United States to the Monroe Doctrine may force the United States, however reluctantly, in flagrant cases of such wrongdoing or impotence, to the exercise of an international police power. If every country washed by the Caribbean Sea would show the progress in stable and just civilization which with the aid of the Platt amendment Cuba has shown since our troops left the island, and which so many of the republics in both Americas are constantly and brilliantly showing, all question of interference by this Nation with their affairs would be at an end. Our interests and those of our southern neighbors are in reality identical. They have great natural riches, and if within their borders the reign of law and justice obtains, prosperity is sure to come to them. While they thus obey the primary laws of civilized society they may rest assured that they will be treated by us in a spirit of cordial and helpful sympathy. We would interfere with them only in the last resort, and then only if it became evident that their inability or unwillingness to do justice at home and abroad had violated the rights of the United States or had invited foreign aggression to the detriment of the entire body of American nations. It is a mere truism to say that every nation, whether in America or anywhere else, which desires to maintain its freedom, its independence, must ultimately realize that the right of such independence can not be separated from the responsibility of making good use of it.

In asserting the Monroe Doctrine, in taking such steps as we have taken in regard to Cuba, Venezuela, and Panama, and in endeavoring to circumscribe the theater of war in the Far East, and to secure the open door in China, we have acted in our own interest as well as in the interest of humanity at large.

Source: Theodore Roosevelt, "1904 Message to the United States Congress" (December 6, 1904), *A Compilation of the Messages and Papers of the Presidents*, edited by James D. Richardson, Vol. XV (New York: Bureau of National Literature), pp. 6894–6930.

ANNUAL MESSAGE from President Theodore Roosevelt to the United States Congress, December 5, 1905:

ONE OF THE MOST effective instruments for peace is the Monroe Doctrine as it has been and is being gradually developed by this Nation and accepted by other nations. No other policy could have been as efficient in promoting peace in the Western Hemisphere and in giving to each nation thereon the chance to develop along its own lines. If we had refused to apply the Doctrine to changing conditions it would now be completely outworn, would not meet any of the needs of the present day, and indeed would probably by this time have sunk into complete oblivion. It is useful at home, and is meeting with recognition abroad, because we have adapted our application of it to meet the growing and changing needs of the Hemisphere. When we announce a policy, such as the Monroe Doctrine, we thereby commit ourselves to the consequences of the policy, and those consequences from time to time alter. It is out of the question to claim a right and yet shirk the responsibility for its exercise. Not only we, but all American Republics who are benefitted by the existence of the Doctrine, must recognize the obligations each nation is under as regards foreign peoples no less than its duty to insist upon its own rights.

That our rights and interests are deeply concerned in the maintenance of the Doctrine is so clear as hardly to need argument. This is especially true in view of the construction of the Panama Canal. As a mere matter of self-defense we must exercise a close watch over the approaches to this canal; and this means that we must be thoroughly alive to our interests in the Caribbean Sea.

There are certain essential points which must never be forgotten as regards the Monroe Doctrine. In the first place we must as a nation make it evident that we do not intend to treat it in any shape or way as an excuse for aggrandizement on our part at the expense of the republics to the south. We must recognize the fact that in some South American countries there has been much suspicion lest we should interpret the Monroe Doctrine as in some way inimical to their interests, and we must try to convince all the other nations of this continent once and for all that no just and orderly government has anything to fear from us. There are certain republics to the south of us which have already reached such a point of stability, order, and prosperity that they themselves, though as yet hardly consciously, are among the guarantors of this Doctrine. These republics we now meet not only on a basis of entire equality, but in a spirit of frank and respectful friendship which we hope is mutual. If all of the republics to the south of us will only grow as those to which I allude have already grown, all need for us to be the especial champions of the Doctrine will disappear, for no stable and growing American Republic wishes to see some great non-American military power acquire territory in its neighborhood. All that this country desires is that the other republics on this Continent shall be happy and prosperous; and they can not be happy and prosperous unless they maintain order within their boundaries and behave with a just regard for their obligations toward outsiders. It must be understood that under no circumstances will the United States use the Monroe Doctrine as a cloak for territorial aggression. We desire peace with all the world, but perhaps most of all with the other peoples of the American Continent. There are of course limits to the wrongs which any self-respecting nation can endure. It is always possible that wrong actions toward this Nation, or toward citizens of this Nation, in some State unable to keep order among its own people, unable to secure justice from outsiders, and unwilling to do justice to those outsiders who treat it well, may result in our having to take action to protect our rights; but such action will not be taken with a view to territorial aggression, and it will be taken at all only with extreme reluctance and when it has become evident that every other resource has been exhausted.

Moreover, we must make it evident that we do not intend to permit the Monroe Doctrine to be used by any nation on this Continent as a shield to protect it from the consequences of its own misdeeds against foreign nations. If a republic to the south of us commits a tort against a foreign nation, such as an outrage against a citizen of that nation, then the Monroe Doctrine does not force us to interfere to prevent punishment of the tort, save to see that the punishment does not assume the form of territorial occupation in any shape. The case is more difficult when it refers to a contractual obligation. Our own Government has always refused to enforce such contractual obligations on behalf of its citizens by an appeal to arms. It is much to be wished that all foreign governments would take the same view. But they do not; and in consequence we are liable at any time to be brought face to face with disagreeable alternatives. On the one hand, this country would certainly decline to go to war to prevent a foreign government from collecting a just debt; on the other hand, it is very inadvisable to permit any foreign power to take possession, even temporarily, of the customhouses of an American Republic in order to enforce the payment of its obligations; for such temporary occupation might turn into a permanent occupation. The only escape from these alternatives may at any time be that we must ourselves undertake to bring about some arrangement by which so much as possible of a just obligation shall be paid. It is far better that this country should put through such an arrangement, rather than allow any foreign country to undertake it. To do so insures the defaulting republic from having to pay debts of an improper character under duress, while it also insures honest creditors of the republic from being passed by in the interest of dishonest or grasping creditors. Moreover, for the United States to take such a position offers the only possible way of insuring us against a clash with some foreign power. The position is, therefore, in the interest of peace as well as in the interest of justice. It is of benefit to our people; it is of benefit to foreign peoples; and most of all it is really of benefit to the people of the country concerned.

This brings me to what should be one of the fundamental objects of the Monroe Doctrine. We must ourselves in good faith try to help upward toward peace and order those of our sister republics which need such help. Just as there has been a gradual growth of the ethical element in the relations of one individual to another, so we are, even though slowly, more and more coming to recognize the duty of bearing one another's burdens, not only as among individuals, but also as among nations.

Source: Theodore Roosevelt, "1905 Message to the United States Congress" (December 5, 1905), *A Compilation of the Messages and Papers of the Presidents*, edited by James D. Richardson, Vol. XV (New York: Bureau of National Literature), pp. 6973–7023.

ANNUAL MESSAGE from President Theodore Roosevelt to the United States Congress, December 3, 1906:

. . . LAST AUGUST an insurrection broke out in Cuba which it speedily grew evident that the existing Cuban Government was powerless to quell. This Government was repeatedly asked by the then Cuban Government to intervene, and finally was notified by the President of Cuba that he intended to resign; that his decision was irrevocable; that none of the other constitutional officers would consent to carry on the Government, and that he was powerless to maintain order. It was evident that chaos was impending, and there was every probability that if steps were not immediately taken by this Government to try to restore order, the representatives of various European nations in the island would apply to their respective governments for armed intervention in order to protect the lives and property of their citizens. Thanks to the preparedness of our Navy, Secretary of War and the Assistant Secretary of State, I was able immediately to send enough ships to Cuba to prevent the situation from becoming hopeless; and I furthermore dispatched to Cuba the army in order that they might grapple with the situation on the ground. All efforts to secure an agreement between the contending factions, by which they should themselves come to an amicable understanding and settle upon some modus vivendi—some provisional government of their own—failed. Finally the President of the Republic resigned. The quorum of Congress assembled failed by deliberate purpose of its members, so that there was no power to act on his resignation, and the Government came to a halt. In accordance with the so-called Platt amendment, which was embodied in the constitution of Cuba, I thereupon proclaimed a provisional government for the island, the Secretary of War acting as provisional governor until he could be replaced by Mr. Magoon, the late minister to Panama and governor of the Canal Zone on the Isthmus; troops were sent to support them and to relieve the Navy, the expedition being handled with most satisfactory speed and efficiency. The insurgent chiefs immediately agreed that their troops should lay down their arms and disband; and the agreement was carried out. The provisional government has left the personnel of the old government and the old laws, so far as might be, unchanged, and will thus administer the island for a few months until tranquillity can be restored, a new election properly held, and a new government inaugurated. Peace has come in the island; and the harvesting of the sugar-cane crop, the great crop of the Island, is about to proceed.

When the election has been held and the new government inaugurated in peaceful and orderly fashion the provisional government will come to an end. I take this opportunity of expressing upon behalf of the American people, with all possible solemnity, our most earnest hope that the people of Cuba will realize the imperative need of preserving justice and keeping order in the Island. The United States wishes nothing of Cuba except that it shall prosper morally and materially, and wishes nothing of the Cubans save that they shall be able to preserve order among themselves and therefore to preserve their independence. If the elections become a farce, and if the insurrectionary habit becomes confirmed in the Island, it is absolutely out of the question that the Island should continue independent; and the United States, which has assumed the sponsorship before the civilized world for Cuba's career as a nation, would again have to intervene and to see that the government was managed in such orderly fashion as to secure the safety of life and property. The path to be trodden by those who exercise self-government is always hard, and we should have every charity and patience with the Cubans as they tread this difficult path. I have the utmost sympathy with, and regard for, them; but I most earnestly adjure them solemnly to weigh their responsibilities and to see that when their new government is started it shall run smoothly, and with freedom from flagrant denial of right on the one hand, and from insurrectionary disturbances on the other.

Source: Theodore Roosevelt, "1906 Message to the United States Congress" (December 3, 1906), *A Compilation of the Messages and Papers of the Presidents*, edited by James D. Richardson, Vol. XV (New York: Bureau of National Literature), pp. 7023–7070.

ANNUAL MESSAGE from President Woodrow Wilson at San Francisco, September 17, 1919:

. . . I WANT TO SAY again that Article X is the very heart of the Covenant of the League, because all the great wrongs of the world have had their root in the seizure of territory or the control of the political independence of other peoples. I believe that I speak the feeling of the people of the United States when I say that, having seen one great wrong like that attempted and having prevented it, we are ready to prevent it again.

Those are the two principal criticisms, that we did not do the impossible with regard to Shantung and that we may be advised to go to war. That is all there is in either of those. But they say, "We want the Monroe Doctrine more distinctly acknowledged." Well, if I could have found language that was more distinct than that used, I should have been very happy to suggest it, but it says in so many words that nothing in that document shall be construed as affecting the validity of the Monroe Doctrine. I do not see what more it could say, but, as I say, if the clear can be clarified, I have no objection to its being clarified. The meaning is too obvious to admit of discussion, and I want you to realize how extraordinary that provision is. Every nation in the world had been jealous of the Monroe Doctrine, had studiously avoided doing or saying anything that would admit its validity, and here all the great nations of the world sign a document which admits its validity. That constitutes nothing less than a moral revolution in the attitude of the rest of the world toward America.

What does the Monroe Doctrine mean in that Covenant? It means that with regard to aggressions upon the Western Hemisphere we are at liberty to act without waiting for other nations to act. That is the Monroe Doctrine. The Monroe Doctrine says that if anybody tries to interfere with affairs in the Western Hemisphere it will be regarded as an unfriendly act to the United States—not to the rest of the world—and that means that the United States will look after it, and will not ask anybody's permission to look after it. The document says that nothing in this document must be construed as interfering with that.

Source: Woodrow Wilson, in a luncheon address in San Francisco (September 17, 1919), *The Papers of Woodrow Wilson*, Vol. 63 (Princeton, New Jersey: Princeton University Press, 1990), pp. 311–322.

✳ PEACE, FRIENDSHIP, LIMITS, AND SETTLEMENT: TREATY OF GUADALUPE HIDALGO 1848

In the name of Almighty God:

The United States of America and the United Mexican States, animated by a sincere desire to put an end to the calamities of the war which unhappily exists between the two Republics, and to establish upon a solid basis relations of peace and friendship, which shall confer reciprocal benefits upon the citizens of both, and assure the concord, harmony and mutual confidence, wherein the two Peoples should live, as good Neighbors, have for that purpose appointed their respective Plenipotentiaries: that is to say, the President of the United States has appointed Nicholas P. Trist, a citizen of the United States, and the President of the Mexican Republic has appointed Don Luis Gonzaga Cuevas, Don Bernardo Couto, and Don Miguel Atristain, citizens of the said Republic; who, after a reciprocal communication of their respective full powers, have, under the protection of Almighty God, the author of Peace, arranged, agreed upon, and signed the following TREATY OF PEACE, FRIENDSHIP, LIMITS AND SETTLEMENT BETWEEN THE UNITED STATES OF AMERICA AND THE MEXICAN REPUBLIC

Article I

There shall be firm and universal peace between the United States of America and the Mexican Republic, and between their respective Countries, territories, cities, towns and people, without exception of places or persons.

Article II

Immediately upon the signature of this Treaty, a convention shall be entered into between a Commissioner or Commissioners appointed by the General in Chief of the forces of the United States, and such as may be appointed by the Mexican Government, to the end that a provisional suspension of hostilities shall take place, and that, in the places occupied by the said forces, constitutional order may be reestablished, as regards the political, administrative and judicial branches, so far as this shall be permitted by the circumstances of military occupation.

Article III

Immediately upon the ratification of the present treaty by the Government of the United States, orders shall be transmitted to the Commanders of their land and naval forces, requiring the latter, (provided this Treaty shall then have been ratified by the Government of the Mexican Republic and the ratifications exchanged) immediately to desist from blockading any Mexican ports; and requiring the former (under the same condition) to commence at the earliest moment practicable, withdrawing all troops of the United States then in the interior of the Mexican Republic, to points, that shall be selected by common agreement, at a distance from the sea-ports, not exceeding thirty leagues; and such evacuation of the interior of the Republic shall be completed with the least possible delay: the Mexican Government hereby binding itself to afford every facility in its power for rendering the same convenient to the troops, on their march and in their new positions, and for promoting a good understanding between them and the inhabitants. In like manner, orders shall be despatched to the persons in charge of the custom houses at all ports occupied by the forces of the United States, requiring them (under the same condition) immediately to deliver possession of the same to the persons authorized by the Mexican Government to receive it, together with all bonds and evidences of debt for duties on importations and on exportations, not yet fallen due. Moreover, a faithful and exact account shall be made out, showing the entire amount of all duties on imports and on exports, collected at such Custom Houses, or elsewhere in Mexico, by authority of the United States, from and after the day of ratification of this Treaty by the Government of the Mexican Republic; and also an account of the cost of collection; and such entire amount, deducting only the cost of collection, shall be delivered to the Mexican Government, at the City of Mexico, within three months after the exchange of ratifications.

The evacuation of the Capital of the Mexican Republic by the troops of the United States, in virtue of the above stipulation, shall be completed in one month after the orders there stipulated for shall have been received by the commander of said troops, or sooner if possible.

Article IV

Immediately after the exchange of ratifications of the present treaty, all castles, forts, territories, places and possessions, which have been taken or occupied by the forces of the United States during the present war, within the limits of the Mexican Republic, as about to he established by the following Article, shall be definitively restored to the said Republic, together with all the artillery, arms, apparatus of war, munitions, and other public property, which were in the said castles and forts when captured, and which shall remain there at the time when this treaty shall be duly ratified by the Government of the Mexican Republic. To this end, immediately upon the signature of this treaty, orders shall be despatched to the American officers commanding such castles and forts, securing against the removal or destruction of any such artillery, arms, apparatus of war, munitions, or other public property. The city of Mexico, within the inner line of entrenchments surrounding the said city, is comprehended in the above stipulations, as regards the restoration of artillery, apparatus of war, etc. The final evacuation of the territory of the Mexican Republic, by the forces of the United States, shall he completed in three months from the said exchange of ratifications, or sooner, if possible: the Mexican Government hereby engaging, as in the foregoing Article, to use all means in its power for facilitating such evacuation, and rendering it convenient to the troops, and for promoting a good understanding between them and the inhabitants.

If, however, the ratification of this treaty by both parties should not take place in time to allow the embarkation of the troops of the United States to be completed before the commencement of the sickly season, at the Mexican ports on the Gulf of Mexico; in such case a friendly arrangement shall be entered into between the General in Chief of the said troops and the Mexican Government, whereby healthy and otherwise suitable places at a distance from the ports not exceeding thirty leagues shall be designated for the residence of such troops as may not yet have embarked, until the return of the healthy season. And the space of time here referred to, as comprehending the sickly season, shall be understood to extend from the first day of May to the first day of November.

All prisoners of war taken on either side, on land or on sea, shall be restored as soon as practicable after the exchange of ratifications of this treaty. It is also agreed that if any Mexicans should now be held as captives by any savage tribe within the limits of the United States, as about to be established by the following Article, the Government of the said United States will exact the release of such captives, and cause them to be restored to their country.

Article V

The Boundary line between the two Republics shall commence in the Gulf of Mexico, three leagues from land, opposite the mouth of the Rio Grande, otherwise called Rio Bravo del Norte, or opposite the mouth of it's deepest branch, if it should have more than one branch emptying directly into the sea; from thence, up the middle of that river, following the deepest channel, where it has more than one to the point where it strikes the Southern boundary of New Mexico; thence, westwardly along the whole Southern Boundary of New Mexico (which runs north of the town called Paso) to it's western termination; thence, northward, along the western line of New Mexico, until it intersects the first branch of the river Gila; (or if it should not intersect any branch of that river, then, to the point on the said line nearest to such branch, and thence in a direct line to the same;) thence down the middle of the said branch and of the said river, until it empties into the Rio Colorado; thence, across the Rio Colorado, following the division line between Upper and Lower California, to the Pacific Ocean.

The southern and western limits of New Mexico, mentioned in this Article, are those laid down in the Map, entitled "Map of the United Mexican States, as organized and defined by various acts of the Congress of said Republic, and constructed according to the best authorities. Revised edition. Published at New York in 1847 by J. Disturnell:" Of which Map a Copy is added to this Treaty, bearing the signatures and seals of the Undersigned Plenipotentiaries. And, in order to preclude all difficulty in tracing upon the ground the limit separating Upper from Lower California, it is agreed that the said limit shall consist of a straight line, drawn from the middle of the Rio Gila, where it unites with the Colorado, to a point on the Coast of the Pacific Ocean, distant one marine league due south of the southernmost point of the Port of San Diego, according to the plan of said port, made in the year 1782, by Don Juan Pantoja, second sailing-master of the Spanish fleet, and published at Madrid in the year 1802, in the Atlas to the voyage of the schooners *Sutil* and *Mexicana*: of which plan a Copy is hereunto added, signed and sealed by the respective Plenipotentiaries.

In order to designate the Boundary line with due precision, upon authoritative maps, and to establish upon the ground landmarks which shall show the limits of both Republics, as described in the present Article, the two Governments shall each appoint a Commissioner and a Surveyor, who, before the expiration of one year from the date of the exchange of ratifications of this treaty, shall meet at the Port of San Diego, and proceed to run and mark the said Boundary in its whole course to the mouth of the Rio Bravo del Norte. They shall keep journals and make out plans of their operations; and the result, agreed upon by them, shall be deemed a part of this treaty, and shall have the same force as if it were inserted therein. The two Governments will amicably agree regarding what may be necessary to these persons, and also as to their respective escorts, should such be necessary.

The Boundary line established by this Article shall be religiously respected by each of the two Republics, and no change shall ever be made therein, except by the express and free consent of both nations, lawfully given by the General Government of each, in conformity with its own constitution.

Article VI

The vessels and citizens of the United States shall, in all time, have a free and uninterrupted passage by the Gulf of California, and by the river Colorado below its confluence with the Gila, to and from their possessions situated north of the Boundary line defined in the preceding Article: it being understood that this passage is to be by navigating the Gulf of California and the river Colorado, and not by land, without the express consent of the Mexican Government.

If, by the examinations which may be made, it should be ascertained to be practicable and advantageous to construct a road, canal or railway, which should, in whole or in part, run upon the river Gila, or upon its right or its left bank, within the space of one marine league from either margin of the river, the Governments of both Republics will form an agreement regarding its construction, in order that it may serve equally for the use and advantage of both countries.

Article VII

The river Gila, and the part of the Rio Bravo del Norte lying below the southern boundary of New Mexico, being, agreeably to the fifth Article, divided in the middle between the two Republics, the navigation of the Gila and of the Bravo below said boundary shall be free and common to the vessels and citizens of both countries; and neither shall, without the consent of the other, construct any work that may impede or interrupt, in whole or in part, the exercise of this right: not even for the purpose of favoring new methods of navigation. Nor shall any tax or contribution, under any denomination or title, be levied upon vessels or persons navigating the same, or upon merchandise or effects transported thereon, except in the case of landing upon one of their shores. If, for the purpose of making the said rivers navigable, or for maintaining them in such state, it should be necessary or advantageous to establish any tax or contribution, this shall not be done without the consent of both Governments.

The stipulations contained in the present Article shall not impair the territorial rights of either Republic, within its established limits.

Article VIII

Mexicans now established in territories previously belonging to Mexico, and which remain for the future within the limits of the United States, as defined by the present Treaty, shall be free to continue where they now reside or to remove at any time to the Mexican Republic, retaining the property which they possess in the said territories, or disposing thereof and removing the proceeds wherever they please; without their being subjected, on the account, to any contribution, tax or charge whatever.

Those who shall prefer to remain in the said territories, may either retain the title and rights of Mexican citizens, or acquire those of citizens of the United States. But, they shall be under the obligation to make their election within one year from the date of the exchange of ratifications of this treaty: and those who shall remain in the said territories, after the expiration of that year, without having declared their intention to retain the character of Mexicans, shall be considered to have elected to become citizens of the United States.

In the said territories, property of every kind, now belonging to Mexicans not established there, shall be inviolably respected. The present owners, the heirs of these, and all Mexicans who may hereafter acquire said property by contract, shall enjoy with respect to it, guaranties equally ample as if the same belonged to citizens of the United States.

Article IX

The Mexicans who, in the territories aforesaid, shall not preserve the character of citizens of the Mexican Republic, conformably with what is stipulated in the preceding article, shall be incorporated into the Union of the United States and be admitted, at the proper time (to be judged of by the Congress of the United States) to the enjoyment of all the rights of citizens of the United States according to the principles of the Constitution; and in the mean time shall be maintained and protected in the free enjoyment of their liberty and property, and secured in the free exercise of their religion without restriction.

Article X

All grants of land made by the Mexican Government or by the competent authorities, in territories previously appertaining to Mexico, and remaining for the future within the limits of the United States, shall be respected as valid, to the same extent that the same grants would be valid, if the said territories had remained within the limits of Mexico. But the grantees of lands in Texas, put in possession thereof, who, by reason of the circumstances of the country since the beginning of the troubles between Texas and the Mexican Government, may have been prevented from fulfilling all the conditions of their grants, shall be under the obligation to fulfill the said conditions within the periods limited in the same respectively; such periods to be now counted from the date of the exchange of ratifications of this treaty: in default of which the said grants shall not be obligatory upon the State of Texas, in virtue of the stipulations contained in this Article.

The foregoing stipulation in regard to grantees of land in Texas, is extended to all grantees of land in the territories aforesaid, elsewhere than in Texas, put in possession under such grants; and, in default of the fulfillment of the conditions of any such grant, within the new period, which as is above stipulated, begins with the day of the exchange of ratifications of this treaty, the same shall be null and void.

The Mexican Government declares that no grant whatever of lands in Texas has been made since the second day of March one thousand eight hundred and thirty six; and that no grant whatever of lands in any of the territories aforesaid has been made since the thirteenth day of May one thousand eight hundred and forty-six.

Article XI

Considering that a great part of the territories which by the present treaty are to be comprehended for the future within the limits of the United States, is now occupied by savage tribes, who will hereafter be under the exclusive control of the Government of the United States, and whose incursions within the territory of Mexico would be prejudicial in the extreme; it is solemnly agreed that all such incursions shall be forcibly restrained by the Government of the United States, whensoever this may be necessary; and that when they cannot be prevented, they shall be punished by the said Government, and satisfaction for the same shall be exacted: all in the same way, and with equal diligence and energy, as if the same incursions were meditated or committed within its own territory against its own citizens.

It shall not be lawful, under any pretext whatever, for any inhabitant of the United States, to purchase or acquire any Mexican or any foreigner residing in Mexico, who may have been captured by Indians inhabiting the territory of either of the two Republics; nor to purchase or acquire horses, mules, cattle or property of any kind, stolen within Mexican territory by such Indians;

And, in the event of any person or persons, captured within Mexican territory by Indians, being carried into the territory of the United States, the Government of the latter engages and binds itself, in the most solemn manner, so soon as it shall know of such captives being within its territory, and shall be able so to do, through the faithful exercise of its influence and power, to rescue them, and return them to their country, or deliver them to the agent or representative of the Mexican Government. The Mexican Authorities will, as far as practicable, give to the Government of the United States notice of such captures; and its agent shall pay the expenses incurred in the maintenance and transmission of the rescued captives; who, in the mean time, shall be treated with the utmost hospitality by the American Authorities at the place where they may be. But if the Government of the United States, before receiving such notice from Mexico, should obtain intelligence through any other channel, of the existence of Mexican captives within its territory, it will proceed forthwith to effect their release and delivery to the Mexican agent, as above stipulated.

For the purpose of giving to these stipulations the fullest possible efficacy, thereby affording the security and redress demanded by their true spirit and intent, the Government of the United States will now and hereafter pass, without unnecessary delay, and always vigilantly enforce, such laws as the nature of the subject may require. And finally, the sacredness of this obligation shall never be lost sight of by the said Government, when providing for the removal of the Indians from any portion of the said territories, or for its being settled by citizens of the United States; but on the contrary, special care shall then be taken not to place its Indian occupants under the necessity of seeking new homes, by committing those invasions which the United States have solemnly obliged themselves to restrain.

Article XII

In consideration of the extension acquired by the boundaries of the United States, as defined in the fifth Article of the present treaty, the Government of the United States engages to pay to that of the Mexican Republic the sum of fifteen Millions of Dollars.

Immediately after this Treaty shall have been duly ratified by the Government of the Mexican Republic, the sum of three Millions of Dollars shall be paid to the said Government by that of the United States at the City of Mexico, in the gold or silver coin of Mexico. The remaining twelve millions of dollars shall be paid at the same place, and in the same coin, in annual installments of three Millions of Dollars each, together with interest on the same at the rate of six per centum per annum. This interest shall begin to run upon the whole sum of twelve millions, from the day of the ratification of the present treaty by the Mexican Government, and the first of the installments shall be paid at the expiration of one year from the same day. Together with each annual instalment, as it falls due, the whole interest accruing on such instalment from the beginning shall also be paid.

Article XIII

The United States engage moreover, to assume and pay to the claimants all the amounts now due them, and those hereafter to become due, by reason of the claims already liquidated and decided against the Mexican Republic, under the conventions between the two Republics, severally concluded on the eleventh day of April eighteen hundred and thirty nine, and on the thirtieth day of January eighteen hundred and forty three: so that the Mexican Republic shall be absolutely exempt for the future, from all expense whatever old account of the said claims.

Article XIV

The United States do furthermore discharge the Mexican Republic from all claims of citizens of the United States, not heretofore decided against the Mexican Government, which may have arisen previously to the date of the signature of this treaty: which discharge shall be final and perpetual, whether the said claims be rejected or be allowed by the Board of Commissioners provided for in the following Article, and whatever shall be the total amount of those allowed.

Article XV

The United States, exonerating Mexico from all demands on account of the claims of their citizens mentioned in the preceding Article, and considering them entirely and forever canceled, whatever their amount may be, undertake to make satisfaction for the same, to an amount not exceeding three and one quarter millions of dollars. To ascertain the validity and amount of those claims, a Board of Commissioners shall be established by the Government of the United States, whose awards shall be final and conclusive: provided that in deciding upon the validity of each claim, the board shall be guided and governed by the principles and rules of decision described by the first and fifth Articles of the unratified convention, concluded at the city of Mexico on the twentieth day of November one thousand eight hundred and forty-three; and in no case shall an award be made in favor of any claim not embraced by these principles and rules.

If, in the opinion of the said Board of Commissioners, or of the claimants, any books, records or documents in the possession or power of the Government of the Mexican Republic, shall be deemed necessary to the just decision of any claim, the Commissioners or the claimants, through them, shall, within such period as Congress may designate, make an application in writing for the same, addressed to the Mexican Minister for Foreign Affairs, to be transmitted by the Secretary of State of the United States; and the Mexican Government engages, at the earliest possible moment after the receipt of such demand, to cause any of the books, records or documents, so specified, which shall be in their possession or power, (or authenticated copies or extracts of the same) to be transmitted to the said Secretary of State, who shall immediately deliver them over to the said Board of Commissioners: *Provided* That no such application shall be made, by, or at the instance of, any claimant, until the facts which it is expected to prove by such books, records or documents, shall have been stated under oath or affirmation.

Article XVI

Each of the contracting parties reserves to itself the entire right to fortify whatever point within its territory, it may judge proper so to fortify, for its security.

Article XVII

The Treaty of Amity, Commerce and Navigation, concluded at the City of Mexico on the fifth day of April A.D. 1831, between the United States of America and the United Mexican States, except the addi-

tional Article, and except so far as the stipulations of the said treaty may be incompatible with any stipulation contained in the present treaty, is hereby revived for the period of eight years from the day of the exchange of ratifications of this treaty, with the same force and virtue as if incorporated therein; it being understood that each of the contracting parties reserves to itself the right, at any time after the said period of eight years shall have expired, to terminate the same by giving one year's notice of such intention to the other party.

Article XVIII

All supplies whatever for troops of the United States in Mexico, arriving at ports in the occupation of such troops, previous to the final evacuation thereof, although subsequently to the restoration of the Custom Houses at such ports, shall be entirely exempt from duties and charges of any kind: the Government of the United States hereby engaging and pledging its faith to establish and vigilantly to enforce, all possible guards for securing the revenue of Mexico, by preventing the importation, under cover of this stipulation, of any articles, other than such, both in kind and in quantity, as shall really be wanted for the use and consumption of the forces of the United States during the time they may remain in Mexico. To this end, it shall be the duty of all officers and agents of the United States to denounce to the Mexican Authorities at the respective ports, any attempts at a fraudulent abuse of this stipulation, which they may know of or may have reason to suspect, and to give to such Authorities all the aid in their power with regard thereto: and every such attempt, when duly proved and established by sentence of a competent tribunal, shall be punished by the confiscation of the property so attempted to be fraudulently introduced.

Article XIX

With respect to all merchandise, effects and property whatsoever, imported into ports of Mexico, whilst in the occupation of the forces of the United States, whether by citizens of either republic, or by citizens or subjects of any neutral nation, the following rules shall be observed:

I. All such merchandise, effects and property, if imported previously to the restoration of the Custom Houses to the Mexican Authorities, as stipulated for in the third Article of this treaty, shall be exempt from confiscation, although the importation of the same be prohibited by the Mexican tariff.

II. The same perfect exemption shall be enjoyed by all such merchandise, effects and property, imported subsequently to the restoration of the Custom Houses, and previously to the sixty days fixed in the following Article for the coming into force of the Mexican tariff at such ports respectively: the said merchandise, effects and property being, however, at the time of their importation, subject to the payment of duties as provided for in the said following Article.

III. All merchandise, effects and property, described in the two rules foregoing, shall, during their continuance at the place of importation, and upon their leaving such place for the interior, be exempt from all duty, tax or impost of every kind, under whatsoever title or denomination. Nor shall they be there subjected to any charge whatsoever upon the sale thereof.

IV. All merchandise, effects and property, described in the first and second rules, which shall have been removed to any place in the interior, whilst such place was in the occupation of the forces of the United States, shall, during their continuance therein, be exempt from all tax upon the sale or consumption thereof, and from every kind of impost or contribution, under whatsoever title or denomination.

V. But if any merchandise, effects or property, described in the first and second rules, shall be removed to any place not occupied at the time by the forces of the United States, they shall, upon their introduction into such place, or upon their sale or consumption there, be subject to the same duties which, under the Mexican laws, they would be required to pay in such cases, if they had been imported in time of peace through the Maritime Custom Houses, and had there paid the duties, conformably with the Mexican tariff.

VI. The owners of all merchandise, effects or property, described in the first and second rules, and existing in any port of Mexico, shall have the right to reship the same, exempt from all tax, impost or contribution whatever.

With respect to the metals, or other property, exported from any Mexican port, whilst in the occupation of the forces of the United States, and previously to the restoration of the Custom House at such port, no person shall be required by the Mexican Authorities, whether General or State, to pay any tax, duty or contribution upon any such exportation, or in any manner to account for the same to the said Authorities.

Article XX

Through consideration for the interests of commerce generally, it is agreed, that if less than sixty days should elapse between the date of the signature of this treaty and the restoration of the Custom Houses, conformably with the stipulation in the third Article, in such case, all merchandise, effects and property whatsoever, arriving at the Mexican ports after the restoration of the said Custom Houses, and previously to the expiration of sixty days after the day of the signature of this treaty, shall be admitted to entry; and no other duties shall be levied thereon than the duties established by the tariff found in force at such Custom Houses at the time of the restoration of the same. And to all such merchandise, effects and property, the rules established by the preceding Article shall apply.

Article XXI

If unhappily any disagreement should hereafter arise between the Governments of the two Republics, whether with respect to the interpretation of any stipulation in this treaty, or with respect to any other particular concerning the political or commercial relations of the two Nations, the said Governments, in the name of those Nations, do promise to each other, that they will endeavor, in the most sincere and earnest manner, to settle the differences so arising, and to preserve the state of peace and friendship, in which the two countries are now placing themselves: using, for this end, mutual representations and pacific negotiations. And if, by these means, they should not be enabled to come to an agreement, a resort shall not, on this account, be had to reprisals, aggression or hostility of any kind, by the one Republic against the other, until the Government of that which deems itself aggrieved, shall have maturely considered, in the spirit of peace and good neighborship, whether it would not be better that such difference should be settled by the arbitration of Commissioners appointed on each side, or by that of a friendly nation. And should such course be proposed by either party, it shall be acceded to by the other, unless deemed by it altogether incompatible with the nature of the difference, or the circumstances of the case.

Article XXII

If (which is not to be expected, and which God forbid!) war should unhappily break out between the two Republics, they do now, with a view to such calamity, solemnly pledge themselves to each other and to the world, to observe the following rules: absolutely, where the nature of the subject permits, and as closely as possible in all cases where such absolute observance shall be impossible.

I. The merchants of either Republic, then residing in the other, shall be allowed to remain twelve months (for those dwelling in the interior) and six months (for those dwelling at the sea-ports) to collect their debts and settle their affairs; during which periods they shall enjoy the same protection, and be on the same footing, in all respects, as the citizens or subjects of the most friendly nations; and, at the expiration thereof, or at any time before, they shall have full liberty to depart, carrying off all their effects, without molestation or hinderance: conforming therein to the same laws, which the citizens or subjects of the most friendly nations are required to conform to. Upon the entrance of the armies of either nation into the territories of the other, women and children, ecclesiastics, scholars of every faculty, cultivators of the earth, merchants, artisans, manufacturers, and fishermen, unarmed and inhabiting unfortified towns, villages or places, and in general all persons whose occupations are for the common subsistence and benefit of mankind, shall be allowed to continue their respective employments, unmolested in their persons. Nor shall their houses or goods be burnt, or otherwise destroyed; nor their cattle taken, nor their fields wasted, by the armed force, into whose power, by the events of war, they may happen to fall; but if the necessity arise to take anything from them for the use of such armed force, the same shall be paid for at an equitable price. All churches, hospitals, schools, colleges, libraries, and other establishments for charitable and beneficent purposes, shall be respected, and all persons connected with the same protected in the discharge of their duties and the pursuit of their vocations.

II. In order that the fate of prisoners of war may be alleviated, all such practices as those of sending them into distant, inclement or unwholesome districts, or crowding them into close and noxious places, shall be studiously avoided. They shall not be confined in dungeons, prison-ships, or prisons; nor be put in irons, or bound, or otherwise restrained in the use of their limbs. The officers shall enjoy liberty on their paroles, within convenient districts, and have comfortable quarters; and the common soldier shall be disposed in cantonments, open and extensive enough for air and exercise, and lodged in barracks as roomy and good as are provided by the party in whose power they are for its own troops. But, if any officer shall break his parole by leaving the district so assigned him, or any other prisoner shall escape from the limits of his cantonment, after they shall have been designated to him, such individual, officer or other prisoner, shall forfeit so much of the benefit of this article as provides for his liberty on parole or in cantonment. And if any officer so breaking his parole, or any common soldier so escaping from the limits assigned him, shall afterwards be found in arms, previously to his being regularly exchanged, the person so offending shall be dealt with according to the established laws of war. The officers shall be daily furnished by the party in whose power they are, with as many rations, and of the same articles as are allowed either in kind or by commutation, to officers of equal rank in its own army; and all others shall be daily furnished with such ration as is allowed to a common soldier in its own service: the value of all which supplies shall, at the close of the war, or at periods to be agreed upon between the respective commanders, be paid by the other party on a mutual adjustment of accounts for the subsistence of prisoners; and such accounts shall not be mingled with or set off against any others, nor the balance due on them be withheld, as a compensation or reprisal for any cause whatever, real or pretended. Each party shall be allowed to keep a commissary of prisoners, appointed by itself, with every cantonment of prisoners, in possession of the other: which commissary shall see the prisoners as often as he pleases; shall be allowed to receive, exempt from all duties or taxes, and to distribute whatever comforts may be sent to them by their friends; and shall be free to transmit his reports in open letters to the party by whom he is employed.

And it is declared that neither the pretence that war dissolves all treaties, nor any other whatever shall be considered as annulling or suspending the solemn covenant contained in this article. On the contrary, the state of war is precisely that for which it is provided; and during which its stipulations are to be as sacredly observed as the most acknowledged obligations under the law of nature or nations.

Article XXIII

This treaty shall be ratified by the President of the United States of America, by and with the advice and consent of the Senate thereof; and by the President of the Mexican Republic, with the previous approbation of its General Congress: and the ratifications shall be exchanged in the City of Washington, or at the seat of government of Mexico, in four months from the date of the signature hereof, or sooner if practicable.

In faith whereof, we, the respective Plenipotentiaries, have signed this Treaty of Peace, Friendship, Limits and Settlement, and have hereunto affixed our seals respectively. Done in Quintuplicate, at the City of Guadalupe Hidalgo, on the second day of February in the year of Our Lord one thousand eight hundred and forty eight.

N. P. TRIST
LUIS G. CUEVAS
BERNARDO COUTO
MIGL. ATRISTAIN

Source: "Treaty of Peace, Friendship, Limits, and Settlement with the Republic of Mexico," 2 February 1848, 9 *Statutes at Large of the United States of America* 922.

✳ BOUNDARIES: GADSEN TREATY 1853

In the Name of Almighty God

The Republic of Mexico and the United States of America desiring to remove every cause of disagreement, which might interfere in any manner with the friendship and intercourse between the two Countries; and especially, in respect to the true limits which should be established, when notwithstanding what was covenanted in the Treaty of Guadalupe Hidalgo in the Year 1848, opposite interpretations have been urged, which might give occasion to questions of serious moment: to avoid these, and to strengthen and more firmly maintain the peace, which happily prevails between the two Republics, the President of the United States has for this purpose, appointed James Gadsden Envoy Extraordinary and Minister Plenipotentiary of the same near the Mexican Government, and the President of Mexico has appointed as Plenipotentiary "ad hoc" His Excellency Don Manuel Diez de Bonilla Cavalier Grand Cross of the National and Distinguished Order of Guadalupe, and Secretary of State and of the Office of Foreign Relations, and Don Jose Salazar Ylarregui and General Mariano Monterde as Scientific Commissioners invested with Full powers for this Negotiation who having communicated their respective Full powers, and finding them in due and proper form, have agreed upon the Articles following.

Article 1

The Mexican Republic agrees to designate the following as her true limits with the United States for the future; Retaining the same dividing line between the two Californias, as already defined and established according to the 5th Article of the Treaty of Guadalupe Hidalgo, the limits between the Two Republics shall be as follows: Beginning in the Gulf of Mexico, three leagues from land, opposite the mouth of the Rio Grande as provided in the fifth article of the treaty of Guadalupe Hidalgo, thence as defined in the said article, up the middle of that river to the point where the parallel of 31°47′ north latitude crosses the same, thence due west one hundred miles, thence south to the parallel of 31°20′ north latitude, thence along the said parallel of 31°20′ to the 111th meridian of longitude west of Greenwich, thence in a straight line to a point on the Colorado river twenty English miles below the junction of the Gila and Colorado rivers, thence up the middle of the said river Colorado until it intersects the present line between the United States and Mexico.

For the performance of this portion of the Treaty each of the two Governments shall nominate one Commissioner to the end that, by common consent, the two thus nominated having met in the City of Paso del Norte, three months after the exchange of the ratification s of this Treaty may proceed to survey and mark out upon the land the dividing line stipulated by this article, where it shall not have already been surveyed and established by the Mixed Commission according to the Treaty of Guadalupe keeping a Journal and making proper plans of their operations. For this purpose if they should Judge it is necessary, the contracting Parties shall be at liberty each to unite to its respective Commissioner Scientific or other assistants, such as Astronomers and Surveyors whose concurrence shall not be considered necessary for the settlement and ratification of a true line of division between the two Republics; that line shall be alone established upon which the Commissioners may fix, their consent in this particular being considered decisive and an integral part of this Treaty, without necessity of ulterior ratification or approval, and without room for interpretation of any kind by either of the Parties contracting.

The dividing line thus established shall in all time be faithfully respected by the two Governments without any variation therein, unless of the express and free consent of the two, given in conformity to the principles of the Law of Nations, and in accordance with the Constitution of each country respectively.

In consequence, the stipulation in the 5th Article of the Treaty of Guadalupe upon the Boundary line therein described is no longer of any force, wherein it may conflict with that here established, the said line being considered annulled and abolished wherever it may not coincide with the present, and in the same manner remaining in full force where in accordance with the same.

Article 2

The government of Mexico hereby releases the United States from all liability on account of the obligations contained in the eleventh article of the treaty of Guadalupe Hidalgo, and the said article and the thirty-third article of the treaty of amity, commerce and navigation between the United States of America and the United Mexican States concluded at Mexico, on the fifth day of April, 1831, are hereby abrogated.

Article 3

In consideration of the foregoing stipulations, the government of the United States agrees to pay to the government of Mexico, in the city of New York, the sum of ten millions of dollars, of which seven millions shall be paid immediately upon the exchange of the ratifications of this treaty, and the remaining three millions as soon as the boundary line shall be surveyed, marked, and established.

Article 4

The Provisions of the 6th and 7th Articles of the Treaty of Guadalupe Hidalgo having been rendered nugatory for the most part by the Cession of Territory granted in the First Article of this Treaty, the said Articles are hereby abrogated and annulled and the provisions as herein expressed substituted therefore The Vessels and Citizens of the United States shall in all Time have free and uninterrupted passage through the Gulf of California to and from their possessions situated North of the Boundary line of the Two Countries. It being understood that this passage is to be by navigating the Gulf of California and the river Colorado, and not by land, without the express consent of the Mexican Government, and precisely the same provisions, stipulations and restrictions in all respects are hereby agreed upon and adopted and shall be scrupulously observed and enforced by the Two Contracting Governments in reference to the Rio Colorado, so far and for such distance as the middle of that River is made their common Boundary Line, by the First Article of this Treaty.

The several Provisions, Stipulations and restrictions contained in the 7th Article of the Treaty of Guadalupe Hidalgo, shall remain in force only so far as regards the Rio Bravo del Norte below the initial of the said Boundary provided in the First Article of this Treaty That is to say below the intersection of the 31°47′30″ parallel of Latitude with the Boundary Line established by the late Treaty dividing said river from its mouth upwards according to the 5th Article of the Treaty of Guadalupe.

Article 5

All the provisions of the Eighth and Ninth, Sixteenth and Seventeenth Articles of the Treaty of Guadalupe Hidalgo shall apply to the Territory ceded by the Mexican Republic in the First Article of the present Treaty and to all the rights of persons and property both civil and ecclesiastical within the same, as fully and as effectually as if the said Articles were herein again recited and set forth.

Article 6

No Grants of Land within the Territory ceded by the First Article of This Treaty bearing date subsequent to the day Twenty fifth of September—when the Minister and Subscriber to this Treaty on the part of the United States proposed to the Govern-

ment of Mexico to terminate the question of Boundary, will be considered valid or be recognized by the United States, or will any Grants made previously be respected or be considered as obligatory which have not been located and duly recorded in the Archives of Mexico.

Article 7

Should there at any future period (which God forbid) occur any disagreement between the two Nations which might lead to a rupture of their relations and reciprocal peace, they bind themselves in like manner to procure by every possible method the adjustment of every difference, and should they still in this manner not succeed, never will they proceed to a declaration of War, without having previously paid attention to what has been set forth in Article 21 of the Treaty of Guadalupe for similar cases; which Article as well as the 22nd is here reaffirmed.

Article 8

The Mexican government having on the 5th of February 1853 authorized the early construction of a plank and railroad across the Isthmus of Tehuantepec, and to secure the stable benefits of said transit way to the persons and merchandise of the citizens of Mexico and the United States, it is stipulated that neither government will interpose any obstacle to the transit of persons and merchandise of both nations; and at no time shall higher charges be made on the transit of persons and property of citizens of the United States than may be made on the persons and property of other foreign nations, nor shall any interest in said transit way, nor in the proceeds thereof, be transferred to any foreign government.

The United States by its Agents shall have the right to transport across the Isthmus, in closed bags, the mails of the United States not intended for distribution along the line of communication; also the effects of the United States government and its citizens, which may be intended for transit, and not for distribution on the Isthmus, free of custom house or other charges by the Mexican government. Neither passports nor letters of security will be required of persons crossing the Isthmus and not remaining in the country.

When the construction of the railroad shall be completed, the Mexican government agrees to open a port of entry in addition to the port of Vera Cruz, at or near the terminus of said road on the Gulf of Mexico. The two governments will enter into arrangements for the prompt transit of troops and munitions of the United States, which that government may have occasion to send from one part of its territory to another, lying on opposite sides of the continent. The Mexican government having agreed to protect with its whole power the prosecution, preservation and security of the work, the United States may extend its protection as it shall judge wise to it when it may feel sanctioned and warranted by the public or international law.

Article 9

This Treaty shall be ratified, and the respective ratifications shall be exchanged at the City of Washington, within the exact period of six months from the date of its signature or sooner if possible.

In testimony whereof, We the Plenipotentiaries of the contracting parties have hereunto affixed our hands and seals at Mexico the—Thirtieth (30th)—day of December in the Year of Our Lord one thousand eight hundred and fifty three, in the thirty third year of the Independence of the Mexican Republic, and the seventy eighth of that of the United States.

JAMES GADSDEN
MANUEL DIEZ DE BONILLA
JOSE SALAZAR YLARREGUI
J. MARIANO MONTERDE

Source: "Gadsden Treaty," 30 December 1853, *Treaties and Other International Agreements of the United States of America, 1776–1949*, Vol. 9, pp. 812–816.

✴ *OUR AMERICA* BY JOSÉ MARTI

Following is Cuban patriot José Martí's famous analysis of the political and governmental problems confronting Spanish America and his perception of the threat of United States imperialism. Published in New York's La revista illustrada *(The Illustrated Review) on January 10, 1891, it forever fixed the idea of two Americas, that of the United States and that of the Latin American countries.*

The conceited villager believes the entire world to be his village. Provided that he can be mayor, or humiliate the rival who stole his sweetheart, or add to the savings in his strong-box, he considers the universal order good, unaware of those giants with seven-league boots who can crush him underfoot, or of the strife in the heavens between comets that streak through the drowsy air-devouring worlds. What remains of the village in America must rouse itself. These are not the times for sleeping in a nightcap, but with weapons for a pillow, like the warriors of Juan de Castellanos weapons of the mind, which conquer all others. Barricades of ideas are worth more than barricades of stone.

There is no prow that can cut through a cloudbank of ideas. A powerful idea, waved before the world at the proper time, can stop a squadron of iron-clad ships, like the mystical flag of the Last Judgment. Nations that do not know one another should quickly become acquainted, as men who are to fight a common enemy. Those who shake their fists, like jealous brothers coveting the same tract of land, or like the modest cottager who envies the squire his mansion, should clasp hands and become one. Those who use the authority of a criminal tradition to lop off the lands of their defeated brother with a sword stained with his own blood, ought to return the lands to the brother already punished sufficiently, if they do not want the people to call them robbers. The honest man does not absolve himself of debts of honor with money, at so much a slap. We can no longer be a people of leaves living in the air, our foliage heavy with blooms and crackling or humming at the whim of the sun's caress, or buffeted and tossed by the storms. The trees must form ranks to keep the giant with seven-league boots from passing! It is the time of mobilization, of marching together, and we must go forward in close order, like silver in the veins of the Andes.

Only those born prematurely are lacking in courage. Those without faith in their country are seven-month weaklings. Because they have no courage, they deny it to others. Their puny arms—arms with bracelets and hands with painted nails, arms of Paris or Madrid—can hardly reach the bottom limb, and they claim the tall tree to be unclimbable. The ships should be loaded with those harmful insects that gnaw at the bone of the country that nourishes them. If they are Parisians or from Madrid, let them go to the Prado under lamplight, or to Tortoni's for a sherbet. Those carpenters' sons who are ashamed that their fathers are carpenters! Those born in America who are ashamed of the mother who reared them, because she wears an Indian apron, and who disown their sick mother, the scoundrels, abandoning her on her sickbed! Then who is a real man? He who stays with his mother and nurses her in her illness, or he who puts her to work out of sight, and lives at her expense on decadent lands, sporting fancy neckties, cursing the womb that carried him, displaying the sign of the traitor on the back of his paper frockcoat? These sons of Our America, which will be saved by its Indians and is growing better; these deserters who take up arms in the armies of a North America that drowns its Indians in blood and is growing worse! These delicate creatures who are men but are unwilling to do men's work! The Washington who made this land for them, did he not go to live with the English, to live with the English at a time when he saw them fighting against his own country? These "iconoclasts" of honor who drag that honor over foreign soil, like their counterparts in the French Revolution with their dancing, their affectations, their drawling speech!

For in what lands can men take more pride than in our long-suffering American republics, raised up from among the silent Indian masses by the bleeding arms of a hundred apostles, to the sounds of battle between the book and the processional candle? Never in history have such advanced and united nations been forged in so short a time from such disorganized elements.

The presumptuous man feels that the earth was made to serve as his pedestal because he happens to have a facile pen or colorful speech, and he accuses his native land of being worthless and beyond redemption because its virgin jungles fail to provide him with a constant means of traveling over the world, driving Persian ponies and lavishing champagne like a tycoon. The incapacity does not lie with the emerging country in quest of suitable forms and a utilitarian greatness; it lies rather with those who attempt to rule nations of a unique and violent character by means of laws inherited from four centuries of freedom in the United States and nineteen centuries of monarchy in France. A decree by Hamilton does not halt the charge of the plainsman's horse. A phrase by Sieyes does nothing to quicken the stagnant blood of the Indian race. To govern well, one must see things as they are. And the able governor in America is not the one who knows how to govern the Germans or the French; he must know the elements that compose his own country, and how to bring them together, using methods and institutions originating within the country, to reach that desirable state where each man can attain self-realization and all may enjoy the abundance that Nature has bestowed on everyone in the nation to enrich with their toil and defend with their lives. The government must originate in the country. The spirit of the government must be that of the country. Its structure must conform to rules appropriate to the country. Good government is nothing more than the balance of the country's natural elements.

That is why the imported book has been conquered in America by the natural man. Natural men have conquered learned and artificial men. The native halfbreed has conquered the exotic Creole. The struggle is not between civilization and barbarity, but between false erudition and Nature. The natural man is good, and he respects and rewards superior intelligence as long as his humility is not turned against him, or he is not offended by being disregarded—a thing the natural man never forgives,

prepared as he is to forcibly regain the respect of whoever has wounded his pride or threatened his interests. It is by conforming with these disdained native elements that the tyrants of America have climbed to power, and have fallen as soon as they betrayed them. Republics have paid with oppression for their inability to recognize the true elements of their countries, to derive from them the right kind of government, and to govern accordingly. In a new nation a governor means a creator.

In nations composed of both cultured and uncultured elements, the uncultured will govern because it is their habit to attack and resolve doubts with their fists in cases where the cultured have failed in the art of governing. The uncultured masses are lazy and timid in the realm of intelligence, and they want to be governed well. But if the government hurts them, they shake it off and govern themselves. How can the universities produce governors if not a single university in America teaches the rudiments of the art of government, the analysis of elements peculiar to the peoples of America? The young go out into the world wearing Yankee or French spectacles, hoping to govern a people they do not know. In the political race entrance should be denied to those who are ignorant of the rudiments of politics. The prize in literary contests should not go for the best ode, but for the best study of the political factors of one's country. Newspapers, universities, and schools should encourage the study of the country's pertinent components. To know them is sufficient, without mincing words; for whoever brushes aside even a part of the truth, whether through intention or oversight, is doomed to fall. The truth he lacks thrives on negligence, and brings down whatever is built without it. It is easier to resolve our problem knowing its components than to resolve it without knowing them. Along comes the natural man, strong and indignant, and he topples all the justice accumulated from books because he has not been governed in accordance with the obvious needs of the country. Knowing is what counts. To know one's country and govern it with that knowledge is the only way to free it from tyranny. The European university must bow to the American university. The history of America, from the Inca to the present, must be taught in clear detail and to the letter, even if the archons of Greece are overlooked. Our Greece must take priority over the Greece which is not ours. We need it more. Nationalist statesmen must replace foreign statesmen. Let the world be grafted onto our republics, but the trunk must be our own. And let the vanquished pedant hold his tongue, for there are no lands in which a man may take greater pride than in our long-suffering American republics.

With the rosary as our guide, our heads white and our bodies mottled, both Indian and Creole, we fearlessly entered the world of nations. We set out to conquer freedom under the banner of the virgin. A priest, a few lieutenants, and a woman raised the Republic of Mexico onto the shoulders of the Indians. A few heroic students, instructed in French liberty by a Spanish cleric, made Central America rise in revolt against Spain under a Spanish general. In monarchic garb emblazoned with the sun, the Venezuelans to the north and the Argentineans to the south began building nations. When the two heroes clashed and the continent was about to rock, one of them, and not the lesser, handed the reins to the other. And since heroism in times of peace is rare because it is not as glorious as in times of war, it is easier for a man to die with honor than to think with logic. It is easier to govern when feelings are exalted and united than after a battle, when divisive, arrogant, exotic, or ambitious thinking emerges. The forces routed in the epic struggle with the feline cunning of the species, and using the weight of realities were under-mining the new structure which comprised both the rough-and-ready, unique regions of our halfbreed America and the silk-stocking and frockcoated people of Paris beneath the flag of freedom and reason borrowed from nations skilled in the arts of government. The hierarchical constitution of the colonies resisted the democratic organization of the republics. The clavated capitals left their country boots in the vestibule. The bookworm redeemers failed to realize that the revolution succeeded because it came from the soul of the nation; they had to govern with that soul and not without it or against it. America began to suffer, and still suffers, from the tiresome task of reconciling the hostile and discordant elements it inherited from a despotic and perverse colonizer, and the imported methods and ideas which have been retarding logical government because they are lacking in local realities. Thrown out of gear for three centuries by a power which denied men the right to use their reason, the continent disregarded or closed its ears to the unlettered throngs that helped bring it to redemption, and embarked on a government based on reason—a reason belonging to all for the common good, not the university brand of reason over the peasant brand. The problem of independence did not lie in a change of forms but in a change of spirit.

It was imperative to make common cause with the oppressed, in order to secure a new system opposed to the ambitions and governing habits of the oppressors. The tiger, frightened by gunfire, returns at night to his prey. He dies with his eyes shooting flames and his claws unsheathed. He cannot be heard coming because he approaches with velvet tread. When the prey awakens, the tiger is already upon it. The colony lives on in the republic, and Our America is saving itself from its enormous mistakes the pride of its capital cities, the blind triumph of a scorned peasantry, the excessive influx of foreign ideas and formulas, the wicked and un-politic disdain for the aboriginal race because of the higher virtue, enriched with necessary blood, or a republic struggling against a colony. The tiger lurks behind every tree, lying in wait at every turn. He will die with his claws unsheathed and his eyes shooting flames.

But "these countries will be saved," as was announced by the Argentinean Rivadavia, whose only sin was being a gentleman in these rough-and-ready times. A man does not sheathe a machete in a silken scabbard, nor can he lay aside the short lance in a country won with the short lance merely because he is angered and stands at the door of Iturbide's Congress, "demanding that the fairhaired one be named Emperor." These countries will be saved because a genius for moderation, found in the serene harmony of Nature, seems to prevail on the continent of light, where there emerges a new realistic man schooled for these realistic times in the critical philosophy which in Europe has replaced the philosophy of guess-work and phalanstery that saturated the previous generation.

We were a phenomenon with the chest of an athlete, the hands of a dandy, and the brain of a child. We were a masquerader in English breeches, Parisian vest, North American jacket, and Spanish cap. The Indian hovered near us in silence, and went off to the hills to baptize his children. The Negro was seen pouring out the songs of his heart at night, alone and unrecognized among the rivers and wild animals. The peasant, the creator, turned in blind indignation against the disdainful city, against his own child. As for us, we were nothing but epaulets and professors' gowns in countries that came into the world wearing hemp sandals and headbands. It would have been the mark of genius to couple the headband and the professors' gown with the founding fathers' generosity and courage, to rescue the Indian, to make a place for the competent Negro, to fit liberty to the body of those who rebelled and conquered for it. We were left with the judge, the general, the scholar, and the sinecure. The angelic young, as if caught in the tentacles of an octopus, lunged heavenward, only to fall back, crowned with clouds, in sterile glory. The native, driven by instinct, swept away the golden staffs of office in blind triumph. Neither the European nor the Yankee could provide the key to the Spanish American riddle. Hate was attempted, and every year the countries amounted to less. Exhausted by the senseless struggle between the book and the lance, between reason and the processional candle, between the city and the country, weary of the impossible rule by rival urban cliques over the natural nation tempestuous or inert by turns, we begin almost unconsciously to try love. Nations stand up and greet one another.

"What are we?" is the mutual question, and little by little they furnish answers. When a problem arises in Cojimar, they do not seek its solution in Danzig. The frockcoats are still French, but thought begins to be American. The youth of America are rolling up their sleeves, digging their hands in the dough, and making it rise with the sweat of their brows. They realize that there is too much imitation, and that creation holds the key to salvation. "Create" is the password of this generation. The wine is made from plantain, but even if it turns sour, it is our own wine! That a country's form of government must be in keeping with its natural elements is a foregone conclusion. Absolute ideas must take relative forms if they are not to fail because of an error in form. Freedom, to be viable, has to be sincere and complete. If a republic refuses to open its arms to all, and move ahead with all, it dies. The tiger within sneaks in through the crack; so does the tiger from without. The general holds back his cavalry to a pace that suits his infantry, for if the infantry is left behind, the cavalry will be surrounded by the enemy. Politics and strategy are one. Nations should live in an atmosphere of self-criticism because criticism is healthy, but always with one heart and one mind. Stoop to the unhappy, and lift them up in your arms! Thaw out frozen America with the fire of your hearts! Make the natural blood of the nations course vigorously through their veins. The new Americans are on their feet, saluting each other from nation to nation, the eyes of the laborers shining with joy. The natural statesman arises, schooled in the direct study of Nature. He reads to apply his knowledge, not to imitate. Economists study the problems at their point of origin. Speakers begin a policy of moderation. Playwrights bring native characters to the stage. Academies discuss practical subjects. Poetry shears off its romantic locks and hangs its red vest on the glorious tree. Selective and sparkling prose is filled with ideas. In the Indian republics, the governors are learning Indian.

America is escaping all its dangers. Some of the republics are still beneath the sleeping octopus, but others, under the law of averages, are draining their lands with a sublime and furious haste, as if to make up for centuries lost. Still others, forgetting that Juarez went about in a carriage drawn by mules, hitch their carriages to the wind, their coachmen soap bubbles. Poisonous luxury, the enemy of freedom, corrupts the frivolous and opens the door to the foreigner. In others, where independence is threatened, an epic spirit heightens their manhood. Still others spawn an army capable of devouring them in voracious wars. But perhaps Our America is running another risk that does not come from itself but from the difference in origins, methods, and interests between the two halves of the continent, and the time is near at hand when an enterprising and vigorous people who scorn or ignore Our America will even so approach it and demand a close relationship. And since strong nations, self-made by law and shotgun, love strong nations, and them alone; since the time of madness and ambition from which North America may be freed by the predominance of the purest elements in its blood, or on which it may be launched by its vindictive and sordid masses, its tradition of expansion, or the ambitions of some powerful leader is not so near at hand, even to the most timorous eye, that there is no time for the test of discreet and unwavering pride that could confront and dissuade it; since its good name as a republic in the eyes of the world's perceptive nations puts upon North America a restraint that cannot be taken away by childish provocations or pompous arrogance or parricidal discords among Our American nations the pressing need of Our America is to show itself as it is, one in spirit and intent, swift conqueror of a suffocating past, stained only by the enriching blood drawn from hands that struggle to clear away the ruins, and from the scars left upon us by our masters. The scorn of our formidable neighbor who does not know us is Our America's greatest danger. And since the day of the visit is near, it is imperative that our neighbor know us, and soon, so that it will not scorn us. Through ignorance it might even come to lay hands on us. Once it does know us, it will remove its hands out of respect. One must have faith in the best in men and distrust the worst. One must allow the best to be shown so that it reveals and prevails over the worst. Nations should have a pillory for whoever stirs up useless hates, and another for whoever fails to tell them the truth in time.

There can be no racial animosity, because there are no races. The theorists and feeble thinkers string together and warm over the bookshelf races which the well-disposed observer and the fair-minded traveler vainly seek in the justice of Nature where man's universal identity springs forth from triumphant love and the turbulent hunger for life. The soul, equal and eternal, emanates from bodies of various shapes and colors. Whoever foments and spreads antagonism and hate between the races, sins against humanity. But as nations take shape among other different nations, there is a condensation of vital and individual characteristics of thought and habit, expansion and conquest, vanity and greed which could from the latent state of national concern, and in a period of internal disorder, or the rapidity with which the country's character has been accumulating be turned into a serious threat for the weak and isolated neighboring countries, declared by the strong country to be inferior and perishable. The thought is father to the deed. And one must not attribute, through a provincial antipathy, a fatal and inborn wickedness to the continent's fairskinned nation simply because it does not speak our language, or see the world as we see it, or resemble us in its political defects, so different from ours, or favorably regard the excitable, dark-skinned people, or look charitably from its still uncertain eminence upon those less favored by history, who climb the road of republicanism by heroic stages. The self-evident facts of the problem should not be obscured, because the problem can be resolved, for the peace of centuries to come, by appropriate study, and by tacit and immediate unity in the continental spirit. With a single voice the hymn is already being sung. The present generation is carrying industrious America along the road enriched by their sublime fathers; from the Rio Grande to the Straits of Magellan, the Great Sem, astride his condor, is sowing the seed of the new America through-out the Latin nations of the continent and the sorrowful islands of the sea!

Source: Jose Marti, "Our America," in *La revista illustrada*, January 10, 1891; reprinted in *Our America: Writings on Latin America and the Struggle for Cuban Independence* (New York: Monthly Review Press, 1977), pp. 84–94.

✳ TREATY OF PEACE [TREATY OF PARIS] 1898

The United States of America and Her Majesty the Queen Regent of Spain, in the name of her August Son Don Alfonso XIII, desiring to end the state of war now existing between the two countries, have for that purpose appointed as Plenipotentiaries: The President of the United States, William R. Day, Cushman K. Davis, William P. Frye, George Gray, and Whitelaw Reid, citizens of the United States; and Her Majesty the Queen Regent of Spain, Don Eugenio Montero Rios, President of the Senate, Don Buenaventura de Abarzuza, Senator of the Kingdom and ex-Minister of the Crown, Don Jose de Garnica, Deputy to the Cortes and Associate Justice of the Supreme Court, Don Wenceslao Ramire de Villa-Ur-

rutia, Envoy Extraordinary and Minister Plenipotentiary at Brussels, and Don Rafael Cerero, General of Division;

Who, having assembled in Paris, and having exchanged their full powers, which were found to be in due and proper form, have, after discussion of the matters before them, agreed upon the following articles:

Article I

Spain relinquishes all claim of sovereignty over and title to Cuba.

And as the island is, upon its evacuation by Spain, to be occupied by the United States, the United States will, so long as such occupation shall last, assume and discharge the obligations that may under international law result from the fact of its occupation, for the protection of life and property.

Article II

Spain cedes to the United States the island of Porto Rico and other islands now under Spanish sovereignty in the West Indies, and the island of Guam in the Marianas or Ladrones.

Article III

Spain cedes to the United States the archipelago known as the Philippine Islands, and comprehending the islands lying within the following line:

A line running from west to east along or near the twentieth parallel of north latitude, and through the middle of the navigable channel of Bachi, from the one hundred and eighteenth (118th) to the one hundred and twenty seventh (127th) degree meridian of longitude east of Greenwich, thence along the one hundred and twenty seventh (127th) degree meridian of longitude east of Greenwich to the parallel of four degrees and forty five minutes (4°45') north latitude to its intersection with the meridian of longitude one hundred and nineteen degrees and thirty-five minutes (119°35') east of Greenwich to the parallel of latitude seven degrees and forty minutes (7°40') north, thence along the parallel of latitude seven degrees and forty minutes (7°40') north to its intersection with the one hundred and sixteenth (116th) degree meridian of longitude east of Greenwich, thence by a direct line to the intersection of the tenth (10th) degree parallel of north latitude with the one hundred and eighteenth (118th) degree meridian of longitude east of Greenwich, and thence along the one hundred and eighteenth (118th) degree meridian of longitude east of Greenwich to the point of beginning.

The United States will pay to Spain the sum of twenty million dollars ($20,000,000) within three months after the exchange of the ratifications of the present treaty.

Article IV

The United States will, for the term of ten years from the date of the exchange of the ratifications of the present treaty, admit Spanish ships and merchandise to the ports of the Philippine Islands on the same terms as ships and merchandise of the United States.

Article V

The United States will, upon the signature of the present treaty, send back to Spain, at its own cost, the Spanish soldiers taken as prisoners of war on the capture of Manila by the American forces. The arms of the soldiers in question shall be restored to them.

Spain will, upon the exchange of the ratifications of the present treaty, proceed to evacuate the Philippines, as well as the island of Guam, on terms similar to those agreed upon by the Commissioners appointed to arrange for the evacuation of Porto Rico and other islands in the West Indies, under the Protocol of August 12, 1898, which is to continue in force until its provisions are completely executed.

The time within which the evacuation of the Philippine Islands and Guam shall be completed shall be fixed by the two Governments. Stands of colors, uncaptured war vessels, small arms, guns of any calibres, with their carriages and accessories, powder, ammunition, livestock, and materials and supplies of all kinds, belonging to the land and naval forces of Spain in the Philippines and Guam, remain the property of Spain. Pieces of heavy ordnance, exclusive of field artillery, in the fortifications and coast defenses, shall remain in their emplacements for the term of six months, to be reckoned from the exchange of ratifications of the treaty; and the United States may, in the mean time, purchase such material from Spain, if a satisfactory agreement between the two Governments on the subject shall be reached.

Article VI

Spain will, upon the signature of the present treaty, release all prisoners of war, and all persons detained or imprisoned for political offenses, in connection with the insurrections in Cuba and the Philippines and the war with the United States. Reciprocally, the United States will release all persons made prisoners of war by the American forces, and will undertake to obtain the release of all Spanish prisoners in the hands of the insurgents in Cuba and the Philippines.

The Government of the United States will at its own cost return to Spain and the Government of Spain will at its own cost return to the United States, Cuba, Porto Rico, and the Philippines, according to the situation of their respective homes, prisoners released or caused to be released by them, respectively, under this article.

Article VII

The United States and Spain mutually relinquish all claims for indemnity, national and individual of every kind, of either Government, or of its citizens or subjects, against the other Government, that may have arisen since the beginning of the late insurrection in Cuba and prior to the exchange of ratifications of the present treaty, including all claims for indemnity for the cost of the war.

The United States will adjudicate and settle the claims of its citizens against Spain relinquished in this article.

Article VIII

In conformity with the provisions of Articles I, II, and III of this treaty, Spain relinquishes in Cuba, and cedes in Porto Rico and other islands in the West Indies, in the island of Guam, and in the Philippine Archipelago, all the buildings, wharves, barracks, forts, structures, public highways and other immovable property which, in conformity with law, belong to the public domain, and as such belong to the Crown of Spain.

And it is hereby declared that the relinquishment or cession, as the case may be, to which the preceding paragraph refers, cannot in any respect impair the property or rights which by law belong to the peaceful possession of property of all kinds, of provinces, municipalities, public or private establishments, ecclesiastical or civic bodies, or any other associations having legal capacity to acquire and possess property in the aforesaid territories renounced or ceded, or of private individuals, of whatsoever nationality such individuals may be. The aforesaid relinquishment or cession, as the case may be, includes all documents exclusively referring to the sovereignty relinquished or ceded that may exist in the archives of the Peninsula. Where any document in such archives only in part relates to said sovereignty, a copy of such part will be furnished whenever it shall be requested. Like rules shall be reciprocally observed in favor of Spain in respect of documents in the archives of the islands above referred to.

In the aforesaid relinquishment or cession, as the case may be, are also included such rights as the Crown of Spain and its authorities possess in respect of the official archives and records, executive as well as judicial, in the islands above referred to, which relate to said islands or the rights and property of their inhabitants. Such archives and records shall be carefully preserved, and private persons shall without distinction have the right to require, in accordance with law, authenticated copies of the contracts, wills and other instruments forming part of notarial protocols or files or which may he contained in the executive or judicial archives, be the latter in Spain or in the islands aforesaid.

Article IX

Spanish subjects, natives of the Peninsula, residing in the territory over which Spain by the present treaty relinquishes or cedes her sovereignty, may remain in such territory or may remove therefrom, retaining in either event all their rights of property, including the right to sell or dispose of such property or of its proceeds; and they shall also have the right to carry on their industry, commerce and professions, being subject in respect thereof to such laws as are applicable to other foreigners. In case they remain in the territory they may preserve their allegiance to the Crown of Spain by making, before a court of record, within a year from the date of the exchange of ratifications of this treaty, a declaration of their decision to preserve such allegiance; in default of which declaration they shall be held to have renounced it and to have adopted the nationality of the territory in which they may reside.

The civil rights and political status of the native inhabitants of the territories hereby ceded to the United States shall be determined by the Congress.

Article X

The inhabitants of the territories over which Spain relinquishes or cedes her sovereignty shall be secured in the free exercise of their religion.

Article XI

The Spaniards residing in the territories over which Spain by this treaty cedes or relinquishes her sovereignty shall be subject in matters civil as well as criminal to the jurisdiction of the courts of the country wherein they reside, pursuant to the ordinary laws governing the same; and they shall have the right to appear before such courts, and to pursue the same course as citizens of the country to which the courts belong.

Article XII

Judicial proceedings pending at the time of the exchange of ratifications of this treaty in the territories over which Spain relinquishes or cedes her sovereignty shall be determined according to the following rules:

1. Judgments rendered either in civil suits between private individuals, or in criminal matters, before the date mentioned, and with respect to which there is no recourse or right of review under the Spanish law, shall be deemed to be final, and shall be executed in due form by competent authority in the territory within which such judgments should be carried out.

2. Civil suits between private individuals which may on the date mentioned be undetermined shall be prosecuted to judgment before the court in which they may then be pending or in the court that may be substituted therefore.

3. Criminal actions pending on the date mentioned before the Supreme Court of Spain against citizens of the territory which by this treaty ceases to be Spanish shall continue under its jurisdiction until final judgment; but, such judgment having been rendered, the execution shall be committed to the competent authority of the place in which the case arose.

Article XIII

The rights of property secured by copyrights and patents acquired by Spaniards in the Island of Cuba, and in Porto Rico, the Philippines and other ceded territories, at the time of the exchange of the ratifications of this treaty, shall continue to be respected. Spanish scientific, literary and artistic works, not subversive of public order in the territories in question, shall continue to be admitted free of duty into such territories, for the period of ten years, to be reckoned from the date of the exchange of the ratifications of this treaty.

Article XIV

Spain shall have the power to establish consular officers in the ports and places of the territories, the sovereignty over which has been either relinquished or ceded by the present treaty.

Article XV

The Government of each country will, for the term of ten years, accord to the merchant vessels of the other country the same treatment in respect of all port charges, including entrance and clearance dues, light dues, and tonnage duties, as it accords to its own merchant vessels, not engaged in the coastwise trade.

This article may at any time be terminated on six months' notice given by either Government to the other.

Article XVI

It is understood that any obligations assumed in this treaty by the United States with respect to Cuba are limited to the time of its occupancy thereof; but it will upon the termination of such occupancy, advise any Government established in the island to assume the same obligations.

Article XVII

The present treaty shall be ratified by the President of the United States by and with the advice and consent of the Senate thereof, and by Her Majesty the Queen Regent of Spain; and the ratifications shall be exchanged at Washington within six months from the date hereof, or earlier if possible.

In faith whereof, we, the respective Plenipotentiaries, have signed this treaty and have hereunto affixed our seals.

Done in duplicate at Paris, the tenth day of December, in the year of Our Lord one thousand eight hundred and ninety eight.

WILLIAM R. DAY
CUSHMAN K. DAVIS
WM. P. FRYE
GEO. GRAY
WHITELAW REID
EUGENIO MONTERO RIOS
B. DE ABARZUZA
J. DE GARNICA
W. R. DE VILLA URRUTIA
RAFAEL CERERO

Source: "Treaty of Peace," 10 December 1898, *Treaties and Other International Agreements of the United States of America, 1776–1949*, Vol. 11, pp. 615–621.

✳ RELATIONS WITH CUBA

Whereas the Congress of the United States of America, by an Act approved March 2, 1901, provided as follows:

Provided further, That in fulfillment of the declaration contained in the joint resolution approved April twentieth, eighteen hundred and ninety-eight, entitled, "For the recognition of the independence of the people of Cuba, demanding that the Government of Spain relinquish its authority and government in the island of Cuba, and to withdraw its land and naval forces from Cuba and Cuban waters, and directing the President of the United States to use the land and naval forces of the United States to carry resolutions into effect," the President is hereby authorized to "leave the government and control of the island of Cuba to its people" so soon as a government shall have been established in said island under a constitution either as a part thereof or in an ordinance appended thereto, shall define the future relations of the United States with Cuba, substantially as follows:

I. That the government of Cuba shall never enter into any treaty or other compact with any foreign power or powers which will impair or tend to impair the independence of Cuba, nor in any manner authorize or permit any foreign power or powers to obtain by colonization or for military or naval purposes or otherwise, lodgement in or control over any portion of said island.

II. That said government shall not assume or contract any public debt, to pay the interest upon which, and to make reasonable sinking fund provision for the ultimate discharge of which, the ordinary revenues of the island, after defraying the current expenses of government shall be inadequate.

III. That the government of Cuba consents that the United States may exercise the right to intervene for the preservation of Cuban independence, the maintenance of a government adequate for the protection of life, property, and individual liberty, and for discharging the obligations with respect to Cuba imposed by the Treaty of Paris on the United States, now to be assumed and undertaken by the government of Cuba.

IV. That all Acts of the United States in Cuba during its military occupancy thereof are ratified and validated, and all lawful rights acquired thereunder shall be maintained and protected.

V. That the government of Cuba will execute, and as far as necessary extend, the plans already devised or other plans to be mutually agreed upon, for the sanitation of the cites of the island, to the end that a recurrence of epidemic and infectious diseases may be prevented thereby assuring protection to the people and commerce of Cuba, as well as to the commerce of the southern ports of the United States and the people residing therein.

VI. That the Isle of Pines shall be omitted from the proposed constitutional boundaries of Cuba, the title thereto being left to future adjustment by treaty.

VII. That to enable the United States to maintain the independence of Cuba, and to protect the people thereof, as well as for its own defense, the government of Cuba will sell or lease to the United States lands necessary for coaling or naval stations at certain specified points to be agreed upon with the President of the United States.

VIII. That by way of further assurance the Government of Cuba will embody the foregoing provisions in a permanent treaty with the United States.

Whereas the Constitutional Convention of Cuba, on June twelfth, 1901, adopted a Resolution adding to the Constitution of the Republic of Cuba which was adopted on the twenty-first of February 1901, an appendix in the words and letters of the eight enumerated articles of the above cited act of the Congress of the United States;

And whereas, by the establishment of the independent and sovereign government of the Republic of Cuba, under the constitution promulgated on the 20th of May, 1902, which embraced the foregoing conditions, and by the withdrawal of the Government of the United States as an intervening power, on the same date, it becomes necessary to embody the above cited provisions in a permanent treaty between the United States of America and the Republic of Cuba;

The United States of America and the Republic of Cuba, being desirous to carry out the foregoing conditions, have for that purpose appointed as their plenipotentiaries to conclude a treaty to that end,

The President of the United States of America, Herbert G. Squiers, Envoy Extraordinary and Minister Plenipotentiary at Havana,

And the President of the Republic of Cuba, Carlos de Zaldo y Beurmann, Secretary of State and Justice,—who after communicating to each other their full powers found in good and due form, have agreed upon the following articles:

Article I

The Government of Cuba shall never enter into any treaty or other compact with any foreign power or powers which will impair or tend to impair the independence of Cuba, nor in any manner authorize or permit any foreign power or powers to obtain by colonization or for military or naval purposes, or otherwise, lodgement in or control over any portion of said island.

Article II

The Government of Cuba shall not assume or contract any public debt to pay the interest upon which, and to make reasonable sinking-fund provision for the ultimate discharge of which, the ordinary revenues of the Island of Cuba, after defraying the current expenses of the Government, shall be inadequate.

Article III

The Government of Cuba consents that the United States may exercise the right to intervene for the preservation of Cuban independence, the maintenance of a government adequate for the protection of life, property, and individual liberty, and for discharging the obligations with respect to Cuba imposed by the Treaty of Paris on the United States, now to be assumed and undertaken by the Government of Cuba.

Article IV

All acts of the United States in Cuba during its military occupancy thereof are ratified and validated, and all lawful rights acquired thereunder shall be maintained and protected.

Article V

The Government of Cuba will execute, and, as far as necessary, extend the plans already devised, or other plans to be mutually agreed upon, for the sanitation of the cities of the island, to the end that a recurrence of epidemic and infectious diseases may be prevented, thereby assuring protection to the people and commerce of Cuba, as well as to the commerce of the Southern ports of the United States and the people residing therein.

Article VI

The Island of Pines shall be omitted form the boundaries of Cuba specified in the Constitution, the title thereof being left to future adjustment by treaty.

Article VII

To enable the United States to maintain the independence of Cuba, and to protect the people thereof, as well as for its own defense, the Government of Cuba will sell or lease to the United States lands necessary for coaling or naval stations, at certain specified points, to be agreed upon with the President of the United States.

Article VIII

The present Convention shall be ratified by each party in conformity with the respective Constitutions of the two countries, and the ratifications shall be exchanged in the City of Washington within eight months form this date.

In witness whereof, we the respective Plenipotentiaries, have signed the same in duplicate, in English and Spanish, and have affixed our respective seals at Havana, Cuba, this twenty-second day of May, in the year nineteen hundred and three.

H.G. SQUIERS
CARLOS DE ZALDO

Source: "Relations with Cuba," 22 May 1903, *Treaties and Other International Agreements of the*

United States of America, 1776–1949, Vol. 6, pp. 1116–1119.

✳ THE "HAY-HERRAN" TREATY, JANUARY 1903

Between the United States and Colombia Signed at Washington, January 22, 1903

Editor's note: This treaty was signed at the convention in Washington, D.C., on January 22, 1903. It was ratified by the United States Senate on March 17, 1903, but later rejected by the Colombian Congress on August 4, 1903, and thus never enforced.

THE UNITED STATES of America and the Republic of Colombia, being desirous to assure the construction of a ship canal to connect the Atlantic and Pacific oceans and the Congress of the United States of America having passed an Act approved June 28, 1902, in furtherance of that object, a copy of which is hereunto annexed, the high contracting parties have resolved, for that purpose, to conclude a Convention and have accordingly appointed as their plenipotentiaries,

The President of the United States of America, John Hay, Secretary of State, and the President of the Republic of Colombia, Thomas Herrán, Charge d'Affaires, thereunto specially empowered by said government, who, after communicating to each other their respective full powers, found in good and due form, have agreed upon and concluded the following Articles:

Article 1

The Government of Colombia authorizes the New Panama Canal Company to sell and transfer to the United States its rights, privileges, properties, and concessions, as well as the Panama Railroad and all the shares or part of the shares of that company; but the public lands situated outside of the zone hereinafter specified, now corresponding to the concessions of both said enterprises shall revert to the Republic of Colombia, except any property now owned by or in the possession of the said companies within Panama or Colon, or the ports and terminals thereof.

But it is understood that Colombia reserves all its rights to the special shares in the capital of the New Panama Canal Company to which reference is made in Article 4 of the contract of December 10, 1890, which shares shall be paid their full nominal value at least; but as such right of Colombia exists solely in its character of stockholder in said Company, no obligation under this provision is imposed upon or assumed by the United States.

The Railroad Company (and the United States as owner of the enterprise) shall be free from the obligations imposed by the railroad concession, excepting as to the payment at maturity by the Railroad Company of the outstanding bonds issued by said Railroad Company.

Article 2

The United States shall have the exclusive right for the term of one hundred years, renewable at the sole and absolute option of the United States, for periods of similar duration so long as the United States may desire, to excavate, construct, maintain, operate, control, and protect the Maritime Canal with or without locks from the Atlantic to the Pacific ocean, to and across the territory of Colombia, such canal to be of sufficient depth and capacity for vessels of the largest tonnage and greatest draft now engaged in commerce, and such as may be reasonably anticipated, and also the same rights for the construction, maintenance, operation, control, and protection of the Panama Railroad and of railway, telegraph and telephone lines, canals, dikes, dams and reservoirs, and such other auxiliary works as may be necessary and convenient for the construction, maintenance, protection and operation of the canal and railroads.

Article 3

To enable the United States to exercise the rights and privileges granted by this Treaty the Republic of Colombia grants to that Government the use and control for the term of one hundred years, renewable at the sole and absolute option of the United States, for periods of similar duration so long as the United States may desire, of a zone of territory along the route of the canal to be constructed five kilometers in width on either side thereof measured from its center line including therein the necessary auxiliary canals not exceeding in any case fifteen miles from the main canal and other works, together with ten fathoms of water in the Bay of Limon in extension of the canal, and at least three marine miles from mean low water mark from each terminus of the canal into the Caribbean Sea and the Pacific Ocean respectively. So far as necessary for the construction, maintenance and operation of the canal, the United States shall have the use and occupation of the group of small islands in the Bay of Panama named Perico, Naos, Culebra and Flamenco, but the same shall not be construed as being within the zone herein defined or governed by the special provisions applicable to the same.

This grant shall in no manner invalidate the titles

or rights of private land holders in the said zone of territory, nor shall it interfere with the rights of way over the public roads of the Department; provided, however, that nothing herein contained shall operate to diminish, impair or restrict the rights elsewhere herein granted to the United States. This grant shall not include the cities of Panama and Colon, except so far as lands and other property therein are now owned by or in possession of the said Canal Company or the said Railroad Company; but all the stipulations contained in Article 35 of the Treaty of 1846–48 between the contracting parties shall continue and apply in full force to the cities of Panama and Colon and to the accessory community lands and other property within the said zone, and the territory thereon shall be neutral territory, and the United States shall continue to guarantee the neutrality thereof and the sovereignty of Colombia thereover, in conformity with the above mentioned Article 35 of said Treaty.

In furtherance of this last provision there shall be created a Joint Commission by the Governments of Colombia and the United States that shall establish and enforce sanitary and police regulations.

Article 4

The rights and privileges granted to the United States by the terms of this convention shall not affect the sovereignty of the Republic of Colombia over the territory within whose boundaries such rights and privileges are to be exercised.

The United States freely acknowledges and recognizes this sovereignty and disavows any intention to impair it in any way whatever or to increase its territory at the expense of Colombia or of any of the sister republics in Central or South America, but on the contrary, it desires to strengthen the power of the republics on this continent, and to promote, develop and maintain their prosperity and independence.

Article 5

The Republic of Colombia authorizes the United States to construct and maintain at each entrance and terminus of the proposed canal a port for vessels using the same, with suitable light houses and other aids to navigation, and the United States is authorized to use and occupy within the limits of the zone fixed by this convention, such parts of the coast line and of the lands and islands adjacent thereto as are necessary for this purpose, including the construction and maintenance of breakwaters, dikes, jetties, embankments, coaling stations, docks and other appropriate works, and the United States undertakes the construction and maintenance of such works and

will bear all the expense thereof. The ports when established are declared free, and their demarcations shall be clearly and definitely defined.

To give effect to this Article, the United States will give special attention and care to the maintenance of works for drainage, sanitary and healthful purposes along the line of the canal, and its dependencies, in order to prevent the invasion of epidemics or of securing their prompt suppression should they appear. With this end in view the United States will organize hospitals along the line of the canal, and will suitably supply or cause to be supplied the towns of Panama and Colon with the necessary aqueducts and drainage works, in order to prevent their becoming centers of infection on account of their proximity to the canal.

The Government of Colombia will secure for the United States or its nominees the lands and rights that may be required in the towns of Panama and Colon to effect the improvements above referred to, and the Government of the United States or its nominees shall be authorized to impose and collect equitable water rates, during fifty years for the service rendered; but on the expiration of said term the use of the water shall be free for the inhabitants of Panama and Colon, except to the extent that may be necessary for the operation and maintenance of said water system, including reservoirs, aqueducts, hydrants, supply service, drainage and other works.

Article 6

The Republic of Colombia agrees that it will not cede or lease to any foreign Government any of its islands or harbors within or adjacent to the Bay of Panama, nor on the Atlantic Coast of Colombia, between the Atrato River and the western boundary of the Department of Panama, for the purpose of establishing fortifications, naval or coaling stations, military posts, docks or other works that might interfere with the construction, maintenance, operation, protection, safety, and free use of the canal and auxiliary works. In order to enable Colombia to comply with this stipulation, the Government of the United States agrees to give Colombia the material support that may be required in order to prevent the occupation of said islands and ports, guaranteeing there the sovereignty, independence and integrity of Colombia.

Article 7

The Republic of Colombia includes in the foregoing grant the right without obstacle, cost, or impediment, to such control, consumption and general utilization in any manner found necessary by the United States to the exercise by it of the grants to, and rights conferred upon it by this Treaty, the waters of the Chagres River and other streams, lakes and lagoons, of all non-navigable waters, natural and artificial, and also to navigate all rivers, streams, lakes and other navigable water-ways, within the jurisdiction and under the domain of the Republic of Colombia, in the Department of Panama, within or without said zone, as may be necessary or desirable for the construction, maintenance and operation of the canal and its auxiliary canals and other works, and without tolls or charges of any kind; and to raise and lower the levels of the waters, and to deflect them, and to impound any such waters, and to overflow any lands necessary for the due exercise of such grants and rights to the United States; and to rectify, construct and improve the navigation of any such rivers, streams, lakes and lagoons at the sole cost of the United States; but any such water-ways so made by the United States may be used by citizens of Colombia free of tolls or other charges. And the United States shall have the right to use without cost, any water, stone, clay, earth or other minerals belonging to Colombia on the public domain that may be needed by it.

All damages caused to private land owners by inundation or by the deviation of water courses, or in other ways, arising out of the construction or operation of the canal, shall in each case be appraised and settled by a joint commission appointed by the Governments of the United States and Colombia, but the cost of the indemnities so agreed upon shall be borne solely by the United States.

Article 8

The Government of Colombia declares free for all time the ports at either entrance of the Canal, including Panama and Colon and the waters thereof in such manner that there shall not be collected by the Government of Colombia custom house tolls, tonnage, anchorage, light-house, wharf, pilot, or quarantine dues, nor any other charges or taxes of any kind shall be levied or imposed by the Government of Colombia upon any vessel using or passing through the Canal or belonging to or employed by the United States, directly or indirectly, in connection with the construction, maintenance and operation of the main work or its auxiliaries, or upon the cargo, officers, crew, or passengers of any such vessels; it being the intent of this convention that all vessels and their cargoes, crews, and passengers, shall be permitted to use and pass through the Canal and the ports leading thereto, subject to no other demands or impositions than such tolls and charges as may be imposed by the United States for the use of the Canal and other works. It

being understood that such tolls and charges shall be governed by the provisions of Article 16.

The ports leading to the Canal, including Panama and Colon, also shall be free to the commerce of the world, and no duties or taxes shall be imposed, except upon merchandise destined to be introduced for the consumption of the rest of the Republic of Colombia, or the Department of Panama, and upon vessels touching at the ports of Colon and Panama and which do not cross the Canal.

Though the said ports shall be free and open to all, the Government of Colombia may establish in them such custom houses and guards as Colombia may deem necessary to collect duties on importations destined to other portions of Colombia and to prevent contraband trade. The United States shall have the right to make use of the ports at the two extremities of the Canal including Panama and Colon as places of anchorage, in order to make repairs for loading, unloading, depositing, or transshipping cargoes either in transit or destined for the service of the Canal and other works.

Any concessions or privileges granted by Colombia for the operation of light houses at Colon and Panama shall be subject to expropriation, indemnification and payment in the same manner as is provided by Article 14 in respect to the property therein mentioned; but Colombia shall make no additional grant of any such privilege nor change the status of any existing concession.

Article 9

There shall not be imposed any taxes, national, municipal, departmental, or of any other class, upon the canal, the vessels that may use it, tugs and other vessels employed in the service of the canal, the railways and auxiliary works, store houses, work shops, offices, quarters for laborers, factories of all kinds, warehouses, wharves, machinery and other works, property, and effects appertaining to the canal or railroad or that may be necessary for the service of the canal or railroad and their dependencies, whether situated within the cities of Panama and Colon, or any other place authorized by the provisions of this convention.

Nor shall there be imposed contributions or charges of a personal character of whatever species upon officers, employees, laborers, and other individuals in the service of the canal and its dependencies.

Article 10

It is agreed that telegraph and telephone lines, when established for canal purposes, may also, under suitable regulations, be used for public and private business in connection with the systems of Colombia and the other American Republics and with the lines of cable companies authorized to enter the ports and territories of these Republics; but the official dispatches of the Government of Colombia and the authorities of the Department of Panama shall not pay for such service higher tolls than those required from the officials in the service of the United States.

Article 11

The Government of Colombia shall permit the immigration and free access to the lands and workshops of the canal and its dependencies of all employees and workmen of whatever nationality under contract to work upon or seeking employment or in any wise connected with the said canal and its dependencies, with their respective families and all such persons shall be free and exempt from the military service of the Republic of Colombia.

Article 12

The United States may import at any time into the said zone, free of customs duties, imposts, taxes, or other charges, and without any restriction, any and all vessels, dredges, engines, cars, machinery, tools, explosives, materials, supplies, and other articles necessary and convenient in the construction, maintenance and operation of the canal and auxiliary works, also all provisions, medicines, clothing, supplies and other things necessary and convenient for the officers, employees, workmen and laborers in the service and employ of the United States and for their families. If any such articles are disposed of for use without the zone excepting Panama and Colon and within the territory of the Republic, they shall be subject to the same import or other duties as like articles under the laws of Colombia or the ordinances of the Department of Panama.

Article 13

The United States shall have authority to protect and make secure the canal, as well as railways and other auxiliary works and dependencies, and to preserve order and discipline among the laborers and other persons who may congregate in that region, and to make and enforce such police and sanitary regulations as it may deem necessary to preserve order and public health thereon, and to protect navigation and commerce through and over said canal, railways and other works and dependencies from interruption or damage.

I. The Republic of Colombia may establish judicial tribunals within said zone, for the determination, according to its laws and judicial procedure, of cer-

tain controversies hereinafter mentioned. Such judicial tribunal or tribunals so established by the Republic of Colombia shall have exclusive jurisdiction in said zone of all controversies between citizens of the Republic of Colombia, or between citizens of the Republic of Colombia and citizens of any foreign nation other than the United States.

II. Subject to the general sovereignty of Colombia over said zone, the United States may establish judicial tribunals thereon, which shall have jurisdiction of certain controversies hereinafter mentioned to be determined according to the laws and judicial procedure of the United States.

Such judicial tribunal or tribunals so established by the United States shall have exclusive jurisdiction in said zone of all controversies between citizens of the United States, and between citizens of the United States and citizens of any foreign nation other than the Republic of Colombia; and of all controversies in any wise growing out of or relating to the construction, maintenance or operation of the canal, railway and other properties and works.

III. The United States and Colombia engage jointly to establish and maintain upon said zone, judicial tribunals having civil, criminal and admiralty jurisdiction, and to be composed of jurists appointed by the Governments of the United States and Colombia in a manner hereafter to be agreed upon between said Governments, and which tribunals shall have jurisdiction of certain controversies hereinafter mentioned, and of all crimes, felonies and misdemeanors committed within said zone, and of all cases arising in admiralty, according to such laws and procedures as shall be hereafter agreed upon and declared by the two Governments.

Such joint judicial tribunal shall have exclusive jurisdiction in said zone of all controversies between citizens of the United States and citizens of Colombia, and between citizens of nations other than Colombia or the United States; and also of all crimes, felonies and misdemeanors committed within said zone, and of all questions of admiralty arising therein.

IV. The two Governments hereafter, and from time to time as occasion arises, shall agree upon and establish the laws and procedures which shall govern such joint judicial tribunal and which shall be applicable to the persons and cases over which such tribunal shall have jurisdiction, and also shall likewise create the requisite officers and employees of such court and establish their powers and duties; and further shall make adequate provision by like agreement for the pursuit, capture, imprisonment, detention and delivery within said zone of persons charged with the commitment of crimes, felonies or misdemeanors without said zone; and for the pursuit, capture, imprisonment, detention and delivery without said zone of persons charged with the commitment of crimes, felonies and misdemeanors within said zone.

Article 14

The works of the canal, the railways and their auxiliaries are declared of public utility, and in consequence all areas of land and water necessary for the construction, maintenance, and operation of the canal and other specified works may be expropriated in conformity with the laws of Colombia, except that the indemnity shall be conclusively determined without appeal, by a joint commission appointed by the Governments of Colombia and the United States.

The indemnities awarded by the Commission for such expropriation shall be borne by the United States, but the appraisal of said lands and the assessment of damages shall be based upon their value before the commencement of the work upon the canal.

Article 15

The Republic of Colombia grants to the United States the use of all the ports of the Republic open to commerce as places of refuge for any vessels employed in the canal enterprise, and for all vessels in distress having the right to pass through the canal and within to anchor in said ports. Such vessels shall be exempt from anchorage and tonnage dues on the part of Colombia.

Article 16

The canal, when constructed, and the entrance thereto shall be neutral in perpetuity, and shall be opened upon the terms provided for by Section I of Article three of, and in conformity with all the stipulations of, the treaty entered into by the Governments of the United States and Great Britain on November 18, 1901.

Article 17

The Government of Colombia shall have the right to transport over the canal its vessels, troops, and munitions of war at all times without paying charges of any kind. This exemption is to be extended to the auxiliary railway for the transportation of persons in the service of the Republic of Colombia or of the Department of Panama, or of the police force charged with the preservation of public order outside of said zone, as well as to their baggage, munitions of war and supplies.

Article 18

The United States shall have full power and authority to establish and enforce regulations for the use of the canal, railways, and the entering ports and auxiliary works, and to fix rates of tolls and charges thereof, subject to the limitations stated in Article 16.

Article 19

The rights and privileges granted to the United States by this convention shall not affect the sovereignty of the Republic of Colombia over the real estate that may be acquired by the United States by reason of the transfer of the rights of the New Panama Canal Company and the Panama Railroad Company lying outside of the said canal zone.

Article 20

If by virtue of any existing treaty between the Republic of Colombia and any third power, there may be any privilege or concession relative to an interoceanic means of communication which especially favors such third power, and which in any of its terms may be incompatible with the terms of the present convention, the Republic of Colombia agrees to cancel or modify such treaty in due form, for which purpose it shall give to the said third power the requisite notification within the term of four months from the date of the present convention, and in case the existing treaty contains no clause permitting its modification or annulment, the Republic of Colombia agrees to procure its modification or annulment in such form that there shall not exist any conflict with the stipulations of the present convention.

Article 21

The rights and privileges granted by the Republic of Colombia to the United States in the preceding Articles are understood to be free of all anterior concessions or privileges to other Governments, corporations, syndicates or individuals, and consequently, if there should arise any claims on account of the present concessions and privileges or otherwise, the claimants shall resort to the Government of Colombia and not to the United States for any indemnity or compromise which may be required.

Article 22

The Republic of Colombia renounces and grants to the United States the participation to which it might be entitled in the future earnings of the canal under Article 1 of the concessionary contract with Lucien N. B. Wyse now owned by the New Panama Canal Company and any and all other rights or claims of a pecuniary nature arising under or relating to said concession, or arising under or relating to the concessions to the Panama Railroad Company or any extension or modification thereof; and it likewise renounces, confirms and grants to the United States, now and hereafter, all the rights and property reserved in the said concessions which otherwise would belong to Colombia at or before the expiration of the terms of ninety-nine years of the concessions granted to or held by the above mentioned party and companies, and all right, title and interest which it now has or may hereafter have, in and to the lands, canal, works, property and rights held by the said companies under said concessions or otherwise, and acquired or to be acquired by the United States from or through the New Panama Canal Company, including any property and rights which might or may in the future either by lapse of time, forfeiture or otherwise, revert to the Republic of Colombia under any contracts of concessions, with said Wyse, the Universal Panama Canal Company, the Panama Railroad Company and the New Panama Canal Company.

The aforesaid rights and property shall be and are free and released from any present or reversionary interest in or claims of Colombia and the title of the United States thereto upon consummation of the contemplated purchase by the United States from the New Panama Canal Company, shall be absolute, so far as concerns the Republic of Colombia, excepting always the rights of Colombia specifically secured under this treaty.

Article 23

If it should become necessary at any time to employ armed forces for the safety or protection of the canal, or of the ships that make use of the same, or the railways and other works, the Republic of Colombia agrees to provide the forces necessary for such purpose, according to the circumstances of the case, but if the Government of Colombia cannot effectively comply with this obligation, then, with the consent of or at the request of Colombia, or of her Minister at Washington, or of the local authorities, civil or military, the United States shall employ such force as may be necessary for that sole purpose; and as soon as the necessity shall have ceased will withdraw the forces so employed. Under exceptional circumstances, however, on account of unforeseen or imminent danger to said canal, railways and other works, or to the lives and property of the persons employed upon the canal, railways, and other works, the Government of the United States is authorized to act in the interest of their protection, without the necessity of obtaining the consent beforehand of the Government of Colombia; and it shall give immediate advice of the measures adopted for the purpose stated; and as soon as sufficient Colombian forces shall arrive to attend to the indicated purpose, those of the United States shall retire.

Article 24

The Government of the United States agrees to complete the construction of the preliminary works necessary, together with all the auxiliary works, in the shortest time possible; and within two years from the date of the exchange of ratification of this convention the main works of the canal proper shall be commenced, and it shall be opened to the traffic between the two oceans within twelve years after such period of two years. In case, however, that any difficulties or obstacles should arise in the construction of the canal which are at present impossible to foresee, in consideration of the good faith with which the Government of the United States shall have proceeded, and the large amount of money expended so far on the works and the nature of the difficulties which may have arisen, the Government of Colombia will prolong the terms stipulated in this Article up to twelve years more for the completion of the work of the canal.

But in case the United States should, at any time, determine to make such canal practically a sea level canal, then such period shall be extended for ten years further.

Article 25

As the price or compensation for the right to use the zone granted in this convention by Colombia to the United States for the construction of a canal, together with the proprietary right over the Panama Railroad, and for the annuity of two hundred and fifty thousand dollars gold, which Colombia ceases to receive from the said railroad, as well as in compensation for other rights, privileges and exemptions granted to the United States, and in consideration of the increase in the administrative expenses of the Department of Panama consequent upon the construction of the said canal, the Government of the United States binds itself to pay Colombia the sum of ten million dollars in gold coin of the United States on the exchange of the ratification of this convention after its approval according to the laws of the respective countries, and also an annual payment during the life of this convention of two hundred and fifty thousand dollars in like gold coin, beginning nine years after the date aforesaid.

The provisions of this Article shall be in addition to all other benefits assured to Colombia under this convention. But no delay nor difference of opinion under this Article shall affect nor interrupt the full operation and effect of this convention in all other respects.

Article 26

No change either in the Government or in the laws and treaties of Colombia, shall, without the consent of the United States, affect any right of the United States under the present convention, or under any treaty stipulation between the two countries (that now exist or may hereafter exist) touching the subject matter of this convention.

If Colombia shall hereafter enter as a constituent into any other Government or into any union or confederation of States so as to merge her sovereignty or independence in such Government, union, or confederation, the rights of the United States under this convention shall not be in any respect lessened or impaired.

Article 27

The joint commission referred to in Articles 3, 7, and 14 shall be established as follows:

The President of the United States shall nominate two persons and the President of Colombia shall nominate two persons and they shall proceed to a decision; but in case of disagreement of the Commission (by reason of their being equally divided in conclusion) an umpire shall be appointed by the two Governments, who shall render the decision. In the event of death, absence or incapacity of any Commissioner or umpire, or of his omitting, declining or ceasing to act, his place shall be filled by the appointment of another person in the manner above indicated. All decisions by a majority of the Commission or by the umpire shall be final.

Article 28

This convention when signed by the contracting parties, shall be ratified according to the laws of the respective countries and shall be exchanged at Washington within a term of eight months from this date, or earlier if possible.

In faith whereof, the respective plenipotentiaries have signed the present convention in duplicate and have hereunto affixed their respective seals.

Done at the City of Washington, the 22d day of January in the year of our Lord nineteen hundred and three.

JOHN HAY
TOMAS HERRAN

Source: "Construction of a Ship Canal," in *Unper-*

fected Treaties of the United States of America: 1776–1976, ed. Christian L. Wiktor (Dobbs Ferry, New York: Oceana Publications, Inc., 1977), Vol. 3, pp. 449–463.

✳ THE "HAY-BUNAU-VARILLA CONVENTION"

Between the United States and Panama, Signed at Washington, November 1, 1903, Isthmian Canal Convention

THE UNITED STATES of America and the Republic of Panama being desirous to insure the construction of a ship canal across the Isthmus of Panama to connect the Atlantic and Pacific Oceans, and the Congress of the United States of America having passed an act approved June 28, 1902, in furtherance of that object, by which the President of the United States is authorized to acquire within a reasonable time the control of the necessary territory of the Republic of Colombia, and the sovereignty of such territory being actually vested in the Republic of Panama, the high contracting parties have resolved for that purpose to conclude a convention and have accordingly appointed as their plenipotentiaries,

The President of the United States of America, JOHN HAY, Secretary of State, and The Government of the Republic of Panama, PHILIPPE BUNAU-VARILLA, Envoy Extraordinary and Minister Plenipotentiary of the Republic of Panama, thereunto specially empowered by said government, who after communicating with each other their respective full powers, found to be in good and due form, have agreed upon and concluded the following articles:

Article 1

The United States guarantees and will maintain the independence of the Republic of Panama.

Article 2

The Republic of Panama grants to the United States in perpetuity the use, occupation and control of a zone of land and land under water for the construction, maintenance, operation, sanitation and protection of said Canal of the width of ten miles extending to the distance of five miles on each side of the center line of the route of the Canal to be constructed; the said zone beginning in the Caribbean Sea three marine miles from mean low water mark and extending to and across the Isthmus of Panama into the Pacific Ocean to a distance of three marine miles from mean low water mark with the proviso that the cities of Panama and Colon and the harbors adjacent to said cities, which are included within the boundaries of the zone above described, shall not be included within this grant. The Republic of Panama further grants to the United States in perpetuity the use, occupation and control of any other lands and waters outside of the zone above described which may be necessary and convenient for the construction, maintenance, operations, sanitation and protection of the said Canal or of any auxiliary canals or other works necessary and convenient for the construction, maintenance, operation, sanitation and protection of the said enterprise. The Republic of Panama further grants in like manner to the United States in perpetuity all islands within the limits of the zone above described and in addition thereto the group of small islands in the Bay of Panama, named Perico, Naos, Culebra and Flamenco.

Article 3

The Republic of Panama grants to the United States all the rights, power and authority within the zone mentioned and described in Article 2 of this agreement and within the limits of all auxiliary lands and waters mentioned and described in said Article 2 which the United States would possess and exercise if it were the sovereign of the territory within which said lands and waters are located to the entire exclusion of the exercise by the Republic of Panama of any such sovereign rights, power or authority.

Article 4

As rights subsidiary to the above grants the Republic of Panama grants in perpetuity to the United States the right to use the rivers, streams, lakes and other bodies of water within its limits for navigation, the supply of water or water-power or other purposes, so far as the use of said rivers, streams, lakes and bodies of water and the waters thereof may be necessary and convenient for the construction, maintenance, operation, sanitation and protection of the said Canal.

Article 5

The Republic of Panama grants to the United States in perpetuity a monopoly for the construction, maintenance and operation of any system of communication by means of canal or railroad across its territory between the Caribbean Sea and the Pacific Ocean.

Article 6

The grants herein contained shall in no manner invalidate the titles or rights of private land holders or owners of private property in the said zone or in or to any of the lands or waters granted to the United States by the provisions of any Article of this treaty, nor shall they interfere with the rights of way over the public roads passing through the said zone or over any of the said lands or waters unless said rights of way or private rights shall conflict with rights herein granted to the United States in which case the rights of the United States shall be superior. All damages caused to the owners of private lands or private property of any kind by reason of the grants contained in this treaty or by reason of the operations of the United States, its agents or employees, or by reason of the construction, maintenance, operation, sanitation and protection of the said Canal or of the works of sanitation and protection herein provided for, shall be appraised and settled by a joint commission appointed by the Governments of the United States and the Republic of Panama, whose decisions as to such damages shall be final and whose awards as to such damages shall be paid solely by the United States. No part of the work on said Canal or the Panama railroad or on any auxiliary works relating thereto and authorized by the terms of this treaty shall be prevented, delayed or impeded by or pending such proceedings to ascertain such damages. The appraisal of said private lands and private property and the assessment of damages to them shall be based upon their value before the date of this convention.

Article 7

The Republic of Panama grants to the United States within the limits of the cities of Panama and Colon and their adjacent harbors and within the territory adjacent thereto the right to acquire by purchase or by the exercise of the right of eminent domain, any lands, buildings, water rights or other properties necessary and convenient for the construction, maintenance, operation and protection of the Canal and of any works of sanitation, such as the collection and disposition of sewage and the distribution of water in the said cities of Panama and Colon, which, in the discretion of the United States may be necessary and convenient for the construction, maintenance, operation, sanitation and protection of the said Canal and railroad. All such works of sanitation, collection and disposition of sewage and distribution of water in the cities of Panama and Colon shall be made at the expense of the United States, and the Government of the United States, its agents or nominees shall be authorized to impose and collect water rates and sewerage rates which shall be sufficient to provide for the payment of interest and the amortization of the principal of the cost of said works within a period of fifty years and upon the expiration of said term of fifty years the system of sewers and water works shall revert to and become the properties of the cities of Panama and Colon respectively, and the use of the water shall be free to the inhabitants of Panama and Colon, except to the extent that water rates may be necessary for the operation and maintenance of said system of sewers and water.

The Republic of Panama agrees that the cities of Panama and Colon shall comply in perpetuity with the sanitary ordinances whether of a preventive or curative character prescribed by the United States and in case the Government of Panama is unable or fails in its duty to enforce this compliance by the cities of Panama and Colon with the sanitary ordinances of the United States the Republic of Panama grants to the United States the right and authority to enforce the same.

The same right and authority are granted to the United States for the maintenance of public order in the cities of Panama and Colon and the territories and harbors adjacent thereto in case the Republic of Panama should not be, in the judgment of the United States, able to maintain such order.

Article 8

The Republic of Panama grants to the United States all rights which it now has or hereafter may acquire to the property of the New Panama Canal Company and the Panama Railroad Company as a result of the transfer of sovereignty from the Republic of Colombia to the Republic of Panama over the Isthmus of Panama and authorizes the New Panama Canal Company to sell and transfer to the United States its rights, privileges, properties and concessions as well as the Panama Railroad and all the shares or part of the shares of that company; but the public lands situated outside of the one described in Article 2 of this treaty now included in the concessions to both said enterprises and not required in the construction or operation of the Canal shall revert to the Republic of Panama except any property now owned by or in the possession of said companies within Panama or Colon or the ports or terminals thereof.

Article 9

The United States agrees that the ports at either entrance of the Canal and the waters thereof, and

the Republic of Panama agrees that the towns of Panama and Colon shall be free for all time so that there shall not be imposed or collected custom house tolls, tonnage, anchorage, lighthouse, wharf, pilot, or quarantine dues or any other charges or taxes of any kind upon any vessel using or passing through the Canal or belonging to or employed by the United States, directly or indirectly, in connection with the construction, maintenance, operation, sanitation and protection of the main Canal, or auxiliary works, or upon the cargo, officers, crew, or passengers of any such vessels, except such tolls and charges as may be imposed by the United States for the use of the Canal and other works, and except tolls and charges imposed by the Republic of Panama upon merchandise destined to be introduced for the consumption of the rest of the Republic of Panama, and upon vessels touching at the ports of Colon and Panama and which do not cross the Canal.

The Government of the Republic of Panama shall have the right to establish in such ports and in the towns of Panama and Colon such houses and guards as it may deem necessary to collect duties on importations destined to other portions of Panama and to prevent contraband trade. The United States shall have the right to make use of the towns and harbors of Panama and Colon as places of anchorage, and for making repairs, for loading, unloading, depositing, or transshipping cargoes either in transit or destined for the service of the Canal and for other works pertaining to the Canal.

Article 10

The Republic of Panama agrees that there shall not be imposed any taxes, national, municipal, departmental, or of any other class, upon the Canal, the railways and auxiliary works, tugs and other vessels employed in the service of the Canal, store houses, work shops, offices, quarters for laborers, factories of all kinds, warehouses, wharves, machinery and other works, property, and effects appertaining to the Canal or railroad and auxiliary works, or their officers or employees, situated within the cities of Panama and Colon, and that there shall not be imposed contributions or charges of a personal character of any kind upon officers, employees, laborers, and other individuals in the service of the Canal and railroad and auxiliary works.

Article 11

The United States agrees that the official dispatches of the Government of the Republic of Panama shall be transmitted over any telegraph and telephone lines established for canal purposes and used for public and private business at rates not higher than those required from officials in the service of the United States.

Article 12

The Government of the Republic of Panama shall permit the immigration and free access to the lands and workshops of the Canal and its auxiliary works of all employees and workmen of whatever nationality under contract to work upon or seeking employment upon or in any wise connected with the said Canal and its auxiliary works, with their respective families, and all such persons shall be free and exempt from the military service of the Republic of Panama.

Article 13

The United States may import at any time into the said zone and auxiliary lands, free of custom duties, imposts, taxes, or other charges, and without any restrictions, any and all vessels, dredges, engines, cars, machinery, tools, explosives, materials, supplies, and other articles necessary and convenient in the construction, maintenance, operation, sanitation and protection of the Canal and auxiliary works, and all provisions, medicines, clothing, supplies and other things necessary and convenient for the officers, employees, workmen and laborers in the service and employ of the United States and for their families. If any such articles are disposed of for use outside of the zone and auxiliary lands granted to the United States and within the territory of the Republic, they shall be subject to the same import or other duties as like articles imported under the laws of the Republic of Panama.

Article 14

As the price or compensation for the rights, powers and privileges granted in this convention by the Republic of Panama to the United States, the Government of the United States agrees to pay to the Republic of Panama the sum of ten million dollars ($10,000,000) in gold coin of the United States on the exchange of the ratification of this convention and also an annual payment during the life of this convention of two hundred and fifty thousand dollars ($250,000) in like gold coin, beginning nine years after the date aforesaid.

The provisions of this Article shall be in addition to all other benefits assured to the Republic of Panama under this convention.

But no delay or difference of opinion under this Article or any other provisions of this treaty shall affect or interrupt the full operation and effect of this convention in all other respects.

Article 15

The joint commission referred to in Article 6 shall be established as follows:

The President of the United States shall nominate two persons and the President of the Republic of Panama shall nominate two persons and they shall proceed to a decision; but in case of disagreement of the Commission (by reason of their being equally divided in conclusion) an umpire shall be appointed by the two Governments who shall render the decision. In the event of the death, absence, or incapacity of a Commissioner or Umpire, or of his omitting, declining or ceasing to act, his place shall be filled by the appointment of another person in the manner above indicated. All decisions by a majority of the Commission or by the umpire shall be final.

Article 16

The two Governments shall make adequate provision by future agreement for the pursuit, capture, imprisonment, detention and delivery within said zone and auxiliary lands to the authorities of the Republic of Panama of persons charged with the commitment of crimes, felonies or misdemeanors without said zone and for the pursuit, capture, imprisonment, detention and delivery without said zone to the authorities of the United States of persons charged with the commitment of crimes, felonies and misdemeanors within said zone and auxiliary lands.

Article 17

The Republic of Panama grants to the United States the use of all the ports of the Republic open to commerce as places of refuge for any vessels employed in the Canal enterprise, and for all vessels passing or bound to pass through the Canal which may be in distress and be driven to seek refuge in said ports. Such vessels shall be exempt from anchorage and tonnage dues on the part of the Republic of Panama.

Article 18

The Canal, when constructed, and the entrances thereto shall be neutral in perpetuity, and shall be opened upon the terms provided for by Section I of Article three of, and in conformity with all the stipulations of, the treaty entered into by the Governments of the United States and Great Britain on November 18, 1901.

Article 19

The Government of the Republic of Panama shall have the right to transport over the Canal its vessels and its troops and munitions of war in such vessels at all times without paying charges of any kind. The exemption is to be extended to the auxiliary railway for the transportation of persons in the service of the Republic of Panama, or of the police force charged with the preservation of public order outside of said zone, as well as to their baggage, munitions of war and supplies.

Article 20

If by virtue of any existing treaty in relation to the territory of the Isthmus of Panama, whereof the obligations shall descend or be assumed by the Republic of Panama, there may be any privilege or concession in favor of the Government or the citizens and subjects of a third power relative to an inter-oceanic means of communication which in any of its terms may be incompatible with the terms of the present convention, the Republic of Panama agrees to cancel or modify such treaty in due form, for which purpose it shall give to the said third power the requisite notification within the term of four months from the date of the present convention, and in case the existing treaty contains no clause permitting its modification or annulment, the Republic of Panama agrees to procure its modification or annulment in such form that there shall not exist any conflict with the stipulations of the present convention.

Article 21

The rights and privileges granted by the Republic of Panama to the United States in the preceding Articles are understood to be free of all anterior debts, liens, trusts, or liabilities, or concessions or privileges to other Governments, corporations, syndicates or individuals, and consequently, if there should arise any claims on account of the present concessions and privileges or otherwise, the claimants shall resort to the Government of the Republic of Panama and not to the United States for any indemnity or compromise which may be required.

Article 22

The Republic of Panama renounces and grants to the United States the participation to which it might be entitled in the future earnings of the Canal under Article 15 of the concessionary contract with Lucien N. B. Wyse now owned by the New Panama Canal Company and any and all other rights or claims of a pecuniary nature arising under or relating to said concessions, or arising under or relating to the concessions to the Panama Railroad Company or any extension or modification thereof; and it likewise renounces, confirms and grants to the United States, now and hereafter, all the rights and property reserved in the said concessions which otherwise would belong to Panama at or before the expiration of the terms of ninety-nine years of the concessions granted to or held by the above mentioned party and companies, and all right, title and interest which it now has or may hereafter have, in and to the lands, canal, works, property and rights held by the said companies under said concessions or otherwise, and acquired or to be acquired by the United States from or through the New Panama Canal Company, including any property and rights which might or may in the future either by lapse of time, forfeiture or otherwise, revert to the Republic of Panama under any contracts or concessions, with said Wyse, the Universal Panama Canal Company, the Panama Railroad Company and the New Panama Canal Company.

The aforesaid rights and property shall be and are free and released from any present or reversionary interest in or claims of Panama and the title of the United States thereto upon consummation of the contemplated purchase by the United States from the New Panama Canal Company, shall be absolute, so far as concerns the Republic of Panama, excepting always the rights of the Republic specifically secured under this treaty.

Article 23

If it should become necessary at any time to employ armed forces for the safety or protection of the Canal, or of the ships that make use of the same, or the railways and auxiliary works, the United States shall have the right, at all times and in its discretion, to use its police and its land and naval forces or to establish fortifications for these purposes.

Article 24

No change either in the Government or in the laws and treaties of the Republic of Panama shall, without the consent of the United States, affect any right of the United States under the present convention, or under any treaty stipulation between the two countries that now exists or may hereafter exist touching the subject matter of this convention.

If the Republic of Panama shall hereafter enter as a constituent into any other Government or into any union or confederation of states, so as to merge her sovereignty or independence in such Government, union or confederation, the rights of the United

States under this convention shall not be in any respect lessened or impaired.

Article 25

For the better performance of the engagements of this convention and to the end of the efficient protection of the Canal and the preservation of its neutrality, the Government of the Republic of Panama will sell or lease to the United States lands adequate and necessary for naval or coaling stations on the Pacific coast and on the western Caribbean coast of the Republic at certain points to be agreed upon with the President of the United States.

Article 26

This convention when signed by the Plenipotentiaries of the Contracting Parties shall be ratified by the respective Governments and the ratifications shall be exchanged at Washington at the earliest date possible.

In faith whereof the respective Plenipotentiaries have signed the present convention in duplicate and have hereunto affixed their respective seals.

Done at the City of Washington the 18th day of November in the year of our Lord nineteen hundred and three.

JON HAY
P. BUNAU VARILLA

Source: "Isthmian Canal," 18 November 1903, *Treaties and Other International Agreements of the United States of America, 1776–1949*, Vol. 10, pp. 663–672.

✳ TREATY OF RELATIONS BETWEEN THE UNITED STATES AND CUBA

Signed at Washington, May 29, 1934

THE UNITED STATES of America and the Republic of Cuba, being animated by the desire to fortify the relations of friendship between the two countries and to modify, with this purpose, the relations established between them by the Treaty of Relations signed at Habana, May 22, 1903, have appointed, with this intention, as their Plenipotentiaries:

[Names of Plenipotentiaries]

Who, after having communicated to each other their full powers which were found to be in good and due form, have agreed upon the following articles:

Article I

The Treaty of Relations which was concluded between the two contracting parties on May 22, 1903, shall cease to be in force, and is abrogated, from the date on which the present Treaty goes into effect.

Article II

All the acts effected in Cuba by the United States of America during its military occupation of the island, up to May 20, 1902, the date on which the Republic of Cuba was established, have been ratified and held as valid; and all the rights legally acquired by virtue of those acts shall be maintained and protected.

Article III

Until the two contracting parties agree to the modification or abrogation of the stipulations of the agreement in regard to the lease to the United States of America of lands in Cuba for coaling and naval stations signed by the President of the Republic of Cuba on February 6, 1903, and by the President of the United States of America on the 23rd day of the same month and year, the stipulations of that agreement with regard to the naval station of Guantanamo shall continue in effect. The supplementary agreement in regard to naval or coaling stations signed between the two Governments on July 2, 1903, also shall continue in effect in the same form and on the same conditions with respect to the naval station at Guantanamo. So long as the United States of America shall not abandon the said naval station of Guantanamo or the two Governments shall not agree to a modification of its present limits, the station shall continue to have the territorial area that it now has, with the limits that it has on the date of the signature of the present Treaty.

Article IV

If at any time in the future a situation should arise that appears to point to an outbreak of contagious disease in the territory of either of the contracting parties, either of the two Governments shall for its own protection, and without its act being considered unfriendly, exercise freely and at its discretion the right to suspend communications between those of its ports that it may designate and all or part of the territory of the other party, and for the period that it may consider to be advisable.

Article V

The present Treaty shall be ratified by the contracting parties in accordance with their respective constitutional methods; and shall go into effect on the date of the exchange of their ratifications, which shall take place in the city of Washington as soon as possible.

In faith whereof, the respective Plenipotentiaries have signed the present Treaty and have affixed their seals hereto. Done in duplicate, in the English and Spanish languages, at Washington on the twenty-ninth day of May, one thousand nine hundred and thirty-four.

CORDELL HULL
SUMNER WELLES
M. MARQUEZ STERLING

Source: "Relations with Cuba," 29 May 1934, *Treaties and Other International Agreements of the United States of America, 1776–1949*, Vol. 6, pp. 1161, 1162.

✳ CONSTITUTIONAL CONVENTION OF PUERTO RICO

Hon. Antonio Fernos Isern, President
Hon. María Libertad Gómez Garriga, First Vice President
Hon. Victor Gutiérrez Franqui, Second Vice President

Delegates and Residences

1. Manuel Acevedo Rosario, Camuy
2. Juan Alemany Silva, Guayama
3. Arcilio Alvarado Alvarado, Santurce
4. Enrique álvarez Vicente, Utuado
5. Francisco L. Anselmi Rodríguez, Coamo
6. Francisco Arrillaga Gaztambide, Hato Rey
7. Carmelo ávila Medina, Naguabo
8. José B. Barceló Oliver, Adjuntas
9. Ramón Barreto Pérez, Hato Rey
10. Ramón Barrios Sánchez, Bayamón
11. Jaime Benítez Rexach, Río Piedras
12. Francisco Berio Suárez, Comerío
13. Virgilio Brunet Maldonado, Hato Rey
14. Agustín Burgos Rivera, Villalba
15. Mario Canales Torresola, Jayuya
16. Angel M. Candelario Arce, Peñuelas
17. Ernesto Carrasquillo Quiñones, Yubucoa
18. Dionisio Casillas Casillas, Humacao
19. José A. Cintrón Rivera, Santurce
20. Luis Alfredo Colón Velázquez, Moca
21. Ramiro Colón Castaño, Ponce
22. Juan Dávila Díaz, Manatí
23. José M. Dávila Monsanto, Guayama
24. Lionel Fernández Méndez, Cayey
25. Antonio Fernos Isern, Santurce
26. Luis A. Ferré Aguayo, Ponce
27. Alcides Figueroa Oliva, Añasco
28. Leopoldo Figueroa Carreras, Cataño
29. Ernesto Juan Fonfrías Rivera, Carretera 2, K-19
30. Jorge Font Saldaña, Santurce
31. Juan R. García Delgado, Hatillo
32. Miguel A. García Méndez, Mayagüez
33. Jenaro Gautier Dapena, Caguas-La Muda
34. Rubén Gaztambide Arrillaga, Río Piedras
35. Fernando J. Geigel Sabat, Santurce
36. José Rosario Gelpi Bosch, Mayagüez
37. Darío Goitía Montalvo, Arecibo
38. María Libertad Gómez Garriga, Utuado
39. Héctor González Blanés, Santurce
40. Andrés Grillasca Salas, Ponce
41. Victor Gutiérrez Franqui, Santurce
42. Celestino Iriarte Miró, Carretera Cataño
43. Jesús Izcoa Mouré, Naranjito
44. Lorenzo Lagarde Garcés, Ponce
45. Ramón Llobet Díaz, Guaynabo
46. Ramiro Martínez Sandín, Vega Baja
47. Juan Meléndez Baez, San Juan
48. Ramón Mellado Parsons, Río Piedras
49. Bernardo Méndez Jiménez, San Sebastián
50. Armando Mignucci Calder, Yauco
51. José Mimoso Raspaldo, Caguas
52. Pablo Morales Otero, Santurce
53. Luis Muñoz Marín, San Juan
54. Luis Muñoz Rivera, Hato Rey
55. Eduardo Negrón Benítez, San Sebastián
56. Luis A. Negrón López, Sabana Grande
57. Abraham Nieves Negrón, Guayama
58. Mario Orsini Martínez, Juncos
59. Benjamín Ortiz Ortiz, Guaynabo
60. Cruz Ortiz Stella, Humacao
61. Lino Padrón Rivera, Vega Baja
62. Santiago R. Palmer Díaz, San Germán
63. Norman E. Parkhurst, Bayamón
64. Francisco Paz Granela, Santurce
65. Santiago Polanco Abreu, Isabela
66. Samuel R. Quiñones Quiñones, Carr. Isla Verde
67. Ubaldino Ramírez de Arellano Quiñones, San Germán
68. Ernesto Ramos Antonini, Hato Rey
69. Ramón María Ramos de Jesús, Aibonito
70. Antonio Reyes Delgado, Arecibo
71. Dolores Rivera Candelaria, Utuado
72. Heraclio H. Rivera Colón, Toa Alta
73. Alejo Rivera Morales, Ceiba
74. Alvaro Rivera Reyes, Rio Grande
75. Carmelo Rodríguez García, Arecibo
76. Carlos Román Benítez, Santurce
77. Alfonso Román García, Fajardo
78. Joaquín Rosa Gómez, Manatí
79. Alberto E. Sánchez Nazario, Santurce
80. Angel Sandín Martínez, Vega Baja
81. Luis Santaliz Capestany, Las Marías
82. Yldefonso Solá·Morales, Caguas

83. Juan B. Soto González, Gurabo
84. Rafael Torrech Genovés, Bayamón
85. Lucas Torres Santos, Orocovis
86. Pedro Torres Díaz, Gurabo
87. José Trías Monge, Guaynabo
88. Augusto Valentín Vizcarrondo, Mayagüez
89. Baudilio Vega Berríos, Mayagüez
90. Sigfredo Vélez González, Arecibo
91. José Veray Hernández, Aguadilla
92. José Villares Rodríguez, Caguas

Officials of the Convention
José Berríos Berdecía, Secretary
Cruz Pacheco Ruiz, Sergeant at Arms
Herminio A. Concepción De Garcia, Assistant Secretary
Nestor Rigual Camacho, Assistant Secretary
Julio Morales Rodríguez, Assistant Secretary
Felipe Jiménez Rivera, Assistant Secretary
Viriato San Antonio Hernádez, Paymaster
Higinia Pastoriza, Property Clerk

Committees of the Constitutional Convention
Rules: Curz Ortiz Stella, President; José Mimoso Raspaldo, Vice President; Luis Alfredo Colón Velázquez, Secretary; Luis Santaliz Capestany, Lionel Fernández Méndez, Eduardo Negrón Benítez, Joaquín Rosa Gómez, Baudilio Vega Berríos, Juan R. García Delgado, José Rosario Gelpi Bosch, Ramón Barrios Sánchez.

Publications and Disbursements: Santiago R. Palmer Díaz, President; Alfonso Román García, Vice President; Juan Dávila Díaz, Secretary; Agustín Burgos Rivera, Dionisio Casillas Casillas, Francisco Arrillaga Gaztambide, Abraham Nieves Negrón, Luis Muñoz Rivera, Norman E. Parkhurst, Juan R. García Delgado, Enrique álvarez Vicente.

Judicial Branch: Ernesto Ramos Antonini, President; José Villares Rodríguez, Vice President; José M. Dávila Monsanto, Secretary; Lorenzo Lagarde Garcés, Santiago Polanco Abreu, Ernesto Juan Fonfrías Rivera, José Trías Monge, Angel M. Candelario Arce, Victor Gutiérrez Franqui, Arcilio Alvarado Alvarado, Miguel A. García Méndez, Juan B. Soto González, Mario Orsini Martínez, Lino Padrón Rivera.

Legislative Branch: Luis A. Negrón López, President; Rubén Gaztambide Arrillaga, Vice President; Francisco L. Anselmi Rodríguez, Secretary; Heraclio H. Rivera Colón, Ramón Barreto Pérez, Augusto Valentín Vizcarrondo, Mario Canales Torresola, Ubaldino Ramírez de Arellano Quiñones, Fernando J. Geigel Sabat, Celestino Iriarte Miró, Lino Padrón Rivera.

Bill of Rights: Jaime Benítez Rexach, President; Ernesto Carrasquillo Quiñones, Vice President; Bernardo Méndez Jiménez, Secretary; Virgilio Brunet Maldonado, Cruz Ortiz Stella, Alvaro Rivera Reyes, Francisco Paz Granela, José A. Cintrón Rivera, Alberto E. Sánchez Nazario, Juan Meléndez Baez, Arcilio Alvarado Alvarado, Rubén Gaztambide Arrillaga, Héctor González Blanés, Leopoldo Figueroa Carreras, Juan B. Soto González, Lino Padrón Rivera, Antonio Reyes Delgado.

Drafting, Style, and Enrollment: Victor Gutiérrez Franqui, President; María Libertad Gómez Garriga, Vice President; Jorge Font Saldaña, Secretary; Samuel R. Quiñones Quiñones, Jaime Benítez Rexach, Benjamín Ortiz Ortiz, Lionel Fernández Méndez, Jesús Izcoa Mouré, Juan Alemany Silva, Celestino Iriarte Miró, Mario Orsini Martínez.

Preamble, Ordinances, and Amendment Procedure: Luis Muñoz Marín, President; José Trías Monge, Vice President; Jorge Font Saldaña, Secretary; Ernesto Ramos Antonini, Ernesto Juan Fonfrías Rivera, Ramón Mellado Parsons, Virgilio Brunet Maldonado, Jenaro Gautier Dapena, Carlos Román Benítez, Luis Alfredo Colón Velázquez, Luis A. Ferré Aguayo, Ramiro Colón Castaño, Antonio Reyes Delgado, Héctor González Blanés, Ramiro Martínez Sandín.

Agenda: Benjamín Ortiz Ortiz, President; Heraclio H. Rivera Colón, Vice President; Sigfredo Vélez González, Secretary; Carlos Román Benítez, Francisco Berio Suárez, Armando Mignucci Calder, Pedro Torres Díaz, Leopoldo Figueroa Carreras, Miguel A. García Méndez, Ramón Barrios Sánchez.

Transitory Provisions and General Matters: Yldefonso Solá Morales, President; Santiago Polanco Abreu, Vice President; Angel Sandín Martínez, Secretary; Francisco L. Anselmi Rodríguez, Carmelo ávila Medina, Andrés Grillasca Salas, José B. Barceló Oliver, Manuel Acevedo Rosario, Alcides Figueroa Oliva, Dolores Rivera Candelaria, Luis A. Ferré Aguayo, Ramón Llobet Díaz, José Veray Hernández, Alejo Rivera Morales, Ramiro Martínez Sandín.

Executive Branch: Samuel R. Quiñones Quiñones, President; Alvaro Rivera Reyes, Vice President; Luis A. Negrón López, Secretary; Darío Goitía Montalvo, Carmelo Rodríguez García, Pablo Morales Otero, Yldefonso Solá Morales, Rafael Torrech Genovés, José Rosario Gelpi Bosch, José Veray Hernández, Antonio Reyes Delgado.

We, the people of Puerto Rico, in order to organize ourselves politically on a fully democratic basis, to promote the general welfare, and to secure for ourselves and our posterity the complete enjoyment of human rights, placing our trust in Almighty God, do ordain and establish this Constitution for the commonwealth which, in the exercise of our natural rights, we now create within our union with the United States of America.

In so doing, we declare:

The democratic system is fundamental to the life of the Puerto Rican community;

We understand that the democratic system of government is one in which the will of the people is the source of public power, the political order is subordinate to the rights of man, and the free participation of the citizen in collective decisions is assured;

We consider as determining factors in our life our citizenship of the United States of America and our aspiration continually to enrich our democratic heritage in the individual and collective enjoyment of its rights and privileges; our loyalty to the principles of the Federal Constitution; the coexistence in Puerto Rico of the two great cultures of the American Hemisphere; our fervor for education; our faith in justice; our devotion to the courageous, industrious, and peaceful way of life; our fidelity to individual human values above and beyond social position, racial differences, and economic interests; and our hope for a better world based on these principles.

Article I

The Commonwealth

Section 1. The Commonwealth of Puerto Rico is hereby constituted. Its political power emanates from the people and shall be exercised in accordance with their will, within the terms of the compact agreed upon between the people of Puerto Rico and the United States of America.

Section 2. The government of the Commonwealth of Puerto Rico shall be republican in form and its legislative, judicial and executive branches as established by this Constitution shall be equally subordinate to the sovereignty of the people of Puerto Rico.

Section 3. The political authority of the Commonwealth of Puerto Rico shall extend to the Island of Puerto Rico and to the adjacent islands within its jurisdiction.

Section 4. The seat of the government shall be the city of San Juan.

Article II

Bill of Rights

Section 1. The dignity of the human being is inviolable. All men are equal before the law. No discrimination shall be made on account of race, color, sex, birth, social origin or condition, or political or religious ideas. Both the laws and the system of public education shall embody these principles of essential human equality.

Section 2. The laws shall guarantee the expression of the will of the people by means of equal, direct and secret universal suffrage and shall protect the citizen against any coercion in the exercise of the electoral franchise.

Section 3. No law shall be made respecting an establishment of religion or prohibiting the free exercise thereof. There shall be complete separation of church and state.

Section 4. No law shall be made abridging the freedom of speech or of the press, or the right of the people peaceably to assemble and to petition the government for a redress of grievances.

Section 5. Every person has the right to an education which shall be directed to the full development of the human personality and to the strengthening of respect for human rights and fundamental freedoms. There shall be a system of free and wholly non-sectarian public education. Instruction in the elementary and secondary schools shall be free and shall be compulsory in the elementary schools to the extent permitted by the facilities of the state. No public property or public funds shall be used for the support of schools or educational institutions other than those of the state. Nothing contained in this provision shall prevent the state from furnishing to any child non-educational services established by law for the protection or welfare of children. *(Editor's note: By Resolution 34, approved by the Constitutional Convention and ratified in the referendum held on November 4, 1952, Section 5 of Article II was amended, adding to such section the following declaration: "Compulsory attendance at elementary public schools to the extent permitted by the facilities of the state as herein provided shall not be construed as applicable to those who receive elementary education in schools established under non-governmental auspices.")*

Section 6. Persons may join with each other and organize freely for any lawful purpose, except in military or quasi-military organizations.

Section 7. The right to life, liberty and the enjoyment of property is recognized as a fundamental right of man. The death penalty shall not exist. No person shall be deprived of his liberty or property without due process of law. No person in Puerto Rico shall be denied the equal protection of the laws. No laws impairing the obligation of contracts shall be enacted. A minimum amount of property and possessions shall be exempt from attachment as provided by law.

Section 8. Every person has the right to the protection of law against abusive attacks on his honor, reputation and private or family life.

Section 9. Private property shall not be taken or damaged for public use except upon payment of just compensation and in the manner provided by law. No law shall be enacted authorizing condemnation of printing presses, machinery or material devoted to publications of any kind. The buildings in which these objects are located may be condemned only after a judicial finding of public convenience and necessity pursuant to procedure that shall be provided by law, and may be taken before such a judicial finding only when there is placed at the disposition of the publication an adequate site in which it can be installed and continue to operate for a reasonable time.

Section 10. The right of the people to be secure in their persons, houses, papers and effects against unreasonable searches and seizures shall not be violated.

Wire-tapping is prohibited.

No warrant for arrest or search and seizure shall issue except by judicial authority and only upon probable cause supported by oath or affirmation, and particularly describing the place to be searched and the persons to be arrested or the things to be seized.

Evidence obtained in violation of this section shall be inadmissible in the courts.

Section 11. In all criminal prosecutions, the accused shall enjoy the right to have a speedy and public trial, to be informed of the nature and cause of the accusation and to have a copy thereof, to be confronted with the witnesses against him, to have compulsory process for obtaining witnesses in his favor, to have assistance of counsel, and to be presumed innocent.

In all prosecutions for a felony the accused shall have the right of trial by an impartial jury composed of twelve residents of the district, who may render their verdict by a majority vote which in no case may be less than nine.

No person shall be compelled in any criminal case to be a witness against himself and the failure of the accused to testify may be neither taken into consideration nor commented upon against him.

No person shall be twice put in jeopardy of punishment for the same offense.

Before conviction every accused shall be entitled to be admitted to bail.

Incarceration prior to trial shall not exceed six months nor shall bail or fines be excessive. No person shall be imprisoned for debt.

Section 12. Neither slavery nor involuntary servitude shall exist except in the latter case as a punishment for crime after the accused has been duly convicted. Cruel and unusual punishments shall not be inflicted. Suspension of civil rights including the right to vote shall cease upon service of the term of imprisonment imposed.

No *ex post facto* law or bill of attainder shall be passed.

Section 13. -The writ of *habeas corpus* shall be granted without delay and free of costs. The privilege of the writ of *habeas corpus* shall not be suspended, unless the public safety requires it in case of rebellion, insurrection or invasion. Only the Legislative Assembly shall have the power to suspend the privilege of the writ of *habeas corpus* and the laws regulating its issuance. The military authority shall always be subordinate to civil authority.

Section 14. No titles of nobility or other hereditary honors shall be granted. No officer or employee of the Commonwealth shall accept gifts, donations, decorations or offices from any foreign country or officer without prior authorization by the Legislative Assembly.

Section 15. The employment of children less than fourteen years of age in any occupation which is prejudicial to their health or morals or which places them in jeopardy of life or limb is prohibited.

No child less than sixteen years of age shall be kept in custody in a jail or penitentiary.

Section 16. The right of every employee to choose his occupation freely and to resign therefrom is recognized, as is his right to equal pay for equal work, to a reasonable minimum salary, to protection against risks to his health or person in his work or employment, and to an ordinary workday which shall not exceed eight hours. An employee may work in excess of this daily limit only if he is paid extra compensation as provided by law, at a rate never less than one and one-half times the regular rate at which he is employed.

Section 17. Persons employed by private businesses, enterprises and individual employers and by agencies or instrumentalities of the government operating as private businesses or enterprises, shall have the right to organize and to bargain collectively with their employers through representatives of their own free choosing in order to promote their welfare.

Section 18. In order to assure their right to organize and to bargain collectively, persons employed by private businesses, enterprises and individual employers and by agencies or instrumentalities of the government operating as private businesses or enterprises, in their direct relations with their own employers shall have the right to strike, to picket and to engage in other legal concerted activities.

Nothing herein contained shall impair the authority of the Legislative Assembly to enact laws to deal with grave emergencies that clearly imperil the public health or safety or essential public services.

Section 19. The foregoing enumeration of rights shall not be construed restrictively nor does it contemplate the exclusion of other rights not specifically mentioned which belong to the people in a democracy. The power of the Legislative Assembly to enact laws for the protection of the life, health and general welfare of the people shall likewise not be construed restrictively.

Section 20. The Commonwealth also recognizes the existence of the following human rights:

The right of every person to receive free elementary and secondary education.

The right of every person to obtain work.

The right of every person to a standard of living adequate for the health and well-being of himself and of his family, and especially to food, clothing, housing and medical care and necessary social services.

The right of every person to social protection in the event of unemployment, sickness, old age or disability.

The right of motherhood and childhood to special care and assistance.

The rights set forth in this section are closely connected with the progressive development of the economy of the Commonwealth and require, for their full effectiveness, sufficient resources and an agricultural and industrial development not yet attained by the Puerto Rican community.

In the light of their duty to achieve the full liberty of the citizen, the people and the government of Puerto Rico shall do everything in their power to promote the greatest possible expansion of the system of production, to assure the fairest distribution of economic output, and to obtain the maximum understanding between individual initiative and collective cooperation. The executive and judicial branches shall bear in mind this duty and shall construe the laws that tend to fulfill it in the most favorable manner possible.

Editor's note: By Resolution 34, approved by the Constitutional Convention and ratified in referendum on November 4, 1962, Section 20 of Article II was eliminated.

Article III

The Legislature

Section 1. The legislative power shall be vested in a Legislative Assembly, which shall consist of two houses, the Senate and the House of Representatives whose members shall be elected by direct vote at each general election.

Section 2. The Senate shall be composed of twenty-seven Senators and the House of Representatives of fifty-one Representatives, except as these numbers may be increased in accordance with the provisions of Section 7 of this Article.

Section 3. For the purpose of election of members of the Legislative Assembly, Puerto Rico shall be divided into eight senatorial districts and forty representative districts. Each senatorial district shall elect two Senators and each representative district one Representative.

There shall also be eleven Senators and eleven Representatives elected at large. No elector may vote for more than one candidate for Senator at Large or for more than one candidate for Representative at Large.

Section 4. In the first and subsequent elections under this Constitution the division of senatorial and representative districts as provided in Article VIII shall be in effect. After each decennial census beginning with the year 1960, said division shall be revised by a Board composed of the Chief Justice of the Supreme Court as Chairman and of two additional members appointed by the Governor with the advice and consent of the Senate. The two additional members shall not belong to the same political party. Any revision shall maintain the number of senatorial and representative districts here created, which shall be composed of contiguous and compact territory and shall be organized, insofar as practicable, upon the basis of population and means of communication. Each senatorial district shall always include five representative districts.

The decisions of the Board shall be made by majority vote and shall take effect in the general elections next following each revision. The Board shall cease to exist after the completion of each revision.

Section 5. No person shall be a member of the Legislative Assembly unless he is able to read and write the Spanish or English language and unless he is a citizen of the United States and of Puerto Rico and has resided in Puerto Rico at least two years immediately prior to the date of his election or appointment. No person shall be a member of the Senate who is not over thirty years of age, and no person shall be a member of the House of Representatives who is not over twenty-five years of age.

Section 6. No person shall be eligible to election or appointment as Senator or Representative for a district unless he has resided therein at least one year immediately prior to his election or appointment. When there is more than one representative district in a municipality, residence in the municipality shall satisfy this requirement.

Section 7. If in a general election more than two-thirds of the members of either house are elected from one political party or from a single ticket, as both are defined by law, the number of members shall be increased in the following cases:

(a) If the party or ticket which elected more than

two-thirds of the members of either or both houses shall have obtained less than two-thirds of the total number of votes cast for the office of Governor, the number of members of the Senate or of the House of Representatives or of both bodies, whichever may be the case, shall be increased by declaring elected a sufficient number of candidates of the minority party or parties to bring the total number of members of the minority party or parties to nine in the Senate and to seventeen in the House of Representatives. When there is more than one minority party, said additional members shall be declared elected from among the candidates of each minority party in the proportion that the number of votes cast for the candidate of each of said parties for the office of Governor bears to the total number of votes cast for the candidates of all the minority parties for the office of Governor.

When one or more minority parties shall have obtained representation in a proportion equal to or greater than the proportion of votes received by their respective candidates for Governor, such party or parties shall not be entitled to additional members until the representation established for each of the other minority parties under these provisions shall have been completed.

(b) If the party or ticket which elected more than two-thirds of the members of either or both houses shall have obtained more than two-thirds of the total number of votes cast for the office of Governor, and one or more minority parties shall not have elected the number of members in the Senate or in the House of Representatives or in both houses, whichever may be the case, which corresponds to the proportion of votes cast by each of them for the office of Governor, such additional number of their candidates shall be declared elected as is necessary in order to complete said proportion as nearly as possible, but the number of Senators of all the minority parties shall never, under this provision, be more than nine or that of Representatives more than seventeen.

In order to select additional members of the Legislative Assembly from a minority party in accordance with these provisions, its candidates at large who have not been elected shall be the first to be declared elected in the order of the votes that they have obtained, and thereafter its district candidates who, not having been elected, have obtained in their respective districts the highest proportion of the total number of votes cast as compared to the proportion of votes cast in favor of other candidates of the same party not elected to an equal office in the other districts.

The additional Senators and Representatives whose election is declared under this section shall be considered for all purposes as Senators at Large or Representatives at Large.

The measures necessary to implement these guarantees, the method of adjudicating fractions that may result from the application of the rules contained in this section, and the minimum number of votes that a minority party must cast in favor of its candidate for Governor in order to have the right to the representation provided herein shall be determined by the Legislative Assembly.

Section 8. The term of office of Senators and Representatives shall begin on the second day of January immediately following the date of the general election in which they shall have been elected. If, prior to the fifteen months immediately preceding the date of the next general election, a vacancy occurs in the office of Senator or Representative for a district, the Governor shall call a special election in said district within thirty days following the date on which the vacancy occurs. This election shall be held not later than ninety days after the call, and the person elected shall hold office for the rest of the unexpired term of his predecessor. When said vacancy occurs during a legislative session, or when the Legislative Assembly or the Senate has been called for a date prior to the certification of the results of the special election, the presiding officer of the appropriate house shall fill said vacancy by appointing the person recommended by the central committee of the political party of which his predecessor in office was a member. Such person shall hold the office until certification of the election of the candidate who was elected. When the vacancy occurs within fifteen months prior to a general election, or when it occurs in the office of a Senator at Large or a Representative at Large, the presiding officer of the appropriate house shall fill it, upon the recommendation of the political party of which the previous holder of the office was a member, by appointing a person selected in the same manner as that in which his predecessor was selected. A vacancy in the office of a Senator at Large or a Representative at Large elected as an independent candidate shall be filled by an election in all districts.

Section 9. Each house shall be the sole judge of the election, returns and qualifications of its members; shall choose its own officers; shall adopt rules for its own proceedings appropriate to legislative bodies; and, with the concurrence of three-fourths of the total number of members of which it is composed, may expel any member for the causes established in Section 21 of this Article, authorizing impeachments. The Senate shall elect a President and the House of Representatives a Speaker from among their respective members.

Section 10. The Legislative Assembly shall be deemed a continuous body during the term for which its members are elected and shall meet in regular session each year commencing on the second Monday in January. The duration of regular sessions and the periods of time for introduction and consideration of bills shall be prescribed by law. When the Governor calls the Legislative Assembly into special session it may consider only those matters specified in the call or in any special message sent to it by him during the session. No special session shall continue longer than twenty calendar days.

Section 11. The sessions of each house shall be open.

Section 12. A majority of the total number of members of which each house is composed shall constitute a quorum, but a smaller number may adjourn from day to day and shall have authority to compel the attendance of absent members.

Section 13. The two houses shall meet in the Capitol of Puerto Rico and neither of them may adjourn for more than three consecutive days without the consent of the other.

Section 14. No member of the Legislative Assembly shall be arrested while the house of which he is a member is in session, or during the fifteen days before or after such session, except for treason, felony or breach of the peace. The members of the Legislative Assembly shall not be questioned in any other place for any speech, debate or vote in either house or in any committee.

Section 15. No Senator or Representative may, during the term for which he was elected or chosen, be appointed to any civil office in the Government of Puerto Rico, its municipalities or instrumentalities, which shall have been created or the salary of which shall have been increased during said term. No person may hold office in the Government of Puerto Rico, its municipalities or instrumentalities and be a Senator or Representative at the same time. These provisions shall not prevent a member of the Legislative Assembly from being designated to perform functions *ad honorem*.

Section 16. The Legislative Assembly shall have the power to create, consolidate or reorganize executive departments and to define their functions.

Section 17. No bill shall become a law unless it has been printed, read, referred to a committee and returned therefrom with a written report, but either house may discharge a committee from the study and report of any bill and proceed to the consideration thereof. Each house shall keep a journal of its proceedings and of the votes cast for and against bills. The legislative proceedings shall be published in a daily record in the form determined by law. Every bill, except general appropriation bills, shall be confined to one subject, which shall be clearly expressed in its title, and any part of an act whose subject has not been expressed in the title shall be void. The general appropriation act shall contain only appropriations and rules for their disbursement. No bill shall be amended in a manner that changes its original purpose or incorporates matters extraneous to it. In amending any article or section of a law, said article or section shall be promulgated in its entirety as amended. All bills for raising revenue shall originate in the House of Representatives, but the Senate may propose or concur with amendments as on other bills.

Section 18. The subjects which may be dealt with by means of joint resolution shall be determined by law, but every joint resolution shall follow the same legislative process as that of a bill.

Section 19. Every bill which is approved by a majority of the total number of members of which each house is composed shall be submitted to the Governor and shall become law if he signs it or if he does not return it, with his objections, to the house in which it originated within ten days (Sundays excepted) counting from the date on which he shall have received it.

When the Governor returns a bill, the house that receives it shall enter his objections on its journal and both houses may reconsider it. If approved by two-thirds of the total number of members of which each house is composed, said bill shall become law.

If the Legislative Assembly adjourns *sine die* before the Governor has acted on a bill that has been presented to him less than ten days before, he is relieved of the obligation of returning it with his objections and the bill shall become law only if the Governor signs it within thirty days after receiving it.

Every final passage or reconsideration of a bill shall be by a roll-call vote.

Section 20. In approving any appropriation bill that contains more than one item, the Governor may eliminate one or more of such items or reduce their amounts, at the same time reducing the total amounts involved.

Section 21. The House of Representatives shall have exclusive power to initiate impeachment proceedings and, with the concurrence of two-thirds of the total number of members of which it is composed, to bring an indictment. The Senate shall have exclusive power to try and to decide impeachment cases, and in meeting for such purposes the Senators shall act in the name of the people and under oath or affirmation. No judgment of conviction in an impeachment trial shall be pronounced without the concurrence of three-fourths of the total number of members of which the Senate is composed, and the judgment shall be limited to removal from office. The person impeached, however, may be liable and subject to indictment, trial, judgment and punishment according to law. The causes of impeachment shall be treason, bribery, other felonies, and misdemeanors involving moral turpitude. The Chief Justice of the Supreme Court shall preside at the impeachment trial of the Governor.

The two houses may conduct impeachment proceedings in their regular or special sessions. The presiding officers of the two houses, upon written request of two-thirds of the total number of members of which the House of Representatives is composed, must convene them to deal with such proceedings.

Section 22. The Governor shall appoint a Controller with the advice and consent of a majority of the total number of members of which each house is composed. The Controller shall meet the requirements prescribed by law and shall hold office for a term of ten years and until his successor has been appointed and qualifies. The Controller shall audit all the revenues, accounts and expenditures of the Commonwealth, of its agencies and instrumentalities and of its municipalities, in order to determine whether they have been made in accordance with law. He shall render annual reports and any special reports that may be required of him by the Legislative Assembly or by the Governor.

In the performance of his duties the Controller shall be authorized to administer oaths, take evidence and compel, under pain of contempt, the attendance of witnesses and the production of books, letters, documents, papers, records and all other articles deemed essential to a full understanding of the matter under investigation.

The Controller may be removed for the causes and pursuant to the procedure established in the preceding section.

Article IV

The Executive

Section 1. The executive power shall be vested in a Governor, who shall be elected by direct vote in each general election.

Section 2. The Governor shall hold office for the term of four years from the second day of January of the year following his election and until his successor has been elected and qualifies. He shall reside in Puerto Rico and maintain his office in its capital city.

Section 3. No person shall be Governor unless, on the date of the election, he is at least thirty-five years of age, and is and has been during the preceding five years a citizen of the United States and a citizen and *bona fide* resident of Puerto Rico.

Section 4. The Governor shall execute the laws and cause them to be executed.

He shall call the Legislative Assembly or the Senate into special session when in his judgment the public interest so requires.

He shall appoint, in the manner prescribed by this Constitution or by law, all officers whose appointment he is authorized to make. He shall have the power to make appointments while the Legislative Assembly is not in session. Any such appointments that require the advice and consent of the Senate or of both houses shall expire at the end of the next regular session.

He shall be the commander-in-chief of the militia.

He shall have the power to call out the militia and summon the posse comitatus in order to prevent or suppress rebellion, invasion or any serious disturbance of the public peace.

He shall have the power to proclaim martial law when the public safety requires it in case of rebellion or invasion or imminent danger thereof. The Legislative Assembly shall meet forthwith on their own initiative to ratify or revoke the proclamation.

He shall have the power to suspend the execution of sentences in criminal cases and to grant pardons, commutations of punishment, and total or partial remissions of fines and forfeitures for crimes committed in violation of the laws of Puerto Rico. This power shall not extend to cases of impeachment.

He shall approve or disapprove in accordance with this Constitution the joint resolutions and bills passed by the Legislative Assembly.

He shall present to the Legislative Assembly, at the beginning of each regular session, a message concerning the affairs of the Commonwealth and a report concerning the state of the Treasury of Puerto Rico and the proposed expenditures for the ensuing fiscal year. Said report shall contain the information necessary for the formulation of a program of legislation.

He shall exercise the other powers and functions and discharge the other duties assigned to him by this Constitution or by law.

Section 5. For the purpose of exercising executive power, the Governor shall be assisted by Secretaries whom he shall appoint with the advice and consent of the Senate. The appointment of the Secretary of State shall in addition require the advice and consent of the House of Representatives, and the person appointed shall fulfill the requirements established in Section 3 of this Article. The Secretaries shall collectively constitute the Governor's advisory council, which shall be designated as the Council of Secretaries.

Section 6. Without prejudice to the power of the Legislative Assembly to create, reorganize and consolidate executive departments and to define their functions, the following departments are hereby established: State, Justice, Education Health, Treasury, Labor, Agriculture and Commerce, and Public Works. Each of these executive departments shall be headed by a Secretary.

Section 7. When a vacancy occurs in the office of Governor, caused by death, resignation, removal, total and permanent incapacity, or any other absolute disability, said office shall devolve upon the Secretary of State, who shall hold it for the rest of the term and until a new Governor has been elected and qualifies. In the event that vacancies exist at the same time in both the office of Governor and that of Secretary of State, the law shall provide which of the Secretaries shall serve as Governor.

Section 8. When for any reason the Governor is temporarily unable to perform his functions, the Secretary of State shall substitute for him during the period he is unable to serve. If for any reason the Secretary of State is not available, the Secretary determined by law shall temporarily hold the office of Governor.

Section 9. If the Governor-elect shall not have qualified, or if he has qualified and a permanent vacancy occurs in the office of Governor before he shall have appointed a Secretary of State, or before said Secretary, having been appointed, shall have qualified, the Legislative Assembly just elected, upon convening for its first regular session, shall elect, by a majority of the total number of members of which each house is composed, a Governor who shall hold office until his successor is elected in the next general election and qualifies.

Section 10. The Governor may be removed for the causes and pursuant to the procedure established in Section 21 of Article III of this Constitution.

Article V

The Judiciary

Section 1. The judicial power of Puerto Rico shall be vested in a Supreme Court, and in such other courts as may be established by law.

Section 2. The courts of Puerto Rico shall constitute a unified judicial system for purposes of jurisdiction, operation and administration. The Legislative Assembly may create and abolish courts, except for the Supreme Court, in a manner not inconsistent with this Constitution, and shall determine the venue and organization of the courts.

Section 3. The Supreme Court shall be the court of last resort in Puerto Rico and shall be composed of a Chief Justice and four Associate Justices. The number of Justices may be changed only by law upon request of the Supreme Court.

Section 4. The Supreme Court shall sit, in accordance with rules adopted by it, as a full court or in divisions. All the decisions of the Supreme Court shall be concurred in by a majority of its members. No law shall be held unconstitutional except by a majority of the total number of Justices of which the Court is composed in accordance with this Constitution or with law. *(Editor's note: As amended in general election of November 8, 1960.)*

Section 5. The Supreme Court, any of its divisions or any of its Justices may hear in the first instance petitions for *habeas corpus* and any other causes and proceedings as determined by law.

Section 6. The Supreme Court shall adopt for the courts rules of evidence and of civil and criminal procedure which shall not abridge, enlarge or modify the substantive rights of the parties. The rules thus adopted shall be submitted to the Legislative Assembly at the beginning of its next regular session and shall not go into effect until sixty days after the close of said session, unless disapproved by the Legislative Assembly, which shall have the power both at said session and subsequently to amend, repeal or supplement any of said rules by a specific law to that effect.

Section 7. The Supreme Court shall adopt rules for the administration of the courts. These rules shall be subject to the laws concerning procurement, personnel, audit and appropriation of funds, and other laws which apply generally to all branches of the government. The Chief Justice shall direct the administration of the courts and shall appoint an administrative director who shall hold office at the will of the Chief Justice.

Section 8. Judges shall be appointed by the Governor with the advice and consent of the Senate. Justices of the Supreme Court shall not assume office until after confirmation by theSenate and shall hold their offices during good behavior. The terms of office of the other judges shall be fixed by law and shall not be less than that fixed for the term of office of a judge of the same or equivalent category existing when this Constitution takes effect. The other officials and employees of the courts shall be appointed in the manner provided by law.

Section 9. No person shall be appointed a Justice of the Supreme Court unless he is a citizen of the United States and of Puerto Rico, shall have been admitted to the practice of law in Puerto Rico at least ten years prior to his appointment, and shall have resided in Puerto Rico at least five years immediately prior thereto.

Section 10. The Legislative Assembly shall establish a retirement system for judges. Retirement shall be compulsory at age of seventy years.

Section 11. Justices of the Supreme Court may be removed for the causes and pursuant to the procedure established in Section 21 of Article III of this Constitution. Judges of the other courts may be removed by the Supreme Court for the causes and pursuant to the procedure provided by law.

Section 12. No judge shall make a direct or indirect financial contribution to any political organization or party, or hold any executive office therein, or participate in a political campaign of any kind, or be a candidate for an elective public office unless he has resigned his judicial office at least six months prior to his nomination.

Section 13. In the event that a court or any of its divisions or sections is changed or abolished by law, the person holding a post of judge therein shall continue to hold it during the rest of the term for which he was appointed and shall perform the judicial functions assigned to him by the Chief Justice of the Supreme Court.

Article VI

General Provisions

Section 1. The Legislative Assembly shall have the power to create, abolish, consolidate and reorganize municipalities; to change their territorial limits; to determine their organization and functions; and to authorize them to develop programs for the general welfare and to create any agencies necessary for that purpose.

No law abolishing or consolidating municipalities shall take effect until ratified in a referendum by a majority of the electors voting in said referendum in each of the municipalities to be abolished or consolidated. The referendum shall be in the manner determined by law, which shall include the applicable procedures of the election laws in effect when the referendum law is approved.

Section 2. The power of the Commonwealth of Puerto Rico to impose and collect taxes and to authorize their imposition and collection by municipalities shall be exercised as determined by the Legislative Assembly and shall never be surrendered or suspended. The power of the Commonwealth of Puerto Rico to contract and to authorize the contracting of debts shall be exercised as determined by the Legislative Assembly, but no direct obligations of the Commonwealth for money borrowed directly by the Commonwealth evidenced by bonds or notes for the payment of which the full faith credit and taxing power of the Commonwealth shall be pledged shall be issued by the Commonwealth if the total of (i) the amount of principal and interest on such bonds and notes, together with the amount of principal of and interest on all such bonds and notes theretofore issued by the Commonwealth and then outstanding, payable in any fiscal year and (ii) any amounts paid by the Commonwealth in the fiscal year next preceding the then current fiscal year for principal or interest on account of any outstanding obligations evidenced by bonds or notes guaranteed by the Commonwealth, shall exceed 15 percent of the average of the total amount of the annual revenues raised under the provisions of Commonwealth legislation and covered into the Treasury of Puerto Rico in the two fiscal years next preceding the then current fiscal year; and no such bonds or notes issued by the Commonwealth for any purpose other than housing facilities shall mature later than 30 years from their date and no bonds or notes issued for housing facilities shall mature later than 40 years from their date; and the Commonwealth shall not guarantee any obligations evidenced by bonds or notes if the total of the amount payable in any fiscal year on account of principal of and interest on all the direct obligations referred to above theretofore issued by the Commonwealth and then outstanding and the amounts referred to in item (ii) above shall exceed 15 percent of the average of the total amount of such annual revenues.

The Legislative Assembly shall fix limitations for the issuance of direct obligations by any of the municipalities of Puerto Rico for money borrowed directly by such municipality evidenced by bonds or notes for the payment of which the full faith, credit and taxing power of such municipality shall be pledged; provided, however, that no such bonds or notes shall be issued by any municipality in an amount which, together with the amount of all such bonds and notes theretofore issued by such municipality and then outstanding, shall exceed the percentage determined by the Legislative Assembly, which shall be not less than five per centum (5 percent) nor more than ten per centum (10 percent) of the aggregate tax valuation of the property within such municipality.

The Secretary of the Treasury may be required to apply the available revenues including surplus to the payment of interest on the public debt and the amortization thereof in any case provided for by Section 8 of this Article VI at the suit of any holder of bonds or notes issued in evidence thereof. *(Editor's note: As amended by the voters at a referendum held December 10, 1961.)*

Section 3. The rule of taxation in Puerto Rico shall be uniform.

Section 4. General elections shall be held every four years on the day of November determined by the Legislative Assembly. In said elections there shall be elected a Governor, the members of the Legislative Assembly, and the other officials whose election on that date is provided for by law.

Every person over twenty-one years of age shall be entitled to vote if he fulfills the other conditions determined by law. No person shall be deprived of the right to vote because he does not know how to read or write or does not own property.

All matters concerning the electoral process, registration of voters, political parties and candidates shall be determined by law.

Every popularly elected official shall be elected by direct vote and any candidate who receives more votes than any other candidate for the same office shall be declared elected.

Section 5. The laws shall be promulgated in accordance with the procedure prescribed by law and shall specify the terms under which they shall take effect.

Section 6. If at the end of any fiscal year the appropriations necessary for the ordinary operating expenses of the government and for the payment of interest on and amortization of the public debt for the ensuing fiscal year shall not have been made, the several sums appropriated in the last appropriation acts for the objects and purposes therein specified, so far as the same may be applicable, shall continue in effect item by item, and the Governor shall authorize the payments necessary for such purposes until corresponding appropriations are made.

Section 7. The appropriations made for any fiscal year shall not exceed the total revenues, including available surplus, estimated for said fiscal year unless the imposition of taxes sufficient to cover said appropriations is provided by law.

Section 8. In case the available revenues including surplus for any fiscal year are insufficient to meet the appropriations made for that year, interest on the public debt and amortization thereof shall first be paid, and other disbursements shall thereafter be made in accordance with the order of priorities established by law.

Section 9. Public property and funds shall only be disposed of for public purposes, for the support and operation of state institutions, and pursuant to law.

Section 10. No law shall give extra compensation to any public officer, employee, agent or contractor after services shall have been rendered or contract made. No law shall extend the term of any public officer or diminish his salary or emoluments after his election or appointment. No person shall draw a salary for more than one office or position in the government of Puerto Rico.

Section 11. The salaries of the Governor, the Secretaries, the members of the Legislative Assembly, the Controller and Judges shall be fixed by a special law and, except for the salaries of the members of the Legislative Assembly, shall not be decreased during the terms for which they are elected or appointed. The salaries of the Governor and the Controller shall not be increased during said terms. No increase in the salaries of the members of the Legislative Assembly shall take effect until after the expiration of the term of the Legislative Assembly during which it is enacted. Any reduction of the salaries of the members of the Legislative Assembly shall be elective only during the term of the Legislative Assembly which approves it.

Section 12. The Governor shall occupy and use, free of rent, the buildings and properties belonging to the Commonwealth which have been or shall hereafter be used and occupied by him as chief executive.

Section 13. The procedure for granting franchises, rights, privileges and concessions of a public or quasi-public nature shall be determined by law, but every concession of this kind to a person or private entity must be approved by the Governor or by the executive official whom he designates. Every franchise, right, privilege or concession of a public or quasi-public nature shall be subject to amendment, alteration or repeal as determined by law.

Section 14. No corporation shall be authorized to conduct the business of buying and selling real estate or be permitted to hold or own real estate except such as may be reasonably necessary to enable it to carry out the purposes for which it was created, and every corporation authorized to engage in agriculture shall by its charter be restricted to the ownership and control of not to exceed five hundred acres of land; and this provision shall be held to prevent any member of a corporation engaged in agriculture from being in any wise interested in any other corporation engaged in agriculture.

Corporations, however, may loan funds upon real estate security, and purchase real estate when necessary for the collection of loans, but they shall dispose of real estate so obtained within five years after receiving the title.

Corporations not organized in Puerto Rico, but doing business in Puerto Rico, shall be bound by the provisions of this section so far as they are applicable.

These provisions shall not prevent the ownership, possession or management of lands in excess of five hundred acres by the Commonwealth, its agencies or instrumentalities.

Section 15. The Legislative Assembly shall determine all matters concerning the flag, the seal and the anthem of the Commonwealth. Once determined, no law changing them shall take effect until one year after the general election next following the date of enactment of said law.

Section 16. All public officials and employees of

the Commonwealth, its agencies, instrumentalities and political subdivisions, before entering upon their respective duties, shall take an oath to support the Constitution of the United States and the Constitution and laws of the Commonwealth of Puerto Rico.

Section 17. In case of invasion, rebellion, epidemic or any other event giving rise to a state of emergency, the Governor may call the Legislative Assembly to meet in a place other than the Capitol of Puerto Rico, subject to the approval or disapproval of the Legislative Assembly. Under the same conditions, the Governor may, during the period of emergency, order the government, its agencies and instrumentalities to be moved temporarily to a place other than the seat of the government.

Section 18. All criminal actions in the courts of the Commonwealth shall be conducted in the name and by the authority of "The People of Puerto Rico" until otherwise provided by law.

Section 19. It shall be the public policy of the Commonwealth to conserve, develop and use its natural resources in the most effective manner possible for the general welfare of the community; to conserve and maintain buildings and places declared by the Legislative Assembly to be of historic or artistic value; to regulate its penal institutions in a manner that effectively achieves their purposes and to provide, within the limits of available resources, for adequate treatment of delinquents in order to make possible their moral and social rehabilitation.

Article VII

Amendments to the Constitution

Section 1. The Legislative Assembly may propose amendments to this Constitution by a concurrent resolution approved by not less than two-thirds of the total number of members of which each house is composed. All proposed amendments shall be submitted to the qualified electors in a special referendum, but if the concurrent resolution is approved by not less than three fourths of the total number of members of which each house is composed, the Legislative Assembly may provide that the referendum shall be held at the same time as the next general election. Each proposed amendment shall be voted on separately and not more than three proposed amendments may be submitted at the same referendum. Every proposed amendment shall specify the terms under which it shall take effect, and it shall become a part of this Constitution if it is ratified by a majority of the electors voting thereon. Once approved, a proposed amendment must be published at least three months prior to the date of the referendum.

Section 2. The Legislative Assembly, by a concurrent resolution approved by two-thirds of the total number of members of which each house is composed, may submit to the qualified electors at a referendum, held at the same time as a general election, the question of whether a constitutional convention shall be called to revise this Constitution. If a majority of the electors voting on this question vote in favor of the revision, it shall be made by a Constitutional Convention elected in the manner provided by law. Every revision of this Constitution shall be submitted to the qualified electors at a special referendum for ratification or rejection by a majority of the votes cast at the referendum.

Section 3. No amendment to this Constitution shall alter
the republican form of government established by it or abolish its bill of rights.

Editor's note: By Resolution 34, approved by the Constitutional Convention and ratified in the referendum held on November 4, 1952, the following new sentence was added to Section 3 of Article VII: "Any amendment or revision of this constitution shall be consistent with the resolution enacted by the applicable provisions of the Constitution of the United States, with the Puerto Rican Federal Relations Act and with Public Law 600, Eighty-first Congress, adopted in the nature of a compact."

Article VIII

Senatorial and Representative Districts

Section 1. The senatorial and representative districts shall be the following:

I. SENATORIAL DISTRICT OF SAN JUAN, which shall be composed of the following Representative Districts: The Capital of Puerto Rico, excluding the present electoral precincts of Santurce and Rio Piedras; 2.—Electoral zones numbers 1 and 2 of the present precinct of Santurce; 3.—Electoral zone number 3 of the present precinct of Santurce; 4.—Electoral zone number 4 of the present precinct of Santurce; and 6.—Wards Hato Rey, Puerto Nuevo and Caparra Heights of the Capital of Puerto Rico.

II. SENATORIAL DISTRICT OF BAYAMON, which shall be composed of the following Representative Districts: 7.—The municipality of Bayamon; 8.—The municipalities of Carolina and Trujillo Alto; 9.—The present electoral precinct of Rio Piedras, excluding wards Hato Rey, Puerto Nuevo and Caparra Heights of the Capital of Puerto Rico; 10.—The municipalities of Catano, Guaynabo and Toa Baja; and 11.—The municipalities of Toa Alta, Corozal and Naranjito.

III. SENATORIAL DISTRICT OF ARECIBO, which shall be composed of the following Representative Districts: The municipalities of Vega Baja, Vega Alta and Dorado; 12.—The municipalities of Manati and Barceloneta; 13.—The municipalities of Ciales and Morovis; 14.—The municipality of Arecibo; and 15.—The municipality of Utuado.

IV. SENATORIAL DISTRICT OF AGUADILLA, which shall be composed of the following Representative Districts: 16.—The municipalities of Camuy, Hatillo and Quebradillas; 17.—The municipalities of Aguadilla and Isabela; 18.—The municipalities of San Sebastian and Moca; 19.—The municipalities of Lares, Las Marias and Maricao; and 20.—The municipalities of Anasco, Aguada and Rincon.

V. SENATORIAL DISTRICT OF MAYAGUEZ, which shall be composed of the following Representative Districts: 21.—The municipality of Mayaguez; 22.—The municipalities of Cabo Rojo, Hormigueros and Lajas; 23.—The municipalities of San German and Sabana Grande; 24.—The municipalities of Yauco and Guanica; and 25.—The municipalities of Guayanilla and Penuelas.

VI. SENATORIAL DISTRICT OF PONCE, which shall be composed of the following Representative Districts: 26.—The first, second, third, fourth, fifth and sixth wards and the City Beach of the municipality of Ponce; 27.—The municipality of Ponce, except for the first, second, third, fourth, fifth and sixth wards and the City Beach; 28.—The municipalities of Adjuntas and Jayuya; 29.—The municipalities of Juana Diaz, Santa Isabel and Villalba; and 30.—The municipalities of Coamo and Orocovis.

VII. SENATORIAL DISTRICT OF GUAYAMA, which shall be composed of the following Representative Districts: 31.—The municipalities of Aibonito, Barranquitas and Comerio; 32.—The municipalities of Cayey and Cidra; 33.—The municipalities of Caguas and Aguas Buenas; 34.—The municipalities of Guayama and Salinas; and 35.—The municipalities of Patillas, Maunabo and Arroyo.

VIII. SENATORIAL DISTRICT OF HUMACAO, which shall be composed of the following Representative Districts: 36.—The municipalities of Humacao and Yabucoa; 37.—The municipalities of Juncos, Gurabo and San Lorenzo; 38.—The municipalities of Naguabo, Ceiba and Las Piedras; 39.—The municipalities of Fajardo and Vieques and the Island of Culebra; and 40.—The municipalities of Rio Grande, Loiza and Luquillo.

Section 2. Electoral zones numbers 1, 2, 3 and 4 included in three representative districts within the senatorial district of San Juan are those presently existing for purposes of electoral organization in the second precinct of San Juan.

Article IX

Transitory Provisions

Section 1. When this Constitution goes into effect all laws not inconsistent therewith shall continue in full force until amended or repealed, or until they expire by their own terms.

Unless otherwise provided by this Constitution, civil and criminal liabilities, rights, franchises, concessions, privileges, claims, actions, causes of action, contracts, and civil, criminal and administrative proceedings shall continue unaffected, notwithstanding the taking effect of this Constitution.

Section 2. All officers who are in office by election or appointment on the date this Constitution takes effect shall continue to hold their offices and to perform the functions thereof in a manner not inconsistent with this Constitution, unless the functions of their offices are abolished or until their successors are selected and qualify in accordance with this Constitution and laws enacted pursuant thereto.

Section 3. Notwithstanding the age limit fixed by this Constitution for compulsory retirement, all the judges of the courts of Puerto Rico who are holding office on the date this Constitution takes effect shall continue to hold their judicial offices until the expiration of the terms for which they were appointed, and in the case of Justices of the Supreme Court during good behavior.

Section 4. The Commonwealth of Puerto Rico shall be the successor of the People of Puerto Rico for all purposes, including without limitation the collection and payment of debts and liabilities in accordance with their terms.

Section 5. When this Constitution goes into effect, the term "citizen of the Commonwealth of Puerto Rico" shall replace the term "citizen of Puerto Rico" as previously used.

Section 6. Political parties shall continue to enjoy all rights recognized by the election law, provided that on the effective date of this Constitution they fulfill the minimum requirements for the registration of new parties contained in said law. Five years after this Constitution shall have taken effect the Legislative Assembly may change these requirements, but any law increasing them shall not go into effect until after the general election next following its enactment.

Section 7. The Legislative Assembly may enact the laws necessary to supplement and make elective these transitory provisions in order to assure the functioning of the government until the officers provided for by this Constitution are elected or appointed and qualify, and until this Constitution takes effect in all respects.

Section 8. If the Legislative Assembly creates a

Department of Commerce, the Department of Agriculture and Commerce shall thereafter be called the Department of Agriculture.

Section 9. The first election under the provisions of this Constitution shall be held on the date provided by law, but not later than six months after the effective date of this Constitution. The second general election under this Constitution shall be held in the month of November 1956 on a day provided by law.

Section 10. Constitution shall take effect when the Governor so proclaims, but not later than sixty days after its ratification by the Congress of the United States.

Done in Convention, at San Juan, Puerto Rico, on the sixth day of February, in the year of Our Lord one thousand nine hundred and fifty-two.

Source: "Constitution of the Commonwealth of Puerto Rico," in *Documents on the Constitutional History of Puerto Rico* (Washington, D.C.: Office of the Commonwealth of Puerto Rico, June 1964), pp. 168–192; and "Constitution of the Commonwealth of Puerto Rico," from http://www.cu-online.com/%7Emaggy/constitu.html.

✳ RESOLUTIONS APPROVED BY THE CONSTITUTIONAL CONVENTION RELATING TO THE CONSTITUTION OF THE COMMONWEALTH OF PUERTO RICO

Resolution No. 22

Approved by the Constitutional Convention of Puerto Rico in the Plenary Session Held February 4, 1952

To determine in Spanish and in English the name of the body politic created by the Constitution of the people of Puerto Rico.

WHEREAS, this Constitutional Convention, in accordance with the mandate of the people, is about to adopt the Constitution by virtue of which the Puerto Rican community will be politically organized;

WHEREAS, it is necessary to give an appropriate name in both English and Spanish to the body politic thus created;

WHEREAS, the word "commonwealth" in contemporary English usage means a politically organized community, that is to say, a state (using the word in the generic sense) in which political power resides ultimately in the people, hence a free state, but one which is at the same time linked to a broader political system in a federal or other type of association and therefore does not have an independent and separate existence;

WHEREAS, the single word "commonwealth", as currently used, clearly defines the status of the body politic created under the terms of the compact existing between the people of Puerto Rico and the United States, i.e., that of a state which is free of superior authority in the management of its own local affairs but which is linked to the United States of America and hence is a part of its political system in a manner compatible with its federal structure;

WHEREAS, there is no single word in the Spanish language exactly equivalent to the English word "commonwealth" and translation of "commonwealth" into Spanish requires a combination of words to express the concepts of state and liberty and association;

WHEREAS, in the case of Puerto Rico the most appropriate translation of "commonwealth" into Spanish is the expression "estado libre asociado", which however should not be rendered "associated free state" in English inasmuch as the word "state" in ordinary speech in the United States means one of the States of the Union;

THEREFORE, Be it resolved by the Constituent Assembly of Puerto Rico:

First: That in Spanish the name of the body politic created by the Constitution which this Convention is adopting for submission to the people of Puerto Rico shall be "Estado Libre Asociado," it being understood that in our case this term is equivalent to and an appropriate translation of the English word "commonwealth."

Second: That, as a consequence, the body politic created by our Constitution shall be designated "The Commonwealth of Puerto Rico" in English and "El Estado Libre Asociado de Puerto Rico" in Spanish.

Third: That the Committee on Style of this Convention is instructed to use these designations in the respective English and Spanish texts of the Constitution when submitting the documents for third reading.

Fourth: That this resolution shall be published in Spanish and in English as an explanatory and authoritative statement of the meaning of the terms "Commonwealth" and "Estado Libre Asociado" as used in the Constitution; and that it shall be widely distributed, together with the Constitution, for the information of the people of Puerto Rico and the Congress of the United States.

Resolution No. 23

Approved by the Constitutional Convention of Puerto Rico in the Plenary Session Held February 4, 1952.

Final declarations of the Constitutional Convention of Puerto Rico.

WHEREAS, the Constitutional Convention of Puerto Rico, in fulfilling the important mission assigned it by the people, has approved a Constitution for the Commonwealth of Puerto Rico within the terms of the compact entered into with the United States of America;

WHEREAS, in accordance with the terms of the compact, said Constitution is to be submitted to the people of Puerto Rico for their approval;

THEREFORE, Be it resolved by this Constitutional Convention:

First: That, pursuant to the relevant regulations, a certified copy of the Constitution as approved be sent to the Governor of Puerto Rico so that he may submit it to the people of Puerto Rico in a referendum as provided by law.

Second: That copies of the Constitution be printed in Spanish and English, respectively, in numbers sufficient for general distribution to the end that it will become widely known.

Third: That the following final declarations of this Convention be entered on its journal and also published:

(a) This Convention deems that the Constitution as approved fulfills the mission assigned it by the people of Puerto Rico.

(b) When this Constitution takes effect, the people of Puerto Rico shall thereupon be organized in a commonwealth established within the terms of the compact entered into by mutual consent, which is the basis of our union with the United States of America.

(c) The political authority of the Commonwealth of Puerto Rico shall be exercised in accordance with its Constitution and within the terms of said compact.

(d) Thus we attain the goal of complete self-government, the last vestiges of colonialism having disappeared in the principle of Compact, and we enter into an era of new developments in democratic civilization. Nothing can surpass in political dignity the principle of mutual consent and of compacts freely agreed upon. The spirit of the people of Puerto Rico is free for great undertakings now and in the future. Having full political dignity the commonwealth of Puerto Rico may develop in other ways by modifications of the Compact through mutual consent.

(e) The people of Puerto Rico reserve the right to propose and to accept modifications in the terms of its relations with the United States of America, in order that these relations may at all times be the expression of an agreement freely entered into between the people of Puerto Rico and the United States of America.

Fourth: That a copy of this resolution be sent to the President of the United States and to the President of the Senate and the Speaker of the House of Representatives of the Congress of the United States.

Source: "Resolution 22" and "Resolution 23," in *Documents on the Constitutional History of Puerto Rico* (Washington, D.C.: Office of the Commonwealth of Puerto Rico, June 1964), pp. 164–167.

✳ THE NORTH AMERICAN FREE TRADE AGREEMENT (NAFTA)

On August 12, 1992, Canadian Minister of Industry, Science, and Technology and Minister for International Trade Michael Wilson, Mexican Secretary of Trade and Industrial Development Jaime Serra, and United States Trade Representative Carla Hills completed negotiations on a proposed North American Free Trade Agreement (NAFTA). The text of the agreement was completed on September 13, 1993 and was presented to Congress in November 1993.

Preamble

The Government of Canada, the Government of the United Mexican States and the Government of the United States of America, resolved to:

STRENGTHEN the special bonds of friendship and cooperation among their nations;

CONTRIBUTE to the harmonious development and expansion of world trade and provide a catalyst to broader international cooperation;

CREATE an expanded and secure market for the goods and services produced in their territories;

REDUCE distortions to trade;

ESTABLISH clear and mutually advantageous rules governing their trade;

ENSURE a predictable commercial framework for business planning and investment;

BUILD on their respective rights and obligations under the General Agreement on Tariffs and Trade and other multilateral and bilateral instruments of cooperation;

ENHANCE the competitiveness of their firms in global markets;

FOSTER creativity and innovation, and promote trade in goods and services that are the subject of intellectual property rights;

CREATE new employment opportunities and improve working conditions and living standards in their respective territories;

UNDERTAKE each of the preceding in a manner consistent with environmental protection and conservation;

PRESERVE their flexibility to safeguard the public welfare;

PROMOTE sustainable development;

STRENGTHEN the development and enforcement of environmental laws and regulations; and

PROTECT, enhance and enforce basic workers' rights;

HAVE AGREED as follows:

Part One: General Part

Chapter One: Objectives

Article 101: Establishment of the Free Trade Area

The Parties to this Agreement, consistent with Article XXIV of the General Agreement on Tariffs and Trade, hereby establish a free trade area.

Article 102: Objectives

1. The objectives of this Agreement, as elaborated more specifically through its principles and rules, including national treatment, most-favored-nation treatment and transparency are to:

(a) eliminate barriers to trade in, and facilitate the cross border movement of, goods and services between the territories of the Parties;

(b) promote conditions of fair competition in the free trade area;

(c) increase substantially investment opportunities in their territories;

(d) provide adequate and effective protection and enforcement of intellectual property rights in each Party's territory;

(e) create effective procedures for the implementation and application of this Agreement, and for its joint administration and the resolution of disputes; and

(f) establish a framework for further trilateral, regional and multilateral cooperation to expand and enhance the benefits of this Agreement.

2. The Parties shall interpret and apply the provisions of this Agreement in the light of its objectives set out in paragraph 1 and in accordance with applicable rules of international law.

Article 103: Relation to Other Agreements

1. The Parties affirm their existing rights and obligations with respect to each other under the General Agreement on Tariffs and Trade and other agreements to which such Parties are party.

2. In the event of any inconsistency between the provisions of this Agreement and such other agreements, the provisions of this Agreement shall prevail to the extent of the inconsistency, except as otherwise provided in this Agreement.

Article 104: Relation to Environmental and Conservation Agreements

1. In the event of any inconsistency between this Agreement and the specific trade obligations set out in:

(a) Convention on the International Trade in Endangered Species of Wild Fauna and Flora, done at Washington, March 3, 1973;

(b) the Montreal Protocol on Substances that Deplete the Ozone Layer, done at Montreal, September 16, 1987, as amended June 29, 1990;

(c) Basel Convention on the Control of Transboundary Movements of Hazardous Wastes and Their Disposal, done at Basel, March 22, 1989, upon its entry into force for Canada, Mexico and the United States; or

(d) the agreements set out in Annex 104.1, such obligations shall prevail to the extent of the inconsistency, provided that where a Party has a choice among equally effective and reasonably available means of complying with such obligations, the Party chooses the alternative that is the least inconsistent with the other provisions of this Agreement.

2. The Parties may agree in writing to modify Annex 104.1 to include any amendment to the agreements listed in paragraph 1, and any other environmental or conservation agreement.

Article 105: Extent of Obligations

The Parties shall ensure that all necessary measures are taken in order to give effect to the provisions of this Agreement, including their observance, except as otherwise provided in this Agreement, by state and provincial governments.

Annex 104

Bilateral and Other Environmental and Conservation Agreements

1. The Agreement Between the Government of Canada and the Government of the United States of America Concerning the Transboundary Movements of Hazardous Waste, signed at Ottawa, October 28, 1986.

2. The Agreement between the United States of America and the United Mexican States on Cooperation for the Protection and Improvement of the Environment in the Border Area, signed at La Paz, Baja California Sur, August 14, 1983.

4

Historic Landmarks

✳ Alabama ✳ Arizona ✳ California ✳ Florida ✳ Georgia ✳ Louisiana ✳ New Mexico
✳ Panama Canal Zone ✳ Puerto Rico ✳ Texas ✳ Virgin Islands

✳ ALABAMA

Apalachicola Fort

One and one-half miles east of Holy Trinity on the Chattahoochee River, Russell County, Alabama. Established in 1690, it was the northernmost Spanish outpost on the Chattahoochee River built to prevent English inroads among the lower Creek Indians.

De Soto Caverns

Childersburg, Alabama; five miles east on state Route 76, southwest of Talladega. These spectacular caverns, which contain 2,000-year-old Indian burials and long stalagmites and stalactites, were visited by Spanish explorer Hernando de Soto.

De Soto Falls

North of Gadsden, Alabama, in DeKalb County. These 100-foot falls were visited by Spanish explorer De Soto and named after him, as were the caverns.

✳ ARIZONA

Ajo

Site of the first commercial copper mine in Arizona, it was founded by Henry Lesinsky in 1855 when he hired Sonoran miners to build and operate the mine and smelter. The open pit can be viewed from a lookout on state Route 85, just past the town of Ajo.

Clifton and Morenci

Sites of copper diggings by Mexican placer miners since the 1860s. Laborers in the copper mines were predominantly Hispanic and were initially subjected to lower wages than those paid to Anglo miners. In 1915, Juan García, R. Rodrigues, Rifino García, and

Adolfo Palacio organized an historic strike against the practice; the result was an end to wage discrimination.

Córdova House

173–177 North Meyer
Tucson, Arizona

This adobe house dates from c. 1750 and is the oldest continuously occupied house in Tucson.

Coronado National Memorial

Hereford, Arizona, 22 miles south of Sierra Vista, five miles from state Route 92 on rural Route 2. This is believed to mark the spot where, in 1540, Spanish explorer Francisco Vásquez de Coronado entered what is today the territory of the United States on his northward search, on behalf of the viceroy of Mexico, for the mythical gold of the Seven Cities of Cíbola. The memorial is on 5,000 acres of land, which provide habitat for many plants and animals. Open daily except major holidays.

Guevavi Mission

Ruins near Tumacacori, Arizona. This was a small mission founded by Father Eusebio Kino in 1692 and abandoned in 1775. The building (probably erected in 1751), is considered the first church erected by Europeans in southern Arizona.

Morenci

See: Clifton and Morenci.

Quiburi

Near Fairbank, Arizona. Site of the Presidio de Santa Cruz de Terrenato established to guard against Apache depredations. It operated from 1775 to 1780. It is also the site of a mission founded by Father Eusebio Kino before 1700.

San Bernardino de Awatobi

In the Painted Desert, east of the Grand Canyon. Visited by Spaniards in 1540 and 1583, the Franciscans founded a Hoi mission here and at four other sites in 1629. All were destroyed in the Rebellion of 1680, although San Bernardino may have functioned until 1700.

San Bernardino Ranch

In Cochise County, 17 miles east of Douglas, Arizona, on the international boundary. Established in 1822 by Ignacio Pérez on the site of a watering hole on the old Spanish military trail, the ranch illustrates the continuity of Spanish and American cattle ranching in the Southwest. Abundant springs made the ranch a stopping place in the era of westward expansion.

San José de Tumacacori Mission

Tumacacori National Monument, Arizona. These are the ruins of the northernmost of the mission chain. It was founded by the Franciscan Father Eusebio Kino in 1696. In 1844, Mexico sold the mission lands to a private citizen and the Tumacacori adobe church subsequently fell into ruins. The national monument, totaling ten acres, was established in 1908.

San Xavier del Bac

San Xavier Road, nine miles southwest of Tucson via Mission Road, Pima County, Arizona (on the Papago Indian reservation). Founded in 1700 by Father Eusebio Kino, it is one of the finest Spanish colonial churches in the United States, having a richly ornamented baroque interior. A good example of Spanish mission architecture, it was completed and consecrated by the Franciscans in 1797. Since 1911, it has been maintained as the primary school and church for the Papago.

Tubac

Tubac Presidio State Park in Tubac, Arizona. The presidio of Tubac was established in 1752 and the Church of Santa Gertrudes in 1754. When Tucson was founded in 1772, the presidio was ordered to move to a new site to protect Tucson and Tubac was virtually deserted and the mission was nearly closed. It survived only to the early 1830s. Museum on-site.

City of Tucson

Founded by Father Garcés in 1776 as the Mission of San José de Tucson, the town was originally surrounded by a high adobe wall to guard against Apache depredations. San José mission stood at the foot of "A" Mountain on the west side of the Santa Cruz River and the presidio was on the east side.

Velasco House

471–477 South Stone
Tucson, Arizona

This was the home of Carlos Ygnacio Velasco, publisher of the Spanish-language newspaper *La Fronteriza* (*The Border Newspaper*) from 1878 to 1914. The house was built in 1878.

✸ CALIFORNIA

Carmel Mission

3080 Río Road
Carmel, Monterey County, California

Also known as the Mission San Carlos Borromeo del Río Carmelo, it was established in 1771 by Father Junípero Serra, who used it as his residence and headquarters until 1784. It became his place of burial. It was the most important of the California missions. The current church dates from 1793 to 1794.

José Castro House

San Juan Bautista State Historic Park
San Benito County, California

Located on the south side of the plaza, it was built in 1840–1841, the adobe structure was owned by the commandant general of the Mexican forces in northern California. On nearby Gabilon Peak, Castro

Carmel Mission.

routed the expedition of John Charles Fremont on March 9, 1846.

Custom House
Maine and Decatur Streets
Monterey, Monterey County, California

Built in 1814, it is the oldest government building in California. It was converted into a lodge in 1848 and opened as a museum in 1930. The custom House Plaza preserves Monterey's heritage as the capital of "Alta California" under Spanish rule.

Elysian Park
Located in Los Angeles, California, this city park is the site of the camp of Don Gaspar de Pórtola and Padre Juan Crespi, who reached the area on August 2, 1769.

Estudillo House
4001 Mason Street
San Diego, California

This 12-room adobe house was built in 1827–1829 by Don José Antonio Estudillo, who eventually became mayor and justice of the peace of San Diego.

Feliciano Canyon
Located near Los Angeles, California. On March 19, 1842, Francisco López discovered gold in profitable quantities here. For the next several years, he worked numerous claims in the area. But his discoveries did not set off the great gold rush.

Flores House
Located in South Pasadena, Los Angeles County. Built c. 1840, it was the site of the withdrawal of the Mexican Army under José Flores after the battle of La Mira in December 1846.

Fort Point National Historic Site
Golden Gate National Recreation Area
San Francisco, California.

This was the site where Juan Bautista de Anza raised the Spanish flag in 1776.

Los Alamos Ranch House
Three miles west of Los Alamos on old U.S. 101, Santa Barbara County. Founded c. 1840, it is a good example of a Spanish Mexican hacienda.

City of Los Angeles
Its formal appellation was "El Pueblo de Nuestra Señora la Reina de los Angeles de Porciúncula" (The Town of Our Lady the Queen of the Angels of Porciúncula). It was founded in 1781, although friars had visited the area and built a chapel there 12 years earlier. Its remaining historic sites in the central area include the Plaza Church (1818) and the Avila House (1818), a typical Hispanic residence of the time, which was the home of the mayor Francisco Avila. It was later used as occupation headquarters by Commander Robert Stockton, and was last surrender to the United States in the Mexican War in 1847.

Monterey Old Town Historic District
Monterey served as the Spanish and Mexican capital of California from 1776 to 1849 and was a center of political, economic, and social activity. There are 43 nineteenth-century adobe structures located in the district, including El Castillo—the fortress built to guard the anchorage in 1794; the Customs House (1828–45); the Presidio Chapel (1790s); and the Casa Alvarado (1836)—home of the poet, revolutionary and governor of California (1836–42), Juan Bautista Alvarado.

Moraga House
Located in Orinda, California, in Contra Costa County, it was built c. 1841 for José Moraga, a descendant of the founder of San Francisco.

New Almadén
Located 14 miles south of San Jose on county Route G8, in Santa Clara County, California, it was the site of the first mercury deposit discovered in North America, in 1824. Mercury from New Almaden's mines was essential to the mining process during the gold rush. The mine town of New Almadén was an early Hispanic population and cultural center.

Peña House
Situated in Vacaville, Solano County, California, it was built in 1842 as the home of Juan Peña, rancher and partner of Juan Manuel Vaca, holder of the 44,000-acre Vaca land grant in this area.

Peralta (Adobe) House
184 West Saint John Street
San José, Santa Clara County, California

The last remaining structure of the San José de Guadalupe Pueblo—the oldest civil settlement and first municipal government in Alta California (established 1777).

Petaluma Adobe State Historic Park

Adobe Road
Petaluma, Sonoma County, California

It was built from c. 1836 to 1846 for General Guadalupe Mariano Vallejo, commandant of the Sonoma Pueblo. The large adobe house served as his home and the hacienda headquarters.

Pico Hotel

430 North Main Street
Los Angeles, California

Constructed in 1859, it was owned and operated by Don Pío Pico, the former governor of Alta California.

Pico House, Mission Hills

1515 San Fernando Mission Boulevard
Mission Hills, Los Angeles County, California

This two-story adobe house was once part of the San Fernando Rey de España Mission. It was sold by the Mexican government in the 1840s to pay for the defense of Alta California against Anglo invaders.

Pico House, Whittier

Located in Whittier, Los Angeles County, California, this was the home of Pío Pico, the last governor of Mexican California, a rancher and a businessman.

The Presidio

Situated on the northern tip of the San Francisco Peninsula on U.S. 101 and Interstate 480 in San Francisco, the fort was established by the Spanish in 1776 to guard the entrance to San Francisco harbor. In 1849, it became the headquarters of the U.S. Army on the Pacific Coast.

La Purísima Concepción Mission State Historic Park

2295 Purisima Road
Lompoc, Santa Barbara County, California 93436
(805) 733–3713

Located four miles east of Lompoc, near the intersection of California 1 and 150. Originally founded in 1787, it was destroyed by an earthquake in 1812. The present buildings are a reconstruction of a second, Franciscan mission, which fell into disrepair after secularization in 1834.

Royal Presidio Chapel, Monterey.

Rancho el Encino

16756 Moorpark Street
Encino, Los Angeles County, California

Located in Los Encinos State Historic Park, this 4,500-acre ranch complex was founded in the 1840s by Don Vicente de la Osa.

Rancho Santa Margarita

Camp Pendelton, Oceanside, California, in San Diego County. This was a home owned by Pío Pico, the last Mexican governor of California. Several buildings and fragments remain.

Royal Presidio Chapel

550 Church Street
Monterey, Monterey County, California

Built in 1789, the chapel was where the royal Spanish governors worshipped and state ceremonies were held. It is the only remaining presidio chapel in California and the sole existing structure of the original Monterey Presidio, now the U.S. Army Language School.

San Carlos Borromeo (del Rio Carvelo) Mission

3080 Río Road
Carmel, Monterey County, California

Founded in 1771 by Father Junípero Serra, it became his place of burial in 1784. The current church dates from 1793–1794.

San Diego de Alcalá Mission Church

10818 San Diego Mission Road
Mission Valley, San Diego, California

Founded in 1769 by Father Junípero Serra and built between 1808 and 1813, it was the first of the 21 California missions.

San Diego Presidio

In Presidio Park, San Diego, California, it is the site of the first permanent European and mestizo settlement on the coast of California. Founded in 1769, it was used as a base for exploratory expeditions into the interior and as the military headquarters for southern California.

San Francisco Bay Discovery Site

Located four miles west of San Bruno via Skyline Drive and Sneath Lane in San Mateo County, California. In 1769, Spanish explorer Gaspar de Pórtola discovered the great inland bay which he named after Saint Francis. The discovery led to the founding of the mission and presidio of San Francisco in 1776.

San Francisco de Asis Mission (Mission Dolores)

16th and Dolores Streets
San Francisco, California

Founded by Father Junípero Serra in 1776, construction began in 1782. Many of the mission's decorations came from Mexico and Spain.

San Francisco de Solano Mission

Located in Sonoma State Historic Park in Sonoma, California, it was the last and most northern of the San Francisco missions to be built (1824), under the direction of Father José Altamira acting in contradiction to government authorities.

San Gabriel Arcángel Mission

Mission and Junípero Serra Drives
San Gabriel, Los Angeles County, California

Founded in 1771, it was operated until 1828; thereafter, it served as a parish church until 1940.

San José Mission

43300 Mission Boulevard
Fremont, Alameda County, California

Established in 1797, the last remaining building is dated c. 1810.

San Francisco de Asís Mission (Mission Dolores).

San Luis Rey de Francia Mission, Oceanside. (Photograph by Henry F. Whitey, 1936.)

San Juan Bautista Mission

Located in San Juan Bautista, San Benito County, California, it was founded in 1797 and finished in 1812. It is the largest of the California missions and is still an active church.

San Juan Bautista Plaza Historic District

In San Juan Bautista, San Benito County, California. It is composed of five buildings, all completed between 1813 and 1874: Plaza Hall, Plaza Stable, Castro House, Plaza Hotel, mission and church.

San Juan Capistrano Mission

Olive Street
San Juan Capistrano, Orange County, California.

Founded on November 1, 1776, by Father Junípero Serra, it was constructed between 1797 and 1806.

San Luis Rey de Francia Mission Church

4050 Mission Avenue
Oceanside, San Diego County, California

Located four miles east of Oceanside on California 76. Founded in 1798 and built between 1811 and 1815, the present building was one of two cruciform mission churches erected in California by the Spanish. Originally named for Louis IX, King of France, it was rededicated in 1893 as a Franciscan college.

San Miguel Arcángel Mission

801 Mission Street
San Miguel, San Luis Obispo County, California

Constructed from 1816 to 1818, this is the third church on the original mission site. Its interior murals were painted by Esteban Munras, aided by Indian assistants.

San Pasqual

Battlefield State Historic Park is located on state Route 78 in San Pasqual, California. It is the site of General Andrés Pico's defeat of General Stephen Watts Kearny on December 6, 1846. A significant battle in the U.S. conquest of California.

Santa Barbara Mission. (Photograph by Henry F. Whitey, 1936.)

Santa Barbara Mission

2201 Laguna Street
Santa Barbara, Santa Barbara County, California

Founded in 1786, it became the Franciscan capital and the seat of the first Spanish bishop. The present church, the fourth on the site, was completed in 1820. This was the only California mission secularized in 1833.

Santa Barbara Presidio

State Historic Park
122–129 East Cañon Perdido
Santa Barbara, Santa Barbara County, California

El Presidio de Santa Barbara was established on April 21, 1782, and was the last presidio built by the Spanish in Alta California.

Vallejo Adobe

Niles Boulevard at Nursery Avenue
Fremont, Alameda County, California

This was the overseer's home, dated 1855, on the estate of José de Jesús Vallejo, the military commander of the Pueblo de San José (1841–1842) and prominent California rancher.

(General) Vallejo House

Third Street, West
Sonoma, Sonoma County, California

Built 1851–1853, it was the house of General Mariano Vallejo, founder of Sonoma.

General Vallejo House. (Photograph by Roger Sturtevant, 1934.)

☀ FLORIDA

Cathedral of St. Augustine

Cathedral Street
Saint Augustine, St. Johns County, Florida

St. Augustine Parish, established in 1594, is the oldest Catholic parish in the United States. The cathedral, first constructed in 1797, is largely a restoration of a church constructed from 1887 to 1888.

Fort San Carlos de Barrancas

Pensacola U.S. Naval Air Station
Pensacola, Florida

Built of earthwork on the beach in 1559 by the Spanish, it was rebuilt of stone in 1696 at its present site. Following the turns of history, it passed from the Spanish to the French to the Spanish to the British and finally it was ceded to the United States in 1821.

Fort San Marcos de Apalche

Situated 18 miles south of Tallahassee on U.S. 319 and Florida 363, St. Marks, Wakulla County. Founded in 1660 by the Spanish, it was captured in 1818 by Andrew Jackson, which facilitated the American acquisition of Florida in 1819.

González-Alvarez House (the Oldest House in the United States

14 St. Francis Street
St. Augustine, St. Johns County, Florida

Built c. 1723, it is a townhouse adapted to Florida's unique climatic conditions. The original one-story structure had *coquina* (broken coral and shell) walls and floors made of tabby (oyster shells mixed with lime).

Plaza Ferdinand VII

South Palafox Street
Pensacola, Escambia County, Florida

It is the site of the formal transfer of Florida from Spain to the United States in 1821. Andrew Jackson, the governor of the territory, officially proclaimed the establishment of the Florida Territory.

St. Augustine Town Plan Historic District

Founded as a Spanish military base in 1565, St. Augustine is the oldest continuously occupied European settlement in the continental United States. Laid out around a central plaza, Plaza de la Constitución, the present streets are all in the original town plan. Additionally, many of the colonial homes and walled gardens have been restored.

San Luis de Apalache

Mission Road
Tallahassee, Leon County, Florida

Located two miles west of Tallahassee on U.S. 90. Founded in 1633 as the administrative center for the Spanish Province of Apalache, it was abandoned in 1702 when Great Britain began the destruction of the Spanish missions in Florida.

☀ GEORGIA

St. Catherines Island

Part of the Sea Islands (the "Golden Isles of Guale") ten miles off the Georgia coast, Liberty County, Georgia, the island was an important Spanish mission center from 1566 to 1684.

☀ LOUISIANA

The Cabildo

Jackson Square
New Orleans, Orleans Parish, Louisiana

Built in 1795, the building originally housed the administrative and legislative council that ruled Spanish Louisiana. The transfer of Louisiana from Spain to France, and the subsequent transfer from France to the United States, both took place in the statehouse in 1803. Now part of the Louisiana State Museum, the structure exhibits the strong influence of Spanish architecture in the territory.

Jackson Square (Place d'Armes)

Located in New Orleans, Orleans Parish, Louisiana, it has been the center of the city since the first plan was drawn up by the Spanish in 1720. Here, in 1803, the American flag was raised for the first time over the newly purchased Louisiana Territory.

Vieux Carré Historic District

Located in New Orleans, Orleans Parish, Louisiana. Known as the "French Quarter," this 85-block district almost coincides with the original city plan laid out by the Spanish in 1721. Despite the name, the architecture is predominately Spanish.

✳ NEW MEXICO

Albuquerque

Located in Bernalillo County, the town was founded in 1706 by Don Francisco Cuervo y Valdés. Old Town is the Spanish center of the city and is a historic zone, telling much about the history of the city through its varied architecture.

Barrio de Analco Historic District

518 Alto Street
Santa Fe, Santa Fe County, New Mexico

This district is unique because it represents a still active, working-class neighborhood of Spanish Colonial heritage that goes back to 1620. The district contains numerous examples of Spanish Pueblo architecture, characterized by the adobe construction indigenous to the Southwest.

Donciano Vigil House

518 Alto Street
Santa Fe, Santa Fe County, New Mexico

The Cabildo in New Orleans.

From 1800 to 1832, this house served as the home of the important political leader Donciano Vigil.

Hawikuh

Located in Valencia County, New Mexico, Hawikuh is a Zuni city and was the largest of the "Cities of Cíbola." It was conquered by Coronado in 1540 and abandoned in 1680.

Las Trampas Historic District

Founded in 1751, the village of Las Trampas, New Mexico, a Spanish-American agricultural community, preserves its eighteenth-century heritage in appearance and culture.

Las Vegas Old Town Plaza

Located in Las Vegas, San Miguel County, New Mexico, the plaza dates from 1835. In 1846, General Stephen Watts Kearny proclaimed New Mexico a U.S. territory here. Once a center of commerce on the Santa Fe Trail, Las Vegas is a modern center of activity.

Laureano Córdova Mill

Located in Vadito, New Mexico, this is a gristmill built c. 1870 in the traditional Mexican fashion, with a horizontal waterwheel; it is the only one of this type still commercially operated in New Mexico.

Mesilla Plaza

Las Cruces

Located two miles south of Las Cruces on New Mexico 28 in Doña Ana County, New Mexico. On July 4, 1854, the American flag was raised over the plaza, confirming the Gadsden Purchase Treaty. The town retains the flavor of a Mexican village. The town was founded by the Spanish in 1598.

"El Morro" National Monument

Located 45 miles southwest of Grants, Valencia County, New Mexico. Site of Inscription Rock, bearing the 1605 graffitto of Juan de Oñate, New Mexico's governor and colonizer. The sandstone mesa was called "El Morro" (or "The Bluff") by the Spanish. Other settlers also carved their inscriptions in the soft rock.

Palace of the Governors

The Plaza
Lincoln and Palace Avenues
Santa Fe, Santa Fe County, New Mexico

Palace of the Governors, Santa Fe.

Originally constructed in 1610–1612, it is the oldest public building in the continental United States. It was used as the territorial capitol and Governor's residence during the Spanish, Mexican and American territorial rules.

San Estevan del Rey Mission Church

On New Mexico 23, Acoma, Valencia County, New Mexico. Constructed from 1629 to 1642, and repaired from 1799 to 1800, San Estevan is an example of Spanish colonial architecture blending a European plan and form with American Indian construction and decorative detail. The mission served the Acoma pueblo.

San Felipe de Neri Church

Old Town Plaza
Albuquerque, Bernalillo County, New Mexico

Founded in 1706, the present building was built in 1793 on the site of the earlier church.

San Francisco de Asís Mission Church

The Plaza
Ranchos de Taos, Taos County, New Mexico

Constructed in c. 1772, it is an example of a New Mexican Spanish colonial church, covered with stuccoed adobe. It was built with exceptionally massive walls.

San Gabriel del Yungue-Ouige

Located four miles north of Española via U.S. 64 and secondary roads in Río Arriba County, New Mexico. The ruins of this Tewa Indian pueblo mark the site of the first Spanish-built capital of New Mexico (1598–1610), established by Juan de Oñate. The capital was removed to Santa Fe in 1610.

San José de Gracia Church

The Plaza
Las Trampas, Taos County, New Mexico

Built from 1760 to 1776, it is one of the best-preserved Spanish Colonial pueblo churches in the state. Its interior features old paintings on the reredos and designs painted under the balcony.

San José de los Jémez Mission

Jémez State Monument
Jémez Springs, San Miguel County, New Mexico

The mission was founded here in 1617 to serve the Pueblo of Giusewa. It was abandoned in 1622 due to Apache depredations.

San Miguel Church

Old Santa Fe Trail and East De Vargas Street
San Miguel of Santa Fe Mission
Santa Fe, Santa Fe County, New Mexico

Built in c. 1636 for the use of Indian slaves and servants, it was almost completely destroyed during the Pueblo Revolt of 1680.

San Miguel Mission, Santa Fe.

Convent of Porta Coeli, San Germán.

San Miguel del Vado Historic District

Located in San José, San Miguel County, New Mexico. Founded in the 1790s as a northern frontier outpost, this is an example of an early Hispanic village.

Santa Fe

Founded by Don Pedro de Peralta in 1610 as a new capital for New Mexico, it was abandoned in 1680 due to the revolt of the Pueblos and re-occupied in 1692. The Fiesta de Santa Fe, held in September, celebrates this reconquest.

Santa Fe Plaza

Founded c. 1610, it was historically the city's commercial and social center and the terminus of the Santa Fe Trail. The Palace of the Governors on the Plaza, was the site of the flag raising in 1846, establishing American rule.

Santuario de Chimayó

Chimayó

Located south of Truchas in Chimayó, Santa Fe County, New Mexico. The sanctuary is a well-preserved, unrestored, small adobe church built in 1816 as an offering of thanks by Don Bernardo Abeyta. Its original wall paintings remain in good condition.

✴ PANAMA CANAL ZONE

Fort San Lorenzo

Near the mouth of the Chagres River on the Atlantic side of the Isthmus of Panama, Panama Canal Zone, the fort was built by Spain between 1597 to 1601 to guard one terminal of the overland route used to avoid the dangerous voyage around Cape Horn.

✴ PUERTO RICO

The Convent of Porta Coeli

Located in San Germán and built in 1530, it is one of the oldest religious structures built by Europeans in all of the Americas. It is the birth place of Santa Rosa de Lima.

La Fortaleza

Located on San Juan Island, San Juan, fort was built by the Spanish between 1533 and 1540, and remodeled and enlarged between 1845 and 1846 as a defense against raids by French and English pirates. It also became the residence of the island's governors.

✴ TEXAS

The Alamo

Alamo Plaza
San Antonio, Bexar County, Texas

Founded by the Spanish in 1718 and built by Franciscans in 1744 as the San Antonio de Valero mission church, it was the site of the 1836 battle between Mexican troops and Texan rebel separatists. The defeat of the Texas rebels here spurred the Texas independence movement. There are two on-site museums.

Camino Real

Located in El Paso, El Paso County, Texas. Because the road was once used by Spanish conquistadors, the "Camino Real" (King's Highway) and "the Old San Antonio Road" were the names given the route connecting settlements on the Rio Grande and the east Texas missions, including Corpus Christi de la Ysleta.

The Alamo, San Antonio.

Chamizal National Monument

700 East Marcial
El Paso, Texas

On the border with Mexico. Locale of the 99-year border dispute between Mexico and the United States. The dispute was settled in 1963.

Concepción Mission

807 Mission Road
San Antonio, Texas

Built from 1731 to 1755 by the Spanish under the leadership of Franciscan friars, it is the best preserved of the Texas missions. The massive church building is designed in Mexican Baroque style, with twin bell towers.

Corpus Christi de la Ysleta Mission

Located in Ysleta, El Paso County, Texas. Established in 1682, the current structure dates from 1744. It has served the Tigua Indians since its founding and adjoins the Tigua Indian Reservation.

Dolores Viejo

On the north bank of the Rio Grande, near Laredo, in Zapata County, Texas. Here are the remains of the oldest Spanish settlement in Texas. It was founded in 1750 by José Vásquez Borrego, lieutenant to José de Escandón.

Espada Aqueduct

San Francisco de la Espada Mission and San Antonio Missions National Historical Park in San Antonio, Bexar County, Texas. Built from 1731 to 1745 by the Spanish, it was once a part of an irrigation system serving five area missions. It is the only remaining Spanish structure of its type in the United States.

José Antonio Navarro House

228 South Laredo Street
San Antonio, Texas

Built c. 1850, it was home to one of two native Texans to sign their names to the 1836 Texas declaration of independence. The house and grounds are now a state historic site.

Laredo (Villa de San Agustin de Laredo)

Laredo, in Webb County, Texas, was founded in 1755 by Tomás Sánchez, an officer of the Royal Army of Spain, the buildings around the old plaza reflect the distinct Spanish/Mexican architectural and cultural heritage. Laredo was also the home to the small stone-and-adobe capitol of the short-lived (1839–1840) Republic of the Rio Grande, which included south Texas and what became three northern states of Mexico.

Los Nogales

Located in Seguin, Guadalupe County, Texas, the house was built prior to 1765 on the Old Spanish Trail. In 1825, it served as a post office operated by Juan Seguín, the Texan freedom-fighter.

Nuestra Señora de la Luz Mission

Located in Wallisville, Chambers County, Texas, the mission and presidio were established in 1756.

Nuestra Señora del Rosario Mission

Established in the 1750s in Goliad County, Texas, it was built to minister to the Karankawan tribes.

Nuestra Señora del Socorro Mission

Moon Road and Farm Road 258
Socorro, Texas

Founded in 1680, the present structure dates from 1840–1848.

Palo Alto Battlefield

Farm Road 511
Brownsville, Texas

Located 6.3 miles north of Brownsville, it is the site of the first of two important Mexican War battles fought in Texas. General Zachary Taylor's victory here in 1846 made the invasion of Mexico possible.

Presidio Nuestra Señora de Loreto de la Bahía

One mile south of Goliad State Park on U.S. 183 in Goliad County, Texas. It was constructed in 1749 to protect the Espíritu Santo de la Bahía Mission. After the 1810 Mexican revolution for independence, its name was changed to Goliad, supposedly an anagram for the patriot of the revolution, (H)idalgo. During the Texas War of Independence, it served as a prison. Execution of the prisoners held there was a rallying point for Texas partisans.

Presidio Saint Louis

Located in Inez, Victoria County, Texas, the fort was established in 1685 by Sieur La Salle's French forces; it was re-founded by Spanish forces from 1722 to 1726 to prevent further French incursions.

Monument honoring the fallen at the Alamo, San Antonio.

Rancho de las Cabras

Located in Floresville, Texas, it is a former stock ranch for the San Francisco de la Espada Mission (established in 1731), which was 30 miles north.

Resaca de la Palma Battlefield

On the north edge of Brownsville on Parades Line Road, Cameron County, Texas. It is the site of the second battle of the Mexican War. On May 9, 1846, the battle involving forces of General Zachary Taylor and the Mexican Army, begun at Palo Alto, continued here. The defeated Mexican force retreated across the Río Grande.

San Antonio

San Antonio, named for the Franciscan mission, San Antonio de Valero, was first settled in 1718 as a way station between the Río Grande and Los Adaes, which was the first capital of Texas. San Antonio developed into an important commercial center and, in 1773, became the capital of Texas. After Mexican independence, it became the headquarters of the lieutenant governor of the state of Coahuila y Tejas. After the war of Texas independence, San Antonio was no longer a political capital, but continued to develop as a commercial center, becoming the most populous city in Texas by the turn of the century. Today, Houston holds that honor.

San Diego

Located in Duval County, Texas. A program was created here for an uprising February 20, 1915, by Mexican Americans along the Mexican border and the creation of a republic, with a possible eventual union with Mexico. The uprising was to be led by the Supreme Revolutionary Congress, which called for the killing of all Anglos over the age of 16, except for the elderly. There was considerable unrest after the plan had been revealed and it led to some Anglo vigilantism against Mexicans. By autumn of 1915, order had been restored.

San Fernando Cathedral

Main Plaza
San Antonio, Bexar County, Texas

It was founded in 1734 by colonists from the Canary Islands, who were sent by King Philip of Spain. The present-day stone church was reconstructed in 1873 after a fire. Alamo heroes are buried here.

San Francisco de la Espada Mission

San Antonio Missions National Historical Park
Espada Road
San Antonio, Bexar County, Texas

Built in the mid-eighteenth century, it was used in 1835 as a fortification against Mexican forces.

San Francisco de los Tejas Mission

Near Weches, Houston County, Texas. Established in March 1690 by Father Massanet to minister to the Caddo Indians and to establish a Spanish presence and ward off French incursions into Texas.

It was the first Spanish mission in Texas. It was abandoned in 1693 after the Indians became hostile. It was re-established in 1716, and in 1721 the Marquis de Aguayo reopened the mission as San Francisco de los Neches a few miles from the original site. Finally, in 1731, the mission was moved to San Antonio and became San Francisco de la Espada. Today, a replica stands on the original site of the San Francisco de los Tejas Mission.

San Jacinto Battleground

Located 22 miles east of Houston on Texas 134 in Harris County, Texas. In 1836, General Sam Houston's forces won the decisive engagement of the Texas Revolution here gaining Texas's independence from Mexico. A heavily monumented Shrine of the Texas Republic now stands on the site.

San José de Palafox

Located 30 miles north of Laredo in Webb County, Texas, are the remains of the Palafox Villa, founded in 1810 by Don Antonio Cordero y Bustamante, Governor of Coahuila, Mexico.

San José y San Miguel de Aguayo Mission. (Photo by Arthur W. Stewart, 1936.)

San José y San Miguel de Aguayo Mission

San Antonio Missions National Historical Park
6539 San Jose Drive
San Antonio, Bexar County, Texas

Founded in 1720, it was one of the most successful and prosperous missions of New Spain. By the time of secularization (1794), it boasted a church, a chapel, Indian quarters, barracks, mill, granary, workshop, and storerooms.

San Juan Capistrano Mission

Olive Street
San Juan Capistrano, Orange County, Texas

Founded on November 1, 1776, by Father Junípero Serra, it was constructed between 1797 and 1806.

San Luis de las Amarillas Presidio

Near Menard, Menard County, Texas. The fort was established in 1758 as a base for Spanish mineral explorations. It was abandoned in 1768.

San Francisco de la Espada Mission, San Antonio.

San Xavier Mission Complex

Located in Rochdale, Texas, is the site of three missions that were later abandoned due to friction between the presidio troops and the missionaries: San Francisco Xavier (1747), San Ildefonso (1749), and Nuestra Señora de la Candelaria (1749).

Socorro Mission

Located in Socorro, El Paso County, Texas, and established in c. 1840, La Purísima Socorro Mission replaced a much earlier mission on this site which had served the Piro, Tano, and Jémez Indians displaced from New Mexico.

Spanish Governor's Palace

105 Military Plaza
San Antonio, Bexar County, Texas

It is the only remaining example in Texas of an aristocratic eighteenth-century Spanish residence. It served as the headquarters for the captain of the presidio.

"La Villita"

Villita Street
San Antonio, Bexar County, Texas

Heart of the original Mexican community, it is made up of a little village of restored houses which now are tourist curio shops.

✳ VIRGIN ISLANDS

Columbus' Landing Site

Located at Salt River Bay, St. Croix Island, this is the earliest site now under the U.S. flag that is associated with Christopher Columbus. The skirmish here with the Carin Indians in 1493 was the first recorded conflict between European explorers and American aborigines.

References

Balseiro, José. *The Hispanic Presence in Florida.* Miami: Seemann Publishers, 1976.

Federal Writers Project. *New Mexico: A Guide to the Colorful State.* New York: Hastings House, 1953.

Forrest, Earle R. *Missions and Pueblas of the Old Southwest.* Cleveland: Arthur H. Clark, 1929.

Johnson, Paul. *Pictorial History of California.* New York: Doubleday, 1970.

National Park Service. *Catalog of National Historic Landmarks.* Washington, D.C.: U.S. Department of the Interior, 1985.

Robinson, W. W. *Los Angeles: A Brief History and Guide.* San Francisco: California Historical Society, 1981.

Welch, June Rayfield. *Historic Sites of Texas.* Dallas: G.L.A. Press, 1972.

Nicolás Kanellos

5

Relations with Spain and Spanish America

❋ Policy Foundations ❋ Developing a Relationship: The Nineteenth Century
❋ A Period of U.S. Dominance: 1903–1954
❋ Suppressing Communism: U.S.-Latin American Relations Since 1954

Because of their colonial experiences, relations between the United States and Latin America began inauspiciously. From the beginning, however, the United States became the dominant player, largely because it had clearly defined foreign policy objectives. As a result, the Latin Americans found themselves responding to U.S. initiatives. Since independence, three distinct time periods characterize inter-American relations. During the nineteenth century each sought its own place in world affairs, but, motivated by similar factors near the end of the century, the United States and Latin America came closer together. During the second time period, from 1903 to 1954, U.S. concern with securing the Panama Canal contributed to its intervention in the internal affairs of the Caribbean nations; its actions increased Latin America's distrust of its northern neighbor. In the final time period, from 1954 to the present, the political leaders in both hemispheres focused their attention on Communist subversion, but in so doing ignored the economic and social disparities that needed to be addressed. As the twenty-first century approaches, the nature of inter-American relations will need to be refocused.

❋ POLICY FOUNDATIONS

From their founding in the sixteenth and seventeenth centuries until U.S. independence in 1783, the British and Spanish New World colonies had little contact with one another. By agreement in 1670, inter-colonial trade required a special license that greatly restricted commerce and led to the development of clandestine trade, particularly between New England and the Caribbean basin region. Beyond this limited commerce there was little interchange and, without it, colonials both north and south knew little about each other.

After 1783, U.S. commercial interests expanded in the Caribbean Basin region. North American merchants took flour, spirits and wine, lumber, iron, shoes, hats, dry goods, and furniture and brought back principally sugar, molasses, brandy, rum, coffee, tobacco, cocoa, and indigo. In this trade, U.S. merchants were often at the mercy of Spanish naval ships sent to intervene on behalf of Madrid's regulations. Looking beyond the Caribbean before 1810, most North Americans anticipated that Latin America would be a marketplace for its eastern manufactures and western agricultural produce.

Also, during the generation following its independence, the United States sought to remove the dangers posed by the presence of the British, French, and Spanish on its borders. The greatest threat came from the Spanish along the southern and western boundaries provided by the 1783 Treaty of Paris.

Like its European neighbors, Spain did not wish the United States to become a strong nation after 1783, nor did Spain want the North Americans to influence its New World colonies. These considerations prompted Spain to contest the generous southern boundary granted the United States at Paris, to stir Indian discontent against U.S. expansion in the old southwest, and to thwart U.S. shipping on the Mississippi River and in the Gulf of Mexico. Part of these difficulties were solved with the Pinckney

Treaty of 1795. But in a weakened position and suspecting that the United States had reached a secret accord with the British in 1794, Spain accepted a diplomatic solution. In the treaty, Spain recognized the 31st parallel as the southern boundary of the United States and granted it free navigation of the Mississippi River with the right of deposit at New Orleans.

Spain's concession did not reduce the U.S. fear that Louisiana and the Floridas might pass to a first-rate European power, specifically Britain or France, either of which could threaten U.S. security, expansion, and prosperity. The U.S. fear became a reality following the 1800 Treaty of San Ildefonso, which provided Napoléon Bonaparte an opportunity to re-establish a French empire in the New World, with an agricultural base in Louisiana and a naval station on Hispaniola in the Caribbean. Haiti's independence in 1802, however, laid waste to Napoléon's plans and made Louisiana expendable. The United States proved to be a willing customer. In 1803, President Thomas Jefferson persuaded a reluctant Congress to pay $15 million to purchase the Louisiana Territory from France in order to expand and secure the nation's western boundary and its use of the Mississippi River.

Still, the Spanish presence in the Floridas made the U.S. southern boundary unsafe. The U.S. efforts to secure the area were piecemeal. In 1804, President Jefferson induced Congress to pass the Mobile Act, which annexed into the Mississippi Territory all navigable waters, rivers, creeks, bays, and inlets that were located within the United States east of the Mississippi River and emptied into the Gulf of Mexico. In 1810, when Spanish authority in west Florida crumbled, President James Madison directed the seizure of the territory between the Mississippi and Perdido Rivers and unsuccessfully urged Spain to temporarily permit the occupation of the remainder of the Floridas in order to prevent its transfer to another power. Congress was more emphatic. In secret session on January 11, 1811, it approved a resolution declaring that the United States could not accept the passing of any part of the Floridas into the hands of a foreign power. It then passed enabling legislation that authorized the president to negotiate with local authorities an agreement that would permit the United States to take custody of east Florida should it be threatened by a foreign power. Known as the "no-transfer resolution," it became a cornerstone of U.S. hemispheric policy.

From 1812 until 1818, the Florida and western boundary questions became peripheral issues to Latin America's independence movements, at which time Great Britain failed to respond to the execution of two of its citizens by General Andrew Jackson during his foray into Florida. The incident served as the final signal that Spain could not obtain European assistance with its New World difficulties and prompted Washington to step up its pressure on Madrid. The result was the 1819 Adams-Onís or Transcontinental Treaty, which granted the remainder of the Floridas to the United States and defined clearly the western boundary of the Louisiana Territory. In return, the United States agreed to pay up to $5 million in claims by U.S. citizens against Spain. With its boundaries secure, the United States increased its interest in Latin America.

By the time of the Adams-Onís Treaty in 1819, Latin America's independence movements had significantly progressed, but the United States had been reluctant to become involved, in part because of the Floridas and in part because of its ignorance about Latin America. The North Americans had little knowledge of Latin America's colonial life or of the independence movements' historical causes. Only a small body of readers were familiar with the few books in English available in the United States during the early nineteenth century. Newspapers and periodicals emphasized the intrigues and complications of the Spanish revolt that Napoléon had stirred in Europe. As a result, U.S. policy evolved only slowly.

On October 22, 1808, Jefferson's cabinet instructed its agents in Cuba and Mexico to express their nation's sympathy with the independence cause, but nothing more. In 1811, motivated by ideological sympathy and commercial prospects, President James Madison appointed consuls to Buenos Aires and Mexico. When the Napoleonic Wars ended in 1815, Madison steered a more neutral course, which did nothing to halt the private assistance that flowed to Latin America from Baltimore and New Orleans. Even the neutrality laws in 1817 and 1818 failed to stem the tide. U.S. public sentiment grew in favor of Latin American independence as émigrés found a sympathetic ear in the newspapers in the eastern U.S. cities. Soon, smaller periodicals throughout the country picked up on the patriotic call against European imperialism. At the same time, Representative Henry Clay of Kentucky began to champion the cause of Latin American independence, paralleling its cause to the lofty ideals of the American Revolution of 1776. Clay engineered a House resolution in 1819 that granted the president authority to send ministers to South American governments that had achieved independence from Spain. Another Clay-sponsored resolution approved by the House in 1820 called for support of Latin

America's independence. The momentum toward recognition culminated on March 8, 1822, when President James Monroe informed Congress that La Plata (Argentina), Chile, Peru, Colombia, and Mexixico[/hid] had sustained independence and were entitled to recognition in order to protect them from European intrigues.

In December 1823 President Monroe, in his annual address to Congress, announced that the Western Hemisphere was off limits to further European expansion and political ideology. Monroe's ideas were not new or novel except for the vague implication that the United States might go to war to defend the Spanish American republics. The Monroe Doctrine expressed the United States' long-standing desire to secure itself from any European threat, but as so often happened in the nineteenth century, U.S. policy was influenced by events in Europe. With the restoration of Ferdinand VII to the Spanish throne in 1823, rumors abounded that a European force would help Spain regain its colonies in the Western Hemisphere. Great Britain, which had placed a heavy financial stake in Latin America's independence movement, wanted no part of any restoration movement and sought a joint declaration to that effect from the United States. Monroe spurned the suggestion and acted alone. In response, the embarrassed British closed their West Indian islands to U.S. merchants for several years. The Latin American leadership gave little credence to Monroe's message because they understood that the British, not the North Americans, had supported their independence movement and possessed a navy second to none.

The United States was not alone regarding Spanish intentions in the New World. Simón Bolívar anticipated a Spanish effort to retake its former New World empire. To meet the challenge and to work together in other common areas of interests, Bolívar envisioned a Latin American League. Toward that end, in 1825 he issued a call for a congress at Panama. Only at the insistence of Colombia, Central America, and Mexico was an invitation extended to the United States. While all shared concern over Spain's intentions, Colombia and Central America appealed to U.S. interests for the preservation of neutral rights on the high seas and its desire for republican governments. President John Quincy Adams immediately expressed interest, but Congress delayed the approval of delegates while it debated (1) concern that any linkage to Latin America would destroy the United States' freedom of action, (2) suspicion that Latin America had already reached a secret agreement with Europe, and (3) fear of Southern congressmen that slavery, already outlawed in Latin America, might be a topic of dis-

cussion. When delegates Richard C. Anderson and John Sergeant were finally appointed, their instructions reaffirmed U.S. opposition to the reestablishment of European colonies in the Western Hemisphere and the transfer of Cuba to a third party, continued commitment to neutral rights on the high seas, and insistence that any transisthmian canal be opened equally to world commerce and be maintained by tolls. While only four Latin American nations sent delegates to the congress, which ended in failure, the arrival of Anderson and Sergeant after the congress had ended only confirmed Latin American suspicion about U.S. indifference toward the Southern Hemisphere.

Throughout this early period, the United States did not have a monopoly on ignorance. Largely because of limited contact with North America during the colonial period and minimal contact after 1776, the Latin American colonials knew little about the United States. In fact, only a few individuals in all of Spanish America had any knowledge of the United States, most of which came to the New World from France in translation. Discussions in Spanish America about U.S. independence focused on Europe, not the revolting colonies. After 1776, a few books dealing with the United States began to filter southward, again mostly via Europe. There is evidence that most of the Spanish American patriots read the Declaration of Independence, federal constitution, and some of Tom Paine's writings. Apparently, works by other U.S. revolutionaries were not read in Spanish America. In short, there was limited knowledge in all of Spanish America about the United States.

Several U.S. agents and consuls, such as Joel Poinsett in Argentina and Chile from 1810 to 1814 and William Shaler in Cuba and Henry M. Brackenridge in Argentina after 1817, often acted as informal cultural emissaries. They also sympathized with the Latin American independence cause. Little is known about the impact that North American mercenaries made when fighting in the armies of Francisco de Miranda, Xavier de Mina, or José Miguel Carrera, and even less is known about the impact made by sailors and merchants who engaged in clandestine trade.

In Latin America, perceptions of the United States varied. Those prone to the Spanish American brand of liberalism looked more favorably upon the United States and its leaders. George Washington, for example, was revered by Ecuadoran Vicente Rocafuerte, Colombian Miguel de Prado, and Argentine Manuel Belgrano. The great liberator Simón Bolívar hoped to be placed in the same pantheon of heroes as Washington, Benjamin Franklin, John Hancock, and John and Sam Adams. Several Spanish American writers, including Rocafuerte, and such travelers as Francisco Miranda, praised the extent of religious, civil, and political freedoms, social equality, literacy, and lack of pomp and ceremony in the United States.

In contrast to the liberals stood the conservatives, who were not convinced that the North American cultural, social, and political institutions were applicable to Spanish Americans. Liberators Bolívar and José San Martin and Colombian statesman José Manuel Restrepo understood that the societies differed and suggested that the federal form of government might not apply to Latin America. In short, the Latin American conservatives feared that any changes in the existing institutions would destroy their orderly world.

When Latin America achieved its independence, it did not have a clearly defined foreign policy. Since the beginning of the nineteenth century, it had focused attention on separation from Spain and the type of government that would replace the Spanish Crown. After independence, the Latin Americans cast about for new friends and found particular solace with the British, who had invested a considerable amount of energy and money in the indepen-

dence movements, which was the primary factor that contributed to Latin America's disdain toward the Monroe Doctrine in 1823. Politically, the liberals and conservatives vied for power and the type of government to be established after independence. There were efforts at a form of federalism adapted to the local cultures, such as the United Provinces of Central America and the Gran Colombia experiment, but during the 1830s, the conservatives held sway and the principles of centralized government with limited participation became the norm across the Southern Hemisphere. Thereafter, until the 1880s, with few exceptions, inter-American relations were unimportant. Europeans, led by the British and followed by the French, Germans, and Dutch, became the beneficiaries of commerce as U.S. consuls and agents across the continent struggled to keep apace.

As the hemispheres drifted apart in the generation following Latin America's independence, the former Spanish colonies struggled to establish stability and new trading partners. The United States engaged in its own struggle for national identity and experienced a surge in social reform, the most important being the slavery issue, and developed an urge

An early rally in East Lower Harlem (El Barrio) in Manhattan in support of the independence of Puerto Rico.

for expansion westward. The latter again brought it into contact with Latin America, this time in the form of a Mexico plagued by political instability.

✳ DEVELOPING A RELATIONSHIP: THE NINETEENTH CENTURY

When the U.S. Senate finally ratified the Adams-Onís treaty, which provided for the acquisition of the Floridas, in 1821, the United States also surrendered its stake in Texas by defining the western boundary of Louisiana. While some western spokesmen, such as Henry Clay, expressed disappointment at the time, the treaty might never have been completed had the United States not yielded on the Texas issue, because the Spanish minister had to show something in exchange for the loss of the Floridas. The loss of Texas did not mean loss of interest. In 1825 and again in 1827, President John Quincy Adams proposed to purchase a portion of the Texas territory. In 1829, President Andrew Jackson made a similar effort, but when his emissary Anthony Butler suggested that $500,000 be used to bribe Mexican officials, the proposal died. Butler's suggestion also infuriated the Mexican government beyond its normal admonishment of U.S. expansionist fever.

In 1821, the Spanish government at Mexico City sowed the seeds for the loss of Texas by granting a huge tract of land to an enterprising Missourian named Austin Moses, with the understanding that he would settle 300 American families on it. Following Austin's death, the actual colonization was begun by his son Stephen. Instead of canceling the contract after its independence, Mexico legalized the pact. By 1835, 14 years after the Austin grant, approximately 30,000 Americans resided in the Texas territory. Friction quickly developed between the newcomers and the Mexicans. The Protestant Americans protested against the requirements to support the Catholic church, to take up Mexican citizenship, and to pay tariffs imposed on goods imported from the United States. Many Texans along the Gulf Coast worried about the precarious status of black slavery, which they deemed essential to their cotton plantations. Finally, the Mexican dictator Santa Ana imposed a centralized government, which the Americans in Texas regarded as a violation of their rights under the 1824 Mexican constitution.

In 1835, the Texans rose in revolt, but Santa Ana led the Mexican forces to brutal victories at the Alamo and Goliad. The massacre of Americans escalated nationalism in the United States, while it gave increased confidence to Santa Ana to drive all the Americans from Texas. Sam Houston's army prevented Santa Ana from achieving his goal. On April 21, 1836, at San Jacinto, Houston routed the Mexicans and forced Santa Ana to sign two vague treaties that ended the conflict and provided for an independent Texas as far as the Rio Grande. Houston's victory was made possible with men and material from the United States, a clear violation of the 1818 neutrality law, contributing to the Mexican government's disavowal of the treaties.

After their independence from Mexico, Texans faced an uphill battle in their desire to be annexed to the United States. The slavery issue impeded the expansionist march. President Jackson understood the impassioned arguments between the pro- and antislavery forces. He also understood that the annexation of Texas might not only split his Democratic party, but also the nation. Thus, he delayed the recognition of Texas until the eve of Martin Van Buren's entry into the White House. The storm passed, and for the next several years the Texas question became a secondary issue as the United States concerned itself with a severe economic downturn.

Infuriated by Washington's failure to annex, the Texans struck an independent course. Plagued by the high cost of maintaining a military to defend the constant threat of Mexican invasion, in 1838 they sent agents to Europe to negotiate treaties of recognition and commerce and to borrow money to develop their economy and build a government. The British, ever anxious to thwart U.S. expansion and in order to safeguard its Caribbean possessions and provide a source of raw cotton for its textile industry, was most receptive. France, not to be outdone by the British, also extended recognition to the Lone Star Republic. The European presence immediately threatened U.S. security and blunted any future expansionist plans.

The issue rested there until the eve of the 1844 presidential contest when President John Tyler submitted an annexation proposal to the Senate. Although the proposal was defeated, Tyler's action threw the issue into the center of the presidential campaign between Henry Clay and James K. Polk. Clay attempted to straddle the issue, but Polk made it clear that he intended to annex Texas (and Oregon). Following Polk's electoral victory, the lame duck incumbent Tyler sought to annex Texas before leaving office. The clever Texans capitalized on the situation, playing British and American interests against each other. Under these conditions Tyler called for a joint resolution, never before used to annex a foreign territory. The House passed the annexation resolution in January 1845, and the Senate a month later. On March 1, 1845, with only three days left in office, Tyler signed the resolution. The annexation resolution so infuriated the Mexicans that its minister in Washington immediately withdrew his credentials and returned home. Several months later the U.S. emissary in Mexico City was obliged to leave. Diplomatic intercourse ceased between Mexico City and Washington.

While attention was focused on Texas, North American traders ventured into New Mexico throughout the first part of the nineteenth century and by the early 1840s became the leading merchants along the northern portion of the Santa Fe Trail, which connected Santa Fe and Albuquerque to Zacatacas and Mexico City. California, whose link to Mexico was tenuous at best, also lured the North Americans. As early as 1835, the Mexican government refused President Jackson's offer of $500,000 for San Francisco and some surrounding areas. Thereafter, hundreds of North Americans migrated to California and, like their Texas brethren in the 1840s, demonstrated contempt for Mexican authority and hinted at a secessionist movement. Other factors increased U.S. interest. A series of treaties in 1843 opened five Chinese ports to international commerce, prompting some New England merchants to call for a U.S. port on the Pacific coast of North America. When British agents appeared in California in the 1840s to promote the territory's annexation to Great Britain, President Polk responded by appointing Thomas O. Larkin as his confidential agent to California to counteract foreign influence. The president also aroused the public against the British by pointing to the Monroe Doctrine.

The expanded U.S. interests in New Mexico and California exacerbated Washington's tenuous relations with Mexico City. Polk sought a favorable diplomatic solution to the growing crisis and dispatched John L. Slidell to Mexico City in 1845 to discuss the claims of U.S. citizens against the Mexican government, the disposition of California, and the Texas boundary. Knowing that the Mexican government was penniless, Slidell carried instructions to settle the Texas boundary at the Rio Grande. In return, the U.S. government would assume its citizens' claims. At most, Slidell was to offer $25 million, if it included California and all intervening territory. The Mexicans refused Slidell when he arrived in their capital on December 6, 1845, and again on January 13, 1846, following the overthrow of the Herrera administration.

Slidell returned to Washington, where he found Polk promoting war against Mexico. But Polk was restrained by his cabinet, which argued that if hostilities were to start, the Mexicans would have to initiate them. Coincidentally, that is what happened. Polk determined to push the issue. He ordered General Zachary Taylor from Corpus Christi, Texas, to move to the Rio Grande, where he threat-ened the town of Matamoros. On April 25, 1846, Taylor reported that Mexican troops had crossed the Rio Grande, attacked his fort, and killed and wounded 16 of his men. The subsequent public anguish and congressional outcry prompted Polk to submit a war message to Congress on May 11, 1845, that summarized 20 years of alleged Mexican offenses against the Americans in Texas. Two days later Congress declared war and appropriated $10 million to cover its costs.

Despite quick victories by Taylor in northern Mexico and General S. W. Kearney in California, the Mexicans refused to capitulate until General Winfield Scott took an expeditionary force from Veracruz to Mexico City, which he captured on September 14, 1847. Accompanying Scott to Mexico City was Minister Plenipotentiary Nicholas Trist, who was to negotiate a settlement, but he was recalled within a month after Scott's victory. The recall notice arrived after Trist had begun negotiations that dragged on to February 2, 1848, when he concluded a peace treaty known as the Treaty of Guadalupe Hidalgo. The treaty met all U.S. objectives at a cost less than the $25 million originally offered. The treaty ceded New Mexico and California to the United States and confirmed the U.S. title to Texas as far south as the Rio Grande. In return, the United States agreed to pay $15 million and assume claims of its citizens up to $3.25 million. The North Americans might have fulfilled their Manifest Destiny, but the event embittered the Mexicans and resulted in charges of U.S. imperialism throughout the remainder of Latin America.

With victory in the Mexican-American War, many North Americans looked as far south as the Central American isthmus in anticipation of an interoceanic canal. Despite a decade-long string of warnings made by U.S. consuls on the isthmus, Washington policymakers expressed surprise in 1848 at the well-entrenched British in the region. British interests in Central America dated to their logging encampments in the 1620s along the ill-defined Mosquito Coast in present-day Belize. Those encampments were secured by a series of agreements with the Spanish Crown in the early 1800s, and the British claimed to inherit them after Central American independence in 1821. Guatemala thought otherwise and unsuccessfully sought U.S. assistance to dislodge the British in 1835. In the 1840s, the British expanded their interests as far south as the San Juan River on the Costa Rican-Nicaraguan border, long the favored site for a transisthmian canal.

Washington's first effort to counter the British came in 1846, when the U.S. chargé d'affaires in Bogotá, Benjamin Bidlack, completed a treaty with

New Granada that granted the United States government and its citizens the right to construct a canal across the isthmus at Panama, provided that the United States guarantee the territory's neutrality and New Granada's sovereignty over it. But Polk hesitated to commit the treaty to the Senate until after the Treaty of Guadalupe Hidalgo was completed. Because the Guadalupe Hidalgo treaty did not contain a provision for canal rights at Tehauntepec, Polk submitted the Bidlack accord instead and the Senate ratified it in March 1848.

Sensing U.S. expansion, the British raised the Union Jack over the Mosquito Territory in June 1848 and claimed a protectorate over the territory under the administration of the governor at Jamaica. To check the British in Central America, Polk dispatched Elijah Hise to the isthmus in June 1848. A year later he returned with a Nicaraguan treaty that granted the United States canal rights along the San Juan River, provided it protect Nicaraguan sovereignty, an indirect reference to the British presence along the Mosquito Coast. Anxious to avoid a debate over an entangling alliance, Polk withheld the treaty from the Senate. But the United States did not alter its strategy with the new administration of Zachary Taylor. He dispatched Ephraim G. Squier to Central America to obtain canal rights for U.S. business interests. Squier quickly reached an agreement with Nicaragua that granted the U.S.-owned (Cornelius Vanderbilt) Atlantic and Pacific Ship and Canal Company exclusive rights along the San Juan River. Squier then moved on to Honduras, where he negotiated a treaty that ceded to the United States Tigre Island in the Gulf of Fonseca, considered to be the western terminus of the Nicaraguan canal. Squier's actions infuriated the British minister in Central America, Frederick Chatfield, who directed the HMS *Gorgon* to the gulf, where he personally led the British troops ashore at Tigre Island. Chatfield's actions were subsequently rebuked because cooler heads prevailed in Washington and London.

In Washington, Secretary of State John M. Clayton recognized that his country's recent diplomatic efforts did not prevent the British or any other power from constructing a canal across the isthmus. At the same time, the British confronted a crisis on the European continent that prompted them to seek an accommodation. Subsequently, Sir Henry Bulwer was dispatched to Washington to work out an agreement. The 1850 Clayton-Bulwer Treaty prevented either nation from constructing a transisthmian canal, but with language deliberately ambiguous that immediately satisfied Washington's desire to curtail British expansion in Central America, while protect-

ing British honor and interests along the ill-defined Mosquito Coast. More significant was the precedent that the treaty set for Central America's tortuous history: during a crisis that involves a foreign power, it usually is settled without Central America's consultation.

In the decade following the Clayton-Bulwer Treaty, Central America remained the focal point of U.S.-Latin American relations. The British slowly extricated themselves from the region, save for the 1859 treaty with Guatemala by which it promised to construct a railroad from the Caribbean coast to Guatemala's interior in return for Guatemala's recognition of a British possession there (Belize). The railroad was never built, provoking a Guatemalan dispute with Belize that has lasted to the present. Meanwhile, the U.S. government did not openly disavow, or even discourage, the attempts of William Walker to establish himself as maximum leader in Nicaragua, from which he planned a Central American confederation under his leadership. Also, during the U.S. Civil War, President Abraham Lincoln proposed the relocation of freed blacks to Central America. Both ventures failed, but they demonstrated the North Americans' lack of sensitivity toward Central America and also served as a basis for the long-standing ill will that the isthmian republics have toward the United States.

In the years immediately after the American Civil War, there was an ebb in inter-American relations. The North American people were more caught up in westward expansion, rapid industrial growth, and Reconstruction in the South than in the possible purchase of the Dominican Republic in 1869 or Mexican border problems in the early 1870s. Even in the 1880s, Secretary of State James G. Blaine received little credit for attempting to serve as an honest broker in the Mexican-Guatemalan border dispute and as a mediator in the War of the Pacific. Both incidents, however, fueled the charges of U.S. interference in Latin America's internal affairs.

These events appeared minor in the context of larger inter-American relations, but not so the Venezuelan boundary dispute that erupted in 1893. The dispute along the Venezuelan border with British Guiana dated to the 1840s, when the British determined a line of demarcation that the Venezuelans refused to accept. The issue was complicated by the discovery of gold in the disputed area, which attracted some 40,000 British subjects that Downing Street felt obliged to protect. A new complication arose in 1895 when the British sent troops to the Bluefields, Nicaragua, to protect its citizens there against the arbitrary rule of José Santos Zelaya. Although the Cleveland administration sided with Zelaya to force out the British, the U.S. press turned the Nicaraguan issue into a question of defending the Monroe Doctrine and made comparisons to the British presence in the disputed Venezuelan territory.

Amidst the jingoism, Cleveland and Secretary of State Richard Olney seized the issue. On July 20, 1895, Olney sent a missive to London reasserting the noncolonial principles of the Monroe Doctrine and demanded that Britain adhere to U.S. arbitration of the dispute. Obviously unimpressed, Lord Salisbury responded with the charge that the Monroe Doctrine was not recognized by international law and that it did not apply to boundary disputes. Not to be outdone, Cleveland asserted that the United States would unilaterally determine the boundary line and would be prepared to defend it. Congress agreed when it approved $100,000 for a boundary commission. Throughout the United States a wave of jingoism followed. Again, Britain was in a vulnerable position, with the rising German power on the European continent and its search for colonies abroad. London backed off and submitted to U.S. arbitration in 1897. When handed down in 1899, the commission's decision favored Venezuela, but was not far out of line with the original British offer. Although the jingoism and public interest had passed, the incident gave recognition to the Monroe Doctrine.

While these issues festered, internal changes in Latin America and the United States brought the two hemispheres closer together by the century's end. In Latin America, liberals returned to the presidential palaces after 1870 and brought with them a desire to modernize their societies. Espousing "positivism," the liberals believed that economic growth and prosperity were essential before true political democracy could take hold. To achieve modernity, these new political leaders directed the construction of modern national capitals replete with theaters, libraries, and universities. As a result, Buenos Aires, Santiago, Guatemala City, and others resembled European cities, but provincial towns remained backwaters. The new political leadership remained obsessed with material development, faith in scientific and technical education, and imitation of U.S. and western European values, but they postponed political democracy. Economically, the liberals focused on the development of an export economy, diversification of agriculture, mining, transportation, communications, and manufacturing. In effect, they opened their doors to foreign investment, but it was the Europeans, primarily the British, not the North Americans, who capitalized on the situation. Argentine beef and wheat, Chilean copper and nitrates, Brazilian sugar and coffee became dependent on the vicissitudes of the world economy. North Americans continued their investments in Cuba and also expanded their interests in Mexico and Central America.

During the latter portion of the nineteenth century, the United States had its own proponents of a larger world policy, such as Albert C. Beveridge, Henry Cabot Lodge, Sr., Alfred T. Mahan, and Theodore Roosevelt. These men advocated that the United States compete with the Europeans in the global economy, construct a two-ocean navy, establish the requisite coaling stations, and build an interoceanic canal. In the diplomatic arena, the leading spokesman was James G. Blaine, who as secretary of state briefly in 1881 and again from 1889 to 1893 advocated an expansion of North American interests in Latin America.

Like Henry Clay, Blaine envisioned a Latin American market awaiting to be tapped. In 1881, he noted the $100 million adverse balance of trade that the United States had with Latin America because the Latin countries shipped large quantities of raw materials to the United States but bought the bulk of their manufactured goods from Europe. Blaine suggested an inter-American conference, but for internal political reasons, Washington did not issue invitations until late 1888. Not until early October 1889 did the delegates of seventeen Latin American nations assemble in Washington to hear Blaine extol the virtues of American industry. Blaine then took his guests on a special 6,000-mile train tour through 41 cities to view giant factories and other mechanical marvels, listen to speeches and brass bands, and witness displays, including the firing of a natural gas well.

The conference failed to achieve Blaine's primary objectives: the creation of an inter-American customs union and the establishment of arbitration machinery. The Latin American delegates were sympathetic to the concept of a customs union, but they thought it impractical and instead favored separate reciprocity treaties. Long-standing mistrust of the United States and mutual jealousies among the Latin American states contributed to defeat the measure to establish an arbitration mechanism. The first inter-American conference resulted in only one tangible achievement: the creation of the agency that came to be called the Pan American Union, which was designed as a clearinghouse for spreading information among the constituent American republics, as well as for encouraging cooperation among them. In 1907, U.S. industrialist Andrew Carnegie donated the money for construction of the building that still houses the Organization of American States (OAS). Despite few tangible results, the 1889 conference momentarily improved inter-American relations.

Blaine moved quickly to capitalize on the reciprocity agreements, asking Congress to give him a free hand in making the necessary arrangements. But the high-tariff Harrison administration was suspicious of attempts to lower trade barriers, and the McKinley Tariff Bill of 1890 was so unsatisfactory to Blaine that he appeared before the Senate committee to forcefully plead for reciprocity. Although he eventually was able to negotiate six such treaties, the Democrats, after returning to power in 1893, reversed the policy to the accompaniment of bitter outcries from the Latin American countries.

While the U.S. Congress continued to debate the nuances of a foreign economic policy after the economic downturn that began in 1893, Cuba came to the center stage of diplomatic interest. Cuba's importance rested with its location at the crossroads of the Caribbean, from which an unfriendly power could bottle up U.S. trade and militarily threaten the U.S. underbelly. U.S. interest in Cuba dated to Thomas Jefferson, who had expressed an interest in acquiring the island. During the wars of Latin American independence, the United States was preoccupied with acquiring the Floridas but was not unhappy that Cuba remained a Spanish colony. In 1823, Secretary of State John Quincy Adams informed the Spanish government that the annexation of Cuba to the United States would be indispensable to the Union's integrity. From then until the Mexican War, the United States remained passive about Cuba.

In 1848, the expansionist-minded President Polk dispatched a special minister to Spain with an offer to pay up to $100 million for the island. But Spain vehemently responded that the island was not for sale at any price. In the 1850s, Cuba again became a focal point of expansion. In anticipation of a congressional imbalance with westward expansion, the Southern slave states looked toward Cuba. Given the Democratic party's Southern proclivity at the time, President Franklin Pierce proposed the purchase of the island for a price of up to $130 million and, if that failed, indicated that the United States would move to detach Cuba from Spanish rule and make the island independent in order to pave the way for annexation. In October 1854, the three U.S. ministers to Europe met at Aix-la-Chapelle, where they affirmed Pierce's proposal. Their declaration, named the Ostend Manifesto, became the object of European vilification of U.S. imperialism and caused Spain to become more recalcitrant than ever in resisting Washington's advance. As the U.S. Civil War approached, Cuba faded into the background.

But events on the island signaled future complications. Many Americans migrated to Cuba and invested in the sugar and tobacco industries, while the Cuban elite developed close ties to the United States. The latter's increased clamor for self-govern-

ment, if not independence, erupted into a war in 1868 that lasted for ten years. During that decade, many North Americans were arrested and executed by Spanish authorities, while others had their properties destroyed for sympathizing with the Cubans. The uprising caused a widespread cry for interference, but Secretary of State Hamilton Fish persuaded Congress not to become involved. When the war ended, the North Americans continued their investment in Cuban agriculture, and the Cuban elite strengthened their informal links to the United States through the large Cuban colony in New York City.

On the island, the spirit of independence did not die. Early in 1895, the Cubans again rose up in rebellion. This time, the insurgents were hardly less ruthless than the Spaniards, who practiced a "scorched earth" policy. The North Americans, who by this time had $50 million invested in Cuba and whose trade totaled some $100 million, were caught in the middle. The insurgents put the torch to U.S. properties in hopes of drawing the North Americans into the fracas, while Cubans in the United States disseminated vicious propaganda about the Spanish. Also, the United States became the center of the rebels' gun-running enterprises.

Madrid decided on harsh measures to quell the insurrection. In 1896, it sent to Cuba General Valeriano Weyler, who rounded up thousands of Cuban men, women, and children in concentration camps. Such barbaric treatment prompted a U.S. congressional resolution calling for recognition of Cuban independence, but national attention was diverted by the 1896 presidential campaign. Following the election of William McKinley, the yellow journalism renewed the call. It portrayed the Spanish atrocities on the island in a most exaggerated fashion. A subsequent change in Spanish government resulted in the recall of Weyler, modification of the reconcentration methods, release of U.S. citizens that were imprisoned, and a grant of partial autonomy to the Cubans. The concessions failed to pacify the island. The Spanish loyalists in Havana rioted in protest of the concessions, while the Cuban nationalists demanded independence. Amidst the tension, the United States dispatched the battleship *Maine* to Havana harbor, hoping to impress both groups. While in port, the *Maine* was ripped by an explosion that took more than 250 lives. Despite cries for reason until an investigation could be completed, the yellow press played into the hands of the Americans already riled at the Spanish.

In the meantime, William Randolph Hearst's *New York Journal* printed a private letter from the Spanish minister in Washington, Dupuy DeLome, that described McKinley as a weak leader. Its publication further irked the public and Congress. Together these events prompted Congress to vote for a declaration of war on March 19, 1898, and appropriate $50 million for its preparations. Nine days later, the Naval Court of Inquiry reported that the *Maine* had been blown up by a submarine mine, leaving the impression that Spain was responsible. The Navy report increased public clamor for some action.

Still, McKinley sought a diplomatic solution. He instructed the U.S. minister in Madrid to determine if Spain would end its reconcentration camps and offer amnesty to the insurgents and accept future U.S. mediation. On April 9, Spain accepted the need for peace but balked at the proposed amnesty. Rather than respond to the Spanish offer, McKinley, caught in the tide of public opinion and its demand for U.S. intervention to liberate Cuba, asked Congress for authority to send troops to the island to bring an end to the hostilities. Congress, also caught up in the war hysteria, passed a four-part resolution on April 19 effectively equivalent to a declaration of war. McKinley approved the resolution on April 29, but stated that war had existed since April 21.

It was not much of a conflict. The war lasted fewer than three months, ending on August 12, 1898. In the subsequent negotiations that led to the Treaty of Paris on December 12, 1898, Spain relinquished her sovereignty over Cuba and opened the door to U.S. tutelage of the island.

In 1898, when President McKinley declared that the nation's objective was to construct a canal under its control, he only reaffirmed his predecessors' proclamations of 30 years. As early as 1869, President Ulysses S. Grant had asserted that a transisthmian canal would be built by the United States. Rutherford B. Hayes repeated the charge 12 years later. Both presidents, like many individuals before them, focused attention on the Nicaraguan route at the San Juan River. Only the attempt by Ferdinand de Lesseps, of Suez Canal fame, momentarily diverted attention to Panama. More important than the location was a round of jingoism it ignited that demanded a U.S.-controlled canal. Writing in the *Nation* in 1881, John A. Kasson warned that U.S. intransigence would permit Europe to turn the Caribbean into another Mediterranean. Although the jingoism subsided after De Lesseps failed in 1881, interest in a transisthmian canal did not.

Since the 1820s, most canal observers and promoters had expected the canal's construction to be a private undertaking. The last such effort was made between 1887 and 1893 by A. G. Menocal's Maritime Canal Company, which spent some $4 million in clearing jungle and doing other preliminary work before collapsing for lack of funding.

In the 1890s, there were increased calls for a U.S.-government canal project. Their position was strengthened by the 98-day trip of the USS *Oregon* from Puget Sound to Cuban waters during the Spanish-American War and the increased call by the business community for access to the Asian and west coast Latin American markets. In addition to the material factors, the expansionists offered an ideological explanation. They pointed to the moral obligation to take western culture to the so-called backward areas of the world. The experience in Cuba reinforced these thoughts, and President McKinley uttered the same to justify the annexation of the Philippines in 1898.

By the century's end, there developed a national demand for an isthmian canal, built, owned, and operated by the U.S. government. What began as a desire to prevent Europeans from building and operating a canal became a national obsession for security and markets and also became a moral crusade. Only the Clayton-Bulwer Treaty stood in the way. The British, suspicious of Germany and experiencing a bogged-down Boer War, were ready to capitulate. The result was the second Hay-Paunceforte Treaty in 1901, which permitted the United States to construct and fortify a transisthmian canal.

That same year the Walker Commission recommended that the United States pursue the Nicaraguan route at an estimated cost of $189 million, as opposed to the $149 million for a route across Panama. The figure did not include the $109 million that the New Panama Canal Company, successor to the De Lesseps company, wanted for its rights and property. In early 1902, the House of Representatives approved the Hepburn bill, putting it on record as favoring the Nicaraguan site. Given this favorable ambiance, Secretary of State John Hay, also an advocate of the Nicaraguan route, and William L. Merry, the minister assigned to both Costa Rica and Nicaragua, commenced negotiations in both Washington and Central America. Like many of their predecessors, Nicaraguan president Zelaya and Costa Rican president Rafael Igesias believed that a canal would bring economic prosperity to their countries. With their hopes raised, the Central Americans signed preliminary protocols that gave the United States the exclusive right to build a canal along their common border and then through Nicaragua.

While Hay and Merry busied themselves, forces favoring the Panama route crystallized, particularly after the New Panama Canal Company dropped its asking price to $40 million. In response, the Walker Commission issued a supplemental report favoring the Panama route, and the Senate Committee on Interoceanic Canals followed suit. At the same time

Hay received a promising proposal from Colombia for the Panama route. The stage was set for a great debate on Capitol Hill. It began in June 1902, and when it ended, the Spooner Amendment to the Hepburn Bill authorized the president to pursue the Panama route first and, only if unsuccessful, to turn to Nicaragua.

The newly elected president, Theodore Roosevelt, was determined to bring the canal project to fruition. Subsequent negotiations resulted in the 1903 Hay-Herrán Treaty. It granted the United States the right to build a canal in a six-mile-wide zone across Panama in return for a $10 million cash payment and an annual subsidy of $250,000. The Colombian senate rejected the treaty but called for new negotiations in the hope of wringing greater financial concessions from the United States.

The displeased North Americans found a willing ally in Panama, where the local citizens resented Bogotá's political domination. The Panamanians also received encouragement from Philippe Bunau-Varilla, who feared losses for the New Panama Canal Company, which he represented. The upshot of this intrigue was a revolt in Panama on November 2, 1903, independence two days later, and U.S. recognition two days after that. Roosevelt did little to conceal his joy for the revolutionary plot, which he at least tacitly encouraged. Bunau-Varilla then negotiated a treaty with Hay in the Waldorf Astoria Hotel in New York City. When completed on November 18, 1903, without Panamanian representation, the Hay-Bunau-Varilla Treaty gave the United States the same privileges as the proposed Hay-Herrán Treaty, except for a ten-mile-wide canal zone.

While Democrats and European leaders criticized Roosevelt's cowboy diplomacy, there was no public outcry against his action. In fact, *Public Opinion* best summarized North American opinion when it wrote that the public "wanted a canal even though this course of action cannot be justified on moral grounds." Latin Americans who had grown impatient with Colombia's dalliance acquiesced to Roosevelt's precipitous diplomacy. While some chastised his questionable tactics, commercial interests generally condemned Colombia, congratulated the Panamanians, and condoned the United States. In Central America, the abrupt change of the canal venue revived latent anti-Americanism. While Costa Rica retreated to its traditional isolationism, the mercurial Nicaraguan president, Zelaya, reacted with a vengeance. He interfered with diplomatic mail, discriminated against North American businessmen, and resisted settling pecuniary claims. The United States did little more than protest until he attempted a Central American union under his leadership.

The selection of Panama also severed U.S.-Colombian friendship. When the Colombians proposed arbitration of their grievance against the United States, the North Americans, long-time advocates of arbitration, demurred. Roosevelt viewed such action as a confession of wrongdoing. Roosevelt's successor, William Howard Taft, made several unsuccessful attempts to placate Colombia, and President Woodrow Wilson sought forgiveness with a 1914 treaty that professed "sincere regret" for the Panama affair and offered $25 million in compensation. But Roosevelt encouraged his fellow Republicans in the Senate to reject the treaty. Finally, in 1921, the William Harding administration dusted off the Wilson treaty and eliminated the "sincere regret" phrase. Colombia accepted the indirect apology and the $25 million.

✳ A PERIOD OF U.S. DOMINANCE: 1903–1954

The acquisition of the Panama Canal Zone marked a major turning point in U.S. relations with the Caribbean region. Under three presidents—Theodore Roosevelt, William Howard Taft, and Woodrow Wilson—the United States actively sought political and financial stability in the region for fear that any instability would threaten the Panama Canal. The navy played an important part in carrying out Washington's assertive Caribbean policies. New facilities were needed to protect regional sea-lanes and the canal. Naval squadrons were upgraded and stood ready to implement Washington's policy. Washington was also motivated by an altruistic crusade to improve the quality of life for the downtrodden and inferior peoples of the Caribbean. At the same time, U.S. businessmen and bankers took advantage of the situation to turn a profit, and in so doing linked themselves to local elites, establishing an informal alliance that sought preservation of the existing social and political system. Although presidential policies differed, the Caribbean region became an American lake by 1920. Because of this, the United States provoked the ire of not only the Caribbean peoples but also all of Latin America.

The character of U.S. policy in the Caribbean was shaped in a large part by the postwar experience in Cuba. Because the Teller Amendment denied the United States the right to annex Cuba after the Spanish-American War, President McKinley, as commander in chief, directed the American presence on the island through Generals John R. Brooke and Leonard Wood. Because Brooke and Wood viewed the Cubans as an inferior people who needed uplifting, they governed them with a paternalistic attitude. With the Panama Canal about to become a reality, Washington determined to protect the island from any foreign intervention. The means came with an amendment to the Army Appropriation Act of 1901 sponsored by Senator Orville Platt of Connecticut. It proscribed postoccupation U.S.-Cuban relations by pledging the republic to a low public debt, preventing it from signing any treaty that impaired U.S. interests, granting the United States intervention rights to protect life, liberty, and property, the right to validate the acts of the military government, and granting the United States the right to construct naval facilities. Before withdrawing from Cuba, U.S. authorities ensured that the Platt Amendment was annexed to the 1901 Cuban constitution and formalized by treaty two years later. Over the next generation, U.S. troops supervised Cuban elections to ensure the peaceful transfer of power. Given the guarantee of security, American investment on the island climbed to $100 million, most of it in tobacco and sugar.

The principles of the Platt Amendment also found their way into the 1903 Hay-Bunau-Varilla Treaty with Panama, which prevented Panama from pursuing an independent foreign policy and incurring excessive foreign debt and granted the United States rights to construct sanitation facilities in the terminal cities and to intervene in Panama to maintain public order. As in Cuba, the marines marched into the Panamanian republic before the decade was out.

In 1904, Roosevelt anticipated new challenges from Europe. In the aftermath of a debt crisis that resulted in an Anglo-German blockade of the Venezuelan coast, The Hague's Court of Permanent Arbitration upheld the right of creditor nations to use force to collect debts from recalcitrant debtor states. In 1903, with the prospect of European creditors intervening in the politically corrupt and financially bankrupt Dominican Republic, Roosevelt had the choice of either accepting European intervention or assuming responsibility for foreign nationals. With the Panama Canal under construction and the assessment that after 100 years of independence, these "incompetent" states would inevitably come under U.S. protection and regulation, Roosevelt chose the latter course. In December 1904, he added a corollary to the Monroe Doctrine, declaring that "chronic wrongdoing" in the Western Hemisphere would force the United States to act as an "international police power." A month later, a protocol with the Dominican Republic provided for the establishment of a U.S.-administered customs receivership by which New York bankers paid off the Dominican debts to Europe and U.S. Marines occupied Dominican customs houses. Part of the money they collected paid off the U.S. bankers, while the remainder was used to improve the island's infrastructure.

In Central America, Roosevelt noted that the inter- and intrastate rivalries and fiscal irresponsibilities that begged European intervention could no longer be tolerated because of their potential threat to the Panama Canal. To ward off the dangers, the Roosevelt administration determined to establish constitutional governments across the isthmus. The opportunity came in 1907 when the machinations of Nicaraguan leader José Santos Zelaya threatened the isthmus with war. In response, Roosevelt and Mexican President Porfirio Díaz called for a general peace conference in Washington. The resultant General Treaty provided for nonrecognition of governments that came to power by coup d'état, banned the Central American governments from interfering in each other's internal affairs, and established the Central American Court of Justice. Roosevelt was pleased with the imposition of constitutional order through a treaty system, but so too were the incumbent Central American leaders, because the treaty system seemed to ensure their terms in office.

Roosevelt's successor, William Howard Taft, entered on a course in Nicaragua that soon became a quagmire from which the United States did not extricate itself until 1933. By 1909, Zelaya had become a hindrance to the American policy of regional stability, and Taft asserted that the United States might support any nation that would force Zelaya's ouster from office. It was the Nicaraguan conservatives who took up the call and, with support from U.S. private interests in the country, ousted Zelaya. As war ensued, Taft sent Thomas C. Dawson to Nicaragua, who worked out a series of agreements that abolished Zelaya's monopolies, established a customs receivership, and created a political arrangement that made liberal Juan B. Estrada president and conservative Adolfo Díaz vice president. Subsequently, the Knox-Castrillo convention put Nicaragua's financial house in order by providing for the refinancing of the country's foreign and domestic debts with a loan from U.S. banking interests secured by a U.S. customs receivership. When the political peace broke down in July, 1912, U.S. Marines were landed to supervise the November election that confirmed Díaz in the presidency. The marines also supervised the 1916 and 1920 elections. To address Nicaragua's financial plight, private bankers advanced loans collateralized by the Nicaraguan national railroad and bank. Nicaragua's financial plight contributed to its acceptance of the Bryan-Chamorro Treaty in 1914. In return for $3 million to pay its creditors, the Nicaraguans granted the United States canal rights in the country, thus securing the route from another canal venture, or at least the sale of the rights to a foreign nation that could then use Nicaragua to threaten U.S. regional security interests. By 1920, Nicaragua had become an American client state.

Taft was not successful in extending "dollar diplomacy" in Honduras or Guatemala. Neither the U.S. Congress nor the Honduran legislature was willing to commit itself to another customs receivership. In Guatemala, President Manuel Estrada Cabrera resisted U.S. pressure for restructuring his nation's foreign debt until 1913, when the British threatened naval intervention. Because the British actions served U.S. interests, the State Department turned its head to this violation of the Monroe Doctrine.

In the first generation of the twentieth century, the most extensive and systematic U.S. intrusion into the internal processes of Caribbean countries came in Haiti and the Dominican Republic. The origins of the Haitian intervention lay in American racial fantasies, economic interests, and strategic requirements. Haiti's independence dated to 1803, but owing to its racial makeup, the United States did not extend recognition until the Civil War. From 1876 to 1910, U.S. Marines landed on eight occasions to protect life and property. An effort was also made to purchase Molé Saint-Nicolas on the island's isolated north coast for a naval coaling station. Despite U.S. disdain for the Haitian blacks, the island's elite lived in a European style, and, in fact, in the first part of the twentieth century the Germans had made significant inroads there. Still, on the eve of intervention, the United States controlled about 60 percent of the republic's import market. For President Woodrow Wilson, the immediate Haitian problems rested with its political turmoil. Haitian presidents were regularly removed forcibly from office and oftentimes assassinated in the process.

By the summer of 1915, the State Department rationalized that some form of intervention was necessary to maintain order and to protect lives and property. The brutal killing of President Guillame Sam and the subsequent threat of revolution became the catalyst to U.S intervention. Admiral William B. Caperton landed bluejackets. Subsequently, the State Department fashioned a treaty that authorized U.S. control of the customs houses, construction of roads and schools, and organization of a constabulary. Under duress, the Haitians accepted the treaty that the North American military implemented, but not without sporadic violence in opposition to its presence. In addition to running the government, the U.S. military administrators demonstrated racism, holding the Haitians to be inferior people.

The origins of the 1916 Dominican occupation lay in the customs receivership established by Theodore Roosevelt in 1905. Financial and political prospects in the republic improved until 1911, when President Ramón Cáceres was assassinated. Subsequently, political rivals vied for office and served in the presidency for short terms, but long enough to loot the treasury. Given this instability, Wilson insisted on new financial and military reforms and that U.S. Marines supervise the 1916 presidential elections. The task fell to General Harry Knapp. He reorganized the government to carry out his reform directives, which included establishing a U.S.-style court system and creating a national guard to act as a local police force. Over time the North Americans modernized the nation's decrepit transportation and communications systems, constructed schools, and carried out fiscal reform. But the countryside remained rich with bandits who continually made life uncomfortable for the North Americans.

Wilson's effort to impose constitutional order took another form in Costa Rica in 1917, when he refused to extend recognition to Costa Rica's Federico Tinoco, who had seized the presidency. Despite appeals from Minor Keith of the United Fruit Company and other U.S. businessmen, authorities in the Panama Canal Zone, and special emissary John Foster Dulles, Wilson refused to budge. He maintained that Tinoco had come to the presidency illegally and was not worthy of recognition. Neither U.S. diplomatic pressure nor the concomitant financial adversity forced Tinoco out, but an unauthorized act by U.S. Naval Commander L. B. Porterfield did. In June 1917, Porterfield took the USS *Castine* to Limón and threatened to land marines. Tinoco feared the worst and resigned. Julio Acosta won the subsequent presidential elections and quickly received U.S. recognition.

Wilson's moralizing was not limited to the smaller states of the Caribbean region. Relations were good with Mexico while Porfirio Díaz ruled for three decades. As a Latin American liberal, Díaz turned Mexico into a safe haven for investment. North American entrepenuers—J. P. Morgan, William Randolph Hearst, James J. Hill, and the Guggenheims—took full advantage of it. By 1913, there were over 500,000 Americans in Mexico, and their investments totaled $1 billion. Despite the outward appearance of order and prosperity, some 15 million Mexicans lived in poverty and were reduced to a state of peonage. Between the poor and the upper class was a growing middle sector that wanted participation in the political process. This group found a leader in Francisco Madero, who led a democratic movement to replace the elderly Díaz in the 1911 presidential sweepstakes. But within two years, Madero was deposed by General Victoriano Huerta, representing the propertied classes. Huerta's action touched off a rebellion by the *caudillos* (chiefs) who represented the rural poor. The Taft administration did respond to the crisis, but the idealistic President Woodrow Wilson determined that nonrecognition would teach the Mexicans to elect a good man. In November 1913, when Huerta refused Wilson's demand that he resign, the United States lifted its arms embargo so that supplies could reach Huerta's two chief opponents, Venustiano Carranza and Francisco "Pancho" Villa. Mexico again plunged into an internal war that wrought much havoc and damage to North American life and property in Mexico.

The hostile atmosphere intensified and on April 9, 1914, a group of U.S. sailors at Tampico were arrested for allegedly violating martial law. Although they were quickly released and an apology was issued, the naval commander there, Admiral Henry T. Mayo, demanded more, and Wilson used the incident to coax congressional approval of U.S. armed intervention. As war seemed inevitable, U.S. investors in Mexico joined with Huerta's political opponents and Latin Americans to protest Wilson's intentions. In face of such opposition, Wilson accepted the ABC powers' (Argentina, Brazil, and Chile) offer to mediate the crisis. Although the Niagara Falls conference met with failure, the Latin American effort prevented another U.S.-Mexican war. Finally, in 1915, Wilson grudgingly extended recognition to the Carranza government, although he still faced the insurrectionist Pancho Villa. When Villa sacked the town of Columbus, New Mexico, on March 9, 1916, killing 17 North Americans, Wilson severed relations and ordered General John J. Pershing to pursue the bandit into Mexico. He never caught up with Villa, but the penetration again brought Mexico and the United States to the brink of war. Events in Europe overtook Wilson, and in February 1917, he ordered Pershing's withdrawal, but confrontation with the Mexican government continued.

The end of the Mexican Revolution brought a new threat to U.S. interests. Carranza's 1917 constitution contained provisions for rural and urban labor and was most anti-Catholic and antiforeign. Most alarming was Article 27, which vested the government with all subsoil properties, including minerals and oil. Carranza declared that this provision was retroactive, a direct threat to U.S. private investment in Mexico. Patient negotiations led to a tacit Mexican government pledge that Article 27 would not be applied retroactively. Satisfied, the United States extended recognition.

The high-water mark of U.S. intervention in Latin America came with the 1923 Central American conference in Washington, D.C. The conference was the product of continued political intrigue that threatened the region with war in August 1922. Still concerned that Central American calamities might spill over into Panama, the United States convened the conference in December 1922. It ended in February 1923 with a series of agreements that more rigidly defined a revolutionary government not worthy of recognition, reiterated promises of not helping revolutionaries, established a new Central American Court, and forced arms limitations. The ink had barely dried on the treaties before the United States again found itself interfering in the internal affairs of Honduras, Nicaragua, El Salvador, and Guatemala. At the same time, currents surfaced that led to a new era in inter-American relations.

In Latin America there was a growing crescendo of opposition to U.S. policies. The Argentines, Brazilians, and Chileans, each viewing themselves as the leader of Latin America, criticized U.S. unilateral actions in the Caribbean. The Central American nations refused to extend the life of the Central American Court after it ruled against the United States over the Bryan-Chamorro Treaty and Washington then ignored the ruling. All of Latin America rushed to join the League of Nations in hopes that it would curtail U.S. domination of the hemisphere. When the United States did not join the world body, the Latin Americans lost interest. Instead, during the 1920s, they used the inter-American conferences at Santiago and Havana to demand U.S. withdrawal from the Caribbean.

Following World War I, the North American public also became tired of conflict and wary of obligations to other governments. It favored withdrawal from world affairs, including staying out of the League of Nations. The war also momentarily ended the European threat to the Caribbean region and weakened its commercial links to Latin America. The decreased European presence contributed to Secretary of State Charles Evans Hughes' belief that inter-American conferences should be gala affairs used to demonstrate harmonious hemispheric relations. The new environment prompted Secretary of Commerce Herbert Hoover to promote withdrawal of U.S. Marines from the several Caribbean countries in order to foster the goodwill that might enhance the North American trading position throughout all of Latin America. The mood change found its way into the 1924 and 1928 platforms of the Democratic party, which condemned intervention, a position repeated by Franklin D. Roosevelt in 1928. Within the State Department there was a growing frustration with U.S. interventions. Successive heads of the Latin American Affairs Division, Francis G. White and Edwin C. Wilson, believed that it was no longer necessary to meddle in the internal affairs of the Latin American states. Others questioned the wisdom of the nonrecognition policy. President-elect Herbert Hoover's goodwill visit to Central and South America in late 1928 was followed by the J. Rueben Clark *Memorandum on the Monroe Doctrine*, which renounced U.S. intervention in Latin American domestic affairs under the terms of the Roosevelt Corollary to the Monroe Doctrine.

In the late 1920s, the public became increasingly frustrated with the continued loss of life in the marines' futile attempt to catch Augusto César Sandino in Nicaragua. The growing forces of change culminated with Roosevelt's 1933 presidential inaugural address, in which he proclaimed the "Good Neighbor" policy. At the 1933 Montevideo and 1936 Buenos Aires Inter-American Conferences, the United States repeated its pledge not to intervene, directly or indirectly, in the domestic affairs of Latin American states. From 1933 to 1954, the State Department only asked that a government control the nation's territory and administrative machinery, have popular support, and be able to meet its international obligations to receive U.S. recognition.

The Good Neighbor policy produced immediate results. The marines were withdrawn from Haiti, the Dominican Republic, and Nicaragua; a new canal treaty was concluded with Panama; the Platt amendment in Cuba was abrogated; and recognition was extended to Jorge Ubico in Guatemala, Maximiliano Hernández Martínez in El Salvador, Tiburcio Carías in Honduras, Anastasio Somoza in Nicaragua, Rafael Trujillo in the Dominican Republic, and Francois Duvalier in Haiti, all of whom illegally extended their presidential terms.

Just as the United States lost interest in its moral crusade in Latin America, changes in the global environment prompted Washington to pursue new policies. For 15 years after Franklin D. Roosevelt announced the Good Neighbor policy, three successive world crises—the Great Depression, World War II, and the onset of the cold war—vaulted the United States into the leadership role in international affairs, and Latin America was incorporated into the larger framework of these global strategies.

The world staggered under economic collapse in 1933. Since 1929, world trade had declined 25 percent in volume and 66 percent in value. During the same period, U.S. trade declined 48 percent in volume and 68 percent in value. Trade with Latin America declined even more drastically: exports dropped 78 percent in value, and imports, 68 percent. The response to the economic calamity was not imaginative. In 1930, the U.S. Congress approved the Hawley-Smoot Tariff Act, which actually increased the cost of foreign imports. Many of the Latin American countries pursued nationalistic policies, including the establishment of a complicated web of monetary devaluations, currency restrictions, higher tariffs, import licensing, exchange controls, quotas, embargoes, and bilateral arrangements with European trading partners. None of these measures stimulated commerce and, in fact, only frustrated it.

Convinced that economic nationalism worsened the depression, Secretary of State Cordell Hull sought to liberalize trade policies in an effort to improve the world's economy and in turn ease world tensions. At home, Hull found a gallery of supporters, including Assistant Secretary of State for Latin American Affairs Adolf A. Berle, Secretary of Commerce Henry A. Wallace, the International Chamber of Commerce, and the American Automobile Association. At the 1933 Montevideo Conference, Hull secured a resolution calling for liberalized trade policies, including the negotiation of reciprocal trade agreements. Congress resisted until June 1934, when it passed the Reciprocal Trade Agreements Act, which provided for the use of the unconditional most-favored-nation clause and the principle of active tariff bargaining. The act also empowered the president to raise or lower tariffs by 50 percent and enabled him to move goods on and off the duty-free list.

Latin America fit neatly into the plan because it did not have a competitive industrial sector, nor did its major exports—flaxseed, cane sugar, cocoa, castor beans, bananas, crude rubber, manganese, bauxite, and platinum—compete with U.S. commodities. In comparison, the United States was in a stronger bargaining position because it could serve as Latin America's chief supplier of manufactured goods, and, given the fact that reciprocal trade agreements favored the principal supplier, tariff negotiations would focus only on those products that constituted the chief source of supply. Because the United States practiced the most-favored-nation principle, it meant that if tariffs were lowered on Brazilian coffee or Guatemalan bananas, the same tariff reductions applied to all other suppliers. In sum, the act placed the State Department in a nonconcessionary negotiating position. Although several agreements were signed with Latin American countries, they failed to break existing trade barriers. Each side contributed to the program's failure. In Washington, the State Department lacked Hull's enthusiasm, while the Latin Americans continued to favor bilateral agreements with the Germans, British, and Japanese. World War II changed that. The world market closed to the Western Hemisphere.

Despite the storm clouds that steadily increased over Europe and Asia during the 1930s, the Latin

Americans did not share the U.S. concern with German, Italian, and, to a lesser degree, Japanese influence in Latin America. The United States first raised the question of hemispheric defense at the Buenos Aires Conference in 1936, when it sought a hemispheric embargo on trade with belligerents. But led by Argentine Foreign Minister Carlos Saavedra Llamas, the Latin Americans accepted only an innocuous agreement to consult when an emergency arose that affected the common defense of the hemisphere.

At the Lima Conference two years later, after Austria and Czechoslovakia had succumbed to Nazi Germany, Spain had come under control of Francisco Franco, and China was engaged in a life-or-death struggle with Japan, the United States still was unable to convince the Latin Americans of the need for mutual defense. While some remained unconvinced of the danger, others charged that Washington was using Germany's aggression in Europe as a backdoor entrance to their internal affairs. Thus, the Latin Americans approved only the establishment of consultative machinery to respond to the threat of any extra-hemispheric threat. The Latin Americans still remained hesitant after Hitler's invasion of Poland in September 1939 and the subsequent outbreak of total war. Not until the fall of France in 1940 did the Latin Americans agree to the U.S.-enforced 300-mile-wide security belt around the hemisphere. They also accepted a U.S. proposal to occupy European colonies in the Western Hemisphere in order to save them from the Axis powers, and they approved a series of measures to combat fifth-column activities in their countries.

Given Latin America's lack of interest and preparedness, the United States acted alone. Its military planners drew their line of defense at a line north of the equator to secure the Caribbean and Panama Canal. With Europe engulfed in war, the United States became determined to establish military missions in each Latin American country to improve the hemisphere's defense capabilities. The 1940 Uruguayan pact became the model. It provided for U.S. funds to construct facilities that remained under the host country's control, but open to the use of all hemispheric nations engaged in the common defense. To carry out military assistance and the construction of defense sites, Latin America was included in the Lend-Lease Act approved by Congress in March 1941. Some $400 million was allocated to Latin America over a three-year period, but only $171.7 million was delivered through May 1945, one month after the European war theater closed. The military assistance emphasized the strengthening of the southern defenses, particularly of the Caribbean and Brazil, and the development and protection of vital military and supply routes by air and water.

Not all Latin American governments quickly joined the Allied cause. Immediately after the Pearl Harbor attack, the five Central American countries, Cuba, and the Dominican Republic declared war on the Axis powers. By March 1942, all but Chile and Argentina had at least severed relations with the Axis countries. Chile demurred, owing to its long, defenseless, coastline. In Argentina, pro-Fascist military officers dominated politics, and they refused to bow to American pressure. Throughout the war, the Latin American nations, save Argentina and Chile, cooperated in stamping out Axis (particularly Nazi) influence by exploiting essential raw materials and by producing war goods for the Allied cause. Brazil, Colombia, Mexico, and Venezuela benefited the most, and the Caribbean and Central American states the least. In fact, Mexico's postwar industrial boom was jump-started by the infusion of U.S. capital during the war. Finally, in 1943, the Chileans succumbed to U.S. pressure and broke relations with the Axis powers. Argentina held out until the inter-American conference at Mexico City in 1945, when a deal was struck to permit its entrance into the United Nations. But Washington's distaste for Argentina's pro-Fascist military leaders prompted Ambassador Spruille Braden to labor unsuccessfully against the election of Juan Perón in 1945. The affair served to embitter U.S.-Argentine relations for some time.

Unfortunately for the Latin Americans, Washington made no plans for postwar economic adjustment. Wartime contracts and subsidies were abruptly canceled. Despite pleas from Latin American political leaders, Washington neglected to address the economic and social dislocations, in contradistinction to what it did with the European Recovery Program (popularly known as the Marshall Plan). Instead, the United States focused on incorporating Latin America into its cold war containment policies, which anticipated Soviet-inspired global expansion. By the Act of Chapultepec, signed in Mexico City in 1945, the American republics agreed to consult before responding to aggressive acts upon any hemispheric nation. Two years later, at Rio de Janeiro, the United States and Latin America agreed, in accordance with individual constitutional requirements, to act jointly in case of an external attack upon one nation. At Bogotá in 1948, the Inter-American Defense Board was established and charged with developing hemispheric defense plans. Finally, in 1951, following six years of debate, the U.S. Congress approved the Mutual Security Act, which initially appropriated $38 million for direct military assistance to Latin America for its participation in hemispheric defense. Through these measures, the United States sought to secure the Western Hemisphere from an external attack, something Washington policymakers considered most remote.

During the same period, 1945–1951, administration spokesmen—Secretaries of State George C. Marshall and Dean Acheson and Assistant Secretary of State for Latin American Affairs Edward G. Miller—continued to espouse traditional themes regarding inter-American relations: pleas for political stability and faith in democracy and promises of nonintervention in Latin America's internal affairs. While preaching such lofty ideals, the United States ignored many Latin Americans' demands for an end to dictatorship and an improvement in the quality of life for the less fortunate. Washington focused its attention on the Communist threat in Europe and Asia.

✳ SUPPRESSING COMMUNISM: U.S.-LATIN AMERICAN RELATIONS SINCE 1954

In the immediate postwar years, U.S. policymakers were quick to compare demands for political and social change in Latin America with the activities of Communist movements in Europe and Asia. For example, during the 1948 Bogotá conference, when Colombia was wreaked by violence, Secretary of State George C. Marshall placed responsibility with the Communists and cautioned that all of Latin America could be victimized. In reality, the violence stemmed from local political passions. That same year, Washington officials did not fully comprehend the nationalistic inclinations of the Costa Rican Civil War, in which José Figueres declared that he had saved the country from communism.

The most striking example of confusing the Communist-nationalist issue came in Guatemala in 1954. Historically, Guatemala's political history had been dominated by strong rulers with the support of the landed elite. At the beginning of the twentieth century, the United Fruit Company (UFCO) was formed and emerged as the dominant economic force in the country. Over time, UFCO and its leaders developed an informal alliance with the elite that prevented the lower socioeconomic groups from advancing economically and socially and denied them political and civil rights. The liberal accomplishments by 1920 and the management opportunities created by UFCO contributed to the development of a broad-based middle sector, which, influenced by U.S. democratic propaganda during World War II, forced the ouster of the last liberal dictator, Jorge Ubico, in 1944. At first, the democratic election of Juan José Arévalo appeared as a triumph for the

middle sector. Arévalo's "spiritual socialism," however, promised economic and social justice for the lower classes at the expense of the elite and the middle sector, prompting the latter to distance themselves from Arévalo. Given this vacuum, Arévalo brought local Communists into government positions. In 1950, when the presidential sash passed to Jacobo Arbenz, Guatemala's leftward political drift accelerated and the alleged influence of Communists in government increased. Arbenz's determination to implement a land reform program that called for the redistribution of idle lands held by the Guatemalan elite and UFCO proved to be his downfall.

Arbenz's actions came at a time when the United States was whipped into an anti-Communist hysteria by the Soviet victories in Europe, the fall of China to Mao Tse-tung, the stalemate in Korea, the anti-Communist moral crusade of President Dwight D. Eisenhower and Secretary of State John Foster Dulles, and the trauma of Senator Joseph McCarthy's Communist witch-hunt. In 1953, Milton Eisenhower and the Commission on Foreign Economic Policy recommended policy changes that gave hope for new directions in Latin American relations. Instead, the president accepted the advice of his closest advisers, businessmen who looked at the world as something that could be managed and who were advocates of private enterprise in a world increasingly turning toward revolution and socialism. Assistant Secretaries of State for Latin American Affairs John M. Cabot, Henry F. Holland, and Roy R. Rubottom echoed similar thoughts. Thus, the United States advised Latin American countries to create an environment conducive to private investment, and, if that was accomplished, the United States would provide funds for the necessary infrastructure.

Compatible with this approach, Secretary Dulles' strident anti-Communist campaign applied to Latin America. According to Dulles, communism, or anything that resembled it, was a threat to U.S. interests. Communists, however identified, were linked to the Soviet Union and viewed as agents of the international Communist conspiracy against the United States. In Guatemala, the Arbenz reform program paralleled what the Communists had done in Eastern Europe and on mainland China. Thus, at the tenth Inter-American Conference meeting in Caracas, Venezuela, in March 1954, Dulles warned that the hemisphere was imperiled by international communism. In response, the Guatemalan representative, Guillermo Toriello, charged that U.S. economic imperialism was responsible for the hemisphere's social and economic injustices. After a spirited debate, the conference adopted a U.S.-sponsored resolution asserting that any hemispheric nation subjected to Communist political control was considered suffering from foreign intervention and a threat to the peace of the Americas. As such, decisive collective action was called for, presumably under the terms of the 1947 Rio Treaty. What the delegates did not know was that the United States had already begun to plan the overthrow of Arbenz.

Without evidence of a clear link to Moscow, the Eisenhower administration began to plot the overthrow of Arbenz in the early summer of 1953. The Central Intelligence Agency (CIA) trained a ragtag army of about 300 men under Colonel Castillo Armas in Honduras and Nicaragua, while at the same time conducting a propaganda campaign inside Guatemala to convince Arbenz that the rebel force was much larger. A shipment of Czechoslovakian small arms to the Arbenz regime on June 18, 1954, became the trigger to action. That same day, Castillo Armas entered Guatemala from Honduras with 150 men, and the U.S. embassy in Guatemala City was turned into an operations center. From the embassy, Ambassador John Puerifoy directed the air assault, and the CIA jammed the Guatemalan airwaves with its own reports of a purported massive invasion by an army of liberation. At the same time, the State Department successfully worked to keep the United Nations and the Organization of American States from intervening in the affair. Arbenz succumbed on June 27 and fled the country. An interim government served until the September presidential election of Castillo Armas. In effect, the United States prevented the advance of the alleged international Communist movement from the Western Hemisphere.

The Latin American nations heaped an avalanche of criticism on the United States for its singlehanded intervention in the domestic affairs of an American republic. But these same governments also maintained that deep-rooted economic and social problems, not communism, threatened their political fabric. Yet, neither U.S. foreign policy nor Latin American domestic policies were aimed at correcting those disparities. Before the decade was out, these issues again surfaced in Cuba.

Throughout the 1950s, the Eisenhower administration indiscriminately granted military assistance to governments that demonstrated a favorable attitude toward the United States and expressed opposition to communism. Such actions contributed to the charge that the United States supported right-wing dictatorships that gave the illusion of stability in Latin America. That illusion was shattered in 1958 during Vice President Richard Nixon's eight-nation goodwill tour of Latin America. Early on, he encountered student demonstrators protesting alleged U.S.

economic imperialism and support of repressive governments. But in Caracas, Venezuela, violence threatened his life. In response, Eisenhower put marines and paratroopers on alert as Nixon sought refuge in the U.S. embassy until the Venezuelan military gained control of the civilian disorders. Without proof, Eisenhower, Dulles, and his brother Allen (head of the CIA) publicly charged that local Communists at Moscow's direction instigated the riots. Privately, they admitted that they had no evidence of a Moscow connection. For the Latin American governments, Eisenhower's preparedness for military intervention gave recall to gunboat diplomacy.

Of greater significance was the rise of Fidel Castro to power in Cuba. Since Cuban independence in 1898, the connection between Cuba and the United States had tightened. North American investment on the island multiplied so much that U.S. private enterprise dominated the sugar industry, transportation, tourism, and the illegal operations in gambling, prostitution, and the like. The privileged position of the Cuban elite also depended on the North American presence. Ever since the "Sergeants Revolt" in 1933, Fulgencio Batista had increased his hold on the country's political apparatus. He controlled presidential elections, dismissed the national congress at will, and brutally suppressed political opposition. In so doing, Batista constructed a powder keg in which both the lower and middle sectors had reason to displace him. They found their catalyst to change in Fidel Castro, a young lawyer who in the early 1950s protested against Batista's political tyranny. Exiled for such activities in 1953, Castro went to Mexico, where he built a rebel force that returned to the island in 1956 to conduct a guerrilla war against Batista. With safe haven provided by the rural poor in the mountains and with financial support from the middle sector for the purchase of arms and other supplies, Castro successfully chipped away at Batista's power until January 1, 1959, when the dictator fled the country and Castro marched into the capital. For the moment, most Cubans and North Americans were happy with the change.

Over the next year, however, Castro moved to consolidate his hold on the nation. He slowly eliminated his political opposition, confiscated property (including North American-owned firms), and implemented social programs that benefited only the poor. Given these conditions, Cuban elites, fearing the loss of all their wealth, and the middle sector became disillusioned at the loss of democracy and fled the island. The Eisenhower administration fretted over the drift leftward and Castro's failure to compensate the North American companies. When Castro demanded a drastic reduction in the size of the U.S.

embassy staff in Havana, Eisenhower imposed a trade embargo against Cuba in hopes that Castro would conform to U.S. wishes. But Castro did not bend, and, in fact, spoke of spreading his revolution elsewhere in the Americas. Near the end of the Eisenhower administration, the president gave his approval for yet another CIA plot. Cuban exiles were assembled in Guatemala and Nicaragua to prepare for an invasion of their homeland.

The invasion of Cuba was left for President-elect John F. Kennedy. When the invasion began at the Bay of Pigs in April 1961, there were hopes that the people within Cuba would rise against Castro and, in combination with the invading brigade, force Castro out of power. But when the plan went awry, Kennedy called off badly needed air cover, leaving the Cuban exiles at Castro's mercy. The Bay of Pigs invasion marked a key turning point in Castro's career. Isolated in the Western Hemisphere, Castro found the essential economic support in Moscow that shortly made Cuba a Soviet client state. In 1962, Khrushchev decided to test the long-standing U.S. defense perimeter in the Caribbean region. He not only introduced Soviet troops to the island but also directed the construction of surface-to-air missile (SAM) sites. At first, the Kennedy administration dismissed the construction reports that came from the exiled Cuban community in the United States because it was the same group that promised an internal uprising at the Bay of Pigs. But when U.S. intelligence planes confirmed the reports, Kennedy quickly acted. He imposed a quarantine on the introduction of offensive weapons into Cuba and clearly indicated that it would be enforced. For 13 days in October 1962, the world appeared poised on the brink of nuclear war between the superpowers before Khrushchev backed off. A subsequent agreement provided the removal of the Soviet missiles from Cuba in return for a promise that the United States would not support an invasion of the island.

In the aftermath of Kennedy's death, the United States determined that economic coercion would ruin Cuba and destroy Castro. The U.S. economic blockade of Cuba became hemispheric policy, and in July 1964 at an Organization of American States (OAS) foreign ministers' meeting in Washington, the delegates voted to sever diplomatic and commercial relations with Cuba, except in food and medicine, and to impose restrictions on travel to Cuba. The Latin American governments went along with U.S. policy because many of them feared a similar revolution themselves.

Nixon's nearly disastrous trip and Castro's success ignited a policy change for the United States, and in Latin America the elite momentarily became more responsive to the need for economic and social change. Late in the Eisenhower administration, Secretary of Treasury C. Douglas Dillon convinced the president to propose the establishment of a hemispheric social progress fund, which Congress subsequently approved. In September 1960, Dillon announced at an OAS meeting a $500 million Social Progress Trust Fund to provide "soft" loans for housing, land settlement and use, water supply, sanitation, and similar social purposes. John F. Kennedy went a step further during the 1960 presidential campaign when he asserted that a joint effort was needed to develop the hemispheric resources, strengthen the democratic forces, and improve the vocational and educational opportunities of every person in the Americas. Kennedy intended to foster a social revolution within a democratic framework by appealing to the lower and middle social groups.

At the White House, before the Latin American diplomatic corps on March 13, 1961—during the same week that 139 years before President James Monroe had urged U.S. recognition of Latin American independence—President John F. Kennedy announced the Alliance for Progress, an ambitious $100 billion, ten-year program to bring political reform and social and economic progress to the Southern Hemisphere. As expressed in the Charter of Punte del Este, the alliance called for 2.5 percent annual economic growth rate, a more equitable distribution of national wealth, trade diversification, emphasis on industrialization, greater agricultural productivity, an end to illiteracy, agrarian reform, increased life expectancy, public housing for the poor, stable price levels, tax reform, and economic development. All these were to be carried out within the processes of political democracy. The alliance failed to achieve its lofty goals, in part because the Latin American elites that controlled the government apparatus resisted social change, tax reform, and democratization, and in part, because the United States lost its idealism as the quagmire in Vietnam and domestic violence engulfed its energies. By 1971, there were few signs of improvement in the quality of life for the masses, and most of the Latin American governments had come under military control.

Despite Kennedy's idealism, he did not lose sight of the Communist military threat. From 1945 to 1961, U.S. military assistance programs to Latin America focused on the prevention of an external attack, security of the Panama Canal and Caribbean sea-lanes, and Mexican and Venezuelan oil. Kennedy altered the emphasis to a concentration on internal aggression. The 1961 Military Assistance Program demonstrated the new emphasis by replacing heavy equipment with mobile light equipment and training troops in counterinsurgency. In its broadest sense, counterinsurgency included a wide range of economic, political, social, psychological, and military activities utilizing several U.S. government agencies. For example, the Agency for International Development (AID) was charged with responsibility for economic programs, and its Office of Public Safety with the training of police forces in interrogation and riot control. The United States Information Agency (USIA) worked with governments to improve the U.S. image both at home and abroad. The CIA engaged in intelligence, covert, and paramilitary activities. U.S. military missions provided training, advice, and supplies to the local armed forces. Emphasis was placed on "civic action" programs that were intended to stimulate counterinsurgency, nation building, and economic development by improving the image of the local military, which would now undertake the construction of bridges, hospitals, and schools, serve as medics for rural civilians, and clear jungle terrain for establishment of small farms. By the time of Kennedy's death, however, it became apparent that the counterinsurgency program had lost its idealistic direction. The military began to assert its independence as it often moved against the non-Communist Left. This was most vivid in Guatemala, where the army turned on rural Indian villages and by the 1970s brought the warfare to the capital at Guatemala City.

As other events demanded more U.S. attention, Presidents Lyndon B. Johnson, Richard M. Nixon, and Gerald R. Ford gave little attention to Latin American affairs, except for isolated incidents of alleged Communist expansion. In March 1964, Johnson signaled his policy change with the appointment of Thomas C. Mann as assistant secretary of state for Latin American affairs. Mann explained that the United States would give greater attention to its own security interests, its investments, and its desire to thwart communism in the hemisphere rather than attempt to promote democracy. Nixon entered the White House in 1969 without a clearly defined Latin American policy. Despite warnings that U.S. military assistance programs had contributed to the increased political role of the military in Latin American politics, Nixon, motivated by profit, not constitutionalism, obtained congressional approval to increase arms sales to the region. In 1974, Ford ignored the recommendation of a 23-member commission that the United States deemphasize hemispheric security as an issue of primary consideration and place greater attention on political and economic relations. Two events, one during Johnson's administration and the other under Nixon, clearly reflected the policy's determinant factor.

Following the assassination of Dominican Republic strongman Rafael Trujillo in 1961, the country was administered by Juan Bosch. In the spirit of the newfound freedom, Bosch permitted the Communists to organize in hope of preventing them from mounting a guerrilla war. Washington opposed the co-opting; and so too did the Dominican generals who ousted Bosch in 1963. The generals installed a triumvirate headed by Donald Reid Cabral. His subsequent austerity measures satisfied Washington's foreign economic policies, but not the Dominican business and professional leaders and the country's socially conscious elements. Soon strikes and demonstrations disrupted the nation. In this environment, a group of younger officers called for the restoration of constitutional order and looked to Bosch as their leader. When they ousted Reid Cabral in April 1965 and announced Bosch's imminent return, Washington officials and the old-line generals feared that Bosch would permit a Communist takeover of the country. In this tense atmosphere, the competing factions exchanged gunfire, prompting President Johnson to dispatch marines, ostensibly to protect U.S. lives and property, but in Johnson's mind to prevent another Cuba. Johnson justified his actions on the grounds, subsequently learned to be exaggerated, that the Communists had already infiltrated the revolution. The unilateral action brought a storm of protest from the Latin American nations. Even the subsequent placement of an Organization of American States (OAS) peacekeeping force in the country did not stem the protest. Eventually, an election was arranged, and Joaquín Balaguer was chosen to guide the U.S.-controlled democratic experiment.

The Dominican experience owed much to the end of the Trujillo regime, but the Chilean experience was quite different. With a long history of political democracy, the system had evolved into coalition politics after World War II, effectively negating the government's opportunity to implement necessary social reform for the urban and rural poor. This void provided the opportunity for a popular coalition front, FRAP, led by a self-proclaimed Marxist, Salvador Allende, to make inroads. As the country stagnated in the late 1950s and early 1960s, Allende's popularity increased. He nearly captured the 1964 presidential contest. Six years later he did, becoming the first freely elected Marxist head of state in Latin America. In Richard Nixon's view, Allende's victory not only threatened U.S. interests in Chile but also served as a symbolic challenge to U.S. political stature elsewhere on the continent.

Allende intended to socialize the economy. He began by nationalizing, without compensation, the largest symbol of U.S. presence in the country, the copper industries. Subsequently, the government intervened in other segments of the foreign-dominated economy. In an appeal to labor, Allende froze prices and decreed hefty wage increases. He implemented an agrarian reform program. Subsequently, he attempted to change the national legislature to one that represented the masses rather than the elite. Such programs prompted wholesale opposition from the foreign-owned companies, the Chilean landowners, the middle sector, and eventually the workers themselves, who could not keep up with inflationary prices for scarce goods. Allende did not help his own image when he invited Fidel Castro to visit Cuba and when he reached a barter trade agreement with mainland China. Nixon's policies exacerbated the situation. He severed U.S trade relations, forbade private bank loans, and used U.S. influence to prevent financial arrangements with the Inter-American and World Banks. Soon the country was beset by political protest, labor discord, and a general strike that led to Allende's ouster by the military in September 1973. In the violence of the coup, Allende lost his life. While the evidence to date does not support the argument that the Nixon administration played a direct role in Allende's overthrow, the administration's policies contributed to the worsening economic conditions that led to the overthrow.

Augusto Pinochet's repressive government in Chile paralleled the experiences of several other Latin American countries in the 1970s and 1980s. Brutal authoritarian regimes were found in Argentina, Brazil, Peru, and El Salvador. In its anxiety to rid their nations of Communists, the military arrested, tortured, exiled, and killed thousands of individuals on the slightest suspicion. Political and civil rights were denied. The U.S. Congress quickly responded to these violations. Provisions in the 1973 Foreign Assistance Act, 1975 Food Assistance Act, and 1976 Security Assistance Act authorized the withholding of aid wherever human rights violations existed. No action was taken, however, until Jimmy Carter moved into the White House in January 1977. He brought with him a commitment to the improvement of human rights not found among his immediate predecessors. Through his assistant secretary of state for Latin American affairs, Terence A. Toddman, Carter made it clear that future U.S assistance would be contingent on improvement in human rights conditions. Subsequently, the administration singled out Argentina, Brazil, Chile, El Salvador, and Guatemala for aid cutoffs. Unfortunately, the aid cutoff did not prevent those governments from securing military assistance elsewhere.

Carter also came to the presidency promising a new era in U.S.-Latin American relations. His intense efforts on behalf of the new canal treaties with Panama in 1977 dramatized that effort. The canal symbolized the highest form of U.S. imperialism in the hemisphere. The Canal Zone, which divided the nation, resembled U.S. suburbia and contrasted greatly with the poverty and injustice that characterized life for most Panamanians. The 1977 treaties provided for turning the canal operation over to Panama in the year 2000. While Latin Americans applauded Carter's work, the treaties deeply divided North Americans. Before the Senate's ratification of the accords, a prolonged debate gripped the nation. Carter's supporters argued that the canal could no longer be defended and that it was of decreased economic and military importance. His opponents viewed the treaties as a sign of weakness, the surrender of a U.S.-owned canal and concomitant rights. The critics incorrectly asserted that the United States owned the Canal Zone even though the 1903 Hay-Herrán Treaty never granted ownership.

If Carter offered new hope to Latin Americans at the start of his administration, he faced a crisis of the old order in Central America before it ended. In Nicaragua and El Salvador leftist guerrilla movements—the Sandinista National Liberation Front and the Farabundo Martí National Liberation Front (FMLN)—had gained much strength in the 1970s. In Nicaragua they challenged Anastasio Somoza, whose family power dated to the 1930s, and in El Salvador the infamous "14 families," who dominated the nation's economic, political, and social structures. At first, Carter expressed a degree of sympathy toward these movements, as they appeared to address the needs of the downtrodden. He resisted Somoza's appeal for support, and only near the end, in May and June 1979, did Carter attempt to broker a settlement. He was too late. Once in power, the Sandinistas moved leftward on the political scale. In actions parallel to Castro in Cuba and Allende in Chile, the Sandinistas nationalized properties, dictated economic policies for the private sector, opened trade with Eastern Europe, curtailed civil rights, and stymied political opposition. His idealism shattered, Carter directed the funding of political opposition groups in Nicaragua before leaving his own presidency.

In October 1979, El Salvador appeared on the verge of civil war when a group of young officers engineered a coup that ousted President Carlos Humberto Romero. The new junta promised an improvement in human rights and an agrarian reform

Archbishop Oscar Romero of El Salvador.

the past as military, not economic and social, solutions received first consideration.

Within this context, Reagan determined to maintain Central America's old order, except in Nicaragua, where he intended to restore it. To carry out this policy, Honduras was turned into an American military outpost, over $300 million in military aid was supplied to the government in El Salvador for its battle against the FMLN, and the Nicaraguan contras were supported in a counterrevolution designed to oust the Sandinistas from power. The policy soon became unpopular, both in the United States and in Central and South America. The U.S. public and Congress debated the righteousness of an armed solution to an indigenous problem and whether the Soviets had any real interest in these conflicts other than supporting opposition to the United States. In Central America, the Guatemalan government refused to be drawn in for fear of becoming a victim of U.S. interference in its internal affairs. Costa Rica, long aloof to isthmian violence, also resisted Reagan's advances in order to maintain its neutrality.

As much as the Central American crisis revived cries of gunboat diplomacy, two other incidents rein-

package. But the violence continued as illustrated by the bloodbath that followed the assassination of Archbishop Oscar Romero. Nor was there any agrarian reform. Late in 1980, Carter lifted the U.S. ban on military assistance so that the Salvadoran government could suppress the violence and implement the agrarian reform package.

Central America appeared on the verge of self-destruction when Ronald Reagan arrived in Washington in January 1980. Reagan was convinced that the malaise of the Carter administration had contributed to a loss of U.S. global prestige and had permitted an advance of international communism. For Latin America, the Reagan administration put its affairs into the context of the East-West struggle, denying that such long-standing issues as the disparity of wealth, deprivation of social mobility, and restriction of political rights were responsible for the contemporary protest and violence. Instead, Reagan argued that the Soviet Union, through its Cuban proxies, capitalized on these issues to vault into political power local Marxists, who would destroy the economies and offer no hope for political reform. From these Communist outposts, Moscow threatened U.S. interests. Human rights became a policy of

Guerrillas of El Frente Farabundo Martí por Liberación Nacional (FMLN) in El Salvador.

Demonstrators on the U.S. capitol steps opposing U.S. military aid to El Salvador in 1980.

forced the perception. Grenada, an island nation of about 110,000 people at the western end of the Antilles, had gained its independence from Great Britain in 1974. Its initial prime minister, Eric Gairy, was overthrown in 1979 by the leftist-leaning New Jewell movement headed by Maurice Bishop. When Bishop identified with the world Socialist movement, the Reagan administration promptly cut off all aid. Bishop visited Washington in 1982 but failed to alter Reagan's course. In the meantime, Bishop had secured Soviet and Cuban assistance for the construction of a runway capable of handling jumbo jets, which Bishop argued were essential for developing the island's tourist industry. U.S. policymakers thought otherwise. They viewed the airstrip as stop-over point for Cuban planes going to and from Africa and for Soviet aircraft to threaten the Caribbean sea routes and the Panama Canal. At the same time, Grenada's political rivalries led to the assassination of Bishop and the emergence of a more leftist faction of the New Jewell movement. Washington panicked. Under the guise of rescuing U.S. medical students from the deteriorating situation on the island, Reagan ordered the invasion of the island on October 25, 1983. Like Lyndon Johnson before him, Reagan was

determined not to have another Cuba in the Caribbean. And like Woodrow Wilson 70 years earlier, Reagan intended to teach the Grenadians to elect good men and in the process prevent the completion of the 10,000-foot runway. The discovery of Soviet and North Korean advisers along with the Cubans and a large arms cache after the invasion was used to justify the U.S. action. Although Reagan subsequently explained that he was invited to act by the Association of Eastern Caribbean nations, in fact the planning for the attack came the day after Bishop's death, and the request for U.S. assistance was drafted in Washington. This explanation was received well only in the United States. Most Latin Americans paralleled the incident to Eisenhower's in Guatemala, particularly when the Reagan administration successfully labored to prevent the United Nations and the Organization of American States from taking any action.

Ever since Great Britain seized the Falklands/Malvinas Islands off the Atlantic coast of Argentina in 1832, the government at Buenos Aires has unsuccessfully sought hemispheric solidarity and the application of the Monroe Doctrine to remove the British from the islands. By 1982 internal factors prompted the Argentine military government to take aggressive action. A decade of repressive government produced political protest amidst a deteriorating economic situation. To divert the public's attention from these issues, Leopoldo Galtieri decided to seize the islands. He believed that the British, more concerned with European affairs, had lost interest in the Falklands/Malvinas, and he also thought that the United States would be neutral because the Argentine army was training the U.S.-backed contras. Despite admonitions to the contrary by Secretary of State Alexander Haig, Galtieri went ahead with the invasion in May 1982. When the British reacted militarily, the United States provided intelligence assistance and refueling of the Royal Navy en route to the South Atlantic. When the crisis was over, the British retained the islands, Galtieri was forced from office, and the United States suffered another setback in its relations with Latin America.

The decade of the 1980s marked a turning point in Central American history, however, when regional initiatives were employed to bring about peace. On January 8–9, 1983, four of the neighboring nations of Central America—Mexico, Venezuela, Colombia, and Panama—met on the Panamanian island of Contadora to negotiate for peace in Central America. By July, the Contadora Group issued its first proposals, which included the withdrawal of all foreign military advisors from Central America the end of all aid to irregular forces, and the cessation of military maneuvers in the border regions. From this beginning the Contadora Group went on to recruit other Spanish American states in the process and to develop a consensus in the Americas that the United States end its militaristic involvement in the area. The process developed over years, continuously hindered by U.S. funding of the Contras, the U.S. mining Nicaraguan ports, the United States invasion of Grenada on October 25, 1983 and U.S. troop maneuvers in Honduras in 1983. Regardless of these obstacles and others, on September 21, 1984, the Nicaraguan government became the first of the Central American nations to sign the Contadora Group's "Draft Act on Peace and Cooperation." But again, the United States pursued a course of undermining the Contadora process.

On November 25, 1986, news of the Iran-Contra scandal broke in the United States: the U.S. National Security Council had been diverting money from secret arms sales to Iran to clandestine support for the Contras, which had been prohibited by Congress under the 1982 Boland Amendment. U.S. policy toward Nicaragua, which had been judged illegal by the International Court of Justice in the Hague, was exposed as possibly illegal within the United States as well. Despite opposition from President Reagan, the Central American governments ratified their own peace plan, based on one developed by Costa Rican President Oscar Arias Sánchez, on August 7, 1987. The plan called for withdrawal of all foreign military advisors from the area, a complete cease-fire and the holding of free and pluralist elections in all of the countries in Central America. Implementation of the accords signed by the five republics was to be overseen by the Group of 8 (the Contadora and Lima Groups), the foreign ministers of the Central American countries and the secretaries general of the United Nations and the Organization of American States. Despite Nicaragua's proceeding to implement the accords and its unilateral declaration of a cease-fire in three of the northern war zones, President Reagan obtained from Congress another $3.2 million for the Contras on September 23, 1987. Later in the year, when Reagan called for more Contra funding, there was a public outcry and defections from his allies in Congress; the administration's policies toward Nicaragua collapsed. Despite continued efforts by the outgoing Reagan administration and the newly elected Bush administration to block the accords, the peace efforts were promoted unilaterally by the Nicaraguan government, which initiated negotiations with the Contras. The efforts were supported regionally and internationally, and eventually resulted in Nicaragua forging a cease fire treaty with the Contras in 1988 and holding free elections in 1990, with both Sandinistas and Contras as political parties. The elections resulted in the Sandinistas losing the presidency and considerable power, and non-violently turning the administration over to the moderates headed by newly elected President Violeta orro, Violeta]. For his efforts in forging a regional peace solution in the face of United States opposition, President Oscar Arias Sánchez was accorded the Nobel Prize.

Many of the ideological struggles that had maintained Central America as a war zone during the 1980s began to dissolve with the dissolution of the Soviet Union, the Soviet bloc and the collapse of Communism in eastern Europe. Nicaragua ceased to be a target for the U.S. struggle against Communism and, in February 1992, the Farabundo Martí National Liberation Front ended its guerrilla movement by signing a peace treaty with the government of El Salvador. One of the bloodiest civil wars, one that had killed some 75,000 people, had finally come to an end. In exchange for the FMNL laying down its weapons and becoming a legal political party, the government agreed to sweeping changes in the military, including the retirement of more than 100 officers believed responsible for widespread human rights abuses. During the 1980's, the United States had poured in more than $6 billion in economic and military aid to defeat the FMLN. On May 24, 1994, the FMLN participated in free and democratic elections as a political party in El Salvador. Former human rights ombudsman, Armando Calderón Sol of the ARENA party became president, although the specter of a still very strong military has maintained an uneasy peace in El Salvador to date.

U.S. adventures in Central America were not completely over, as the U.S. turned to an increasing domestic and international problem: the so-called "war on drugs." In December, 1989, President Bush took a definitive and unusual move against a dictator formerly supported by the United States: the United States invaded Panama, captured, removed to the United States, tried and imprisoned President Manuel Noriega, whom it accused of masterminding an international drug trafficking ring and laundering money. The U.S.-backed Guillermo Endara was made provisional president until truly open and democratic elections on May 8, 1994, resulted in a candidate from Noriega's old party, Ernesto Pérez Balladares, winning the presidency.

At the close of the century, Central America seems to have the greatest opportunity in its history for peace and stability, although economic instability still remains a fact of life and a threat to long-lasting peace in the volatile region.

Whereas the end of the Cold War and the dissolution of the Soviet Bloc had resulted in growing peace and stability in Central America, the converse was true in Cuba. The change in government in Russia, coupled with Russia's economic crises, led to a withdrawal of support to the Cuban economy. Cuban Communism and Castro were not only destabilized, but the Cuban economy rapidly took a nosedive, which eventually led to new waves of Cubans abandoning the country and attempting to enter the United States. The outflow taking the form of a flotilla of home-made rafts in 1994 was so intense and threatening to the capability of social services to deal with them in Florida, that the United States changed its decades-long policy of automatically accepting Cuban refugees and began to interdict them at sea. The Unites States Coast Guard eventually returned some 60,000 refugees to the Guantanamo Naval Base and made arrangements for as many as possible to be readmitted to Cuba, with the cooperation of the Cuban government, anxious to better relations with the U.S. The Clinton administration, while preparing a policy for warming relations with Cuba and facilitating U.S. business investment there, was faced with mounting opposition from Cuban exile groups and, early in 1996 was forced into a corner by hardline Cuban exiles who provoked an international incident during this election year by repeatedly flying over Cuban national air space. After repeated warnings from the Cuban government, the Cuban air force finally shot down two light commuter craft. Conservatives in Congress, led by Senator Jesse Helms, jumped at the opportunity to increase sanctions against Cuba and force the president to do likewise, thus once again straining U.S.-Cuban relations for the foreseeable future.

During the 1990s, relations with Mexico have become closer, principally through the signing of the North American Free Trade Agreement (NAFTA) by Canada, Mexico and the United States. On January 1, 1994, NAFTA went into effect to eliminate all tariffs between the three trading partners within 15 years. The measure is a first step toward integrating the economies of the three countries and possibly toward the creation in the future of an American common market which will include the whole hemisphere. Regarding Mexico and the United States, on this date 53.8 percent of U.S. imports from Mexico became duty free, while 31 percent of imports from the U.S., excluding those imported by *maquiladoras*, became duty free. The most effected industries immediately were energy, automobiles, textiles, agriculture, electricity, banks and insurance, bus and trucking services, ports, railroads and telecommunications. NAFTA passage was opposed in the United States by labor unions, which feared the continuing loss of jobs to Mexico, and domestic industries artificially protected by tariffs, such as textiles. In Mexico, well-planned and executed revolutionary outbreaks by Mayan peasant farmers in Chiapas were timed to coincide with the beginning of NAFTA, and, in fact, they began shortly after 12:00 A.M. New Years Day. As many as 2,000 Mayan guerrillas, baptizing themselves the Zapatista National Liberation Army (in honor of the revolutionary general Emiliano Zapata), with some of them uniformed and well armed, took over the important southern city of San Cristóbal de las Casas, as well as the towns of Ocosingo, Las Margaritas, Altamirano and others. This led to bloody confrontations with and repression by the Mexican Army until a cease fire was accepted by both sides on January 12, with a an agreement to dialog on the problems of the Mayas in Chiapas. The dialogs and negotiations continue to this day. Mayas of southern Mexico, who have suffered poverty and dispossession of their communal lands for years, were now faced with the prospect of imported corn displacing their main farm product and dietary staple. All of this crystallized in a recent environment of increasing indigenous overpopulation, poverty and exploitation as Mexico bowed to the demands of foreign debtors and the constraints of the International Monetary Fund to control inflation and recent devaluations of the peso. With the economic policy of President Carlos Salinas de Gortari straining to bring Mexico into the "first world," the gap between the select few rich, and getting richer under new economic programs, and the poor in Mexico had become accentuated. The euphoria in Mexico upon signing of the NAFTA agreement was short-lived, as fundamental weaknesses in the economy came to light and the peso was forced to take some of its steepest devaluations in history. The Mayan uprising had contributed to the international loss of confidence in the Mexican economy, as did protest by farmers who were unable to pay off their loans and were otherwise to be adversely affected by NAFTA, beginning on February 24, 1994. Further instability followed when the Institutional Revolutionary Party (PRI) candidate for the presidency was assassinated in Tijuana on March 23, 1994; the assumed motive was protest to NAFTA. On March 24, acting unilaterally, the United States extended a $6 billion-line of credit to Mexico. This was followed later by both NAFTA partners, the United States and Canada, moving rapidly to create a multimillion-dollar fund to stabilize Mexico's currency and protect it from onslaughts from global speculation. The centerpiece of the fund was a $6.7 billion line of credit for the Central Bank of Mexico. All three parties to the treaty see their economies as intertwined and interdependent. Critics have charged that the United States has repeatedly shored up and supported the Institutional Revolutionary Party (PRI) with loans and lines of credit during elections and political transitions to ensure stability. In 1995, considerable corruption, including possible involvement in political assassinations and the misappropriation of millions of dollars, among the family of ex-president Carlos Salinas de Gortari led to arrest of family members and the flight into exile in the United States of Salinas de Gortari himself. With the Mexican economy plummeting into a serious depression, once again undocumented immigration of Mexican laborers into the United States skyrocketed, with the result that throughout 1995 and into the 1996 U.S. electoral campaign, restricting immigration of all sorts has became a hotly contested issue, one even straining the NAFTA accord.

References

Connel-Smith, Gordon. *The United States and Latin-America: An Historical Analysis of Inter-American Relations.* New York: Wiley, 1974.

Gil, Federico. *Latin American-United States Relations.* New York: Harcourt, Brace, Jovanovich, 1975.

Kryzanek, Michael. *U.S.-Latin American Relations.* New York: Praeger, 1985.

Leonard, Thomas M. *Central America and the United States: the Search for Stability.* Claremont, California: Regina Books, 1985.

Leonard, Thomas M. *The United States and Central America, 1944–1949: Perceptions of Political Dynamics.* Tuscaloosa: University of Alabama Press, 1984.

Lowenthal, Abraham. *Partners In Conflict: The United States and Latin America.* Baltimore: John Hopkins University Press, 1987.

Mecham, J. Lloyd. *A Survey of United States-Latin American Relations.* Boston: Houghton, 1965.

Stuart, Graham H., and James L. Tigner. *Latin America and the United States,* sixth edition. Englewood Cliffs, New Jersey: Prentice Hall, 1975.

Thomas Leonard

6

Hispanics and Race

✳ Racial Ideas among the Spaniards ✳ European Americans and the Racialization of Hispanics
✳ The Hispanic "Race" Today: Self-Perceptions and Anglo Impressions

The great Cuban philosopher and patriot José Martí stated in a 1894 speech he gave in New York City, "There are no races. There are only a number of variations in Man, with reference to customs and forms, imposed by the climatic and historical conditions under which he lives, which do not change that which is identical and essential." Despite U.S. thinkers, writers, and propagandists having for the preceding century proclaimed the superiority of Anglo-Saxons and "Americans" as a race over all other peoples of the world, Martí sustained this position. He would be vindicated in the late twentieth century by biologists and anthropologists, who have proved beyond a doubt that there are no species of men, that all peoples are identical in their genetic and intellectual potential, that only culture and history have produced different customs and lifestyles and that, in reality, all peoples descended from the same prehistoric Cro-Magnon progenitors in Africa and later migrated to the various regions of the world. Unfortunately, it was only after most of the world's population had been colonized and stigmatized as inferior by Europeans, and that Jews and Gypsies had suffered genocide under the perverse delusions of Nazi superiority, that the intellectual and scientific bases of racism have been eroded. But as all socially conscious individuals must know, racism is still very much a part of popular thought and attitudes and still very much a part of societal institutions in the United States and other countries. Hispanics in the United States today occupy a precarious position, for in great part their very existence is the negation of racism: as a whole they have developed out of the conscious interbreeding of distinct peoples, that is, peoples from geographically and culturally separate parts of the world. On the other hand, in the United States, Hispanics are often perceived as a race, usu-
ally by European Americans, but at times even by themselves.

✳ RACIAL IDEAS AMONG THE SPANIARDS

Of all Europeans, it was the Spaniards of the Renaissance who were truly aware of their having developed as a people out of the cohabitation and mixing of culturally and religiously distinct peoples. On a base of prehistoric peoples that had inhabited the Iberian Peninsula, Spanish identity developed out of conquest and colonization by Romans, Germanic peoples, Celts and then from the diverse peoples of northern Africa who believed in Islam. During 700 years, Spanish culture evolved under one of the most tolerant theocracies: early Islam. Latinized Visigoths lived side-by-side with Moors and Jews; and more than that, they intermarried and eventually developed the basis of what became one of Europe's first nation states. The considerable mixing and hybridization that took place over the 700 years, it is believed (Morner, 14), later facilitated and influenced the hybridization that took place under the Spanish in the New World.

This notable tolerance ended, however, with the process of nation building, which was spearheaded and carried out by Christian monarchs who rallied their kingdoms to rid the peninsula of the infidels, that is the Moorish rulers who were not Christian. Thus, the Reconquest and eventual national unity of the Iberian Peninsula was effected through a crusade by Christians on their own soil. When the two strongest Christian kingdoms united in 1492 through the marriage of the Catholic Kings Ferdinand and Isabel and they defeated the last Moorish stronghold, Granada, Ferdinand and Isabel created a nation-state that was politically and religiously unified. They then set about consolidating their nation state by making Spanish the official language, suppressing the political power and ethnic diversity of the other Visigothic kingdoms they had conquered in the peninsula, and forcing the Jews and Moslems to convert to Christianity or abandon the peninsula. The Spanish Inquisition (actually of Italian origin) was used to ferret out people who practiced Judaism and Islam underground, and a social environment of suspicion and persecution developed where people's ethno-religious lineage became a cause for doubt of their loyalty to the state and the Church. However, such doubts could easily by assuaged through the purchase of certificates from the Church, which verified the "purity" of lineage—more a cultural and religious assessment than a racial one.

The Spanish term *raza* among the Renaissance Spaniards was more akin to our use today of the term *culture* and it is still used frequently with that meaning. At the time of the exploration and colonization of the Americas, there was no belief that Spaniards were biologically or even culturally superior to other peoples. In fact, their history contradicted any such sentiments, as the peninsula had continuously been overrun by diverse peoples who not only conquered the residents militarily, but also had brought the residents advanced institutions in government, education, science, commerce and the arts—such was especially the case of the Moors and the Jews. What the Spanish believed was fundamental, if not superior, was their religion, which was destined to be shared by all of the peoples of the world. They continued the Crusade against the Moor and the Turk in Africa and the Middle East and, of course, they set about the immense task of evangelizing man of the Americas. In their conquest and colonization of the Americas, they unknowingly facilitated the hybridization of peoples from four of the continents of the world: Africa, Europe, North and South America.

Whereas Spanish policy and law toward the American Indians evolved over a period of some 300 years, the common denominator of their official positions and their actions was that the Amerindians were seen as human beings whose souls could be saved through the Catholic religion. Following the customs instituted during the Reconquest of the peninsula, the Spanish could claim the lands conquered from the Indians, as they had those conquered from the Moslem caliphates, and they set about converting the natives of the New World to Catholicism. What is also clear is that over time, both policy and practice encouraged intermarriage among Spaniards and Indians, at the elite levels of society among the Spanish captains and the Indian royalty to facilitate the transfer of power, and at the lower levels at least to further Hispanization of the Indians as well as to inhibit illegitimacy and stabilize the colonies through the building of families.

With the conquest and colonization, many free Africans were introduced into the Americas by the Spaniards. When the diseases brought by the Europeans (as well as abuse of the natives) took extremely high tolls from the native populations, African slaves were also introduced. Again, interbreeding was fostered indirectly for the slaves and directly for the free Hispanicized Africans and mulattoes. By the sixteenth century, a class of mixed castes had grown so large and complex with all the diverse interbreeding that it was practically impossible to perceive or track the genetic lineage of the mixed Spanish, African (mostly West African) and American Indian peoples. The Hispanic peoples that settled in Florida and the Southwest not only brought this varied genetic legacy with them, they also continued to interbreed with resident indigenous groups.

One of the greatest features of Hispanic culture over the ages has been the ability to incorporate peoples from various other ethnic and national cultures and still maintain its Hispanic identity—although freely acknowledging and proclaiming an African, Amerindian, or Asian subculture within its Hispanism.

All of the above is not to say that there were no class distinctions between the Europeans, the Indians, Africans and mixed castes in colonial Spanish America. While the Medieval distinction between Christian and heathen had facilitated the conquest and colonization, as well as servitude and enslavement of native peoples, as the natives became Christianized, this distinction became undermined. According to Morner, the distinction gave way to "the typically colonial dichotomy between conquerors and conquered, masters and servants or slaves" (Morner 1967: 6). The Negro and the mulatto were stigmatized for having been or having descended from slaves; and many of the mixed castes were stigmatized because of the predominance of illegitimacy of so many people of mixed ancestry. Because of the make-up of Spanish laws and the distribution of work in colonial society, both Spaniard and Indian were privileged in many ways that mixed castes and African slaves were not. In the course of development of colonial society, it was, however, the Spaniards born in Spain who enjoyed the most privileges and the highest positions. They were followed by the Criollos, Spaniards born in the Americas, who were somewhat discriminated against. In practical terms, there appeared only three really definable groups: Spaniards, castes (mestizos) and Indians. But in reality there were hierarchical subdivisions to these as seen by the law and as perceived in social status (Morner 1967: 60):

Legal condition:

1. "Spaniards"
2. Indians
3. Mestizos
4. Free Negroes, mulattoes, zamboes (African-Indian)
5. Slaves

Social status:

1. Peninsular Spaniards
2. Criollos
3. Mestizos
4. Mulattoes, zamboes, free Negroes
5. Slaves
6. Indians (if not chiefs or royalty, etc.)

In the breakdown of social functions, the peninsular Spaniards headed the institutions of the society and were the bureaucrats and merchants. Criollos were large landowners and the mestizos were the artisans, shopkeepers and tenants. Mulattoes were the urban manual workers and the Indians became the peasants and the unskilled labor (Morner 1967: 61). African slaves, of course, served as manual laborers, as well as artisans and soldiers. It is worth noting that slavery in Spanish America was not as rigidly defined and maintained as in the United States, and Hispanic slaves enjoyed written rights and more liberal customs and access to manumission—even the widespread ability to earn money to purchase their manumission—than did slaves in the United States. Also, it became a practice to free the children of master-slave unions. Furthermore, there was never developed a body of ideology regarding the inferiority of the African slaves to justify their enslavement as had occurred in the U.S. And slavery was abolished in the Spanish American republics almost immediately after their independence from Spain.

As for the Criollos (Spanish born in the Americas) and the mixed castes (*mestizos*), they eventually became resentful enough of their limited opportunities in the society to lead the fight for independence from Spain. In Mexico, this independence movement was forged through an alliance with the Indians. (In Cuba and Puerto Rico, the independence movement was not only linked to the movement to abolish slavery but was also led by such free blacks as General Antonio Maceo.) The history of most of the countries of Latin America really can be traced as the ascendance of the mestizo, not only in the political sense but also in the growth of the mestizo population to be the largest segment of the society—with Argentina and southern Chile the two most obvious exceptions.

At first, the mestizo population grew dramatically in comparison to the indigenous and the Spanish segments because of the demographic disaster that came about with the European-origin diseases that devastated indigenous populations at the precise moment when the greatest interbreeding was beginning. But over the course of the centuries, the mestizo identity came not to be based on genetic or physical features of individuals, but on their assimilation to or participation in the national culture (Knight, 73)—thus the ranks of mestizos grew as Indians and freed slaves became acculturated. For example, a "full-blooded" Indian would be considered a mestizo if acculturated enough to speak Spanish, use the national dress and participate in the common national life outside of the tribe (this is especially salient to the development of Mexican American heritage among the descendants of Indians who had been acculturated at missions throughout the Southwest). Likewise, blacks and mulattoes were "whitened" as they ascended to positions of greater economic and social prestige.

Although prejudice existed against the mestizo during colonial times because of a background of illegitimacy, today no significant prejudice in this regard remains in the countries of large indigenous or African populations, such as those that give origin to the bulk of U.S. Hispanics: Mexico, Cuba, and Puerto Rico. Rather Mexico, in particular, has made the mestizo its national archetype and has forged a national culture that is mestizo—despite the greatest genetic base of the population being indigenous. Likewise, due to the large plantation economy that developed in the Spanish Caribbean, the long history of cohabitation and mixing of Africans and Spaniards has given rise to societies that have a mixed culture as well as mixed genetic ancestry. In the same Cuban or Puerto Rican family live individuals that are perceived by Anglo-Americans as black, white, or mulatto—not to mention the vestiges of Caribbean Indian ancestry that still may remain in physical features.

In the course of the ascendancy of mestizos (including mulattoes), not only were the highest governmental and entrepreneurial levels of society in Mexico, Central America, and the Caribbean attained, but also in what became the Southwest of the United States. Even Pío Pico, the governor of California just prior to the United States takeover, had African ancestry. And despite the claims of Californios and New Mexican founding families when faced with Anglo-American race and class systems, their ancestry is just as mixed as that of the people in central Mexico. Through this process of ascendancy of the mestizo, ethnic and genetic lines were blurred and a class system was established along economic lines. But throughout Spanish America, nevertheless, ethnic and physical features still can be seen in class divisions, the most obvious of which result in the unassimilated Indians and poor blacks predominating at the bottom of the social ladder. And while "race" distinctions and prejudice exist in Spanish America, they do not, nor ever have they, taken the form of institutionalized discrimination as in the United States; they are more subtly expressed (some glaring exceptions are to be found in the history of Cuba and Puerto Rico under U.S. domination).

✳ EUROPEAN AMERICANS AND THE RACIALIZATION OF HISPANICS

Among the English who colonized North America there was no overriding desire to evangelize the Indians or to inter-marry with them or with African slaves or free men; to the contrary, laws were passed prohibiting intermarriage. Both Indians and Africans were seen as savages whose inferiority justified their enslavement or, as in the case of the Indians, their expulsion. In the ideology and imagery that developed as slavery grew in the British colonies, dark skin color soon became a symbol of savagery and heathenism, as well as many other negative attributes, and the savagery of the dark-skinned peoples was intrinsic and terminal; it could not be mediated or changed (Smedley, 107). By the late eighteenth century, precisely the time when the American Republic was being founded, *race* was seen not just as a division of the diverse populations who were in contact in the colonies, but as (1) an intellectual construct about human differences and power relationships, and (2) a novel and unprecedented quality introduced into structuring the social status. By keeping blacks, Indians, and whites socially and spatially separated and enforcing endogamous mating, they were making sure that the visible physical differences would be preserved as the premier insignia of unequal social statuses. In this way they institutionalized exclusive group membership and paved the way for later rationalizations of group distinctiveness in terms of natural, inbred inequality (Smedley, 109).

Throughout the eighteenth and nineteenth centuries, Anglo-Saxon theorists, pseudo-scientists and legislators furthered a concept whose origins date back to the Germanic tribes of the Middle Ages: God had chosen the northern European peoples to be the most intelligent and physically robust, and to be the practitioners of the highest forms of government.

The apex of this northern European race was thought to be the Anglo-Saxons, whose providential mission was to supplant the other, inferior peoples of the world or bring them under the enlightened Anglo-Saxon domination. In the nineteenth century, this doctrine of Manifest Destiny was popularized by both statesmen and the press and institutionalized as the basic philosophy of American expansionism southward and westward. In the path of the Americans lay not only vast populations of Indians but also Spaniards and the mixed breeds they had forged, what the Anglo-Saxon ideologues came to call the "mongrel races." Later, after the United States had won the Mexican War and incorporated northern Mexico into its territories and states, Social Darwinist theories of "natural selection" and "survival of the fittest" also helped to justify dispossessing, subduing and controlling the native populations of the Southwest.

In the Anglo-Saxon cosmology of peoples, Spaniards had already been to some extent racialized in their eyes by the time of the Renaissance. The British brought with them to North America an image of the Spaniards as inordinately cruel, greedy, and lazy, as well as highly interbred with Jews and infidels while supporting a papist, obscurantist religion. In rejection of Spain's imperialist reach over the Lowlands and Italy, British and other northern European writers constructed their case for Spanish brutality on the abuses of Spanish soldiers in Europe as well as on the abuses visited on the Indians in the Caribbean. Propagandists wishing to justify British rights to challenge Spain's colonial hegemony in the New World latched onto Friar Bartolomé de las Casas' written exposes of Spanish enslavement and torture of the Indians and built them into what has come to be known as the "Spanish Black Legend."

England and Spain continued to be rivals, if not enemies, into the nineteenth century. The Enlightenment in Europe conveniently chose Spain and its Catholicism as targets for derision and symbols of obscurantism. Of course, these attitudes were passed on to England's colonies in North America, and even despite Spain's assistance to the 13 colonies in their war of independence, the intellectuals in the newly founded United States not only harbored the hispanophobic attitudes of their ancestors, but also proceeded to treat Spain and its New World colonies as, if not enemies, rivals—rivals for hegemony in the Western Hemisphere. Already in 1648 with the publication of Thomas Gage's *The English-American,* the idea was becoming widely disseminated that the iniquitous Spanish rule in the New World could easily—militarily—be replaced by that of the virtuous English Protestants. As Powell in his study of the Spanish Black Legend goes at length to emphasize, "Our ancestors established themselves in America during the seventeenth century, and this colonization process was nourished by their hatred of Spain and their desire to break the Spanish New World monopoly" (102). And, with the rise of the American Republic, the Spanish Black Legend provided the ugly image of the Hispanic enemy that would fuel hateful speeches in Congress, yellow journalism and popular culture to justify the expansion of the United States westward and southward.

In the intellectual modes that crystallized in the United States during the nineteenth century and often have extended to the present, there are several main lines in which popularization of hispanophobic biases is clearly seen. Some of our frontier clashes were still, irritatingly, with the Spanish (or Mexicans), and in the Texan-Mexican struggle and then in our war with Mexico, we transferred some of our ingrained antipathy toward Catholic Spain to her American heirs. And Spain continued ruling and fighting rebellions in nearby Cuba, leading to disagreeable incidents that kept alive the ancient antagonisms. This abrasive proximity to persons of Spanish speech, especially a darker-hued Mexican (remember those long-ago German disparagements of the smaller, darker men of Iberia?), encouraged our faith in Nordic superiority. It was a small step, really, from "Remember the Armada" to "Remember the Alamo." Highly intemperate utterances in the U.S. Congress and elsewhere contained abusive references to Latin America's Spanish past and advocated the takeover of those lands, at least as far as Panama and sometimes beyond. And, at the century's end a heady mixture of Darwinism, war with Spain, and faith in a kind of Nordic "manifest destiny" heightened superior race concepts in the Anglo-American mind (Powell, 118).

The early Americans soon found an ideology that would allow them to replace the "iniquitous Spanish" and their bastard progeny, at least in North America—Manifest Destiny. And this doctrine inevitably and permanently to the present racialized Hispanics, all Hispanics, that is, except for a thin veneer of upper class wealthy and powerful, often landholding families in California who were thought to have European ancestry. The racial superiority of the Anglo-Saxons not only allowed them to conquer and incorporate northern Mexico into the Union but also to colonize part of the Hispanic Caribbean and imperialistically determine and intervene in the internal politics of the other nations of the Caribbean, Mexico and Central America. It further allowed the great entrepreneurs of the society to develop immigration policies and programs that facilitated the importation of Hispanic American laborers to work the factories and fields that would make the United States the agricultural and industrial powerhouse that is today. The late nineteenth century history of the Southwest is dominated by the theme of conversion of Mexican Americans into a proletariate, while the twentieth century is dominated by that of Mexican and later Puerto Rican, Cuban, Dominican and Central American mass migration to the United States, determined by economic cycles dependant on cheap labor and a foreign policy designed to ensure Spanish American dependency on the United States. The Hispanics, with their mixed racial heritage, came into the bipolar racial system of the United States—whites and non-whites. Without doubt, Hispanics became non-whites, despite laws, court decisions, census descriptors and even pronouncements by civil rights groups that have stated the contrary at one time or another.

What has muddied the legal waters concerning Hispanic racial status is the 1790 U.S. Immigration Act, which prohibited U.S. citizenship from being extended to non-whites. Despite this law, the Treaty of Guadalupe Hidalgo (See chapter on Documents), which ended the Mexican War in 1848, extended U.S. citizenship to all Mexicans residing in the Southwest. Citizenship was one privilege conceded to the "mongrel" Mexican, but statehood for the territories in which they predominated was another matter.

After the Mexican War, Texas and the other territories of the Southwest pursued admission to the Union as states, but debate ensued as to whether they would individually enter as "free" or "slave" states. Complicating the issue was the fact that New Mexico and southern Texas were populated predominantly by Mexicans. In 1850, the United States Congress passed a series of laws, known as the Compromise of 1850, to defer the divisiveness of the slavery issue as regarded the admission of states to the Union. The compromise consisted in California—which had been overrun by so much Anglo migration that Mexicans rapidly became the minority population—being admitted as a state and New Mexico remaining as a territory. The New Mexicans were especially disappointed by the denial of statehood, which was not approved until 1912. But the fear in the United States Congress of having inferior races as citizens and legislators was considerable. Typical of the statements in opposition to New Mexican statehood were Floridian Senator James D. Westcott's, who did not want to be "compelled to receive not merely the white citizens of California and New Mexico, but the peons, Negroes, and Indians of all sorts, the wild tribe of Comanche, the bug-and-liz-ard-eating 'Diggers,' and other half-monkey savages in those countries, as equal citizens of the United States" (Cited in the *Congressional Globe,* 30th Congress, first session, appendix, [July 17, 1850], pp. 48–49).

The resistance to extending citizenship to peoples of other races had come early on in Congress from both the Whig and Democratic parties. Such statements as, "I do not want any mixed races in our union, nor men of any color except white, unless they be slaves. Certainly not as voters or legislators" (as stated by Congressman William Wick of Indiana, according to the *Congressional Globe,* 29th Congress, first session, January 30, 1846, p. 184) typified Congressional sentiment, which explains somewhat the policies set for facilitating settlement of Anglo-Americans in the West and resisting New Mexico's statehood until Anglos were in controlling majority of the territory.

The slavery issue also determined the direction of the discussion over annexation of Cuba and its eventual statehood. In 1854, President Franklin Pierce offered Spain $130 million for the island and threatened U.S. support of the Cuban independence movement in what is known as the Ostend Manifesto presented by U.S. representatives at Aix-la-Chapelle, France. This declaration brought a hostile reaction against United States imperialism from the European powers and caused Spain to resist the United States initiatives even more strenuously. But in the United States, the debate over Cuba was even more complicated in that Southern congressmen were hoping to add another "slave" state to the union. The Civil War put these initiatives to rest for a period. Nevertheless, U.S. expansionism under Manifest Destiny was striking out in all directions and even was manifested as far south as Nicaragua in 1856, when U.S. citizen William Walker seized the presidency of Nicaragua and made English the official language of the country. Once again it was President Franklin Pierce who exploited feelings about slavery and Manifest Destiny and officially recognized Walker's short-lived government during Pierce's re-election bid. After Pierce was not even nominated by his party at the Democratic convention, he withdrew what came to be an increasingly embarrassing and blatantly imperialistic recognition of Walker's government.

But with the annexation of the territories and states of the Southwest, the United States had indeed expanded to the sea, to be sure at the expense of Mexicans and Indians who, as the ideology of Manifest Destiny had predicted, had to surrender their space to a superior and divinely favored race.

In fact, Horseman argues that it was the very confrontation with Mexicans that had led Anglo-Saxons to see themselves as a race:

By the 1830s the Americans were eagerly grasping at reasons for their own success and for the failure of others. Although the white Americans of Jacksonian America wanted personal success and wealth, they also wanted a clear conscience. If the United States was to remain in the minds of the people a nation divinely ordained for great deeds, then the fault of the suffering inflicted in the rise to power and prosperity had to lie elsewhere. White Americans could rest easier if the suffering of other races could be blamed on racial weakness rather than on the whites' relentless search for wealth and power. In the 1830s and 1840s, when it became obvious that American and Mexican interests were incompatible and that Mexicans would suffer, innate weaknesses were found in the Mexicans. Americans, it was argued, were not to be blamed for forcibly taking the northern provinces of Mexico, for Mexicans, like Indians, were unable to make proper use of the land. The Mexicans had failed because they were a mixed, inferior race with considerable Indian and some black blood. The world would benefit if a superior race shaped the future of the Southwest (Horseman, 210).

It is in this period that many of the stereotypes of Mexicans are solidified in the literature of travelers, pioneers and later politicians and policy makers, and also in the popular entertainments and media such as the dime novel. Mexicans were pictured as a mongrel race, cowardly, cruel, lazy, superstitious and shiftless, which of course was an inheritance of the stereotypes created in the Spanish Black Legend. As Horseman notes, the process of dehumanizing the people who would be misused rapidly preceded the expropriation of their lands (Horseman, 211).

The next Hispanics to become subjects of U.S. expansionism resided close to the borders of the United States: in the Caribbean. The relationship between the Spanish colonies in the Caribbean and the British colonies of New England actually began in the sixteenth century as a by-product of war and competition between England and Spain; the Spanish colonies from that time were plagued by attacks and had various of their port cities occupied by the British navy and privateers—by the likes of Francis Drake both as pirate and privateer. It must also be remembered that natives of Cuba, and to lesser extent Puerto Rico, have resided in territories that are now part of the United States since the 1560s in such colonies as St. Augustine, Florida. The rudiments of an illicit trade between the Hispanic and British colonies began when Spanish American goods and merchants ended up in New England. In 1670, Spain and England finally abated some of their competition with each other upon signing an accord which recognized each others' presence in the Caribbean: the Treaty of Madrid. The Treaty further sanctioned England's holdings in the Americas. But trade between the Spanish and British colonies was only permitted with a special license; this restricted commerce severely and led to the development of smuggling between these colonies. Then, later, England became a major supplier of slaves to the Americas, even to the Spanish colonies. In 1717, England's South Sea Company obtained permission to bring 144,000 African slaves into the Spanish colonies at a rate of 4800 per year for 30 years. The trade rapidly expanded, and grew into a link in the economies of Cuba and especially the Southern plantation states of the U.S. in the nineteenth century.

During the first half of the nineteenth century, the trading relationship expanded dramatically, leading as well to the beginning of the Cuban communities in New Orleans, Philadelphia and New York. Many Cubans began coming to the United States to pursue their education, and the United States became a refuge for Cuban dissidents, exiles and revolutionaries plotting the independence of their homeland. Many Cubans also furthered the idea of annexation of Cuba to the United States, and both annexationists and revolutionaries continuously prevailed upon U.S. leadership to support and underwrite separation from Spain. But even the revolutionaries seeking independence foresaw a close relationship with the United States in governing their own republic.

As Cuba became the world's largest producer of sugar in the nineteenth century and southern states were anxious to increase the number of "slave" states, American designs on Cuba, which dated back to Thomas Jefferson's interest in acquiring the island, intensified and led to, as mentioned above, various attempts by the United States to purchase Cuba from Spain. Also, after somewhat of a reconciliation with Spain in the 1850s, the Cuban revolutionary movement once again gained strength for another 30 years, causing a surge in immigration to the United States corresponding with their wars—the Ten Years' War (1868–1878) and the Independence War (1895–1898)—and the growth of the cigar industry in Florida, Louisiana, and New York. Beginning in the 1860s, a large segment of the tobacco industry relocated from Cuba to the United States to

get around the protectionist tariffs of the U.S. and to avoid the turbulence of the wars of independence and a very active labor movement; in addition, the factories would be closer to the primary markets. At the same time, Cuba drew large investors in its agriculture from the United States. In 1890, the McKinley Tariff practically curtailed cigar shipments from Cuba to the United States and benefitted even more the Cuban cigar industry located within the United States.

By 1895, the year of the outbreak of the final phase of the war of Cuban independence, North Americans had invested $50 million in Cuba and trade with Cuba amounted to over $100 million per year (See Chapter on Relations with Spain and Spanish America). Following the election of William McKinley, yellow journalism promoted U.S. intervention in Cuba on behalf of its independence, by invoking every anti-Spanish slur and racial attack that had been passed on through the Black Legend and Manifest Destiny. William Randolph Hearst and Joseph Pulitzer built up such an hispanophobic frenzy through the press that preachers directed their sermons against Spain, anti-Spanish demonstrations were held by Princeton University students and Leadville miners, and the Youngstown, Ohio, Chamber of Commerce even boycotted the Spanish onion (Horseman, 122–123). There was even a new edition of Bartolomé de las Casas' sixteenth-century *Brief Relation* published in 1898 under the inflammatory title of *An Historical and True Account of the Cruel Massacre and Slaughter of 20,000,000 People in the West Indies by the Spaniards.*

The U.S. Congress declared war on Spain on March 19, 1898. After much of the war had been fought and won by Cuban insurgents, the United States conducted negotiations with Spain without the Cubans, and forced Spain through the Treaty of Paris, signed December 12, 1898, to relinquish its dominion over Cuba, Puerto Rico, the Virgin Islands, Guam, and the Philippines. In effect, these islands had unwittingly traded one colonial ruler for another. In one felt swoop, the United States became a colonial empire and its Manifest Destiny had brought it to the doorstep of the Far East; it would govern the various and disparate races that had been feared earlier—in 1898 Hawaii also became a protectorate of the United States. The objections to governing territories that were filled with "black, mixed, degraded, and ignorant, or inferior races" had lost out to more important geo-political concerns and trade issues. The ideological line, however, that covered this change from expanding borders to appropriation of the colonial model was that the United States had a moral obligation to extend the benefits of Anglo-Saxon culture to backward areas of the world. And, there was an added imperial goal for dominion over the Caribbean islands: the impending construction of a trans-isthmian canal in Central America, a canal that had been discussed and negotiated for half a century. The last piece in the puzzle that made the United States into a colonial power in Spanish America was Panama; it was added—although not as a star on our flag; none of these colonies became stars—after the United States fomented Panama's revolution and separation from Colombia in 1903 to acquire better control of the intended canal zone along with better terms for lease of the zone—all the while staving off British and other European interests by invoking the Monroe Doctrine.

Thus, the United States went into the twentieth century with a military government in place in Cuba and Puerto Rico, and poised for numerous military interventions in the Caribbean, Mexico and Central America in the name of the Monroe Doctrine, a soon-to-be-added Corollary to the Monroe Doctrine by President Theodore Roosevelt, and the obligation to extend the benefits of Anglo-American freedom and liberty to inferior peoples who had such a difficult time in governing themselves. Throughout the century, the numerous interventions in the internal politics of Santo Domingo, Mexico and Central America favored and protected U.S. business interests in these countries and extended the power and control of the United States over their economies. Puerto Ricans became citizens of the United States in 1917 under the Jones Act and lived under U.S. military government until 1953. Cuba became nominally independent and elected its own president in 1901, but through the Platt Amendment forced into its constitution by the United States, Cuba was compelled to accept United States intervention at any time. Part of the relationship that developed was the dependency that developed by both the sender countries and the United States on e/immigrant labor, both legal and illegal, to the United States; the laborers became a natural resource, in effect, imported by United States industries.

During the twentieth century, further expansionism would come through trade and investment, not territorial expansion, and it would always be protected by the "big stick": gunboat and dollar diplomacy. In the twentieth century, the moral imperative of the Anglo-American empire became the incorporation and maintenance of the Spanish American countries within the U.S. economic and political sphere while fashioning an immigration policy that treated the inferior races of these societies as the unskilled manpower to develop the agribusiness and manufacturing industries at home so as to further elaborate the economic miracle that was the United States. In essence, the greatest resources that Mexico, Puerto Rico and, to some extent, Cuba had to offer the United States was the low-wage labor that would be needed to supplant that great institution that had enriched the South: slavery. During times of war, also, the resident Hispanic workers and their children—and the entire male citizenry of Puerto Rico—would make an excellent non-commissioned fighting force. In effect, the U.S. system of races had effectively converted the African, Indian and mixed-blood working and peasant classes of its nearest Hispanic neighbors into a caste of laborers on which the United States could base its economic development. Ubiquitous segregation practices in employment, housing and schooling ensured that the Hispanic caste, from the turn of the century to the present making up the majority of Hispanics in the United States, would remain available in times of economic expansion; in times of recession, the Hispanics were easily deported.

✳ THE HISPANIC "RACE" TODAY: SELF-PERCEPTIONS AND ANGLO IMPRESSIONS

As previously mentioned, in the United States there predominates two large categories of race division, white and non-white, the first attended by privileges and the second by disadvantages. The non-white category is further divided by tradition and such institutions as the census into four sub-categories: black, red, yellow and brown. Race is strictly genealogical in the United States and permanent, as long as one drop of non-white blood persists in the individual family line. In Latin America, however, race, if seen at all, is seen as a continuum with no fixed demarcation between categories, and there are many more categories perceived based on class, education and many other social variables (Rodríguez 1994: 131). Thus Hispanics from a culturally and genetically mixed racial background entered a biologically based biracial structure in the United States, where European Americans were at one end of the pole and African Americans were at the other end. Native Americans and Asians occupied "ambiguous gray positions vis-a-vis the dichotomy," and Hispanics were expected to fit into the same space (Rodríguez 1994: 132).

As noted above, in the nineteenth century, Mexicans were considered white and eligible for citizenship because of the stipulations of the Treaty of Guadalupe Hidalgo, and in the mid-twentieth century, some Mexican American civil rights groups were able to fight being segregated with blacks by claiming this whiteness under the law. In 1917, in a step towards incorporating Puerto Rico as a colony of the United States, the United States Congress extended U.S. citizenship to all Puerto Ricans. It was not until the case of *Hernández v. Texas* and the passing of civil rights legislation during the 1960s, however, when Hispanics were legally recognized as a separate and unique group.

Hernández v. Texas was the first Mexican American discrimination case to reach the U.S. Supreme Court. The suit against Texas claimed that Pete Hernández, a convicted murdered had been denied equal protection under the law because he had faced a jury that did not include Mexican Americans. The court found that Jackson County, Texas, had not chosen a Mexican American juror in 25 years, despite its having a Mexican American population of 14 percent. The decision was the first to recognize Hispanics as a separate class of people suffering profound discrimination. Previously, Hispanics were officially recognized as "white" and, therefore, not a separate, minority class. The 1954 decision paved the way for Hispanic Americans to use legal means to attack all types of discrimination throughout the United States. Thus, Mexicans, and all Hispanics, had gained the right to be seen as a separate category; in effect, through this case and the Hispanic civil rights movements of the 1960s and 1970s, Hispanics had become brown. By the 1980 census, Hispanics were allowed to identify themselves as Hispanics. Today, there is still no identifier on the census for biracial or multiracial individuals— despite considerable mixing of all groups progressing in the United States at probably the fastest rate in history.

Under the influence of the racial system of the United States, Hispanics here perceive themselves along a color line in reference to three poles: more white, more Indian or more black, with the perception of greater stigma being attached going from the white extreme to the black. And, it is believed, that greater discrimination is experienced the closer an individual's skin color approaches the black pole. Hispanics are helpless within the racial system to define themselves; living in the United States means being defined by color rather than by culture for the vast majority of Hispanics. Only those very few that are perceived as completely white are approached by Anglos as *culturally* rather than racially distinct. But in either case—that of being perceived as white or that of being perceived as black—the Hispanic individual experiences a great deal of confusion and anger, for the resultant identification can have the effect of isolating him from his family or community

on purely superficial grounds. "Identification by white Americans as black, or even as racially mixed or white appearing . . . has had economic, residential, social, and even political results" (Rodríguez 1994: 136). Moreover, occupying the intermediate ground can make the Hispanic acutely aware of the bi-polar world of the United States and feel that he or she really has no place here and is not part of the national identity (or debate, in questions of entitlement and policy on civil rights, affirmative action, representative politics, etc.).

Rodríguez theorizes that Hispanics have not accepted U.S. racial standards, as evidenced by their responses on the U.S. censuses of 1980 and 1990. She points out that more than 40 percent of Hispanic respondents did not identify themselves as white or black (nor indigenous or Asian), but chose the last category, titled "other," and then further specified that they were Puerto Rican or Mexican American, Chicano, Spanish, etc. (Rodríguez 1994: 137). Predictions that "white" Hispanics would assimilate into the white population of the United States and that "black" Hispanics would also assimilate into the black populations, leaving only a "brown" people to identify as Hispanics or Latinos, have not been borne out (Rodríguez 1980: 29). But, how long and to what extent Hispanics will continue in the future to identify themselves as a culture in the United States is unknown. There is great pressure in education and politics to convert Hispanics into a race. However, continued immigration, as well as travel and communications with Latin America, may also have the effect of reinforcing Latin American standards among Hispanics in the United States.

References

Almaguer, Tomás. *Racial Fault Lines: The Historical Origins of White Supremacy in California.* Berkeley: University of California Press, 1994.

Barrera, Mario. *Race and Class in the Southwest: A Theory of Racial Inequality* Notre Dame: University of Notre Dame Press, 1979.

History Task Force of the Centro de Estudios Puetorriqueños. *Labor Migration under Capitalism: The Puerto Rican Experience.* New York: Monthly Review Press, 1979.

Hoffman, Abraham. *Unwanted Mexican Americans in the Great Depression: Repatriation Pressures.* Tucson: University of Arizona Press, 1974.

Horseman, Reginald. *Race and Manifest Destiny. The Origins of American Racial Anglo-Saxonism.* Cambridge: Harvard University Press, 1981.

Kanellos, Nicolás, with Cristelia Pérez. *Chronology of Hispanic American History.* Detroit: Gale Research, 1995.

Kanellos, Nicolás, and Claudio Esteva-Fabregat, general editors. *Handbook of Hispanic Cultures in the United*

States. four volumes. Houston: Arte Público Press, 1994–95.

Knight, Alan. "Racism, Revolution, and *Indigenismo*: Mexico, 1910–1940." In *The Idea of Race in Latin America, 1870–1940,* edited by Richard Graham. Austin: University of Texas Press, 1990: 71–113.

Meier, Matt S., and Feliciano Rivera. *Dictionary of Mexican American History.* Westport, Connecticut: Greenwood Press, 1981.

Montes Huidobro, Matías, ed. *El laúd del desterrado.* Houston: Arte Público Press, 1995.

Morner, Magnus. *Race and Class in Latin America.* New York: Columbia University Press, 1970.

——. *Race Mixture in the History of Latin America.* Boston: Little, Brown and Company, 1967.

Powell, Philip Wayne, *Tree of Hate. Propaganda and Prejudices Affecting United States Relations with the Hispanic World.* New York: Basic Books, 1971.

Rodríguez, Clara. "Challenging Racial Hegemony: Puerto Ricans in the United States." In *Race.* Steven Gregory and Roger Sanjek, eds. New Brunswick, New Jersey: Rutgers University Press, 1994: 131–145.

——. *The Ethnic Queue in the U.S.: The Case of Puerto Ricans.* San Francisco: R & E Associates, 1974.

——. "Puerto Ricans: Between Black and White." In *The Puerto Rican Struggle: Essays on Survival in the U.S.* New York: Puerto Rican Migration Research Consortium, 1980; 47–57.

Ruiz de Burton, María Amparo. *The Squatter and the Don.* Houston: Arte Público Press, 1993.

Smedley, Audrey. *Race in North America: Origin and Evolution of a Worldview.* Boulder, Colorado: Westview Press, 1993.

Varela, Félix. *Jicoténcal.* Houston: Arte Público Press, 1995.

Nicolás Kanellos

Population Growth and Distribution

※ Census Bureau Statistics and the Hispanic Population ※ Demographics ※ Hispanic Diversity

In the last three decades Hispanics have received a great deal of attention and have become part of the national consciousness for several reasons. One is the rapid increase in the size of the Hispanic population. As can be seen from the statistics presented in this chapter, Hispanics are increasing at a much higher rate than the total population and are expected to become the nation's largest minority group sometime early in the next century.

A second reason for the increased attention is immigration to the United States, especially undocumented migration from Mexico. The size of the immigrant population and its effects on society have been intensely debated. The political turmoil in Central America, especially in El Salvador, has added to the debate as Central Americans have migrated to the United States to escape the crises in their countries.

The bilingual-bicultural movement has also focused attention on Hispanic demands that society's institutitons, especially those devoted to education, develop programs in Spanish as well as in English to meet their needs and reflect their culture. These programs are controversial among many non-Hispanics.

A fourth reason for the expanded awareness of Hispanics is the economic and political power that Hispanics have gained as their numbers have grown. The sheer size of the Hispanic population makes it an important economic group in areas where Hispanics are concentrated. Hispanics are also an important voting bloc and now elect members of their own to political positions in states such as Florida, California, Texas, New Mexico, and New York. In other states, Hispanics play an important role in electing non-Hispanics to office.

These issues, amont others, are pushing many Hispanic concerns to the forefront, and for many ob-
servers of American society portend a national minority group whose economic, political, and social influence can only continue to increase.

※ CENSUS BUREAU STATISTICS AND THE HISPANIC POPULATION

Most of the statistics presented in this chapter are taken from U.S. Census Bureau publications. Census Bureau information about Hispanics is controversial because of undercounting, the criteria used to identify Hispanics, and the presence of undocumented immigrants.

Generally speaking, persons from the working class tend to be undercounted to a greater degree than others. Since most Hispanics tend to be working-class, they are likely to be affected disproportionately by an undercount. The Census Bureau estimates that approximately 5.8 percent of the total Hispanic population, or 1.2 million people, were not counted in the 1990 census.

The criteria used by the Census Bureau to identify the Hispanic population has changed over time. Such categories as foreign birth or parentage, Spanish mother tongue, Spanish language, Spanish surname, and Spanish heritage are some of the ways in which Hispanics have been identified since 1850. These different identifiers make it difficult to make comparisons over time because they do not precisely define the same population. Also, the various definitions have not always been used on a national basis. The Spanish surname criteria, for example, was restricted to the five southwestern states of Texas, New Mexico, Arizona, Colorado, and California, where Mexican Americans constitute the main Hispanic group. Currently the Census Bureau uses a self-identification method. Persons are asked if they are of Spanish or Hispanic origin. If they answer yes, they are then asked to identify themselves as Mexican, Mexican American, Chicano, Puerto Rican, Cuban, or other Spanish/Hispanic origin.

While the U.S. Census is broken down according to a system of race designation, it does request that individuals self-identify. The census form is biased against individuals choosing the "Other" category, and the census does not allow for biracial or multiracial designations. Although the majority of Hispanics are mestizos or of mixed heritage, the census form encourages the individual to identify with a racial designation. However, Hispanics have more and more resisted racial identification and chosen instead to check the "Other" box and fill in the blank by writing in such designations as Mexican American, Puerto Rican, Cuban, etc., which are cultural designations. The number of people who checked the box marked "Other" on the census forms increased 45 percent between the 1980 and 1990 censuses, to 9.8 million—about one in 25 Americans. Out of that group, 98 percent claimed Hispanic origin or ethnicity. That means that more than 40 percent of the nation's 22 million self-identified Hispanics were not

willing to identify themselves as either black or white.

Generally speaking, persons from the working class tend to be undercounted to a greater degree than others. Since most Hispanics tend to be working-class, they are likely to be affected disproportionately by an undercount. The Census Bureau estimates that approximately 5.8 percent of the total Hispanic population, or 1.2 million people, were not counted in the 1990 census.

The presence of undocumented immigrants is an issue not only because of the debate over their economic and social impact because no one really knows how many reside in the United States. Estimates of their number have ranged from half a million to 12 million. The Census Bureau estimates that there were approximately 3.3 million undocumented immigrants in the United States in 1989. Undocumented migrants from Mexico constitute the largest portion of such immigrants, but there are other undocumented immigrants from other countries as well, but again no one knows precisely how many.

In addition to uncertainty over the size of the undocumented population, there is also uncertainty about its demographics. For instance, undocu-

Senior citizens at the Domino Park in Little Havana, Miami.

Undocumented workers entering the United States at El Paso, Texas, 1990.

mented immigrants tend to be young males, but the proportion of young males, relative to females and older people is not known.

These problems with undercounting, identifying criteria, and undocumented immigrants indicate that census information about Hispanics should be interpreted cautiously. Nevertheless, despite the limitations, the Census Bureau is the main source of such information, and much can be learned about the Hispanic population from analyzing the data. Also, the Census Bureau continues to refine its counting and reporting techniques in order to ensure a more accurate count of not only the Hispanic population but other groups as well.

✳ DEMOGRAPHICS

Hispanics and Non-Hispanics: Growth Rate

The Hispanic population is growing at a faster rate than the non-Hispanic. Between 1980 and 1990, it increased by 53 percent, in comparison with only 6.8 percent for non-Hispanics.

In 1991, Hispanics numbered approximately 22 million people and composed approximately 9 per-

cent of the total U.S. population of 249 million. If the number of undocumented Hispanic immigrants could be accurately counted, the growth rate and size of the Hispanic population would be greater.

The ten states with the largest increase in the number of Hispanics are California, Texas, New York, Florida, Illinois, New Jersey, Arizona, New Mexico, Colorado, and Massachusetts, in that order. The increase in the size of California's Hispanic population is particularly noteworthy. It increased dramatically, from approximately 4.5 million in 1980 to 7.6 million in 1990, or by 69 percent. This rate of increase exceeded the national Hispanic increase of 53 percent. The size of California's Hispanic population is in fact larger than the total population of all but nine states.

Factors in Population Growth

A population increases its size through net migration and natural increase. Net migration is the number of immigrants minus the number of emigrants. Natural increase is defined as the number of births minus the number of deaths. One-half of the growth rate among Hispanics is attributed to net migration and one-half to natural increase. In comparison, 21 percent of the increase in the number of non-Hispanics is attributed to net migration and 7.9 percent to natural increase. Again, the contribution of net migration to the growth of the Hispanic population is probably greater because of the number of undocumented immigrants.

Population Predictions

At the current rates of growth, Hispanics will double in size by the year 2020 and will number approximately 43 million people. Most of the growth rate will occur among those 35 years of age and older. In contrast, it will take the non-Hispanic population 160 years to double. Non-Hispanics may peak in size by the year 2020 and then begin to decline in relative as well as absolute numbers.

In 1996, the U.S. Census Bureau predicted that Latinos and Asians would account for more than half of the growth in the population of the United States every year for at least 50 years. The result will be a great change in the ethnicity of the United States. By the year 2050, non-Hispanic whites will only be a bare majority. As of July, 1995, the total population of the United States was 262.8 million, but is estimated to climb to 393; 9 million by the year 2050. While the rate of general population growth will shrink over the next 50 years, the rate of growth of the Hispanic population will actually increase. By the year 2050, the Hispanic population is predicted to make up 24.5 percent of the total population, making Hispanics by far the largest minority group in the United States, and almost half of the size of the non-Hispanic white population. The Bureau of the Census expects immigration of 820,000 per year, including about 225,000 undocumented persons. The Hispanic population in 1996 was growing at a rate of 900,000 per year, including net immigration of 350,000. Even without immigration, the Hispanic population would be the fastest growing because it is younger and has a higher fertility rate. Hispanics will become the United States' largest minority in the year 2009 by surpassing the black population. The largest growth in the Hispanic population will take place in the states of California, Texas, New York, Florida, Illinois and New Jersey, in that order. However, there is now a spill-over effect, with immigrant communities growing in such areas as Atlanta, Minneapolis, and Washington state.

States with Large Hispanic Populations

The majority of Hispanics are concentrated in the five southwestern states of California, Colorado, New Mexico, Arizona, and Texas. Approximately 63 percent of the total U.S. Hispanic population reside

A group of Hispanics have just been issued their temporary residence cards, 1991. (Photograph by Les Fetchko.)

in these five states. Four states outside the Southwest account for 26 percent of the Hispanic population: New York (12.3 percent), Florida (8 percent), Illinois (4 percent), and New Jersey. Puerto Ricans are the largest group in New York and New Jersey, and Cubans are the largest in Florida. Puerto Ricans and Mexican Americans are the largest groups in Illinois.

Hispanics are more geographically concentrated than the total population. Approximately 53 percent of the population lived in California and Texas in 1990. In comparison, a majority of the total population of the United States lived in nine states.

Age

Hispanics are younger than the non-Hispanic population. The median age of Hispanics, according to a 1991 census report, is 26.2 years, compared with 33.8 years for non-Hispanics. Another indicator of the youthfulness of the Hispanic population is the relative number of people under five and 15 years of age. Hispanics under age five make up 11 percent of the population, and people under age 15 make up 30 percent. Among non-Hispanics the respective figures are 22 percent and 7 percent.

Birth Rates

Hispanics are younger than non-Hispanics because they have a higher birthrate. The average number of children among Hispanics is 3.6, in comparison with 2.4 for non-Hispanics. The high birthrate of Hispanic women is emphasized when different age groups are considered. Hispanic women between ages 15 and 24 have 43 percent more children than non-Hispanic women of the same age group. Hispanic women between ages 25 and 34 have 30 percent more children than non-Hispanic women of the same age group, and Hispanic women 35 to 44 have 29 percent more children than non-Hispanic women.

Educational Attainment

Educational attainment differences between Hispanics and non-Hispanics are glaring. Approximately 12.5 percent of Hispanics over age 25 have completed fewer than five years of education, compared with 1.6 percent for non-Hispanics. In regard to high school, 51.3 percent of Hispanic adults have a high school education, in comparison with 80.5 percent of non-Hispanics. Only 9.7 percent of Hispanics have a college education, in contrast to 27.3 percent of non-Hispanics.

Labor Force Participation

The civilian labor force is defined as persons 16 years of age and over who are employed or are actively seeking employment. According to this criteria, 78 percent of Hispanic males and 51 percent of Hispanic females were in the labor force in March 1991. The respective figures for non-Hispanic males and females were 74 percent and 57 percent.

Occupation

The occupational status of Hispanics is not as high as that of non-Hispanics. Over twice as many non-Hispanic males (27.6 percent) hold managerial and professional jobs as do Hispanic males (11.4 percent). At the lower end of the occupational hierarchy, there are more Hispanics (29.1 percent) than non-Hispanics (19.1 percent) working as operators, fabricators, and laborers.

A similar picture emerges when the occupational distribution of Hispanic and non-Hispanic females is

The drive to legalize undocumented workers in Houston, Texas. (Photograph by Curtis Dowell.)

Mexican Independence Day Parade, Houston, Texas, 1982. (Photograph by Curtis Dowell.)

compared. Approximately 15.8 percent of Hispanic females in the labor force hold managerial and professional occupations, in contrast to 28 percent of non-Hispanic females. At the lower end, Hispanic females make up 14 percent of the operators, fabricators, and laborers, in comparison with 7.6 percent of non-Hispanic females.

Unemployment

Unemployment rates are greater for Hispanics than for the white population. In November of 1992, 12 percent of the Hispanic population was unemployed compared to only 6.3 percent of the white population. In the same year, the Bureau of Labor Statistics reported that the unemployment rate of blacks was, however, greater than that of the other two groups at 13.8 percent. While the percentages of unemployed were different in November of 1991, the same trend held in regard to percentages.

Income

Given the relatively low educational-attainment level and occupational status of Hispanics, it is not surprising that they earn less income than non-His-

panics. The median family income of Hispanics is $23,400, in comparison with $36,300 for non-Hispanics, or 64 percent of the non-Hispanic median family income.

The median income of Hispanic males is $14,100, and $22,000 for non-Hispanic males. Hispanic males are earning 64 percent of what non-Hispanic males earn.

Hispanics females earn 81 percent of what non-Hispanic females earn. The median income figures are $10,100 for Hispanic females and $12,400 for non-Hispanic females.

Poverty

More Hispanic than non-Hispanic families live in poverty. According to 1990 U.S. Census income figures, 25.2 percent of all Hispanic families were classified as living in poverty, compared with 9.4 percent of non-Hispanic families. Further, 17 percent of the Hispanic families living in poverty were headed by persons 65 years of age or older, 48.3 percent were headed by females, and 35.7 percent of the heads of household were high school dropouts. The rates for non-Hispanic families were 9.5 percent, 31.7 percent, and 21.2 percent, respectively.

✳ HISPANIC DIVERSITY

The Hispanic population is not a homogeneous group. It shares a common culture, but beyond this, the groups that make up the Hispanic population differ significantly in many important ways. The three major groups are Mexican Americans, Puerto Ricans, and Cubans. Other Hispanic groups are the Central and South Americans and people of various other Hispanic origins. There are major historical, cultural, and demographic differences between these groups.

History

The history of Mexicans, Puerto Ricans, and Cubans is radically different. The Spaniards conquered the Indians of Mexico, and by mating with them, produced the mestizo or Mexican people. Mexicans, therefore, have a strong Indian as well as Spanish heritage.

The islands of Cuba and Puerto Rico were also conquered by the Spaniards. Both islands were originally populated with the Arawak and Carib Indians, whom the Spaniards forced into slavery to work in the mines and fields in Puerto Rico and the sugarcane fields in Cuba. The Spaniards began importing slaves from Africa to Cuba and Puerto Rico, and eventually the African slaves outnumbered and began to marry into the Indian population. Thus, Cubans and Puerto Ricans not only have an Indian and Spanish heritage but a strong African ancestry as well.

Immigration

Immigration patterns to the United States are also different for Mexican Americans, Cubans, and Puerto Ricans. The number of people who migrated to the United States from Mexico was small prior to 1900. After 1900, Mexican immigration began to increase. The factors that stimulated emigration from Mexico were the Mexican Revolution, poor economic conditions, and a rapid increase in the size of the population. The primary factor which pulls Mexican immigrants to the United States today is the demand for cheap labor. Constant migration from Mexico means that within the Mexican American community there is always a large number of Mexican immigrants.

Prior to 1959, the number of Cubans who migrated to the United States was very small. In 1959, Fidel Castro overthrew the Fulgencio Batista dictatorship, declared Cuba a socialist state, and began implementing measures that outlawed private property and individuals' accumulation of large amounts of wealth. Many Cubans fled Cuba and immigrated to Florida. This was the first wave of Cubans to migrate, and the majority were educated professionals and skilled technicians. A second wave of Cubans migrated to the United States in 1980. Unlike the first wave, most of these immigrants were from the poorer classes and were not as welcome or as well treated.

As a result of these two immigration movements, the number of Cubans in the United States increased rapidly. In 1959, there were only 30,000 Cubans in the United States, and in 1991 there were 1.1 million. Cubans have become a major economic, political, and cultural force in Florida, especially in Miami, which has the largest concentration of Cubans in the United States.

The pattern of migration from Puerto Rico to the United States is different from that of either Mexico or Cuba. Puerto Rico became a possession of the United States in 1899, and Puerto Ricans were granted United States citizenship in 1917. Thus, Puerto Ricans who migrate to the United States are not considered immigrants in the same sense as Mexicans and Cubans. Prior to 1940, Puerto Ricans did not immigrate to the United States in large numbers. After World War II, the economy of Puerto Rico began to deteriorate, and migration to the United States increased and has been constant ever since. Today there are approximately 2.4 million Puerto Ricans living in the United States and 3.5 million living on the island of Puerto Rico.

Geographical Concentration

Mexican Americans, Puerto Ricans, and Cubans tend to reside in different parts of the United States. The majority of Mexican-origin people live in the five southwestern states of Texas, New Mexico, Colorado, Arizona, and California. Puerto Ricans tend to live in New York, New Jersey, and Illinois, while the majority of Cubans reside in Florida.

Age and Birthrate Variations

Cubans are the oldest Hispanic population, and Mexican Americans are the youngest. The median age for Cubans is 39.3 years, in comparison with 24.3 years for Mexican. Puerto Ricans are also a young population, but not as young as Mexican Americans; their median age is 26.7 years.

Mexican Americans have the highest birthrate of the three groups, followed by Puerto Ricans and then Cubans, according to 1987 reports. Mexican American women between the ages of 35 and 44, for exam-

A mass citizenship swearing-in ceremony at Hoffheinz Pavilion, University of Houston, 1987. (Photograph by Curtis Dowell.)

ple, have given birth, on the average, to 3.6 children. The average for Puerto Rican women in the same age group is 3.2 children, and for Cuban women, 2.0 children. The Cuban average is even lower than the 2.6 average of the total U.S. population.

Education, Occupation, and Income Variations

Cuban Americans are primarily a middle-class population with relatively high levels of education, occupational status, and income. Mexican Americans are primarily a working-class population holding blue-collar occupations and have low levels of education and income. Generally, Puerto Ricans rank in between Cubans and Mexican Americans, but are closer to Mexican Americans than Cubans in terms of their educational attainment, occupational status, and income.

The high educational level of Cubans is seen in the number of Cuban high school and college graduates: 61 percent have a high school education and approximately 19 percent have a college education. Among Puerto Ricans, 58 percent have a high school education and 10 percent have completed college. Among Mexican Americans, 44 percent have com-

pleted high school and only 6 percent are college graduates.

The high level of education among Cubans reflects the middle-class status of the Cubans who migrated to the United States in the early 1960s. Later generations of Cubans, however, are continuing to achieve high levels of education as well. Among Cubans ages 25 to 34, for example, approximately 78 percent are high school graduates and 20.4 percent have a college education.

Mexican American males are in the labor force in a larger proportion than either Cuban or Puerto Rican males; 80 percent of all Mexican American males over age 16 are participating in the nations' work force, in comparison with 73 percent of the Cuban and 66 percent of the Puerto Rican males. What Mexican American, Puerto Rican, and Cuban males have in common is being concentrated in the skilled and semiskilled occupations. Approximately 50 percent of all Mexican American males and 43 percent of all Cuban and Puerto Rican males hold skilled and semiskilled occupations. Where the groups differ is in managerial and professional and technical sales and administrative support occupations. Cubans hold more of these types of occupations than either Puerto Ricans or Mexican Americans.

There are more Cuban females in the labor force than either Puerto Rican or Mexican American females. Approximately 55 percent of all Cuban females over age 16 are in the civilian labor force, compared with 42 percent of Puerto Rican females and 51 percent of Mexican American females.

The female occupational distribution resembles that of the males in that Cuban females have a higher occupational status than Puerto Rican and Mexican American females. One significant difference is the higher proportion of Mexican American females in service occupations. Approximately 27 percent of the Mexican American females hold service occupations, compared with 16 percent of Puerto Rican and Cubans females.

Cubans have the highest average family income and Puerto Ricans have the lowest. The figures for the three groups are $38,144, $27,879, and $25,066 for Cuban, Mexican American and Puerto Rican families, respectively.

There are more Puerto Rican families living in poverty than either Mexican American or Cuban families. Approximately 38 percent of all Puerto Rican families live in poverty, 65 percent of these, families are headed by a female, and 55 percent of the females are high school dropouts.

Mexican Americans have the second-highest proportion of families living in poverty, approximately 28 percent. Of these 46 percent are headed by a female, with 34 percent of the females being high school dropouts.

Only 14 percent of all Cuban families live in poverty. Unlike the Puerto Rican and Mexican Americans, relatively few of the poor Cuban families are headed by females. Rather, most are headed by males who are high school dropouts.

Central and South Americans and Other Hispanics

In addition to Mexican Americans, Puerto Ricans, and Cubans, the Hispanic population consists of Central and South Americans and people who are classified by the U.S. Census Bureau as "other Hispanic origins." This latter category includes those whose origins are in Spain and those identifying themselves generally as Hispanic, Spanish, Spanish American, Hispano, Latino, and so on. Central and South Americans make up 13.8 percent of the total Hispanic population, and those of "other Hispanic origins" make up 7.6 percent.

Generally, Central and South Americans and "other" Hispanics tend to have characteristics that resemble the Cubans rather than the Mexican Ameri-

can or Puerto Rican populations. The median age of Central and South Americans and "other" Hispanics is 27.9 and 31.0 years, respectively. Both groups tend to be highly educated. Approximately 15.1 percent of Central and South Americans and 16.2 percent of "other" Hispanics have four or more years of college.

Both groups also have a relatively high occupational status, with 12.7 percent of males and 14.5 percent of females of the Central and South American groups holding managerial and professional occupations; the respective figures for "other" Hispanics is 20.5 percent for males and 19.8 percent for females. At the lower end of the occupational hierarchy, Central and South Americans and "other" Hispanics tend to mirror the situation of Cubans, Mexican Americans, and Puerto Ricans in that there is a relatively large number of males concentrated in the operators, fabricators, and laborers category and a large number of females concentrated in the service occupations.

The average family income of Central and South Americans is $31,415 and for "other" Hispanics the average is $35,474. These averages are higher than the averages for Mexican Americans and Puerto Ricans but lower than the average for Cubans.

Approximately 27.2 percent of Central and South American families are classified as living below the poverty level. Approximately 33.3 percent of the families who live in poverty are headed by a high school dropout, and 39.3 percent are headed by females. Among "other" Hispanics, 19.4 percent of the families live in poverty, 49.1 percent are headed by females, and 38.7 percent are headed by a high school dropout. These percentages are closer to the rates for Mexican Americans and Puerto Ricans than to those for Cubans.

References

American Statistical Association. *Estimating Coverage of the 1990 United States Census: Demographic Analysis.* Atlanta, Georgia: U.S. Government Printing Office, 1991.

Bean, Frank D., Barry Edmonston, and Jeffrey S. Passel, *Undocumented Migration to the United States: IRCA and the Experience of the 1980s.* Santa Monica, California: Rand Corporation, and Washington, D.C.: The Urban Institute, 1990.

Bouvier, Leon F., and Cary B. Davis. *The Future Racial Composition of the United States.* Washington, D.C.: Demographic Information Services Center (DISC) of the Population Reference Bureau, 1982.

Flagin, Joe R. *Racial and Ethnic Relations.* Englewood Cliffs, New Jersey: Prentice Hall, 1989.

Hogan, Howard. *The 1990 Post-Enumeration Survey: Operations and Results.* Washington, D.C.: Bureau of the Census, 1991.

Passel, Jeffrey S. "Undocumented Immigration." *Annals, AAPSS,* 487, September 1986.

Portes, Alejandro, and Robert L. Bach. *Latin Journey: Cuban and Mexican Immigrants in the United States.* Los Angeles: University of California Press, Berkeley, 1985.

U.S. Bureau of the Census. *The Hispanic Population in the United states: March 1986 and 1987.* Current Population Reports, Series P-20, No. 434. Washington, D.C.: U.S. Government Printing Office, 1988.

U.S. Bureau of the Census. *The Hispanic Population in the United States: March 1991.* Current Population Reports, Series P. 20, No. 455. Washington, D.C.: U.S. Government Printing Office, 1991.

U.S. Bureau of the Census. *Projections of the Hispanic Population: 1983 to 2080.* Gregory Spencer, Current Population Reports, Series P. 25, No. 995. Washington, D.C.: U.S. Government Printing Office, 1986.

U.S. Department of Commerce. *1990 Census of Population and Housing: Puerto Rico.* Washington, D.C.: U.S. Government Printing Office, 1991.

U.S. Department of Commerce, Economics and Statistics Administration, Bureau of the Census. *1990 Census Profile. Race and Hispanic Origin,* No. 1. Washington, D.C.: U.S. Government Printing Office, 1991.

Warren, Robert, and Jeffrey S. Passel. "A Count of the Uncountable: Estimates of Undocumented Aliens Counted in the 1980 United States Census." *Demography,* Vol. 24, No. 3., 1987.

Tatcho Mindiola

8

Language

❋ Variations of Spanish Spoken ❋ English Usage among Hispanics
❋ Spanish in Business, the Media, and in Other Social Environments ❋ Bilingualism and Code-Switching

❋ VARIATIONS OF SPANISH SPOKEN

To a large extent, the varieties of Spanish spoken in the United States reflect the countries of origin of the Spanish-speaking communities and the conditions under which their language has evolved in the U.S. setting. It is frequent for groups sharing common national and social origins to live in the same neighborhoods, which reinforces the use of regional language features. If immigration continues in significant numbers, and new arrivals gravitate toward already established Hispanic communities, regional tendencies are further reinforced. Hispanic groups living in rural areas of the United States are nearly homogeneous with respect to country of origin, which, due to historical patterns of migration, is usually Mexico. In large urban areas many Spanish-speaking groups may coexist, sometimes even in the same neighborhoods. If one Hispanic group is numerically and economically predominant, other groups usually make some accommodation to the leading variety of Spanish, which sets the standard in local advertising, communications media, and education. Such is the case for Mexican American Spanish in the Southwest and in some Midwestern cities, for Cuban Spanish in South Florida, and for Puerto Rican Spanish in some northeastern cities. In Chicago, for example, several varieties of Spanish compete, and there is more variation in usage, even among speakers of a single ethnic community.

Spanish-speaking communities in the United States are, in approximate descending order of size, of the following origins: Mexican, Puerto Rican, Cuban, and Central American. In the latter category, Nicaraguans and Salvadorans are the most numerous. The Dominican population of New York City is rapidly growing; Dominican Spanish is quite similar to that of Puerto Rico, although members of each

group are aware of differences. Large numbers of Colombians are found in Miami, New York City, and elsewhere, but they come from many dialect zones of Colombia and do not exercise a strong centralizing influence on any variety of U.S. Spanish. Finally, there are several small but close-knit Spanish-speaking groups whose use of Spanish does not fall under the four large categories previously mentioned. These include Sephardic (Judeo-) Spanish-speakers in New York, Miami, and other urban areas, the *Isleños* of southeastern Louisiana, descendants of Canary Island settlers who arrived at the end of the eighteenth century, and the pre-Castro Cuban-Spanish communities of Key West and Tampa, which have been overshadowed by more recent Cuban immigration.

Spanish of Caribbean Origin

Cubans, Puerto Ricans, and Dominicans can instantly identify their own form of Spanish, but outsiders note more similarities than differences among the varieties of Spanish that originate in the Caribbean. Pronunciation is the single most important unifying factor, since Caribbeans are known for "swallowing" the final consonants, which are clearly heard, for example, in Mexican Spanish and parts of Central America. This slurring over final sounds also contributes to the impression that Caribbean Spanish is spoken faster than other varieties. For example, final *s* may sound somewhat like English *h*, or may disappear altogether. *Mis vecinos americanos* "my American neighbors" may come out as *mih vecinoh americano*. In careful speech, *s* may be pronounced more frequently, since schools often insist on giving the "correct" pronunciation to every written letter, but in colloquial speech the nearly total lack of final *s* is often baffling to students of Spanish who have

195

The Teatro Puerto Rico in October 1960, where Spanish-language vaudeville and films survived into the 1960s.

learned only a "spelling-pronunciation," and even Spanish-speakers from Mexico and Central America often find Caribbean Spanish hard to decipher.

Many Puerto Ricans pronounce trilled *rr* rather like English *h*, causing *Ramón* and *jamón* "ham" to practically fall together. This pronunciation of *rr* is often identified with rural regions; among Puerto Ricans in the United States, this type of *rr* is more frequent among families that have migrated from interior regions of the island, although it crops up from time to time in all Puerto Rican communities. More recently in Puerto Rico, this pronunciation has undergone a partial reevaluation, and some consider it a unique symbol of Puerto Rican cultural identity. Educated urban speakers may pronounce *rr* like *h* in circumstances which only a decade or two ago would have been unthinkable.

Also found in the Caribbean, particularly among Puerto Ricans, is the replacement of *r* by *l* at the end of words or before consonants; *trabajar* "to work" becomes *trabajal*, *carta* "letter" becomes *calta*, and *verdad* "true" may sound like *velá*. Even the most educated speakers utilize this pattern at times, but conscious attempts are usually made to avoid it. Since this pronunciation does not occur in Mexican

or Central American Spanish, even a few instances of *l* for *r* among Puerto Ricans are enough to create the stereotype that the entire Puerto Rican community speaks this way. Among Cubans, the change of *r* to *l* is rare among the first generation of highly educated immigrants, most of whom came from Havana. Among more recent arrivals, representing rural regions and the urban working class, this change is found, alongside what sounds like a doubling of the following consonant: *algo* "something" becomes *aggo*, *puerta* "door" becomes *puetta*, and so forth.

A few key words also set Caribbean Spanish-speakers apart from their mainland counterparts. *Guagua* "city bus," *goma* "automobile tire," and *chiringa* "kite," are ready identifiers of Caribbean origin. Words like *ají* "hot or sweet pepper," *maní* "peanut," and *caimán* "alligator" have spread to other Spanish-speaking countries, but are seldom used in Mexico or Central America.

Several words are unique to Puerto Rico, and sometimes also the Dominican Republic. As in other countries, many involve food and cultural practices. Beans, the staple food of the Caribbean, are known as *habichuelas* in Puerto Rico. These habichuelas are pink, as opposed to the black (Cuban) or red

(Mexican) *frijoles*. Puerto Ricans also eat *gandules*, small greenish-brown beans, the same way they eat *habichuelas* with rice. Puerto Ricans refer to oranges as *chinas*; orange juice is, predictably, *jugo de china*. Bananas of the eating variety are *guineos*, while cooked bananas are more frequently *plátanos*. Fried banana slices are *tostones*. The word *pastel*, which in other Spanish-speaking countries refers to sweet cakes or cookies, is in Puerto Rico a type of meat pie prepared with mashed tubors. The colloquial term for money is *chavos*, coming from the old Spanish *ochavos* "pieces of eight." As in other Latin American countries where the U.S. dollar is in common circulation, *peso* refers to the U.S. dollar, while *peseta* is a U.S. quarter. *Escrachao* means "ruined, destroyed," and a common interjection upon discovering something in this condition is *ay bendito!* Puerto Ricans joke among themselves that this expression is sometimes an alternative to taking action, calling this attitude *aybenditismo*. In Puerto Rico, a *jíbaro* is a "hillbilly" from the mountainous interior of the island; the recent cultural revival is bringing more respect and even veneration to this term, which in the past was used only derisively to describe rustics who failed to cope with urban customs. In Puerto Rico, *aguinaldos* are Christmas carols, and *mahones* are blue jeans. The latter word comes from the name of a town on the Spanish island of Menorca, where the blue denim cloth was originally produced. A wastebasket or garbage can is a *zafacón* in Puerto Rico; some have suggested English "safety can" as the source, but this is doubtful.

Cuban Spanish contains many local words. Unlike fellow Antilleans, Cubans often prefer the diminutive *-ico* instead of the more general Spanish *-ito*: *momentico* "just a minute," *chiquitico* "very little," and so on. Cubans use *chico* as a common form of address, at times even when speaking to more than one person. Neither excessive familiarity nor a male listener is necessarily assumed; the usage is similar to colloquial American English *man*, or *hombre* as used in Spain. Corresponding to the Puerto Rican *jíbaro*, or "hillbilly," is the Cuban *guajiro*, the country dweller immortalized in the popular song "Guantanamera." Cubans refer to small sacks or bags, such as used in grocery stores, as *cartuchos*. More recent arrivals from Cuba might have heard of the *por si acaso*, a bag carried (in Cuba) in case an unexpected supply of a rationed product is found. In western Cuba, including Havana, *papaya* is a taboo word, and this fruit is known as *fruta bomba*. Producers of tropical juices that are marketed among Cuban Americans carry two versions of papaya juice, *jugo de papaya* for the general Latin American clientele, and *jugo de fruta bomba*

for the Cuban population. Among other uniquely Cuban culinary terms are *arroz congrí*, prepared with red beans and rice in eastern Cuba, and *tocino del sol*, a type of custard. The *sandwich cubano* is a well-known food item in Cuban American communities, as is the *café cubano*, a tiny cup of highly sweetened espresso coffee. In Cuban Spanish, twins are colloquially referred to as *jimaguas*, a word of African origin. A *chucho* is a light switch, much to the surprise of Spanish-speakers from other regions, where the term has much different meanings. Cubans use *fajarse* for "to fight," *fastidiarse* for "to break, become ruined, run into trouble," and *me luce* for "it seems to me." A highly charged issue among Cuban Americans is the word used to refer to those who arrived via the Mariel boatlift of 1980, among whom the lower socioeconomic classes and rural regions were strongly represented. At the early stages, the term *marielero* was used, in reflection of Cuban place-naming patterns, but this has been replaced by *marielito*, a term that most Cubans regard as at least mildly pejorative.

Central American Spanish

People frequently refer to "Central America" as though it were a single entity. Indeed, the countries that form modern Central America (with the exception of Belize) did enjoy a fleeting moment of unity: following independence from Spain in the early 1820s, the Central American republics formed the ill-fated Central American Union, an attempt to federate five tiny nations into a significant regional power. After several unsuccessful trial marriages, the union was definitively dissolved in 1854, and the Central American republics have gone their own ways ever since. Even during the colonial period there were striking differences in the Spanish spoken in different regions of Central America, in fashions that do not always correspond to what might be supposed by looking at a map. For instance, Costa Rica, the southernmost Central American nation, shares more similarities with Guatemala, at the far north, than with neighboring Nicaragua. Honduran and Salvadoran Spanish blend together smoothly, but the contrast with Guatemalan Spanish is striking, and Nicaraguan Spanish is also rather different. Costa Rican Spanish bears no resemblance to neighboring Panamanian Spanish to the south, which is not surprising in view of the fact that Panama was formerly a province of Colombia, administered from Bogotá and largely populated from Colombia's coastal provinces, whose speech even today is very similar to that of Panama. Guatemalan Spanish, on the other hand, is similar to the Spanish of Mexico's Yucatán region, largely due to the common Mayan heritage.

All Central American nations have contributed to the U.S. Hispanic populations, in differing proportions and for different reasons. The Costa Rican contribution has been the least noticeable; this may perhaps reflect Costa Rica's relative prosperity and political stability within Central America. The Honduran contingent in the United States is also small, scattered across Miami, Houston, New York, and Los Angeles, but the largest group is found in New Orleans. This community results from the early years of the Central American banana industry, when companies based in New Orleans administered plantations on Honduras' northern coast.

Although there have always been Guatemalans from the middle and professional classes in the United States, the heaviest immigration has come in the form of political refugees from a nation torn by civil war. Many of these refugees are Mayan-speaking native Americans who speak little or no Spanish. Guatemalan communities are concentrated in Los Angeles, Miami, Houston, and New York. Small rural groups are found, for example, in southern Florida.

The Nicaraguan population in the United States is large, due mainly to the political uncertainty in Nicaragua. Prior to the Sandinista revolution of 1979, there were significant groups of Nicaraguans living in Miami and Los Angeles, but the mass exodus to the United States began in the 1980s, bringing tens of thousands of Nicaraguans, most of whom settled in Los Angeles, San Francisco, and particularly in Miami. In the latter city, Nicaraguans live in several well-defined neighborhoods, in which they have transplanted social, cultural, and economic structures from their homeland. Nicaraguan restaurants, stores, travel agencies, beauty shops, and medical facilities serve to reinforce the "little Nicaragua" image; several newspapers are published within the Nicaraguan community, and local radio stations air special programs produced by and for local Nicaraguans. Nicaraguan holidays are celebrated as fervently in Miami as in Nicaragua, and nearly any product or food found in Nicaragua can be found in the transplanted colonies in the United States. As with the Cubans, the first Nicaraguans to leave following the Sandinista revolution were the professionals, or those who had held high posts in the previous government. Subsequent arrivals include citizens from all walks of life, including English-speaking residents of the Caribbean shore, as well as Miskito Indians. Small communities of seafaring coastal Nicaraguans are found in Florida and along the coast of Texas, and even within Miami the *costeños* "coastal people" live and work in parts of the city different from those where the *ladinos* or Spanish-speakers from the highlands live. Although the post-Sandinista Nicaraguan government has put out a call for the return of all those who left during the previous regime, the Nicaraguan community in the United States shows no signs of shrinking, and may actually be growing larger.

The largest Central American group in the United States is the Salvadoran, concentrated in Los Angeles, Houston, Chicago and, Miami. Although the prolonged civil war in El Salvador has caused many professional and middle-class residents to move to the United States, there has not been a mass exodus such as occurred in Cuba and Nicaragua following the overthrow of earlier governments. Most of the several hundred thousand Salvadorans living in the United States come from the poorest groups, from rural areas of El Salvador and from squatter communities in San Salvador and other cities. They frequently have little or no formal education, and their speech patterns combine regional features with the results of social and cultural isolation. The contrast with Nicaraguans is striking; for the latter, it is the speech of the middle and professional class that sets the standard, while among Salvadorans, when a voice is raised to speak for the entire community, it is often from the opposite end of the social spectrum. Within the United States, the precarious situation of Salvadorans has kept many of their children from entering the school system, with the result that education in English or Spanish is comparatively limited. For these reasons, Salvadoran Spanish as found in the United States contains a high proportion of words and grammatical patterns representative of less-educated groups.

The pronunciation of Nicaraguan Spanish is in many ways similar to Cuban and Puerto Rican Spanish, particularly in the weak pronunciation of final *s*. Unlike Caribbean Spanish-speakers, Nicaraguans never interchange or drop *l* and *r*. On the other hand, Nicaraguans pronounce the Spanish *j* very weakly, and for example *trabajo* "work" may come out like *trabao*. Even more characteristic of Central American Spanish is the weak pronunciation of *y*; *gallina* "chicken" sounds like *gaína*, and *silla* "chair" like *sía*. Overcompensation is also heard, especially among Nicaraguans, so that *María* and *frío* "cold" sound like *Mariya* and *friyo*. None of this occurs in the Spanish-speaking Caribbean, and this difference is a major contributor to the unique accent of the *nicas* "Nicaraguans" and *guanacos* "Salvadorans."

To the casual listener, Salvadoran Spanish is closer to Mexican Spanish than to any of the Caribbean varieties, an impression that is confirmed by history. Salvadoran and Mexican Spanish share a large quantity of vocabulary items derived from Native American languages, principally Nahuatl and to a much lesser extent Mayan. Like Nicaraguans, Salvadorans weaken *y* and *j*. Among many rural speakers, a heavy nasalization is noted, with entire words and even phrases being pronounced "through the nose." This nasality, easy to detect and imitate but difficult to describe in technical terms, is not heard among other U.S. Hispanic groups. Another idiosyncratic feature of many Salvadorans is the occasional and sporadic pronunciation of *s* like English *th* in *thick* or the *z* of Castilian Spanish *zapato* "shoe." Salvadorans weaken final *s*, but not to the extent found among Nicaraguans and speakers from the Caribbean. On the other hand, many Salvadorans pronounce *s* like *h* at the *beginning* of words, something not heard in other varieties of Spanish. This causes *la semana* "the week" to sound like *la hemana*, and *cómo se llama* "what is your name" like *cómo he llama*. Sometimes this change affects *s* in the middle of a word; *presidente* "president" frequently comes out as *prehidente*, *necesario* "necessary" is heard as *nehesario*, and *nosotros* "we" as *nojotros*. Many rural Mexican and Nicaraguan speakers also say *nojotros*, but this is hardly ever found in the Caribbean. All these factors combine to make rural Salvadorans difficult for other Spanish-speakers to understand. Mexicans, for example, claim that Salvadorans speak f3.4]entre dientes "mumbling"; Salvadorans in turn say that Mexicans "sing" instead of talk! Cubans in Miami often make similar remarks.

All Central Americans share a word that is puzzling for other Spanish-speakers in the United States, although it is well known, for example, in Argentina. It is *vos*, used instead of *tú* as the familiar "you." This pronoun is accompanied by different verb conjugations, for example, *comés* instead of *comes* "you eat," *tenés* for *tienes* "you have," *decí* for *di* "say," *sos* for *eres* "you are." Nicaraguans, like all other Central Americans, prefer *vos* when speaking to one another, but many Nicaraguans in the United States comfortably switch to *tú* when speaking with non-Central Americans. Salvadorans may also use *tú*, sometimes even among one another, when a less-familiar relationship is perceived, but this is limited to more sophisticated urban speakers. Salvadorans from rural areas use *vos* nearly exclusively, and also use the formal *usted* to a greater extent than other Hispanic groups in the United States. Rural Salvadorans frequently use *usted* with small children to train them the respectful forms of address, and also use *usted* in situations where other groups would use a familiar pronoun. Central Americans in the United States who wish to conceal their origin or simply avoid misunderstandings when talking to other Spanish-speakers avoid using *vos*, although some

speakers cling to this word precisely because of its strong regional identification.

Nicaraguan Spanish has many unique words, some of which are becoming well known in Miami. These include such food items as *gallo pinto* "red beans and rice," *vigorón* "type of salad," and *pinol* "a drink made from toasted corn." Nicaraguans colloquially refer to themselves as *pinoleros*, reflecting their fondness for this drink, and this term vies with *nica* as a general reference to Nicaraguans. Like Salvadorans, Nicaraguans often refer to a turkey as *chompipe*, use the term *chele* to refer to blond-haired or fair-skinned individuals, and call dogs *chuchos* (which to Cubans means electric light switches). Nicaraguans employ the common interjection *idiay*, "wow" or "gosh." To a Nicaraguan, *arrecho* means "angry" and *dundo* means "stupid"; neither term is used in this fashion by non-Central Americans.

Although sharing many similarities with both Mexico and Nicaragua, Salvadoran Spanish also has words not used by other U.S. Hispanic groups (although they may be used elsewhere in Central America). Some such words are *andar* "carry, take along" (for example, *no ando mi cédula* "I don't have my identification card with me"), *suelto* "loose change," *chompa* "sweater," *bolo* "drunk," *pisto* "money," *cipote* "small child," *pupusa* "food made of tortillas filled with cheese or meat," *andén* "sidewalk," *chero* "friend, buddy," *chinear* "to baby-sit," and *colocho* "curly, unkempt hair." Many Salvadorans use expressions like *un mi amigo* "a friend of mine, my friend," where other Spanish-speakers would leave out *un*. They often use *hasta* "until" to refer to the *beginning* of an event, rather than to the end: *Abrimos hasta las ocho* thus means "we open *at* 8:00" and not "we are open *until* 8:00." This may cause confusion when Salvadorans talk to other Spanish-speakers, particularly in making and keeping appointments.

Mexican Spanish

Mexican varieties of Spanish share more similarities with Central American speech, particularly Salvadoran, than with any Caribbean dialects. The same native American language families had a strong influence on Mexican Spanish, and the patterns of colonial administration resulted in similar profiles in central Mexico and the highland capitals of Central America. "Mexican" Spanish existed in what is now U.S. territory several centuries before the nations of Mexico and the United States came into being. More Mexican Spanish was incorporated through U.S. territorial expansion (the Texas revolution and the Mexican-American War), and still more Mexican varieties are the result of twentieth-century immigration. Each stage of Mexican Spanish presence in the United States has its own peculiarities, although the similarities outweigh the differences.

The Spanish expedition of Juan de Oñate eventually settled in what is now New Mexico in the 1600s, and "Spaniards" have lived in this region ever since. When Mexico won its independence from Spain, the lives of the "Spaniards" in New Mexico and southern Colorado scarcely changed, and when this region became a U.S. territory following the Mexican-American War, the effects were again minimal. When New Mexico and Colorado attained statehood, following the migration of English-speaking settlers, the original Spanish began to recede, but even today it is possible to find speakers of what is regarded as the oldest variety of Spanish continuously spoken in North America. Families who identify with the earliest Spanish settlements refer to themselves as "Spaniards," and reject labels such as "Mexican," "Latin," and "Chicano." In its purest form, the speech of these "Spaniards" provides a window to the past, a taste of the speech of Spanish settlers during the Formative period of Latin American dialects.

More so than most Mexican dialects of today, the old Spanish of New Mexico and Colorado weakens word-final *s*, as in the Caribbean. Spanish *j* and *y* are also weakened. The intonation is less typically "Mexican" than other "Mexican American" varieties; in particular, the characteristic *norteño* accent is virtually absent. The old-Spanish-speakers of New Mexico and southern Colorado use words and expressions that have long since disappeared in other varieties of Spanish (*cócono* "turkey" is a typical example), at the same time using fewer native American borrowings than does modern Mexican Spanish.

Another group of U.S. Spanish-speakers, all but unknown and rapidly disappearing, represents a somewhat later stage of Mexican Spanish. Long before the Mexican Wars of Independence, the Texas revolution, or the Mexican-American war, *mestizo* soldiers from Mexico were sent to fortify the border between Texas and the French territory of Louisiana. In the early 1700s Spain established outposts at Los Aes (presently San Augustine, Texas), at Nacogdoches, Texas, and at Los Adaes, near modern-day Robeline, Louisiana; by the second half of the eighteenth century, the settlements were well established and the residents knew no other home. Spain had intended to settle eastern Texas to create a buffer zone against intrusion from French Louisiana, particularly the outpost at Natchitoches, but when the Louisiana territory was ceded to Spain, these defenses were no longer needed, and the Spanish government decided to withdraw all settlers. In 1773, the order arrived in eastern Texas to abandon

the settlements, for immediate resettlement in San Antonio, and despite bitter protests most residents were forced to abandon homes and crops and make an onerous journey of more than three months to the principal Spanish settlement in Texas. Upon arrival, the newcomers were treated poorly, given inferior land, and left to languish, and immediately they began planning for a return to the only place they knew as home. Many settlers managed to move back to eastern Texas, founding the town of Nacogdoches in 1779 at the site of an old mission. Louisiana once again came under French sovereignty in 1800, and the United States purchased the Louisiana Territory in 1808, but the Spanish settlers remained.

When Mexico won independence from Spain in 1821, only three significant Spanish-speaking settlements remained in what is now Texas: San Antonio, Bahía del Espíritu Santo (Goliad), and Nacogdoches. By the time that Texas joined the United States in 1845, massive immigration of English-speaking residents into Nacogdoches was well established, and before long the population balance had tipped completely in favor of the Anglo-Americans. In Louisiana, the arrival of Anglo-Americans had begun following the Louisiana Purchase, and the Hispanic character of the old Los Adaes settlement soon became a thing of the past. Despite these adverse circumstances, tiny pockets of Spanish-speakers, descendants of the original expeditions, survived well into the second half of the twentieth century, in small communities deep in the pine woods of northern Louisiana and east Texas. The residents use rustic implements such as the *molcajete* "mortar," *comal* "griddle for cooking tortillas," and "grinding stone"; they make *nixtamal* "hominy," tie up objects with a *mecate* "rope," cut *zacate* "grass" and raise *guajolotes* "turkeys." The names of Mexican animals have been applied to similar small animals found in Texas and Louisiana: *tacuache* "possum," *tejón* "raccoon," *coquena* "Guinea hen." Other old or rustic words still remembered by old residents are *mercar/ marcar* "to buy," *calzón/calzones* "pants," *túnico* "ladies' dress," *calesa* "horse-drawn buggy," *la provisión* "supplies, provisions," *noria* "water well," *truja / troja* "barn," *palo* "tree," *encino* "oak tree," *peje* "fish," *fierro* "iron, tool," *lumbre* "fire," *prieto* "black." Currently only a handful of the oldest residents still speak Spanish, but a generation ago the total was much higher, and two generations ago there were still monolingual Spanish-speakers living in rural northwestern Louisiana, unknown even to their most immediate neighbors. A tiny settlement near Zwolle, Louisiana, bears the name Ebarb, a name still shared by some community residents; this is simply the Anglicized version of Antonio Gil Ybarbo, the leader of the rebellious settlers who returned to their homes more than two centuries ago.

Additional groups of Mexican speakers were incorporated into the United States as a result of the Mexican-American War, and their speech represents northern Mexican Spanish. Emigration across the Rio Grande, which was an artificial border at best, never slowed down following the Mexican-American War, so that until the turn of the twentieth century the Spanish spoken in the southwestern United States was identical with that of Mexico. The U.S.-Mexican border began to tighten up during the first decades of the twentieth century, creating the beginnings of a real separation between Mexicans and Mexican Americans. This gap was further widened with the advent of *bracero* recruitment programs in the 1930s, which recruited labor forces not from the nearby northern Mexican states, but from poorer central and southern areas such as Guanajuato, Michoacán, and Guerrero. These laborers, many of whom ended up staying in the United States, spoke Spanish differently from natives of the border regions. Although the braceros passed through the southwestern United States on their way to sources of employment, a large number of these Mexicans from the south ended up working in the Midwestern states. The original braceros were principally agricultural workers, giving rise to the waves of migrant farm workers that even today travel across the country, following the harvest patterns of seasonal crops such as orchard fruits, melons, and truck vegetables. Many of these Mexicans settled in northern cities such as Chicago, Detroit, Milwaukee, and Cleveland, so that "northern" Spanish in the United States was actually from southern Mexico, and vice versa.

At the same time as immigrants from central Mexico were arriving in the Midwest, an increasing number of Mexicans from the border region were arriving in southwestern cities, a change from the predominantly rural settlement of the past. As emigration from Mexico came under tighter control, an urban language began to evolve. During this same period, negative feelings grew in Mexico toward compatriots living in the United States. A new vocabulary derisively referred to these expatriates or foreign-born Mexicans. One such word was *pocho*, a strongly derogatory term referring to Mexicans who, it was thought, had lost their identity in a hostile foreign environment. The old Spanish word *gabacho*, originally applied by Spaniards to the French, was revived by Mexicans to refer to Americans. The term *bolillo* was also used with the same meaning, presumably because of the white color of the bread referred to. This use of *bolillo* is not recent; it is found among the Spanish-speakers in northwestern

Louisiana, representing Mexican Spanish of more than 200 years ago. Mexicans and Mexican Americans began to use the word *chicano*, an old colonial word dating back to the time when *México* was pronounced as *Méshico* and *mexicano* as *meshicano*. In Mexico, this word continues to carry negative connotations, while in the United States it has undergone a more complex evolution. Its use by political and social activists, along with such terms as *La Raza* and *Aztlán*, has polarized feelings toward the word *chicano*, which many Mexican Americans do not accept. Even for those who accept *chicano*, the term is used freely only by members of the group in question, but is not so readily tolerated when used by outsiders, least of all by those who are perceived as unsympathetic to Mexican American culture.

Within Mexico, there are many regional dialects, just as occurs with English in the United States. In the United States, Mexican American Spanish is best divided along rural-urban lines, together with degree of fluency in English. Pronunciation is relatively uniform, representing a broad cross section of northern and central Mexican dialects. Some Mexican Americans pronounce Spanish *b* as *v*, not always in accordance with Spanish spelling. In Spanish, the letters *b* and *v* represent the same sound, and some have viewed the use of *v* among Mexican Americans as a carryover from English. This is unlikely, however, since the same pronunciation is also found within Mexico, while not used by bilingual Cubans and Puerto Ricans. Also found in some Mexican American communities is the pronunciation of Spanish *ch* as *sh*.

The vocabulary of Mexican Spanish differs from textbook versions of the language, principally due to the huge number of indigenous elements absorbed over a period of more than four centuries. Most such items are of Nahuatl origin, and a few have passed into general Spanish: *tomate* "tomato," *aguacate* "avocado," *chocolate*, *chile* "green pepper." The majority of indigenous borrowings are confined to Mexico and neighboring Central America; their number runs into the hundreds, but most refer to flora and fauna found in rural areas of Mexico, or to implements and objects used in rustic life. In the United States, these words are easily replaced by English equivalents, or dropped altogether. Some indigenous words are found in all varieties of Mexican and Mexican American Spanish: *zacate* "grass, lawn," *elote* "corn," *papalote* "toy kite," *guajolote* (*jolote*) "turkey," *tecolote* "owl," *zopilote* "vulture," *camote* "sweet potato," *cuate* "friend, buddy" (literally, "twin"), *hule* "rubber," and many more. Other characteristic Mexicanisms found in the United States include: *camión* "bus," *combi* "van, station wagon," *güero* "blond, fair

In downtown El Paso, Texas, and all along the border, Spanish is just as much the language of business as English, and bilingualism is even more valued in business than either language alone.

complexioned," *chamaco* and *huerco* "child, baby," *feria* "loose change," *chamba* "job," *nieve* "ice cream," *aventón* "pick up, ride," *banqueta* "sidewalk," *raspa/raspada* "snow-cone," and many others. Mexican Spanish commonly uses *ándale* "let's go, OK" (and many other items ending in *-le*, such as the expression of surprise *híjole*, *órale* "come on, get going," f3.4]dale "do it," and so on). For many observers, *ándale* is as synonymous with Mexican Spanish as *chévere* is with Caribbean varieties. Vulgar/slang terms also strongly identified with Mexican Spanish, whose omission would seriously distort any account of Mexican American Spanish, include *pinche* "cursed, damned," *lana* "money," *mordida* "bribe," *padre* "excellent, great," and that most Mexican of all the *malas palabras*: *chingar* and its derivatives, originally referring to sexual intercourse and now reduced to insults. Mexican Spanish uses *no más* in the sense of "only, just" as in *no más quería platicar contigo* "I just wanted to talk with you." *Mero* is used where *mismo* occurs in other Spanish dialects, meaning "very, same, one and only": *aquí mero* "right here," *él es el mero jefe* "he's the boss," *el mero mero* "the big boss, the big cheese." *Ya mero* means

"almost." *Se me hace* means "it seems to me," and *qué tanto?/qué tan?* is preferred to *cuánto?* "how much"; for example *qué tanto ganas?* "how much do you earn?" *qué tan viejo es tu carro?* "how old is your car?" Also typical of Mexican Spanish is *puro* in the sense of "only, exclusively, predominantly": *son puras mentiras* "nothing but lies," *ahí va pura raza* "only Mexican Americans go there." All of these expressions are frequent in Mexican American speech.

✷ ENGLISH USAGE AMONG HISPANICS

The majority of Hispanics born or raised in the United States speak English, as a home language or a strong second language. Arrivals from Spanish-speaking countries also learn English, to a greater or lesser extent depending on such factors as age upon arrival, previous study of English, urgency of using English in the workplace or in the home environment, children in school who bring English into the home, and economic conditions that provide opportunities for acquiring English. As happens with speakers of other languages, Spanish-speakers who learn English during adolescence or later frequently retain an "accent," regardless of the level of fluency eventually attained. Even in bilingual communities where most residents learned English in childhood, a slight "Hispanic" flavor is often found in English. This ranges from a different intonation, to pronunciation shifts such as *v* to *b* (*bery* for *very*), *y* to *j* (*jes* for *yes*), *th* to *t* (*tank* for *thank*), *z* to *s* (making *does* sound like *duss*), and *sh* to *ch* (*chip* to *ship*), reflecting the phonetics of Spanish.

Grammatical interference from Spanish is only found among those who have never fully learned English. Some features of "Hispanic" English are also found in the speech of other Americans, such as pronunciation of *-ing* endings as *-in*, or the use of double negatives as in *I'm not doin "nothin."* Not all Hispanics use this ethnic variety of English; many speak the prevailing regional form of English and cannot be distinguished from non-Hispanics. There are many reasons for the continued existence of Hispanic English among speakers who have spoken English since early childhood. In large bilingual communities, this may be the sort of English heard most often, so that speakers reinforce one another's use of English. Even in school, use of non-Hispanic English may be only passive, and there may be no attempt by teachers to change pronunciation patterns. Much as has happened in other ethnic neighborhoods in the United States, the Hispanic accent can persist for many generations, only fading away as the ethnic group itself becomes more integrated into the wider community, marriages take place outside the group, children interact at school with members of other groups, and so forth.

Traditionally, Hispanic English has been seen in a negative light, as a way of speaking that needs to be corrected. More recently, linguists have studied Hispanic English as it is actually used, without preconceived notions, and have discovered that it also has a role in maintaining community solidarity. The shift from Spanish to English is affecting all Hispanic groups in the United States, and maintaining an ethnically marked form of English is sometimes a semiconscious way of resisting total assimilation to the American "melting pot." Research has demonstrated that some speakers deliberately switch varieties of English depending on whether they are inside the ethnic neighborhood or in an Anglo-American setting. Community activists and grass roots political campaigners often find it more effective to use ethnic varieties of English, which arouse a more favorable response from their audience. Among educators and community leaders, there is ongoing debate as to the desirability of Hispanic English. Some feel that it is an impediment to economic and social advancement, while others insist that it is the attitudes of society that must be changed first. This controversy shows no signs of being resolved in the near future.

Whether or not they speak a Hispanic variety of English, Hispanics in the United States inevitably use more English as they enter wider economic and social structures, and when they work and live in the midst of non-Hispanics. Eventually, the daily use of Spanish becomes of secondary importance in defining and maintaining Hispanic identity, and many individuals who identify strongly with Hispanic culture prefer to use English in most of their activities. Older, Spanish-dominant community members may feel that this represents alienation and loss of cultural identity, while those who take a negative attitude toward maintenance of Spanish see increased use of English as an encouraging sign of social integration. Neither viewpoint is necessarily correct, and the history of the United States provides many examples that show that the shift away from an ancestral language does not automatically entail abandonment of ethnic identity. A significant proportion of literature written by U.S. Hispanics is in English, and peer role models adopted by young Hispanic Americans freely speak English without compromising their ethnicity. In the United States, the concept of being Hispanic does not necessarily require frequent use of, or even fluency in Spanish. At the same time, given the increasingly large numbers of non-Hispanics learning Spanish, in New York City, south Florida, and the Southwest, speaking Spanish is no longer the exclusive property of Hispanics, either.

✳ SPANISH IN BUSINESS, THE MEDIA, AND IN OTHER SOCIAL ENVIRONMENTS

Spanish as used in radio, television, and the written media parallels regional varieties found throughout the United States, particularly in areas where a single Spanish-speaking group prevails. As in other Spanish-speaking nations, radio and television announcers adopt a "neutral" speech, including careful articulation, precise grammar, and few regional or colloquial words. Many Spanish-speaking news announcers and talk-show hosts have received broadcast training or professional experience in other countries. It is not uncommon to find announcers in Miami with experience in Cuba, announcers in New York who have worked in Puerto Rico, or broadcast personnel in the Southwest who have worked in Mexico. This collective experience gives U.S. Spanish-language broadcasting a professional sound and an international flavor. Not all Spanish-speakers in the United States prefer this approach; some feel that the unique situation of the Spanish language in the United States and the people who use it should receive greater emphasis. In response to this need, Spanish-language broadcasting in the United States comes into its own with community action programs, popular music programs, political and social commentary, and programs with an artistic focus. In such programs, regional and casual varieties of Spanish are used more prominently. Broadcast personnel may accentuate regional features of their speech to strengthen the emotional bond with their audience. Many community-oriented programs include participation by individuals not involved in broadcasting and media production, who bring to the airwaves the speech of all segments of the community. Talk shows and call-in programs are particularly representative of community-wide speech patterns, and by listening to these programs the "special" nature of U.S. Hispanic broadcasting can be appreciated.

The use of English and of anglicisms varies widely in Spanish-language broadcasting. When programs aimed at U.S. Spanish-speakers were first aired, they were entirely in Spanish, and public pressure to maintain "pure" Spanish resulted in avoidance of anglicisms. As U.S. Hispanic broadcasting developed its own profile, closer approximations to community language usage became more frequent. This can be clearly seen in advertising, where products, services, and brand names with no easy Spanish equivalent require borrowing from English. Sportscasting is also instrumental in enhancing the use of Anglicisms, but the most important single factor that has put U.S. varieties of Spanish on the airwaves is audience participation. Active community involvement has even brought language-switching to the airwaves, and popular programs on many Hispanic radio stations freely use this format.

The language styles used in U.S. Hispanic broadcasting are frequently a factor of the commercial orientation. Large, powerful stations in big cities are often conservative in matters of language. Such stations may discourage all but the most neutral forms of Spanish, may have a high proportion of advertising and prerecorded material produced in other cities, or overseas, and may downplay controversial social issues in favor of a more consumer-oriented menu of news, musical variety, and sports. Small stations, publicly sponsored stations, and stations run by colleges and universities may have more flexible programming, including announcers (sometimes unpaid volunteers) with little professional training in broadcasting. Such stations tend to have a higher percentage of locally produced material, some of which is aired without rehearsal. Although the most

Two scenes from the "Villa Alegre" television series, which used scripts with extensive code-switching.

powerful Spanish-language stations are as slickly modern as their English-language counterparts, U.S. Hispanic broadcasting as a whole retains a "family" sound that has largely been lost in mainstream commercial broadcasting in English.

Spanish-language newspaper and magazine publishing in the United States affords a wide range of options of language usage, given the relatively small capital investment needed to publish a local newspaper or newsletter and the lack of government licensing requirements, which have often impeded the establishing of Hispanic broadcasting stations. A Spanish-language press has existed in the United States for more than a century. Many of the early newspapers, concentrated along the Mexican border, have long since disappeared. Innumerable parish papers and bulletins have appeared; labor unions, political action groups, and social organizations have also produced Spanish or bilingual publications. The language of all these publications has followed the same evolution as English-language newspapers. The earliest publications used a stiffly formal language based on European Spanish, and some current papers still do. The articles in the early publications

A customer buying *La prensa,* the Spanish-language daily newspaper, which survives today as *El diario-La prensa* in New York City.

were directed to an elite, socially active sector of the community, the assumption being that less affluent community members could not read well enough to benefit from such publications. News reporting was confined to local affairs and personalities, and with the exception of such major events as wars, depressions, or natural disasters, nothing beyond the pale of the ethnic community was included. Such papers continue to exist, in areas where the Hispanic community is small and localized, or where recent immigrants from a single region attempt to recreate a bit of their homeland. For example, the Nicaraguan community in Miami publishes several small newspapers. There have also been, from time to time, Salvadoran newspapers in Houston and Los Angeles, Honduran newspapers in New Orleans, aapers[/hid]s aimed at Mexicans and Puerto Ricans in the Midwest. The language used by these small newspapers varies widely. Some use highly formal, journalistic prose, while others use a closer approximation to community language.

In the United States today, there are numerous large Spanish-language newspapers with regional or national circulation. The language used in these papers is professional and international, reflecting the standards of Spanish-language journalism worldwide and not giving preference to any regional variety of Spanish. Common to all Hispanic newspapers in the United States is use of anglicisms, particularly in advertising. Most Spanish-speakers born and raised in the United States use English words for many items advertised in newspapers, and may fail to recognize "legitimate" Spanish equivalents. Advertisers and publishers must balance the attitudes of educators and community leaders and the reality of effective communication; the results vary widely. Some advertisers invent new Spanish expressions, in hopes that they will be accepted as translations of English terms, while others go to the opposite extreme, including more English words than would ever be done by a bilingual speaker. In general, the language of advertising, classified announcements and editorial commentary as found in Spanish-language newspapers provide a good window on actual usage.

Many Hispanics in the United States use English in business and professional activities, particularly if they are surrounded by English-speaking co-workers and clients, but in cities with large Spanish-speaking populations, professional services are also offered in

A typical Hispanic grocery store in New York City.

Spanish. Bilingualism is a highly desirable commodity for companies doing business with an increasingly affluent Hispanic community, and non-Hispanics in cities like Miami find that learning and using Spanish is advantageous. Commerce with Latin America is also a major source of revenue for many American cities, and financial and industrial transactions conducted in Spanish represent hundreds of millions of dollars for American businesses. Finally, at the neighborhood level, Spanish is used in thousands of small businesses, such as grocery stores, gas stations, travel agencies, banks, restaurants, and any place that provides products and services to a Hispanic clientele. It is difficult to calculate the volume of trade that these businesses involve, but taken as a whole, the Spanish-speaking market represents a large and important share of the American economy.

✳ BILINGUALISM AND CODE-SWITCHING

Except for recent arrivals, or in a few isolated rural areas, the majority of Hispanics in the United

States speak English. A gradual but definite shift from Spanish to English occurs in most Hispanic communities, the same course followed by every other immigrant language brought to the United States, and the speed with which this language shift takes place is increasing. Europeans arriving in the nineteenth and early twentieth centuries often settled in rural areas of the United States and were able to maintain their own languages and traditions for a considerable time, while experiencing little pressure to learn English. Immigrants who moved to urban areas learned English, as did their children, but settlement in ethnic neighborhoods made retention of the ancestral language easy. With the breakup of the tight mosaic of ethnic neighborhoods, the increase of mixed-ethnic marriages, and the greater penetrating power of public education, radio, and television, the shift to English is increasingly rapid among new immigrants, and the period of stable bilingualism is steadily decreasing. Often one generation is sufficient for the ancestral language to disappear from a family and even from a neighborhood.

Hispanics currently have a higher retention rate of the ancestral language than any group in the United States. Ironically, at a time when the United States is emphasizing international economic and political cooperation and promoting proficiency in foreign languages to gain a competitive edge, the high rate of retention of Spanish is viewed by some Americans as threatening. Throughout the country, nearly all "English only" campaigns and amendments have targeted Spanish-speakers, and in many cities there is strong public sentiment against bilingual education, the use of Spanish in official government documents and institutions, and the high priority accorded to bilingual fluency in job descriptions.

There is no single answer to the question of why Spanish-speakers have successfully maintained their language in the United States, but there are several obvious contributing factors. Circumstance of arrival in the United States is a major influence on language retention. The original Mexican Americans did not move to the United States, but were enveloped by a new government and language following U.S. territorial expansions. The same occurred with Puerto Ricans, whose government and citizenship changed due to circumstances beyond their control. The first migrations from Puerto Rico to the mainland United States did not fit the pattern of European immigration, which had a much higher voluntary component, although most European arrivals in the nineteenth and twentieth centuries were impelled by economic necessity. Beginning in 1901, Puerto Ricans were recruited as sugar plantation laborers in Louisiana and, in much greater numbers,

in Hawaii. Descendants of the original Puerto Rican cane-cutters are found in Hawaii even today, and Puerto Ricans contributed words and cultural items to Hawaiian life. The Puerto Ricans became known as *Pokoliko, Poto Riko,* or *Borinki,* and the Puerto Rican *arroz y gandules* "small green beans cooked with rice" became transmuted to *gandude rice.*

From the end of the Spanish-American War (1898) to the present, the Puerto Rican population in the United States has steadily grown. While the community in New York had its origins in the revolutionaries who were organizing the rebellion from Spain, by the beginning of the twentieth century there were numbers of Puerto Ricans (and Cubans) in the cigar manufacturing industry in New York. Puerto Ricans involved in service and manufacturing industries grew, with greater migration spurred by the authorization of U.S. citizenship in 1917, under the Jones Act. U.S. trade and business relationships during the twentieth century continued Spain's practices of encouraging mono-culture in one failing agricultural product after another: coffee, tobacco, sugar. Each failed industry produced greater waves of labor migration. But the largest mass migration, which was stimulated by labor recruiters and free airfare, took place during World War II labor shortages in the United States. From the 1940s to the middle 1950s, one-third of Puerto Rico's population migrated to the continental United States. These landless and homeless Puerto Ricans ended up in the cold, industrialized cities of the Northeast, where they frequently suffered even worse conditions than those left behind in Puerto Rico. The plight of these displaced Puerto Ricans, who cannot be considered voluntary immigrants in the true sense of the word, is poignantly covered in many literary works, including the collection of stories *Spiks,* by Pedro Juan Soto, and the play *La carreta,* by René Marqués. Forced by economic hardship and racial prejudice to live in ghettos and tenements, and deprived of the opportunity to be educated in their home language, many Puerto Ricans dropped out of school, and by returning to their home neighborhoods, consolidated the retention of Spanish.

The landless Mexicans recruited in the bracero program of the 1950s also fail to fit the definition of voluntary immigrants, and their retention of Spanish is a natural outgrowth of the circumstances of their life in the United States. Recent immigrants from border regions of Mexico maintain close contacts with their original homeland, through visits and additional migration, and a sense of continuity with Mexico can be maintained indefinitely under such conditions.

The large number of Spanish-speakers who immi-

A voter-registration drive in New York City, where Hispanics cherish the right to vote in the Spanish language.

grated to the United States because of political or social problems in their homelands constitutes another source of Spanish-language retention, since such groups initially harbor the intention to return to their country of origin, and see their presence in the United States as transitory. At first, some may even consciously resist learning English or teaching it to their children, since learning English symbolically represents accepting a prolonged stay outside their homeland. Cubans arriving in the 1960s and 1970s were predominantly from the professional classes, and insisted that their children learn and retain Spanish. These same Cubans intended to return to their homeland shortly, and the awareness that this would not be possible in the near future came only slowly and painfully. The relatively positive reception given to these Cubans in the United States, in contrast to the harsh treatment often afforded to Puerto Rican, Mexican, and Central American arrivals, might have added to the feeling of self-assurance in maintaining Spanish as the language of the community as well as of the home. To this day, more than 30 years after the first immigration of Cubans spurred by the Cuban Revolution, young Cuban Americans, particularly in South Florida,

continue to learn and use Spanish at a higher rate, and with less shift in the direction of English, than many other U.S. Hispanic groups.

The Nicaraguan community in the United States shows patterns similar to those of Cuban Americans. The Sandinista Revolution of 1979 brought several hundred thousand Nicaraguans to the United States, most from professional and middle classes, although in recent years the number of rural and working-class residents has increased. Most Nicaraguans, planning to return to their homeland, have maintained a high level of Spanish. Although their children learn English in school, Spanish is maintained without difficulty. This situation is different among Salvadorans who come from the ranks of the rural poor. In cities with a large Salvadoran population, Salvadorans live and work in Spanish-speaking neighborhoods and drift toward jobs that do not require learning English. However, those young Salvadorans who do go to school may shift to English faster than other Hispanic groups, at times with the active encouragement of their parents.

Even though Spanish remains a strong home language in U.S. Hispanic communities, English is always present. It is the first language for some, the second language for others, and for most U.S.-born Hispanics, bilingualism begins in earliest childhood. Spanish and English in such close contact inevitably influence one another, but despite this natural process, any evidence of language mixing is often criticized and ridiculed. It is the hybrid varieties of Spanish that receive the most criticism; terms like "Tex-Mex," "Spanglish," and "pocho" are used to describe a wide range of language, ranging from only limited abilities in Spanish by English-dominant speakers, to fully fluent Spanish that has simply absorbed some English words. Although often based on prejudice and intolerance, these terms do arise from several types of English influence that can be noticed in U.S. Spanish.

Spanish has borrowed many words from English. At first, English words were modified to fit Spanish patterns, sometimes capitalizing on already existent patterns. *Lunch* became *lonche*, a term that is now found well into South America. In all instances, *lonche* refers to the light lunch eaten in the United States, for example, by schoolchildren or by employees at work, and not to the large *almuerzo* or *comida* consumed at midday in Hispanic countries. *Lonche*

therefore represents a borrowing for a new cultural concept. Derived from *lonche* are *lonchera* "lunch box," *lonchar* "to eat lunch," and *lonchería* "lunchroom, cafeteria," all words based on productive patterns of Spanish word formation. Sometimes an existent Spanish word was replaced for no apparent reason. For example, in many countries *estacionar* "park an automobile" has been replaced by *parcar*, *aparcar*, or *parquear*, all derived from "park." This extends to *parquímetro* "parking meter," and *parqueo* or even *parking* "parking lot." Other anglicisms widely known in Latin America are *líder* "leader" (together with *liderar* "to lead" and *liderazgo* "leadership"), *guachimán* "watchman," *flirtear* "to flirt," *esnob* "snob" (together with *esnobismo* "snobbishness"), *esquí* "ski," *esmóquin* "tuxedo" (from "smoking jacket"), *bluyíns* "blue jeans." *livin* "living room," *estándar* "standard," *sanuiche* (with variants *sánuich*, *sánuiche*, *sanduche*, and so on) "sandwich," and so on. Sports terminology is full of anglicisms, some of them unmodified. This is particularly true in baseball, where Spanish terms (all of which were originally translated from English) are largely replaced by English

Catholic churches in Hispanic-populated areas quite often offer masses in both English and Spanish, as does Our Lady of Guadalupe Church in Queen Creek, Arizona.

words in live commentary, although the Spanish forms may be used in written form: *pícher (lanzador), cácher (receptor), lef fílder (jardinero de izquierda), jonrón* "home run" *(cuadrangular)*, and so forth. Some baseball terms were made over into plausible-sounding Spanish words right from the beginning: *base* "base," *bate* "bat," *bateador* "batter."

In the United States, borrowing from English is naturally more frequent and penetrates further into Spanish. Early borrowings like *troca* "truck" have spread into Mexico, but most remain confined to the United States. Verbs are usually formed by adding *-ear* or *-iar*: *güeldiar* "to weld," *taipiar* "to type," *espelear* "to spell." *Frizar* "to freeze," *tochar* "to touch," *fixar* "to fix," and so forth, add only *-ar*. Sometimes Spanish *hacer* "to make, to do" is followed by an English word: *hacer fix* "to fix," but this is not done often. Anglicisms in U.S. Spanish do not detract from the communicative potential of the language, and are in no way different from indigenous words in Latin American Spanish, which are often not understood outside a limited region. Most U.S. Hispanics who use the words just mentioned alternate with words from the general Spanish vocabulary.

Another common aspect of language appropriation is word-by-word translation. Colorful expressions like "kick the bucket," "spill the beans," and "toe the line" started out with concrete meanings, but ended up signifying something that cannot be predicted by looking at the individual words. On the other hand, an expression like "think it over" is also idiomatic, since "over" is not operating with its normal meaning. Colorful idiomatic expressions are seldom translatable, although cultural contact may cause some to enter another language. For example, *patear el balde* "kick the bucket" is sometimes used outside the United States. In Texas, "redneck" is often semiseriously rendered as *pescuezo colorado* or *nuca colorada*. Speakers who use such expressions are aware of their idiomatic nature and usually do so jokingly, and only with other bilingual speakers who will appreciate the humor. In expressions that are part of everyday language, speakers may not be aware that a word-by-word translation is not possible. In bilingual communities, word-by-word translations are used more frequently, but grammatical rules of Spanish are hardly ever broken. What does change is the meaning of individual words. Thus, when a bilingual speaker says that a politician *está corriendo para sheriff* "is running for sheriff," nothing about the Spanish expression is out of place, except that *correr* ordinarily refers to the physical act of running, and not to a political campaign. Spanish-English bilinguals in the United States frequently use expressions based on *para atrás* (usually

pronounced *patrás*) as a translation of English "back": *te llamo patrás* "I'll call you back," *fuimos patrás* "we went back," *no me hables patrás* "don't talk back to me." *Para atrás*, is a legitimate Spanish combination, but only in the sense of backward motion: *el hombre se echó para atrás* "the man jumped backward." The "new" use of *patrás* has occurred under the influence of English. The grammar is Spanish, the words are Spanish, but the meaning can only be interpreted in a bilingual environment.

Among fluent bilinguals, rapid switches between languages commonly occur in a single conversation. Linguists refer to this behavior as "code-switching," where "code" refers to the language or communicative system that is changed. This may happen at a logical break in the conversation, for example when answering the telephone or welcoming a newly arrived participant. Language switching also takes place in direct quotes, or to underscore a personal identification with the group represented by the language in question. This is a strategy used by bilingual speakers worldwide, and even individuals with only a slight knowledge of a second language engage in this strategy (for example, in the foreign language classroom). Bilinguals may slip in short tag expressions in the opposite language: *tú sabes* "you know," *ándale* "OK, right," *de acuerdo* "all right," *ay bendito* "my goodness," *qué chévere* "that's great," and in English, "wow, right on," "that's incredible," and so forth. These switches are not always conscious, but they are invariably short and colloquial, a way of reaffirming one's identity and of reassuring the listener of solidarity and intimacy. In the U.S. setting, inclusion of Spanish phrases in the midst of a conversation in English is the more common case, even among English-dominant bilinguals. In these circumstances, English is perceived as the neutral language, spoken by everybody and carrying no connotations of ethnicity, while Spanish is the "special" half of a bilingual conversation.

The type of language shifting that arouses the most controversy is the switch in the middle of a sentence. The titles of recent research articles illustrate the process: "Sometimes I'll Start a Sentence in English *y termino en español* [and I finish up in Spanish]." "*Ta bien* [it's OK], you can answer me *en cualquier idioma* [in either language]." Such combinations are baffling to the outsider, incomprehensible to the monolingual speaker of either language, and bewildering to foreign language learners. This fluent switching in midsentence has been taken by many as the deterioration of English and Spanish, evidence of the undesirability of bilingualism. Some have even used bilingual language switching as an argument to convince Spanish-speakers to abandon their native language, on the assertion that it is already corrupted beyond reclamation. Midsentence language shifting is the sort of shift most often associated with pejorative terms like "Spanglish" and *pocho*.

Although bilingual code-switching has often been criticized when practiced by Hispanics in the United States, language switching is not regarded so negatively in all other bilingual communities throughout the world. It is an effect of the lopsided social status accorded to English, as opposed to Spanish, in the United States. In bilingual societies where a more nearly even balance exists between languages, switching, even in midsentence, is seldom criticized. The residents of Gibraltar, nearly all of whom are Spanish-English bilinguals (although English is the only official language), switch languages in the same fashion found in the United States, arriving at many of the same bilingual combinations. During the height of the Napoleonic Empire, aristocratic Russians freely switched in and out of French, which was regarded as highly prestigious behavior, since in Russia, only the elite knew French. Code-switching is the order of the day in countries such as India and the Philippines, and in areas of Belgium, Switzerland, the former Soviet Union, and Canada. During the Norman occupation of England, Anglo-Saxons who were forced to learn the French of their conquerors actually spoke a code-switched mixture. French and English intellectuals of the time condemned this mixed language as vulgar and depraved, but after withstanding the test of time, it went on to become a world language—modern English—with its hundreds of French words. Spanish absorbed hundreds of Arabic words during the nearly eight centuries of Moorish occupation of Spain, from 711 to 1492, during which time bilingualism was the rule in southern Spain, and language shifting undoubtedly occurred. Attitudes toward language mixing and shifting reflect social power rather than actual communicative value. Languages of powerful nations are respected and imitated, and when a nation or society loses power, its language loses prestige and is learned by fewer people.

After the fact, a bilingual speaker may not be exactly sure where in a sentence the shift occurred, and may even be unaware (until reminded) of having switched languages at all. This is not evidence of confusion or the inability to keep the two languages apart, since bilinguals take care to not shift languages with nonbilinguals or those who object to this style of speaking. This crucial fact, combined with the maintenance of grammatical rules during language shifting, is evidence that bilingual speakers are manipulating two separate language systems. Serious research into bilingual code-switching re-

veals that, far from being a random jumble of two languages, this way of speaking is governed by the same types of rules that determine the acceptability of sentences in Spanish or English. Bilingual language shifting is not a "mix and match" strategy of randomly alternating Spanish and English words. Segments in Spanish and segments in English contain no internal grammatical errors; each portion is a mini-sentence produced in a single language. The transition from one language to the other creates no grammatical violation; the same parts of speech are used in the same basic order, and in general the only thing that changes is the language from which they are taken. The transition is smooth, and each half of the sentence sounds acceptable with respect to the language in which it was produced. When the beginning of a sentence in one language would not be compatible with a continuation in the other language, the shift does not occur. For example, one might say in English, "This is the record that I was telling you about" ending with "about." In Spanish this word order is not possible: *Este es el disco de que te hablaba*. If languages were to be switched in such a sentence, likely possibilities would be *Este es el disco que I was telling you about*, or *This is the record de que te hablaba*, since the same grammatical patterns are followed after the language shift as would have been had the sentence remained in the first language. However, *This is the record that te hablaba*, would hardly ever occur, because there would be no way of adding the meaning of English "about" in an acceptable way in Spanish. Similarly, we might hear *my red carro*, but not *mi carro red*, since in English the adjective does not usually follow the noun that it modifies.

The reasons for language switching in the middle of a sentence are complex and not yet fully understood. One common cause is unavailability of a word in the initial language due to a momentary memory lapse, a word with no equivalent in the first language, or a proper name. The switch will often "pull" the rest of the sentence along; it may not occur exactly at the point where a word from the second language is introduced, but may anticipate the triggering element. A typical example is *Mucha gente no sabe where Magnolia Street is* "Many people don't know where Magnolia Street is," where the speaker, thinking of a street name in English, switched languages at the first clause boundary before the English name. Although some language switching is triggered by words or expressions that are untranslatable or momentarily forgotten, many more cases simply reflect the expanded combinations available to bilingual speakers during a relaxed conversation. Such switching reinforces ethnic solidarity, allows for greater subtlety of expression, and gives bilingual speakers the pleasure of having an additional "language" of their own, not shared by monolingual speakers of either language.

Bilingual language switching is not simply a way of speaking, it is a way of writing, and the use of Spanish-English alternations is increasingly common in literature written by bilingual authors. This strategy is most frequently used in poetry but has also found its way into novels and stories depicting the life and language of Spanish-speakers in the United States. One of the best-known novelists to extensively use language switching is Rolando Hinojosa (for example in *Mi querido Rafa*). Many prominent poets and playwrights also use this technique, reflecting the real language of U.S. Hispanic communities.

It is frequently asked whether or not there is a uniquely "U.S." variety of Spanish. It seems, after considering the full panorama of Spanish language usage in the United States, that the answer in general is no. Spanish in the United States continues to be divided mainly according to the country of ancestral origin: Mexican, Puerto Rican, Cuban, and so forth. Even in cities where more than one large Hispanic group is found, a single language variety usually prevails. In a few cities, such as Chicago, more than one variety of Spanish is represented in the communications media, but this has little effect on Spanish used in individual neighborhoods. Similarly, and despite dictionaries that claim to describe such dialects, it is almost impossible to justify the existence of "American" varieties of Spanish: "Mexican American," "Puerto Rican American," "Cuban American," and so forth. What is found in the United States is greater use of English, and shifting of some Spanish words to match equivalent English terms. This does not make for separate dialects of Spanish, especially since the use of English elements is not consistent from speaker to speaker. In fact, the claim of a special U.S. Spanish is often a by-product of negative attitudes toward Spanish-speakers in the United States, as held by Spanish-speakers from other nations as well as by many Americans.

The nonexistence of a unique U.S. Spanish dialect is not a negative result. Spanish use in the United States is expanding rather than shrinking, and this expansion involves styles and ranges of language in addition to the number of speakers. U.S. Spanish is, more than ever, closely tied both to the international Spanish-speaking community and to American society and culture. What *is* uniquely American U.S. Spanish is the complex pattern of bilingual language usage, which finds its highest form of expression in bilingual literature. By being able to communicate bilingually, U.S. Spanish-speakers command an extraordinarily rich language repertoire, which is at once part of Latin American and U.S. society and also uniquely Hispanic American.

References

Amastae, John, and Lucía Elías-Olivares, eds. *Spanish in the United States: Sociolinguistic Aspects.* Cambridge: Cambridge University Press, 1982.

Berger, John, ed. *Spanish in the United States: Sociolinguistic Issues.* Washington, D.C.: Georgetown University Press, 1990.

Elías-Bowen, J. Donald, and Jacob Ornstein, eds. *Studies in Southwest Spanish.* Rowley, Massachusetts: Newbury House, 1976.

Elías-Olivares, Lucía, ed. *Spanish in the U.S. Setting: Beyond the Southwest.* Rosslyn, Virginia: National Clearinghouse for Bilingual Education, 1983.

——, Elizabeth Leone, René Cisneros, and John Gutiérrez, eds. *Spanish Language Use and Public Life in the U.S.A.* The Hague: Mouton, 1985.

Fishman, Joshua, Roxanna Ma, and Eleanor Herasimchuk, eds. *Bilingualism in the Barrio.* The Hague: Mouton, 1972.

Hernández Chávez, Eduardo, Andrew Cohen, and Anthony Beltramo, eds. *El lenguaje de los chicanos.* Arlington, Virginia: Center for Applied Linguistics, 1975.

Lipski, John. "Spanish World-wide: Toward a More Perfect Union." *Revista Chicano-Riqueña,* 12, No. 1, 1984: 43–56.

——. "Central American Spanish in the United States: El Salvador." *Aztlán,* 17, 1986: 91–124.

——. *Linguistic Aspects of Spanish-English Language Switching.* Tempe: Arizona State University, Center for Latin American Studies, 1985.

——. "Salvadorans in the United States: Patterns of Sociolinguistic Integration." *National Journal of Sociology,* 3, 1989: 97–119.

Metcalf, Allan. *Chicano English.* Arlington, Virginia: Center for Applied Linguistics, 1979.

Ornstein-Galicia, Jacob, ed. *Form and function in Chicano English.* Rowley, Massachusetts: Newbury House, 1980.

Peñalosa, Fernando. *Chicano Sociolinguistics.* Rowley, Massachusetts: Newbury House, 1980.

——. *Central Americans in Los Angeles: Background, Language, Education.* Los Alamitos, California: National Center for Bilingual Research, 1984.

Poplack, Shana. "Sometimes I'll Start a Sentence in English y termino en español." *Linguistics,* 18, 1980: 581–618.

Sánchez, Rosaura. *Chicano Discourse.* Rowley, Massachusetts: Newbury House, 1983.

Timm, Leonra. "Spanish-English Code-Switching: el porque y how-not-to." *Romance Philology,* 28, 1975: 473–82.

Zentella, Ana Celia. "Ta bien, You Could Answer Me en cualquier idioma: Puerto Rican Code-Switching in the Bilingual Classroom." In *Latino Language and Communicative Behavior,* edited by Roberto Durán, 95–107. Norwood, New Jersey: Ablex, 1981.

John M. Lipski

9

The Family

✸ The Institutions of the Hispanic Family ✸ Puerto Ricans: Born in the United States ✸ Dominicans ✸ Cubans ✸ Mexican Americans

The United States harbors one of the most diverse Hispanic populations in the world. Large urban populations are present on both the Pacific and Atlantic coasts, rural pockets dot every state of the union, and large expanses of Hispanics are found in the major states from California to New York. The first impression a person gets of this population is the basic similarity that is expressed in social and cultural behavior regardless of urban or rural setting. The entire population is Spanish-language oriented, and indeed many newcomers and settlers speak nothing but Spanish.

Cultural manifestations expressed in dance, music, fiestas, and so forth, help paint a picture of similarity. The broad similarities in culture and language, however, mask a diverse people that represent every Hispanic-Latino country and group of people in the world. This diversity is a product of widespread Hispanic immigration and the different ways Hispanics have adapted to the United States. These are complex processes in which Hispanics, like other immigrant and settler groups, have relied on both traditional and hybrid cultural institutions in relating, adapting, and surviving in the new cultural milieu that is the United States.

Fundamental to this adaptation process, and indeed to Hispanic culture in general, is the institution of the family. The family is considered the single most important institution in the social organization of Hispanics. It is through the family and its activities that all people relate to significant others in their lives and it is through the family that people communicate with the larger society.

Although these primary functions of the family are evident among all peoples, the family among Hispanics has been a central thread that connects a multitude of strands that make up their social world. The central importance in social-cultural functions and the values of cultural life expressed through the family are emphasized in all studies focusing on Hispanics both in the United States and throughout the Hispanic world. There is no argument that when compared to the U.S. population in general, Hispanics place special emphasis, sentiment, and value on the family.

The Hispanic family is organized around a group of primary institutions that are common to all Hispanic groups in the United States, but the family is expressed in different ways. The Hispanic family structure is composed of elements (institutions) that provide important social and cultural meaning and to one degree or another are identifiable in all groups. But this hides the specific and rich cultural diversity and the complex cultural adaptations of Mexicans, Puerto Ricans, Cubans, Dominicans, and Central and South Americans to the United States. Each of these cultural groups exhibits a broadly identifiable "Hispanic family" that is organized around a number of supportive institutions. These variations, however, of the Hispanic family are seen both within and across all groups.

Understanding the diversity of the family among Hispanics requires a fundamental understanding of the different Hispanic groups in the United States. Each group has a particular history within the United States that has affected the manner in which the family and its supportive institutions have been expressed. Only one group, Mexican Americans/Chicanos, originates in the area that is the continental United States, but the bulk of the Hispanic population, like Puerto Ricans, Cubans, Dominicans, and Central and South Americans, immigrated to this country. Puerto Ricans on the other hand are the only "colonized" group that has migrated and settled in the United States in mass. Significantly, Puerto Ricans are U.S. citizens and move freely between the

The Lugo Family at Bell Gardens, California, circa 1888.

island of Puerto Rico and the mainland. The adaptation of the Hispanic population in both urban and rural settings stems from the socioeconomic and historical relations of home countries with the United States, a continuing migration based primarily on labor needs, and, to varying degrees, a continued relationship with home regions. Hispanics have used and generated new social processes based on the traditional family patterns in the migration process and in adapting to life in the United States.

Understanding the family as it has evolved among Hispanics in the United States requires a consideration of the societal contexts that influence and condition Hispanic socialization in the United States. The settlement of Puerto Ricans in New York and the creation of urban barrios in Spanish Harlem, Brooklyn, and Manhattan have been conditioned by continuous high unemployment, lack of housing, and poverty, which are exacerbated by the dense population in the city. This is very different from the Cuban settlement in Miami, where strong economic enclaves of primarily middle-class entrepreneurs are thriving in what is now known as Little Havana.

Additional social factors differentiating the Hispanic family include race and class. Although Hispanics stem from a similar origin, their ethnic/racial makeup differs because of the historical patterns in their countries of origin. Among those groups from the Caribbean (Dominicans, Puerto Ricans, Cubans), for example, a rich African element exists in the population that stems from the importation of slaves in early colonial periods. Mexicans, on the other hand, are primarily mestizo, rich in Indian (Native American)

background mixed with descendants from Spain. And Hispanics come from every socioeconomic class that is represented in the United States. The majority of Hispanics, however, are to be found in the lower economic strata of society, and a great percentage continue to remain below the poverty line. Racial attitudes toward people of color in the United States have had a great influence on their adaptation. Discrimination toward blacks and Hispanics and others has restricted access to employment, education, and housing, and in turn has influenced patterns of family and household development.

Although Hispanics are among the newest groups of immigrants to the United States, they are also some of the first settlers. Indeed, the ancestors of the populations in the southwestern United States (California, Arizona, New Mexico, Colorado, and Texas) settled in these states long before the U.S. colonies severed their ties from England. There have also been successive waves of immigrants for many generations. The Puerto Rican migration began at the turn of this century, after the United States took that island from Spain, and Mexican immigration began in great earnest early in the century and escalated after the Mexican Revolution of 1911. The long-time residence and established settlements mean that many generations of Hispanics can be counted in the United States. The family must be viewed across these generations as well as within the generations to fully appreciate its role. For example, early settlers and migrants created and utilized social networks based on family relations, while later generations illustrate a more nuclear family preference and

A child's birthday party in New York City.

maintain family values and kin extensions in different ways.

The focus here is not just the different elements but the primary processes that together make up the family. The idea of a static and unchanging family, although once a major depiction in scholarly literature, is not accepted by current scholars and practitioners. (This is partly because of the emergence of critical research that has reanalyzed and often interpreted social science from a Hispanic perspective, by Chicano, Puerto Rican, Cuban, and other Hispanic scholars who are focusing on their own communities and people.) In the past, the family has been viewed as an archaic vestige of former societies to which men, women, and children were tied. The sense of a "traditional family" among Hispanics emphasized a nonchanging and out-of-date institution that kept Hispanics from becoming productive and contributing to the larger U.S. society. The contrary, however, is in fact the rule. The Hispanic family is an institution that provided the social mechanisms which helped people, at least initially, in the processes of migration and settlement. It is the one institution, in varying forms, that provided the initial contacts and ties to employment, friends, kin, and new settle-

ments in the United States. There are, to be sure, elements that have not fit certain aspects of the larger U.S. Hispanic society, but these elements appear generally after initial settlement, in later generations. A high rate of divorce, for example, is found among the second-generation population compared to first pioneers.

✳ THE INSTITUTIONS OF THE HISPANIC FAMILY

What are the primary elements that make up the social-cultural "machinery" of the Hispanic family in the United States? The concept of "family" among all Hispanics refers to more than just the nuclear family that consists of a household of man and wife with their children. Rather, the family incorporates the idea of *la familia* (the greater family), which includes, in addition to the immediate nuclear household, relatives that are traced on both the female and male sides. There include parents, grandparents, brothers and sisters, cousins, and to a certain extent any blood relatives that can be identified through the hierarchy of family surnames. This broad-ranging concept has important consequences for actual social and cultural behavior. It places individuals as well as nuclear families into a recognizable network of social relations within which mutual support and reciprocity occur.

Before describing the particular aspects of each of the major groups of Hispanics in the United States, the distinction between household and family needs to be made. "Household" has been a focus of anthropological inquiry because households are the entities in which people actually live. According to Maxine Baca-Zinn in *The State of Chicano Research in Family, Labor, and Migration Studies* (1983), families are groups of persons bound together by ties of kinship both real and fictive and households are groups of persons bound to place. Households are the units within which people pool resources and perform specific tasks. They are units of production, reproduction, and consumption. They are residential units where persons and resources are connected and distributed.

Important supportive institutions of la familia include the extended family, *parentesco* (the concept of familism), compadrazgo (godparenthood), confianza (trust), and family ideology. Family ideology is more

Community action through family and parent power: United Bronx Parents, Inc.

than just the way people think about family. Family ideology among Hispanics sets the ideal and standards to which individuals aim; it is the guiding light to which all look and attempt to shape their behavior for themselves as well as for the perception others have of them. Family ideology consists of the conceptual rules that people try to maintain, the values that are expressed about what the family should be and how it is maintained. For Hispanics, the ideal of family is that it is the central and most important institution in life. It holds all individuals together and all individuals should put family before their own concerns. It is the means of social and cultural existence. Ideology also defines the ideal roles and behaviors of family members. Although there is truth to family ideology in that it influences actual behavior, this ideology is never totally realized among Hispanics. Like all ideology, the ideology of la familia is a guide for behavior, a basis from which to act.

Family ideology defines the ideal roles and behaviors of family members. The ideal family is a patriarchy that revolves around a strong male figure who is ultimately responsible for the well-being of all individuals "under his roof." The concept of "machismo" is embedded in this ideal, in which men are viewed as virile, aggressive, and answerable only to themselves. In real life, however, this is rarely realized. There are degrees of male authoritarianism that vary both within and across groups, but for the most part women are strong contributors to decision making and are often the internal authority figures in the family. In both subtle and direct ways, women not only contribute to decision making but often have the authority in the family. This is contrary to the stereotype in which the woman is viewed as subservient and deferent to "her man" and that child rearing and household chores should be her main concern. In fact, one of the greatest of changes in the Hispanic family in the United states is in the woman's role. There is a very high percentage of woman-headed households, especially among Puerto Ricans in New York. A high percentage of women in all Hispanic groups are employed and are the primary household wage earners. This, as might be expected, has caused tremendous changes in family structure and role behavior. However, family ideology continues to be verbally expressed as a value and cultural norm, often in contradiction to actual family behavior.

The role of children in the family ideology is one in which they, as stated in the age-old dictum, "are to be seen but not heard." Children should be subservient and show respect to all elders, *respeto* (respect) being a concept held by all individuals. In a variety of studies in education, Hispanic children, especially those of new migrants, do behave in a "culturally prescribed manner" that is congruent with family ideology. However, as in all other aspects of family ideology among Hispanics, children's roles have experienced drastic changes. Education in the American system and exposure to people outside the immediate family and network of relatives has affected children in many ways. Hispanic children often become the social brokers between their parents and the outside world. They are the best speakers of English and know the outside more thoroughly than parents.

Among all Hispanics some form of the extended family is present. The extended family is an important part of the la familia concept, because it includes more than one generation of individuals that are related, and who express immediate support to one another as a primary value. The ideal extended family includes a husband and wife, their children, grandparents (mothers and fathers of husband and wife), and siblings of the husband and wife. Many members of this extended family live together under one roof and share economic and social activities. Although a number of variants to the ideal type do exist, Hispanic groups in the United States do not generally live in an extended family household. The reality is that Hispanics tend to favor the nuclear family and a separate household. This is especially true of later settlers and individuals born in the United States. The extended family living in single households is generally a transitory stage in family and household development. It is seen primarily during the migrant stages of first arrival when newcomers need support and help in adjusting and finding their way in a new environment. The reality of the extended Hispanic family is that it transcends geographical barriers and has functioning units in both the country of origin as well as in the United States. It is in this sense that the institution of the family has taken on a hybrid form through the strategic expression of migrants adapting to a new environment.

Hispanics have used the extended family in conjunction with other kinship institutions that form part of the greater familia and family ideology. As in the family in general, the Catholic religion has had a very strong influence in familia institutions. Religious rites of baptism and marriage take on special meaning that have evolved into sociocultural expressions important among Hispanics in the United States. Compadrazgo, marriage, and *parentesco* are primary institutions that need to be understood in relation to the family. These are multidimensional elements that together help maintain la familia. Compadrazgo is formed usually through the baptism of a child, with parents choosing *padrinos* (godpar-

A Puerto Rican mine worker at home with his family after work in Bingham Canyon, Utah.

ents) from close friends or relatives. Compadrazgo is the extension of kinship to nonrelatives and the strengthening of responsibilities between kin. Padrinos sponsor the child in baptism and confirmation ceremonies. They are also chosen to be best man and bridesmaid at weddings. Compadres (co-parents) ideally have special responsibilities toward the godchild and in the past have been expected to take the parental role if parents were to pass away, except in the case of marriage sponsorship. This special parental relationship is maintained throughout life. In addition, the *ahijado/a* (godchild) has a special responsibility towards the padrino/a. This is manifested in varying degrees, but can be seen when the padrino/a is elderly; ahijados may pay such individuals special attention almost as though the padrino/a were a grandparent. However, the strongest relationship in compadrazgo is that between the child's parents and godparents, who call each other compadres. Godparents often address each other as *comadre* (co-mother) or *compadre* (co-father), illustrating the special relationship they have toward one another. Compadrazgo forms an intimate relationship in which those sharing the role have specific expectations of each other. The reciprocal nature of the relationship between compadres is especially strong in the early period of adaptation to the United States. Compadres are expected to provide each other with mutual help, to care for one another in time of need, and to be readily available in times of crisis. Compadrazgo has been, as might be expected, a key institution embraced by migrants from all the Hispanic countries. Compadres, as kin, have provided shelter for newcomers, access to jobs, and a base from which people can become acclimatized to the new environment. Compadrazgo is a means to further "extend" the family by adding new members and ensuring support in times of need.

In addition to the compadrazgo, which extends reciprocity to nonrelatives, *parentesco* has been an important institution that has taken on new meaning in the early periods of migration and settlement. Parentesco has been especially utilized by Mexican immigrants. As used in the border area, it became a broader concept than that understood in the home region, where parentesco was reserved for kin. In the United States it was expressed on the basis of regional affiliation, the migration experience, or the mutual settlement in a foreign environment. Families did not just extend parentesco to other migrants; they were extending parentesco to families and individuals who shared a specific history in the country of origin. Parentesco is not familism, which is the recognition of the importance of family, family ties, family honor, and the ideal of respect. Familism incorporates the altruistic value that the family is more important than any of its members. This recognition carries a responsibility to kin in general. Parentesco is a kinship sentiment used by Hispanics to incorporate kin as well as nonkin into family networks. It is the extension of family sentiment to kin and nonkin.

Parientes (blood relatives), because of their natural relation as bloodkin, are automatically part of a family network. Similarly, compadres, if not already kin, are brought into the network as well. However, among Hispanics in the United States, the sentiment of parentesco is extended to individuals who share regional or specific geographic origins, especially a town or township in the country of origin. This was especially evident among early migrants to the United States who came from primarily rural backgrounds; often similar origins in towns did indicate kinship even if distant. The new environment in the United States utilized the sentiment toward kin and friends from home regions to build the support and reciprocity networks needed in the new settlements. Kin terms are used to express this relationship—*primo/a* (cousin), *tío/a* (uncle/aunt), for example.

Confianza is of particular importance to both the institutions of compadrazgo and parentesco among Hispanics in the United States, and is the basis of the relationships between individuals in many spheres of social activity. It is evident in business relations among entrepreneurs who work on the basis of trust and among friendships in which trust is fundamental. But confianza goes beyond relationships between individuals and forms the underlying base of reciprocity of all types. Confianza is the underlying factor that builds relationships and forms the basis for trust in the institutions of parentesco and compadrazgo. In a sense, the combined expression and practice of compadrazgo and parentesco produce the continued trust that is expressed as confianza. To have confianza with an individual is not just to regard that person with trust, but it signifies a relationship of special sentiment and importance involving respect and intimacy. Confianza developed in friendship can, for example, lead to a relationship of compadrazgo and to expressing parentesco to individuals who are not kin, as for example an individual who is from a home region and is a friend or compadre of kin.

A unique characteristic of the extended family among Hispanics in the United States is regionalism. Because of the migration over time of different generations from specific home regions, the family has been extended to include both U.S. and home country components. The family has become in many instances a binational or transnational institution even after several generations of time. Among Dominicans and Mexicans this is especially evident, but it is true to varying degrees among all Hispanics in the United States. Extensions of the family in the United States form part of a social network that includes not just regions but actual ties to specific hometowns. Among early pioneers and first migrants, kinship forms the basis for help in settling and finding jobs in the United States; later as settlements became more established, these early migrants host and assist both relatives and friends from their home areas. And migrants themselves return to home countries and regions, setting up a back-and-forth flow that depends on the support of family members in both areas. This actually extends the family across geographic space, creating the reciprocity, mutual help, and parentesco in the country of origin as well as in the United States. Hence the extended regional family becomes a basis of reciprocity between families in the home and the country of origin, as well as a potential basis for continuing migration to and from the United States.

The institution of marriage varies tremendously among Hispanics in the United States, and like the family in general has been adapted to a number of different socioeconomic conditions. The value of a religious wedding is not, nor has it ever been, the sole means for recognizing unions between men and women. Among Dominicans, for example, marital unions consist of *matrimonio por la iglesia* (church wedding), *matrimonio por ley* (civil marriage), and *union libre* (free union). Church weddings carry higher prestige and are more prevalent among persons of higher socioeconomic status, but free unions allow for early cohabitation in the migrant settlement. Marriage, however, has been an institution that strengthens extended family ties and incorporates individuals and their kin into network alliances under parentesco. Marriage, in addition to its important function of uniting conjugal pairs in critical household formation and procreation of children, is an institution used in the primary adaptive processes to the United States. Marriage among Hispanics continues to be within their own group (endogamous), that is, Mexicans marrying Mexicans, Puerto Ricans marrying Puerto Ricans, and so on. There is some intermarriage between groups, but this is infrequent, and there is a growing rate of intermarriage with Anglo-Americans, especially among second-generation Hispanics. This is especially true of Mexican Americans.

La familia incorporates the institutions of ideology, parentesco, compadrazgo, marriage, and confianza that together have formed the basis of migration and settlement in the United States. Through the variant forms of the extended family, Hispanics have adjusted and adapted to a new environment. The family, however, continues changing as seen in the shift from extended to nuclear family preference in later generations and among U.S.-born persons. This, however, is not an indication of abandoning extended family ties, but a change in the manner in which extended ties and relations are expressed that are congruent with life in the United States. Although these institutions can be viewed as separate strands of a single thread, they are strands that together form the social fabric in unique products of expression. Social networks composed of extended families are the basis of communities in urban and rural barrios of Chicanos, Mexicans, Puerto Ricans, Cubans, and the other Latinos in the United States.

Because families live in households, they are often taken as one and the same thing. Hispanics make the differentiation clearly, as they refer to the nuclear family living under one roof as *la casa*, as opposed to the broader institution la familia. Households, however, are a good indication of the changing nature of adaptation and settlement of Hispanics in the United States. Households include the extended family as people first migrate and begin to settle in the United States. It is the first step in becoming permanent settlers.

❋ PUERTO RICANS: BORN IN THE UNITED STATES

Puerto Ricans are the second-largest Hispanic group in the United States and have been migrating to the mainland United States since the turn of the century. In 1917, the Jones Act granted all Puerto Ricans born on the island U.S. citizenship. This is a striking difference to all other Hispanic immigrants to the country, as Puerto Ricans can move freely between their country of origin without the legal restrictions and entanglements of U.S. immigration law.

Migration to the continental United States became a viable alternative to the deteriorating economic and social situation on the island. Economic changes on the island brought about by foreign control of land for sugar, coffee, and tobacco plantations caused high unemployment and consequently, a steady stream of Puerto Ricans migrated to the United States. One of the first casualties of this economic change was the incremental decline of family patterns that were based on subsistence. High unemployment coupled with a gradual industrialization caused both increased unemployment and dependence on outside commodities. This imbalance created surplus labor at a time when jobs in New York City and elsewhere on the mainland needed to be filled. Puerto Ricans began migrating to the United States and, in particular, to New York City. Initially, as is the case with the majority of Hispanics in the United States, the early migration was intended to be only temporary. Puerto Ricans did not want to leave the island, but high unemployment and the draw of jobs in New York encouraged a steady flow of people between the mainland and the island.

In the late 1890s, during the Spanish American War, a small group of Puerto Ricans fled the island and sought refuge in New York City where they sought support for Puerto Rico's independence. Most of these people returned after the United States obtained the island from Spain and felt somewhat betrayed when the United States maintained jurisdiction over the island and did not support the liberation movement. Nonetheless, the early colony helped establish New York as a receiving area, and it grew geometrically in the following years. In the early part of the century, migration to the United States continued and New York became the preferred area for the majority of migrant Puerto Ricans, establishing one of the largest concentrations of Hispanics in the United States. Early migration was composed of people moving from rural to urban areas in Puerto Rico as well as people who immigrated to New York directly from rural areas of the island. Of importance here is the fact that these people maintained what might be called the traditional family as it was known in Puerto Rico. Some of these people joined the migrant labor circuits on the mainland doing agricultural work, but the majority went to the city of New York. The early conditions of this migration created a relationship that was to have enduring consequences for settlement and adaptation of Puerto Ricans and their families as well as for the subsequent forms the family would take in the United States.

In the 1940s, airline flights between the island and New York became regular, were relatively inexpensive, and travel time was short. Air travel became the common means of leaving and returning to the island and paved the way for what was to become the "Great Migration" from the mid 1940s to the 1970s. The decades before 1945 are considered the period of pioneer migration. Many of the people emigrating from Puerto Rico during this time were contract laborers who came to work in industry and agriculture. These individuals provided the foundation for many Puerto Rican communities that currently exist outside New York City. However, the majority of migrants continued to pour into New York City. By 1940, there was a total of almost 70,000 Puerto Ricans in the United States; more than 87 percent, or almost 61,000, were living in New York City.

During the war years, there were not many migrants who crossed from the island because of the danger in the Atlantic. But when the war ended, there was a sizable unemployed population looking to leave for jobs in the United States. It was at this time that the Great Migration began. The economic situation in Puerto Rico had worsened before this period and the island fell further under the domination of a market economy controlled by U.S. interests. By 1960, a total of 887,662 Puerto Ricans had migrated to the United States; 69 percent of these people, or about 612,000, resided in New York City. By the end of the next decade, a total of 1,391,463 people left the island and had become residents of the United States, with 817,712 of them residing in the city of New York.

Like other Hispanic immigrants, Puerto Ricans did not travel together in family groups at the beginning of the migration. Usually, young men immigrated to find work, then began sending for spouses and families. But the social conditions in the United States, especially in New York, where new communities were established, set parameters that changed family patterns and conditioned the adaptation of Puerto Ricans to the city.

In Puerto Rico, unemployment in these later years continued to worsen, and the educational system was not meeting the needs of the island's growing population. The majority of people worked *la zafra* (the sugar harvest), but this work lasted only five months of the year. Workers were idle for the remaining seven months. Unemployment was further heightened by a growing working-age population; a rising population coupled with a drop in the death rate created a large, young, unemployed working class.

Poverty became a significant factor in the lives of families in both Puerto Rico and the United States. It is impossible to discuss the Puerto Rican family in the United States without discussing the extreme conditions that have pervaded the Puerto Rican community here. From a historical perspective, Puerto Ricans have never recovered from the early colonial period when U.S. capital interests took over the ownership of the majority of land on the island and created a labor force that was dependent on cash crops. Puerto Rico had one of the highest infant mortality rates in the world and one of the lowest rates of average income per worker during the early years of U.S. jurisdiction over the island. Consider for example that in 1899 Puerto Ricans maintained ownership of 93 percent of all farms, but by 1930 foreign (U.S.) interests controlled 60 percent of sugar cultivation, 80 percent of tobacco lands, 60 percent of all banks, and 100 percent of maritime lines that controlled commodities entering and leaving the island. Prior to the capitalist sugar economy, the family was very important in the subsistence economy. Diminished ownership of agriculture, continued unemployment, and poor education in Puerto Rico resulted in severe poverty on the island. Similar factors account for continued poverty in the United States. People arrived in the States with low skills due to their rural background and little or no schooling and consequently, found jobs that were poor-paying. Of all Hispanic groups in the United States Puerto Ricans continue to be the most socioeconomically disadvantaged group in the country, especially in New York City. In 1980, the median family annual income for Puerto Ricans was $9,900, compared to $15,000 for all Hispanics and $19,500 for all U.S. families. In New York City, 45 percent of Puerto Ricans live below the poverty level. Much of this poverty is found among female-headed households, a family configuration that is increasing among Puerto Ricans, Dominicans, and other Hispanics in the United States. Poverty, then, is a consistent factor and an underlying force among the Puerto Rican families in the United States. It has conditioned change and the adaptation of families to the social and cultural environment of the United States.

At the end of the 1960s and into the early 1970s, what has become known as "revolving door" migration began. This is a back-and-forth stream of people moving between the United States and Puerto Rico. It is no longer focused in New York, although a majority of Puerto Ricans continue to migrate and settle in the Northeast.

This back-and-forth movement has encouraged

the unification and extension of families on the mainland with those in Puerto Rico. Travel of family members to and from households on the island and on the mainland is now a natural part of the migration cycle. Even "Nuyoricans," Puerto Ricans born in New York, have migrated to the island and have begun to adapt to life there.

A significant problem in New York and in other urban areas that has greatly influenced Puerto Rican families and individuals is access to housing. Housing in New York has always been a problem, but among Puerto Ricans who earn low wages and are often unemployed in the city, housing is poor, crowded, and a major adaptational factor, especially for those Puerto Ricans who are on the lowest rung of the socioeconomic ladder. In Hartford, Connecticut housing problems are contributing to household fragmentation. Two of every three Puerto Rican households were reported to lack employment, even part-time. This has contributed to a number of household types: dual-parent households where at least one of the two parents is employed; households with two parents but with neither employed; and single-parent households where the parent is not employed. These variations, however, illustrate the workings of the extended family in that the households with two unemployed parents are often helped by other relatives living in the Hartford area. Similarly, among single-parent households, there are relatives in the city who appear to be providing help and support. Here again the range of assistance received from others outside the household demonstrates the general patterns of exchange and reciprocity. It is clear, then, that the urban milieu in the United States has influenced Puerto Rican family patterns and households.

Although poverty among Puerto Ricans is a significant factor, not all Puerto Ricans are suffering from unemployment and poverty. Although the majority of early migrants were unskilled, Puerto Ricans have slowly penetrated the white-collar world associated with the middle class in the United States. Even with great poverty, the children of migrants, the second generation, are improving their socioeconomic position. Less unemployment, higher educational achievement, and higher incomes are not the rule but are evident in the population as a whole.

The ideal of the family as a cultural expression is still adhered to and the institutions of *parentesco, comadrazgo, confianza,* and varying degrees of patriarchy are maintained among Puerto Ricans in the United States. One significant change among the general population is the increasing influence of the role of women. This has been a direct result of women working, often when the male in the house is

Mexican Mother of the Year, 1969: Dolores Venegas and her husband, Miguel, Houston, Texas.

unemployed. Women in many cases have become the breadwinners of the household. This has led to an increasing trend toward stronger egalitarian relations among spouses, but this generally means that the wife has taken on traditional male tasks, not that men have taken on the wives' roles and tasks in the household. Marriage preference continues to be a religious ceremony in the Catholic church, and there is a low rate of Puerto Ricans marrying outside the community, although this has increased among second-generation U.S.-born persons.

Puerto Ricans continue to identify strongly with their cultural and ethnic past. A study by Lloyd H. Rogler and Rosemary Santana Cooney, entitled *Puerto Rican Families in New York City* (1984), of 100 parents and their married children (a total of 200 married couples) in New York reported that not one member of the children's generation, almost all born in the United States, reported feeling closer to Anglo-Americans than to Puerto Ricans, nor did anyone in their generation consider Anglo-Americans to be his or her real people.

What we see in the family among Puerto Ricans in the United States is a great variation in form, but it is still based in part on the ideal type of Hispanic family. Major institutions appear to be alive and well, but the dearth of research in this area of family life does not allow any assured conclusions. Research and documentation of the Puerto Rican family centers around the revolving-door migration between the island and the mainland United States and focuses on New York City. However, the extreme socioeconomic conditions in which Puerto Ricans have lived are significant factors in the formation of variant types of households. The extended family is an important institution that has been utilized in situations of mutual help and reciprocity, but the preferred family living pattern is the nuclear family with a woman, man, and children living in one household. The variety of family types include intergenerational forms where the nuclear family enjoys considerable autonomy from kin, but where frequent visits and exchanges of gifts and help, especially on ceremonial occasions, keep the extended nature of the family alive. Also, there are families in which married children are completely dependent on their parents and where the younger generation is almost totally absorbed and nurtured by the parents. The range of behavior includes situations where strong mothers have created matriarchal patterns of organization in which they control and bind the family together. Although there is variation among households and families in general, there are strong underlying bonds that maintain the norms that bind the family together, allowing a flexibility that has provided for successful adaptation in numerous areas of the United States.

✳ DOMINICANS

The Dominican population in the United States, like Puerto Ricans and Mexicans, began arriving at the turn of the twentieth century, but the political and economic conditions in the Dominican Republic fostered a pattern of migration and settlement in the United States that affected the formation and structure of families differently from the way it did other groups. The Dominican Republic has had a history of strong economic and political dependency on the United States that, as in other Caribbean nations, began around 1900. However, unlike Puerto Rico, the Dominican Republic experienced an internal domination during the "Trujillato," the reign of dictator Molina Trujillo from 1930 to 1960, that created a constriction of the migrant flow from the Republic. After the death of Trujillo in 1960, a surge of Dominicans began leaving for the United States. Throughout this period and into the present, the family and its constituent institutions have been a major factor

for Dominicans in both initiating migration to the United States and in the initial settlement and adaptation to the United States. Through the institution of the family, Dominicans have maintained a continuous chain of movement between the Republic and the mainland United States. Understanding the basic causes of the migration helps comprehend the development of the Dominican family as an institution responding to socioeconomic circumstances in both the United States and the Republic.

According to Eugenia Georges in *The Making of a Transnational Community: Migration, Development and Cultural Change in the Dominican Republic* (1990), Dominicans are the fourth-largest Hispanic group in the United States, but, like Puerto Ricans, in New York City and the northeastern United States they are the second-largest group. Estimates of their numbers range for 300,000 to over 500,000, but the actual figure is probably closer to 300,000. In 1981, Dominicans in the United States represented 5 to 8 percent of the total Dominican Republic's work force. Dominicans are primarily working-class. Of all the major immigrant groups (Hispanics and others) who entered the United States between 1970 and 1980, Dominicans had the lowest family income ($9,569). Like the majority of Hispanics, they are a young population.

The presence of the United States was felt in the Dominican Republic early in the century and continues to the present. This influence helped set the economic structure that was to change the basic pattern of subsistence in the island, convert land to foreign interests, and create a labor force that was initially confined to work in the Dominican Republic. However, after the death of dictator Molina Trujillo in 1960, that labor force poured into the United States.

At the turn of the century, there was little migration to the United States from the Dominican Republic. By the second quarter of the century, sugar, as in the other Caribbean islands, became an important crop that attracted investors to the island. North Americans, Europeans, Cubans, and others looking for expanded or new areas in which to invest went to the island. In addition, investment in coffee, cacao, and cattle ranching became popular. These investments created a demand for land and, as in Puerto Rico, people were forced out of subsistence agriculture and into a labor force that was dependent primarily on sugar cultivation.

The early part of the century was marked by economic distress and political instability, opening the way for U.S. intervention. The intervention took the form of an eight-year occupation that became the basis for major changes in Dominican health services, education, and public works. Under U.S. guidance, schools and hospitals were built where they had never existed; new roads and bridges connected once remote areas. One of the lasting results of the public works program was political centralization. Unification of the country neutralized the power of local political leaders. These processes helped form a new relationship with the United States and created a mass of people who came to rely on wage labor, first in the Republic itself and then, as unemployment became a serious problem, in the urban Northeast of the United States.

By the end of the U.S. occupation in 1924, sugar companies controlled almost a quarter of all agricultural land; 80 percent of this control was by U.S. companies. During this period, the Dominican National Guard was created, which came to have lasting effects on the Republic. The guard was trained by the United States, and it produced a military establishment that was strongly favorable to the United States. A result of this establishment was the rise of Trujillo, who worked his way from a guardsman into the presidency of the Republic.

President Trujillo instilled a strongly pronational industry that relied on a large and stable work force. During his reign from 1930 to 1960, migration to the United States was a mere trickle; the population was restricted to the Dominican Republic. Trujillo also encouraged population growth to both counter a long-standing territorial conflict with Haiti and to boost the national labor force. During the period form 1930 to 1961, the population of the Dominican Republic doubled from 1.5 to 3 million people. Some of this growth was, to be sure, the result of improved health. The result, however, at the time of Trujillo's death, was a sizable population that was dependent on wage labor.

In the early 1960s, constraints in the agricultural sector created a massive rural-urban migration. In 1970, over one-half of the population of the capital city, Santo Domingo, was composed of migrants from the countryside. By the end of the following presidential period (of Joaquín Balaguer), a 1980 study reported that in the five poorest neighborhoods around Santo Domingo, 91 percent of household heads were migrants, most from rural areas. This migration became international as household heads and families left the Republic for Puerto Rico and the United States.

In the final years of Trujillo's dictatorship between 1950 and 1960, 9,800 people immigrated to the United States. In the next two-year period, from 1960 to 1962, this number increased six-fold, and in almost every year after 1962, a number equal to or greater than the total for the previous decade migrated to the United States. Between 1966 and 1980, the number of legal immigrants admitted to the United States averaged about 14,000 per year. It is obvious that both legal and undocumented migration became a partial solution to a growing unemployment problem in the Republic.

A significant aspect of the Dominican migration that affects the settlement of families in the United States is the influx of undocumented migrants, or migrants that enter on tourist or other types of temporary visas and remain in the United States illegally. By the mid-1960s, more than 150,000 nonimmigrants were being admitted annually, and between 1961 and 1978 approximately 1,800,000 entered the United States on nonimmigrant visas. Although most of these people did not choose to stay in the United States, some did indeed regularize their status through marriages and other means. Estimates of the undocumented migrants are between 14 to 17 percent of the total Dominican U.S. population.

The closeness of the Republic to Puerto Rico and the mainland has made travel back and forth to the island relatively easy. Most immigrants travel directly to the United States, others go first to Puerto Rico. Recently, undocumented Dominicans have begun to enter the United States through Mexico, crossing into the United States as do many Mexicans and Central Americans at the U.S.-Mexican border. The migrant stream between the Dominican Republic and the United States has become one social field in which family connections at both ends of the stream are important. Indeed, it is the family in its extended form that helps initiate the migration to the United States and helps in initial adaptation and settlement. Once settlement is accomplished, the connection to the Republic is maintained.

In many ways, Dominican migration to the United States illustrates in dramatic fashion how Hispanics strategically use *familia* institutions in new ways. Although all Hispanic groups utilize *parentesco, compadrazgo,* extended kin, and *confianza,* the massive and direct migration of Dominicans from the Republic in a relatively short time period to dense urban areas in the United States shows an intense use of these institutions.

Because of the direct contact with the home country, modern transportation, and the proximity of the Republic to the United States, Dominicans have maintained a very strong ethnic identity in the United States. In addition, the recent immigration of numerous first-generation Dominicans has helped transfer social patterns from the Republic to the United States. The large, existing Hispanic population in the northeastern United States has been a further incentive both to keep cultural ties alive and to settle in Hispanic neighborhoods where identity and adaptation appear to be easier than in purely Anglo areas.

The household based on the ideal of the nuclear family with two spouses and children is the elementary unit of social and economic relationships in the Dominican Republic. This ideal has been carried over to the United States, but it is not realized. What has occurred is a hybrid form of the family that is begun in the Dominican Republic. The basis of this new form is reciprocal exchange and mutual help. As with other Hispanic groups, individuals in the household are connected through the extended family and network of friends traced through both spouses. Compadrazgo, confianza, parentesco, and marriages unite and extend reciprocal relations and sentiment between individuals and groups of individuals. The principal relationships of the extended family play an important role in connecting individuals not only at local and regional levels, but also beyond national boundaries.

When migration to the United States began in earnest, individuals relied on the extended family for support in initiating the move. Branches of the (kindred) extended family were sent first to the cities of the Republic or to the United States to secure contacts there. Once in the United States, family members and kindred branches utilized the institutions of confianza and parentesco with other Dominicans, forming large networks of mutual support that led to the extension of kinship ties through marriage and other familial institutions. In 1974, Hendricks reported that in the village he studied in the Republic, 65 percent of families had immediate family members living in the United States and 87 percent of these families were receiving money from kin in the United States. The extended family has become so important that seldom do immigrants leave home without some assurance of help from contacts in the United States.

Because individuals have traveled to the United States often without spouses, household and marriage relations have been adapted to the new environment. In the Dominican Republic and in the United States, the authority of the male is an ideal standard in which the man of the house is the final authority and decision maker. There are few households, however, in which this form is evident. Circumstances in the United States and in the Republic are encouraging change in sex roles, especially among women.

Because of migration and settlement in the United States, the role of women is the most affected and changed in family relationships. In the Dominican Republic, as men leave, women are left as the main authority figures in the households. Although many women were always in the position of head of household, this seems to have increased because of migration. The greatest change, however, is seen in the United States. Here women have the opportunity to work, changing the traditional roles they occupy, but also influencing the role of the male as provider and principal head of the household. Women are becoming heads of household primarily because of their financial contributions to the home, which, in the absence of a male head, is often essential in maintaining family needs, goals, and even survival. Women are being exposed to the outside environment, and new social situations are providing them with important social skills that many men do not have.

Not all women, however, are becoming more independent. Those women who do not work are confined to the household to care for children. This encourages the strengthening of the male's authority and the isolation of women, who, unlike those in the Dominican Republic, have less freedom in general. They are confined to the household, seldom have outside contacts, and are the caretakers of children.

In addition to the change in women's roles, a significant change in the Dominican family in the United States is the number of children in families. In the United States, Dominicans have fewer children than in the Republic, primarily due to financial constraints. Economic restrictions in housing, food, clothing, and child care limit the ability of women to work. Parents are often brought from the Dominican Republic to help with children, and other kin in the United States are often caretakers of children while parents work, thus making the extended family a further support. Interestingly, migration has increased the likelihood that children will live with or be cared for by a variety of individuals.

Heads of household are often those individuals who are the financial providers, are proficient in English, and are the ones to whom the family is obligated because of financial support. Glenn Hendricks has shown in *The Dominican Diaspora* (1974) that this is often not the man in the household, especially if he has come to the United States as a mature adult. For many U.S. households, the father or elderly male is often the least able to perform this role.

The Dominican acceptance and acknowledgment of different conjugal unions has been a factor in U.S. settlement and continued ties to the Republic. Three types of marriage are acknowledged by Dominicans: *matrimonio por iglesia*, *matrimonio por ley*, and *unión libre*. According to Glenn Hendricks in *The Dominican Diaspora* (1974), all three are legitimate types of conjugal unions that cut across all classes, legitimizing the children of the unions. In addition to accommodating U.S. legal requirements for securing visas, these three types of marital unions help Dominicans to adapt socioeconomically to the United States. Religious marriages are often forgone because they are more expensive than civil unions. Civil unions are legal in the United States and help unite conjugal pairs. Free unions have played a significant role in maintaining family connections in the Republic because they allow individuals to cohabit and share households and expenses in the United States while maintaining legal spouses and households in the Republic. In the Dominican Republic, polygamous marriage, that is, men having more than one "wife," and men supporting and having a union with more than one woman, is socially and legally approved. Although not approved legally in the United States, the acceptability of these norms allows men and women to engage in relations in the United States while families are maintained in the home country.

✳ CUBANS

The experience of Cubans in the United States has been markedly different, although there are similarities they share with other Hispanics. The Cuban immigration and settlement in the United States was primarily a politically instigated migration caused by the Cuban Revolution of 1959 headed by Fidel Castro. Prior to the revolution there had been some migration into Florida and New York. At the turn of the century tobacco workers were relocated to work in Tampa in companies that had been moved from Cuba. According to Joan Moore and Harry Pachón in *Hispanics in the United States* (1985), there were some 18,000 to 19,000 Cubans living in the United States in 1930 and a slow trickle of Cubans who entered the United States prior to the 1950s. But of the total, now nearing 1,000,000 Cubans in the United States, more than half have arrived since 1959.

The United States played a significant role in the early history of the Republic of Cuba and established strong economic ties there early in the century. This history, like that of other Hispanics, is important in understanding the Cuban immigration to the United States and the sentiment that Cubans hold for their home country. As in Puerto Rico and the Dominican Republic, the United States played a significant role in bringing Cuba into the new industrial epoch of the twentieth century and a world economy (dominated by capital interests primarily from the United States).

Just before the turn of the century, Cuba had begun to resist the Spanish government and rebelled. In 1898, the United States intervened, supported the Cuban revolutionaries who were fighting Spain for independence, and began the Spanish American War. (The U.S. entrance into the war was justified by blaming Spain for sinking the battleship *Maine* in Havana Harbor in February 1898.) In December 1898, the conflict ended and a treaty was signed in which Spain relinquished sovereignty over Cuba. The United States ruled until 1902, when the Cuban Republic was formally instituted. However, political unrest continued and the United States, with the right of intervention secured in the original Cuban constitution, intervened from 1906 to 1909 and again in 1912. During this period and after World War I, U.S. interests dominated Cuba's economy through the control of land dedicated to the production of sugar. Through the next 30 years and into the decade of the 1950s, Cuba experienced continued economic instability and unrest.

During the Second World War, Cubans experienced continued food shortages and political instability owing to fluctuations in world sugar prices, the primary export crop of the Cuban nation. High costs of living and continued inflation led to unrest and political violence in the late 1940s. In 1952, Fulgencio Batista, the head of the Cuban Army, seized power, suspended the constitution, dissolved the Cuban Congress, and set up a provisional government. Batista, running unopposed, held elections in 1954 and was inaugurated in February 1955. The entire first half of the twentieth century had been marked by unrest, economic instability, and a strong foreign interest that controlled sugar production and export. Batista's strong hand, in conjunction with the stabilization of world sugar prices, brought initial suppression of the political unrest and economic stability through an economic development program supported by the United States.

During the later years of Batista's dictatorship, 10,000 to 15,000 Cubans entered the United States annually. This early migration was composed of ruling elite and the politically and socially alienated, as well as individuals who were unemployed. But it was overrepresented by the upper classes. This migration was to continue in earnest after the next Cuban revolution that brought Fidel Castro into power in 1959.

That early period of Cuban history set up a stratified society favoring the ruling class and foreign interests in sugar, primarily from the United States. Although initially stymied by Batista, unrest grew and erupted in the Cuban Revolution of 1959, led by Fidel Castro. It was this revolution that initiated the first major wave of exiles into the United States. The revolution was supported by all classes and all generations in Cuba. In "Dilemmas of a Golden Exile" (1969), Alejandro Portes, a well-noted Cuban sociologist, states that "seldom has history seen a more complete example of social consensus." However, Castro's plan was to return Cuba to the ordinary people, and he began a program of socialization in which the powerless working class took control. Castro initiated agrarian reform affecting plantations controlled by U.S. companies. The operation of plantations by non-Cuban stockholders was prohibited and Castro eventually deemphasized sugar for food crops. Upper-class Cubans, the wealthy, the educated, and the powerful saw their status challenged and their influence radically curtailed. The lower strata of Cuban society was now in control and in power.

This restructuring of Cuban society resulted in the first massive immigration of Cubans to the United States in 1960. Between 1959 and 1962, more than 155,000 people left the island. This migration was slowed because of a three-year suspension of airline flights from Cuba to the United States. But in 1965, when the airlift was reestablished, daily flights brought some 257,000 Cubans to the United States between December 1965 and December 1972. These individuals were fleeing the Castro government and felt betrayed by the revolution. They brought a fierce hostility toward the Castro regime, but also an attachment and pride to their values and style of life, a clearly defined identity as Cubans, and a strong desire to return to Cuba.

The majority of this first wave of Cubans went to Miami, Florida. In Miami, they were close to Cuba and were in a climate that was very much like home. In addition, the previous tobacco-worker immigration to Florida had established communities there. This first wave of refugees was followed by a subsequent group of people who left Cuba in the 1980s. In April 1980, 10,000 people took refuge in the Peruvian embassy in Havana, hoping to leave Cuba. The Castro regime allowed these people and an additional 118,000 others to leave. The majority of them left from the port of Mariel and are known as the Marielitos. Hence, the prerevolution, the immediate postrevolution, and the Mariel migrations constitute the three waves of migrations for Cubans entering the United States.

Most Cuban immigrants settled in Miami, although there are smaller communities in Los Angeles, New York City, and Union City, New Jersey. In addition to having a history of settlement in Miami, the first wave of refugees who had come from the professional and entrepreneurial classes came equipped to begin new businesses and prosper from the economy. Unlike many other Hispanic groups, most of the Cubans arrived with resources in the form of capital, education, and both professional and semiprofessional skills, allowing them to take advantage of their new situation in the United States. In addition, there were many political groups in the United States who provided help and resources because of their anti-Communist sentiments. The result was a strong economic foothold in Miami. The success of the early immigrants provided fertile ground for the successive immigrant waves in the form of jobs and opportunities that were not available to other groups. This has been described as an ethnic economic enclave in which Cubans have provided viable alternatives to the U.S. labor market. The enclave is characterized by ethnic (Cuban) businesses that employ and do business within the ethnic community and provide upward mobility for labor. Hence, the early immigrants were able to get a strong foothold, with succeeding waves providing continued input into the enclave in the form of resources and labor. The result in Miami is a strong Cuban community that has influenced not only the economy but also politics. Spanish, for example, is the primary language spoken, making it possible even for monolingual Spanish-speakers to succeed. This environment has had strong binding effects on the families of Cubans in the United States.

In "Dilemmas of a Golden Exile" (1969), Alejandro Portes has shown the adaptive nature of Cuban immigrants in Milwaukee. He noted that educational attainment, occupational skills that were in demand in the United States, and a middle-class ethic and style of life combined to produce a fast process of adaptation. Significantly, the adaptation of Cuban families in Milwaukee was generally not a problem. They had come with strong values in individualism, self-concept, personal rights, and belief in the improvement of one's position in the stratification system. The satisfaction and attraction to life in the United States was almost an exclusive result of the level of socioeconomic rewards these people received. These socioeconomic rewards were the only factors that overcame old attachments among the families studied, which, according to Portes, is in "perfect agreement with the beliefs they supported and the role they played during the revolutionary process."

The individuals who are now in the United States are primarily exiles, but there is a significant difference in the people who arrived in the United States at different times. During the first waves just before and during the revolution in 1959, Cubans coming to the United States were primarily the more privileged classes consisting of managers, entrepreneurs, and landowners. Later, after a decade of socialism, immigrants of lower-middle and working-class backgrounds predominated. This resulted in a U.S. population that was truly historically representative of Cuban society, a factor that is not seen in the other Hispanic groups who have come to the United States.

Cubans in the United States are also different in other ways from Mexicans, Puerto Ricans, Dominicans, and other Hispanic immigrants and settlers. Although the exiled population represents all sectors of the prerevolutionary society, it is overrepresented by professionals and semiprofessionals. In general, the upper occupational strata of the Cuban population are overrepresented. Because the Caucasian population in Cuba was in the upper strata, Cuban Caucasians are also overrepresented in the United States. A 1953 Cuban census indicated that 72 percent of the population was Caucasian; in the 1970 U.S. census, the Cuban Caucasian population was 95 percent. In addition, the Cuban population is disproportionately elderly. Currently, 10 percent of Cubans in the United States are over 65, a proportion three times larger than for other Hispanic groups. When viewed as a whole, Cuban Americans are also a highly educated group. Of the pre-1953 population, only 4 percent had completed the twelfth grade or more, but the later post-Castro group reported that 36 percent of the immigrant group had completed 12 or more years of schooling. These factors along with settlement patterns illustrate a highly adapted and successful population. As with Puerto Ricans, Dominicans, and Mexicans, however, the family played an initially important role in adjustment.

As in pre-Castro Cuba, the family and its structure varies according to class. Since the 1930s, according to Magaly Queralt in *Understanding Cuban Immigrants: A Cultural Perspective* (1984), Caucasian Cubans have been oriented toward the nuclear family, with both spouses and children living together as the norm. The immigration and consequent adaptation to the United States has encouraged this trend even more. The middle and lower classes have relied more on the extended family because of its supportive nature in initial settlement and employment. But the trend is toward a nuclear family household for all Cubans in the United States.

There is no doubt that family ideology is of central importance among Cubans in the United States. The concept of a good family, in particular in the value placed on conserving and exhibiting a strong and good family name, has helped keep the traditional family ideology among Cubans. One example of this has been the reestablishment of strict chaperoning

of daughters. Although changes in family relationships and roles are taking place, Cubans continue to uphold the ideals of male authority and paternally centered families. The traditional view of the role of children and adolescents, however, has begun to cause conflict between the generations. A study in west New York and Union City, New Jersey, indicated that 86 percent of parents interviewed reported having great difficulty accepting similar freedom and independence enjoyed by other U.S. teenagers for their own children (*The Cuban Experience*, 1980). It appears that the trend and focus on the nuclear family has had influences on more traditional institutions of Hispanic family structure among Cubans. According to Queralt, compadrazgo, for instance, does not appear as strong or pervasive an institution as for other Hispanic groups. Marriages appear to have remained primarily within the Cuban community, but this appears to be changing. Parental pressure, intergenerational language barriers, and the tightness and completeness of the Cuban community help keep marriages within the group. The immigration of more women in recent years as compared to men of marriageable age has not yet had an impact on marriage patterns. The Cuban law prohibiting the emigration of males of military service age has resulted in an uneven distribution of the sexes among U.S. Cubans of marital age. In 1970, in the age category of 20–29, there were 76 males for each 100 females in the United States. Although marriages continue to be within the group (called endogamy), the rate of divorce among Cubans is higher than for other Hispanic groups and in fact is higher than for the U.S. population in general. According to the *Harvard Encyclopedia of Ethnic Groups* (1980), between 1960 and 1970, there were 6.2 divorces per 100 marriages among Cubans, 5.3 for the general population, and only 2.9 for other foreign-born immigrants.

The generational differences produced by the different waves of immigrants from both prerevolutionary Cubans who adhere to traditional values and those who have been exposed to the socialist change are significant to family and sex roles in the United States. Generally speaking, Cubans in the United States continue to hold a stronger traditional value about the family when compared to Anglo-Americans. For example, emphasis on the male authority is still present. However, the Castro regime placed considerable emphasis on incorporating more women into the labor force and has questioned the norms about sex roles. Individuals who have entered the United States more recently have been exposed to these and other more liberal ideas. A consequence has been a more open attitude toward women in the work force and change in the family. Cuban women have the highest rate of participation, 54 percent, in the labor force among Spanish-speaking women. Cuban women actually have a higher rate of participation than do Caucasian women as a percentage of the total U.S. population.

Although working women appear to have more freedom and access to social relations outside the family, work for Cuban women also has negative consequences. Work can be an increased burden, as men have yet to take on any of the domestic responsibilities of women in the household. In addition, for Cuban women the lack of domestic help increases their responsibility in the home. However, there continues to be an increase in the percentage of working wives. As with many other Latino groups in the United States, those in the grandparental generation serve as baby-sitters and instillers of traditional values.

In general, it appears that when compared to other Hispanic groups in the United States Cubans are adapting successfully to American life. They have not exhibited the severe poverty nor severe socioeconomic constraints suffered by Puerto Ricans, Mexicans, and Dominicans. Their adaptive success is the result of a strong and viable economic structure that is based within the community itself and a set of values based on individualism that parallel those of the United States generally.

Although the majority of Cuban Americans tend to favor a nuclear family, this does not discount the importance of the use of the extended family and its institutions in adapting to the United States. In fact, when viewed from a sociological point of view, the extended family in the form of social networks is a prevailing institution that has had significant impact for Cubans. This may in fact be stronger for Cubans than for other Hispanic groups. Dense kinship networks provide the basis for a pattern of social relationships that revolve around the ethnic community. In fact, according to Alejandro Portes and Robert L. Bach's book *Latin Journey (1985)*, Cuban refugees in 1976 reported that 87 percent had received help from relatives living in the United States. The social world of Cuban immigrants is one that is full of kin and ethnic ties. In 1973, on arrival to the United States, Cuban exiles reported having an average of 10 relatives and friends awaiting them. Three years later, they reported an average of 4 relatives living in the same city and 2.5 relatives living elsewhere in the United States. This was true for both men and women. Cuban wives had numerous relatives in cities where they lived. Similarly, Cubans reported an average of 8 close friends living in the same city, 7 of which were Cuban. Of these, 93

percent stated they had no American friends. These figures illustrate of the thick kinship and friendship networks to which Cuban immigrants belong and upon which they depend. Although the family has taken different forms, its role as an adaptive institution continues to be a significant factor in the U.S. Cuban community.

✳ MEXICAN AMERICANS

The Mexican-origin population is the largest Hispanic group in the United States, numbering over 12 million according to the 1990 U.S. census. Because of its size and geographic range both in the United States and in Mexico, this population is also the most diverse. Indeed, some of the Mexican regions from which immigrants have come are larger than any of the other Hispanic-origin countries. The U.S. East Coast is represented by Mexicanos from Tamaulipas, Saltillo, Torreón, and the southeastern seaboard of Mexico, including Vera Cruz and other Caribbean-like regions. The core sending area of Mexico, however, is the central states of Durango, Zacatecas, San Luis Potosí, Guanajuato, Jalisco, and Michoacán. The majority of these people from the core sending states have come to the southwestern United States, principally to California and Texas. But people from throughout Mexico are represented in all areas of the United States. People have also migrated from the northern Mexican border states of Sonora, Chihuahua, Coahuila, Nuevo León, and the states of the Pacific coast, Sinaloa and Nayarit. Even remote Mexican areas and regional cultures are represented in the United States. In fact, Mexican colonies in the United States are often dense settlements of people from specific Mexican regions and states. Neighborhoods in Los Angeles, for example, are made up of people from Sonora, others from Michoacán and Sinaloa. Each group expresses a regional pride and specific cultural practices. Neighborhoods exhibit commercial establishments that boast native restaurants and shops specializing in regional specialties. This variety, a product of recent immigration, is complicated by the fact that many Mexican Americans were also original populations in much of the Southwest.

The historical conditions between the United States and Mexico set the tone for current relationships. Of extreme importance in these relationships are the southwestern borderlands, which were first Spanish outposts in the New World, then Mexican territory before the Mexican-American War of 1846. This is the area currently separated by a 2,000-mile border. It consists of the U.S.-Mexican border states of Texas, New Mexico, Arizona, and California. Although indigenous Americans first lived in this region and continue to do so, each state is historically Spanish Mexican. Unlike the political-economic influence and domination of the United States in other countries of Hispanic origin, the United States conquered the Southwest and took it from Mexico. This conquest was the beginning of a U.S.-Mexican relationship that shaped present attitudes, economic dependencies, and immigration. The Southwest borderlands, currently the area of the highest density of the Mexican-origin population, stretches from the Pacific Ocean at San Diego, California, to the Gulf of Mexico at Texas. This 2,000-mile zone has been a frontier since indigenous periods when trade routes between the civilizations in Mexico and the Pueblo Indians in the north were established before the arrival of the Spanish. It is an area of immense geographic variety and isolation. The history of settlement here reflects this diversity, a long-standing Mexican and Spanish heritage. The names of states, major settlements, and geographic sites bear witness to this heritage.

However prominent the Spanish Mexican heritage of the Southwest, the population, both native and immigrant, has been subordinate to the dominant Anglo and has lived a history of segregation and racial conflict that only recently has begun to change in meaningful ways. Before the Anglo arrived, there were only outpost settlements in the region that had very small populations. According to Moore and Pachón (1985), Texas had some 5,000 Mexicans; New Mexico, the farthest outpost yet the largest, had some 60,000; California, around 7,000; and Arizona, perhaps 1,000 people. Each of these states has a specific history of Mexican and Anglo social interaction that conditioned the modern incorporation and adaptation of Mexicans, both U.S.-born and immigrants.

The adaptive response of the family during this early period was conditioned both by the frontier nature of the Mexican settlements and the ensuing conflict of conquest and entrance of the Anglo population. The long-standing Hispanic presence in the United States is exemplified by New Mexican settlements around Albuquerque and Santa Fe. New Mexicans to this day consider themselves Hispanos, direct descendants of the original Spanish settlers who arrived in the seventeenth century. Similarly, the towns along the Texas Rio Grande frontier had been settled early in the original Mexican settlement. And in California, the Spanish-Californio families became landowners and ranchers, establishing a specific culture that was a product of their lives there.

It was the early Spanish and Mexican settlements that were the basis for the Mexican American and Hispanic Southwest. Mexico had lost nearly one-third of its territory in the Mexican-American War. The Treaty of Guadalupe Hidalgo set both the boundaries for the international border separating the United States and Mexico and outlined the rights of the Mexican population that remained in the territory ceded to the United States. In each region and state, the new American presence capitalized on a variety of economic pursuits. Mexicans, once landowners and dominant entrepreneurs throughout the region, fell prey to the new economies and became wage laborers, although a few upper-class families survived. The overall result was the subjugation of the Hispanic population from a dominant economic and political entity to one of a prevailing wage labor in which Anglo economic interests controlled the regions. In Arizona, mining became a major resource for American capitalists that depended on Mexican labor, both native and immigrant. Agriculture became prominent in both California and Texas, establishing the migrant streams of Mexican workers.

In the late 1880s, the termination of the transcontinental railroad brought an onslaught of Americans from the eastern seaboard who made the Southwest their home. According to Moore and Pachón (1985), in 1887 the railroad brought in 120,000 Anglo settlers to southern California when the total population was only 12,000 for all Mexicans. The early families of these Mexican populations slowly lost power and social status. To Anglos they became socially indistinguishable from the Mexicans who began arriving in great numbers after the turn of the century.

The historic connection of the Southwest and Mexico continues to be prominent. Spanish is still spoken in much of the area, the geographic proximity makes travel back and forth to Mexico easy, and many of the border towns became truly a part of both cultures. The names for Calexico (California-Mexico) and Mexicali (Mexico-California), for example, were derivatives of the frontier and binational status along the California-Mexico border.

Small Mexican settlements developed throughout the Southwest and became the basis for the onslaught of Mexican immigration that was to begin in the early 1900s. The early settlements, however, had been closely tied to specific regions in Mexico. In California, for example, the regional ties between Baja California and Alta California during Spanish and Mexican periods provided traditional patterns of movement for families migrating into the United States. These regional ties helped people maintain affiliation to hometowns and kin in the south. By the 1900s, colonies of Mexicans from specific regions of

Mexico had established themselves in southwestern towns and cities, providing links to hometowns and the country of origin. Many of these settlements were agricultural camps, others the result of mining, and many Mexicans began moving to the growing cities of the West.

Mexican immigration has been the result, as in other Hispanic immigration and settlement, of the ongoing economic and political relationship of the home country with the United States. The concurrent conditions in Mexico, coupled with the demand for wage labor in the United States, and the history of the Spanish Mexican Southwest, influenced the massive and continuous movement of people between the two countries. The development of Mexican railroads, financed and controlled by American capitalists in the early 1900s, provided access to raw resources and human labor. The railroads made labor accessible to every major economic center in the United States. Mexican labor was contracted for work in the Southwest and later in the industrial middle-eastern states.

The onslaught of the Mexican Revolution, a result of the tyrannical control of Porfirio Díaz, uprooted and literally opened the doors for mass migration from the previously landlocked peasantry. Díaz, who was dictator of Mexico from 1887 to 1911, ruled Mexico with an iron hand. He took millions of acres from the Mexican *campesino* and fostered a laissez-faire development program that favored foreign interests in the republic. Díaz gave up huge land grants to foreign capitalists under the rubric of development. Many of these schemes were in the mining industry. One of his most amazing land grants was to an American company that went by the name of the International Company of Mexico in Baja California; the company was given some 18 million acres (28,000 square miles). The confinement and destitution of the major Mexican population, together with continued land takeover, led to civil disorder and finally the Mexican Revolution of 1911. Many people fled Mexico at this time, many with hopes of returning.

At the end of the revolution, the migration to the United States did not abate, and through 1930 continued in a steady stream, with only brief stoppage during the First World War. In 1930, the Great Depression in the United States caused economic upheaval and the Mexicans became a threat to the nation's unemployed and were displaced by Anglo Dust Bowl migrants. Mexicans became the scapegoats for the economic crisis in America. Then, President Hoover initiated a repatriation program aimed at returning the Mexican-origin population to Mexico. The result was the deportation of almost one-half million Mexicans and Mexican Americans to Mexico.

Much of this was voluntary, but social pressures and the country's mood influenced the return of many Mexican Americans, even some who had been born U.S. citizens. The 1940s reversed this pattern and the Second World War provided new opportunities for Mexican Americans in the United States. This period was characterized by a move out of agriculture, railroad work, and mining. Significantly, 300,000 to 500,000 Mexican American men served in the U.S. armed forces during the war. This was also a period in which the majority of Mexican people made a shift from a basic rural to an urban existence. In 1950, about 25 percent of Mexican Americans were rural; by 1970 only 15 percent were rural. In some areas, 90 percent of the Mexican population today is urban.

What has occurred is a slow movement into the middle class for many Mexican Americans. Even though immigrant Mexicans have continued to be primarily unskilled, there has been a steady incorporation of Mexican Americans into the primary labor market of the United States. Immigrants and undocumented Mexicans continue to be at the bottom strata of the labor market, filling nonskilled jobs primarily in the service sectors. However, Mexican Americans now represent three and four generations in the country; many are U.S.-born citizens. This residential longevity has provided for a basic adaptation and slow movement into the mainstream of American society.

The 1950s through the present has seen the continued movement of Mexicans into the United States. Much of the migration has been the result of voluntary immigration by Mexicans who come in search of better jobs that will help support their families and kin in home areas; others arrive with hopes of settlement. U.S. programs have also influenced the migration. For example, the Bracero Program, a labor contract program for agricultural workers in the United States, brought hundreds of thousands of Mexicans into the Southwest in the early 1960s. Many Mexicans returned to Mexico when the program was ended, but many "braceros" had made their home in the United States. This period (the 1960s) also saw the beginnings of real political involvement. Mexican Americans became involved in the Chicano movement and in politics in general. Ethnic identity became an important issue for Mexican Americans/Chicanos and brought visibility to the population as a national minority. It was no longer perceived as an isolated population of the Southwest but recognized as the fastest-growing minority in the United States.

This brief outline provides some idea of the complexity of the immigration and origin of the Mexican

American population in the United States. There are major differences in Mexican immigration from that of other Hispanic groups, and these discrepancies explain how these processes have influenced family patterns of socialization and change among Mexicans. In the first place, it is easy for Mexicans to get to the major cities of the United States. All are accessible by inexpensive travel (car, bus, and railroad) in addition to air travel. Mexicans and Mexican Americans often return to Mexico to visit relatives and to enjoy cultural and social events not available in the United States. These and other factors have had an impact on the development and change of the family and its institutions among Mexican Americans.

Mexican traditions, including the family, have survived more widely among Mexican Americans because of the historic isolation of the southwestern settlements and the geographic proximity to Mexico. The earliest of settlements as well as newcomer *colonias* (settlements) are rejuvenated by the continuing migration and the easy access to the border and the home regions of early pioneers. Furthermore, the residential segregation of Mexican communities and neighborhoods has fostered strong ethnic ties and boundaries to the greater society. These factors, along with racial conflict and discrimination toward Mexicans, have sustained a fierce pride and commitment to sociocultural institutions, which have in many ways become cultural symbols among Mexican Americans.

The family continues to be held as a particularly important institution among Mexican Americans. But family and familism is also a source of stress and conflict. Although the extended family is instrumental in socialization, especially in early settlement, it is also seen as creating inner barriers to adaptation to the outside world. The concept that family is all-important and that the individual should sacrifice for the good of the family has its costs, especially if individuals forgo immediate opportunities that may aid in long-term adaptation. Education is one example. Among migrant farm labor families, the economic necessity of having all family members participating and contributing to the family helped lead to one of the worst dropout rates for Hispanics in the country. Among second- and third-generation Mexican Americans, the traditional family values can be sources of stress in that they are not congruent with modern life-styles. However, the values of *la familia* are still adhered to by many, albeit only ideologically.

However, as with other groups of Hispanics, the family has played an instrumental role in the early adaptation and settlement of Mexicans to the United States. Among Mexican and Mexican Americans, the concept of the family is rooted in Mexico's agrarian past. This concept was emphasized first by the severance of the original native Mexican population from political and economic standing, then with the continuing entrance of rural immigrants from across the border. Once pioneer migrants settled in the United States, loved ones were brought north. This began a migration stream that included whole branches of families, representing the towns and regions to which they were connected. It is not uncommon for migrations between specific Mexican and U.S. regions to have three and four generations of continual back-and-forth flow, with established U.S. branches that receive and aid newcomers from Mexico.

Familism is perhaps the single most consistent aspect of Mexican American culture. The strong sentiment toward family, family cohesiveness, and incorporation of the individual into family membership has provided a base for settlement in the form of community for people in the United States. Migrants faced with strange and often threatening social environments naturally sought each other out and extended the relationships used in home regions. These were the institutions of ideology, *confianza, compadrazgo, parentesco,* and marriage. In some U.S. areas, migrants maintained strong regional ties through these institutions, whereas people who had migrated out of the same home regions and remained in Mexico did not maintain the regional and familial ties. These latter individuals were absorbed into new Mexican regions as Mexicanos, but in the United States the socioeconomic environment incurred a boundary maintenance and cohesiveness. People count on their personal connections in the United States for housing, help in finding jobs, and in adapting.

Although the nuclear family and household is preferred to the extended family household, connections to kin and the relations of the extended family continue to play important roles in the lives of Mexicans and Mexican Americans in the United States. There is a great range here, however, especially when one considers the generational differences of family branches in the United States. Recent and early immigrants rely on kin and the extended family for the majority of their social relationships, while individuals born as U.S. citizens have less extended kin relations (especially after the second generation). Education in the United States, geographic and social mobility, and economic stability have all contributed to strengthen the nuclear family and household for Mexican Americans. The nuclear family is in fact the desired type of family for both Mexican Americans and Mexicans.

The relationships of the extended family often

take different forms for these more acculturated individuals. Frequent visiting between immediate kin and special celebrations such as birthdays, baptisms, marriages, and funerals serve to bring kin together and rekindle family ties, whereas among newer immigrant Mexicanos the extended family is the center of social and kin relations. Marriage has continued to be primarily within the group, but a growing number of Mexican Americans have wed non-Mexican-origin individuals. This is greatest among Chicanos in California, but it is not uncommon among all the U.S.-born Latinos, especially after the first generation.

Mexicans, as with other ethnic groups, first live in segregated neighborhoods and are schooled with peers of the same ethnic background. However, as families get better jobs, the first priority is to move out of the ethnic neighborhoods, thus ensuring more exposure to American society for offspring. Schooling and the continued upward mobility of families has resulted in the economic severance from the reciprocity and mutual help among kin, so needed in early settlement and adaptation. The reciprocal duties of kinship obligations through compadrazgo, for example, continue to be ideological values that are not expressed or carried out as in previous periods. But it must be remembered that the migration from Mexico continues to emphasize these values and the actual expression of compadrazgo and other kin institutions in social behavior.

Compadrazgo has been a very strong institution among Mexican Americans. The *compadre/comadre* relationship often stands above even sibling relationships. The asking of individuals to be padrinos in baptisms or marriage is a high honor that brings with it kin-like obligations that are often considered of special importance. Compadres are expected to provide help and advice in time of crisis, and in the migration process the compadre/comadre is often the central individual who provides mutual help in the first stages of settlement. These are life long relationships in which compadres provide help such as needed information, access to jobs, and other essential social-economic benefits. As with all Latinos and other family institutions, compadrazgo varies within the generations. As with marriage and familism in general among second and later U.S.-born generations, compadrazgo has lost much of its reciprocal obligatory and mutual help functions, and when it is still practiced, this is sometimes only symbolic and expressive of ethnic pride and identity.

Although the actual role of the male in the family has changed, the ideals of the patriarchical family with father as decision maker and authoritarian is still expressed. Respect and deference to the male is expected ideal behavior. Children, especially, are expected to regard the father as the final voice and decision maker without exception. However, in actual behavior, fathers and mothers have taken on a more dualistic role in the management of the family, with the mother having increasingly more responsibility, especially regarding economics.

Children have been exposed to American education and have had much more exposure to the outside world than parents. The natural outcome of this exposure and education is the acceptance of mainstream values and goals for normalized American life-styles. This, as with other Hispanic groups, has been the root cause of conflict within the home and family. Mexican American youths, like other youths, now spend most of their time being schooled in an educational system that stresses the norms and values of American society. These norms are often in conflict with the expected behavior of the family and its institutions.

Women's roles have changed the most dramatically among Mexican Americans. As with the other Latino groups, it is the female's entrance into the work force that has initiated the major changes in sex roles and division of labor. Mexican women have a long history of working in various industries in the United States. In southern California during the Second World War, Mexican American women worked in the aviation industry on assembly lines and afterward in the canneries throughout the state. Their history as migrant laborers throughout the United States is also well noted. The garment industry and other industries employed Mexican women as well.

Working women have gained more access to society in general and more of an egalitarian role in the household. As with other Hispanic groups, however, Mexican American families exhibit change in women's roles but not necessarily in those of men. Men generally continue not to participate in the sharing of household duties. It is the woman who has taken on some of the male responsibilities. Although these are generalizations about the changes taken place in sex roles, women, regardless of the value and ideal of the father-centered household, in the past have had a strong input into decisions and acted as the final authority within the family and household. In fact, women are often seen as central individuals who are primary catalysts and authoritarian figures in family relationships.

As with other groups, Mexican Americans must be viewed in the range of their historical experiences and relationships in the United States. A look at any single region, town, or neighborhood that is characterized as Mexican or Mexican American/Chicano will illustrate many inter- and cross-generational differences. Families of well-adapted and acculturated individuals who hold strong Mexican familial patterns live side by side with families who have opted for more nuclear family patterns. In addition, bilingual families can be found in neighborhoods where monolingual Spanish- and monolingual English-speakers are also residents. Some values are held on to more stringently than others, as for example the respect held for the elderly. This continues to be a strong value among Mexicans and Mexican Americans, illustrated by the low rates of elderly in nursing or old-age homes. They continue to be cared for in the homes of kin and children.

When compared to other Hispanic groups and to the U.S. population in general, Mexican Americans have the largest family size, averaging almost five people per family. Puerto Ricans have almost four (3.67) people per family, and Cubans, 3.5. These averages illustrate a growing population and, when viewed in conjunction with the median age of Hispanics, indicate very high population projections for the future. It is estimated, for example, that by the turn of the next century, Hispanics will be the largest minority population in the United States. The Mexican-origin population is currently 60 percent of this total.

The fact that the Mexican American and Hispanic population is growing and will have a greater impact on the United States in the future is obscured by the fact that Hispanics continue to be at the bottom rungs of the economic and social classes. Poverty among Mexican Americans, as with other Hispanic groups and particularly Puerto Ricans, is a continuous problem that affects family life-styles and well-being. A full quarter of Mexican Americans in the late 1970s were living in poverty. What is shocking is that it appears that instead of decreasing, poverty is increasing. The Mexican American family will continue to be an important adaptive mechanism, utilizing the support institutions and evolving in ways that fit the sociocultural milieu of the United States.

References

Alvarez, Robert R., Jr. *Familia: Migration and Adaptation in Alta and Baja California 1850–1975.* Berkeley: University of California Press, 1987.

Baca-Zinn, Maxine. "Marital Roles and Ethicy: Conceptual Revisions and New Research Dimensions." In *Hispanic Report on Families and Youth.* The National Coalition of Hispanic Mental Health and Human Services Organizations. Washington, D.C.: Cosmho, 1978.

——. "Ongoing Questions in the Study of Chicano Families." In *The State of Chicano Research in Family, Labor, and Migration Studies,* edited by Armando Valdez, Albert Camarillo, and Tomas Almaguer. Palo Alto, California: Stanford University, Center for Chicano Research, 1983.

Casal, Lourdes, and Andrés R. Hernández. "Cubans in the United States: A Survey of the Literature." In *The Cuban Experience, edited by Carlos E. Cortez.* New York: Arno Press, 1980.

Cross, Harry E., and James A. Sandos. *Across the Border: Rural Development in Mexico and Recent Migration to the United States.* Berkeley: University of California, Institute of Governmental Studies, 1981.

Fitzpatrick, Joseph P. *Puerto Rican Americans. The Meaning of Migration to the Mainland,* second edition. Englewood Cliffs, New Jersey: Prentice-Hall, 1987.

Gallagher, P. *The Cuban Exile.* New York: Academic Press, 1980.

Galarza, Ernesto. *Merchants of Labor: The Mexican Bracero Story.* San Jose, California: Rosicrucian Press, 1965.

García, Mario T. *Mexican Americans.* New Haven: Yale University Press, 1989.

Georges, Eugenia. *The Making of a Transnational Community: Migration, Development and Cultural Change in the Dominican Republic.* New York: Columbia University Press, 1990.

Harvard University. *Harvard Encyclopedia of American Ethnic Groups.* Cambridge: Harvard University Press, 1980.

Hendricks, Glenn. *The Dominican Diaspora.* New York: Teachers College of Columbia University, 1974.

Moore, Joan, and Harry Pachón. *Hispanics in the United States.* Englewood Cliffs, N.J.: Prentice-Hall, 1985.

Morales, Julio. *Puerto Rican Poverty and Migration: We Just Had to Try Elsewhere.* New York: Praeger, 1986.

Pelto, Pertti J., Maria Roman, and Nelson Liriano. "Family Structures in an Urban Puerto Rican Community." *Urban Anthropology,* 11, spring 1982: 39–58.

Portes, Alejandro. "Dilemmas of a Golden Exile: Integration of Cuban Refugee Families in Milwaukee." *ASR,* 34, 1969: 501–518.

Portes, Alejandro, and Robert L. Bach. *Latin Journey: Cuban and Mexican Immigrants in the United States.* Berkeley: University of California Press, 1985.

Queralt, Magaly. "Understanding Cuban Immigrants: A Cultural Perspective." *Social Work,* March-April 1984: 111–51.

Rodríguez, Clara. *Born in the U.S.A.* Boston: Unwin Hyman, 1989.

Rogler, Lloyd H., and Rosemary Santana Cooney. *Puerto Rican Families in New York City.* New York: Intergenerational Processes, 1984.

Zaragoza, Alex. "The Conceptualization of the History of the Chicano Family." In *The State of Chicano Research in Family, Labor and Migration Studies,* edited by Armando Valdez, Albert Camarillo, and Tomas Almaguer. Palo Alto, California: Stanford University, Center for Chicano Research, 1983.

Robert R. Álvarez, Jr.

10

Women

※ Hispanic Women in Society ※ Women Making History ※ Women Inscribe Their Identity
※ Selected Outstanding Hispanic Women

Hispanic women are those women whose ancestors or they themselves were born in Spain or Spanish America. Until recently, the use of the rubric Hispanic was only limited to the government or to academia, and few people used it for self-identification. Some among the Hispanic group, seeing this as a strategy of control, have refused to self-identify as such, and prefer the label of Latino or Latina. The reason for this is that many women identify primarily with their own or their ancestors' country of origin rather than with the pan-Hispanic label preferred by those who keep track of the population of Hispanics. Therefore, Latina and Hispana are both inexact descriptors at best in that they are supposed to tell us who we are talking about. In actuality they are very general terms used to define many different groups of women that are assembled under that term: *Méxicoamericanas* (Mexican American women), *chicanas, puertorriqueñas* or *boricuas* (Puerto Rican women), *nuyorriqueñas* (Nuyorican women), *cubanas* (Cuban women), *dominicanas* (Dominican women), *nicaragüenses,* and women from other Central and South American countries.

Some of the these women are descendants of the Spanish settlers in the Southwest; some arrived on ships at the turn of the century. By the 1980s there were millions of Hispanics living permanently in the United States and today they continue to travel from very far to reach the border, often at great personal risk and sacrifice through the shark infested Florida straits, or the swift currents of the Rio Grande with thieves and murderers along the way always at the ready to prey on the weak and desperate. Along the Texas-Mexico border alone, the University of Houston's Center for Immigration found in their ten year study, 1985 to 1994, that some 1,900 to 3,200 migrants died. Some two-thirds of the bodies disappeared before a death certificate was issued. Autopsies are not routinely performed as they are too costly, so the exact cause of death goes undetermined. Sometimes a picture is taken of the deceased to be used for identification purposes, but most often they are buried in unmarked graves, and attempts to contact next of kin are limited. Those who do survive the journey from outside U.S. borders often travel with their friends and families: fathers, husbands, siblings, children, or other relatives.

Hispanic women are from all walks of life. Some are highly educated, some are unable to read or write, some speak Spanish with great difficulty, some are old, some are young. They hail from urban as well as rural settings; they represent many ethnic backgrounds, many racial groups, and have widely varying ideologies. Some are highly skilled or have professional credentials, while others are unskilled laborers whose primary jobs may be either agricultural or domestic employment.

For sociologists it is not an easy task to study this female population. The complexity, made difficult by the mix of factors that bring together national origin, education and class, linguistic and cultural capacities, and self-identification, is further complicated by the fact that the women comprising this population are subordinated doubly—by being Hispanic and by being female. It is similar to the difficulty explained by Nathan Glazer in his comments regarding the study of European migrations at the turn of the nineteenth and twentieth centuries, where all the nationalities and social classes, together with the melange of languages, became hard to assimilate into the description of one group of immigrants—Europeans.

※ HISPANIC WOMEN IN SOCIETY

Sociological and historical literature describes this aggregate group of women by studying their

235

characteristics and behavior. It is important to take into account that most of the sociological and historical literature on Hispanic women is derivative of studies concerning the general Hispanic population. Specific studies on women have only begun to emerge recently, and these are not always at the level they should be. They are sometimes more revealing of the authors' point of view about contextual topics than about the subjects of the investigation. Nevertheless, the existing studies, both the general and the specific, regarding Hispanic women are of interest.

Historical Presence and Evolution of Hispanic Groups

Most of the studies concerning the historical presence and evolution of each national group within the general category of Hispanics concern the nineteenth-century origins of the population under scrutiny and their subsequent behavior and development. Mexican American women were part and parcel of the U.S. population when, after the Mexican War of 1846, and the Treaty of Guadalupe Hidalgo (1848), the north of Mexico became the Southwest of the United States. The border, however, was always a permeable divider for both countries, and women did migrate north with their families. In the nineteenth century the migrations included groups motivated by economic factors. But it was after the Mexican Revolution of 1910 that many women crossed the border for political reasons. Subsequent migrations in the 1940s and 1950s were a prelude to the deluge of the 1960s, 1970s, 1980s, and 1990s.

The literature regarding Puerto Ricans was created primarily by researchers in the United States. Most studies conducted by island Puerto Ricans have concentrated on their political status vis-a-vis the United States, and have left no track on the bibliographies about migration. Prior to Operation Bootstrap, there were 100,000 Puerto Ricans in the United States, half of whom were women. However, after the great migration of the 1940s, these women were joined by an enormous horde of migrant women and men for the next three decades. It was a one-way migrant stream until reverse migration began in the 1970s and more Puerto Ricans returned to the island than came to the mainland.

Cuban women began coming in significant numbers to the United States in the nineteenth century. Some, like Janeta Loreta Velázquez who wrote her autobiography, integrated it into the story of the U.S. Civil War. Others, like Evangelina Cosío y Cisneros, wrote her autobiography, but her story was connected to the Spanish-American War. These women were not representative of most of the women who worked in the cigar-rolling factories in New York, Tampa, and Key West, but they mark extraordinary roles in the development of U.S. society.

Determinants of Migration

The students of why women and men take the risk of such difficult journeys have consistently found three theses that have helped to debunk intuitive comments about migration: (1) the very poor are unable to undertake the journey of migration due to a severe lack of both financial and intellectual resources; (2) the reasons for migration very often have to do with structural factors which limit access to agricultural land, to underemployment or to a widening of income and expenditures due to wage dislocation or to inflation or both; and (3) the people feel that the political circumstances of their society make it impossible for them to continue to live in it. Women have migrated to the United States from Hispanic countries for all of these reasons, and it was never the intractable lumpenproletariat that migrated. Rather the contrary has been true. Women who have undertaken the journey of migration have had the mettle to deal with all the hardships of the trip and all the difficulties of adapting to a new society and environment. This is true for Mexican American women, for Puerto Rican women, for Cuban American women and for all the other women who have migrated.

Demographics

The themes that are explored in demographic studies regard regional distribution, housing segregation, fertility and the rate of intermarriage. These studies tend to view the group as a whole due to the fact that the main source of data, the U.S. Bureau of the Census, has kept it in that manner until the 1990 census. An important contribution to that literature in 1989 was the excellent book by Clara Rodríguez, *Puerto Ricans: Born in the U.S.A.,* which examines that group with detail. In 1980 anthropologist Margarita Melville wrote *Twice a Minority: Mexican American Women,* which analyzed the specific population of women, following the 1979 *La Chicana: The Mexican-American Woman* by A. Mirandé and E. Enríquez. These books detail struggle for adaptation of women in American society.

Economic Situation of Women

Regarding the economic situation of women and the labor market in which they may be able to find employment, one of the base studies is the 1966 Equal Employment Opportunity Commission's *Job Patterns for Minorities and Women in Private Indus-*

Traditional roles for women still hold a great deal of influence in the community. A beauty queen for the Fiestas Patrias celebration, Houston, Texas. (Photograph by Curtis Dowell.)

try. Among the interesting studies is Ruth Zambrana's *Latina Women in Transition* (1982). The story of being seen as only a domestic worker or a field worker has plagued women as they have tried to break the barriers erected at the office, the school and the corporation.

Use of Language

Among some of the first considerations is that the women migrants from abroad knew Spanish better than English, while for native-born women, the reverse was true: they confessed to having difficulty with Spanish, but their knowledge of English was unquestioned except by the school systems. This points to the issues of language and schooling with which women have to cope in fulfilling their expected roles as heads of household. There have been a host of studies showing that women head Hispanic households in at least 25 percent of the cases, with Puerto Rican women having to shoulder the burden in 45 percent of the families, Central and South American women in 26 percent, other Hispanic women in 23 percent, Mexican American women in 19 percent, and

Cuban women in 18 percent of the cases. The figure of 16 percent, however, is the norm for the rest of the U.S. population. So Hispanic women are carrying a disproportionate burden on their economic backs.

Political Behavior and Status

Mexican American women have a historical pattern of participation as demonstrated in novels such as *The Squatter and the Don* (1885) and *Who Would Have Thought It?* (1872), that María Amparo Ruiz de Burton penned in San Diego, the dispossession of the land is foremost in her mind, together with the stripping of civil rights for the women and their families. Without an elite, she intuited that there would be no community, except a community of poverty without rights or recourses. No less impressive is the account of the women that crossed the border after the 1910 Mexican Revolution. Leonor Villegas de Magnón's *The Rebel* speaks about some of the problems at the time. So for Chicanas and Mexican American women, in general, the discourse of reclamation of their rights has been at the forefront of the movement. Together with their having to fight for the rights of their children in schools, since the 1960s

Poster advertising a Hispanic women's conference in Texas in 1987.

they have had to take on the whole issue of bilingual education as well.

❋ WOMEN MAKING HISTORY

The historical record leaves much to be desired in terms of the representation of women as forgers of their communities. Yet, it is indisputable that they had a strong hand in the development of their homes, their schools, their workplace, and their places of worship. In short, they were, alongside the men, making a new community for themselves, their families and their children. Some historians that have taken time to look at the history of the Hispanic people of the United States have occasionally noted the presence of women whose leadership has served as a model for other women and men to follow in their tracks. The following is a recounting of the deeds of some of these important women in their communities.

Within the world of the Mexican Americans there have been a number of notable women who have left their mark on the historical record, despite the easy gender blindness of most male historians. The Spanish arrived in Mexico, renaming it New Spain, in 1519. Shortly thereafter they sent expeditions to what would be the Southwest of the United States to pacify the many indigenous inhabitants of that region. There are chronicles (Álvar Núñez Cabeza de Vaca's *The Account,* for example), diaries (as is Hernando de Escalante Fontaneda's *Memorial de las cosas, costa e indios de la Florida* [Memories of the Things, the Coast and the Indians of Florida]), and even epic poems (Gaspar de Villagrá's *Historia de la Nueva México* [History of New Mexico], for instance) written by men that record what they did, where they went, who was there and what happened. Women, on the other hand, were not discussed much, which made it difficult to almost impossible to ascertain the roles of women during this very early period. For those scholars interested in the lives of women of the nineteenth century this seems to be changing, however, as they search through church records, court documents, diaries, letters, and fiction of the period. They are beginning to provide a clearer picture. There were women who were doctors, shopkeepers, landowners, midwives, business women, religious workers, servants, barmaids, etc. By the nineteenth century, many Hispanas were working outside their homes as servants to the wealthy, in canneries or packing enterprises, because they needed to supplement the household income. They sometimes joined their husbands in the fields picking crops and took the children along. While child labor laws were finally passed in 1919, farm workers were not included in the provisions. One of the first Mexican American women of note was Lucía Eldine González, who was born in 1853, in Johnson County, Texas. She married Albert Parsons in Austin and they moved to Chicago and had two children. She did sewing in her home to help with the household expenses and became aware of the impossible plight of women workers who were not protected by existing unions because they were not allowed to join them. So Lucía founded the Chicago Working Woman's Union. The union not only included homemakers, but also called for housework to be compensated, and for equal pay for equal work. By 1882 the Knights of Labor decided to allow women to join. In 1885, she participated in the effort to organize Chicago seamstresses, who worked 16-hour days in the typical basement sweatshop for next to nothing.

Workers were striking all over the United States for a reduction in the daily work hours, from 12- to 16-hour days to an eight-hour work day. The labor organizations decided that if there were no law establishing the eight hour work day, there would be a nationwide strike on May 1, 1886. Chicago was the hub of labor organizing and had 40,000 striking workers. Lucy González Parsons' husband Alfred was arrested, along with other labor leaders, for his participation in the Haymarket Riot and hanged by the courts, even though he was seen at a tavern with Lucy, the children and some friends by many people. Lucy continued to work and organize. She was a founder of the International Labor Defense, which specialized in providing legal help to laborers and political dissidents. She continued to march, lead hunger strikes, and speak in union halls, lumber camps, and mining communities. She also spent much time in jail. When the International Workers of the World was formed in 1905, Lucy González Parsons insisted that women, Mexican migrant workers, and all other nationalities and races, and even the unemployed, be full and equal members. Lucy Parsons died penniless in a fire in her home at the age of 89 in 1942.

Many women were active in the Mexican Liberal Party (PLM). Juana Bélen Gutiérrez de Mendoza, born in Durango, Mexico in 1875, was a teacher concerned with indigenous groups and working people. She founded a newspaper in 1901 called *Vésper* in which she attacked the Catholic Church and defended the miners. She was often jailed by the Porfirio Díaz regime in Mexico, finding herself in the company of Dolores Jiménez y Muro, Inés Malváez, and Elisa Acuña y Rossetti. Juana and Elisa went into exile together in San Antonio, and with Dolores, they organized a feminist group, Hijas de Cuauhtémoc, which dedicated itself to the bettering

A workshop at the Chicana Issues Conference, California, 1980.

of women both economically and intellectually. After a time, Juana and Elisa went back to Mexico and joined Zapata's revolutionary army. Juana was a troop commander and had the rank of colonel. Another PLM member, Sara Estela Ramírez, represented the revolutionary party on the U.S. side. She was born in Mexico in 1881, graduated from normal school in Saltillo and moved to Laredo in 1898. She worked as a Spanish teacher and was well known as a labor organizer, poet, human rights activist, and woman who encouraged political activity in other women. She was only 29 when she died in 1910.

On September 11, 1911, Mexican American leaders met for El Primer Congreso Mexicanista (the First Mexicanist Congress). La Liga Femenil Mexicanista (Mexican Woman's League) was created at this meeting. The membership consisted mostly of teachers who received daily reports from their students regarding the violence, beatings and shootings, against Mexicans. In 1929, however, when the League of United Latin American Citizens (LULAC) was created in Corpus Christi, Texas, for the purpose of defending the civil rights of Mexican Americans and other Hispanic citizens, women were not allowed to join as full-fledged members. In 1934

LULAC still continued to bar women's full participation among its ranks, although, technically, they were allowed to vote. The LULACs, however, responding to the pressure of the women who had helped so much in the struggles, introduced the Ladies Councils as a way of incorporating women more fully into the organization. It was not, however, until 1994 that the LULAC elected its first woman president, Belén Robles, a chief inspector with the U.S. Customs Service. She seeks to separate immigration issues from the political rhetoric which so often governs the passage of new laws regarding immigration.

Puerto Rican women left their mark both on the history of the island and on that of the mainland. On the island, of course, there are many outstanding cases of important women. Chief among them was Lola Rodríguez de Tió, who was a rebel against Spanish oppression and wrote the national anthem of Puerto Rico, "La Borinqueña." She was also a strong feminist who fought for many of the rights sought by women in the nineteenth century. On the island, also fighting the Spanish at the Grito de Lares, the Puerto Rican cry of independence and rebellion of 1868, were Mariana Bracetti, Eduvigis Beauchamp, and Rosa María de Font. These women joined their fathers, husbands, and brothers in the struggle for freedom.

In the Puerto Rican community on the mainland, a number of significant women were involved in the development of the community. Luisa Capetillo was one such woman who bridged the distance between her native homeland, New York, Florida, and even Cuba. In 1912, Capetillo settled in Tampa as an activist involved in the battle for worker's and women's rights. She was an unusual type of person in that she donned men's clothing, was divorced, abandoned the Catholic Church, and became a labor organizer of some repute. Capetillo was an outstanding leader who was so visible that her co-workers elected her the first woman ever to occupy the position of *lector* (reader) at a cigar factory. This was a job given to educated men, usually, who could read works of literature alongside works of some social importance for the workers while they rolled cigars. Capetillo, using her distinguished position, called on her co-workers to support women's suffrage, but her call fell on deaf ears. Her other call for action regarding women, however, did not. She crusaded for working women's rights, and this call resonated with her colleagues, both young and old. The younger women workers were inspired by Capetillo and sought gender equality in union ranks, and in 1916 they led a wildcat strike, calling the men who refused to join them "women" and offering them their skirts.

In New York, meanwhile, two other important women made their contribution to the building of their community. They were the Reverend Leoncia Rosado Rousseau, who was known as Mamá Leo, and Carmela Zapata Bonilla Marrero, called Sister Carmelita. These women were from the ranks of the religious community, the former a Pentecostal minister and the latter a Trinitarian nun. Mamá Leo organized drug rehabilitation centers from the 1930s to the 1950s. Sister Carmelita, for her part, coordinated the resources available through the Catholic church and other prominent donors in the community in order to develop health care, adequate housing, and effective schools for Puerto Rican children.

Throughout the many periods of time in which Cubans arrived in the United States, women have contributed importantly to the construction of a new home for their exile activities. This is also true in the labor force. Although the percent of women who worked outside the home in Cuba was very low, emigré and exile women have always kept a high profile in the labor force in the United States. Women workers made up 9 percent of cigar rollers in Key West in the 1890s and 25 percent of the workforce in the Tampa cigar factories during the same period; the percentage has grown to over 55 percent participa-

tion in the labor force by 1980. In the aftermath of the Cuban Revolution, women, both on the island and in exile, have increased their participation in the world of work outside the home, making them more active even than Anglo-American women, who have some of the highest work force participation in the world.

From the 1870s to the 1930s, women played a key role in the political life of Cuban communities in the United States. Shortly after the formation of the first exile juntas, women created their own organizations in order to get fully involved in the support of the political goals of the banished group. Emilia Casanova de Villaverde, for example, founded the Liga de Hijas de Cuba (League of Daughters of Cuba) in New York. In Florida, the women organized social clubs and schools to promote community and educational goals. Among the institutions that they founded were the Casa Cubana (Cuban House) and the San Carlos School in the Instituto San Carlos in Key West. An important Afro-Cuban leader was Paulina Pedroso, who was an activist for the movement of independence from Spain. When José Martí was obtaining support from the cigar workers in Florida, he often stayed with her and her husband as a guest in their home.

From the 1960s to the present, Cuban American women have continued to work on behalf of their communities, forming political associations such as the Unión de Mujeres (Women's Union), the Cruzada Femenina Cubana (Cuban Women Crusade), and the Movimiento Femenino Anticomunista de Cuba (Women's Anti-Communist Movement). Other organizations that began as social clubs became more committed to political activity later on. This was the case with the Cuban Women's Club, which was founded in 1969 in order to promote artistic, social and cultural events. As time passed, the group became more involved in the support of issues, such as bilingual education and other political issues, that impacted their families and their community.

These women were so committed to the development of their ideas and causes that they were able to have the first Hispanic and Cuban American woman ever elected to the U.S. Congress: Ileana Ros-Lehtinen. Katherine Fernández-Rundle became the first Cuban American woman state attorney, following in the footsteps of Janet Reno, who left the post to become the first woman attorney general of the United States.

✴ WOMEN INSCRIBE THEIR IDENTITY

An important frontier in the consideration of Hispanic women is the fact that they have traditionally been treated as objects that are depicted by male writers, artists, and journalists. As such they occupy the stereotypical roles assigned by them: virgin, mother, and whore. It has been an uphill battle for women to recreate their sense of identity through their active participation in the creative arts, particularly those like writing and painting that inscribe anew their identities as they are, as subjects, not vice-versa. Many are the cases, however, in which women have been witnesses to their own protagonistic roles in history and in everyday life, giving testimony of who they were and are, what they thought and think, and what they wanted and need.

Literature

As mentioned above, María Amparo Ruiz de Burton wrote several books. Among these is *Who Would Have Thought It?* (1872), an historical romance which discusses gender, race, the disenfranchisement of women, northern racism, nationality myths in the United States prior to and during the Civil War, and the opportunism and hypocrisy of the dominant society. In *The Squatter and the Don,* first published in San Francisco in 1885, she addresses the issues of the Californios, land loss, redress of grievances, U.S. expansionism and the rise of corporate monopolies with their power over government policy. Despite the Treaty of Guadalupe-Hidalgo of 1848, the Californios found themselves subordinated and marginalized as a national minority. All of this was documented by Ruiz de Burton.

For Leonor Villegas de Magnón, her book *The Rebel* is at once an autobiography, the story of the nursing corps *La Cruz Blanca* (The White Cross), and the story of women who supported the Mexican Revolution on both sides of the border. This narrative documents the heroic action of women who participated in the Mexican Revolution, risked their lives and were never acknowledged between the years of 1876 through 1920.

Josephina Niggli (1910) also relates the Mexican experience in the America after 1848 in her novels *Mexican Village* (1945) and *A Miracle for Mexico.* Fabiola Cabeza de Baca's (1920) *We Fed Them Cactus* (1954) is less a conventional narration and more of a family memoir. Estela Portillo-Trambley (1936) is the author of many plays, including *The Day of the Swallows* (1971), *Sun Images* (1979), and *Sor Juana* (1989). She has also written a novel, *Trini* (1986), and short fiction. Portillo-Trambley received the national award for Chicano literature, the Premio Quinto Sol (Fifth Sun Award), in 1972. Her literature discusses the issues of women's rights and freedom to choose a career instead of marriage, to create a personal identity instead of accepting the expected role, to choose non-patriarchal solutions to domestic violence. She also discusses the difficulties and dangers inherent in lesbian expression within misogynistic societies and many other feminist concerns.

Other important writers who have struggled with the re-inscription of the image of women over the stereotypical reductions fashioned by male authors are Cherríe Moraga, Gloria Anzaldúa, Evangelina Vigil-Piñón, Mary Helen Ponce, Helena María Viramontes, Sandra Cisneros, Ana Castillo, Pat Mora, Denise Chávez, and Roberta Fernández.

The Puerto Rican women who have put pen to paper in the service of their own personalities and identities have made their mark on the literary scene. Among them is Nicholasa Mohr, who was born in New York City's El Barrio (Spanish Harlem) of immigrant Puerto Rican parents. Her first book, *Nilda* (1973), is a novel composed of a series of vignettes related to her growing up in El Barrio. She has published *El Bronx Remembered* (1975), a novella with other stories for which she also did the jacket illustrations, and three semi-autobiographical books: *In Nueva York* (1977), *Felita* (1979), *Going Home* (1986), all for juvenile audiences. Her first adult-audience book is *Rituals of Survival: A Woman's Portfolio* (1985), a series of stories and a novella that are powerfully written. Mohr's work endures as a testimony of Puerto Rican life in Spanish Harlem since World War II.

Another interesting writer, Sandra María Esteves, was born in the Bronx. Esteves wrote her first poetry collection, *Yerba buena* (Mint) in 1980. It contains her explorations of self and community in terms of being a Puerto Rican born on the mainland. Her second and third books, *Tropical Rains: A Bilingual Downpour* (1984) and *Bluestown Mocking Bird Mambo* (1992) continue her mythmaking and her debunking of identity myths in the United States.

Another important writer, Judith Ortiz Cofer, was born in Hormigueros, Puerto Rico. Facing the problem of living in the world as a woman, Judith Ortiz Cofer proposes her conditions in the 1987 poetry collection *Terms of Survival*. Having received recognition in her collection, *Reaching for the Mainland* (1987), which constituted a part of the very successful title *Triple Crown*, Ortiz Cofer followed her poetic tour de force with her first novel, *The Line of the Sun* (1989). In it she portrays the migration from a Puerto Rican village to a tough immigrant community in New Jersey. This fictional reflection led her to a reexamination of her own personal memory in her award-winning autobiography *Silent Dancing: A Partial Remembrance of a Puerto Rican Childhood* (1990). Her *The Latin Deli* was published in 1994.

An important poet and editor is Gloria Vando, who was born in New York. As an editor, she created in 1977 the celebrated *Helicon Nine: The Journal of Women's Art and Letters,* named after the muses. As a poet, Vando has published much of her work in numerous literary magazines and anthologies, including the *Kenyon Review, El Gato tuerto* (The One-Eyed Cat), *Women of the 14th Moon,* and *Seattle Review.* After being awarded a poetry fellowship from the Kansas Arts Commission in 1989, she won the Billee Murray Denny Poetry Prize in 1991. Her first book of poetry, *Promesas: Geography of the Impossible,* was published in 1993.

Among the Cuban American women who have left their mark is Lydia Cabrera (1900–1991), who completed her first volume of short stories, *Contes negres de Cuba* (Black Stories from Cuba; 1936 in French, 1940 in Spanish) while a young woman visiting France. *Por qué . . . cuentos negros de Cuba* (1948) was her second volume of stories. To these we must add *Ayapá: cuentos de Jicotea* (1971), a volume of Afro-Cuban trickster tales, and *Cuentos para grandes, chicos y retrasados mentales* (Stories for adults, children and the mentally retarded; 1979), a collection of stories heard during her childhood. *Francisco y Francisca: chascarrillos de negros viejos* (Francisco and Francisca: Old Black Anecdotes; 1976), is a delightful conversation that reveals what life was like during the Cuban colonial period. In addition, she has written several important books about Afro-Cuban folklore, including *El monte: notas sobre las religiones, la magia, las supersticiones y el folklore de los negros criollos y del pueblo de Cuba* (The Country: Notes About Religions, Magic, Superstitions and the Folklore of the Black Creoles and of the Cuban People; 1954), *Refranes de negros viejos* (Old Black Proverbs; 1955), *La sociedad secreta Abakuá* (The Abakuá Secret Society; 1958), and a number of other books on *santería* (Afro-Cuban religion), *palo mayombé* (Afro-Cuban religion), and several glossaries of African languages used in Cuba for religious purposes.

Another important writer has been Dolores Prida, a playwright and a screenwriter, whose work has been produced in the United States, Puerto Rico, the Dominican Republic, and Venezuela. In 1977, the Duo Theater produced *Beautiful Señoritas.* Since then she has had more than ten plays produced, including scripts that represent several types of theater. Prida has adapted international texts, such as *The Three Penny Opera,* and she has also experimented with the Broadway-musical form in plays like *Savings* (1985). In *Coser y cantar* (Sewing and Singing; 1981), she created a bilingual text that reflects, with measured doses of humor and pathos, the difficulties experienced by Hispanics living in the United States. *Botánica* (The Herbal Shop) debuted in 1990 with the Spanish Repertory Theater and has continued to run perennially since then. In it Prida examines Puerto Rican life in New York by portraying the intergenerational conflict that marks a family of women. In 1991, Arte Público Press collected her works in book form with the title *Beautiful Señoritas and Other Plays.* As a poet, Prida led the group of young poets Nueva Sangre (New Blood) in the 1960s. She has published several poetry collections, including, with Roger Cabán, *The IRT Prayer Book* and her own *Treinta y un poemas* (Thirty One Poems; 1967) and *Women of the Hour* (1971).

Belonging to the younger generation is Achy Obejas, whose poetry has appeared in several magazines, journals, and anthologies. She has edited a special issue of *Third Woman* and has published a collection of short stories, *We Came All the Way From Cuba So You Could Dress Like This?* (1994). In it she explores with enormous humor, wit, and sensibility the trials and tribulations of growing up in two cultures, in two languages, and as a lesbian.

Of that same generational group is Carolina Hospital, a poet whose work appears in magazines throughout the United States, including the *Americas Review* and *Bilingual Review.* She also has compiled an interesting anthology of Cuban American writers, *Cuban American Writers: Los Atrevidos* (1989), and served as a guest editor of one of the issues of *Cuban Heritage Magazine* in 1989. Hospital has worked on a translation of poetry by Tania Díaz Castro and has written for *Linden Lane* magazine, where she has served as an editor on several occasions.

Another important talent is Cristina García, the journalist who wrote *Dreaming in Cuban,* an interesting novel which combines *santería,* the revolution and exile. It is worth mentioning fiction writers such as Hilda Perera, Margarita Engle, Uva Clavijo, Marcia del Mar, and poets such as Juana Rosa Pita, Eliana Rivero, Ana Rosa Núñez, Belkis Cuza Malé, Rita Geada, Gladys Zaldívar, Isel Rivero, Magaly Alabau, Lourdes Gil, Iraida Iturralde, and Mireya Robles.

Art

Part of the Chicano Movement during the late 1960s and the early 1970s was the creation of nontraditional places where this cultural identity and search for a true worldview or self-definition could be exhibited and supported. These organizations received funding from their communities, the Expansion Arts division of the National Endowment for the Arts and state councils for the arts. In the early days of the movement, murals were the medium of expression and artists like Judith Baca of the Artes Guadalupanas de Aztlán (Guadalupe Arts of Aztlán) in Santa Fe demonstrated a clear influence from Siqueiros in their work. Baca directed the Citywide Murals Program in Los Angeles and founded Neighborhood Pride: Great Walls Unlimited in 1976. One of its projects, the *Great Wall of Los Angeles,* was a mural a half-mile long, which depicts the history of minority groups in California up to 1960. The Great Wall was created between 1978 and 1983, and required the work of 100 young people under the supervision of some 30 artists all of whom were directed by Baca. She and ten other artists were commissioned in 1984 to create murals for the Olympic Games. She has also designed a portable canvas mural dealing with world peace, *World Wall,* which was installed in several countries and ended up at the Smithsonian Institute in 1991.

Yolanda López, Yreina Cervántez and Juana Alicia are also outstanding muralists. Celia Múñoz, a conceptual artist, explores folk narrative and adult life as viewed by a child. Carmen Lomas Garza is inspired by the daily-life themes of her Texas youth. Patricia Rodríguez began as a muralist, but objected to the political topics addressed in such a macho way, so she and three other students founded *Mujeres Muralistas* (Women Muralists). Their work pays homage to women's culture by employing religious rituals and communal life as points of departure. Of late, Rodríguez has dedicated herself to making assemblages that express the cultural as well as the personal.

In the Puerto Rican art scene, we find a different group of artists. Myrna Báez was trained by Lorenzo Homar, known as the father of the Puerto Rican poster movement and its most accomplished artist. Not only is she a talented printmaker, but she is also well recognized in the area of socially concerned figurative painting. An active participant in the *Taller Boricua* (Puerto Rican Workshop), Nitza Tufiño, a ceramicist and activist, has also engaged young people in the making of ceramic murals. Marina Gutiérrez explored the political and the personal through the use of folk art. Olga Albizú was moderately successful in New York showings in the 1950s with her colorful abstracts. In the 1960s, she became quite well known when her art work was used on record jackets.

Among the Cuban American women, art has been one of the most important means of expression. Ana Mendieta trained at the Center for the New Performing Arts at the University of Iowa. After using canvas as a space for expression, she switched to ephemeral art using her own body. She was widely recognized during her brief career and received two National Endowment for the Arts visual art grants and a Guggenheim Fellowship before her untimely death in 1985. María Brito-Avellano creates strange environments through sculpture that express feelings of alienation and fragmentation that are part and parcel of the exile's psyche. Among the more interesting new arrivals from Cuba is Ana Albertina Delgado. Trained at the Fine Arts Institute in Havana, she was a member of *Puré,* a group of young painters and sculptors whose images revolutionized the art scene in Cuba. Now in Miami, Delgado conceives of haunting visions of women in different circumstances of their life.

Film

Despite enormous economic restrictions, Chicana filmmakers have excelled in portraying the feminine point of view in their communities as well as their particular problems. Sylvia Morales, in *Chicana* (1979), reviews the history of Chicanas since pre-Hispanic times and emphasizes the contributions made and the role of women. Esperanza Vásquez and Moctezuma Esparza review the life of an older Chicana in New Mexico, in *Agueda Martínez* (1977), who is a weaver that shuns the submissive role of a dependent woman for that of a hard-working rancher, raising her children well.

Elvia Alvarado discusses sexual abuse among Chicana women in *Una Mujer* (A Woman; 1984). In short-length feature films, Esperanza Vásquez' *Tabla Rasa* (Clean Slate; 1973) and Lourdes Portillo's *Después del Terremoto* (After the Earthquake; 1979) offer a promising future. Other filmmakers are Olivia Chumacero, Salomé España, Osa Hidalgo de la Riva and Beverly Sánchez-Padilla.

Among Puerto Rican women, film has often been linked to their own political and economic struggle. It is for this reason that the documentary has been a favorite type of film. In 1981, for instance, Lillian Jiménez co-produced *What Could You Do with a Nickel?,* which tells the story of how a labor union was formed in the South Bronx, New York. *La Operación* (The Operation; 1982), directed by Ana María Garía is the story of the sterilization of thousands of Puerto Rican women. In 1986, *The Battle of Vieques* by Zydnia Nazario depicted the U.S. military maneuvers off the Puerto Rican coast. In the area of narrative film stands *Reflections of Our Past* (1979) by Angela Fontánez and Luis Soto, a collective night journey that visits Puerto Rican history, culture and identity. In the category of full-length feature films, María Norman directed *The Sun and the Moon* (1987), a film exploring the search for identity of a Puerto Rican woman.

Cuban American women have not yet entered the world of filmmaking fully, and very few of them have participated in the projects of the Instituto Cubano de Artes Cinematográficas (Cuban Institute of Cinematographical Arts; [ICAIC]). One of them, Saba Cabrera Infante, was responsible, together with Orlando Jiménez Leal, for issuing the controversial *PM* (1961), which aired once on Cuban television, but never reached the cinemas throughout the island due to its view of the alienated poor, even in revolutionary Cuba. While many of the ICAIC filmmakers have left for the United States, women have yet to make their mark in this area.

Journalism

Together with the creative artists, who work images and words, there exists another group that shapes the image of women; they are those women who work in the media. Although mostly men labor in the field of print and broadcast journalism, some women have toiled also in that calling to issue forth a different voice and to reshape the image of working women and homemakers. Among them, Isidra T. de Cárdenas founded and directed *La Voz de la Mujer* (Woman's Voice) in El Paso in 1907, thus assuring the readership that women were committed to the revolutionary movement against the oppressive dictatorship of Porfirio Díaz. In 1909, Teresa Villarreal started *El Obrero* (The Worker), calling for the involvement of everyone, male and female, in the new social order. Andrea Villarreal González and her sister Teresa published and managed *La Mujer Moderna* (The Modern Woman) in San Antonio in 1910.

Blanca de Moncaleano positioned the emancipation of women at the center of its anarchist agenda in *Pluma roja* (The Red Pen), published in Los Angeles from 1913 to 1915. Juana Gutiérrez de Mendoza and Elisa Acuña y Rosetti established the militant newspaper *Vésper* (Eventide; 1901). Sara Estela Ramírez worked on newspapers, including *La Corregidora* (The Magistrate), *La Guillotina* (The Guillotine), *La Lucha de Clases* (Class Struggle; San Antonio, 1915), and *El Defensor del Pueblo* (Defender of the People; Laredo). In contemporary times Betita Martínez published *El Grito del Norte* (The Cry of the North; 1968–1973) in Las Vegas, a city in northern New Mexico. It was a bilingual, as well as a progressive, newspaper that covered injustices suffered by the Chicano population. Academics such as Norma Alarcón began the publication of *Third Woman* in 1981 at Indiana University; Sylvia Castillo started a newsletter *Intercambios Femeniles* (Womanly Exchanges) at Stanford University, which later became a magazine, and Rosaura Sánchez, for her part, encouraged the literary criticism in the journal *Crítica: A Journal of Critical Essays* at the University of California, San Diego. Radio reporter, author and artist María de Lourdes Hinojosa is a well known personality on National Public Radio. In New York, she is also a recognized television talk show host and, as an artist, Hinojosa creates altars to commemorate the Day of the Dead, always relating them thematically to social ills in need of redress, such as undocumented workers or AIDS.

Among Puerto Rican women there are also interesting journalists. Franca de Armiño, a feminist labor leader, in 1937, wrote *Los Hipócritas* (The Hypocrites) a dramatic comedy, and published commentary in *Gráfico* (Graphic), a newspaper in New York. Little is known about her other writings, poems and essays that she mentions. We know she was involved in the *Federación Libre de los Trabajadores de Puerto Rico* (Free Federation of Puerto Rican Workers) and the *Liga de la Mujer Obrera* (League of Women Workers), that she also participated in the First Congress of Women Workers in 1919, and that she was a leader, along with Carmen Gaetán. Both of these women were presidents of two tobacco strippers' unions in the *Asociación Femenista Popular* (Popular Feminist Association) organized in 1920 by women laborers who were active in the Puerto Rican Socialist Party to defend the working conditions of Puerto Rican women and universal suffrage. During the 1930s, De Armiño lived in New York, but there are few details regarding her life.

Another Puerto Rican labor organizer, Luisa Capetillo, arrived in New York in 1912. *Cultura Obrera* (Worker Culture) published her articles dealing with women's emancipation. In Ybor City, Florida, where she worked in cigar factories, she published the second edition of *Mi opinión* (My Opinion) in 1913 and wrote several essays which she later included in *Influencia de las ideas modernas* (The Influence of Modern Ideas) published in 1916.

Julia de Burgos, an often studied feminist poet, also contributed to *Pueblos Hispanos* (Hispanic Peoples) newspaper in New York between 1946 and 1953, and Josefina Silva de Cintrón edited *Revista de Artes y Letras* (Review of Arts and Letters) from 1933 until 1945.

Conclusion

This chapter is an attempt to represent Hispanic women in an informative manner, though it does so by bringing to the reader but a small glimpse of that experience. This representation tells their stories through a small sample of their own biographies and, too often, lost accomplishments. Any accounting of their deeds, their courage, and their inventiveness, or of their collective lives, is but a reduction of their own experience. There is still much to be uncovered about them in both formal repositories of information (libraries, archives, institutional records of all sorts) and in informal resting places of forgotten papers, photographs and other paraphernalia of family histories (attics, basements, garages). The bibliography that follows may serve as an invitation for learning more about these women, even as research on their participation in the building of American society continues.

✳ SELECTED OUTSTANDING HISPANIC WOMEN

Deborah Aguiar Vélez

See Chapter 14.

Norma Alarcón

See Chapter 17.

Lupe Anguiano (1929–)

Born on March 12, 1929, in La Junta, Colorado, Anguiano received her M.A. degree from Antioch University in 1978. She taught at Our Lady of Victory Missionary Sisters from 1949 to 1965. She was the East Los Angeles coordinator of the Los Angeles Federation of Neighborhood Centers, from 1965 to 1966; a presidential appointee to the U.S. Office of Education, from 1967 to 1969; the Southwest regional director for the National Association for the Advancement of Colored People, Legal Defense and Educational Fund in 1969; a civil rights officer for the U.S. Department of Health, Education and Welfare, from 1970 to 1972; the Southwest regional director for the National Conference of Catholic Bishops, from 1973 to 1977; and president of the National Women's Program Development, from 1977 to 1978. She is also the founder and, since 1979, president of National Women's Employment and Education, Inc., and president/consultant of Lupe and Associates since 1982. She is the author of *Women's Employment and Education Model Program* (1982) and the editor and publisher of *Comunidad Newsletter* (1975–77) and *Women's Employment Newsletter* (1978–80). Her many honors include being named one of the *Ladies' Home Journal*'s 100 Most Important Women (1988) and receiving the Soroptimist International of Auburn (Tacoma, Washington) Women Helping Women Award (1985).

Polly Baca-Barragán (1943–)

Polly Baca-Barragán was born in La Salle—a small town near Greeley, Colorado—in 1943. She

Polly Baca-Barragán.

received a degree in political science form Colorado State University and later worked as an editor for two union publications. During the 1960s, Baca-Barragán was active in the Democratic party and worked on the presidential campaigns of President John F. Kennedy, President Lyndon B. Johnson, and Senator Robert F. Kennedy. From 1971 to 1972 she was Director of Spanish Speaking Affairs for the Democratic National Committee. In 1974, she was elected to the Colorado House of Representatives and in 1978 to the state senate. She was the first Hispanic woman to be elected to those offices. Baca-Barragán was re-elected to Colorado's state senate in 1982. She remains active in politics working on behalf of Mexican Americans and dealing with housing issues. Baca-Barragán served as Special Assistant to President Bill Clinton and Director of the U.S. Office of Consumer Affairs until November 1995, when she was named as the new regional administrator for the General Services Administration in Denver.

Mary Helen Barro

See Chapter 27.

Teresa Bernárdez.

Teresa Bernárdez (1931–)

Born on June 11, 1931, in Buenos Aires, Argentina, Bernárdez received her B.A. degree from Liceo No. 1 de Señoritas in 1948 and her degree in medicine form the School of Medicine, University of Buenos Aires, in 1956. Her internship was at *Hospital de Clinicas* (University Hospital) in Argentina, and her residency was in psychiatry at the Menninger School of Psychiatry, Topeka State Hospital, Topeka, Kansas. She was a staff psychiatrist at the Menninger Memorial Hospital, 1960–65; a staff psychiatrist at the Menninger Foundation, Department of Psychotherapy, 1965–71; a professor in the Department of Psychiatry at Michigan State University, 1971–89; and has taught at Tavistock Clinic, Adult Psychiatry Department, London, England (1977–78) and the Mary Ingraham Bunting Institute, Radcliffe College (1984–85). She has been a consultant to many national and international groups and has done a great deal of research and publishing on the subject of women. Her awards and honors include the Distinguished Faculty Award, Michigan State University Faculty Women's Association (1982), the first Leadership Workshop Award from the American Medical Women's Association (1977), and the Peace Award from the Pawlowski Foundation (1974).

Gloria Bonilla Santiago

See Chapter 27.

Lynda Córdoba Carter

See Chapter 27.

Margarita Hortensia Colmenares (1957–)

Born on July 20, 1957, in Sacramento, California, Colmenares was educated at Stanford University, where she received her B.S. degree in civil engineering in 1981. She has worked for Chevron as an environmental affairs air quality specialist, lead engineer on the Subsurface Recovery Project, compliance specialist in marketing operations, foreign training representative, recruiting coordinator, and field construction engineer. She has been the national president of the Society of Hispanic Professional Engineers since 1989 and a member of the board of directors of the Hispanic Women's Network of Texas. Her honors include Leadership America, Training Program Participant (1990); National Hispana Leadership Initiative, Training Program Participant (1989); Hispanic Engineer Magazine Community Service Award (1989); and Hispanic Role Model of the Year, Society of Hispanic Professional Engineers (1989).

Gilda Cruz-Romo

See Chapter 27.

Margarita Fernández Olmos

See Chapter 27.

Beatriz Angela Ginorio (1947–)

Born on January 30, 1947, in Hato Rey, Puerto Rico, Ginorio received her B.A. and M.A. degrees in psychology from the University of Puerto Rico (1968 and 1971) and her Ph.D. degree in social psychology from Fordham University (1979). She has taught at the University of Puerto Rico (1970–71), the University of Illinois (1976–78), Bowling Green State University (1978–80), and the University of Washington (1981–82). She was a counselor in the Special Services Program (1981–83), served as director of the Women's Information Center (1983–87), and is currently the director of the Northwest Center for Research on Women (1987) at the University of Washington. She has published extensively and is active in the American Psychological Association and the Mexican American Women's National Association. She is the first Puerto Rican to direct a center for research on women in the United States. She has been recognized by the campus chapter of the Business and Professional Women with a Woman of the Year award (1986) and by the Mexican American Women's National Association, Seattle Chapter, with a Certificate of Appreciation (1987).

Maria Elena Girone (1939–)

Born on March 31, 1939, in Puerto Rico, Girone was educated at the Universidad de Puerto Rico, where she received a B.A. degree in psychology (1964) and a Master's degree in social work (1967). She has taught at the Puerto Rico University and is currently the national executive director of the

Puerto Rican Family Institute. She is on the executive committee of the National Puerto Rican Coalition and has been recognized for her outstanding work by the New York City Hispanic Heritage (1986), the Institute Cultura (1988), and the National Coalition of Hispanics Health and Human Services Organizations (1990).

Elsa Gómez

See Chapter 27.

Deena J. González (1952–)

Born on August 25, 1952, in Hatch, New Mexico, González received her B.A. degree from New Mexico State University (1974) and her M.A. degree (1976) and Ph.D. degree (1985) from the University of California, Berkeley. She was a professor of history and Chicano studies at Pomona College (1983–91), acting chair of Chicano studies (1990), visiting associate professor in history and women's studies at the University of New Mexico (1991–92), and visiting associate professor at University of California, Santa Barbara (1992). She is currently an associate professor at Pomona College. She has received grants from Hewlett Packard and the National Endowment for the Humanities, and her publications include a *The Spanish-Mexican Women of Santa Fe* (1993) and *On Their Own* (1988). She has served on numerous committees for universities and other organizations and currently serves on advisory and editorial boards for *Signs,* Women of the West Museum, and Program in Collegiate Scholars in History at the University of Florida.

Lucía Parsons González (1852–1942)

Born in a small town south of Fort Worth, Texas, in 1852, González grew up to become a labor leader. During the early 1880s, she joined the Chicago Working Women's Union and led marches for women's rights and an eight-hour workday. Her husband, Albert Parsons, was executed for being part of the Haymarket riot, a labor demonstration. After his execution, González continued to be active in the radical labor movement and the women's movement and was one of the founders of the International Labor Defense and the Industrial Workers of the World. Even through her eighties, González was an active figure in the International Labor Defense. She died at 90 as a result of a fire that destroyed her home.

Suzanna Guzman

See Chapter 27.

Carolina Herrera

See Chapter 27.

Dolores Huerta

See Chapter 27.

Marci-Luci Jaramillo (1928–)

Born in Las Vegas, New Mexico, in 1928, Jaramillo received her A.B. (1955), M.A. (1959), and Ph.D. (1970) degrees from New Mexico Highlands University, Las Vegas. From 1972 to 1977, she was a professor education at the University of New Mexico and became a well-known speaker and educational researcher. In 1977, President Jimmy Carter appointed her U.S. ambassador to Honduras, and she became deputy assistant secretary for inter-American affairs at the U.S. Department of State in 1980. In 1982, she was named associate dean for the University of New Mexico's College of Education and in 1985, the university's vice president for student affairs. Two years later, Educational Testing Services hired Jaramillo as vice president for its San Francisco Bay office. She is the recipient of numerous awards, including the 1986 Harvard Graduate School of Education's Anne Roe Award for contributions to women's professional growth in the field of education.

Olga Jiménez de Wagenheim

See Chapter 17.

Olga Mapula (1938–)

Born on January 30, 1938, in Williams, Arizona, Mapula received her B.A. degree from Texas Western College (1958) and her M.A. degree from the University of Texas at El Paso (1973). She was an El Paso public school teacher (1958–60), field representative for the Social Security Administration (1960–71), lecturer for the University of Texas at El Paso (1973–75), program evaluator for the Bilingual Consortium (1975–78), consultant for Educational Consulting (1979–86), and marketing director for KXCR/ETCOM, Inc. (1983–85). At present she is president of The Communications Group sits on the board of directors for the El Paso Chamber of Commerce, the Minority Business Council, and the Private Industry Council. She is director of the El Paso Certified Development Corporation, Hispanic Women's Network of Texas, and the Hispanic Leadership Institute. She is vice president of the University of Texas, El Paso, Alumni Fund for Excellence and a trustee for the El Paso Community College. She has been recognized for her outstanding work by El Paso Women in Education/Employment (1986),

Hispanic Women in Communications (1988), and Texas Teachers of English to Speakers of Other Languages (1989). She was a nominee to the Texas Women's Hall of Fame (1987), and received the Adelante Award from the Nations Bank and *Hispanic Magazine* for outstanding leadership and business success (1994).

Vilma Martínez

See Chapter 13.

Antonia Coello Novello

See Chapter 27.

Ellen Ochoa

See Chapter 27.

Graciela Olivárez (1928–)

Born near Phoenix, Arizona, in 1928, Olivárez worked in the radio industry as Phoenix's first female disc jockey before becoming the first woman to graduate from the University of Notre Dame Law School in 1970, receiving her juris doctor degree in 1978. Active in the civil rights movement in the Southwest, she was appointed director of planning for New Mexico (1975–77). President Jimmy Carter appointed her director of the Community Services Administration in Washington, D.C. (1977–80). In 1980, she returned to her home in New Mexico to run her own business, the Olivárez Television Company, and served as a senior consultant for the United Way of America. Olivárez was the recipient of many honors for her work: the American Cancer Society presented her with an Outstanding Leadership Award in 1960; during the early 1970s the League of Mexican American Women named her an Outstanding Woman of the Southwest; Amherst College in Massachusetts awarded her with an honorary doctorate in 1973, and she went on to receive others from Michigan State University in 1976 and Notre Dame in 1978; the Woodlawn Organization honored her with its Leadership Award in 1978; she won the Mexican American Opportunity Foundation's Aztec Award in 1979; and in December of 1985, Olivárez was honored by the Mexican American Legal Defense and Educational Fund for her contributions to the Latino community.

Katherine D. Ortega

See Chapter 27.

Vilma Ortiz

See Chapter 13.

Gaudalupe C. Quintanilla

See Chapter 27.

Tey Diana Rebolledo (1937–)

Born on April 29, 1937, in Las Vegas, New Mexico, Rebolledo received her B.A. degree from Connecticut College (1959), her M.A. degree from the University of New Mexico (1962), and her Ph.D. from the University of Arizona (1979). She has taught at the University of North Carolina, Chapel Hill (1977–78), and the University of Nevada, Reno (1978–84). She has been a professor at the University of New Mexico since 1984. She is editor of *Las mujeres hablan: An Anthology of Nuevo Mexicana Writers* (1988) and author of numerous articles. She serves on the editorial boards of El Norte Publication, and Arte Público Press. She was designated an eminent scholar by the New Mexico Commission on Higher Education (1989) and is a member of the Group Project of the University of New Mexico in India, Fulbright Foundation (1988); a fellow of the Aspen Institute (1987); and a recipient of a research grant from the National Endowment for the Humanities (1984–87).

Eliana Rivero

See Chapter 17.

Emyré Barrios Robinson (1926–)

Born on March 23, 1926, in El Paso, Texas, Robinson received her B.A. degree in Spanish from the University of Houston (1971). She was a data services manager and later business manager for Kentron International from 1976 to 1980, when she founded and became president of Barrios Technology, Inc. In 1993, she founded and became C.E.O. of Condor Trading International Ltd. She is chair of the Texas Space Commission (1990); president of Armand Bayou Nature Center (1989–90); a member of the University of Houston Development Board (1986–90) and the University of Houston, Clear Lake, Development and Advisory Council (1985–90); a member of the board of directors of the Bay Area Bank and Trust (1985–90); and a member of the board of trustees of the United Way, Gulf Coast (1985–90). She has been recognized for her outstanding work by the Small Business Administration, Texas Executive Women, NASA, and the Houston Hispanic Chamber of Commerce.

Elizabeth Rodríguez (1953–)

Born on March 18, 1953, in San Benito, Texas, Rodríguez was educated at the University of New Mexico, where she received her B.S. (1975) and M.A. (1976) degrees in mathematics and her Ph. D. degree

(1980) in program management and development/ experimental statistics. She was a mathematician and program manager for the Pacific Missile Test Center (1980–88) and an instructor for Oxnard Community College (1981–84). Currently, she is a research analyst for RAM/suitability for the Office of the Secretary of Defense/Director of Operational Test and Evaluation. A member and leader of numerous organizations and author of numerous articles, Rodríguez has been honored for her work by the Pacific Missile Test Center, *Gente* magazine, and Ventura County, California, Commission for Women.

Gloria C. Rodríguez

See Chapter 27.

Ileana Ros-Lehtinen

See Chapter 13.

Vicki L. Ruiz (1955–)

Born on May 21, 1955, in Atlanta, Georgia, Ruiz received her B.S. degree from Florida State Univer-

Emyré Barrios Robinson.

sity (1977) and her M.A. degree (1978) and Ph.D. degree (1982) from Stanford University. She was director of the Institute of Oral History at the University of Texas from 1982 to 1985 and has taught at the University of California, Davis, since 1985. In 1992 she became Andrew W. Mellon Professor in the Humanities at the Claremont Graduate School; and since 1993, she has chaired the history department. She is an active leader in the Organization of American Historians, the Immigration History Society, and the American Studies Association. Moreover, Ruiz is an editorial board member of the *NWSA Journal;* author of *Cannery Women, Cannery Lives: Mexican Women, Unionization and the California Food Processing Industry, 1930–1950* (1984); and coeditor of *Women on the U.S.-Mexico Border* (1977), *Western Women* (1988), and *Unequal Sisters* (1990).

Virginia Korrol Sánchez (1938–)

Born in New York City, Virginia Korrol Sánchez received her B.A. degree from Brooklyn College, City University of New York (1960), and her M.A. degree (1972) and Ph.D. degree (1981) from the State University of New York, Stony Brook. She taught in the public schools of Chicago and is currently a professor of Puerto Rican Studies at Brooklyn College, City University of New York. She is author of *From Colonia to Community: History of Puerto Ricans in New York City: 1917–1948* (1983); coeditor of *The Puerto Rican Struggle: Essays on Survival in the U.S.* (1984); coauthor of *Restoring Women to History: Women in the History of Africa, Asia, Latin America and the Caribbean and the Middle East*; and author of numerous articles on the history of Puerto Rican women and Latinos in the United States.

Cristina Saralegui

See Chapter 27.

María-Luisa Urdaneta (1931–)

Born on October 2, 1931, in Cali, Colombia, Urdaneta received her professional nursing degree from Methodist Hospital, Dallas, Texas (1956), her R.N. degree from Baylor University (1958), her B.A. degree in psychology (1965) and M.A. degree in sociology (1969) from the University of Texas, Austin, and her M.A. degree in anthropology (1974) and Ph.D. degree in anthropology (1976) from Southern Methodist University, Dallas. She was a staff anesthetist at Methodist Hospital of Dallas (1958–59) and Brackenridge Hospital (1960–69 and 1972–74); a research associate at the University of Texas Health Science Center at San Antonio (1974–75); and since 1975 has been a professor at the University of Texas, San Antonio. Author of numerous articles on Mexican Americans and health, Urdaneta has been recognized by the San Antonio Women's Hall of Fame, the Texas Diabetes Council, the National Institutes of Health, the Mexican American Business and Professional Women's Club of San Antonio, and the National Chicano Research Network.

Paquita Vivó (1935–)

Born in San Juan, Puerto Rico, Vivó was educated at the University of Puerto Rico (1953–55). She was assistant to the under secretary of the commonwealth Department of State (1955–60); staff writer and researcher for the Puerto Rico News Service (1960–62); public affairs officer for the Organization of American States (1962–80); and independent consultant of Public Relations, Public Affairs (1970–80). She has been president of ISLA, Inc., since 1980 and president of the Institute for Puerto Rican Affairs, Inc., since 1988. She has been president, treasurer, and secretary of the National Conference of Puerto Rican Women (1972–89); member of the boards for the National Urban Coalition (1980–86) and the National Puerto Rican Coalition (1976–79); and member of the Women's Research and Education Institution and the Council for Puerto Rico-U.S. Affairs. She is author of *The Puerto Ricans: An Annotated Bibliography*, selected by the American Library Association as one of the outstanding reference books of 1974. Her awards include the Center for Women Policy Studies, Wise Women Award (1989); the National Urban Coalition, Distinguished Community Service Award (1986); the National Conference of Puerto Rican Women, Isabel Award (1988); and the National Council of Negro Women, International Women of Distinction Award.

Carmen Delgado Votaw (19?–)

Born in Humacao, Puerto Rico, Votaw was educated at The American University in Washington, D.C., where she received her B.A. degree. She was vice president and member of the board of directors of the Overseas Education Fund of the League of Women Voters (1964–81). She has served as Federal Programs Specialist, Office of the Commonwealth of Puerto Rico, Washington, D.C. (1972–76); cochair of the National Advisory Committee on Women (1977–79); U.S. representative to the Inter American Commission of Women and its Executive Committee (1977–81); president of the Inter American Commission of Women of the Organization of American States (1978–80); vice president of ISLA, Inc. (1981–84); administrative assistant to Congressman Jaime B. Fuster (1985–91); and is currently director of the Washington office of Girl Scouts U.S.A. She is author

Carmen Delgado Votaw, Director, Washington Office, Girl Scouts, U.S.A.

of *Puerto Rican Women: Some Biographical Profiles* (1978) and numerous articles. She has received numerous awards and honors, including the National Council of Hispanic Women Award for Outstanding Achievement (1991); was profiled in the *Maryland Women's History Resource Packet* (1987 and 1990); and received an honorary doctorate of humanities from Hood College, Frederick, Maryland (1982).

Maxine Baca Zinn (1942–)

Born on June 11, 1942, in Santa Fe, New Mexico, Zinn was educated in sociology at California State College (B.A., 1966), the University of New Mexico (M.A., 1970), and the University of Oregon, where she received her Ph.D. degree in 1978. She has taught women's studies at the University of Delaware (1988–89) and has been a professor at the University of Michigan-Flint, since 1975. She is the author of numerous articles on the Hispanic family and is an associate editor of the *Social Science Journal*. She was a recipient of a Ford Foundation fellowship (1973–75) and is acknowledged as an outstanding sociology scholar.

References

Acosta-Belén, Edna, ed. *The Puerto Rican Woman,* second edition. New York: Praeger, 1986.

Chacón, María A., Elizabeth G. Cohen, Margaret Camarena, Judith Gonzales, and Sharon Strover. *Chicanas in Postsecondary Education.* Stanford, California: Center for Research on Women, Stanford University, 1982.

Cortina, Rodolfo J., and Alberto Moncada, eds. *Hispanos en los Estados Unidos.* Madrid: Ediciones de Cultura Hispánica, 1988.

Cotera, Martha P. *Latina Sourcebook: Bibliography of Mexican American, Cuban, Puerto Rican and Other Hispanic Women Materials in the U.S.A.* Austin, Texas: Information Systems Development, 1976.

——. *The Chicana Feminist.* Austin, Texas: Information Systems Development, 1977.

——. *Diosa y Hembra: The History and Heritage of Chicanas in the United States.* Austin, Texas: Information Systems Development, 1976.

Elsasser, Nan, Kyule Mackenzie, and Yvonne Tixier y Vigil. *Las Mujeres: Conversations from a Hispanic Community.* Old Westbury, New York: Femenist Press, 1980.

Garza, Hedda. *Latinas: Hispanic Women in the United States.* Chicago: Franklin Watts, 1994.

Kanellos, Nicholás, and C. E. Fabregat, general eds., *Handbook of Hispanic Cultures in the United States,* four volumes. Houston: Arte Público Press, 1994.

McKenna, Teresa Flora, and Ida Ortiz, eds. *The Broken Web: The Education Experience of Hispanic American Women.* Berkeley, California: Floricanto Press and The Tomás Rivera Center, 1988.

Melville, Margarita, ed. *Twice a Minority: Mexican American Women.* St. Louis: Mosby, 1980.

Mirandé, Alfredo, and Evangelina Enríquez. *La Chicana: The Mexican American Woman.* Chicago: University of Chicago Press, 1979.

Norwood, Vera, and Janice Monk, eds. *The Desert Is No Lady: Southwestern Landscapes in Women's Writing and Art.* New Haven: Yale University Press, 1980.

Portes, Alejandro and Robert Bach. *Latin Journey: Cuban and Mexican Immigrants in the United States.* Berkeley: University of California Press, 1985.

Rodríguez, Clara E. *Puerto Ricans Born in the U.S.A.* Boston: Unwin Hyman, Inc., 1989.

Zambrana, Ruth E., ed. *Work, Family, and Health: Latina Women in Transition.* New York: Hispanic Research Center, Fordham University, 1982.

Zavella, Patricia. *Women's Work and Chicano Families: Cannery Workers of the Santa Clara Valley.* Ithaca: Cornell University Press, 1987.

Lynn E. Cortina

⑪

Religion

✳ The Beginnings ✳ Instruments of Religious Conversion ✳ Our Lady of Guadalupe and the Saints
✳ Florida ✳ New Mexico ✳ Texas ✳ Arizona ✳ California ✳ The Anglo Conquest
✳ Developing a Pastoral Approach ✳ A Search for Parity ✳ Protestantism and Hispanics
✳ Popular Religiosity ✳ Beyond Orthodoxy

Hispanics are an eminently religious people. Throughout the centuries, regardless of the accessibility of priests or places of worship, or the availability of religious instruction, they have maintained their faith through the nurturing of their families and villages. Often misunderstood and chastised as ignorant, retrograde, or pagan, they have clung to the symbols of a deep spirituality received from their elders. Religious expression is apparent in the exchanges of everyday life—in the readiness with which Hispanics add the expressions Gracias a Dios *(Thanks be to God) or* Si Dios quiere *(God willing) and the ever-present invocations to God, the Virgin, and the saints. That the manner of religious expression for U.S. Hispanics is fundamentally Christian and Catholic is natural; Catholicism is still the religion of choice of Hispanics everywhere. The most recent surveys reveal that 75 percent of U.S. Hispanics consider themselves Catholic, 19 percent Protestant, and 5 percent "other" (Jewish, Jehovah's Witnesses, Mormon, to name a few).*

Hispanics brought Christianity to present-day Florida and the Southwest 250 years before the Pilgrims landed at Plymouth Rock. This period of Christianity on U.S. soil is largely ignored by mainstream church historians. A 1989 five-volume work on this subject commissioned by the U.S. Conference of Catholic Bishops devotes only nine pages to Hispanics. It places them exclusively in the context of an "immigrant" church. As Moisés Sandoval explains in On the Move, *a history of the Hispanic church in the United States, "There is great ignorance about Hispanics in the Church, extending not only to their past and current religious contributions but even to their very existence." Hispanic religious contributions are*

worthy of examination, however, if prejudice is to be dispelled.

✳ THE BEGINNINGS

Catholicism, the religious affiliation of the majority of U.S. Hispanics, came to the New World with Christopher Columbus in 1492. The Spanish conquerors, imbued with the religious ardor of their day, were not content with seizing and claiming kingdoms and treasures in the name of the Spanish sovereigns; they also wanted to win over the inhabitants of the newly discovered territories to Christianity. This was a natural development, for Spain had just fought for seven centuries a religious crusade against the Moors on its own soil. Throughout the first two centuries of European presence in the Americas, Spain was the most zealous daughter of the Roman church.

Uniformity of religious belief, in this case Catholicism, was one of the main pillars on which the Spanish Empire rested. At the time of the discovery of the Americas, Spain was preoccupied with uniting into one nation and under one monarch the various medieval kingdoms into which the Iberian Peninsula was divided. Roughly 20 years before, through the marriage of Isabella of Castile and Ferdinand of Aragon, all but the southern, Muslim-occupied territories came under the royal couple's joint reign. Religious diversity, which provided for the more or less peaceful, if not totally tolerant, coexistence of Christians, Muslims, and Jews, seemed ill-advised to the monarchs; they were already having a difficult enough time coping with the behind-the-scenes machinations of noblemen who resented surrendering their prerogatives as feudal overlords to a centralized government.

The significance of the year 1492 goes far beyond the fateful encounter with the Americas; it constitutes the boundary between religious plurality and uniformity for Spain. Following that date, Spain tolerated no religion other than Catholicism on its soil or in the vast lands it set forth to bring beneath its imperial mantle. In January 1492, Isabella and Ferdinand captured Granada, the last Moorish stronghold in Iberia. This put an end to the 700-year-long Reconquest, which had begun shortly after 711 when the Moors invaded all but the extreme northern regions of Spain. In April, the monarchs gave notice to the Jews that they had until July to repudiate their faith or leave Spain. An estimated 140,000 chose the road to exile. Thenceforth, only the Cross would follow the sword of the Spanish soldiers, both to the European battlefields, where the Spanish Hapsburg kings fought their religious wars against Protestants, and to the remote jungles and deserts of the newly discovered regions of the Americas and Asia.

Father Virgilio Elizondo pointed out in his book *Galilean Journey* (1985) that in matters of religion the attitudes of the Spanish conquistador and his English counterpart were worlds apart. Early in the period of conquest and discovery, theologians like Father Francisco Vitoria, a Spanish Dominican, settled the question as to whether Indians were human. Indians, they determined, were made in God's image and likeness and were endowed with an immortal soul. Converting them to Christianity became a sacred mandate for the Spaniards. According to Elizondo, the Spanish conquerors were not concerned about their own personal salvation, of which they felt assured. Whenever they sought royal permission and support for their enterprises, they listed the evangelization of the native populations as a goal. In Bernal Díaz del Castillo's account of Hernán Cortés' conquest of Mexico, he states that after each village and town surrendered to the conquistadors, the Spaniards immediately took time to destroy the pagan idols and temples and in their place erected crosses and shrines in honor of the Virgin Mary. To Cortés and most Spaniards of his day, the conquest was not merely a political and economic enterprise but a religious crusade.

Their English counterparts, on the other hand, coming from the austerity of Protestant Europe, were obsessed with achieving their own salvation and gave no thought to the spiritual well-being of the American native. From their standpoint, the natives were less than human, unworthy of the Christian promise, children of the Devil. They were not to be evangelized, but rather destroyed; thus, the expression popular during the conquest of the American Far West, "The only good Indian is a dead Indian."

✳ INSTRUMENTS OF RELIGIOUS CONVERSION

Conversion of the Indians facilitated interbreeding of the Spanish and the Indians. The Spaniards, Virgilio Elizondo explained in *Galilean Journey: The Mexican American Promise* (1985), contrary to the early English colonists, considered sexual relations with the native women as something natural. The conquistadors took them as mistresses, concubines, and wives and accepted both their legitimate and illegitimate children, producing almost from the outset a generation of Christian mestizos.

On a less fortunate note, converting the Indians mandated the development of systems and strategies that would render them receptive to Christian teachings or force them into accepting them. In the name of evangelization, the unscrupulous or overzealous committed abuses never intended by either the Crown or the church. From the first, the Indians were exploited, enslaved or forced into some sort of servitude. The church consistently censured these excesses; the Spanish Crown attempted to prevent and remedy them, as the passing of the *Leyes de Indias* (Laws of the Indies) makes evident. This body of laws, among other things, recognized the natives as subjects of the Crown and forbade their forced conversion and enslavement. Unfortunately, the Spanish monarchs and their courts were an ocean away, and more often than not the letter of the law was executed rather than its intent.

The first approach to the orderly evangelization of the natives, the *encomienda,* further opened the door to the inhumane excesses that would characterize the colonization of the New World. The encomienda entrusted a group of Indians to a colonist, known as the *encomendero* (trustee), who was responsible for providing for the material needs and religious instruction of his charges. In exchange for his paternalism, the encomendero was entitled to work the Indians. The provisions of the laws that set down in detail the responsibilities of the encomendero and regulated the conditions under which the Indians would labor were largely ignored. The *repartimiento,* a variation of the encomienda, offered no relief to the sufferings of the newly conquered peoples. It merely placed colonial authorities instead of individuals in charge of the natives. The latter, when not forced to work in Crown-owned mines, farms, or other projects, were apportioned out to private citizens as laborers.

The Franciscan methold of teaching the Indians by pictures. (From an engraving based on Fray Diego Valdés, O.F.M., in his *Rhetorica Christiana,* Rome, 1579.)

tives. The vulnerability of the unarmed, nonthreatening padre was often his greatest strength. Missionaries could succeed where the conquistadors failed. Such was the case in the Sonora region of northern Mexico (southern Arizona today) and in the peninsula of Baja California, where the hostility of the natives prevented the soldiers from making inroads. After several failed attempts, the Mexican viceroy entrusted the Jesuits with this conquest, which they performed successfully with no other weapon than the Cross.

The mission, in most cases, served as a center for religious instruction and a beachhead from which the padre could set out to scout for other promising mission sites, where another beachhead in the evangelization process could be established. Missions, therefore, as was the case in Florida and the Southwest, tended to stretch out over a territory much like the links of a chain. This arrangement, in turn, facilitated the logistics of supplying and defending them. The Texas and California missions established by the Franciscan friars were rather ambitious institutions. Some were villages unto themselves. The Indians learned Christian doctrine and a variety of skills—farming, animal husbandry,

In either case, whether as part of an encomienda or a repartimiento, the Indians were brutalized, starved, and often worked to death. Whole populations were wiped out in the West Indies, where the encomiendas and the repartimientos were first imposed. Preeminent among the voices that rose to the defense of human rights for the Indians was Father Bartolomé de las Casas (1474–1566), a Spanish-born Dominican priest and historian. To his protests and pleas can be attributed the above-mentioned Laws of the Indies enacted by the Crown.

A vastly more humane instrument of evangelization, and the one most widely utilized in the Spanish territories now encompassed by the United States, was the mission, a temporary institution established and run by priests who resided among or in proximity to native populations. The missionary usually came right on the heels of the conquistador and built his rudimentary chapel and convent at a reasonable distance from the military garrison, once the area was somewhat pacified. Instead of force, it was the missionary's works of mercy and his teachings that often brought about the evangelization of the na-

Bartolemé de las Casas (1474–1566).

San Juan Capistrano Mission in San Antonio, Texas. (Photograph by Silvia Novo Pena.)

weaving, metalwork, leather craft, carpentry, and masonry—aimed at bringing about economic self-sufficiency to populations that once depended on collecting, hunting, or fishing for their sustenance. These missions became very wealthy, supplying not merely their own residents but the garrisons and townships in the immediate area.

The missions were secularized during the first part of the nineteenth century, either for political reasons or because their original aims had been achieved. By this time and because in most cases their residents had fused with the people of the surrounding townships and farms, missions became the nuclei for modern-day parishes. It is not uncommon for the descendants of the first Indian neophytes baptized within mission walls to still flock to the same old church buildings generation after generation.

In light of this, the assertion that missions and missionaries served the purposes of the empire cannot be denied. The missions contributed to the pacification of the Indians, and in so doing facilitated the process of colonization. They fostered the development of townships in their immediate vicinity. Furthermore, by Christianizing and Hispanicizing the Indians, the missionaries transformed entire populations into loyal subjects of the Spanish kings and obedient children of the Roman church.

One of the services offered by the church, which served to both Christianize and Hispanicize the native and mestizo populations, was formal education. In townships and missions, the clergy was expected to establish schools, both for boys and girls, to teach the children to read and write and learn the catechism. The curriculum sometimes included Indian languages. As early as 1534, archbishop of Mexico Juan de Zumárraga had a school built at Tlatelolco, the first in the Americas. Countless Indian children spent their mornings reading, writing, and singing and their afternoons involved in religious instruction. Zumárraga, an indefatigable worker for the education of the Indians, published numerous books on the subject, paying special attention to the education of girls.

✳ OUR LADY OF GUADALUPE AND THE SAINTS

The spiritual conquest of Mexico served as the first chapter in the spiritual conquest of the Hispanic territories now encompassed by the United States, Florida and Louisiana being the exceptions. As Carey McWilliams aptly underscores in his book *North from Mexico* (1968), the Spanish-speaking colonists who settled Texas and the Southwest were, but for rare exceptions, mestizos, second generation and beyond, born of Spanish fathers and Mexican Indian mothers; the balance was constituted by Christianized Mexican Indians (the ductile Tlaxcalans, in particular), blacks, and mulattoes. The Catholic religiosity of the Mexican mestizo would come to predominate in this area even after the final invasion of northern Mexico by the United States in 1846. This religiosity continues to be reaffirmed by the various waves of Mexican immigrants that have entered the United States since the late nineteenth century.

A providential event that contributed to the conversion of the native population of Mexico and Central America to Roman Catholicism was the alleged miraculous apparition of the Virgin Mary in Tepeyac in the environs of Moctezuma's vanquished capital of Tenochtitlán shortly after the conquest of the Aztec Empire by Hernán Cortés in 1521. In the early morning hours of December 9, 1531, Juan Diego, a converted Indian, was on his way to mass when he was surprised by the sound of beautiful singing voices coming from a hill. As he approached the site, he saw a woman enveloped by a brilliant aura. She identified herself as the Virgin Mary. In the course of several apparitions, she requested that Juan Diego inform Archbishop Zumárraga of what he had seen and heard and that she wished for a temple to be built on the hill at Tepeyac so that she could communicate all her love and compassion, help and defend all the inhabitants of the land, and remedy their misery, pain, and suffering. The archbishop refused to believe Juan Diego's story. Finally, so that he could prove his veracity, the Virgin performed a miracle. She instructed Diego to gather roses from a bush that would not normally bloom that time of year and take them to the archbishop. When the humble messenger unfolded his cloak before Zumárraga, so as to put before him the roses the Lady was sending, the image of the Virgin Mary appeared imprinted on the cloth.

Detractors have claimed that the clergy perpetrated a hoax on the credulous natives in order to speed up their conversion. It was too much of a coincidence that the apparition took place on a site dedi-

The image of Our Lady of Guadalupe on tour from Mexico at Our Lady of Guadalupe Church in Houston, Texas, 1992. (Photograph by Curtis Dowell.)

cated to the cult of the Aztec mother goddess Tonantzin. The image, however, displayed to this day in the basilica of Our Lady of Guadalupe in Mexico City, has not disintegrated in over four centuries, even though it is imprinted on a highly perishable cloth made of agave fibers. Furthermore, scientific testing has failed to explain the origin of the image or its durability.

News of the miracle spread throughout the colony, bringing about mass conversions. To the natives, the fact that the Virgin had chosen to appear before one of the oppressed and the vanquished, that she had adopted the physical appearance of a brown woman, and that she communicated in Nahuatl, the language of the Indians, established a bond between them and Christianity. The fact that her body blocked the face of the sun, the focal point of the native religions, established the precedence of the new faith brought by the Spaniards over the old faith of the Aztec.

Noted Mexican writer Carlos Fuentes observed in a 1992 presentation at the University of Houston that mestizo artisans invariably portrayed Christ as a broken, bleeding god suffering on the Cross. The Virgin of Guadalupe, on the other hand, appears surrounded by flowers, rays of sunlight, and all of nature triumphant. As he explained it, the first Indian converts identified the death of their old gods with Christ. He was a god who was willing to be destroyed to save his people. The Virgin, on the other hand, surrounded by all the symbols of a joyous nature, brought the hope for a new beginning.

The colorful liturgy of Catholicism and its doctrine of the veneration of saints further paved the way for native conversions. The Mexican Indians were accustomed to paying tribute to a wide variety of deities. Each clan, each site, each day, week, and month was the purvey of a god or goddess whose favor was sought to ensure the happy outcome of events. They felt quite at home with the feast days assigned by the church calendar to holy men and women of the past, who were also named patrons for townships and villages, professions and trades and protectors for individuals. By the same token, elaborate priestly vestments, music, incense, candles, ornate sacred vessels, and other external aspects of the Catholic church must have appeared to the Indians as echoes of their past devotions.

✳ FLORIDA

The first chapter of the Christian saga in present-day Florida began shortly after the Easter season—*la Pascua Florida*—of 1513 with the arrival of Juan Ponce de León. Although no priest is known to have accompanied this expedition, the customs of the day presupposed that there was an act of thanksgiving to God for the safe arrival of the conquistadors. Ponce de León returned in 1526 as military escort for a contingent of secular and regular priests. He was commissioned by the Crown to establish mission posts for the dual purpose of affirming Spain's presence in the newly discovered territories and spreading the gospel. Finding armed resistance from the Indians of the Gulf Coast area where they landed, the Spaniards retreated to Cuba, Ponce de León dying en route from wounds he sustained.

After several failed attempts, Spain abandoned all efforts to colonize Florida until 1564, when a handful of French soldiers, some of them Protestant Huguenots, founded Fort Caroline on the Saint John's River near present-day Saint Augustine. Pedro Menéndez de Avilés, a man known for his zeal and cruelty, was dispatched by the government to protect its claims against the intruders and to destroy the fort. Carried away by the religious fanaticism typical of the day, Menéndez ordered the non-Catholic French soldiers put to the sword even after they had surrendered. Three years later, the Spanish garrison that held the little fort, by then renamed San Mateo, was subjected to the same fate at the hands of the Frenchman Dominique Gourges.

The establishment of Saint Augustine in 1565 by Menéndez was pivotal to the evangelization efforts. Using Saint Augustine as a base, the handful of diocesan priests who first accompanied Menéndez—Jesuits from the order's province of Andalusia after 1566 and Franciscans after 1587—sailed north along the Atlantic coast, establishing and operating missions among the Indians. The diocesan priests also ministered to the white settlers in garrisons and outposts. Time and conditions permitting, they also saw to the spiritual welfare of neighboring Indian tribes. By 1647, a chain of missions and forts spanned from Saint Augustine in the south to Fort San Felipe on Parris Island, South Carolina.

Beginning in 1607, the Franciscans, with Father Francisco Prieto in the role of pioneer, ventured into northwestern Florida to do missionary work among the Apalache Indians. Their dedication bore fruit, and by 1655 the friars could claim 26,000 converts. Their missions in the Gulf and northwestern areas of Florida stretched from the Suwannee River in the south to the Apalachicola River in the northwest.

The state of the church in Florida in 1674 was recorded by Bishop Gabriel Díaz Vara Calderón of Santiago de Cuba, who, at the insistence of Queen Mariana, made an episcopal visit there. Upon his return, after confirming 13,152 Christianized Indians and Spaniards and traveling hundreds of leagues to visit every one of the 36 missions in the province, Bishop Calderón gave a detailed account of his observations in a letter to the pious Spanish queen. His assessment was that despite the hardships and the indifference and sometimes cruelty of the civil authorities, the missionaries had succeeded. The missions, although poor, served as firm bulwarks of the faith upon which the empire rested.

Less than 50 years later, beginning with the outbreak in 1702 of the War of Spanish Succession, which pitted France and Spain against England, the network of Florida missions was laid to waste. When in 1763, at the end of the war, Spain ceded Florida to France according to the terms of the Treaty of Paris, only two parish churches and a handful of mission buildings still stood.

❋ NEW MEXICO

As in Florida, the early expeditions or *entradas* into New Mexico from Mexico were of little consequence to the efforts of evangelization. From 1536, when Álvar Núñez Cabeza de Vaca, after years of captivity among the Karankawa Indians of Texas, heard of the big Zuni pueblos of New Mexico and mistook them for the legendary Seven Cities of Gold, until 1598, when Juan de Oñate led his group of settlers northward along the banks of the Rio Grande, New Mexico remained virtually unaffected by religious campaigns elsewhere. Heroes, cowards, martyrs, and scoundrels crossed from Mexico into the northern frontier, with or without permission from the Crown, leaving behind nothing but their failed hopes, a few relics, the carcasses of their beasts, their fallen comrades, and their rusting swords.

The course of religious history took a turn with Oñate's entrada of 1598. Oñate, a silver miner and the wealthiest man in Mexico, like Ponce de León in Florida, had a mandate from the Crown to Christianize the native people of New Mexico, among which his settlers were to dwell. Consequently, he took—in addition to his 83 oxcarts of goods, 7,000 head of stock, and 400 soldiers—a handful of priests and a plan that called for the creation of seven mission districts, each to be headed by a Franciscan friar. By 1630, 25 missions had been founded among the various settled tribes known collectively as the Pueblos.

As would be the case wherever sword and Cross ventured jointly, a conflict soon developed between the priests and the civil and military authorities. Abuse and exploitation of the natives were the order of the day. The military, sent to establish an orderly government among the Indians, stole from them, did them all sorts of violence, and raped the women.

The Pueblos were an agricultural people. They raised corn, beans, and a variety of foodstuffs. As the newcomers saw their own supplies dwindle, they robbed the Pueblos of their stores. Oñate, an irascible man who had little patience with either the settlers or the Pueblos, ordered the removal of grain from the Indians, even when it meant destroying villages and injuring the defenders.

The clergy protested. They described the excesses and the sufferings of the Pueblos at the hands of the Hispanic contingent in official reports to the civil and ecclesiastic authorities in Mexico. Fray Francisco de Zamora, to give an example, wrote that the depredations of the Hispanics against the Pueblos were a discredit to Christian teaching. He said that the natives were "stabbed and knifed when things were taken from them" and that the women were often raped by the soldiers. Echoing the feelings of other friars, he recommended that New Mexico be abandoned, so that the Pueblos might live in peace and the Word of God not be further dishonored.

Needless to say, Oñate's supporters countered these reports to the authorities with accusations of sloth on the part of the clergy and recommendations that the colony not be abandoned. They made these arguments hypocritically in the name of Christian evangelization. A later report to the viceroy that the conversion of 7,000 Indians had been accomplished was instrumental in saving the colony, pointing to the fact that religious accomplishments were vital to determining the success or failure of the colonizing enterprise. The viceroy made provisions to ensure against any further injustices and ill treatment of the natives. These included replacing Oñate as governor with Pedro de Peralta in 1609 and limiting the largest military garrison to 50 married soldiers.

The Pueblos were not willing converts to Christianity. They had their own cults to ancestors and to various natural forces that had to be propitiated to ensure abundant crops. They worshiped the sun and the mother earth and believed in life after death. Their ceremonial life was rich and colorful. To give in to the missionaries, as they saw it, could result in famine and many other calamities. Conversions were seldom totally sincere, and apostasy was quite common. Those who were outwardly Christianized more than likely practiced the old rituals secretly. For these infractions they were routinely punished by the friars. The troublemakers were sold into slavery along with Apache caught raiding the settlements. The yearly trade caravan from Santa Fe to Mexico City led them tethered like cattle, a human chain of captives to be sold in the marketplace along with the buffalo hides and wool of the New Mexican Hispanos.

The excesses of the civilian population and the unbending zeal of the Franciscan friars brought about the Pueblo Revolt of 1680. Fanning the fires of religious discontent, Popé, a Pueblo chieftain from Taos, organized the villages against the Hispanics. An initial bloody rampage forced 1,500 settlers and Christianized Indians to retreat South to Isleta, near present-day El Paso. Upriver, Popé and his men ransacked the churches of the hated religion, burning vestments, defacing statues, and destroying sacred vessels and ornaments. Furthermore, in an effort to remove all traces of Christianity, they rubbed themselves with a solution made out of yucca to erase the waters of baptism from their bodies.

The Cross and the sword, however, did not concede defeat. On September 13, 1893, a well-armed detachment of soldiers headed by Diego de Vargas, a deeply religious man, arrived outside Santa Fe after an almost bloodless campaign to retake New Mexico. Popé, seen as the devil incarnate, was dead. Under his reign the Pueblos had suffered almost as much as under the Hispanics. The Pueblo delegation that had met with Vargas initially argued that if it surrendered, their people would be subjected to forced labor, put to work in encomiendas as slaves, and be made to rebuild the churches. Vargas assured them that the people who had abused them would not return. He further gave them one hour to abjure their pagan beliefs, to pledge their allegiance to the Spanish king, and to be willing to adopt Christianity. The alternative was destruction. The Pueblos acceded. On December 16, a vanguard of soldiers and priests, which was part of a long column of more than 800 colonists and 18 supply wagons, arrived at the outskirts of Santa Fe. The priests entered the city singing hymns while the sullen Indians watched. Christianity was permanently implanted on New Mexican soil, even though it would never succeed in eradicating the ancient Pueblo beliefs.

✳ TEXAS

Altogether, 20 expeditions are known to have entered Texas before the threat of French encroachment forced the Spanish Crown to think of making good its territorial claims over the region.

In 1685, Robert Cavalier, sieur de la Salle, established Fort Saint Louis on Matagorda Bay. The Spanish, having word of this development ordered the colony found and destroyed. Four consecutive expeditions by Alonso de León searched the upper Gulf Coast of Texas before the ruins of the French fort were found. In the course of the fourth expedition, a Franciscan from the College of Querétaro, Father Damián Massenet, was invited by an Indian chief whom he met near the Guadalupe River to visit his people. He indicated that they dwelled further east. The Indian's invitation, according to some accounts, came from the tradition among his people of a lady in blue who had appeared to their ancestors and had recommended they go seek priests that would bring the true faith to them.

The story of the lady in blue first surfaced among the Jumano Indians near Isleta. In 1639, 50 Jumanos appeared before missionaries in Isleta, requesting instruction in the Christian faith so that they could eventually be baptized. After some investigation, it was determined that the lady in blue was Sor María de Jesús, a cloistered nun who had never gone beyond the confines of her convent in Agreda, Spain. A mystic, she was so well known for her piety that on occasion King Philip IV visited and consulted her. Sor María is said to have experienced in her mystical trances the phenomenon of bilocation, whereby she found herself in the New World teaching religion to the Indians.

Father Massenet was enthusiastic in responding to the Indian chief. For years the competing Franciscan colleges of Querétaro and Zacatecas, in Mexico, had sought the opportunity of opening Texas as a new mission field, but the Crown had only lent a deaf ear to their pleas. No missions had been allowed north of the Rio Grande. The implications of La Salle's failed expedition changed the political picture. The expedition pointed to the fact that the French, who already had claimed the valley of the Mississippi River, were harboring imperial designs for Texas. Consequently, in 1690 Alonso de León was sent at the head of a fifth expedition into Texas. He was accompanied by Father Massenet and three other Franciscans sent to establish missions in the easternmost region of Texas and evangelize the Hasinai Indians (incorrectly labeled "Tejas" by the first explorers). The underlying purpose was to buttress Spanish claims to the territory. The Franciscans founded two missions: San Francisco de los Tejas and El Santísimo Nombre de María. The missions were short-lived. Constant bickering between the friars and the military authorities over the treatment of the Indians, poor crops, the inability to make a settled people out of the nomadic eastern Texas tribes, and the easing of tensions with France brought about their closing in 1593.

In 1714, a French trader, Louis Juchereau de St. Denis, appeared at the San Juan Bautista mission on the southern bank of the Rio Grande. That a foreigner could openly enter Mexico through the back door instilled fear in the Spanish authorities. Once again they decided to establish missions along the eastern Texas border as a buffer against the

French. "By this means similar incursions will be prevented and, what is more important, these Indians will obtain instruction in our Holy Catholic Faith and the spiritual welfare of their souls," the viceroy wrote in 1715, outlining the plan for resettlement of eastern Texas.

The following year, Captain Domingo Ramón, commandant of the San Juan Bautista presidio, led the expedition aimed at founding the new missions. Altogether, 25 soldiers and their families, 11 Franciscans, from both the Colleges of Querétaro and Zacatecas, and 1,000 head of cattle traveled to eastern Texas. Among the missionaries was a leading figure who would come to be known as the Father of Texas Missions, Fray Antonio Margil de Jesús. Already 60 years of age when he joined the expedition, Margil had previously established missions in Guatemala, founded the Franciscan College of Zacatecas, and helped establish its rival institution in Querétaro. Years later, Margil would be the founder of Mission San José y San Miguel de Aguayo in San Antonio, Texas, which is reputedly the best example of Spanish missionary architecture in the United States. In a flurry of activity fired by evangelical zeal, Margil and his brethren built six missions among the Hasinai between July 1716 and the early part of 1717. Once the task was completed, it became evident that the logistics of supplying eastern Texas called for the establishment of another outpost midway between the Rio Grande and this distant frontier.

A proposal made by Father Antonio de Olivares, who had long strived to establish a mission on the San Antonio River, paved the way for the new foundation. Over 20 years before, Father Olivares swam across the Rio Grande into Texas and ambled north to the site occupied today by the city of San Antonio. The good friar was overcome with excitement by the sight of thousands of Indians congregated on the banks of San Pedro Springs. Having assumed these to be permanent Indian settlements, Fray Olivares set off on a campaign to establish missions in their midst, projecting a plentiful harvest of converts to the faith. He returned years later with Captain Diego Ramón on a journey of exploration geared to whetting the appetite of the Crown on behalf of his missionary project. In the course of this expedition, the river was given the name San Antonio de Padua. In December 1716, Olivares' proposal was approved with additions that provided for a presidio and a township to house the relatives of the garrison soldiers. In 1718, Mission San Antonio de Valero, the fateful Alamo of Texas revolutionary history, was founded, together with the presidio and the township.

The height of missionary activity in Texas followed the inspection tour of the royal visitor the Marquis de Aguayo in 1720. After assessing the situation in Texas, Aguayo granted permission to build Mission San José in San Antonio and the Presidio La Bahía near the mouth of the San Antonio River on Matagorda Bay. From San José, missionaries would subsequently set off to evangelize the Lipan Apache Indians, who eventually made peace with the Hispanic population. In the environs of La Bahía, missions were founded to attempt the conversion of the Karankawa and the Apache.

Missions in Texas were never truly successful. The Apache, for instance, are said to have assisted in the building process to please the friars, but they were never willing to give up their nomadic life and their horse-thieving ways. Time and again they made promises of settling down "next season" or "after the hunt," but they never remained for long. Like migratory birds, their sojourns were brief. As to the other Indians, mission life was never too attractive. At its peak, Mission San José had no more than 1,400 native dwellers. Their lack of success notwithstanding, some of the missions became wealthy in terms of arable lands and herds, awakening the greed of the authorities. By the time of Mexican independence in 1821, they all had been secularized, their lands and herds had been forfeited, and their buildings had fallen into disrepair. The settled areas of Texas at the time, however—Nacogdoches, San Antonio, and La Bahía (Goliad)—owed their existence to the efforts of the old friars.

✳ ARIZONA

The name of Jesuit Father Eusebio Kino, a German-educated Italian, pervades the history of evangelization in southern Arizona. Kino, a cartographer, among other things, had labored in the missions of Baja California, which he succeeded in proving was a peninsula rather than an island.

In 1687, he was sent to the northern Sonoran Desert to work in the conversion of the region known as Pimería Alta. In the course of the next 24 years, until his death in 1711, Kino established 29 missions, using the Mission Nuestra Señora de los Dolores in Sonora as his base of operations. Three of these missions—Guevavi, Tumacacori, and San Xavier de Bac—were located within the borders of the modern state of Arizona.

Kino was first and foremost a diplomat. He succeeded where others failed in winning the goodwill of Indian chieftains. Kino's mediation succeeded in bringing peace to the region in 1695, when war broke out among the Indian tribes divided over the issue of loyalty to the Spanish newcomers. As a missionary, Kino developed in the people a desire for conversion.

In the course of developing a mission, and before settling down to the task of religious instruction, he routinely introduced cattle ranching to the Indians. Then, after convincing the chieftains of the advantages of Christianity, he would have them travel to the Jesuit superior to request missionaries for their people. Unfortunately, there were never enough missionaries to satisfy the demands. The Hispanic settlers, on the other hand, were always eager to dismantle the missions. They wanted control of the herds and wanted Indian labor in the form of repartimientos to support work in the mines.

A second Pima uprising in 1751 and the expulsion of the Jesuits from all Spanish territories left little of Father Kino's work intact. The Franciscans who were entrusted with the Arizona missions were largely confined to Tumacacori and San Xavier. The Pimas for the most part returned to their ancient pagan ways.

✳ CALIFORNIA

The last mission territory to be opened in the northern frontier of Mexico was California. On July 1, 1769, more than 200 years after the Portuguese Juan Rodríguez Cabrillo, sailing under the flag of Spain, first discovered it, Franciscan Father Junípero Serra celebrated a solemn mass of thanksgiving on the shores of the Bay of San Diego. Months before, four expeditions, two by sea and two by land, had left Baja California for San Diego for the purpose of initiating the missionary process.

The original force behind this effort was Don José de Gálvez, visitor general for King Charles III, a man as visionary and driven by faith as Fray Junípero. As part of his duties, Gálvez visited in 1767 a handful of desolate missions in the rugged peninsula of Baja California. Built by the Jesuits, upon their expulsion these missions were entrusted to the Franciscans. Gálvez had a plan for Father Serra. Worried about the activities of Russian fur trappers who traveled into North America through the Bering Straits, the Spanish Crown began to look with interest at long-neglected California. Gálvez's proposal to Serra, the president of the Baja California missions, was a plan to establish a series of missions along the coast of northern California.

Junípero Serra (1713–1784) was born on the island of Mallorca, off the southern coast of Spain. Shunning the opportunity for further training as a theologian, for which he was eminently qualified, he offered himself for mission work and was sent to Mexico in 1747. From that date forward, Serra tirelessly traveled through Mexico giving himself completely to the task of evangelization and, as a result,

putting his health at serious risk. Needless to say, José Gálvez's mission plan was earmarked for the indefatigable padre, and during the late spring of 1769, the visitor general and Serra, undertaking the task of stevedores, personally packed and loaded on board a ship bound for San Diego chalices, vestments, altar cloths, and other items for the churches soon to be built in the northern California frontier.

July 16, 1769, marks the foundation of the first California mission, San Diego de Alcalá, on a hill overlooking the beautiful bay of the same name; and 54 years later, in 1823, the last of a chain of 21 missions, San Francisco Solano, was established north of the city of San Francisco. The missions were joined by the Camino Real, or Royal Road. They achieved, as nowhere else, great prosperity, with some of the missions owning over a dozen cattle ranches. Vineyards, orchards, vast fields of grain dotted the landscape surrounding the mission buildings.

Within their confines life was orderly, the ringing of bells dividing the day into work, rest, instructional, and devotional periods. Artisans and craftsmen brought from Mexico taught the residents a wealth of skills. Additionally, the missions operated schools and hospitals. The role that the missions played in the development of California cannot be overexaggerated. The development of a population from the fusion of the Hispanic mestizo settlers that came from Mexico and the native populations, the founding of townships and villages, and the emergence of a prosperous agricultural and cattle industry are primarily owed to the missions.

✳ THE ANGLO CONQUEST

By the time of the Treaty of Guadalupe Hidalgo in 1848, the mission system had disappeared, but the faith was kept alive by the people. Secular priests belonging to the northern dioceses of Mexico ministered to the needs of the faithful as well as they could, considering the vast distances they had to travel and the sparseness of their numbers. In distant villages and ranches, months and years would pass without a visit from a priest. In northern New Mexico, the Brotherhood of the Penitente s (Fraternidad Piadosa de Nuestro Padre Jesús Nazareno—the Pious Fraternity of Our Father Jesús the Nazarene) filled in the spiritual vacuum. These penitential organizations, which, according to some historians, have their roots in the Third Order of St. Francis, a lay arm of the Franciscans, practiced scourging and a rigorous piety centered on the sufferings of Christ. In the absence of clergy, they organized liturgies for the different feasts in the church calendar and taught religion to the young.

Although originally Rome had intended for the bishops of northern Mexico to continue administering the affairs of the church in what had now become the southwestern frontier of the United States, the North American bishops protested, voicing the displeasure of their government and probably their own jealousy. Political expediency forced the Vatican to bow before the pressures of the new rulers and appoint foreign bishops to each newly erected diocese or vicariate. The effects of this decision are still felt in our day. Texas, which fell under the diocese of Coahuila, was made a missionary vicariate under Rome in 1841. In 1847, the diocese of Galveston (now Galveston-Houston) was erected by the Vatican. It encompassed the entire state and its first bishop was Jean Marie Odin, a native of Lyon, France. The spiritual needs of the thousands of European Catholic immigrants that poured into Texas became the primary concern of the local church. Neglect of the Hispanic faithful became the norm.

The fate of the church in Texas was repeated in New Mexico, Arizona, Colorado, and California. Vicariates and dioceses were erected in all conquered territories, and with rare exceptions non-Hispanic bishops were appointed to head them. The new bishops and vicars, in turn, brought in almost exclusively European priests and congregations of religious men and women. The disdain that the newcomers felt toward the native population was reflected in the myth that its clergy were worthless and lazy. Underlying this assumption was the fear of the authorities that Hispanic priests were by virtue of their place in the community natural leaders who could induce their flocks to rebellion. Their fears materialized in the person of Father Antonio José Martínez of Taos, New Mexico.

Father Martínez (1793–1868), a native of Río Arriba County, New Mexico, was ordained to the priesthood after being widowed and fathering a daughter. His defense of the rights of Hispanic clergy before the unreasonable demands of French-born bishop Jean Baptiste Lamy of Santa Fe and his resistance to the suppression of the Penitente brotherhood led to his excommunication. Lamy's attitude toward the Hispanic faithful was typical of the church leaders sent to the conquered territories at the bequest of the U.S. bishops. The religious traditions of the people were shunned. The beautiful old adobe churches were allowed to decay. Plaster religious images replaced the colorful hand-carved cottonwood santos. Popular Hispanic religiosity was attacked as superstitious or pagan. To be Catholic you first had to be American, you had to pray in English, you had to give up your traditional religious practices.

By the end of the nineteenth century, Father

Moisés Sandoval states, Hispanic Americans in the Southwest had no institutional voice in the church. The native Hispanic priests who had been their spokesmen in mid-century had all been purged or had died of old age. The Hispanic laity returned to their homespun religious traditions, which had served them well throughout the centuries.

Ironically enough, during this same period a Hispanic priest was working on behalf of the destitute Irish Catholic immigrants who were arriving in droves to this country. Cuban-born Father Félix Varela (1778–1853) was a political exile living in New York when Catholicism was the faith of a minority. The plight of the poor Irish, who would become the backbone of the church in the United States, was a catalyst that drove this intellectual into active social ministry. His acts of charity on behalf of the Irish and the sensitive and intelligent manner in which he defended and promoted Catholicism—he established the second Catholic newspaper in the United States—have served to bolster the cause for his canonization.

✳ DEVELOPING A PASTORAL APPROACH

Although the original attitude of the English-speaking conquerors of the Mexican Southwest was that Hispanics would eventually disappear, migrations from Mexico, Cuba, and Puerto Rico in the latter part of the nineteenth century and the early years of the twentieth mandated a new approach on the part of the church. The church now saw herself as an instrument in the process of integrating Hispanics into the mainstream. For this purpose, national parishes were established for Hispanics, an approach utilized with other ethnic groups, such as the Polish, the Italians, and the Germans. Contrary to other nationalities, however, native Hispanic priests who could supply leadership and role models for their own people were seldom available. One of the salient reasons for this absence was the failure by church authorities to promote vocations among Hispanics, who, because of prevalent social and economic conditions, could seldom meet the educational standards required by seminaries and novitiates. The gap was filled by Spanish-speaking priests of other national origins. In Texas, two religious orders, the Oblates of Mary Immaculate and the Claretians, were invited in by the different bishops specifically to minister to Hispanics.

In the meantime, Hispanics grew in number and began to settle in areas other than the Southwest. Waves of migration came from Mexico and, after 1917, when its people were granted U.S. citizenship, from Puerto Rico. By the 1920s, it was evident that more than a diocesan approach was needed to serve this population. In 1923, the U.S. bishops established an immigration office in El Paso, Texas, aimed at ministering to the large number of Mexicans fleeing the revolution, which had begun in 1910. In 1944, Archbishop Robert E. Lucey of San Antonio held a seminar for the Spanish-speaking to discuss the needs of the Hispanic faithful. In 1945, the Bishops Committee for the Spanish-speaking was created to establish programs, both of a social and a pastoral nature, in Texas, California, Colorado, and Santa Fe. One of its goals was to put an end to prejudice and discrimination against Hispanics in the church. The catalyst for these measures was the increasing proselytism of Hispanics by Protestant churches.

✳ A SEARCH FOR PARITY

Although in the 1950s and 1960s the number of Hispanic priests and nuns increased, they were often not allowed to work with their own people. Archbishop Patrick Flores, the highest-ranking Hispanic in the U.S. Catholic church today, likes to recall how as a young priest assigned to a predominantly Hispanic parish in Houston, Texas, he was forbidden by his pastor the use of Spanish except in the confessional.

The reforms imposed on the church by the Second Vatican Council in the early 1960s, particularly those calling for the use of the vernacular rather than Latin in the celebration of the Mass, and the activism among minority groups in the period that followed brought to a head the silent struggle of Hispanic Catholics. Demands that the Mass and the sacraments be offered in Spanish mounted. In 1967, Henry Casso of San Antonio was named executive director of the Bishops Committee for the Spanish-speaking, a position occupied by Anglos from its inception. In 1969, Hispanic priests organized Priests Associated for Religious, Educational and Social Rights (PADRES), and in 1971 Hispanic sisters followed suit with the creation of Las Hermanas, an organization representing 20 religious orders. The same year saw the creation in San Antonio of the Mexican American Cultural Center (MACC), a Hispanic pastoral institute aimed at training clergy and lay leaders to serve the spiritual needs of Hispanics. The moving force behind MACC was Father Virgilio Elizondo, a native of San Antonio and a leading Hispanic theologian. Hispanic offices at the regional and diocesan level were also established about this time. Finally, in 1974, the U.S. bishops, at the instance of PADRES, created the Secretariat for Hispanic Affairs as a permanent office within the U.S. Catholic Conference. The secretariat is charged with assisting and advising the bishops.

Three Encuentros, or national meetings, of delegates representing Hispanic Catholics from throughout the land have been held in the nation's capital, in 1972, 1977, and 1985. The Encuentros served to voice the needs and expectations of Hispanic Catholics and were instrumental in promulgating the U.S. bishops' pastoral letter, "The Hispanic Presence: Challenge and Commitment" (1983), and a national plan for Hispanic ministry approved by the bishops in 1987.

The first Hispanic to be ordained bishop was Patrick Flores, the son of poor migrant workers from Ganado, Texas. Flores was ordained on May 5, 1970, and named auxiliary bishop of San Antonio and later installed as bishop of El Paso, Texas. With his appointment in 1979 to the archdiocese of San Antonio, which heads the ecclesiastical province of Texas, he became the first Hispanic to be installed as an archbishop in this country. Since 1971, the Vatican has appointed more Hispanics as auxiliary bishops, but only infrequently as full bishops to U.S. dioceses. Their numbers, however, fail to reflect demographic reality. Although population projections indicate that by the year 2000 the majority of U.S. Catholics will be Hispanic, as of 1992 only 19 out of more than 360 bishops and only one out of some 45 archbishops in the United States were Hispanic—of these, two were Cubans, two Puerto Ricans, one Ecuadorian, one Venezuelan, two Spaniards, and two Mexicans. The balance were U.S.-born Hispanics.

In 1991, the Missionary Catechists of Divine Providence, the only religious order of Mexican American women, was granted total independence by the Vatican. Having begun as an organization for lay catechists in Houston, Texas, in the 1930s, the missionary catechists are dedicated to foment leadership among Hispanics in different dioceses of the Southwest.

✳ PROTESTANTISM AND HISPANICS

Latin America was missionary territory for the nineteenth-century U.S. Protestant churches. As the Latin American nations gained their independence from Catholic Spain, Protestant England's traditional foe, English-speaking missionaries, aware of the anticlericalism present in the independence movements south of the border decided that the time had come for the spiritual conquest of the region. Proselytism of Hispanics born in the United States was now a goal of the Protestant ministers who traveled south to the lands newly conquered from Mexico. Those who converted were valuable as Spanish-speaking leaders who could be sent to the promising mission fields of Mexico. A case in point was Alejo Hernández, a former Catholic priest who had converted to the Methodist faith and was ordained deacon in Corpus Christi, Texas, in 1871. Shortly after his ordination, he had to abandon the work he had begun in Texas among his own people to become a missionary in Mexico City. As in the case of the Catholic church after the U.S. takeover of Texas and the Southwest, the Protestant churches assumed that the native Hispanic population would disappear in time. Ministering to U.S. Hispanics also helped Anglo missionaries to learn the ways and the language of the people south of the border, whose conversion was their ultimate goal.

The level of preparation for Hispanic ministers was lower than that of their Anglo counterparts. A system of patronage developed in Texas and the Southwest whereby Hispanic congregations and ministers were made to depend upon their more enlightened and wealthier Anglo counterparts. According to Methodist Church Historian Edwin E. Sylvester, the essential patterns and structures of Hispanic American Protestantism in this region were fixed in the second half of the nineteenth century. Anglos controlled the churches and their institutions. Hispanic churches were not encouraged to develop self-determination, but to assimilate and accommodate to the customs and the institutional interests of the conquering culture. Hispanic leaders were trained out of expediency rather than out of respect for the values that their culture could bring to the churches.

In 1898, after the end of the Spanish-American War, Protestant missionaries descended upon Cuba and Puerto Rico, where they achieved a modicum of success. Some were born in Cuba or Puerto Rico and had converted as exiles in the United States. Catholicism was seen by many as the faith of the old oppressive order and Protestantism as a more enlightened faith.

Conversion, however, implied relinquishing traditional values. Cuban-born Protestant theologian and church historian Justo González explains in his book *Mañana* (1990) that for Hispanics to become Protestant entailed a surrender of their identity similar to that expected of Hispanic Catholics in the United States. Becoming Protestant required Americanization, partly because Catholicism was so ingrained in Hispanic culture. As González points out, when these Cuban and Puerto Rican Protestants migrated to the United States, they had a sense of alienation from both the Anglos and their own compatriots.

The seeds planted during the first part of the twentieth century began to root and by the 1930s a Spanish-speaking Protestant clergy was emerging. For Methodists and Presbyterians, a big stumbling block, then as now, was the integration of Hispanics into national conferences of their respective churches. Hispanics, wishing to preserve their cultural and linguistic identities, often fear being absorbed by the non-Hispanic majority in the conferences. One of the most successful of the mainstream Hispanic churches has been the Rio Grande Conference, which includes Hispanic Methodists in Texas and New Mexico. Its roots date back to the early 1930s when Alfredo Náñez, the first Hispanic to receive his B.D. degree from Southern Methodist University, and Francisco Ramos were selected as presiding elders of the Texas American Conference. In 1939, it became the Rio Grande Conference, a powerful group of churches that has chosen, in spite all pressures, to remain independent. Under similar historical circumstances, the Latin American Conference of Southern California opted to merge with the Anglo conferences, a move that has resulted in declining membership. The less structured nature of the Southern Baptists and the Pentecostals, whereby each congregation retains partial or total autonomy, has contributed to their increasing Hispanic membership, the only mainstream churches to experience such growth.

Pentecostalism, a brand of evangelical Christianity that is sweeping Central and South America, is growing in leaps and bounds among U.S. Hispanics. Its popularity seems to rest in the small-community atmosphere of the individual churches, which allows Hispanics a feeling of belonging. More particularly, because Pentecotalism does not dismantle for Hispanics the building blocks of their religious expression, Hispanic converts to Pentecostalism find in their new church room to express their religiosity. According to a study done in Chile by Lalive d'Epinay, although Pentecostalism disallows Catholic traditions such as processions and other external religious manifestations, it provides the convert with a highly emotional form of worship. The place that the saints and the Virgin occupied as protectors, intercessors, and healers of suffering humanity is now replaced with the healing powers of the Holy Spirit. Catholic clerical authority finds its counterpart in the authority that those who have received the baptism of the Holy Spirit acquire. Interestingly enough, the charismatic renewal movement in the Roman Catholic church, which like the Pentecostals stresses the worship of the third person of the Trinity (God the Holy Spirit), is most popular among Hispanics.

During the period of brown power activism in the 1960s, Hispanic Protestants tended to remain on the sidelines. But it must be noted that two of the early leaders of the Chicano movement were Reies Tijerina, a Pentecostal minister who fought for the rights of New Mexicans to their ancestral land grants, and Rudolfo "Corky" González, a Presbyterian leader. González, a former boxer who had served time for his political involvement in the struggle for Mexican American rights, was an early Chicano literary figure, having authored the important epic poem "Yo soy Joaquin."

✳ POPULAR RELIGIOSITY

Hispanics who lived in the territories occupied by the United States in the nineteenth century and those who migrated from Mexico and the other Spanish American countries have succeeded in preserving the religious traditions of their forefathers. Perhaps because of the almost universal scarcity of priests in the Spanish-speaking Americas, the family and the home have always been at the center of Hispanic religiosity. This religiosity is not necessarily derived from the teachings of childhood catechisms nor the homilies of parish priests. It is formed by assimilating and adapting the private religious practices that individuals observe within their extended family, which includes not only relatives, but friends and neighbors as well.

The religious instruction of the children, rosaries, novenas, *promesas* or *mandas* (the practice of making sacrificial offerings for some specific purpose), and the wearing of scapulars and medals occur or are promoted in the home usually at the behest of the grandmother or some other elderly female figure. For Hispanics, religion is often the concern of the women, who must look out for the spiritual well-being and even the salvation of their menfolks. In this context, it should be noted that in some cultures, particularly among Hispanics of Mexican origin, the *quinceañera* (fifteenth birthday) celebration, which marks the coming of age of the young girls, involves a mass or prayer service with a sermon that usually reminds the young woman of her future responsibilities as a Christian wife and mother.

Within the Hispanic household it is not unusual to find a place that functions as an altar. In creating the altar, the Hispanic woman tries to gather within the confines of her private domain symbols of the spiritual forces on which she depends for assistance in fulfilling her primary responsibility as caretaker of a family. The home altar might be nothing more than a religious picture before which candles are lit in a wordless form of prayer; it can be a statuette of a saint, of Christ or the Virgin on a table or a television set accompanied by a vase filled with flowers; or it can be elaborate, attempting to approximate an altar within a church, with a profusion of religious images, hand-embroidered cloths, candles, incense, holy water, and other objects of the Roman Catholic worship.

Veneration of the Virgin Mary in her different aspects is foremost for most Hispanic groups: Our Lady of Guadalupe and Our Lady of San Juan de los Lagos for the Mexicans, Our Lady of Providencia for the Puerto Ricans, La Caridadholid del Cobre for the Cubans, and Altagracia for the Dominicans, to name a few. Veneration of Our Lady of Sorrows (Dolores) is prevalent among all groups, particularly among women, who as mothers identify with the Virgin suffering for her son. The degree of identification with this aspect of the Virgin is manifest in a tradition observed by some Mexican Americans that involves visitation of a local image of the Virgin on Good Friday to offer condolences for the death of Christ. Another tradition that reveals the intimacy of the people with their celestial Mother is observed on February 2, the feast of the Purification of Mary. For Mexican Americans this is the day when the Holy Infant first sits up—"El Asentamiento del Niño." A *madrina* (godmother) is selected for the

Feast of the Crowning of Mary, Sacred Heart Cathedral, Houston, 1987. (Photograph by Curtis Dowell.)

Annual mass on the feast day of Our Lady of Guadalupe, Houston, Texas.

Child. She thus strengthens her bonds through godparenting with Our Lady. The madrina, often a young girl, dresses a doll-like image of the Infant with new clothes and helps him sit up. This feast concludes for the Mexicans the Christmas season, which begins with the apparition of Our Lady of Guadalupe on December 12.

The special meaning of the Virgin for Hispanics cannot be stressed enough. For the males she is the understanding mother who forgives and intercedes for her errant sons; for the women she sympathizes with the earthly travails of a mother, sister, or daughter. Even Protestants are not immune to the appeal of this veneration. Justo González, the Protestant historian, recounts how in his seminary days some of the students, wanting to ingratiate themselves with their teacher, began to mock the cult of Our Lady of Guadalupe. The old professor, a Mexican, stopped them with the admonition that they were free to tear down Roman Catholic dogma, but they should be careful of being disrespectful toward "mi virgencita" (my little Virgin).

Adoration of particular images of Christ is traditional among certain national groups: for Guatemalans there is El Cristo Negro de Esquipulas (The

Black Christ of Esquipulas); for Colombians, El Señor de los Milagros (The Lord of Miracles); and for Salvadorans, Cristo El Salvador (Christ the Savior). Additionally, the cult of the Sacred Heart of Jesus, representing the suffering aspect of Christ's human love for people, is universally popular. As noted previously, these cults invariably center on a bleeding, wounded representation of Jesus. It is not unusual for theologians or priests to bemoan Hispanics' stress on the dead rather than on the resurrected Christ.

Hispanics worship Jesus as a child, frequently under the name El Santo Niño de Atocha (The Holy Child of Atocha). This traditional cult dates back to the time of the Reconquest of Spain, when allegedly a child brought a basket of bread to Christian captives held in a Moslem prison. The child revealed himself to them as Jesus, who had come to bring them the bread of Holy Communion. Theorists claim that the fear of the early explorers and settlers of falling captive to the Indians is responsible for the popularity of the Niño de Atocha in the Americas. Similar reasons are adduced for the popularity of El Niño Perdido (Jesus lost and found in the temple by his parents).

According to Father Virgilio Elizondo, in a 1990 speech at Peabody University, the most popular saint among U.S. Hispanics is Martin of Porres, a seventeenth-century Dominican lay brother who was the illegitimate son of a black woman and a Spaniard. Martin chose to perform the most menial tasks at his convent and to personally feed and heal the poor.

The veneration of different Franciscan saints was propagated by the early missionaries, a great many of whom were members of the Franciscan order. Saint Francis of Assisi, founder of this order, and his close friend Saint Anthony of Padua have been popular since colonial days. Veneration of Saint Joseph dates back to the days of exploration and colonization, because he is the patron saint of expeditions. The same can be said about Saint Christopher, protector of travelers. Among Cuban Americans, the veneration of Saint Lazarus and Saint Barbara are very popular and more than likely related to the phenomenon of religious syncretism evident in Santería. *Velorios de santos*, celebrations on the eve of either saint's feast day, are often held in the homes of devotees.

Processions, pilgrimages, and other external manifestations are an important element of religious expression for Hispanics. In the United States, the feast of the patron saint of a national group or a town still calls for a solemn mass followed by different forms of merriment. Processions sometimes are held, but seldom do they go beyond the grounds of the church. Exceptions to this rule are the processions of Our Lady of Guadalupe in the Southwest and of La Caridad del Cobre in the Miami area.

Pilgrimages to the shrine of Our Lady of Guadalupe in Mexico City are routinely organized wherever large groups of Mexican Americans reside. Of great interest are the pilgrimages to the shrine of Our Lady of San Juan de los Lagos in Jalisco, Mexico, which dates back to colonial times and is popular among people in northern Mexico and the U.S. Southwest. The subject of this veneration is an image of the Immaculate Conception that since the early 1600s has been said to possess healing powers. Today a large shrine to the Virgin in the Texas border town of San Juan attracts many pilgrimages from within the United States. The shrine to La Caridad del Cobre facing Biscayne Bay in Coral Ga-

The celebration of the feast day of Our Lady of Caridad del Cobre, the patron of Cubans, in Houston, 1986. (Photograph by Curtis Dowell.)

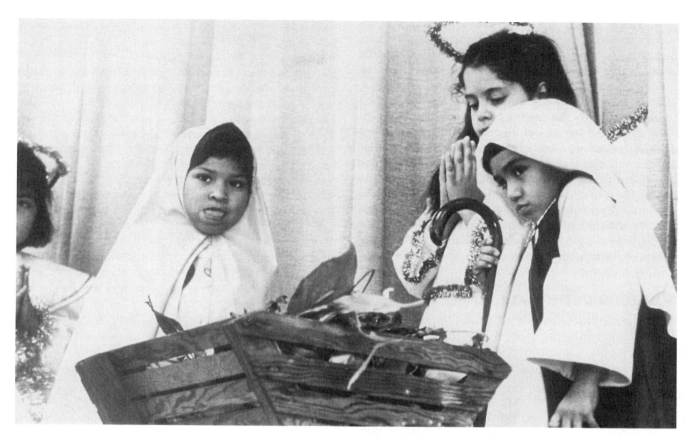

A Christmas *posada* sponsored by the Club Sembradores de la Amistad in Houston, 1988. (Photograph by Curtis Dowell.)

bles, Florida, built with funds collected among Cuban exiles in the 1960s, attracts Cuban American pilgrims from throughout the United States.

An integral part of many pilgrimages is the fulfilling of vows made by the faithful. This may involve making the final part of the journey on one's knees. Among Mexican Americans and some Central Americans, the tradition of the ex voto (gifts presented to a saint as a show of gratitude for a favor conceded) still remains. Colonial ex votos were often primitive drawings on tin or wood depicting the miracle performed by the saint and often included a written explanation. Modern ex votos can be photographs, bridal wreaths, baby shoes, letters of gratitude, and, in many cases, the traditional *milagrito* (a charm made out of tin, gold, or silver and shaped in the form of an arm, a leg, a baby, or a house, for instance). More graphic ex votos are crutches, leg braces, eyeglasses, and other devices that through supernatural intercession the presenter was able to discard. Both the magnificent shrine in San Juan, Texas, and the quaint Sanctuary of Chimayo in Chimayo, New Mexico, where the soil behind the chapel is said to have curative powers, are excellent examples of churches where this practice flourishes.

Mexican Americans have preserved to this day the traditional *posada,* a novena that ends on Christmas eve and dates back to colonial days. For nine nights a different neighborhood family serves as host for the posada. The "pilgrims," reenacting Mary and Joseph's search for lodging, knock at the designated home, singing a traditional hymn and asking for shelter, but are refused repeatedly. Finally, an innkeeper allows them into a home, a rosary is said, and refreshments are served. The *Pastorela*, a folk play dating to the colonial period that reenacts the adoration of the shepherds, is still presented in some Mexican American communities during this season.

In northern New Mexico, despite periods of persecution, the *penitentes* continue to observe their Holy Week traditions. The brothers, all laymen, gather in the "moradas," or secret meeting places. They still practice some sort of corporal punishment, if not the extreme forms of flagellation and crucifixion observed up through the nineteenth century. After commemoration of the death of Christ on Good Friday, "tinieblas" is observed. In the completely dark morada, fearful sounds meant to instill in the faithful a contemplation of the horrors of hell are made with traditional wood and metal noisemakers.

Mexican Americans as a whole reflect, less severely perhaps, the spirit of the penitentes. Without question, Ash Wednesday draws the biggest crowds of faithful to Catholic churches in Mexican American neighborhoods. According to Virgilio Elizondo's, 1990 speech at Peabody University, this penitential tendency reveals the feelings of inferiority of the Indian and the mestizo before the Spanish conquistador. At the opposite end of the spectrum is December 12, the feast of Our Lady of Guadalupe, which also draws multitudes to the churches. The faithful come to this feast to rejoice in their new hope, according to Elizondo. Symbols of this joy and this hope are the flowers with which they shower the Virgin and the traditional singing of "Las Mañanitas" (Morning Songs) by mariachi groups at the break of dawn.

✳ BEYOND ORTHODOXY

Despite all precautions by church authorities, pagan or non-Christian cults have always coexisted with orthodox practices. Herb shops known as "yerberías" by Mexican Americans and "botánicas" by people of Hispanic-Caribbean descent offer not only medicinal plants but also a variety of products used or recommended by spiritualists and faith healers.

Yerberos are herb specialists who know the medicinal qualities of plants and utilize them to cure physical ailments. They claim that the roots, leaves, and seeds of many herbs can offset snakebite, infertility, arthritis, kidney stones, and any other conceivable illness.

The *curandero* is also a folk healer, but one who can cure ailments of a physical and a spiritual nature. He can also remedy just about any human condition by utilizing the forces of good and evil. To bring about the desired results, the *curandero* uses, among other things, medicinal plants, eggs, candles, spells, perfumes, prayers, incense, holy water, and religious images. The curandero can, to name a few gifts, remove a spell that renders a person physically ill, make an unfaithful husband return to his wife, cure a child of "ojo" (the effects of someone's covetousness) or "susto" (fright), help someone have good luck in business or gambling, prevent or terminate pregnancies, and prepare amulets, oils, ointments, and charms. A curandero who does evil is technically a witch, a *brujo* or *bruja*. He uses the tools of his trade to do harm to others. Most curanderos, however, practice both white and black magic.

Spiritism and spiritualism sometimes coexist with curanderismo. Spiritism is a pseudoscience developed in Europe in the last century by Alan Kardec. By the 1860s it had reached Latin America. Spiritists invoke the spirits of the dead through me-

Diversity in Hispanic evangelism. (Photograph by Curtis Dowell.)

diums. They seek through these communications to give guidance, advice, and revelations of a supernatural nature. Spiritists may pride themselves in having access to the spirits of famous persons, such as Napoleon, Moctezuma, or Cleopatra, or they may "work" through ordinary spirits—a black slave, a great-grandmother, a fisherman. The services performed by a spirit relate to characteristics it allegedly had while alive. In this context it should be noted that Pancho Villa, the Mexican bandit and revolutionary, is a favorite among U.S. Hispanic spiritists. Villa, who was known for his hot temper, is called upon to chase away all evil spirits.

Spiritualism is a cult developed in Mexico, also during the nineteenth century. Spiritualists, unlike spiritists, are usually practicing Catholics. They consider themselves vehicles or "cajas" (boxes) for great religious figures and utilize these powers to heal. Among Mexican Americans, spiritualists often serve as channels for two late spiritualists: Don Pedrito Jaramillo, a curandero from Falfurrias, Texas, and the Niño Fidencio, from a village outside Monterrey, Nuevo León, Mexico. Today there is a popular movement of canonization of these healers by the Catholic church. Others have created separate cults. In the case of Fidencio, his devotees display images of Our Lady of Guadalupe and the Sacred Heart of Jesus bearing the healer's face where the face of Mary or Jesus would normally appear.

Santeros and *babalaos* are the curanderos and brujos of Caribbean Hispanics. They are the spiritual healers, advisers, and witches of the cults brought from the western coast of Africa by the Yoruba slaves, who were imported in large numbers to Cuba and Puerto Rico during the last century. Today Miami, Tampa, New York, and San Juan, Puerto Rico, are centers of this religious cult. Santería in the United States has spread beyond the Cuban and Puerto Rican communities to people of other national origins. It is already influencing and being influenced by Mexican American curanderismo. Santería merges elements from different Yoruba cults and Catholicism. African slaves, often forced to accept baptism by their masters, continued to worship their African gods under the external cult of the Christian saints. A less complex form of Santería is practiced by people from the Dominican Republic. This cult is a modified form of the Haitian voodoo.

A Catholic charismatic prayer meeting.

Santería is a cult of the *orishas* (deities), who control the forces of nature. The most popular of these gods are portrayed on candles and icons labeled Las Siete Potencias (the Seven Powerful Spirits). Ruling over all of these spiritual forces is Olofin, God the Creator. His son, Obatala, takes the form of Our Lady of Mercy, although he is also worshiped in his male aspect as Christ, and in some Mexican American areas as Our Lady of San Juan. Obatala is vengeful, powerful, and indifferent, and his devotees wear white. Chango, the god of war, snakes, storms, and thunder, takes the form of Saint Barbara. Her color is red, the color of blood. Babalu-aye, the god of healing, is Saint Lazarus, portrayed as a leper on crutches, often accompanied by two dogs. Ogun is John the Baptist, a wild man of the forest who controls things made out of iron. Ochun, Our Lady of la Caridad del Cobre, is the goddess of love. Yemaya rules the waters. She is Our Lady of Regla. Orula, St. Francis of Assisi, can see the future.

The babalaos are the diviners of Ifa, a system they learn after many years of study. Their powers come from the god Orula. They use the so called Rosary of Ifa (16 cowrie shells, mango seeds, or pieces of coconut shell) to determine which god or orisha is affecting a person's life. The babalao casts the shells or seeds and determines which of the possible 16 x 16 patterns they follow. Each pattern asks for a verse the babalao recites by rote and then interprets for the client. The babalao further determines what sacrifice must be offered to the orisha to appease him or win his favor and performs it. The client must pay him for both the divination and the sacrifice. The sacrifice varies. Different gods like different gifts in terms of food, perfumes, ornaments, and so forth. Before reaching most of these gods, however, one must appeal to Elegua, who under the guise of Saint Christopher, rules road crossings. Some of the saints demand animal sacrifices. In the case of Obatala, for example, because his favorite color is white, it must be a white hen or dove.

Santeros are the devotees of the different gods. After rigorous initiation, they become the son or daughter of the orisha and are endowed with special faculties. The orisha lives in a container within the santero's house (in the United States it is usually an expensive soup tureen in the orisha's favorite color). The santero wears the orisha's color, builds him elaborate altars, and celebrates his feast day with great fanfare and at great expense. The priests and priestesses of Santería are charged with directing the liturgy.

There are three "reglas," or ways to practice Santería. The one described above is the regla of Obatala, the most widespread. The regla Lucumi is similar to the regla Obatala, although there is less syncretism between African and Christian saints. The third way is the regla Mayombera or Palo Mayombé, which intermingles Congolese rites with spiritism or the cult of the dead. It is similar to Haitian voodoo in that it works more with the *ngangas* (the spirits of the dead) than with the orishas or deities. The practitioners (*mayomberos*) are feared as powerful magicians. They can exorcise evil spirits, cast spells, and make amulets. A client may chose to consult a babalao to determine the nature of his problem and go to a mayombero for the cure or solution.

A cult incorrectly connected with Santería is Nañiguismo. Nañigos are members of the Sociedad Abakúa, a secret society that combines religious elements of the Carabalí (Efik people from the coast of Calabar in southern Nigeria) and Freemasonry. Nañiguismo has its roots in the early days of slavery. Encouraged by the church, slaves grouped themselves into cabildos (religious brotherhoods dedicated to promoting the veneration of a saint). The cabildos helped slaves from the same African nations to maintain their ties unbeknownst to their white masters. The Sociedad Abakúa developed from a cabildo formed by the Carabalí. Nañiguismo, as it is commonly known, has survived to this date, thanks to its elaborate secret rules and rituals.

References

Bolton, Herbert Eugene. *Rim of Christendom: A Biography of Fray Eusebio Kino.* Tucson: University of Arizona Press, 1984.

Castañeda, Carlos. *Our Catholic Heritage in Texas,* seven volumes. Austin: Von Boeckmann-Jones, 1936–41.

Diaz Del Castillo, Bernal. *La verdadera historia de la conquista de la Nueva España.* México City: Porrúa, 1966.

Elizondo, Virgilio. *Galilean Journey: The Mexican American Promise.* Maryknoll, New York: Orbis Books, 1985.

Gannon, Michael V. *The Cross in the Sand: The Early Catholic Church in Florida, 1513–1870.* Gainesville: University Presses of Florida, 1983.

González, Justo. *Mañana: Christian Theology from a Hispanic Perspective.* Nashville: Abingdon Press, 1990.

Goodpasture, H. McKennie. *Cross and Sword: An Eyewitness History of Christianity in Latin America.* Maryknoll, New York: Orbis Books, 1989.

Kessell, John L. *Kiva, Cross and Crown: The Pecos Indians and New Mexico, 1540–1840.* Albuquerque: University of New Mexico Press, 1987.

McWilliams, Carey. *North From Mexico: The Spanish-Speaking People of the United States.* Westport, Connecticut: Greenwood Press, 1968.

Macklin, June, and Margarite B. Melville, eds. "All the Good and Bad in this World." In *Twice a Minority: Mexican American Women.* St. Louis: Mosby, 1980: 127–148.

Mirandé, Alfredo. *The Chicano Experience: An Alternative Perspective.* Notre Dame: University of Notre Dame Press, 1985.

Palou, Fr. Francisco. *Vida de Fr. Junípero Serra y Misiones de la California Septentrional.* Mexico City: Editorial Porrúa, 1975.

Pena, Silvia Novo, and Robert Flores, eds. *Interiors: Secular Aspects of Religion.* Houston: Houston Public Libraries, 1982.

Pollak-Eltz. *Cultos afroamericanos.* Caracas: Universidad Católica Andrés Bello, 1977.

Sandoval, Moisés. *On the Move: A History of the Hispanic Church in the United States.* Maryknoll, New York: Orbis Books, 1990.

Steele, Thomas J. *Santos and Saints: The Religious Folk Art of Hispanic New Mexico.* Santa Fe, New Mexico: Ancient City Press, 1974.

Terrell, John Upton. *Pueblos, Gods and Spaniards.* New York: Dial Press, 1973.

Silvia Novo Pena

12

Military

✳ U.S. Revolutionary War ✳ Mexican War for Independence from Spain ✳ Mexican-American War
✳ U.S. Civil War ✳ World War I ✳ World War II ✳ Conflicts in Korea and Vietnam
✳ Outstanding Hispanics in the Military

The history of Hispanics in military service in North America begins before the founding of the 13 British colonies. It includes service under at least five flags: those of the King of Spain, the Republic of Mexico, the Republic of Texas, the Confederacy and the United States of America—not to mention the Hispanics that lived in the southern portions of what would become the United States under British and French rule. The exploration and colonization of the areas of today's United States that were once New Spain and later Mexico—much of the Southeast, Southwest and West (See chapter on Spanish Explorers and Colonizers)—was accomplished by soldiers in the service of Spain. Although many of the first explorers of the Floridas and the Atlantic and Gulf coasts were military men from Spain, later exploration and especially colonization was effected over a period of three centuries by people born in the Americas, many of whom already were the product of mixed racial heritage, such as mestizos and mulattoes, as well as full-blooded American Indians and Africans who had been Hispanicized. The Spanish pattern of settling the frontier was to establish a military fort, or presidio *alongside a mission for evangelizing and acculturating the natives, as well as to lay out towns as population centers for the agricultural exploitation of the surrounding fields. This basic pattern not only led to extensive military presence throughout the Southwest and Southeast, but also to the development of a racially mixed population, including the ranks of the military.*

There were other Spanish traditions and practices, moreover, that also led to racial and ethnic diversity in the military. The Spanish attitude about race was quite distinct from that of the British. Since the Roman domination of the Iberian Peninsula, slavery was seen as the result of spoils of war—not as an elaborate ideology of inferiority of the enslaved. Under Spanish law and practice, slaves had certain rights, and Spanish culture and the Catholic church were more disposed to releasing slaves than was British culture and Protestant religions. Slaves were seen as people who should share in the salvation of the Christian religion. They could have the opportunity to earn their freedom, progress independently in trades and professions, and, while still being slaves, even move up in the ranks of the military. By the year 1600, there already existed a black Spanish militia in Florida. Many of the colonists of Florida were free black craftsmen and black soldiers in the Spanish army. The black militia comprised both free and enslaved blacks serving as soldiers and officers. In fact, by 1738, the first black commander of a Spanish regiment had been named in lands that would become part of the United States. He was a runaway slave by the name of Francisco Menéndez. Originally a Mandingo from West Africa, Menéndez escaped from English slavery in the Carolinas. After assisting Yamassee Indians in battle, they helped him to reach the Spanish sanctuary for runaway slaves in St. Augustine, Florida. He was betrayed by an Indian and sold into Spanish slavery as a soldier. He became an officer while still a slave, and in 1738 was freed and made commander of the all-black regiment of soldiers at Fort Mose, just north of St. Augustine. Captain Menéndez held the position until 1763, when Florida became a British colony and the inhabitants of Ft. Mose were evacuated to Cuba.*

✳ U.S. REVOLUTIONARY WAR

During the Revolutionary War, the Spanish army assisted the cause of U.S. independence from England by engaging in direct combat with the British

273

in the South and especially in the Gulf of Mexico, cutting off supply lines and otherwise harassing the "Redcoats." One of the most outstanding and effective supporters of the revolutionary effort was governor of Louisiana Bernardo de Gálvez, who engaged British forces repeatedly for three years along the Gulf of Mexico, destroying their forts, capturing Mobile and Pensacola, and generally rendering great support to the Continental Army. Gálvez's victory at Pensacola, in particular, made the American victory at Yorktown possible. (In 1980, the U.S. government commemorated the Hispanic contribution to the American War of Independence by issuing a stamp recognizing General Bernardo de Gálvez's 1780 victory at the Battle of Mobile.)

One of the first, if not the first, Hispanic Revolutionary War hero was Jorge Farragut, a seaman born on the Spanish island of Minorca who joined the South Carolina Navy as a lieutenant and fought at the battle of Savannah (1779) and at the second defense of Charleston (1780), where he was captured. After being freed, Farragut joined the Continental Army and earned the rank of major. He stayed in the newly independent United States, married and fathered a son who would become the first admiral of the United States Navy—David Farragut.

✳ MEXICAN WAR FOR INDEPENDENCE FROM SPAIN

Hispanics not only played a role in the American Revolution, but Hispanics from the Southwest also participated in the war to free Mexico from Spain. In fact, in 1811, a captain in the militia in Texas, Juan Bautista Casas, became the first martyr for Mexican independence from areas that would become the United States. Casas led a local revolt in San Antonio, Texas, against the Spanish governor, Colonel Manuel de Salcedo. Casas seized the governor and officials, proclaiming support for Mexico's revolution and declaring himself the governor of Mexican Texas. Casas was captured and executed by Spanish soldiers and his head was exhibited at the central plaza as a warning to other sympathizers of the revolution led by Miguel Hidalgo (See Historical Overview chapter). In 1812, Bernardo Gutiérrez de Lara became the first hero from the area in the struggle for Mexican independence. In June, Gutiérrez de Lara led his men in taking the towns of Nacogdoches and Salcedo from the royalist garrison. Gutiérrez also sent emissaries to other parts of Texas and to the Rio Grande Valley to spread the word of the revolution.

✳ MEXICAN-AMERICAN WAR

Later, in 1836, when Texas sought its independence from Mexico, numerous Hispanic soldiers distinguished themselves in battles against the central government in Mexico, with Lorenzo de Zavala and Juan N. Seguín emerging as leaders; later the former was elected vice president of the Texas Republic and the latter mayor of San Antonio. Mexico lost Texas and, in the 1846–1848 war, the rest of what would become the Southwest and West of the United States, with Hispanics often ambivalent or engaged in fighting with relatives and friends. Some of the Mexican commanders of forces in California and New Mexico, despite their defeat, often made a successful transition to American rule, and served in the territorial and state governments and their militia.

✳ U.S. CIVIL WAR

Soon after the Mexican War, the United States engaged in its own Civil War. This again had the effect of dividing the Hispanics of the Southwest, with some from Texas, such as Santos Benavides (who rose to become the highest ranking Hispanic in the Confederate Army), distinguishing themselves in service to the Confederacy, while others, especially in New Mexico and California, served the cause of the Union. In 1863, the U.S. government authorized the formation of the first Hispanic battalion during the Civil War. The First Battalion of Native Cavalry was formed to take advantage of the extraordinary horsemanship of the Mexican American Californians, under the command of Major Salvador Vallejo. Some 469 Mexican Americans served in the four companies of the battalion throughout California and Arizona. Also for the Union, four independent militia companies were formed in New Mexico, known by their commanders' names (Gonzales, Martínez, Tafolla, and Perea). Hispanics served significantly in southern battalions in Alabama, Florida, Louisiana, and South Carolina for the Confederacy. Because the noteworthy horsemanship of Hispanics during the Civil War had become legendary, Teddy Roosevelt later recruited many of his Rough Riders for the Spanish-American War from Hispanics in New Mexico and Texas.

In 1864, Diego Archuleta (1814–1884) became the first Hispanic Brigadier General of the United States, commanding the New Mexican militia during the Civil War. Archuleta was born into a prominent New Mexican family and was educated in Durango, Mexico. From 1843 to 1845, he served in the Mexican National Congress as a delegate from New Mexico. After conquest of New Mexico by the United States, Archuleta took part in two unsuccessful rebellions in 1846 and 1847. After the Mexican-American War, Archuleta took the oath of allegiance to the United States, served in the state assembly and became a brigadier general for the Union. In 1857, he was appointed a U.S. Indian agent, a position to which he was reappointed by President Abraham Lincoln after the Civil War.

During the Civil War, Hispanics also emerged in the intelligence service for the first time. The first Hispanic spy for the United States was Captain Román Antonio Baca, an officer in the New Mexico Volunteers—a unit that was incorporated into the Union forces during the Civil War. The first Hispanic female spy in U.S. history was the Cuban-born woman who disguised herself as a Confederate soldier and served as Lieutenant Harry Buford. Loretta Janet Vásquez left her married, domestic life in San Antonio, Texas, without her husband's knowledge, and fought at such battles as Bull Run, Ball's Bluff, and Fort Donelson. After her female identity had been detected twice and she was discharged, she began her life as a spy working in male and female guise.

During the Civil War, the long tradition of extraordinary valor of Hispanics in combat for the United States began. In 1865, the first Hispanic Medal of Honor winner in history was awarded to Philip Bazaar, a seaman born in Chile, South America, who on January 15, 1865, courageously engaged in an assault on a fort from a six-man boat. It was during the Civil War, too, that the first Admiral of the United States Navy, David, G. Farragut (1801–1872), the son of a Spanish immigrant, was commissioned, on July 26, 1866. Farragut was appointed a midshipman at the age of nine. As a commander during the Civil War, Farragut was engaged in numerous battles, including the capture of New Orleans, Vicksburg, and Mobile. It was after the tremendous victory that he had led at Mobile Bay (where he is reported to have said, "Damn the torpedoes! Full speed ahead!") that he was commissioned an admiral. In today's Navy, the guided missile destroyer USS *Farragut, DDG-37,* bears his name.

✳ WORLD WAR I

Hispanics have fought bravely in every war in which the United States was engaged. As mentioned above, their service was distinguished in the Spanish-American War, despite the popular press questioning their loyalty to the United States because of confronting an Hispanic enemy. During World War I, Hispanics again rendered extraordinary service; but at least one Hispanic soldier who deserved the Medal of Honor was denied the nation's highest award. Private Marcelino Serna was awarded the Distin-

guished Service Cross for single-handedly capturing 24 German soldiers on September 12, 1918. The Albuquerque native was not recommended for a Medal of Honor because he was only a "buck" private and could not read and write English well enough to sign reports.

✳ WORLD WAR II

It was during World War II, however, that Hispanic soldiers as a group made military history. Hispanics enlisted in force, perhaps as means of proving their Americanism; for to that date, many in the United States persisted in looking upon Hispanics as foreigners. So many Hispanics enlisted and were drafted, in fact, that entire neighborhoods were depopulated of their young men. In Silvis, Illinois, just west of Chicago, eight young Mexican American men on one short street gave up their lives for their country in World War II. A total of 84 men from this street saw action in World War II, the Korean war and the Vietnam war. This street reportedly contributed more men to service, 57, during World War II and the Korean war, than any place of comparable size in the United States. The street, which was once Second Street, was renamed Hero Street.

During World War II, Mexican American soldiers, in particular, won proportionately more Medals of Honor and other recognition for valor than any other ethnic group—far exceeding their percentage of the population of the armed services or Hispanic population of the United States. The first Hispanic Medal of Honor winner of World War II was Private José P. Martínez, who took part in the American invasion of the Aleutian Islands in May 1943. The Taos, New Mexico, native led his out-numbered platoon in fighting Japanese soldiers in their trenches, and was finally mortally wounded in his valiant attacks. A Disabled American Veterans chapter in Colorado and an American Legion Post in California are named in his honor. Another Mexican American made national news and passed into folklore and popular culture for his valor in action. He was Guy Gabaldón (1927–), a Mexican American born in Los Angeles who was adopted by a Japanese American family. His heroism was demonstrated at the battle for Saipan Island, and later became the subject of a Hollywood film: *From Hell to Eternity*. In 1970, Gabaldón returned his Navy Cross and Purple Heart to the government in protest of discrimination against minorities in the United States.

The story of Hispanic valor in American wars, and particularly World War II (when Mexican American youth, for example, were being used as scapegoats by the press and subjected to street violence at the hands of soldiers and sailors in southern California) had been a well-kept secret. And even when the documentation was finally available, there was very little support for publicizing it. Raúl Morín (1913–1967), a Mexican American veteran and commercial artist from Lockhart, Texas, researched and wrote *Among the Valiant,* the first book to document the heroism and valor of Mexican Americans in the armed services during World War II. However, Morín was denied publication of the book for ten years until the American G.I. Forum, a civil rights organization made up of Mexican American veterans, backed its publication and distribution in 1963. After the book's successful publication, Morín remained active in Mexican American and Democratic political organization and in veterans affairs. In 1968, a veterans' memorial in East Los Angeles was officially named Raúl Morín Memorial Square.

World War II was a watershed in Mexican American history. After so many young men from the barrios across the Southwest had fought so bravely on foreign soil for *their* country, they believed they had earned the right to enjoy the full benefits of American citizenship. The veterans returned to the Southwest, many of them furthering their education under the G.I. Bill, and pursued the American Dream. They were now unwilling to tolerate discrimination, the way many of their parents were forced to as immigrants. More than ever before in history, thus, Mexican Americans founded and supported a wide range of civil rights and political organizations, and it was the World War II veterans that took the lead. One of the sparks that ignited the post-war Mexican American civil rights movement was the refusal of authorities in Three Rivers, Texas, to allow the burial in the city cemetery of Private Félix Longoria, who had lost his life in the Pacific. This outrageous case of segregation became notorious among Mexican American veterans, whose American G.I. Forum, a nascent political action group formed by veteran Dr. Héctor García Pérez, protested to Congressman Lyndon Baines Johnson. The congressman, who later as president would further the cause of civil rights for Hispanics, had Longoria's remains flown to Washington, D.C., and buried at Arlington National Cemetery. The American G.I. Forum grew into one of the largest civil rights organizations in U.S. Hispanic history; it is still very active today.

✳ CONFLICTS IN KOREA AND VIETNAM

As mentioned above, the Korean war saw continued Hispanic valor and leadership, with Hispanics becoming more represented among the ranks of officers and even the prestigious and previously segregated Air Corps. The Korean war saw the emergence of the first Hispanic "ace": Colonel Manuel J. Fernández Jr., who from September 1952 to May 1953 flew 125 combat missions in an F-86, engaging Communist MIG aircraft. On his fifth victory, he became an "ace" and ended the war with 14.5 "kills" to his credit. His 14.5 air victories placed him sixtieth among the top U.S. Air Force aces of the two world wars and the Korean conflict combined. During the Vietnam war, another pilot, Lieutenant Junior Grade Everett Alvarez Jr. became the longest held POW in U.S. history. He was also the first U.S. serviceman shot down over North Vietnam. The Salinas, California, native was captured after his plane was shot down over the Gulf of Tonkin, North Vietnam, and remained imprisoned for eight and a half years. He was repatriated by the North Vietnamese in February 1973. In 1981, President Ronald Reagan appointed war hero Everett Alvarez the first Hispanic deputy director of the Veterans Administration. The previous year, the president had appointed him deputy director of the Peace Corps.

Beginning during the Korean conflict, and continuing to the present, more and more Hispanics were promoted to officer rank in the armed services. It was not until the mid-1970s, however, that the military academies began graduating Hispanic officers regularly. Currently, there are many Hispanic officers commanding soldiers of all ethnic backgrounds; and there are Hispanics represented at the highest ranks among generals and admirals. In 1964, Horacio Rivero became the first Hispanic four-star admiral in the Navy. The native of Puerto Rico graduated from the United States Naval Academy, saw action, and was decorated in World War II. He later rose to Commander of Allied Forces in Southern Europe for NATO. In 1976, Richard E. Cavazos became the first Hispanic general in the United States Army. A Texas native, Cavazos distinguished himself as a commander in Vietnam and later served extensively in the Pentagon and as a commander at Fort McPherson, Georgia. In 1979 also, Hispanics saw one of their own named to the highest armed service position ever: Edward Hidalgo became the first Hispanic to serve a Secretary of the Navy. His two-year stint followed a career in which he had served as special assistant to the Secretary of the Navy, special assistant for economic affairs to the Director of the U.S. Information Agency and General Counsel, and congressional liaison for the Agency. From 1977 to 1979, he served as assistant secretary of the Navy. Hidalgo was born in Mexico City and immigrated to the United States as a child.

Santos Benavides.

✱ OUTSTANDING HISPANICS IN THE MILITARY

Roy P. Benavides (1935–)

Born on May 8, 1935, in Cuero, Texas, Benavides was educated in southeastern Texas and received his B.A. degree in 1981 from Wharton County Junior College. He served as a Green Beret in the U.S. Army from 1952 to 1976, when he retired as a master sergeant. One of the country's most decorated soldiers of the Vietnam War, his medals include the Congressional Medal of Honor, the Purple Heart with an Oak Leaf Cluster, the Defense Meritorious Service Medal, and the Army Commendation Medal. His valor and life story have been celebrated in books and in the founding of the Roy P. Benavides Airborne Museum. Benavides, with coauthor Oscar Griffin, published his autobiography, *The Three Wars of Roy Benavides*, in 1986.

Santos Benavides (1823–?)

Born on November 1, 1823, in Laredo, Texas, Benavides became the patriarch of a family that would render military service and even service in the Texas Rangers for generations. As a young man he partici-

pated in Mexican civil war battles in the Rio Grande Valley. In 1856, he became mayor of Laredo and a leading financial figure. When the Civil War broke out, he rose rapidly to the rank of colonel, thus becoming the highest rankling Hispanic officer in the Confederacy. He commanded his own regiment, known as the "Benavides Regiment"; it was the only sizable force defending Texas from the Union. And he used that force to drive Union forces back from Brownsville, Texas. After the war, he and his brothers, who fought alongside him, returned to civilian life.

Robert Léon Cárdenas (1920–)

Air Force Brigadier General Robert León Cárdenas was born in Mérida, Yucatán, Mexico, on March 10, 1920. He received his early education in San Diego and his B.S. degree in Mechanical Engineering from the University of New Mexico in 1955. Cárdenas served in the Army from 1941 until 1989. Among his many military awards are the Air Medal with four oak leaf clusters, Joint Service Commendation Medal, Air Force Outstanding Unit Award with two oak leaf clusters, Legion of Merit with oak leaf cluster, Distinguished Flying Cross, the Purple Heart, and others. He also received the Spanish

Robert Léon Cárdenas.

Grand Cross of the Order of Aeronautical Merit. Since his retirement in 1989, Cárdenas has served as a member of the California Veterans Board.

Richard E. Cavazos (1929–)

Richard E. Cavazos became the first Hispanic general in the United States Army in 1976. A Texas native, Cavazos distinguished himself as a commander in Vietnam and later served extensively in the Pentagon and as a commander at Fort McPherson, Georgia. Born in Kingsville, Texas, on January 31, 1929, he received a Bachelor of Science degree in Geology at Texas Tech University and was commissioned a second Lieutenant in 1951. During his 30 years of military service, he attended various military training schools and commanded forces in Vietnam as well as served in the Pentagon. In 1976, he became commanding general of the 9th Infantry Division and Post Commander of Fort Lewis, Washington. From 1982 to 1984, General Cavazos was Commander of the United States Armed Forces Command, Fort McPherson, Georgia. Under his command, combat troops were deployed to Grenada. He retired in June, 1984. During his career, he re-

Richard E. Cavazos.

ceived the Distinguished Service Cross with oak leaf cluster, the Silver Star with oak leaf cluster, the Defense Superior Service Medal, the Legion of Merit with oak leaf cluster, the Distinguished Flying Cross, the Purple Heart, and many others.

Pedro A. del Valle (1893–)

The first Hispanic to rise to the rank of general in the United States Marine Corps was Pedro A. del Valle, who was born on August 28, 1893, in San Juan, Puerto Rico. Del Valle graduated from the U.S. Naval Academy in 1915 and served on the USS *Texas* during World War I. During his career at a variety of duty posts in the U.S. and abroad, including service in Nicaragua and Cuba, Del Valle rose up through the ranks. During World War II, he served as Commanding Officer, 11th Marines (Artillery), and assisted in the seizure and defense of Guadalcanal, for which he was awarded the Legion of Merit. From May to July, 1943, he served as Commander of Marine forces, less aviation, on Guadalcanal, Tulagi, Russel and Florida Islands. In 1944, he served as Commanding General, Third Corps Artillery, Third Amphibious Corps. He participated in the Guam operation and was awarded the Gold Star. He received a Distinguished Service Medal for his command in the Okinawa operation in 1945. After the war, Del Valle served as Inspector as General and later as Director of Personnel for the Marine Corps. He retired in 1948; whereupon he was advanced to lieutenant general on the retired list.

Francisco de Miranda (1756–1816)

Francisco de Miranda was a Venezuelan officer who served under Bernardo de Gálvez in the gulf campaigns in support of the American Revolution. Educated and trained as an officer in Spain, he served as a captain under Gálvez in the campaign which returned the lower Mississippi River to Spanish control. He later participated in the siege and capture of Pensacola. From Cuba, he was instrumental in obtaining supplies for the French Admiral de Grasse, who sailed to the Chesapeake Bay to assist in the American capture of Yorktown. After participating in the American Revolution and becoming inspired by all of those ideas of "liberty, fraternity, equality," Miranda founded the American Lodge in London in 1797, whose membership swore allegiance to democracy and was to work for the independence of the Spanish American colonies. In 1806, Miranda tried to liberate Venezuela by embarking from New York with a group of 200 soldiers. When they disembarked in Coro, Venezuela, they did not find the necessary support and the mission failed. Miranda returned to England, and from there pre-

Francisco de Miranda.

tion he held until his retirement in 1957. General Quesada died on March 12, 1958.

David G. Farragut (1801–1872)

The most distinguished Hispanic soldier in the Union forces during the Civil War was David G. Farragut, who became the first Admiral of the United States Navy. Born in Campbell's Station, Tennessee, on July 5, 1801, the son of an Hispanic immigrant, Jorge Farragut, who had distinguished himself in the American Revolution and the War of 1812, David G. Farragut was appointed a midshipman in the U.S. Navy at the age of nine. At the age of 13, he served aboard the USS *Essex* during the War of 1812. During the Mexican War, he commanded a sloop-of-war, the Saratoga, but saw no action. In 1854, Farragut established the Mare Island Navy Yard near San Francisco. During the Civil War, he took New Orleans after a furious battle in 1862, and then proceeded up the Mississippi River to capture Vicksburg and, through attacks on Port Hudson, was able to break the Confederate supply routes. Farragut returned to Gulf action and, in 1864, despite heavy defense from forts, torpedoes and iron-clads, Farragut took Mobile, Alabama. It was at this battle

pared the liberation of his country with Simón Bolívar. When Miranda returned to Venezuela in 1810, he was arrested and sent to Spain, where he died in a Cádiz jail on July, 14, 1816.

Luis R. Esteves (1893–1958)

Luis R. Esteves was the first Puerto Rican to graduate from the United States Military Academy at West Point, in 1915. Born in 1893 in Aguadilla, Puerto Rico, before the American occupation, he obtained his elementary and secondary education under American military rule of the island and, without his parents' knowledge, took the test and was admitted to West Point. After graduating, he rose through the ranks to become a Brigadier General in 1937. During World War I, he served in Puerto Rico training officers for service—the draft laws had recently been applied to Puerto Rico, and he served as instructor and commander of three officer training camps which produced the officers who led more than 20,000 men from the island. In 1919, he organized the first Puerto Rican National Guard, commanding its first battalion and its first regiment. In 1937, Esteves was made Adjutant General, a posi-

Luis R. Esteves.

David G. Farragut.

that he was reported to have uttered the famous phrase, "Damn the torpedoes! Full speed ahead!" Farragut was commissioned Admiral of the Navy on July 26, 1866, and took command of the European Squadron.

Héctor García Pérez (1914–)

Héctor García Pérez, the Mexican American civil rights leader, was born on January 17, 1914, in Llera, Tamaulipas, Mexico. Educated in the United States, after his parents immigrated to Texas, he received his B.A. in 1936 and his M.D. in 1940, both from the University of Texas. During World War II he served with distinction in the Army Medical Corps, earning the Bronze Star and six Battle Stars. At the end of the war, he opened a medical practice in Corpus Christi and, outraged at the refusal of local authorities to bury a Mexican American veteran in a local city cemetery, he organized the American G.I. Forum, which is still one of the largest and most influential Hispanic civil rights organizations. García became the most effective Hispanic veteran in working for the peacetime advancement of his people. Besides becoming active in a wide variety of

civil rights organizations, García also became active in the Democratic Party and was appointed to the Democratic National Committee in 1954. In the 1960 presidential campaign, García became the national coordinator of the Viva Kennedy Clubs, and he was later appointed to various national positions by presidents Kennedy and Johnson. In 1967, President Johnson named García alternate delegate to the United Nations with the rank of ambassador, and he also appointed him the first Mexican American member of the United States Commission on Civil Rights. In 1965, the president of Panama awarded García the Order of Vasco Núñez de Balboa in recognition of his services to humanity. In 1984, he was awarded the United States of America Medal of Freedom.

Diego E. Hernández (1934–)

Vice Admiral Diego E. Hernández was born in San Juan, Puerto Rico, on March 25, 1934. He graduated from the Illinois Institute of Technology in with a B.S. in 1955 and also received an M.S. in International Affairs in 1969 from George Washington University; that same year he also attended the U.S. Naval War College. Among his important command

Diego E. Hernández.

Edward Hidalgo.

posts was that of Commanding Officer on the aircraft carrier USS *John F. Kennedy* from 1980 to 1981, after which he served as chief of staff of the Naval Air Forces Atlantic Fleet until 1982. From 1986 to 1989, he served as deputy commander-in-chief, U.S. Space Command. Hernández became a vice admiral in 1955. Among his decorations are the Distinguished Service Medal with Gold Star, the Distinguished Flying Cross, the Purple Heart and numerous others. He also holds decorations from abroad: The Venezuelan Naval Order of Merit and the Peruvian Cross of Naval Merit.

Edward Hidalgo (1912–

In 1979, Edward Hidalgo became the first Hispanic to serve as Secretary of the Navy. Born in Mexico City on October 12, 1912, he came with his family to the United States as a child. He graduated from Holy Cross College in 1933 and from Columbia Law School in 1936. In 1959, he also received a degree in Civil Law from the University of Mexico. From 1942 to 1943, Hidalgo was assigned to the State Department as a legal advisor to the U.S. Ambassador in Montevideo, Uruguay. From 1943 to 1945, he served

as an air combat intelligence officer on the carrier USS *Enterprise,* and later served as Special Assistant to the Secretary of the Navy. From 1946 to 1965, he developed his private law practice in Mexico City, but then in 1965 was named Special Assistant to the Secretary of the Navy. He later took on positions at the U.S. Information Agency, and was back as an Assistant to the Secretary of the Navy when he, himself, was named Secretary in 1979.

Benjamin F. Montoya (1935–)

Rear Admiral Benjamin F. Montoya was born in Indio, California, on May 24, 1935. He graduated with a B.S. degree in Naval Science from the U.S. Naval Academy in 1958; he also received a B.S. degree in Civil Engineering from Rensselaer Polytech in 1960 and an M.S. degree in Environmental Engineering from Georgia Institute of Technology in 1968. He received his law degree from Georgetown University in 1981. Montoya served as a rear admiral from 1958 to 1989, whereupon he retired from the service and became the manager of the Sacramento division of the Pacific Gas and Electric Company. Since 1991, he has served as senior vice president and general manager of Gas Supply for the same

Benjamin F. Montoya.

Horacio Rivera.

company. Among his military honors are the following: Legion of Merit, Meritorious Service Medal, Bronze Star with Combat V, the Navy Commendation Medal and the Vietnam Service Medal with three bronze stars. In 1989, he was named Hispanic Engineer of the Year.

Horacio Rivera (1910–)

Horacio Rivera became the first Hispanic to rise to the rank of four-star admiral in modern times (Farragut has the distinction of being the first U.S. admiral). Born in Ponce, Puerto Rico, on May 16, 1910, Rivero graduated from the United States Naval Academy in 1931, and began serving on a variety of cruisers and battleships. During World War II, he saw considerable action in the Pacific, and participated in the Iwo Jima and Okinawa campaigns and the first carrier raids on Tokyo. He was awarded the Legion of Merit for saving his ship and preventing loss of life during a fierce typhoon in 1945. In 1955, he was promoted to Rear Admiral and to Vice Admiral in 1962. In 1964, he was promoted to Admiral and became Vice Chief of Naval Operations. In 1968, he commanded NATO forces as Commander in Chief of

Allied Forces, Southern Europe. He retired in 1972 and was later named ambassador to Spain.

Carmelita Schemmenti (1936–)

Carmelita Schemmenti is the first Hispanic female general in the armed services. Born in Albuquerque, New Mexico, on December 16, 1936, she received a Nursing degree from the Regina School of Nursing in Albuquerque and a B.S. in Nursing from the University of Pittsburgh; she also received a Master of Public Health degree from the University of North Carolina. Today she is a Brigadier General in the United States Air Force and has won numerous awards, including the Legion of Merit, the Air Force Commendation Medal, the Air Force Outstanding Unit Award, the National Defense Service Medal and others.

Juan N. Seguín (1806–1890)

One of the founders of the Republic of Texas, Juan N. Seguín was born into a prominent family of French extraction in San Antonio, Texas. At the age of 18, he was elected mayor of San Antonio. One of the developers of a nationalist spirit in Texas, Seguín led Texans in opposition to the centrist

Carmelita Schemmenti.

Juan N. Seguín.

Antonio, where he commanded the military post there and served as mayor. In 1838, he was elected to the Texas senate, and in 1840 again to the mayoralty if San Antonio. He was active in defending Tejanos against profiteering Anglos that were rushing into the state to make their fortune at all costs. Unjustly accused of favoring invading Mexican forces and betraying the Santa Fe Expedition to foment revolt in New Mexico against Mexico, Anglos forced Seguín to resign as mayor in April, 1842. He moved with his family across the Río Grande into Mexico in fear of reprisals. In Mexico, he was jailed and forced to serve in the Mexican army, including in battle against the United States during the Mexican War. In 1848, he once again moved to Texas, only to return to live out his days in Nuevo Laredo, Mexico, from 1867 until his death in 1890.

References

Gleiter, Jan, and Kathleen Thompson. *David Farragut.* Milwuakee, WI: Raintree Publications, 1989.

Gómez-Quiñones, Juan. *Roots of Chicano Politics, 1600–1940.* Albuquerque: University of New Mexico Press, 1994.

Henderson, Ann L., and Gary R. Mormino, eds. *Spanish Pathways in Florida.* Sarasota, FL: Pineapple Press, 1991.

Hispanics in U.S. History. 2 vols. Englewood Cliffs, NJ: Globe Book Company, 1989.

Kanellos, Nicolás. *Hispanic Firsts.* Detroit: Gale Inc., forthcoming.

Kanellos, Nicolás, with Cristelia Pérez. *Chronology of Hispanic American History.* Detroit: Gale Inc., 1995.

Meier, Matt S., and Feliciano Rivera. *Dictionary of Mexican American History,* Westport, CN: Greenwood Press, 1981.

Office of the Secretary of Defense, *Hispanics in America's Defense.* Washington, DC: U.S. Printing Office, 1990.

Nicolás Kanellos

government of Antonio López de Santa Anna in the 1830s. In the struggle for independence from Mexico, Seguín served as a captain in the Texas cavalry, eventually achieving the rank of lieutenant colonel. He fought with distinction at the Battle of San Antonio in 1835 and at the Battle of San Jacinto in 1836. He was among the defenders of the Alamo, but averted his demise because he was sent for reenforcement. After the war, Seguín returned to San

⓭

Law and Politics

✳ Origins of Hispanics in the United States ✳ The Development of U.S. Immigration Law
✳ The Current Debate over U.S. Immigration Law ✳ The Legalization Program
✳ Employment Discrimination ✳ Police Brutality ✳ Federal Legislation Affecting Hispanic Americans
✳ Important Cases Affecting Hispanic Americans ✳ Hispanics in the Legal Profession
✳ Hispanics in the U.S. Judiciary ✳ Presidential Appointment of Hispanics to the Courts
✳ Hispanics in the Political Process ✳ Hispanic Voting and the Voting Rights Act of 1965
✳ Congressional Hispanic Caucus ✳ Hispanics in Congress
✳ Selected Prominent Hispanic Federal Officials ✳ Prominent Hispanic Politicians in State Government
✳ Prominent Hispanic Metropolitan Leaders ✳ Legal and Political Organizations

The Hispanic experience is unique in U.S. history. U.S. Hispanics are at once the oldest and the newest immigrants to the United States. In a nation of immigrants from all over the world, Hispanic immigrants have endured a long history of obstacles.

To understand the problems facing many Hispanics, how those problems arose and why they still exist today, we must first examine the Hispanic American experience in history. Unique historical milestones have colored the collective experience of Hispanics and have influenced American attitudes and decisions throughout the past. Unlike any other ethnic group in the United States, Hispanics are the only people to become citizens by conquest, with the exception of certain Native Americans.

✳ ORIGINS OF HISPANICS IN THE UNITED STATES

From the landing of Christopher Columbus on October 12, 1492, until the early nineteenth century, the entire Spanish-speaking world was controlled by Spain. The Spanish settled in North America long before the American Revolution, with the earliest settlement established at Saint Augustine, Florida, in 1563. Spanish settlers then began immigrating to the Southwest and founded El Paso, Texas, in 1598 and Santa Fe, New Mexico, in 1609. By 1760, there were an estimated 20,000 settlers in New Mexico and 2,500 in Texas. In 1769, the mission at San

Diego, California, was established and the colonization of California began.

In 1810 in Mexico, Father Miguel Hidalgo y Castilla led the revolt against Spain, and Mexico gained its independence in 1821. Soon after Mexico became independent, Anglo-American settlers began to move into the Mexican territories of the present-day U.S. Southwest, especially Texas. In 1836, the Anglo settlers declared the Republic of Texas independent of Mexico. In 1846, the United States invaded Mexico under the banner of Manifest Destiny. The treaty of Guadalupe Hidalgo ended the Mexican War that same year. Under the treaty, half the land area of Mexico, including Texas, California, most of Arizona and New Mexico, and parts of Colorado, Utah, and Nevada, was ceded to the United States. The treaty gave Mexican nationals one year to choose U.S. or Mexican citizenship; 75,000 Hispanic people chose to remain in the United States and become citizens by conquest. James Gadsden was later sent to Mexico to complete the U.S. acquisition of the Southwest and negotiated the purchase of an additional 45,532 square miles, which became parts of Arizona and New Mexico. As more Anglos settled in the newly acquired lands, the new Hispanic Americans gradually became a minority population in the Southwest. The 1848 gold rush lured a flood of Anglo settlers to California, which became a state in 1850. Settlement in Arizona and New Mexico occurred at a slower pace, and they both became states in 1912.

The Treaty of Guadalupe Hidalgo guaranteed the property rights of the new Hispanic American landowners by reaffirming land grants that had been made by Spain and Mexico prior to 1846. However, the treaty did not explicitly protect the language or cultural rights of these new U.S. citizens. Over the next 50 years, most Southwestern states enacted language laws inhibiting Hispanic participation in voting, judicial processes, and education. More devastating, the Reclamation Act of 1902 dispossessed many of these same Hispanic Americans of their land. Only in New Mexico were the civil rights of the descendants of the original Spanish-speaking settlers protected.

Such conditions of discrimination discouraged immigration to the United States for most of the late nineteenth century, even though the United States had no immigration statutes relating to the admission of foreign nationals until 1875. In fact, entering the country without a visa was not a punishable offense until 1929. However, in the 1890s there was a demand for low-wage laborers to construct American railroads, and Mexican immigration was encouraged, especially after 1882, when Congress passed the Chinese Exclusion Act of 1882, which virtually ended immigration from China to the United States.

By 1910, conditions in Mexico deteriorated under the considerable political repression of the dictatorship of President Porfirio Díaz, who ruled Mexico for 34 years, from 1876 to 1910. Dispossession of property, widespread poverty, and runaway inflation forced many Mexicans to join forces in revolt. After the Mexican Revolution began in 1910, hundreds of thousands of people fled north from Mexico and settled in the Southwest. Between 1910 and 1930, about 10 percent of the entire population of Mexico immigrated to the United States, including 685,000 legal immigrants. They were welcomed during this period because of the labor needs of the expanding U.S. economy. Special rules were developed in 1917, during World War I, to permit "temporary" Mexican farm workers, railroad laborers, and miners to enter the United States to work. By the late 1920s, as much as 80 percent of the farm workers in southern California were of Mexican descent.

The Great Depression of the 1930s brought rapid change to Mexican immigration. From 1929 to 1934, more than 400,000 persons were "repatriated" to Mexico without any formal deportation proceedings. Thousands of U.S. citizens were illegally deported because they were of Mexican descent.

During World War II, the United States again needed workers and immigration was encouraged. In 1942, an arrangement was made with the Mexican government to supply temporary workers, known as "braceros," for American agriculture. Formalized by legislation in 1951, the Bracero Program brought an annual average of 350,000 Mexican workers to the United States until its end in 1964.

Mexican Americans again faced economic difficulties and discrimination because of competition for jobs during the late 1950s. This led to Operation Wetback, in which 3.8 million persons of Mexican descent were deported between 1954 and 1958. Only a small fraction of that amount were allowed deportation hearings prior to being deported. Thousands more legitimate U.S. citizens of Mexican descent were also arrested and detained.

In 1965, the United States enacted a law placing a cap on immigration from the Western Hemisphere for the first time, which became effective in 1968. Immediate family members of U.S. citizens were not subject to the cap and could legally immigrate. Legal immigration from Mexico averaged about 60,000 persons per year from 1971 to 1980. A substantial number of undocumented persons entered the United States from Mexico during those years, and that number has increased dramatically since. Estimates of the number of undocumented immigrants in the United States often range from three to five million people. In the early 1980s, programs to apprehend undocumented immigrants were again implemented, and once more there were reports of violations of civil rights of U.S. citizens and lawful permanent residents of Mexican descent.

Mexican Americans are only a part of the entire U.S. Hispanic population. Many other Spanish-speaking peoples became U.S. citizens under different circumstances. For example, Florida, Puerto Rico, and Cuba were possessions of Spain until the nineteenth century. Florida was claimed for Spain after its discovery by Juan Ponce de León in 1513. Saint Augustine in Florida was the earliest settlement established in North America, founded in 1563. It remained a possession of Spain until 1819. After Andrew Jackson led a U.S. military force into Florida, capturing two Spanish forts, Spain sold Florida to the United States for $5 million under the Onís Treaty.

Puerto Ricans, like the first Mexican Americans, became U.S. citizens through conquest. In 1898, following the brief Spanish-American War, Puerto Rico became a U.S. possession through the Treaty of Paris. Many Puerto Ricans assumed that annexation meant that all Puerto Ricans were U.S. citizens, thus entitling them to all the rights and privileges of citizenship. However, that was not the case. Many Puerto Ricans were denied the right to vote, and many were prevented from moving to the U.S. mainland.

Nearly 20 years later, the Jones Act of 1917 finally resolved this problem, making all Puerto Ricans U.S. citizens. Since then, Puerto Ricans have had the unrestricted right to travel between the island and the mainland. By the early 1920s, there were a significant number of Puerto Rican communities in U.S. cities, most notably New York.

Cuba also became a U.S. possession in 1898 through the Treaty of Paris, which ended 387 years of Spanish rule. However, Cuba was a possession only for a brief time and became independent in 1902. In the late nineteenth century, a small number of Cubans migrated to the United States, mainly to Florida and New York. By 1930, only about 20,000 Cubans lived in the United States, and by 1950, only about 35,000.

The vast majority of Cuban Americans immigrated to the United States after 1959, when Fidel Castro took power in Cuba. Between 1959 and 1962, 25,000 Cubans were "paroled" to the United States using a special immigration rule. The immigration laws did not provide for special refugee status without proof of physical persecution until 1965. In 1966, a program was initiated to airlift Cubans to the United States, but it was halted by Castro in 1973. Over 250,000 Cubans were airlifted to the United States during that period. About 10 percent of the island's population immigrated to the United States between 1966 and 1973.

Throughout the remainder of the 1970s, many Cubans immigrated to the United States by routes through other Latin American countries. In 1980, a boatlift of Cubans from Mariel Harbor was permitted by Castro, and about 130,000 refugees arrived in the United States. Controversy surrounded this boat-lift because a small percentage of the refugees were from Cuban prisons and institutions for the mentally ill.

Today, about one million Cuban Americans live in the United States, with the majority residing in Florida, although there are increasing numbers in California, Illinois, Massachusetts, New York, and New Jersey. While many early Cuban refugees expected to return to Cuba, the continuation of the Communist regime under Castro has led many to conclude that they will not be able to return. They have become naturalized citizens at a much higher rate than any other Hispanic immigrant group.

At different times in U.S. history, waves of immigrants have arrived from other Latin American countries, such as Nicaragua, Colombia, the Dominican Republic, Guatemala, Honduras, and El Salvador, as well as many others. More than half of these immigrants have come to the United States since 1970. Often they have entered the United States through Mexico. Some have entered legally under established immigration quotas, others have come as students or tourists and stayed in this country after their temporary legal status expired. Many immigrants from the Caribbean and Central and South America have come through circuitous and difficult routes to escape civil war, poverty, and repression.

More recent Central American immigration can be traced largely to economic and political conditions in the source countries, especially during the past two decades. During the 1960s, the establishment of the Central American Common Market led to economic growth and improved conditions in the region. In 1969, however, the border war between Honduras and El Salvador led to the collapse of the common market and the rapid decline of economic conditions in Central America.

Since 1979, political upheaval and civil wars in Nicaragua, El Salvador, and Guatemala have contributed to large migrations of refugees to the United States. The number of Central and South Americans in the United States in 1950 was about 57,000. Estimates in 1985 ranged from 1.4 million to 1.7 million, but these figures may be low because of difficulties in accurately counting large numbers of undocumented emigrants from Central and South America.

✳ THE DEVELOPMENT OF U.S. IMMIGRATION LAW

Americans have always taken pride in their immigrant heritage but ironically have feared new immigration at the same time. Since the United States declared its independence from Great Britain in 1776, protectionism has had its place in the population's subconscious. In later years it was often used as justification for restricting immigration.

Article I of the U.S. Constitution entrusted Congress with the power to regulate immigration and "to establish an uniform Rule of Naturalization." During the first 100 years following the American Revolution, the United States had an open-door policy with regard to immigration, which meant that immigrants from any country in the world were allowed to enter the United States unimpeded.

The first legislation to limit immigration to the United States came during the administration of President John Adams; it did not, however, limit the numbers or the origin of immigrants. The Naturalization Act of 1798 raised the number of years an immigrant had to live in the United States to be eligible for citizenship from five years to 14. The Alien Act of 1798 granted the president the authority to expel any alien he deemed dangerous. Opposed by President Thomas Jefferson, the Alien Act expired under its own terms in 1800, during his presidency.

Although the United States had a neutral immigration policy with few restrictions, some state legislatures enacted laws restricting immigration, most notably denying entry to Catholic immigrants in the early 1800s owing to fear of being dominated by the pope. These fears were used in 1854 by the American party, better known as the Know-Nothing party, which mounted successful local campaigns by denouncing immigration of Catholics and other groups. The Know-Nothing party won 40 seats in the Congress that year. In 1856 the party launched a national campaign and nominated former president Millard Fillmore for the presidency. Fillmore suffered defeat and won only 8 of 296 electoral votes.

In 1875, the U.S. Supreme Court in *Henderson v. Mayor of New York,* 92 U.S. 259, ruled that all power to regulate immigration was held solely by the federal government and struck down state restrictions as unconstitutional. However, Congress passed the first major federal immigration restrictions during the ensuing years.

The first statutes aimed at excluding certain persons from immigrating to the United States denied admission to convicts and prostitutes. In 1882, the first general federal immigration law was enacted, which included an entry tax of 50 cents per person and denied entry to the United States to "idiots, lunatics, convicts and persons likely to become public charges." But the first major legislation to reverse the century-old tradition of free and open immigration to the United States was the Chinese Exclusion Act of 1882. By its terms, the Exclusion Act put an end to Chinese immigration to the United States for ten years; later laws extended the ban indefinitely and prohibited the naturalization of Chinese persons already in the United States. It was not repealed until 1943.

The first literacy test law to restrict immigration was enacted in 1917, over the veto of President Woodrow Wilson. The literacy test acted to limit immigration from areas outside northern Europe, requiring literacy in some language for immigrants over age 16. Ironically, that same year the Jones Act of 1917 was passed, which extended U.S. citizenship to all Puerto Ricans.

By 1920, Congress had passed about a dozen major immigration laws that restricted certain kinds of individuals from immigrating to the United States, such as criminals, persons with chronic diseases, and persons with unacceptable moral or political beliefs. In 1921, limits on the number of immigrants allowed to enter the United States during a single year were imposed for the first time in the country's history. This legislation limited immigration from Europe to 3 percent of each European nationality present in the United States in 1910, a sharp reduction from previous immigration levels. The National Origins Quota Law of 1924 restricted the immigration of southern and eastern Europeans even more, and immigration from Asia was banned.

Immigration from Latin American countries was exempt from the quota restrictions that Congress created for two reasons. The first, and most important, was that farmers and manufacturers in the southwestern states had become dependent on cheap, plentiful labor from Mexico. The second reason was that the United States was attempting to emerge as a leader of cooperative spirit among its neighbors in the Western Hemisphere under the banner of Pan-Americanism. Even without the quota restrictions, immigration from Latin America, excluding Mexico, remained low from the 1930s through the 1950s.

Following World War II, President Harry Truman allowed large numbers of displaced persons from Europe to enter the United States far in excess of the countries' quotas. In response to Truman's action, Congress passed the Immigration and Nationality Act of 1952, also known as the McCarran-Walter Act. The act reaffirmed the basic features of the 1924 quota law (the Immigration Act of 1924) by maintaining a restrictive limit on immigration from particular countries. Immigration from Asia was legalized, but only at very low levels. England, Ireland, and Germany represented two-thirds of the yearly quota for the entire world. Immigration from the Western Hemisphere remained exempt, except that applicants had to clear a long list of barriers devised to exclude homosexuals, Communists, and others.

Immigration from Latin America increased following the enactment of the McCarran-Walter Act. During the 1950s, immigration from Mexico doubled from 5.9 percent to 11.9 percent, and in the 1960s it rose to 13.3 percent of the total number of immigrants to the United States. Immigration from Cuba during this same period was 7.75 percent of the total. The total number of immigrants from Latin American countries during this time, including Mexico and Cuba, was 39 percent of all immigrants entering the United States

In 1965, a major revision of immigration law resulted when Congress amended the Immigration and Nationality Act of 1952. The national origin quota system was abolished. A complex seven-category preference system for granting visas was created in its place. The 1965 amendments gave preference to family reunification. Spouses, parents, and children of U.S. citizens were given preference in awarding visas and were not bound by a quota. The amendments maintained limits on immigration through the seven-category preference system, providing for immigration from each country of no more than 20,000 immigrants per year. Race or national origin was no longer a consideration. More important, the 1965 amendments imposed a quota ceiling on immigration from countries in the Western Hemisphere as well. This marked the first time in U.S. history that such a numerical restriction was placed on immigration from these countries.

Amendments to the law passed in 1978 removed the ceilings for each hemisphere and established a worldwide competition for 290,000 visas granted each year. Every country in the world was subject to the seven-category preference system and to the 20,000-per-year limit. The 1965 and 1978 amendments led to a dramatic shift in immigration. No longer were Europeans, formerly favored by law, the largest group of immigrants. They now represented only 13 percent of the total. Asians benefited most, representing 21 percent of the total number of immigrants entering the United States per year. Immigration from Latin American countries and the Caribbean remained at about 40 percent of the total.

The Immigration Act of 1990 continues to permit immigration of immediate relatives of U.S. citizens without numerical limitation but sets a "pierceable" overall cap on worldwide immigration of 700,000 for fiscal years 1992 through 1994, and of 675,000 for fiscal year 1995. The seven-category preference system has been replaced by one based on family relationships, employment, and diversity. The per-country limit is 25,000.

The 1970s and early 1980s brought a different kind of immigration problem to the attention of the American public. The rise in politically motivated violence in Central America spurred a massive increase in undocumented immigration to the United States. The flight of "boat people" from Indochina following the Vietnam War created an enormous refugee settlement challenge for the United States. In a six-month period alone in 1980, some 125,000 Cubans arrived in Florida in an uncontrolled sea migration to the United States. At about the same time, over 10,000 Haitians fled the repressive regime of dictator Jean Claude Duvalier and sailed to the United States in overcrowded fishing boats.

These immigrants, or more appropriately, refugees, created a problem for U.S. immigration authorities. They were not eligible to enter the United States under established quotas without visas, nor could many of them meet the requirements to enter the United States under an exemption to the quota system as "refugees." Previous U.S. law provided for the admission of persons fleeing persecution or having a well-founded fear of persecution from Middle Eastern Communist-dominated countries. This was advantageous to the Cubans fleeing Communist dictator Fidel Castro and the Vietnamese fleeing the Communist regime in Vietnam but was no help to the thousands of Central Americans who were fleeing political violence. The Refugee Act of 1980 removed the ideological definition of refugee as one who flees from a Communist regime, thus allowing thousands to enter the United States as refugees who otherwise would have been excluded.

✳ THE CURRENT DEBATE OVER U.S. IMMIGRATION LAW

The high level of illegal immigration from Mexico and other Latin American countries has fueled continuing debate about U.S. immigration policies. Beginning in the early 1970s, Congress, along with Presidents Nixon and Ford, assembled high-level commissions to study the problem, with no tangible results.

President Jimmy Carter appointed the bipartisan Select Commission on Immigration and Refugee Policy to forge a consensus in Congress and to propose solutions. The commission went through hundreds of reports on trends in immigration and their effects on the nation and held a long series of hearings throughout the country. The commission's final report was issued in 1981 and is entitled *U.S. Immigration Policy in the National Interest.* The report states, "The United States is disturbed by immigration. The very fact that so many come outside of the law or abuse their nonimmigrant visas is troubling in a nation which prides itself on respect for law generally, and for its legal immigration system specifically."

Once separated from the fear and deception of racist sentiments, the current immigration policy debate involves three key issues: control of U.S. borders, economic interests of the United States, and enforcement of U.S. immigration law. There is genuine concern over the nation's ability to humanely control immigration at its borders. As the number of undocumented immigrants apprehended at the U.S.-Mexican border rises, so does concern over regaining control of the rate of immigration. There is also illegal immigration from the north, but the numbers are smaller, and there is a higher proportion of native English-speakers who look American in appearance.

If the United States is to maintain an immigration policy consistent with the American notion of an open society, while at the same time limiting immigration to serve the national interest, most national policymakers believe that immigration must be controlled. But border enforcement must also be equitable and must maintain an open society. Limits imposed because of color, race, nationality, or religion are not fair. Moreover, those who are admitted must be allowed the full rights of participation in U.S. society.

The U.S. economy is a key force behind illegal immigration as well as a major cause for American concern about it. In much of Mexico, especially in rural areas, finding employment is extremely difficult, and a job pays only a small fraction of the minimum wage in the United States. Similar economic pressures encourage immigration from other countries, but illegal immigration is most practical for Mexicans and Central Americans, who can reach the United States by land. In southwestern states, certain U.S. industries depend on undocumented laborers, who work hard for very low pay and who seldom complain. Thus, illegal immigration is welcomed by many employers. As history demonstrates, the United States typically welcomes immigrants in times of economic growth and labor shortages, and repels them during economic hard times.

The economic effects of illegal immigration are intensely argued today. Some argue that undocumented laborers steal jobs from American workers and that undocumented aliens abuse the welfare and social services system. However, others argue and several studies demonstrate that undocumented laborers actually create jobs and thereby bolster the national economy. Furthermore, the data show that undocumented aliens rarely use any form of public assistance and, for the most part, are ineligible for government assistance because of their immigration status. Immigration policy should take into account the economic impact on the national economy, but it must first carefully examine labor needs and the actual effects of illegal immigration.

Enforcement of U.S. immigration law is a key issue in the immigration debate. Once policy is set and law is enacted, it should be enforced fairly. Our immigration laws should reestablish and maintain a consistent, practicable and humane rule of law.

✳ THE LEGALIZATION PROGRAM

The Immigration Reform and Control Act of 1986 created a major alien legalization program. Under the act, legal status was given to applicants who had held illegal status in the United States from before January 1, 1982, until the time of application. The act also offered legal status to Special Agricultural Workers (SAW) who could prove they had spent at least 90 days during a qualifying period doing agricultural work in specific crops. The Immigration and Naturalization Service (INS) accepted legalization applications between May 5, 1987, and May 4, 1988, and SAW applications from June 1, 1987, to November 30, 1988.

It is estimated that approximately three to five million undocumented immigrants lived in the United States at the time the legalization program began. On a case-by-case basis, the program has allowed those undocumented immigrants who could demonstrate continuous residence in the United States since 1982 and who would otherwise be admissible as immigrants to become legal residents. The program dealt with a complex statute and was often the subject of intense controversy, particularly over who was eligible and what documentation was needed. Disputes with the INS over the regulations led many applicants to the courtroom, where the INS usually lost.

Despite these problems, the program was successful and brought major benefits to a large number of Hispanics. More than three million applicants applied for legal status under the program, and over 90 percent of such applicants received at least temporary legal status. The largest number of applicants, about 69 percent, was from Mexico. Approximately 11 percent were from Central America, 2 percent from Caribbean countries, and about 1.5 percent from South America. The remaining applicants were from various countries around the world.

Among the most obvious and immediate benefits is the ability of applicants to cross borders legally. Additionally, the massive number of applicants has been vital in unscrambling close to two million Social Security accounts that were incorrect or fraudulent. Applicants who had acquired a false or incorrect Social Security card had the opportunity to correct their Social Security account. One subtle change has been in the behavior of the newly legalized. Many are showing an increased willingness to use public health facilities and to assert legal rights they always had but were afraid to invoke for fear that it would lead to questions about their immigration status. Many have left the very worst jobs and are now able to seek higher-paying employment.

The legalization program might not have been without its difficulties, but the program has made a necessary difference for a powerless class of individuals. It has improved the lives of millions of Hispanics and provided them with the opportunity to obtain full U.S. citizenship.

✳ EMPLOYMENT DISCRIMINATION

As demonstrated by the history of U.S. immigration law, employment has always been closely related to patterns of immigration by Hispanics. Mexican American workers suffered widespread abuses after the Southwest was ceded to the United States by Mexico. Mexican American workers endured various forms of mistreatment, including intolerable working conditions, substandard pay, and extended work hours.

Following the conquest of the Southwest, Hispanic Americans, deprived of virtually any means of building a decent economic base, were forced to work in the employ of newly arrived Anglo-Americans. During the 1800s, many Mexican Americans worked 12-hour days, six days a week, in mines, yet they were paid only half the wages paid to white miners. Mexican American workers were denigrated and were always the most poorly paid.

Mexican American farm workers in Texas were described as subhuman by historian Pauline Kibbe in 1946. She referred to this population of laborers as "but a species of farm implement that comes mysteriously into being coincident with the maturing of the cotton, that requires no upkeep or special consideration during the period of usefulness, needs no protection from the elements, and when the crop has been harvested, vanishes into the limbo of forgotten things, until the next harvest season rolls around."

Hispanic American citizens historically have always faced employment discrimination on the basis of their national origin. Such discrimination is comparable to that experienced by members of other minority groups. It was not until the landmark case of *Hernández v. Texas* (1954) that the nation's highest court acknowledged that Hispanic Americans were not being treated as "whites." The Supreme Court recognized Hispanics as a separate class of people suffering profound discrimination. The 1954 decision paved the way for Hispanic Americans to use legal means to attack all types of discrimination throughout the United States.

Among the most important legislation enacted to end employment discrimination against all minorities was the Civil Rights Act of 1964, which made it illegal for an employer to discriminate on the basis of race, color, religion, sex, or national origin. The statute was designed to protect Hispanic Americans and other minorities. It is still often used to challenge unlawful denial of jobs to Hispanic Americans.

Today, the law of employment discrimination is complex, and there are many relevant federal statutes. An important development regarding employment discrimination against immigrants was the enactment of antidiscrimination provisions in the Immigration Reform and Control Act of 1986. As noted earlier, the immigration laws were amended in 1986, making it unlawful for employers to hire undocumented persons. However, Congress believed, when passing this legislation, that the threat of sanctions created the risk that employers might refuse to hire or might discriminate against persons who appear to be foreign, have foreign-sounding names, or speak in a foreign language or with a foreign accent. Consequently, Congress included the antidiscrimination provisions in the act as a counterbalance to employer sanctions. These provisions created a new legal tool for Hispanic Americans who have experienced discrimination on the basis of national origin. The law states that it is an unfair immigration-related employment practice to discriminate in hiring, recruitment, or discharge because of a person's national origin or citizenship status. Protection against discrimination arising from citizenship status extends to all citizens, as well as to other classifications of immigrants who are legally in the United States.

✳ POLICE BRUTALITY

In the 1800s, brutality against Mexican Americans in the Southwest territories was commonplace. In fact, lynchings and murders of Mexican Americans became so common in California and Texas that, in 1912, the Mexican ambassador formally protested the mistreatment of Mexicans and cited several brutal incidents that had recently taken place.

The prevailing conditions in the 1920s along the Texas-Mexico border were intolerable. Texas Rangers killed Mexicans along the border without fear of penalty. No jury along the border would ever convict a white man for shooting a Mexican. Abuse of Mexican Americans by rangers and police continued unchecked in the 1930s.

In 1943, *Time* magazine reported that 200 navy men, angered by scuffles with Hispanic youth, commandeered taxicabs and began attacking Mexican Americans in East Los Angeles. The Los Angeles police followed the caravan of navy men and watched them beat the Hispanics and did nothing to stop them. Mexican American boys were dragged from movie theaters, stripped of their clothing, beaten, and left naked in the streets. Police did nothing to stop the attacks.

Courts of law were rarely a source of justice for Mexican American victims of such abuse. In 1947, for example, a 19-year-old Mexican American was convicted of murder in Hudspeth County, Texas. He was blind and mentally retarded, and had retaliated to an attack on his elderly father. He was not proved to have the legally necessary intent to kill to justify first-degree murder, but an all-white jury found him guilty of first-degree murder anyway. He was sentenced to death. The ruling was appealed on the grounds that some Mexican Americans should have been on the jury because the population of Hudspeth County was 50 percent Hispanic. The appellate court held that the Fourteenth Amendment, which prohibits discrimination on the basis of race or color, did not protect Mexican Americans, and the young man was executed.

As late as 1970, brutality against Mexican Americans continued. In *López v. Harlow,* a case filed in an attempt to bring the violence under control, a police officer shot and killed López, a Mexican American, allegedly in self-defense, because he thought López was about to throw a dish at him.

Since the 1970s, Hispanics have come forward in greater numbers and have documented abuses by police, abuses that include unreasonable seizures, physical brutality, and incarceration without cause. Ammunition against police abuse is growing, but the fight on this issue is destined to be a long one.

✳ FEDERAL LEGISLATION AFFECTING HISPANIC AMERICANS

Reclamation Act of 1902

From a Hispanic perspective, the Reclamation Act of 1902 is among the most devastating pieces of legislation in history. This law dispossessed Hispanic Americans of their land in the Southwestern territories 50 years after the Treaty of Guadalupe Hidalgo ceded these lands to the United States in 1846. Only in New Mexico were the civil rights of the descendants of the original Spanish-speaking settlers protected.

Jones Act of 1917

The Jones Act of 1917 gave residents of Puerto Rico full U.S. citizenship. Puerto Rico had been annexed by the United States in 1898 following the Spanish-American War. With the enactment of this law, Puerto Ricans were granted the unrestricted right to travel between the island and the U.S. mainland.

Civil Rights Act of 1964

Among the most important laws enacted to end discrimination against all minorities, the Civil Rights Act of 1964 made it illegal to discriminate on the basis of race, color, religion, sex, or national origin. The statute was designed to protect Hispanic Americans and other minorities, and it is often used to challenge unlawful denial of jobs for Hispanic Americans.

Immigration and Nationality Act of 1965

In 1965, Congress, for the first time in history, placed a limitation on the number of persons allowed to immigrate to the United States from Western Hemisphere countries, which had always been exempt from quotas until the enactment of this law. The abolition of the national origins system brought greater equality to the American immigration system.

Voting Rights Act of 1965

Although the single aim of the Voting Rights Act of 1965 was African American enfranchisement in the South, obstacles to registration and voting faced by all minorities were affected. Its potential as a tool for Hispanic Americans, however, was not fully realized for nearly a decade.

Voting Rights Act of 1970

The 1970 amendments constituting the landmark Voting Rights Act of 1970 added a provision that was designed to guard against inventive new barriers to political participation. It requires federal approval of all changes in voting procedures in certain jurisdictions, primarily southern states. This act prevents minority votes from being diluted in gerrymandered districts or through at-large elections.

Equal Educational Opportunity Act of 1974

Congress passed the Equal Educational Opportunity Act of 1974 to create equality in public schools by making bilingual education available to Hispanic youth. According to the framers of the act, equal education means more than equal facilities and equal access to teachers. Students who have trouble with the English language must be given programs to help them overcome their difficulties with English.

Voting Rights Act Amendments of 1975

The Voting Rights Act Amendments of 1975 extended the provisions of the original Voting Rights Act Voting Rights Act of 1965 and made permanent the national ban on literacy tests. Critical for Hispanic Americans, the amendments made bilingual ballots a requirement in certain areas.

Refugee Act of 1980

Under previous U.S. law, persons fleeing persecution or having a well-founded fear of persecution in Middle Eastern or Commmunist-dominated countries could be admitted to the United States despite any applicable restrictions. This was advantageous to Cubans fleeing Communist dictator Fidel Castro and the Vietnamese fleeing the Communist regime in Vietnam, but it was no help to the thousands of Central Americans who were fleeing political violence. The Refugee Act of 1980 removed the ideological definition of refugee as one who flees from a Communist regime, thus allowing thousands who otherwise would have been excluded to enter the United States as refugees.

Voting Rights Act Amendments of 1982

The Voting Rights Act Amendments of 1982 prohibit any voting law or practice created by a state or political subdivision that "results" in denial of the right of any citizen of the United States to vote on account of race, color, or language minority status. This amendment also eliminates the need to prove that the state or political subdivision created a voting law with the "intention" of discriminating against minority voters.

Immigration Reform and Control Act of 1986

The Immigration Reform and Control Act of 1986 created a major alien legalization program. Lawful resident status was extended to applicants who had held illegal status in the United States from before 1982 until the time of application. The Immigration and Naturalization Service (INS) accepted applications for one year, from May 1987 until May 1988. The program was successful and brought legal status to a large number of undocumented Hispanics. More than three million applicants applied for lawful residence under the program, and over 90 percent of them received at least temporary legal resident status.

Additionally, the act made it unlawful for employers to hire undocumented workers. However, because of the threat that sanctions might deter employers from hiring or cause them to discriminate against persons appearing to be foreign, Congress included antidiscrimination provisions in the Immigration Reform and Control Act.

Immigration Act of 1990

The Immigration Act of 1990 continued to permit immigration of immediate relatives of U.S. citizens without numerical limitation but set a "pierceable" overall cap on worldwide immigration to the United States of 700,000 for fiscal years 1992 through 1994, and 675,000 for fiscal year 1995. The seven-category preference system has been replaced by allocation of visas based on family relationships, employment, and diversity. The per-country limit is now 25,000.

✳ IMPORTANT CASES AFFECTING HISPANIC AMERICANS

Hernández v. Texas
347 U.S. 475 (1954)

A crucial case argued in 1954, *Hernandez v. Texas* was the first Mexican American discrimination case to reach the nation's highest court. It was also the first U.S. Supreme Court case to be argued and briefed by Mexican American attorneys. The case was brought by lawyers Carlos Cadena and Gus García. It was an important victory.

The defendant, Pete Hernández, had been tried and convicted for murder in Jackson County, Texas. Jackson County was 14 percent Hispanic, but the jury panel that found Hernández guilty did not include any Hispanics. In fact, no Spanish-surnamed person had served on any jury of any sort in Jackson County for 25 years prior to the trial.

Chief Justice Earl Warren, speaking for the Supreme Court, held that the Texas court was in error by "limiting the scope of the equal protection clause to the white and negro classes" and that Mexican Americans were entitled to the protection of the Fourteenth Amendment of the U.S. Constitution. The Court had acknowledged that Mexican Americans were not being treated as "whites" in the Southwest. Mexican Americans were recognized as a separate class of people who were suffering profound discrimination. The 1954 decision paved the way for Hispanic Americans to use legal means to attack discrimination throughout the country.

Allen v. State Board of Elections
393 U.S. 544 (1969)

In *Allen v. State Board of Elections,* the U.S. Supreme Court extended federal authority to object to discriminatory alterations in voting districts, the introduction of at-large voting, and other such changes, in addition to reaffirming the original power to object to discriminatory innovations involving registration and voting.

Graham v. Richardson
403 U.S. 365 (1971)

Graham v. Richardson was a decision involving application of the equal protection clause of the U.S. Constitution to state welfare laws discriminating against aliens in Arizona and Pennsylvania. The Supreme Court held that provisions of state welfare laws conditioning benefits on citizenship and imposing durational residency requirements on aliens violated the equal protection clause.

San Antonio Independent School District v. Rodríguez
411 U.S. 1 (1973)

A suit brought on behalf of poor schoolchildren, *San Antonio Independent School District v. Rodríguez,* challenged the Texas system of financing its school system based on local property taxation. The Supreme Court held that the system did not violate the constitutional right of the children to equal protection under the Fourteenth Amendment. By a five-to-four majority, the Court ruled that education is not a fundamental right and poverty is not a reason to hold otherwise.

Espinoza v. Farah Manufacturing Company
411 U.S. 86 (1973)

An employment discrimination case, *Espinoza v. Farah Manufacturing Company* was brought against Farah for discrimination toward an employee, Espinoza, on the basis of his citizenship status under the Civil Rights Act. However, the Supreme Court held that there was nothing in Title VII, the equal employment opportunities provisions of the Civil Rights Act of 1964, that makes it illegal to discriminate on the basis of citizenship or alienage.

Lau v. Nichols
414 U.S. 563 (1974)

Lau v. Nichols was brought before the Supreme Court by students who did not speak English. The Court held that the California school system's failure to provide English-language instruction to the students denied meaningful opportunity to participate in public educational programs and was in violation of Title VI of the Civil Rights Act of 1964.

Matthews v. Díaz
426 U.S. 67 (1976)

Resident alien Díaz, age 65, brought suit challenging the constitutionality of the Social Security Act provision requiring resident aliens to have resided in the United States for five years before they are eligible for Medicare. The U.S. district court in Florida held that it was an unconstitutional requirement, but the Supreme Court reversed, holding that Congress may condition aliens' eligibility for participation in Medicare, or any other federal program, on citizenship or continuous residence in the United States.

Plyler v. Doe
457 U.S. 202 (1982)

Plyler v. Doe was brought on behalf of Mexican children who had entered the United States illegally and resided in Texas. The suit challenged a Texas statute excluding the children from attending public schools. The Supreme Court struck down the Texas statute as unconstitutional and in violation of the equal protection clause, which provides that no state shall deny to any person the equal protection of the laws.

League of United Latin American Citizens v. Pasadena Independent School District
662 F. Supp. 443 (S.D. Tex. 1987)

In the *League of United Latin American Citizens v. Pasadena Independent School District,* the League of United Latin American Citizens (LULAC), on behalf of undocumented aliens who were terminated from their employment as Pasadena school district custodial workers because they provided false Social Security numbers, brought suit against the school district. The U.S. District Court for the Southern District of Texas held that the aliens were entitled to their jobs because the termination violated the anti-discrimination provision of the Immigration Reform and Control Act of 1986.

Hernández v. New York
111 S. Ct. 1859 (1991)

In *Hernández v. New York,* Hernández appealed a conviction by a New York State court on the basis that the prosecutor had discriminated against him by dismissing two prospective Spanish-speaking jurors. The prosecutor argued that he doubted the jurors' ability to defer to the official translation of anticipated Spanish-language testimony. The Supreme Court held that the state trial court was justified in concluding that the prosecutor did not discriminate on the basis of race.

✳ HISPANICS IN THE LEGAL PROFESSION

As early as the 1730s, with the formation of the Society of Gentlemen Practisers in the Courts of Law and Equity, attorneys have established organizations for the purpose of improving standards in the American legal profession. Historically, however, such professional have established an elite class of lawyers who are able to maintain control over the legal profession and its development. These lawyers came to represent the bar and established the rules and guidelines affecting the entire legal community.

In particular, they were able to limit participation by defining the qualifications for admission to the bar, thereby maintaining the status quo. The early legal profession was designed to promote certain political views and to resist change. Such standards were effectively, if not intentionally, racist and served to restrict access to the powerful bar. The American Bar Association, established in 1878, itself has recognized its unenviable history of inaction in reaching out to minorities.

Adoption of the Fourteenth Amendment to the U.S. Constitution in 1868 marked a turning point. This constitutional amendment, along with civil rights legislation, helped the United States move toward equality. The road was difficult, and even after a century had passed, discrimination and inequality still existed.

Congress enacted the first comprehensive civil rights law since the Reconstruction period when it passed the Civil Rights Act of 1964. One result of the act was the establishment of affirmative action programs. During the early years of affirmative action, equal opportunity plans were an effective way of ending employment discrimination. The U.S. Supreme Court supported this view, in many cases striking down employment and hiring practices that discriminated on the basis of race, color, gender, or national origin. As a result, civil rights legislation and affirmative action programs were pivotal in providing minorities with equal opportunities in professions from which they were previously barred.

Despite these legislative advances, Hispanic Americans continue to be underrepresented in the legal profession, especially in the nation's largest law firms. To increase Hispanic representation, large law firms must recognize that a greater, more concerted effort is needed to assist Hispanic Americans in getting through the subtle acculturation process found within law firms.

The number of Hispanic attorneys working for U.S. corporations is 50 percent greater than the number of Hispanic attorneys in the nation's largest law firms. A survey conducted by the *National Law Journal* reported that Hispanics represent 1.2 percent of all the attorneys in the 251 largest law firms in the United States. In large part, the reason for underrepresentation of Hispanic Americans in the legal profession, especially in large law firms, is that Hispanics are not attending law schools in numbers proportionate to the Hispanic population in the United States.

Hispanics and Legal Education

Despite many advances, Hispanic American representation in the legal profession, as in most prestigious fields, is still not proportionate to the number of Hispanics in the general population. The low number of Hispanics admitted to U.S. law schools is the major barrier.

The American Bar Association (ABA) reported that Hispanic American enrollment in ABA-ap-

proved law schools was 1.5 percent of all law students in 1975. About ten years later, the ABA reported that the number had increased slightly to 2 percent. Although this is an improvement, it is far from representative of the Hispanic presence in the general population. Hispanic American law school enrollment is also adversely affected by a high attrition rate, much higher than that of law students overall. Even more devastating is the high dropout rate among Hispanic youth in high school and college; almost half of all Hispanic college students drop out during their first two years, which has prevented large numbers of them from reaching law school or other professional schools.

Another commonly noted problem of Hispanic students is a deficiency in academic background. This often requires a long academic adjustment period, private tutoring, or some other form of academic support to assist the student in completing law school. This may often be the case for Hispanic students who speak Spanish as their native language. Many Hispanic students also experience pressure from peers who attempt to dissuade them from pursuing higher education. These academic problems are often accompanied by financial difficulties. Unfortunately, many, if not most, law schools do little to accommodate Hispanic students' needs.

Obstacles to financing the high costs of a legal education may be a significant reason for the high number of law school dropouts. Many of the resources that helped Hispanic Americans to attain higher education in the 1970s are becoming more and more scarce. Financial aid has been decreasing because of government cutbacks, and the political climate has become less receptive to affirmative action and other programs that had previously facilitated the higher education of Hispanics and other minorities.

Hispanic Americans who do graduate from law school may face additional obstacles before entering law firms. Perhaps the most significant one is the bar examination, which all attorneys must pass to practice law. The bar is a hurdle for all would-be attorneys, but is a more significant impediment for Hispanics. In California, which has a large Hispanic population, scores for the California Bar Examination in July 1985 showed that while 61.5 percent of whites passed, only 33.5 percent of Hispanics did. Whether the bar examination is discriminatory against minorities is a volatile issue that is hotly debated.

Hispanics in Large Law Firms

As attorneys, Hispanics face formidable obstacles in joining law firms. According to a survey conducted by Stanford Law School in 1987, Hispanic American

TRENDS IN LAW SCHOOL ENROLLMENT

J.D. Enrollment
1981-82 to 1990-91

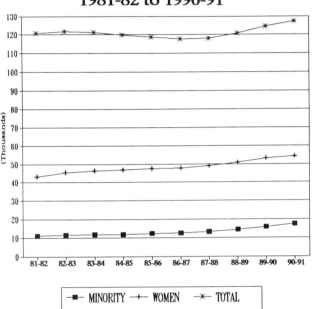

MINORITY ENROLLMENT COMPOSITION
1981-82

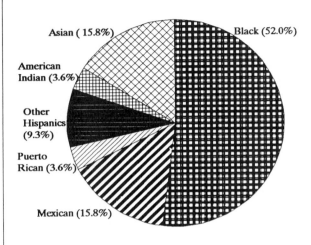

J.D. Enrollment
Women and Minorities
1981-82 to 1990-91

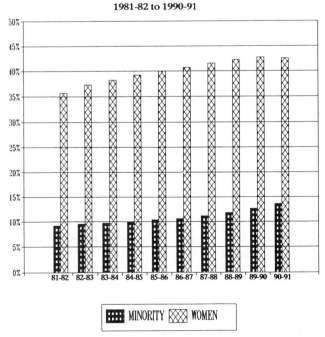

MINORITY ENROLLMENT COMPOSITION
1990-91

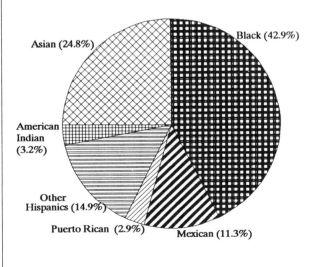

Four charts on law school enrollment. (*Consultant's Digest*, May 1991.)

graduates reported they felt they had to overcome barriers when joining law firms that nonminorities do not face. At the interviewing stage of the hiring process, Hispanics must confront the preconceptions many interviewers will have of them, preconceptions that large law firm interviewers may not even be aware of. Hispanic students are often stereotyped as being oriented more to public service careers than to careers with large law firms. In the past, Hispanic law school graduates have generally gravitated toward government jobs, poverty law, or legal services. This phenomenon is largely the result of greater opportunity in those types of law practice. Today, however, many Hispanics are pursuing careers in large law firms more aggressively.

Overcoming preconceptions about the kind of law Hispanics want to practice is not the only problem facing Hispanic American law graduates. Although major law firms are gradually opening up opportunities for minorities, they usually hire only attorneys, including minorities, with outstanding academic records who have attended top law schools.

The problems Hispanics face in getting jobs at the country's major law firms do not end with the first job after law school. Having been barred from entry-level positions at large law firms, Hispanics are effectively prevented from joining firms later as lateral hires, because few Hispanics have substantial legal experience in corporate law or in other fields of law in which many large firms specialize. As long as Hispanics have difficulty joining these firms at entry level, the number gaining experience at large law firms will continue to be minimal. Because the firms tend not to hire lawyers without that required experience, Hispanic representation in large law firms is not likely to be improved through lateral hiring.

Increasingly, however, Hispanic attorneys are overcoming the entry barriers and joining large law firms. Even for some of these attorneys, disadvantages may appear within the law firm in the form of additional barriers or added pressures. Breaking the racial barriers of a firm by being the first or only Hispanic attorney is not an easy task. Culture shock for Hispanics entering corporate law firms may not be an uncommon experience. A feeling of isolation may result and is often enhanced by the lack of Hispanic mentors within the law firm. Mentors serve as role models and advisers, and many attorneys think not having a minority mentor hurts their progress within the firm.

Hispanics in the Public Interest

A great number of Hispanic attorneys have chosen a career in the public interest. Many serve at government posts or with nonprofit legal organizations established to aid underprivileged and disenfranchised clients. Many attorneys who enter service in the public interest do so because they have a desire to aid other Hispanic Americans with legal, social, and cultural problems.

In public interest service, Hispanic attorneys have the opportunity to make gains for not only themselves and their community but also all Americans. They take pride in the victories made in the struggle for equal rights at a time when the tide is running against civil rights efforts of minorities. Public interest firms often act as watchdogs that monitor government action to see that public resources are effectively channeled into the Hispanic community. By monitoring these agencies, they can ensure that programs they devise realistically account for the needs of Hispanics. However, public interest firms and organizations are plagued by insufficient funding and staff. Despite these limitations, those people who join the public interest have achieved a great deal in this country.

Issues often monitored by public interest groups include immigration, employment, education, housing, voter registration and elections, public funding, discrimination, and civil rights. In the past two decades, there has been dramatic growth in the number of public interest organizations specifically created to assist Hispanics with legal problems and to advocate political involvement. Some of the most well known and effective national public interest groups in the United States include local offices funded by the Legal Services Corporation; Migrant Legal Action Program; Mexican American Legal Defense and Educational Fund; Puerto Rican Legal Defense and Education Fund; and the National Immigration Law Center.

Selected Prominent Hispanic Attorneys and Law Professors

Michael J. Aguirre (1949–)

Civil Litigation Attorney

Born in San Diego, California, on September 12, 1949, Aguirre was educated in California, earned a bachelor of science degree at Arizona State University in 1971, a law degree from the University of California, Berkeley, in 1974 and a master of public administration degree from Harvard University in 1989. He has worked as deputy legislative counsel for the California legislature, 1974–1975; as assistant U.S. attorney, 1975–76; assistant counsel for the U.S. Senate Subcommittee on Investigations, 1976–77; and as special reports legal counsel for the C.B.S. network, 1977. Since that time he has worked in private practice.

In 1980, he became the president of his own law

Michael J. Aguirre.

ation in 1988. He is currently a partner with the firm of Mitchell, Silberberg & Knupp in Los Angeles.

Wilfredo Caraballo (1947–)

Public Advocate / Public Defender, State of New Jersey

Caraballo was born in Yabucoa, Puerto Rico, and grew up in a tough neighborhood in New York City. He attended St. Joseph's University and went on to New York University Law School, receiving his law degree in 1974. He then worked the streets of New York City as a community activist and a legal aid lawyer. Caraballo was also active in the Puerto Rican Legal Defense and Education Fund. In 1975, he joined Seton Hall Law School in Newark, New Jersey, as a clinical professor. During his 15 years at Seton Hall, Caraballo specialized in teaching contract, commercial, and bankruptcy law. He was a visiting professor at New York University, the City University of New York, and Pace College law schools. In 1982 he was named associate dean of Seton Hall Law School. Caraballo took a leave of absence from his post as associate dean in 1990. Governor James Florio appointed Caraballo to the Office of Public Advocate and Public Defender in 1990, a cabinet post he served until 1992.

firm, Aguirre and Meyer, A.P.C., which specializes in civil litigation. He has also been an adjunct professor and lectured in law at the University of California, San Diego, and at the University of Southern California. Aguirre is active in the community and has also been the author of various laws passed by the California legislature. His awards include the Wille Velásquez Community Service Award, given by the Chicano Federation in San Diego in 1989. In 1987, he was voted the most distinguished name in the San Diego legal community by the readership of the *San Diego Daily Transcript*.

James E. Blancarte (1953–)

Litigation Attorney

Blancarte was born in 1953 in Pomona, California, and graduated from Pomona College. He received his law degree from the University of California School of Law and was admitted to the bar in 1979. Blancarte's current areas of practice are litigation and entertainment and business law. Blancarte was president of the Mexican American Bar Association of Los Angeles in 1983 and was president of the western region of the Hispanic National Bar Associ-

Wilfredo Caraballo.

Daniel P. García (1947–)

Attorney

García was born in Los Angeles. He attended Loyola University, where he received a degree in business in 1970, and went on to the University of Southern California, earning his M.B.A. in 1971. García then attended U.C.L.A. School of Law and was awarded a law degree in 1974, at which time he joined the prestigious firm of Munger, Tolles & Olson in Los Angeles and became a partner. Since 1991, he has served as an attorney for Warner Brothers in Burbank, California. He is a member of the board of the Mexican American Legal Defense and Education Fund and has been active in Los Angeles politics. García was a member of the Los Angeles Planning Commission from 1976 to 1988 and was its president from 1978 to 1988. He has served as president of the Mexican American Bar Association.

Antonia Hernández

President and General Counsel, Mexican American Legal Defense and Educational Fund (MALDEF)

Born in Coahuila, Mexico, Hernández earned her B.A. at U.C.L.A. in 1968, a teaching credential at the university's School of Education, and her law degree at the U.C.L.A. School of Law in 1974. Hernández began her legal career as a staff attorney with the Los Angeles Center for Law and Justice that same year. In 1977, she became the directing attorney for the Legal Aid Foundation office in Lincoln Heights. An expert in civil rights and immigration issues, Hernández worked with Senator Edward M. Kennedy and the U.S. Senate Committee on the Judiciary in 1979 and 1980. She was also the Southwest regional political coordinator of the Kennedy for President campaign in 1980. Active in community affairs, she presently serves on the board of directors of several organizations, including the National Hispanic Leadership Conference, the Latino Museum of History, Art & Culture, and the Independent Sector.

Hernández has been the president and general counsel of MALDEF since 1985, served as its vice president from 1984 to 1985, as employment program director from 1983 to 1984, and as an associate counsel from 1981 to 1983. As president of MALDEF, she directs all litigation and advocacy programs, manages a $4.5 million budget and a 65-person staff, and is responsible for the organization's long-range plans and goals. In 1992 after the Los Angeles riots, Hernández was appointed by Mayor Tom Bradley to the Rebuild L.A. Commission.

Antonia Hernández.

Gerald P. López (1948–)

Law Professor

López attended the University of Southern California and received his law degree from Harvard Law School in 1974. He then served as law clerk to U.S. District Court Judge Edward Schwartz from 1974 to 1975 in San Diego. López has taught at California Western School of Law, U.C.L.A. Law School, and Harvard Law School. He has been a professor at Stanford School of Law since 1985.

Vilma Socorro Martínez (1943–)

Former General Counsel, Mexican American Legal Defense and Educational Fund (MALDEF)

Martínez is a partner in the firm of Munger, Tolles & Olson in Los Angeles. Born in San Antonio, Texas, in 1943, she attended the University of Texas and went on to Columbia University Law School, where she received her law degree in 1967. As general counsel of MALDEF from 1973 to 1982, Martínez was an influential advocate during the congressional hearings for the Voting Rights Act of 1975, which opened the door to greater access to political participation by Hispanics. Martínez also served as a consultant to the U.S. Commission on Civil Rights from 1969 to 1973. In the 1990s, Martínez returned to MALDEF, this time as a member of its board of directors. In 1978 and 1992, Martínez received the medal of excellence from the Columbia Law School as a major figure in civil rights.

Miguel Angel Méndez-Longoria (1942–)

Professor

Méndez-Longoria attended Texas Southmost College and received his law degree from George Washington University Law School in 1968. He was admitted to the Texas bar that same year. He served as a law clerk for the U.S. Court of Claims in Washington, D.C., from 1968 to 1969. He then was legal assistant to U.S. Senator Alan Cranston (D-California) from 1969 to 1971. He was a staff attorney for the Mexican American Legal Defense and Educational Fund (MALDEF) in San Francisco from 1971 to 1972 and was deputy director of California Rural Legal Assistance in San Francisco from 1972 to 1974. From 1975 to 1976, he served as deputy public defender for Monterey County, California. Since 1976, Méndez-Longoria has taught law at the University of Santa Clara Law School, University of California at Berkeley Law School (Boalt Hall), Vermont Law School, University of San Diego Law School, and Stanford University Law School, where he has been a professor since 1984.

Mario G. Obledo (1932–)

Cofounder, Hispanic National Bar Association (HNBA) and Mexican American Legal Defense and Educational Fund (MALDEF); Past President, League of United Latin American Citizens (LULAC)

Born in San Antonio, Texas, Obledo attended the University of Texas, where he was awarded a degree in pharmacy. After serving in the Korean war, he returned to Texas and received his law degree from St. Mary's University Law School in 1961. Obledo has been active in Hispanic affairs for over 30 years. In LULAC he has held local, district, state, and national offices, including the presidency. He was also active in the Southwest Voter Registration Project. Obledo has been active in government and is a former Secretary of the California Health and Welfare Agency, where he was instrumental in bringing thousands of Hispanics into state government. Obledo was also assistant attorney general for the state of Texas and has lectured at Harvard Law School. Currently, Obledo is chairman of the National Rainbow Coalition. He has offices in Austin,

Mario G. Obledo.

Texas, Sacramento, California, and Washington, D.C., where he remains active in national politics.

Michael A. Olivas (1951–)

Professor

Olivas attended Pontifical College in Columbus, Ohio, where he was awarded a B.A. degree in 1972 and an M.A. degree in 1974. He then went on to Ohio State University to receive his Ph.D. degree in 1977. Olivas received his law degree from Georgetown University Law School in 1981. He served as director of resources for the League of United Latin American Citizens (LULAC) Education Resource Center in Washington, D.C., from 1979 to 1982. In 1982, he began teaching law at the University of Houston Law School. He is director of the Institute for Higher Education Law and Governance there and was named associate dean in 1990.

Andrea S. Ordin (1940–)

Former U.S. Attorney, District of California

Ordin was born in 1940 and attended the University of California, where she received her B.A. degree in 1962 and her law degree in 1965. She served as deputy attorney general for California from 1965–72; she then worked as legal counsel for Fair Employment Practices Commission, 1972–73; she served as assistant district attorney for Los Angeles County, 1973–77, and U.S. attorney for the central district of California, Los Angeles, 1977–81; she taught as an adjunct professor at U.C.L.A. law school in 1982; between 1983–90, she was chief assistant attorney general, Los Angeles; and since 1993, she has been a partner in the firm of Morgan, Lewis & Bockius in Los Angeles.

Leo M. Romero (1943–)

Dean, University of New Mexico Law School

Romero is the only Hispanic dean in the United States. He attended Oberlin College and received his J.D. degree from Washington University Law School in St. Louis, Missouri, and his LL.M. degree from Georgetown University Law School in Washington, D.C. Romero was associate editor of the *Washington University Law Quarterly,* and was editor-in-chief of the *Urban Law Review* at Washington University. Romero has taught law at Dickinson University Law School, the University of Oregon Law School, and the University of New Mexico Law School. He became associate dean at the University of New Mexico Law School in 1989 and was named dean in 1991.

Gerald Torres (1952–)

Professor

Torres was born in Victorville, California, in 1952. He attended Stanford University, where he received his B.A. in 1974. He received his J.D. degree from Yale Law School in 1977 and his LL.M. degree from the University of Michigan Law School in 1980. He was admitted to the bar in 1978. Torres was staff attorney for the Children's Defense Fund in Washington, D.C., from 1977 to 1978. He began teaching law in 1980 and has taught at the University of Pittsburgh Law School, the University of Minnesota Law School, and Harvard Law School. He now teaches jurisprudence, environmental law, property law, and agricultural law, at the University of Texas School of Law. Since 1993, he has served as head of the U.S. Justice Department's Environmental Division.

Abelardo López Valdez (1942–)

Attorney, Former Presidential Aide, and Governmental Official

Valdez was born in Floresville, Texas, and attended Texas A & M University. He received a J.D. degree from Baylor University Law School and an LL.M. degree from Harvard Law School. He was admitted to the bar in 1970. Valdez served as an aide to President Lyndon Johnson from 1965 to 1967. He was an attorney for the Overseas Private Investment Corporation from 1971 to 1973 and was general counsel for the Inter-American Foundation from 1973 to 1975. Under President Carter, Valdez was assistant administrator of the Latin American and Caribbean region for the U.S. Agency for International Development from 1977 to 1979. He served as U.S. ambassador and chief of protocol for the White House from 1979 to 1981. In 1981, Valdez joined the law firm of Laxalt, Washington, Perito and Dubuc in Washington, D.C., where he is a partner. Valdez specializes in administrative, regulatory, and international law.

✳ HISPANICS IN THE U.S. JUDICIARY

The U.S. federal court system was created by the Constitution of the United States. Article III of the Constitution states that the "judicial Power of the United States, shall be vested in one supreme Court" and authorizes the Congress to create lower federal courts, which the first Congress did in 1789. Congress created federal trial courts, which are known as district courts and, later, intermediate appellate courts, which are called circuit courts. Article II provided that all federal judges, including Supreme Court justices, are to be appointed by the president and confirmed by the U.S. Senate. Article III provides that federal judges hold their offices for life terms. The American judiciary has great independence, yet its judges are carefully selected through the process of presidential nomination and Senate confirmation.

Almost all of the nation's judicial business was handled by state courts in the early years of the country, partly because there were few federal judges and their jurisdiction was limited. Each state system differed, but nearly all had lower courts to hear trials and appellate courts to hear appeals. Even today, most of the nation's judicial business is handled by state rather than federal courts.

The federal government expanded significantly after the Civil War ended in 1865, and the federal courts grew along with it. In 1891, Congress created the tier of regional appellate courts called courts of appeals, to which appeals of the decisions of the federal trial courts could be taken. These appellate courts, more commonly known as circuit courts, were so named from the days when a judge used to ride a "circuit" on horseback.

The growth of the federal courts was gradual but accelerated after 1958, when the number of cases filed in federal court increased at a rapid pace. Between 1958 and 1988 Congress responded by doubling the number of judges serving in the district courts and courts of appeals. Additionally, Congress created a host of diverse judicial adjuncts, such as magistrates and administrative law judges, to which some of the caseload is delegated.

The Supreme Court, the nation's highest court, consists of the chief justice and eight associate justices. The Supreme Court has original jurisdiction in all cases involving "ambassadors, other public Ministers and Consuls" and those arising from disputes between the states. The Supreme Court can also hear appeals of decisions of the courts of appeals, the intermediate court, and the final decisions of the highest courts of each state if they involve federal questions. The Supreme Court may choose which cases it wants to hear and generally limits its review to cases involving national questions or to issues on which different courts of appeals have reached conflicting results.

There are currently 13 courts of appeals, or circuit courts. The United States is divided into 12 geographical circuits. In addition to these, there is a U.S. Court of Appeals for the Federal Circuit, a specialized court that hears appeals from the Court of Claims and the Court of Customs and Patent Appeals. Each circuit court of appeals is headed by a chief judge and has between six and 26 judges. They usually sit in three-judge panels to review decisions of lower courts, but occasionally meet in greater numbers in important cases. In rare cases, all the judges of the circuit will preside *en banc* to hear an appeal.

U.S. district courts have been established in every state, the District of Columbia, and the U.S. territories. Each state has at least one U.S. district court, and states with large populations are divided into two or more subdistricts. For example, the heavily populated states of California, New York, and Texas are each divided into four subdistricts, while the states of Alaska, Arizona, Montana, and New Mexico each contain one district despite their enormous size.

Hispanic Judges in Federal Courts

Almost all Hispanic judges currently sitting on the bench at all levels of the judiciary received their appointments in the last three decades. Hispanics now sit on both the U.S. district courts and the U.S. courts of appeals. However, no Hispanic has yet sat on the U.S. Supreme Court.

In 1985, the Fund for Modern Courts conducted a study identifying minority judges in all 50 states, excluding Puerto Rico and the District of Columbia. According to that study, there was a total of 24 Hispanic judges in the federal courts at all levels, representing 3.2 percent of the 753 federal judges nationwide. Two of the 24 Hispanic judges were court of appeals judges and 22 were district court judges.

According to the *Directory of Hispanic Judges of the United States,* there were 85 Hispanic members of federal tribunals in 1991, but this includes judges in the District of Columbia and Puerto Rico as well as U.S. magistrates and administrative law judges.

Today seven Hispanic judges sit on the court of appeals, the second-highest federal court in the united States. Arthur L. Alarcón and Ferdinand Fernández sit on the Ninth Circuit for California, Arizona, Nevada, Washington, Oregon, Idaho, Montana, Alaska, Hawaii, Guam and the Northern Mariana Islands. Fortunato P. Benavides, Emilio M. Garza, and Reynaldo G. Garza sit on the Fifth Circuit for Texas, Louisiana and Mississippi. Carlos Lucero sits on the Tenth Circuit for Colorado and New Mexico.

There are 27 Hispanic judges who have been appointed to U.S. district courts across the country. They sit on district courts in Arizona, California, Connecticut, Florida, Illinois, Indiana, Michigan, Missouri, New Jersey, New Mexico, New York, Pennsylvania, Rhode Island, Texas, Washington, D.C., and Puerto Rico.

Additionally, eight Hispanic judges serve as U.S. magistrates, four serve on the U.S. Bankruptcy Court, and 43 currently serve as administrative law judges for various federal agencies, such as the Executive Office for Immigration Review (special inquiry officers), the Social Security Administration, and the Federal Communications Commission (FCC).

Hispanic Judges in State Courts

Currently 90 percent of the nation's judicial business is handled by state rather than federal courts. Each state system differs, but nearly all have trial courts, intermediate courts, and a court of last resort. Those states that mirror the federal three-tier court system generally have district or superior courts in each county, intermediate courts of appeals to review decisions of the trial courts, and state supreme courts, which provide the ultimate review of decisions of the lower courts.

Hispanic Americans have made the greatest inroads at the state, county, and municipal court levels, where hundreds have been appointed or elected to these courts. Hispanic judges have served on state courts throughout the history of the United States, but almost always at the lowest levels. In recent years this trend has changed, as large numbers of Hispanics have been both appointed and elected to all levels of state courts.

In its 1985 study, the Fund for Modern Courts found that there were approximately 163 Hispanic state court judges across the country, representing 1.3 percent of the 12,093 full-time judges of state courts. In 1992, the Hispanic National Bar Association found that over 600 Hispanic Americans are judges on state tribunals of all kinds, including state supreme courts, state appeals courts, and state trial courts.

The growing number of Hispanic judges can be attributed to the increasing Hispanic population as well as to favorable legislation such as the Civil Rights Act of 1964 and the Voting Rights Act of 1965, which have enabled Hispanics to become full participants in the U.S. political and judicial process.

Today, Hispanics serve on some of the highest state courts in the nation. Five Hispanics are state supreme court justices, in Colorado, Michigan, New Mexico, and Texas. There are 14 Hispanics serving

TABLE 13.1
HISPANIC JUDGES IN STATE COURTS

COURT	HIGHEST (A)	INTERM. (B)	TRIAL (C)	MUNICIPAL (D)	MAGISTRATE/JOP (E)	OTHER (F)
AL	0	0	1	0	0	0
AK	0	0	1	0	0	0
AZ	0	2	42	18	19	0
CA	0	3	86	41	0	9
CO	1	1	14	3	0	1
DC	0	0	3	0	0	0
FL	0	0	25	0	0	0
HI	0	0	1	0	0	0
IL	0	0	16	0	0	0
IN	0	0	2	0	0	0
KS	0	0	1	0	0	0
LA	0	0	4	0	0	0
MD	0	0	1	0	0	0
MI	1	0	2	0	0	1
MN	0	0	2	0	0	0
MO	0	0	1	0	0	0
MT	0	0	1	0	1	0
NV	0	0	7	0	2	0
NJ	0	0	13	5	0	0
NM	1	4	86	35	18	1
NY	0	1	25	11	0	0
OH	0	0	2	0	0	0
OR	0	0	1	0	0	0
PA	0	0	2	0	0	0
TX	2	3	280	93	114	0
UT	0	0	1	0	0	0
VA	0	0	1	0	0	0
WA	0	0	4	0	0	0
TOTAL	5	14	625	206	154	12

Source: Hispanic National Bar Association Nationwide Summary of Hispanics in the State Judiciary (1992). This summary excludes judges sitting in Puerto Rico courts.

A. Judges in state courts of last resort; in most states, such courts are called supreme courts

B. State appellate or intermediate court judges   D. Municipal or metropolitan court judges

C. State judges in trial courts of general jurisdiction   E. Local magistrates, or justices of the peace

as state appeals court judges in the states of Arizona, California, Colorado, New Mexico, New York, and Texas.

Most dramatic are the large numbers of Hispanic Americans serving in lower state courts—625 Hispanics serve on various state trial courts. Table 13.1 lists the number of Hispanic judges in each state.

Critics of the process of selecting judges charge that the system is subject to a wide range of problems and abuses, including discrimination against minorities. The appointment process, critics charge, is also subject to political interference from special interest groups, influence peddling, and highly inflammatory campaigning by opposition groups. The nominee's qualifications are rarely the test of whether he or she should be a judge. For example, a 1988 analysis of U.S. Supreme Court appointments published in *Texas Lawyer* found that of 27 failed nominations to the Court, only five were denied because of qualifications or ethical concerns. Political concerns were the primary reasons the other nominees were not confirmed.

Discrimination is a serious problem in the appointive system. The Mexican American Legal Defense and Educational Fund (MALDEF) recently concluded that the appointive system is discriminatory. According to MALDEF, approximately 97 percent of all individuals making judicial appointments are white, which consequently tends to limit the opportunities for minority nominees. (MALDEF states that the elective system is of the greatest benefit to Hispanics and other minorities.) Instead of taking politics out of the system, the appointive process takes the voter out of the system.

Fortunately, today the majority of states select judges through the election process. Eight states choose all their judges in partisan elections; 12 use nonpartisan elections. One state, Virginia, uses legislative election exclusively to select its judges. Another 13 states have variable procedures, appointing judges to certain courts and electing them to others.

The elective franchise is a fundamental and cherished right for all Americans. Advocates of the election process state that judicial officeholders should be held accountable to voters in the same manner as legislators. Proponents of an appointive system often state that areas of the country with small Hispanic populations would be better served by the appointment process. Election advocates charge that the underlying assumption of those who promote an appointive system is that the voters cannot be trusted to select good judges. Regardless of which method is used, if the courts of the United States are to reflect the population they serve, Hispanic lawyers must be included in greater numbers among those who become members of the judiciary.

✳ PRESIDENTIAL APPOINTMENT OF HISPANICS TO THE COURTS

The president appoints federal judges, with the advice and consent of the U.S. Senate. The presidential appointment process has had varied success in elevating Hispanics to the federal courts during the last three decades. The most significant progress for Hispanic Americans was seen during the administration of President Jimmy Carter.

Presidents generally receive district court recommendations for nominations from the senior home-state senator of the president's party, or if there is no such senator, from the state's governor, senior member of Congress of the president's party, or party leader. President Lyndon B. Johnson, whose presidency was from 1963 to 1968, appointed three Hispanic Americans to the district court. President Richard M. Nixon appointed two Hispanics to the court during his presidency, from 1968 to 1974. President Gerald R. Ford appointed one Hispanic American to the district court during his brief presidency, from 1974 to 1977.

The years of the presidency of Jimmy Carter, from 1977 to 1981, were years of change in the judicial selection process. Carter issued an executive order creating a U.S. Circuit Judge Nomination Commission in 1977, modeled after the merit selection system he established while governor of Georgia. The president's order resulted in the appointment of 16 Hispanic Americans to federal courts, nearly thrice the total appointed by Presidents Johnson, Nixon, and Ford combined, and more than all previous presidents of the United States combined throughout the history of the country. Of these, 14 were appointed to the district court and two to the court of appeals.

President Ronald Reagan did not continue the nomination commission begun by President Carter and reverted to the old system used by earlier presidents. During the Reagan years, from 1981 to 1989, ten Hispanic Americans were appointed to the district court and one to the court of appeals. President George Bush did not change the old system used by President Reagan.

From the time Bush became president in 1989 through December of 1991, he had appointed only two Hispanic Americans to the district court and two to the court of appeals. After Supreme Court Justice Thurgood Marshall announced his retirement in mid-1981, there was intense speculation that Bush might nominate the first Hispanic to the Supreme Court. Speculation ended when he nominated Judge Clarence Thomas, an African American, to the Court.

Prominent Hispanics at the Federal and State Judicial Levels

Raymond L. Acosta (1925–)

Acosta was born in New York City and grew up in Teaneck, New Jersey. After graduating from high school in 1943, Acosta joined the U.S. Navy during World War II and took part in the Normandy invasion. He returned to New Jersey after the war and graduated from Princeton University in 1948. Acosta received his law degree in 1951 from Rutgers University Law School in Newark, New Jersey. From 1951 to 1954, he was in private practice in Hackensack, New Jersey, and worked for the Federal Bureau of Investigation in Washington, D.C., from 1954 to 1958. In 1958, he moved to Puerto Rico to serve as assistant U.S. attorney there. From 1962 to 1980, he was in the private sector, practicing law in San Juan, Puerto Rico, with the firm of Igaravídez and Acosta, and held posts with various real estate and banking interests. From 1980 to 1982, Acosta was the U.S. attorney for Puerto Rico. In 1982, President Reagan appointed Acosta to the U.S. District Court for the District of Puerto Rico.

Arthur L. Alarcón.

Raymond L. Acosta.

Robert P. Aguilar (1931–)

Former judge of the U.S. District Court for the Northern District of California, Aguilar attended the University of California, Berkeley, where he received his B.A. degree in 1954. He then went on to receive his law degree from the University of California Hastings College of Law. He practiced law with the firms of Mezzetti and Aguilar, Aguilar & Aguilar, and Aguilar & Edwards from 1960 to 1979. In 1979 Aguilar was appointed a California Superior Court judge for Santa Clara County. He was later appointed to the U.S. District Court for the Northern District of California by President Jimmy Carter in 1980, where he remained until his resignation in 1991.

Arthur L. Alarcón (1925–)

Alarcón received his B.A. degree in 1949 and his LL.B. degree in 1951, both from the University of Southern California. President Carter appointed him to the U.S. Court of Appeals for the Ninth Circuit in 1979.

John Argüelles (1927-)

Former supreme court justice for the state of California, Argüelles was born in Los Angeles, California, to Arturo Argüelles, a Mexican American who graduated from Columbia University with an accounting degree, and Eva Powers, the daughter of an Oklahoma judge. Argüelles was educated in public schools in Los Angeles and went on to U.C.L.A. where he received a degree in economics in 1950. He continued his education at the U.C.L.A. law school and received his degree in 1954. Argüelles practiced law in East Los Angeles and Montebello, California, from 1955 to 1963. During that time, he was president of the local bar association and was elected to the Montebello City Council with the largest vote in that city's history. In 1963 Governor Edmund G. Brown, Sr., appointed Argüelles municipal court judge for the East Los Angeles Municipal Court. He was then elevated to the Los Angeles Superior Court by Governor Ronald Reagan in 1969. Argüelles was appointed to the California Court of Appeal for the Second District in 1984 by Governor George Deukmejian. Three years later, Deukmejian named Argüelles to the California Supreme Court, where he served until his retirement in 1989. At the end of 1989, Argüelles joined the law firm of Gibson, Dunn & Crutcher.

Joseph Francis Baca (1936-)

Baca was born in Albuquerque, New Mexico, to Mexican American parents. He graduated from the University of New Mexico in 1960 with a degree in education and studied law at George Washington University in Washington, D.C., receiving his degree in 1964. Baca served as assistant district attorney in Santa Fe from 1965 to 1966, then as special assistant to the attorney general of New Mexico from 1966 to 1972. He also established a private law practice in Albuquerque during this time. In 1972 Baca was appointed by Governor Bruce King to fill a vacancy in the New Mexico District Court for the Second District in Albuquerque. Baca was elected to six-year terms in 1972, 1978, and 1984. In 1988, Baca was elected to an eight-year term as justice of the New Mexico Supreme Court. In 1989, Baca was named Judge of the Year by the People's Commission for Criminal Justice.

Juan C. Burciaga (1929-)

Burciaga attended the U.S. Military Academy at West Point, where he received his B.S. degree in 1952. He then served in the U.S. Air Force from 1952 to 1960. He received his law degree from the University of New Mexico School of Law in 1963. Burciaga was in private practice from 1964 to 1979 with the firm of Ussery, Burciaga & Parrish. In 1979, President Jimmy Carter appointed Burciaga to the U.S. District Court for the District of New Mexico. Burciaga became chief judge of that court.

José A. Cabranés (1940-)

Born in Mayagüez, Puerto Rico, Cabranés is the first native Puerto Rican appointed to the federal court within the continental United States. Cabranés moved with his family to New York from Puerto Rico when he was only five. After attending public schools in the Bronx and Flushing, Queens, he graduated from Columbia College in 1961. He received his law degree from Yale University Law School in 1965, and an LL.M. degree in international law from the University of Cambridge in Cambridge, England, in 1967. Cabranés served as general counsel of Yale University from 1975 to 1979. Previously he had practiced law at the firm of Casey, Lane & Mittendorf in New York City from 1967 to 1971; taught law at Rutgers University School of Law in New Jersey from 1971 to 1973; and served as special counsel to the governor of Puerto Rico and as administrator, Office of the Commonwealth of Puerto Rico, Washington, D.C.

Cabranés also served in the administration of President Jimmy Carter as a member of the President's Commission on Mental Health from 1977 to 1978; as a member of the U.S. delegation to the Belgrade Conference on Security and Cooperation in Europe from 1977 to 1978; and as consultant to U.S. Secretary of State Cyrus Vance in 1978. In 1979, Carter appointed Cabranés to the U.S. District Court for the District of Connecticut; he served as chief judge from 1992 to 1994, when he was named judge of the U.S. Court of Appeals. In December 1988 U.S. Supreme Court Chief Justice William H. Rehnquist named Judge Cabranés as one of five federal judges for the 15-member Federal Courts Study Committee, created by an act of Congress "to examine problems facing the federal courts and develop a long-range plan for the future of the federal judiciary."

Santiago E. Campos (1926-)

Campos served in the U.S. Navy during World War II. He attended Central College in Fayette, Missouri, and received his law degree from the University of New Mexico in 1953. Campos was assistant attorney general for the state of New Mexico from 1954 to 1957 and from 1971 to 1978 he was a New Mexico district judge. President Carter appointed Judge Campos to the U.S. District Court for the District of New Mexico in 1978; he became a senior judge in 1992.

John M. Cannella (1908–)

Cannella is a Colombian American who played professional football for the New York Giants from 1933 to 1935. He attended Fordham University, where he received his B.A. degree in 1930 and his law degree in 1933. Cannella was assistant U.S. attorney for the Southern District of New York from 1940 to 1942. In 1963 President Kennedy appointed him to the U.S. District Court for the southern district of New York.

Carmen C. Cerezo (1940–)

Cerezo attended the University of Puerto Rico, where he received his B.A. degree in 1963 and his LL.B. degree in 1966. He was a judge on the Puerto Rico Court of Inter Appeals from 1976 to 1980, and was on the Superior Court of Puerto Rico from 1972 to 1976. President Carter appointed Judge Cerezo to the U.S. District Court for the District of Puerto Rico in 1980; and in 1993, he became chief judge.

James DeAnda (1925–)

Born in Houston in 1925, DeAnda received his B.A. degree from Texas A & M University and his J.D. degree from the University of Texas in 1950. He was in private practice from 1951 until 1979. In 1979, Judge DeAnda was appointed to the U.S. District Court for the Southern District of Texas where he subsequently became chief judge.

Ferdinand Francis Fernández (1937–)

Fernández attended the University of Southern California and was awarded his B.A. degree in 1958 and his J.D. degree in 1962. He was in private practice from 1964 to 1980 with the law firm of Allard, Shelton & O'Connor in Pomona, California. Fernández was on the U.S. District Court for the Central District of California from 1985 to 1989. In 1989, Fernández was appointed to the U.S. Court of Appeals for the Ninth Circuit by President Bush. Fernández was reportedly considered as a potential replacement for retiring U.S. Supreme Court Justice Thurgood Marshall.

José Antonio Fuste (1943–)

Fuste attended the University of Puerto Rico, where he received his B.A. degree in 1965 and his LL.B. degree in 1968. He was in private practice from 1968 to 1985 with the law firm of Jiménez and Fuste. Fuste was appointed to the U.S. District Court for the District of Puerto Rico by President Reagan in 1985. President Bush appointed Gaitán to the U.S. District Court for the Western District of Missouri in 1991.

Fernando J. Gaitán, Jr.

President Bush appointed Gaitán to the U.S. District Court for the Western District of Missouri in 1991.

Edward J. García (1928–)

García attended the Sacramento City College and graduated in 1951. He received his law degree from the McGeorge School of Law in 1958. García was deputy district attorney for Sacramento County from 1959 to 1964, supervising deputy district attorney from 1964 to 1969, and chief deputy district attorney from 1969 to 1972. He was a Sacramento Municipal Court judge from 1972 until 1984. President Reagan appointed Judge García to the U.S. District Court for the Eastern District of California in 1984.

Hipolito Frank García (1925–)

García served in the U.S. Army during World War II. He then attended St. Mary's University, where he received his B.A. degree in 1949 and his LL.B. degree in 1951. He was a Texas county court judge from 1964 to 1980. In 1980 President Carter appointed García to the U.S. District Court for the Western District of Texas.

Ferdinand Francis Fernández.

Emilio M. Garza (1947–)

Garza attended the University of Notre Dame and was awarded his B.A. degree in 1969 and M.A. degree in 1970. He received his law degree from the University of Texas in 1976. He was in private practice from 1976 to 1987 with the law firm of Clemens, Spencer, Welmaker & Finck. Garza was a judge for the U.S. District Court for the Western District of Texas from 1988 to 1991. President Bush appointed Judge Garza to the U.S. Court of Appeals for the Fifth Circuit in 1991.

Reynaldo G. Garza (1915–)

Garza was born in Brownsville, Texas, in 1915. His parents were both born in Mexico and had immigrated to the United States in 1901. Garza attended the University of Texas, where he received his law degree in 1939. He practiced law in Brownsville as a solo practitioner until he joined the air force during World War II. After the war, he resumed his private practice until 1950, when he joined the firm of Sharpe, Cunningham & Garza.

President Kennedy in 1961 appointed Garza to the U.S. District Court for the Southern District of Texas; in 1974 he became chief judge of that court. In 1979, Garza was appointed to the U.S. Court of Appeals for the Fifth Circuit by President Jimmy Carter. In 1987, U.S. Supreme Court Chief Justice William H. Rehnquist appointed Garza to the Temporary Emergency Court of Appeals of the United States. He was later named by Rehnquist as chief judge of that court.

Garza has often been recognized for his active role in education, community affairs, and the law. He was honored when a small law school opened its doors in Edinburg, Texas, and was named the Reynaldo G. Garza School of Law. Pope Pius XII twice decorated Garza for his work with the Knights of Columbus, conferring on him the Medal Pro Ecclesia et Pontifice in 1953 and recognizing him as a Knight of the Order of St. Gregory the Great in 1954. Garza received the American Association of Community and Junior Colleges Alumnus of the Year Award in 1984, and in 1989 he was given the Distinguished Alumnus Award of the University of Texas.

President Carter offered the position of attorney general of the United States to Judge Garza. Garza declined the cabinet post because he would have had to resign from his position as a federal judge, which is a lifetime appointment. Today, Judge Garza is on reduced duty and close to retirement.

Gilberto Gierbolini (1926–)

Gierbolini attended the University of Puerto Rico, where he received his B.A. degree in 1951 and his LL.B. degree in 1961. He was a captain in the U.S. Army and served during the Korean War from 1951 to 1957. Gierbolini served as assistant U.S. attorney for Puerto Rico from 1961 to 1966, as a superior court judge from 1966 to 1969, as assistant secretary of justice for Puerto Rico from 1969 to 1972, and as solicitor general of Puerto Rico from 1970 to 1972. Gierbolini was in the private practice of law between 1972 and 1980. In 1980, President Carter appointed Judge Gierbolini to the U.S. District Court for the District of Puerto Rico.

Ricardo H. Hinojosa (1950–)

Hinojosa attended the University of Texas, where he received his B.A. degree in 1972. He received his law degree from Harvard University Law School in 1975 and was in private practice as a partner in the law firm of Ewers & Toothaker in McAllen, Texas, from 1976 until 1983. From 1975 to 1976, Hinojosa served on the Texas Supreme Court. In 1983, Hinojosa was appointed by President Reagan to the U.S. District Court for the Southern District of Texas.

Ricardo H. Hinojosa.

Héctor M. Laffitte (1934–)

Héctor M. Laffitte was born in Ponce, Puerto Rico. Laffitte received his B.A. from the Interamerican University in 1955, his law degree from the University of Puerto Rico in 1958, and his LL.M. degree from Georgetown University in 1960. He was the Civil Rights Commissioner for the commonwealth of Puerto Rico from 1969 to 1972. He was in private practice from 1972 to 1983 with the firm of Laffitte, Domínguez and Totti. President Reagan appointed Laffitte to the U.S. District Court for the District of Puerto Rico in 1983.

George La Plata (1924–)

La Plata was born in 1924 in Detroit to Mexican American parents. He attended Wayne State University, where he received his B.A. degree in 1951. He received his law degree from the Detroit College of Law in 1956. La Plata also served in the U.S. Marine Corps during World War II, reaching the rank of colonel. La Plata, in conjunction with George Menéndez, adviser to the Republic of Mexico, helped pioneer the representation of migrant workers in Michigan, Ohio, and Indiana during the 1950s. From 1956 to 1979, La Plata was in private practice. He served as a Michigan county judge from 1979 to 1985, making him the first Hispanic judge in Michigan history. President Reagan appointed Judge La Plata to the U.S. District Court for the Eastern District of Michigan in 1985. He remains active in providing pro bono services to Hispanics in his community.

Rudolpho Lozano (1942–)

Lozano attended Indiana University, where he received his B.A. degree in 1963 and his law degree in 1966. He was in private practice with the law firm of Spangler, Jennings, Spangler, & Dougherty in Merrillville, Indiana, from 1966 to 1988. In 1988 President Reagan appointed Lozano to the U.S. District Court for the Northern District of Indiana.

Alfredo C. Márquez (1922–)

Márquez served in World War II as an ensign in the U.S. Navy. After the war, he attended the University of Arizona, where he received his B.S. degree in 1948 and his law degree in 1950. Márquez served as assistant attorney general for the state of Arizona from 1951 to 1952, as prosecutor for the city of Tucson and assistant county attorney for Pima County from 1953 to 1954, and as an aide to Congressman Stewart Udall (D-AZ) in 1955. Márquez was in private practice with the firm of Mesch, Márquez and Rothschild from 1957 until 1980. Márquez was appointed by President Carter in 1980 to the U.S. District Court for the District of Arizona.

Harold R. Medina, Sr. (1888–1991)

Former U.S. circuit court judge, Harold Medina was born in Brooklyn, New York, on February 16, 1888, of Mexican American and Dutch American parents. His father, Joaquín Medina, came to the United States as a refugee from a bitter civil and race war in the Yucatan Peninsula. Harold Medina attended Princeton University, where he graduated with honors in 1909. He went on to Columbia University Law School and received his law degree in 1912. Medina began practicing law and also lectured at Columbia Law School at the invitation of Dean Harlan Fiske Stone. In 1918, Medina formed his own law firm and specialized in appeals. The most famous case argued by Medina was the Cramer treason case during World War II. Anthony Cramer, of Brooklyn, was accused of helping two Nazi spies who had landed from a submarine. Medina initially lost the case in the lower courts but won it on appeal to the U.S. Supreme Court. After World War II ended, Medina was appointed to the U.S. District Court for the District of New York by President Harry Truman. In 1951 President Truman appointed Medina to the U.S. Court of Appeals for the Second Circuit.

Harold R. Medina, Sr.

Federico A. Moreno, Sr. (1952–)

Moreno was born in Caracas, Venezuela, and immigrated to the United States with his family in 1963. In 1974, Moreno graduated from the University of Notre Dame, where he received his B.A. degree in government. He worked as a janitor and in restaurants to pay his way through college. After graduating, he taught at the Atlantic Community College in Mays Landing, New Jersey, and at Stockton State College in Pomona, New Jersey, in 1975 and 1976. In 1978, Moreno received his law degree from the University of Miami School of Law. Moreno was an associate with the law firm of Rollins, Peeples & Meadows in 1978 and 1979, and served as an assistant federal public defender from 1979 to 1981. He was a partner in the law firm of Thornton, Rothman & Moreno from 1982 to 1986. He served as Dade County judge in 1986 and 1987. Moreno was a Florida Circuit Court judge from 1987 until 1990. President Bush appointed Moreno to the U.S. District Court for the Southern District of Florida in 1990.

Philip Newman (1916–)

The first Mexican-born U.S. judge, Newman was born in Mexico City to a German American father and a Mexican mother. His family fled Mexico in the 1920s during the Mexican civil war and settled in California. Arriving destitute in the United States, Newman's father put himself through law school at night and became an attorney. Newman also became an attorney in 1941. He won landmark cases protecting the rights of individuals against unwarranted searches and seizures and leading to changes in immigration law. He was also the founder of the Community Services Organization in Los Angeles. In 1964, Newman was appointed by Governor Edmund G. Brown to a Los Angeles municipal judgeship, where he remained until his retirement in 1982.

Juan M. Pérez-Giménez (1941–)

Pérez-Giménez received his B.A. degree in 1963 and his LL.B. degree in 1968 from the University of Puerto Rico; his M.B.A. degree was conferred by George Washington University in 1965. He was an assistant U.S. attorney for Puerto Rico from 1971 to 1975. President Carter appointed Pérez-Giménez to the U.S. District Court for the District of Puerto Rico in 1979.

Jaime Pieras, Jr. (1924–)

Pieras served in the U.S. Army during World War II. He received his B.A. degree from Catholic University in 1945 and his J.D. degree from Georgetown University in 1948. Pieras was in private practice from 1949 until 1982. In 1982, Pieras was appointed to the U.S. District Court for the District of Puerto Rico by President Reagan.

Edward C. Prado (1947–)

Prado attended the University of Texas, where he received his B.A. degree in 1969 and his J.D. degree in 1972. In 1984, President Reagan appointed Prado to the U.S. District Court for the Western District of Texas.

Raul Anthony Ramírez (1944–)

After receiving his law degree from the University of the Pacific, McGeorge School of Law, Ramírez went into private practice. He served as a municipal court judge in Sacramento from 1977 until 1980. In 1980, he was appointed by President Carter to the U.S. District Court for the Eastern District of California. Since 1990, he has been a senior partner in the firm of Orrick, Herrington & Sutcliffe in Sacramento.

Manuel L. Real (1924–)

Real's parents immigrated to the United States from Spain. His mother was born in 1924 in Albunol, Granada, Spain, and his father was born in Sierra de Yegas, Malaga, Spain. Real was educated in California and received his B.S. degree from the University of California in 1944 and his LL.B. degree from Loyola University in 1951. Real also served as assistant U.S. attorney from 1952 to 1955 for the Southern District of California. He was in private practice from 1955 to 1964 in San Pedro, California, and was assistant U.S. attorney for the Southern District of California from 1964 to 1966. In 1966, Real was appointed to the U.S. District Court for the Central District of California by President Johnson. He was named chief judge of that court in 1982.

Cruz Reynoso (1931–)

A former state supreme court justice for California, Reynoso was born on May 2, 1931, to farm worker parents in the small town of Brea, California, where he was raised and received his early education. He attended Fullerton Junior College and Pomona College, where he earned his B.A. degree in 1953. From 1953 to 1955, he served in the U.S. Army. After his discharge, Reynoso began studying law at the University of California, Berkeley, and was awarded his degree in 1958. That same year he began a private law practice in El Centro, California. During the 1960s, Reynoso acted as assistant chief of the Division of Fair Employment Practices for California. From 1967 to 1968, he was associate general

Cruz Reynoso.

counsel to the Equal Employment Opportunity Commission in Washington, D.C., returning to California to become the first deputy director and then director of California Rural Legal Assistance. In 1972, he accepted a position at the University of New Mexico Law School, where he served for four years.

In 1976, Reynoso was appointed to the California Court of Appeals in Sacramento as an associate justice. Governor Jerry Brown then appointed him to the California Supreme Court in 1982. Reynoso became the first Hispanic on the court and served until 1986. In 1987, he entered private practice with the firm of O'Donnell & Gordon in Los Angeles and subsequently was of counsel to Kaye, Scholer, Fierman, Hays & Handler in Sacramento. Reynoso has been honored with appointments to four presidential commissions, including the Select Commission on Immigration and Refugee Policy and the UN Commission on Human Rights. He was appointed to the law faculty of the University of California, Los Angeles, in 1990.

Dorothy Comstock Riley (1924–)

Supreme court justice for the state of Michigan, Dorothy Riley was born to Hispanic parents in De-

troit in 1924. She attended Wayne State University, where she received both her B.A. degree in politics and her law degree. She went into private practice in 1950 and established the firm of Riley and Roumell in 1968. Riley sat on the Michigan Court of Appeals from 1976 until 1982, when she was elevated to the Michigan Supreme Court as an associate justice. Riley was named chief justice in 1987 and remains in that position.

Joseph H. Rodríguez (1930–)

Rodriguez received his B.A. degree from LaSalle University in 1955 and his J.D. degree from Rutgers University in 1958. He was in private practice from 1959 to 1982 with the firm of Brown, Connery, Kulp, Wille, Purcell, & Greene and was also an instructor at Rutgers University School of Law from 1972 to 1982. In 1982, Rodriguez was appointed New Jersey public advocate, a state cabinet position, and served until 1985. He litigated landmark cases in the areas of education and housing. President Reagan appointed Rodriguez to the U.S. District Court for the District of New Jersey in 1985. Rodriguez is active in community affairs.

Dorothy Comstock Riley.

Luis D. Rovirá (1923–)

Supreme court justice for the state of Colorado, Rovirá was born in San Juan, Puerto Rico. His family moved to Colorado, where he was educated. Rovirá attended the University of Colorado and received both B.A. and law degrees. He was in private practice with the firm of Rovirá, DeMuth & Eiberger until 1976. In 1976, Rovirá was appointed to the Colorado District Court for the second district. In 1979, he was elevated to the Colorado Supreme Court as an associate justice and became chief justice in 1990.

Ernest C. Torres (1941–)

Torres graduated from Dartmouth College in 1963 and received his law degree from Duke University School of Law in 1968. He was in private practice from 1968 to 1974. In 1975, Torres was elected to the Rhode Island House of Representatives, where he served until 1980. After leaving the state house, he went into private practice. Torres was appointed by President Reagan in 1988 to the U.S. District Court for the District of Rhode Island.

Juan R. Torruella (1933–)

Torruella received his B.A. degree from the University of Pennsylvania in 1954 and his LL.B. degree from Boston University in 1957. He was appointed by President Ford to the U.S. District Court for the District of Puerto Rico in 1974 and was chief judge of that court from 1982 to 1984. In 1984, President Reagan appointed Torruella to the U.S. Court of Appeals for the First Circuit.

Filemón B. Vela (1935–)

Vela graduated from the University of Texas and received a J.D. degree from St. Mary's University in 1962. He was in private practice from 1962 to 1975 and also served as an attorney for the Mexican American Legal Defense and Educational Fund (MALDEF) from 1962 to 1975. He was a Texas district court judge from 1975 to 1980. President Carter appointed Vela to the U.S. District Court for the Southern District of Texas in 1980.

✳ HISPANICS IN THE POLITICAL PROCESS

Widespread political activity at the national level by Hispanic Americans has been intermittent since the first Hispanic was elected to Congress. Joseph Marion Hernández was elected to Congress representing Florida in 1822 as a member of the Whig party. No other Hispanic held national office for 30 years. A total of 11 Hispanics were elected to the U.S. Congress in the entire nineteenth century, all from New Mexico, except for one from California and Congressman Hernández from Florida. From the turn of the century until the 1950s, there were a total of 15, five from New Mexico, two from Louisiana, and eight resident commissioners from Puerto Rico, which became a U.S. possession in 1898. Since the 1960s, the number of Hispanic Americans elected to Congress has been steadily increasing. In 1996, there were 17 Hispanics serving in Congress, representing constituents from Arizona, California, Florida, Illinois, New Jersey, New Mexico, New York and Texas. All are congressmen and women; none are senators. In addition, there are three non-voting representatives from Puerto Rico, Guam, and the U.S. Virgin Islands.

For a century, the majority of Hispanic Americans holding political office at the local level was limited to southwestern states, southern Florida, and New York City. Since the 1960s, growth in the population of Hispanics and favorable civil rights legislation, such as the Voting Rights Act of 1965, have combined to create opportunity for Hispanic candidates to win public office in other areas of the country. Hispanic Americans have made the greatest inroads at the municipal level. In 1991, Hispanics held elected office at the local level in 35 of the 50 states.

Harry P. Pachón, national director of the National Association of Latino Elected and Appointed Officials (NALEO), stated that in 1990 NALEO identified "4,004 Hispanic Americans holding publicly elected offices throughout the country." Pachón stated that "although this number is only a small fraction of the nation's 504,404 elected officials, less than one percent, the number of Hispanic elected officials for various states is quite large."

In the past 30 years, Hispanic Americans have become one of the largest and fastest-growing groups of elected officials in the United States. Congressman Bill Richardson (D-New Mexico) states, "National candidates and both major political parties are undertaking major campaigns to woo Hispanic American support. We are recognized as the nation's fastest growing minority group and are being courted as such. This attention will only increase our political strength."

✳ HISPANIC VOTING AND THE VOTING RIGHTS ACT OF 1965

The primary aim of the Voting Rights Act of 1965 was African American enfranchisement in the South. Specifically, obstacles to registration and voting faced by African Americans were the major concern of those who framed the statute in the 1960s. Its potential as a tool for Hispanic Americans was not fully realized until the act was extended and amended in 1970.

The 1970 amendments to this landmark legislation added a provision that was designed to guard against inventive new barriers to political participation by requiring federal approval of all changes in voting procedure in certain jurisdictions, primarily southern states. Disgruntled officials in Mississippi and other southern states embarked on schemes to dilute African American voter impact in elections by eliminating single-member districts and creating at-large voting.

The U.S. Supreme Court responded, in *Allen v. State Board of Elections,* 393 U.S. 544 (1969), by extending federal authority to object to proposed discriminatory alterations in voting districts, the introduction of at-large voting, and other such changes, in addition to reaffirming the original power to object to discriminatory innovations involving registration and voting.

Until 1980, the U.S. Census Bureau had historically classified Hispanic Americans as "white," with the single exception of the 1930 census, and many argued that to extend coverage of the Voting Rights Act to a class of people who considered themselves white was unjustifiable. The Fifteenth Amendment rights secured by the statute protected against denial of the right to vote only on account of "race, color or previous condition of servitude." If Hispanic Americans were white, they were ineligible for the special protection of the Voting Rights Act.

During congressional hearings to extend the Voting Rights Act in 1975, J. Stanley Pottinger, assistant attorney general of the U.S. Justice Department's Civil Rights Division, saw the labeling problem as inconsequential and told Congress that the Justice Department's practice "has been to treat Indians, Puerto Ricans, and Mexican Americans as racial groups." His argument hardly settled the matter for everyone, but Congress agreed to amend the act to include "language minorities," which specifically included Spanish-speakers.

Vilma S. Martínez, president of the Mexican American Legal Defense and Educational Fund (MALDEF), testified before Congress in 1975 about voting districts in Texas where assistance to non-English-speaking voters was being denied. She testified further that Texas had been gerrymandering voting districts to give unfair advantage to English-speaking residents. State action creating at-large voting, annexations to voting districts, and redistricting plans fragmented Hispanic voting strength. Additionally, majority vote requirements, numbered posts, and other confusing procedural rules diminished the likelihood that a Hispanic American would gain an elected office.

Congress acted decisively. The Voting Rights Act Amendments of 1975, which extended the provisions of the Voting Rights Act of 1965, made permanent the national ban on literacy tests. The amendments condemned any action by states, which was no longer limited to southern states, to realign voting districts to dilute the impact of minority voters who resided within the district. Any redistricting plan would have to be approved by the federal government.

In 1980, the U.S. Supreme Court, in *City of Mobile v. Bolden,* 446 U.S. 55, rejected a challenge to at-large elections in Mobile, Alabama, because the Court was not convinced that the city had acted with the purpose of discriminating against minority voters. The Court, in its sharply divided decision, found that the city had not violated the Voting Rights Act.

Congress reacted to the Supreme Court decision with the important Voting Rights Act Amendments of 1982. The amendments, under Section 2, prohibit any voting law or practice created by a state or political subdivision that "results" in denial of the right of any citizen of the United States to vote on account of race, color, or language-minority status. The amendments eliminated the need to prove that the state or political subdivision created a voting law with the "intention" of discriminating against minority voters.

In one of the first cases to be tried under Section 2 of the 1982 amendments, *Velásquez v. City of Abilene,* 725 F.2d 1017 (5th Cir. 1983), prominent judge Reynaldo G. Garza delivered the opinion of the U.S. Court of Appeals for the Fifth Circuit. Garza stated for the court that the intention of Congress was clear in cases of vote dilution, referring to the 1982 amendments. Garza stated that the city of Abilene's use of at-large voting, bloc voting, and other voting mechanisms resulted in vote dilution and had a discriminatory effect on Hispanic American voters in the city.

A year later, the Fifth Circuit Court made a similar ruling in *Jones v. City of Lubbock,* 727 F.2d 364 (5th Cir. 1984). The city of Lubbock, Texas, a medium-sized city with a diverse population, had a clear white majority. Under an at-large voting scheme, the majority uniformly elected an all-white city council. The court found that the voting method used by the city polarized voting between the white majority and minority voters, and the result was discrimination against minority voters.

In the last decade, holdouts of racially discriminatory electoral patterns have been coming under intense pressure from the courts to end discrimination against minority voters. The success in the courts has contributed to the growing numbers of Hispanic Americans holding elected offices across the United States. In 1991, for the first time in history, the city of Abilene had two Hispanics on its city council; the city of Lubbock had one Hispanic on its city council, as well as a Hispanic county commissioner.

✳ CONGRESSIONAL HISPANIC CAUCUS

The Congressional Hispanic Caucus, organized in December 1976, is a bipartisan group of 12 members of Congress of Hispanic descent. The caucus is dedicated to voicing and advancing, through the legislative process, issues affecting Hispanic Americans in the United States and its territories.

Organized as a legislative service organization under the rules of Congress, the caucus is composed solely of members of the U.S. Congress. Under these rules, associate membership is offered to dues-paying members of Congress who are not of Hispanic descent. With its associate members, caucus membership represents 20 states, Puerto Rico, Guam, and the U.S. Virgin Islands.

Although every issue that affects the quality of life of all U.S. citizens is a Congressional Hispanic Caucus concern, there are national and international issues that have a particular impact on the Hispanic community. The caucus monitors legislative action as well as policies and practices of the executive and judicial branches of government that affect these issues.

In 1995, Congress abolished funding for the minority caucuses. The overwhelmingly conservative Congress eliminated its funding for what the Republics saw as the opposition; the majority of minority congressmen and senators are Democratic and liberal.

✳ HISPANICS IN CONGRESS

The growing Hispanic population remains significantly underrepresented in the U.S. Congress today. Hispanic American voting levels have traditionally fallen well below the national average. In spite of favorable legislation, advocates actively seeking to increase Hispanic American voter registration still cite poverty, inadequate education, language barriers, and alienage as critical obstacles that have discouraged voting. Despite these problems, Hispanic Americans have been going to the polls in increasing numbers. This is evident at the national level, where, in 1991, 13 Hispanic Americans were serving in the U.S. House of Representatives.

Of the 20 Hispanic representatives currently hold-ing office, 17 have full voting privileges and represent districts in the states of Arizona, California, Florida, Illinois, New Jersey, New Mexico, New York, and Texas. The three nonvoting members are resident commissioners of Puerto Rico, Guam and the U.S. Virgin Islands. Of the 17 congressmen, 14 are Democrats. Three congressmen are Republicans: Henry Bonilla of Texas, and the two Florida congressmen, Lincoln Díaz-Balart, and Ileana Ros-Lehtinen.

No Hispanic American candidate has been elected to the U.S. Senate since 1970, when New Mexico Democrat Joseph Manuel Montoya won his second and last election. Senator Montoya served in the Senate from 1964 to 1977. The only other Hispanic American to be elected to the Senate was New Mexico Democrat Dennis Chávez, who served with great distinction from 1935 to 1962. Both Senators Chávez and Montoya served as members of the U.S. House of Representatives prior to being elected to the Senate.

Xavier Becerra (1958–)

(D-California)

Born on January 26, 1958, in Sacramento, California, Becerra received his B.A. from Stanford University in 1980 and his law degree from Stanford in 1984. He served as deputy attorney general in the California Department of Justice from 1987 to 1990, when he was elected to the state legislature. In 1994, Becerra was elected to represent Los Angeles' Thirtieth Congressional District; he is currently in his second term.

Henry Bonilla

(R-Texas)

Born in Calvert, Texas, Bonilla received his B.A. degree from the University of Texas in 1968 and his law degree from Texas in 1971. After working in private practice since graduation, he served as the state director of the League of United Latin American Citizens (LULAC) from 1977 to 1979. From 1979 to 1980, he served as president of LULAC and then from 1980 to 1985 as its general counsel. From 1985 to the president, he has been the chairman of the Mexican American Democrats of Texas. Bonilla is in his second term of serving the Twenty-third District of Texas, which covers San Antonio.

E. (Kika) de la Garza (1927–)

(D-Texas)

De la Garza was born on September 22, 1927, in the Mexican border town of Mercedes, Texas. He comes from a family with roots in the Rio Grande Valley that go back to the 1700's. After graduating from high school, de la Garza, by struggle and perseverance, obtained his education at Edinburg Junior

College and St. Mary's University in San Antonio. His education was interrupted by the Korean War, in which he served as an artillery officer from 1950 to 1952. He then earned his B.A. degree from St. Mary's in 1952 and later received his law degree from St. Mary's Law School.

With heavily Mexican American Hidalgo County as his base of support, de la Garza was elected to the Texas House of Representatives in 1952. He was reelected for another five terms. De la Garza was first elected to Congress in 1964 as a Democrat from the Rio Grande Valley's Fifteenth District. His election was a milestone for Texas Mexican Americans.

De la Garza is chairman of the House Agriculture Committee and an ex officio member of all its subcommittees. He is also a member and former chairman of the Congressional Hispanic Caucus. He is an active member of the League of United Latin American Citizens (LULAC) and a host of other organizations. In 1978 Mexican President José López Portillo awarded de la Garza Mexico's highest award to a foreigner, the order of the Aztec Eagle.

Lincoln Díaz-Balart (1961–)

(R-Florida)

Díaz-Balart was born on August 25, 1961, in Havana, Cuba. He received his B.A. from the New College University of Southern Florida in 1976 and his law degree from Case Western Reserve University in 1969. After entering the private practice of law, Díaz-Balart served as a state representative from 1986 to 1989 and as a state senator from 1989 until his election to the U.S. Congress in 1992. He represents the Twenty-first Congressional District of Miami.

Henry Barbosa González (1916–)

(D-Texas)

González was born on May 3, 1916, in San Antonio, Texas, to Mexican refugees. He grew up in a family that stressed education and intellectual pursuits. González received his early education in San Antonio public schools. He went on to attend San Antonio Junior College and the University of Texas at Austin, where he received his bachelor's degree. He then attended St. Mary's University Law School, where he received his law degree in 1943. After graduation, González worked at a variety of jobs, including teaching and social services. In 1950, González entered the political arena and ran for San Antonio City Council. He lost narrowly, but won in his second bid three years later. González fought for a city ordinance ending segregation in city facilities. In 1956, he was elected to the Texas Senate. González was the first Mexican American Texas state senator in

Henry Barbosa González.

110 years. He attracted national attention as an outspoken advocate of equal rights for minorities and as an opponent of racist legislation.

In 1960 González was elected to Congress for the first time, as a Democrat representing the Twentieth District of Texas. He has been overwhelmingly reelected to Congress for each subsequent term. Congressman González is currently the chairman of the influential House Banking, Finance and Urban Affairs Committee and is also chairman of the Housing and Community Development Subcommittee. The first Texan of Mexican descent to serve in the U.S. House of Representatives, he has fervently defended civil rights, distinguishing himself nationally as a liberal Democrat during the 1960s and 1970s. He was chairman of the Viva Kennedy campaign in 1960 and the Viva Johnson campaign in 1964. In 1964, he contributed significantly to the termination of the infamous Mexican Bracero Program.

Luis Gutiérrez (1953–)

(D-Illinois)

Gutiérrez was born in Chicago on December 10, 1953. He received his B.A. from Northeastern Illinois University in 1976 and worked as a teacher in the Chicago public schools until 1984, when he became an administrative assistant to the mayor of Chicago. In 1986, Gutiérrez became an alderman for the Twenty-sixth Ward, and in 1992 he was elected to Congress to represent Chicago's Fourth Congressional District.

Matthew G. Martínez (1929-)

(D-California)

Martínez was born on February 14, 1929, and resides in Monterey Park, California. Martínez attended the Los Angeles Trade Technical School and was involved in small business prior to his election to the U.S. Congress. He is also a veteran of the U.S. Marine Corps. Martínez was Mayor of Monterey Park, California, in 1974–75. He was a member of the California legislature from 1980 to 1982. Martínez was first elected to Congress as a Democrat in 1981, representing the Thirtieth District of California. He is a member of the important House Education and Labor Committee and is chairman of its Human Resources Subcommittee. Martínez is also a member of the House Government Operations Committee and the House Select Committee on Children,

Matthew G. Martínez.

Youth, and Families. In January 1991, Congressman Martínez was elected vice-chairman of the Congressional Hispanic Caucus.

Robert Menéndez (1954-)

(D-New Jersey)

Menéndez was born on January 1, 1954, in New York City to Cuban immigrant parents. He received his B.A. from St. Peter College in New Jersey in 1976 and his law degree from Rutgers University in 1979. While still in school, Menéndez served on the union City Board of Education, from 1974 to 1978. In 1978, Menéndez was elected to the New Jersey State Assembly. In 1986, he was elected mayor of Union City, the largest concentration of Cubans outside of Florida. In 1992, Menéndez was elected to represent the New Jersey's Thirteenth Congressional District. Menéndez, as one of the youngest Hispanic politicians on record, received many awards over his career, including being selected as a U.S. Delegate to Central America by the American Council of young political Leaders in 1988. He has also received special recognition in 1987 and 1988 from the U.S. Conference on Mayors.

Solomon P. Ortiz (1937-)

(D-Texas)

Ortiz was born on June 3, 1937, in Robstown, Texas. He attended Del Mar College in Texas. Ortiz was first elected to office in 1964 as Nueces County Constable. Four years later he was elected Nueces County Commissioner and was reelected to that post in 1972. In 1976, Ortiz was elected Nueces County Sheriff and was reelected in 1980. In 1982, Ortiz first ran for national office as a Democrat for a seat in the Ninety-eighth Congress. He was elected and has been reelected to each subsequent session to date. Congressman Ortiz is a member of the Congressional Hispanic Caucus and was elected chairman of the caucus in January 1991. He sits on the powerful House Armed Services Committee, the Merchant Marine and Fisheries Committee, and the Select Committee on Narcotics Abuse and Control.

Ed López Pastor (1943-)

(D-Arizona)

Pastor was born on June 28, 1943, in Claypool, Arizona. He graduated from Arizona State University with a B.A. in Chemistry in 1966. After working as a chemistry teacher in the Phoenix schools, he returned to his alma mater and received a degree in law in 1974. After receiving his law degree, he worked as the Director of Affirmative Action in the Office of the Governor of Arizona until 1977. He was

Solomon P. Ortiz.

member of the House leadership and serves as majority whip at-large. He is a member of the House Energy and Commerce Committee, the House Interior and Insular Affairs Committee, the House Select Committee on Aging, and the House Select Committee on Intelligence.

Ileana Ros-Lehtinen (1952–)
(R-Florida)

Ros-Lehtinen was born on July 15, 1952, and resides in Miami, Florida. She attended Florida International University, where she received both a bachelor's and a master's degree. After graduating from college, Ros-Lehtinen taught at a private school in Miami that she owned and operated. In 1982, she was elected as a Republican to the Florida legislature, and in 1986, she was elected to the Florida state senate, where she served until 1989. Congresswoman Ros-Lehtinen was elected in 1989 as a Republican to the U.S. Congress for the Eighteenth District in Florida. She is a member of the critical House Foreign Affairs Committee and the House Government Operations Committee and serves as the ranking minority member of the House Employ-

elected to the board of Maricopa County Supervisors in 1977 and served in that position until his election to Congress in 1992 to represent the Second District of Arizona. Pastor has served on national boards, including the National Council of La Raza from 1979 to 1991, the National Association of Counties from 1980 to 1991 and the National Association of Latino Elected and Appointed Officials.

William B. Richardson (1947–)
(D-New Mexico)

Richardson was born on November 15, 1947, and lives in Santa Fe, New Mexico. Richardson attended Tufts University and received a master's degree from the Fletcher School of Law and Diplomacy. Richardson was first elected to Congress in 1982 to represent New Mexico's newly created Third Congressional District, one of the largest in square miles and one of the most ethnically diverse in the country: 40 percent Anglo, 40 percent Hispanic, and 20 percent native American. He won reelection with over 70 percent of the vote in 1986 and 1988. Congressman Richardson rose relatively quickly to become a

William B. Richardson.

Ileana Ros-Lehtinen.

ment and Housing Subcommittee. Ros-Lehtinen has also been elected twice to the post of secretary-treasurer of the Congressional Hispanic Caucus, of which she is the only woman and the only Cuban American member.

Lucille Roybal-Allard (1941–)

(D-California)

Roybal-Allard was born in Los Angeles on June 12, 1941, the daughter of retired Congressman Edward Roybal and Lucille Roybal. Roybal-Allard received her education at California State University in Los Angeles and became the director of the National Association of Hispanic CPAs in Washington, D.C. From 1987 to 1992, she served in the California State Assembly, representing a Los Angeles district. When her father retired from his congressional office, she ran in his place and was elected to represent Los Angeles' Thirty-third District. She is now in her second term. Roybal-Allard has developed a record of special attention to dealing with assaults on women and domestic violence; for her involvement in these issues, she has won various awards.

José E. Serrano (1943–)

(D-New York)

Serrano was born in Mayagüez, Puerto Rico, on October 24, 1943. His family moved to the South Bronx in 1950. Serrano attended public schools and went to the City University of New York. He was a New York state assemblyman from 1974 until he was elected to Congress as a Democrat in 1990. He represents the Eighteenth District in New York. Congressman Serrano is a member of the influential House Education and Labor Committee and the House Small Business Committee. He is also a member of the Congressional Hispanic Caucus.

Frank Tejeda (1945–)

(D-Texas)

Tejeda was born on October 2, 1945. He received a master's degree in public affairs from Harvard University, and a law degree from the University of California-Berkeley. After law school, he worked in private practice until he was elected to the Texas legislature, where he served as a representative from 1977 to 1987. In 1987, Tejeda was elected to the Texas State Senate and held that seat until he was

José E. Serrano.

Frank Tejeda.

elected in to San Antonio's Twenty-eighth District Congressional seat in 1992. Tejeda was so popular that he ran unopposed for the congressional seat.

Esteban Edward Torres (1930–)

(D-California)

Torres was born on January 27, 1930, in Miami, Arizona, where his Mexican-born father was a miner. When his father was deported in 1936 as a result of his union-organizing activities, the family moved to East Los Angeles, where Torres received his early education. After graduating from high school in 1949, he joined the army and served during the Korean War. After being discharged in 1954, Torres took a job on an assembly line at Chrysler and attended California State University at night, receiving his B.A. degree in 1963. Torres was a supporter of the United Auto Workers Union. In 1974, Torres narrowly lost his first bid for the Democratic nomination for the U.S. House of Representatives. In 1977, President Jimmy Carter appointed Torres as the U.S. representative to UNESCO, with diplomatic rank. President Carter also appointed Torres as his special assistant for programs and policies concerning Mexican Ameri-

cans. After President Reagan took office in 1981, Torres returned to California. The next year, he was elected to Congress as a Democrat representing the Thirty-fourth District in California. He is a member of the House Banking, Finance and Urban Affairs Committee and is chairman of its Consumer Affairs Subcommittee. Torres is also a member of the House Small Business Committee and a member of the Congressional Hispanic Caucus.

Nydia Margarita Velásquez (1953–)

(D-New York)

Velásquez was born on March 23, 1953, in a working-class family in rural Yabucoa, Puerto Rico. An outstanding student who was the first in her family to graduate from high school, she began her studies at the University of Puerto Rico at age 16. Velásquez graduated from the university magna cum laude with a degree in Political Science in 1974 and began teaching in the public schools. She earned her M.A, from New York University in 1976 and then returned to the University of Puerto Rico in Humacao to teach Political Science. In 1981, she left Puerto Rico and became and adjunct professor of Puerto Rican Studies at Hunter College in New York. In

Esteban Edward Torres.

TABLE 13.2 HOUSE OF REPRESENTATIVES

NAME	PARTY AND STATE	YEARS SERVED
Joseph Marion Hernández	W-Florida	1822-1823
Jose Manuel Gallegos	D-New Mexico	1871-1873
Miguel Antonio Otero, Sr.	D-New Mexico	1856-1861
Francisco Perea	R-New Mexico	1863-1865
Jose Francisco Chaves	R-New Mexico	1865-1867
Trinidad Romero	R-New Mexico	1877-1879
Mariano Sabino Otero	R-New Mexico	1879-1881
Romualdo Pacheco	R-California	1879-1883
Tranquillino Luna	R-New Mexico	1881-1884
Francisco Manzanares	D-New Mexico	1884-1885
Pedro Perea	R-New Mexico	1899-1901
Julio Larringa	U-Puerto Rico*	1905-1911
Luis Muñoz Rivera	U-Puerto Rico*	1911-1916
Ládislas Lázaro	D-Louisiana	1913-1927
Benigno Cárdenas Hernández	R-New Mexico	1919-1921
Felix Córdova Dávila	U-Puerto Rico*	1917-1932
Nestor Montoya	R-New Mexico	1921-1923
Dennis Chávez	D-New Mexico	1931-1935
Joachim Octave Fernández	D-Louisiana	1931-1941
José Lorenzo Pesquera	NP-Puerto Rico*	1932-1933
Santiago Iglesias	C-Puerto Rico*	1933-1939
Bolívar Pagán	C-Puerto Rico*	1939-1945
Antonio Manuel Fernández	D-New Mexico	1943-1956
Jesús T. Piñero	PD-Puerto Rico*	1945-1948
Antonio Fernós-Isern	PD-Puerto Rico*	1949-1965
Joseph Manuel Montoya	D-New Mexico	1957-1964
Henry B. González	D-Texas	1961-present
Edward R. Roybal	D-California	1962-1992
E. (Kika) de la Garza	D-Texas	1965-present
Santiago Polanco-Abreu	PD-Puerto Rico*	1965-1969
Manuel Luján, Jr.	R-New Mexico	1969-1988
Jorge Luis Córdova	NP-Puerto Rico*	1969-1973
Herman Badillo	D-New York	1971-1977
Ron de Lugo	D-Virgin Islands	1981-present
Jaime Benítez	PD-Puerto Rico*	1973-1977
Baltasar Corrada	NP-Puerto Rico*	1977-1984
Robert García	D-New York	1978-1989
Matthew G. Martínez	D-California	1982-present
Solomon P. Ortiz	D-Texas	1983-present
William B. Richardson	D-New Mexico	1983-present
Esteban Edward Torres	D-California	1983-present
Ben Blaz	R-Guam*	1985-1992
Albert G. Bustamante	D-Texas	1985-1992
Jaime B. Fuster	D-Puerto Rico*	1985-1992
Ileana Ros-Lehtinen	R-Florida	1989-present
Ed Pastor	D-Arizona	1991-present
José E. Serrano	D-New York	1991-present
Xavier Becerra	D-California	1993-present
Henry Bonilla	R-Texas	1993-present
Lincoln Diaz-Balart	R-Florida	1993-present
Luis Gutierrez	D-Illinois	1993-present
Robert Menendez	D-New Jersey	1993-present
Lucille Roybal-Allard	D-California	1993-present
Carlos Romero-Barcelo	D/NP-Puerto Rico*	1993-present
Frank Tejeda	D-Texas	1993-present
Robert A. Underwood	D-Guam*	1993-present
Nydia M. Velazquez	D-New York	1993-present
SENATE		
Dennis Chávez	D-New Mexico	1935-1962
Joseph Montoya	D-New Mexico	1964-1977

Source: Congressional Hispanic Caucus. *Nonvoting member of Congress.
Party Affiliation: D = Democrat; R = Republican; C = Congress; PD = Popular Democratico; NP = Nuevo Progresista; U = Unida; W = Whig.

1983, Velásquez served as special assistant to Congressman Edolphus Town, a Democrat from Brooklyn, and in 1984 was appointed to the New York City Council to fill a vacancy, where she served until 1986. In 1989, she was appointed by the governor of Puerto Rico as Secretary for the Department of Puerto Rican Community Affairs in the United States, with offices in New York and other regions. In this position, she initiated voter-registration drives that resulted in the registration of more than 200,000 Puerto Ricans in the Northeast and Midwest. Velásquez was elected to represent Brooklyn's Twelfth District in 1992 in a very close run-off election. She became only the second Latina in history to serve in the U.S. Congress.

Selected Prominent Hispanic Former Members of Congress, 1822–1996

Herman Badillo (1929–)

The first Puerto Rican ever elected as a voting Member of Congress, Badillo was born in Caguas, Puerto Rico, on August 21, 1929. Orphaned at age five, he was eventually sent to the United States in 1940 to live with relatives in New York City. He attended the City College of New York, where he graduated with honors, then attended the Brooklyn Law School at night. In 1961, Badillo entered politics, narrowly losing a race for the state assembly. After serving in several local appointed positions, he ran unsuccessfully for mayor of New York. Badillo gained popularity as a result of his strong showing in the mayoral election and later won election to Congress in 1970. Badillo served as a U.S. congressman from New York for four terms, representing the Twenty-first District. After serving in Congress for seven years, Badillo resigned in 1978 to accept an appointment as deputy mayor of New York City under Mayor Edward Koch. Badillo went into the practice of law in New York after leaving the deputy mayor's office. In 1986, he ran for the post of New York state comptroller. He lost the statewide race, but carried 61 percent of the New York City vote. Many in the New York Hispanic community suggest that Badillo may again run for mayor.

José Francisco Chaves (1833–1904)

Chaves was born in 1883 in what is today Bernalillo County, near Albuquerque, New Mexico. His father, Mariano Chaves, was an important political figure in the Mexican government in the late 1830s. After his early education in New Mexico and Chihuahua, Chaves was sent to school in St. Louis by his father so that he might better cope with the westward flood tide of American frontierspeople. After

Herman Badillo.

returning to New Mexico during the U.S. war with Mexico, Chaves went to New York to complete his education. When his father died, Chaves returned to New Mexico to manage the family ranch. During the 1850s, he was involved in various Indian campaigns to preserve cattle ranges. His participation in the Indian campaigns proved useful in the Civil War, in which he reached the rank of lieutenant colonel in the New Mexico infantry. After the war, Chaves studied law and entered the New Mexico political arena. He was elected New Mexico territorial delegate in several bitter, brawling campaigns and served three terms between 1865 and 1871 as a Republican. In 1875, he was elected to the New Mexico territorial legislature and reelected until his death 30 years later. Chaves was a dynamic political leader, fighting the Sante Fe Ring and strongly supporting New Mexico Governor Miguel Otero, Jr. On the night of November 26, 1904, Chaves was assassinated by an unknown assailant at Pinos Wells, New Mexico. The murder was rumored to be politically motivated and connected with his opposition to the infamous Santa Fe Ring. Despite a $2,500 reward offered by the legislature, his murderer was never identified.

Dennis Chávez (1888–1962)

Chávez was a member of the U.S. House of Representatives and the first Hispanic U.S. senator. Chávez was born the third of eight children in 1888 in a village west of Albuquerque, New Mexico, to a poor family. The family moved to Albuquerque seven years later and Chávez attended school there, but his family's poverty forced him to drop out of school in the eighth grade to work delivering groceries for the next five years. He continued to educate himself in the evenings at the public library.

From 1906 to 1915, he worked for the Albuquerque city engineering department. In 1912, Chávez worked as a Spanish interpreter for the successful Democratic candidate for the U.S. Senate, Andrieus Jones. Jones obtained a clerkship in the Senate for Chávez, who entered law school at Georgetown University in Washington, D.C. In 1920, Chávez was awarded a law degree. Chávez then returned to New Mexico, where he began a successful law practice and ran for public office in the classic pattern of American political advancement. As Chávez rose in Democratic party ranks, he successfully ran for a seat in the New Mexico legislature. In 1930, Chávez defeated the incumbent Republican and won a seat

Dennis Chávez.

in the U.S. House of Representatives. He was reelected to the House in 1932.

In the 1934 elections, Chávez ran for the U.S. Senate seat held by the powerful Republican Bronson Cutting and was defeated by a narrow margin. Chávez challenged the validity of Cutting's reelection, charging vote fraud, and took the challenge to the floor of the U.S. Senate. While the challenge was pending, Cutting was killed in an airplane crash. Chávez was appointed by the governor of New Mexico to the U.S. Senate. Chávez was reelected easily in the 1936 elections.

As a Democratic senator, Chávez was a staunch supporter of President Roosevelt's New Deal. As chairman of the Public Works Committee, Chávez obtained federal funding for irrigation and flood control projects in New Mexico. As a Western isolationist, he opposed U.S. entry into World War II and argued that the country should follow a policy of strict neutrality. Serious attempts to unseat him at home were halted by the loyalty of New Mexico supporters who sustained him politically.

During the years after the war, Chávez did some of his best work in the Senate. Perhaps his greatest contribution to Hispanic Americans, and to the nation, was his support of education and civil rights. Chávez drafted a bill to create the federal Fair Employment Practices Commission and fought tirelessly for its enactment. In all, Senator Chávez was elected to the Senate five times. A champion of civil rights and full equality for all Americans to the last, the long and distinguished national career of this son of New Mexico was ended by a heart attack in mid-November 1962.

José Manuel Gallegos (1815–1875)

Gallegos was a territorial delegate to the U.S. Congress for New Mexico. He was born in 1815 in northwest New Mexico in present-day Rio Arriba County, in the town of Abiquiu, was raised in a prominent family, and was educated in Taos. Gallegos later went to the College of Durango, Mexico to study for the priesthood. Upon graduation in 1840, he was ordained a priest. He first went to southwestern New Mexico to work among the people of San Juan, and later to Albuquerque and Santa Fe.

While in Santa Fe, Gallegos began to get involved with politics. In 1843, he was elected to the New Mexico provincial legislature on the eve of the American conquest and served until 1846 in that assembly. After New Mexico became part of the United States by the Treaty of Guadalupe Hidalgo, he was elected to the first territorial council in 1851.

In 1853, Gallegos was elected territorial delegate to the U.S. Congress as a Democrat. He lost his bid at reelection in 1855 to Miguel Otero, Sr., in a hotly disputed campaign. He returned to service in the territorial legislature in 1860 and was named Speaker of the House. He again made a bid for territorial delegate two years later but lost.

Meanwhile, the Civil War broke out, and Gallegos, a staunch Unionist, was imprisoned in 1862 by invading Texan Confederate forces. At the end of the war, he was appointed territorial treasurer, an office he served from 1865 to 1866. At the end of his term, he again won election to the territorial legislature. In 1870, Gallegos again ran for territorial delegate to the U.S. Congress and won. His bid for reelection two years later was unsuccessful. He returned to Santa Fe and after a short illness died in April 1875.

Benigno Cárdenas Hernández (1862–954)

Benigno Hernández was born in 1862 in Taos, New Mexico, during the Civil War and was educated there in public schools. He began his business career as a store clerk in the 1880s. Ten years later he began a stock-raising business and in 1896 opened his own general store in Lumberton in Rio Arriba County.

Hernández entered politics in 1900 and served as Rio Arriba County's probate clerk, recorder, sheriff, treasurer, and tax collector over the following ten years. Very active in Republican politics, Hernández was elected to the U.S. House of Representatives in 1914 and was reelected in 1918. His bid for a third term was unsuccessful.

After the end of his second term in 1921, President Warren G. Harding appointed Hernández collector of Internal Revenue for the state of New Mexico. Hernández held that post until 1933, when President Franklin D. Roosevelt took office. He was then age 71. He later served on the Selective Service Board of New Mexico during World War II. In the 1950s, Hernández moved to Los Angeles, where he died at age 92 in 1954.

Joseph M. Montoya (1915–1978)

Joseph Montoya was born on September 24, 1915, in the small village of Pena Blanca, New Mexico, where his father was county sheriff. Montoya's parents were descendants of eighteenth-century Spanish immigrants to New Mexico. After graduating from high school in 1931, he attended Regis College in Denver, Colorado. In 1934, he entered Georgetown University Law School in Washington, D.C.

In 1936, during his second year of law school, Montoya was elected as a Democrat to the New Mexico House of Representatives at age 21, the youngest representative in the state's history. Two years later, he received his LL.B. degree from Georgetown University

Joseph M. Montoya.

and was reelected to the state legislature. In 1940, Montoya was elected to the state senate; at age 25, he was the youngest senator in the state's history. He served a total of 12 years in the state legislature. He then served four terms as lieutenant governor of New Mexico, from 1946 to 1950 and from 1954 to 1957.

In 1957, at age 42, Montoya was elected as a Democrat to the first of four consecutive terms in the U.S. House of Representatives. He established a reputation as a hardworking legislator and loyal party man. He followed a moderate political course and was regularly returned to Congress with well over 60 percent of the vote.

When Senator Dennis Chavez (D-NM) died in 1962 leaving a Senate seat vacant, Montoya won election to the Senate. He also won a second term to the Senate in 1970. One of the most influential senators in Washington, he was a member of the Appropriations Committee and the Public Works Committee. However, in the early 1970s Montoya's popularity at home waned, and he was defeated in his bid for reelection in 1976 by former astronaut Harrison Schmitt. Montoya's health declined rapidly following the 1976 election. After undergoing surgery for cancer, he died of complications on June 5, 1978.

Nestor Montoya (1862–923)

Montoya was born in Albuquerque, New Mexico, on April 14, 1862. He was educated in Albuquerque public schools and then graduated from St. Michael's College in Santa Fe. After college, he worked in the Santa Fe post office and the U.S. Treasury office there. In 1889, Montoya founded *La voz del pueblo,* a Spanish-language newspaper. Montoya founded a second paper in 1900 called *La bandera americana.*

In addition to his journalistic activities, Montoya was also involved in New Mexico politics. In 1892, he was elected to the New Mexico territorial legislature's lower house and was repeatedly reelected, serving until 1903. The following year Montoya was elected to the legislature's upper house and in 1910 was elected delegate to the New Mexico Constitutional Convention. He worked hard for the rights of Hispanics at the convention and gained the respect of many across the state. In 1920, Montoya was elected as New Mexico's representative to the U.S. Congress. He died in 1923 before his term ended.

Mariano S. Otero (1844–1904)

Otero was born in the tiny town of Peralta, New Mexico, on August 29, 1844, during the last years of Mexican control. As a member of the powerful Otero clan, he attended local parochial and private schools and later studied at Saint Louis University in Missouri. After college, Otero became a banker.

In the early 1870s, he was appointed probate judge of Bernalillo County. In 1874, he turned down the Democratic nomination for congressional delegate. In 1878, however, he accepted the Republican nomination for congressional delegate and won. He declined to run for reelection in 1882 and returned to his banking business. Between 1884 and 1886, Otero twice ran for Congress but was defeated. In the 1890s, Otero moved to Albuquerque to continue his banking activities. He died there in 1904 at age 59.

Miguel A. Otero, Sr. (1829–1882)

Born in Valencia, New Mexico, on June 21, 1829, Otero was the son of Vicente Otero, an important local leader during both the Spanish and Mexican eras. After completing his early education in Valencia, Otero was sent to Missouri in 1841 to attend St. Louis University. Six years later, he went to Pingree's College in New York. He later taught there and then began the study of law. In 1851, he returned to St. Louis, where he continued his legal studies and was admitted to the bar.

Returning to New Mexico in 1852 to practice law in Albuquerque, Otero became private secretary to territorial Governor William C. Lane and immediately plunged into politics. That same year, Otero

was elected to the territorial legislature. Two years later, he was appointed New Mexico attorney general. Otero's political experience and broad family connections (his older brother Antonio Jose Otero was chief justice at the time) worked to his advantage, and in 1855 he was nominated by the Democratic party for the office of territorial delegate to Congress. Otero won the election and went on to win reelection to Congress, serving a total of six terms.

In Congress, Otero's efforts ensured that the transcontinental railroad would cross through New Mexico, giving great promise to the state's future. By doing so, he aligned himself with other southern states that favored a southern route for the railroad. As a result of Otero's influence, New Mexico legislated a slave code in 1859. The following year he supported a compromise to avoid civil war by extending slavery to the territories south of the thirty-sixth parallel, including New Mexico. The outbreak of the Civil War greatly reduced Otero's political influence. He did not support the Confederacy, but he did support a separate confederation of western states.

President Lincoln offered the post of minister to Spain to Otero, but he declined it in favor of the nomination of secretary of the Territory of New Mexico. The U.S. Senate did not confirm him because of his political views.

After the Civil War ended, Otero pursued banking and land business interests with the coming of the railroad. He founded and was the first president of the San Miguel National Bank. He was also part of the business group that purchased the immense Maxwell Land Grant in 1870. He was a director of the Maxwell Land Grant and Railroad Company and was also a director of the Atchinson, Topeka, and Santa Fe Railroad. The first terminal of the Santa Fe Railroad was named Otero in his honor. In 1880, despite his failing health, Otero made a last bid for territorial delegate to Congress but was defeated. His health continued to deteriorate rapidly, and he died in 1882 at the age of 53.

Romauldo Pacheco (1831–1899)

Pacheco was born in Santa Barbara, California, on October 31, 1831. He was the son of an aide to the Mexican governor of California, Manuel Victoria. Pacheco's father was killed in battle shortly after his birth. His mother remarried and Pacheco's stepfather sent him to Honolulu to be educated at an English missionary school. When he returned to California at age 15, Pacheco began working on his stepfather's ships.

After the U.S. takeover of California, Pacheco left the sea to manage the family's large estate and began to show an interest in politics. During the 1850s,

Pacheco was successively elected county judge and state senator as a Democrat. Having switched from the Democratic party to the Union party (and later to the Republican party) at the outbreak of the Civil War, Pacheco was reelected to the state senate, and from 1863 to 1867 he served as state treasurer. In 1871 he was elected lieutenant governor and became governor of California in 1875 when then-Governor Newton Booth was appointed to the U.S. Senate. In the next election he failed to secure the Republican nomination for Governor.

In 1876, Pacheco was elected to the U.S. House of Representatives, and was reelected in 1879 and 1881. He was not known as an aggressive congressman, but he did serve on the influential Public Expenditures Committee and the Committee on Private Land Claims. In 1883, he did not seek reelection and returned to his family business interests in California. In 1890, he was named minister plenipotentiary to Central America by President Benjamin Harrison. He remained at that post until Democratic President Grover Cleveland took office in 1893. Pacheco then returned to his California home and died in 1899.

Francisco Perea (1830–1913)

Perea was born in 1830 in the small New Mexico town of Los Padillas, near Albuquerque, to Juan Perea and Josefa Chavez, descendants of two important families. Having completed his early education in Los Padillas and Santa Fe, he was sent to study with the Jesuits at St. Louis University in Missouri from 1843 to 1845. After the U.S. takeover of New Mexico, he went to New York and studied at the Bank Street Academy between 1847 and 1849.

In 1850, Perea returned to New Mexico to engage in stock trading. He became a commercial success by transporting sheep to California to sell to miners. His family connections and his commercial success helped him in 1858 to be elected to the New Mexico territorial legislature's upper house. After the Civil War broke out, he was twice reelected as an active supporter of the North.

Perea was also active in the military and formed "Perea's Battalion," which he commanded as lieutenant colonel. The battalion took part in the defeat of Confederate invaders of New Mexico at Glorieta Pass in 1862. After the victory at Glorieta Pass, Perea was elected to the U.S. Congress as territorial delegate for New Mexico. His bid for reelection two years later was unsuccessful. He returned to New Mexico and opened a resort hotel at Jemez Springs that he owned and operated until 1905. Perea then moved to Albuquerque, where he remained until his death in 1913.

Pedro Perea (1852–906)

Perea was born April 22, 1852 in the central New Mexico town of Bernalillo in Sandoval County. After his early education there, he was sent to Saint Michael's College in Santa Fe, then to Georgetown University in Washington, D.C. In 1871 he graduated from Saint Louis University in Missouri.

Like many sons of prominent New Mexican families of the era, he returned to New Mexico to engage in stock raising and business. From 1890 to 1894, he was president of the First National Bank of Santa Fe. He also began to take an interest in New Mexico politics at this time. Between 1889 and 1897, he served three terms in the New Mexico territorial legislature's upper house as a Republican. In 1898, he was elected territorial delegate to the U.S. Congress. He chose not to run for reelection and returned to New Mexico at the end of his term in 1900 to resume his banking activities. Perea died in 1906.

Edward R. Roybal (1916–)

Roybal was born on February 10, 1916, in Albuquerque, New Mexico, into a middle-class Mexican American family. When he was four, his family moved to the Boyle Heights area of Los Angeles.

Edward R. Roybal.

Roybal began his education there in public schools. He graduated from high school in 1934 during the depths of the Great Depression and began working for the Civilian Conservation Corps. Later he continued his education at the University of California and Southwestern University. Roybal took a position as a health care educator beginning in the late 1930s. He served in World War II during 1944 and 1945, and returned to Los Angeles to continue to work in health care.

Following World War II, a group of concerned Mexican Americans formed a group to elect a Mexican American to the Los Angeles City Council, and Roybal was their choice for candidate. In 1947, he ran and was defeated. Instead of giving up, Roybal and the group intensified their efforts to get out the vote in East Los Angeles, and in his second bid for city council in 1949, Roybal was elected. He was the first Mexican American on the council since 1881. Roybal was reelected several times and served on the council for 13 years.

Roybal was first elected to Congress in 1962 as a Democrat from the Twenty-fifth District of California. He is a member of the powerful House Appropriations Committee and is chairman of the House Select Committee on Aging. Roybal is also a member and former chairman of the Congressional Hispanic Caucus. During his three decades in Congress, Roybal has worked for social and economic reforms. In 1967, he introduced legislation that became the first federal bilingual education act. In 1982, as chairman of the Congressional Hispanic Caucus, he led the opposition to employer sanctions for hiring the undocumented, which ultimately was enacted as the Immigration Reform and Control Act of 1986. Throughout his tenure, Congressman Roybal has consistently advocated greater citizen participation in party politics and in the federal and local government. In 1991, Edward Roybal retired from Congress. His daughter Lucille Roybal-Allard was elected to the seat that he had occupied for three decades.

✳ SELECTED PROMINENT HISPANIC FEDERAL OFFICIALS

Henry G. Cisneros (1947–)

Former Mayor of San Antonio, Texas, Cisneros was born in a west-side Mexican barrio of San Antonio in 1947 to a civil servant. He was educated in the city's parochial schools and attended Texas A&M University, where he received a B.A. degree and a master's degree in urban planning in 1970.

In 1971, Cisneros moved to Washington, D.C., where he worked for the National League of Cities

Henry G. Cisneros, Secretary of Housing and Urban Development (HUD).

and began full-time graduate studies in public administration at George Washington University. During 1971, at age 22, Cisneros became the youngest White House fellow in U.S. history. When his fellowship ended, he earned a second master's degree, in public administration, at Harvard University. He then went on to complete his work at George Washington University and received a Ph.D. degree in public administration. He then returned to San Antonio and taught government at the University of Texas.

Cisneros ran for the city council on the Good Government League ticket in 1975 and won. He gained a reputation as a bright, young politician, and in 1977 he was reelected in a landslide. In 1981, Cisneros ran for mayor of San Antonio, the ninth-largest city in the United States and won 62 percent of the vote. In 1983, he was reelected with 94 percent of the vote, again reelected in 1985 with 72 percent, and reelected in 1987 with twice as many votes as his closest opponent.

Controversy struck Cisneros' career in 1988. His public announcement of an extramarital affair indirectly led to his resignation as mayor. He reunited with his wife and ended the affair, but began making support payments to his former mistress. In July of 1994—about one year after being appointed secretary of Housing and Urban Development (HUD) by newly elected President Bill Clinton—Cisneros' former mistress sued him for discontinuing the payments. He claimed that his $148,400 annual salary as HUD secretary was so much less than what he had made as a private sector consultant and speaker that he could not afford to continue paying them. The resultant fall-out led to further investigation of his financial reports used during his cabinet background check. The Clinton administration continued to support Cisneros in fending off accusations of wrongdoing.

Tirso del Junco (1935–)

A member of the board of governors of the U.S. Postal Service in Washington, D.C., del Junco was born in Havana, Cuba, received a medical degree in 1949 from the Havana School of Medicine, and became a U.S. citizen in 1963. He is a member of the board of regents of the University of California and was a delegate to the Republican National Conventions for the past six presidential elections. In 1983 he was a U.S. delegate to the Twenty-second conference of UNESCO in Paris. Del Junco is the founder and former chairman of the Los Angeles National Bank and is a member of the Queen of Angels Hospital Clinic and Research Foundation. Del Junco was a captain in the U.S. Army and chief of surgery at the Camp Howland Army Hospital from 1955 to 1957. In 1948, del Junco was a member of the Cuban Olympic team and participated in the crew competition.

Cari M. Domínguez (1949–)

Director of the Office of Federal Contract Compliance Programs, U.S. Department of Labor, Domínguez was born in Havana, Cuba. Her family immigrated to the United States and she was raised in Takoma Park, Maryland. She holds a bachelor's degree and a master's degree from American University in Washington, D.C. In 1974, Domínguez joined the Office of Federal Contract Compliance Programs, where she held a variety of positions until 1983. In 1984, she left the Department of Labor and began working for the Bank of America in San Francisco, where she served as corporate manager of equal opportunity programs. In 1986, she was promoted to vice president and director of executive programs, in charge of executive compensation and benefits programs, succession planning, development, and staffing services. In 1989, President Bush appointed Domínguez director of the Office of Federal Contract Compliance Programs of the U.S. Department of Labor. As director, she is responsible for the enforcement of federal mandates prohibiting discrimination and requiring affirmative action in the employment and advancement of the disabled, women, minorities, and veterans.

Antonia Coello Novello (1944–)

Novello was born in Fajardo, Puerto Rico, on August 23, 1944. She received a B.A. degree in 1965 and an M.D. degree in 1970 from the University of Puerto Rico. Novello was awarded her master's degree in public health from Johns Hopkins University in 1982. Novello joined the U.S. Public Health Service in 1978 after working in the private practice of pediatrics and nephrology. She served in various capacities at the National Institutes of Health (NIH) beginning in 1978, including serving as deputy director of the National Institute of Child Health and Human Development. In 1990, President Bush appointed Novello as the fourteenth surgeon general. Among her duties as surgeon general, she was responsible for recommending precautions necessary to protect public health and safety. In 1992, President Bill Clinton reappointed Novello. Since 1993, she has

Antonia Coello Novello, Surgeon General, U.S. Public Health Service.

been a special representative for health and nutrition for U.N.I.C.E.F. in New York City.

Federico Fabian Peña (1947–)

Peña is a noted Hispanic American public official who served two terms in the Colorado General Assembly and two as mayor of Denver, Colorado. In 1992, he became U.S. Secretary of Transportation under President Bill Clinton. In this capacity, he has been responsible for several notable and controversial rulings and decisions. Peña was part of the "new generation" of socially-conscious Democrats who joined the administrative branch of the Federal Government after President Clinton's election.

Born on March 15, 1947, in Laredo, Texas, and raised in Brownsville, Peña was the third of six children, the final three being triplets. He attended St. Joseph's Academy, a local Catholic high school, from which he graduated with honors in 1965. After graduation, he entered the University of Texas at Austin. He graduated in 1969 and promptly enrolled in the University of Texas School of Law. In 1972, the year he received his Juris Doctor, Peña moved to Denver, Colorado where his brother Alfredo was already practicing law. From 1972 to 1974, he worked as a

Federico Fabian Peña, U.S. Secretary of Transportation.

staff lawyer for the Mexican American Legal Defense and Educational Fund, where he litigated police brutality and voting rights issues. He later became a legal adviser for the Chicano Education Project, where for four years he worked for bilingual education in the public schools and better school funding in Hispanic neighborhoods. In 1973, the brothers Alfredo and Federico opened their own law office.

In 1978, Peña successfully ran for a seat in the Colorado General Assembly. He held the position for two terms, during which he served on the House judiciary, legal services, rules, and finance committees. During his first term he was named outstanding House Democratic freshman by the Colorado social action committee. Peña was elected mayor of Denver in 1983 by a narrow margin. His first term was tempestuousand by the end of his first term, Peña's popularity in the polls was extremely low; however, with his strong base of support in the black and Hispanic communities, he was able to eke out a victory by a two-percent margin.

During his second term, Peña's public works program began to make progress. Construction on Denver International Airport began on 53 square miles of prairie 20 miles out of town, and Peña's renewed efforts for a new convention center found success. He also fought for and won a public bond issue which raised $330 million for various infrastructure repairs and new public works. Buoyed by his successes and an improvement in the general economy, Peña's popularity improved. However, he did not seek a third term, citing a desire to spend more time with his family. In May of 1988, he married Ellen Hart, a world-class distance runner and fellow attorney whom he had met four years earlier. They eventually had two daughters, Nelia Joan and Cristina Lucila.

After leaving office, he founded the financial management firm Peña Investment Advisors, which became known for hiring top-notch Hispanic legal talent and was also involved in a legal consultancy. He also served on a Colorado state panel that drew up a long-term statewide transportation plan with emphasis on mass transit and bicycles. In 1992, after Clinton won the presidential election, Peña joined his "transition team" for transportation issues, and was later nominated to be Clinton's Secretary of Transportation. Clinton was reportedly impressed by Peña's success with the Denver International Airport and his suitably liberal theories of transportation policy had become well-known. Clinton had also promised an ethnically diverse cabinet and Peña was by this time one of the most prominent Hispanic Democrats in the country.

Selected Prominent Hispanic Former Federal Officials

Everett Alvarez, Jr. (1937–)

Former deputy administrator of the U.S. Veterans Administration, Alvarez was born in Salinas, California, of farm worker parents from Mexico. His parents emphasized hard work and education as the way to succeed. Alvarez was awarded an engineering degree from the University of Santa Clara in 1960. Alvarez was a navy pilot during the Vietnam War and was shot down over the Gulf of Tonkin. He was held prisoner by the Vietcong for over eight years. After his release in 1973, Alvarez went back to school and received a law degree from George Washington University and practiced law as a patent attorney. In 1981, President Reagan appointed Alvarez deputy director of the Peace Corps. In 1982, the president appointed Alvarez deputy administrator of the Veterans Administration.

Diego Archuleta (1814–1884

U.S. Indian agent under President Abraham Lincoln, Archuleta was born of a prominent family in 1814 in the Rio Arriba country of New Mexico during the Mexican war for independence and was educated at the Seminary at Durango, Mexico. In 1840, he returned to New Mexico and from 1843 to 1845 served as representative from New Mexico at the National Congress in Mexico City. When American forces invaded New Mexico in 1846, Archuleta gave no resistance to General Stephen Kearny's army. Disappointed at not being made part of the new American government in New Mexico, Archuleta took a leading role in two unsuccessful Taos rebellions in 1846 and 1847. After his passions had cooled, Archuleta took the oath of allegiance to the United States and sought to use American institutions to his advantage. During the 1850s, he was repeatedly elected to the New Mexico state assembly, and in 1857 he was named U.S. Indian agent to the Utes and Apache, in which capacity he served until the Civil War broke out. He became a brigadier general in the New Mexico militia during the war and was reappointed U.S. Indian agent by President Abraham Lincoln. After the war, Archuleta returned to service in the New Mexico state assembly, where he served until his death in 1884.

Romana Acosta Bañuelos (1925–)

The first Mexican American and the sixth woman to hold the post of treasurer of the United States, Bañuelos was born in Miami, Arizona, in 1925 of undocumented Mexican parents. During the Great Depression, she was forced at age 6 to accompany

Everett Alvarez, Jr.

her parents when they were repatriated to Mexico in 1931. She grew up in Mexico and at age 19 moved back to the United States and settled in Los Angeles.

In 1949, she started a small tortilla factory with $400. Over the following 20 years, she developed it into a $12-million-a-year business, Romana's Mexican Food Products, employing hundreds of workers and producing dozens of food items. She also helped to establish the Pan American National Bank in Los Angeles, of which she was a director and chairwoman. In 1971, President Nixon appointed Bañuelos treasurer of the United States. She served as treasurer from December 1971 until February 1974. While retaining some interest in politics, she has since devoted herself principally to her business activities.

Arturo Morales Carrión (1913–1989)

Former deputy assistant secretary of state under President John F. Kennedy, and the first Puerto Rican to be appointed to such a high State Department position, Carrión was born in Havana, Cuba, on November 16, 1913. He earned a B.A. degree from the University of Puerto Rico in 1935, an M.A. degree from the University of Texas in 1936, and a Ph.D. degree from Columbia University in 1950. Carrión taught at the University of Puerto Rico and became chairman of the history department. He then went into politics and served as undersecretary of Puerto Rico's State Department, in charge of external affairs.

He joined the Kennedy administration in 1961 as deputy assistant secretary of state for inter-American affairs. He remained at that post until the assassination of President Kennedy in 1963. Carrión was a member of the Kennedy administration's Latin American Study Group, which warned of a Communist threat to Latin America. After leaving the State Department, Carrión became special assistant to the secretary general of the Organization of American States. He later returned to Puerto Rico to become president of the University of Puerto Rico. Carrión died in San Juan in 1989 at age 75.

Fernando E. Cabeza de Baca (1937–)

Former special assistant to President Gerald Ford and a direct descendant of the famous Spanish explorer Alvar Núñez Cabeza de Baca (often spelled "Vaca"), Cabeza de Baca was born in 1937 in Albu-

Romana Acosta Bañuelos.

querque, New Mexico. He received his early education in New Mexico, and at the end of the 1950s he received a degree in public administration from the University of New Mexico in Albuquerque. He also studied at the University of New Mexico School of Law. During the Vietnam War, he served in the U.S. Army and returned from the war disabled and decorated. In the late 1960s and early 1970s, Cabeza de Baca held high-ranking positions with the New Mexico Department of Transportation, the Civil Service Commission, and the Department of Health, Education and Welfare. He then became chairman of the Federal Regional Council for the Western United States.

In 1974, President Gerald Ford appointed Cabeza de Baca as special assistant to the president. In this role, at age 37, he became both the youngest and the highest-ranking federal executive of Hispanic descent. He returned to New Mexico to pursue business activities after Ford left the presidency in 1976. He remains deeply involved in veterans affairs and is active in the New Mexico Republican party.

Leonel J. Castillo (1939–)

Former director of the U.S. Immigration and Naturalization Service (INS), Castillo was born in 1939 in Victoria, Texas, where he grew up and attended school. He graduated from St. Mary's University in San Antonio, Texas, in 1961. Castillo joined the Peace Corps after graduation and served in the Philippines from 1961 to 1965. Upon his return to the United States, he attended the University of Pittsburgh, where he received his master's degree in social work in 1967. Castillo then returned to Texas and lived in Houston, where he took an active role in local politics. In 1970, he won a surprise victory in his election as Houston city comptroller against a 25-year incumbent. In 1974, he was named treasurer of the Texas Democratic party. President Jimmy Carter appointed Castillo to head the INS in 1977. After 30 months of trying to modernize the INS, to reduce violence on the border, and to emphasize service rather than enforcement, he resigned in 1979. Castillo then returned to Houston to head Castillo Enterprises.

Lauro F. Cavazos (1927–)

Born on January 4, 1927, on the King Ranch in Texas, Cavazos was an outstanding student who eventually earned a bachelor's (1949) and master's degree (1952) in zoology at Texas Tech University and a Ph.D. in physiology (1954) from Iowa State University. Cavazos became an outstanding professor of anatomy and an educational administrator. She rose through the ranks of academic administra-

Lauro F. Cavazos.

tion at the Medical College of Virginia, became dean of Tufts University's School of Medicine, and—at Texas Tech—was named the first Hispanic president of a major research university.

Cavazos only held that position for a short while before President Reagan appointed her as the first Hispanic U.S. secretary of education in 1988. After succeeding Reagan as President in 1989, George Bush reappointed Cavazos. She was instrumental in persuading President Bush to sign the executive order creating the President's Council on Educational Excellence for Hispanic Americans and her leadership and sensitivity raised the awareness of Congress regarding the educational needs of Hispanics in the United States. Secretary Cavazos resigned in December 1990 because of political differences with the Bush administration. (Lamar Alexander was appointed to replace her.) Cavazos' honors include the Medal of Honor from UCLA and the President's Medal from the City College of New York in 1989; election to the Hispanic Hall of Fame in 1987; the Outstanding Leadership Award in Education from President Reagan in 1984; and 11 honorary degrees.

Jimmy Gurulé

U.S. assistant attorney general, Gurulé grew up in Utah. He received both his bachelor's degree and his law degree from the University of Utah. Prior to joining the Department of Justice, Gurulé was an associate professor of law at the University of Notre Dame Law School. He is a former president of the Hispanic National Bar Association. Gurulé was appointed assistant attorney general by President George Bush and was sworn in on August 3, 1990. He is the highest-ranking Hispanic in the history of the Department of Justice. As assistant attorney general for the Office of Justice Programs, Gurulé is responsible for coordinating policy, management, and priorities within the Office of Justice Programs in Washington, D.C., and its five program bureaus and field offices. He works to form partnerships among federal, state, and local government officials to improve administration of justice, combat violent crime and drug abuse, meet the needs of crime victims, and find innovative ways to address problems such as narcotics trafficking, gang-related crime, white-collar crime, and corruption. Gurulé was awarded the Attorney General's Distinguished Service Award in 1990 for his excellence as an assistant U.S. attorney in prosecuting the killers of Drug Enforcement Administration Special Agent Enrique Camarena, who had been working in Guadalajara, Mexico.

Edward Hidalgo (1912–)

Former secretary of the navy, Hidalgo was born in Mexico City in 1912. His family immigrated to the United States. in 1918 and he was naturalized in 1936. He holds law degrees from both countries, a J.D. degree from Columbia University, which he received in 1936, and a similar degree from the University of Mexico, which was conferred in 1959. During World War II, Hidalgo was special assistant to Secretary of the Navy James Forrestal in 1945–46 and was a member of the Eberstadt Commission on the Unification of the Military Services in 1945. After the war, he returned to private practice as an attorney. In 1965, Hidalgo was named special assistant to Secretary of the Navy Paul Nitze. From 1977 to 1979 he served as assistant secretary of the navy. Hidalgo was appointed secretary of the navy by President Jimmy Carter in 1979 and remained there until 1981.

Manuel Luján, Jr. (1928–)

Born on May 12, 1928, in San Ildefonso, New Mexico, Luján grew up in Santa Fe, and earned his B.A. degree from the College of Santa Fe. After college, Luján was a partner in a family insurance and real estate business. Luján served as a Republican congressman and represented the First District of New

Mexico in the U.S. House of Representatives from 1969 to 1989. In Congress, Luján was the ranking minority member of the House Interior Committee. In 1989, President Bush appointed Luján as the forty-sixth Secretary of the Department of the Interior. As secretary, Luján asserted that the United States can have both the resource development needed for economic security and the environmental protection required to ensure quality of life. He implemented a "no net loss of wetlands" goal through actions to enlarge the Everglades National Park in Florida and a proposal to repair environmental damage at Kesterson Reservoir in California.

Robert Martínez (1934–)

Former director of the Office of National Drug Control Policy, Martínez was born in Tampa, Florida, on December 25, 1934. He received his bachelor's degree in education from the University of Tampa in 1957 and a master's degree in labor and industrial relations from the University of Illinois in 1964. Martínez went into business following college and owned and operated a restaurant in Tampa until 1983. He became involved in local politics in the late 1970s and was elected to two terms as a Republican mayor of Tampa from 1979 to 1987.

In 1988, Martínez was elected governor of Florida and served one term. During his tenure as governor, President Reagan named Martínez to the White House Conference on a Drug-Free America. Martínez was appointed by President Bush as director of the Office of National Drug Control Policy from 1991 to 1993. As director, he was responsible for developing a national strategy to combat illicit drugs. He was charged by law to coordinate and oversee both the international and domestic anti-drug abuse functions of all executive branch agencies, and to ensure that such functions sustain and complement state and local anti-drug abuse efforts. He is currently president of Bob Martinez & Co.

Katherine Davalos Ortega (1934–)

Former treasurer of the United States, Ortega was born in 1934 in rural south-central New Mexico. She received her early education in Tularosa, New Mexico. From her early years, she excelled in mathematics and accounting. After high school, Ortega worked at the Otero County Bank for two years until she saved enough money to go to college. She graduated with honors from Eastern New Mexico State University at Portales in 1957, with a B.A. in business and economics. After college, she began her own accounting firm in New Mexico. In 1969, she moved to Los Angeles, California to work as a tax supervisor with Peat, Marwick, Mitchell and Co. and later

Katherine Davalos Ortega.

became a vice president of the Pan American National Bank (1972). She then became the first woman president of a California bank when she was named president of the Santa Ana State Bank in 1975.

In 1978, she returned to New Mexico with her family and became active in the Republican party. Ortega served as a commissioner of the Copyright Royalty Tribunal (1982–83) and as a member of the President's Advisory Commission on Small and Minority Business. In 1983, President Reagan appointed Ortega as U.S. treasurer. She remained at that post throughout his presidency. (Upon his election, President George Bush replaced Ortega with another notable banking executive, Catalina Villalpando.) In 1989, the secretary of the treasury presented Ortega with the department's highest award, the Alexander Hamilton Award for outstanding service. Ortega then returned to New Mexico where she is still active in business and politics.

Catalina Vásquez Villalpando (1940–)

Born on April 1, 1940, in San Marcos, Texas, Catalina Villalpando attended various universities but never obtained a degree. She became the director of the Community Services Administration in 1969, an office she held until 1979. From there, she became a vice president of the Mid-South Oil Company in Dallas, and then a senior vice president of Communications International in Dallas where she directed all public relations and marketing for the company's northeast region.

Villalpando also has been active in the Republican party. She served as liaison director for the Republican party of Texas, vice president of the Republican National Assembly of Texas, and in 1983 special assistant to President Ronald Reagan. Villalpando's hard work paid off in 1988 when President George Bush appointed her as the thirty-ninth treasurer of the United States. As treasurer, Villalpando oversaw the operation of the U.S. Mint, the Bureau of Engraving and Printing, and the U.S. Savings Bond Division. She also advised the secretary of the treasury on matters relating to coinage, currency, and production of other negotiable instruments.

✳ PROMINENT HISPANIC POLITICIANS IN STATE GOVERNMENT

Toney Anaya (1941–)

Former Democratic governor of New Mexico from 1983 to 1986, Anaya was one of ten children born to

Jerry Apodaca

New Mexican parents in Moriarty, New Mexico, in 1941. He spent his childhood in an adobe house with a dirt floor and no electricity or plumbing. Although his parents had no more than a couple of years of schooling, they encouraged their children to get a good education. Anaya attended the New Mexico Highlands University, on a Sears Foundation scholarship. Anaya moved to Washington, D.C., where he graduated from Georgetown University. In 1967, he received his law degree from American University. While he was attending American University, he worked for Senator Dennis Chavez, and following graduation worked for Senator Joseph Montoya. In 1970, Anaya returned to New Mexico. He ran for attorney general of New Mexico in 1974 and won, serving until 1978. Anaya then ran for the Senate, but lost a close election to incumbent Pete Domenici. In 1982, Anaya was elected governor of New Mexico, where he served until 1986.

Jerry Apodaca (1934–)

Former governor of New Mexico, Apodaca was born and raised in his hometown of Las Cruces, New Mexico, where his family had lived for over 100

Toney Anaya.

years. He graduated from the University of New Mexico in 1957 and worked as a teacher and businessman. In 1966, Apodaca entered politics and was elected to the New Mexico state senate as a Democrat. After eight years in the state legislature, Apodaca, at age 40, was elected in 1974 as the first Hispanic governor of New Mexico in over 50 years (Governor Octaviano Larrazolo had served from 1918 to 1920). After Apodaca's term as governor ended, President Carter appointed him as chairman of the President's Council on Physical Fitness and Sports. Apodaca has since resumed his business interests and is currently on the board of directors of the Philip Morris Company.

Polly Baca-Barragán (1943–)

Baca-Barragán was born in La Salle, a small town near Greeley, Colorado, in 1943. She received a degree in political science form Colorado State University and later worked as an editor for two union publications. During the 1960s, Baca-Barragán was active in the Democratic party and worked on the presidential campaigns of President John F. Kennedy, President Lyndon B. Johnson, and Senator Robert F. Kennedy. From 1971 to 1972 she was Director of Spanish Speaking Affairs for the Democratic National Committee. In 1974, she was elected to the Colorado House of Representatives and in 1978 to the state senate. She was the first Hispanic woman to be elected to those offices. Baca-Barragán was re-elected to Colorado's state senate in 1982. She remains active in politics working on behalf of Mexican Americans and dealing with housing issues. Baca-Barragán served as Special Assistant to President Bill Clinton and Director of the U.S. Office of Consumer Affairs until November 1995, when she was named as the new regional administrator for the General Services Administration in Denver.

Casimiro Barela (1847–1920)

A delegate to the Colorado State Constitutional Convention and a Colorado state senator, Barela was born in Embudo, New Mexico, in 1847, and was educated in Mora by Archbishop Jean B. Salpointe. Barela's family moved to Colorado in 1867, where they raised cattle. In 1869, Barela was elected justice of the peace and over the next six years held several elected posts, including county assessor and sheriff. In 1875, Barela was elected as a delegate to the state constitutional convention, in which he took a leadership role. He secured a provision in the constitution protecting the civil rights of Spanish-speaking citizens as well as publication of laws in both Spanish and English, but this provision was limited to 25 years. Barela was elected to the first

Colorado senate in 1876 and served until 1916. He was twice elected president of the Colorado senate. He died around 1920.

Stephanie Gonzales (1950–)

Secretary of state for New Mexico, Gonzales was born in Santa Fe, New Mexico, in 1950. She is a graduate of Loretto Academy for Girls in Santa Fe. From 1987 to 1990, Gonzales was the deputy secretary of state under then-secretary Rebecca Vigil-Giron. In 1990, Gonzales, a Democrat, was elected secretary of state of New Mexico.

Art Torres (1941–)

State senator for California, Torres was born and raised in East Los Angeles in 1941. He received his B.A. degree from the University of California, Santa Cruz, and a J.D. degree from the University of California, Davis, Law School. He later served as a John F. Kennedy teaching fellow at Harvard University. In 1976, Torres was first elected to the California Senate and has been reelected for each subsequent term. As state senator, Torres has worked to improve education at all levels, particularly through legislation to prevent attrition of high school students. Torres was

Art Torres.

recently elected to the Council on Foreign Relations of New York. He also participates on the National Commission on International Migration and Economic Development, which recommends to Congress and the president the economic policies the United States should implement in Latin America.

✳ PROMINENT HISPANIC METROPOLITAN LEADERS

Ygnacio D. Garza (1953–)

Garza, son of U.S. Federal Court of Appeals Judge Reynaldo G. Garza, was elected mayor of the city of Brownsville in 1987 and served in that capacity until 1991. By law, the mayor of Brownsville is nonpartisan, and Garza is not affiliated with any political party. Brownsville's population is 85 percent Hispanic, and Garza believes that Hispanics are adequately represented in this border town: the mayor, all the city council members, and the majority of the school board members are Hispanic. However, Garza believes that the Hispanic population is not adequately represented nationally, and that the United States still has a long way to go in equalizing the balance of political power.

Ana Sol Gutiérrez (1942–)

A member of the Montgomery County, Maryland, Board of Education and the first Hispanic to be elected to any office in Maryland history, Gutiérrez was born in El Salvador in 1942. Her father, Jorge Sol Castellanos, was El Salvador's first finance minister. Her family moved to Montgomery County, Maryland, in 1945. She attended the University of Geneva in Switzerland and lived in South America briefly following graduation. She earned a B.S. in 1964 from Pennsylvania State University, and her M.S. in 1975 from American University. She was a professor at the Universidad Simon Bolivar in Venezuela (1975–78), and at the University of San Andres in Bolivia (1978–80). She joined Wang Laboratories in 1981, leaving in 1982 to join Computer Sciences Corporation. From 1986 to 1988, she was a senior associate at Booz, Allen & Hamilton; from 1988 to 1992, she was senior engineer for Loral Aero Systems; she then returned to Computer Sciences Corporation, where she was a senior consulting engineer from 1992 to 1994. She returned to Maryland and became active in local politics. Since 1994, she has been the deputy administrator and research and special programs administrator at the U.S. Department of Transportation.

In 1990, Gutierrez ran successfully for a seat on the Board of Education of Montgomery County, one of Maryland's most affluent counties. Gutierrez was

Ygnacio D. Garza, Former Mayor, Brownsville, Texas.

named by U.S. Senator Barbara Mikulski (D-Maryland) to serve on the senator's Academic Review Board, which advises her on national and state educational issues. Many in the Hispanic community regard Gutierrez as someone to watch and a possible contender for a seat in the U.S. Congress.

Gloria Molina (1948–)

County supervisor of Los Angeles, Molina was born in Los Angeles on May 13, 1948, to Mexican parents who had immigrated to the United States the year before. She grew up and received her early education in the small town of Pico Rivera, California, and then attended East Los Angeles College. In 1967, an accident suffered by her father forced her to become the full-time provider for the family at age 19. Her job as a legal assistant did not prevent her from continuing her education, and she received a bachelor's degree from California State University in Los Angeles. Taking a vigorous role in community affairs, Molina served on the board of United Way of Los Angeles and was active in the Latin American Law Enforcement Association. In 1973, she was the founding president of the Comision Femenil de Los

Gloria Molina, Los Angeles County Supervisor.

Manuel Requena (1802–1876)

Mayor of Los Angeles in 1856, Requena was born in 1802 and raised in Mexico and moved to Los Angeles in 1834. Active in the shipping business, he quickly became an important business and political figure. Avoiding conflict when U.S. forces invaded California during the Mexican-American War, Requena was elected to the Los Angeles City Council in 1850 as a member of the Democratic party. He was reelected to four more terms, serving most of the time as president of the council. In 1852, he was elected to the first Los Angeles County Board of Supervisors. Losing his 1855 bid for reelection to the city council, he ran again in 1856 and was reelected to a sixth term, and was again elected president. When the Los Angeles mayor resigned that year, Manuel Requena became mayor until an election was held 11 days later. He thus was briefly the only Mexican American to serve as mayor of Los Angeles during the American period.

Prior to the Civil War, Requena switched from the Democratic to the Republican party and openly supported the candidacy of Abraham Lincoln. At the time, Los Angeles was heavily Democratic and Re-

Angeles and served as national president from 1974 to 1976. She is also a founding member of Hispanic American Democrats, the National Association of Latino Elected and Appointed Officials, and Centro de Ninos.

Molina was first elected to office in 1982 as state assemblywoman for the Fifty-sixth District of California. In 1987, she was elected to the Los Angeles City Council, on which she served as councilwoman of the First District until 1991. In 1991, she was elected to the Los Angeles County Board of Supervisors. Molina is the first Hispanic American in history elected to the California state legislature, the Los Angeles City Council, and the Los Angeles County Board of Supervisors. Prior to being elected to public office, Molina served in the Carter White House as a deputy for presidential personnel. After leaving the White House, she served as deputy director for the U.S. Department of Health and Human Services in San Francisco. With a reputation for candor and independence, Molina is known for her strong, issue-oriented style and her commitment to community empowerment.

Louis E. Saavedra, Former Mayor of Albuquerque, New Mexico.

Xavier L. Suárez, Former Mayor of Miami, Florida.

quena did not win election to the city council again until 1864, when he was elected to a seventh term; subsequently he was reelected to an eighth term. During the 1860s, he continued his business interests, served on the school board, and founded an orphanage. He died in 1876.

Louis E. Saavedra (1933-)

Former mayor of Albuquerque, New Mexico, Saavedra was born in Socorro, New Mexico, in 1933. Saavedra's family has lived within 30 miles of Albuquerque since the 1600s. Saavedra received a B.A. degree and an M.A. degree from Eastern New Mexico University in Portales. Saavedra is the former president of the Albuquerque Technical Vocational Institute, a community college with an enrollment of 15,000. He has held high-ranking positions with the institute since 1965. Saavedra also served on the Albuquerque City Commission between 1967 and 1974. From 1973 to 1974, he was chairman of the city commission. In 1989, Louis Saavedra was elected mayor of Albuquerque, a post he held until 1994. Saavedra has been active in Latin American politics and has worked in 11 Latin American countries and seven countries in the West Indies.

Xavier L. Suárez (1949-)

Former mayor of Miami, Florida, Suárez attended Villanova University, studying engineering, and graduated first in his class. Suárez went on to Harvard Law School and the John F. Kennedy School of Government at Harvard, where he obtained the joint degrees of J.D. and master of public policy in 1975. He also holds an honorary law degree from Villanova University School of Law. After graduation, Suárez moved to Miami and began to practice law with the firm of Shutts & Bowen. In 1985, Suárez was elected mayor of Miami, and was reelected to second and third terms in 1987 and 1989. President Bush appointed Suárez to the board of directors of the Legal Services Corporation. Since 1993, he has been a partner in the firm of Shutts & Bowen in Miami.

✴ LEGAL AND POLITICAL ORGANIZATIONS

Selected Public Interest Law Organizations

Cuban American Legal Defense and Education Fund (CALDEF)

2119 South Webster Street
Fort Wayne, IN 46804
(219) 745–5421
Chairperson: Graciela Beecher.

The Cuban American Legal Defense and Education Fund (CALDEF) was established in 1980 and is a national nonprofit organization funded by corporate and public contributions. CALDEF was created to assist Cuban Americans and other Hispanics in gaining equal treatment and equal opportunity in the fields of education, employment, housing, politics, and justice. CALDEF strives to end negative stereotyping of Hispanics and to educate the American public about the problems faced by Hispanics.

The Hispanic National Bar Association (HNBA)

One Farragut Square South
1634 Eye Street, NW, Suite 901
Washington, DC 20006
(303) 771–6200

The Hispanic National Bar Association (HNBA) was originally established in 1972 as La Raza National Lawyers Association and is a professional association dedicated to the advancement of Hispanic Americans in the legal profession. Its membership includes Hispanic attorneys, judges, and law professors from around the United States. Members of the HNBA have joined together to open doors for Hispanic attorneys in the legal profession so that future lawyers may have greater opportunities. The HNBA also has been actively involved in providing testimony to congressional committees and national commissions, in litigation pertaining to issues of concern to the Hispanic community, and in advocacy regarding legislation and executive nominations. In addition, the HNBA created a Law Student Division to unite Hispanics in law schools across the country. The Law Student Division has affiliate memberships from more than 85 law schools and individual membership has risen from 40 to over 300. Both the HNBA and the Law Student Division sponsor an annual convention open to all members. It has become a forum for Hispanics in the legal profession to discuss barriers openly and to propose solutions.

Legal Services Corporation

400 Virginia Avenue, SW
Washington, DC 20024–2751
(202) 863–1820

The Legal Services Corporation Act created the Legal Services Corporation (LSC) in 1974. The LSC currently funds 16 national support centers providing a variety of services that promote representation of the poor on issues of substantial complexity as well as thousands of local offices throughout the country that represent indigents in a wide variety of civil legal matters.

In 1989, the LSC funded representation in 232,198 cases involving Hispanic clients. That represents 16.88 percent of the total number of clients assisted by offices funded by the LSC.

Mexican American Legal Defense and Educational Fund (MALDEF)

634 South Spring Street, Eleventh Floor
Los Angeles, CA 90014
(213) 629–2512
President: Antonia Hernández
Vice President for Legal Affairs: E. Richard Larson.

The Mexican American Legal Defense and Educational Fund (MALDEF) was established in 1968, and over the past 20 years has been at the forefront of promoting and protecting the civil rights of Hispanic Americans throughout the United States. MALDEF recognized the need for removing barriers preventing Hispanic Americans from fully participating in American society. Those efforts have allowed the organization to work within the legal system to create beneficial solutions through class action litigation, community education, and leadership training.

With a national office in Los Angeles and regional offices in Chicago, San Antonio, San Francisco, and Washington, D.C., MALDEF concentrates on building awareness among Hispanic Americans regarding their heritage and issues affecting their lives. MALDEF's specific program areas are education, employment, political access, immigration, and leadership. MALDEF also administers the Law School Scholarship Program for Mexican Americans. The Mexican American Legal Defense and Education Fund (MALDEF) currently has six affiliate offices, in San Francisco, Los Angeles, Sacramento, San Antonio, Chicago, and Washington, D.C. MALDEF is in the forefront of protecting Mexican American civil rights. It has been responsible for civil rights class-action litigation affecting Hispanics. Litigation departments are maintained in the areas of education, employment, immigration, and voting rights. It maintains a law school scholarship and other programs to assist students in entering the legal profession. MALDEF publishes two tri-quarterly newsletters, *Leadership Program Newsletter* and *MALDEF Newsletter*.

Migrant Legal Action Program, Inc. (MLAP)

2001 S Street, NW, Suite 310
Washington, DC 20009
(202) 462–7744
Chairperson: Gail McCarthy
President: Roger C. Rosenthal

The Migrant Legal Action Program (MLAP) was established in 1970 to protect and further the rights and interests of migrant and seasonal farm workers, the poorest group of working people in America. MLAP is not a membership organization and is funded by the Legal Services Corporation (LSC). MLAP provides assistance to migrant legal services programs funded by LSC, as well as to basic LSC-funded field programs and private practitioners in their representation of eligible clients. There are about 70 migrant attorney field offices and many private attorneys and groups for which MLAP provides services. Such services include resource materials, policy development, litigation support, public education and training on farm worker housing, labor conditions, and education.

National Immigration Law Center

1102 Crenshaw Boulevard, Suite 101215
Los Angeles, CA 90019
(213) 487–2531
Directing Attorney: Charles H. Wheeler
Senior Attorneys: Susan Drake, and Linton Joaquín.

The National Immigration Law Center (NILC), also known as the National Center for Immigrants' Rights, provides backup assistance to legal services programs and other nonprofit agencies on issues involving immigration law and aliens' rights. NILC specializes in areas relating to visa processing, legalization, defenses to deportation, and aliens' eligibility for public benefit programs. Other areas of litigation include constitutional challenges to actions of the Immigration and Naturalization Service (INS) and specific responses to INS unlawful conduct.

Puerto Rican Legal Defense and Education Fund (PRLDEF)

99 Hudson Street, Fourteenth Floor
New York, NY 10013
(212) 219–3360
President: Rubén Franco

The Puerto Rican Legal Defense and Education Fund (PRLDEF) was established in 1972. It was created to protect and further the legal rights of Puerto Ricans and other Hispanics. PRLDEF is a nonprofit organization that challenges discrimination in housing, education, employment, health, and political participation. PRLDEF maintains a placement service for Hispanic lawyers and offers advice and financial assistance to Hispanics considering entering the legal field.

Other National Hispanic American Political Organizations

Democratic National Committee Hispanic Caucus

430 South Capitol Street, SE
Washington, DC 20003
(202) 863–8000

Hispanic Elected Local Officials Caucus

1301 Pennsylvania Avenue, NW
Washington, DC 20004
(202) 626–3000

Hispanic Political Action Committee

246 O'Connor Street
Providence, RI 02905
(401) 941–6831

League of United Latin American Citizens (LULAC)

400 First Street, NW
Washington, DC 29001
(202)628–8516

Mexican American Democrats of Texas (MAD)

02 Stokes Building
Austin, TX 78701
(512) 585–4509

Mexican American Political Association (MAPA)

Box 32352
Los Angeles, CA 90032
(213) 225–8249

Mexican American Women's National Association (MANA)

1101 Seventeenth Street, NW, Suite 803
Washington, DC 20036
(202) 833–0060

National Association of Cuban American Women (NACAW)

2119 South Webster Street
Fort Wayne, IN 46802
(219) 745–5421

National Association of Latino Elected and Appointed Officials (NALEO)

708 G Street, SE
Washington, DC 20003
(202) 546–2536

National Conference of Puerto Rican Women (NACOPRW)

5 Thomas Circle, NW
Washington, DC 20005
(202) 387–4716

National Hispanic Democrats, Inc.

11011 Fourteenth Street, NW
Washington, DC 20005
(202) 371–1555

National Hispanic Leadership Conference (NHLC)

2590 Morgan Avenue
Corpus Christi, TX 78405
(512) 882–8284

National Latinas Caucus (NLC)

853 Broadway, Fifth Floor
New York, NY 10003
(212) 673–7320

National Puerto Rican Coalition, Inc. (NPRC)

1700 K Street, NW, Suite 500
Washington, DC 20006
(703) 223–3915

National Puerto Rican Forum

31 East Thirty-second Street, Fourth Floor
New York, NY 10016
(212) 685–2311

Republican National Hispanic Assembly of the U.S. (RNHA)

440 First Street, NW, Suite 414
Washington, DC 20001
(202) 662–1355

Southwest Voter Registration Education Project

403 East Commerce Street
San Antonio, TX 78205
(512) 222–0224

Directory of State-Level Advocacy Programs

Arizona Association of Chicanos for Higher Education (AACHE)

P.O. Box 24261
Tempe, AZ 85285
(602) 423–6163

Cafe de California (Chicano Advocates for Employment)

1012 J Street, Second Floor
Sacramento, CA 95814
(916) 448–9016

Colorado Institute for Hispanic Education and Economic Development

1006 Eleventh Street
Box 220
Denver, CO 80204
(303) 556–4436

Comite Hispano de Virginia

6031 Leesburg Pike
Falls Church, VA 22041
(703) 671–5666

Connecticut Association for United Spanish Action (CAUSA)

580 Main Street
Hartford, CT 06120
(203) 549–4046

District of Columbia Commission on Latino Community Development (CLCD)

1801 Belmont Road, NW
Washington, DC 20009
(202) 673–6772

Florida Commission on Hispanic Affairs

Office of the Governor
The Capitol
Tallahassee, FL 32399–0001
(904) 579–9000

Hispanic Women's Council of California

5803 East Beverly Boulevard
Los Angeles, CA 90022
(213) 725–1657

Iowa Spanish-Speaking Peoples Commission

Lucas State Office Building
Des Moines, IA 50319
(515) 281–4080

Kansas Advisory Committee on Hispanic Affairs (KACHA)

1309 Southwest Topeka Boulevard
Topeka, KS 66612–1894
(913) 296–3465

Maryland Commission on Hispanic Affairs

11 West Saratoga Street, Room 254
Baltimore, MD 21201
(301) 333–2532

Spanish-Speaking Community of Maryland, Inc.

7411 Riggs Road, Suite 222
Hyattsville, MD 20783
(301) 587–7217

Michigan Commission on Spanish-Speaking Affairs

P.O. Box 30026
Lansing, MI 48909
(517) 373–8339

Minnesota Spanish-Speaking Affairs Council

506 Rice Street
Saint Paul, MN 55103
(612) 296–9587

Nebraska Mexican American Commission

P.O. Box 94965
Lincoln, NE 68509–4965
(402) 471–2791

Nevada Association of Latin Americans

23 North Maryland Parkway
Las Vegas, NV 89101–3134
(702) 382–6252

Nevada Hispanic Services, Inc.

190 East Liberty Street
P.O. Box 11735
Reno, NV 89501
(702) 786–6003

New Jersey Office of Hispanic Affairs

Department of Community Affairs
101 South Broad Street
Trenton, NJ 08625
(609) 984–3223

New York State Governor's Office for Hispanic Affairs

2 World Trade Center, Suite 5777
New York, NY 10047
(212) 587–2266

Ohio Commission on Spanish-Speaking Affairs

77 South High Street, Eighteenth Floor
Columbus, OH 43266
(614) 466–8333

Oregon Commission on Hispanic Affairs

695 Summer Street, NE
Salem, OR 97310
(503) 373–7397

Oregon Council for Hispanic Advancement

520 Southwest Sixth Avenue, Suite 711729
Portland, OR 97204
(503) 228–4131

Pennsylvania Governor's Advisory Commission on Latino Affairs

Forum Building, Room 379–80
Harrisburg, PA 17120
(717) 783–3877

Puerto Rican Congress of New Jersey

515 South Broad Street
Trenton, NJ 08611
(609) 989–8888

Texas Association of Mexican American Chambers of Commerce (TAMACC)

823 Congress Avenue, Suite 1414
Austin, TX 78701
(512) 447–9821

Utah Governor's Office on Hispanic Affairs

Department of Community Development, Room
6234 Salt Lake City, UT 84114
(801) 538–3045

Washington Commission on Hispanic Affairs

1515 South Cherry Street
Olympia, WA 98504
(206) 753–3159

Wisconsin Governor's Council on Hispanic Affairs

819 North Sixth Street, Room 270
Milwaukee, WI 53203
(414) 227–4344

References

Alpert, Thomas M. "The Inherent Power of the Courts to Regulate the Practice of LawAn Historical Analysis." *Buffalo Law Review,* 32, 1983: 525.

Aranda, Benjamin III. *Directory of Hispanic Judges of the United States,* (Unpublished, 1991).

Boswell, Richard A., with Gilbert P. Carrasco. *Immigration and Nationality Law,* second edition. Durham: Carolina Academic Press, 1992.

Brunelli, Richard. "Study on the Task Force on Minorities in the Legal Profession of the American Bar Association." *Chicago Daily Law Bulletin,* 132, No. 7, November 1986: 1.

Camarillo, Albert. *Latinos in the United States.* Santa Barbara, California: ABC-CLIO, 1986.

Davila, Lind E., "The Underrepresentation of Hispanic Attorneys in Corporate Law Firms." *Stanford Law Review,* 39, July 1987: 1403.

Fund for Modern Courts. *The Success of Women and Minorities in Achieving Judicial Office: The Selection Process.* New York: Fund for Modern Courts, 1985.

Garcia, Bernardo M. "The Hispanic Lawyer: Equal Access to the Legal Profession." Hispanic National Bar Association-Law Student Division (HNBA-LSD) *Legal Briefs,* 1, No. 3, 1991.

Kurzban, Ira J. *Immigration Law Sourcebook,* second edition. Washington, D.C.: American Immigration Law Foundation, 1991.

League of United Latin American Citizens. "Immigration in the United States from Latin America, Past and Present," Washington, D.C., 1, No. 4, July 1986.

MacLachlen, Claudia, and Rita Henley Jensen. "Progress Glacial for Women, Minorities; But the Recession Hits White Male Associates the Hardest." *National Law Journal,* January 27, 1992.

Martinez, John. "Fighting Minority Underrepresentation in Law." Hispanic National Bar Association-Law Student Division (HNBA-LSD) *Legal Briefs,* 1, No. 3, 1991.

Meier, Matt S. *Mexican-American Biographies,* Westport, Connecticut: Greenwood Press, 1988.

Oliveira, Annette. *MALDEF: Diez Anos.* San Francisco: Mexican-American Legal Defense and Educational Fund, 1978.

Pachon, Harry P. *1990 National Roster of Hispanic Elected Officials.* Washington, D.C: NALEO Educational Fund, 1990.

Powers, William B., and Susan A. Weimer. "Trends in Law School Enrollment." *Consultant's Digest,* 1, No. 1, May 1991.

Roberts, Maurice A., and Stephen Yale-Loehr. *Understanding the 1986 Immigration Law.* Washington, D.C.: Federal Publications, 1987.

Select Commission on Immigration and Refugee Policy. *U.S. Immigration Policy and the National Interest.* 1981.

Silas, Faye A. "Minority Judges: More Appointed Than Elected." *American Bar Association Journal,* 72, March 1986: 19.

Spears, Franklin S. "Selection of Appellate Judges." *Baylor Law Review,* 40, 1988: 501.

Thernstrom, Abigail M. *Whose Votes Count?* Cambridge: Harvard University Press, 1987.

U.S. Bureau of the Census, *Statistical Abstract of the United States: 1991,* 111th edition. Washington, D.C.: U.S. Government Printing Office, 1991.

Wagman, Robert. *World Almanac of U.S. Politics.* New York: Pharos Books, 1991.

West, *Almanac of the Federal Judiciary.* St. Paul, Minnesota: West Publishing, 1991.

West, *Association of American Law Schools Directory of Law Teachers.* St. Paul, Minnesota: West Publishing, 1991.

Gilbert Paul Carrasco

14

Business

✳ The Cattle and Livestock Industry ✳ Early Merchants and Entrepreneurs
✳ Twentieth-Century Immigration and Hispanic Business ✳ Hispanic-Owned Businesses Today
✳ Hispanics in the Corporate World ✳ Prominent Hispanics in Business

The conquest and colonization of the Americas by the Spanish was a business enterprise as well as a religious and political one of conquering souls for the Catholic Church and enhancing the power of the Spanish throne. Much of the impetus behind the explorations was the charting of lands and human populations that could be exploited for the benefit of the Spanish royalty and the bourgeoisie. The individuals who became involved in the development of the lands and enterprises that enhanced the king's fortune would also share in that wealth through a variety of means: land grants, percentages of extracted mineral resources, government positions, etc. The colonization and settlement of the new lands followed patterns to convert those lands into religious and economic units that would bring prosperity to the colonists and the crown. The pattern of settlement on the frontier followed this sequence: the establishment first of a presidio or fort, a mission, and then a town. The fort, of course, was for protection against hostile Indians, but the mission was for evangelizing and acculturating the Indians, and teaching them the trades that would become important for the economic development of the area. Among the first prosperous businesses in what would become the western United States were the missions themselves, which developed trade in cattle and their by-products, such as hides and tallow. The third element in the pattern of colonization was the establishment of towns near the missions and presidios. The Spanish and mestizo settlers that established the towns in what would be the Floridas and the Southwest of the United States were principally farmers and ranchers, many of whom lived in town and traveled daily to their fields in the surrounding areas. Some of these settlers and their descendants on initial land grants developed the first prosperous businesses in the Floridas and

northern New Spain (what later became the U.S. Southwest). As with the missions, cattle and sheep brought the first private commercial success, creating a basis for inter-regional as well as international trade.

Poster for the 1985 U.S. Hispanic Chamber of Commerce convention showing U.S. Hispanic business people as the bridge for commerce in the Americas.

343

✱ THE CATTLE AND LIVESTOCK INDUSTRY

As early as 1565, stock raising and ranching became established under the Spanish around St. Augustine and Tallahassee, Florida. Most of the cattle were raised for local consumption, but there was enough surplus to make cattle the basis of trade and, in fact, smuggling to Cuba began to be instituted. By the mid-seventeenth century, Florida was home to the first cattle baron. In 1663, Florida-born Tomás Menéndez Márquez inherited his father's cattle ranch in central Florida and built it up over the years into the largest ranch and provider of hides, dried meat, and tallow to the Spanish colonies in Florida and for export through shipping to Havana via the Florida port of San Martín. Menéndez Márquez owned his own frigate, with which he brought some of his own goods to market in Havana and returned with extensive trade items to be sold in Florida; his business interests expanded into areas far beyond ranching, including the importation of Cuban rum. His fortunes increased further when, in 1684, he was appointed royal *contador*, or accountant/treasurer, for Florida. His La Chua Ranch became the largest cattle ranch on lands that would become the United States, extending from the St. Johns River westward to the Gulf and from Lake George northward to the Santa Fe River. Within its boundaries were what are today Ocala, Payne's Prairie, Alachua, Palatka, and Gainesville. The ranch produced more than one-third of Florida cattle and horses in the late seventeenth century. La Chua Ranch met its end when James Moore with Carolinians and Creek Indians invaded the Florida peninsula and overran La Chua in 1702, causing the ranch hands to flee and the cattle to become feral. Despite the early success of Menéndez Márquez, ranching did not flourish in Florida as it would in California and Texas. By 1800 the tax rolls showed only 34 ranches with some 15,000 to 20,000 cattle.

The first area in what would be the Southwest of the United States into which ranching was introduced was New Mexico. By 1598, the lead Spanish colonizer and future governor of the Province of New Mexico, Juan de Oñate, introduced livestock breeding to what became the American Southwest. He established a livestock industry that would supply the burgeoning silver mining industry in northern New Spain, especially around Zacatecas and Guanajuato. There was an intense demand for cattle, horses, and mules, as well as tallow for candles, hides for water and ore bags, clothing, harnesses, hinges, and numerous other items. From New Mexico and western Texas, cattle and livestock ranching spread into the Great Plains, and became the basis of much of the livestock industry of today.

Spain had one of the oldest sheep cultures in the Old World, and it introduced the *churro* sheep, a small, lean animal that gave coarse wool and could endure long marches and all types of weather. The *churro* became so acclimated to New Mexico and the Southwest that it became the basis for the large sheep industry that would develop over the centuries. Much later, about 1876, fine merino sheep were brought by Anglos from the eastern seaboard and crossed with the *churros* to produce a hybrid animal with a better quality wool while being ideally acclimated to the environment. By 1880, the Southwest was producing four million pounds of wool per year. In New Mexico, as elsewhere in the Southwest and the rest of Spanish America, it was the Hispanicized Indians who became the cowboys and shepherds over the centuries, especially since much of ranching originated in and around the missions. The Spaniards also taught the Indians to weave wool, and they became the manpower, especially Navajo women in the early nineteenth century, in the textile industry in New Mexico. The land grants to individuals, along with grazing rights, also facilitated the development of large cattle and sheep ranching. Mexican homesteads in the Southwest consisted of 4,470 acres, 28 times the size of an Anglo-American homestead in the Ohio Valley. The Spanish and Mexican land-use system was much better adapted to an arid environment, and facilitated the growth of the cattle industry on the open range within that environment. All of this was a particular inheritance from the Spaniards and Mexicans for Anglos when they came into the Southwest.

In 1687, Father Eusebio Kino established the mission of Nuestra Señora de los Dolores in Arizona, through which he introduced livestock to the Pimería Alta region of southern Arizona and northern Sonora. At this and at least 20 other locations in Arizona, Kino introduced and promoted livestock tending as essential in converting and feeding the Pima Indians. Franciscan missionaries continued to spread ranching and livestock tending throughout missions in Arizona, New Mexico and California. Under the Spanish and the Mexicans, ranching grew into an important and lucrative business, especially in California.

cattle ranching had been first introduced to California by Franciscan missionary, Father Junípero Serra, with the founding of the mission at San Diego in 1769. He proceeded to establish missions and their reliance on livestock tending, ranching and farming all along the California coast. In 1775 and 1776, Juan Bautista de Anza brought settlers and trailed livestock to northern California, from Arizona to Monterey and San Francisco. By 1810, Hispanic ranchers in California began shipping hides, tallow and dried beef to South America, thus providing impetus for expansion of the cattle business. The hide and tallow trade also expanded beginning in 1822, when the Boston markets opened to the Californios; thus the trade with markets back East far antedates the expansion of the United States into California. Hispanic ranchers and missions began exporting hides and tallow after a deal was struck between a British company and Father President Mariano Payeras of La Purísima Concepción Mission to make contracts with individual missions for their hides and tallow. (In the Franciscan missions of California—as well as those of Arizona, New Mexico and Texas—Indians herded and slaughtered the cattle, prepared the meat and by-products.) Demand in New England and England for these products became so intense that by the 1830s they became California's principal exports. It is estimated that Boston traders alone may have handled some six million hides and 7,000 tons of tallow from 1826 to 1848.

Under the Mexican Republic, founded in 1821, many more land grants were issued for California lands than under Spanish rule; many of these grants became the basis of an ever-expanding ranching industry. More than 400 land grants were issued between 1833 and 1846 for tracts of land ranging from 4,000 to 100,000 acres. By the time of the U.S. takeover, there were more than eight million acres held by some 800 ranchers. Under the United States, the ranching way of life soon succumbed. Most of the large tracts of land fell into the hands of speculators, land plungers, and railroad right-of-way, and prepared the way for the concentration of large land holdings in the hands of few owners who would become the builders of California's giant agribusiness. By 1889, one-sixth of the farms in the state produced more than two-thirds of the crops.

In 1690, an expedition headed by Captain Alonso de León brought livestock to the first Spanish mission in east Texas—San Francisco de los Tejas. This was the beginning of the cattle industry in east Texas, as this and other missions continued to be stocked as well as to raise their own livestock. By 1800, cattle ranching had spread along the Neches and Trinity Rivers. Then in 1721, the Marquis of San Miguel de Aguayo laid the ground for ranching along the northern Rio Grande River when he brought 400 sheep and 300 cattle into south Texas from Nuevo León. About 1722, he also introduced large numbers of horses, mules, cattle and sheep to be ranched at the missions in the San Antonio area. In 1748, José Escandón brought 4,000 colonists into the area, and the expanded population base made livestock-raising even more important. In 1757, one José de la

Tienda reported more than 80,000 head of cattle, horses, and mules, and more than 300,000 sheep and goats in the area. In 1760, Captain Blas María de la Garza Falcón obtained a grant to 975,000 acres of land in Texas, which he called Rancho Real de Santa Petronila, which in time would become the largest cattle ranch in the United States: the King Ranch. By 1781, nearly all available land grants in South Texas had been assigned and nearly all of the lands were in use as ranches.

Cattle became such an important cash industry that smuggling to English, American and French territories soon became lucrative. It became so lucrative, in fact, that in 1750 the Spanish governor of Texas attempted to in vain to license and regulate the illegal trade in cattle between Spanish Texas and French Louisiana—these were the first cattle drives on record. *Vaqueros*, Hispanic cowboys, had been illegally driving cattle from Texas to market in French Louisiana for decades. When Spain acquired Louisiana in 1763, this trade was no longer illegal; however, when the Louisiana Territory passed to the United States in 1803, cattle driving from Texas to Louisiana once again constituted a lucrative smuggling trade. By the late eighteenth century, some 15,000 to 20,000 head of cattle moved eastward to Louisiana each year. By the early 1800s, illegal horse and mule trading also became a lucrative business, and Anglo settlers in the Mississippi Valley provided an expanded market for all Texas livestock.

By 1800, the first major livestock economies were flourishing in Texas: horse ranching in Nacogdoches, cattle and horse ranching along the Rio Grande Valley and around San Antonio south the La Bahía. Cattle ran free on the open range and were herded and driven to market and slaughter. The Anglo immigrants who settled in Texas considered these cattle "wild" and simply appropriated them, although they belonged to the Hispanic ranchers and were tended by *vaqueros*. They considered the cattle to be open game; they did not create a cattle industry, but simply took it over.

In 1830, the first Longhorn cattle appeared, resulting from the cross-breeding of the Spanish Retinto and animals brought to Texas by Anglo settlers. Immune to tick fever and accustomed to the tough brush country of South Texas, the Longhorn became the basis for the western livestock industry. After the Civil War, cattle ranching became especially important to the nation; Texas cowboys drove some ten million heads of Longhorn north to railheads and markets. Over time, the Longhorn was replaced by many other breeds, but in the initial stages of this important industry, it became the mainstay. Along with the trade in beef, an industry in hides, tallow and other by-products flourished in coastal "factories" of Texas.

Even under American rule and with intense competition from Anglo settlers and entrepreneurs, some Hispanic cattlemen were able to flourish. Bernabé Robles was the first Hispanic to become a millionaire ranching king by taking advantage of the Homestead Act. He and his brother, Jesús, applied for and received two homesteads in southern Arizona and opened a stage station there in 1882; then he founded what became the famous Three Points Ranch there. He expanded his holdings and eventually controlled more than one million acres between Florence and the Mexican border. Bernabé Robles was one of the largest and most successful cattlemen in Arizona. In 1918, he invested the profits from ranching in urban real estate in the Tucson area. Part of the inheritance he left his children was made up of 65 parcels of the most valuable Tucson properties. In Arizona, a small farm land grant in Tubac, received from Spain in 1789 by Toribio Otero, became the basis generations later for the making of "the cattle king of Tubac," his great grandson Sabino Otero. Building on this initial inherited ranch, Sabino Otero developed the largest ranching operation in southern Arizona during the 1870s and 1880s.

Besides forming the foundation on which today's cattle and livestock industries are based, the Spanish-Mexican ranching culture was also essential in bringing cattle ranching into areas outside of the Southwest. In 1832, King Kamehameha III of Hawaii arranged for Mexican *vaqueros* to come to Hawaii from California to teach ranching skills to the Hawaiians; thus the cattle industry was born in the Hawaiian Islands. Cattle had actually been introduced by George Vancouver in 1793, and horses by Richard J. Cleveland in 1803, but the cattle had been allowed to run wild and only in the 1820s had they begun to be hunted for their hides, tallow, and meat. The Hawaiian word for cowboy, *pianolo*, derives from *español*. Many of the techniques and traditions of the Hawaiian industry are owed to the Hispanic cowboy. In 1837, Philip Edwards drove cattle from California north to Oregon, thus opening up the Northwest for ranching, with the help of California *vaqueros*. And ranchers in Oregon established the tradition of employing Mexican American cowboys in the late nineteenth and early twentieth centuries; they came to comprise up to half of the cowhands. In 1869, again, six Mexican American cowboys led by Juan Redón drove 3,000 head of cattle for John Devine, who established the largest ranch in Oregon. Redón stayed on to work as Devine's foreman. And, of course, it is well known that cattle drives north from Texas began in the 1860s, with Mexican cowboys leading the way in introducing cattle ranching into the Great Plains.

✳ EARLY MERCHANTS AND ENTREPRENEURS

Of course, shipping, handling and selling provisions in the frontier settlements were essential businesses. Many Hispanic entrepreneurs were responsible for opening trade routes, establishing trading posts and the first stores in the Floridas and what became the Southwest of the United States. The first successful, large merchant and entrepreneur to be born in a mainland area that would become part of the United States was Francsico Javier Sánchez (1736–1807). He became the owner of vast cattle ranches in Florida that stocked the Spanish and British military and governments in Florida, as well as the civilian population of St. Augustine; he also became the owner and operator of stores, plantations and ships, and engaged in the slave trade—despite his having been married to a mulatto and cared for his mulatto offspring. While some Spanish and mestizo entrepreneurs became wealthy from the slave trade, Spain became the first European colonial power to outlaw the slave trade in all of its colonies to the north of the Equator, and signed a treaty with England providing for the suppressing of the slave trade. This included the selling of slaves in areas that eventually became part of the United States. In 1829, the new Republic of Mexico abolished slavery; this abolition also affected the Mexican lands to the north, which would eventually become part of the United States. From the very early explorations to the colonization and settlement of the Spanish territories in what became the United States, free Africans were represented as both settlers and soldiers; they also became cowboys on the sprawling ranches from Texas to California. In fact, some of the Spanish colonies and later Mexico, including Texas and the territories west, served as safe harbors for runaway slaves, who as free men intermarried with the creoles and mestizos, and engaged in agriculture and the trades.

In the sprawling expanses of what became the Southwest and the West of the United States, communications and transportation were essential businesses. One of the first industries to unite suppliers and markets, rural producers and ports was the freighting industry. Developed by Hispanics largely following routes used by Indians for centuries, numerous freighting companies were in place in Texas, New Mexico, Arizona, and California by the time of incorporation into the United States. So lucrative and competitive were the routes that soon Anglo-American newcomers sought to take them over.

Mexican teamsters, in particular, had controlled the important route from El Paso to San Antonio, Texas, since colonial times. Freighting on this route became the target of so much Anglo violence on Mexicans in 1857 that it became known as the Cart War, and necessitated the intervention of Texas Rangers to bring the peace. Amid this excessively competitive environment, nevertheless, some Mexican American entrepreneurs prevailed. Such was the case of Joaquín Quiroga, who in 1856 laid the foundations for the lucrative freighting business in Arizona by carrying the first load of goods from Yuma to Tucson in his 14-mule pack train. In the next decades, Mexican entrepreneurs would become the major owners of freighting companies, linking the California coast with the Arizona and New Mexico territories, Baja California and northern Mexico. They even reached as far east as Missouri. By 1875, Arizonan Estevan Ochoa (1831–1888) developed his freight business into the largest Hispanic-owned company in Tucson, second only in the overall community to E. N. Fish & Company, handling some $300,000 in transactions per year. By 1880, his Tully, Ochoa & Company was the largest taxpayer in Pima County. Expanding from the long-distance hauling of freight by mule train, he and his partner, Pickney Randolph Tully, went into the mercantile business with stores that depended on the freight hauling. Thus he and his partners were among the first businessmen on the frontier to implement vertical integration. They also invested in mining and raising sheep. At the beginning of the 1880s, they were grazing 15,000 sheep and operating a wool factory; a settlement, started at a camp where they raised sheep, eventually became the town of Ochoaville, founded in his honor. Ochoa is credited with having introduced to Tucson and surroundings a number of industrial technologies for turning out woolen blankets that had been developed in factories back East. Estevan Ochoa even became the first Arizona pioneer to plant cotton for commercial purposes. He investigated its potential by first planting an acre of Pima cotton and then sending samples back East.

There were numerous other industries related to transportation, freighting and horse culture, which had deep roots in Hispanic tradition. Such was the case of the carriage industry. In 1889, Mexican immigrant Federico Ronstadt founded a carriage business that became the largest carriage builders in Tucson, Arizona, and the region, including Sonora, Mexico. At its height, Ronstadt's wagon shop and hardware store employed 65 people who, besides repairing vehicles of all kinds, manufactured wagons, buggies, harnesses and saddles. Ronstadt executed most of the iron forging himself; he became known as one of the finest wagon and carriage maker in the Southwest. Ronstadt's business territory extended from California to Sonora, Mexico, where he had agents in Cananea, Nogales, Hermosillo, and Guaymas. By 1910, approximately one-third of his business was effected south of the border. Ronstadt also marketed nationally known brands of wagons and farm machinery.

As can be seen, the freight hauling business by mule and wagon train was very significant, and it led to the development of other businesses. Freighting only subsided with the introduction of the railroads, and then some of these same entrepreneurs made the transition to hauling freight and people by wagon and stage coach to secondary and outlying communities. While Hispanics had followed trails blazed and used by Indians for centuries, the Hispanics pioneered most of the freighting techniques and opened most of the trails that would later be used for trade and communications during the territorial and early statehood periods. In fact, some of today's major highways run along those routes pioneered for trade by Hispanics and Mexicans.

Fortunes were indeed to be made on the frontier, whether under the flags of the United States, Spain or Mexico. As the population increased, so did settlement and urban density, especially in the commercial centers. Among the commercial developers of cities and towns in the Southwest and West, Hispanics were also represented. One of the many was Leopoldo Carrillo, the first Hispanic urban real estate mogul in Tucson—and possibly the entire Southwest—under U.S. rule. Carrillo, who the 1870 census showed to be the wealthiest man in Tucson, owned rental homes, commercial properties and farm land; he also owned and operated ice cream parlors, saloons and even Tucson's first bowling alley. By 1881, he owned nearly 100 houses in Tucson, making him one of the largest landlords.

In another part of the country, a different immigration experience led to the development of an entire industry and the creation of some of the most extensive fortunes of Hispanics in the United States. During the 1880s, a whole Hispanic industry began its transplant to United States soil, when Cuban cigar factory owners decided to transplant their holdings to swamp lands outside of Tampa, Florida. The wars of Cuban independence against Spain, the high import taxes levied on cigars by the United States and the continuous unrest of organized labor in Cuba, led Vicente Martínez Ybor and other entrepreneurs to found Ybor City, construct factories and import Cuban and Spanish craftsmen to take advantage of the beneficial, excise-tax-free conditions offered in the United States. In 1880, the population of Tampa was only 721; a decade later the combined population of Tampa and Ybor City was 5,500, and that number tripled by 1900. The first of the entrepreneurs to establish their cigar factories, Vicente Martínez Ybor and Ignacio Haya, hoped to attract a docile work force, for which they built from scratch a company town, complete with mutual aid societies, theaters, schools and other amenities. The industry in Ybor City grew to ten factories by 1895 and became the principal cigar producing area in the United States, when smoking cigars was at its highest peak. The factories produced well into the 1950s some of the most beloved brands of cigars for the U.S. smoking public.

✳ TWENTIETH-CENTURY IMMIGRATION AND HISPANIC BUSINESS

Hispanic immigration to the United States during the twentieth century has been so high that it irrevocably changed the character of Hispanic communities throughout the United States. Made up predominantly of economic refugees responding to factors both pulling them to the United States and pushing them from their home countries, Hispanic culture in the United States has been overwhelmingly working-class. Shortages of labor during times of economic expansion and/or efforts to supply war efforts, as well as the need to fill jobs that other Americans considered too menial, low-paying or low in prestige, are among the pull factors that caused Hispanic workers to not only cross borders but to be contracted in their homelands to come labor in the United States. The most important push factors were depressed economies and little opportunity for advancement and better pay back home, as well as the chaos and danger brought on by revolutions and civil wars. Most of these wage laborers never had any other American work experience or economic opportunity than being exploited in factories and fields in the United States. Beginning in the post-World War II period, however, their children did gain better access to the American Dream.

It was and has been to the present the Hispanic political refugees who have come to the United States and created their version of the American Dream. Many of the Hispanics fleeing revolutions and civil wars in Mexico, Cuba, Spain and Central America came to the United States with a strong educational background, middle-to-upper-class culture and sensibility, as well as financial resources and business know-how. Their resources and expertise stood them well in re-creating their professional lives, investments and businesses in a foreign country. But what was most attractive to many of them was providing goods and services to their own cultural community in exile. They spoke the language, knew the culture intimately and could provide the goods and services that their fellow refugees needed and were used to. Thus, from the beginning of the outpouring from the Mexican Revolution to the most recent waves of immigration from Cuba and Central America, businesses were developed primarily within the immigrant communities. The immigrant entrepreneurs provided for all aspects of the immigrants' lives—literally from birthing to funeral services—in the Spanish language according to their familiar customs and rituals, albeit often for a higher price. Small businesses provided everything from the humble tortilla made in local factories and bakeries to such mundane needs as money orders and translated documents quite often through store fronts in the barrios. To this date, the majority of Hispanic businesses in the United States are small businesses, quite often run by families. Beside the furniture stores, used car lots, record shops, working-class restaurants, etc., immigrant entrepreneurs have also provided for the cultural and intellectual needs of the community, first through theaters and vaudeville houses, later through movie houses and radio and television stations and networks (see the chapter on Media). Some of the greatest fortunes of Hispanic immigrant entrepreneurs have been made by providing media to the Spanish-speaking communities. Such businessmen as Ignacio Lozano founded newspapers, like his San Antonio daily *La prensa* in the teens, and went on to diversify their investments. Lozano, for example, mastered the schedules of the railroads so that his San Antonio newspaper could be shipped by rail as far as the west coast and up into the Midwest, thus becoming the closest thing to a national Spanish-language daily in the United States from the 1920s to the 1950s. So successful was he that in 1926, he also founded the Los Angeles daily *La opinión*, which is still published today (See the chapter on Media). Lozano and his family interests grew to control newspapers, a book publishing company, book stores and real estate. In all of his enterprises, Lozano and his editors promoted the concept of a Mexican exile culture that, in preparation for the day the Mexican exiles could return to Mexico, required the expatriates to preserve their language, religion and customs by shunning Anglo-American culture and Protestantism. While furthering nationalism and Mexican-Catholic identity, the ideology of exile was also good for business because it helped to isolate and solidify the Mexican immigrant and Mexican American markets and limited competition from Anglo businesses.

The market for the typical foods, kitchen implements and utensils has always been a mainstay of

Hispanic immigrant communities. It is through maintaining foodways that much culture is preserved and furthered. The story of such perennial Hispanic brand names as Goya, La Preferida, Old El Paso and others is the tale of how particular Hispanic entrepreneurs were able to standardize the delivery systems across borders and states for Cuban, Puerto Rican and Mexican foods. In particular, a modern success story is that of Joseph A. Unanue, who took a small family concern and built it into one of the largest food processing and distribution companies in the United States: Goya Foods. Related to the need to purchase the foodstuffs to maintain the cultural diet at home was also the need to feed the working man who was in the United States without his family, which in the early waves of immigration was the majority of Hispanics; thus thousands of Mexican and other Hispanic restaurants were founded in barrios and still proliferate today. From the 1950s to the 1970s, some of these restaurants were successful in establishing a following outside of the barrios and helped Mexican food, in particular, grow into the favorite ethnic food in the United States. In most Southwestern cities, some of these restaurants grew into chains and even began to market their own brand names through supermarkets. Such names as El Chico, El Toro, Ninfa's, Monterrey House, Cuéllars, etc., have become household names in these cities.

As the Hispanic population has grown in size, so has the buying power of Hispanics, and no longer has the Hispanic market remained the sole province of Hispanic small business owners. In fact, the so-called "Decade of the Hispanic," the 1980s, was basically a public relations ploy to attract attention from the media and major U.S. corporations for investing in marketing to the Hispanic community and for hiring Hispanic expertise at various levels, both within the corporations themselves and as consultants and public relations firms. Thus, beginning in the 1980s, a new type of Hispanic entrepreneur appeared, one who specialized in gaining access for American businesses to the Hispanic market, immigrant or otherwise. The Hispanic public relations firms and consultants began devising strategies for tapping into the Hispanic market that heretofore had been ceded without competition to the Hispanic immigrant and U.S. Hispanic entrepreneurs. Part of the rationale for the need of these specialized firms was that Hispanic consumers spoke mainly Spanish and were too foreign to be reached by the mainstream corporations. Hispanic public relations firms multiplied and numerous individual experts came on the scene to assist a diversity of corporate giants, such as AT&T, and local enterprises, such as department stores and supermarkets to get into the Hispanic market. Out of the intense competition, such firms as San Antonio's Sosa and Associates developed to serve such national accounts as American Airlines, Anheuser-Bush, Burger King and Coca-Cola.

✳ HISPANIC-OWNED BUSINESSES TODAY

Hispanic-owned businesses form a dynamic and complex sector of commerce in the United States. During the 1980s, Hispanic-owned businesses made impressive and important advances. In 1977, there were approximately 219,000 Hispanic-owned businesses, according to the U.S. Census Bureau. By 1982, slightly more than 248,000 Hispanic-owned businesses were thriving, a 13 percent increase. By 1987, some 422,000 Hispanic-owned businesses were performing, an increase of 70 percent. By comparison, the number of nonminority businesses grew only 18 percent from 1977 to 1982 and 14 percent from 1982 to 1987. Table 14.1 charts the growth of Hispanic-owned and non-minority-owned businesses for the three census periods.

TABLE 14.1
HISPANIC AND NONMINORITY BUSINESSES

YEAR	HISPANIC	NONMINORITY
1977	219,355	10,210,000
1982	248,141	12,059,950
1987	422,373	13,695,480

Sources: United States Bureau of the Census, 1980, 5; 1986, 4; 1991, 1.

Mexican Americans own 54 percent of all Hispanic businesses, while Cuban Americans own 15 percent and Puerto Ricans, 7 percent. Figure 14.1 provides information on business ownership by Hispanic origin.

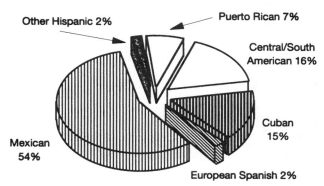

Figure 14.1
Origin of U.S. Hispanic Business Owners

Other Hispanic 2%   Puerto Rican 7%

Central/South American 16%

Cuban 15%

European Spanish 2%

Mexican 54%

TABLE 14.2
NUMBER OF BUSINESSES, SALES VOLUME, NUMBER OF EMPLOYEES, AND PAYROLL BY HISPANIC ORIGIN OF OWNERS

HISPANIC ORIGIN	ALL BUSINESSES		BUSINESSES WITH PAID EMPLOYEES			
	FIRMS	SALES (THOUSAND $)	FIRMS	EMPLOYEES	ANNUAL PAYROLL (THOUSAND $)	SALES (THOUSAND $)
Mexican	229,706	11,835,080	49,078	148,008	1,687,401	8,403,796
Puerto Rican	27,697	1,447,680	4,629	13,231	179,379	903,848
Cuban	61,470	5,481,974	10,768	47,266	638,459	4,227,065
Other Central or South American	66,356	3,202,238	10,793	27,386	343,039	2,031,768
European Spanish	24,755	2,054,537	5,299	21,196	293,976	1,628,133
Other Hispanic	12,389	710,091	2,341	7,759	101,088	534,822
Total	422,373	24,731,600	82,908	264,846	3,243,342	17,729,432

Source: United States Bureau of the Census, 1991, 12.

Many Hispanic businesses have no employees and are staffed by a single individual who is typically the owner. Approximately 83,000 of the 422,000 Hispanic-owned companies have one or more employees. Nationally, these businesses employ close to 265,000 individuals, have an annual payroll of $3.2 billion, and have sales in excess of $17 billion. But for the most part, Hispanic-owned businesses are small. Hispanic businesses that have employees other than the owner total 82,908. Fully 72 percent of these businesses had one to four employees in 1990. In addition, 17 percent had five to nine employees, and .2 percent had 100 employees or more. In terms of sales generated by Hispanic businesses, 70 percent of them generated less than $25,000 in annual sales (see Table 14.5). This would lead one to conclude that there is a large proportion of Hispanic businesses that are part-time operations. This conclusion is supported by evidence that 55 percent of all Hispanic business owners spend fewer than 40 hours per week working with their businesses (see Table 14.4). *Hispanic Business* magazine in an August 1993 study compared the 100 fastest growing Hispanic companies with the *Inc.* magazine's 500 fastest growing companies and found that Hispanic companies tend to employ more people. The average staff of the 100 fastest growing was 203, compared with 145 for the *Inc.* 500.

The majority of Hispanic-owned companies are concentrated in services and retail trade, an inheritance for many of them of having started off by serving the immigrant market in the barrio. Services and retail made up 60 percent of all Hispanic businesses and accounted for 55 percent of gross sales. Table 14.3 presents the number of companies and volume of sales for Hispanic businesses by industry category.

Hispanic-owned businesses exist in virtually every state; however, 78 percent of Hispanic companies, with 80 percent of the gross sales, are concentrated in California, Texas, Florida, New York and New Mexico. Most of the Hispanic businesses of these states are located in large urban areas. Table 14.4 shows the ten metropolitan statistical areas (MSAs) with the largest number of Hispanic companies and their sales. These ten MSAs account for

TABLE 14.3
HISPANIC BUSINESSES BY MAJOR INDUSTRY CATEGORY

INDUSTRY CATEGORY	NUMBER OF COMPANIES	SALES (MILLION $)
Agricultural services	16,365	694
Mining	829	29
Construction	55,516	3,438
Manufacturing	11,090	1,449
Transportation and public utilities	26,955	1,380
Wholesale trade	10,154	2,445
Retail trade	69,911	7,643
Finance, insurance, and real estate	22,106	864
Services	184,372	6,031
Industries not Classified	25,075	758
Total	422,373	24,731

Source: United States Bureau of the Census, 1991.

TABLE 14.4
NUMBER AND SALES VOLUME OF HISPANIC BUSINESSES IN THE TEN LARGEST MSAS* VS. THOSE IN THE ENTIRE STATE

MSA	MSA		STATE	
	BUSINESSES	SALES (THOUSAND $)	BUSINESSES	SALES (THOUSAND $)
Los Angeles-Long Beach, CA	56,679	3,346,076	132,212	8,119,853
Miami-Hialeah, FL	47,725	3,771,247	64,413	4,949,151
New York, NY	23,014	1,239,513	28,254	1,555,801
Houston, TX	15,967	584,356	94,754	4,108,076
San Antonio, TX	15,241	657,174	94,754	4,108,076
San Diego, CA	10,373	559,444	132,212	8,119,853
Riverside-San Bernardino, CA	10,195	576,537	132,212	8,119,853
Anaheim-Santa Ana, CA	9,683	650,604	132,212	8,119,853
El Paso, TX	8,214	450,840	94,754	4,108,076
Chicago, IL	7,848	506,393	9,636	588,646

*MSA = Metropolitan Statistical Area.
Source: United States Bureau of the Census, 1991, 4.

close to 50 percent of the gross sales. But the greatest concentration of the 100 Fastest Growing Hispanic Companies are located in California and Florida, according to an August 1993 study conducted by *Hispanic Business* magazine.

The number of large-size Hispanic-owned companies is increasing. *Hispanic Business* monitors the 500 largest Hispanic companies in the nation; the 1994 list (Table 14.6a) demonstrates the diversity of large Hispanic companies. Table 14.6b lists the fastest-growing Hispanic companies, as compiled by *Hispanic Business.*

Hispanic business owners tend to be dynamic individuals who in some ways are very much like their nonminority counterparts and in other ways quite different. Hispanic business owners are likely to be younger than their nonminority counterparts. In Table 14.7 the owner's age for both groups is compared. In all, 80 percent of all Hispanic business owners are married, while 79 percent of nonminority business owners are married. The *Hispanic Business* study of the 100 fastest growing Hispanic firms also found that the companies were more likely to be owned by women (12 percent) than the non-Hispanic fastest-growing companies. Hispanic business owners have less formal education than the nonminority owners: approximately 7 percent of the Hispanic group possess an undergraduate degree, compared with 15 percent of the nonminority group. On the other hand, 27 percent of all Hispanic business owners possess a high school diploma or equivalent, as opposed to 32 percent of their nonminority counterparts. In Table 14.8, the formal education of Hispanic business owners is compared with their nonminority counterparts. Generally, a larger percentage of Hispanic business owners are first-time entrepreneurs, compared with their

nonminority counterparts. Approximately 15 percent of Hispanic business owners have previously owned a business, while 21 percent of their nonminority counterparts have. In addition, 28 percent of Hispanic business owners have close relatives who own a business, while 40 percent of nonminority business owners do. Hispanic business owners as a group also possess less managerial experience prior to establishing their businesses than their nonminority counterparts; approximately 10 percent have ten or more years as managers before starting a business, while 21 percent of their nonminority counterparts possess such experience. Finally, 30 percent of Hispanic businesses were established prior to 1976, compared with 42 percent of the nonminority businesses. These data confirm that Hispanic business owners as a group tend to have less business experience and tend to be more recent entrants into the world of business than their nonminority counterparts. Variations between Hispanic and nonminority business owners across several dimensions are shown in Table 14.9.

TABLE 14.5
SALES VOLUME OF HISPANIC BUSINESSES

PERCENTAGE OF BUSINESSES	SALES ($)
34	Less than 5,000
35	5,000–24,999
20	25,000–99,999
7	100,000–249,999
3	250,000–999,999
1	1,000,000 or more

Source: United States Bureau of the Census, 1987, 140.

TABLE 14.6a
THE THIRTY LARGEST HISPANIC BUSINESSES

RANK	COMPANY AND LOCATION	CHIEF EXECUTIVE	TYPE OF BUSINESS	NUMBER OF EMPLOYEES	YEAR STARTED	SALES ($ MILLIONS)
1	Goya Foods, Secaucus, NJ	Joseph A. Unanue	Hispanic Food Mfg./Mktg.	1,600	1936	453.00
2	Burt on Broadway Auto. Grp. Englewood, CO	Lloyd G. Chavez	Automotive Sales & Svc.	600	1939	422.76
3	Sedano's Supermarkets Miami, FL	Manuel A. Herren	Supermarket Chain	1,500	1962	224.56
4	Galeana's Van Dyke Dodge Inc. Warren, MI	Frank Galeana	Automotive Sales & Svc.	334	1977	186.30
5	Cal-State Lumber Sales Inc. San Diego, CA	Benjamin Acevedo	Wood Products Sales	98	1984	169.64
6	Ancira Enterprises Inc. San Antonio, TX	Ernesto Ancira Jr.	Automotive Sales & Svc.	300	1983	168.00
7	International Bancshares Corp. Laredo, TX	Dennis E. Nixon	Financial Svcs.	650	1979	160.70
8	Handy Andy Supermarkets San Antonio, TX	A. (Jimmy) Jimenez	Supermarket Chain	1,705	1983	148.00
9	Frank Parra Autoplex Irving, TX	Tim & Mike Parra	Automotive Sales & Svc.	284	1971	146.62
10	Normac Foods Inc. Oklahoma City, OK	John C. Lopez	Meat Products Mfg.	255	1970	142.77
11	Lloyd A. Wise Inc. Oakland, CA	A.A. Batarse Jr.	Automotive Sales & Svc.	291	1914	137.21
12	Infotec Development Inc. Santa Ana, CA	J. Fernando Niebla	Aerospace Engr./Systems Devel.	600	1978	126.03
13	CTA Inc. Rockville, MD	C.E. (Tom) Velez	Aerospace/Defense Systems	1,280	1979	115.94
14	Capital Bancorp Miami, FL	Abel Holtz	Financial Svcs.	632	1974	114.17
15	COLSA Corp. Huntsville, AL	Francisco J. Collazo	Engineering Svcs.	700	1980	112.00
16	Troy Ford Troy, MI	Irma B. Elder	Automotive Sales & Svc.	115	1967	111.09
17	CareFlorida Inc. Miami, FL	Paul L. Cejas	Health Care Svcs.	194	1986	110.60
18	Gaseteria Oil Corp. Brooklyn, NY	Oscar Porcelli	Gasoline Stations	450	1972	108.00
19	Eagle Brands Inc. Miami, FL	Carlos M. de la Cruz Sr.	Beer Dist.	200	1984	97.95
20	Precision Trading Corp. Miami, FL	Israel Lapciuc	Consumer Electronics	35	1979	96.00
21	Condal Distributors Inc. Bronx, NY	Nelson Fernandez	Food Dist.	250	1968	95.00
22	TELACU Industries City of Commerce, CA	David C. Lizarraga	Economic Devel./Financial Svcs.	600	1968	93.00
23	Rosendin Electric Inc. San Jose, CA	Raymond J. Rosendin	Electrical Contracting	650	1919	91.00
24	Mexican Indust. in Michigan Inc. Detroit, MI	Henry J. Aguirre	Automotive Trim Mfg.	800	1979	87.50
25	Vincam Group Inc. Miami, FL	Carlos A. Saladrigas	Employee Leasing	6,500	1985	85.30
26	Ruiz Food Products Inc. Dinuba, CA	Frederick R. Ruiz	Mexican Food Mfg.	1,123	1964	83.26
27	United Poultry/Belca Foodservice Atlanta, GA	Alfredo Caceres	Foodservice Dist./Export	108	1976	78.22
28	Pan American Hospital Miami, FL	Carolina Calderin	Health Care Svcs.	600	1963	76.00
29	H & H Meat Products Co. Inc. dba H & H Foods, Mercedes, TX	Liborio E. Hinojosa	Meat Packing/Dist.	310	1947	68.79
30	Advanced Sciences Inc. Albuquerque, NM	Ed L. Romero	Environ. Engineering Svcs.	492	1977	66.59

Source: *Hispanic Business,* January 1994.

TABLE 14.6b
THE FASTEST GROWING HISPANIC-OWNED COMPANIES

RANK	COMPANY AND LOCATION	TYPE OF BUSINESS	NUMBER OF EMPLOYEES	YEAR STARTED	SALES ($ MILLIONS)	COMPOUND GROWTH RATE 1988–1992
1	**Superior Tomato and Avocado Co. Inc.** San Antonio, TX	Fresh Vegetables & Fruit Dist.	175	1988	30.10	250.25
2	**Shadrock Petroleum Products Inc.** San Antonio, TX	Petroleum/Natural Gas Products Dist.	9	1946	41.69	243.31
3	**Research Management Consultants Inc.** Camarillo, CA	Environ. Engineering Svcs./Info. Syst.	188	1987	16.00	216.70
4	**Stature Construction Co.** Houston, TX	General Contracting	8	1987	11.45	178.87
5	**HJ Ford Associates Inc.** Arlington, VA	Systems Engineering/Integ.	105	1981	9.21	152.95
6	**PCI International** Lafayette, LA	Food Ingredient/Coconut Export	5	1981	4.54	134.44
7	**Trandes Corporation** Lanham, MD	Transport. Engr./Logistics/Mgmt.	180	1980	11.17	132.00
8	**O.I.V. Systems Inc.** San Antonio, TX	Computer Programming	76	1988	7.65	127.94
9	**Oasis Technology Inc.** Camarillo, CA	Computer Software/System Design	5	1979	4.78	124.52
10	**Cal-State Lumber Sales Inc.** San Diego, CA	Wood Products Sales	98	1984	169.64	121.88
11	**Compu-Centro USA Inc.** El Paso, TX	Computer Sales/Svc./Training/Net.	39	1986	8.03	118.85
12	**MVM Inc.** Falls Church, VA	Investigation/Security Svcs.	1,152	1979	24.45	117.43
13	**Compatible Micro Solutions Inc.** dba CMS, El Paso, TX	Computer Sales/Syst. Integ.	23	1987	3.29	111.01
14	**HBLF** Jacksonville, FL	Translations/Typesetting/Printing	76	1986	2.72	105.36
15	**Certified Abatement Systems Inc.** Houston, TX	Asbestos & Lead Abatement	50	1987	5.00	101.03
16	**Perii Systems Inc.** Ho-Ho-Kus, NJ	Systems Engineering/Integ.	30	1987	2.18	99.66
17	**Scientech Inc.** Idaho Falls, ID	Environ. Safety/Waste Mgmt.	257	1983	20.43	89.64
18	**Sani Serv Inc.** Indianapolis, IN	Ice Cream/Yogurt Machine Mfg.	96	1977	28.00	88.88
19	**Maria Elena Toraño and Assos. (META)** Miami, Fl	Mgmt. Consulting Svcs.	228	1980	15.45	88.84
20	**Operational Technologies Corp.** San Antonio, TX	Environ. Engineering Svcs.	156	1986	6.96	88.61
21	**Vincam Group Inc.** Miami, FL	Employee Leasing	6,500	1985	85.30	87.51
22	**Tru & Associates Inc.** Vista, CA	Petrol./Lubricant/Coal Prod. Dist.	3	1983	5.20	86.06
23	**Montoya & Sons Construction Co. Inc.** Schiller Park, IL	General Contracting	55	1986	10.31	84.28
24	**Shifa Services Inc.** Hackensack, NJ	Janitorial Svcs./Plant Maintenance	800	1980	13.80	84.15
25	**C.P.F. Corporation** Washington, DC	Janitorial/Painting Svcs.	417	1984	5.10	81.81
26	**Copier Depot Inc.** Miami, FL	Copier Equipment and Sales	23	1972	3.80	80.25
27	**Film Roman** N. Hollywood, CA	TV/Theater Anim. Entertain. Dist.	210	1984	25.00	77.83
28	**Pinto Brothers Construction Inc.** Chicago, IL	General Contracting/Painting	100	1987	7.20	73.21
29	**JC's Mid America Building Services Inc.** Carol Stream, IL	Janitorial/Painting Svcs.	480	1979	10.40	71.58
30	**Comprehensive Technologies Internatl. Inc.** Chantilly, VA	Software Develop./Systems Integ.	490	1980	39.23	70.57

Source: *Hispanic Business,* January 1994.

Figure 14.2
Sources of Start-up Capital for Hispanic and Nonminority Business Owners

Hispanic

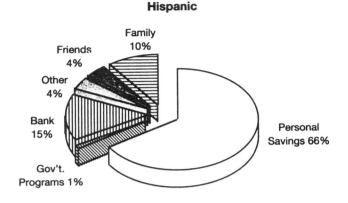

Family 10%
Friends 4%
Other 4%
Bank 15%
Gov't. Programs 1%
Personal Savings 66%

Nonminority

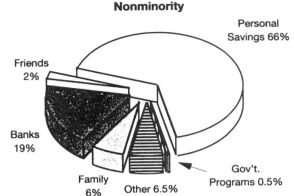

Personal Savings 66%
Friends 2%
Banks 19%
Family 6%
Other 6.5%
Gov't. Programs 0.5%

TABLE 14.7
HISPANIC AND NONMINORITY BUSINESS OWNERS BY AGE

	UNDER 25	25–34	35–44	45–54	55–64	OVER 65
Hispanic business owners	4%	22%	28%	24%	14%	4%
Nonminority business owners	3%	20%	25%	22%	18%	9%

Source: United States Bureau of the Census, 1987, 10.
Note: 4 percent of Hispanic business owners and 3 percent of nonminority business owners did not report age.

Other interesting similarities exist between the groups. Slightly over 76 percent of Hispanic business owners used $10,000 or less in capital to start or acquire their businesses, while 72 percent of nonminority businesses required $10,000 or less. Start-up capital requirements for Hispanic and nonminority businesses are illustrated in Table 14.10.

The sources of start-up capital for Hispanic and nonminority business owners are varied. The major portion for both groups has come from personal savings. However, 19 percent of nonminority business owners borrowed the capital from commercial banks, while 15 percent of Hispanic business owners did so. Approximately 8 percent of nonminority business owners obtained capital from family and friends, compared with 13 percent of Hispanic business owners. Sources of start-up capital for Hispanic and nonminority business owners are illustrated in Figure 14.2.

Some indication of business productivity can be obtained by examining net profit or loss of Hispanic businesses and comparing them to nonminority businesses. More than 4 percent of Hispanic-owned businesses generated net profits of $50,000 or more, compared with 6 percent for nonminority businesses. Approximately 14 percent of Hispanic businesses reported a loss, while 16 percent of nonminority businesses did. In terms of productivity when measured by profit or loss, it can be concluded that minority businesses are as productive as nonminority ones. Profit and loss for Hispanic and nonminority businesses are compared in Table 14.11

TABLE 14.8
HISPANIC AND NONMINORITY BUSINESS OWNERS BY YEARS OF EDUCATION

	LESS THAN 9 YEARS	9–11 YEARS	HIGH SCHOOL DIPLOMA	1–3 YEARS OF COLLEGE	COLLEGE DEGREE	MORE THAN 5 YEARS OF COLLEGE
Hispanic business owners	19%	11%	27%	20%	7%	12%
Nonminority business owners	5%	8%	32%	20%	15%	18%

Source: United States Bureau of the Census, 1987, 18.
Note: 4 percent of Hispanic business owners and 2 percent of nonminority business owners did not report education.

The dominant form of Hispanic-owned business is the sole proprietorship; this is also the dominant form of all U.S. businesses. The majority of Hispanic companies—94 percent—are sole proprietorships, compared to 92 percent for nonminority businesses, according to the Bureau of the Census. Hispanic-owned corporations, on the other hand, account for 2 percent of the total number of Hispanic companies, while 3 percent of nonminority firms are corporations. Approximately 4 percent of Hispanic businesses are partnerships, compared with 5 percent of nonminority businesses.

Hispanic-owned businesses tend to differ from their nonminority counterparts in at least one area; they tend to hire other Hispanics or minorities. Approximately 67 percent of Hispanic businesses report that their work force consists of 75 to 100 percent minority employees. This contrasts with the 14 percent of nonminority businesses that reported their work force to consist of 75 to 100 percent minority employees. The percentage of minority employees in both Hispanic and nonminority businesses is summarized in Table 14.12.

TABLE 14.9
HISPANIC AND NONMINORITY BUSINESS OWNERS ACROSS FOUR CHARACTERISTICS

	HISPANIC BUSINESS OWNERS (%)	NONMINORITY BUSINESS OWNERS (%)
College education	7	15
First-time entrepreneur	85	79
Management experience of 10 years or more	10	21
45 years of age or older	42	49

Source: United States Bureau of the Census, 1987, 10, 18, 37, 74.

No clear and consistent information is available, but what little research does exist indicates that Hispanic-owned businesses fail at a rate slightly higher than those of similar nonminority firms. There is some evidence that minority firms are burdened by higher debt structure, resulting in more problems, especially during recessions or tight money periods.

TABLE 14.10
START-UP CAPITAL REQUIRED FOR HISPANIC AND NONMINORITY BUSINESS OWNERS

	NONE	$1–4,999	$5,000–9,999	$10,000–24,999	$25,000–49,999	$50,000–99,999	$100,000–249,000	$250,000 OR MORE
Hispanic Businesses	27%	37%	12%	11%	4%	2%	6%	4%
Nonminority Businesses	27%	34%	10%	11%	6%	3%	2%	6%

Source: United States Bureau of the Census, 1987, 82.
Note: 6 percent of Hispanic business owners and 6.4 percent of nonminority business owners did not respond.

TABLE 14.11
PROFIT AND LOSS FOR HISPANIC AND NONMINORITY BUSINESSES

	PROFIT								
	LESS THAN $5,000	$5,000–9,999	$10,000–19,999	$20,000–24,999	$25,000–29,999	$30,000–49,999	$50,000–74,999	$75,000–99,999	$100,000–249,000	$250,000 or More
Hispanic	26%	14%	12%	4%	2%	4%	2%	1%	1%	0.5%
Nonminority	27%	11%	11%	4%	3%	5%	2%	1%	2%	1%

	LOSS		
	LESS THAN $5,000	$5,000–9,999	$10,000–24,999	$25,000 OR MORE
Hispanic-Owned Businesses	11%	2%	1%	0.6%
Nonminority-Owned Businesses	12%	2%	1%	1%

Source: United States Bureau of the Census, 1987, 114.
Note: 18.9 percent of Hispanic businesses and 17 percent of nonminority businesses did not respond.

TABLE 14.12
MINORITY EMPLOYEES IN HISPANIC AND NONMINORITY BUSINESSES

	NO MINORITY EMPLOYEES	1–9%	10–24%	25–49%	50–74%	75–100%
Hispanic Businesses	11	2	4	5	11	67
Nonminority Businesses	65	6	6	5	4	14

Source: United States Bureau of the Census, 1987, 130.

✳ HISPANICS IN THE CORPORATE WORLD

With higher college graduation rates and the implementation of Affirmative Action programs since the 1970s, more and more Hispanics are succeeding in entering corporate management, but as yet there are very few of them at the highest managerial levels and in the board rooms. In its January/February 1996 issue, *Hispanic Business* magazine reported on the 20 largest companies for employment of Hispanic managers, illustrated by Table 14.13.

Hispanics that are in the corporate world, like women in the corporate world, have hit a "glass ceiling," an invisible barrier that has to date stopped their advancement up the corporate ladder. While a Hispanic, Roberto C. Goizueta, is the President and CEO of one of the world's largest corporations, *Hispanic Business* magazine has shown that in 1995 its Corporate Elite directory included only 217 executives at 118 *Fortune* 1,000 companies. Hispanics remain far below parity with their 10 percent of the

TABLE 14.13
RANKING THE 20 LARGEST CORPORATIONS
ANALYSIS OF EMPLOYMENT REPORTS FOR 18 OF THE 20 LARGEST U.S. COMPANIES
AS LISTED BY *FORTUNE* MAGAZINE.

RANK OVERALL	COMPANY	RANK BY PERCENT OF HISPANICS IN WORK FORCE	RANK BY PERCENT OF OFFICIALS/ MANAGERS WHO ARE HISPANIC	RANK BY PERCENT OF PROFESSIONALS WHO ARE HISPANIC	RANK BY PERCENT OF HISPANIC EMPLOYEES WHO ARE OFFICIALS/ MANAGERS	RANK BY PERCENT OF HISPANIC EMPLOYEES WHO ARE PROFESSIONALS	TOTAL SCORE
1	Citicorp	2	1	1	3	7*	14
2	Exxon	8	5	7	4	5	29
3	Texaco	9	9	3	8	3	32
4	Mobil	7	7*	5	9	6	34
5	Chevron	5	6	6	7	11	35
6	AT&T	10	7*	8	1	10	36
7*	IBM	11*	11	10	6	1	39*
7*	Sears	3	3	2	13	18	39*
9	PepsiCo	1	2	4	18	16	41
10	Philip Morris	6	10	9	14	14	53
11*	General Electric	14	13*	12	11	4	54*
11*	Prudential	11*	12	11	5	15	54*
13	Procter & Gamble	17*	13*	13*	2	12	57
14*	Du Pont	17*	16	13*	10	2	58*
14*	Kmart	4	4	18	15	17	58*
16	Ford	15*	17	17	12	7*	68
17	Chrysler	15*	18	13*	16	9	71
18	General Motors	13	13*	16	17	13	72

*Indicates tie in vertical column. Note: Total score is based on sum of rankings in five categories; each category carries equal weight. Wal-Mart Stores Inc. and State Farm Mutual Automobile Insurance Company did not release employment reports to HISPANIC BUSINESS. The top three companies in each category are denoted by special type.
Hispanic Business, January–February, 1996.

U.S. population. The Hispanic percent of the 15,000 senior executives at these 1,000 corporations is thus only 1.4 percent. White males hold 95 percent of these senior positions, while white females hold 2 percent and all minorities account for only 3 percent. Among the diverse industries in the *Fortune* 1,000, pharmaceuticals has the highest representations of Hispanic senior executives; this lead is followed by telecommunications. Other companies employing above the average of Hispanic senior executives are beverages, entertainment, toys/sports, and soaps and cosmetics. Table 14.14 shows the corporations with the most Hispanic senior executives.

In the rarified air of the corporate board room, Hispanics have barely arrived. According to the January/February 1996 issue of *Hispanic Business*, there are only 62 Hispanics serving on the boards of a total of 85 *Fortune* 1,000 corporations and their divisions or subsidiaries. Anheuser-Bush Companies Inc. is the corporation with the most Hispanics on its board: five. The following corporations have three Hispanics on their boards: Barnet Bank of South Florida, Sun Trust Banks of Atlanta, and Miami and the Public Services Company of New Mexico. Utility and finance companies are the industrial sectors that have companies with two Hispanic board members, most of these located in New Mexico and California. Three Hispanic individuals serve on the most boards, each with five directorships, according to the *Hispanic Business* survey: Katherine Ortega, the former Treasurer of the United States; Armando Codina, chairman of Codina Group Inc. in Miami, and Roberto C. Goizueta, CEO of the Coca-Cola Co.

Despite the relative absence of Hispanics from most of the major board rooms in the United States, Hispanic businessmen and corporate executives have made some major advances in the corporate world in the last two decades. Included among those historical landmarks in Hispanic business history are the following: In 1977, Carlos José Arboleya became the first Cuban president and CEO of a major bank in the United States—Barnet Banks of Miami. Thanks to Arboleya and other Cuban American businessmen and bankers, Miami has become a major banking center for Latin America. In 1979, Humberto Cabañas became the first Hispanic CEO of a major corporation in the hospitality industry when he assumed the position of CEO and founding president of Benchmark Hospitality Group in the Woodlands, Texas. He was also the first U.S. Hispanic president of the International Association of Conference Centers, from which he received a distinguished service award in 1988. In 1980, Frank Lorenzo became the first U.S. Hispanic to serve as the

TABLE 14.14
TOP COMPANIES OF THE CORPORATE ELITE

COMPANY	NUMBER OF EXECUTIVES
American Telephone & Telegraph (AT&T)	9
Xerox Corp.	8
Dole Food Co. Inc.	7
CoreStates Financial Corp.	5
SBC Communications Inc.	5
Turner Broadcasting System Inc.	5
Viacom International Inc.	5
Colgate-Palmolive Co.	4
Gannett Co. Inc.	4
Mattel Inc.	4
Motorola Inc.	4
Philip Morris Cos. Inc.	4
US WEST Inc.	4
Chrysler Corp.	4
Dayton Hudson Corp.	3
Dial Corp.	3
International Business Machines (IBM)	3
Johnson & Johnson	3
Knight-Ridder Inc.	3
McDonald's Corp.	3
Northrop Grumman Corp.	3
PepsiCo Inc.	3
Principal Financial Group	3
Schering-Plough Corp.	3
WMX Technologies Inc.	3

Note: No other company placed more than two executives on this year's list.
Hispanic Business, January–February, 1996.

president of a major national and international airline, Continental Airlines, headquartered in Houston, Texas. From 1986 to 1990, Lorenzo served as chairman and CEO of Continental Airlines. A graduate of the Harvard M.B.A. program, Lorenzo served as president and chairman of the board of Texas International Airlines (TII), from 1972 to 1980; TII became the holding company for Continental Airlines. In 1981, Roberto C. Goizueta became the first U.S. Hispanic to lead one of the largest corporations in the world, Coca-Cola, when he became the company's CEO and chairman of the board. One of the highest paid CEOs, if not the highest, in the United States, the Cuban-born Goizueta started out as a Coca-Cola bottler in Miami, after receiving his B.S. degree in engineering from Yale University in 1953. In 1989, Edgar J. Milán became the first New York Puerto Rican to serve as controller and vice president of one of the largest U.S. corporations, Tenneco Inc. Raised in New York City, where he received a degree in accounting from Hunter College, Milán rose in the ranks of the oil industry, serving in the United States, Canada, England, Peru, and Nicaragua. In 1990, Sosa and Associates, the San Antonio advertising agency founded and headed by Lionel Sosa, became the first Hispanic concern to be named Agency of the Year and the Hottest Agency in the Southwest by *Adweek* magazine. In 1989, Sosa and Associates had billings of $54.8 million. There is certainly room for more of these success stories of Hispanics in the world of business.

✱ PROMINENT HISPANICS IN BUSINESS

Deborah Aguiar-Vélez (1955–)

Born on December 18, 1955, in New York City, Aguiar received a B.S. degree in chemical engineering from the University of Puerto Rico in 1977 and a certificate from the University of Virginia Entrepreneurial Executive Institute in 1989. In her early career, she was a systems analyst for Exxon and then worked in the small-business division of the New Jersey Department of Commerce. After that she founded and was president of her own business, Sistemas Corporation. Her honors include selection in 1990 as the Outstanding Women Entrepreneur Advocate by American Women in Economic Development and selection for Coca-Cola commercials as a Hispanic woman entrepreneurial role model. Aguiar has served on the boards of the Hispanic Women's Task Force, the Hispanic Leadership Opportunity Program, and the New Jersey Women's Business Advisory Council, which she chaired from 1987 to 1988.

Linda Alvarado (1951–)

Raised in Albuquerque, New Mexico, Alvarado was a good student and an outstanding athlete in basketball, volleyball and soft ball in both high school and college. After graduating from Pomona College in California, she became a contract administrator for a California development company and learned all aspects of the construction business. After some formal education in blue printing and other skills necessary for construction, she and a partner founded the Martínez Alvarado Construction Management Corporation in 1974. In 1976, she bought out her partner and became the sole general contractor under the title of Alvarado Construction Inc. The company experienced great success in constructing high rise office structures, commercial buildings, airport hangars and a convention center. In 1993, Alvarado became a partner in the Colorado Rockies franchise, a new major league baseball team. As such, she became the first Hispanic team owner in the history of baseball in the United States, a sport that has always been important to Hispanics. In addition to running her construction business and helping to administer the baseball franchise, Alvarado is a member of the board of directors of several *Fortune* 500 corporations.

Gabriel Eloy Aguirre (1935–)

Born on January 12, 1935, in Akron, Ohio, Aguirre worked for SaniServ in Indianapolis in the service and sales divisions from 1957 to 1977; in 1977, he became the owner of the company. For his outstanding success with the company, he was named the 1987 Minority Entrepreneur of the Year by the president of the United States. Aguirre has been very active in the community, serving on numerous boards and as president of school boards and police commissions. Since 1988, he has been a member of the board of the U.S. Senate Task Force on Hispanic Affairs.

Carlos José Arboleya (1929–)

Born on February 1, 1929, in Havana, Cuba, Arboleya is a graduate of the University of Havana who developed his early career in banking as the Havana manager of the First National City Bank of New York. After the Cuban Revolution of 1959, he immigrated to the United States and worked at a number

Gabriel Eloy Aguirre.

Carlos José Arboleya.

of banks in Miami, moving up the ranks from clerk to bank administrator. By 1966, he was executive vice president of the Fidelity National Bank of South Miami; by 1973, the co-owner, president, and director of the Flagler Bank; and by 1977, president and CEO of the Barnett Banks of Miami. Since 1983, he has been vice chairman of the Barnett Bank of South Florida. Arboleya has remained active in the profession and the community, serving as vice president of the American Institute of Banking and on the boards of such organizations as the Inter-American Affairs Action Committee, the National Advisory Council for Economic Opportunity, the American Arbitration Association, and the Cuban American Foundation. Among his many honors are the American Academy of Achievement Gold Plate Award in 1974, the Horatio Alger Award of the American Schools and Colleges Association in 1976, and the American Red Cross Man of the Year Award in 1988.

Humberto Cabañas (1947–)

Hotel Management

Born on September 3, 1947, in Havana, Cuba, Cabañas received a B.S. degree in hotel and restau-

rant management from Florida International University in 1974 and went on to rise through the ranks at Sheraton, Doral, and Stouffer hotels until becoming the founding president and CEO of the Benchmark Hospitality Group in Woodlands, Texas, in 1979. Benchmark properties include the Woodlands Executive Conference Center and resort, the Woodlands Country Club, the Exxon Conference Center, the Tournament Players Golf Course, and the San Luis Resort Hotel on Galveston Island. He has been a president of the International Association of Conference Centers from which he received a Distinguished Service Award in 1988. Cabañas serves on the industry advisory committee for the Conrad Hilton School of Hotel and Restaurant Management of the University of Houston and is a past president of the International Association of Conference Centers.

Gilbert Cuéllar, Jr.

Restaurant Chain Executive

Cuéllar is the chairman and CEO of the 50-year-old restaurant chain founded by his family. Formerly known as El Chico Corporation, the Dallas-based chain is now Southwest Cafes and has, under Cuéllar's direction, expanded to various states under

Gilbert Cuéllar, Jr.

such local names as Cantina Laredo, Cuéllar's Cafe, Casa Rose, and El Chico Restaurants. First becoming associated with the corporation in 1970, he has served in various capacities, including manager of quality control, product research and development, and director of marketing research. In 1977, Campbell Taggart acquired the restaurant chain and Cuéllar enrolled at North Texas State University and received an M.B.A. degree. After founding various restaurants of his own, he and his father were able to repurchase El Chico Corporation in 1982. In 1986, Cuéllar was named chairman of the corporation.

Remedios Díaz-Oliver (1938–)

The president and CEO of one of southern Florida's top companies, Díaz-Oliver was born on August 22, 1938, in Cuba, the daughter of a hotel owner. Her early experience in business was fostered by her father who often took his daughter along with him on business trips around the island and to the United States and Spain. She obtained a Master's degree from Havana Business University and a Ph.D. in Education from the university of Havana. After becoming a wife and mother, she was jailed by the Communist regime in Cuba in 1961 for her protesting government mail inspections; on her release later that year, she immigrated to the United States with her husband and daughter. Her first job in the United States was working as an accounting clerk in the Emmer Glass company of Miami for $55 a week. Within a year she founded an international division for Emmer and took charge of exporting glass containers. In 1976, Díaz-Oliver and her husband Fausto founded American International Container with Frank H. Wheaton Jr., one of the most respected names in U.S. glass manufacturing. By 1991, American International Container was grossing $90 million in revenues and was listed thirty-third on the list of top privately-owned companies in southern Florida by the *Florida Business Journal*. In 1991, she founded All American Container with her husband and two children, which distributes packaging products and materials, including plastic and glass bottles for such companies as Coca-Cola. Pepsi, McCormick and Kraft. Her sales offices are located throughout South America and in London and Sydney.

Roberto C. Goizueta (1931–)

Beverage Company Executive

Born on November 18, 1931, in Havana, Cuba, Goizueta received a B.S. degree in chemical engineering in 1953 from Yale University. He began at the Coca-Cola Company as an assistant vice president of research in 1964; by 1981, he had become the chairman of the board and CEO of Coca-Cola, one of the world's largest corporations. Goizueta has been active in service nationally and internationally. He is the founding director of the Points of Light Initiative and sits on the boards of the Ford Motor Company and Eastman Kodak, among others. Since 1980, he has been a trustee of Emory University. Among his many honors are being chosen a Gordon Grand fellow of Yale University in 1984, the 1984 Herbert Hoover Humanitarian Award of the Boys Clubs of America, and the 1986 Ellis Island Medal of Honor.

Fredrick J. González (1949–)

Design Engineering Executive

Born on June 28, 1949, in Detroit, Michigan, González received a B.S. degree in engineering and an M.S. degree in architecture and urban planning from Princeton University in 1971 and 1972, respectively. After working for three years as an architect for Smith Himchman Gryllis Associates, in 1975 he and his father founded their own firm, González Design Engineering in Madison Heights, Michigan, for which he has served as CEO since 1977, when his

Roberto C. Goizueta.

Fredrick J. González.

father died. In 1979, he also became the president of Semi-Kinetics, a printed circuit board assembly line in Laguna Hills, California. Since a 1968 automobile accident, González, who had been a high school football star, has been paralyzed from the waist down. Among his and his company's honors are being named by the White House as the National Minority Service Firm of the Year in 1975, selection as the 1989 Minority Businessman of the Year, and selection as the 1989 Minority Supplier of the Year by the National Minority Business Development Council. González participates on many boards, including the board of directors of the U.S. Hispanic Chamber of Commerce. González and his brother/partner, Gary, have been featured in full-page ads by General Motors as successful suppliers to the car company.

Frank A. Lorenzo (1940–)

Former Airline Company Executive

Born on May 19, 1940, in New York City, Lorenzo received a B.S. degree from Columbia University in 1961 and an M.B.A. degree from Harvard University in 1963. He began his career in air transportation as a financial analyst for Texas World Airlines from 1963 to 1965; and by 1966, he had founded and become chairman of his own company, Lorenzo Carney and Company. From 1972 to 1980 he served as president and chairman of Texas International Airlines, which eventually became a major national and international holding company for Continental Airlines, for which he served as president from 1980 to 1985, and then as chairman and CEO from 1986 to 1990. After developing the company into the world's largest carrier through the purchase of various other carriers, Lorenzo was embattled by strikes, rising costs, and competition, and the problems of deregulation, and he was eventually forced to resign.

Edgar J. Milán (1934–)

Controller

Born on November 23, 1934, in New York City, Mílan received a B.S. degree in accounting from Hunter College in 1957 and pursued additional courses toward an M.S. degree at the City College of New York. He rose through the ranks as a career accountant in oil companies, serving in the United States, Canada, England, Peru, and Nicaragua. After serving in a number of vice presidential positions in the financial divisions of Tenneco Oil, one of the

Edgar J. Milán.

largest U.S. corporations, Mílan was named vice president and controller in 1989. Mílan serves on a number of advisory boards, including those of Arte Público Press and the accounting programs for Texas Tech and Texas A & M Universities. Mílan was also an outstanding college basketball player; and in 1957, he was selected Hunter College Athlete of the Year; and in 1991, he was inducted into the Hunter College Athletic Hall of Fame.

Luis Nogales (1943–)

Known as one of the most outstanding Hispanic businessmen in the United States, Luis Nogales was born on October 17, 1943, in Madera, California, to migrant farm workers. His early years were spent picking crops in southern California, but he nevertheless was able to complete his education and go on to college and eventually graduate from Stanford Law School in 1969, whereupon he was hired by the university as an assistant to the president. He later went on to serve as a White House fellow and to travel to Europe and Asia in that capacity. Throughout his university education and his early career, Nogales was an advocate for Hispanic civil and educational rights. From 1973 to 1980, Nogales worked as vice president for Golden West Broadcasters and served on the board of directors of the Levi-Strauss corporation; he also served on the board of the Mexican American Legal Defense and Education Fund (MALDEF). In 1983, he assumed the position of executive vice president for United Press International (UPI), the second largest news agency in the world. Nogales resigned from UPI in 1985 and in 1987 became the president of the Univisión television network, a position which he kept for only one year. After that he continued his work in community projects and on the board of directors of Lucky Stores, Bank of California and Southern California Edison Company. In 1988, he became a member of the board of trustees of Stanford University.

Robert Ortega, Jr. (1947–)

Construction Company Executive

Born on February 1, 1947, in El Paso, Texas, Ortega received B.S. and M.S. degrees in civil engineering from the University of Texas at El Paso in 1970 and 1980, respectively. He worked as an engineer in the U.S. Public Health Service, the U.S. Bureau of Reclamation, and the El Paso Housing Department before founding Construction Management Associates in 1983. In 1988, his company was rated the fifth-fastest-growing Hispanic company in the United States by *Hispanic Business* magazine. In 1989, the company was named the Outstanding Small Business for the City of El Paso by the Small

Business Administration. In 1980, Ortega was named Young Engineer of the Year, and in 1989, Engineer of the Year by the Texas Society of Professional Engineers. He is a past president of the Texas Society of Civil Engineers and of the Associated Builders and Contractors.

Carlos D. Ramírez (1946–)

See Chapter 27.

Emyré Barrios Robinson (1926–)

See Chapter 10.

John Rodríguez (1958–)

Advertising and Public Relations

Born on August 9, 1958, in New York City, John Rodríguez is cofounder and president of AD One, an advertising and public relations firm in Rochester, New York. Rodríguez completed his bachelor's degree at the Rochester Institute of Technology, where he majored in advertising and photography. He continues his education by attending classes at local universities and is currently working toward a master's degree in communications. As a young entrepreneur, he has built his company, AD One, into a successful firm that specializes in international sales promotion, recruitment, and the Hispanic market. Their clients have included Eastman Kodak Company, Bausch and Lomb, Preferred Care, the University of Rochester, the Girl Scouts, Rochester City School District, and Mobil Chemical.

Oscar Rodríguez

Computers

Oscar Rodríguez was born and raised in San Antonio, Texas. He spent 17 years as a very successful entrepreneur in Boston, Massachusetts. He obtained his master's of business administration degree at Harvard University and then sold three successful computer-oriented companies. In 1985, after a highly successful business career, Rodríguez returned to San Antonio and, with Héctor Dávila, bought out a failing computer services company. The new company, Antares Development Corporation, assumed the computer support responsibility for 60 of San Antonio's most respected firms. By the end of 1988, the company had become one of the premier suppliers of computer services in San Antonio.

Eduardo G. Santiago (1949–)

Controller

Born on September 26, 1949, in Ponce, Puerto Rico, Santiago earned a B.S. degree in accounting from Baruch College in 1975 and a M.B.A. in finance from Pace University in 1979. He began his career as an accounting clerk for Guy Carpenter & Co. in 1969. He worked for American International Marine and for MacMillan until 1975, when he became the controller of Philip Morris International.

Lionel Sosa (1939–)

Advertising

Born on May 27, 1939, in San Antonio, Texas, Sosa became a graphic artist who developed a career in advertising, founding his own company, Sosart, in 1966. In 1974, he became a partner of Ed Yardang and Associates. In 1984, he founded Sosa and Associates, for which he serves as chairman and CEO. Sosa and Associates is the leading firm in handling national accounts targeted at Hispanic consumers. In 1990, *Adweek* magazine named Sosa and Associates the Agency of the Year and the Hottest Agency in the Southwest, with 1989 billings of $54.8 million. Sosa's clients include American Airlines, Anheuser-Busch, Burger King, Coca-Cola USA, Montgomery Ward, and Western Union. Among his many awards are the 1990 Entrepreneur of the Year, the 1989 Marketing Person of the Year Award, the 1989 Silver Award from the Public Relations Society of America, and the Gold ADDY from the American Advertising Foundation in 1988. Sosa is active in the community, participating on many local and national boards.

Jospeh A. Unanue (1926–)

Joseph A. Unanue took his father's company, Goya Foods Inc., and built it into the largest Hispanic-owned company in the United States. After his father's death in 1976, Unanue took over the chain that his father built from an importing business. Under his guidance, the company grew to sell more than 800 products. It's revenue rose to $453 million by 1992, a growth rate of some 12% annually. Unanue had refocused the company from principally serving Puerto Ricans and Cubans on the east coast of the United States to serving all Hispanics in the United States. The company then began importing and processing foods to cater specifically to Mexicans and Central Americans precisely at the time that these populations within the United States were experiencing their greatest growth. Despite this success, Goya has remained loyal to its initial customers and has been able to retain them even while faced with increasing competition from other Hispanic companies and mainstream corporations attempting to acquire a piece of the Hispanic market. While under Unanue the company has become one of the largest food pro-

Clifford Lane Whitehill.

cessors in the United States, Goya has remained a family-owned and operated; there are eight Unanues running the company across the U.S. today.

Clifford Lane Whitehill (1931–)

Corporate Attorney

Born on April 14, 1931, the son of Catalina Yarza and Clifford Whitehill, Whitehill earned a B.A. from Rice University in 1954, a LL.B. from the University of Texas, and a LL.M. from Harvard University in 1957 and 1958, respectively. He became a corporate attorney, working for various companies in Houston and New York until joining General Mills in Minneapolis as an attorney in 1962. He moved up the ranks to vice presidential positions and attained his present position of senior vice president, general counsel, and secretary in 1981. Among his honors is the 1988 Whitney North Seymour Sr. Award from the American Arbitration Society. Among the many boards and directorates on which Whitehill serves are the National Hispanic Scholarship Fund and the United Nations Association of the USA, both of which he directs.

References

Chipman, Donald E. *Spanish Texas, 1519–1821*. Austin: University of Texas Press, 1992.

Fontana, Bernard L. *Entrada: The Legacy of Spain and Mexico in the United States*. Albuquerque: University of New Mexico Press, 1994.

Henderson, Ann L., and Gary R. Mormino, eds. *Spanish Pathways in Florida*. Sarasota, FL: Pineapple Press, 1991.

Kanellos, Nicolás, with Cristelia Pérez. *Chronology of Hispanic American History*. Detroit: Gale Research, 1995.

Rosaldo, Renato, Robert A. Calvert, and Gustav L. Seligmann, *Chicano: The Evolution of a People*. Minneapolis: Winston Press, 1973.

Sheridan, Thomas E. *Los Tucsonenses: The Mexican Community in Tucson*. Tucson: University of Arizona Press, 1986.

Simmons, Helen, and Cathryn A. Hoyt, eds. *Hispanic Texas: A Historical Guide*. Austin: University of Texas Press, 1992.

Slatta, Richard W. *Cowboys of the Americas*. New Haven: Yale University Press, 1990.

"Special Report on Corporate America." *Hispanic Business* (January/February 1996).

Tardiff, Joseph C., and L. Mpho Mabunda, eds. *Dictionary of Hispanic Biography*. Detroit: Gale Research, 1996.

"The 100 Fastest Growing Hispanic Companies." *Hispanic Business* (August 1993).

"The Fastest Growing Hispanic-Owned Companies." *Hispanic Business* (January 1994).

Nicolás Kanellos

15

Labor and Employment

✳ Hispanics in Organized Labor ✳ Immigration and Migration ✳ Hispanic Employment in Industry
✳ Federal Employment Programs and Laws ✳ Youth Employment ✳ Women's Employment
✳ Government Programs ✳ Income, Poverty, and Unemployment

Hispanics are the fastest-growing major group in the labor force of the United States. Between 1980 and 1988, the number of Hispanics in the work force increased by 48 percent, representing 20 percent of U.S. employment growth. The employment of Hispanic women during this period increased by 56 percent, or more than two and one-half times the rate of other women.

Between 1980 and 1990, Hispanics increased from 6.1 percent to slightly more than 9 percent of the nation's work force. Their youth relative to other groups in the work force and continued high rates of immigration indicate that Hispanics will continue to increase their representation in the nation's work force in the foreseeable future.

Although the numbers have increased rapidly, conditions of employment for Hispanics have deteriorated during the 1980s. Many worker protections and benefits have been lost, incomes have declined in absolute terms, and the gap between Hispanics and whites has widened sharply.

In the final quarter of 1990, the median weekly earnings of Hispanic men were $331, compared with $370 for black men and $502 for white men. Hispanic women's weekly earnings were $283, compared with $313 for black women and $363 for white women. This means that white women and black men earned 74 percent, black women 62 percent, Hispanic men 66 percent, and Hispanic women 56 percent of that earned by white men. By March 1991, unemployment among Hispanics had reached 10.3 percent, roughly double the rate for whites.

Federal policy is partly responsible for the declining conditions, as the strategies of the Reagan-Bush era have resulted in the government's altering its priorities and shirking its earlier responsibilities. It has consciously adopted employment policies fa-voring large employers and higher income groups at the expense of the poor, particularly blacks and Hispanics. Employer abuses have even extended to child labor. In the four-year period from 1986 to 1990, child labor violations increased by 128 percent.

Brief History of Hispanics in the Labor Force

Between the late 1500s and the incorporation of northern Mexico into the United States at the end of the Mexican-American War in 1848, workers of Mexican birth who resided in the present-day Southwest worked largely in agricultural tasks. Most of them held land on which they grew and raised most of their sustenance, which they often supplemented by working for others. As they lost their lands after the war, the majority of them became wage laborers. They were employed as field hands, cowboys, railroad maintenance workers, ditch-diggers, and miners.

The movement of Mexican American workers out of rural and agricultural tasks was relatively slow. As their numbers gradually increased in cities and towns, they found employment in service and manufacturing occupations. Yet, in contrast to the overall trend among whites, they experienced a marked downward mobility during the last half of the nineteenth century.

Another Hispanic group also appeared in the late nineteenth century. A small Cuban population migrated to Florida, partly in response to the independence movement against Spain, as exiles, revolutionaries, and workers. Applying skills they learned in Cuba, they were engaged largely in the tobacco industry, as field owners and workers, and in cigar factories of the State.

A new phase of the labor history of Hispanics in

365

César Chávez exhorting people to start a new grape boycott in 1986.

wage worker in the United States can earn approximately ten times as much as in Mexico, although the differences are largely offset by much higher prices for food, rent, and other living expenses in the United States.

In the early twentieth century, Mexicans were recruited largely for agricultural, railroad maintenance, and mining enterprises. Smaller numbers found employment in domestic and other service occupations, and in manufacturing. Mexican immigrant families often worked as a single unit in cotton, sugar beet, and fruit and vegetable planting, cultivation, and harvesting operations, especially in the Southwest. In other occupations, including mining, manufacturing, and most service occupations, adult workers were the rule, as child labor laws were harder to evade, restricting the employment of children.

As a result of the patterns of labor recruitment that evolved in the early twentieth century, cities and towns on and near the Mexican border, and eventually throughout the Southwest and in many Midwestern settings, developed large labor pools of Mexican workers who were available to perform un-

the United States began around the turn of the twentieth century, when employers in the Southwest, and soon afterward in the Midwest, began to recruit workers from the Mexican border. Their efforts set in motion a movement that has shaped migration patterns from Mexico throughout the twentieth century. Using labor contractors and other recruiters, they brought in workers from Mexico to perform largely unskilled, low-paying tasks. This planned labor migration quickly stimulated another pattern of individual migration that took on an independent character of its own and outpaced the rate of migration by labor recruitment. During the early twentieth century, the majority of Hispanic workers in the United States were Mexican immigrants and their children. In sheer numbers, the new arrivals soon overwhelmed the older Mexican-descent residents in most parts of the Southwest and Midwest, except New Mexico.

Mexico offered employers a reservoir of workers because of its high level of unemployment and very low incomes. The wage differential between Mexico and the United States throughout the century has always been very sharp. At present, an unskilled

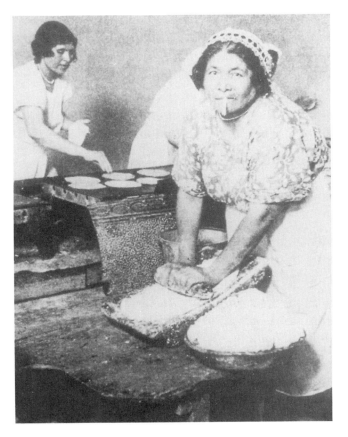

Mexican women working at a commercial tortilla factory in the 1930s.

A cotton picker in 1933. (Photograph by Dorothea Lange.)

skilled, low-paying jobs throughout the year. Characteristically, the Mexican workers found employment largely in seasonal tasks and experienced high rates of unemployment and frequent changes in employers. Although many of them brought skills from Mexico, few of the tasks they performed in the United States required high levels of training or English-language proficiency to perform.

The Spanish-American War in 1898 resulted in the incorporation of Puerto Ricans into the work force of the United States. As continental-based corporations quickly gained control of the best agricultural lands in Puerto Rico, they displaced many small landholders, offering them the alternatives of wage work in the fields or unemployment. By 1930, four U.S. corporations controlled about three-fifths of sugar production in Puerto Rico, and the sugar industry was responsible for more than two-thirds of all employment on the Island.

Because of World War I, Puerto Ricans were made citizens of the United States in 1917. The war also stimulated a modest migration from the island to New York City and environs, where the new arrivals worked in textiles and other low-wage industrial and service occupations.

Conditions of employment for all workers, but Mexicans in particular, deteriorated rapidly with the onset of the Great Depression in 1929. Immigration to the United States virtually ceased, and return migration to Mexico increased sharply. Mexican workers were singled out by employers and quickly fired or laid off, particularly in and near urban centers in both the Southwest and the Midwest.

In many cities, government agencies and employer groups collaborated to conduct organized repatriation drives that involved publicity and propaganda campaigns intent on convincing the English-speaking public that Mexicans were taking jobs away from U.S. citizens. Although the propagandists argued that repatriation would provide employment to unemployed citizens, most Mexicans had already lost their jobs. The underlying motive in the campaigns was to remove unemployed Mexicans from public welfare rolls. The intensity of the drives varied in different locations, but they were partly responsible for the reduction of the Mexican-descent population in the United States by about 25 percent during the early years of the Great Depression. Almost all the formal repatriation drives ended with the election victory of President Franklin D. Roosevelt and the ascendancy of the Democratic party in Congress in 1933. Unlike the Republicans, they did not consider Mexican workers a major cause of the depression.

In 1940 and 1941, the war in Europe stimulated production, and the demand for labor in the United States rose sharply. Employers wanted even more workers from Mexico, but the Mexican government opposed their efforts, concerned that another humiliating repatriation campaign might again occur at the time of the first economic downturn after the war. A compromise was reached in 1942 when employers convinced the U.S. government to make an agreement with the Mexican government to initiate a formal program of recruitment of contract laborers from Mexico for agricultural and railroad work. This new program included guaranteed minimum wages, worker protection, and an organized procedure for workers to return to Mexico on termination of the contract. The Mexican Labor Agreement was popularly called the Bracero Program. The war also stimulated labor migration from Mexico and the Caribbean to the United States via other formal programs and informal recruitment mechanisms.

World War II hastened changes in the employment profile of Hispanic workers in the United States. The agricultural industry, which was the major single employer prior to the Great Depression, had been declining in relative terms throughout the century. It peaked in absolute numbers shortly after

Mexican mine workers in the early 1900s.

the end of World War II. With the onset of the war, employment for Hispanics expanded more rapidly in several areas of manufacturing and in the services. Hispanic workers continued to concentrate in unskilled and semiskilled employment, largely in extractive agriculture, mining, and unskilled production tasks, especially as operatives, and in services.

The labor demands of World War II also stimulated a major wave of migration of Puerto Rican workers to the United States, largely through the auspices of Operation Bootstrap, a program initiated by the Puerto Rican government in 1944. Its major concern was to encourage industrialization in Puerto Rico and thereby diminish unemployment on the island. To further accomplish its goal of reducing the number of unemployed, it promoted a program of labor migration to the United States that involved arranging for labor recruiters to visit the island and also entailed working with airline companies to arrange for cheap flights from Puerto Rico to New York City. The labor migration program was aimed mostly at securing employment in urban locations, but as part of the plan the Puerto Rican Department of Labor also devised arrangements with agricultural employers to hire seasonal agricultural work-

ers under contract. Most of the agricultural workers went to eastern seaboard locations between Florida and New England to work in fruit and vegetable harvesting and canning operations. During the heyday of Operation Bootstrap, a net migration of at least 100,000 workers came to the United States from Puerto Rico each year, seeking permanent residence and employment principally in manufacturing and service industries.

A third phase of labor migration to the United States began in the 1960s, when the established patterns of movement from Mexico and Puerto Rico to the United States were modified, and migration from other countries increased. The Bracero Program ended in 1964, and after a brief decline in immigration, workers from Mexico increasingly arrived to work under the auspices of the H-2 Program of the Immigration and Nationality Act of 1952, as well as for family unification purposes or as undocumented workers. Workers from Puerto Rico continued to migrate to the United States, most often without promises of employment, but their migration at this time was increasingly offset by a massive return migration to Puerto Rico.

Another feature of this later labor migration has

Puerto Rican garment workers in New York City.

been the inclusion of people from a much wider range of countries in Latin America, and with a greater diversity of working backgrounds. Whereas Mexicans and Puerto Ricans continue to migrate for the most part as unskilled, semiskilled, or skilled workers, immigrants from other parts of the Caribbean and Central and South America have a wide range of backgrounds, including business and professional. This is particularly true of Cubans, the third most numerous Hispanic group in the United States. Their major wave of immigration occurred following the victory of the Cuban Revolution in 1959, and it included many prominent professionals and businesspeople. Later waves of Cuban immigrants were not as prosperous. The highly publicized Mariel boatlift in 1980 included many individuals from very poor, unskilled backgrounds, and with a lack of adequate job training. Many of them have had great difficulty becoming incorporated into the work regimen of the United States.

✴ HISPANICS IN ORGANIZED LABOR

As a predominantly working people, Hispanics have long been involved in efforts to organize as workers. One of their earliest groups, the Caballeros de Labor (Knights of Labor), was active in the Southwest in the late nineteenth century. Modeled after the American organization by the same name, Knights of Labor, its major stronghold was in New Mexico. It was never formally chartered, and it was more interested in land loss to recently arriving whites than labor issues. Other important cases of labor organizing in the late nineteenth century included Mexican cowboys in Texas and Cuban cigar workers in Florida.

During the late nineteenth and early twentieth centuries, a much greater number of Hispanic workers organized their own *mutualistas*, or mutual aid societies. These organizations engaged in social activities and provided for basic needs of workers, including insurance and death benefits for members. Mutualistas functioned largely as self-help organizations and did not threaten employers, which helps explain their greater success than unions. In the early twentieth century, a plethora of mutualistas appeared, especially among groups of recent immigrants, who were encouraged by the local Mexican consular officials. They continued to represent the most widespread form of worker organization.

Apart from the mutualistas, labor organizing among Hispanics in the late nineteenth and early twentieth centuries was hindered by several factors. Hispanics were concentrated geographically in largely antiunion settings in the South and Southwest. They also faced hostility and discrimination because of societal attitudes, which often portrayed them as taking jobs away from white workers. The major labor organization in the nation, the American Federation of Labor (AFL), tended to be craft-exclusive and structurally not interested in the participation of largely unskilled Hispanic workers. More important, the AFL itself could not resolve internally the nativism and racism pervasive in American society that often led it and its local unions to adopt exclusionary policies. These problems severely reduced Hispanic participation in organized labor and resulted in significant organizing efforts outside the mainstream labor federation.

In the early twentieth century, union organizing among Hispanic workers increased in many areas. The most notable efforts took place in agriculture, which was still the most important single occupation. Most organizing took place under the auspices of independent Mexican unions, while in some cases there were either independent interethnic unions or multiethnic organizations, often with support from the radical Industrial Workers of the World. Railroad and other urban workers joined together for brief periods under the leadership of independent or

Socialist organizations and, occasionally, the AFL. Many miners formed union organizations with the support and encouragement of the Western Federation of Miners in the early years of the twentieth century.

The most concentrated labor activity among the Spanish-speaking under the flag of the United States took place in Puerto Rico, led by the Federación Libre de los Trabajadores (Workers Labor Federation), or FLT, formed shortly before the turn of the century. In 1901, it affiliated with the American Federation of Labor, which broke from its more common policy of exclusivism toward non-whites. It accepted Puerto Rican workers because of its concern that they could enter freely into the United States and compete in the labor market and because of its fear of being overshadowed by rival organizations that also appeared in Puerto Rico. Important and widespread strikes in the sugar cane fields occurred in 1905 and 1906, and even larger ones took place in 1915 and 1916. After the early years of the century, however, the FLT organizing efforts turned more from the fields to the political arena.

Following a low point during the 1920s, labor organizing among Hispanic workers reached new peaks during the Great Depression. Independent organizations not affiliated with mainstream organized labor were most active and more typically composed of independent Mexican groups, Socialists, and members of the Communist party. In the later 1930s, leaders in the newly formed Congress of Industrial Organizations (CIO) also exhibited interest in organizing unskilled workers, and the CIO participated in the famous pecan shellers' strike in San Antonio in 1938, involving mostly young Mexican and Mexican American women. Organizers Emma Tennayuca and Manuela Solis Seger gained attention in Texas at that time and remained active in labor for many years afterward.

Organizing and strikes in the 1930s also occurred among mining, industrial, and agricultural workers throughout the country. Mexican farm workers in California were particularly active throughout the decade. Their efforts were highlighted by the Central Valley cotton strike of 1933, in which several groups of independent Mexican union organizers and radicals offered support. The AFL considered these activities a serious challenge to its dominance, and in many occupations it permitted the formation of local unions for the first time to attract Mexican workers into its fold.

In Puerto Rico, workers—upset with what they considered a sellout agreement between the FLT and U.S. owners—who belonged to the Association of Sugar Producers staged a massive but unsuccessful

Unemployed workers waiting in line at a relief office during the Depression.

spontaneous strike in 1933–34 to protest the arrangement. Their strike was the beginning of a long and protracted struggle against traditional FLT leadership that led to a sharp decline in the AFL-affiliated organization.

The turbulence of the 1930s reflected a sharp increase in expressions of sympathy toward unionism and unions among Hispanic workers. Much of the support had been latent but untapped until that time. Immigrants from Mexico frequently had strong union sympathies because of their earlier experiences before they arrived in the United States. Yet, traditional unions made only partial inroads into the Hispanic working population during the decade, hindered by continued employment discrimination, the success of employer efforts to pit workers against each other, and divisions within organized labor.

World War II served as a partial brake to direct labor organizing among Hispanic workers. But progressive elements within organized labor remained active, particularly in the struggle to eliminate many of the statutory forms of employment discrimination that Hispanics and other workers continually faced. Their efforts contributed to the formation of the Fair Employment Practices Committee (FEPC) in 1941. The FEPC investigated discrimination throughout the country by private companies with government contracts. Over a third of its cases in the Southwest involved Mexicans. Despite the efforts of President Truman, the FEPC was terminated at the end of World War II. It stands as an important predecessor to the corrective legislation and administrative bodies formed in the 1960s, particularly the Equal Employment Opportunity Commission.

Unionization among Hispanic workers increased rapidly in the 1940s and 1950s, as Hispanic workers and sympathizers within both the AFL and CIO struggled for reforms that permitted them equal access and fair treatment. In many local unions they formed their own caucuses to demand representation and changes in discriminatory procedures by the union hierarchy and to encourage the union to challenge discriminatory practices by employers. They demonstrated union loyalty, sympathy, and a class-consciousness reinforced by their work experiences and treatment in the workplace. During this period they participated in many notable strikes, perhaps the best known of which was the "salt of the earth" strike by miners in Silver City, New Mexico, led by the International Mine, Mill and Smelter Workers Union between 1950 and 1953. The efforts of the National Farm Labor Union, later called the National Agricultural Workers Union, to organize in California during the 1940s and 1950s were also noteworthy. Union leader Ernesto Galarza demonstrated keen insight as a union leader, scholar, and role model for a later generation of Chicano activists.

In Puerto Rico, the independent Confederación de Trabajadores Generales, or CGT, formed in 1940, but it quickly affiliated with the CIO. It soon replaced the Federación Libre de los Trabajadores (FLT) as the major labor organization on the island. Through its close links to the government, it attained its greatest influence and membership during the 1940s and 1950s.

Among Hispanics, a number of independent unions again began to form in both Puerto Rico and in the continental United States. The most notable was the National Farm Workers Association in California, led by César Chávez. It began as an independent organization in 1962 and became part of the AFL-CIO in 1966. It is now known as the United Farmworkers of America. During its numerous strikes and boycotts of table grapes, wines, and lettuce, it popularized many tactics involving ethnic alliances, community organizing, and a focus on protecting the environment that suggest alternative organizing strategies for organized labor in the future. Another creative venture, The East Los Angeles Community

Union (TELACU), was formed in 1971 as the result of cooperative efforts between the United Auto Workers and community organizers in East Los Angeles to build a "community" union.

Union-organizing activity in the United States peaked in the 1950s. From the early 1960s through the 1970s, the number of union members in the nation increased, though at a much slower rate than overall employment. The decrease in the rate of unionization during this period resulted from the reduction of jobs in highly unionized sectors, the growth of employment in traditionally nonunion occupations, the lack of vigilance of union leadership, increasingly sophisticated antiunion activities among employers and hostile government policy not enforcing protective labor legislation.

From the beginning of the Reagan Presidency in 1981 until 1985, union membership fell rapidly while total employment rose. Between 1985 and 1990, union membership declined more slowly, while total employment continued to rise. The decline in the 1980s is due to factors unfavorable to unions during the past generation, coupled with the most hostile federal government policy toward labor organizing and unions since the 1920s.

Unionization levels vary according to geography and occupation. Rates are highest in the Northeast and Midwest, and lowest in the South and Southwest, where Hispanic workers are most concentrated. In 1989, unionization in the public sector stood at 37 percent of workers, compared with 12 percent in private industry. It seems that private employers had a greater ability than the government to thwart worker organization despite the more rigid laws restricting labor organizing in the public sector. In the private arena, the more highly unionized sectors include transportation and public utilities at 32 percent, construction and manufacturing at 22 percent, and mining at 18 percent. In other major areas of private employment, union membership ranged from only 1 to 6 percent.

Union membership in 1990 was 16.1 percent of the working population over age 15, reflecting the continued decline over the past three decades. Unionization stood at 20 percent for men and 13 percent for women. By ethnicity, it was 22 percent among blacks, 16 among whites, and 15 percent among Hispanics. Among Hispanic men, 18 percent belonged to unions, compared to 20.8 percent of white men and 27.5 percent of black men. Among women, 14.2 percent of Hispanics, compared with 14 percent of whites and 21.2 percent of blacks, were union members.

Union benefits typically include better working conditions; a greater range of such benefits as health care, vacation, and leave policy; worker protection;

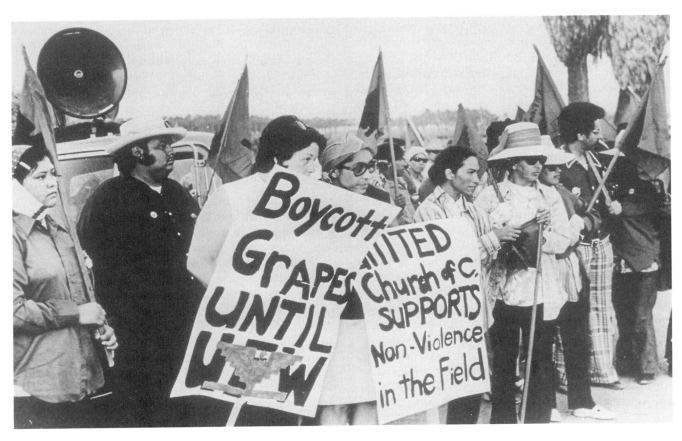

A United Farm Workers picket line in Coachella, California, 1973.

and higher wages. In 1990, union members earned an average of $420 per week, compared with $276 for nonunion members.

In 1991, there were approximately 1.3 million Hispanic union members. Although there are many union officers, vice presidents and directors, there are only two Hispanic presidents or directors among the 88 unions of the AFL-CIO: Arturo Rodríguez of the United Farm Workers (who succeeded César Chávez upon his death in 1993) and Dennis Rivera of the National Health and Human Services Employees Union, with 117,000 members. In 1973, the Labor Council of Latin American Advancement (LCLAA) formed to promote the interests of Hispanics within organized labor.

✳ IMMIGRATION AND MIGRATION

Since the late 1960s, two major factors affecting immigration to the United States have become clear: an increase in the rate of undocumented immigration and a shift from Europe to Asia as the predominant source of immigration. Despite annual fluctuations, Latin America, dominated by Mexico, has maintained its proportionate contribution, while it has increased its total contribution of immigrants to the United States substantially, both in legal and undocumented immigration.

In the period from 1955 to 1964, 50.2 percent of all legal immigrants to the United States were from Europe, with rates declining to 10.1 percent in 1988. Immigration from Asia, meanwhile, increased from 7.7 percent during 1955–64 to 41.1 percent in 1988. Immigration from the Americas during this period increased from 41.1 percent to 44.3 percent. In 1989, immigration from the Americas rose to 61.4 percent. Of the major countries, Mexico accounted for 37.1 percent of total documented immigration to the United States, the next highest number of immigrants being from El Salvador, 5.3 percent, the Philippines, 5.2 percent, Vietnam, 3.5 percent, Korea, 3.1 percent, and China, 3.0 percent.

Between 1985 and 1989, immigration accounted for 2.7 percent of the nation's net population growth, with rates varying from 1.8 percent of whites, 2.1 percent of blacks, 15.5 percent of Hispanics, and 29.7 percent of the increase for other races.

Several formal and informal programs have been established to encourage immigration of workers to the United States. The best-known forms of organized labor recruitment have involved agricultural workers from Mexico and Puerto Rico. These include the mechanisms in the Bracero Program and Operation Bootstrap. Labor recruitment by the U.S. Farm Placement Service to encourage labor migration for temporary seasonal employment has also influenced permanent settlement patterns. The H-2 Program within the Immigration and Nationality Act of 1952, as amended by the 1986 Immigration Reform and Control Act of 1986 (IRCA), continues to guide immigration patterns to the United States.

Immigration from Mexico, Central and South America, and the Caribbean has also been encouraged by labor recruiters and by informal networks that link individual families and communities in Latin America and the United States together.

Internal migration has greatly affected the population patterns of Hispanics within the United States. The most general patterns of migration include the dispersal of Mexicans from their historic concentrations in the Southwest to the Midwest, the Pacific Northwest, and recently to Florida and the East Coast; the spread of Puerto Ricans beyond New York to other areas of the country; and the relocation of Cubans to places other than Miami. Most of this migration has been through informal mechanisms, established at the level of individuals and families, and by word of mouth.

The major net flows of Hispanics within the United States are from the Northeast and Midwest to Florida, Texas, and California; from New York to neighboring states in the Northeast; and from California to neighboring states in the West. Cuban Americans are becoming increasingly concentrated at somewhat higher levels in Florida, while Central and South Americans are becoming more concentrated in California and New York. People of Mexican origin are tending to disperse from the Southwest, while Puerto Ricans are moving away from their center of concentration in New York City.

The total impact of migration and immigration in the 1970s and 1980s has been twofold. In absolute numbers, Hispanics have dispersed to a greater number of states and in wider areas within those states. In proportionate terms, they have concentrated at somewhat higher rates in the states already having large Hispanic populations. In 1970, 82 percent of the Hispanic population of the nation lived in nine states, with the proportion rising to 86 percent in 1990. The major recipients of Hispanic immigrants are California, Texas, and New York, and to a lesser degree Florida, Illinois, and New Jersey.

Hispanics born in the United States or residing in the country many years are more likely to migrate than are recent immigrants, who typically know less about the country, are less familiar with English, and generally of lower socioeconomic status. The recent immigrants are more likely to concentrate in ethnic enclaves for social and economic support.

Immigration remains an important factor accounting for the expansion of the labor force in the United States. The rates of immigration in the 1980s approached the levels of the early 1900s. Legal immigration during the first decade of the century reached 8.8 million, while during the 1980s 6.3 million immigrants were granted permanent residence. The immigrants are overwhelmingly young and in search of employment, and Hispanic immigrants continue to account for more than 40 percent of the total.

The Bracero Program

The term *bracero*, (from the Spanish *brazo*, meaning arm) applied to day laborers, generally; is sometimes used to refer to any Mexican worker in the United States under legal auspices. In this sense it includes workers entering the country under the H-2 Program of the Immigration and Nationality Act of 1952 and the H-2A Program of the Immigration Reform and Control Act of 1986, as well as to Mexican

A scene from the Bracero Program.

commuters often referred to as "green carders." "*Bracero*" is also occasionally used to refer to any unskilled Mexican workers brought into the United States.

The most popular use of "*bracero*" applies to the temporary Mexican agricultural and railroad workers first brought into the United States under contract in 1942 as an emergency measure to meet the temporary labor shortage of World War II. These braceros were an important part of the nation's agricultural labor force for almost a generation afterward. They dominated the harvest labor force in many parts of the Southwest and Midwest, particularly in sugar beets, cotton, pickles, tomatoes, and several other vegetable crops.

The Bracero Program, also referred to as the Mexican Farm Labor Supply Program and the Mexican Labor Agreement, began as a bilateral agreement between the governments of Mexico and the United States. It was given congressional sanction in 1943 as Public Law 45. Both governments considered it an important part of the Mexican contribution to the war effort.

The program was very popular among agricultural employers, who quickly organized and lobbied

A migrant work camp.

Congress to ensure its continuation beyond the end of the war. They were able to extend it temporarily several times, claiming a shortage of able and willing workers in the United States. Opponents of the Bracero Program, however, were able to reduce the scale of bracero employment in the late 1940s by demonstrating sufficient domestic worker availability. The outbreak of the Korean War in 1950, nevertheless, thwarted their efforts. In response to labor demands stemming from the war, agricultural employers convinced Congress in 1951 to pass Public Law 78, which renewed and expanded the program. On behalf of organized farm employers, the legislature passed several temporary extensions until 1964.

At the peak of the program in the late 1950s, the United States admitted more than 400,000 contract workers each season, almost twice as many as the number entering the country during the entire wartime emergency from 1942 to 1947.

The program was anathema to Mexican Americans and labor groups, who eventually gathered convincing evidence that, despite contract guarantees, braceros were not protected against abuses by employers and labor contractors, their working conditions were not adequate, and they frequently were not paid the wages guaranteed them by contract. The opposition also demonstrated the program had an adverse effect on wages and working conditions of domestic workers and stifled unionization efforts not only in agriculture, but also in southwestern industry. The struggle against the program in the 1950s focused largely on its adverse effects, seeking reforms requiring employer compliance with contract guarantees and permitting braceros joining unions. This effort, nevertheless, failed, convincing opposition later in the decade to conduct an all-out attack on the program. Ultimately a combined group of labor union representatives, Mexican American groups, religious and civic organizations, and their allies

A field worker in the Bracero Program.

The interior of a migrant labor shack.

gained the support of a more pro-labor Democratic administration and obtained Congressional termination of the temporary program in 1964.

Since 1964, employer groups in agriculture have initiated several efforts in Congress to pass new and modified versions of the Bracero Program by hiring temporary seasonal contract workers from Mexico. As of 1991, none of their efforts have succeeded.

Termination of Public Law 78 was an important victory for Mexican American and labor groups and helped pave the way for a flurry of labor organizing efforts in agriculture in the late 1960s.

The Maquiladoras

The abolition of the Bracero Program in 1964 demanded greater efforts by the Mexican government to relieve its own unemployment via industrialization. The most important element of its border industrialization program is the *maquiladora* (assembly plant) program, initiated in 1965. Mexico found industrialists and politicians in the United States very interested in the industrialization program. Mexico hoped that it could raise the standard of living in the northern border region, while both the

U.S. and Mexican governments were concerned about the possible negative political and economic consequences of leaving hundreds of thousands of Mexican workers stranded on the border without employment when the Bracero Program was ended. Industrialists were eager to reap the benefits offered by tax and tariff breaks and by the availability of unemployed and underemployed workers in Mexico.

The central feature of the plan established "twin plants" on both sides of the Mexico-U.S. border. It also set up a duty-free zone which permits industrialists in the United States to ship unfinished goods to Mexico under bond for partial assembly or completion. The goods are then returned duty free to the "twin plant" on the U.S. side, to complete the manufacturing process. In the early years of the program, about two-thirds of the products involved in the program were electric and electronic goods. As the program expanded in the 1970s and 1980s, the range of products expanded rapidly. By 1987, electric and electronic goods represented only about 35 percent of the total; textiles, clothing, and shoes, 18 percent; furniture, 10 percent; transportation equipment (including car motors), 9 percent; and a range of other goods, 28 percent.

The scale of production in the maquiladora industry also grew impressively. In 1966, it comprised 57 plants with about 4,000 workers. By 1979, it had about 540 plants hiring 120,000 workers, and by 1986 there were 844 plants employing 242,000 workers. By 1990, there were more than 1,000 plants employing about 450,000 workers. It is estimated that by 1995 there will be at least 1,500 plants with more than one million workers engaged in the program.

The maquiladora program in its actual operation is not at all as it was initially conceived. Its original intent was to alleviate the unemployment of male workers stranded at the end of the Bracero Program. Yet, the work force in the maquiladoras from the beginning has been approximately 85 percent female, mostly teenage women with very high rates of turnover. In sum, the program does not offer steady employment or work to unemployed men.

Another discrepancy is that the program was initially restricted to a 12.5-mile-wide strip along the Mexican-U.S. border. A 1972 amendment, however, permitted its expansion into the Mexican interior. As a result, plants are now located throughout northern and central Mexico.

Still yet another flaw in the original plan is that the "twin plant" concept never became operational. While the production phase was conducted in the Mexican plants, the "plants" on the U.S. side were essentially warehouses. Like their counterparts in Mexico, the operations in the United States offered low-wage, unskilled employment. The maquiladora program in effect, thus, became a runaway shop taking advantage of cheap Mexican labor and exemption from tariffs.

U.S. companies involved in maquiladora operations assert that the program enables them to produce in Mexico rather than transfer their operations to Asia. Yet, during the 1980s, Japanese industrialists took advantage of the maquiladoras to send greater amounts of raw materials to Mexico to have them finished, then shipped duty free into the United States. This led to a storm of protest in the United States, because, as Representative Duncan Hunter complained, "the Japanese can essentially use the program simply as a conduit into American markets without conferring benefits on American businessmen." In their discussion of the maquiladora program, very few politicians have considered the adverse impact on the much larger group of workers in the United States continuously displaced by the program.

The North American Free Trade Agreement (NAFTA) went into effect on January 1, 1994. Prior to its going into effect, various mechanisms were insisted upon by the U.S. Congress as well as trade unions and environmental groups to regulate the abuses that have characterized the maquiladoras to this date: the relocation of factories attempting to avoid unions in the U.S., abuses of workers and degradation of the environment under Mexico's more lax laws. Whether the new regulations and American observers as watchdogs will succeed in improving labor and environmental standards in Mexico is still being debated. What is certain is that with the economic downturn and crisis in the values of the peso in Mexico, following the NAFTA pact, the maquiladoras are experiencing an even greater boom.

Although supporters of the Free Trade Agreement maintain that it expands the size of markets in both Mexico and the United States, the sharp wage differential between Mexico and the United States makes it very difficult for Mexicans to afford to purchase the goods produced for export to the United States. In terms of worker protection, environmental damage, and the threat to the unity of Hispanic and Latin American workers on both sides of the border, the maquiladora program and the Free Trade Agreement pose even greater threats than the Bracero Program.

Migrant Farm Labor

A migrant worker is a person employed at a job temporarily or seasonally and who may or may not have a permanent residence in another community, state, or nation. It is a misconception to portray farm workers solely as migrants or Hispanics, or to portray all migrant workers as farm workers. Migrants comprise only a small portion of the total of the ethnically diverse farm labor force of the United States. Seasonal migrant workers are employed in a wide range of occupations, including mining, forestry, and fishing, in addition to agriculture, which is the best-known form of migrant labor in the United States.

Most people who work on farms are either families who own or rent them or residents of nearby farms and communities who travel to work and return home at the end of the workday. Migrant farm workers are concentrated in the harvest operations of fruit and vegetable crops in several locations throughout the United States. At other times of the year, they seek employment in agricultural or other occupations, often where they are permanently settled.

The number of agricultural migrant laborers has declined sharply since the late 1930s, when about four million people worked each season. Because of the problems of keeping track of them, it is very difficult to make an accurate estimate of their numbers. It is likely that about one million people were employed as migrant farm workers in the United States annually during the 1980s.

In the late nineteenth and early twentieth centuries, the size of the migrant labor force expanded rapidly owing to the introduction of large-scale commercial agriculture that was linked to the industrialization and urbanization of the nation's population. Millions of people left the farms and joined immigrants in the cities, augmenting the demand for foods they could not produce themselves.

Agricultural migrants at the turn of the century frequently were foreign immigrants who worked on farms temporarily while saving money to buy farms or seeking more permanent employment in nearby cities. On the West Coast, a large portion of the migrant farm workers at the end of the nineteenth and early twentieth centuries were Asians, while in other parts of the country most were Europeans and their children. With the expansion of the sugar beet, vegetable, and cotton industries in the early twentieth century, Mexican migrant workers increasingly took over seasonal farm labor, frequently returning to the Mexican border or nearby cities at the end of work in a crop or at the end of the season.

With the onset of the Great Depression, many Mexican migrant workers were displaced by southern whites and blacks, who dominated the migrant agricultural labor force in the 1930s and 1940s. In the 1950s and 1960s, black workers continued as the most numerous migrants along the eastern seaboard states, while Mexican and Mexican American workers soon dominated the migrant paths between Texas and the Great Lakes, the Rocky Mountain region, and the area from California to the Pacific Northwest. Some observers noted very rough patterns of movement referred to as "migrant streams" that went northward from Florida, Texas, and Southern California each season in the 1940s and 1950s; but these became increasingly blurred over time.

A very large portion of the migrant agricultural labor force that traveled long distances eventually settled permanently wherever they could find higher-paying and more steady employment, especially in nearby towns and cities. Sometimes they continued to work in agricultural or food-packing or food-processing activities, but more often they left agriculture entirely. As a result of this unstable movement, there was a very rapid movement into and out of agriculture. Migrant workers who left agriculture were constantly replaced by new workers.

Despite more sophisticated government programs on behalf of farm workers and governmental efforts to coordinate the needs of workers with the demands of employers since the 1950s, the movement of migrant workers between jobs remains very haphaz-

ard. Migrant and seasonal farm workers continue to experience long periods of unemployment, and are among the worst-paid and least-protected workers in the nation. They suffer high rates of illness, retain low levels of education, and they find few advocates within political circles. As outsiders to local communities, often separated by language and ethnic barriers, they seldom participate in decisions affecting the communities where they are employed.

In the 1960s and 1970s, the migrant agricultural work force changed rapidly. With the rise of the black power and Chicano movements, the appearance of modest protective legislation, and the increasingly successful unionization efforts of farm workers, employers increasingly sought to recruit and hire foreign workers to replace the citizens. Along the East Coast, they recruited increasingly from the Caribbean, and supplemented with workers from Mexico and Central America. In other parts of the country, they recruited mostly from Mexico and Central America. In the 1980s and 1990s, the vast majority of migrant farm workers in the United States have been foreign-born. Many of them migrate seasonally from Mexico and the Caribbean to the United States through the H-2 Program, which became an important mechanism of labor recruitment following the termination of the Bracero Program. In 1992 it still held that the majority of migrant workers were of Hispanic origin. Of these workers, the majority were of Mexican origin. In recent decades, undocumented workers from Latin America have become the most important part of the migrant labor force in many locations.

✹ HISPANIC EMPLOYMENT IN INDUSTRY

Service Industries

The employment profile of workers in the U.S. has changed sharply in recent decades. The major category of service is increasing, while that of manufacturing is declining.

The service industries include a wide range of activities, from private household work, restaurant, hotel, and food services, and health and personal service occupations. Employment in service industries, which nearly doubled between 1970 and 1990, is high among females in most areas. The rate of Hispanic employment in service occupations is about double that of the non-Hispanic population for males, and about 40 percent higher for females.

In March 1989, 17.7 percent of employed Hispanic men worked in service industries, compared with 9 percent for non-Hispanic men. The rates were 24.1

percent for Hispanic women and 17.1 percent for non-Hispanic women.

Manufacturing and Basic Industries

Manufacturing and basic industries, traditionally the mainstay of the U.S. economy and historically the indicator of the leading economic nations in the world, are declining rapidly. Manufacturing occupations include precision production workers, craft and repair people, as well as operators, fabricators, and laborers. Both Hispanic males and females are highly overrepresented in this category, males by almost 25 percent and females at rates roughly double those of non-Hispanic females.

In 1989, about 47.9 percent of Hispanic males were employed in the broad category of manufacturing, compared with 39.8 percent of non-Hispanic males. Among females, 21.3 percent of Hispanics worked in manufacturing, compared with 10.5 percent of non-Hispanics.

✳ FEDERAL EMPLOYMENT PROGRAMS AND LAWS

Title VII and the Equal Employment Opportunity Commission

The Economic Opportunity Act (EOA) of 1964 was the centerpiece of President Lyndon B. Johnson's War on Poverty. The philosophy behind the War on Poverty espoused private initiative and local efforts had not resolved longstanding problems of discrimination and poverty during the postwar boom in the United States. Furthermore, the government believed efforts to improve conditions were consistently thwarted by private interests, often in conjunction with local and state governmental authorities, where the poor, blacks and, Hispanics were seldom represented. The federal government, thus, decided to initiate a program to provide training for workers, to encourage recruitment, and to monitor hiring practices of public and private employers across the nation.

The EOA also created the Office of Economic Opportunity (OEO) to administer a number of programs on behalf of the nation's poor. These included the Job Corps, the Community Action Program (CAP), and the Volunteers in Service to America (VISTA).

The Job Corps is a job-training program whose goal seeks to help disadvantaged youths aged 16–21 find employment. In 1990, the typical Job Corps enrollee was 18 years old, 83.5 percent were high school dropouts, 75 percent were minorities, 75 percent had never had a prior full-time job, 67 percent were male,

and almost 40 percent came from families on public assistance.

VISTA, conceived as a domestic equivalent to the Peace Corps, worked with the poor in urban and rural locations. CAP was the primary OEO program, in which local groups combined the efforts of local government, business, labor, civic, and religious organizations and the poor to mobilize local resources to alleviate poverty.

Title VII of the Civil Rights Act of 1964 comprised the most important statute of the War on Poverty addressing employment discrimination. It prohibits discrimination on the basis of gender, creed, race, or ethnic background, "to achieve equality of employment opportunities and remove barriers that have operated in the past." Discrimination is prohibited in advertising, recruitment, hiring, job classification, promotion, discharge, wages and salaries, and other terms and conditions of employment.

Title VII also established the Equal Employment Opportunity Commission (EEOC) as a monitoring device to prevent job discrimination. In effect, it renewed and expanded the Fair Employment Practices Committee, which had been dismantled at the end of World War II. The EEOC works in conjunction with state agencies in investigating charges of discrimination.

The issue of employment discrimination has led to a great deal of litigation. Many important cases defined the scope of discrimination and employee protection under Title VII of the Civil Rights Act of 1964. In the key case of *Griggs v. Duke Power Company* (1971), Chief Justice Warren Burger, speaking for a unanimous Supreme Court, ruled that employers could not create screening devices in employment that operated as "built-in headwinds" for minority groups. The Court required employers to initiate practices that considered their impact on minorities. The ruling encouraged many employers in public and private sectors to devise programs encouraging the hiring of women and non-Euro-Americans.

Several of the important employment lawsuits directly involved Hispanics. *Espinoza v. Farah Manufacturing Company* (1973) held that Title VII does not protect discrimination against aliens. The Court also held, however, that Title VII prohibits practices that have "the purpose or effect of discriminating on the basis of national origin." In *Carino v. University of Oklahoma* (1984), the Court held that an employer cannot refuse to hire an individual "because the individual has the physical, cultural or linguistic characteristics of a particular national origin group," or discriminate "because of the individual's accent or manner of speaking."

In reaction to equal employment legislation and

the increasing presence of Hispanics and other non-English-speaking people in the workplace, some states in the past several years have enacted so-called English-only amendments to their constitutions. Collectively they imposed English as the official language of their state.

Following the spirit of this legislation, many employers attempted to restrict the use of foreign languages by imposing "English-only" rules in the workplace. Such actions are prohibited under Title VII, which prohibits discrimination on the basis of national origin. EEOC policy provides that rules "which require employees to speak English only at all times are presumptively unlawful because they unduly burden individuals whose primary language is one other than English, and tends to create a hostile or discriminatory environment based on national origin."

Language rights have thus become an important employment issue challenging Hispanic workers in the 1990s, particularly where their numbers are high. Public and private employers commonly engage in hiring Hispanic employees because of their special skills as translators, but seldom grant them compensation or consider such skills as important factors in job promotion. In *Pérez et al. v. Federal Bureau of Investigation* (1988), Hispanic FBI agents offered their special skills to the FBI more than Anglo Spanish-speakers and non-Spanish-speakers, but did not receive compensation. The federal district court held that by being concentrated in interpreting tasks, the Hispanic agents were treated differently from and denied promotional opportunities offered to Euro-American agents.

As a result of positive legislation and court interpretations, conditions of employment for Hispanics registered significant improvements in several areas during the 1960s and much of the 1970s.

The Office of Economic Opportunity (EEOC) and Comprehensive Employment and Training Administration (CETA) Under Nixon and Carter

During the Nixon presidency, the first efforts to dismantle the War on Poverty began. The Nixon administration did not overtly attack the concept of equal opportunity, nor did it challenge the theories or actual programs already established to deal with the chronically unemployed. Rather, its desire for changes focused on attempts to realign political relationships involving federal, state, and local governments and community organizations.

Its remedies were part of its "New Federalism" program. The Great Society programs in the Office of Economic Opportunity (OEO) were centralized, with training programs and a strong oversight mechanism headed by the federal government. Local involvement was conceived largely through participation in the organizations where citizens were directly involved, especially through the Community Action Program (CAP). The New Federalism sought to reduce federal involvement and place the programs in the hands of state and local governments.

While in theory local control should be superior in meeting local needs, the creators of the New Federalism conceived the change in political terms. The political problem they perceived was that under the War on Poverty programs, there was a modest shift in local power away from the old elites, particularly white politicians, in the direction of the poor, particularly Hispanics and blacks. They believed they could return power to the old elites by removing the presence of the federal government and eliminating the community organizations.

The poor were justifiably dubious of Nixon's argument that local officials were most responsive to those most in need, having recent memories of breaking down local barriers to education and employment, with the assistance of federal government intervention.

The Nixon administration placed all employment and training programs, previously in the OEO, into the new Comprehensive Employment and Training Administration (CETA), created in 1973. The major difference between the old and the new poverty efforts was that the earlier employment and training programs were clearly targeted to specific population groups and allocated as "categorical" grants, on the basis of national and local considerations. Under CETA, allocations were granted directly to local politicians in the form of "bloc" grants to state and local governments, which could then make decisions on the kinds of programs to establish. Another change was that the CETA plan reduced the power of the federal government's regulations, standards, and other monitoring mechanisms created to ensure the efficacy of the local programs. Furthermore, although the new plan intended to allow local people to determine needs locally, no affirmative action guidelines were established to ensure that the poor and, especially, women, blacks, and Hispanics—the people for whom the programs were intended—would be represented in the decision-making process. This was particularly evident as CAP was severely weakened. The success of CETA rested on the goodwill of federal and local authorities. During the Nixon administration, many of the community leaders were removed and CETA programs were made increasingly the province of local politicians.

During the Carter presidency, the federal government expressed an increased commitment to equal opportunity, and CETA was strengthened. It is no coincidence that at this time the economic well-being of Hispanics and other non-whites peaked and the gap with the white population narrowed.

Furthermore, CETA was considered a success by most of its Hispanic participants. In fiscal year 1978, 142,000 youths, or slightly more than one-tenth of those enrolled in CETA programs, were Hispanics. Overall, approximately 5 percent of the country's white youth, 19 percent of blacks, and 13 percent of Hispanic youth participated in CETA programs that year. Hispanic participation ranged from 23 percent of Puerto Ricans, 13 percent of Mexican Americans, and 7 percent of Cubans. Interviews conducted that year indicated that more than 87 percent were satisfied with the program, and more than 70 percent believed that it improved their job chances. Nevertheless, CETA and government training programs for the unemployed were being more strongly criticized than ever before by their nonparticipant detractors, who found their own opportunity when Reagan was elected president.

The Job Training Partnership Act

The Reagan administration philosophy led to a profound change in government policy on job training programs based on both political and economic thought. Politically, the Reagan administration adopted the position that although it must still provide a "safety net" to assist the needy poor, such assistance should be distinguished from support, and that support is not a federal government responsibility. It also carried the New Federalism concept much further politically and economically than Nixon by reducing the amount of federal assistance for job creation and other social service programs.

The federal government also reduced its direct involvement by operating more in "partnership" with private as well as state and local government bodies. The impact of government philosophy and policy is clearly evident in the Job Training Partnership Act (JTPA) of 1983, the central employment training program of the Reagan and Bush years. The JTPA, like its predecessor, CETA, delivers employment and training services to the economically disadvantaged in need. Compared with CETA, the JTPA depends much more on the private sector to deliver these services.

The new program departs sharply from earlier direct job creation strategies that were central to projects of the 1960s and the 1970s. Federally funded jobs created by the Public Service Employment, offering employment to both the cyclically and structurally unemployed, were eliminated under the JTPA. Part of the concept of less government support

for the poor, it represented a 60 percent reduction in subsidies for youth employment. It severely reduced employment prospects for many disadvantaged youth whose first full-time employment had come from CETA and its predecessors.

In effect, the JTPA is designed to serve the demands of employers rather than the needs of unemployed workers. It is performance-driven and is structured to reward programs with high placement rates and low costs. In practice however, its standards are ignored. Furthermore, government monitoring devices established by earlier programs have been virtually dismantled.

The JTPA, as an example of the New Federalism, has failed to meet its mandate of providing for the training needs of the unemployed. Its structure is flawed, does not meet the interests of society generally, and is riddled with corruption.

Several structural problems in the Job Training Partnership Act specifically hinder Hispanic participation. A high proportion of Hispanics are needy, in part because of a nearly 50 percent high school dropout rate and because over one-fourth are not fully proficient in English but they are vastly underserved. The JTPA penalizes these people more than any other among the poor by not including precisely those who are most disadvantaged and harder to place. In addition, the JTPA has income-based eligibility stipulations requiring that people must either be receiving food stamps or not have more than a specific level of income. Many Hispanics who are eligible for JTPA, however, are imbued with a work ethic and are unwilling to accept food stamps. Still others are not eligible because they are willing to accept jobs that place them in an income level slightly above the sharply increased level of eligibility requirements. Another problem is that the JTPA has increased requirements for documentation of eligibility beyond those of CETA—a policy that has been criticized as unduly burdensome. Furthermore, Mexican Americans, in particular, lack familiarity with government programs, and the means of informing them about JTPA programs are woefully lacking. Finally, Hispanics lack a presence in most JTPA policy-making forums, and thus lack consistent advocates to set policies.

Beyond their structural problems, the cutbacks in job training efforts caused by the JTPA program have even broader negative consequences for the society at large. The reduction in training has been criticized by proponents of human capital, who argue that the reduced investment in training workers will have a costly long-term impact by reducing federal revenues and entitlement expenditures in the future. The disinvestment will also contribute to high unemployment and an inadequately trained work force. Society benefits, such as income tax and revenues for programs like Social Security, will decline, while costs for public assistance will increase.

The impact of Reagan job training policy, continued under the Bush administration, is further evident in the case of the Job Corps, created under the EEOC, and presently part of the JTPA. The Job Corps has residential and nonresidential centers where enrollees take intensive programs in education, vocational training, work experience, and counseling. It is popular in both parties of Congress, and the U.S. Department of Labor (USDL) has acknowledged its success. A 1985 USDL study determined that the Job Corps returns $1.38 to the U.S. Treasury in only three years for each $1 invested by the federal government. The funds come from continuing taxes paid by former Job Corps trainees once they begin employment and from reduced welfare payments. The Job Corps, serving the most disadvantaged, nonetheless, was among the programs cut most sharply by the JTPA.

Even the inadequate funds for the program are not being utilized effectively. Congress established specific levels of spending to ensure sufficient funding establishing adequate programs for the needy; yet in many areas the funds are not being spent.

Congressional hearings in 1990 found that corruption abounds in the training process itself. Many private schools, so-called "proprietary schools," replaced government-trained OEO and CETA workers providing training. The proprietary schools are for-profit institutions set up specifically to receive government grants, and are paid to train workers. The recipients of the funds seldom have competent training in operating educational institutions. Many of the courses their schools teach lack rigor, are taught by untrained and uncertified teachers, prepare the workers for nonexistent jobs and are not placement driven.

The structural design of the incentives process created by the JTPA reveals severe difficulties in the program. Local JTPA offices are motivated by incentives based on the actual number of people hired by private employers. This has led to the process of "creaming" in client selection. Creaming selects the least-disadvantaged individuals because they are the easiest to place. The programs have targeted services primarily to in-school youth or high school graduates; thus, service to high school dropouts has declined sharply.

Furthermore, local employers are paid by JTPA funds to hire employees. This leads to widespread abuse, for it allows employers to receive government funds to "hire" individuals they would have other-

wise hired without JTPA "incentives" of several weeks' or months' pay. The JTPA has become a major government subsidy for private employers, not a training program for those most in need.

The "New Federalism" originally was designed to transfer power from the federal government to local agencies and employers. In effect, it has taken away power from the poor and from community organizations, remaining largely pushed out of the decision-making process. In the past, community organizations worked in conjunction with federal government administrators. Under the JTPA, however, funding is granted directly to governmental agencies and private proprietors as rewards for their support. Because the monitoring system is so lax and community participation dismantled, efforts to expose the JTPA have been long delayed. As a result, the JTPA has shortchanged the needs of Hispanics, blacks, and others most in need of training, as well as society at large, while serving the narrow interests of employers in the private sector and their allies.

Employment Rights

During the 1980s, the Reagan and Bush administrations launched an attack on civil rights legislation as it extended to the workplace. The new Supreme Court justices appointed by Reagan and Bush helped change the direction of court protection of employees. In effect, its rulings have relaxed the duties of employers and have made it much more difficult for women and non-whites to convince the courts that violations of civil rights laws have taken place. The attack peaked in a series of 1989 Supreme Court decisions relating to employment law. In *Patterson v. McLean Credit Union* (1989), the Supreme Court ruled that an individual could no longer sue for racial harassment at work under a 1966 civil rights statute: "A practice of racial harassment adopted after an employee was hired does not by itself violate that employee's rights under the statute." In effect, it permitted the employer to hound Ms. Patterson out of her job because of race.

In *Wards Cove Packing Co. v. Antonio* (1989), the Court ruled that a group of employees who were able to demonstrate that an Alaska cannery that hired whites for well-paid and skilled jobs and minorities for low-paid, unskilled jobs, and even segregated employees by race in mess halls and dormitories, did not offer sufficient evidence of employment discrimination. It reversed 28 years of well-established law in its holding by imposing a heavier burden on employees in proving its employer did not have legitimate business reasons for engaging in such practices.

During the same period, other Supreme Court cases severely limited the filing of discrimination charges, and further ruled that a civil rights statute could not be used to sue local governments for damages for acts of discrimination. These and other cases successfully narrowed the coverage of civil rights statutes, making it extremely difficult for women and minorities to prove discrimination, simultaneously making it easier for those opposed to civil rights to post challenges.

The erosion of past civil rights legislation by the Supreme Court during the Reagan and Bush administrations resulted in efforts by representatives of civil rights, black, and Hispanic organizations to initiate a push for a new Civil Rights Act in 1990 to return to previous standards. The legislation sought to redress the discriminatory impact of recent Supreme Court decisions that in sum eliminated much of the thrust of equal employment opportunity law established in the previous generation. Although the 1990 bill had overwhelming support in both houses of Congress, the Bush administration vetoed the legislation on the grounds that it promoted quotas. A series of compromises produced a watered-down Civil Rights Act in 1991.

The Clinton administration was unable to improve the civil rights situation despite liberal appointments, such as that of Norma Cantú (the former director of MALDEF), to the position of Assistant Secretary for Civil Rights in the Department of Education, and Antonio Califa as Director of Civil Rights, Department of Transportation, among many other liberal civil rights and labor appointments. The very conservative Republic majority in Congress as of Clinton's second year in office curtailed all progressive legislation.

Affirmative Action

Affirmative action, centering on the Civil Rights Act of 1964, was a central concept of the Great Society programs of the Johnson administration. It accepted the premise that the high levels of unemployment and ongoing discrimination that women and many non-white groups encountered were impediments to the vision of the Great Society. The federal government accepted the responsibility to devise "affirmative action" programs to remedy such discriminatory practices and their consequences.

Affirmative action is designed to counter the effects of practices that exclude individuals from the workplace and other settings because of race, color, creed, gender, and national origin. It accepts the assumption that because of their background, many highly qualified people have been passed over in hiring and promotion practices and that steps should be taken to rectify exclusionary practices. The federal mandate was to encourage employers to volun-

tarily increase the presence of underrepresented minorities in the work force to levels commensurate with their presence in the local community. Compliance officers in the Equal Employment Opportunity Commission (EEOC) and the Department of Labor set goals, targets, and timetables for employers. For example, Executive Order 11246 in 1972 established two requirements: nondiscrimination, or "the elimination of all existing discriminatory conditions whether purposeful or inadvertent," and affirmative action, whereby employers are to take positive efforts "to recruit, employ and promote qualified members or groups formerly excluded." It also encourages individual employers to voluntarily adopt affirmative action programs.

Affirmative action programs were immediately criticized by some conservative elements in the country who argued that affirmative action favored minorities over more "qualified" whites. The struggle over affirmative action continued into the 1970s, when opponents coined the term "reverse discrimination," by which they suggested that white males were victims of discrimination as a result of affirmative action on behalf of women, blacks, Hispanics, and other underrepresented groups.

Within the federal government, the Reagan and Bush administrations in the 1980s intensified the attack and engaged in a systematic dismantling of affirmative action programs. The Reagan administration promoted the argument that affirmative action programs entailed quotas, constituting a form of reverse discrimination. The Justice Department under Reagan also spearheaded opposition to affirmative action, claiming that the administration "has profound doubts whether the Constitution permits governments to adopt remedies involving racial quotas to benefit persons who are not themselves the victims of discrimination." In essence it denied that broad discrimination against a group of people as a class could in theory exist. A highlight of the Reagan-Bush administration success was the Supreme Court decision in *City of Richmond v. Croson* (1989), which struck down an ordinance that set aside 30 percent of Richmond Virginia's construction contracts for minority businesses.

The attacks on affirmative action have had a profound impact on hiring policies in many sectors of private and public employment. They have contributed to the overall decline of the economic position of Hispanics and other ethnic minorities during the 1980s, both in absolute levels and in comparison with whites. It is most telling in top management positions in large corporations, where most surveys indicate that at least 95 percent of positions are still held by white males.

The federal government has failed not only to abide by its responsibility to serve as watchdog over affirmative action policies in the private sector but also to take affirmative steps itself. Although the Reagan administration could point to an increase in Hispanic representation in the federal work force from 4.3 percent to 4.8 percent between 1980 and 1988, the Hispanic population during that period increased from 6.4 percent to 8.1 percent. Thus, Hispanic underrepresentation in federal employment during the Reagan administration increased sharply, from 50 percent to 69 percent. The underrepresentation was most stark in the highest levels. At the top scale of government, senior executive service, Hispanics accounted for only 1 percent of the employees.

With the rise of conservatism in the 1990s, further empowered by a conservative take-over in 1994 of the U.S. Congress, affirmative action programs have been targeted for elimination. Politicians throughout the country, led by California Governor Pete Wilson, have made affirmative action an issue related to waste in government and economic recessions. Wilson and others have even linked the issue to the cost of serving immigrants, legal as well as undocumented. In 1995, empowered by various propositions on the California ballot, Wilson began tearing down the state's affirmative action structure, beginning with admissions and hiring at the University of California. Conservative governors in other states were soon announcing their following Wilson, while the House of Representatives utilized the budget negotiations to eliminate many affirmative action programs. President Clinton was forced to follow suit by announcing some the appointment of commissions to reform affirmative action. All of this came to a head in the election year of 1996, in which conservative candidates, such as Pat Buchanan and Robert Dole, demonized affirmative action and swore to eliminate it.

Undocumented Workers

Use of the term "undocumented" to refer to people who are in the United States without proper immigrant papers was established by the International Labor Organization in 1974. It was meant to be descriptive and neutral, in contrast to the term "illegal," which has negative connotations and implies criminality. The presence of undocumented aliens in the United States violates civil statutes but does not violate criminal laws. Some undocumented workers enter the country without legal authorization, while others enter under temporary permits but then extend their stay.

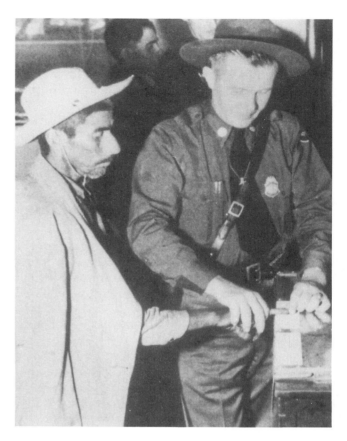

A Mexican worker being finger-printed for deportation.

Immigration and Naturalization Service

The number of undocumented aliens in the United States cannot be precisely determined, and is the subject of intense debate. In the 1970s, Immigration and Naturalization Service (INS) Commissioner Leonard Chapman, seeking to increase funding and expand the power of his organization, claimed that there were as many as 12 million undocumented workers in the country. Other observers most commonly place the number in the range of 3.5 million to five million people.

Popular perceptions and the press portray almost all undocumented workers as Mexicans. This is further bolstered by the policies of the INS, whose enforcement efforts are concentrated along the land border between Mexico and the United States, rather than at seaports and airports, or along the United States' northern border. About 95 percent of INS apprehensions are Mexicans, yet it is likely that only about half of all undocumented workers in the United States are Hispanics, the remainder being mostly natives of Europe and Asia.

In addition to their numerical importance, undocumented workers have been at the center of several political battles. On several occasions in recent decades, a national hysteria among citizens developed over their presence, typically during periods of economic recession and depression. Debates intensified during those periods over whether the undocumented take jobs away from U.S. citizens.

Operation Wetback, which occurred during a time of recession in 1954, involved a concerted campaign by the federal government that successfully apprehended more than one million undocumented Mexican workers. The frenzy subsided when the government and private employers expanded the scale of the bracero program, reducing the demand of agricultural employers for undocumented workers.

Following abolition of the bracero program in the mid-1960s, the number of undocumented workers again began to increase, and a new hysteria appeared in public circles, accompanied by increased activity by the border patrol. By 1977, the INS was again apprehending more than one million undocumented workers each year.

The hysteria over the undocumented intensified during the 1980s. Several ultraconservative and nativist groups attempted to stir up the nation. In 1986, for example, the Ku Klux Klan announced that the influx of "illegal aliens" was responsible for Texas' economic problems, including its high level of unemployment, and vowed to hunt down illegal aliens and turn them over to the border patrol.

The effect of undocumented workers on the economy has stirred a wide-ranging debate in the nation. One side of the argument is that they are a major drain on public services and that they displace U.S. citizens by accepting low-paying jobs. These arguments frequently are based on stereotypes and ethnic biases, and they seldom address the related issue of why employers are permitted to disregard protective labor statutes and immigration law.

An opposing position is that the undocumented pay taxes, and because they seldom use available social services, they make a very positive contribution to the nation's economy. Further, the jobs in which they are employed typically are those that others are unwilling to perform.

Undocumented workers enter the United States for various reasons. The most important are to escape political and social turmoil in their native country, to escape poverty and poor living conditions, and to achieve a better life in the United States. These are combined with active and aggressive recruitment by employers, often with the implied consent of the U.S. government.

Undocumented Hispanic immigrants are concentrated geographically in the South and Southwest and employed largely in service occupations, manufacturing, and agriculture. While their average earnings exceed the minimum wage, their wages are significantly lower than legal residents and citizens in the same occupations. Furthermore, they are commonly hired at wages below the legal minimum, working in unsafe conditions and facing inhumane and discriminatory treatment. Politically, they are vulnerable, and either unaware of their rights, or because of fear of deportation and loss of jobs, apprehensive about exerting the rights to which they are entitled under protective labor legislation.

Undocumented workers retain most employment rights of citizens, including those of minimum wage, joining and participating in union activities, the right to sue over contracts, and other protection under federal labor law. They are also deemed "employees" within the meaning of the National Labor Relations Act, and are protected under its provisions. Legal cases have also recognized the right to worker's compensation and protection under the Fair Labor Standards Act. Yet, employers frequently use the INS to escape their responsibilities under these laws and report for deportation workers who attempt to organize unions or assert other employment rights.

The anti-immigrant sentiments are often used by INS officials to increase their own power and that of the organization beyond its constituted civil authority. In its increasing exercise of violence, clearly in opposition to statutes that govern its operation, it is becoming a paramilitary organization. The tactic of INS workplace raids to apprehend undocumented workers has enabled the agency to violate workers' rights. In the 1984 INS Operation Jobs campaign, INS agents even raided businesses without valid search warrants or the consent of the employer.

In *Immigration and Naturalization Service v. Delgado* (1984), the Supreme Court ruled that workers were not subject to seizures as a result of INS raids on the workplace because the workers were "free to leave." Yet the raids occurred in the "presence of agents blocking each exit, armed with badges, walkie-talkies and guns and roving agents in open view questioning workers and taking some of them away." The INS has also intensified its border activities, increasing the use of force, intimidation, and other forms of violence.

Several observers, including the American Friends Service Committee, have reported widespread harassment and cases of assault by INS officers. They have documented "sexual abuse of undocumented immigrants, particularly refugee women," "beating undocumented immigrants, or those suspected of being undocumented immigrants," and the "deliberate destruction of immigrants' property or documents." Several tragedies occurred in the 1980s because of violent tactics of INS officials, including the deaths of at least 14 farm workers seeking to escape apprehension by the Border Patrol during field operations. Civil rights and other organizations have exposed cases of inhumane treatment, including strip searches, beatings, unprotected exposure to the direct sun for several hours, lack of medical attention, denial of visitation by family members, and denial of counsel. In defense of their tactics, INS officials have criticized individuals and groups seeking to educate undocumented immigrants about their rights as "incredible" and "against America."

Hostility directed against foreign workers, particularly the undocumented, surfaced again in the 1970s and 1980s in congressional circles, and demands for a change in the nation's immigration laws intensified.

The hostility came to a boil in 1994, 1995 and during the election year of 1996, when both legal and undocumented immigrants (especially Hispanics and Asians) were targeted for control. California passed various referenda to limit immigration, and the conservative Republican governors California and Florida filed suit against the federal government to recoup monies spent on providing services to immigrants. So intense was the immigrant bashing and increase of negative sentiments nationally toward immigration that President Bill Clinton named a commission, headed by Barbara Jordan, to study and revamp the policy on immigration, and Clinton changed the United States' 30-year policy of automatically accepting Cuban immigrants during the 1994–95 exodus of Cuban rafters—thousands of them were turned back to Cuba or placed in refugee camps in Guantanamo, Panama and neighboring Caribbean islands. Under Clinton's commission, as well, decades-old policies about re-uniting families through immigration was also threatened. The issue intensified in 1995 and 1996 during the campaign for the presidency, with Pat Buchanan, among other conservatives, bashing immigrants and swearing to close the borders.

The Immigration Reform and Control Act of 1986

Sensitive to the increased immigration that began in the 1960s and the economic uncertainty of the 1970s, the Ford administration appointed several task forces to address the issue of undocumented entry into the United States. It encouraged several congressional representatives to introduce new legislation to control immigration to the United States. After more than a decade of debate, Congress enacted the Immigration Reform and Control Act of 1986, popularly referred to as IRCA.

The proponents of IRCA argued that the legislation was necessary to reverse the perceived accelerated immigration of the undocumented, to "save jobs for Americans," and to halt the perceived drain on social services. Numerous careful studies produced since that time have demonstrated that none of the above perceptions was accurate.

IRCA contains three major provisions. First, it establishes civil and criminal penalties, referred to as employer sanctions, on employers who fail to verify the documentation of employees hired since 1986 whether they are eligible to work. This marks the first time in the history of the United States that employers have been prohibited by law from hiring undocumented workers. Second, IRCA provided a one-time provision to legalize undocumented workers in the United States. The legalization process included a separate program to legalize seasonal agricultural workers (SAWs) in the United States. Third, the law specifically prohibits several forms of employment discrimination. In response to the concerns of Hispanic and civil rights groups that the employer sanctions would result in discrimination, the law mandated that the General Accounting Office (GAO) conduct in an ongoing investigation of the impact of IRCA for three years. IRCA specifically provides Congress with the statutory authority to repeal employer sanctions if the GAO's final report were to conclude that widespread discrimination existed. To facilitate the provisions of the law, Congress also strengthened the power and personnel of the INS.

The GAO made its final report on IRCA to Congress on March 29, 1990. It observed that the implementation and enforcement of employer verification and sanctions provisions were not carried out satisfactorily, that they had caused a widespread pattern of discrimination against members of minority groups, and that they caused unnecessary regulatory burdens on employers. Many employers were confused about the law and its application and initiated illegal discriminatory hiring practices against Hispanics, Asians, and other people who appeared "foreign." Even white workers experienced discriminatory practices. The GAO concluded that there was a "widespread pattern" of discrimination based on national origin, practiced by 19 percent of the employers surveyed, that included not hiring foreign-appearing or foreign-sounding job applicants for fear of noncompliance with the law. In a "sting" operation involving pairs of Hispanic and Anglo "testers," it found that "Anglo testers received 52 percent more job offers than the Hispanic testers with whom they were paired."

The GAO investigation was narrow in its view of

what constituted "widespread discrimination" and did not support repealing employer sanctions. Other agencies and civil rights activists documented cases of discrimination, such as employers' firing applicants for legalization along with undocumented workers, depriving them of seniority and other benefits, imposing English-only rules, withholding paychecks, failing to pay overtime, harassing them sexually, assaulting them physically, and violating other civil and constitutional rights. In effect, IRCA pushed undocumented workers into even less regulated and more exploitative jobs.

Employers have also suffered the impact of employer sanctions. Estimates of total costs to businesses to perform record-keeping required by employer sanctions vary from $182 million to $675 million per year. Furthermore, businesses are paying millions of additional dollars in fines and otherwise suffering financially because of loss of workers and INS intrusions into the workplace.

In meeting one of its original goals, preventing the entry of undocumented workers into the United States, IRCA appears to have been successful in its first two years. Since that time, the entry of undocumented workers has increased sharply. In the early 1990s, it appears that the prohibitions of IRCA have not had a long-term impact on rates of undocumented entry into the country. They have proved to be a nuisance to employers and an additional burden to all workers—undocumented, legal residents, and citizens alike.

Thus, the GAO report and other evidence confirmed the fears of Hispanic groups before its enactment—that the law would intensify discrimination against Hispanics. On the basis of the GAO report and other evidence, employer sanctions are causing widespread discrimination. Hispanic activists are trying to convince Congress to comply with its own mandate and repeal employer sanctions.

✳ YOUTH EMPLOYMENT

The Hispanic work force is younger than other major work force groups, and in the future it will represent an even greater portion of the work force. Hispanics have lower levels of schooling than other groups. Among youths ages 16–21 not attending college, more than two-fifths of employed blacks and whites are high school graduates, compared with less than one-third of Hispanics. Because government job training programs are being cut back, the nation's future work force may be inadequate.

Hispanic youths are more likely to work full time and year round than either white or black youths. Employed Hispanic male youths are also more likely to be married than black and white males. As with other groups, Hispanic male youths are more likely to be employed than females.

Youths of all backgrounds tend to have much higher unemployment rates than older workers, and their rate of unemployment is more sensitive to business cycles. White youths have the lowest unemployment level, while blacks have the highest rate of unemployment, which tends to be less sensitive to changes in the economy than either the white or Hispanic rates. Unemployment rates for Hispanics fluctuate between the two others. During upturns in the economy, the rate of unemployment declines more sharply for Hispanic youths, while during downturns, it rises much more rapidly than for either whites or blacks.

In 1988, the unemployment rate for youths ages 16–19 was 12.7 percent for whites. For blacks it was 32.4 percent, and for Hispanics, 19.4 percent.

In the third quarter of 1990, the median weekly earnings for full-time male workers ages 16–24 were $283 for whites, $255 for blacks, and $238 for Hispanics. Among female youths, the earnings were $250 for whites and $225 for blacks and Hispanics.

✳ WOMEN'S EMPLOYMENT

During the past decade, the number of Hispanic women in the work force increased more rapidly than any other major population group, and by the end of the decade their rate of participation nearly equaled those of women in other groups. The distinctiveness of Hispanic women in employment has been largely erased. Between 1978 and 1988, Hispanic female participation in the work force more than doubled, from 1.7 million to 3.6 million. In 1988, 56.6 percent of Hispanic women were in the work force, compared with 66.2 percent of white women and 63.8 percent of blacks. The lower rate for Hispanic women can be attributed largely to their younger age and higher number of children than black and white women.

Hispanic women in 1988 formed 6.5 percent of the civilian labor force. Of the total of 3.6 million Hispanic women workers, 58.5 percent were of Mexican origin, 10.4 percent were Puerto Rican, 6.6 percent were of Cuban origin, and the other 24.5 percent were of other Hispanic backgrounds. By ethnicity, 53.9 percent of women of Mexican origin, compared with 54.9 percent of Cuban origin and 41.4 percent of Puerto Rican origin, were employed.

In March 1988, 41.1 percent of working Hispanic women were employed in technical, sales, and administrative support occupations, rates not much different from those of other women. At that same date, there were sharper differences in occupations of high and low pay and status. In the higher-status managerial and professional jobs, 15.7 percent of Hispanic women found employment, versus 25.3 percent of all women. Meanwhile, 16.6 percent of Hispanic women worked as lower-paid operators, fabricators, and laborers, compared with only 8.8 percent of all women. There were very few Hispanic women in extractive occupations, in mechanic and repairer jobs, or in most construction trades.

In the fourth quarter of 1990, the median weekly earnings of Hispanic women was $283, compared with $313 for black women and $361 for white women. Because of sharp increases in the work force, Hispanic women in the 1990s are about as likely to be employed in wage labor as other women. But their incomes remain substantially below those of women in the other major groups.

✳ GOVERNMENT PROGRAMS

The federal government committed itself to eliminating discrimination in employment when it passed the Fair Employment Practices Act in 1941. The act created a monitoring mechanism in the Fair Employment Practices Commission (FEPC), which went out of existence in 1945. Despite its ongoing commitment, the federal government made little systematic effort to address fair employment practices again until the Kennedy administration.

The Manpower Development and Training Act (MDTA), passed in 1962, initially offered vocational training for unemployed adult workers displaced by automation, and later it was expanded to include youth training programs. The government effort increased with the enactment of the Economic Opportunity Act (EOA) of 1964, the flagship of the War on Poverty. Among the programs included in the act aimed at the poor, including Hispanics, were the Neighborhood Youth Corp, the Job Corps, the Community Action Program, and VISTA. The EOA also had a section dealing specifically with migrant and seasonal farm workers.

The War on Poverty held a philosophical position that a culture of poverty existed. Leaders of the New Frontier and Great Society considered it the responsibility of the federal government to take steps to eradicate poverty through a centralized program of training and other forms of direct action. They were convinced that eliminating poverty and discrimination would not succeed if responsibilities remained in the hands of local authorities and employers, or if left to the individual efforts of the poor.

The New Frontier and Great Society were also responding to the needs of their own constituencies among labor, community, black, and Hispanic groups. Part of the EEOC thrust was directed toward Hispanics because of the efforts of the two most important Mexican American organizations in the country, the American G.I. Forum and the League of United Latin American Citizens (LULAC). Immediately after the EOA was passed, the two initiated an independent program, Jobs for Progress, commonly known as SER (service, employment, redevelopment; in Spanish *ser* means "to be"). SER began as a voluntary job placement center in Washington, D.C., and through its close ties to the government, soon expanded. By 1966, SER was receiving funds from the Office of Economic Opportunity, the Department of Health, Education and Welfare, the Department of Labor, and private sources to meet its goals of providing skills training and related services to the Hispanics of the Southwest. In 1970, SER became a categorical program under the Department of Labor. By 1972, it had expanded to 13 states in the Southwest and Midwest, plus the District of Columbia. SER is a nonprofit corporation whose principal objectives are to assist the disadvantaged, with a priority given to Hispanics and emphasis on manpower and related programs to upgrade educational and vocational skills and open career opportunities. It is the closest link between a Hispanic job training organization and the federal government.

The direction of government action and philosophy has undergone two major changes since the EOA was enacted in 1964. In 1973, the government created the Comprehensive Employment and Training Administration (CETA), an effort to alter the direction of government programs that it felt were gaining too much power. CETA, which was to be the major federal legislation governing employment and training programs for the next decade, offered a decentralized delivery system that gave state and local governments a greater degree of control over the programs, the original intent being to allow the poor, blacks, and Hispanics to have a direct voice in their own affairs.

The direction of CETA was sharply altered in 1983 when the Job Training Partnership Act (JTPA) was initiated. It became an employer-oriented organization in which the demands of local employers were given priority over the specific needs of the unemployed and poor.

Occupations

The occupational distribution of the Hispanic work force is highly overrepresented in manufacturing, operator, and service jobs, including semiskilled and clerical positions. Hispanics are highly underrepresented in managerial, sales, technical, and administrative areas. In 1989, 27 percent of Hispanic men were employed in managerial, sales, technical, and administrative positions, compared with 48 percent of non-Hispanic men. They were twice as likely to be employed in service occupations as non-Hispanics (18 percent versus 9 percent).

In 1989, Hispanic women were more likely than non-Hispanic women to be employed in service occupations (24 percent versus 17 percent), and less likely to work in managerial or professional occupations (15 percent versus 27 percent).

✳ INCOME, POVERTY, AND UNEMPLOYMENT

Median family income in 1989 for white families was $35,210; for blacks, $20,210; and for Hispanics, $23,450. Per capita income was $14,060 for whites, $8,750 for blacks, and $8,390 for Hispanics. Among Hispanics, family income was highest among Cuban and lowest among Mexican families. In 1988, non-Hispanics were twice as likely as Hispanics to earn more than $25,000 per year (42.7 percent versus 21.5 percent).

As individual workers, the incomes of Hispanic men and women in the late 1980s and early 1990s were lower than either blacks or whites. Between 1982 and 1988, the income gap between Hispanic and non-Hispanic families increased as median family income for Hispanic families fell from 68 percent to 57 percent of non-Hispanic family incomes.

Between 1978 and 1988, the proportion of Hispanic children living in poverty rose more than 45 percent, and by 1989, 38 percent of Hispanic children were living in poverty. Between 1978 and 1988, the rate of poverty for all whites rose from 8.7 percent to 10.1 percent; for blacks it rose from 30.6 percent to 31.6 percent; and for Hispanics it rose from 21.6 percent to 26.8 percent. During this same period, poverty rates for white children under age 18 rose from 11.3 percent to 14.6 percent; for black children from 41.5 percent to 44.2 percent; and for Hispanic children from 28 percent to 37.9 percent.

The poverty rates for married-couple Hispanic families are higher than for other major groups. Between 1978 and 1988, poverty rates for white families remained constant at 5 percent, fell for blacks from 13 percent to 11 percent, and for Hispanics increased from 13 percent to 16 percent. The median income of Hispanic families below the poverty level fell from $7,238 in 1978 to $6,557 in 1987, controlling for inflation.

In 1987, 70.1 percent of Hispanic female-headed households with children were living in poverty.

In 1988, the unemployment rate for whites was 4.5 percent, compared with 11.4 percent for blacks, and 8.0 percent for Hispanics. By December 1990, the rate for whites rose to 5.3 percent, for blacks to 12.2 percent, and for Hispanics to 9.3 percent. By January 1991, the highest rate of unemployment in the United States was in Puerto Rico, with a rate of 15.1 percent.

Hispanics are more than three times as likely as non-Hispanic Whites to be poor. In 1988, 26.7 percent of Hispanics, versus 10.1 percent of Whites and 31.3 percent of Blacks, lived below the poverty level. Between 1982 and 1988, the number of Hispanic families in poverty increased from 875,000 to 1.1 million. During the 1980s, the number of poor Hispanic families increased by 30 percent, while the number of poor White families declined by 10.3 percent.

Selected Labor Facts

Fact 1

Total Hispanic employment grew by 43 percent between 1980 and 1987. Rates of growth varied, from 48 percent for individuals of Mexican origin, to 24 percent for Puerto Ricans, 27 percent for Cubans, and 44 percent for other Hispanics. The rate of growth was almost three times the rate for other workers.

Fact 2

Hispanic men in the labor force is at 80 percent, compared with 74 percent for all other U.S. men.

Fact 3

Unemployment for Hispanics fell from 16.5 percent in March 1983 to 8.5 percent in March 1988. It then rose to 9.3 percent for whites and 12.2 percent for blacks.

Fact 4

Median weekly earnings in the third quarter of 1990 for white men were $492; for white women, $350; for black men, $438; for black women, $302; for Hispanic men, $317; and for Hispanic women, $302. In percentages, white women earned 71 percent of the amount earned by white men; black men earned 89 percent, Hispanic men 64 percent, and black and Hispanic women 61 percent of that amount. The earnings discrepancies between men and women of the same background were 71 percent for whites, 69 percent for blacks, and 95 percent for Hispanics. Of the three groups, income disparities between women and men were greatest among whites, and least among Hispanics.

Fact 5

In 1988, one-third of white and Hispanic union members were women, while 44 percent of black union members were women. Union membership among all women declined from 14.6 percent to 12.6 percent between 1983 and 1988.

Fact 6

In 1988, 6.5 percent of women in the labor force, or 3.6 million women, were of Hispanic origin. Of the total, 58.5 percent were of Mexican origin, 10.4 percent of Puerto Rican origin, 6.6 percent of Cuban origin, and 24.5 percent were of other Hispanic origin. Of all Hispanic women age 16 and over, 53.2 percent were in the labor force in 1988, compared with 36.6 percent for non-Hispanic women.

Fact 7

In 1988, labor force participation for all Hispanics was 67.4 percent, compared with 66.2 percent for whites and 63.8 percent for blacks.

Fact 8

In 1988, the mean family income for non-Hispanic families was $34,563; for those of Mexican origin it was $25,051; for those of Puerto Rican origin it was $21,963; for those of Cuban origin it was $33,350; and for those of Central and South American origin it was $30,641. On a per capita basis, income for non-Hispanics was $13,449; for Mexicans, $6,627; for Puerto Ricans, $7,652; for Cubans, $13,241; for Central and South Americans, $9,342; and for other Hispanics, $9,441.

Fact 9

In March 1989, 9.4 percent of non-Hispanic families were below the poverty line, compared with 23.7 percent of Hispanic families. Among specific groups, the rates were 24.9 percent for Mexicans, 30.8 percent for Puerto Ricans, 16.9 percent for Cubans, 16.6 percent for Central and South Americans, and 20.6 percent for other Hispanic families.

Fact 10

In March 1989 per capita earnings for individuals in non-Hispanic families was $12,701, compared with $7,287 for all individuals in Hispanic families. Among the different Hispanic groups, the amounts were $6,325 for Mexicans, $7,293 for Puerto Ricans, $12,855 for Cubans, $8,855 for Central and South Americans, and $8,925 for other Hispanics. The per capital earnings for Hispanics was 57.3 percent of that of non-Hispanics, 49.8 percent for Mexicans, 57.4 percent for Puerto Ricans, 101.2 percent for Cubans, 69.7 percent for Central and South Americans, and 70.2 for other Hispanics.

References

Acuña, Rodolfo. *Occupied America: A History of Chicanos,* third edition. New York: Harper and Row, 1988.

Bean, Frank D., and Marta Tienda. *The Hispanic Population of the United States.* New York: Russell Sage Foundation, 1988.

Cattan, Peter. "The Growing Presence of Hispanics in the U.S. Work Force." *Monthly Labor Review,* 111, No. 8, August 1988: 9–14.

McHugh, Kevin E. "Hispanic Migration and Population Redistribution in the United States." *Professional Geographer,* 41, No. 4, November 1989: 429–439.

Miranda, Leticia, and Julia Teresa Quiroz. *The Decade of the Hispanic: An Economic Retrospective.* Washington, D.C.: National Council of La Raza, 1990.

Portes, Alejandro, and Robert L. Bach. *Latin Journey: Cuban and Mexican Immigrants in the United States.* Berkeley: University of California Press, 1985.

Santos, Richard. *Hispanic Youth: Emerging Workers.* New York: Praeger, 1987.

U.S. Bureau of the Census. *Statistical Abstract of the United States: 1990,* 110th edition. Washington, D.C.: GPO, 1990.

U.S. Department of Labor. *Women of Hispanic Origin in the Labor Force.* Washington, D.C.: U.S. Department of Labor Women's Bureau.

Valdés, Dennis Nodín. *Al Norte: Agricultural Workers in the Great Lakes Region, 1917–1970.* Austin: University of Texas Press, 1991.

Dennis Valdez

16

Education

* Education of Hispanics in the Spanish Period, 1540–1821
* Education of Hispanics in the Mexican Period, 1821–1848
* Education of Hispanics: The American Period in the Nineteenth Century, 1850–1900
* Education of Hispanics in the Twentieth Century

The roots and patterns of contemporary Hispanic education can be found in the Spanish, Mexican, and Anglo conquests of North America. The original Spanish influence extended from the Carolinas and Florida on the East Coast, down through the Gulf Coast and on to the western part of the United States. By the end of the Spanish period in the early 1800s, the vast majority of Spanish subjects were concentrated in Indian-controlled lands of what we know today as the American Southwest: California, Arizona, New Mexico, and Texas. Informal rather than formal learning was the norm during the first 300 years of Spanish rule.

Formal learning, or schooling as it is more commonly known in today's world, began to emerge during the nineteenth century to meet the increasing needs of the Hispanic population for literacy and socialization. A variety of public, parochial, and private secular schools were established during this period. The schools provided, however, were limited in many respects. They were segregated, assimilationist, nonacademic in orientation, and inferior to those provided for other children. No higher education facilities were provided for Hispanic children. In the early twentieth century and until 1965, public education became the dominant form of learning in the Hispanic community. Private forms of schooling existed, but the community, augmented by an influx of Puerto Ricans from the island, began to increasingly support public education over other types of schooling. Due to their subordinate status in the society where they were concentrated, Mexican Americans and Puerto Ricans were provided with segregated and inferior forms of public education.

During the contemporary period, from 1965 to the present, public education continues to be the domi-

nant form of schooling for the Hispanic population. As a result of various pressures, the schools have become more sensitive to the academic, cultural, and linguistic needs of the Hispanic population during this period. However, the patterns of inequality have

Children during recess at the Guadalupe Aztlán alternative school in Houston, 1981. (Photograph by Curtis Dowell.)

continued. Unequal access to unequal schools contin-
ues to characterize the schooling of Hispanics. Unlike
the past, the Hispanic community is now more di-
verse and includes a significant number of immi-
grants from all areas of the Spanish-speaking world,
including Mexico, Puerto Rico, the Caribbean, Cen-
tral America, and the rest of Spanish America.

✳ EDUCATION OF HISPANICS IN THE SPANISH PERIOD, 1540–1821

During the years from 1540 to 1821, education in
Spain's far northern frontier was a function of the
Crown, the church, and, to some extent, the settlers.
As in most agricultural societies, education was
broadly conceived as an informal aspect of institutional life and included at least three elements:
knowledge, skills, and behaviors needed in making a
living, in maintaining a household, and in satisfying
personal wants. Education, however, was not conducted in schools. Schools were available in the far
northern region of the Spanish regime but they were
rare. The missions at times established schools, but
only sporadically. The missions in California and especially in New Mexico made reference to formal
instruction in them. There is no mention of schooling
in any of the Texas missions. The primary reason
given was that Texas Indians were more nomadic
than those in other parts of the Southwest. Sedentary groups such as those found in New Mexico were
easier to teach than nomadic ones. Schooling in the
missions was for the benefit of the Indians. Basic
literacy skills were taught in them. Schools outside
the mission were rarely found. The sons and daughters of the Spanish settlers, including the military
personnel, rarely received formal instruction on the
frontier.

The diverse population that came to comprise the
Hispanics, that is, the indigenous groups, the Spaniards, and the mestizos or other racially mixed
groups, acquired basic literacy skills and knowledge
or behaviors necessary for adult life not from schools
per se but from other institutions. Education was an
informal process that occurred in the three major
institutions established in the far northern frontier:
the missions, the settlements, and the presidios. The
primary purposes of these institutions were to conquer, civilize, and control the Indian population in
this part of the Americas in order to exploit their
resources for the benefit of Spain. These institutions,
however, served an educational purpose. This is especially the case with the missions. They provided
informal instruction on political culture, moral, and
religious values, and attitudes and skills needed for
adult life in Spanish America.

Missions, presidios, and pueblos in the far northern frontiers were established decades after Spaniards in search of gold, glory, and new trade routes
explored the area. Spaniards, for instance, explored
Florida and the Atlantic coast from 1513 to the 1540s
and both New Mexico and Arizona in the late 1530s.
But after finding no gold or precious minerals, they
left. Although Spain decided to withdraw from the
area once it realized that there were no precious
minerals to be found, the Jesuits and other religious
orders stayed to convert the Indians. They made
religious arguments for colonization, but their pleas
went unheeded for nearly half a century.

Serious colonization of the far northern frontier
began in the seventeenth century. These efforts were
led by the missionaries who established a large number of missions to convert the Indians to Christianity, that is, to a Spanish way of life. The missions
were initially financed by the state, but eventually
became self-supporting. Most missionaries were
scholarly and literate "men of high calibre" who
wrote many historical tracts, scientific documents,
ethnographically rich reports and translations of Indian languages. Unlike those in central Mexico, the
missionaries in this far northern frontier, comprised
of both Jesuit and Franciscans, requested the presence of soldiers in their colonization efforts. Fear for
their lives because of hostile Indians provided the
rationale for such actions. Some of the soldiers assigned to protect them, however, were a hindrance to
their educational endeavors, since they mistreated
the Indians.

Settlement efforts were first initiated in New
Mexico during the 1590s. In 1595, a large force of
missionaries, soldiers, and settlers set off to colonize
New Mexico. The first permanent settlement was in
1598. However, by 1601 there was no missionary
work done; it was mostly military. Missionary work
and the construction of missions began in earnest
between 1605 and 1608. By 1626, there were more
than 25 missions, 43 churches, and more than 36,000
new converts.

Between 1659 and 1665, the new civil governors
established a reign of tyranny and alienated all
groups in the far northern frontier. They also did
irreparable harm to the missions. Eventually these
actions led to the 1680 Pueblo revolt and to the
killing of the missionaries. The area was recon-
quered by Spain between 1695 and 1698. Continuing
conflict and tensions for the next decade, including a
second rebellion involving at least 15 pueblos,
slowed down but did not stop the Franciscans from
doing their missionary work. However, the success of
the past was not equaled. By 1774, some success in
conversion, mission and church establishment, and

in teaching the practical arts and education was made. The missions continued to decline after 1775 owing to insufficient number of missionaries and to friction between missionaries and local Spanish officials.

Arizona was the second area settled by the Spanish government. As in New Mexico, the missionaries led the way. Due to Indian resistance, this area was not settled until the late 1600s, although it had been explored in the 1630s. By 1680, there were six Franciscan missions in northeast Arizona. After the Pueblo revolt of 1680, these missions were abandoned and never rebuilt. In the south, the Jesuits founded several missions in 1700. During the next 67 years two missions and 11 visitas (substations) were founded. The Jesuits were expelled in 1767 and the missions were assigned to the Franciscans, but the hostility of Indians forced them to close five visitas. Two additional ones were established under them. Despite this activity, the missionaries were unable to establish more missions because of the Indian raids and the area's lack of strategic value. Few settlers went to Arizona. By the end of the colonial period, it contained a sparse Mexican population centered in the Santa Cruz Valley.

Defense against foreign powers rather than economic considerations was the major reason for settling California and Texas. Religious conversion, however, was still a primary goal of the missionaries. Successful missions were established in the El Paso region between 1659 and 1684. Missionaries explored east Texas in the 1670s but no missions were established until 1690, and then largely due to fears of French activity in that area. But Indian raids slowed the growth of a Spanish presence. For this reason missionary activity in Texas was more uneven and at times less successful than in New Mexico. By 1690, the missions were abandoned because of Indian resistance to missionary activity and agriculture. Some scholars have reported the founding of many more missions than originally suspected in other parts of the state. Sister Mary Stanislaus Van Well, in her *The Educational Aspects of the Missions of the Southwest* (1942), stated that as many as 50 of them were founded during the late 1600s and early 1700s. In San Antonio, more than five missions were founded. The first and longest-lasting one, San Antonio Mission, was founded in 1718.

Spain colonized California for defensive reasons, too, but missions came to dominate the life of the province. Fear of Russian traders in the north in 1769 encouraged Spanish authorities in Mexico to settle California. Between 1769 and 1823, for instance, 21 missions and a large number of presidios were constructed. Despite the large number of missions and the excellent climate, few individuals settled in California. Those who did settled in widely scattered pueblos throughout California. By 1821, the non-native population was located in pueblos scattered along the coast.

During this period, education occurred in the missions and in the pueblos. The mission community was considered a school of civilization. In a San Antonio mission founded in 1718, for instance, the missionaries taught Indian children and adults Catholic religious and moral instruction, adherence to Spanish custom and law, and training in agriculture and the domestic arts. All the Indians knew the Christian doctrine (prayers, beliefs, and so on) and spoke Spanish, and most played musical instruments or sang. They also dressed with "decency," assisted in making furniture, raised their own food, and went to school. The missionaries likewise taught the Indians family living, stock raising, European farming techniques, church construction, and furniture making.

Education also occurred in the Spanish settlements and to some extent in the presidios. As in most agricultural societies, the family and the community were the primary vehicles for teaching non-Indian youths in the pueblos and presidios the values and skills needed to survive. People also learned from other sources of nonformal education, including textbooks, folklore, oral history, drama, traveling puppet shows, and the Spanish mail service.

By the end of the Spanish period, several patterns of educational development were discernible. First, formal instruction was not an integral aspect of community development. If present, it was peripheral to other community institutions. Second, the primary goal of education in the mission was to assimilate, forcefully if need be. Education was for the purpose of teaching Indians the dominant political and religious values of Spanish culture. In the process of teaching Christianity and Spanish ways, the missionaries either showed contempt or else disregarded the population's native language and culture. Under the Spaniards, most of the indigenous institutions, including the educational traditions and native languages, were trampled and destroyed. The government's official policy toward language, for instance, called for the abolition of the native language in instruction and the sole use of Spanish in religious conversion. In 1793, King Carlos IV decreed that schools in the American empire should replace the Indian languages with Castilian. This did not occur because of the special linguistic circumstances faced by the missionaries. Third, the informal curriculum that was provided, especially in the mission, emphasized vocational or industrial education at the expense of academic instruction. Fourth, there was disagreement among the missionaries over the role that the native language would play in Christianization. Most of the Franciscans, for instance, strongly believed in Spanish and failed to learn the native languages of the Indians. The Jesuits, on the other hand, were supportive of native languages in conversion. They used Spanish whenever possible and learned the languages of those whom they sought to convert. But, the Jesuits, for the most part, were not in support of native language maintenance. They, like the Spanish Crown, believed that Spanish should replace the Indian languages. The use of the Indians' native language in instruction was a temporary measure aimed at more easily assimilating them into Spanish culture. Fifth, a distinct pattern of community distrust of educators and educational institutions emerged during this period. Owing to the foreign teachings and the mistreatment by soldiers and some missionaries, the Indian community began to distrust Spanish institutions and leaders. In New Mexico, especially, missionaries destroyed native religious objects, built the church away from the Indian community, utilized soldiers to ensure compliance with their rules, and imposed harsh discipline on Indians for failing to adhere to Spanish religious and work practices. These teachings and mistreatment were for the most part rejected or resisted by the native populations. These incipient patterns of educational development in the Spanish period were modified and eventually strengthened in the decades to come, especially with the emergence of schooling as an important socialization agency in the nineteenth and twentieth centuries.

✳ EDUCATION OF HISPANICS IN THE MEXICAN PERIOD, 1821–1848

During the latter part of the eighteenth and early nineteenth centuries, the family and the parish church replaced the missions as the key educational institutions in the northern provinces. The focus and objectives of instruction also shifted from teaching Indians to teaching non-Indian children, from propagating Spanish political, economic, and cultural values to preserving them, and from teaching religious values to teaching basic literacy skills. The decline in the number of missionaries and in the Indian population, as well as the increase in the non-Indian population (for instance, it nearly trebled in New Mexico from 1750 to 1800), led to increasing pressure to better serve the spiritual needs of the colonists who were concentrated in certain parts of the northern frontier. This period also led to the emergence of schools as important frontier institutions.

The Decline, Collapse, and Weakening of Frontier Institutions

The missions and pueblos of the American Southwest began to decline in significance in the late eighteenth century. Their complete collapse occurred under independent Mexico. The lack of federal funds, the shortage of priests, ideological opposition to missions, and various local conditions led to their eventual decline.

The order to secularize the missions led to their eventual demise. This order, issued originally in 1813 but resurrected in 1821 once Mexico gained its independence, was based on the notion that all men, including Indians, were equal before the law. These sentiments were embodied in the government's Plan of Iguala in 1821. It called for the elimination of all distinctions on the basis of race or class. The missions were antiquated institutions that oppressed Indians and had to be eliminated. The missions also aided the church in amassing immense wealth and property and in maintaining its influence in secular affairs. The need to undercut the church's power, both economic and political, thus served as a rationale for secularization.

Within a decade and a half after Mexico declared its independence, the missions of the far northern provinces fell to pieces. After secularization, Indians deserted the missions, the buildings began to decay, the fields lay bare, and the Franciscans disappeared from sight. With secularization, the colonizers became parishioners. This led to the emergence of the Catholic parish church as one of the most significant institutions involved in educating the population, composed now primarily of mestizo settlers.

The secularization of the missions brought an end to the influence of missionaries on the frontier and to the weakening of the Catholic church. The church remained strong in central Mexico, but weak in the frontier during the period of Mexican independence. It failed to fill the void created by the dismantling of the missions and the departing of the Franciscans for several reasons. First, its leadership decreased due to the expulsion of all Spaniards from Mexico during the 1830s. Second, there was a shortage of priests and funds. Mexico did not train its own priests and the Vatican forbade sending any new ones to Mexico. The church also abolished all tithes and service fees, for example for marriages, births, and deaths. The major result of the church's weakened leadership and lack of funds or priests was the neglect of the spiritual welfare of the mestizos and the decline in the morale and morality of frontier clerics.

In addition to the church's collapse, the military supremacy over the frontier also slipped away. In many areas of the frontier, the decades following independence saw relations worsen with the Indians, who rejected Christianity and much of Hispanic culture. The Indians increased their attacks on Mexican settlements for various reasons. According to David J. Weber, in *The Mexican Frontier, 1821–1846* (1982), missionaries had forcibly recruited Indian neophytes for missions or for slavery and settlers sought their land after secularization in 1830. But most important, Indian resistance to the Spanish/Mexican presence increased due to the influx of Anglos who upset the balance of power in the frontier, while the Mexican government failed to strengthen its military and economic posture. Anglo traders as well as some Mexican ones, in some cases, provided firepower to Indians in return for stolen goods and encouraged them to attack Mexican settlements and missions. Firepower upset the balance of power on the frontier. Anglo settlers also pushed Indians out of traditional areas in their westward expansion, especially in Texas.

The new resistance by Indians led to discussions of how best to deal with them. Mexicans for the most part were in disagreement whether Indians should be assimilated and provided with gifts to maintain the peace or whether they should be annihilated or removed, as in the United States. The former view prevailed, although it was perceived to be a failure.

The decline of these frontier institutions led to a disruption in the education of the population in the northern provinces. Other frontier institutions, especially the family, the Catholic parish church, and the state-sponsored public schools, began to replace the missions as key educational institutions. The emergence of these institutions accompanied the secularization of the missions and the growth of ranches and pueblos in the far northern provinces.

The Emergence of New Frontier Institutions and the Education of Hispanics in the Early Eighteenth Century

Ranches and pueblos emerged in California during the period of Spanish control. In addition to land provided for the establishment of the missions, the Spanish government also allotted land to private individuals. Independent Mexico confirmed these grants and distributed many more. The numbered ranches increased after the secularization of the missions in 1834. Similar to the early Spanish missions, the ranches provided most of the daily needs of their owners and workers. They raised sheep and hogs and cultivated grapes, fruit, wheat, and other grains.

Towns also were established during the Spanish period, but did not expand until the latter part of the 1700s, when Indian raids were halted and local economies began to expand. Pueblo life revolved around the plaza, a park-like square that formed the center of town. On one side of the plaza stood the church. Opposite the church was the town government building, known as the *cabildo,* and on the remaining two sides local ranchers built their town houses on lots referred to as *solares.*

In both the ranch and pueblo the extended family pattern was the norm. A typical household included parents, children, grandchildren, in-laws, other relatives, occasionally orphans, and Indian servants all living together. The children learned obedience, respect, political values, religious beliefs, and cultural traditions. The families in the ranches likewise taught routine household tasks such as cooking, washing, and the making of candles, soap, cloth, and wine. They also taught the planting of crops, the raising of cattle and sheep, and the making of clothing and other goods needed for survival on these ranches.

The church was another important institution that taught the knowledge, skills, and attitudes necessary for Christian living in these areas. It served an educational function through such activities as mass, religious rituals, weddings, christenings, wakes, and celebrations of town saints. The education of Indians decreased but learning among non-Indians increased.

In addition to the informal education provided by the church and the family residing in the ranches and pueblos, the state, especially in the form of the federal and provincial governments, began to express an interest in the formal instruction of the population. The declining influence of the church, as well as pressure from the settlers, encouraged the federal government late in the colonial period and in the Mexican era to support the establishment of public schools.

The Emergence of Schooling in the Far Northern Provinces

The initial interest for public education was expressed by the King of Spain in 1793 when he mandated the establishment of public schools in the colonies. High illiteracy among soldiers prompted the king to pass this mandate. However, nothing concrete was done to promote schooling in the far northern provinces until the early part of the 1800s. In 1802, for instance, Governor Juan Bautista Elguezábal of Texas issued a compulsory school attendance law for children up to age 12. This law however could not be enforced. As a result, no new schools were produced and existing ones were eradicated. Social and economic factors, compounded by political unrest, during these years ended the period of Spanish rule without a semblance of an educational system.

In California, two governors—Governor Diego de Borica and Pablo Vicente de Solá—promoted schooling in the latter part of the Spanish period. During Governor Borica's administration, from 1794 to 1800, approximately ten schools in five different cities were established. Under Governor Solá's administration, from 1815 to 1822, nine schools in two different cities were established. These schools, however, did not last long and had a negligible effect on the population. Public officials were unsuccessful in establishing a viable public school system in California during the Spanish period for many reasons, including the lack of public education tradition among the settlers, the isolation and sparseness of the population, general indifference, financial problems, shortage of funds, poor quality of teachers, external threats from foreign powers and rivalries, and internal bickering among state and local officials. No publicly sponsored schools were established in New Mexico during this same period.

Government leaders continued to support the establishment of public schools after Mexican independence. In Texas, for instance, state officials prodded local authorities and provided them with some financial assistance for the establishment of schools. In 1827, the state of Coahuila-Texas formulated a state constitution that required all municipalities to establish primary schools. Between 1828 and 1833, state officials issued several decrees attempting to encourage local authorities, usually known as *ayuntamientos,* to establish schools. Local officials, however, faced many obstacles in establishing schools, including individual and municipal poverty, lack of qualified teachers and lack of commitment to the importance of education among "ordinary" folks. In 1833, the state issued land grants for the support of local schools, but political unrest in central Mexico once again ended all efforts at establishing public schools. As in prior years, then a variety of social, political, and economic factors deflected government interest in formal education and prevented officials from establishing public schools.

In New Mexico, government officials were temporarily successful in establishing schools during the Mexican period. Between 1825 and 1827, for instance, 18 schools were established in New Mexico. Efforts by Mexican government officials to establish more schools were thwarted by indifference, political turmoil, and poverty.

Government officials were not the only ones interested in the establishment of schools in the far northern provinces of the Mexican nation. There was also a fluctuating interest in schooling on the part of religious leaders and private individuals. Anglo settlers in Texas, for instance, established some private schools. These private schools started by American settlers in Texas during the Mexican period fared better than public ones.

Formal education for the most part was not an important component of learning for the majority of the population during the latter part of the eighteenth and the first half of the nineteenth centuries. It nevertheless assumed an increasingly important part in the lives of Hispanics and other school children with the coming of Anglos and American rule after 1848.

✳ EDUCATION OF HISPANICS: THE AMERICAN PERIOD IN THE NINETEENTH CENTURY, 1850–1900

During the first half-century of American rule in the "Southwest," Hispanic traditions and institutions were trampled upon, modified to meet new needs, or gradually replaced by American ones. After the signing of the Treaty of Guadalupe Hidalgo in 1848, Americans introduced new political, economic, cultural, and social institutions and organized the society on the basis of certain Protestant, capitalist, republican, gender, and racial ideals. They sought to create a world in their own image, but encountered passive or active resistance by significant numbers of Hispanics. A few wealthy Hispanics initially supported these efforts, but by the turn of the century they had been dispossessed of their fortunes, had been relegated to wage earners in seasonal or low-paying jobs, and had lost any semblance of political influence and social status. Many of the Hispanic elite then joined the majority of the population as members of a cheap labor force, a politically powerless group, and the victims of social and cultural discrimination.

The family during this period continued to be the central agency for educating Hispanic children. The family assumed greater importance in many respects because of the rapid changes occurring in the society, for example, immigration and the transformation of the pueblos into barrios, the Americanization of the Catholic church, the emergence of Protestantism in the Southwest, and the decline of the ranches and the emergence of farming in the rural areas. Of primary importance to Hispanic education was the emergence of the institution of schooling. Schools were established during this period by private individuals, the Catholic church, Protestant groups, and public officials to meet the increasing needs of developing an American social order.

By the middle of the 1800s, schools had undergone

a significant transition from transmitter of basic literacy skills to the agency of socialization. This change was due to the desires of one group to assert control over others and to improve the lives of those viewed as racially or culturally inferior. The changed mission of the school touched off a debate between Hispanics and school-based reformers over who would decide the education of these children and what role would be assigned to the native languages and cultures.

Reformers believed that the school was to shape desirable behaviors for functioning in American society. More specifically, its purpose was to promote uniformity and eliminate all differences, including regional, class, and ethnic. Hispanics disagreed with this view and argued that the role of the schools was to teach these youngsters, but not at the expense of their cultural identity. Hispanics generally opposed school reforms if they were aimed at the elimination of their cultural and linguistic heritage.

During the first half-century of American rule, then, schools became increasingly important to Hispanics, but unlike in earlier decades, they were not viewed as supplementary to education or as part of community life. For most Hispanics, the schools became alien institutions aimed at controlling them. This was especially the case with public forms of schooling, which were vehement in their insistence on cultural assimilation. In many respects, the school became the setting for a struggle for the loyalties of the next generation as reflected in important controversies, such as English-language school laws and sectarian influences in public schools.

Schools established by individuals from the community and by the Catholic church were very much a part of Hispanic culture and continued in the United States after 1848. The number of Catholic schools expanded significantly during the second half of the nineteenth century. Ironically, increased Catholic education among Hispanics came to be associated with cultural tolerance at a time in which the Catholic church was undergoing its own transformation and becoming an instrument of Americanization. This apparent association of an Americanizing Catholic church with cultural tolerance was due to the large number of Spanish-speaking parishioners and the willingness by individual priests, nuns, and religious orders to accommodate to these differences. Demography and individual initiative rather than policy were the driving forces behind this apparent contradiction in church behavior. It is important to note that the Catholic church did not specifically create schools for Hispanic children. It founded schools that turned out to be attended primarily by Hispanics. Quite often it was residential segrega-

tion, not policy, that accounted for the development of "Hispanic" Catholic schools throughout the Southwest.

Reasons for the transformation of the Catholic church and for the expansion of its school system were varied. The emergence of secular institutions, especially public school systems, the growing educational needs of an increasing Catholic population, the anti-Catholic sentiments prevalent during the second quarter of the nineteenth century, and the proselytizing efforts made by various Protestant denominations acted as catalysts for the extension of Catholic parochial schooling in the Southwest. In response to these various forces, the Catholic church encouraged ecclesiastical authorities to promote the construction of additional parishes and schools by which an American Catholicism could be propagated.

Catholic education for Mexican children developed at uneven rates in the different states of the Southwest. In New Mexico, four religious orders came to dominate Catholic schooling during the period from 1851 to 1874: the Sisters of Loretto, the Christian Brothers, the Sisters of Charity, and the Jesuits. The Sisters of Loretto first came to the New Mexico territory in 1853. The Christian Brothers came from France to New Mexico in 1859. The other two religious orders, the Sisters of Charity and the Jesuits, arrived in New Mexico in 1865 and 1870, respectively. Together they established between 15 and 20 schools in as many cities.

In California, beginning in 1854 and continuing into 1889, ecclesiastical authorities encouraged the construction of additional parishes and schools by which an American Catholicism could be propagated. In order to staff these new parochial schools, at least nine religious orders were recruited. They established parochial schools for Catholic children in Santa Barbara, Ventura, Los Angeles, and throughout other parts of the state where the majority of the Mexican population was concentrated.

In Texas, religious orders also were requested to assist in the establishment of parochial schools. In some cases, Catholic parishes initially established these schools with the support of their parishioners. Carlos E. Castañeda, in his massive study of the Catholic heritage in Texas, identified more than 20 important religious orders that came to this state to establish missions, convents, and schools during the second half of the nineteenth century. The Catholic church, with the assistance of these religious orders, established some of the more well-known Catholic parochial schools attended by Mexican children in cities such as El Paso, Brownsville, Corpus Christi, and San Antonio.

Protestant denominations established schools for Hispanic children during the first half-century of American rule. Unlike the Catholic church, Protestant denominations acknowledged the presence of racially and ethnically distinct Hispanic children and took specific actions to encourage the establishment of schools for them.

Protestant schools varied tremendously within regions and across time, but they shared the common goals of Christianization and Americanization. The primary purpose of their elementary schools was, in the words of Melinda Rankin (1881), a prominent lay missionary of the 1850s, to "give them the Gospel, which is the antidote for all moral evils." In addition to these goals, the Protestant schools also promoted community leadership development. This task was assigned to the secondary schools established throughout the Southwest. One of the major goals of these schools was to train a Spanish-speaking Christian leadership that would propagate the Protestant faith and American ideals in their own communities. For this reason, some Protestant schools allowed for the use of the Spanish-language and Mexican cultural instruction in them. However, cultural and language diversity were viewed as means to an end, that is, as instruments for the more effective evangelization of the Mexican American population. Despite this end, ethnicity in education became one of the major distinguishing characteristics of Protestant secondary schooling.

Protestants have a long history of involvement with Spanish-speaking individuals in the Southwest. In the New Mexico territory, for instance, Protestant groups, including Presbyterians, Congregationalists, Baptists, and Methodists, all sponsored ambitious evangelization and educational programs during the second half of the nineteenth century. Presbyterian ministers began to conduct missionary work and organize schools in their missions in various cities as early as 1860. But they were unsuccessful in these early efforts because of lack of funds and support among the population. Despite these early setbacks, Presbyterian and other Protestant missionaries continued to evangelize and to establish schools. During the entire territorial period, from 1850 to 1912, they succeeded in establishing five major boarding schools and more than 40 mission day schools. The latter were commonly known as plaza schools. Most of this growth was spurred by favorable church policies and financial assistance from national lay and religious organizations, as well as by the determination of individual missionaries. Catholic opposition to Protestant schools, as well as Mexican American distrust of non-Catholic

missionaries, acted as barriers to the establishment and growth of some of these schools.

While Presbyterians were the most active Protestant sect, important educational institutions were also founded by other denominations. The Baptists, for instance, preceded the Presbyterians and began to establish churches and schools as early as 1849. Several efforts were made to establish Baptist schools in Santa Fe during the 1850s and early 1860s. Other New Mexico Baptist schools operated briefly at Alcalde (1851), Albuquerque (1851, 1855), Peralta (1852), Cubero (1854), and Socorro (1857). Since few Anglos were located in the New Mexico territory, one can assume that all of these schools were for the conversion of Mexican children to Protestantism. These schools were vigorously opposed by the Catholic clergy and rapidly were forced to close their doors because of the lack of students.

Congregationalists in 1880 started several rural schools and academies. According to Jerry L. Williams, in *New Mexico in Maps* (1986), the Congregationalists opened more than a dozen schools between 1878 and 1891. Four of these were still in operation by 1911. The Methodists also conducted missionary work and educational development in New Mexico. They worked in New Mexico in the late 1840s and even established two mission schools in 1854. But these were not permanent ventures. In total, the Methodists opened approximately 11 schools during the second half of the nineteenth century. Three of them were still in operation by 1911.

In Texas, Presbyterians dominated, but occasionally a group such as the Methodists established lasting schools. During the period from 1845 to the early decades of the twentieth century, individual Protestant missionaries led the way in providing educational opportunities for native Mexican children. Of primary importance were the Presbyterians. In total, individual missionaries sponsored by Presbyterians established seven major schools.

Methodists also conducted "Spanish work" in Texas. Their major achievements were in the area of church development. Between 1874 and 1884, for instance, they organized four Mexican American districts in west Texas. To complement their ministry to Mexican Americans, the Methodists established several schools. Three major educational institutions for Mexican children were founded between 1880 and 1914: the Holding Institute, the Lydia Patterson Institute for Boys, and the Effie Eddington School for Girls. The former was founded in Laredo in 1880. The latter two were founded in El Paso in 1914. In addition, there was also a school called the Anglo-Mexican Mission Institute founded in El Paso in

1907. This school was built by the Baptists in the heart of "Mexican El Paso."

Probably owing to the presence of public schools at an early period and to the dominance of the Catholic church, few Protestant groups other than the Methodists established schools in California during the nineteenth century. The Methodists were the most prominent group in this state. They did not begin to minister to Spanish-speaking Catholics until 1879. In this year the Southern California Conference of the Methodist Episcopal Church appointed a committee to investigate the possibility of starting "Spanish work." This work began in Los Angeles in 1880 and had spread by 1900 to include missions in all three of the conference's districts. During this period of growth, the Methodist church established the Forsythe Presbyterian Memorial School in 1884. Several years later, in 1900, the Francis de Pauw Methodist School for Mexican Girls was founded. The Spanish American Institute for Boys was founded by the Presbyterians 11 years later.

Public officials began to establish schools in the second half of the nineteenth century. Unlike the religious groups or private individuals, public officials sought to develop a public school system that would eventually enroll all children residing in each state. Racial discrimination, ideological differences, and political tensions based on conflicts of heterogeneous values and different power relations, however, affected the development of Hispanic public education so much that by the end of the nineteenth century several distinct patterns had emerged. By 1900, Hispanic education was characterized by the following patterns: (1) denial of equal access to public schools, (2) the establishment of segregated facilities, (3) an absence of Hispanic individuals in decision-making positions, and (4) an assimilationist goal aimed at replacing Hispanic socioeconomic, political, moral, cultural, and linguistic ideologies with Anglo ones.

Denial of Equal Access to Public Schools

Local educators for the most part did not provide Mexican children with access to public school facilities until the post-Civil War period and usually years or decades after schools for white children had been established. During the period from 1836 to the late 1860s, they established a system of public education for the school-age population, but limited it only to white or Anglo students. Increasing financial ability and willingness, new state mandates, and local demands for education led to the establishment of public school facilities for the population. Political pressures from powerful economic interests and biased Anglo parents, local official indifference, and

racial discrimination served to deny Hispanics full access to the emerging public school system. Some local communities, such as those in Santa Barbara and Los Angeles, California, did provide public school facilities for Hispanics during the 1850s and 1860s. But whenever enrollment occurred it was on Anglo terms. That is, access was based on the understanding that the Hispanic children's language and culture would be excluded from the schools.

Various means were used to deny Hispanics equal access to public schooling during these early years. Local officials either built public schools in Anglo communities and away from the Hispanic community or else allowed only members of the elite to enroll in the schools that were established. Once large numbers of working-class Hispanics were present and both the commitment and the resources were available, local officials began to provide Hispanics with their own school facilities.

The variety of conditions thus led to differential rates of public school access by Hispanics living in different parts of the Southwest. In California, Hispanics were allowed access to the public schools in the 1850s. Schools for Mexican children in Arizona were established in 1872, ten years after it became a territory. In Texas, public schools for Hispanic children in the urban areas were provided in the 1860s; rural school children were provided access to the schools in the 1880s. New Mexico officials failed to provide any significant access to public education until after 1872. The lack of finances, legal authority, and controversies over the issues of language, religion, and politics slowed educational developments in that territory.

Segregation

Although Hispanics were provided with increased access to public schools, the facilities provided in most cases were segregated owing to a combination of both race and residence. In most areas, residence played a large role in the establishment of segregated facilities. But in some districts race became a determining factor in the establishment of segregated schools for Mexican children. These segregated facilities were expanded over the years as the number of Hispanic children in the districts increased. Local officials expanded segregation through the use of containment and dispersal policies. In many cases, local officials prohibited the growing numbers of Hispanic children from enrolling in non-Mexican schools and kept assigning them to segregated facilities. If more Hispanic children enrolled, they usually added rooms to the existing school or purchased portables. Anglos on the other hand were provided with a greater number of school facilities that were dispersed throughout the local districts.

Absence of Hispanics in Decision-Making Positions

During the early years of American rule, Hispanics, especially members of the elite, were allowed to participate in the development of public education policy and in the establishment and operation of these schools. These individuals ran for political office and assumed important decision-making positions at various levels of government, including state or territorial legislatures, county boards of education, and local city councils and boards of education. In California, for instance, nine Hispanics were elected to the state senate and 12 to the state assembly during the years from 1849 to 1864. In the New Mexico territory, Hispanics were more fortunate, due to their numerical superiority and to the presence of a social and economic elite that was granted some political power. From 1850 to 1912, 177 Hispanics served in the territorial council and 531 served in the territorial house of representatives. Hispanics in the New Mexico territory also held other important legislative positions. Several of them were elected to the presidency of the upper chamber and nine were chosen to be Speaker of the House.

During the territorial period, from 1850 to 1912, Mexican Americans likewise assumed a few positions in the other branches of state government as well as in the federal government. Two Hispanics served as governor of the territory, one in the beginning of American rule and the other one at the turn of the century. Only one individual, Antonio José Otero, sat on the supreme court during the period from 1850 to 1912. Of the 18 individuals who were elected territorial delegates to the United States Congress from 1851 to 1908, 11 were Hispanics, including José M. Gallegos, Mariano A. Otero, Francisco Perea, J. Francisco Chávez, Mariano S. Otero, Tranquilino Luna, F. A. Manzanares, Antonio Joseph, and Pedro Perea.

Hispanics for a short period of time during the 1850s and 1860s also occupied on occasion a few important regional decision-making positions, including those of county superintendent and positions on county school boards and local boards of education. In California, for instance, approximately 6 out of 293 county superintendents serving between 1852 and 1865 were Hispanics. In New Mexico, the native Mexican population in the early decades of American rule made up a significant proportion of those elected to the office of county superintendent and county school boards. For example, in the 1873–74 school year, Mexican Americans comprised slightly over 75 percent of the total number of county superintendents in the territory. Out of 13 county superintendents, ten of these then were Hispanics.

By the latter part of the nineteenth century, Hispanics were relatively absent from the schools. Their involvement, for all intents and purposes, ceased to exist largely due to the relative increase of Anglo immigration, racial gerrymandering, vote-diluting policies and practices, structural changes in institutional life, and changing school policies and practices on governance and hiring. California legislators, for example, established citizenship and residency requirements for voting, used English-only ballots and voting procedures, and constantly changed registration procedures. They also enacted English literacy requirements for voting and holding office in the 1870s. This culminated in a constitutional amendment making English the official language of the state in 1890. Texas legislators voted to charge a poll tax for voting in the state beginning in the 1840s. They also established citizenship and literacy requirements for participation in the governmental process. Other forces, including the declining status of the Mexican population, the increasing proportions of non-Chicano immigrants to the areas, poverty, nonfamiliarity with the English language, and the legacy of distrust, acted to discourage any further participation and contributed to the decline of Mexican American officeholders.

The actions taken by school officials also played an important role in the decline in leadership positions by Hispanics. Local and state officials, for the most part, made no serious efforts to encourage the continuation of Hispanic participation in the shaping of public educational structures, policies, or practices. They did little to encourage the election, selection, or hiring of Hispanics to important positions of authority in the school structure. With one minor exception at the turn of the century, no Hispanics, for instance, were appointed to important statewide positions in education. Few if any Hispanics were hired to be administrators or teachers in the public schools during this period. In the case of New Mexico, where Hispanics played important roles in local and county government, their numbers decreased appreciably over time so that by 1912, when the territory became a state, the vast majority of the teachers, administrators, and school board members were Anglos. This was true even in areas that were predominantly Hispanic.

The decreasing political influence and voting power of Hispanics in general made it nearly impossible for them to elect their own members to important state positions, such as those of the superintendency or the board of education. No Hispanic, for instance, was elected to a state superintendent position during the second half of the nineteenth century in any of the southwestern states or territories. With the exception of New Mexico, no Hispanics served in the state boards of education either.

Assimilationism and School Content

The schools provided for Hispanics became rigidly assimilationist over the years and highly intolerant of cultural differences. They inculcated the dominant political, social, and moral ideologies through the use of English; they also devalued and excluded the Hispanic heritage from the curriculum. Between 1848 and 1900, three key aspects of Hispanic heritage were excluded from the schools—the Catholic heritage, the Hispanic cultural traditions, and the Spanish language.

Public policy toward Hispanic education was based on a developing and strengthening notion of the American national cultural identity that evaluated the religious, cultural, and linguistic heritage of Hispanics and rejected it from the schools. In its place, educators and political authorities proposed an "essentially American" identity that was comprised of Pan-Protestantism, republican values, and core British values, especially the ability to speak English. The schools were to embody and reproduce these ideological notions of American culture. Alternative forms of cultural identity, especially those based on Catholicism, non-English languages, Mexican cultural traditions, and racially distinct individuals who embraced these cultural traits, were to be replaced with American ideals, traditions, and individuals. Political leaders thus developed educational policies that promoted and transmitted the essential elements of an American cultural identity to the multitude of culturally diverse children, including Hispanics.

These assimilationist ideals, nevertheless, were internally inconsistent and at times in conflict with each other. Various groups of political authorities and educators in the Southwest supported different strands of these ideals with varying intensities. In the early decades of American rule, most Anglo rulers in the Southwest supported cultural pluralist policies and practices, primarily out of political expediency. But toward the latter part of the nineteenth century, officials began to support more assimilationist policies in the schools and to devalue cultural diversity in education. The stated purpose of these assimilationist policies was to facilitate the entry and success of Mexican immigrant children into mainstream society. However, the underlying reason was to structurally exclude them from participating in the society and to reproduce the dominant cultural ideology.

The process of cultural intolerance in the schools is reflected in the history of Catholic exclusion from the schools in the New Mexico territory and other areas, of cultural exclusion in the textbooks, and of school language policies in the Southwest.

School Language Policies

School officials at the state level at first tolerated Spanish in the schools, primarily out of political expediency. During the early years of American rule, political leaders enacted educational policies in the Southwest that were tolerant of language differences and accepted Spanish as an appropriate medium for conducting public affairs. For example, Texas legislators in the late 1830s tolerated Spanish and encouraged the printing of the republic's laws in that language. In California, legislators included in the 1849 constitution a provision requiring that all laws be printed both in English and Spanish. Prominent school leaders such as State Superintendent of Public Instruction John G. Marvin and San Francisco educator John Pelton also supported the teaching of Spanish and other modern languages in the public schools. Los Angeles city officials, as early as 1851, enacted a school ordinance supportive of bilingualism. It provided that "all the rudiments of the English and Spanish languages should be taught" in all the schools subsidized by public funds. In the Colorado territory, a school law of 1867 mandated the establishment of bilingual schools with at least 25 non-English-language children present.

The language policies developed during this early period of American rule were, in the words of H. Kloss in his *The Bilingual Tradition* (1977), "designed to serve certain ends of the government rather than the concerns of the minority." The use of Spanish in the conduct of local government agencies ensured their operation during a period in which many individuals lacked knowledge of English. It was in the interests of the state itself therefore to accommodate the first generation of non-English-speakers with respect to the language of public affairs. Publicly sponsored bilingualism also served to facilitate and accelerate the assimilation of culturally distinct groups.

The basis of this initial accommodation was power. Expediency-based language policies were based on the political balance of power between Anglos and Mexican Americans. Once Anglos consolidated their political control of state institutions, educational authorities began to enact subtractive school language policies (that is, policies that strengthened the use of English while weakening the use of Spanish). The primary purpose of these policies was to reproduce the dominant ideological and cultural order in the schools, not, as Arnold Leibowitz in his *Educational Policy and Political Acceptance* (1971) has argued, to deny Mexican children access to them or to their content. School language policies sought to reproduce the dominant cultural order by promoting English and simultaneously eliminating the use of Spanish in the schools. By the end of the century, nearly all the southwestern states that had at one time provided for the use of Spanish in public institutions, such as schools, had effectively converted to using English only. At the turn of the century, only New Mexico still formally recognized Spanish as a medium of communication in the schools and in other public institutions.

But within a decade after assuming political control of state institutions, educational authorities began to develop policies and practices that were subtractive. The policies strengthened the use of English by at first prescribing, then mandating it. They weakened Spanish by neglecting to use it in public life or by prohibiting its use in public and private institutions.

The establishment of subtractive policies and the shift to English in the Southwest began as early as 1841, when the Texas legislature adopted a resolution that suspended the printing of the laws in the Spanish language, and continued into the 1920s. During this period, policymakers eliminated Spanish-language use in the courts, the legislature, and the public schools and strengthened the use of English in public affairs. This is most apparent in the area of education, as school authorities enacted subtractive language policies that prescribed English as the language of instruction in education while simultaneously rejecting Spanish and other "foreign languages" in the schools. In some cases, Spanish and other non-English languages were rejected as academic subjects.

Policy decisions favoring the elimination rather than the preservation of the Spanish language in the Southwest were part of a larger national campaign against cultural and linguistic pluralism initiated at mid-century. The annexation of the Southwest in the late 1840s coincided with and probably facilitated the emergence of this campaign for conformity to American cultural and linguistic mores. This campaign deemphasized diversity of cultures and languages while it promoted the understanding of idealized American customs and the speaking of English. Strong assimilationist views motivated school leaders to seek the reduction or elimination of Spanish in public life. For the most part, Anglo officials and

laypersons viewed non-English-language use among culturally different groups as a strong indicator of their "foreignness" and their unwillingness to adopt "American" ways over time. Elimination of non-English languages from all public institutions such as the schools was a sure way of encouraging the cultural incorporation of a group perceived to be "foreign" and unAmerican. It also served to maintain the cultural hegemony of white America while the diversity of this nation was increasing significantly during the second half of the nineteenth century.

These subtractive language policies, enacted in response to political pressure from groups with varying intensities of nationalist and racialist ideologies, did not go unchallenged. Hispanics and other groups supportive of cultural diversity sought to challenge, resist, and modify them over the years. At certain historical moments, changing political and economic circumstances created conditions that led to increasing degrees of tolerance and further modifications of these types of exclusionary policies. In most cases, however, these policies were ignored by the masses of Hispanics. The majority did not attend public or private schools during the nineteenth century and thus paid no attention to them. Those enrolled in the public schools also initially ignored the English-language policies and the culturally biased textbooks. They continued to speak their language in the schools, to overlook the demeaning comments made about their heritage in the curriculum, and to participate in the governance and administration of the public schools. Over the years, however, the exclusionary and assimilationist measures were strengthened. The increasing loss of wealth, political clout, and prestige made Hispanics unable to mount an effective challenge to them.

✳ EDUCATION OF HISPANICS IN THE TWENTIETH CENTURY

In the twentieth century, Hispanic education underwent many significant transformations. In many ways it reflected the tremendous social, economic, political, and cultural changes underway in American life and both affected and was affected by these developments. Despite these changes, the patterns of Hispanic education formed in the latter part of the nineteenth century did not change significantly. The schools continued to be exclusionary, discriminatory, and assimilationist.

During this century, Hispanics continued to be educated by a variety of formal and informal institutions. Parochial, Protestant, and private secular schools provided essential knowledge, values, and skills for Hispanic achievement. Hispanics also were

Mexican fourth-graders at Drachman School (circa 1913).

"taught" by new institutions, such as radio, TV, industry, the armed forces, the federal government, and their peers. Schooling, especially public education, assumed a new importance as it became the dominant form of education for all groups, including Hispanics. Increased state support for public schooling, as well as pressures from industry and from Hispanics, made this institution the dominant form of education in the twentieth century.

As did most institutions during the twentieth century, public education changed dramatically. So did the composition, status, and ideological orientation of the Hispanic population.

Between 1900 and 1980, the goals, structure, and content of public education were transformed as a result of pressures from various sources. Education was extended to individuals from all racial, national, gender, and age groups. Governance structures were altered to benefit middle-class individuals. New innovations in educational administration, such as standardized testing, were introduced. The curriculum was diversified to meet the varied needs of the heterogeneous student population. Educational programs were standardized. Instructional methodology was revolutionized through the introduction of a

new psychology and more sophisticated learning theories. One-room schools in rural areas were consolidated into larger units for efficiency, and schools became articulated from elementary to the postsecondary grades.

The Hispanic population changed and became more diversified during the twentieth century. Between 1900 and 1980, the composition, social class status, and ideological orientation of the Hispanic population underwent dramatic transformation. The Hispanic population became more heterogeneous and included multiple groups with a range of views and experiences with education.

Between 1848 and 1940, Mexican-descent individuals were the predominant and, in some areas, the only group of Hispanics in the United States. Most of these individuals were concentrated in the Southwest. During the 1920s, Mexican-descent individuals began to migrate to other parts of the United States, especially the Midwest. During the 1940s, the United States experienced a tremendous influx of Hispanics from Puerto Rico. Beginning in 1959, the United States again experienced another tremendous influx of Hispanics. This time it was from Cuba. Beginning in the mid-1960s and spurred by political conflict and economic instability in their homelands during the 1970s, there was a tremendous influx of immigrants from Central and South American countries, such as Guatemala, Nicaragua, and Peru. Despite the tremendous growth of this group in the last three decades, Mexicans, both citizen and noncitizen, continued to be the largest and oldest residing group of Hispanics in the United States.

The Hispanic population, with the exception of Cubans, is composed of a large poor and working-class sector and a small but increasing group of middle-class individuals. As a group, Hispanics are politically powerless, economically impoverished, and socially alienated. Most of them live in highly segregated communities, tend to speak Spanish as a group, and live in dismal housing conditions. Hispanics are predominantly a cheap source of labor for American industry.

Despite their "common lot," the Hispanic population has a range of views and experiences with education that has affected their schooling in this country. Some, such as the first wave of Cuban immigrants in 1959, were middle class in status and had benefited from education in their country. They embraced all forms of education and actively sought schooling in the United States. Others, such as Mexicans and Puerto Ricans, have more diverse experiences that range from no schooling of any sort to college degrees. They, unlike the Cubans, are more ambivalent about education in general and public schools in particular. A large proportion of those who migrated from poor rural areas in Mexico have no formal school traditions and tend to be indifferent or distrustful of education in this country. Still others, including the small but growing middle class and the more stable sectors of the working class, actively seek educational opportunities and take whatever measures are needed to obtain them.

The range of views and experiences with education, as well as the diversity of Hispanic groups, posed significant challenges for public schools over the decades. They, however, did not meet these challenges. For the most part, schools and those who shaped them ignored the special needs of the heterogeneous Hispanic student population or else interpreted them in such a way that the differences brought by these children had to be eliminated. In many cases, the schools responded not to the genuine needs of this diverse group of children but to those of other stronger political and economic interests. As a result of these contextual realities, the nineteenth-century pattern of inequitable, segregated, and inferior schooling was extended and strengthened over time. Hispanic students were provided with access to schools but it was inequitable.

The schools they were provided with also were segregated and inferior, discriminating, assimilationist, and academically weak.

School Access in the Twentieth Century, 1900–1990

In the twentieth century, Hispanics were provided with increasing albeit inequitable access to the elementary, secondary, and postsecondary grades of the public schools. In the first half of the century, Mexican American school-age children gained access to public education in large part owing to the increasing availability of school facilities, their migration to urban areas, greater economic stability, and, especially, their resolve and desire to educate their young.

Increased access to public education became apparent by 1930. In 1900, for example, slightly less than 50 percent of the Hispanic scholastics, that is, school-age children between five and 17 in New Mexico were enrolled in the public schools. By 1930, Hispanic enrollment in the public schools had increased to 74 percent in New Mexico. Data from other parts of the Southwest, although incomplete, show that

A poster encouraging Hispanics to register to vote, which shows education to be a top priority.

the proportion of Hispanic children enrolled in school also increased during these 30 years. In Texas at the turn of the century, for instance, less than 18 percent of the Hispanic scholastics were enrolled in any type of school, much less public ones. By 1930, close to 50 percent of Hispanic school-age children in Texas were enrolled. In that same year, the proportion of Hispanic scholastics enrolled in public schools of California stood at 58 percent.

Access to public education stemmed from a variety of forces, including increased district ability to finance the establishment of schools, local willingness to expand educational opportunities to all levels of society, and political support for the enactment and enforcement of child-labor and school-attendance laws. Community resolve was also an important factor in increased school enrollment. Hispanics had, as did most other groups, diverse views toward education. Some Hispanics, especially those from the poorer classes and recent immigrants from Mexico, were unaware of the importance of education as an instrument of mobility. They were distrustful of the assimilationist role of public education. They were unable to send their children to school for economic reasons. But there were other Hispanic individuals and groups within the community who were supportive of education and took whatever actions they could to enroll their children in the schools. Although the majority of those in support of education came from the wealthier sector of the community, there were also working-class individuals. The number of working-class Hispanic individuals and groups who, despite their dire circumstances, made great sacrifices to educate their children increased over time. During the latter part of the nineteenth and early twentieth centuries, a larger number of them began to send their children to the public schools. An increasing stability in employment, migration to urban areas within the Southwest, and a slight increase in their ability to send their children to school encouraged these trends.

Despite the increasing access to education, a large proportion of Hispanic students continued to be out of school, largely because of poverty, mobility associated with rural employment, and discrimination on the part of educational policymakers. Three major groups of students were denied full access to public education during the first half of the twentieth century: agricultural migrants, secondary school-age students, and postsecondary school-age students. School officials excluded these children from the public schools or else took little positive action to encourage their enrollment. In the 1920s and early 1930s, for instance, local officials refused migrant and rural children admission to the elementary

grades. Although special laws were passed in areas such as California and New Mexico for the education of migrant children, no significant action was taken by public officials to ensure their enrollment. During the second quarter of the twentieth century, largely from 1925 to 1950, local officials also excluded older Hispanic students from gaining access to the secondary and postsecondary grades. Local officials refused to allow Hispanic students admission into Anglo high schools or failed to establish sufficient secondary schools for them. Higher-education officials also failed to recruit or allow Hispanics entry to postsecondary educational institutions.

After World War II, Hispanic access to the public schools increased so significantly that by the third quarter of the twentieth century this group gained parity in elementary and secondary school enrollment. Data from Texas, for instance, indicate that between 1942 and 1960 the proportion of Hispanic school-age children enrolled in public schools skyrocketed from 53 percent to 79 percent. Hispanic enrollment in the other states also became significant and ranged between 84 percent in Arizona to 91 percent in California.

Enrollment continued to increase so that by 1980 the overwhelming majority of Hispanic scholastics in the Southwest were enrolled in the elementary and secondary grades. By 1980, the proportion of Hispanic school-age children enrolled in the public schools increased to slightly over 91 percent.

Increased educational access during this period was spurred by a variety of forces, including the continued expansion and extension of public educational opportunities to all levels of society, the vigorous enforcement of child-labor and school-attendance laws, and the addition of new curricula aimed at working-class children. Added vigor in Hispanic resolve was also an important factor in increased school enrollment. The increased support by Hispanics for public education as well as their greater involvement in challenging the exclusionary and discriminatory character of public education likewise led to increased access.

Despite the increased access by Hispanics during the post-World War II period, there was still a significant proportion of these children who were not enrolled in the public schools. Two major groups of students continued to be excluded or denied full admission to the schools: noncitizens and college students. In the early 1970s, local officials, led by the state of Texas, excluded the children of undocumented workers from enrolling in public schools. Although this exclusionary practice was challenged and overturned by the courts, there were still thou-

Children at the Guadalupe Aztlán alternative school in Houston in 1981, when public school education was denied to children of undocumented workers. (Photograph by Curtis Dowell.)

sands of children, both citizens and noncitizens, who were not allowed in the schools.

As noted earlier, by the 1970s, notwithstanding lingering inequities, Hispanics had reached parity with the total school-age population in the elementary and secondary grades, but not in postsecondary school enrollment. For this reason, the central issue by the 1970s was no longer access to the elementary and secondary grades but rather access to quality educational services within the public schools and access to higher education.

The Quality of School Facilities in the Twentieth Century: Separate and Unequal

Access to public schools for Hispanic children increased over time, but owing to their subordinate status, they were provided with segregated and unequal facilities. Although segregation originated in the mid-nineteenth century, it expanded significantly between 1890 and 1980. Segregation grew in existing communities in the Southwest in the first quarter of the twentieth century and expanded to the rest of the country by mid-century. Because of the high withdrawal rates of Hispanic children from the public schools in the early decades of the twentieth century, segregation was confined to the elementary grades. But once Hispanic children began to seek access to secondary schooling, local officials established segregated facilities in these grades. The number of segregated secondary schools increased significantly after World War II. Today, Hispanics are now the largest single racial group in five of the 50 largest school districts in the country and more segregated than Afro-Americans.

Politics and prejudice were key in establishing segregated facilities, but culture and class became crucial in maintaining and extending this practice over time. State officials played an important role in the expansion of school segregation by sanctioning its presence and by funding local requests for increased Hispanic segregation. Residential segregation, demographic shifts in the population, and economic conditions likewise greatly affected the expansion of segregation in the twentieth century.

In addition to being separate, these schools were unequal in many respects to those provided for Anglo children. The facilities, for the most part, were older

A sixth-grade classroom in the Huelga School, an alternative school set up in St. Patrick's Chapel, Houston, when public education was denied children of undocumented workers. (Photograph by Curtis Dowell.)

and more dilapidated than those for Anglos. Recreation space was usually minimal and substandard in comparison to Anglo schools. The school equipment was generally less adequate for the students' needs. Per pupil expenditures in the Hispanic schools was extremely low. Finally, the staff of these schools were less appropriately trained, qualified, and experienced than those in Anglo schools. In many cases, the teachers were sent to the Mexican schools as a form of punishment or to introduce them to the teaching profession.

Discrimination in School Administration in the Twentieth Century

The third major pattern of Hispanic education was in school administration. Local officials developed administrative measures that were discriminatory toward these children. This can be seen in the evolution of assessment and placement practices and in the pattern of interaction between Hispanic students, their peers, and the teaching staff.

Hispanic children, similar to other working-class, immigrant, and racially different children, were con-

sistently diagnosed as inferior, retarded, or learning-disabled, channeled into low-track classes, and deprived of opportunities for success. Their mental, emotional, and language abilities were assessed on the basis of biased instruments and used to classify Hispanic children as intellectually inferior, culturally backward, and linguistically deprived. These assessments were shaped by class and racial biases and economic imperatives. Once classified as inferior, Hispanic children were systematically placed in "developmentally appropriate" instructional groups, classes, or curricular tracks. At the elementary level, Hispanics were assigned to mostly slow-learning or nonacademic classes. At the secondary level, administrators assigned these culturally different children to vocational or general education courses (tracks) and discouraged them from taking academic classes. Tracking of Hispanics originated in the late 1920s and expanded after World War II. The policies, procedures, and practices utilized by school administrators to assess and classify students, place them in classes, or promote them through the grades served to stratify the student population according to various catego-

A poster encouraging affirmative action and equal opportunity in education in California.

ries and to reproduce the existing relations of social and economic domination in the classroom.

The discriminatory treatment of Hispanic children was also apparent in the interaction between them, the instructional staff, and their peers. Generally speaking, local educators provided Hispanic children with schools that were staffed by instructors who were insensitive or oblivious to the cultural and special educational needs of these children. Although some of these teachers were caring instructors, the majority had low expectations of the children's learning abilities, and they discouraged, at times unwittingly, Hispanics from achieving. They also ridiculed them for their culturally distinctive traits. Many a Hispanic child was punished simply for speaking Spanish at school or in the classroom. Teachers also interacted with Anglo students more and had less praise for Hispanic children.

The peers of Hispanic students likewise mistreated and ostracized them over time. Paul Taylor quoted, in *An American Mexican Frontier: Nueces County, Texas* (1934), Mexican students in the 1920s to illustrate what he called their severe "hazing" by Anglo children: "Some Americans don't like to talk to

me," said one Hispanic youth in 1929. "I sat by one in high school auditorium and he moved away. Oh my god, it made me feel ashamed. I felt like walking out of school." Another student commented, "In grammar school they used to call us 'dirty Mexicans,' 'pelados' and greasers. A few times they moved away from me."

Curricular Policies

During the twentieth century, public officials continued to provide Hispanic children with a curriculum that was culturally partial toward Anglos and linguistically subtractive, despite minority efforts to reintroduce language and culture into the schools. Local educators also provided these children with a curriculum that was academically imbalanced.

The curriculum for Hispanic schoolchildren originally was comprised of the three Rs (reading, writing, and arithmetic) and some socialization, but in the early decades of the twentieth century it began to change. Sometime between 1880 and 1930, the Hispanic curriculum began to emphasize socialization and nonacademic concerns at the expense of academic ones. At the elementary level, it shifted its emphasis from the three Rs to the three Cs, that is, it focused more on the teaching of common cultural norms, civics instruction, and command of the English mother tongue. At the secondary grades, the emphasis was shifted to vocational and general education. Although composed of some elements of the three Rs, the curriculum for Hispanics in the secondary grades came to have larger doses of more practical instruction.

In addition to becoming academically imbalanced, the curriculum also was assimilationist. More particularly, it was linguistically and culturally intolerant. The latter was reflected in instructional materials and school textbooks, which, for the most part, either omitted or distorted the Hispanic cultural heritage. Linguistic intolerance was reflected in the English-only policies and anti-Spanish practices found in most public school systems throughout the country. Both cultural and language exclusion were opposed by Hispanics and other groups and at times challenged by them. The history of language policy in the United States illustrates this process of Hispanic challenges to assimilationism in the schools.

The curriculum for Hispanics was by the second decade of the twentieth century increasingly intolerant of diversity. It had negatively evaluated and rejected the Spanish language and the Hispanic cultural background of these children. This form of intolerance was reflected in curricular language policies and in the passage of English-only laws. English-language policies, however, were consistently questioned or challenged over the years by various groups, including Hispanics. The repeal of prescriptive laws by the Supreme Court in the 1920s, the modification of prescriptive English-only laws in the Southwest during the 1930s and 1940s, and the introduction of foreign languages into the elementary schools during the 1950s illustrate the result of these new pressures in support of language diversity in American public life. The most significant attempt to confront the ideology of assimilationism in the schools and in American life was initiated by various groups, especially Hispanics, during the period from 1965 to 1980. These groups viewed political empowerment and cultural resurgence as the key to academic and socioeconomic success. As a result of their resurgent awareness and their growing political strength, these new forces began to challenge the cultural and political hegemony of the dominant groups by promoting significant educational reforms and by supporting the reintroduction of language, culture, and community into the public schools. Specific language reforms were proposed by activists, including the elimination of the English-only laws and the enactment of federal and state legislation supporting the use of non-English languages in the conduct and operation of public institutions, especially the schools.

Hispanics and their allies were quite successful in accomplishing these goals and in promoting increased tolerance toward Spanish and other non-English languages in the schools, as well as in other aspects of government. Their efforts more particularly led to the repeal of subtractive language policies and to the enactment of more tolerant ones. Federal policies, for instance, began to recognize and urge the utilization of non-English languages in the schools. The United States Congress enacted bilingual education legislation, the Supreme Court forbade English-only instruction and sanctioned the use of native-language instruction in the schools, and the executive branch of government issued various documents supporting the use of non-English languages in educational services.

These actions served as catalysts for the increased support of bilingualism in the schools at the state and local levels. Between 1967 and 1980, for instance, more than 24 states passed some form of legislation either permitting or requiring the use of a language other than English in its public institutions, especially the public schools.

The increased use of non-English languages in the public schools led to much confusion over the goals of bilingual education and whether this program should be aimed at promoting bilingualism or English fluency. Although prominent educators and government officials argued that the ultimate goal of bilingual education was to promote bilingualism and biculturalism among schoolchildren, formal policy was geared toward the learning of English. The first piece of federal legislation, in 1968, for instance, said nothing about bilingualism. The reauthorized bills of 1974 and 1978 allowed for the use of two languages in instruction but underscored the importance of becoming proficient in English. The latter, especially, deemphasized the use of the primary language or of the minority culture in the instructional program. It also limited funding to accomplish this goal of English fluency. Even the Supreme Court decision *Lau v. Nichols,* as well as a variety of executive pronouncements, were aimed at promoting English fluency, not bilingualism.

In practice, English became the dominant language used in bilingual education programs. During the last two decades, various reports found empirical evidence of this fact. According to these reports, the vast majority of bilingual programs in the United States, usually over 80 percent of them, discouraged the use of minority children's native language and helped to facilitate language shift among them. Non-English languages then were rarely used in bilingual programs.

Manuel Pacheco, president of the University of Arizona.

Despite the dominance of English in bilingual policy and practice, even during its heyday in the 1970s, individuals and groups began to oppose the idea of non-English-language use in public life. In the 1980s, assimilationism once again, as in the 1920s, resurfaced with a vengeance, owing to, in many respects, the growing number of individuals and groups, such as the U.S. English and English First, who are opposed to pluralist and egalitarian ideologies. They have successfully led efforts to repeal bilingual policies and have enacted English-only laws. Although Hispanics continue to support bilingualism in American institutional life, the forces of assimilation have become once again dominant in today's world, including the public schools.

The Pattern of School Performance in the Twentieth Century

In the twentieth century, the major educational consequence of inferior schooling as well as unfavorable socioeconomic circumstances was the establishment of a pattern of skewed academic performance characterized by a dominant tradition of underachievement and a minor one of success.

The pattern of poor school performance has been documented over the decades by social scientists and scholars in general. The dimensions of the pattern of poor school performance can be documented by analyzing various measures, such as achievement test scores, withdrawal rates from school, and the median number of school years for the population age 25 years and older. For the most part, Hispanics have had lower test scores, higher withdrawal rates, and lower median number of school years than Anglos or the general population. Although there has been some improvement in these scores over the decades, the gap between these two groups has not changed significantly over time and continues into the contemporary period. Additionally, according to reports in 1991, the Hispanic dropout rate was significantly higher than that of other groups at 35.3 percent compared to 8.9 percent of whites and 13.6 percent of blacks.

The case of Hispanics in Texas illustrates this continuing pattern of poor school performance. In the 1920s, an overwhelming majority of Hispanics in Texas, approximately 75 percent of them, withdrew from school by the third grade. During the 1940s, half of the Hispanic student population withdrew from the public schools before reaching the secondary grades. Withdrawal rates were still abysmally high in the 1960s and 1970s, ranging anywhere from 40 percent to 80 percent, depending on local and state circumstances.

Not all Hispanic students have done poorly in school. Contrary to popular and scholarly opinion, a small proportion of them have done extremely well in achievement test scores, received a high school diploma, and continued into postsecondary education. This small group, of which we know little, experienced a pattern of school success, not academic failure. This group is composed of those individuals who completed secondary school during the interwar years, from 1917 to 1940, and of those who completed postsecondary education during the 1960s and 1970s. Considering that the overwhelming majority of Hispanic students dropped out between the third and sixth grades prior to the 1950s, completion of secondary school can be viewed as one aspect of academic achievement. The emergence of a professional and intellectual group of Hispanics likewise indicates scholastic achievement that has gone unrecorded. The existence of high school graduates in the past and college graduates in the contemporary period refutes the myth of unprecedented underachievement and suggests a more diverse pattern of school performance in the Hispanic community.

Hispanics, then, have had a checkered pattern of academic performance, not merely one of underachievement. The pattern of success should be explored further in order to better understand how these students overcame what were obviously tremendous odds.

References

Carter, Thomas P., and Roberto Segura. *Mexican Americans in the Public Schools: A History of Neglect.* Princeton, New Jersey: College Entrance Examination Board, 1979.

Castañeda, Carlos. *Our Catholic Heritage in Texas, 1519–1936.* New York: Arno Press, 1976.

Comptroller General of the United States. *Bilingual Education: An Unmet Need.* Washington, D.C.: GPO, 1978.

Crawford, James. *Bilingual Education: History, Policy, Theory and Practice.* Trenton, New Jersey: Crane Publishing, 1989.

De León, Arnoldo. *The Tejano Community.* Albuquerque: University of New Mexico Press, 1982.

"From a Dual to a Tri-partite School System." *Integrated Education,* 17, 1979: 27–38.

Gallegos, Bernardo P. *Literacy, Society and Education in New Mexico, 1693–1821.* Albuquerque: University of New Mexico Press, 1991.

Kloss, Heinz. *The Bilingual Tradition.* Rowley, Massachusetts: Newberry House, 1977.

Leibowitz, Arnold. *Education Policy and Political Acceptance.* Washington, D.C.: ERIC, 1971.

Manuel, Herschel T. *Spanish-Speaking Children of the Southwest.* Austin: University of Texas Press, 1965.

Meier, Kenneth J., and Joseph Stewart. *The Politics of Hispanic Education.* New York: Russell Sage Foundation, 1987.

Rankin, Melinda. *Twenty Years Among the Mexicans: A Narrative of Missionary Labor.* Cincinnati: Central Book Concerns, 1881.

San Miguel, Guadalupe, Jr. *Desegregation of Black and Hispanic Students from 1968 to 1980.* Washington, D.C.: Joint Center for Political Studies, 1981.

Schneider, Susan G. *Reform, Revolution, or Reaction.* New York: Las Americas Publishing Company, 1976.

Taylor, Paul S. *An American Mexican Frontier: Nueces County, Texas.* Chapel Hill: University of North Carolina Press, 1934.

Van Well, Sister Mary Stanislaus. *The Educational Aspects of the Missions of the Southwest.* Milwaukee: Marquette University Press, 1942.

Weber, David J. *The Mexican Frontier, 1821–1846: The American Southwest under Mexico.* Albuquerque: University of New Mexico Press, 1982.

Weinberg, Meyer. *A Chance to Learn.* New York: Cambridge University Press, 1977.

Williams, Jerry L., ed. *New Mexico in Maps.* Albuquerque: University of New Mexico, 1986.

Guadalupe San Miguel, Jr.

Scholarship

The biographies in this chapter are of scholars not covered in other chapters of this almanac, such as the ones on science, law and politics, and other chapters where scholars are studied or mentioned. Scholars that have become university presidents are included in the chapter on prominent Hispanics. Primarily, the scholars here have made their careers in the humanities and social sciences and have been pioneers in Hispanic studies, a field of scholarship that did not exist two decades ago. Many of them were involved in the civil rights movement of the late 1960s and were among the first scholars to research the history and culture of Hispanics in the United States. They were actively involved in creating the intellectual and structural bases for the creation of Mexican American, Puerto Rican, and Cuban studies departments and centers, as well as bilingual education programs at universities throughout the country. Many of them took as their models and mentors such early pioneer scholars as María Teresa Babín, Arthur León Campa, Carlos Castañeda, Luis Leal, Américo Paredes, and George I. Sánchez, who were among the extremely few Hispanic researches in academia during the 1940s, 1950s, and early 1960s. Today, most of them are tenured associate and full professors, continuing their efforts to broaden the curriculum so that Hispanic history and culture are not only taught but also attain their rightful place as a substantial part of the cultural identity of the United States as a whole. In addition, many of the social scientists are working toward alleviating many of the social and educational problems that continue to afflict Hispanics in American society. As a group, their research is contributing to the information about Hispanics that appears today in textbooks at every curricular level, from preschool to graduate school, and to the policies and practices of government at every level as well.

Edna Acosta-Belén (1948–)

Literature

Born on January 14, 1948, in Hormigueros, Puerto Rico, Acosta-Belén received her B.A. and M.A. degrees from the State University of New York, Albany, in 1969 and 1971, respectively, and her Ph.D. degree from Columbia University in 1977. She has been a National Endowment for the Humanities summer fellow at the University of Massachusetts (1982) and Princeton University (1978) and a visiting fellow at Yale University (1979–80). From 1972 to the present, she ascended the ranks from instructor to full professor with joint appointments in the Department of Latin American and Caribbean Studies and the Department of Women's Studies. From 1989 to the present, she has served as the director of the Center for Latin American and Caribbean Studies and, from 1983 to 1986 and again from 1988 to 1989, as chair of the Department for Latin American and Caribbean Studies. From 1987 to 1991, she was the cofounding associate director of the Institute for Research on Women. Acosta-Belén is one of the founders of the Puerto Rican Studies Association and has served as its president. She is also the recipient of numerous awards, including the New York State Chapter of the National Organization of Women's Making Waves Award (1991), the Chancellor's Award for Excellence in Teaching (1989), and the President's Award for Excellence in Teaching (1988). Her books include *In the Shadow of the Giant: Colonialism, Migration and Puerto Rican Culture* (1992), the co-edited *Integrating Latin American and Caribbean Women into the Curriculum and Research: Perspectives and Sources* (1991), *The Hispanic Experience in the United States* (1988), and *The Puerto Rican Woman: Perspectives on Culture, History and Society* (1979, 1986).

Rodolfo Acuña (1932–)

History

Born on May 18, 1932, in Los Angeles, California, Acuña received his B.A. and M.A. degrees from Los Angeles State College in 1957 and 1962, respectively, and his Ph.D. degree from the University of Southern California in 1968. He began his teaching career in 1962, at Mount St. Mary's as an instructor and has risen to the rank of full professor at California State University, Northridge. He is the founder of the Chicano studies department at Northridge and the author of the standard Chicano history textbook, *Occupied America: the Chicano's Struggle Toward Liberation* (1972, 1981, 1987). Acuña is a dynamic speaker and teacher as well as an assiduous researcher whose articles have been published far and wide.

Norma Alarcón (1948–)

Chicano Studies

Born in Mexico, Alarcón received her B.A., M.A., and Ph.D. degrees in Spanish from Indiana University in 1970, 1972, and 1983, respectively. From 1983 to 1987, she was an assistant professor at Purdue University. From 1987 to the present she has been a member of the Chicano studies department at the University of California, Berkeley. In 1991, she was promoted to associate professor with tenure. Alarcón has been an outstanding editor and promoter of Hispanic women's literature. From 1981 to the present, she has been the founding editor of Third Woman Press, and from 1975 to the present, a contributing editor of *The Americas Review*. She is the author of *La póetica feminista de Rosario Castellanos* (1992) and various articles on feminist literary theory, especially as it relates to women of color.

Fernando Alegría (1918–)

Literature

Born on September 26, 1918, in Santiago, Chile, Alegría received his early education in Chile, his M.A. degree from Bowling Green State University in 1941 and his Ph.D. degree in Spanish from the University of California, Berkeley in 1947. After receiving his doctorate, he made his entire career at Stanford University, where he ascended the ranks to full professor with a chair, and finally professor emeritus, which is his current status. Alegría has been a pioneer in the study of Hispanic American literature, in which his books have concentrated on narrative, and he has also been a novelist, essayist, and poet, recognized in both the Spanish- and English-speaking world. His book *Historia de la novela hispanoamericana* (*History of the Spanish American Novel,* 1965) has gone through various editions and served as a standard text of Latin American literature.

Noted for his important critical works on Latin American literature, his poetry, and his novels, Alegría has been living in exile since a military junta overthrew Chilean President Salvador Allende's government on September 11, 1973. *The Chilean Spring,* is Alegría's fictionalized account of a young photographer's ordeal and death at the hands of the junta. Alegría has received a Guggenheim Fellowship and has won numerous other awards and distinctions. He was also one of the first and most influential scholars to acknowledge and promote Hispanic literature of the United States in academia.

Rodolfo Alvarez (1936–)

Sociology

Born on October 23, 1936, in San Antonio, Texas, Alvarez received his B.A. degree in 1961 from San Francisco State University and his M.A. and Ph.D. degrees from the University of Washington in 1964 and 1966, respectively. He served as an assistant professor at Yale University from 1966 to 1972, after which he moved to the University of California, Los Angeles, as an associate professor; in 1980 he became a full professor. From 1972 to 1974, he served as the director of the Chicano Studies Research Center at U.C.L.A., and from 1973 to 1975 he served as the founding director of the Spanish-Speaking Mental Health Research Center. Alvarez has been active in his profession and in the community, serving on numerous boards and committees, including the board of the Mexican American Legal Defense and Education Fund (1975 to 1979), the presidency of the ACLU of Southern California (1980 to 1981), and the presidency of the Society for the Study of Social Problems (1985–86). He has served as a management fellow at the University of California since 1994, and has coedited various books, including *Racism, Elitism, Professionalism: Barriers to Community Mental Health* (1976) and *Discrimination in Organizations* (1979).

María Teresa Babín (1910–)

Literature

Born in Ponce, Puerto Rico, in 1910, Babín received her early education in Ponce, her M.A. degree from the University of Puerto Rico in 1939, and her Ph.D. degree from Columbia University in 1951. She served for many years as the director of the Spanish-language program of the Puerto Rican Department of Public Instruction and the Hispanic Studies Program at the University of Puerto Rico at Mayagüez. During the 1970s, Babín finished her career as a pioneer in Puerto Rican studies at the City College of New York, where she taught some of the first courses in Puerto Rican literature and culture. Her best-known and most important book is her pioneering history and overview of Puerto Rican culture, *Panorama de la cultura puertorriqueña* (1958). Another pioneering work by Babín is the anthology that she cowrote with Stan Steiner, *Borinquen: An Anthology of Puerto Rican Literature* (1974), which is one of only two anthologies of Puerto Rican literature in the English language and which includes works by Puerto Rican (Nuyorican) writers of the United States. Babín's other books include *Introducción a la cultura hispánica* (*Introduction to Hispanic Culture,* 1949), *El mundo poético de García Lorca* (*The Poetic World of García Lorca,* 1954), and *García Lorca: Vida y obra* (*García Lorca: His Life and Works,* 1955). Babín is also a creative writer, the author of local-color essays, *Fantasía Boricua: Estampas de mi tierra* (*Puerto Rican Fantasy: Scenes from My Land,* 1956, 1957); a play, *La hora colmada* (*The Over-Filled Hour,* 1960); and a book of poems, *Las voces de tu voz* (*The Voices of Your Voice,* 1962).

Maxine Baca-Zinn (1942–)

Sociology

Born on June 11, 1942, in Santa Fe, New Mexico, Baca-Zinn received her B.A. degree from California State College in 1966, her M.A. degree from the University of New Mexico in 1970, and her Ph.D. degree from the University of Oregon in 1978. Since 1975 to the present, Zinn has taught at the University of Michigan, Flint. In 1988–89, she served as a visiting professor in the Women's Studies Program at the University of Delaware. She is the author of numerous articles on the Hispanic family. Baca-Zinn is currently the associate editor of the *Social Science Journal* and is acknowledged as an outstanding sociology scholar.

Frank Bonilla (1927–)

Political Science

Frank Bonilla received his B.B.A. from City College of New York in 1949, his M.A. in sociology from New York University in 1954, and his Ph.D. from the Department of Social Relations, Harvard University in 1959. From 1960 to 1963, Bonilla was a member of the American Universities Field Staff on a contract to be carried out on behalf of UNESCO, investigating the relations between social development and education in Argentina, Chile, Mexico, and Brazil. In 1963, he became an associate professor of political science at Massachusetts Institute of Technology; in 1967, he was promoted to full professor. In 1969, he be-

came a professor of political science at Stanford University. In 1973, he became a full professor of political science at the City University of New York, where he served as director of the Center for Puerto Rican Studies until 1993. He retired from teaching in 1994. Bonilla is a pioneer in Puerto Rican studies and is known for helping develop some of the most important scholars in the field and for administering the leading program in the field. His awards include the 1986 Ralph C. Guzmán Award from CUNY. He is the author of numerous articles, books, and monographs, including *The Failure of Elites,* (1970) and *Industry and Idleness,* (1986). He coauthored *Labor Migration under Capitalism* (1979).

Gloria Bonilla-Santiago (1954–)

Social Work

Bonilla-Santiago received her B.A. degree in political science from Glassboro State College in New Jersey in 1976, her M.S.W. degree from Rutgers University in 1978, her M.A. degree in philosophy from the City University of New York in 1986, and her Ph.D. degree in sociology from the City University of New York in 1986. In 1991, Bonilla-Santiago became a tenured professor in the Graduate School of Social Work at Rutgers University; she is also chairperson of the Hispanic Women's Task Force of New Jersey, and director of the Hispanic Women's Leadership Institute at the Graduate School of Social Work. In 1992, she received the Warren I. Sussman Excellence in Teaching Award at Rutgers. She is the author of numerous reports, articles, book chapters, monographs, and two books: *Hispanic Women Leaders Breaking Ground and Barriers* (1993) and *Organizing Puerto Rican Migrant Farmworkers: The Experience of Puerto Ricans in New Jersey* (1988). In addition to her academic career, Bonilla-Santiago has been instrumental in passing legislation for Hispanic women in New Jersey.

Juan David Bruce-Novoa (1944–)

Literature

Born on June 20, 1944, in San José, Costa Rica, Bruce-Novoa received his Ph.D. degree from the University of Colorado in 1974. He has taught Chicano literature at Yale University, Trinity University, and, since 1990, at the University of California, Irvine, as a full professor. In 1993, Bruce-Novoa became chairman of the Department of Spanish and Portuguese at U.C.-Irvine. In that department, he has coordinated the UC-Irvine Prize for Chicano Literature and sponsored numerous Chicano and Latin American literature conferences. In 1994, Bruce-Novoa began publishing commercial fiction, with his first novel in

English, *Only the Good Times,* being offered by Arte Público Press. Bruce-Novoa is a leading scholar in literary theory as applied to Chicano literature. His books include *Chicano Authors: Inquiry by Interview* (1980), *Chicano Poetry: A Response to Chaos* (1982), and *Retrospace* (1990). Bruce-Novoa has been particularly active in developing a following among European scholars for Hispanic literature of the United States by participating in the organization of conferences in Germany, France, and Spain.

Pastora San Juan Cafferty (1940-)

Social Work

Born on July 24, 1940, in Cienfuegos, Las Villas, Cuba, Cafferty received her B.A. degree in English from St. Bernard College and her M.A. and Ph.D. degrees in American literature and cultural history from George Washington University in 1966 and 1971, respectively. Cafferty served as assistant to the secretary of the U.S. Department of Transportation and the U.S. Department of Housing and Urban Development from 1967 to 1969 and from 1969 to 1970, respectively. Since 1971, Cafferty has been a professor in the School of Social Service Administration of the University of Chicago. Included among her honors are the following: Doctor in Humane Letters, Columbia College (1987), White House Fellow (1969), Smithsonian Research Fellow (1966), Woman of the Year, Operation PUSH (1975), and Award of Achievement, U.S. Girl Scouts (1987). Cafferty has cowritten various books: *Hispanics in the USA: A New Social Agenda,* with William McCready (1985); *The Dilemma of Immigration in America: Beyond the Golden Door,* with Barry Chiswick, et al. (1983); *The Politics of Language: The Dilemma of Bilingual Education for Puerto Ricans,* with Carmen Martínez (1981); and others.

Albert Michael Camarillo (1948-)

History

Born on February 9, 1948, in Compton, California, Camarillo received his B.A. and his Ph.D. degrees from the University of California, Los Angeles, in 1970 and 1975, respectively. Camarillo has taught at Stanford University, where he has risen in rank to full professor. From 1983 to 1988, he served as the executive director of the important Inter-University Program for Latino Research. From 1980 to 1985, Camarillo served as the director of the Stanford Center for Chicano Research. In 1988, he received the Lloyd W. Dinklespiel Award for Outstanding Service to Undergraduate Education at Stanford. He is the author of *Chicanos in a Changing Society* (1979), *Chicanos in California* (1984), and various coedited books.

Albert Michael Camarillo.

Arthur León Campa (1905-1978)

Folklore, Literature

Born on February 20, 1905, in Guaymas, Sonora, Mexico, of American parents (his father was a Methodist missionary killed by Francisco Villa during the revolution), Campa was raised in El Paso, Texas. He received his B.A. and M.A. degrees from the University of New Mexico in 1928 and 1930, respectively,

Arthur León Campa.

and his Ph.D. degree in Spanish from Columbia University in 1940. From 1933 to 1942 Campa rose from instructor to full professor at the University of New Mexico. From 1942 to 1945, he served in World War II as a combat intelligence officer, suffering a back injury and winning a Bronze Star. After the war, he returned to the University of New Mexico. During the postwar years he served as a State Department lecturer in Spain (1953) and as a cultural affairs officer at the U.S. embassy in Lima, Peru. During the 1960s he served as a language training coordinator for the Peace Corps and as a director of Peace Corps Training Projects in Peru, Ecuador, and Venezuela. Included among his many fellowships are the Guggenheim and the Rockefeller. He was named to the national academies of scholars in Argentina, Brazil, Chile, Mexico, Peru, and Spain. Campa also served as the regional editor for *Western Folklore* and on various other editorial boards. He won many awards for his numerous books, most of which were pioneering collections and analyses of Hispanic folklore of the Southwest. His last, all-embracing vision is represented by his book *Hispanic Culture in the Southwest* (1978).

Antonia I. Castañeda (1942–)

History

Born into a migrant labor family in Texas in 1942, Castañeda's family moved to the state of Washington while following the crops. In 1966, she received her B.A. degree in Spanish and in education from Western Washington State University; she received her M.A. degree in Latin American studies from the University of Washington in 1970 and her Ph.D. degree in American history from Stanford University in 1990. She has been the recipient of various fellowships, including the Ford (1976), the Whiting (1980), the American Association of University Women (1981), and the University of California, San Diego, chancellor's fellowship (1990). From 1971 to the present, she has taught Chicano, Latin American, and Women's history at various universities and colleges, including the University of Washington, Stanford University, Foothills Community College, University of California, Davis, Sacramento City College, and Pomona College. In 1991, she began as an assistant professor with a joint appointment in the Departments of Women's Studies and Chicano Studies at the University of California, Santa Barbara. In 1994, Castañeda relocated to the history department of the University of Texas at Austin. She is the author of numerous research articles and papers and the coeditor of the important historical anthology *Chicano Literature: Text and Context* (1972).

Carlos Eduardo Castañeda (1896–1958)

History

Born in 1896 in Ciudad Camargo, Chihuahua, Mexico, Castañeda moved with his family to Brownsville, Texas in 1906, where he received his early education, graduating valedictorian from Brownsville High School in 1916. After high school, his scholarship studies at the University of Texas were interrupted by his service in World War I. He received his B.A. and M.A. degrees from the University of Texas in 1921 and 1923, respectively. In 1923, he was appointed associate professor at William and Mary College in Virginia. He returned to the University of Texas in 1927 as a librarian and received his Ph.D. degree in history there in 1932. Castañeda is best known for his *Our Catholic Heritage in Texas,* a six-volume history of Texas from 1519 to 1836 and a history of the Catholic church in Texas from 1836. Castañeda worked on the voluminous history book from 1936 to 1950. It was in 1939 that he joined the faculty of the history department at the University of Texas, and in 1946 he became full professor. Over the course of his career, he served at various times as editor of the *Hispanic American Historical Review, The Americas Review,* and *The Handbook of Latin American Studies.* Over all, Castañeda produced 12 books and more than 80 articles on Mexican and Southwest history. He died on April 3, 1958.

Carlos E. Cortés (1934–)

History

Born on April 6, 1934, in Oakland, California, Cortés received his B.A. degree in communications and public policy from the University of California, Berkeley, in 1956, his M.S. degree in journalism from Columbia University in 1957, his M.A. degree in Portuguese and Spanish from the University of New Mexico in 1956, and his Ph.D. degree in history from the University of New Mexico in 1969. Since 1961, Cortés has developed his teaching and research career at the University of California, Riverside; since 1968, he has been a full professor there. Cortés has lectured widely throughout the United States, Latin America, Europe, and Asia. His honors include numerous fellowships and honors, including the 1980 Distinguished California Humanist Award, conferred by the California Council for the Humanities, and the 1974 Herring Award, conferred by the Pacific Coast Council on Latin American Studies. His books include *Three Perspectives on Ethnicity: Blacks, Chicanos and Native Americans; Understanding You and Them; Gaucho Politics in Brazil* (1974); *A Filmic Approach to the Study of Historical*

Carlos E. Cortés.

Dilemmas (1976); and *Images and Realities of Four World Religions* (1986).

Rodolfo J. Cortina (1946–)

Literature

Born on February 23, 1946, in Cuba, Cortina received his B.A. degree in Spanish and economics from Texas A & I University in 1966 and his M.A. and Ph.D. degrees from Case Western Reserve University in 1968 and 1972, respectively. In 1971, he began his career as an assistant professor of Spanish at the University of Wisconsin, Milwaukee, and was promoted to associate professor in 1977. In 1986, he moved to Florida International University as an associate professor and was promoted to full professor in 1989. At the University of Wisconsin, Milwaukee, he served in various administrative positions, including chair of the Department of Spanish, director of the Spanish-Speaking Outreach Institute, and chair of the Latin American Studies Program. At Florida International University from 1985 to 1989, he was the director of the Center for Multilingual and Multicultural Studies, and from 1989 to 1995, the director of Hispanic Research Programs. In 1995, Cortina relo-

cated to the University of Houston as a full professor and director of the bibliographic subproject for Recovering the Hispanic Literary Heritage, a national research program centered at the University of Houston. Cortina is the recipient of various awards, including the Jaycees Outstanding Young Man of America (1979), the Special Award of the Governor of Wisconsin (1980), and the Five Year Service Award at Florida International University (1991). He has coedited various anthologies of scholarly articles and is the editor of *Cuban American Theater* (1992). He is the author of *El lenguaje poético de Federico García Lorca* (*The Poetic Language of Federico García Lorca,* 1985) and *Blasco Ibáñez y la novela evocativa* (*Blasco Ibánez and the Evocative Novel,* 1973).

Rodolfo de la Garza (1942–)

Political Science

Born on August 17, 1942, in Tucson, Arizona, de la Garza received his B.S. and M.A. degrees in marketing from the University of Arizona in 1964 and 1967, respectively, and his Ph.D. degree in Latin American Studies from Arizona in 1972. He also studied foreign trade and political research at the American Institute of Foreign Trade and at the University of

Rodolfo J. Cortina.

Michigan Inter-University Consortium for Political Research in 1965 and 1971. From 1974 to 1980, he served as an assistant dean and, from 1978 to 1980, as director of the Southwest Studies Program at Colorado College. From 1981 to 1985 and again in 1987, he served as the director of the Center for Mexican American Studies at the University of Texas. Since 1983, he has been the codirector of the Inter-University Project of the Ford Foundation at the University of Texas, where he is a full professor. Among his many awards are the following: (University of Texas) Dean's Award for Outstanding Classroom Performance, 1987–88; University of Colorado Outstanding Faculty Award, 1980; Western Political Science Association Best Paper on Chicano Politics, 1979. De la Garza has also been a productive researcher and author on Hispanic political topics and has served on the editorial boards of the *Western Political Science Quarterly,* the *Social Science Quarterly,* the *Journal of Politics,* and the *Hispanic Journal of Behavioral Science.* He is the editor of two books: *The Mexican American Experience: An Interdisciplinary Anthology* (1985) and *Ignored Voices: Latinos and Public Opinion Poles in the United States* (1986). Since 1988, De la Garza has directed the National Latino Political National Survey.

Jorge I. Domínguez (1945–)

Government

Born on June 2, 1945, in Havana, Cuba, Domínguez received his B.A. degree from Yale University in 1967, and his M.A. and Ph.D. degrees from Harvard University in 1968 and 1972, respectively. From 1972 on, Domínguez developed his teaching career at Harvard University, becoming a full professor in 1979; in 1993, he became the Frank G. Thomson professor of government, and chair of the Latin American and Iberian studies department. Domínguez is a member of the editorial boards of *Political Science Quarterly, Mexican Studies, Journal of Inter-American Studies and World Affairs,* and *Cuban Studies,* for which he has served as coeditor since 1990. Domínguez's books include *To Make a World Safe for Revolution* (1989), *U.S. Interests in the Caribbean and in Central America* (1982), *Cuba: Internal and International Affairs* (1982), and *Insurrection or Loyalty: The Breakdown of the Spanish American Empire* (1980).

José B. Fernández (1948–)

History, Literature

Born on August 20, 1948, in Sagua la Grande, Cuba, Fernández received his B.A., M.A., and Ph.D. degrees in Spanish and history from Florida State

University in Tallahassee in 1970, 1971, and 1973, respectively. From 1973 to 1976, he served as an assistant professor and, from 1976 to 1979, as associate professor at the University of Colorado at Colorado Springs, where he also served as chairman of the Department of Foreign Languages. From 1981 to the present, he has been a professor of history and foreign languages at the University of Central Florida in Orlando. Fernández has been a Fulbright Lecturer in Argentina (1984) and has received various other awards, including the University of Colorado (Colorado Springs) Outstanding Teaching Award (1977) and the Chancellor's Award (1979). Fernández is the author of numerous articles and books, including *Alvar Núñez Cabeza de Vaca: The Forgotten Chronicler* (1975), *Indice bibliográfico de autores cubanos* (*Bibliographic Index of Cuban Authors,* 1983), and (with Nasario García) *Nuevos Horizontes: Cuentos chicanos, puertorriqueños y cubanos* (*New Horizons: Chicano, Puerto Rican and Cuban Stories,* 1982).

Margarita Fernández Olmos (1949–)

Literature

Born in 1949 in New York City, Fernández Olmos received her B.A. degree from Montclair State Col-

Margarita Fernández Olmos.

lege in New Jersey in 1970 and her M.A. and Ph.D. degrees in Spanish from New York University in 1972 and 1979, respectively. Following her graduate studies, Fernández Olmos was able to develop her career at Brooklyn College of the City University of New York, where she rose to he present rank of full professor. Fernández Olmos has written extensively on Latin American and U.S. Hispanic literature, with a special interest in women's literature. Her books include *La cuéntistica de Juan Bosch* (*The Short Story Art of Juan Bosch*, 1982), *Sobre la literatura puertorriqueña de aquí y de allá: aproximaciones feministas* (*On Puerto Rican Literature from the Mainland and the Island: Feminist Approaches*, 1989), and two coedited anthologies of Latin American women's literature: (with Doris Meyer) *Contemporary Women Authors of Latin America: New Translations and Introductory Essays* (1983) and (with Lizabeth Paravisini-Gebert) *El placer de la palabra: literatura erótica femenina de América Latina* (*The Pleasure of the Word: Erotic Women's Literature of Latin America*, 1991).

Juan Flores

Literature, Sociology

Born in New York City, Flores received his B.A. degree in German from Queens College in 1964 and his M.A. and Ph.D. degrees in German from Yale University in 1966 and 1968, respectively. He began his career as an assistant professor of German at Stanford University in 1968, but in 1975 redirected his career toward Puerto Rican studies when he became the research director and consultant for the Center for Puerto Rican Studies at Hunter College, CUNY. From 1981 to 1989, he worked as an associate professor in the Department of Sociology of Queens College, CUNY; from 1990 to the present, he has been a member of the graduate faculty in the sociology program of the Graduate Center of CUNY. In 1994, Flores became the director of the Center for Puerto Rican Studies of the City University of New York. Flores is a distinguished researcher whose books have won important awards. His *Insularismo e ideología burguesa: Nueva lectura de Antonio S. Pedreira* (*Insularism and Bourgeois Ideology: A New Reading of Antonio S. Pedreira*, 1980) won the prestigious international Casa de las Americas prize. His other books include *Divided Borders: Essays on Puerto Rican Identity* (1992) and (with Jean Franco and George Yúdice) *On Edge: The Crisis in Contemporary Latin American Culture* (1992). His introduction and edition of Jesús Colón's *A Puerto Rican in New York* (1984) won the American Book Award.

Juan Gómez-Quiñones (1940–)

History

Born in 1940 in Parral, Chihuahua, Mexico, Gómez immigrated to the United States with his family as a young child and became a naturalized citizen. He received his B.A. degree in English, his M.A. degree in Latin American Studies, and his Ph.D. degree in history from the University of California, Los Angeles in 1962, 1974, and 1972, respectively. He is a full professor of history at the University of California, Los Angeles, where he has developed his entire career and served for many years as the director of the Chicano Research Center. He is a cofounder/codirector of the Mexican American Legal Defense and Education Fund and is a board member of the Los Angeles Urban Coalition. He is the author of numerous articles and books, including *Sembradores: Ricardo Flores Magón y El Partido Liberal: A Eulogy and a Critique* (1973), *Roots of Chicano Politics, 1600–1940* and *Chicano Politics: Reality and Promise, 1940–1990* (1995).

Deena J. González (1952–)

History

See Chapter 10.

Erlinda González-Berry (1942–)

Literature

The native New Mexican, born in 1942, received her B.A., M.A., and Ph.D. degrees from the University of New Mexico in 1964, 1971, and 1978, respectively. In 1974, she began as an assistant professor in Earlham College in Indiana, moved to New Mexico State University in 1978, and then to the University of New Mexico in 1979, where she has risen in rank to her present full professorship. González-Berry is an outstanding teacher and researcher. In 1984, she received the University of New Mexico President's Award as Outstanding Teacher of the Year and, in 1991, the Outstanding Teacher of the Year Award from the "Hispanics at UNM." González has published numerous articles on Chicano literature and is the editor of two books: *Pasó por Aquí: Four Centuries of New Mexican Hispanic Literature* (1989) and (with Tey Diana Rebolledo and Teresa Márquez) *Las mujeres hablan: An Anthology of Nuevomexicana Writings* (1988).

Richard A. Griswold del Castillo (1942–)

History

Born on October 26, 1942, in Los Angeles, California, Griswold received his B.A., M.A., and Ph.D. degrees from the University of California, Los Angeles, in 1968, 1969, and 1974, respectively. From 1974 to the present, he has taught at San Diego State University, where he is currently a full professor and chair of the Mexican American Studies. From 1985 through 1988, he was the recipient of the San Diego State Outstanding Faculty Award. Among his many publications are the following books: *The Treaty of Guadalupe Hidalgo* (1990), *La Familia Chicana: Chicano Families in the Urban Southwest, 1848 to the Present* (1984), and *The Los Angeles Barrio, 1850–1890: A Social History* (1980).

Ramón Gutiérrez (1951–)

History

Born on April 19, 1951, in Albuquerque, New Mexico, Gutiérrez obtained his B.A. degree from the University of New Mexico in 1973 and his M.A. and Ph.D. degrees from the University of Wisconsin in 1976 and 1980, respectively. Beginning in 1980, he served as an assistant professor at Pomona College; since 1982, he has taught at the University of California, San Diego, becoming a professor in 1988. His honors include a prestigious MacArthur Fellowship, 1983–88, as well as the Best Book Award for 1991

Erlinda González-Berry.

from the American Historical Association, Pacific Coast Branch, the Best Article Award from the AHA Conference on Latin American History in 1986, and the Hubert Herring Prize for the Best Dissertation in Latin American Studies in 1981. In 1994, President Clinton appointed Gutiérrez to the National Council on the Humanities. He has won numerous fellowships, including the Fulbright, Danforth, and National Defense Education Act. Gutiérrez is the author of numerous ground-breaking articles in Latin American and Chicano history and a book, *When Jesus Came the Corn Mothers Went Away: Marriage, Sexuality and Power in New Mexico, 1500–1846.*

José Hernández (1935–)

Puerto Rican Studies

Born on August 22, 1935, in Jersey City, New Jersey of Puerto Rican parents, José Hernández is one of the first Puerto Ricans to develop a career as a professor of Sociology in the United States. He received his B.A. and M.A. degrees from Fordham University in 1958 and 1960, respectively, and went on toe earn his Ph.D. at the University of Minnesota in 1966. After an initial position of assistant professor at the university of Arizona from 1970 to 1974, he served as the research director for the United States Civil Rights Commission for two years. Thereafter, he was an associate professor at the University of Wisconsin until 1983. He is currently a full professor in the Department of Black and Puerto Rican Studies at Hunter College in New York. His published research includes *Latinos in Metropolitan Chicago* (1983), *Hispanics in Higher Education: New Jersey* (1986) and numerous published articles and reports. From 1975 to 1980, Hernández served as the chair of the Spanish Origin Advisory Committee to the U.S. Census.

José Manuel Hernández (1925–)

History

Born on February 18, 1925, in Cuba, Hernández received his law degree from the University of Havana in 1947 and his M.A. and Ph.D. degrees in history from Georgetown University in 1969 and 1976, respectively. From 1973 to 1980, he served as assistant dean of the School of Languages and Linguistics at Georgetown University, and since 1980, as associate dean. From 1984 to 1987, he served as the director of the Latin American Studies Program at Georgetown. Included in his many honors is the Georgetown University Vicennial Medal. His published scholarship includes the book *ACU, los primeros cincuenta años* (*ACU, the First Fifty Years,* 1981).

María Herrera-Sobek

Literature

Born in Mexico, Herrera-Sobek received her B.A. degree in chemistry from California State University, Northridge, in 1974, her M.A. degree in Latin American studies from the University of California, Irvine, and her Ph.D. degree from the University of California, Los Angeles, in 1975. From 1975 to the present, she has developed her entire career at the University of California, Irvine, rising in rank from assistant to full professor as of 1987. Included among her honors are the Orange County Book of the Year Award (1980), the Hispanic Woman of the Year Award from the League of United Latin American Citizens, Orange County (1981), and the Educator of the Year Award given by the Mexican American Educators Association, Orange County chapter (1990). Herrera-Sobek has published numerous articles, edited various anthologies, and written the following books: *The Bracero Experience: Elitelore versus Folklore* (1979), *The Mexican Corrido: A Feminist Analysis* (1990), and *Northward Bound: The Mexican Immigrant Experience in Corridos and Canciones* (1993).

Olga Jiménez-Wagenheim.

Olga Jiménez-Wagenheim (1941–)

History

Born in Camuy, Puerto Rico, on September 24, 1941, Jiménez received her B.A. degree from the Inter-American University in Puerto Rico in 1970, her M.A. degree from the State University of New York at Buffalo in 1971, and her Ph.D. degree from Rutgers University in 1981. After achieving the Ph.D. degree, she has developed her university career at Rutgers University, where she has served as an associate professor since 1986. Her honors include the Hispanic Association for Higher Education Scholarly Achievement Award (1989), the Hispanic Women's Task Force of New Jersey Award (1988), and the Outstanding Teacher of the Year Award (1991) at Rutgers University-Newark. Jiménez's books include *Puerto Rico's Revolt for Independence: El Grito de Lares* (1985), *El grito de Lares: Sus causas y sus hombres* (*The Shout of Lares: Its Causes and Its Men,* 1984) and her coedited *The Puerto Ricans: A Documentary History* (1973).

Luis Leal (1907–)

Literature

Born on September 17, 1907, in Linares, Mexico, Leal received his B.A. degree from Northwestern University in 1940 and his A.M. and Ph.D. degrees from the University of Chicago in 1941 and 1951. Leal is one of the most productive, most respected, and most honored scholars of Latin American and Chicano literature, a true pioneer in both disciplines. In his long career, he has taught at the University of Chicago, the University of Mississippi, Emory University, the University of Illinois, where he has been professor emeritus since 1976, and the University of California, Santa Barbara, where he has served as a visiting professor and acting director of Chicano studies since 1980. He is the author of some 16 books, including his important *El cuento hispanoamericano* (*The Spanish American Short Story,* 1967) and his *Breve historia de la literatura hispanoamericana* (*Brief History of Spanish American Literature,* 1971). He has also edited some 21 anthologies and other books, besides publishing scores of articles. In 1978, a conference was held and a book published in his praise: *Homenaje a Luis Leal* (*Homage to Luis Leal*), edited by Donald W. Bleznick and Juan O. Valencia.

Francisco A. Lomelí (1947–)

Literature

Born on April 13, 1947, in Sombrerete, Zacatecas, Mexico, Lomelí received his B.A. and M.A. degrees from San Diego State University in 1971 and 1974,

Luis Leal.

respectively, and his Ph.D. degree from the University of New Mexico in 1978. Since 1978, he has ascended the ranks at the University of California, Santa Barbara, where he became a full professor in 1989. Lomelí has won numerous fellowships, including the Rotary International (1983), Fulbright (1969), Ford (1974), and Rockefeller (1989). He is the author of numerous articles of literary criticism and the editor of various reference works: *Dictionary of Literary Biography: Chicano Writers* (1989), *Chicano Literature: A Reference Guide* (1985), and *Aztlán: Essays on the Chicano Homeland* (1989). Lomelí also serves on the editorial board of various journals, including *The Americas Review, The Bilingual Review, Discurso Literario,* and *The Latino Studies Journal.*

Roberto Márquez (1942–)

Latin American Studies

Born on July 14, 1942, in New York City, Márquez received his B.A. in comparative literature from Brandeis University in 1964, and his M.A. and Ph.D. degrees in romance languages and literatures from Harvard University in 1970 and 1975, respectively.

From 1970 to 1986, he taught at Hampshire College in Hispanic American and Caribbean literatures, where in 1983 he was named the first incumbent of the Harold F. Johnson Professorial Chair. From 1986 to 1989, he was the Robinson Professor at George Mason University and, from 1989 to the present, the William F. Kenan Professor of Latin American studies at Mount Holyoke College. Márquez is the author of numerous articles, anthologies of Latin American poetry, which he also translates, and the book, *The Third World: The Dialectic of Culture* (1978). He is also the founder and editor of *Caliban: A Journal of New World Thought and Writing* (1975–1982).

Oscar Martínez (1943–)

History

Born in Mexico on March 4, 1943, Martínez received his B.A. degree from California State University in Los Angeles in 1969, his M.A. degree from Stanford in 1970, and his Ph.D. degree from the University of California, Los Angeles, in 1975. From 1975 to 1988, he ascended the ranks from assistant to full professor at the University of Texas at El Paso. From 1975 to 1988, he served as the director of the Institute for Oral History at U.T.E.P. In 1988, he became a full professor at the University of Arizona. He has served as president of the Association of Borderland Scholars and is a member of various editorial boards, including the *Journal of Borderland Studies,* the *Latin American Research Review,* and the *Journal of the Southwest.* He has won two book awards, 1978 and 1988, from the Border Region Library Association. His books include *Border Boom Town* (1978), *Fragments of the Mexican Revolution* (1983), *Across Boundaries* (1986), and *Troublesome Border* (1988).

Alfredo Matilla (1937–)

Puerto Rican Studies

Born in Valencia, Spain, on July 31, 1937, Matilla was raised in Puerto Rico. He received his B.A. from the University of Puerto Rico in 1959, his M.A. and Ph.D. from New York University in 1961 and 1967, respectively. From 1965 to 1968, he served as an assistant professor of Spanish at Goucher College; in 1968 he moved to Rutgers University as an associate professor, and then in 1980 to Brooklyn College. Since 1982, he has taught at the State University of New York, Buffalo, and was named full professor of Puerto Rican studies/American studies in 1988. Matilla is the author of various books and articles primarily on Puerto Rican and Nuyorican literature. With Iván Silén, he edited a ground-breaking anthology in bilingual format, *The Puerto Rican Poets/Los poetas puertorriquenos,* 1972. He is also a respected poet, author of *Catálogo de locos (Catalog of Insane People,* 1977), and translations.

Carmelo Mesa-Lago (1934–)

Economics

Born on August 11, 1934, in Havana, Cuba, Mesa-Lago received his LL.M. degree in civil law from the University of Havana in 1965, his LL.D. degree from the University of Madrid in 1958, his M.A. degree in economics from the University of Miami in 1965, and his Ph.D. degree in labor economics from Cornell University in 1968. From 1967 on, Mesa-Lago developed his career at the University of Pittsburgh, beginning as an assistant professor in economics and rising to the rank of full professor in 1980. During his tenure there, he also served as the director of the Center for Latin American Studies (1974 to 1986). He has lectured and taught in Europe and Latin America as well and has held prestigious fellowships, including the Ford, Rockefeller, and Tinker. Mesa-Lago has also served as the president of the Latin American Studies Association (1980) and as regional advisor for the United Nations on Social Security and Development (1983–84). Included among his many honors is the Alexander von Humbolt Senior Research Award on Social Security (1990–92), the Bicentennial Medallion of the University of Pittsburgh (1987), and the Hoover Institution Prize for Best Article on Latin America (1986). Included among his many books are *Cuba after the Cold War* (1993), *Health Care for the Poor in Latin America and the Caribbean: Problems, Cases and Solutions* (1992), *Social Security and Prospects for Equity in Latin America* (1991), and *Portfolio Performance of Selected Social Security Institutes in Latin America* (1991), to name just some of the most recent.

Raúl Moncarraz

Economics

Born in Cuba, Moncarraz received his B.S. degree in business administration from Florida Atlantic University in 1965 and his M.B.A. and Ph.D. degrees in economics from Florida State University in 1966 and 1969, respectively. From 1969 to 1972, he rose from an assistant professorship to associate professor at Louisiana State University. From 1972 to the present, he has taught at Florida International University, where he became a full professor and chairman of the Department of Economics in 1988. Among his many honors is a Gold Medal from the Consulate of Venezuela in Miami (1984) and various scholarships and fellowships. Moncarraz is the author of numerous publications on development issues in Central America and the Caribbean and on labor market issues.

Sonia Nieto (1943–)

Children's Literature

Nieto received her B.S. degree in Education from St. John's University in 1965, her M.A. degree in Spanish from New York University in 1966, and her Ed.D. degree in curriculum with minors in bilingual and multicultural education from the University of Massachusetts, Amherst, in 1979. From 1972 to 1975, Nieto was and instructor and deputy chairperson of the Department of Puerto Rican Studies, Brooklyn College; from 1979 to 1980, the LAU Coordinator for the Massachusetts Department of Education; and in 1980, she began her career at the University of Massachusetts, rising to her present rank of associate professor and program director of Cultural Diversity and Curriculum Reform in 1988. Nieto received the Human and Civil Rights Award from the Massachusetts Teachers Association in 1988 and the Outstanding Accomplishment in Higher Education Award from the Hispanic Caucus of the American Association of Higher Education in

Raúl Moncarraz.

Sonia Nieto.

1991. Nieto is an expert on Hispanic and culturally diverse children's literature, which is reflected in her many articles, book chapters, lectures, and papers. She is the author of *Affirming Diversity: The Sociopolitical Context of Multicultural Education* (1992) and coauthor (with Roberto Márquez) of *Puerto Rican Literature and Society: A Curriculum for the Secondary School* (1986).

Julián Olivares (1940-)

Literature

Born on December 6, 1940, in San Antonio, Texas, Olivares received his B.A. degree from California State University at Los Angeles in 1968 and his M.A. and Ph.D. degrees from the University of Texas in 1974 and 1977, respectively. He served as an assistant professor at Bridgewater State College from 1978 to 1981, when he relocated to the University of Houston, becoming professor of Spanish in 1993. In 1994, Olivares became the chair of the Department of Modern and Classical Languages at the University of Houston, where he also served from 1981 to 1994 as the editor of the prestigious *The Americas Review* and senior editor of Arte Público Press. Ol-

ivares is a respected scholar in two fields: Golden Age Spanish literature and Chicano literature. He has won numerous fellowships, including the Ford (1975), National Endowment for the Humanities (1984), and National Research Council/Ford (1985). As editor of *The Americas Review,* he has won two unprecedented Citations of Achievement from the Council of Literary Magazines and Presses. His books include *Tras el espejo la musa escribe: Lírica femenina del Siglo de Oro* (Behind the Looking Glass the Muse Writes: Women's Lyrics of the Golden Age, 1992) and *The Love Poetry of Francisco de Quevedo* (1983). His edited books include *Hispanic Short Fiction* (1992), *International Studies in Honor of Tomás Rivera* (1985), and all of the works of Tomás Rivera (in four separate volumes).

Vilma Ortiz (1954-)

Social Psychology

Ortiz received her B.A. degree in psychology from the City College of New York in 1976 and her M.A. and Ph.D. degrees in social psychology from New York University in 1979 and 1981, respectively. From 1981 to 1985, she has had three postdoctoral fellowships at Fordham University, the University of Michigan, and

Julián Olivares.

the University of Wisconsin, respectively. From 1985 to 1987, she served as a visiting scholar at the Educational Testing Service in Princeton, New Jersey. She began her teaching career in 1988 as an assistant professor in the Department of Sociology, University of California, Los Angeles, where she has been an associate professor since 1990. Since 1990, Ortiz has been the director of the Interdepartmental Program in Chicana and Chicano Studies at U.C.L.A. Ortiz's specialties are urban poverty and social welfare policy, race and ethnicity, Puerto Rican migration, and Hispanic women, among other research interests that form the bases of her numerous articles and book chapters.

Harry Pachón (1945-)

Political Science

Born on June 4, 1945, in Miami, Florida, Pachón received his B.A. and his M.A. degrees from California State University in Los Angeles in 1967 and 1968, respectively, and his Ph.D. degree from the Claremont Graduate School in 1973. He served as an assistant professor at Michigan State University from 1974 to 1976 and as an administrative assistant at the United States House of Representatives from 1977 to 1981. From 1981 to 1986, he was an associate professor at the City University of New York, and since 1986, the Kenan Professor of Political Science at Pitzer College. Pachón is a founding board member of the National Association of Latino Elected and Appointed Officials (since 1981), and since 1983 he has served as its national director. Pachón has been a fellow of the National Endowment for the Humanities and has published research articles and two books: *Hispanics in the U.S.* (1985) and *Mexican Americans* (1975).

Amado Manuel Padilla (1942-)

Psychology

Born on October 14, 1942, in Albuquerque, New Mexico, Padilla received his B.A. degree in 1964 from New Mexico Highlands University, his M.S. degree in 1966 from Oklahoma State University, and his Ph.D. degree in 1969 from the University of New Mexico. He was an assistant professor at the State University of New York from 1967 to 1971 and at the University of California, Santa Barbara, from 1971 to 1974. He moved to the University of California, Los Angeles, in 1974, where he rose to the rank of full professor. From 1988 to the present, he has been a full professor at Stanford University. Padilla has been a Fulbright Scholar and is the recipient of the American Educational Research Association Distinguished Scholar Award (1987). His books include

Crossing Cultures in Therapy (1980), *Chicano Ethnicity* (1987), *Foreign Language Education: Issues and Strategies* (1990), and *Bilingual Education: Issues and Strategies* (1990).

Américo Paredes (1915-)

Folklore

Born on September 3, 1915, in Brownsville, Texas, Paredes received his B.A., M.A., and Ph.D. degrees from the University of Texas in 1951, 1953, and 1956, respectively. After working at a variety of jobs, including journalist, and serving in the armed forces, Paredes received an advanced education later in life and became one of the most distinguished Hispanic scholars in U.S. history. Paredes has taught at the University of Texas from 1951 on and is currently professor emeritus of English and anthropology there. He has been instrumental in the development of the field of folklore in academia as well as in the field of Mexican American studies. He has served as president of the American Folklore Society and been recognized for his leadership internationally. In the United States, he was awarded one of the nation's highest awards for a humanist, the Charles Frankel Prize given by the National Endowment for the Arts (1989), and in Mexico, the highest award given a foreigner by the Mexican government, the Aguila Azteca (the Aztec Eagle) medal (1991). Besides publishing numerous research articles, he is the author of *With a Pistol in His Hand: A Border Ballad and Its Hero* (1958), *Folktales of Mexico* (1970), *A Texas Mexican Cancionero* (1976), *Uncle Remus con chile* (title means "Uncle Remus with Chile," 1992), *Folklore and Culture on the Tex-Mex Border* (1993), and *The Hammon and the Beans and Other Stories* (1994). He is also the author of a novel, *George Washington Gomez* (1990) and a book of poems, *Between Two Worlds* (1991).

Gustavo Pérez-Firmat (1949-)

Literature

Born on March 7, 1949, in Havana, Cuba, Pérez-Firmat received his B.A. degree in English and M.A. degree in Spanish from the University of Miami in 1972 and 1973, respectively. He received his Ph.D. degree in comparative literature from the University of Michigan in 1979. Since 1979, he has developed his career at Duke University, where he has risen in rank from assistant to full professor in Spanish and in the Graduate Literature Program. Pérez-Firmat has created a dual career as a literary historian and critic and as a creative writer. His academic books include *Idle Fictions: The Hispanic Vanguard Novel, 1926–1934* (1982), *Literature and Liminality: Fes-*

tive *Readings in the Hispanic Tradition* (1986), *The Cuban Condition: Translation and Identity in Modern Cuban Literature* (1989), and *Life on the Hyphen: The Cuban American Way* (1994). His creative books include two collections of his poems: *Triple Crown: Chicano, Puerto Rican and Cuban American Poetry* (1987) and *Equivocaciones* (*Mistakes*, 1989). He is also the author of numerous articles and poems for journals and magazines.

Guadalupe C. Quintanilla (1937–)

Language

See Chapter 27.

Tey Diana Rebolledo (1937–)

Literature

See Chapter 10.

Eliana Rivero (1940–)

Literature

Born in Cuba in 1940, Rivero immigrated to the United States in 1961. She received her Ph.D. degree in Spanish from the University of Miami in 1968, and from that time on has developed her career at the University of Arizona, where she is currently a full professor in the Spanish department. Her specialties are Latin American and U.S. Hispanic literatures and women's literature and feminist criticism. Rivero is the author of *El gran amor de Pablo Neruda: estudio crítico de su poesía* (*The Great Love of Pablo Neruda: A Critical Study of His Poetry,* 1971), *Cuban American Women Writers: Breaking Boundaries,* (1989), *Isabel Allende's Storytelling: Splintering Darkness,* (1990), and numerous articles. She is also the coeditor (with Tey Diana Rebolledo) of *Infinite Divisions: An Anthology of Chicana Literature* (1993). Rivero is also a respected poet whose books include *De cal y arena* (*Of Lime and Sand,* 1975) and *Cuerpos breves* (*Brief Bodies,* 1977).

Sergio G. Roca

Economics

Born in Cuba, Roca received his B.A. degree in economics from Drew University in 1965 and his Ph.D. degree from Rutgers University in 1975. From 1971 to the present, he has developed his career at Adelphi University; he has been a full professor there since 1984. In 1988, he received the Adelphi University Merit Award for Scholarship. He is the author of numerous articles and two books: *Socialist Cuba: Past Interpretations and Future Challenges* (1988) and *Cuban Economic Policy and Ideology: The Ten Million Ton Sugar Harvest* (1976).

Clara Rodríguez (1944–)

Sociology

Born on March 29, 1944, Rodríguez received her B.A. degree in sociology from the City College of New York in 1965, her M.A. degree in Latin American studies from Cornell University in 1969, and her Ph.D. degree in sociology and urban and regional studies from Washington University in St. Louis in 1973. From 1974 to 1976, Rodríguez served as chair of the Department of Puerto Rican Studies at Lehman College, CUNY; beginning in 1976, she was dean of general studies at Fordham University, after which she took leaves of absence and visiting fellowships at the Massachusetts Institute of Technology and Yale University. From 1981 to the present, she has been a full professor at Fordham University. Rodríguez has presented numerous lectures and papers and published many articles on the sociology of race, ethnicity, and gender, especially as such subjects relate to Puerto Ricans. Her books include *Puerto Ricans: Born in the USA* (1989, 1991), *The Ethnic Queue in the United States: The Case of Puerto Ricans* (1974), and two coedited books: (with Virginia Sánchez Korrol and Oscar Alers) *The Puerto Rican Struggle: Essays on Survival in the U.S.* (1979) and (with Edwin Meléndez and Janice Barry-Figueroa) *Hispanics in the Labor Force: Issues and Policies* (1991).

Ricardo Romo (1943–)

History

Born on June 23, 1943, in San Antonio, Texas, Romo received his B.A. degree from the University of Texas in 1967, his M.A. degree from Loyola University of Los Angeles in 1970, and his Ph.D. degree from the University of California, Los Angeles, in 1975. From 1974 to 1980, he was an assistant professor at the University of California, San Diego, and from 1980 to the present, a full professor at the University of Texas at Austin. Since 1988, he has also been the director of the Tomás Rivera Center, a research institute in San Antonio. He has been a member of the board of editors of *Social Science Quarterly* since 1982 and has been the managing editor of the Mexican American Monograph Series at the University of Texas since 1981. Romo has received various fellowships during his career and he is the author of *East Los Angeles: A History of a Barrio* (1983) and coeditor of *The Mexican American Experience: An Interdisciplinary Anthology* (1985) and *New Directions in Chicano Scholarship* (1978).

Ricardo Romo.

Ramón Eduardo Ruiz

History, Literature

Ruiz received his Ph.D. degree in history from the University of California, Berkeley, in 1954. He began his career as an assistant professor at the University of Oregon in 1956–57 and Southern Methodist University in 1957–58. He moved to Smith College in 1958 as an assistant professor and was promoted to associate professor in 1961 and to full professor of Latin American History in 1963. Since 1970, he has been a full professor at the University of California, San Diego. Among his many awards are the 1981 Hubert C. Herring Prize from the Pacific Coast Council on Latin American Studies for his *The Great Rebellion, Mexico, 1905–1924* (1980) and various fellowships, including the Fulbright. Included among his 13 books are *Triumphs and Tragedy: A History of the Mexican People* (1991), *The People of Sonora and Yankee Capitalists* (1988), and *Labor and Ambivalent Revolutionaries: Mexico, 1905–1924* (1976).

Vicki L. Ruiz (1955–)

History

See Chapter 10.

Julián Samora (1920–)

Sociology

Born on March 1, 1920, in Pagosa Springs, Colorado, Samora received his B.A. degree from Adams State College in 1942, his M.S. degree from Colorado State University in 1974, and his Ph.D. degree from Washington University in 1953. From 1955 to 1957, he was an assistant professor at the University of Colorado Medical School, associate professor at Michigan State University from 1957 to 1959, and a full professor at the University of Notre Dame from 1959 to 1985, when he became professor emeritus. Samora is one of the pioneer Hispanic sociologists and has trained a whole generation of important sociologists whose ranks include the noted Mexican sociologist Jorge Bustamante. Among his many awards is the White House Hispanic Heritage Award (1985) and the Mexican government's highest award given to a foreigner, the Aguila Azteca (Aztec Eagle) medal (1991). Included among his books are *A History of the Mexican-American People* (1977) and *Gunpowder Justice: A Reassessment of the Texas Rangers* (1979). In 1991, a research center at the Michigan State University was named in his honor.

Ramón Eduardo Ruiz.

George I. Sánchez (1906–1972)
Educational Administration

Born on October 4, 1906, in Albuquerque, New Mexico, to parents with long histories in the territory, Sánchez became a teacher while he was still a student at the University of New Mexico, which he attended only during the summer months. He graduated from the University of New Mexico in 1930 with a B.A. degree in Spanish. After that he received an M.S. degree in educational psychology at the University of Texas and then his Ed.D. in educational administration from the University of California, Berkeley, in 1934. During the next 35 years Sánchez became the foremost expert on the education of Hispanic children and a tireless and effective civil rights leader on their behalf. He also became an expert on Latin American education and a pioneer in bilingual, bicultural education. Since the early 1990s, Sánchez conducted research into Hispanic literary history, and, with Beatriz Pita, has prepared critical editions of two works by nineteenth-century California novelist María Amparo Ruiz de Burton: *The Squatter and the Don* (1992) and *Who Would Have Thought It?* (1994). Sánchez is also the editor of the journal *Crítica*, through which she has also published recovered nineteenth-century texts. Among his many writings are *Mexico: A Revolution by Education* (1936) and *Forgotten People* (1940), the latter a work that documents the educational neglect of Mexican American children in New Mexico during the 1930s. After working in the state of New Mexico educational administration, Sánchez joined the faculty of the University of Texas in 1940, and in 1941, became the president of the League of United Latin American Citizens. From then on, he used LULAC as a forum to struggle against the practices that were inhibiting the civil and educational rights of Hispanics. In 1951 he founded a national organization to bring together all of the civil rights-oriented Hispanic organizations and focus their efforts, the American Council of Spanish-Speaking People. It was this council that experienced early civil rights legal victories and prepared the way from many of the gains made during the 1960s and for the later emergence of the Mexican American Legal Defense and Education Fund. Because of his many pioneering studies, articles, and books, as well as the very important role he played in preparing the ground for the Hispanic civil rights and educational movements, George I. Sánchez has been the subject of numerous books, articles, and homages, and there is many a school named in his honor today.

Rosaura Sánchez (1941–)
Linguistics, Literature

Born on December 6, 1941, in San Angelo, Texas, Sánchez received her B.A. degree in Spanish and English in 1963, her M.A. degree in Spanish in 1969, and her Ph.D. degree in Romance Linguistics in 1974 from the University of Texas. Since 1972, Sánchez has developed her entire teaching career in the Literature Department at the University of California, San Diego, where she serves as a full professor. Sánchez is the author of *Chicano Discourse,* a fundamental book for the understanding of Mexican American Spanish and English patterns. She is also the author of numerous articles in linguistics and literature, as well as the author of short stories. Sánchez's work in linguistics has involved both the theoretical and the applied; she has been a pioneer in the teaching of Spanish to Spanish-speakers. In her literary studies, she has also concentrated on literary theory and feminist theory, as well as conducted critical studies of works by such writers as Gina Valdez, Arturo Islas, and Rolando Hinojosa.

José Sánchez-Boudy (1928–)
Literature

See Chapter 19.

Virginia Sánchez-Korrol (1936–)
History

See Chapter 10.

Saskia Sassen (1947–)
Economics, Sociology

Born on January 5, 1947, in The Hague, Netherlands, Sassen received first-year certificates from the University of Buenos Aires, Argentina, and the Universitá degli Studi in Rome in 1966 and 1968, respectively. She received her M.A. degree in sociology and her Ph.D. degree in economics and sociology from the University of Notre Dame in 1968 and 1971, respectively. From 1974 to 1975, she was a postdoctoral fellow at the Harvard Center for International Affairs, and she climbed the ranks at the City University of New York from assistant to full professor from 1976 to 1985. Since 1985, she has been a full professor of urban planning in the Department of Architecture at Columbia University. Sassen has been a consultant and member of policy groups on Hispanic social and political issues for the Ford Foundation, the Rockefeller Foundation, the Inter-University Group in Latino Research, the Russell Sage Foundation, and on women's and other issues for the United Nations. In 1986, Sassen was awarded the American Institute of Certified Planners National Award. She is the author of *The Mobility of Labor and Capital* (1988) and *The Global City: New York, London, Tokyo* (1990), as well as numerous research articles.

Adljiza Sosa-Riddell (1937–)
Political Science
    See Chapter 10.

References

Martínez, Julio A. *Chicano Scholars and Writers. A Bio-Bibliographic Directory.* Metuchen, New Jersey: Scarecrow Press, 1979.

Meier, Matt S. and Feliciano Rivera. *Dictionary of Mexican American History.* Westport, Connecticut: Greenwood Press, 1981.

Unterberger, Amy L., ed. *Who's Who among Hispanic Americans 1991–92.* Detroit: Gale Research, 1991.

Nicolás Kanellos

18

Science

❋ A General Overview ❋ Prominent Hispanic Scientists

The story of Hispanics in the sciences is really a bittersweet tale of outstanding achievement, on the one hand, and underrepresentation of U.S. Hispanics in math and science careers, on the other. Hispanics have contributed to world scientific and classical learning since the Middle Ages in Spain, developed excellent medical schools in Spain and Spanish America, and founded the first universities in the New World. The American Indian tradition, which enriched the culture of the Spanish and Europeans that settled in the New World, was also one of achievement in such sciences as astronomy and horticulture. However, today the record of Hispanics born or raised in the United States shows high dropout rates, and low college admission and retention rates, with dismally few Hispanic students going into math and science. While there are many Hispanic scientists, engineers, and mathematicians, many of these were born and educated in Spain and Spanish America and have come to the United States to benefit from our excellent graduate schools or the excellent research institutions and industries here that can provide the intellectual communities, resources, and salaries that their own countries cannot. Many of these scientists remain in the United States, contribute greatly to world knowledge, become citizens here, and enrich all of our lives in and out of the Hispanic communities.

❋ A GENERAL OVERVIEW

Deeply ingrained in Spanish and Hispanic cultures are the attitudes about the natural world and the sciences that the Arabs brought to the Iberian Peninsula during their 800 years of living there, from the beginning of the eighth century until 1492. Arab civilization was a crucial link with the classical learning of the Greeks, whose work they translated, advanced, and began to introduce to medieval Europe. Furthermore, the Arabs established universities, academies, and seats of learning long before such institutions were established in Europe. In extending their commerce to the far reaches of Asia and Africa, they learned many things from the cultures that they encountered. The expansion and domination by Islam of lands and peoples far and wide during the Middle Ages was built on the bedrock of solid technological and scientific knowledge. In Spain, the Arab cities of Córdoba, Sevilla, and Toledo became centers of learning that drew students from the rest of western Europe. Arabs were the inventors of algebra, and they were able to apply the principles of mathematics to everything that they did, including architecture, design, and landscaping. Originating in arid climates, they became superb horticulturists and agronomers, and developed systems of water management and irrigation that still survive in many parts of the Americas today. Their advances in the medical sciences even extended to mastering delicate corneal operations. All of this and much more is part of the Arab contribution to Hispanic culture everywhere.

The native peoples of the Americas had also advanced scientific knowledge and its application long before the arrival of the Europeans. In particular, the Native Americans were outstanding horticulturists and agronomists. Over thousands of years, they took the wild plants of the Americas and developed them into foodstuffs that eventually would revolutionize the diet of the whole planet. The native Americans took a wild grass and a variety of tubers and developed them into foods that would become staples for millions upon millions of people around the world: corn and potatoes. In addition, they developed myriad varieties of other foods that are common parts of our diets today, including beans, tomatoes, squash, and many fruits. The native Americans were ecologists and land and game managers who respected the wildlife and all of the natural world in everything that they did. Only recently has modern man really begun to learn from them in this regard, now that we are suffering so much from the degradation of the natural environment that has come with wasteful industrial overdevelopment and pollution.

Native Americans throughout the hemisphere were attentive astronomers who arrived at complex calculations that even modern scientists cannot achieve by using the types of instruments that were available to these native peoples. Achievements by such cultures as the Mayan even included the construction of modern-looking observatories. The Mayan mathematicians even invented the concept of zero. Little is known of the medical advances and the medicines developed from plants of the Americas by these peoples, except what little has come down to us in the techniques and folk medicines of such healers as *curanderos* (folk healers). We cannot be sure today how many scientific and medical advances were achieved by the peoples of the Americas before the arrival of the Spaniards, for these Europeans burned the Mayan books and destroyed temples with hieroglyphs throughout Mesoamerica and the Andes, the seats of highest learning, in their fervor to convert the "Indians" to Christianity.

Of course, much of the exploration and colonization of the New World can be seen as a scientific adventure. The Spaniards, including Hispanicized Indians and Africans, who explored these lands became superb cartographers and geographers, leaving us a legacy of minutely detailed maps and descriptions not only of the topography, but also of the fauna and flora and of the human inhabitants. Besides being the first to chart all of the coasts of what became the United States, they were also the first to map ocean currents, islands, rivers and mountain ranges. One such discovery was that of the Gulf Stream on February 4, 1513, by pilot Antonio de Alaminos, during Juan Ponce de León's voyage to Florida. Antonio de Alaminos had served as the pilot on Columbus' fourth voyage (1502–1504). This discovery resulted in Havana becoming a major port of assembly and Florida becoming a strategic stopping place for voyages. The current runs from the Florida Strait into the Bahamas Channel, past the coast of the Carolinas into the open ocean, where it forks northward to Norway and east to the Azores. Spanish ships, thus, headed for the Azores, refitted, and returned to Spain. One of the most important maps was the one developed in 1562 by Diego Gutiérrez (b. 1485), a pilot, chart- and instrument-maker in Seville, who created the largest, most complete print map of the Americas, relying on the data collected by Spain during its explorations. The map included in-

formation on the people and settlements, fauna and flora from Tierra del Fuego all the way up to Labrador on the east coast of the Hemisphere and to California on the west coast. This was the largest printed map of the Hemisphere known up to that time.

Many of the explorers wrote reports, diaries and chronicles describing the life of the Native Americans, and in this they became the first ethnographers and anthropologists. The first social science and biological document for the study of the flora and fauna of the South and Southwest, particularly Texas and the Mariam, Avavar, Karankawa, and other Indians of the region, is the 1536 "Joint Report," which was written in 1536 in Mexico City by three shipwrecked Europeans and an Afro-European, including Álvar Núñez Cabeza de Vaca. No other region in today's United States was described so early with so much detail. In 1541, Rodrigo Rangel and a soldier known only as the Gentleman of Elvas were the first to describe the culture of the Caddo Indians, which they observed on the expedition of Hernando de Soto to southern Arkansas and east Texas.

Álvar Núñez Cabeza de Vaca (1490–1557) may be considered to have become the first anthropologist and ethnographer of the New World in studying the Indians of the South and Southwest of what would later become the United States. He documented his observations and experiences in his book, *The Account,* which was published in Spain in 1542 after his return from the New World. In the winter of 1528, Núñez Cabeza de Vaca was only one of 15 survivors from a shipwreck off the coast of Florida. The Indians, who were suffering from illness, forced the survivors to become "healers," and Cabeza de Vaca began his career as a renowned physician among the Indians. During the six years that he remained among the Indians along the Gulf Coast, as far west as Texas, Cabeza de Vaca also became a merchant, a translator. He recorded in great detail for the first time many observations about the Indians of the South and Southwest. In 1534, he and four other marooned survivors set out on a march west in search of New Spain. They marched on foot completely across Texas and into New Mexico, going from one tribe to the next as healers and traders. They finally encountered Spaniards in what is today northwestern Mexico in 1536. Cabeza de Vaca's ten-year journey from Florida to New Mexico ended when he set sail in April 1537, for Spain. His memoir, *La relación* ("The Account"), may be considered the first ethnographic study of the Americas, as well as a literary masterpiece, possibly the first book "American literature" written in a European language.

The first European to study and translate the languages of Indians residing in what is today the United States was Father Francisco Pareja who, from 1595 until his death sometime after 1626, became an expert in the Timicuan language and published four works on the language. These studies are the basic texts used by modern linguists to understand the now extinct language. Father Pareja was a missionary to the Timicuan Indians at the San Juan del Puerto Mission, founded in 1587, in what is now Georgia.

Much of the agricultural technology was developed and introduced to North America by the Spaniards, including the breeding and raising of the basic livestock, such as cattle, sheep, horses, hogs, and goats, on which much of the economy of the Southwest was once almost entirely based. The Spanish were the first to introduce the plow, systems of irrigation and farm-land distribution, but especially important was the heritage that they brought from the Arabs of farming in arid climates. The Spanish, Hispanicized Indian and mestizo colonizers were the first engineers to come to lands that would become the United States. By 1610, they had built the first irrigation canals and irrigation systems north of the Rio Grande, in Santa Fe, New Mexico. They dug two *acequias madres* (main ditches) on each side of the small river which passed through the center of the town they were establishing. The Spanish had strict codes and plans for the construction of irrigation systems for the towns they were founding in the arid Southwest; such systems were constructed often in advance of the building of the forts, houses and churches. The undertaking was quite often massive, calling for the digging, dredging, transportation of materials and feeding of humans and animals. This was the case in the founding of Albuquerque in 1706, that of San Antonio in 1731, and of Los Angeles in 1781. The canals of San Antonio were so well planned, lined with stone and masonry as they were, that many of them are still functioning today.

Other Hispanic engineers saw the feasibility of linking the two main coasts of North America. Around 1790, the idea for a transcontinental road first occurred to the Spanish governor of California, Pedro Fages, who wrote his viceroy for permission to contact George Washington about constructing a continental trail from Virginia to California, with the roads meeting in the Spanish fort at Saint Louis. The idea did not take hold until 1869 when the transcontinental railroad finally linked East and West.

As early as the nineteenth century, Hispanic engineers began to immigrate to the United States and left their mark on our society as it developed. In 1885, Spanish immigrant Rafael Guastavino (1842–1908) obtained the first of his 25 patents, this one for new mortars he developed for tiled floor and ceiling vaults, partitions and stairs. Over the years this architect and contractor developed fireproofing innovations and perfected traditional cohesive masonry for modern use; he was responsible for building the tiled vaults for such New York City monuments as Grand Central Station, Carnegie Hall, the old Penn Station, the Metropolitan Museum of Art, the Plaza and Biltmore hotels, the Cathedral of St. John the Divine, and many others. Born in Valencia, Spain, Guastavino studied architecture in Barcelona, where he built factories, houses, and theaters by using many of the traditional technologies of Mediterranean architecture. Guastavino immigrated to the United States in 1881 in search of broader markets and better mortars, and went on to become one of the most recognized designers and builders of vaults, domes and tiled surfaces, promoting their acoustics, elegance and economy. By 1891, Guastavino's company had offices in New York, Boston, Providence, Chicago and Milwaukee. In 1892, Guastavino documented his successful system of construction in his book, *Essay on the Theory and History of Cohesive Construction*. After his death, Guastavino's business was continued by his son Rafael II, who expanded the company and was responsible for numerous patents of his own. In all, the Guastavinos were responsible for domes built at state capitals, major universities, museums and railroad stations throughout the United States, including the United States Supreme Court building and the Natural History Museum in Washington, D.C.

Today there are many outstanding universities and research institutions in the Hispanic world, especially in Argentina, Chile, Cuba, Mexico, Puerto Rico, and Spain. But many of the countries in Spanish America suffer from economic and industrial underdevelopment as a result of at least four centuries of European and U.S. colonialism and exploitation of their natural resources, including the export and exploitation of their human resources, be they laborers or intellectuals. Many foreign students are drawn to the excellent graduate schools of the United States, quite often with scholarships and support from their home countries. After becoming scientists or doctors here, it is often quite difficult for them to return to their homelands because of the superior research facilities and resources here, and the greater opportunities for teaching and making a comfortable living within the relatively prosperous economy of the United States.

Also, the scientific and scholarly community of the United States is very rich, drawing on scientists and teachers from throughout the world and boasting the most advanced communications, publications, and conferences. Many other doctors and scientists from Spanish America and Spain, without having been trained in the United States, are drawn to these benefits and come to make their homes here. Then, too, political disruptions have also precipitated the immigration to the United States of many intellectuals and scientists from Spanish America and Spain: the Spanish Civil War, the Mexican and Cuban Revolutions, and periodic violent dictatorships in Argentina, Chile, Nicaragua, El Salvador, and elsewhere.

One of the most recent Nobel Prizes was authorized to a scientist born and educated in Mexico, but working in a U.S. institution. Mario Molina, a researcher and professor at the Massachusetts Institute of Technology, shared the Nobel Prize in Chemistry with two others for their work that led to the international ban on chemicals believed to be depleting the ozone protective layer of the earth. A native of Mexico with a B.S. in chemical engineering from the National Autonomous University of Mexico (1965) and a Ph.D. in physical chemistry from the University of California-Berkeley (1972), he has taught and conducted research at various universities in the United States.

What is certain is that the United States has benefited greatly from this "brain drain," often at the expense of the home countries that, as Third World nations, direly need physicians, scientists, and teachers. The Hispanic communities within the United States have always benefited as well from this continued source of renewal of creative and intellectual membership. The Hispanic medical and scientific community has always actively contributed to community life in the large urban areas of Hispanic concentration. In fact, it is precisely Hispanic community life that quite often draws these doctors and scientists to settle in such communities as Houston, Los Angeles, Miami, New York, or San Antonio. The Houston Medical Center, for example, is not only replete with doctors and researchers from throughout the Hispanic world, but it has also become one of the principal medical centers for all of Latin America.

While there are many doctors and researchers that have moved to the United States from Spain and Spanish America—thus proving that Hispanics can indeed become successful doctors and scientists—Hispanics raised and educated in the United States have had a dismal record of entering the medical and scientific professions. Hispanic students tend to have high dropout rates and low college admission and graduation rates. The rate of their going

on to and graduating from graduate and medical schools is far worse. All of the effects of poverty, discrimination, and culture clash, poor schools and educational tracking, as well as many other barriers have resulted in a serious lack of doctors and scientists coming out of the Hispanic communities of the United States.

There are programs and organizations today that aim to provide greater opportunities for Hispanics in these fields. And there are outstanding teachers, such as Jaime Escalante, who are proving that students—even from the poorest and most crime-ridden neighborhoods—can be outstanding achievers in math and science. Even the College Board has taken on as its number one priority equity in admissions and graduation rates for minorities by the year 2000.

Despite these problems, the scientists and doctors that Hispanic communities have produced, and the ones that have come from their homelands to make their careers in the United States, have achieved a record of outstanding success, working within the most respected hospitals, universities, laboratories, and research institutes we have to offer.

✳ PROMINENT HISPANIC SCIENTISTS

Carlos Alberto Abel (1930–)
Medicine

Born in Argentina on May 7, 1930, Abel graduated from the medical school of the University of Buenos Aires in 1957. He began his career at the Children's Hospital in Buenos Aires, but by 1959 had moved to Providence, Rhode Island, as an intern at St. Joseph's Hospital. Through years of residencies and further scientific study in Maryland, California, and England, Abel became a specialist in biophysics and genetics and became a noted immunologist. From 1970 to 1984, he taught at the University of Colorado Medical Center, rising to the rank of full professor. From 1984 until 1992, he was a senior scientist in immunology at the Institute for Cancer Research of the Medical Research Institute of San Francisco, where since 1993 he has served as chair of the research council. His research has centered on lymphocytes and the relationships of their components with various immunological functions. In particular, he has been researching the AIDS virus and how to combat it. He is a member of the University of California Task Force on AIDS.

Daniel Acosta, Jr. (1945–)
Pharmacology

Born on March 25, 1945, in El Paso, Texas, Acosta received his B.S. degree from the University of Texas in 1968 and his Ph.D. degree in pharmacology from the University of Kansas in 1974. He began as an assistant professor at the University of Kansas, and is currently a full professor at the University of Texas. He has been an Eli Lilly Centennial Fellow and a Ford Fellow. Acosta's research is in cell toxicology, particularly studying the effects of drugs and toxicants at the cellular and subcellular levels; he is particularly interested in heart cells and injury to them.

Francisco José Aisle (1934–)

Genetics

Born on March 12, 1934, in Madrid, Spain, Aisle received his B.S. degree from the University of Madrid in 1955 and his M.S. and Ph.D. degrees from Columbia University in 1963 and 1964, respectively. Since 1964, he has worked as a researcher and professor at various universities and institutes. Since 1974, he has been a professor of genetics at the University of California, Davis. He is the associate editor of *Molecular Evolution and Paleobiology,* a research journal. He also serves as the chairman of boards at the National Academy of Sciences and the National Research Council. His research concentrates on evolution, population genetics, and fitness of natural and experimental populations, among other subjects.

José Ramón Alcalá (1940–)

Anatomy, Biochemistry

Born in Ponce, Puerto Rico, on May 1, 1940, Alcalá began his high school education in Santurce, Puerto Rico, and finished it in Waynesville, Missouri, where he graduated in 1957. His stepfather, a career army man had been transferred to Fort Leonard Wood in 1956. Alcalá went on to receive his B.A. and M.A. degrees in Zoology from the University of Missouri in 1964 and 1966, respectively. He received his Ph.D. degree in anatomy from the University of Illinois Medical Center in 1972. Since 1972, he has taught and conducted research at the School of Medicine at Wayne State University, where he has been a full professor since 1987. Since 1990, he has been the director of the gross anatomy programs of the School of Medicine. Alcalá specializes in the anatomy of the eye, studying the biochemistry and immunochemistry of lens plasma membranes. This research has had great methodological and conceptual impact in the field of lens research for its first clear delineation of the protein composition of lens fiber plasma membranes. His continued work in this area has had impact on research on cataracts. In 1992, Alcalá returned to Puerto Rico to become chair of the anatomy

department at the Ponce School of Medicine in Ponce, where he continued his studies of lens proteins. He is supervisor of the school's body donation program and a member of the state anatomy board of the Commonwealth of Puerto Rico.

Kenneth B. Alonso (1942–)

Pathology, Nuclear Medicine

Born in Tampa, Florida, on November 26, 1942, Alonso received his A.B. degree from Princeton University in 1964 and his M.D. degree from the University of Florida in 1968. He has worked as an intern, resident, and pathologist at various hospitals around the country from 1968 to 1976. In 1976, he became the director of laboratory procedures for Upjohn South Company in Georgia, and from 1978 to 1984, he worked as chief of staff and pathology for two hospitals. Since 1984, he has been the director of Lab Atlanta in Riverdale, Georgia. His research interests include immunological disorders, especially receptors, membrane transport, human tumor stem cell assay, and monoclonal antibodies.

Anne Maino Alvarez (1941–)

Plant Pathology

Born on April 14, 1941, in Rochester, Minnesota, Alvarez received her B.S. degree from Stanford University in 1963 and her M.S. and Ph.D. degrees from the University of California, Berkeley, in 1966 and 1972, respectively. Since that time she has worked at the University of Argentina in Nequen, from 1969 to 1970, and at the University of Hawaii, where she is currently a researcher and educator in plant pathology. Alvarez has done field research in Argentina, Costa Rica, and Mexico on bacterial diseases in fruits and crops and on epidemiology and disease control. She has particularly studied the orchard and postharvest diseases of the papaya.

Luis Walter Alvarez (1911–1988)

Experimental Physics

Born in San Francisco, California, on June 13, 1911, Luis Alvarez was one of this country's most distinguished and respected physicists. In addition to B.S. (1932) and Ph.D. (1936) degrees from the University of Chicago, Alvarez received a number of honorary degrees from universities in the United States and abroad. He developed most of his work at the University of California, Berkeley, beginning in 1936. From 1954 to 1959 and from 1976 to 1978, he served as associate director of the prestigious Lawrence Berkeley Lab. In 1986, Alvarez was awarded the Nobel Prize in physics; he also received the Collier Trophy (1946), the Scott Medal (1953), the Einstein

Medal (1961), the National Medal of Science (1964), and many other awards. Alvarez was a pioneer in particle physics, astrophysics, ophthalmic and television optics, geophysics, and air navigation. He died on September 1, 1988, in Berkeley, California.

Angeles Alvariño de Leira (1916–)

Marine Biology

Born on October 3, 1916, in El Ferrol, Spain, Alvariño received her master's (1941) and doctorate degrees in chemistry and sciences in 1951 and 1967, respectively, from the University of Madrid. From 1941 to 1957, she worked at universities and institutes in Spain as a biological oceanographer. In 1957, she began her career in the United States as a biologist at the Scripps Institute of Oceanography of the University of California, La Jolla. In 1970, she assumed her current position of fishery research biologist at the National Marine Fisheries Service in La Jolla. Alvariño has held concurrent positions at universities in England, Mexico, and Venezuela, and she has been a Fulbright scholar and a National Science Foundation fellow a number of times. Alvariño has been the discoverer of 11 new species of chaetognatha and three new species of syphono-

Angeles Alvariño de Leira.

phorae, which are her specialty, along with zooplankton and medusae. Although Alvariño officially retired in 1987, she continues to conduct research on zooplankton. In 1993, she was awarded the Great Silver Medal of Galicia by King Juan Carlos I.

Ralph Amado (1932–)

Theoretical Physics

Born in Los Angeles on November 13, 1932, Amado received his B.S. degree from Stanford University in 1954 and his Ph.D. degree from Oxford University, England, in 1957. After graduating, he began his career as a research associate at the University of Pennsylvania and has remained at that institution; his current title is professor of physics. Besides research and teaching duties at Penn, Amado has worked as a consultant to the Arms Control and Disarmament Agency. His specialties are theoretical nuclear physics, many-body problems, particle physics and scattering theory.

Elías Amador (1932–)

Medicine, Pathology

Born in Mexico City, Mexico, on June 8, 1932, and educated at the Central Mexico University (B.S. degree, 1959) and the National University of Mexico (M.D. degree, 1956), immediately after becoming a doctor, Amador relocated to the United States and developed his career here at various hospitals and universities. Since 1972, he has served as professor and chairman of the Department of pathology of the Charles R. Drew Postgraduate Medical School, professor at the University of Southern California, and chief of pathology of the Martin Luther King, Jr., General Hospital, all three positions held concurrently. He has been a teaching fellow at Harvard Medical School (1957–58) and at the Boston University School of Medicine (1959–60). His research concerns the development of accurate and sensitive methods for diagnosis and detection of disease.

Alberto Vinicio Baez (1912–)

Physics

Born in Puebla, Mexico, on November 15, 1912, Baez received his B.S. degree from Drew University in 1933, his M.A. degree from Syracuse University in 1935, and his Ph.D. degree from Stanford University in 1950. Over his long career he has taught and conducted research at various universities, including Cornell, Drew, Stanford, Wagner (New York), and Redlands and Harvey Mudd (both in California). Between 1961 and 1974, he worked for UNESCO in New York and Paris in science education. He has also held various international board and committee

Alberto Vinicio Baez.

positions, and from 1974 to 1978, served as the chairman of the Committee on Teaching Sciences of the International Council of Science Unions. Since 1984, he has been chairman emeritus of Community Education, International Union for the Conservation of Nature and Natural Resources, Glantz, Switzerland. In 1991, the S.P.I.E. conferred the Dennis Gabor Award on Baez and his coresearcher, Paul Kirkpatrick, in recognition of their pioneering contributions to the development of X-ray imaging microscopes and telescopes. The Kirkpatrick-Baez Lamar X-ray telescope was approved for use on the Freedom Space Station. In his research, Baez specialized in x-ray radiation, optics, and microscopy, as well as in science and environmental education.

Teresa Bernárdez (1931–)

Medicine, Psychiatry

See Chapter 10.

Caridad Borras (1942–)

Radiological Physics

Born in Spain on February 18, 1942, Borras received her M.S. and Ph.D. degrees from the Univer-

sity of Barcelona in 1964 and 1974, respectively. Until 1966, she worked in Barcelona in hospitals; in 1967, she relocated to Thomas Jefferson University in Philadelphia as an assistant physicist. Since 1974, she has served as a radiological physicist at the West Coast Cancer Foundation. Since 1982, she has also been a clinical assistant professor at the University of California. Borras studies the radioembryopathological effects of high LET nuclides, as well as the physics of diagnostic radiology and radiation therapy.

César A. Cáceres (1927–)

Medicine, Computer Science

Born on April 9, 1927, in Puerto Cortés, Honduras, Cáceres received his B.S. and M.D. degrees from Georgetown University in 1949 and 1953, respectively. He then served as an intern and resident in Boston hospitals, but returned as a fellow in cardiology to George Washington University from 1956 to 1960, and from 1960 to 1971 he moved up the ranks there from assistant professor of medicine to full professor and department chairman. From 1960 to 1969, he was also chief of the Medical Systems Development Lab for the United States Public Health Service. In 1971, he founded his own company, Clinical Systems Associates, for which he still serves as president to date; he also worked concurrently as a professor of electrical engineering at the University of Maryland from 1971 to 1976. Cáceres specializes in electrocardiography, cardiology, medical diagnosis, and computers in medicine.

Marta Cancio (1928–)

Biochemistry

Born in San Sebastián, Puerto Rico, on December 8, 1928, Cancio received her B.S. degree from the University of Puerto Rico in 1949 and her M.S. and Ph.D. degrees from the University of Missouri in 1952 and 1954, respectively. In 1954, she began as an associate biochemist at the University of Puerto Rico School of Medicine and moved up the ranks. Since 1966, she has served as the supervisory research chemist for the Veterans Administration Hospital, and since 1971, as associate professor of biochemistry and nutrition at the University of Puerto Rico Medical School. Her research concerns lipid and protein chemistry, malabsorption, and immunochemistry.

Graciela Candelas (1922–)

Molecular Biology

Born in Puerto Rico in 1922, Candelas received her B.S. degree from the University of Puerto Rico in

Graciela Candelas.

1944, her M.S. degree from Duke University in 1959, and her Ph.D. degree from the University of Miami in 1966. Since 1966, she has moved up the ranks at the University of Puerto Rico; since 1971, she has been a full professor of cell and molecular biology there. She has also held visiting and concurrent positions at the University of Syracuse, Rockefeller University, City University of New York, and the Medical College of Georgia. She was given the Special Science Award by the Puerto Rican Institute in New York in 1985 and the Distinguished Alumnus Award by the Alumni Organization of the University of Puerto Rico in 1988. One of her research interests is fibroin synthesis and its regulation using a pair of glands from the spider *Nephila clavipes*.

Oscar A. Candia (1935–)

Physicology, Biophysics

Born in Buenos Aires, Argentina, on April 30, 1935, Candia received his M.D. degree from the University of Buenos Aires in 1959. After working as a researcher in Buenos Aires, he relocated to the University of Louisville in 1964 as a research associate and moved up the ranks there to full professorship.

Since 1984, he has been professor of opthalmology and physiology at Mt. Sinai School of Medicine in New York. He received career development awards from 1966 to 1971 from the National Institutes of Health. He is an associate editor of *Investigations in Opthalmology and Visual Science*, a research journal. In 1985, he won the Alcon award. His principal research concern is ion transport in biological membranes.

Fernando Caracena (1936–)

Atmospheric Physics, Physics

Born on March 13, 1936, in El Paso, Texas, Caracena received his B.S. degree from the University of Texas at El Paso in 1958 and his M.S. and Ph.D. degrees from Case Western Reserve in 1966 and 1968, respectively. From 1958 to 1961, he worked as an atmospheric physicist for the Department of Defense at White Sands Missile Range, and from 1969 to 1976, he worked as an assistant professor at Metropolitan State College, Denver, Colorado. Since 1976, he has been working as an atmospheric physicist at the Environmental Research Labs of the National Oceanic and Atmospheric Administration. His research concerns air safety, especially clear air turbulence, low altitude wind shear, and the meteorology of wind-shear-related aircraft accidents.

Mary Janet M. Cárdenas (1942–)

Biochemistry

Born in Miami, Oklahoma, on January 31, 1942, Cárdenas received her B.A. degree from Oklahoma State University in 1963 and her M.S. and Ph.D. degrees from the University of Illinois in 1965 and 1967, respectively. From 1967 through 1981, she taught at various universities, achieving the rank of associate professor of chemistry at the University of North Carolina. Since 1981, she has been health science administrator at the National Eye Institute of the National Institutes of Health. Her research concerns the sensorimotor aspects of vision, especially culomotor disorders.

Manuel Cardona (1934–)

Physics

Born in Barcelona, Spain, on September 7, 1934, Manuel Cardona received his B.S. degree in physics from the University of Barcelona in 1955 and his Ph.D. degree in applied physics from Harvard University in 1959. After graduation, he worked until 1964 at RCA Laboratories in Switzerland and in Princeton, New Jersey. Since then he has been a researcher associated with various universities and institutes, most notably as professor of physics at

Manuel Cardona.

Brown from 1964 to 1971, and, since 1971, as the director of the Max-Planck-Institut for Solid State Research in Stuttgart, Germany. In 1967, Cardona became a naturalized citizen of the United States. He is the author of some 700 scientific publications in journals and nine monographs on solid-state physics. Among his many awards are the Frank Isakson Prize from the American Physical Society (1984), the Grand Cross of Alfonso el Sabio from Spain (1987), the Príncipe de Asturias Prize from Spain (1988), the Kronland Medal from Czechoslovakia (1988), and the Excellence in Superconductivity Award of the World Congress on Superconductivity (1992). He is a member of both the American and European Academies of Science.

David Cardús (1922–)

Cardiology, Biomathematics

Born on August 6, 1922, in Barcelona, Spain, Cardús received his M.D. degree from the University of Barcelona in 1949. He did his internship and residency in Barcelona and postgraduate work in cardiology and physiology there. In 1960, Cardús relocated to Texas and embarked on a career at the

Baylor University College of Medicine as a professor and researcher in cardiology and rehabilitation. He moved up the ranks to his present positions: professor of physiology, professor of rehabilitation, head of the cardiopulmonary lab, and director of biomath. Among his many awards are a Gold Medal from the Sixth International Congress on Physical Medicine in 1972, a Licht Award for Excellence in Science Writing in 1980, and the Narcis Monturiol Medal from Catalunya, Spain, in 1984. In 1993, Cardús was elected president of the International Society for Gravitational Physiology. He has researched experimental exercise and respiratory physiology, mathematical and computer applications to the study of physiological systems, and rehabilitation medicine.

Alberto Castro (1933–)

Biochemistry, Endocrinology

Born on November 15, 1933, in San Salvador, El Salvador, Castro received his B.S. degree from the University of Houston in 1958 and his Ph.D. degree in biological chemistry from the University of El Salvador in 1962. He moved up the ranks from assistant to full professor at the University of El Salvador from 1958 to 1966. From 1966 to 1970, he was an

David Cardús.

NIH fellow at the University of Oregon, and from 1970 to 1973, he was a lab director at the United Medical Lab. From 1973 to 1977, he once again moved up the ranks to full professor of medicine, pathology and microbiology at the University of Miami Medical School. Since 1973, he has been the director of the Hormone Research Lab there. His primary work is in carbohydrate biochemistry, metabolism, and modes of action, and hormone mechanisms and their interrelationship to hypertension.

George Castro (1939–)

Physical Chemistry

Born February 23, 1939, in Los Angeles, California, Castro received his B.S. degree in chemistry from the University of California, Los Angeles, in 1960 and his Ph.D. degree in physical chemistry from the University of California, Riverside, in 1965. He has been a postdoctoral fellow at the University of Pennsylvania, Cal Tech, and Dartmouth, but has worked as a researcher for IBM since 1968. Since 1986, he has been the manager of Synchrotron Studies for IBM at the Almaden Research Center. In 1978, he received the Outstanding Innovation Award from IBM, and in 1990, he was elected a fellow of the American Physical

George Castro.

Society. Castro is the discoverer of the mechanism of the intrinsic charge carrier of organic photoconductors. Years later, such materials in the form of organic polymeric films became the basis for flexible photoconductors that are used in photocopying machines and high-speed printers. Castro assumed the leadership of the physical sciences of the IBM San Jose Research Lab in 1975, three years after its formation. He has built the organization into one that is world-famous for its scientific discoveries. These include the discovery of the first superconducting polymer, novel organic metals and superconductors, high-resolution laser techniques, and new methods of investigating magnetic materials.

Peter Castro (1943–)

Zoology, Parasitology

Born on July 20, 1943, in Mayagüez, Puerto Rico, Castro received his B.S. degree from the University of Puerto Rico at Mayaguez in 1964, and his M.S. and Ph.D. degrees in zoology from the University of Hawaii in 1966 and 1969, respectively. From 1970 to 1975, he worked as a teacher and researcher in the biology department of the University of Puerto Rico at Mayaguez. Since 1975, he has been an associate professor of Biological Sciences at California State Polytechnical Institute in Pomona. Castro has been a fellow and visiting researcher at Stanford, the Smithsonian Institute, and Moss Landing Marine Labs. Castro's research concerns ecological, physiological, and behavioral aspects of marine symbiosis.

Asunción Elena Charola (1942–)

Analytical Chemistry, Physical Chemistry

Born in Argentina on February 23, 1942, Charola received her Ph.D. degree in analytical chemistry from the National University of La Plata in 1974. After receiving a fellowship to New York University from 1974 to 1976, Charola remained in the United States as an assistant professor of chemistry at Manhattan College from 1978 to 1981 and at the Metropolitan Museum of Art from 1981 to 1985. Since 1985, she has been an associate scientist at the IC-CROM in Rome, Italy. Her research concerns solid-state chemistry, polymorphism, and x-ray crystallography, among other subjects.

Guillermo B. Cintrón (1942–)

Medicine

Born on March 28, 1942, in San Juan, Puerto Rico, Cintrón received his B.S. degree from the University of Puerto Rico in 1963 and his M.D. degree from Loyola-Stritch School of Medicine in Chicago in 1967. After residencies in Washington, D.C., Cintrón

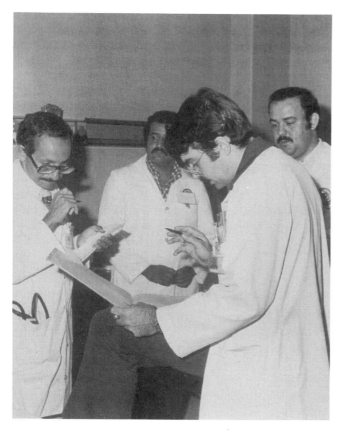

Guillermo B. Cintrón.

returned to Puerto Rico, where from 1975 to 1983, he taught and conducted cardiac research at the University of Puerto Rico Medical School. Since 1983, he has been an associate professor at the University of Southern Florida School of Medicine. Since 1987, he has been the associate director of cardiology there. His principal research concerns heart disease and its causes and prevention.

Antonio E. Colás (1928–)

Biochemistry

Born on June 22, 1928, in Muel, Spain, Colás received his B.S. degree from the University of Zaragoza in 1951 and his M.D. degree from the University of Madrid in 1953. In 1955, he received his Ph.D. degree in biochemistry from the University of Edinburgh in Scotland. Following his studies at Edinburgh, Colás took various teaching and research positions in Spain, Colombia, and finally, in 1960, in the United States at the University of Oregon Medical School, where he served as professor of obstetrics and gynecology until 1968. Since then, he has been professor of obstetrics and gynecology and physiological chemistry at the University of Wisconsin Medi-

cal School. His research interests include the biochemistry and metabolism of steroid hormones; he has published more than 80 research articles.

Julio Cordero (1923–)

Fluid Engineering

Born on January 10, 1923, in San José, Costa Rica, Cordero received his B.S. degree from Wayne State University in 1948 and his M.S. degree from the University of Minnesota in 1951. From 1951 to 1976, he worked as a research scientist at a number of universities and industries. Since 1976, he has been chief engineer at the Magnetohydrodynamics Research Facility of the Massachusetts Institute of Technology. His principal research concerns shock wave phenomena and supersonic and hypersonic aerodynamics.

Francisco Dallmeier (1953–)

Wildlife Biology

Born on February 15, 1953, in Caracas, Venezuela, Francisco Dallmeier received his licentiate in biology from the Central University of Venezuela in 1979 and his M.S. and Ph.D. degrees in wildlife biology from the

Antonio E. Colás.

Francisco Dallmeier.

University of Colorado in 1984 and 1986, respectively. From 1973 to 1977, he was the director of the La Salle Museum of Natural History and a member of the ecology team of the Institute of Tropical Zoology of the Central University of Venezuela. From 1977 to 1986, he worked as a biologist and researcher in various positions in Venezuela and the United States. Since 1986, he has worked for the Smithsonian Institute in Washington, D.C., for which he has served as director of the Man and the Biosphere Biological Diversity Program since 1989. In that capacity, he coordinates field biodiversity research and training in Bolivia, Brazil, Peru, Ecuador, Guatemala, Panama, Puerto Rico, the Virgin Islands, Tennessee, and Washington, D.C. His major research focuses on the integration of biological diversity and natural resources and conservation and management programs. His latest studies concern neotropical waterfowl and wetlands ecology and management.

Henry Frank Díaz (1948–)

Atmospheric Sciences

Born in Cuba on July 15, 1948, Díaz received his B.S. degree from Florida State University in 1971,

his M.S. degree from the University of Miami in 1974, and his Ph.D. degree in geology and climatology from the University of Colorado in 1985. From 1974 through 1985, Díaz worked as a meteorologist at the Environmental Data Service, the National Climate Center, and the Environmental Research Lab. Since 1985, he has been acting director of the Climate Research Program of the National Oceanic and Atmospheric Administration. In 1977 and 1983, he received awards for outstanding achievement at the Environmental Research Lab. Díaz researches climatology and climatic variation, developing long-term historical climatic data bases. He is especially recognized for his 1992 study *El Niño: Historical and Paleoclimatic Aspects of the Southern Oscillation.*

Javier I. Escobar (1943–)

Psychiatry, Psychopharmacology

Born on July 26, 1943, in Medellín, Colombia, Escobar received his M.D. degree from the University of Antioquia in Colombia in 1967; in 1969, he became a resident at the University of Minnesota Hospitals, and by 1976, had attained the rank of associate professor of psychiatry there. From 1976 to 1979, he worked at the University of Tennessee, and in 1979, he became an associate professor of psychiatry at the University of California, Los Angeles. Today he is a full professor at that institution. Escobar has worked with many hospitals and numerous research projects on a regional and national level. His research concerns clinical projects in schizophrenia and affective disorders, including testing for new treatments. He is also a specialist in cross-cultural psychiatry as it concerns somatization traits across different cultures.

José Alberto Fernández-Pol (1943–)

Medicine

Born on March 17, 1943, in Buenos Aires, José Alberto Fernández-Pol received his M.D. degree from the University of Buenos Aires in 1969. From then until 1971, he was affiliated with various hospitals in Buenos Aires; in 1971, he became a resident physician at the State University of New York, Buffalo. After that he worked at various microbiology and cancer research labs in the United States, notably at the National Cancer Institute of the National Institutes of Health from 1975 to 1977. In 1977, he began as an assistant professor of medicine at St. Louis University; since 1985, he has been a full professor there. Fernández's research concerns growth control mechanisms in normal and cancerous cells, oncogenies.

Jorge Fischbarg (1935–)

Opthalmology

Born on August 14, 1935, in Buenos Aires, Argentina, Jorge Fischbarg received his early education there and graduated with a B.S. degree from the Colegio Nacional de Buenos Aires in 1953. He received his M.D. degree from the University of Buenos Aires in 1962 and his Ph.D. degree in physiology from the University of Chicago in 1971. From 1961 to 1969, he held various postdoctoral fellowships and traineeships in Buenos Aires, Louisville, Kentucky, and Chicago. Since 1970 he has pursued a career in physiology (ophthalmology) research and teaching at Columbia University. In 1984 he became head of the Membrane Biology Laboratory (Eye Research Division) at Columbia. He has received research awards from and worked closely with the National Institute of Health, and has been a visiting scientist in France (1974 and 1978) and England (1976–1977). In 1986, he was awarded the Alcon Recognition Award from the Alcon Research Institute. Fischbarg has been a member of the editorial board of *Experimental Eye Research* since 1986. His research interests include the transport of fluid and electrolytes across epithelial membranes, corneal physiol-

José Alberto Fernández-Pol.

ogy, and molecular biophysics of water channels in cell membranes.

Alfredo Mariano García (1927–)

Biology, Anatomy

Born on September 12, 1927, in Itati-Corrientes, Argentina, García received his M.D. degree from the University of Buenos Aires in 1953 and a Ph.D. degree in zoology from Columbia University in 1962. Since 1957, he has worked in the United States at various hospitals and research institutes. Since 1964, he has been a professor of anatomy at the State University of New York Upstate Medical Center in Syracuse; he achieved full professorship status in 1974. His research concerns quantitative cytochemistry and fine structure and nucleic acid metabolism of mammalian blood cells.

Carlos Ernesto García (1936–)

Mechanical Engineering

Born on May 14, 1936, in Las Vegas, New Mexico, García received his three degrees from New Mexico State University: B.S. (1958), M.S. (1962), and D.Sc. (1966). He has worked as a research engineer at a variety of government institutions and private industries, including the Atomic Energy Commission, from 1971 to 1973, as a weapons development engineer. Since 1984, he has been the director of the environmental safety and health division of the U.S. Department of Energy. His specialty is hydromechanical missile control systems and shock wave phenomena, including the study of underground nuclear explosions.

Celso Ramón García (1921–)

Obstetrics and Gynecology

Born on October 31, 1921, in New York City, García received his B.S. degree from Queens College in 1942 and his M.D. degree from the State University of New York in 1945. He has worked as a professor and researcher at various hospitals and universities, including Harvard and the University of Puerto Rico. He held the William Shippen Jr. Chair in Human Reproduction at the School of Medicine at the University of Pennsylvania until 1992, when he became professor emeritus. From 1973 to 1978, he was the vice chairman of the Department of Obstetrics and Gynecology and the director of the Division of Human Reproduction. Since 1978, he has been the director of reproductive surgery. Included among his many awards are the Carl Harman Award from the Human Fertility Society (1961), Extraordinary Professor, University of San Luis Potosí, Mexico (1974), and the Pincus Lecturer, School of Medicine, Wayne

Celso Ramón García.

State University (1974). His specialty is reproductive physiology and infertility.

José D. García (1936–)

Physics

Born in Santa Fe, New Mexico, on January 3, 1936, García received his B.S. degree from New Mexico State University in 1957, his M.A. degree from the University of California, Berkeley, in 1959, and his Ph.D. degree from the University of Wisconsin, Madison, in 1966. In 1967, he joined the faculty of the University of Arizona; since 1975, he has been a full professor of physics at Arizona. He has a been a Fulbright fellow (1957), a NASA postdoctoral fellow (1963), a NORDITA visiting fellow in Stockholm (1972), and an elected fellow of the American Physical Society since 1979. His principal research concerns quantum theory and ion-atom and ion-surface interactions.

Elma González (1942–)

Cell Biology

Born in the United States on June 6, 1942, González received her B.S. degree from Texas

Woman's University in 1965 and her Ph.D. degree in cell biology from Rutgers University in 1972. After working with a fellowship in plant physiology at the University of California, Santa Cruz, from 1972 to 1974, González became an assistant professor of cell biology at the University of California, Los Angeles in 1974. Since 1981, she has been an associate professor there. Her research concerns the mechanisms and regulation of the formation of microbodies and other metabolic compartments.

Paula González (1932–)

Environmental Science, Bioethics

Born on October 25, 1932, in Albuquerque, New Mexico, González received her A.B. degree from the College of Mt. St. Joseph in 1952, her M.S. degree from the Catholic University of America in 1962, and her Ph.D. degree in cell physiology from there in 1966. González has taught at high schools, schools of nursing, and at the university level. From 1965 to 1982, she moved up the ranks from assistant professor to full professor at the College of Mt. St. Joseph; from 1968 to 1973, she served as the chairman of the Department of Biology. Her research concerns nucleolar changes during the cell cycle, energy and environment, and biomedical advances and their human implications.

Richard Rafael González (1942–)

Physiology

Born on September 15, 1942, in El Paso, Texas, González received his B.S. degree from the University of Texas in 1962, his M.S. degree from the University of San Francisco in 1966, and his Ph.D. degree in Physiology and Biophysics from the University of California-Davis in 1970. After spending two years as a U.S. Public Health Service fellow at Yale University, during the next four years he went from assistant professor to associate professor of environmental physiology at Yale University. Since 1976, he has worked in ergonomics and environmental medicine at the U.S. Army Research Institute. His research concerns thermal physiology, peripheral circulation, and environmental physiology.

Enrique Hernández (1951–)

Medicine

Born on October 25, 1951, in Vega Baja, Puerto Rico, Hernández received his B.S. and M.D. degrees from the University of Puerto Rico in 1973 and 1977, respectively. From then until 1981, he was a fellow, intern, and resident at the Johns Hopkins Hospital. After academic appointments at the Johns Hopkins

University School of Medicine and the College of Osteopathic Medicine of the Pacific, he joined the faculty of the Medical College of Philadelphia, where he has been a full professor since 1989. In 1987, Hernández became the director of the Division of Gynecological Oncology at the college. He has had a number of hospital appointments in Philadelphia and Hawaii, as well as numerous consulting positions. In 1985, he became a fellow of the American College of Obstetricians and Gynecologists, and in 1986, a fellow of the American College of Surgeons. One of his main research interests is cancer of the female reproductive tract; he is the coauthor of the *Manual of Gynecological Oncology,* as well as of many other studies published in medical journals. Among his numerous awards are the 1994 Award for Excellence in Teaching at the Medical College of Pennsylvania. He was also named "Top Doctor" by *Philadelphia Magazine* in 1991 and 1994.

Gonzalo J. Hernández (1936-)

Optics, Atmospheric Physics

Born in San José, Costa Rica, in 1936, Hernández received his B.S. degree from the University of Notre Dame in 1958 and his Ph.D. in physical chemistry from the University of Rochester in 1962. From 1961 to 1969, he worked as a physicist at the Cambridge Research Lab of the air force, and from 1970 to 1985, he was the director of the Fritz Peak Observatory. From 1985 to 1987, he was a research scientist at the Space Physics Research Lab of the University of Michigan. He has been professor in the graduate program in geophysics at the University of Washington since 1988. Hernández has been a physicist for the Environmental Research Labs of the National Oceanic and Atmospheric Administration since 1969. He is a specialist in upper atmosphere physics and high-resolution spectroscopy.

Michael Louis Ibáñez (1916-)

Pathology

Born on November 9, 1916, in Havana, Cuba, Ibáñez received his M.D. degree from the University of Havana in 1948. He became an intern at Hermann Hospital in Houston in 1949–50 and developed a career in pathology there and at other hospitals. Since 1975, he has been professor of pathology, and since 1974, pathologist for the Cancer Center of the M. D. Anderson Hospital and Tumor Institute in Houston. Ibáñez has researched the pathologic anatomy of cancer and the pathology of the thyroid gland.

Vicente José Llamas (1944-)

Solid-State Physics

Born on February 15, 1944, in Los Angeles, California, Llamas received his B.S. degree from Loyola University of Los Angeles in 1966 and his M.S. and Ph.D. degrees from the University of Missouri, Rolla, in 1968 and 1970, respectively. From 1970 to 1984, he went from assistant to full professor of physics at New Mexico Highlands University. Since 1984, he has been chairman of the Department of Physics and Math. His research concerns surface studies of alkali halides in the infrared, as well as the atmospheric study of air pollutants.

Joseph Llauradó (1927-)

Nuclear Medicine, Biomedical Engineering

Born on February 6, 1927, in Barcelona, Spain, Llauradó received both M.D. (1950) and Ph.D. (1960) degrees from the University of Barcelona. After teaching and researching in countries around the world, including England, Italy, Holland, New Zealand, and Venezuela, he became a senior endocrinologist for Pfizer and Co. in Connecticut from 1959 to 1961. From 1963 to the present, he has been a researcher and professor at universities in the United States. Since 1983, he has been professor of radiation science at the Loma Linda School of Medicine and chief of nuclear medical services of the Veterans Administration Hospital in Loma Linda. Llauradó researches radionuclides in cardiology and radionuclide treatment of pulmonary cancer.

Rodolfo Llinas (1934-)

Neurobiology, Electrophysiology

Born on December 16, 1934, in Bogotá, Colombia, Llinas received his M.D. degree from the Pontifical Universidad Javierana in Bogotá in 1959 and a Ph.D. degree in neurophysiology from the Australian National University in 1965. He has worked at the National University of Colombia, the University of Minnesota, the American Medical Association, and the University of Iowa. Since 1976, he has been professor and chairman of physiology and biophysics at New York University Medical Center. Since 1975, he has been the editor-in-chief of *Neuroscience Journal.* He conducts structural and functional studies of neuronal systems and also studies the evolution and development of the central nervous system.

Diana Montes de Oca López (1937-)

Microbiology, Immunology

Born on August 26, 1937, in Havana, Cuba, López received her B.S. degree from the University of Havana in 1960 and her M.S. and Ph.D. degrees in microbiology from the University of Miami in 1968 and 1970, respectively. From 1970 to 1983, she went from research associate to full professor of microbiology at the University of Miami School of Medicine, where she continues to pursue her career. Since 1980, she has been the section leader in tumor virology and immunology for the state of Florida Comprehensive Cancer Center. Her research concerns tumor immunology, viral oncogenesis, and cell kinetics.

Cynthia Luz Marcelo (1945-)

Cell Physiology

Born on August 13, 1945, in New York City, Marcelo received her B.S. degree from Mt. St. Vincent College in 1967 and her M.S. and Ph.D. degrees in cell physiology from the State University of New York at Buffalo in 1969 and 1973, respectively. From 1975 to 1983, she went from assistant to associate professor of physiology in dermatology at the University of Michigan; since 1983, she has been the director of the research division of dermatology there. Her research concerns the control of epidermal cell function and the use of tissue culture technology to study growth factors and the effects of hormones and vitamin A on growth and function.

Michael Allen Mares (1945-)

Mammalian Biogeography

Born on March 11, 1945, in Albuquerque, New Mexico, Mares received his B.S. degree from the University of New Mexico in 1968, his M.S. degree from Kansas State University in 1969, and his Ph.D. degree in zoology from the University of Texas in 1973. He went from assistant to associate professor of ecology at the University of Pittsburgh from 1973 to 1981. In 1981, he went to the University of Oklahoma; he is currently a professor of zoology there and director of the Stovall Museum. Mares has been a fellow and fieldworker in Argentina as well as in the Southwest of the United States. In his research, he examines convergent evolution, adaptation and community organization of desert rodents of the world, as well as ecology, conservation, evolution, and systematics of South American mammals.

Richard Isaac Martínez (1944-)

Physical Chemistry

Born on August 16, 1944, in Havana, Cuba, Martínez received his B.S. degree from McGill University in 1964 and his Ph.D. degree in chemistry from the University of California, Los Angeles, in 1976. Martínez has worked as a research chemist at San Diego State University, Shell Oil, and UCLA. Since 1976, he has been a research chemist for the National Bureau of Standards of the U.S. Department of Commerce. In 1981, he was the recipient of the Bronze Medal Award from the Department of Commerce, and in 1983, he received the Independent Research 100 Award. He has worked on the development and application of tandem mass spectrometry MS/MS to the study of kinetics of complex organic reaction systems relevant to oxidation and atmospheric chemistry.

José Méndez (1921-)

Physiology, Nutrition

Born on August 17, 1921, in Tapachula, Mexico, Méndez received his B.S. degree from the Universidad de San Carlos in Guatemala City in 1947, his M.S. degree from the University of Illinois in 1948 and his Ph.D. degree in physiology from the University of Minnesota in 1957. From 1965 to 1966, he was associate professor of nutrition at the Massachusetts Institute of Technology; since 1966, he has been professor of health and applied physiology at Penn State University. He is a specialist in nutrition studies and nutrition training in developing countries and the adaptation of man to different environmental stresses.

Manuel Gaspar Meléndez (1935-)

Atomic Physics, Molecular Physics

Born in New York City on June 15, 1935, Meléndez received his B.Ch.E. and his Ph.D. degrees in chemical physics from the University of Florida in 1958 and 1963, respectively. From 1965 to 1966, he worked as an atomic physicist at the National Bureau of Standards and as a staff scientist at Martin Marietta from 1966 to 1969, when he relocated to the University of Georgia. He is currently professor of physics at Georgia. His research concerns ionization mechanisms at intermediate and low energies.

Teresa Mendoza

Engineering

Teresa Mendoza was born in Oakland, California, and brought up in a bilingual environment. She received her primary education there and later her B.S. in Civil Engineering from San Jose State University in 1979. Subsequently, she received training in Environmental Studies and Program Management with the state of California Department of Transportation. In 1980, Mendoza joined the U.S. Army Corps of Engineers' Rotational Engineering Program, and by 1986 became the chief of the Emergency Management Branch, supervising the Emergency Management Center, which deals with such natural disasters as earthquakes and floods. She is a founder and serves as the Chief of the Earthquake Preparedness Center for the U.S. Army Corps of Engineers. Among her many honors is the 1988 Emergency Manager of the Year Award from the U.S. Army Corps of Engineers and the 1993 Hispanic Engineer Award for Professional Achievement.

Teresa Mercado (1921–)

Histochemistry, Cytochemical Pathology

Born on October 15, 1921, in Ponce, Puerto Rico, Mercado received her B.S. degree from the College of Mt. St. Vincent in 1947 and her M.S. and Ph.D. degrees in biological physiology from the Catholic University of America in 1947 and 1950, respectively. Since 1949, she has been a research physiologist at the National Institute for Allergy and Infectious Diseases of the National Institutes of Health. Her research is in pathologic physiology, histochemistry, biochemistry, and cytochemistry of parasitic diseases, especially experimental malaria and trypanosomiases.

Mario Molina. (Photograph by Donna Coveney.)

Teresa Mercado.

Mario Molina (1943–)

Chemistry

Mario Molina was born in Mexico City on March 19, 1943. In 1995, as a researcher and professor at the Massachusetts Institute of Technology, Molina shared the Nobel Prize in Chemistry with two others for their work that led to the international ban on chemicals believed to be depleting the ozone protective layer of the earth. The native of Mexico earned his B.S. degree in Chemical Engineering from the National Autonomous University of Mexico in 1965 and his Ph.D. in Physical Chemistry from the University of California-Berkeley in 1972. Molina has taught and conducted research at various universities in the United States. From 1982 until 1989, Molina was a Senior Research Scientist at the Caltech Jet Propulsion Laboratory. In 1989, he was appointed Professor in the Department of Earth, Atmospheric and Planetary Sciences at the Massachusetts Institute of Technology. In 1992, he became the Lee and Geraldine Martin Professor of Environmental Sciences at MIT. Molina has been a world leader in developing scientific understanding of the chemistry of the stratospheric ozone layer and its susceptibility to man-made perturbations. He has explained through his laboratory experiments new reaction sequences that enable the catalytic processes which account for most of the observed ozone destruction in the Antarctic stratosphere. Dr. Mario J. Molina became the first Hispanic scientist to receive the NASA Medal for Exceptional Scientific Achievement. That same year he was also the first Hispanic to receive the United Nations Environmental Programme Global 500 Award. His other awards include the United Nations Environment Programme Global 500 Award (1989) and the Pew Scholar on Conservation, the Environment (1990–92) and the Hispanic Engineer National Achievement Award (1992).

Héctor Rolando Nava-Villarreal (1943–)

Medicine, Oncology

Born in Nuevo Laredo, Tamaulipas, Mexico, on May 23, 1943, Nava received all of his education in Mexico, including his M.D. degree from the Universidad de Nuevo León in 1967. He did his internship in Corpus Christi and his residency at the Roswell Park Cancer Institute in Buffalo, New York, where he also served as a fellow in surgical oncology from 1974 to 1976. From 1968 to 1970, he served in active duty in the U.S. Army, spending time from 1969 to 1970 as a battalion surgeon in Vietnam. From 1976 to the present, he has been a cancer researcher at the Roswell Park Cancer Institute. From 1991 to the present, he has been the vice chairman of the surgical oncology program there. Nava has been a pioneer in the use of lasers to treat cancer.

Isabel Cristina Pérez-Farfante (1916–)

Zoology

Born on July 24, 1916, in Havana, Cuba, Pérez received her B.S. degree from the University of Havana in 1938 and her M.S. and Ph.D. degrees in biology from Radcliffe College in 1944 and 1948, respectively. From 1948 to 1960, she was a professor of invertebrate biology at the University of Havana. Since 1966, she has worked as a systematics zoologist at the National Marine Fisheries Service. Her research interests include systematics, morphology, and distribution of decapod crustacea, with special reference to western Atlantic and eastern Pacific regions.

Víctor Pérez-Méndez (1923–)

Physics

Born on August 8, 1923, in Guatemala City, Guatemala, Pérez received his B.S. degree in 1947 from the Hebrew University in Jerusalem and his Ph.D. degree in physics from Columbia University in 1951.

He became a research scientist at the Lawrence Berkeley Lab in 1953 and has remained there until this date. Since 1969, he has been a professor of physics (radiology) at the University of California, San Francisco; from 1969 to 1977, he was the head of that department. Pérez has published more than 300 papers on his research in the fields of nuclear and high-energy physics, radiation detectors, and medical imaging.

David Pimentel (1925–)

Ecology, Entomology

Born on May 24, 1925, in Fresno, California, Pimentel received his B.S. degree from the University of Massachusetts in 1948 and his Ph.D. degree in entomology from Cornell University in 1951. From 1951 to 1953, he was chief of the Tropical Research Lab at the U.S. Public Health Service in San Juan, Puerto Rico. From 1955 to 1976, he moved up the ranks from assistant to full professor of insect ecology at Cornell University, which is his current position. He has had a number of prestigious fellowships in the United States and Europe, and from 1964 to 1966, he was a member of the President's Science Advisory Council; he has also worked extensively

Isabel Cristina Pérez-Farfante.

with the United Nations, UNESCO, the National Academies of Science, HEW, USAID, the Environmental Protection Agency, and the Department of Energy. He has also been a lecturer and keynote speaker at the principal biological and entomological societies in Africa, Europe, Canada, and the United States. His research concerns ecology and genetics of insect-plant, parasite-host, and predator-prey population systems. In 1992, Pimentel received the Award for Distinguished Service to rural Life from the rural Sociological Society Council. In addition, he has been selected to present numerous keynote speeches prestigious scientific organizations in the United States and abroad. In addition to his more than 400 scientific publications, of which 17 are books, Pimentel has served on the editorial boards of such journals as *Ecological Economic, Journal of Sustainable Agriculture,* and *Crop Protection.*

Fausto Ramírez (1923–)

Organic Chemistry

Born on June 15, 1923, in Zulueta, Cuba, Ramírez received his B.S., M.S., and Ph.D. degrees from the University of Michigan in 1946, 1947, and 1949, respectively. He made his career at the University of Virginia, Columbia University, the Illinois Institute of Technology, and the State University of New York at Stoney Brook, where he was professor from 1959 to 1985; today he is professor emeritus there. Ramírez developed a record of lectures, fellowships, and honors around the world. In 1969, he was awarded the Silver Medal of the City of Paris, and in 1968, the Cresy-Morrison Award from the New York Academy of Sciences. His research concerns the theoretical and practical aspects of the chemistry of phosphorus and sulfur compounds, organic synthesis, and molecular biology.

Mario E. Ramírez (1926–)

Medicine

Mario Ramírez was born in Roma, Texas, on April 3, 1926. He received his early education there and went on to graduate from the University of Texas with a B.A. in 1945; after that he received his M.D. degree from the University of Tennessee College of Medicine in 1948. Since that time he has led a distinguished career in family practice and in medical education, rising to the governing boards of medical institutions in the state of Texas and to membership on the Coordinating Board of Texas Colleges and Universities (1979–85) and the Board of Regents of the University of Texas System (1988–95). Throughout his career he has won numerous awards, including the American Academy of Family Physicians and

the *Good Housekeeping* magazine Family Doctor of the Year Award (1978) and the Bicentennial Dr. Benjamin Rush Award of the American Medical Association (1985).

Marian Lucy Rivas (1943–)

Medical Genetics, Computer Systems

Born on May 6, 1943, in New York City, Rivas received her B.S. degree from Marian College in 1964 and her M.S. and Ph.D. degrees in medical genetics from Indiana University in 1967 and 1969, respectively. After serving with a fellowship at Johns Hopkins University from 1969 to 1971, Rivas worked as an assistant professor of biology at Douglas College of Rutgers University from 1971 to 1975; thereafter, she was an associate professor from 1975 to 1982 at the Hemophilia Center of the Oregon Health Science University. Since 1982, she has been a full professor there, and since 1978, an associate scientist at the Neurological Science Institute of Good Samaritan Hospital. She has served in genetics committees at the National Institutes of Health and in adjunct positions at universities in the United States and in Venezuela. Her research concerns human gene mapping, genetic aspects of epilepsy, computer applications in clinical genetics, and genetic counseling.

Evelyn Margaret Rivera (1929–)

Endocrinology, Cancer

Born on November 10, 1929, in Holister, California, Rivera received her A.B., M.A., and Ph.D. degrees in zoology from the University of California, Berkeley, in 1952, 1960, and 1963, respectively. She was a fellow of the American Cancer Society in England from 1963 to 1965. From 1965 to 1972, she went from assistant to associate professor of zoology at Michigan State University; from 1972 on, she has been a full professor. In her research she has worked for the National Cancer Institute and held fellowships for her work on cancer and endocrinology from a number of institutions. In 1965, Rivera was given the UNESCO Award from the International Cell Research Organization. Rivera's research interests include cell transformation and the biology of tumors.

Eloy Rodríguez (1947–)

Biology

Born in Edinburg, Texas, on January 7, 1947, Rodríguez is the founder of the discipline of zoopharmacognosy, or self-medication by primates and is a world-renown expert on natural products chemistry and biology. He received his B.A. in Biology and his Ph.D. in phytochemistry and plant biology in

Eloy Rodríguez.

1969 and 1975, respectively, from the university of Texas at Austin. He followed these degrees with post-graduate work at the University of British Columbia in Vancouver, Canada. From 1976 to 1995, he served as a professor with a joint appointment in the Toxicology Program and the Department of community and Environmental Medicine at the University of California-Irvine. In 1995, Rodríguez was selected for the Jane Perkins Chair of Environmental Studies at Cornell University. Rodríguez has conducted research and served as a consultant all over the world. He is the discovered of numerous important organic chemicals from tropical and desert plants, which are being tested as drugs in the fight against cancer and other diseases. Included among his many awards are the *Los Angeles Times* Professional Research Accomplishment Recognition (1989) and the First Hispanic Educator Award from the League of United Latin American Citizens (1984). Rodríguez has raised millions of dollars in grants to fund his extensive research projects. Among his professional activities, he has served as the chair of a special study section for the National Cancer Institute, Director of the National Chicano Council on Higher Education and Vice President of the Society

for Advancement of Chicanos and Native Americans in Science. Rodríguez is has also the been the editor of various newsletters and served on the editorial boards of scientific journals, such as *Phytochemical Analysis* (1989–1992).

Juan Guadalupe Rodríguez (1920–)

Entomology

Born on December 23, 1920, in Española, New Mexico, Rodríguez received a B.S. degree from New Mexico State University in 1943 and M.S. and Ph.D. degrees from the University of Ohio in 1946 and 1949, respectively. From 1949 to 1961, he went from associate entomologist to full professor of Entomology at the University of Kentucky, where he still does research and teaches in the College of Agriculture. He has been awarded the Thomas Poe Cooper Award for Distinguished Research by the University of Kentucky. Rodríguez's research concerns axenic culture of arthropods, insect and mite nutrition, and insect pest management.

Juan Carlos Romero (1937–)

Animal Physiology, Computer Science

Born on September 15, 1937, in Mendoza, Argentina, Romero received his B.S. degree from San José College in Argentina in 1955 and his M.D. degree from the University of Mendoza in 1964. From 1968 to 1973, Romero worked as a research associate physiologist at the University of Michigan. From 1973 to 1980, he ascended the ranks to become a professor of physiology at the Mayo School of Medicine of the Mayo Foundation, a position he still holds today. Since 1982, he has also served as the director of the Hypertension Research Lab. He has been associated with and served on numerous committees that deal with heart disease and hypertension, including the Pan American Council on High Blood Pressure, the National Heart, Lung and Blood Institute of the NIH, the American Heart Association, and NASA. In his research, Romero studies mechanisms by which the kidney can produce high blood pressure; he identifies hormones that control renal circulation and excretion of salt. Among Romero's numerous awards are the Teacher of the Year Award from the Mayo School of Medicine in 1981. In 1991, he was elected by the Council on High Blood Pressure Research to give the Lewis K. Dahl Memorial Lecture in the American Heart Association's 464th scientific session.

Albert William Saenz (1923–)

Theoretical Physics

Born in Medellín, Colombia, on August 27, 1923, Saenz received his B.S., M.S., and Ph.D. degrees in physics from the University of Michigan in 1944, 1945, and 1949, respectively. He then worked at the Naval Research Laboratory, where he later became head of the theory consulting staff in the condensed matter and radiation science division. He has been a visiting scientist at the Oak Ridge National Lab, the Massachusetts Institute of Technology, Johns Hopkins University, Princeton University, and elsewhere. In 1969, he was the recipient of the Pure Science Award at the Naval Research Lab. His research interests include special and general relativity, symmetry and degeneracy in quantum mechanics, and quantum scattering theory.

Pedro Antonio Sánchez (1940–)

Agronomy, Soil Fertility

Born on October 7, 1940, in Havana, Cuba, Sánchez received his B.S., M.S., and Ph.D. degrees in soil science from Cornell University in 1962, 1964, and 1968, respectively. From 1968 to the present, he has been associated with North Carolina State University, where he has been a professor of soil science and leader of the Tropical Soils Program since 1979.

Pedro Antonio Sánchez.

His research and consultancies have taken him abroad, most frequently to Latin America. For his outstanding service, the government of Peru awarded him the Orden de Mérito Agrícola Medal. Currently, Sánchez is professor emeritus from North Carolina State and director of the International Centre for Research in Agroforestry (ICRAF), Nairobi, Kenya. ICRAF is devoted to alleviating poverty, tropical deforestation, and land degradation, through improved agroforestry systems. He also serves as chairman of the board of the worldwide Tropical Soil Biology and Fertility Program and as chairman of the National Academy of Sciences panel on sustainable agriculture and the environment in the humid tropics. Sánchez's research concerns the fertility and management of tropical soils, especially rice soils and tropical pastures.

Alberto Serrano (1931–)

Psychiatry

Born on April 7, 1931, in Buenos Aires, Argentina, Serrano was raised and educated in Argentina, where he became a medical doctor after graduating from the Buenos Aires School of Medicine in 1956. He did his internship at the Clínica Córdoba and at the National Institute of Mental Health, both in Buenos Aires. In 1957, he immigrated to the United States and began developing his career in is psychiatry as a resident in the Department of Neurology and Psychiatry at the University of Texas Medical Branch in Galveston, Texas. Since that time he has grown to become one of the finest psychiatrists and professors of psychiatry, specializing in child psychiatry in the United States. He rose the ranks at the University of Texas, first in Galveston, then in San Antonio, where he became the director of child and adolescent psychiatry. From 1986 to the present, he has served as professor of psychiatry and pediatrics and director of the Division of Child and Adolescent Psychiatry at the University of Pennsylvania School of Medicine. In the communities that he has lived, Serrano has been a director of various mental health clinics; since 1986, he has been the medical director of the Philadelphia Child Guidance Clinic and the psychiatrist-in-chief and director of the psychiatry division of the Children's Hospital of Philadelphia. In 1991, he became associate chairman of the Department of Psychiatry of he University of Pennsylvania School of Medicine. Among his various international recognitions, the American Family Therapy Association recognized him in 1986 for his "Pioneering Contribution to Family Therapy."

Margarita Silva-Hunter (1915-)

Mycology, Microbiology

Born on November 28, 1915, in Río Piedras, Puerto Rico, Silva received her B.A. degree from the University of Puerto Rico in 1936 and her M.S. and Ph.D. degrees from Harvard University in 1945 and 1952, respectively. From 1945 to the present, she has worked in the College of Physicians and Surgeons of Columbia University, where she has been an associate professor of dermatology since 1963. She has worked as a consulting mycologist and researcher at a number of hospitals and institutes, including the U.S. Public Health Service, the Squibb Institute for Medical Research, and the American Board of Medical Microbiology. Her research concerns the morphology, taxonomy, and biology of pathogenic fungi.

Aída R. Soto (1931-)

Organic Chemistry, Biochemistry

Born on December 3, 1931, in Havana, Cuba, Soto received her B.S. degree from the University of Havana in 1953 and her M.S. and Ph.D. degrees in chemistry from the University of Miami in 1962 and 1966, respectively. After serving as an instructor in the Department of Pharmacology and the School of Medicine of the University of Miami, in 1969 Soto became a researcher for the Dade division of the American Hospital Supply Company, where she has been a section head since 1984. Among her research interests are clinical enzymology, radioimmunoassays, and the use of immunologic techniques in clinical chemistry.

John Taboada (1943-)

Physical Optics, Applied Physics

Born on September 8, 1943, in Tampico, Mexico, Taboada received his B.A. degree from Trinity University (San Antonio) in 1966 and his M.S. and Ph.D. degrees in physics from Texas A & M University in 1968 and 1973, respectively. Since 1966, he has worked for the U.S. Air Force, first in the radiation science division, and since 1968 in the data Science division. In 1915, he received the Outstanding Technical Achievement Award, and in 1975, the Outstanding Science Achievement Award from the air force. Taboada's research concerns the biophysics of ultrashort pulsed lasers, laser spectroscopy, nonlinear optics, and applied optics.

Frank Talamantes (1943-)

Biology

Frank Talamantes was born on July 8, 1943 and raised in El Paso, Texas. He received his B.A. in biology from the University of St. Thomas in Houston, his M.A. in Biology from Sam Houston State University in 1970 and his Ph.D. in Endocrinology from the University of California-Berkeley in 1974. From 1974 on, Talamantes developed his research and teaching career at the University of California-Santa Cruz, where he became a full professor in 1984. Talamantes' research concerns the endocrine function of the placenta and the structure and regulation of various hormones, including the growth hormone. His work in reproductive endocrinology is internationally recognized. In recognition of his achievement, in 1991 he was selected to give the Transatlantic Medal Lecture by the Society for Endocrinology of the United Kingdom. In 1993, he also received the Research award from the Society for the Study of Reproduction. From 1986 to 1988, Talamantes served as the associate editor of the journal *Endocrinology*.

Gladys Torres-Blasini

Microbiology

Born in Ponce, Puerto Rico, Torres received a B.S. degree from the University of (San Antonio) Puerto Rico in 1948 and M.S. and Ph.D. degrees in bacteriology from the University of Michigan in 1952 and 1953, respectively. From 1952 on, she made her career at the Medical School of the University of Puerto Rico, where she has been head of the Department of Microbiology and Medical Zoology since 1977. She has held grants from the U.S. Public Health Service, Hoffman-LaRoche, the National Institutes of Health, and Veterans Administration hospitals. Her research in bacteriology includes the comparison of the phagocytosis of various candid species.

Pedro Ramón Urquilla (1939-)

Clinical Pharmacology

Born on July 18, 1939, in San Miguel, El Salvador, Urquilla received his M.D. degree from the University of El Salvador in 1965. From 1966 to 1969, he held fellowships from the Pan American Health Organization and from the National Institutes of Health. From 1969 to 1979, he developed a career as a professor of pharmacology at the University of Madrid. Since 1979, he has worked in private industry in the United States; since 1981, he has been the associate director of clinical research for Pfizer, Inc. His research concerns the analysis of the pharmacological receptors of the cerebral arteries.

James J. Valdés (1951–)

Biotechnology

Born on April 25, 1951 in San Antonio, Texas, Valdés received his B.S. degree in psychology and biological sciences from Loyola University in Chicago in 1973. He received an M.S. degree in physiological psychology from Trinity University in San Antonio in 1976 and a Ph.D. degree in neuroscience from Texas Christian University in 1979. From 1979 to 1982, he did postgraduate work in toxicology and environmental health sciences at Johns Hopkins University. In 1982 he began working as a researcher for the Department of the United States Army in Maryland. Valdés has won many awards from the army for his achievements as a researcher. His research interests include biosensors, receptor and ion channel response to toxic commands, and mechanisms of neurotransmission.

Gaspar Rodolfo Valenzuela (1933–)

Electronic Engineering

Born on January 6, 1933, in Coelemu, Chile, Valenzuela received his B.S. and M.S. degrees in electrical engineering from the University of Florida in 1954 and 1955, respectively; he received his Dr. Eng. degree from Johns Hopkins University in 1965. Between 1957 and 1968, he worked as a research engineer at Johns Hopkins. Since 1968, he has been a research electronic engineer for the Naval Research Lab in Washington, D.C. His research concerns electromagnetic theory, rough surface scattering theory, and the interaction of electromagnetic waves with the ocean.

Carlos Vallbona (1927–)

Community Medicine

Born on July 29, 1927, in Granollers, Barcelona, Spain, Vallbona received all of his primary education there, and his B.S. and M.D. degrees from the University of Barcelona in 1944 and 1955, respectively. He did postgraduate work in Barcelona, Paris, and Louisville, Kentucky. Vallbona began at the Baylor College of Medicine in Houston, Texas, as a pediatric resident in 1955 and has remained with that institution throughout his career. There he has served as service professor and chairman of the Department of Community Medicine at Baylor and chief of staff of the Community Health Program of the Harris County Hospital District. He has received numerous awards for his contributions to academic medicine and to community health. Moreover, Vallbona has done extensive research on the applications of computers in medicine, cardiorespiratory problems of disabled persons, community medicine, and the control of hypertension and diabetes in the community.

Lydia Villa-Komaroff (1947–)

Biology

Biologist Lydia Villa-Komaroff was born in 1947 in Las Vegas, New Mexico, the oldest of six children. While still in high school, she began studying biology in a Texas college program sponsored by the National Science Foundation during summers. Villa-Komaroff received her B.A. degree from Goucher College in Maryland in 1970 and her Ph.D. in cell biology from M.I.T. in 1975. Following her studies, she became an assistant professor at the University of Massachusetts and, since 1986, has been an associate professor at the Harvard Medical School. Villa-Komaroff's research in molecular biology focuses on cloning and on how bacteria can produce insulin brought her national attention. Her current research deals with the development of the brain. Villa-Komaroff has been selected to give major lectures at scientific conferences and, in 1992, she received the Hispanic Engineer National Achievement Award. She serves on the editorial boards of *Journal of molecular Evolution, BioTechniques* and *Journal of Women's Health.*

References

Jaques Catell Press, eds. *American Men and Women of Science,* 16th edition. New York: R. R. Bowker, 1986.

Amy L. Unterburger, ed. *Who's Who among Hispanic Americans.* Detroit: Gale Research, 1991.

Nicolás Kanellos

Literature

**✳ The Colonial Period ✳ The Nineteenth Century ✳ The Early Twentieth Century
✳ World War II to the Present ✳ Outstanding Hispanic Literary Figures**

Hispanic literature of the United States is the literature written by Americans of Hispanic descent. It includes the Spanish-language literature of what became the U.S. Southwest before this territory was incorporated through war and annexation. It thus incorporates a broad geographic and historical space, and even includes the writings of early explorers of the North American continent as well as Spanish-speaking immigrants and exiles who made the United States their home. It is a literature that reflects the diverse ethnic and national origins of Hispanics in the United States, and thus includes writers of South and Central American, Caribbean, and Spanish descent, as well as writers of Afro-Hispanic and Indo-Hispanic literatures; it may also include writers of Sephardic (exiled Spanish Jews) origins who identified themselves as Hispanic, should their works be brought to light in the future. Finally, Hispanic literature of the United States is a literature that also reflects the linguistic diversity of the people and has been written and published in both Spanish and English and even bilingually.

✳ THE COLONIAL PERIOD

The roots of Hispanic literature were planted north of the Rio Grande long before the landing of the Mayflower at Plymouth Rock. Juan de Oñate's 1598 colonizing expedition up from central Mexico into what is today New Mexico is doubly important as the beginning of a written and oral literary tradition in a European language, Spanish. The written tradition is represented by the landmark epic poem *La conquista de la Nueva México* (*The Conquest of the New Mexico*), by one of the soldiers on the expedition, Gaspar Pérez de Villagrá. The oral Spanish literary tradition was introduced with the improvised dramas, songs, ballads, and poetic recitations of the soldiers, colonists, and missionaries, some of which have survived in New Mexico and the Southwest to this date.

The Northeast of what is today the United States, on the other hand, can point to its earliest written and oral expression in Spanish with the founding of the colony of Sephardic Jews in New Amsterdam in 1654. Both the Northeast and Southwest can boast an unbroken literary tradition in Spanish that predates the American Revolutionary War. Much of this early literary patrimony from the colonial period has been lost or has not been collected and studied; the same can be said of all periods of literature except for contemporary Hispanic literature in the United States. A missionary and colonial literature of historical chronicles, diaries, and letters and an oral literature developed in the Southwest until the Mexican-American War of 1846–48.

✳ THE NINETEENTH CENTURY

Following the Mexican-American War and up to 1910, the foundation was really laid for the creation of a true Mexican American literature, a U.S. Hispanic literature, with the resident population of the Southwest adapting to the new U.S. political and social framework. It was the period when many Spanish-language newspapers begin publishing throughout the Southwest and when they and the creative literature they contained became an alternative to Anglo-American information and cultural flow. During this period the important commercial centers of San Francisco and Los Angeles supported numerous newspapers, which, besides fulfilling their commercial and informational functions, also published short stories, poetry, essays, and even serialized novels, such *Las aventuras de Joaquín Murieta* (*The Adventures of Joaquín Murieta*), a

455

novel of the legendary California social bandit, published in 1881 by the Santa Barbara newspaper *La gaceta.* Among the more important newspapers in California were Los Angeles' *El clamor público* (*The Public Clamor*) and *La estrella de Los Angeles* (*The Los Angeles Star*), issued in the 1850s, and *La crónica* (*The Chronicle*), from the 1870s to the 1890s, and San Francisco's *La voz del Nuevo Mundo* (*The Voice of the New World*), *La sociedad* (*Society*), *La cronista* (*The Chronicles*), and *La República* (*The Republic*), issued during the last four decades of the century. In New Mexico, *El clarín mexicano* (*The Mexican Clarion*) and *El fronterizo* (*The Frontier*), in the 1870s, *El nuevomexicano* (*The New Mexican*), from the 1850s to the turn of the century, and *El defensor del pueblo* (*The People's Defender*), in the 1890s, were important. Among Texas' contributions during this period were San Antonio's *El bejareño* (*The Bejar County*) during the 1850s, El Paso's *Las dos Américas* (*The Two Americas*) in the 1890s, and *El clarín del norte* (*The Northern Clarion*) in the 1900s. These were but a few of the literally hundreds of newspapers that provided for the cultural enrichment and entertainment of the Mexican American communities while they provided information, helped to solidify the community, and defended the rights of Mexican Americans in the face of the growing influence of Anglo-American culture.

During the latter part of the nineteenth century various literary authors were published in book form. In southern California, María Amparo Ruiz de Burton was one of the first writers to contribute important novels in the English language. Writing under the pseudonym C. Loyal, she published *The Squatter and the Don* in 1881, a novel that effectively exploits the genre of the romance to document the loss of family lands by many Californios to squatters and other interests supported by the railroads, corrupt bankers and politicians in the newly acquired American territory and later the new state of California. From a wealthy California family herself, she underwrote the cost of publication of *The Squatter* and of her other novel, *Who Would Have Thought It?* (1872), which satirizes Yankee attitudes toward Indians, Mexicans and blacks during and after the Civil War.

Also in 1881, New Mexican Manuel M. Salazar published a novel of romantic adventure, *La historia de un caminante, o Gervacio y Aurora* (*The History of a Traveler on Foot, or Gervacio and Aurora*), which creates a colorful picture of the pastoral life in New Mexico at this time. Another New Mexican, Eusebio Chacón (1869–1948) published two short novels in 1892 that are celebrated today: *El hijo de la tempestad* (*Child of the Storm*) and *Tras la tormenta*

Miguel A. Otero.

la calma (*The Calm after the Storm*). New Mexican Miguel A. Otero (1859–1944) issued a three-volume autobiography, *My Life on the Frontier* (1935), in English, in which he covers his life from age five until just after his term as governor of New Mexico ended in 1906.

During the late 1870s, California bookseller and historian Hubert H. Bancroft had numerous autobiographies transcribed from oral dictation in his research for writing the history of California. In the process, some 15 Hispanic women of early California were able to dictate their autobiographies, some of which are literary documents that reveal women's perspectives on life, culture, politics and gender roles. Notable among these autobiographies are those of María Inocenta Avila's *Cosas de California* (*Things of California*), Josefa Carrillo de Fotch's *Narración de una californiana* (*Narration by a California Woman*), Apolinaria Lorenzana's *Memorias de una beata* (*Memories of a Pious Woman*), Eulalia Pérez's *Una vieja y sus recuerdos* (*An Old Woman and Her Memories*) and Felipa Osuna de Marrón's *Recuerdos del pasado* (*Memories of the Past*).

During the nineteenth century, poetry was primarily lyric, amorous, and pastoral and appeared regularly in the newspapers, with very few authors ever collecting their works in books. Among the most frequently appearing poets were the Texan E. Montalván in *El bejareño,* Felipe Maximiliano Chacón and Julio Flores in New Mexico papers, and Dantés in Santa Barbara's *La gaceta (The Gazette).* One of the most interesting poets of the turn of the century was Sara Estela Ramírez, who published her poems and some speeches in Laredo's *La crónica (The Chronicle)* and *El demócrata (The Democrat)* and in her own literary periodicals, *La corregidora (The Corrector)* and *Aurora,* between the years 1904 and 1910. In her life and in her literary works, Ramírez was an activist for the Mexican Liberal Party in its movement to overthrow dictator Porfirio Díaz, and for workers' and women's rights. But much work needs to be done in collecting and analyzing Ramírez's works and the thousands upon thousands of other poems that were published throughout the Southwest during the nineteenth century.

On the other hand, the late nineteenth century is the period when the Mexican *corrido,* (a folk ballad related to the *romance* introduced by the Spanish colonists and missionaries) came into maturity and proliferated throughout the Southwest. In particu-

Title page of *El hijo de la tempestad* by Eusebio Chacón.

Eusebio Chacón.

lar, the border ballad, which chronicled the adventures of social bandits, like Joaquín Murieta, Aniceto Pizaña, and even Billy the Kid, became a popular anvil on which was forged a Mexican American identity. The corrido increased its popularity in the twentieth century and became a living historical and poetic document that records the history of the great Mexican immigrations and labor struggles between the two world wars.

During the nineteenth century, the New York area sustained various Hispanic literary activities and cultural institutions. The newspapers came to play a key role in providing a forum for literary creation for a community that at that time was made up principally of Spaniards and Cubans. Such newspapers as *El menasajero semanal (The Weekly Messenger)* and the weekly *El mercurio de Nueva York (The New York Mercury),* during the late 1820s and the 1830s published news of the homeland, political commentary and poetry, short stories, essays, and even excerpts of plays. One of the first novels to be written and published in the United States by an Hispanic was also the very first historical novel written in the Spanish language: *Jicoténcal,* written by Father Félix Varela, the Cuban religious philosopher and publisher of Philadelphia's newspaper, *El habanero*. A promoter of Cuban independence from Spain, Varela details the treachery of Spanish conquistadors in Mexico during the early colonial period, probably as an ideological basis for Cuban separation from Spain. Two other early newspapers were *La crónica* (*The Chronicle*) and *La voz de América* (*The Voice of America*), appearing in the 1850s and 1860s, respectively. Among the poets publishing at this time were Miguel Teurbe Tolón (1820–1858), who was born in the United States, educated in Cuba, and became a conspirator for Cuban independence from Spain. One of the few books of poetry in Spanish was published in 1828: *Poesías de un mexicano* (*Poems by a Mexican*), by Anastacio Ochoa y Acuña.

But it was not until the late nineteenth century that newspaper, magazine, and book publishing really began to expand, because of increased immigration and the political and cultural activity related to the Cuban, Puerto Rican, and Dominican independence movements and the Spanish-American War. In this regard, the most noteworthy institution was the Cuban newspaper *La patria,* in whose pages could be found essays by the leading Cuban and Puerto Rican patriots. Furthermore, numerous essays, letters, diaries, poems, short stories, and literary creations by some of Puerto Rico's most important literary and patriotic figures were written in New York while they worked for the revolution. Included among these were Eugenio María de Hostos, Ramón Emeterio Betances, Lola Rodríguez de Tió, and Sotero Figueroa. Active as well in literature and political organizing were the revolutionary leaders Francisco González "Pachín" Marín, a Puerto Rican, and the Cuban José Martí. Marín, a typesetter by trade and an important figure in Puerto Rican poetry for his break with romanticism, left us an important essay, "Nueva York por dentro; una faz de su vida bohemia" ("New York on the Inside; One Side of Its Bohemian Life"), in which he sketches New York from the perspective of a disillusioned immigrant; this is perhaps the earliest document in Spanish that takes this point of view and can be perhaps considered the beginning of Hispanic immigrant literature. Martí was an international literary figure in his own right, and his writings are still studied today in Latin American literature classes throughout the world; he has left us a legacy of many essays and other writings that relate directly to his life in New York and elsewhere in the United States.

Also of importance as the most widely circulated weekly was *Las novedades* (1893–1918, *The News*), whose theater, music, and literary critic was the famed Dominican writer Pedro Henríquez Ureña.

Cuban literary and patriotic figure, José Martí.

An early Puerto Rican contribution was *La gaceta ilustrada* (*The Illustrated Gazette*), edited in the 1890s by writer Francisco Amy. Many of the Spanish-language literary books published in New York were also related to the Cuban independence struggle, such as Luis García Pérez's *El grito de Yara* (1879, *The Shout at Yara*) and Desiderio Fajardo Ortiz's *La fuga de Evangelina* (1898, *The Escape of Evangelina*), the story of Cuban heroine Evangelina Cossío's escape from incarceration by the Spaniards and her trip to freedom and the organizing effort in New York.

✸ THE EARLY TWENTIETH CENTURY

The Southwest

The turn of the century brought record immigration from Mexico to the Southwest and Midwest because of the Mexican Revolution of 1910. During the period from 1910 until World War II, immigrant workers and upper-class and educated professionals from Mexico interacted with the Mexican-origin residents of the Southwest, who had been somewhat cut off from the evolution of Mexican culture inside Mexico. During this period Hispanic newspaper and book publishing flourished throughout the Southwest. Both San Antonio and Los Angeles supported Spanish-language daily newspapers that served diverse readerships made up of regional groups from the Southwest, immigrant laborers, and political refugees from the revolution. The educated, political refugees played a key role in publishing, and in light of their upper social class, they created an ideology of a Mexican community in exile, or "México de afuera" [Mexico on the outside].

In the offices of San Antonio's *La prensa* (*The Press*) and Los Angeles' *La opinión* (*The Opinion*) and *El heraldo de México* (*The Mexican Herald*), some of the most talented writers from Mexico, Spain, and Latin America, such as Miguel Arce, Esteban Escalante, Gabriel Navarro, Teodoro Torres, and Daniel Venegas, earned their living as reporters, columnists and critics. These and many others wrote hundreds of books of poetry, essays, and novels, many of which were published in book form and marketed by the newspapers themselves via mail and in their own bookstores. Besides the publishing houses related to these large dailies, there were many other smaller companies, such as Laredo Publishing Company, Los Angeles' Spanish American Printing, and San Diego's Imprenta Bolaños Cacho Hnos.

The largest and most productive publishers resided in San Antonio. Leading the list was the publishing house founded by the owner, of *La prensa* and Los Angeles' *La opinión*, Ignacio Lozano. The Casa Editorial Lozano was by far the largest publishing establishment ever owned by a Hispanic in the United States. Among the San Antonio publishers were the Viola Novelty Company, probably a subsidiary of P. Viola, publisher of the satiric newspapers *El vacilón* (*The Joker*) and *El fandango* (*The Fandango*), active from 1916 until at least 1927; the Whitt Company; and the Librería Española, which still exists today as a bookstore. Many of the novels produced by these houses were part of the genre known as "novels of the Mexican Revolution"; the stories were set within the context of the revolution and often commented on historical events and personalities. In the United States, the refugees who wrote these novels were very conservative and quite often attacked the revolution and Mexican politicians, which they saw as the reason for their exile. Included among these were Miguel Bolaños Cacho's *Sembradores de viento* (1928, *Sewers of the Wind*), Brígido Caro's *Plutarco Elías Calles: dictador volchevique de México* (1924, *Plutarco Elías Calles: Bolshevik Dictator of Mexico*), and Lázaro Gutiérrez de Lara's *Los bribones rebeldes* (1932, *The Rebel Rogues*). Many were the authors of this very popular genre, including Miguel Arce, Conrado Espinosa, Alfredo González, Esteban Maqueo Castellanos, Manuel Mateos, Ramón Puente, and Teodoro Torres. The most famous has become Mariano Azuela, author of the masterpiece that is one of the foundations of modern Mexican literature, *Los de abajo* (*The Underdogs*), which was first published in 1915 in a serialized version in *El Paso's* newspaper El paso del norte (*The Northern Pass*) and was issued later by the same newspaper in book form.

Although most of the novels published during these years gravitated toward the political and counterrevolutionary, there were others of a more sentimental nature and even some titles that can be considered forerunners of the Chicano novel of the 1960s in their identification with the working-class Mexicans of the Southwest, their use of popular dialects, and their political stance in regard to U.S. government and society. The prime example of this new sensibility is newspaperman Daniel Venegas' *Las aventuras de Don Chipote o Cuando los pericos mamen* (1928, *The Adventures of Don Chipote or When Parakeets May Suckle Their Young*), a humorous picaresque account of a Mexican immigrant, Don Chipote, who travels through the Southwest working here and there at menial tasks and running into one misadventure after the other, suffering at the hands of rogues, the authorities, and his bosses while in search of the mythic streets of gold that the United States is supposed to offer immigrants. *Don Chipote* is a novel of immigration, a picaresque novel, and a novel of protest all wrapped into one, and furthermore, it is the one clear forerunner of today's Chicano literature.

One of the most important literary genres that developed in the newspapers at this time was *la crónica*, (chronicle). It was a short satirical column that was full of local color, current topics, and observation of social habits. It owed its origins to Addison and Steele in England and José Mariano de Lara in Spain, but was cultivated extensively throughout Mexico and Latin America. In the Southwest it came to function and serve purposes never before thought of in Mexico or Spain. From Los Angeles to San Antonio, Mexican moralists satirized the customs and behavior of the colony whose very existence was seen as threatened by the dominant Anglo-Saxon culture. It was the *cronista's* (cronicler's) job to enforce the ideology of "México de afuera" and battle the influence of Anglo-American culture and the erosion of the Spanish language caused by the influence of speaking English. The cronistas, using such pseudonyms as El Malcriado (The Spoiled Brat—Daniel Venegas), Kaskabel (Rattler—Benjamín Padilla),

Az.T.K. (Aztec), and Chicote (The Whip), were literally whipping and stinging the community into conformity, commenting on or simply poking fun at the common folks' mixing of Spanish and English and Mexican women's adapting American dress and more liberalized customs, such as cutting their hair short, raising the hemlines, and smoking.

First and foremost behind the ideology of the crónica writers and the owners of the newspapers was the goal of returning to the homeland; as soon as the hostilities of the revolution ended, the immigrants were supposed to return to Mexico with their culture intact. Quite often the target of their humorous attacks were stereotyped country bumpkins, like Don Chipote, who were having a hard time getting around in the modern American city. They also poked fun at the Mexican immigrants to the United States who became impressed with the wealth, modern technology, efficiency, and informality of American culture, to the extent that they considered everything American superior and everything Mexican inferior. In some of his chronicles, Jorge Ulica satirized women who made much to do about throwing American-style surprise parties and celebrating

The cover of Daniel Venegas' satirical newspaper, *El Malcriado.*

Thanksgiving, and criticized their taking advantage of greater independence and power at the expense of men's machismo. The cronistas quite often drew from popular jokes, anecdotes, and oral tradition to create these tales. Two of the most popular cronistas, who saw their columns syndicated throughout the Southwest, were the aforementioned Benjamín Padilla, an expatriate newspaperman from Guadalajara, and Julio Arce, who was also a political refugee from Guadalajara and used the pseudonym Jorge Ulica for his "Crónicas Diabólicas" (Diabolical Chronicles). So popular was this type of satire that entire weekly newspapers, usually of no more than eight pages in length, were dedicated to it. Daniel Venegas' weekly *El Malcriado* (*The Brat*) and P. Viola's *El vacilón* (*The Joker*) are prime examples of these.

Clustered around the publication of newspapers in the Southwest were communities of women intellectuals who not only aimed their journalism at the service of the Mexican Revolution and women's empowerment, but also penned and published some of the most eloquent editorials, speeches and poems in support of their liberal causes. Most noteworthy were Sara Estela Ramírez's newspapers and magazines, mentioned above; Andrea and Teresa Villarreal's *El obrero* (*The Worker*), founded in San Antonio in 1910; Isidra T. de Cárdenas' *La voz de la mujer* (*The Woman's Voice*), founded in El Paso in 1907; and *Pluma roja* (*Red Pen*), edited and directed by Blanca de Moncaleano from 1913 to 1915 in Los Angeles. In the anarchist *Pluma roja,* there was a consistent editorial articulation of reconfiguring the role of women in society as central to the struggle for social, political and economic freedom; it was presented as an integral part of the ideal of anarchism. Blanca de Moncaleano addressed both men and women, urging them to free women of their enslavement and to encourage their education and politicization. In a February 1, 1914, editorial entitled "Hombre, educad a la mujer" ("Man, Educate Woman"), she pled for men to let women obtain an education.

One of these women activists, Leonor Villegas de Magnón (1876–1955), was born and raised in Mexico, but emigrated to Laredo, Texas. She provided one of the very few autobiographies of the Mexican Revolution to be written by a woman: *The Rebel,* which was finally published posthumously in 1994 after the author was unsuccessful in having it published in her Spanish and/or English versions during her lifetime. Villegas de Magnón was associated with the ideological precursors of the Mexican Revolution, the Brothers Flores Magón, and in fact spent her inherited fortune in support of the revolutionary forces. Villegas was the founder of a women's nursing corps, made up mostly by women from the Texas side of the border, which tended to the wounded in Venustiano Carranza's army. As such, she worked side-by-side with the future victor of the Revolution and president of the republic. Upon seeing how fast official sources had ignored the women's contribution, she specifically created her two autobiographies to document the role of women in Mexico's cataclysmic insurgency. Villegas was both an heroic figure and a dramatic writer, one who wrote with documentary care, but with literary style and flair.

Much of this literary activity in the Mexican American Southwest came to an abrupt halt with the Great Depression and the repatriation, forced or voluntary, of a large segment of that society back to Mexico. Some writers during the depression, like Américo Paredes, began to write in both Spanish and English and to express a very pronounced and politicized Mexican American sensibility. His English novel *George Washington Gómez* was written from 1936 to 1940 (but not published until 1990), and during the 1930s and 1940s he was a frequent contributor of poetry in Spanish, English, and bilingual format to newspapers in Texas, including *La prensa*. In 1937, he published a collection of poems, *Cantos de adolescencia (Songs of Adolescence)*, at age 22, but it was not until 1991 that his collected poems were issued, under the title *Between Two Worlds,* a collection containing works selected from his writings from the late 1930s to the 1950s.

Another very important literary figure who emerged during the depression and began to publish poetry and tales based on New Mexican folklore was Fray Angelico Chávez. A Franciscan monk, Chávez's poetry books are principally made up of poems to Christ and the Virgin Mary: *Clothed with the Sun* (1939), *New Mexico Triptych* (1940), *Eleven Lady Lyrics and Other Poems* (1945), *The Single Rose* (1948), and *Selected Poems with an Apologia* (1969). From the 1930s to the 1950s there appeared a number of short story writers who succeeded in publishing their works in mainstream English-language magazines. Most of these, such as Texas' Josefina Escajeda and Jovita González, based their works on folktales, oral tradition, and the picturesque customs of Mexicans in the Southwest. Robert Hernán Torres, who published some of his stories in *Esquire* magazine, focused his works on the cruelty and senselessness of the revolution in Mexico. Another prose writer in English who experienced relative success was Josephina Niggli; she focused many of her novels and short stories on life in Mexico after the revolution. Despite the significance of Chávez, Paredes, Niggli, and the others, it

Fray Angelico Chávez.

was not until the 1960s that there was a significant resurgence of Mexican American literary activity, except that by the end of that decade it was called Chicano literature.

Josephina Niggli was successful in having a number of her works published by general market presses in the United States. While writing as an adult, Niggli was able to vividly recreate the small-town settings of her rural upbringing in Mexico. Although born in 1910, she was somewhat of a nineteenth-century regionalist in her descriptions and evocations. Her *Mexican Village* (1945), for example, portrays the power of land and locale over individuals and community, in this case a fictional town on the northern border of Mexico. Like many of the New Mexico writers, Niggli was also concerned with tradition and the passage of customs and worldview from one generation to the other.

Emerging in the English-language literary world at the same time as Angélico Chávez was a group of New Mexican women writers who sought to examine the colonial and territorial past and preserve the folkways and customs that were fast passing away. Their contributions ranged from fiction and literary folklore to personal narrative and social history. Included among their works are: Nina Otero Warren's *Old Spain in Our Southwest* (1936); Cleofas Jaramillo's *The Genuine New Mexico Tasty Recipes: Old and Quaint Formulas for the Preparation of Seventy-five Delicious Spanish Dishes* (1939), a kind of culinary autobiography; Aurora Lucero White Lea's *Literary Folklore of the Hispanic Southwest* (1953); Fabiola Cabeza de Vaca's *The Good Life: New Mexico Traditions and Food* (1949) and *We Fed Them Cactus* (1954). Many of the personal reminiscences in these books are framed within the traditional practices of telling stories within the family, of passing recipes down from mother to daughter and relating them to life experiences and family history, of preserving the songs and other oral lore of the family and the region. In these women, we find a somewhat nostalgic recreation of the past that is an embryonic resistance to the Anglo-American ways that were eroding traditional New Mexican culture.

An English-language short fiction writer, María Cristina Mena (1893–1965), was also born and raised in Mexico and moved to the United States at age 14. In New York from 1913 to 1916, Mena published a series of short stories in *The Century Illustrated Monthly Magazine*. In 1927, many of these stories, along with new ones, were published in a collection under her husband's name, Henry K. Chambers, a dramatist and journalist. In the 1940s, she developed into a prolific novelist: *The Water Carrier's Secret* (1942), *The Two Eagles* (1942), *The Bullfighter's Son* (1944), *The Three Kings* (1946), and *Boy Heroes of Chapultepec: A Story of the Mexican War* (1953). Behind all of her writing was her desire to inform the public in the United States of the history and culture of Mexico, proposing to correct the negative image that Mexico has held in the popular media.

The Northeast

In New York, the period from the turn of the century up into the Great Depression was one of increased immigration and interaction of various Hispanic groups. It was a period of increased Puerto Rican migration, facilitated by the Jones Act, which declared Puerto Ricans to be citizens of the United States, and later of immigration of Spanish workers and refugees from the Spanish Civil War. Artistic and literary creation in the Hispanic community quite often supported the Puerto Rican nationalist movement and the movement to reestablish the Spanish republic.

At the turn of the century, Cuban and Spanish writers and newspapers still dominated the scene. The first decade of the century witnessed the founding of *La prensa* (*The Press*), whose heritage continues today in *El diario-La prensa* (*The Daily-The Press*), born of a merger in 1963. Also published during the decade were *Sangre latina* (*Latin Blood*), out of Columbia University, *Revista Pan-Americana* (*Pan American Review*), and *La paz y el trabajo* (*Peace and Work*), a monthly review of commerce, literature, science, and the arts. Even places as far away as Buffalo began to support their own publications, such as *La hacienda* (*The State*), founded in 1906.

Spanish-language literary publishing did not begin to expand until the late teens and early twenties. By far the most interesting volume that has come down to us from the teens is an early example of the immigrant novel. Somewhat similar in theme to *Don Chipote*, Venezuelan author Alirio Díaz Guerra's *Lucas Guevara* (1917) is the story of a young man who comes to the city seeking his fortune, but is ultimately disillusioned. While *Lucas Guevara* was probably self-published at the New York Printing Company, there were several Spanish-language publishing houses functioning during the teens in New York. One of the most important and long-lived houses, Spanish American Publishing Company, began issuing titles at this time and continued well into the 1950s. It too was an early publisher of books on the theme of Hispanics in New York, such as Puerto Rican playwright Javier Lara's *En la metrópoli del dólar* (*In the Metropolis of the Dollar*), circa 1919. *Las novedades* newspaper also published books, including Pedro Henríquez Ureña's *El nacimiento de Dionisos* (1916, *The Birth of Dionysus*).

Although during the 1920s the Spanish American Publishing Company, Carlos López Press, The Phos Press, and others were issuing occasional literary titles, it was not until the late twenties and early thirties that there was an intensification of activity. To begin with, various specialized newspapers began to appear. Probably as an outgrowth of the very active theatrical movement that was taking place in Manhattan and Brooklyn, *Gráfico* (*Graphic*) began publishing in 1927 as a theater and entertainment weekly newspaper under the editorship of the prolific writer Alberto O'Farrill, who was also a playwright and a leading comic actor in Cuban blackface farces (*teatro bufo cubano*). As was also the custom in the Southwest, *Gráfico* and the other newspapers and magazines published numerous poems, short stories, literary essays, and crónicas by the leading New York Hispanic writers. Among the most notable cronistas were those unknown writers using the pseudonyms Maquiavelo (Machiavelli) and Samurai; O'Farrill himself was an important contributor to the tradition, signing his columns "Ofa." As in the Southwest, these cronistas labored in their writings

Cover of the first issue of *Gráfico* newspaper.

to solidify the Hispanic community, which in New York was even more diverse than in the Southwest, drawing from many ethnic and national backgrounds. They too were protecting the purity of Hispanic culture against the dangers of assimilation, as they voiced the political and social concerns of the community and corrected and satirized current habits. While in the Southwest the cronistas promoted a "México de afuera," York they often attempted to create a "Trópico en Manhattan" (A Tropical [or Caribbean] Culture in Manhattan).

Unlike in the Southwest, there were no massive repatriations and deportations disrupting the cultural life in the Hispanic community during the Great Depression. In fact, New York continued to receive large waves of Hispanics during the depression and World War II: refugees from the Spanish Civil War, workers for the service and manufacturing industries flown in from Puerto Rico during World War II in the largest airborne migration in history, and Hispanics from the Southwest. Newspapers were founded that reflected this renewed interest in Spanish, Puerto Rican, and working-class culture: *Vida obrera* (1930, *Worker's Life*), *Alma boricua* (1934–35, *Puerto Rican Soul*), *España libre* (1943,

Free Spain), and *Cultura proletaria* (1943, *Proletariat Culture*). The pages of these newspapers are valuable sources of an important body of testimonial literature that reflected the life of the immigrant. They frequently took the form of autobiographical sketches, anecdotes, and stories, quite often in a homey, straightforward language that was also replete with pathos and artistic sensibility. Despite the many sources available in print, a large part of Puerto Rican, Cuban, Dominican, and Spanish literature in New York is an oral literature, a folk literature, completely consistent with and emerging from the working-class nature of the immigrants. For the Caribbean peoples there is an immense repository of lyric and narrative poetry that is to be found in their songs, such as the *décimas, plenas,* and *sones,* and in the popular recorded music of such lyrical geniuses as Rafael Hernández, Pedro Flores, and Ramito, whose compositions began appearing on recordings in the 1930s and continue to influence Puerto Rican culture on the island and in New York to the present. Of course, the compositions of Hernández and Flores have influenced Hispanic popular music around the world.

As the Puerto Rican community grew in the late 1920s and into World War II, Puerto Rican literature began to gain a larger profile in New York, but within a decidedly political context. It also seems that the literature with the most impact for the Puerto Rican community was dramatic literature, if published books are a measure. Poet Gonzalo O'Neill (1867–1942) was a businessman who, during the 1920s and 1930s, was at the hub of Puerto Rican and Hispanic cultural life, not only as a writer, but as a cultural entrepreneur, investing his money in the theater and protecting and offering support to other writers. O'Neill began his literary training and career in Puerto Rico as a teenager in association with a magazine, *El palenque de la juventud* (*The Young People's Arena*), which featured the works of some of the most important writers in Puerto Rico, such as Luis Muñoz Rivera, Lola Rodríguez de Tió, Vicente Palés, and many other notables. O'Neill's first published book was a dramatic dialogue in verse, more appropriate for reading aloud than staging: *La indiana borinqueña* (1922, *The Puerto Rican Indians*). Here O'Neill revealed himself to be intensely patriotic and interested in Puerto Rican independence from the United States. His second published book was the three-act play *Moncho Reyes,* named after the central character, issued by Spanish American Publishing in 1923. In 1924, O'Neill published a book of nationalistic poetry, *Sonoras bagatelas o sicilianas* (*Sonorous Bagatelles or Sicilian Verses*), of which Manuel Quevedo Baez stated in the prologue

Lola Rodríguez de Tió.

that "Gonzalo is a spontaneous and ingenuous poet. . . . He is a poet of creole stock, passionate, tender, and as melancholic as Gautier Benítez" (Gautier Benítez was Puerto Rico's greatest poet to date). Although all of his plays, even *La indiana borinqueña,* enjoyed stage productions, it was his third play, *Bajo una sola bandera* (1928, *Under Only One Flag*), that won critical acclaim and was produced on stages in New York as well as in Puerto Rico. *Bajo una sola bandera* examines the political options facing Puerto Rico, as personified by down-to-earth flesh-and-blood characters. A glowing review in San Juan's *La democracia (Democracy)* on April 16, 1929, marveled at O'Neill's conserving perfect Spanish and his Puerto Rican identity, despite having lived in the United States for 40 years. O'Neill certainly continued to write, although the remainder of his work is unknown or has been lost. Newspapers report that another play of his, *Amoríos borincanos (Puerto Rican Loves)*, was produced for the stage in 1938.

Following the example of Gonzalo O'Neill, there were many other Puerto Ricans who wrote for the stage and even published some of their works from the late 1920s to the 1940s, such as Alberto M. González, Juan Nadal de Santa Coloma, José Enamorado Cuesta, Frank Martínez, and Erasmo Vando. But one poet-playwright stands out among the rest as a politically committed woman, although the major portion of her work has been lost: Franca de Armiño (probably a pseudonym). Franca de Armiño wrote three works that have been lost and are inaccessible today: *Luz de tienieblas (Light of Darkness)*, a book of poems on various themes; *Aspectos de la vida (Aspects of Life)*, philosophical essays; and *Tragedia puertorriqueña (Puerto Rican Tragedy)*, a comedy of social criticism. Her one published and available play, *Los hipócritas: comedia dramática social (The Hypocrits: A Social Drama)*, self-published in 1937 at the Modernistic Editorial Company, is a major work that demands critical attention. Dedicated to "the oppressed and all those who work for ideas of social renovation," the work is set in Spain during the time of the republic and is openly anti-Fascist and revolutionary, calling for a rebellion of workers. *Los hipócritas,* which begins with the 1929 stock market crash, deals with a daughter's refusal to marry her father's choice, the son of a duke. Rather, she is romantically involved with a man of the working class, Gerónimo, whom her father calls a Communist and who has led her into atheism. The plot is complicated, with Gerónimo organizing workers for a strike, a Fascist dictatorship developing in Spain, and a corrupt priest trying to arrange for Gloria to become a nun so that the church will receive her dowry. The play ends with Gloria and Gerónimo together, the traitors unmasked, and the workers' strike prevailing over police, who attack them brutally. While full of propaganda and stereotyped characters, *Los hipócritas* is a gripping and entertaining play that reflects the tenor of the times, as far as the Great Depression, labor organizing, and the Spanish Civil War are concerned.

A cigar roller who settled in New York in 1916, Bernardo Vega reconstructed life in the Puerto Rican community during the period between the two great wars. Written in 1940, his *Memorias de Bernardo Vega* was published in 1977, and its translation was published in English as *The Memoirs of Bernardo Vega* in 1984. Valuable as both a literary and a historical document, Vega's memoirs make mention of numerous literary figures, such as poet Alfonso Dieppa, whose works were either not published or are lost to us. Vega is an important forerunner of the Nuyorican writers of the 1960s because he wrote about New York as a person who was there to stay, with no intention to return to live in Puerto Rico.

A figure similar to the women activists of the Hispanic Southwest was Luisa Capetillo, who came to New York from Puerto Rico in 1912 and wrote for various labor publications. In *Cultura obrera* (*Worker Culture*), she consistently built a case for women's emancipation. She re-emerged in the cigar factories of Tampa and Ybor City and continued her intellectual as well as her activist life there, and later in Puerto Rico. In Tampa, she published the second edition of her book, *Mi opinión* (*My Opinion*) in 1913, and published a new book of essays, *Influencia de las ideas modernas* (*The Influence of Modern Ideas*) in 1916.

The literature of this period is also represented by a newspaper columnist who wrote in English and was very active in the Communist Party: Jesús Colón, author of columns for the *Daily Worker*. Colón's was a heroic intellectual battle against the oppression of workers and racial discrimination; he nevertheless wrote about and supported Puerto Rican culture and literature, even to the extent of founding a small publishing company that has the distinction of issuing some of the first works of the great Puerto Rican novelist and short story writer José Luis González. In 1961, Colón selected some of the autobiographical sketches that had appeared in newspapers and published them in book form in *A Puerto Rican in New York,* which was perhaps the one literary and historical document that was accessible to young Nuyorican writers and helped to form their literary and social awareness, as well as stimulate their production of literature. Colón, a black Puerto Rican, had created a document that, tempered with his political ideology, presented insight into Puerto Rican minority status in the United States, rather than just immigrant or ethnic status. In this it was quite different from all that had preceded it.

✳ WORLD WAR II TO THE PRESENT

Chicano Literature

Scholars consider the year 1943 as the beginning of a new period in Mexican American history and culture. This is the year when the so-called Zoot Suit Riots occurred in the Los Angeles area; they mark a stage in the cultural development of the Mexican American in which there was a consciousness of not belonging to either Mexico or the United States. Rather, Mexican Americans began to assert a separate independent identity, just as the zoot-suiters in their own subculture were doing by adopting their style of dress, speech, and music (zoot-suiters were Mexican American youth who used baggy pants and long, feathered, wide-brimmed hats—elements that made up a zoot suit—as symbols of their subculture.) Then, too, Mexican American veterans serving in and returning from World War II, where they proportionately suffered more casualties and won more medals for valor than any other group in U.S. society, now felt that they had earned their rights as citizens of the United States and were prepared to assert that citizenship and to reform the political and economic system so that they could participate equitably. Thus, the quest for identity in modern American society was initiated, and by the 1960s, a younger generation made up of children of veterans, not only took up this pursuit of democracy and equity in the civil rights movements but also explored the question of identity in all of the arts, paramount of which was literature.

Because of the interruption caused by the depression, repatriation, and World War II, and the decreased production of literature that ensued during the 1940s and 1950s, the renewed literary and artistic productivity that occurred during the 1960s has often been considered a Chicano renaissance. In reality, it was an awakening that accompanied the younger generation's greater access to college and its participation in the civil rights movements as well as the farm-worker labor struggle and the protest movement against the Vietnam War. For Chicano literature the decade of the 1960s was characterized by a questioning of all the commonly accepted truths in society, foremost of which was the question of equality. The first writers of Chicano literature in the 1960s committed their literary voices to political, economic, and educational struggles. Their works were frequently used to inspire social and political action, quite often with poets reading their verses at organizing meetings, at boycotts, and before and after protest marches. Many of the first writers to gain prominence in the movement were the poets who could tap into an oral tradition of recitation and declamation, such as Abelardo Delgado, Ricardo Sánchez, and Alurista (Alberto Urista), and create works to be performed orally before groups of students and workers, in order to inspire them and raise their level of consciousness.

The most important literary work in this period that was used at the grass roots level as well as by university students to provide a sense of history, mission, and Chicano identity was an epic poem written by an ex-boxer in Denver, Colorado: Rodolfo "Corky" González's *I Am Joaquín/Yo Soy Joaquín* (1964). The short, bilingual pamphlet edition of the poem was literally passed from hand to hand in the communities, read from at rallies, dramatized by street theaters, and even produced as a slide show on film with a dramatic reading by none other than Luis

Valdez, the leading Chicano director and playwright. The influence and social impact of *I Am Joaquín* and poems such as "Stupid America," by Abelardo Delgado, which was published and reprinted in community and movement newspapers throughout the Southwest, and later cut out of those papers and passed hand to hand, is inestimable. "Stupid America" was included as well in Abelardo's landmark collection, *Chicano: 25 Pieces of a Chicano Mind* (1969). This period was one of euphoria, power, and influence for the Chicano poet, who was sought after, almost as a priest, to give his blessings in the form of readings at all cultural and Chicano movement events.

The 1960s was an era of intense grass roots organizing and cultural fermentation, and along with this occurred a renewed interest in publishing small community and workers' newspapers and magazines, such as the California farm workers' *El Malcriado* (*The Brat*) and Houston's *Papel Chicano* (*Chicano Newspaper*), which were now quite often published bilingually. During the late 1960s and early 1970s, literary magazines proliferated, from the academic, such as Berkeley's *El grito* (*The Shout*

[for independence]), to the grass roots type printed on newsprint and available for 25 cents, such as San Antonio's *Caracol* (*Shell*), to the artsy, streetwise, avant-garde, and irreverent, such as Los Angeles' *Con Safos* (*Safety Zone*).

In 1967 appeared the most influential Chicano literary magazine, *El grito,* which initiated the careers of some of the most prominent names in Chicano literature and, along with the publishing house Editorial Quinto Sol, which it established in 1968, began to delineate the canon that is the official identity of Chicano literature by publishing those works that best exemplified Chicano culture, language, themes, and styles. The very name of the publishing house emphasized its Mexican/Aztec identity, as well as the Spanish language; the "quinto sol" (fifth sun), referred to Aztec belief in a period of cultural flowering that would take place some time in the future, in a fifth age that conveniently coincided with the rise of Chicano culture. In 1968 Quinto Sol published an anthology, *El espejo / The Mirror,* edited by the owners of Quinto Sol, Octavio Romano and Herminio Ríos. It included works by such writers as Alurista, Tomás Rivera, and Miguel Méndez, who are still

(Left to right) Albelardo Delgado, Ron Arias, and Rolando Hinojosa at the Second National Latino Book Fair and Writers Festival, Houston, Texas, 1980.

models of Chicano literature today. *El espejo* recognized the linguistic diversity and the erosion of Spanish literacy among the young by accompanying works originally written in Spanish with an English translation; it even included Miguel Méndez's original Yaqui-language version of his short story "Tata Casehue." In *El espejo* and in later books that Quinto Sol published, there was a definite insistence on working-class and rural culture and language, as exemplified in the works of Tomás Rivera, Rolando Hinojosa, and most of the other authors published in book form. Also, there was not only a tolerance but a promotion of works written bilingually and in—the code of street culture that switches between both English and Spanish in the same literary piece—as in the poems of Alurista and the plays of Carlos Morton.

In 1970, Quinto Sol, a Chicano publishing house founded in 1968 by Octavio Romano and Herminio Ríos, reinforced its leadership in creating the concept of Chicano literature by instituting the national award for Chicano literature, Premio Quinto Sol (Fifth Sun Award), which carried with it a $1,000 prize and publication of the winning manuscript. The first three years of prizes went to books that today are still seen as exemplary Chicano novels and, in fact, are still among the best-selling Chicano literary texts: Tomás Rivera's *. . . y no se lo tragó la tierra/ . . . And the Earth Did Not Part* (1971), Rudolfo Anaya's *Bless Me, Ultima* (1972), and Rolando Hinojosa's *Estampas del valle y otras obras/ Sketches of the Valley and Other Works*. Rivera's outwardly simple but inwardly complex novel is much in the line of experimental Latin American fiction, demanding that the reader take part in unraveling the story and in coming to his own conclusions about the identity and relationships of the characters, as well as the meaning. Drawing upon his own life as a migrant worker from Texas, Rivera constructed a novel in the straightforward but poetic language of migrant workers in which a nameless central character attempts to find himself by reconstructing the over-heard conversations and stories as well as events that took place during a metaphorical year, which really represents his whole life. It is the story of a sensitive boy who is trying to understand the hardship that surrounds his family and community of migrant workers; his path is first one of rejection of them only to embrace them and their culture dearly as his own at the end of the book. In many ways, *. . . y no se lo tragó la tierra* came to be the most influential book in the Chicano search for identity.

Rivera, who became a very successful university professor and administrator—he rose to the position of chancellor of the University of California, Riverside, before his death in 1984—wrote and published other stories, essays, and poems. Through such essays as "Chicano Literature: Fiesta of the Living" (1979) and "Into the Labyrinth: The Chicano in Literature" (1971) and his personal and scholarly activities, he was one of the prime movers in the promotion of Chicano authors, in the creation of the concept of Chicano literature, and in the establishment of Chicano literature and culture as legitimate

The original manuscript of the Tomás Rivera poem, "When love to be?"

Evangelina Vigil-Piñón, reciting at the Third National Hispanic Book Fair, Houston, 1987. (Photograph by Julián Olivaries.)

his attempts to understand good and evil and his role in life by the folk healer, Ultima, who passes on many of her secrets and insights about life to Antonio. Anaya puts to good use his knowledge of the countryside of New Mexico in fashioning this novel full of mystery and symbolic references to American Indian, Asian, and Spanish culture.

Anaya went on to become celebrated in his home state and to head the creative writing program at the University of New Mexico. His subsequent novels, all dealing with Chicano/Indian culture in New Mexico, have not been as well received by the critics: *Heart of Aztlán* (1976), *Tortuga* (1979, *Tortoise*), *The Silence of the Llano* (1982), and *Lord of the Dawn: The Legend of Quetzalcoatl* (1987). As can be seen from these titles, Anaya is a promoter of the concept of Aztlán, the mythical place of origin of the Aztec, supposedly located in what has become the five states of the Southwest. He and numerous other Chicano writers have derived both poetic inspiration and a sense of mission in reviving the cultural glories of Mexico's indigenous past. For Anaya and especially for poets and playwrights such as Alurista and Luis Valdez, the Aztec and Mayan past has been a

academic areas in college curriculum. In 1989, his stories were collected and published under the title *The Harvest,* and in 1990 his poems were collected and published under the title *The Searchers,* both by Arte Público Press, which has also kept his first novel in print and has recently published *Tomás Rivera: The Complete Works* (1990). In 1987, *. . . y no se lo tragó la tierra* was given a liberal translation into Texan dialect under the title *This Migrant Earth* (1987) by Rolando Hinojosa; the translation that accompanies the Arte Público bilingual edition was done by poet Evangelina Vigil-Piñón. By any accounts, Tomás Rivera remains the most outstanding and influential figure in the literature of Mexican peoples in the United States.

Rudolfo Anaya's *Bless Me, Ultima* is a straightforward novel about a boy's coming of age. Written in a poetic and clear English, it has reached more readers, especially non-Chicano readers, than any other Chicano literary work. In *Bless Me, Ultima,* again we have the search for identity, but this time the central character, Antonio, must decide between the Spanish heritage of the plainsman-rancher or the Indian heritage of the farmer; he is guided and inspired in

The cover of Rudolfo Anaya's best-selling novel, *Bless Me, Ultima.*

A vendor at the First National Latino Book Fair in Chicago, 1979.

source of imagery, symbols, and myths that have enriched their works.

Rolando Hinojosa is the most prolific and probably the most bilingually talented of the Chicano novelists, with original creations in both English and Spanish, published in the United States and abroad. His Quinto Sol Award-winning *Estampas del valle y otras obras/Sketches of the Valley and Other Works* is a mosaic of the picturesque character types, folk customs, and speech of the bilingual community in the small towns along Texas' Rio Grande valley. His sketches and insights, at times reminiscent of the local color of the *crónicas* of the 1920s, are considered among the most sophisticated contributions to Chicano literature.

Estampas consists of the first portion of a continuing novel that has become a broad epic of the history and culture of the Mexican Americans and Anglos of the valley. It takes place in the fictitious Belken County and centers on two fictitious characters and a narrator—Rafa Buenrostro, Jehú Malacara, and P. Galindo—all of whom may be partial alter egos of Hinojosa himself. What is especially intriguing about Hinojosa's continuing novel, which he calls the Klail City Death Trip Series, is his experimentation

with various forms of narration—derived from Spanish, Mexican, English, and American literary history—in respective installments of the novel. *Klail City y sus alrededores* (1976, *Klail City and Surroundings*) owes much to the picaresque novel, *Korean Love Songs* (1980) is narrative poetry, *Mi querido Rafa* (1981, *Dear Rafe*) is part epistolary novel and part reportage, *Rites and Witnesses* (1982) is mainly a novel in dialogue, *Partners in Crime* (1985) is a detective novel, *Claros varones de Belken* (1986, *Fair Gentlemen of Belken*) is a composite, and *Becky and Her Friends* (1990) continues the novel in the style of reportage, but with a new unnamed narrator, P. Galindo having died.

While there have been translations by others of his works, Hinojosa has penned and published recreations in English and Spanish of all of these books, except for the English titles *Korean Love Songs, Rites and Witnesses,* and *Partners in Crime.* *Mi querido Rafa* is especially important because it represents the first novel to experiment with bilingual narration and demands of the reader a good knowledge of both English and Spanish and their south Texas dialects.

Because of his many awards—including the inter-

Ana Castillo, 1979.

national award for Latin American fiction given in Cuba, Premio Casa de las Americas, 1976—his academic background and doctorate in Spanish, and the positive response to his sophisticated art from critics and university professors, in particular, Hinojosa is one of the few Hispanic writers in the country to teach in creative writing programs at a high level. In holding the distinguished title Ellen Clayton Garwood Professor of English and Creative Writing at the University of Texas, Hinojosa is the most recognized and highest-ranking Chicano/Hispanic author in academia.

It was not until 1975 that the Quinto Sol Award—an annual award given by Editorial Quinto Sol for outstanding Chicano literature—was given to a woman, Estela Portillo Trambley, for her short story collection *Rain of Scorpions,* and it marked the ascendancy of women's voices in Chicano literature, which had previously been dominated by males. Portillo Trambley's strong feminist and irreverent stories did much both to sensitize the publishing powers in Chicano literature and to encourage a new generation of women writers to persevere in getting their works published; their works were soon to change the character of Chicano literature in the

1980s. In nine finely crafted stories and a novella, Portillo Trambley presents a series of female characters who draw from an inner strength and impose their personalities on the world around them. In the novella that gives title to the collection, a fat and unattractive central character overcomes her own dreams of beauty and social acceptance to prevail as a woman capable of controling and determining the action around her. She has chosen her life and how to live it, refusing to be imposed upon by others. In the most feminist of the short stories, "If It Weren't for the Honeysuckle," the eldest of three women being oppressed and enslaved by a drunk and irrational male succeeds in poisoning him and in freeing the women. In this, as in the other stories, as well as in her books to follow—*The Day of the Swallows* (1971), the collection of plays *Sor Juana* (1983, *Sister Juana*), and the novel *Trini* (1986)—Portillo Trambley has created strong women who prevail in a male-dominated world. Her work, *Trini,* is the story of a Tarahumara woman who leaves her Indian life behind and, after numerous tragedies and betrayals, crosses the border to give birth to her child in the United States, where she is able to control her life for

Helena María Viramontes, 1986. (Photograph by Georgia McInnis.)

herself and even become a landowner. In all of her work Portillo Trambley has demonstrated an uncompromising pursuit for equality and liberation for women.

By the end of the 1970s most of the literary magazines and Chicano literary presses had disappeared, including Editorial Quinto Sol and *El grito*. Fortunately, since 1973 a new Hispanic magazine, *Revista Chicano-Riqueña* (*Chicano-Rican Review*), edited by Nicolás Kanellos and Luis Dávila in Gary, Indiana, had been operating and making greater incursions into academia than any other Hispanic literary publication. In 1979, Kanellos founded Arte Público Press as an outgrowth of the magazine and relocated both to Houston, Texas, just in time to carry on where Quinto Sol had left off and to assume the leadership in publishing the works of a blossoming Hispanic women's literary movement. During the 1980s, Arte Público published books of poetry by San Antonio poets Evangelina Vigil and Angela de Hoyos, Chicago poets and prose writers Ana Castillo and Sandra Cisneros, San Francisco Bay Area novelist and poet Lucha Corpi, Los Angeles short story writer and former editor of the magazine

ChismeArte, and New Mexico novelist and playwright Denise Chávez, who were to produce some of the best-selling and most highly reviewed Chicano books of the decade.

Along with Arte Público and *Revista Chicano-Riqueña,* which in 1987 became *The Americas Review* and was edited by Julián Olivares and Evangelina Vigil, *Third Woman,* the magazine/book publisher directed by Norma Alarcón, was founded in Indiana in 1980 and relocated to the University of California, Berkeley, in 1985. Around the same time, another Hispanic book publisher with an academic base, *Bilingual Review Press,* also relocated, from Binghamton, New York to Arizona State University in Tempe. Supported by these three establishments and various other presses that were occasionally issuing women's titles, this first full-blown generation of Chicana writers flourished, finding a welcome space for their books in the academic curriculum, not only in Chicano literature courses but also in women's studies programs and American literature courses. The majority of the women were more educated than the 1960s and 1970s writers; most of them were college graduates—two of its representa-

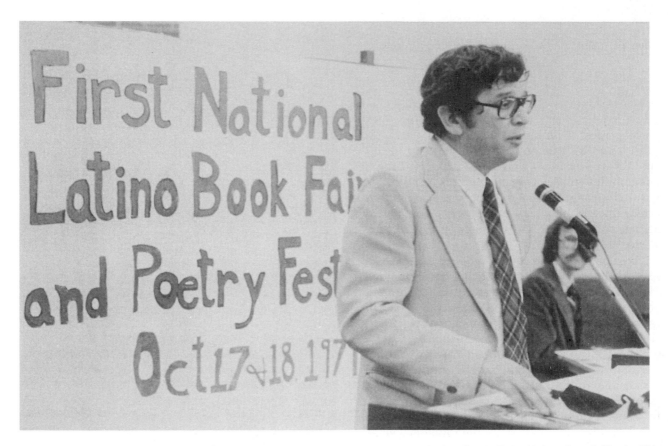

Luis Dávilla, co-editor of *Revista Chicano-Riquería,* at the First National Latino Book Fair, University of Illinois-Chicago Circle, 1979.

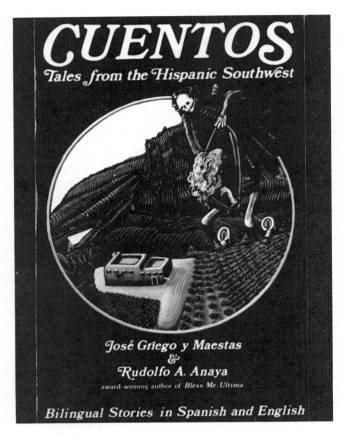

The cover of Rudolfo Anaya's *Cuentos: Tales from the Hispanic Southwest.*

tives, Denise Chavez and Sandra Cisneros, had even obtained master's degrees in creative writing—and they were mostly dominant in English, thus the Spanish language was no barrier to their works' entering literature courses and becoming accessible to broader circles of the reading public. As a whole, they were thoroughly versed in the mainstream feminist movement while preserving their own Chicana identities and culture and developing their literature from it.

At the close of the decade, mainstream textbook publishers began responding to the reform movements occurring in academia and also to the new demographic statistics relating to the public school markets in the most populous states, which demonstrated overwhelming Hispanic enrollments. As a result, most of the textbook publishers have begun to desperately search out and include Hispanic writers. In 1990, the nation's largest textbook publisher, Harcourt Brace Jovanovich, in fact, even went so far as to issue a high school English anthology titled *Mexican American Literature,* which includes selections of works from the colonial period to the present in its more than 700 pages. Some of the most success-

ful writers in being chosen for the general American literature textbooks and for such canonizing texts as *The Norton Anthology of American Literature* include Pat Mora and Denise Chávez. Mora is the author of three books of poetry, her first two winning the Southwest Book Award: *Chants* (1984), *Borders* (1986), and *Communion* (1991). Drawing upon the desert landscape and a Mexican Indian sensibility, *Chants* is a richly textured exploration, in beautiful whispered tones, of the desert as a woman and of women as holders of the strength and endurance of the desert. In *Borders,* Mora, an El Paso native, continues in the same vein, drawing upon folk customs and the insight of healers as she explores all types of borders: the political and cultural ones between the United States and Mexico, the borders between the sexes, and so forth. Her latest book, *Communion,* is about communion with other women and other peoples of the earth, as she expands her vision to Asia and Africa.

Denise Chávez is a talented actress and a prolific playwright, but it is as a novelist that she has gained a deserved place in Chicano and American literature as a whole. For Chávez, as for Rolando Hinojosa, literature is very much the art of writing about lives,

Pat Mora, 1986.

The cover of Denise Chávez's *The Last of the Menu Girls.*

about individuals, and about the stories they have to tell. Both of her novels, *The Last of the Menu Girls* (1986) and *Face of an Angel* (1993), present series of lives and characters talking for themselves within a loose biographic structure. In the case of her first novel, the unifying structure is the life of Rocío Esquivel, who, through a series of interconnected stories gains maturity by rebelling against the social roles created for her. *Face of an Angel,* on the other hand, centers on the life of a waitress and the unfortunate and tragicomic amorous relationships that she has with men; in the midst of the narration are brought in various types of unlikely elements, such as a manual on how to become a good waitress that the protagonist is writing. Both Mora and Chávez have won attention from the world that was previously off-limits to Chicano writers: the pages of the *New York Times Book Review* and the Norton anthologies, important fellowships, and awards.

While women were ascending in the world of Chicano literature, so was a younger generation of male writers who were the products of creative writing programs at universities, through which they gained access to opportunities for study, travel, and publishing never before had by Chicanos (nor Chicanas).

To date, theirs is the only Chicano poetry that has begun to become part of the American literary establishment. Of this new cadre of American poets who no longer speak or write in Spanish and no longer derive sustenance from the oral tradition, recitation, and political action, the most famous and prolific is Gary Soto, currently a tenured associate professor in creative writing and ethnic studies at the University of California, Berkeley. He is the winner of numerous prestigious awards, including the Academy of American Poets Prize (1975), the *Discovery-Nation* Award (1975), a Guggenheim fellowship (1979), an American Book Award, and many other prizes. His poetry is finely crafted, down-to-earth, and rigorous, mostly inspired by the life of the common working man in the fields and factories.

Quite often, as in his book *The Elements of San Joaquin,* published, as are most of his other poetry books, by the prestigious University of Pittsburgh Press poetry series, his work is a recollection of growing up in Fresno. While dealing with very real and concrete pictures of life in a particular time and setting, such as his youth in the agricultural San Joaquin Valley, Soto frequently approaches his subject from a classical frame of reference. For instance, in the second section of the book, the Valley is envisioned according to the four universal elements of the Greek philosophers: earth, air, water, and fire. He takes these elements and transforms them into the particular sights, smells, and labors of the Valley.

Among Soto's other books of poetry are *The Tale of Sunlight* (1978), *Where Sparrows Work Hard* (1981), *Black Hair* (1985), and *Who Will Know?* (1990). In 1985, Soto also began publishing autobiographical prose essays, which have met with a great deal of success, his first three books winning an American Book Award: *Living Up the Street* (1985), *Small Faces* (1986), and *Lesser Evils: Ten Quartets* (1988).

Among other writers who have made it into university creative writing programs as professors are Arizonan Alberto Rios and Californians Ernesto Trejo and Lorna Dee Cervantes. Cervantes did not follow the usual trek through master of fine arts programs in creative writing for entrance into her career. She was very much a product of the 1970s and the Chicano literary movement, during which she began reading her poetry in public at a theater festival in 1974, published her first works in *Revista Chicano-Riqueña* in 1975, and shortly thereafter founded and edited a literary magazine, *Mango,* which was free-form and experimental and not limited to publishing Chicanos. By 1981, her first book of poems, *Emplumada (Plumed),* was published by the University of Pittsburgh Press. Despite her many publications in magazines and success as a

Gary Soto and Evangelina Vigil-Piñón at the Third National Hispanic Book Fair and Writers Festival in Houston, Texas, 1987.

performer of poetry, it was not until 1986 that she finished her B.A. degree. In 1990, she earned a Ph.D. in the history of consciousness at the University of California, Santa Cruz. She currently teaches creative writing at the University of Colorado.

Perhaps better than anyone yet, Lorna Dee Cervantes has described the pain of separation from family in such poems as "Refugee Ship" and "Oaxaca, 1974." Her work also deals with the dehumanizing landscape and the dehumanization that is caused by racism and sexism. Today she is still very much a hard-driving poet who takes risks and is not afraid to deal with taboo topics and violence, whether it be racist, sexist, or psychological, as can be seen in her book *From the Cables of Genocide* (1991).

Today, as greater opportunities in academia have opened up for both Hispanic students and writers, the larger commercial world of publishing is beginning to open its doors to a few more Chicano writers.

The 1990s have seen the "discovery" by large commercial presses of Chicano literature as represented by a generation of Chicano authors who are the product of creative writing departments at universities. During this decade, such publishers as Random

House and simon and Schuster have published their the most recent works of handful of these newer writers, such as those of Sandra Cisneros, Ana Castillo, Denise Chávez, Gary Soto and others. More importantly, these publishers also re-issued some of their earlier works. After this incursion by the younger generation, some of the publishers began to take notice of the older pioneers and re-issued the works of Oscar Zeta Acosta, Rudolfo Anaya and others. The mainstream publishing houses also began publishing works by similarly educated Puerto Ricans, Dominicans and Cubans, such as Esmeralda Santiago, Julia Alvarez, Oscar Hijuelos and Virgil Suárez. They also reissued works by such pioneers as Piri Thomas and Nicholasa Mohr. Then, too, the Hispanic publishers were also growing, with Arte Público Press not only capable of creating bestsellers such as Victor Villaseñor's *Rain of Gold* but also of selling the lucrative paperback rights to such giants as Bantam Doubleday Dell. In fact, after Arte Público registered the success with *Rain of Gold,* Bantam Doubleday Dell made the unprecedented move of buying back rights from Arte Público to Villaseñor's book, *Macho,* which Dell had originally published only to let go out-of-print. Today, Chicano authors have greater alternatives for publication through both the commercial and non-commercial presses.

Nuyorican Literature

In 1898, Puerto Rico became a colony of the United States and in 1917, Puerto Ricans became citizens of the United States. Since that time, Puerto Ricans have never really been immigrants to the United States, but migrants. Puerto Ricans on the island and those on the continent, despite geographic separation, hold in common their ethnicity, history, and their religious and cultural traits and practices. They also both deal with the confrontation of two languages and cultures. Thus, whether they reside in the continental United States or on the island of Puerto Rico, Puerto Ricans are one people. That is true whether they prefer the Spanish language or English, whether they were born on the island or not. Thus, most attempted divisions of the people are for vested interests, whether political or prejudicial.

Puerto Rican culture today is the product of powerful political, economic, and social forces who descended upon the small native population and at-

tempted to evangelize, assimilate, decimate, or otherwise transform them. Christopher Columbus first initiated this process when he discovered the island in 1493. It was this act of "discovery" that resulted in Puerto Rico's becoming a colony in the Spanish Empire until 1898, when it passed into the possession of the United States. Puerto Rico is therefore a land that has been and still is subject to overseas rule—politically and economically, as well as artistically.

Despite being an island geographically cut off from the rest of Latin America and despite being ruled as a colony and not enjoying complete self-determination, Puerto Rican literature has been rich, for it has developed out of the many cultures and experiences that make up its peoples. In the middle of the nineteenth century, it assumed a creole, Hispanic American identity, emphasizing the new speech, customs, and history of people in this hemisphere as opposed to the Spanish in Europe— Puerto Rico and Cuba were among the very last remnants of Spain's colonial empire, the rest of Spanish America having gained its independence at the beginning of the nineteenth century. After 1898,

(Central figures) Ricardo Sánchez, Alejandro Morales, critic Salvador Rodríguez del Pino, and Victor Villaseñor at a book fair in Mexico City in 1979.

Puerto Ricans began emphasizing their Latin American, Spanish-speaking identity as separate from the Anglo-American United States. Therefore, while Puerto Rican artists initially sought to create a nationalism or an ethnic identity based on *mestizaje,* a blending of the cultures and the values of the New World, but due to the presence of the United States, Puerto Ricans have since insisted on the use of the Spanish language and on maintaining their relationship with Latin America, its cultures and arts.

At the turn of the century, the island's literature began developing along the lines of Latin American modernism, which was heavily influenced by French, peninsular Spanish, and Latin American models. As was the case in Mexico, Peru, Argentina, and Cuba, Puerto Rican artists and writers turned to the indigenous people of the island, their folklore, and national models in an effort to define the true identity of their national culture.

Although he was one of Puerto Rico's master poets, Luis Llorens Torres (1878–1944) was a European-educated intellectual who adapted the verse forms of the plaintive mountain songs (*décimas*) and folk speech of the jíbaros, or highlanders, in poems that took pride in rural life and its values rather

Julia de Burgos.

than in the sophistication and modern advances of the city. His jíbaros were always skeptical and unmoved by the bragging and showing off of Americanized Puerto Ricans who believed in Yankee ingenuity and progress. Puerto Rico's greatest and most universally studied poet, Luis Palés Matos (1898–1959), was the first Puerto Rican literary figure to achieve a lasting impact on the evolution of Latin American literature, principally through the development of a poetic style that was inspired by the rhythms and language of Africa and the black Caribbean. His landmark book, *Tun tun de pasa y grifería* (1937), whose onomatopoic title has no translation, openly claimed a black African heritage and presence for the cultural makeup of Puerto Rico. Like Torres, the primitivism, vigor, and freedom of his black verses represent his critical stance toward Europe and the United States. In Palés Matos' master poem, "La plena de menéalo" ("The Dance of Shake It"), Puerto Rico is personified by a seductive *mulata* who sweats rum as she erotically dances close to, but just out of reach of, a drooling Uncle Sam.

Two figures are essential in recognition of the transition of Puerto Rican literature from the island to the continent: Julia de Burgos (1914–1953) and René Marqués (1919–1979). The former cultivated beautiful, sensuous verses, odes to her beloved countryside, only to die tragically on the streets of New York. Her lyricism served the parallel desires for personal as well as national liberation. René Marqués, the most widely known Puerto Rican playwright, spent time in New York as well, and was able to capture the true meaning of the dislocation of the native populations from Puerto Rico and their relocation to foreign lands and values. Even more moving than John Steinbeck's *Grapes of Wrath* is the plight of the family of displaced mountain folk in Marqués' *La carreta* (*The Oxcart*), which was first produced on stage in New York in 1953 and then published in Spanish in 1961 and in English in 1969. *La carreta,* which dramatizes the tragic life of this family as they are forced to move from their farm to a San Juan slum and then to New York, ends with an appeal to Puerto Ricans not to leave their homeland and to return to the island and the values of the countryside.

To a great extent, today's major Puerto Rican writers on the island still draw upon Marqués' spirit, style, and message in their attempt to preserve the integrity of the Puerto Rican culture and in their call for the political independence of the island. Prose writers like José Luis González, Pedro Juan Soto, Luis Rafael Sánchez, and Jaime Carrero satirize the complacency of the Americanized middle class, which would like Puerto Rico to become a U.S. state.

enced by roving bards, reciters, storytellers, salsa music composers, and the popular culture and commercial environment of New York City.

Thus Nuyoricans are typically the children of working-class Puerto Rican migrants to the city; they are generally bilingual and bicultural, and so is their literature. During the search for ethnic roots and the civil rights movements of the 1960s, young Puerto Rican writers and intellectuals began using the term *Nuyorican* as a point of departure in affirming their own cultural existence and history as divergent from that of the island of Puerto Rico and that of mainstream America, much as the Chicanos were doing. A literary and artistic flowering in the New York Puerto Rican community ensued in the late 1960s and early 1970s as a result of greater access to education for Puerto Ricans raised in the United States and as a result of the ethnic consciousness movement. Although the term "Nuyorican" was first applied to literature by playwright-novelist Jaime Carrero in his poem "Neo-Rican Jetliner/Jet neorriqueño" in the late 1960s when he resided in New York, and the term finds some stylistic and thematic development in his plays *Noo Jall* (a blending of the Spanish pronunciation of "New York" and

José Luis González.

They also develop the themes of Puerto Rico's past as Edenic and the jíbaro as a child of nature, with his intense code of honor and decency. Most of today's island novelists, while romanticizing the island's past, have, however, also created a one-dimensional image of Puerto Ricans in New York, only focusing on the tragedy of the rootlessness, poverty, and oppression of the second-class citizens who seem to by lost in the labyrinth of the monster city.

Puerto Rican writing in New York dates back to the end of the nineteenth century, and writing in English begins about the time that Jesús Colón was writing his columns for the *Daily Worker*. This seems to be a rather appropriate beginning, given that most of the Puerto Rican writers in English that followed identify with the working class. Unlike the writers of the island, who largely are members of an elite, educated class and many of whom are employed as university professors, the New York writers, who came to be known as Nuyoricans, are products of parents transplanted to the metropolis to work in the service and manufacturing industries. These writers are predominantly bilingual in their poetry and English-dominant in their prose; they hail from a folk and popular tradition heavily influ-

Luis Rafael Sánchez.

Pedro Juan Soto.

the word "jail") and "Pipo Subway no sabe reír" (Pipo Subway Doesn't Know How to Laugh), it was a group of poet-playwrights associated with the Nuyorican Poets' Café in the lower East Side of New York who later defined and exemplified Nuyorican literature in their works. Included in the group were Miguel Alagarín, Lucky Cienfuegos, Tato Laviera, and Miguel Piñero. Two members of the group, Cienfuegos and Piñero, were ex-convicts who had begun their writing careers while incarcerated and associating with Afro-American convict-writers; they chose to concentrate on prison life, street life, and the culture of poverty and to protest the oppression of their peoples through their poetry and dramas. Algarín, a university professor, owner, and operator of the Nuyorican Poets' Café, contributed a spirit of the avant-garde for the collective and managed to draw into the circle such well-known poets as Alan Ginsberg. Tato Laviera, a virtuoso bilingual poet and performer of poetry (*declamador*), contributed a lyrical, folk, and popular culture tradition that derived from the island experience and the Afro-Caribbean culture but was cultivated specifically in and for New York City.

It was Miguel Piñero's work (and life), however,

that became most celebrated, his prison drama, *Short Eyes,* having won an Obie and the New York Drama Critics Award for Best American Play in the 1973–74 season. His success, coupled with that of the autobiography of fellow Nuyorican writer and ex-convict Piri Thomas and that of poet Pedro Pietri, who developed the image of a street urchin always high on marijuana, resulted in Nuyorican literature and theater's often being associated with crime, drugs, abnormal sexuality, and generally negative behavior. Thus, many writers who in fact were affirming Puerto Rican working-class culture did not want to become identified with the movement. Still others wanted to hold onto their ties with the island and saw no reason to emphasize differences, but, rather, wanted to stress similarities.

What exacerbated the situation was that the commercial publishing establishment in the early 1970s was quick to take advantage of the literary fervor in the Puerto Rican community by issuing a series of ethnic autobiographies that insisted on the criminality, abnormality, and drug culture of New York Puerto Ricans. Included in this array of mostly paperbacks was, of course, Piri Thomas' *Down These Mean Streets* (1967, issued in paper in 1974),

Thomas' *Seven Long Times* (1974), Thomas' *Stories from El Barrio* (1978, issued in paper in 1980), Lefty Barreto's *Nobody's Hero* (1976), and a religious variation on the theme: Nicky Cruz's *Run Nicky Run.* So well worn was this type of supposed autobiography that it generated a satire by another Nuyorican writer, Ed Vega, who comments in the introduction to his novel *The Comeback* (1985) as follows:

> I started thinking about writing a book, a novel. And then it hit me. I was going to be expected to write one of those great American immigrant stories, like *Studs Lonigan, Call It Sleep,* or *Father. . . .* Or maybe I'd have to write something like *Manchild in the Promised Land* or a Piri Thomas' *Down These Mean Streets. . . .* I never shot dope nor had sexual relations with men, didn't for that matter, have sexual relations of any significant importance with women until I was about nineteen. . . . And I never stole anything. . . . Aside from fist fights, I've never shot anyone, although I've felt like it. It seems pretty far-fetched to me that I would ever want to do permanent physical harm to anyone. It is equally repulsive for me to write an autobio-

Bernardo Vega, 1948.

graphical novel about being an immigrant. In fact, I don't like ethnic literature, except when the language is so good that you forget about the ethnic writing it.

The Comeback is the story of a confused college professor who creates for himself the identity of a Puerto Rican-Eskimo ice hockey player; he suffers a nervous breakdown and is treated for the classical symptoms of an identity crisis. Throughout the novel, Vega satirized all types of characters that populate the barrio as well as popular culture, such as Puerto Rican revolutionaries, psychiatrists, and a Howard Cosell-type sportscaster. In his interrelated collection of stories told by fictitious narrator Ernesto Mendoza, *Mendoza's Dreams* (1987), Vega surveys the human comedy of everyday barrio life and relates tales of success in small ways in reaching for the American Dream. In his collection *Casualty Report* (1991), he shows us the inverse: the physical, psychological, and moral death of many who live within the poverty and deprivation of the Puerto Rican barrio, as well as in the larger ghetto of a racist society.

More than anything else, the first generation of

Jesús Colón, circa 1950s.

Nuyorican writers was one that was dominated by poets, many of whom had come out of an oral tradition and had honed their art through public readings; thus the creation of the Nuyorican Poets' Café was a natural outcome of the need to create a specific space for the performance of poetry. Among the consummate performers of Nuyorican poetry were Victor Hernández Cruz, Tato Laviera, Miguel Piñero, and Miguel Algarín. Like his fellow poets, Cruz's initiation into poetry was through popular music and street culture; his first poems have often been considered to be jazz poetry in a bilingual mode, except that English dominated in the bilingualism and thus opened the way for his first book to be published by a mainstream publishing house: *Snaps: Poems* (Random House, 1969). It was quite a feat for a 20-year-old from an impoverished background. In *Snaps* were the themes and styles that would dominate and flourish in his subsequent books; in all of Hernández Cruz's poetry sound, music, and performance are central. He also experiments with bilingualism as oral poetry [and written symbols of oral speech], and he searches for identity through these sounds and symbols. His next two books were odysseys that take the reader back to Puerto Rico and primordial Indian and African music and poetry (*Mainland,* 1973) and across the United States and back to New York, where the poet finds the city transformed by its Caribbean peoples into their very own cultural home (*Tropicalization,* 1976). *By Lingual Wholes* (1982) is a consuming and total exploration of the various linguistic possibilities in the repertoire of a bilingual poet, and *Rhythm, Content and Flavor* (1989) is a summary of his entire career.

Tato Laviera's bilingualism and linguistic inventiveness have risen to the level of virtuosity. Laviera is the inheritor of the Spanish oral tradition, with all of its classical formulas, and the African oral tradition, which stresses music and spirituality; in his works he brings both the Spanish and English languages together as well as those of the islands of Puerto Rico and Manhattan—a constant duality that is always in the background. His first book, *La Carreta Made a U-Turn* (1979) was published by Arte Público Press, which has become the leading publisher of Nuyorican literature, despite its location in Houston. *La Carreta Made a U-Turn* uses René Marqués' *Oxcart* as a point of departure but redirects back to the heart of New York, instead of back to the island, as Marqués had desired; Laviera believes that Puerto Rico can be found here too. His second book, *Enclave* (1981) is a celebration of diverse heroic personalities, both real and imagined: Luis Palés Matos and salsa composers, the neighborhood gossip and John Lennon, Miriam Makeba and

Tito Madera Smith, the latter being a fictional, hip offspring of a jíbara and a southern American black. *AmeRícan* (1986) and *Mainstream Ethics* (1988) are surveys of the lives of the poor and marginalized in the United States and a challenge for the country to live up to its promises of equality and democracy.

One of the few women's voices to be heard in this generation is a very strong and well-defined one, that of Sandra María Esteves, who from her teen years has been very active in the women's struggle, Afro-American liberation, the Puerto Rican independence movement, and, foremost, the performance of poetry. In 1973, she joined El Grupo, a New York-based touring collective of musicians, performing artists, and poets associated with the cultural wing of the Puerto Rican Socialist party. By 1980, she had published her first collection of poetry, *Yerba Buena,* which involves the search for identity of a colonized Hispanic woman of color in the United States, the daughter of immigrants from the Caribbean. All three of her books, *Yerba Buena, Tropical Rains: A Bilingual Downpour* (1984), and *Mockingbird Bluestown Mambo* (1990), affirm that womanhood is what gives unity to all of the diverse characterizations of her life.

Sandra María Esteves, 1979.

(Left to right) Nicholasa Mohr, Publisher Nicolás Kanellos, and Ed Vega on the occasion of their reading at the Bookstop in Houston, Texas, 1985.

The most productive and recognized Nuyorican novelist is Nicholasa Mohr. Her works, *Nilda* (1973), *El Bronx Remembered* (1975), *In Nueva York* (1986), were all published in hardback and paperback editions by major commercial publishing houses and are still in print, three of them having been reissued by Arte Público Press. Her books have entered the mainstream as have no other books by Hispanic authors of the United States. They have won such awards as the *New York Times* Outstanding Book of the Year, the *School Library Journal* Best Children's Book, and many others, including a decree honoring her by the state legislature of New York. Her best-loved novel, *Nilda,* traces the coming of age of a young Puerto Rican girl in the Bronx during World War II. Unlike many other such novels of development, Nilda gains awareness of the plight of her people and her own individual problems by examining the racial and economic oppression that surrounds her and her family, in a manner that can be compared to Tomás Rivera's central character in . . . *y no se lo tragó la tierra.*

In two of her other books, *In Nueva York* and *El Bronx Remembered,* Mohr examines through a series of stories and novellas various Puerto Rican neighborhoods and draws sustenance from the common folks' power to survive and still produce art, folklore, and strong families in the face of oppression and marginalization. *Rituals of Survival: A Woman's Portfolio* (1985), in five stories and a novella, portrays six strong women who take control of their lives, most of them by liberating themselves from husbands, fathers, or families that attempt to keep them confined in narrowly defined female roles. *Rituals* is the book that the mainstream houses would not publish, wanting to keep Mohr confined to what they saw as immigrant literature and children's literature, as in her *Felita* and *Going Home.*

While not banding together with groups and collectives, Mohr has been one of the most influential of the Nuyorican writers out of sheer productivity and accomplishment. She has also led the way to greater acceptance of Nuyorican and Hispanic writers in creative writing workshops, such as the Millay Colony, in Poets, Editors and Novelists (PEN), and on the funding panels of the National Endowment for the Arts and the New York State Council on the Arts.

Another Nuyorican writer who has not participated in nor benefitted from collective work is Judith Ortiz Cofer, who grew up in Paterson, New Jersey, and has lived much of her adult life in Georgia and Florida. Cofer is one of the few Nuyorican products of the creative writing programs, and much of her early poetry was disseminated through establishment small presses in the South that may have been intrigued by the exoticism of her Puerto Rican subjects, packaged in finely crafted verses, with a magic and mystery that is similar to that of Pat Mora's poetry.

Her first book of poems, *Reaching for the Mainland* (1987), is a chronicle of the displaced person's struggle to find a goal, a home, a language, and a history. In *Terms of Survival* (1987), she explores the psychology and social attitudes of the Puerto Rican dialect and how it controls male and female roles; in particular she carries on a dialogue with her father throughout the poems of the book. In 1989, Cofer published a highly reviewed novel of immigration, *Line of the Sun,* through the University of Georgia Press and in 1990 an even more highly reviewed book, made up of a collection of autobiographical essays, in the style of Virginia Wolf, *Silent Dancing: A Remembrance of Growing Up Puerto Rican,* through Arte Público Press.

In 1988, Cofer and five other writers—Nicholasa Mohr, Tato Laviera, Rolando Hinojosa, Alberto Ríos, and Lorna Dee Cervantes—were featured reading and performing their works in a historic documentary, *Growing Up Hispanic,* directed by Jesús Treviño, presented on national television by the Corporation for Public Broadcasting. The future of Hispanic literature in the United States promises to be very fruitful, and more and more segments of the population are getting the message.

Cuban American Literature

Cuban culture and literature in the United States dates back to the nineteenth century when writer-philosopher José Martí and other patriots plotted from the U.S. mainland for Cuban independence from Spain. During the first half of the twentieth century, Cubans and Spaniards dominated Hispanic arts and media in New York. While Cuban culture was on the ascendancy in New York, its island literature had already joined that of Mexico and Argentina in the leadership of Spanish American letters since the nineteenth century, with such internationally acknowledged masters as Gertrudis Gómez de Avellaneda, José Echeverría, Julián del Casal, and José Martí, and in the twentieth century with such leaders as patriarch Nicolás Guillén, who has taken Spanish American poetry from a markedly Afro-Caribbean to a Pan Hispanic vision in support of universal socialist revolution. Cuban writers who have contributed to the Latin American literary boom include Alejo Carpentier, José Lezama Lima, and Gabriel Cabrera Infante.

It is no wonder then that the inheritors of such a rich and dynamic tradition would contribute so greatly to Hispanic culture in the United States, especially given the fact that their mass immigration took place so recently, beginning in 1959 as refugees from the Cuban Revolution. In contrast, whereas Puerto Rican mass migration really had begun during World War II, when the American economy drew heavily on its island territory for workers, the Cubans came as political refugees from a land that had never been a colony of the United States, although it had been a protectorate and an economic dependent since the Spanish-American War. Most of the Puerto Ricans had come as workers and generally did not have the level of education nor the financial resources and relocation services that the Cubans did. This first mass of Cubans came with an outstanding written tradition well intact. And the Cuban literary aesthetic, unlike the Puerto Rican one, had never been so obsessed with protecting the

Virgil Suárez, 1991.

Spanish language and Hispanic culture while defending itself against Anglo-American culture and language. Numerous writers and intellectuals immigrated to the United States as refugees; many of them were able to adapt to and become part of the U.S. Hispanic and mainstream cultural institutions.

Today, after three decades of new Cuban culture in New York, New Jersey, Miami, and dispersed throughout the United States—in contrast to the older Cuban communities in New York City and Tampa—a Cuban American literary and artistic presence has developed. Younger writers are no longer preoccupied with exile, with eyes cast only on the island past; instead they are looking forward to participating in the English-language mainstream or serving the intellectual and cultural needs of the U.S. Cuban and Hispanic communities. Thus, there has developed a definite separation of purpose and aesthetics between the younger writers—Roberto Fernández, Iván Acosta, Virgil Suárez, and Oscar Hijuelos, for instance—and the older writers of exile—Lydia Cabrera, Matías Montes Huidobro, José Sánchez Boudy, and so on. Also, there continues to be an influx of exiled writers, disaffected with Cuban communism, like Heberto Padilla, who must be viewed differently from the earlier generation of exiles who have already created for themselves a solid niche within Hispanic and mainstream institutions such as publishing houses and universities.

What we have seen during the last decades is a literature that almost exclusively attacked the Cuban Revolution and Marxism. The novel of exile became another weapon in the struggle. Following the first antirevolutionary novel, *Enterrado vivo* (*Buried Alive*), published in Mexico in 1960 by Andrés Rivero Collado, were a host of others published in the United States and abroad by minor writers, such as Emilio Fernández Camus, Orlando Núñez, Manuel Cobo Souza, Raúl A. Fowler, Luis Ricardo Alonso, and many others. When they were not openly propagandistic and rhetorical, they were nostalgic for the homeland to the point of idealization. Poetry and drama followed the same course, for the most part. Later, political verse would come to form a special genre of its own, what has been called by critic Hortensia Ruiz del Viso "poesía del presidio político" (political prisoner poetry), as in the works of Angel Cuadra, Heberto Padilla, and Armando Valladares, who resides in Spain but is quite active in the United States.

A key figure in providing a new direction for Cuban literature in the United States has been Celedonio González, who, beginning with *Los primos* (1971, *The Cousins*), changed ssiofocus to concentrate on Cuban life and culture in the United States.

José Sánchez Boudy.

Later, in *Los cuatro embajadores* (1973, *The Four Ambassadors*) and *El espesor del pellejo de un gato ya cadáver* (1978, *The Thickness of the Skin on a Cat Already a Corpse*), he not only examined culture shock and conflict between Cubans and Americans, but he also treated a very taboo topic: criticism of the economic system of the United States, especially in its exploitation of Cuban workers. González presents us with Cubans who do not yet see themselves as Americans but who are also conscious that Cuba is no longer theirs.

Ironically, one of the most important writers in forging a Cuban American literature and in breaking new ground in his use of the English language is a professor of Spanish, Roberto Fernández. Through his novels, Fernández not only touches upon all the taboo subjects in the Cuban community of Miami— the counterrevolutionary movement in the United States, racism, acculturation, and assimilation—but also helps the community to take them in a less serious vein and to laugh at itself. In his two open-form mosaiclike novels, *La vida es un special* (1982, *Life Is on Special*) and *La montaña rusa* (1985, *The Roller Coaster*), Fernández presents a biting but loving satire of a community transformed by the materialism and popular culture of the United States, but somewhat paralyzed by the nostalgia and political obsession with a Communist Cuba. In 1988, Fernández continued the community saga in English, with the publication of *Raining Backwards,* which has become his best known and most regarded novel. Here as in his other works, the hilarious parade of characters, language styles—with quite a bit of bilingual humor—and diverse social events are aimed at encouraging the community to take stock of its present circumstances and reckon with a future here in the United States.

One of the most influential literary magazines of Cuban literature in the United States has been *Linden Lane,* which is published in Spanish. Published by writer Heberto Padilla and edited by poet Belkis Cuza Malé, who is a professor at Princeton University, the magazine has created a forum for the whole Cuban writing community, both the generation of exile and the new Cuban American generation. In 1990, the magazine formally announced the advent of a Cuban American literature with its publication of an anthology containing works in both English and Spanish and entitled *Los atrevidos: Cuban American Literature,* edited by Miami poet Carolina Hospital, also an editor of *Linden Lane.* In 1991, Arte Público Press published an anthology that also proclaimed a Cuban American identity, *Cuban American Theater,* edited by critic Rodolfo Cortina. Both collections draw upon writers dispersed throughout the United States, not just from the Miami and New York communities.

Among the new generation of Cuban American writers growing up in the United States, there are a few who have gone through creative writing programs at universities and who thus have had access to mainstream publishing opportunities. A graduate of the important writing program at Louisiana State University, Virgil Suárez has had two novels published, *Latin Jazz* (1989) by Morrow and *The Cutter* (1991) by Ballantine Books. His third book, a very fine collection of short stories, *Welcome to the Oasis,* was not accepted by commercial publishers who prefer novels; it was published in 1991 by Arte Público Press. *Latin Jazz* is a somewhat different type of ethnic biographical novel, portraying a whole Cuban family, instead of just one individual; in alternate chapters devoted to each of the family members, Suárez provides their respective histories, hopes, and desires as they wait for a missing family member to arrive in Miami with the Mariel boat-lift.

Probably the most important of the Cuban American writers to come out of the creative writing schools is Oscar Hijuelos, who is not the son of refu-

gees from the Cuban Revolution, but of earlier immigrants to New York. Nevertheless, Hijuelos' first offering, *Our House in the Last World* (1983), is a typical ethnic autobiography and may be seen as a symbol of Cuban assimilation in that it is one of the few novels that negatively portrays the island culture, as personified by an alcoholic and machistic father, while developing the common theme of the American dream. His novel *The Mambo Kings Play Songs of Love* (1990) made history; it is the first novel by a Hispanic writer of the United States to win the Pulitzer Prize. It is also the first time that a major publishing house, Simon and Shuster, has ever invested heavily in a novel by a Hispanic writer, bringing it out at the top of its list and promoting the book very heavily. *The Mambo Kings* is the story of two musician brothers during the prime of mambo music in the 1950s. The novel thus has a historical background that lends it a rich texture; it allows us to see a portion of American popular culture history through the eyes of two performers very wrapped up in the euphoria of the times and then the waning of interest in things Latin in the United States. The story of the tragic ending of the duo is very touching, but offers hope for the potential of Hispanic culture to influence the mainstream. In fact, Hijuelo's book and the recognition that it has won may open the door to mainstream publishing for other U.S. Hispanic writers.

✳ OUTSTANDING HISPANIC LITERARY FIGURES

Iván Acosta

See Chapter 21.

Miguel Algarín (1941–)

A native of Santurce, Puerto Rico, Algarín grew up in a hardworking family that loved music and the arts. His parents passed on to their children an appreciation of opera and classical music; Miguel's father taught him to play the violin. The Algaríns moved to New York City in the early 1950s; they settled in Spanish Harlem for a while, and then moved to Queens. Miguel Algarín began his higher education at City College and finished his B.A. degree at the University of Wisconsin in 1963; in 1965, he graduated with a master's degree in English from the Pennsylvania State University. After teaching English literature at Brooklyn College and New York University for a time, Algarín went on to teach at Rutgers, where he is an associate professor in the English department.

Algarín is the founder and proprietor of the

Miguel Algarín reciting his poetry at the First National Latino Book Fair, Chicago, 1979.

Algarín published translations of the poetry of Chilean Nobel Prize winner Pablo Neruda, under the title *Canción de gesta / A Song of Protest*.

Alurista (Alberto Baltazar Urista) (1947–)

Alurista is considered one of the pioneers of Chicano literature. He was one of the first poets to support the Chicano movement through his poetry, a writer and signer of important manifestoes of the movement, a founder of the Moviemiento Estudiantil de Aztlán (MECHA, Chicano Student Movement of Aztlán) in 1967, and one of the first to establish the concept of Aztlán in literature, which forecasts a return to the glories of Aztec civilization by the Chicanos in the mythic homeland of the Aztec, what is today roughly the five states of the Southwest.

Born in Mexico City on August 8, 1947, Alberto Baltazar Urista spent his early years in the states of Morelos and Guerrero. At age 13 he immigrated to the United States with his family, which settled in San Diego, California. He began writing poetry at an early age and was a restless and widely-read student. He began Chapman College in 1965 and transferred to and graduated from San Diego State Uni-

Puerto Rican Poets' Café, which is dedicated to the support of writers performing their art orally. It was especially important as a gathering place of young writers during the early 1970s when Nuyorican literature was being defined. Algarín played an important leadership role in the definition of that literature by compiling, with Miguel Piñero, an important anthology, *Nuyorican Poetry: An Anthology of Puerto Rican Words and Feelings* (1975). He also founded a short-lived publishing house, the Nuyroican Press, which only issued one book, his own *Mongo Affair* (1978). One year later, he took part in the launching of Arte Público Press, which became the leading publisher of Nuyorican literature.

Algarín has written plays, screenplays, and short stories, but is principally known as a poet. His books include *Mongo Affair, On Call* (1980), *Body Bee Calling from the 21st Century* (1982), and *Time's Now / Ya es tiempo* (1985). Algarín's poetry runs the gamut from jazz-salsa poetry to the mystical and avant-garde. He is one of the foremost experimenters with English-Spanish bilingualism and has even penned trilingual works that incorporate French. In 1976,

Alurista, 1980.

versity in 1970 with a B.A. degree in psychology. He later obtained an M.A. degree from that institution and a Ph.D. degree in literature from the University of California, San Diego, in 1983. Around 1966, he began writing poetry seriously for publication and assumed the pen name Alurista, which is virtually the only name he uses now.

Alurista is a consummate reader and performer of his poetry, which has led to many travels to fulfill invitations nationally and internationally to read his works. He was the founder and coeditor, with his wife, Xelina, of the literary magazine *Maize* and the publishing house associated with it; both ceased to exist after he became an associate professor of Spanish at California State Polytechnic, San Luis Obispo, in 1986. In 1992, he became a professor of Chicano Studies at the University of California, Santa Barbara. Alurista is a prolific and talented poet, a pioneer of bilingualism in Chicano poetry. Throughout his career, his study of the Nahuatl and Mayan languages and mythology have enriched his poetic works and inspired his promotion of the ideology of Aztlán. But it is his bilingualism that has opened new frontiers in poetry, with his free experimentation in combining the sounds, meanings, and graphic representations of Spanish and English in the same poem, quite often achieving surprising and beautiful effects.

Alurista has published the following books of poetry: *Floricanto en Aztlán* (1971), *Nationchild Plumaroja, 1967–1972* (1972), *Timespace Huracán: Poems, 1972–1975* (1976), *A'nque* (1979), *Spik in Glyph?* (1981), and *Return: Poems Collected and New* (1982).

Julia Alvarez

Novelist and poet Julia Alvarez was born to Dominican parents in New York City. She received her early education in the Dominican Republic, but returned with her family to the United States when she was ten years old. Alvarez's narratives are loosely based on her growing up between the two cultures of the United States and the Dominican Republic, although her perspective has always been one of growing up in privilege as the daughter of a successful medical doctor with political connections both in the United States and in her parents' homeland. However, when her father became involved in a plot to overthrow dictator Rafael Trujillo, the failed coup led to her father's exile in the United States and Julia Alvarez's permanent residence here. She thus finished her education in the United States, earning college degrees in literature and writing. She went on to become an English professor at Middlebury College and receive grants from the National En-

dowment for the Arts and the Ingram Merrill Foundation. After publishing stories and poems in literary magazines, she published a book of verse, *Homecoming* in 1984 and, in 1991, the novel that brought her to a national audience: *How the García Girls Lost Their Accents*. She thus joined the wave of Hispanic writers with creative writing degrees that were making their way into mainstream presses. These were followed in 1994 with her second novel, *In the Time of the Butterflies* and, in 1995 with another collection of poems, *The Other Side/El Otro Lado*. The largely favorable reviews in the press have tended to cast her works as immigrant literature, and her second novel reinforces this judgment, as it engages a theme of political assassination back in the Dominican Republic.

Rudolfo A. Anaya (1937–)

Rudolfo A. Anaya was born on October 30, 1937, in the village of Pastura, New Mexico, in surroundings similar to those celebrated in his famous novel about growing up in the rural culture of New Mexico: *Bless Me, Ultima*. He attended public schools in Santa Rosa and Albuquerque and earned both his B.A. (1963) and his M.A. (1968) degrees in English from the University of New Mexico. In 1972, he also earned an M.A. degree in guidance and counseling from the same university. From 1963 to 1970, he taught in the public schools, but in 1974 he became a member of the English department of the University of New Mexico; in 1993, he became professor emeritus. With the success of his writing career, Anaya has risen to become the head of the creative writing program at the University of New Mexico. Included among his many awards are the following: an honorary doctorate from the University of Albuquerque, the New Mexico Governor's Award for Excellence, the President's National Salute to American Poets and Writers in 1980, and the Premio Quinto Sol in 1972 for his novel *Bless Me Ultima*. Since 1989, Anaya has been the founding editor of *Blue Mesa Review*. Anaya is also a fellow of the National Endowment for the Arts and the Kellogg Foundation through whose auspices he has been able to travel to China and other countries for study.

Anaya is very much a believer and promoter of a return to pre-Columbian literature and thought through the reflowering of Aztec civilization in Aztlán, the mythic homeland of the Aztec, which corresponds to the five states of today's Southwest. He sees his role in literature as that of the shaman; his task as a storyteller is to heal and reestablish balance and harmony. These ideas are present throughout his works, but are most successfully represented in his prize-winning novel *Bless Me, Ul-*

Rudolfo A. Anaya.

tima, in which the folk healer Ultima works to reestablish harmony and social order in the life of the Mares family and to bring psychological well-being to Antonio, the protagonist, who is struggling to understand the roles of good and evil in life. Anaya's other books are *Heart of Aztlán* (1976), *Tortuga* (1979), *The Silence of the Llano* (1982), *The Legend of La Llorona* (1984), *The Adventures of Juan Chicaspatas* (1985), *A Chicano in China* (1986), *The Farolitas of Christmas* (1987), *Lord of the Dawn: The Legend of Quetzalcoatl* (1987), *Alburquerque* (1992), *Zia Summer* (1995), and *Jalamanta: A Message from the Desert* (1996). He is also the author of plays and screenplays and has coedited three literary anthologies: with Simon Ortiz, *Ceremony of Brotherhood, 1680–1980* (1980); with José Griego y Maestas, *Cuentos: Tales from the Hispanic Southwest* (1980), and with Antonio Márquez, *Cuentos Chicanos* (1980, *Chicano Stories*).

In 1995, Anaya signed a multi-book contract with giant Warner Books to reissue all of his novels as well as to publish his new works. This is the first time that such financial and marketing commitment has been extended to an Hispanic creative writer.

The first new title of Anay's issued by Warner was a detective novel, *Zia Summer,* in 1996.

Jimmy Santiago Baca (1952–)

Jimmy Santiago Baca is one of the most successful Chicano poets to come out of the oral tradition, tempered by prison experiences and the Chicano Movement; in this and other aspects, his background is similar to that of Ricardo Sánchez. Baca was born in Santa Fe, New Mexico, in 1952 to Mexican and Apache-Yaqui parents who abandoned him to be raised by his Indian grandparents; he was later raised in an orphanage. In 1973, Baca was sentenced to five years imprisonment for narcotics possession. In the a maximum security prison in Arizona, Baca taught himself to read and write and he passed his G.E.D. exam. In prison, Baca discovered poetry and began penning his first compositions. While still serving time, *Mother Jones* magazine published his first poems. By the time of his release in 1978, his first book of poems, *Immigrants in Our Own Land* had been accepted for publication by the prestigious Louisiana State University Press, which issued the book in 1979. Baca's poems were highly polished, but naturalistic, and met with immediate critical approval; the accolades from mainstream critics expanded with his next books: *What's Happening* (1982), *Martin and Meditations on the South Valley* (1987) and *Black Mesa Poems* (1989), the latter two published by one of the most important literary houses in the United States: New Directions. In 1993, Baca also published a book of autobiographical essays, *Working in the Dark: Reflections of a Poet in the Barrio* and, in 1993, wrote a screenplay for a film, *Bound by Honor,* which was released by Disney's Hollywood Pictures. For *Black Mesa Poems,* Baca became the first Hispanic poet to win the important Wallace Stevens Poetry Award. Baca has served as a poet in residence at Yale University and the University of California-Berkeley.

Lorna Dee Cervantes (1954–)

Lorna Dee Cervantes was born into an economically deprived family of Mexican and American heritage, on August 6, 1954, in the Mission District of San Francisco. At age five she moved with her mother and brother to San Jose to live with her grandmother when her parents separated. Cervantes began writing poetry when she was six years old; poems written when she was 14 were eventually published in a magazine after Cervantes had established her career as a writer. She later attended college, but did not finish her B.A. degree from California State University until after she had initiated her writing career; in 1990 she obtained a Ph.D.

degree from the University of California, Santa Cruz, where she studied philosophy and aesthetics. She then went on to teach creative writing at the University of Colorado in Denver.

Emplumada (1981, *Plumed*), Cervantes' first collection of poems, is made up of works published in literary magazines throughout the Southwest. The book's popularity has made it the best-selling title in the University of Pittsburgh's prestigious poetry series. *Emplumada* presents a young woman coming of age, discovering the gap that exists in life between one's hopes and desires and what life eventually offers in reality. The predominant themes include culture conflict, oppression of women and minorities, and alienation from one's roots. Cervantes' poetry is very well crafted and has the distinction of using highly lyrical language while at the same time being direct and powerful. The same can be said of her second book, *From the Cables of Genocide,* which is very much the work of a mature poet dealing with the great themes of life, death, social conflict, and poverty. *From the Cables of Genocide* won the Paterson Poetry Prize and the national Hispanic Poetry Prize given by New York's *La Brújula / The Compass* magazine.

Angélico Chávez (1910–)

Fray Angélico Chávez is one of the most renowned religious poets in the United States. The author of some 19 books, Chávez is also a historian of his order, the Franciscan brothers, and of the Catholic church in New Mexico. Born on April 10, 1910, in Wagon Mound, New Mexico, he was named Manuel Chávez by his parents. Chávez was raised in Mora and attended St. Francis Seminary in Cincinnati, Ohio, and colleges in the Midwest. In 1937, he became the first New Mexican to become a Franciscan friar. From the time of his ordination at age 27, until age 62, he served as a pastor in several towns and Indian pueblos of New Mexico.

What unifies Chávez's large output as a poet and historian is his interest in New Mexico's past, the work of his order in New Mexico, and his own Catholicism. Beginning as essentially a religious poet, he later took an interest in historical fiction and, finally, in the history of the region itself, as in his most famous historical essay, *My Penitente Land: Reflections on Spanish New Mexico* (1974). Other historical writings by Chávez were intended to provide an accurate understanding of Hispanic New Mexico; these include *Our Lady of the Conquest* (1948), *Origins of New Mexico Families in the Spanish Colonial Period* (1954), *Coronado's Friars* (1968), *But Time and Chance: The Story of Padre Martínez of Taos, 1793–1867* (1981), and other edited books.

His works of historical fiction include *New Mexico Triptych: Being Three Panels and Three Accounts: 1. The Angel's New Wing, 2. The Penitente Thief, 3. Hunchback Madonna* (1940), *La Conquistadora: The Autobiography of an Ancient Statue* (1954), *From an Altar Screen / El retablo: Tales from New Mexico* (1957), and *The Lady from Toledo* (1960).

Chávez's reputation as a creative writer rests upon an important body of poetic works that include *Clothed with the Sun* (1939), *Eleven Lady Lyrics, and Other Poems* (1945), *The Single Rose; the Rose Unica and Commentary of Fray Manuel de Santa Clara* (1948), and *The Virgin of Port Lligat* (1959). Although Chávez's poetry and all of his works are grounded in New Mexico Catholicism, his poems are not local-color pieces celebrating New Mexico's picturesque landscape; instead they depict Chávez's inner life. In *The Single Rose,* Chávez was so intent on communicating the poems' inner religious meaning that he included commentary in the book, which studies the rose as an allegorical figure for human and divine love. Chávez's last poetry collection was *Selected Poems, With an Apologia* (1969), which

Lorna Dee Cervantes, 1990. (Photograph by Georgia McInnis.)

brought together some of his most successful poems along with an apologia that announced that he would no longer publish poetry, due to changing fashions in poetry and his loss of excitement in writing verse.

Denise Chávez (1948–)

Denise Chávez is a novelist, playwright, and poet who, through her writings, has brought to life entire populations of memorable characters of the Southwest, both Mexican American and Anglo-American. Born on August 15, 1948, in Las Cruces, New Mexico, Chávez was raised principally by her mother Delfina, a teacher; her father had abandoned the family while she was still young. After attending schools and colleges in Las Cruces, Chávez obtained a master's degree in theater arts from Trinity University in San Antonio, Texas, in 1974, and a master's degree in creative writing from the University of New Mexico in Albuquerque in 1984. During her career she has taught and been a writer in residence at numerous institutions in New Mexico and elsewhere. She taught in the drama department of the University of Houston from 1988 to 1993, when she

Denise Chávez.

became a visiting professor of creative writing at New Mexico State University.

Denise Chávez has won numerous awards and fellowships, including Best Play award for *The Wait* from New Mexico State University in 1970, the Steele Jones Fiction Award in 1986 for her story "The Last of the Menu Girls," two fellowships from the National Endowment for the Arts (in 1981 and 1982), a Rockefeller Foundation fellowship in 1984, and the Creative Writing Arts fellowship from the Cultural Arts Council of Houston in 1990.

As a playwright, Chávez has written numerous plays, many of which have been produced on the stage but not published. Her writings include *Novitiates* (1971), *Elevators* (1972), *The Mask of November* (1977), *Nacimiento* (1979, *Birth*), *Santa Fe Charm* (1980), *Sí, Hay Posada* (1980, *Yes, There Is Room*), *El Santero de Córdova* (1981, *The Saint-maker of Córdova*), *Hecho en México* (1982, *Made in Mexico*) (with Nita Luna), *The Green Madonna* (1982), *La Morenita* (1983, *The Little Brown Girl*), *Francis!* (1983), *How Junior Got Throwed in the Joint* (1981), *Plaza* (1984), *Novena Narrativa* (1986, *A Narrative Novena*), *The Step* (1987), *Language of Vision* (1987), and *The Last of the Menu Girls* (1990).

She has also had three of her children's plays produced on stage: *The Adobe Rabbit* (1979), *El Más Pequeño de Mis Hijos* (1983, *The Smallest of My Children*), and *The Flying Tortilla Man* (1975), which was also published in a high school textbook, *Mexican American Literature,* edited by Charles Tatum (1990). Chávez has also edited an anthology of plays, *Plays by Hispanic Women of the United States* (1991).

Despite Chávez's high productivity as a playwright, it is her published works of fiction that have contributed most to her national reputation. Chávez has published short stories in magazines and has two novels in print, *The Last of the Menu Girls* (1986) and *Face of an Angel* (1993). The first of these is a series of stories, centering on the coming of age of Rocío Esquivel, that come together to form a novel. As Rocío compares her own life to that of her mother and as she encounters a wide range of characters in her neighborhood and at work, she begins to formulate her own identity. By the end of the book, we realize that we have been participating in the making of a novelist, and that what we have been reading is the product of Rocío's creative and psychological exploration.

While still centering on the life of a female central character and her development, *Face of an Angel* is completely different from Chavez's first novel. It is an unrestrained, bawdy, irreverent, and hilariously funny novel that explores some of the major themes of the women's liberation movement as represented in the life of a waitress, Soveida Dosamantes, who is an author in her own right (of a manual on waitressing that is included in the novel). Dosamantes is depicted as someone who repeatedly gets involved with the wrong men. The novel consists of her experiences with a number of lazy, good-for-nothing men who are irresistible to her. *Face of an Angel* is populated with a host of humorous and tragic figures that represent a cross section of life in the Southwest.

Sandra Cisneros (1954–)

Sandra Cisneros was born in Chicago, the daughter of a Mexican immigrant father and a Mexican American mother. A graduate of Loyola University in Chicago and of the prestigious University of Iowa Writers' Work with an M.F.A., Cisneros began publishing her poems while she was working at an alternative high school in Chicago, teaching English and creative writing to barrio children. From those days almost to the present, she has developed a creative persona of a young girl and has maintained a youthful reader as her ideal audience. Not only do such essays as her "Notes to a Young Writer" cultivate this relationship, but her most important book, *The House on Mango Street,* casts a teenager, Esperanza, as the narrator and protagonist coming of age with the desire to become a writer. *The House on Mango Street,* published in 1984 by what eventually became the leading Hispanic press, Arte Público Press, became an underground best seller, principally among college and high school students and won the Before Columbus Foundation American Book Award, despite the book having received very few reviews. Today, the loosely framed, novelistic collection of poetic stories is a mainstay on college English and ethnic studies curricula. More importantly, the book became Cisneros' calling card for entrance into mainstream presses. Her next prose venture was a highly regarded collection of essays and stories, *Woman Hollering Creek,* published in 1991 by Random House, which had also bought the rights for and re-issued *The House on Mango Street.* Cisneros published her first full-length collection of poems, *My Wicked Wicked Ways* in 1987 with a Hispanic feminist press, Third Woman Press, of Berkeley, California. In 1995, Cisneros became the first Hispanic writer to win the highly funded and prestigious MacArthur fellowship.

Judith Ortiz Cofer (1952–)

Judith Ortiz Cofer was born in Hormigueros, Puerto Rico, on February 24, 1952, into a family that was destined to move back and forth between Puerto Rico and Paterson, New Jersey. Her father, Jesús Ortiz Lugo, was in the navy, first assigned to the Brooklyn Navy Yard and then other points around the world. In Puertro Rico, the young Judith attended San José Catholic School in San Germán, and in Paterson she went to public schools at first and then to Saint Joseph's Catholic School. In 1968, after her father had retired from the navy with a nervous breakdown, the family moved to Augusta, Georgia, where she attended high school and Augusta College. She met John Cofer at the college and they were married. After graduation and the birth of her daughter, they moved to West Palm Beach, Florida, and she earned an M.A. degree at Florida Alantic University. She was also awarded a scholarship to do graduate work at Oxford University by the English-Speaking Union of America. Included among many other awards were fellowships from the Florida Arts Council (1980), the Bread Loaf Writers Conference (1981), and the National Endowment for the Arts (1989).

While teaching English in south Florida colleges, Cofer began writing poetry, and her works were soon appearing in such magazines as the *New Mexico Humanities Review, Kansas Quarterly, Prairie Schooner, Revista Chicano-Riqueña, Southern Hum-*

Judith Ortiz Cofer.

anities Review, Southern Poetry Review, and else-where. Her collections of poetry include four chapbooks—*Latin Women Pray* (1980), *Among the Ancestors* (1981), *The Native Dancer* (1981), *Peregrina* (1986)—and two full-length books—*Reaching for the Mainland* (1987) and *Terms of Survival* (1987). Her well-crafted poetry reflects her struggle as a writer to create a history for herself out of the cultural ambiguity of a childhood spent traveling back and forth between the United States and Puerto Rico. Through her poetry she also explores from a feminist perspective her relationship with her father, mother, and grandmother, while also considering the different expectations for the males and females in Anglo-American and Hispanic cultures. In particular, her book of autobiographical essays, *Silent Dancing: A Remembrance of a Puerto Rican Childhood* (1990), pursues this question. Her novel *The Line of the Sun* (1990) is based on her family's gradual immigration to the United States and chronicles the years from the Great Depression to the 1960s. Since 1992, she has been writing and teaching full-time at the University of Georgia.

Jesús Colón (1901–1974)

Jesús Colón's writings are considered to be landmarks in the development of Puerto Rican literature in the continental United States because he is one of the first writers to become well known through his use of English, because of his identification with the working class, and because of his ideas on race. These three factors in the essays that he was already writing in the 1940s and 1950s make him a clear forerunner of the Nuyorican writers who began to appear two decades later.

Colón was born in 1901 into a working-class family in Cayey, Puerto Rico. At age 16, he stowed away on a ship that landed in Brooklyn. In New York, he worked in a series of jobs that exposed him to the exploitation and abuse of lower-class and unskilled workers. He became involved in literary and journalistic endeavors while working as a laborer, trying to establish a newspaper and writing translations of English-language poetry. As he strived to develop his literary and journalistic career, he encountered racial prejudice, mainly because of his skin color, for Colón was of Afro-Puerto Rican heritage. Despite discrimination, Colón became active in community and political activities. He became a columnist for the *Daily Worker,* the publication of the national office of the Communist party, as an outgrowth of these activities and his literary interests. Colón also founded and operated a publishing house, Hispanic Publishers (Editorial Hispánica), which published history and literary books, as well as political infor-

mation in Spanish. In 1952 and 1969, he ran for public office on the Communist party ticket, but was unsuccessful.

A selection of Colón's newspaper columns and essays was collected and published in 1961 in book form under the title *A Puerto Rican in New York and Other Sketches.* In this work, Colón's major themes are (1) the creation and development of a political consciousness, (2) his own literary development and worth, (3) advocacy for the working-class poor, and (4) the injustices of capitalist society in which racial and class discrimination is all too frequent and individual worth does not seem to exist. The collection as a whole is richly expressive of a socially conscious and humanistic point of view. He died in 1974. In 1994, a second collection of his journalistic columns was published: *The Way It Was and Other Writings.*

Victor Hernández Cruz (1949–)

Victor Hernández Cruz is the Nuyorican poet most recognized and acclaimed by the mainstream. Born on February 6, 1949, in Aguas Buenas, Puerto Rico, he moved with his family to New York's Span-

Victor Hernández Cruz.

ish Harlem at age 5. Cruz attended Benjamin Franklin High School, where he began writing poetry. In the years following graduation, his poetry began to appear in *Evergreen Review, New York Review of Books, Ramparts, Down Here,* and in small magazines. In 1973, Cruz left New York and took up residence in San Francisco, where he worked for the U.S. Postal Service. In 1989, he moved back to Puerto Rico, where he currently resides.

Cruz's poetry books include *Papa Got His Gun* (1966), *Snaps* (1969), *Mainland* (1973), *Tropicalization* (1976), *By Lingual Wholes* (1982), and *Rhythm, Content and Flavor* (1989). Classifying his poetry as Afro-Latin, Cruz has developed as a consummate bilingual poet and experimenter who consistently explores the relationship of music to poetry in a multiracial, multicultural context. Cruz has often been considered a jazz poet or an African American poet. The April 1981 issue of *Life* magazine included Cruz among a handful of outstanding American poets.

Abelardo Delgado (19311–)

Abelardo "Lalo" Delgado is one of the most renowned and prolific Chicano poets, a pioneer of bilingualism in Hispanic poetry and a consummate oral performer of his works. Delgado was born in the small town of La Boquilla de Conchos in northern Mexico on November 27, 1931. At age 12 he and his mother immigrated to El Paso, Texas. In El Paso, he lived in a poor Mexican barrio until 1969. Despite early problems in school with the English language, Delgado excelled as a student, and by graduation in 1950 from Bowie High School, he had become vice president of the National Honor Society chapter there. He went on to college while working at a variety of jobs and graduated from the University of Texas, El Paso, in 1962. Since that time he has earned his living as a counselor for migrant workers and as a teacher in Texas and later in Colorado. During the late 1960s and throughout most of the 1970s, Delgado was also one of the most popular speakers and poetry readers in the Southwest, which translated into a life of frequent tours and engagements. This was the height of the Chicano movement, and Delgado was one of its most celebrated animators and poet laureates.

Besides writing numerous poems, essays, and stories that have been published in literary magazines and anthologies nationwide, Delgado is the author of some 14 books and chapbooks; many of these were published through his own small printing operation known as Barrio Press. Delgado's first book, *Chicano: 25 Pieces of a Chicano Mind* (1969), is his best known, containing many of the poems that were

Abelardo Delgado.

performed personally in the heat of the protest movement and that subsequently received widespread distribution through small community newspapers and hand-to-hand circulation throughout the Southwest. Poems such as his "Stupid America" not only embodied the values of life in the barrio but also called for the types of social reform that became anthems for the Chicano movement. Other noteworthy titles include *It's Cold: 52 Cold-Thought Poems of Abelardo* (1974), *Here Lies Lalo: 25 Deaths of Abelardo* (1979), and his book of essays, *Letters to Louise* (1982), which ponder the feminist movement and the social roles of women and men and was awarded the Premio Quinto Sol, the national award for Chicano literature. In all, Delgado is a remarkably agile bilingual poet, an outstanding satirist and humorist, an undaunted and militant protester and pacifist, and a warmhearted and loving narrator and chronicler of the life and tradition of his people.

Roberto Fernández (1951–)

Roberto Fernández is in the vanguard of Cuban American literature, having made the transition from a literature of exile to a literature very much a part of the culture and social conditions of Cubans in the United States, and having made the transition from producing works in Spanish to writing in English. Born in Sagua la Grande, Cuba, on September 24, 1951, just eight years before the Cuban Revolution, he went into exile with his family at age 11. His family settled in southern Florida, not in the Cuban community of Miami but in areas where Anglo-American culture was dominant. This required adjustment to an apparently hostile environment, which accounts for some of the culture conflict that is depicted in his writings. The Fernández family did maintain close ties with the Miami community, and this too became subject matter for the writer. Fernández became interested in writing as an adolescent, and this interest led him to college and graduate school. In 1978, he completed a Ph.D. degree in linguistics at Florida State University; by that time he had already published two collections of stories, *Cuentos sin rumbo* (1975, *Directionless Tales*) and *El jardín de la luna* (1976, *The Garden of the Moon*). At this point he also began his career as an academic, teaching linguistics and Hispanic literature at Florida State University in Tallahassee.

Fernández is the author of three novels that have created for him the reputation of being a satirist and humorist of the Miami Cuban community. In all three, he is a master at capturing the nuances of Cuban dialect in Spanish and English. *La vida es un special* (1982, *Life Is on Special*), *La montaña rusa* (1985, *The Roller Coaster*), *Raining Backwards* (1988), and *Holy Radishes!* (1995) are all mosaics made up of monologues, dialogues, letters, phone conversations, speeches, and other types of oral performance that, in the composite, make up a continuing tale of the development of the exile community and its younger generations of increasingly acculturated Cuban Americans. Through the pages of these books the author charts the goings-on at social clubs and coming-out parties, follows counterrevolutionary guerrilla movements in the Florida swamps and the emergence of a Cuban pope, plots a mystery novel, discusses a poetry and art contest, and gives many other episodic bits and pieces that create a broad spectrum of a dynamic community caught between two cultures, two sets of values, two languages, and two political systems. *Raining Backwards,* Fernández's first book to be published in English, became something of a small press hit, receiving outstanding reviews from coast to coast in major newspapers and magazines (including *The New York Times, USA Today, San Francisco Chronicle*), and was optioned to become a feature film.

Lionel G. García (1935–)

Lionel G. García is a novelist who has created some of the most memorable characters in Chicano literature in a style that is steeped in the traditions of Texas tall-tales and Mexican American folk narratives. Born in San Diego, Texas in 1935, García grew up in an environment in which Mexican Americans were the majority population in his small town and on the ranches where he worked and played. García grew up in a middle-class family; his father was an auto body worker and his mother was a teacher. He excelled in school and became one of the few Mexican Americans admitted to Texas A & M University. He majored in biology, but was encouraged by one of his English professors to write. After graduating he attempted to become a full-time writer but was unsuccessful in getting his works published. He served in the army, and after being discharged honorably, he returned to Texas A & M and graduated from that institution in 1969 as a doctor of veterinary science. Since then he has developed a successful career as a veterinarian.

Throughout this time he continued to write. In the early 1980s, he once again attempted to publish, and he found that there were many more opportunities. In 1983, he won the PEN Southwest Discovery

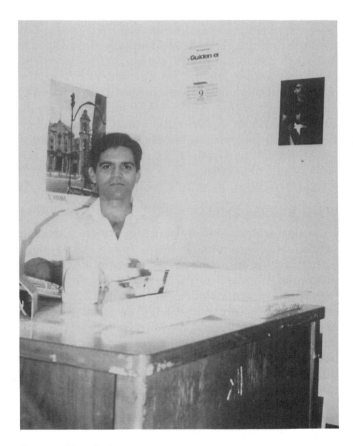

Roberto Fernández.

Lionel G. García.

Award for his novel in progress, *Leaving Home,* which was published in 1985. This and his second novel, *A Shroud in the Family* (1987), draw heavily on his family experiences and small-town background. In part, *A Shroud in the Family* also de-mythologizes the "great" Texas heroes, such as Sam Houston and Jim Bowie, who have become symbols of Anglo-Texans' defeat of and superiority over Mexicans; this was García's contribution to the Texas sesquicentennial celebrations. His novel *Hardscrub* (1989) is a departure from his former works; it is a realistically drawn chronicle of the life of an Anglo child in an abusive family relationship. García has also published short stories in magazines, newspapers, and anthologies. Lionel García's latest works are a novel, *To a Widow with Children* (1994) and a collection of short stories, *I Can Hear the Cowbells Ring* (1994).

Celedonio González (1923–)

Celedonio Gonzalez has been known as "el cronista de la diáspora" (the chronicler of the Cuban diaspora or flight from Cuba). Of all of the Cuban exile novelists, he is the one who has turned his attention most to the trials, tribulations, and successes of the Cuban refugees and their children in the United States. Born on September 9, 1923, in the small town of La Esperanza in central Cuba, González began his education in the neighboring city of Santa Clara at a Catholic school and later graduated from a Protestant high school in the city of Cárdenas. Upon returning to La Esperanza he began working in his family's farming enterprises, which he eventually came to manage. He was a supporter of progressive causes and of Castro's revolution, but by 1960 he had become disillusioned with the revolution and was imprisoned for two months as a counter-revolutionary. Upon release, he immigrated to the United States with his wife and children. In Miami he eked out a living at a number of odd jobs. In 1965, he and his family resettled in Chicago in search of a better living.

It was there that he began writing, but it was not until his return to Miami at age 41 that he wrote his first successful novel, *Los primos* (1971, *The Cousins*), a mirror of Cuban life in Miami during the 1960s. The same year, his short stories depicting the loneliness of Cuban exile life in the United States, *La soledad es una amiga que vendrá* (*Solitude Is a Friend Who Will Come*), were published in book form. His novel *Los cuatro embajadores* (1973, *The Four Ambassadors*) criticizes American capitalism and the dehumanization in American life. His greatest work to date is his *El espesor del pellejo de un gato ya cadáver* (1978, *The Thickness of Skin of a Dead Cat*), a call for Cubans to give up their dreams of returning to the island of their birth and to make the best of life in the United States. González's short stories also deal with American life from the vantage point, quite often, of the Cuban laboring classes and small-scale shopkeepers.

Oscar Hijuelos (1951–)

Born on August 24, 1951, to Cuban American working-class parents in New York City, Hijuelos was educated in public schools and obtained a B.A. degree in 1975 and an M.A. degree in 1976, both in English, from City College of the City University of New York. While at City College he studied creative writing with the noted novelist Donald Barthelme. Hijuelos is one of the few Hispanic writers to have formally studied creative writing and to have broken into the Anglo-dominated creative writing circles, participating in prestigious workshops such as the Breadloaf Writers Conference, and benefiting from highly competitive fellowships, such as the American Academy in Rome fellowship from the American Academy and the Institute for Arts and Letters

(1985), the National Endowment for the Arts fellowship (1985), and the Guggenheim fellowship (1990).

Hijuelos is the author of numerous short stories and four novels, *Our House in the Last World* (1983), *The Mambo Kings Play Songs of Love* (1989), *The Fourteen Sisters of Emilio Montez O'Brien* (1993), and *Mr. Ives' Christmas* (1995). His first novel follows in the tradition of ethnic autobiography as it chronicles the life and maladjustment of a Cuban immigrant family in the United States during the 1940s. *The Mambo Kings Play Songs of Love* examines a time period in which Hispanic culture was highly visible in the United States and was able to influence American popular culture: it takes place during the 1950s at the height of the mambo craze and the overwhelming success of Desi Arnaz's television show, "I Love Lucy." Written in a poetic but almost documentary style, the novel follows two brothers who are musicians trying to ride the crest of the Latin music wave. While providing a picture of one segment of American life never seen before in English-language fiction, the novel also indicts, as does *Our House in the Last World,* womanizing and alcoholism as particularly Cuban flaws.

Rolando Hinojosa (1929–)

Rolando Hinojosa is the most prolific and well-respected Hispanic novelists in the United States. Not only has he created memorable Mexican American and Anglo characters, but he has completely populated a fictional county in the lower Rio Grande Valley of Texas through his continuing generational narrative that he calls the Klail City Death Trip Series.

Born in Mercedes, Texas, on January 21, 1929, to a Mexican American father and an Anglo-American mother, his paternal ancestors arrived in the lower Rio Grande Valley in 1749 as part of the José Escandón expedition. Hinojosa received his early education in Mexican schools in Mercedes and later in the segregated public schools of the area where all his classmates were Mexican Americans. His classes were not integrated until his junior high years. It was in high school that Hinojosa began to write, publishing his first English pieces in an annual literary magazine entitled *Creative Bits.* Hinojosa left the valley in 1946 when he graduated from college, but the language, culture, and history of the area form the substance of all his novels. The ensuing years saw a stretch in the army, studies at the University of Texas, reactivation into the army to fight in the Korean War (an experience that informs his poetic narrative *Korean Love Songs*), graduation form the University of Texas in 1954 with a degree in Spanish, and back to Brownsville as a teacher,

Rolando Hinojosa.

among a variety of other jobs, and finally, on to graduate school. In 1969 he obtained his Ph.D. degree in Spanish from the University of Illinois and returned to teach at Texas colleges. Hinojosa has remained in academia in a variety of positions at several universities; today he serves as Ellen Clayton Garwood Professor of English and Creative Writing at the University of Texas.

Although he has written throughout his life, Hinojosa did not begin publishing until 1973, his first work being *Estampas del Valle y otras obras,* which he recreated in English and published as *The Valley* in 1983. The book won the national award for Chicano literature, Premio Quinto Sol. Since then, he has become one of the most prolific Chicano novelists, publishing one novel after another in his generational narrative that centers on the lives of two of his alter egos, Rafa Buenrostro and Jehú Malacara, in individual installments that vary in form from poetry and dialogue to the picaresque novel and the detective novel. His titles in English alone include *Korean Love Songs* (1980), *Rites and Witnesses* (1982), *Dear Rafe* (1985), *Partners in Crime: A Rafe Buenrostro Mystery* (1985), *Claros varones de*

Belken/Fair Gentlemen of Belken County (1986, bilingual edition), *Klail City* (1987), *Becky and Her Friends* (1989), and *The Useless Servants* (1993). His original Spanish version of *Klail City,* entitled *Klail City y sus alrededores* (1976), won an international award for fiction, Premio Casa de las Américas, from Cuba in 1976; it was issued there under this title and one year later, a version was published in the United States under the title *Generaciones y semblanzas.* The book was also published in German two years later. In addition, Hinojosa has published several short stories and essays, as well as installments of a satirical running commentary on life and current events in the United States, known as "The Mexican American Devil's Dictionary," supposedly created by another of his alter egos who is also one of the narrators of the Klail City Death Trip Series: P. Galindo (meaning "right on target" in Spanish).

Hinojosa has been hailed as a master satirist, an acute observer of the human comedy, a Chicano William Faulkner for his creation of the history and people of Belken County, and a faithful recorder of the customs and dialects in Spanish and English of both Anglos and Mexicans in the lower Rio Grande Valley. One of the best-loved and most highly regarded Hispanic writers, Hinojosa is universally lauded for his commitment to and realistic portrayal of Mexican American life.

Jesús Abraham "Tato" Laviera (1951–)

Jesús Abraham "Tato" Laviera is the best-selling Hispanic poet of the United States, and he bears the distinction of still having all his books in print. Born in Santurce, Puerto Rico, on May 9, 1951, he migrated to New York at age ten with his family, which settled in a poor area of the lower East Side. After finding himself in an alien society and with practically no English, Laviera was able to adjust and eventually graduate high school as an honor student. Despite having no other degrees, his intelligence, aggressiveness, and thorough knowledge of his community led to his developing a career in the administration of social service agencies. After the publication of his first book *La Carreta Made a U-Turn* (1979), Laviera gave up administrative work to dedicate his time to writing. Since 1980, his career has included not only writing but touring nationally as a performer of his poetry, directing plays, and producing cultural events. In 1980, he was received by President Jimmy Carter at the White House gathering of American poets. In 1981, his second book, *Enclave,* was the recipient of the American Book Award of the Before Columbus Foundation.

All Tato Laviera's books have been well received by critics, most of whom place him within the context of Afro-Caribbean poetry and U.S. Hispanic bilingualism. *La Carreta Made a U-Turn* is bilingual, jazz- or salsa-poetry that presents the reader with a slice of life drawn from the Puerto Rican community of the lower East Side. As such, it examines both oppression of the migrant community and its alienation through such popular culture forms as soap operas; it probes crime and drug addiction while affirming the spiritual and social values of the community and the place of art, poetry, and music in what many may consider to be the unlikeliest of social environments. Laviera, here as in the rest of his books, acknowledges and supports the existence of a true Puerto and Latino culture within the heart of the metropolis and within the very belly of the United States. He further affirms that there is no need to return to a homeland on an island or south of the border, for Latinos have made their home here and are transforming not only mainstream culture in the United States, but throughout the hemisphere.

In *Enclave,* Laviera celebrates such cultural heroes, both real and imagined, as Alicia Alonso, Suni Paz, John Lennon, Miriam Makeba, the fictitious

Tato Laviera, 1990. (Photograph by Georgia McInnis.)

half-southern black, half-Puerto Rican Tito Madera Smith, the barrio gossip Juana Bochisme, and the neighborhood tough Esquina Dude. As in *La Carreta Made a U-Turn,* Laviera acknowledges his debt to Afro-Caribbean music and poetry in his eulogies of salsa composer Rafael Cortijo, the famed poetry reciter Juan Boria, and master poets Luis Palés Matos and Nicolás Guillén. *AmeRícan* (1986), published on the occasion of the centennial celebration of the Statue of Liberty, is a poetic reconsideration of immigrant life in New York City and the United States. *Mainstream Ethics* (1988) proposes transforming the United States from a Eurocentric culture to one that is ethnically and racially pluralistic in its official identity. *Continental* (1992), published during the Columbus quincentenary, extends these themes and imperatives to the whole hemisphere.

Despite Laviera's outstanding publishing record, the sophistication of his vision, and his artistic bilingualism, he is an oral poet, a consummate performer of his poetry, which slowly but surely is constituting a living epic of the Hispanic peoples of the United States. Even Laviera's written and published poems have been created out of a process that attempts to re-create as much as possible the oral performance. For Laviera, part of that oral tradition and performance are the structures, spirit, and rhythms of popular and folk music, especially those drawn from Afro-Puerto Rican music.

Julio Matas

See Chapter 21.

Nicholasa Mohr (1935–)

To date, Nicholasa Mohr is the only Hispanic American woman to have developed a long career as a creative writer for the major publishing houses. Since 1973, her books for such publishers as Dell/Dial, Harper & Row, and Bantam Books, in both the adult and children's literature categories, have won numerous awards and outstanding reviews. Part and parcel of her work is the experience of growing up a female, a Hispanic, and a minority in New York City.

Born on November 1, 1935, in New York City, Nicholasa Mohr was raised in Spanish Harlem. Educated in New York City schools, she finally escaped poverty after graduating from the Pratt Center for Contemporary Printmaking in 1969. From that date until the publication of her first book, *Nilda* (1973), Mohr developed a successful career as a graphic artist. *Nilda,* a novel that traces the life of a young Puerto Rican girl confronting prejudice and coming of age during World War II, won the Jane Addams Children's Book Award and was selected by *School*

Nicholasa Mohr, 1990.

Library Journal as a Best Book of the Year. After *Nilda*'s success, Mohr was able to produce numerous stories, scripts, and the following titles: *El Bronx Remembered* (1975), *In Nueva York* (1977), *Felita* (1979), *Rituals of Survival: A Woman's Portfolio* (1985), *Going Home* (1986), *All for the Better* (1992), *Isabel's New Mom* (1993), *Jaime and His Conch Shell* (1994), and *Old Letivia and the Mountain of Sorrows* (1994). Selections from all these story collections have been reprinted widely in a variety of anthologies and textbooks.

Mohr's works have been praised for depicting the life of Puerto Ricans in New York with empathy, realism, and humor. In her stories for children, Mohr has been able to deal with the most serious and tragic of subjects, from the death of a loved one to incest, in a sensitive and humane way. Mohr has been able to contribute to the world of commercial publishing—where stereotypes have reigned supreme—some of the most honest and memorable depictions of Puerto Ricans in the United States. In this and in her crusade to open the doors of publishing and the literary world to Hispanics, Nicholasa Mohr is a true pioneer.

Matías Montes Huidobro

See Chapter 21.

Cherríe Moraga (1952–)

The works of Cherríe Moraga have opened up the world of Chicano literature to the life and aesthetics of feminism and gay women. Moraga's works are well known in both feminist and Hispanic circles for their battles against sexism, classism, and racism. Born in Whittier, California, on September 25, 1952, to a Mexican American mother and an Anglo father, Moraga was educated in public schools in the Los Angeles area, after which she graduated from college with a B.A. degree in English in 1974. While working as a teacher she discovered her interest in writing, and in 1977 moved to the San Francisco Bay Area, where she became acquainted with the Anglo lesbian literary movement. In part to fulfill the requirements for a master's degree at San Francisco State University, Moraga collaborated with Gloria Anzaldúa in compiling the first anthology of writings by women of color, *This Bridge Called My Back: Writings by Radical Women of Color* (1981), which has become the most famous and best-selling anthology of its kind and has inspired a movement of Hispanic feminist and lesbian writers. In her writings here and in other books, Moraga explains that her understanding of racial and class oppression suffered by Chicanas only came as she experienced the prejudice against lesbians. In 1983, Moraga edited another ground-breaking anthology with Alma Gómez and Mariana Romo-Carmona, *Cuentos: Stories by Latinas. Cuentos* attempts to establish a poetics or a canon of Hispanic feminist creativity, a canon where there is room for, and indeed, respect for, the insights of lesbianism. In 1983, Moraga published a collection of her own essays and poems dating back to 1976, *Loving in the War Years: (lo que nunca pasó por sus labios),* in which she explores the dialectical relationship between sexuality and cultural identity. Her conclusion here, as elsewhere, is that women must be put first. Moraga is also a playwright whose work *Giving Up the Ghost* was produced in 1984 and published in 1986. Her latest produced play, *The Shadow of a Man,* was published in 1991. To date, Moraga remains one of the most militant and controversial of the Hispanic literary figures.

Alejandro Morales (1944–)

Alejandro Morales is one of the leading Chicano novelists, having published substantial novels in both Spanish and English in the United States and Mexico and having created through them a better understanding of Mexican American history, at least as seen from the vantage point of working-class cul-

ture. Born in Montebello, California, on October 14, 1944, Morales grew up in East Los Angeles and received his B.A. degree from California State University, Los Angeles. He went on to complete an M.A. degree (1973) and a Ph.D. degree (1975) in Spanish at Rutgers University in New Jersey. Today Morales is a full professor in the Spanish and Portuguese department at the University of California, Irvine.

Morales is at once a recorder of the Chicano experience, basing many of his narratives on historical research, and he is also an imaginative interpreter of that experience by creating memorable and dynamic characters and language. His first books were written in Spanish and published in Mexico, due to the lack of opportunity here in the United States. *Caras viejas y vino nuevo* (1975, translated as *Old Faces and New Wine,* 1981), examines the conflict of generations in a barrio family. *La verdad sin voz* (1979, translated as *Death of an Anglo,* 1988) is a continuation of the earlier novel, but is created against the backdrop of actual occurrences of Chicano-Anglo conflict in the town of Mathis, Texas. The novel also includes autobiographical elements in the form of a section that deals with racism in academia, which

Alejandro Morales.

comes to a head when a Chicano professor goes up for tenure. *Reto en el paraíso* (1983, *Challenge in Paradise*) is based on more than 100 years of Mexican American history and myth, as it centers on a basic comparison of the decline of the famed Coronel family of Californios and the rise of the Irish immigrant Lifford family. The novel charts the transfer of power and wealth from the native inhabitants of California to the gold-and land-hungry immigrants empowered by Manifest Destiny. *The Brick People* (1988) traces the development of two families connected with the Simons Brick Factory, one of the largest enterprises of its type in the country. Again, Morales uses the technique of comparing the lives of two families, those of the owners of the factory and those of an immigrant laborer's family. Morales' novel *The Rag Doll Plagues* (1991), while still incorporating a historical structure, follows the development of a plague and a Spanish Mexican doctor who is forever caught in mortal battle with this plague in three time periods and locations: colonial Mexico, contemporary Southern California, and the future in a country made up of Mexico and California united together.

In all, Morales is a meticulous researcher and a creator of novelistic circumstances that are symbolic of Mexican American history and cultural development. His novels have an epic sweep that are cinematic and highly literary.

Alberto O'Farrill

See Chapter 21.

Josephina Niggli (1910–1983)

Josephina Niggli demonstrated many of the sensibilities that would develop into a full-blown literary movement in the 1960s and 1970s. Born on July 13, 1910, in Monterrey, Mexico, she came to the United States with her parents in 1913 during the Mexican Revolution. Educated in American schools, she attended a Catholic high school in San Antonio, received her B.A. degree from Incarnate Word College (1931), and an M.A. degree from the University of North Carolina (1937). During her adolescence she began her writing career, publishing short stories and poems in such magazines as *Ladies' Home Journal* and *Mexican Life*. By age 18, she had published her first collection of poetry, *Mexican Silhouettes* (1928). She later received training in playwriting and had various plays produced and some screenplays made into Hollywood films. The following plays have been published in anthologies: *Soldadera* (1938), *This Is Villa* (1939), *Red Velvet Goat* (1938), *Sunday Costs Five Pesos* (1939), *Miracle at Blaise* (1942), *The Ring of General Macías* (1943), and *This Bull Ate Nutmeg* (1945). In 1945, the University of North Carolina Press published her novel *Mexican Village*. The press had already published her collection of *Mexican Folk Plays* in 1938; from 1942 on, Niggli embarked upon a career as an instructor and later, a professor of radio, television, theater arts, and speech at the University of North Carolina. While working as a professor at the University of North Carolina, Niggli also published another novel, *Step Down, Elder Brother* (1947), which was so successful that it was distributed by the Book-of-the-Month Club. In 1964, she published a young adult book, *A Miracle for Mexico*. Niggli died in 1983.

Niggli's writings reveal a thorough knowledge of Mexican customs, traditions, and history. Some of her works also analyze the role of women in Mexican life, especially from her bicultural perspective. All of her work set in Mexico can been seen as a mosaic of Mexican life and character types; her depiction of the Mexican Revolution is realistic and epic in nature, acquainting her readers with the struggles that would bring about the birth of modern Mexico.

Gustavo O'Neill

See Chapter 21.

Américo Paredes

See Chapter 17.

Pedro Pietri (1943–)

Pedro Pietri is famous for the literary persona of street urchin or skid-row bum that he has created for himself. His works are characterized by the consistent perspective of the underclass in language, philosophy, and creative and psychological freedom. Pietri was born in Ponce, Puerto Rico, on March 21, 1943, just two years before his family migrated to New York. He was orphaned of both parents while still a child and raised by his grandmother. Pietri attended public schools in New York City and served in the army from 1966 to 1968. Other than his having taught writing occasionally and participated in workshops, very little else is known about this intentionally mysterious and unconventional figure.

Pietri has published collections of poems and poetry chapbooks: *The Blue and the Gray* (1975), *Invisible Poetry* (1979), *Out of Order* (1980), *Uptown Train* (1980), *An Alternate* (1980), and *Traffic Violations* (1983). Nevertheless, it was his first book of poetry, *Puerto Rican Obituary* (1971), that brought him his greatest fame and a host of imitators. In 1973, a live performance by him of poems from this book was recorded and distributed by Folkways Records. In 1980, Pietri's short story *Lost in the Museum of Natural History* was published in bilingual format in Puerto Rico. Pietri has also had numerous unpublished, but produced, plays and one published collection, *The Masses Are Asses* (1984). Always a master of the incongruous and surprising, Pietri has created unlikely but humorous narrative situations in both his poetry and plays, such as that in his poem "Suicide Note from a Cockroach in a Low Income Housing Project" and in a dialogue between a character and her own feces in his play *Appearing in Person Tonight—Your Mother*. Pietri's work is one of a total break with conventions, both literary and social, and it is subversive in its open rejection of established society and its hypocrisies.

Miguel Piñero

See Chapter 21.

Dolores Prida

See Chapter 21.

Tomás Rivera

See Chapter 17.

Richard Rodríguez (1944–)

Essayist Richard Rodríguez was born on July 31, 1944, in San Francisco, the son of Mexican immigrants. Having begun school as a Spanish-speaker, he had to make the difficult transition to English in order to progress in school. As he recalled in his autobiographical book-length essay, *Hunger of Memory,* he came to believe that English was the language of U.S. school and society and that the Spanish language and Hispanic culture were private matters, for the home. Rodríguez went on to have outstanding success in school and eventually received a B.A. in English from Stanford University in 1967, and M.A. from Columbia University in 1969 and doctoral work at the University of California, which he never terminated because his writing career had begun and he had not submitted his dissertation. In 1981, Rodríguez published the above mentioned autobiography which received praise from mainstream critics across the nation for its elegant and passionate prose as well as for its rejection of bilingual education and affirmative action programs. Rodríguez immediately was seen by Hispanics as an Uncle Tom or Tío Taco for having bought success at the price of attacking Hispanic language, culture and programs aimed to assist Hispanics in education and employment. To this date, despite a successful career as an essayist, television commentator and opinion writer for newspapers, Rodríguez is not embraced by Hispanic critics as an authentic or valuable voice. His second book, *Days of Obliga-*

tion: An Argument with My Mexican Father (1992), which does not have the political content of *Hunger of Memory,* received fewer, but generally good reviews and passed with very little criticism by from Hispanic quarters.

Ricardo Sánchez (1941–1995)

Ricardo Sánchez was one of the most prolific Chicano poets, one of the first creators of a bilingual literary style, and one of the first to be identified with the Chicano movement. Born the youngest of 13 children on March 21, 1941, he was raised in the notorious Barrio del Diablo (Devil's Neighborhood) in his hometown of El Paso, Texas. He was a high school dropout, an army enlistee, and later a repeat offender sentenced to several prison terms in both Soledad Prison in California and Ramsey Prison Farm Number One in Texas; at these prisons he began his literary career, shortly before his last parole in 1969. Much of his early life experience, which includes oppressive poverty, overwhelming racism, suffering in prisons, and his self-education and rise to a level of political and social consciousness, is chronicled in his poetry, which although very lyrical, is considered the most autobiographical of all the Hispanic poets. Once his writing career was established and Sánchez began to publish his works with both mainstream and alternative literary presses, he assumed a number of visiting appointments as a professor or writer in residence at various universities. He was a founder of the short-lived Mictla Publications in El Paso, editor of various special issues of literary magazines, such as *De Colores* and *Wood/Ibis,* a columnist for the *San Antonio Express,* a bookseller, a migrant worker counselor, and remains an active performer of his poetry on tours in the United States and abroad.

Sánchez's poetry is characterized by an unbridled linguistic inventiveness that not only calls upon both English and Spanish lexicon but is also a source of neologisms and surprising combinations of the sounds and symbols of both languages in single works. His work can be virile and violent at one moment and delicate and sentimental at the next, as he follows the formulas and dictates of a poetry written for oral performance. His is often the exaggerated gesture and emotion of the *declamador* (poetic orator), whose works are performed to inspire a protest rally, inaugurate a mural, celebrate a patriotic holiday, or eulogize the dead. Most of all, Sánchez was an autobiographical poet who cast himself as a Chicano Everyman participating in the epic history of his people through his poetry. His bilingual facility and immense vocabulary and inventiveness were legendary in Chicano literature.

Ricardo Sánchez.

Besides publishing hundreds of poems in magazines and anthologies, Sánchez was the author of the following collections: *Canto y grito mi liberación (y lloro mis desmadrazgos)* (*I Sing and Shout for My Liberation [and Cry for My Insults]*, 1971), *Hechizospells: Poetry/Stories/Vignettes/Articles/ Notes on the Human Condition of Chicanos & Pícaros, Words and Hopes within Soulmind* (1976), *Milhuas Blues and Gritos Norteños* (1980), *Amsterdam cantos y poemas pistos* (1983), *Selected Poems* (1985), and *American Journeys* (1995).

Gustavo Solano

See Chapter 21.

Gary Soto (1952–)

In academic and creative writing circles, Soto is considered the most outstanding Chicano poet; he is certainly the most widely known Hispanic poet in the Anglo-American poetry establishment, as represented by creative writing departments, magazines, and workshops. Born to Mexican American parents in Fresno, California, on April 12, 1952, Soto was raised in the environs of the San Joaquin Valley and attended Fresno City College and California State University in Fresno, where he came under the guidance of poet Philip Levine and his creative writing career was born. Soto graduated magna cum laude from California State University in 1975, and in 1976 he earned an M.F.A. degree in creative writing from the University of California, Irvine. From 1977 until 1993, when he began writing full-time, he taught at the University of California, Berkeley, in the English and ethnic studies departments.

Soto has more prestigious awards than any other Hispanic poet in the United States, including the Academy of American Poets Prize in 1975, the

Gary Soto, 1991. (Photograph by M. L. Marinelli.)

Discovery-Nation Award in 1975, the United States Award of the International Poetry Forum in 1976, the Bess Hopkins Prize from *Poetry* magazine in 1977, a Guggenheim fellowship in 1979, a National Association fellowship in 1981, the Levinson Award from *Poetry* magazine in 1984, and the American Book Award from the Before Columbus Foundation in 1984.

Soto's books of poetry include the following: *The Elements of San Joaquin* (1977), *Father Is a Pillow Tied to a Broom* (1980), *Where Sparrows Work Hard* (1981), *Black Hair* (1985), *Who Will Know Us?* (1990), *Home Course in Religion: New Poems* (1991), and *New and Selected Poems* (1995). Soto has also published three collections of autobiographical essays and stories: *Living Up the Street: Narrative Recollections* (1985), *Small Faces* (1986), *Lesser Evils: Ten Quartets* (1988), *A Summer Life* (1990), and *The Bike* (1991). During the 1990s, Gary Soto launched a new career as a prolific writer for young adults and children, largely through commercial houses that were seeking to serve the burgeoning Hispanic school-age population. From 1990 to 1995 along, he published 12 such titles, including the highly regarded *Baseball in April and Other Stories* (1990), *The Pool Party* (1993), *Too Many Tamales* (1993), *Jesse* (1994), and *Chato's Kitchen* (1995). He has also produced two short films: *The Pool Party*, based on his book of the same title (1993), and *Novio Boy* (1994).

All of Soto's works are highly autobiographical and characterized by a highly polished craft. In his poetry and prose, there is also a great attention paid to narration and characterization; whether he is writing a poem or an essay, Soto is always cognizant of telling a story. Critics have always stated that Soto has something important and human to say, and it is poignantly said in well-crafted writing. While writing from his particular ethnic stance and worldview, he also maintains that there are certain values, experiences, and feelings that are universal.

Piri Thomas (1928–)

Piri Thomas is one of the most widely known cultivators of ethnic autobiography; his *Down These Mean Streets* (1976) was so successful as a powerful chronicle of growing up in the barrio that it spawned a host of Puerto Rican imitators. Piri (John Peter) Thomas was born on September 30, 1928, in New York City, to a Puerto Rican mother and a Cuban father. Thomas grew up during the Great Depression, facing both poverty and racism in New York's East Harlem. American society perceived Thomas as black, while his family perceived him as Puerto Rican and encouraged his identification with the

island that he had never seen. However, out on the streets and later in prison, he began to see himself as an African American, and to take pride in that identity, even becoming a Black Muslim for a while.

Thomas entered a life of theft, gang violence, and criminality in adolescence, and he eventually landed in prison. After serving seven years of a 15-year term, he was paroled at age 28. While in prison he had obtained his high school equivalency diploma and also had begun to learn to express himself in writing; he also developed a sense of dignity and self-respect. After returning to his old neighborhood and then to his family, who now lived in Long Island, he worked at a variety of jobs, but eventually developed his career as a writer.

All of Thomas' literary works are highly autobiographical, dealing mostly with his upbringing in the atmosphere of poverty, racism, and culture conflict in the barrio. In addition to his well-known *Down These Mean Streets,* Thomas also wrote a sequel, *Saviour, Saviour Hold My Hand* (1972), and a book on his seven-year imprisonment, *Seven Long Times* (1974). He has also published a collection of stories, *Stories from el Barrio* (1978). In addition, Thomas has written numerous articles and essays and has written plays that have been produced on stage. Thomas' works are important for having entered the mainstream, with all of his books issued by major publishers, and *Down These Mean Streets* was so highly reviewed that it projected Thomas into the television talk-show circuit and instant celebrity. A powerful and charming speaker, Thomas became an important spokesperson for the Puerto Rican community. In his books and in his public presentations he became identified with the search for identity, and to many readers and critics of the time this became the most important characteristic of Hispanic literature in the United States.

Omar Torres

See Chapter 21.

Estela Portillo Trambley (1936–)

Estela Portillo Trambley is one of the first women writers to successfully publish prose in the early male-dominated stages of the Chicano literary movement. Born in El Paso, Texas, on January 16, 1936, she was raised and educated in El Paso, where she attended high school and the University of Texas, El Paso, for her B.A. degree (1957) and her M.A. degree (1977). After graduation from college, she became a high school English teacher and administrator. Since 1979, she has been affiliated with the Department of Special Services of the El Paso Public

Schools. From 1970 to 1975, she served as dramatist in residence at El Paso Community College.

Trambley was the first woman to win the national award for Chicano literature, Premio Quinto Sol, in 1973, for her collection of short stories and novela *Rain of Scorpions and Other Writings,* which was published in 1975. Besides stories and plays published in magazines and anthologies, Portillo Trambley has written a collection of plays, *Sor Juana and Other Plays* (1981), and a novel, *Trini* (1983). In both her prose and drama, Portillo Trambley develops strong women who resist the social roles that have been predetermined for them because of their sex. In her fiction, women command center stage and achieve a level of self-determination and control over social and cultural circumstances. The culmination of her pursuit of strong women is represented in her exploration of the life of the eighteenth-century poet and essayist Sor Juan Inés de la Cruz in her play *Sor Juana.* The protagonist of her novel, *Trini,* is a fictional character who struggles against poverty and adversity to make her way in life; she eventually leaves Mexico and crosses the border illegally to find the power over her own life for which she has been searching.

Sabine Ulibarrí (1919–)

Short story writer, poet, and essayist Sabine Ulibarrí has had one of the longest and most productive literary careers in Chicano literature. He is a well-known and highly respected chronicler of the way things once were in his beloved New Mexico. Born on September 21, 1919, in the small village of Tierra Amarilla, New Mexico, he was raised on a ranch by his parents, both of whom were college graduates. Besides learning the ways of rural life and the rugged countryside, Ulibarrí also experienced firsthand the folk culture of the area, which included not only the full repository of oral literature but also a strong connection to the language and oral literature of Spain and the Spanish-speaking Americas. His early love for the Spanish language and Hispanic literature took Ulibarrí to college and eventually to a Ph.D. degree in Spanish. Over the years he taught at every level, from elementary school to graduate school, except during World War II, when he flew 35 combat missions as an air force gunner. Today he is a professor emeritus of the University of New Mexico, where he spent most of his academic career as a student and professor.

Among Ulibarrí's awards are the following: Governor's Award for Excellence in Literature (1988), Distinguished Alumni Award and Regents' Medal of Merit, University of New Mexico (1989), and the White House Hispanic Heritage Award (1989). Uli-

Sabine Ulibarrí.

barrí has had published two books of poems, *Al cielo se sube a pie* (1966, *You Reach Heaven on Foot*) and *Amor y Ecuador* (1966, *Love and Ecuador*), and the following collections of short stories in bilingual format: *Tierra Amarilla: Stories of New Mexico / Tierra Amarilla: Cuentos de Nuevo México* (1971), *Mi abuela fumaba puros y otros cuentos de Tierra Amarilla / My Grandma Smoked Cigars and Other Stories of Tierra Amarilla* (1977), *Primeros encuentros / First Encounters* (1982), *El gobernador Glu Glu* (1988, *Governor Glu Glu*), and *El Cóndor and Other Stories* (1989).

In all of his work, Ulibarrí preserves a style, narrative technique, and language that owes much to the oral folk tradition. Through his works he has been able to capture the ethos and the spirit of rural New Mexico before the coming of the Anglo. His works memorialize myths and legends and such distinctive characters of the past as cowboys, sheriffs, folk healers, penitents, and just the common everyday folk. Quite often writing two versions of the same story, in English and Spanish, in all of modern Chicano literature his works are among the most direct and accessible to broad audiences.

Luis Valdez

See Chapter 21.

Ed Vega (1936–)

Ed Vega is a Puerto Rican fiction writer who bases many of his works on life in New York City's Spanish Harlem. Edgardo Vega Yunqué was born in Ponce, Puerto Rico, on May 20, 1936, where he lived with his family until they moved to the Bronx, New York, in 1949. He was raised in a devout Baptist home, his father having been a minister of that faith; today, Vega and his wife and children have adopted the Buddhist faith. As a child, books were very accessible at home, and he began both his education and writing at an early age in Spanish in Puerto Rico. After moving to New York and going through the public education system of the city, he served in the air force and studied at Santa Monica College in California under the G.I. Bill. In 1963, Vega almost graduated as a Phi Beta Kappa from New York University with a major in political science; he was short three hours of credit and did not actually graduate until 1969. He did not return to finish until that date because he had become disillusioned after personally experiencing racism at the university. After leaving

Ed Vega.

there in 1963, he worked in a variety of social service programs. In 1969, he returned to academic life as a lecturer for Hunter College and thereafter assumed various other lecturing and assistant professor positions at other colleges. From 1977 to 1982, he worked at such community-based education programs as ASPIRA of New Jersey. From 1982 to the present, he has been a full-time writer.

Vega is one of the most prolific Hispanic prose writers, although much of his work remains unpublished. In 1977, his short stories began to be published by Hispanic magazines, such as *Nuestro, Maize* and *Revista Chicano-Riqueña.* In 1985, his novel *The Comeback,* a rollicking satire of ethnic autobiography and the identity crisis, as personified by a half-Puerto Rican, half-Eskimo ice hockey player who becomes involved in an underground revolutionary movement for Puerto Rican independence, was published. In 1987, a collection of interconnected short stories, *Mendoza's Dreams,* narrated by a warmhearted observer of the human comedy, Alberto Mendoza, was published. An additional common thread holding these barrio stories together is their charting of various Puerto Ricans on the road to success in the United States; thus, once again we have a Puerto Rican interpretation of the American dream. Vega's third book, *Casualty Report* (1991), is just the opposite; for the most part the collection of stories included here chronicle the death of dreams, as characters faced with racism, poverty, and crime succumb to despair in many forms: violence, alcohol and drug abuse, withdrawal, and resignation.

Daniel Venegas

Daniel Venegas was a harbinger of today's Chicano writers not only in openly proclaiming a Chicano identity and pursuing working-class language but also in generating a style and a literary attitude that would come to typify the Chicano novels of the late 1960s and the 1970s. Very little is known of his life. Born and raised in Mexico, his level of formal education is uncertain. In Los Angeles, he maintained an active life in the world of Mexican journalism and the theater during the 1920s and 1930s. There he founded and edited a weekly satirical newspaper, *El malcriado (The Brat),* from 1924 into the 1930s. He was the director of a popular vaudeville theatrical company and the author of numerous plays, short stories, and one novel that relates to the language, customs, and values of working-class Mexican immigrants, who at that time were known as *chicanos.*

All of his theatrical works have been lost, only one issue of *El malcriado* has been located (this containing two short stories by Venegas). His novel, *Las aventuras de Don Chipote o Cuando los pericos mamen* (1928, *The Adventures of Don Chipote or When Parakeets Suckle Their Young*), was rediscovered and reissued in 1985. *Don Chipote* is the humorous tale of the trials and tribulations of one Don Chipote, who immigrates to the United States from Mexico believing naively that he can shovel up the gold from the streets and send it back to his family. The novel becomes a picaresque story of Chipote's struggle to survive in the alien environment while facing oppression and exploitation from foremen and representatives of industry and the legal authorities. In the course of the novel Chipote also serves as a target for con men and other underworld characters bent on fleecing him. The satirical tale ends with a moral that warns Mexicans not to come to the United States in search of riches. What is important about *Don Chipote* is the identification of the author-narrator with Chicanos and his having as ideal readers the Chicanos themselves. Not only does it imply that a good portion of those workers knew how to read, but also that those workers, like the author himself, were capable of producing literature and art.

Víctor E. Villaseñor (1940–)

Víctor Villaseñor is a novelist and screenwriter who has brought Chicano literature to mainstream audiences through his novel of immigration, *Macho!,* issued in 1973 by the world's largest paperback publisher, Bantam Books; through the epic saga of his own family in *Rain of Gold* (1991); and through the television screenplay *The Ballad of Gregorio Cortez,* the miniseries *Rain of Gold,* and the feature film, *Macho.* Born on May 11, 1940, in Carlsbad, California, the son of Mexican immigrants, Villaseñor was raised on a ranch in Oceanside and experienced great difficulty with the educational system, having started school as a Spanish-speaker and dyslexic. He dropped out of high school and worked on the ranch and in the fields and as a construction worker. After attempting college at the University of San Diego for a brief period, he again dropped out and went to live in Mexico, where he discovered the world of books and learned to take pride in his identity and cultural heritage. From then on he read extensively and taught himself the art of writing fiction. During years of work in California as a construction worker, he completed nine novels and 65 short stories, all of which were rejected for publication, except for *Macho!,* which launched his professional writing career. His second publishing venture was the nonfiction narrative of the life and trial of a serial killer, *Jury: The People versus Juan Corona* (1977). Negative experiences with stereotyping and discrimina-

Víctor E. Villaseñor.

tion of Hispanics in the commercial publishing world led Villaseñor to publish his most important literary effort with a small, not-for-profit Hispanic press, Arte Público Press of Houston.

Macho! tells the tale of a young Mexican Indian's illegal entry into the United States to find work; it is in many ways a classic novel of immigration, though it departs from the model in that, upon return to his hometown in central Mexico, the protagonist has been forever changed. He is unable to accept the traditional social code, especially as it concerns *machismo. Rain of Gold* is the nonfiction saga of various generations of Villaseñor's own family, their experiences during the Mexican Revolution, and their eventual immigration to California. The saga is narrated in a style full of spiritualism and respect for myths and oral tradition, derived not only from Villaseñor's own childhood but also from the years of interviews and research that he did in preparing the book. The popularity of *Rain of Gold* has brought to millions of Americans one family's stories of the social, economic, and political struggles in Mexico that have resulted in widespread Mexican immigration to the United States, a place where new stories of racism, discrimination, and the triumph over these barriers continue to develop in the epic of Mexican American life. In 1994 and 1996, respectively, Villaseñor published two sequels to *Rain of Gold* featuring his parents and grandparents in Mexico—*Walking Stars and Other Stories* and *Wild Steps of Heaven*—the former to glowing reviews and the latter to very mixed commentary.

Jose Yglesias (1919–1995)

Jose Yglesias was born in the Ybor City section of Tampa, Florida, and grew up within the tradition of Cuban cigar rollers. As a young man he moved to Grenwich village, New York City, to become a writer. From his early twenties on, he became politically engaged; his politics would initiate him in the groups of writers and artists who militated against fascism in Spain under Franco, who promoted Socialism in the United States and who were the first supporters of Fidel Castro in Cuba. His early journalistic writing, in the *Daily Worker* and elsewhere, during the late 1940s and early 1950s eventually led to his opening several journalistic books on Spain and Cuba, such as *The Goodbye Land* in 1967, *In the Fist of the Revolution: Life in a Cuban Country Town* in 1968, *Down There* in 1970 and *The Franco Years* in 1977. But it is Yglesias' work as a novelist that is most enduring, with his very humane narrators, eloquent prose and sly humor as noteworthy. Moreover, Yglesias is one of the very first U.S. Hispanic writers to be published by mainstream presses in the United States. His first novel, *A Death in Ybor City* is considered to be a classic of U.S. Hispanic literature. His other novels include *The Kill Price* (1976) and *Tristan and the Hispanics*. Yglesias was a working writer until his death from cancer in 1995. Two important new and highly received novels were published posthumously: *Break-in* (1996), set in Tampa and exploring the theme of race relations, and *The Old Gent* (1996), set in New York and dealing with the final days of an aging novelist. Jose Yglesias is the father of novelist and screen writer Rafael Yglesias.

Jose Yglesias.

References

Kanellos, Nicolás. *Biographical Dictionary of Hispanic Literature in the United States.* Westport, Connecticut: Greenwood Press, 1989.

Lomelí, Francisco, and Julio A. Martínez, eds. *Chicano Literature: A Reference Guide.* Westport, Connecticut: Greenwood Press, 1985.

——, and Carl F. Shirley, eds. *Chicano Writers: First Series.* Detroit: Gale Research, 1989.

Tatum, Charles M. *Chicano Literature.* Boston: Twayne, 1982.

Nicolás Kanellos

20

Art

✳ The Sources of Hispanic Art ✳ Exploration, Settlement, and History of Hispanics in the United States
✳ New Spaniards and Mexicans: 1599 to 1848
✳ Hispanics and Mexican Americans: 1848 to the Present
✳ Hispanic American Artists: 1920s through the 1950s ✳ Hispanic American Artists: 1960s and 1970s
✳ Hispanic American Artists: 1970s to the Present ✳ Chicano Murals

Hispanic American art is art produced by American artists who have a Hispanic background. "Hispanic" in this context refers to individuals whose antecedents are traced to Spanish America, where most of the people speak Spanish and their culture is related to that of Spain, the American Indians, or the African slaves introduced by Europeans. The development of these cultures was determined greatly by a long history of exploration, settlement, and control of the area by Spain.

Each region in Spanish America developed its own variant of Hispanic culture because of local conditions, resources, and people. Mountains, jungles, and other natural barriers isolated settlements and affected communications between them. Cultural differences also resulted from differences in the size of the indigenous populations and their level of civilization at the time of European contact. Finally, the history of the areas determined how the peoples of Spanish America developed as nations following their independence from Spain in the early nineteenth century.

The Spaniards encountered highly developed civilizations in central and southern Mexico, Guatemala, and the Andean region now divided into the countries of Ecuador, Bolivia, and Peru. The large populations in these regions served the needs of the colonial empire established by Spain in Latin America. In the Caribbean basin and other coastal areas of Central and South America, where the population was smaller, the Spaniards brought in slaves from Africa.

The result is that Hispanic American cultures have been tempered by European, indigenous, and African peoples. There is no single Hispanic American culture because Hispanic Americans trace their antecedents to *Spanish America, where each country has its own individual culture and history, influenced by African, indigenous, and/or European peoples.*

✳ THE SOURCES OF HISPANIC ART

The sources of Hispanic art in the United States are found primarily in Mexico and the Caribbean basin as well as in the regions where most Hispanics reside (Texas, Colorado, New Mexico, Arizona, California, New York, and Florida). The countries or territories to the immediate south of the United States—Mexico, Puerto Rico, and Cuba—have had a greater influence on the art of Hispanic Americans than others because of their geographical proximity and the result of wars between Spain, Mexico, and the United States in the nineteenth century. There are fewer people from other parts of Latin America, and as a result, their impact on Hispanic art in the United States has not been as great.

Mexico, the largest country south of the border, is the place of origin for the vast majority of Hispanics in the United States, who identify themselves as Mexican Americans, Hispanos (Spanish Americans), or Chicanos. They are found primarily in the Southwest, Pacific Southwest and Pacific Northwest, and Great Lakes regions. They are related to the people of Mexico and share their history, religion, and culture. They therefore identify with Mexican history, which began with the Indian civilizations of the pre-Columbian epoch and continued through the colonial period under Spanish rule, which lasted three centuries. The modern period began in 1821 with Mexican independence from Spain and the rise of a civilization that combines Indian and Spanish roots. Thus, the overriding Spanish influence in the northern territory was tempered by the Mexican experience, which began with Mexican independence and continued into the twentieth century with constant immigration caused by economic necessity and the Mexican Revolution of 1910. Anglo-American influence began in the middle of the nineteenth century and has continued unabated throughout the area.

Continued American expansion toward the end of the nineteenth century led to the acquisition of Puerto Rico following the war between the United States and Spain in 1898. By 1917, Puerto Ricans were made citizens of the United States and thus were able to travel freely and to settle in the United States without any immigration restrictions. Cubans have lived in the United States since the nineteenth century, but extensive Cuban immigration began after the takeover of Cuba by Fidel Castro and his partisans in 1959 and the failed Bay of Pigs invasion of 1962. They and other Hispanic American groups from all over Latin America have continued to immigrate to the United States. Thus, the largest groups of Hispanics in the northeastern and southeastern parts of the United States are from Puerto Rico, Cuba, and other nations in the Caribbean area, and to a lesser extent from the rest of Latin America.

✳ EXPLORATION, SETTLEMENT, AND HISTORY OF HISPANICS IN THE UNITED STATES

Spanish presence in the area now encompassed by the states of Florida, Texas, and California began in the early sixteenth century. The first explorations were carried out by Spaniards based in the Caribbean region following the discovery of the New World in 1492, and later by Spaniards from Mexico (named New Spain by the Spaniards) after the fall of the Aztec Empire in 1521. The Spaniards were seeking a northern passage to the South Sea (Pacific Ocean) that would lead them to the fabled cities of the Far East. The newly discovered lands were not immediately settled because the Spaniards were busy exploring, conquering, and consolidating their holdings in Central and South America as well as in the far western reaches of the Pacific Ocean.

By the end of the sixteenth century, the settlements in New Spain had reached what is today the state of New Mexico. Other parts to the east and west of this vast area were settled over the next several centuries, largely as the result of competition between the Spanish, French, Dutch, English, and the Russians. Most of New Mexico was settled toward the end of the seventeenth century but was temporarily lost following the Pueblo Indian revolt of 1682. The Spaniards resettled the area in 1692. In the meantime, French incursions into the Gulf Coast of Texas prompted the Spaniards to establish settlements in eastern Texas in 1690. Their reinforcement in 1715 and the establishment of other settlements in central Texas (San Antonio) firmed up the territory for the Spaniards. Similar incursions in California by the Russians stimulated the Spaniards to settle that territory in the 1770s from San Diego to San Francisco. The entire area from Florida to California formed the northern reaches of the Spanish Empire from the late fifteenth century to the beginning of the nineteenth century.

Spain lost most of its colonies when Mexico and other Spanish American countries declared and gained their independence in the early nineteenth century. Following Mexican independence in 1821, the southern border of the new nation included most of the Yucatán Peninsula southward to the Pacific Ocean, limited by the border with Guatemala. Its northern border stretched from Texas to California and included the area now encompassed by those states along with New Mexico, Arizona, and parts of Colorado, Utah, and Nevada. The loss of the northern territories began with Texas independence in 1836 and continued when Texas joined the United States ten years later. This led to war between Mexico and the United States and the subsequent loss of the northern territory.

In summary, the earliest Hispanics were the New Spaniards who settled New Mexico, Arizona, Texas, and California during the seventeenth and eighteenth centuries, when the area was claimed by Spain. Other Hispanics began to arrive in the nineteenth and twentieth centuries. Most arrived as a result of conquest (New Spaniards and Mexicans in the Southwest in the middle of the nineteenth century, and Puerto Rico at the turn of the century) or upheavals in their countries in the twentieth century (Mexicans following their revolution and on up to the present, and Cubans since the 1960s).

What brings these disparate groups together? How do they differ? What distinguishes one from the other?

✳ NEW SPANIARDS AND MEXICANS: 1599 TO 1848

The Missions

The missions built from Texas to California in the seventeenth and eighteenth centuries were intended to serve as Christianizing outposts as well as economic, social, and political units. The Franciscan friars in charge of the northernmost missions were sometimes the sole Europeans along the frontier. The missions, therefore, had to serve the many assigned functions and be relatively independent, self-contained units.

The northern missions are related to the architectural complexes built by the friars in central New Spain in the sixteenth century. These complexes, known as *conventos*, always included a single-nave church and the various units associated with it, such as the sacristy (a small room next to the altar for storage of religious vestments), the friars' quarters, the cloister, the refectory or dining room, the kitchen, and other areas. The friars also included a large open space in front of the church, known as the *atrio* (atrium), with small chapels called *posas* at each of the four corners and a cross in the center. The posas were used for religious processions and the cross was used to teach the Indians about the new religion.

The seventeenth- and eighteenth-century missions in the Indian pueblos of New Mexico follow the same arrangement used in the conventos of central New Spain. Examples are found in New Mexico at the Indian pueblos of Laguna (San José, about 1700) and Acoma (San Esteban del Rey, 1629–41).

By the eighteenth and early nineteenth centuries, the standard arrangements seen in the sixteenth-century conventos were no longer strictly followed in the northern territories. They varied from region to region. The church no longer seemed to be the focal point of the complex, since the various units were not clustered around it as in central New Spain, nor did they have the standard east-west orientation of the earlier churches. Most churches had Latin cross plans, which also correspond to examples found in central New Spain. Examples are seen in the churches of Nuestra Señora de la Purísima Concepción(1755) in San Antonio, Texas, San Xavier del Bac (1783–97), south of Tucson, Arizona, San Juan Capistrano (1796–1806) in California, and San Francisco de Assís (1813–15) in Ranchos de Taos, New Mexico.

The facades of the mission churches also followed examples seen in the churches of central New Spain. The early convento churches have a vertical extension of the facade sometimes used as a belfry (*espadaña*), as in the churches of the Indian pueblos of Laguna and Picuris, New Mexico, and in the San Francisco de la Espada church in San Antonio. Another type of belfry is the bellwall (*campanario*), a wall with one or more openings for bells. A campanario was added to one of the walls of the nave of the San Juan Capistrano church in San Antonio (Figure 20.1). Another was built as an independent tower or wall adjacent to the facade but not part of it

Figure 20.1. Bell wall, San Juan Capistrano Mission, 1760–87. San Antonio, Texas. (Photograph by Jacinto Quirarte.)

as in the churches of the San Diego, San Gabriel, and Santa Inés missions in California.

The bell towers of the later colonial period and a dome over the crossing of the nave and transept are seen in the San José and Concepción churches in San Antonio, and the San Xavier church in Arizona. Bell towers but not the domes are seen in the Acoma and Ranchos de Taos churches in New Mexico, and the Santa Barbara, Carmel, San Buenaventura, and San Luis Rey churches in California.

Although the missions of the Southwest have *espadañas,* campanarios, bell towers, and domes, each region or mission field has its own characteristics due to the local conditions and the time that the building programs began. The style of the New Mexico missions, built in adobe, remained unchanged over a period of several hundred years. The others differ only slightly, owing to the differences in style (baroque in Texas and Arizona and neoclassical in California) and distance from the central part of New Spain.

The primary function of the mission churches and chapels was to provide an area for religious celebrations carried out on a daily, weekly, and annual

Figure 20.2. Facade, San José y San Miguel de Aguayo Mission, 1768–82. San Antonio, Texas. (Photograph by Kathy Vargas.)

and the niche-pilasters provide its outer frame. Inner pilasters extend up to the entablature beyond the jambs of the doorway, which has a mixtilineo arch. The second-story bay, narrower than the first, has an entablature with supporting pilasters and a choir window, which are in line with the inner dimensions of the main doorway. The pedestals with sculptures are in line with the inner pilasters of the first story. Mixtilineo brackets provide the frame for the ensemble and a transition to the cornice topped by a stone cross.

Figural sculptures are on each side of the doorway, and above it under the cornice of the entablature. The same arrangement is seen around the choir window of the second story (Figure 20.2).

The main doorway is flanked by sculptures of Saint Joachim on the left and Saint Anne on the right (Figures 20.3 and 20.4). A sculpture of Our Lady of Guadalupe is seen over the doorway. There is a sculpture of Saint Dominic on the left side of the choir window and one of Saint Francis on the right. A sculpture of Saint Joseph holding the Christ Child is seen above the choir window. The arrangement of

basis. The images on the exterior portal facades and the altarpieces placed inside these sacred areas were meant to be viewed and experienced for their religious meaning, with the devout using them for veneration and supplication purposes. Thus, purpose and function were related to the religious content and meaning the images conveyed, rather than their being created for purely artistic or aesthetic reasons.

The best examples of portal facades with figural and architectural sculptures are found in the mission churches of San José y San Miguel de Aguayo (1768–82) in San Antonio and San Xavier del Bac (1783–97) near Tucson. Figural sculptures are placed in niches framed by columnar supports, known as *estipites,* at San Xavier and on pedestals placed within niche-pilasters at San José. The pilaster is so named because it functions as a background for the sculptures.

San José and San Miguel de Aguayo

The architectural frame of the San José church portal has a single bay that spans its two stories. The entablature of the first story establishes its width

Figure 20.3. *Saint Joachim* portal sculpture (left side of the doorway), 1768–82, San José y San Miguel de Aguayo Mission. San Antonio, Texas. (Photograph by Kathy Vargas.)

rounding spaces than those at the San José mission in San Antonio.

Other Mission Church Portals

The few sculptures that may have been placed in the portal niches of the California mission churches have long since disappeared. As an example, the three sculptures on the portal of the Santa Barbara church are modern replacements of those that were destroyed by an earthquake in 1925. The sculptures of the San Luis Rey church have disappeared. Those that were undoubtedly on the portal of the San Juan Capistrano church were destroyed by the earthquake of 1812. And finally, the sculpture in a niche on the portal of the San Gabriel church is a modern addition.

The mission churches of New Mexico did not have figural or architectural sculptures on the facades, owing to the use of adobe, which does not lend itself to this type of decoration. The primary focus in these churches was on the interior walls used for paintings and individual panels hung as pictures. Every church had an altar screen, known as *reredos* in New Mexico (and *retablo* in Mexico), on the back wall of

Figure 20.4. *Saint Anne* portal sculpture (right side of the doorway), 1768–82, San José y San Miguel de Aguayo Mission. San Antonio, Texas. (Photograph by Kathy Vargas.)

the sculptures by threes at each level of the portal is in keeping with other similar ones found throughout New Spain. There is no other example like this one in the mission churches of New Mexico, Arizona, or California. The closest to this arrangement is found at San Xavier, where the sculptures are located in niches on each side of the door and choir window. However, there are no sculptures along the central axis.

San Xavier del Bac

The estipite columns and the entablatures of the San Xavier del Bac portal are arranged in a rectangular grid (Figure 20.5). This is contrasted by the third story, framed by the curvilinear frame known as a reretted cornice. There is a sculpture of Saint Francis of Assisi in the central part of the cornice, known as a chamfered center. The sculptures on either side of the doorway are Saint Catherine of Siena on the left and Saint Lucy on the right (Figure 20.6). The sculptures on the second story are Saint Barbara on the left and Saint Cecilia on the right. These are much smaller in relation to their sur-

Figure 20.5. Facade, 1783–97, San Xavier del Bac Mission. Tuscon, Arizona. (Photograph by Jacinto Quirarte.)

the sanctuary and numerous freestanding sculptures of holy images, known as *santos* (literally, saints), placed in front of it on altar tables.

Architectural Polychromy

Some of the mission churches featured painted decorations on the exterior surfaces to enhance their appearance, particularly in those cases where it was too expensive to add architectural and figural sculptures on the portals. A good example of this practice is seen on the facade of Nuestra Señora de la Purísima Concepción de Acuña Mission (1755) in San Antonio (Figure 20.7). All the windows and the portal and tower bases and the belfries were painted to simulate stone masonry frames and belfry arches. Simulated masonry was also painted on each side of the portal to give the illusion of tower bases. Simulated fluted pilasters were painted near the corners of each side of the belfry towers. Finally, a sun and a moon were painted on the upper part of the portal with the letters "AE" (Ave María). Other examples are found at San José y San Miguel de Aguayo mission church in San Antonio, where a quatrefoil pattern was painted over the entire facade along with simulated block frames on the tower base windows and zig-zags on the dome (Figure 20.8). Examples of architectural painting in California are seen in the mission churches of Santa Clara de Asís (1822–23) and Santa Inés.

The use of colors on the facades of the Texas and California churches reflects the interest in creating dramatic effects of light and color seen in the churches of central Mexico (New Spain), where glazed tiles were used on domes and, on occasion, on facades as well. The best example of this practice is seen at the church of San Francisco Acatepec, Puebla.

Altarpieces

Few of the mission churches in Texas and California have sculptures or paintings on canvas that are original or date from the mission period. Those seen in some of the churches may not be from that period but are recent additions. Others that are from the mission period, as in the case of the San Antonio missions, are no longer in their original locations because the altarpieces in which they were placed disappeared in the nineteenth century.

Most of the sculptures and paintings of the altarpieces in Texas and California were probably brought in from central New Spain where they were Spanish art produced. Some wood sculptures originally located in altarpieces or altar areas of the Texas mission churches are now placed on pedestals (altars), in museum exhibitions, or in storage. There

Figure 20.6. *Saint Lucy.* Portal sculpture (right side of the doorway), 1783–97, San Xavier del Bac Mission. Tucson, Arizona. (Photograph by Jacinto Quirarte.)

are also isolated sculptures and paintings in the California mission churches and museums. Some are placed in modern altarpieces.

Only the church of San Xavier del Bac and others in New Mexico have their original altar screens in place. Those at San Xavier cover the altar area and the transepts (the arms of a Latin cross). The apostles are represented in the nave and chancel (the area in front of the altar at the crossing of the transepts and the nave). The focus is on man's salvation (entrance to the chancel), and within the chancel are references to the missionary work of Saint Francis Xavier, the birth of the Virgin Mary, the earthly experience of Adam's offspring, and God the Father giving his benediction.

The altarpieces of the New Mexico mission churches were painted by local artisans in a folk art style. The sculptures made of wood and painted in different colors were also done by local craftsmen. Some mission altar screens are now found in museums in Santa Fe (Museum of New Mexico) and Colorado Springs, Colorado (Taylor Museum).

Alteration and Restoration of Mission Churches

Many of the original churches have been altered over the years as a result of neglect and, in some cases, restorations carried out in the nineteenth and twentieth centuries. In the nineteenth century, some of the New Mexico churches were altered when Victorian-style decorations were added to the adobe structures. Most of these additions were removed in the twentieth century and efforts were made to restore the churches to their original configurations. Unfortunately, the need to continually maintain the adobe surfaces because of the fragile nature of the material has led to unintended changes in the details of the structures.

More durable materials were used in Texas and Arizona, and to some extent in California. It is on the portal facades of these structures that figural and architectural sculptures are more apt to be found than on the adobe churches of New Mexico. However, these sculptures have suffered as a result of abandonment and vandalism in the nineteenth century. This began when the missions were secularized a few years after Mexico gained its independence

Figure 20.8. Polychromy (reconstruction, 1948), south tower, 1768–82, San José y San Miguel de Aguayo Mission, San Antonio, Texas. (Photograph by Kathy Vargas.)

from Spain in 1821. Political turmoil and war between Texas and Mexico eventually led to the partial destruction of some of the sculptures found on these facades. Some of them have been restored in the twentieth century.

New Mexico Santeros

The relatively isolated New Mexicans developed a folk art independent of academic models far to the south during the first half of the nineteenth century. That style, generally dated from 1810 to 1850, is characterized by the work of holy image makers known as *santeros* (literally makers of saint images—sculptures and paintings). The paintings on panels were called *retablos;* the sculptures were called *bultos.* However, they were not totally isolated. Works by masters from the metropolitan cities were available in such places as the church at Pecos Pueblo and the church of Our Lady of Guadalupe in Santa Fe. In addition, the earlier paintings and sculptures produced in New Mexico during the eighteenth century are derivative of academic styles.

Figure 20.7. Main portal, 1755, Nuestra Señora de la Purisma Concepción de Acúna Mission. San Antonio, Texas. (Photograph by Kathy Vargas).

The Laguna Santero

The unique style of painting and sculpture in New Mexico began with the work of the anonymous Laguna santero who worked there from 1796 to 1808. The design of his altar screens and paintings indicate that he may have been from the provinces of Mexico. His work is clearly derived from Mexican provincial sources, specifically paintings and engravings, but is simplified to such an extent (all the forms are flattened out) that the figures appear weightless. The facial expressions are neutral in contrast to the more animated baroque examples from central New Spain. The baroque image and its variety of poses and expressions was meant to accentuate the ecstasy or other states of the saintly or holy person portrayed. The expression of religious piety in the works by the Laguna santero are closer to the images of medieval Europe.

A good example of the santero's work is the Laguna altar screen, dated 1800 to 1808. It has three bays on the first story and a single one on the second story. Solomonic columns frame each of the side bays and solomonic balusters top the two outer columns on the second story. (Other santeros painted altar screens in a similar style, that is, they emphasized the architectural frame for the images as in the examples found in central New Spain.) Altar screens attributed to the Laguna santero are found in Pojoaque (about 1796–1800), Santa Fe (around 1796 and 1798), Zia and Santa Ana (both about 1798), and Acoma (1802). The altar screens have three bays and usually two stories.

The Laguna santero had several followers, among them Molleno, who may have worked in the santero's workshop. Among Molleno's works is the altar screen at the church in Rio Chiquito (1828). Another santero, known as the Quill Pen Santero, was a follower of Molleno. These two artists, like the Laguna santero, emphasized the linear treatment of all forms and details.

José Aragón

José Aragón differed from the other santeros because he could read and write, and this ability was reflected in his work. He used engravings as models for his paintings, signed them, and even included lengthy prayers in them. While his work can be considered folk in style, it has a relationship to academic sources. It is sophisticated in its definition of form and the proportions of the human figure.

A good example of Aragón's *reredos* (altar screen) paintings is the one of Our Lady of Guadalupe, now in the Taylor Museum in Colorado Springs. The iconographic program is clearly based on the well-known conventional sources, but Aragón emphasized the formal rather than the narrative qualities of the image. There is a fine linearity that permeates all of the narrative panels and the spaces between them as well as the frame that contains them all. The Virgin is represented in the center, and her appearance to Juan Diego and the events subsequent to it are depicted in the four corners of the painting. Christ is seen in the top center, and the church that the Virgin ordered built in her honor is seen at the bottom center.

The Truchas Master

Another of the anonymous santeros working in the first quarter of the nineteenth century was initially identified as the Dot-Dash Painter, then later as don Antonio Fresques, and more recently as the Truchas Master. Works by this artist are dated between 1790 and 1830

The *reredos* painting of Our Lady of Guadalupe, now in the Taylor Museum in Colorado Springs, is also a good example of the Truchas Master's work. This painting is unlike most representations of the Virgin, which are based on the original in the basilica of Guadalupe near Mexico City. The artist ignored the standard proportions of the slender figure of the Virgin and did away with all semblance of naturalism in the depiction of her downward gaze. The eyes are simple crescent shapes and each iris is indicated by a black dot. The other features are defined with an equal economy of means. The figure and the slender form of the original have been transformed into a schematic rendition in which there is an emphasis on the colors and the vigorous line used to outline all forms.

José Rafael Aragón

José Rafael Aragón was born in 1796 or 1797 and died in 1862. His earliest dated altar screen (1825) is found in the pueblo church of San Lorenzo de Picuria. Other works are in Chimayo, Taos, Talpa, and the Cordoba Santa Cruz area.

Aragón was the major artist from around 1820 to 1860, and his *reredos* panel paintings, altar screens, and sculptures are the finest examples of the local folk art style.

Aragón took all the abstracting tendencies of his predecessors and created even finer examples of this type of art. His work is known for bold use of line and pure color, and although he used late baroque models, his work did not depend on them. Typical of his mature work is the altar screen originally in the chapel of Our Lady of Talpa (near Taos) and now in the Taylor Museum in Colorado Springs. It was completed in 1838. The style is softer than his earlier works. The faces tend to be round instead of elongated ovals, and the figures are relatively static in presentation.

A fine example of Aragón's sculpture is a *bulto* (religious sculpture) from the Talpa chapel, now in the Taylor Museum collection of Our Lady of Talpa. She is crowned and holds the Christ Child in her left arm. As in the retablo and altar screen paintings, the artist created a fine balance between the decorative and figural elements in the sculpture.

✳ HISPANICS AND MEXICAN AMERICANS: 1848 TO THE PRESENT

1848 to 1920

There is little information on the art of Hispanos (Spanish Americans) and Mexican Americans dating from the period immediately following 1848, when the northernmost territories of Mexico became part of the United States. The process of bringing the entire area into the economic, political, and cultural life of the United States was begun at this time and continued during the remainder of the nineteenth century and the first two decades of the twentieth. The area became known as the Southwest and Pacific Southwest of the United States. Its incorporation into the country's economic system was hastened by the building of railroads in the area. Cultural changes were eventually brought about by the people who began migrating into the area from the eastern seaboard and other parts of the country.

Modernization in Mexico and the United States during the last decades of the nineteenth century led to a period of consolidation on both sides of the border. There were no great movements of people in either direction. On the American side, the modernization affected various regions of the area during the second half of the nineteenth century. The most apparent changes took place in New Mexico, where new churches were built on American and European models, and the old ones were changed with the addition of wood siding, pointed spires, and a general refurbishing consistent with the eclectic tastes of the nineteenth century. Plaster saints and inexpensive religious prints were also introduced into the area. The latter supplanted the retablo painting tradition but the former did not stop the production of bultos. A few of the artists who continued to produce santos were "discovered" in the twentieth century.

Santos and Santeros

The production of santos in New Mexico declined in number and in style, as well as technical quality, after the 1850s. The changes were the result of a change in patronage of the church, first under the Spanish Crown and later Mexico, and the importation of plaster saints and inexpensive prints after 1848. The few santos produced for Spanish Americans in the isolated communities of northern New Mexico are the work of less technically proficient artists. Santos were made for the oratories and *moradas* (meeting houses) and were used by the Penitente Brotherhood for the first time in 1833, when they were condemned by the Mexican church. The Penitentes eventually became the first of many groups of Hispanics who sought to retain the integrity of their culture against the attacks of Protestant Americans and the Catholic church in the 1850s. Although the Penitentes had been condemned by the Mexican Catholic church, their persecution by American Catholics and Protestants in the mid-1850s eventually led to their activities becoming more and more secretive. The Penitentes provided the patronage as well as the selection of certain subjects that were an essential part of their religious observances and practices. The subjects most often represented were the death figures and the suffering Christ of the Passion.

Miguel Herrera (1835–905)

Miguel Herrera, a resident of Arroyo Hondo in Taos County, was among the several santeros serving the needs of the Penitentes and others in the area. He worked in the 1870s, 1880s, and possibly later as a bulto maker. (No retablos are known to have been produced by him, but this is not surprising, since religious prints were readily available.) The tall figures with attention paid only to the head and hands were meant to be dressed in fabric clothing. His santos are noted for small seashell ears set too low on the head. Much of his work was done for the moradas of the Penitentes. A fine example of his work is the *Christ in the Holy Sepulchre,* in the Taylor Museum (Colorado Springs) collection. It is a life-sized work with articulated knees, shoulders, neck, and jaw.

José Benito Ortega (1858–1941)

José Benito Ortega traveled from town to town, a true itinerant artist, to seek out potential patrons. He was one of several such artists serving the needs of the Hispanos in northern New Mexico. When Ortega received an order, he stayed in the town until he finished the work. He also made death figures for use in the moradas. His santo figures are very simple and stylized with sharply defined Spanish features and painted in bright colors.

An example of Ortega's work is *San Isidro Labrador (Saint Isidro the Farmer)* in the Denver Art

Figure 20.9. José Benito Ortega. *Saint Isidore the Farmer,* 1880s–1907.

Museum, made of wood and gesso, and painted (Figure 20.9). The work is modeled on the traditional representations of this saint in the tin paintings of northern Mexico, in which the size of the figures is based on their importance rather than on how they would appear in nature. The saint towers over all the other figures in the group. The winged angel behind the plow is slightly less than half the size of Saint Isidor! The oxen are also less than half the size of the angel, thereby creating a pronounced distortion of scale in the work.

Traditional Arts from 1920 to the Present

By the 1920s, the Hispanic communities in various parts of the Southwest had begun to change as a result of American cultural dominance in the area and the increased immigration from Mexico following the political and economic chaos caused by the Mexican Revolution of 1910. The most immediate changes occurred in northern New Mexico following World War I, when the traditional arts of santo (saint) making were brought to an end as a result of economic changes in the area. They were revived but in different form and to serve other than religious purposes. However, the traditional arts were strengthened in other parts of the Southwest by the new arrivals from Mexico. Their strong devotion to the saints and Our Lady of Guadalupe, to whom they prayed for salvation and assistance in resolving problems, especially in time of crisis, led to the creation of private oratories, known as yard shrines and home altars. The latter have inspired contemporary Chicano artists who call themselves *altaristas* (altar makers). The former have inspired contemporary santeros in New Mexico. Both are expressions of the Hispanic experience in the Southwest and Pacific Southwest.

The new emphasis on santo making was created by a number of American artists who began to arrive in Santa Fe and Taos in the 1920s. The craftsmen were encouraged to continue making furniture and other domestic products as well as sculptures that were similar to the traditional santos of the nineteenth century. Unlike the earlier pieces, however, the new santos were not painted in different colors, nor were they intended for chapels or churches. They were produced for collectors and tourists who acquired such objects as mementos of a trip through the area. Another change was seen in the production of the santos. Entire families were now involved in making santos, in contrast to the production of works by single artists in the past.

The revival of santo making took place primarily in the small community of Cordoba, New Mexico. However, the impetus for it can be found in Santa Fe, where the needed mechanisms were instituted starting in 1919 with the "revival" of the Santa Fe Fiesta and culminating in 1929 with the incorporation of the Spanish Colonial Arts Society, which had an impact on the making of santos in northern New Mexico. An annual fiesta exhibition was adopted in the late 1920s in which the works of Hispanic craftsmen were included. These exhibitions were variously called Spanish Colonial Handicrafts, Spanish Fair, and Spanish Arts and Crafts Exhibition. In 1929, the Spanish Arts Shop was established by the Spanish Colonial Arts Society in Sena Plaza, Santa Fe. During the time it lasted, through the early 1930s, it served as an impetus to some of the santeros, such as José Dolores López and others, who began to concentrate on the production of objects that were acceptable to Anglo patrons. As patrons, the Anglos determined questions of quality and originality of craftsmanship. Santos were no longer produced on the basis of the Hispanics' own understanding of their heritage.

Figure 20.10. José Dolores López. *Expulsion from the Garden of Eden.*

José Dolores López (1868–1937)

One of the most important of the new santeros was José Dolores López, whose works date from about 1929 to 1937, the year of his death. He was primarily a furniture maker from 1917 to about 1929. He also did carpentry work—window and door frames, roof beams and corbels, crosses for grave markers, coffins, and chests—and small wooden figures, primarily for relaxation and as gifts for neighbors and relatives. He began to carve birds and animals as well as santos after 1929 because he could no longer earn a living from his fields and livestock and his carpentry work. This new endeavor coincided with the emerging interest in Hispanic culture and handicrafts generated by a few Anglo artists. They were interested in revitalizing Hispanic "traditional," "colonial," and "Spanish" crafts. These external factors created new markets for Hispanic crafts and competition between artists. At the same time, the new patrons taught the Hispanic artists to be "selective" in their work, that is, to produce objects for the non-Hispanic market.

López made several changes in his work during the period of transition from an older Hispanic tradition to the new one created by Anglo patrons. The furniture he produced in painted and unpainted versions was changed exclusively to the latter because the painted pieces were too "gaudy" for Anglo patrons. He then turned to making unpainted santos at the prodding of Frank Applegate, who was in charge of arts and crafts for the Spanish Colonial Arts Society. Another reason for the change had to do with the success of the image carvings by Celso Gallegos, who was awarded several prizes for his work in 1926 and 1927. Gallegos, a santero from Agua Fria who was slightly older than José Dolores López, carved sacred images and animals in stone and wood and, like López, served as *sacristan* (caretaker) for his church. He was among the last of the pious santeros. Both santeros were deeply religious.

The santos by López demonstrate an interest in narrative content. This differs from the emphasis on local prototypes of favored saints and other religious figures represented in the traditional santos. López used several sources for his images, among them an old book of French drawings that he displayed with pride to visitors. He was also influenced by the work of José Rafael Aragón, which he saw in the Cordova church in the course of his work as a sacristan of the sanctuary. He is known to have overpainted and repaired several worn traditional images during that period.

Among the subjects López portrayed in his work are Saint Anthony, Saint Peter, Saint Michael with the dragon, a *nacimiento* (nativity) in which all the appropriate figures are included, a *muerte* (death cart), and Adam and Eve, in which the Garden of Eden and the Tree of Life with the Serpent are included. The latter is a formal extension of earlier trees with birds made by the artist. A good example of the Adam and Eve theme is the piece in the Taylor Museum (Colorado Springs) collection entitled *Adam and Eve in the Garden of Eden.* It is composed of three separate units that can be moved around to create different arrangements. The figures of Adam and Eve are placed on a long, narrow base, which allows a frontal presentation of the two figures. Behind them is a stylized representation of the garden, composed of vertical plants inserted onto a similar base, which is used as a backdrop for Adam and Eve. To the side is the Tree of Life with the forbidden fruit and the Serpent. "The Tree of Life of the Good and the Bad" is inscribed on its base in English and Spanish. López made other elaborate santos, such as *The Expulsion from the Garden of Eden* (Figure 20.10), the collections of the Museum of International Folk Art, Santa Fe; in the *Michael the Archangel and the Dragon,* in the Taylor Museum (Colorado Springs); *The Expulsion from Paradise,* in the collections of the Museum of International Folk Art, Santa Fe, and in the same museum, the *Flight into Egypt.*

Patrocino Barela (1908–1964)

The work of Patrocino Barela, a Taos wood-carver, was supported by the Federal Art Project (FAP), part of the Works Progress Administration, from 1936 to 1943. He began to carve santos in 1931, and his work was later exhibited nationally under the auspices of the FAP. His benefactors had an even greater impact on his work than was the case with the López family. Barela broke away from the santero tradition and began to carve figurative works that have an overall organic quality usually suggested by the grain of the woods he used for his works.

A good example of Barela's work is *Saint George,* in the National Museum of American Art in Washington, D.C. It was carved from a single piece of cedar. The helmet-like nose and brow of the saint form one continuous shape that is echoed by the figure's legs. The saint's expression is characterized by a stern projecting chin and the gentle slit of the mouth, set off to one side. Through a dynamic series of directions and counter-directions—created by the play between positive and negative form and space— Barela adroitly depicted the slaying of the dragon.

George López (1925–)

The increased markets and competition between artists led to an increase in the number of people making santos in the 1930s. The children of José Dolores López began to make santos at this time. Among them was George López, who began carving objects in 1925 but was not able to devote full time to it until 1932. Eventually, his work became more widely known than that of the other Cordova santeros. By the 1960s, he was considered the best of the santeros.

Outdoor Shrines and Home Altars

The yard shrines or private oratories found in the barrios of the Southwest are similar to the folk art produced in New Mexico in terms of genesis, purpose, function, and meaning. These private oratories are called *capillas* (chapels) in San Antonio, *nichos* (niches) in Tucson, and *grutas* (grottoes) in Los Angeles. They express the deeply held religious beliefs of the people who made them. In their genesis they are related to the *exvotos* of northern New Mexico painted in the nineteenth century. Both are responses to a time of crisis experienced by individuals who promised to paint an image (exvoto) as an offering or as a testament of their salvation or to build a shrine (oratory) for similar reasons, if their prayers were answered. The words in Spanish for these acts of devotion and thanksgiving are *promesa* (promise) and *manda* (gift, offering).

The exvoto paintings and shrines testify to relief from an illness, a malady, financial problems, accidents, robberies, pursuit by enemies or the police, and so on. The nature of the problem determined the manner of supplication: through prayer at the time and place of the natural or man-made catastrophe or in a formal setting, such as a church, for a long-standing illness, or prayer coupled with the use of milagros placed on the saint selected for the occasion. Milagros are small sculptures made of various metals (brass, tin, nickel, silver, or gold) into numerous configurations (natural and man-made objects) that can be used to point to the problem. All the body parts are represented, as are the human figure, animals, automobiles, houses, and so forth. The images were used for relief from some illness, such as an arthritic arm, leg, or other part of the body, or a financial problem, such as an outstanding debt or a pending mortgage on a house.

Milagros have been used traditionally in Latin American and some European countries where Catholicism is practiced. Parishioners routinely place milagros on favored saints found in the chapels. Devout parishioners continue to use milagros in some of the mission churches of the Indian pueblos, such as San Xavier del Bac. Mexican Americans use milagros in the shrines and home altars, which are usually comprised of a small sacred image on a shelf or framed for placement on a wall.

San Antonio, Texas

As of the early 1980s, there were more than 175 oratories in the west side of San Antonio. Some were built as early as the 1940s. Many of them have deteriorated because the younger residents have not maintained them when the owners or builders died. Some have suffered from vandalism. Enough remain, however, to demonstrate the survival of a strong tradition of folk art.

The oratories are made of concrete, wood, mirror fragments, tile, brick, stone, pebbles, aluminum, plexiglass, seashells, cement, or other materials. The sacred images placed inside them can be lighted with Christmas lights, plain light bulbs, or even neon light. In most cases, the oratory was built from scratch by the person who made the promise; in other cases, the individual embellished a ready-made oratory available in west-side shops that also sell figurines and flowerpots. In both cases, the individuals placed the sacred image of the saint to whom it was dedicated along with other sacred images inside the shrine. These were decorated with plants, flowers (real, paper, or plastic), candles, seashells, and assorted Christmas decorations.

The shrines vary in size from relatively small constructions (no more than one foot in height) to highly elaborate structures (12 feet in height, nine feet wide, and eight feet in depth), in which the sacred image was placed. The two most popular images used were Our Lady of Guadalupe and Our Lady of San Juan de los Lagos. Oratories for the latter were modeled on the miraculous statue in the town of San Juan de los Lagos in the state of Jalisco, Mexico.

A good example of the shrines in San Antonio is the one dedicated to Our Lady of San Juan, built in the mid-1950s by Ramiro Rocha as a manda (offering) to the Virgin. The shrine had a statue of Our Lady in the front central part of the niche, and statues in the corners in the back—the Sacred Heart, left, and San Martín de Porres, right. An electric light was suspended directly above the Virgin. The niche was protected by a glass door. Rocha built the shrine on the property of Elia González, who paid for the materials (the reason is unknown, since Rocha is deceased). González, who allowed her mother, María Garza, to live there, maintained the shrine by looking after it and repainting and clean-

ing it. González was also responsible for the neon that spelled out the name of the Virgin as follows: "San Juanita de los Lagos," with "viva" in front of it. The shrine was, therefore, appropriately identified by its makers and its location as the Garza/González/Rocha shrine. The property was later sold, and the shrine was destroyed.

Tucson, Arizona

The private oratories in Tucson, Arizona, are called *nichos* by the residents of the barrio. Most feature representations of Our Lady of Guadalupe. Some of the yard shrines are as elaborate as the shrines of San Antonio. Most were built of brick or stone, and on occasion embellished with tiles to enhance the appearance of the image placed inside the shrine.

There is an unusual example in which holy images are placed inside a square niche and on a shelf above it (Figure 20.11). The shrine was built out of a discarded refrigerator in 1957 on Theodora Sánchez's front lawn by her husband as a fulfillment of a promise made to Saint Dymphna, the patron

Figure 20.11. Theodora Sánchez. *Nicho* (Yard Shrine), dedicated to Saint Dymphna, 1957. Tucson, Arizona. (Photograph by Jacinto Quirarte.)

saint of lunatics. This was in response to their prayers to the saint to save their son's girlfriend, who went crazy when she visited his grave five years after his death in Korea in the early 1950s. When she got well, they fulfilled their promise to build the shrine.

Framed pictures of Our Lady of Guadalupe are propped up in each corner of the lower niche, in which the statue of Saint Dymphna is placed. On the top shelf there is a statue of Saint Francis Xavier lying in a glass box. This shrine is reminiscent of the work *Christ in the Holy Sepulchre,* by Miguel Herrera, in the Taylor Museum (Colorado Springs) collection.

Austin, Texas

In Austin, yard shrines differ from the small oratories constructed inside the home, appropriately called home altars by those who study them, and *altares* (altars) or *altarcitos* (little altars) by those who build them. The former are "public" and the result of a manda (offering), the latter are "private" and are not tied down to a specific promise given in a time of "need." Both serve a religious function and can be equally complex. Home altars, however, are probably found over a wider area.

The most frequently used image in the Austin home altars is Our Lady of Guadalupe, although other sacred images are also used. The altars include votive candles, flowers, milagros (small sculptures), family photographs, ceramic birds, shells, stones, stuffed animals, bottles full of buttons, ribbons, tea cups, and even photographs of John Kennedy and Bobby Kennedy (both martyred) and other political figures. The altars, therefore, provide the focus for religious as well secular concerns.

✱ HISPANIC AMERICAN ARTISTS: 1920s THROUGH THE 1950s

Throughout the period from World War I through the 1950s, most Hispano (Spanish American), Mexican American, and other Hispanic American artists were part of mainstream art in the United States. Their work was part of the figurative and regionalist traditions that dominated such art in the 1920s through the 1940s. Among the noted artists whose works are characteristic of the period are the Mexican American artists Octavio Medellín, Antonio García, José Aceves, and Edward Chávez. Other important Hispanic artists of the period are Francisco Luis Mora, born in Uruguay, and Carlos López, born in Cuba. Among the Spanish-born artists are José Moya del Pino and Xavier González. The latter two are also associated with Mexico, González through immigra-

tion before entering the United States, and Moya del Pino through the subjects and style of his work.

The Mexican American artists were primarily found in the Southwest, and other Hispanics lived in the Great Lakes and northeastern regions. Medellín, García, and Aceves were based in Texas; Chavez in New Mexico, Colorado, and New York; López in Michigan; and Mora in New York and Connecticut. González was initially based in Texas and later in Louisiana, and Moya del Pino in California.

Mexican American Artists

The subject matter of most of the works by Mexican American and other Hispanic artists was primarily American, particularly in the murals they painted in the 1930s under the auspices of the Works Progress Art Project (WPAP). However, some of the Mexican American artists focused on their Mexican as well as American background in their work, as in the case of García and Medellín.

Antonio García (1901–)

Antonio García, born December 27, 1901 in Monterrey, Mexico, moved with his family to San Diego, Texas around 1911. He studied at the Chicago Art Institute from 1927 to 1930 and taught art at Del Mar College, Corpus Christi, Texas, from 1950 to 1970. García's art is recognized for containing elements derived from his Mexican heritage, although some of his works reveal American influence. Among his most famous works is *Aztec Advance* (1929), a piece based upon the Spanish Conquest of Mexico, and *Our Lady of Guadalupe* (1946–47), a mural inspired by the Mexican national and religious icon.

Octavio Medellín (1907–)

Octavio Medellín, born in Matehuala, Mexico in 1907, moved to San Antonio, Texas in 1920, where he studied painting under José Arpa and drawing under Xavier González at the San Antonio School of Art from 1921 to 1928. In 1928 Medellín ventured to Chicago where he studied at the Chicago Art Institute. He traveled the Gulf Coast of Mexico from 1929 to 1931 and the Yucatán in 1938. He taught at North Texas State College (now the University of North Texas), Denton, from 1938 to 1942, and at Southern Methodist University, Dallas, from 1945 to 1966. In 1969 he opened his own art school in Dallas. Medellín's art generally covers the entire scope of Mexican history, from pre-Columbian times to the 1940s, as in his sculpture *History of Mexico* (1949). He is also highly regarded for his series of prints, *Xtol: Dance of the Ancient Maya People* (1962), in which he treats the pre-Columbian Maya and Toltec, based

Figure 20.12. Octavio Medellín, *Xtol* print.

upon research he carried out in the Yucatán (Figure 20.12). He is retired and lives in Bandera, Texas.

José Aceves (1909–)

José Aceves painted murals (framed oil paintings) for the post offices in Borger and Mart, Texas (both in 1939). The mural in Borger, titled *Big City News,* deals with the mail service's delivering news to the most remote and isolated regions of the country. The mural in Mart, titled *McLennan Looking for a Home,* focuses on the arrival in 1841 of Neil McLennan and his family in the Bosque River Valley, eight miles east of Waco, Texas. The latter is typical of the idealized portrayals of the pioneers in the Southwest seen in post office murals of that period. Aceves was influenced by the muralist Edward Holsag in the development of the western subject matter in the Mart painting.

Aceves was born in Chihuahua, Mexico, in 1909, and moved with his family to El Paso in 1915 as a result of the chaos created by the Mexican Revolution. He studied art at the Museum of Fine Arts in Dallas and at the Chicago Art Institute in the 1930s.

Edward Chávez (1917–)

Edward Chávez painted murals for post offices and other government buildings from 1939 to 1943 in Denver, Colorado, Geneva, Nebraska, Center, Texas, and Fort Warren, Wyoming. His murals deal with a direct portrayal of life and industry in each of the areas where he received commissions for his work. He turned to abstraction in the 1950s and 1960s.

For the Denver Center High School panels, titled *The Pioneers* (1939), Chávez focused on the daily chores of tending the oxen on the wagon trail and chopping down trees. He chose the actual building of a sod house as the subject for his Geneva, Nebraska, mural, *Building a Sod House* (1941). He portrayed the early method of hauling logs in the lumber industry around Center, Texas, for that city's post office mural, *Logging Scene* (1941). He focused on the Indians and the first white men in Wyoming for the mural in Fort Warren, *Indians of the Plains* (1943) (Figure 20.13). All his works were painted with oil on canvas except for the one in Wyoming, which was painted with egg tempera on plywood.

The large wall of Chávez's mural in the Fort Warren Service Club measures 18 feet high by 40 feet wide (Figure 20.13). It has double doors in the lower center and stairs on each side that break up the rectangular format of the mural. A large Indian in the central part of the mural over the doors kneels on one leg, holds a peace pipe in one hand, and gestures with the other. There are numerous scenes in which hunting and other everyday activities of the Indians are depicted in two horizontal registers to the left and right of the large Indian. American soldiers standing by a tent are seen on the lowermost panel on the left, and Indians are standing by a tepee on the right.

Edward Chávez was born in New Mexico in 1917 and now lives in Woodstock, New York. Although he studied at the Colorado Springs Fine Arts Center, he considers himself to be largely self-taught as an artist. He taught at the Art Students League, New York City in 1954 and from 1955 to 1958; Colorado College, Colorado Springs in 1959; Syracuse University in New York from 1960 to 1961, and Dutchess Community College, Poughkeepsie, New York in 1963. He was appointed artist in residence at the Huntington Fine Arts Gallery in West Virginia in 1967.

Other Mexican American Artists

From the 1940s through the 1950s, other Mexican American artists continued to reflect regional concerns in their work in a figurative or realistic style. Others worked in the abstract and nonfigurative styles of the same period. There was an emphasis on

Figure 20.13. Edward Chávez, *Indians of the Plains,* 1943. Egg Tempera on Plywood. 18′ high × 40′ wide. Service Club, Fort Warren, Wyoming.

regionalism in the landscapes of the New Mexican artist Margaret Herrera Chávez and the Texas bluebonnet painter Porfirio Salinas. Other regionalists, such as Pedro Cervantes of New Mexico, painted still lifes.

Herrera Chávez was born in Las Vegas, New Mexico, in 1912. Salinas, born in Bastrop, Texas, in 1912, was raised in San Antonio, where he died in 1973. Cervantes, born in Wilcox, Arizona, in 1915, has spent most of his life in Clovis, New Mexico.

Chelo González Amezcua, a contemporary of Antonio García and Octavio Medellín, devoted the last ten to 20 years of her life to her art and poetry. Most of her work was based on a highly personal ichnography in which there are depictions of numerous birds and exotic places and personages. Amezcua was born in Ciudad Acuña, Mexico, in 1903, but lived most of her life in Del Rio, Texas, where she died in 1975.

Other Hispanic American Artists

The murals painted by other Hispanic artists in the 1930s were similar to those painted by Aceves,

Chávez, and other Mexican American artists. The subjects portrayed invariably dealt with the history, industry, identity, or landscape of the city or region for which they were painted.

Francisco Luis Mora (1874–1940)

Francisco Luis Mora painted murals for the Orpheum Theatre in Los Angeles, the reading room of the Lynn Public Library in Lynn, Massachusetts, the central building of the Red Cross in Washington, D.C., and in Clarksville, Tennessee (1938). Among his earliest public works was a large decoration for the Missouri State Building for the Saint Louis Fair of 1904, for which he received a Bronze Medal.

The Clarksville mural deals with the settlement of the area by Moses Renfroe and his family, who arrived there in April 1779, and modern Tennessee, its resources, and its industries. The subjects were depicted in two panels. The first focuses on the first settlement of the area. A group of settlers is seen on the top of a bank overlooking the Red River. Colonel Donaldson, who had brought them there, is shown in conversation with the elder Renfroe. Most of the settlers were later killed by the Indians in the area. The second panel focuses on the many resources of modern Tennessee—tobacco, corn, cotton, lumber, and marble—and its mills and factories. According to the artist, the first panel deals with "sacrifice," the second with "a sense of achievement."

Mora was born in Montevideo, Uruguay, in 1874, and his family immigrated to the United States in 1880. He studied with his father, a sculptor, and at the Museum of Fine Arts School in Boston and at the Art Students League in New York. He taught painting and drawing for many years at the Chare School and the Art Students League in New York. He died in New York City in 1940.

José Moya del Pino (1891–1969)

Throughout the 1930s, Moya del Pino painted murals under the auspices of the Works Progress Art Project (WPAP) and for private corporations. In 1933, he painted murals and did the decorations, in Aztec and Mayan motifs, for the rathskeller of the Aztec Brewery in San Diego, California. In the mid 1930s, he worked on the WPAP-sponsored murals painted in San Francisco's Coit Tower. He also painted murals in Stockton (1936), Redwood City (1937), and Lancaster, California (1937), and Alpine, Texas (1940).

As in the case of other Hispanic American muralists, Moya del Pino focused on the industries and landscapes of the cities where his works were placed. The Redwood City mural, *Flower Farming and Vegetable Raising,* deals with the important activities of the county—agriculture, horticulture, industry, maritime trade, and leisure. The Lancaster mural, *Hauling Water Pipe Through Antelope Valley,* focuses on the characteristic view of this desert valley with a long mule team hauling a wagon filled with water pipe for irrigation. The Alpine, Texas, mural, *View of Alpine,* emphasizes the vast landscape, with placement of the town of Alpine in the middle distance, and in the foreground, students with their books, cattle, horses, and a cattleman reading his farm journal.

In 1988, Moya del Pino's murals and decorations in the rathskeller of the Aztec Brewery in San Diego were threatened with destruction when the brewery was targeted for demolition to make way for the construction of a $10-million concrete warehouse. The brewery had been closed for more than 30 years. When Salvador Roberto Torres, a leading Chicano activist from the Barrio de la Logan, learned of the demolition, he sought to have the murals saved.

José Moya del Pino, born in Cordova, Spain, in 1891, studied art in his native country and settled in San Francisco, California, in 1928. He died in Ross, outside San Francisco, in 1969. Most of his work was done in California.

Xavier González (1898–1993)

In 1930, Xavier González won third prize in a national competition for murals on the subject "The Dynamic of Man's Creative Power." The winning entries were installed in the Los Angeles Museum. He later painted murals for the post offices in Hammond and Covington, Louisiana (1936 and 1939), the federal courtroom in Huntsville, Alabama (1937), and the post offices in Kilgore and Mission, Texas (1941 and 1942).

Typical of González's work is the mural for the Huntsville federal courtroom, titled *Tennessee Valley Authority.* The five figures in the painting symbolize, according to the artist, "a community devoted to the activities of a well-organized society." The figures are independent of each other but were drawn to the same scale. The arrangement of the figures creates a circular motion on the frontal plane. Each figure represents an aspect of human endeavor in the scientific, agricultural, economic, or artistic sphere and the social organization needed to coordinate these spheres. A standing woman in the center with a basket of fruit represents youth and fertility, and a man on the upper right represents work. A young man holding a plant of corn below him represents "scientific agriculture." A woman making pottery on the upper left represents artistic endeavor, and the woman holding a child in the lower center of the painting represents motherhood. They are placed within a landscape that is characteristic of Huntsville.

Xavier González was born in Almeira, Spain, in 1898, and received his art training at the Chicago Art Institute. He taught art in San Antonio, Texas, in the early 1920s and at Newcomb College, Tulane University, from 1929 to 1943. He died on January 1, 1993.

Carlos López (1908–1953)

Carlos López painted murals under the WPAP from 1937 to 1942. His first mural was painted in Dwight, Illinois (1937), followed by three others in the Michigan cities of Plymouth (1938), Paw Paw (1940), and Birmingham (1942).

The Dwight mural, *The Stage at Dawn,* depicts a Wells Fargo stagecoach being harnessed for its journey to the western boundaries of the United States. The Plymouth mural, *Plymouth Trail,* represents a passenger coach arriving in Plymouth around the mid-1860s. The focus is on the transportation link between Indiana and Illinois and the east. The Paw Paw mural, *Bounty,* depicts the agricultural industries (fruit and vegetables) and recreations of the people of Paw Paw (grape festival with square dancing, and an ice-skating scene).

Throughout the 1940s, López received numerous commissions from several federal agencies and from private companies to portray various aspects of American life: American industries at war for the War Department, a pictorial record of the war for *Life* magazine, the amphibious training activities for the navy, and the project "Michigan on Canvas," for the J. L. Hudson Company. After World War II, López's work turned toward fantasy and symbol, conveyed by figures that always appear to stand alone, lonely and sad.

López, born in Havana, Cuba, in 1908, spent his early years in Spain and lived in South America before immigrating to the United States when he was 11 years old. He studied at the Art Institute of Chicago and the Detroit Art Academy and taught art at the University of Michigan from 1945 until his death in 1953.

Rufino Silva (1919–)

The work of Rufino Silva, a Chicago-based artist, belongs to the Chicago school of social realism in a surrealistic vein. His work is similar to that of Jack Levine, but less trenchant.

Silva was born in Humacao, Puerto Rico, in 1919. He studied at the Chicago Art Institute from 1938 to 1942 on a fellowship from the Puerto Rican government. He taught at the Layton School of Art, Milwaukee, from 1946 to 1947 and studied abroad for four years, 1947–51, in Europe and South America on grants from the art institute. He returned to Chicago in 1952 and joined the faculty. He retired in the 1970s.

✳ HISPANIC AMERICAN ARTISTS: 1960s AND 1970s

In the 1960s, the art of Mexican American and other Hispanic American artists continued to reflect the many current styles of art, from figurative to abstract, to pop, op, and funk, to destructive and all the others. Some of the artists who had painted murals in the 1930s and 1940s turned to abstraction, as in the case of Edward Chávez. However, he continued to make references in his abstract works to his background by using Mexican place-names, such as Xochimilco in one of his paintings.

Among the Mexican American and Chicano artists who matured in the 1960s are Michael Ponce de León of New York, Eugenio Quesada of Phoenix, Arizona, Peter Rodríguez of San Francisco, Melesio Casas of San Antonio, Texas, Manuel Neri of San

Francisco, Ernesto Palomino of Fresno, California, and Luis Jiménez of Hondo, New Mexico. Puerto Rican artists who matured during the same period include New York-based artists Olga Albizu, Pedro Villarini, Rafael Montañez-Ortiz (Ralph Ortiz), and Rafael Ferrer. There were many other artists from Latin America working in New York and other U.S. cities at the time, but their work falls outside the confines of this study because their formative years as artists were spent in their country of origin. Their presence, however, has not gone unnoticed by Hispanic American and other American artists. Some remained in the United States for many years and then returned to their native countries. Others stayed to continue their careers.

Among those who stayed and attained national and international status for their work is the Argentine printmaker Mauricio Lasansky, who immigrated to the United States in 1943 and taught printmaking at Iowa State University, Ames. He influenced generations of American printmakers through his teaching and his work. He was born in Buenos Aires in 1914 and became a U.S. citizen in 1952. Marisol Escobar, born to Venezuelan parents in Paris in 1930, has resided in New York City since 1960. She became internationally famous in the 1960s with her sculptures of well-known personalities, such as Lyndon Baines Johnson and John Wayne. Fernando Botero, known for his paintings of overblown figures used in satirical contexts, arrived in New York City in 1960. He was born in Medellín, Colombia, and now resides in New York City and Paris.

Mexican American Artists

Michael Ponce de León (1922–)

The work of New York printmaker Michael Ponce de León was in keeping with the new styles of the 1960s. He used a raised surface (relief) and objects to create works that were expressive of his feelings toward words, places, conditions, and events.

Ponce de León was born in Miami, Florida, in 1922 and spent his early years in Mexico City. He joined the U.S. Air Force during World War II. After working as a cartoonist in New York in the 1940s and early 1950s, he turned to printmaking in the late 1950s. He has taught printmaking at the Pratt Graphic Center in New York.

Peter Rodríguez (1926–)

Peter Rodríguez of California spent several years in Mexico, and his work reflects that experience. He used Mexican place-names in some of his abstract works, such as *Tlalpan*. In recent years, he has concentrated on making altars that have a closer relationship to his background as a Chicano in northern California. He was born in Stockton, California, in 1926 and received all his schooling in that city. As founder of the Mexican Museum in San Francisco in 1972, he has had a great impact on the development of the Chicano art movement in the San Francisco Bay area.

Eugenio Quesada (1927–)

Eugenio Quesada of Arizona spent several years in Mexico, and his work reflects that experience. Quesada's drawings of Mexican American children are similar in form and subject to the paintings and drawings of Mexican artists such as Raúl Anguiano. He was born in Wickenburg, Arizona, in 1927, and studied at Mesa Community College and Arizona State University, where he received a bachelor of arts degree. He taught at Santa Paula High School, California, in 1954, Glendale Community College, Arizona, in 1972, and has taught at Arizona State University since 1972.

Manuel Neri (1930–)

Manuel Neri of the San Francisco Bay area was at the forefront of the art movements of the 1960s, especially funk art. Although his work was based primarily on the human figure defined in plaster and selective polychromy, he referred to pre-Columbian architectural forms, such as the pyramid, in other works.

Neri, born in Sanger, California, in 1930, received all his early schooling in Los Angeles. He studied ceramics from 1949 to 1953 at San Francisco City College, the University of California, and the Bray Foundation in Helena, Montana. He also studied at the Oakland School of Art and Crafts from 1955 to 1957 and at the California School of Art, now the San Francisco Art Institute, from 1957 to 1959. He has taught at the University of California, Davis, for many years.

Chicano Artists

Melesio Casas (1929–)

Melesio Casas of Texas, was among the pioneers of the Chicano art movement. Although he began to include references to the United Farm Workers' eagle logo and pre-Columbian motifs in his work as early as 1970, the way in which these were used reflects the pop art style of the early 1960s. Typical of these works is the 1970 painting *Brownies of the Southwest.*

Casas was born in El Paso, Texas, in 1929. He attended Texas Western University, where he received his bachelor of arts degree in 1956, and the University of the Americas in Mexico City, where he

received his master of fine arts degree in 1958. As a teacher and an artist at San Antonio College for almost 30 years, he had a strong impact on the training and education of many Chicano artists in San Antonio. He is retired and presently lives in southern Italy.

Ernesto Palomino (1933–)

Ernesto Palomino was among the first of the Chicano muralists to use pre-Columbian and Mexican as well as Chicano motifs in murals, such as the one he painted in Fresno, California, in 1971. Before he began work as a muralist, Palomino made constructions of various materials that were characteristic of the works being produced in the San Francisco Bay area in the mid-1960s.

Palomino, born in Fresno, California, in 1933, has spent most of his life in that city as an artist, and has been a professor at Fresno State University since 1970. He attended the San Francisco Art Institute, 1954, Fresno City College, 1957, and San Francisco State University, 1960–65.

Luis Jiménez (1940–)

Luis Jiménez, of El Paso, Texas, is primarily known for his sculptures made of resin epoxy coated with fiberglass. Jiménez paraphrased Mexican art, American Western art, and used pre-Columbian concepts in his works of the late 1960s and early 1970s. Since then, he has concentrated on the Southwest for a series of sculptures and colored-pencil drawings. Among the early works are *Man on Fire* (1969–70), *The End of the Trail* (1971), *The American Dream* (1967–69), and *Indians to Rockets* (1972).

Jiménez initially selected the many post office murals found all over the country as a source for the imagery in the *Indian to Rockets* project. The murals in the Southwest invariably deal with the history of the region or its industries. What struck the artist most was the emphasis in all of these murals on the notion of progress, exemplified by the machine. Starting in the early 1970s, he did studies on the history of the Southwest that were eventually used for a series of sculptures on that subject, titled *Progress I, Progress II,* and so on.

Toward the end of the 1970s, Jiménez began to concentrate more specifically on regional subjects in which the Chicano, the Anglo, and others were represented in their natural surroundings. A good example of these works is the drawing of a man and woman dancing while an onlooker watches, titled *Honky Tonk* (1981–86).

Jiménez was born in El Paso, Texas, in 1940. He attended the University of Texas, Austin, where he received his bachelor of fine arts degree in 1964. He received a fellowship from the National University of Mexico. Shortly afterward, he moved to New York, where he worked and exhibited in several galleries. He now resides in Hondo, New Mexico, for half the year, and Houston, Texas, for the other half. In 1995, he was named to an academic chair in the Art Department of the University of Houston. He is the first U.S. Hispanic artist to earn such a distinction.

Puerto Rican Artists

Olga Albizu (1924–)

Olga Albizu is an abstract painter who became widely known for her paintings for RCA record covers for the music of Stan Getz in the late 1950s. Albizu was born in Ponce, Puerto Rico, in 1924 and has lived in the United States since 1956. She first arrived in New York City in 1948 with a University of Puerto Rico fellowship for postgraduate study. She studied with the well-known abstract expressionist Hans Hoffmann at the Art Students League, from 1948 to 1951, and that experience is evident in her work. She also studied in Paris and Florence in 1951.

Rafael Ferrer (1933–)

In the 1960s, Rafael Ferrer was at the forefront of the movement in New York City that dealt with temporary installations and other ephemeral works and deemphasized "the object" as a work of art. He experimented with a variety of media and methods, from assemblages, constructions, and freestanding sculpture to lengths of chain-link fence, blocks of ice, bales of hay, and masses of dry leaves used to create environments for indoor and outdoor exhibitions. These temporary installations were related to the nonobject events of conceptual art of the early 1970s.

In the early 1970s, Ferrer began to focus on imaginary voyages and the apparatus used to carry them out—maps, kayaks, tents, and boats—in works assembled or constructed of steel, wood, and other materials.

Ferrer was born in Santurce, Puerto Rico, in 1933. He studied at the Shunton Military Academy, Virginia, from 1948 to 1951 and at Syracuse University, New York, from 1951 to 1952. He abandoned his studies at Syracuse to study art in Puerto Rico, where he was introduced to the work of the surrealists by the Spanish painter E. F. Granell. From then on he spent part of the year in Puerto Rico and part in the United States until 1966, when he settled in Philadelphia.

Pedro Villarini (1933–)

Pedro Villarini defines all the motifs in his paintings with great precision. There is a stillness and an air of calm in his painting *La Fortaleza* (1968). The peaceful effect is enhanced by the horizontal directions established by the fortress wall and the buildings in the middle ground, and by the clouds in the sky. They are balanced by the turret of the fortress on the left side of the painting.

Villarini was born in 1933 in Hato Ray, Puerto Rico, and has lived in New York City since 1947. He is a self-taught painter.

Ralph Ortiz (1934–)

The work of Rafael Montañez-Ortiz (Ralph Ortiz), was part of the European and American movement known as destructive art. His best-known piece, *Piano Destruction Concert,* was performed on BBC television in 1966 and later presented on national and local television in the United States (Figure 20.14). The extreme gestures in Ortiz's work have their source in the work of the European Dadaists, who emerged during World War I. In one of their events, they invited viewers to use an ax placed next to a small exhibit to destroy the art. This was only one of many antiart gestures of the Dadaists. Ortiz

Figure 20.14. Ralph Ortiz, *Piano Destruction Concert Duncan Terrace.* Destruction in Art Symposium, September 1966, London.

focused on the violence itself in order to emphasize its pervasive presence in our lives. This was unlike the "happenings" of Claes Oldemburg, Allan Kaprow, and others, which were essentially formalist events.

Ortiz also used pre-Columbian references in a series he called Archaeological Finds, in order to focus on his non-European roots and the destruction wrought by the first Europeans who arrived in the Americas. A typical piece in this series is an upholstered chair that was torn apart—destroyed—and titled *Tlazolteotl* (1963, a manifestation of the Aztec earth goddess).

Ortiz was born in New York City in 1934. He studied at the High School of Art and Design, the Brooklyn Museum of Art, and the Pratt Institute, where he received a bachelor of science degree and a master of fine arts degree in 1964. He received the doctorate of fine arts and fine arts higher education degrees from Columbia University in 1967. He taught at New York University, 1968, and was an adjunct professor at Hostos Community College, in the Bronx in 1970.

✳ HISPANIC AMERICAN ARTISTS: 1970s TO THE PRESENT

Chicano Artists

There were many Chicano artists who matured in the 1970s and 1980s. Some were muralists or public artists, others were not. There were many easel painters, sculptors, printmakers, and poster artists who were also interested in the Chicano movement as a source of their work. Some of them started as muralists and then turned to painting easel pictures, making altars, or creating other nonmural work. The greatest number of Hispanic artists are found in California, followed by Texas and then the other states where Mexican Americans and Chicanos reside. Many have received recognition for their work through regional, national, and international exhibitions that have focused on their background as Mexican Americans, Chicanos, or Hispanics. In the late 1960s and early 1970s, exhibitions of Chicano art were strictly local and regional events. By the late 1970s, major exhibitions that included all Hispanic groups were being organized and presented in the United States and abroad.

Los Angeles, California

In Los Angeles, there were numerous muralists as well as easel painters, sculptors, and printmakers. Those who painted murals in the 1970s concentrated more and more on nonmural work by the 1980s.

Among the artists who did both are Carlos Almaraz, Gilbert Sánchez Luján (Magú), Frank Romero, John Valadez, and Gronk. Almaraz, Sánchez Luján (Magú), and Romero were members of the group called Los Four. The other member was Beto de la Rocha. They focused on Mexican icons and the Chicano political movement in their work. Gronk was a member of ASCO (nausea) along with Willie Herrón, Harry Gamboa, and Patssi Valdez. They were conceptual and performance artists as well as muralists in the 1970s.

Gilbert Sánchez Luján (Magú) (1940–)

Sánchez Luján is known for his pastel paintings and painted wood sculptures that deal with barrio life in southern California. In some of the wood sculptures, he combines brightly colored cactus and palm trees in tableaus that include smartly dressed figures with dog faces! Their activities on the street, at the beach, or elsewhere in the barrio strike a responsive chord in the viewer who reacts to the humor in the scenes. A good example of his work is the sculpture *Hot Dog Meets La Fufu con su Poochie* (1986). The wood cutouts of the two figures, the dog, the plants, and the small fence were painted in different colors and constructed to create a whimsical street scene with two young people in the barrio reacting to each other.

Luján was born in French Camp (Stockton), California, in 1940. He attended East Los Angeles Junior College and Long Beach State College, where he received his bachelor of arts degree. He received his master of fine arts degree at the University of California, Irvine, and made a commitment to Chicano art at this time. He joined Almaraz and Romero to form the exhibiting group known as Los Four. Their first show went up at Irvine in 1974. He taught ethnic studies at Fresno City College, 1976–81, and then returned to Los Angeles, where he taught at the Municipal Art Center at Barnsdall Park.

Carlos Almaraz (1941–)

Carlos Almaraz was deeply involved with the Chicano movement in the 1970s, doing volunteer work with the United Farmworkers Union from 1972 to 1974, and graphic designs for the Teatro Campesino, which was formed to promote the farm worker cause. He was also a counselor and program director for the All Nations Neighborhood Center, helping "hard core" youth from 1974 to 1976. He also painted murals in East Los Angeles during the same period until 1978. Since the 1980s, he has concentrated on painting nonmural works of art that focus on his background as a Chicano. A good example of his nonmural work is the painting *Europe and the Jag-*

uar (1982), in which the two major strands of Mexican and Mexican American or Chicano culture—the European and the indigenous—are woven into a complex pictorial statement. A woman and a jaguar walking hand in hand are in front of a backdrop full of isolated motifs—a house, a train, a quarter moon, human heads in profile—painted in an explosive style. A man between them on a lower level stands calmly smoking a cigarette. The backdrop seems to be full of multicolored sparks that give the surface a luminous effect. Almaraz was born in Mexico City in 1941. His family moved to Chicago when he was one year old, and to California when he was eight. He attended Loyola University in New Orleans, California State University, Los Angeles, East Los Angeles College, and Los Angeles Community College. He also attended the New School of Social Research and the Art Students League in New York City. Almaraz received his master of fine arts degree from the Otis Art Institute in 1974. He exhibited as a member of Los Four in 1974 at the University of California, Irvine and the Los Angeles County Museum.

Rupert García (1941–)

The precisely defined flat areas that are characteristic of the silk-screen process make the work of Rupert García immediately recognizable. The unvarying fields of color, which are also part of this process, carry over into some of his painting. This aspect of his work is so strong that a design he provided for a mural in Chicano Park, San Diego, retained the look of a silk-screen print. The pylon mural, actually painted by Víctor Ochoa and the Barrio Renovation Team, focuses on *Los Tres Grandes* (Diego Rivera, José Clemente Orozco, and David Alfaro Siqueiros) and *Frida Kahlo* (1978).

García was born in French Camp, California, in 1941. He attended Stockton College and San Francisco State University, where he received his bachelor of arts degree, in painting in 1968 and a master of arts degree in printmaking (silk-screen) in 1970. He pursued his doctoral studies in art education at the University of California, Berkeley, from 1973 to 1975, and received another master of arts degree, in the history of modern art, in 1981. He taught at San Francisco State University, 1969–81; the San Francisco Art Institute, 1973–80; the University of California, Berkeley, 1979 to the present; Mills College, 1981; Washington State University, 1984; and the Mexican Museum, San Francisco, 1986.

Frank Romero (1941–)

Frank Romero, another member of the Los Four, has often focused on street scenes in his paintings, in which automobiles are prominently displayed.

Sometimes he makes a statement about barrio life in Los Angeles. He works in various media other than painting and drawing—photography, graphics, ceramics, and textile design. A good example of his work is the painting *The Closing of Whittier Boulevard* (1984). The night scene includes a bird's-eye view of a street corner in East Los Angeles where the police have set up barricades to stop the flow of traffic. The two streets leading up to the corner are filled with cars with their lights illuminating the police behind the barricades, who are holding billy clubs. The toy-like appearance of the figures and the cars gives the entire scene an eerie effect.

Romero was born in East Los Angeles in 1941. He attended the Otis Art Institute and California State University, Los Angeles, where he met Carlos Almaraz in the 1960s. He met Gilbert Luján and Beto de la Rocha in 1969 during a sojourn in New York (1968–69) during which he stayed with his friend Almaraz. Throughout the early 1970s, he was involved in the Chicano movement.

Yolanda López (1942–)

López used Our Lady of Guadalupe in a series of works that emphasize Chicano culture and identity. She substituted human figures and an Aztec deity for Our Lady of Guadalupe in several works, including her grandmother, Tonantzin (Our Mother), a small sculpture of Coatlicue (Serpents her Skirt), an Indian woman nursing her child, and the artist herself. Her self-portraits include a performance piece and a painting. In the former, the artist was photographed moving toward the viewer armed with paint brushes and wearing blue shorts, a sleeveless undershirt with stars painted on it, and sneakers. In the latter, the artist is shown appropriating the attributes of Our Lady of Guadalupe and her pre-Columbian counterpart. She runs toward the observer with an expression of triumph while holding a serpent in one hand and a mantle with a star-studded blue field in the other.

López was born in San Diego in 1942. She received her master of fine arts degree from the University of California, San Diego in 1978.

Amalia Mesa-Baines (1943–)

Although the altar installations by Amalia Mesa-Baines (b. 1943) are not directly religious in content, their format has allowed her to attain a spiritual sensibility that is in tune with her personal and cultural life. She has used these altars to pay homage to ancestors and Mexican historical figures in the arts, religion, and the cinema, such as Frida Kahlo, Sor Juana de la Cruz, and Dolores del Rio.

Mesa-Baines uses Mexican symbols in her altars,

such as *calaveras* (skulls), *corazones* (hearts), crosses, and images of the Virgin in her many manifestations. She also cuts her own paper (*papel picado*), makes the altar cloths and paper flowers, and builds the *nichos* and the *retablo* boxes with the help of a carpenter.

One of her major works, *Altar for San Juana Inés de la Cruz* (1981), a mixed-media construction, was shown in the Made in Aztlán exhibition at the Centro Cultural de la Raza in San Diego in 1986.

Mesa-Baines first exhibited an altar in the annual show at the Galería de la Raza in 1976 and later at the San Francisco Museum of Art in 1980. She has since exhibited altars in several national and international exhibitions. Mesa-Baines received her doctor of philosophy in psychology with an emphasis on culture and identity. In 1994, Mesa-Baines became the first Hispanic artist to win a prestigious MacArthur fellowship ("genius grant").

Ester Hernández (1944–)

Ester Hernández used her painting and graphic work to make statements about Chicano culture and the economic forces that have had a negative impact on one segment of it: the farm-working communities in California. One of the most controversial works by Hernández is a print that was published on the cover of *En frecuencia,* a guide for public radio in Santa Rosa, California. The primary focus of the image was on Our Lady of Guadalupe, but instead of using the traditional image of the Virgin, she used a woman in a karate stance to make a statement about the liberation of Chicanas.

Hernández was born in Dinuba, California, in 1944 to farm-worker parents. She moved to the San Francisco Bay area in 1971 to continue her studies. She met and worked with other Chicano artists, among them Malaquías Montoya, and became involved with Mujeres Muralistas (Women Muralists). She teaches at an art center for the developmentally disabled in San Francisco.

Patricia Rodríguez (1944–)

Patricia Rodríguez was one of the leading muralists in the Bay Area in the 1970s. In 1972, she organized the group known as Mujeres Muralistas, and with them painted murals from 1972 to 1977. Its members were Consuelo Méndez, Irene Pérez, and

Figure 20.15. Judy Baca, *The Great Wall of Los Angeles,* "350 Mexicans Deported and Dustbowl Refugees." Detail of the Great Wall of Los Angeles, 1980. Mural program was begun in 1976. (Photograph by Jacinto Quirarte.)

Figure 20.16. Carmen Lomas Garza, *Lotería—Table Llena,* 1974.

Graciela Carrillo. In 1980, she began working on box constructions, inspired by the traditional *nichos* that serve a religious function for the Chicano family. She focused on religious prejudice, cultural identity, and the world around her. The boxes or nichos, made with found and handmade objects, are based on Catholic traditions as well as on the myths, legends, and magic of Mexican culture dating all the way back to the Aztec and the Mayan.

Rodríguez was born in Marfa, Texas, in 1944. She was raised by her grandparents, and at age 11 lived with her parents, who worked as migrants throughout the Southwest. At age 13, in the 1950s, she attended public schools in California. She later attended junior college and the San Francisco Art Institute on a scholarship. She taught at the University of California from 1975 to 1980.

Judy Baca (1946–)

Judy Baca one of the pioneers of the mural movement in Los Angeles. She founded the first city of Los Angeles mural program in 1974, and in 1976 she cofounded the Social and Public Art Resource Center (SPARC) in Venice, California, where she served as artistic director throughout the 1970s and 1980s. Her best-known work is *The Great Wall of Los Angeles* (Figure 20.15). Painted over five summers, the half-mile long mural employed 40 ethnic scholars, 450 multicultural neighborhood youth, 40 assisting artists, and more than 100 support staff.

She is currently working on a mural program that addresses issues of war, peace, cooperation, interdependence, and spiritual growth. It is titled World Wall: A Vision of the Future Without Fear and consists of seven portable panels that measure ten feet by 30 feet each.

Baca was born in Los Angeles in 1946. She attended California State University, Northridge, where she received her bachelor of arts degree in 1969, a master's degree in art, and completed an intensive mural techniques course in Cuernavaca, Mexico. She is a full professor of art at the University of California, Irvine.

Carmen Lomas Garza (1948–)

Carmen Lomas Garza, a painter and printmaker, uses her Chicano background as the primary focus of her work. Her images, based on recollections of her childhood in south Texas, are used to heal the wounds she suffered as a result of racism and discrimination.

One of Lomas Garza's most widely known series is the one based on the game Lotería (the Lottery). In the work, titled *Lotería—Tabla Llena* (Figure 20.16), she consciously used an exaggerated perspective, reminiscent of the works of native artists, because it allowed her to present all the thematic elements in the work in as clear a fashion as possible. The large table is presented as if seen from above, and everything else—the figures, the animals, furniture, plants, and trees—is represented as if seen head-on. The only exception is the walkway at the bottom of the print, also shown as if seen from above.

Garza was born in Kingsville, Texas, in 1948. She attended Texas Arts and Industry University in Kingsville, where she received her bachelor of arts degree in 1972. She attended Antioch Graduate School of Education, Juarez Lincoln Extension (Austin), where she received her master of arts degree in 1973. She received another master of arts degree from San Francisco State University in 1980. In the 1990s, Lomas Garza has become a much sought-after illustrator of picture books for children.

San Francisco, California

In San Francisco since the 1960s, artists have focused on social, political, cultural, and feminist issues in their nonmural works. Malaquías Montoya and Rupert García were two of the most active political artists in the Bay Area. Their comments against American involvement in the internal affairs of Latin American countries appeared repeatedly in their silk-screen prints, posters, and paintings of the 1970s and 1980s. Many women artists dealt with cultural and feminist issues during the same time. Yolanda López focused on the family and Our Lady of Guadalupe in her drawings, paintings, and installations of the late 1970s. Amalia Mesa-Baines dealt with similar issues in her altar installations. Ester Hernández dealt with feminist and environmental issues in her prints and paintings. Patricia Rodríguez, a muralist in the 1970s, turned to cultural issues in the 1980s, with boxes that have their genesis in the home altars found in many Chicano homes. Carmen Lomas Garza focused on her childhood in south Texas in her prints and paintings of the 1970s and 1980s.

Figure 20.17. Victor Ochoa, *Gerónimo,* 1981. Centro Cultural de la Raza, Balboa Park, San Diego, California.

San Diego, California

Many Chicano artists in San Diego were at the forefront of the Chicano mural movement. Their struggle to create Chicano Park in the Barrio de la Logan and the Centro Cultural in Balboa Park has been recounted in numerous local, national, and international publications. The story has even been told in an hour-long video that has been telecast over National Public Television. Among the pioneers of that struggle were Salvador Roberto Torres, Víctor Ochoa, David Avalos, and others who were members of the group called Toltecas en Aztlán, initially, and later Congreso de Artistas Chicanos en Aztlan. (See the section later in this chapter on Chicano murals for more information.)

Víctor Ochoa (1948–)

Víctor Ochoa, who is one of the pioneers of the Chicano art movement in San Diego, has concentrated primarily on mural painting. A good example of his work is the mural *Gerónimo* (1981) on one part of the wall of the Centro Cultural in Balboa Park (Figure 20.17). It is a gigantic depiction of the late-nineteenth-century Apache warrior Gerónimo. It is a faithful rendition of a well-known photograph of the Apache leader. Ochoa saw him as a freedom fighter, with whom he identified as a Chicano fighting for his rights in his community. This is in contrast to the view of Gerónimo in traditional American history as a renegade. The other figures on either side are also rendered from photographs. There is a potter on the left and a woman in a skeletal costume on the right. Behind her is a view of Chicano Park with the kiosk where celebrations take place (Figure 20.18). The Coronado Bridge is seen in the background.

San Antonio, Texas

Although Chicano murals were painted in San Antonio, most of the artists in that city concentrated on nonmural work as painters, sculptors, printmakers, and photographers. Among the best-known Chicano artists in San Antonio are César Martínez, Rudy Treviño, Jesse Treviño, and Adán Hernandez.

César Martínez (1944–)

In the late 1970s, César Martínez dealt with specific Chicano motifs other than the usual Huelga eagle and the Chicano triface. He was fascinated with

Figure 20.18. Victor Ochoa, *Chicano Park,* 1981. Centro Cultural de la Raza, Balboa Park, San Diego, California.

Figure 20.19. Cesar Martínez, *La Pareja,* 1979.

the pachuco (zoot-suiter) as an important icon in Chicano culture. As a teenager in the 1950s and 1960s, he saw individuals who adopted the dress of the pachucos. He also included other figures in his works that he classified as batos locos (pachucos) and *mujeres* (women). Since he did not have any other visual information, other than his memory and photographs (snapshots and high school annual pictures), he used them as sources for some of his paintings. He was interested in these types as individuals rather than as a social phenomenon. An example of these works is *La Pareja (The Couple;* 1979) (Figure 20.19).

Aside from these Chicano subjects, Martínez also did a painting of Our Lady of Guadalupe under the guise of Leonardo's Mona Lisa; it was a bizarre juxtaposition of motifs. The work, titled *Mona Lupe,* demonstrates the power that each of its sources has to evoke emotions and to function within several levels of meaning. First of all, there is the antiart posture first articulated by Marcel Duchamp in his work of 1919 titled *L.H.O.O.Q.* (a reproduction of Leonardo's Mona Lisa with a mustache and beard added in pencil), and second, there is the entire realm of Chicano identity, exemplified by the reli-

gious, national, and political icon of Our Lady of Guadalupe. Martínez was born in Laredo, Texas, in 1944. He attended Texas A&I University in Kingsville, where he received his bachelor of science degree in 1968. He resides in San Antonio.

Rudy Treviño (1945–)

Rudy Treviño worked in an abstract style in the 1960s and in a more figurative one in the 1970s and 1980s in which he used pre-Columbian, Mexican, and Chicano subjects. An example of Chicano ichnography is his work titled "George Zapata." The work refers to the Mexican revolutionary hero, Emiliano Zapata and to the American revolutionary hero, George Washington, both of which are components of Chicano culture and identity.

Jesse Treviño (1946–)

Jesse Treviño used everyday scenes and places in the barrio for works that have been included in photorealism exhibitions in San Antonio and elsewhere. An example of the very matter-of-fact portrayals of the barrio is the painting *La Panaderia (The Bakery)* (Figure 20.20.)

Treviño was born in Monterrey, Mexico, in 1946. His family moved to San Antonio in 1948. From 1965 to 1966, he attended the Art Students League in New York City on an art scholarship and studied portrait painting under William Draper. He also studied at Our Lady of the Lake University in San Antonio, where he received his bachelor of arts degree in 1974, and the University of Texas, San Antonio where he received his master of fine arts degree in 1979.

Brownsville, Texas

George Trúan (1944–)

George Trúan used the altar format in the late 1970s in a series of works he called Altares Chicanos. Among those works is *Self-Portrait,* which includes a statue of Our Lady of Guadalupe in the center of the tabletop with a backdrop filled with numerous photographs of the artist taken at different ages. Next to the image of Our Lady of Guadalupe is a photograph of John Kennedy, and above that, a print of the Santo Niño de Atocha (The Christ Child of Atocha). Flowers were placed in vases on the left and right sides of the tabletop.

Trúan was born in Kingsville, Texas, in 1944. He attended Texas A&I University in Kingsville, where he received his bachelor of arts degree in 1968 and his master of arts degree in 1974. He resides in Brownsville, Texas, where he is an art professor at Southmost College.

Figure 20.20. Jesse Treviño, *Panadería,* late 1970s.

Santa Fe, New Mexico

The artists in Santa Fe are unique because they have been able to build on the santero tradition as well as the Chicano muralist movement that was central to Chicano art in the 1970s and 1980s. No other region where Chicanos reside has santeros. (For more information on the Chicano murals in Santa Fe, see the section on Chicano murals later in this chapter.)

The resurgence of the santo-(saint)making tradition dates from the 1960s when New Mexico artists looked to their own past for inspiration for their work. They ignored the work of the López family and other twentieth-century santeros and turned to the use of colors to make the pieces closer to the traditional ones produced in the nineteenth century. Among the well-known new santeros are Luis Tapia of Santa Fe and Félix A. López of Española.

Félix A. López (1942–)

Typical of the new works are the sculptures of Saint Michael by Félix López and Luis Tapia. *San Miguel* (1984) by López, in a private collection, shows the saint with his sword in one hand and the scales in the other. This is the traditional image of the saint. The other way in which Saint Michael was portrayed is seen in the elaborate image of *St. Michael and the Dragon* by Tapia in the collection of the Museum of International Folk Art, Santa Fe. These and other pieces by these santeros are generally larger than the unpainted santos made in Cordova and are meant to be taken more seriously as images related to the Hispanic tradition in New Mexico.

López was born in Gilman, Colorado, in 1942. He attended New Mexico Highlands University, where he received his bachelor's degree with a major in Spanish and a minor in German in 1965. He taught high school in Corcoran and Orange, California, in the late 1960s. He continued his studies and received his master's degree in Spanish literature in 1972 from the University of New Mexico, Albuquerque. He began making santos in 1977.

Luis Tapia (1950–)

Tapia was born in Santa Fe, New Mexico, in 1950. He attended New Mexico State University for a year and began making santos around 1970 when he became aware of the Hispanic issues related to the civil rights movement. Unlike the earlier santeros, he began to use bright colors for the figures; this was shocking to viewers in the early 1970s. He also paints altar screens in the old style.

Chicago, Illinois

As in other regions where Hispanics are found, Chicago is home to numerous Chicano artists who painted murals during the late 1960s through the 1970s and part of the 1980s and now devote their energies to producing portable objects or nonmural art. Some have turned to painting, printmaking, or sculpture. (See the section on Chicano murals later in this chapter for more information on the murals of the Chicago area.)

José Gonzalez (1933–)

José González of Chicago, Illinois, is a multitalented painter, photographer, and arts administrator who has been at the forefront of the muralist movement in that city since the early 1970s. He has also worked with the publication *Revista Chicano Riqueña,* now *The Americas Review,* published in Houston, Texas, by Nicolás Kanellos. Among the designs by González for *The Americas Review* is the one titled *Barrio murals* (1976; Figure 20.21). The cover design is a photo collage composed of the many murals painted in Chicago in the early 1970s.

González, born in Iturbide, Nuevo León, Mexico, in 1933, has lived most of his life in the United States. He studied and received a diploma from the Chicago Academy of Fine Arts in the mid-1950s and continued his studies at several institutions in the 1960s: the Instituto Allende, San Miguel Allende, Mexico; the University of Chicago; the School of the Art Institute of Chicago, where he received his bachelor of fine arts degree in 1970; and the University of Notre Dame, where he received his master of fine arts degree in 1971. He devoted all his energies to the Chicano movement throughout the 1970s and 1980s as a muralist, organizer of exhibitions, and founder of organizations, such as Movimiento Artístico Chicano (MArCh) and others.

Marcos Raya (1948–)

One of the most prolific painters of murals and easel pictures is Marcos Raya, who was a full participant in the Chicano mural movement in Chicago and in recent years has also made altars with secular subjects, such as *Frida and Her Nurse* (1987).

Raya's murals deal with political issues in Chicago and abroad, with particular emphasis on Central America. This is seen in his panel for the mural program *Stop World War III* (1980) (Figure 20.22), in which six other artists participated. The mural project was initiated by the Chicago Mural group under the leadership of John Weber. The block-long mural includes different panels framed in accordance with a series of curvilinear formats. Raya's work is seen on the upper left of the mural. The motifs include the fallen statue of a Central American dictator and a group of figures above it holding banners and flags with the image of Che Guevara and references to El Salvador and Guatemala.

Raya was born in Irapuato, Guanajuato, Mexico, and moved to Chicago in 1964. He studied drawing and painting for two years with Allan Thiekler.

Other Hispanic American Artists

Puerto Ricans in the United States, Cuban Americans, and non-Mexican Hispanics are found primarily in New York, New Jersey, Miami, and Chicago. Their work is varied and represents the many styles that are found in the United States, Europe, and Latin America. It is difficult, therefore, to distinguish their work as being distinctively Puerto Rican, Cuban, and so forth. A few of the better-known artists and their works are discussed below.

Figure 20.21. José González, *Barrio Murals,* 1976. Cover design for *Revista Chicano-Riquería.*

Figure 20.22. Marcos Raya, *Stop World War III*. Mural, Chicago, Illinois.

Rafael Colón-Morales (1941–)

Rafael Colón-Morales was a member of Borinquen 12, an artists' group formed to find venues for their work. The artists did not have a unifying goal in their work other than a practical aim to have their art exhibited, and the group no longer exists. Colón-Morales' early work was primarily geometric abstraction. His later works bear a resemblance to the Cuban surrealist painter Wifredo Lam, with crescent shapes and spiked projections within a dense thicket of forms. An example is *Apestosito* (*Stinker*) (1969).

Colón-Morales was born in 1941 in Trujillo Alto, Puerto Rico. He has lived in New York since 1970.

Luis Cruz Azaceta (1942–)

The Cuban American artist Luis Cruz Azaceta, like other Hispanic artists in New York, has been concerned with the brutalizing effects of violence in his work, in which cartoon-like characters are often presented as victims. According to Azaceta, "My art takes the form of violence, destruction, cruelty, injustice, humor, absurdity and obscenity, as a revolt against our condition and man's evil instincts. I want my paintings and drawings to be an outcry, to awaken man's deepest feelings. Feelings of love, nobility and brotherhood."

Azaceta, born in Havana, Cuba, in 1942, arrived in the United States in 1960 and settled in Hoboken, New Jersey. He began to take life-drawing lessons at an adult center in Queens in the mid-1960s. While working nights as a clerk in the library of New York University, he enrolled in the School of Visual Arts in 1966 and received the equivalent of a bachelor of arts degree in 1969. He has taught at the University of California, Davis (1980), Louisiana State University, Baton Rouge (1982), the University of California, Berkeley (1983), and Cooper Union, New York (1984). He lives in Queens, New York.

Jorge Soto (1947–1986)

Jorge Soto of New York, became identified with the Taller Boricua (Puerto Rican Workshop), established in the barrio, where he distinguished himself as an artist. Like many self-taught artists, Soto defines his forms with very elaborate linear patterns. A good example is an untitled work on canvas painted in acrylic and ink. The two meticulously defined nude figures, a female and a male, are armless and shown standing in a frontal position on a green field with a few tropical plants around their legs. He is concerned with recovering an African and Taino Indian aesthetic in his works.

Soto was born in New York City in 1947 and died in 1986.

Alfonso Carlos (1950–1992?)

Carlos Alfonso, a Miami-based Cuban American artist, drew his images from the Afro-Cuban religious tradition. Among the motifs he used was the knife, which stands for protection against the evil eye. The knife through the tongue is intended to keep evil quiet. He used such motifs for their connotations as well as for formal reasons. His paintings include numerous references to the human figure presented in simplified configurations that recall the jungle paintings (1943) of Wifredo Lam. They are shown within a flattened-out visual field full of crescent shapes that can be used to define large mouths with toothy grins, tongues, large leaves, and eye masks.

Alfonso was born in Cuba in 1950. He studied painting, sculpture, and printmaking at the Academia de Bellas Artes San Alejandro in Havana (1969–73) and art history at the University of Havana (1974–77). He began a teaching career at the Academia San Alejandro as instructor in art history (1971–73), and then taught studio courses in art schools of the Ministry of Culture (1973 and 1980). He immigrated to the United States in 1980 for ideological and professional reasons.

Arnaldo Roche Rabell (1955–)

Arnaldo Roche Rabell, a Chicago-based Puerto Rican artist, has a unique style of painting in which the figures and their surroundings are almost overwhelmed by a densely painted surface. An overall fur-like effect is the result of the paint being applied and then scratched with a sharp instrument. Rubbings and projections are the two methods he uses in his work. He lays a piece of canvas or paper over a model or an object that has been smeared with paint. He then rubs it and elaborates upon the distorted image. His projections of face-only self-portraits are presented in frontal view.

Roche Rabell was born in Puerto Rico in 1955. He studied architecture but gave it up for painting. He studied at the Chicago Art Institute, where he received a bachelor of fine arts degree and later a master of fine arts degree in 1984. He continues to live much of the year in Chicago.

✳ CHICANO MURALS

Although there is great diversity in the works of the Chicano muralists, they shared a desire to paint walls in the barrios where large numbers of Hispanics reside. Their aim was to provide images that were acceptable to that community. Finally, they all had an affinity for the Mexican muralists of the 1920s through the 1950s.

Chicano murals are found over a vast area in the barrios of the Southwest, Pacific Southwest, Northwest, and the Great Lakes region. The number of murals in each community varies from just a few in some cities, like Houston, Texas, to the many hundreds in Los Angeles, California. Only a few of the most representative murals are included in this discussion because of limited space. The intent is to give the reader an understanding of the form, content, and meaning of the murals rather than a full survey of all the murals that were painted from the late 1960s through the early 1990s. The murals selected for discussion are among the most complex in thematic and formal terms. They are not the best, nor do they represent all the regions, but they span the decade of the 1970s, the period of greatest activity in the mural movement. Many of the artists have since worked on easel paintings and other portable works.

Diagrams of the murals are provided in the text, where appropriate, with captions listing the motifs used by the artists. The murals are discussed in chronological order as follows:

1. *History and Heroes,* by Congreso de Artistas Chicanos en Aztlán and Toltecas en Aztlán. 1973, Chicano Park, San Diego, California.
2. *Black and White Mural,* by Willie Herron and Gronk. 1973 and 1978, Los Angeles, California.
3. *History of the Mexican American Worker,* by Vicente Mendoza, José Nario, and Raymond Patlán. 1974–75, Blue Island, Illinois.
4. *La Raza Cosmica (The Cosmic Race),* by Raúl Valdez. 1977, Austin, Texas.
5. *En la lucha . . . ponte trucha, (In the struggle . . . Beware),* by Rogelio Cárdenas. 1978, Hayward, California.
6. *Multicultural Mural,* by Gilberto Garduño and others. 1980, Santa Fe, New Mexico.

San Diego, California

Some of the earliest murals were painted in the San Diego area known as Chicano Park, in the Barrio de la Logan, and at the Centro Cultural de la Raza in Balboa Park, near downtown. Although murals were painted in other barrios of the city, it is in these two places that most of the murals were painted by local artists as well as by those who came in from other parts of California over a period of ten years in the 1970s.

Chicano Park exemplifies the mural movement, in which the community, artists' groups, students, and others were involved in efforts to give the area cohesiveness, direction, and meaning. The story behind the movement, which began in earnest in 1970 in the Barrio de la Logan (named after the street that runs through it), was reported in the local press and in several books.

The Barrio de la Logan was first altered when a freeway was built through its center in a north-south direction in the early 1960s. By 1969, the completion of the Coronado Bridge, running in an east-west direction, fragmented it further. Many residents lost their homes as a result of such massive construction. Despite these changes, Salvador Roberto Torres, a former resident and a graduate of the Oakland School of Arts and Crafts, returned to the barrio in 1968 and began planning the concept he had been formulating to turn the area under the bridge into a Chicano park. The plan was to make it a green corridor all the way to the waterfront and thereby open up the area to the sky and the bay for the people. In order to achieve this, the refuse dump under the bridge had to be cleaned up and murals painted along the way. The waterfront itself also had to be cleaned up.

By early 1970, Torres, along with other Chicano artists who called themselves Toltecas en Aztlán, began to discuss ideas regarding the bridge, the community, and their role as artists in it. This led to the discussion of murals in Chicano Park. Among those involved in the planning were Guillermo Aranda, Mario Acevedo, Víctor Ochoa, Tomás Castañeda, and Salvador Barajas.

While Torres and others were continuing with their plans to revitalize the barrio, an event that was to activate the entire community took place in April 1970. The California Highway Patrol moved in with a bulldozer to clear the topsoil under the bridge for the construction of a parking lot for 30 patrol cars. In addition, Chicano artists found out that the highway patrol had plans for a small brick building once used by the bridge engineer, which they wanted for themselves. The response was immediate. Artists, students, families, and children occupied the Ford Building in Balboa Park to emphasize the need for a Chicano cultural center. The area under the bridge was eventually turned over to the community piece by piece, and an abandoned water tank in Balboa Park was turned over to the group for a cultural center in 1971.

Chicano Park has more than 18 concrete pillars,

which have been painted on both sides since 1973. The area is bounded by the approaches to the bay bridge (completed in 1969) connecting Coronado Island to the mainland and Interstate Highway 5, and the freeway running perpendicular to it. More than 30 individual panels were painted during the 1970s and early 1980s by artists from San Diego and other California cities. The pillars supporting the bridge approaches are T-shaped and of varying heights. Almost all the pillars on the various ramps between National and Logan Avenues have been painted.

History and Heroes, Congreso de Artistas Chicanos en Aztlán and Toltecas en Aztlán, 1973.

The *History and Heroes* painting program began on the most eastern side of the area on two of the off-ramps flanking Logan Avenue. The triangular-shaped ramps were painted during the months of March and April 1973 by artists and people from the community. Both murals were coordinated by Congreso de Artistas en Aztlán and Toltecas en Aztlán. Among the artists who worked on both panels were Guillermo Aranda, Víctor Ochoa, Abraham Quevedo, Salvador Barajas, Arturo Román, Guillermo Rosete, Mario Acevedo, Tomas Castañeda, and Salvador Roberto Torres.

The off-ramp mural on the west side of Logan Avenue is typical of what was painted in the early 1970s in the Chicano barrios everywhere. It includes references to all three Mexican epochs (pre-Columbian, colonial, and modern) and recent Chicano history. In addition, there are references to contemporary events, such as space travel and civil rights demonstrations. It is immediately apparent that the entire mural was painted by several different artists. There are sharp lines of demarcation, with panels having little or no relation to others on either side, and the themes are not fully articulated.

To make the description and discussion of the mural easier to follow, a diagram in which all the motifs and themes are numbered and identified in the caption is included. Also listed are the names of the artists and the portions each one painted.

The people represented along the upper portion of the mural, numbered from 1 to 17, represent historical as well as contemporary figures and are the work of several artists. The first four heads were painted by Guillermo Aranda: Pablo Picasso (1), included because he died when the mural was being painted; Jose Clemente Orozco (2) and David Alfaro Siqueiros (4), two of the Mexican muralists most admired by the Chicano artists; and *La Niña Cosmica,* or the Cosmic Child (3), a reference to the people of Mexican descent and their future.

Carlos Santana (5), the rock music star, and Che Guevara (6), the Cuban-based Communist leader, were painted by an unknown artist, possibly Guillermo Rosete.

Víctor Ochoa painted César Chávez (7), the head of the United Farmworkers Union, and Joaquín Murrieta (10), a folk hero and bandit in nineteenth-century California. Chávez was a key figure in the Chicano movement for equal rights along economic, political, and educational lines.

The next heads were painted by Salvador Barajas. Rubén Salazar (8), a well-known newspaperman, was accidentally killed by police during the National Chicano Moratorium demonstration against the Vietnam War that took place in East Los Angeles on August 29, 1970. Salazar was considered the first martyr of the Chicano movement. Ramón Ortiz (9), born in Santa Fe, New Mexico (1813–96), was a diplomat and priest who worked for better U.S.-Mexican relations during the 1840s. He was also appointed to oversee the removal of those New Mexicans who wished to live in Mexico after the war between Mexico and the United States. The next heads represent heroes of Mexican history: Miguel Hidalgo y Costilla (11) and José Guadalupe Morelos (13), heroes of the War of Independence (1810–21); Benito Juárez (14), the leading figure during the War of Reform of the 1850s and in the struggle against the French occupation of the 1860s; and the key figures of the Mexican Revolution of 1910: Venustiano Carranza (12), Francisco Villa (15), Rojas (16), and Emiliano Zapata (17).

There are panels from the extreme left to right beneath the heads appearing on the upper register. The first one on the left (18), painted by Guillermo Aranda and Guillermo Rosete, is a reference to the conquest of Mexico by the Spaniards. Skeletal figures wearing Spanish helmets are engulfed by flames and a jaguar is shown in their midst. The jaguar refers to the pre-Columbian peoples of Mexico. The flames, a paraphrase of José Clemente Orozco's murals in Mexico and the United States, refer to destruction as well as regeneration or rebirth. The skeletal figures are also a reference to Mexican art in general and to the work of José Guadalupe Posada in particular.

The next set of panels, also painted by Guillermo Aranda, focus on the future, the present, and the past. The first panel (19) deals with outer space with some celestial bodies, and the present—the Chicano struggle for economic parity with other Americans—directly below it with the inclusion of the United Farmworkers' eagle symbol. The pyramid (20) refers to the ancient past of Mexico, with which Chicanos identify.

The next two panels, painted by Arturo Román, focus on Chicano identity and the struggle to save the Barrio de la Logan from destruction by local and state authorities. Our Lady of Guadalupe (21), a reference to Mexican and Chicano identity, has religious as well as political meaning. The demonstration by barrio residents (22) includes banners of Our Lady of Guadalupe and United Farmworkers flags. The stylized rainbow and workers in the fields above the demonstration scene were painted by Guillermo Rosete.

The Olmec colossal head (23) was painted by Víctor Ochoa, and the two *soldaderas* (female soldiers of the Mexican Revolution) (24) were painted by Arturo Román. The final two motifs, the man on horseback and the flag (25 and 26) were painted by Guillermo Rosete and Sal Barajas. The man on horseback started out as a portrait of Francisco Villa carrying a Mexican flag and was later changed to a member of the Brown Berets, a paramilitary group of young Chicano militants, and the triface motif in the center of the flag is a reference to the mestizo, part Spanish, part Indian.

Los Angeles, California

Hundreds of murals were painted in Los Angeles over an extremely large area and on every conceivable type of surface (brick, wood, stucco, and concrete) and building (end walls of housing project buildings, in back alleys, concrete stairways, park pavilions, side walls of grocery stores, pharmacies, launderettes, cultural centers, and many other structures). Although most were painted in East Los Angeles, some were painted in other parts of the city, such as the Tujunga Wash murals by Judy Baca, miles away from the barrio. The earliest murals date from 1972 and are found in Estrada Courts and at the Mechicano Art Center.

Among the many artists who painted murals in East Los Angeles, starting in 1972, were Leonard Castellanos, who directed the Mechicano Art Center on Whittier Boulevard, and Charles Félix, who was associated with the Goez Gallery and others. Judy Baca founded and headed the arts organization known as SPARC (Social and Public Art Resource Center) for many years. Many of the artists worked as members of groups such as ASCO (Distasteful), Los Dos (The Two) Streetscapers, Los Four (The Four), and others.

Castellanos was committed to finding ways to initiate and implement programs emanating from the Mechicano Art Center and introducing them into the barrio. The murals were part of the center's stated reasons for being. Eventually 25 murals were painted in Echo Par and 15 in Ramona Gardens, a federal housing project of 600 families.

The most extensive mural project at one location in the barrios of East Los Angeles is found at the Estrada Courts housing complex. The work, under the direction of Charles Félix, was begun in the summer of 1973. Materials for the project were provided by the Los Angeles City Housing Authority and the Los Angeles Fire Department, initially, and also by the Board of Public Works.

The murals designed by Charles Félix and other community artists were painted by youths living in the housing complex and surrounding community. About 125 of the more than 150 youngsters who participated in the project during the first summer were paid by the Los Angeles Housing Authority with funds from the Neighborhood Youth Corps.

There is great variety in the murals of Estrada Courts. The subjects portrayed range from the usual pre-Columbian references to historical and contemporary ones relating to Mexico and the United States. The subjects had to be approved by a group of residents, organized under the name of Residentes Unidos (United Residents). Among the artists who painted murals at the courts are Willie Herron and Gronk, and Mario Torero of San Diego, as well as

other members of the San Diego artist's group Congreso de Artistas Chicanos en Aztlán. Nearly 60 panels were painted by 1977. Many others were painted after that date.

Black and White Mural, by Willie Herrón and Gronk, 1973 and 1978.

Black and White Mural, Figures 20.23 and 20.24, by Willie Herrón and Gronk has various narratives and is composed of heads and massed figures that were placed in interlocking squares and rectangular units. There are long views of street scenes, as in the upper central part interspersed with other smaller units in which groups of figures are also shown at various eye levels. These are contrasted with individual heads that fill up the square formats and extreme close-ups of only the eyes of a human head presented upside down and right side up to the right of center.

The artists focused on their community, the Chicano movement, and their own lives as well as on their own artwork in the mural. The panels were evenly distributed in terms of space allotted to each artist. Herrón painted a baboon (1) on the upper left,

Figure 20.23. Willie Herrón and Gronk, *Black and White Mural,* 1973 and 1978. Estrada Courts, Los Angeles, California. (Photograph by Jacinto Quirarte.)

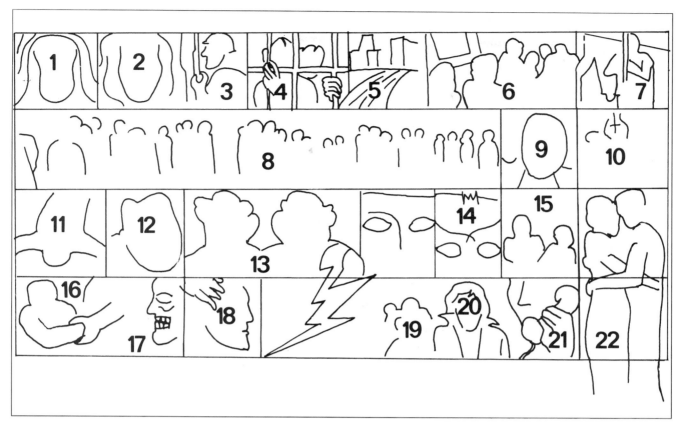

Figure 20.24. Willie Herrón and Gronk, *Black and White Mural,* 1973 and 1978. Estrada Courts, Los Angeles, California. (Diagram by Jacinto Quirarte.)

and Gronk painted a head of a long-haired youth (2) next to it. The rest of the panels on this register and most of the next one below it deal with East Los Angeles in general and the National Chicano Moratorium in particular. Herron painted a Los Angeles street scene (5), demonstrators carrying placards (7), and the largest panel, in which the demonstration itself is depicted (8). Gronk presents a helmeted soldier with rifle (3), figures behind bars (4), and women and children who may have sat and stood on the sidelines during the demonstration (6).

The remaining panels on the second through the fourth registers deal with terror, religion, death, Chicano art, portraiture, and the family in the barrio. Herron painted the remaining two panels of the second register from the top, which represent a terror-struck screaming woman (9) and the Catholic Sacred Heart (10). He also painted two panels in the third register, which represent a work performed by members of the artist's group ASCO in the early 1970s, known as the *Walking Mural* (13), and a self-portrait with his sister based on a photograph taken of them when they were children (15). Herron also painted panels on the fourth register. On the ex-

treme lower left a figure is being pulled by another by the arm (16), and next to it there is a long-haired head in profile with skeletal attributes (17). Toward the right there are demonstrators reacting to tear gas (19), a portrait of Patssi Valdés (20), a member of ASCO (Herron, Gronk, and Harry Gamboa were the other members), and a woman using a telephone (21).

On the extreme left of the third register, Gronk painted a sprawled dead figure (11) seen from above and only from the waist up, and the face of a clown (12) next to it. To the right of center on the same register, he painted two different views of the same set of eyes framed by barbed wire and a crown of thorns (14). On the fourth register, he painted a profile head (18), which has a somber aspect and the young couple (22) seen on the extreme right in the only vertical format used in the mural.

Gronk's young couple embracing each other and Herron's self-portrait with his sister were added in the late 1970s. They worked on the mural for the last time in 1980. The mural remains untitled. (*Black and White Mural* is used for convenience only).

Figure 20.25. Raymond Patlán and others, *History of the Mexican American Worker,* 1974–75. Blue Island, Illinois. (Photograph by Jose Gonzales.)

Chicago and Blue Island, Illinois

In Chicago, most of the artists were grouped around three organizations: The Public Art Workshop, The Chicago Mural Group, and Movimiento Artistico Chicano (Chicano Artistic Movement, MARCH).

The first Hispanic murals were painted in 1968 and 1969 by Mario Castillo, a Mexican-born artist. He used pre-Columbian references in both murals, which are essentially nonfigurative works. In the first mural, *Metafísica,* the artist used enamel paints on a brick wall. In the second mural, *Wall of Brotherhood,* he used acrylic paints.

Raymond Patlán was an early muralist who painted on the inside and outside walls of Casa Aztlán (Aztlán House) cultural center. The murals deal with Mexican and Mexican American history. The first was painted by the artist in the auditorium of Casa Aztlán in 1970–71. Titled *From My Fathers and Yours,* it deals with Mexican history from the time of the Spanish conquest of Mexico to the Revolution of 1910 and with Mexican American history in the United States. The narrative is carried primarily

by the portraits of historical figures, such as Moctezuma, Hernán Cortes, Miguel Hidalgo y Costilla, Emiliano Zapata, César Chávez, and Rodolfo "Corky" González. There are thematic references to the War of Independence, the Revolution of 1910, and the Mexican American worker. The latter is

Figure 20.26. Raymond Patlán and others, *History of the Mexican American Worker,* 1974–75. Blue Island, Illinois. (Diagram by Jacinto Quirarte.)

conveyed by three figures in procession wearing hardhats, blue pants, work shoes, no shirts, and holding tools of their trade in the right hand, while the one leading the trio points with his left. The viewer's attention is drawn to a portrait of César Chávez shown in profile and placed in a cartouche.

History of the Mexican American Worker, by Vicente Mendoza, José Nario, and Raymond Patlán, 1974–75.

One of the most ambitious murals in thematic and formal terms was painted in Blue Island (a suburb of Chicago), Illinois, by Raymond Patlán, Vicente Mendoza, and José Nario in 1974 and 1975. *History of the Mexican American Worker,* Figures 20.25 and 20.26, has allegorical and historical figures, Mexican and Chicano icons, medicine, and a pre-Columbian life-death symbol along the upper register. Farm workers, steelworkers, and meat-packers were represented along the lower register. The discussion of the themes and motifs corresponds to the numbers shown in the diagram.

There is a gigantic figure on the extreme upper left of the mural shown lunging forward (1). Only the upper half of the figure, from the waist up, is represented. Its greatly foreshortened arms and hands hold two cog wheels with interlocking sprocket gears in which there are representations of Our Lady of Guadalupe (greatly simplified) and the Huelga eagle. The large figure is reminiscent of the many lunging figures in the works of the Mexican muralist David Alfaro Siqueiros.

The next cluster of motifs to the right of the lunging figure is comprised of an open book (2) flanked by two gigantic figures presented in bust form (head and shoulders only). The two figures presented in frontal view have their arms around each other as evidenced by the hands shown on each figure's shoulder. The man is a blue-collar worker and the woman is his counterpart. The open book has quotes from the writings of Abraham Lincoln and José Vasconcelos, who was the minister of education in Mexico (1921–24) and the man responsible for the government support that helped initiate the mural movement in Mexico.

To the right of center there is a large hand shown in the open position with fingers spread apart and, directly below it, the other one shown extended toward the viewer (3). These are the hands of Benito Juárez, the president of Mexico who led the fight against French intervention in the 1860s. Right next to him is a three-quarter view of Abraham Lincoln's face.

A profile head next to Lincoln draws the viewer's attention to the last scene on the right side of the mural. It includes a physician on the left side holding a newborn child by the ankles with his left hand and a nurse behind him (5). The physician extends his arm in a gesture of offering to a woman in white on the right side who appears to be reaching for the baby (6). There is an American flag behind the physician and the nurse, and a very large life-death head in the midst of the offering scene.

Mexican American workers picking grapes in the fields are seen on the extreme left of the lower register (7). A railroad worker and machinist are seen to the immediate right below a man and woman flanking an open book (8). A Mexican flag and the American Bicentennial logo (9) are seen below Benito Juárez. Molten steel spills out of a tilted vat (10), and next to it are the meat-packers (11) and other workers (12) that complete the scene on the right side of the mural.

History of the Mexican American Worker generated controversy even before it was completed. This was not unusual. Opposition to murals led to confrontations all over the Southwest. Opposition, regardless of the reasons for it, was expressed through direct action (vandalism and defacement of murals), pressure through the press or local governments, by petitions, and even by legal action. Such opposition occurred in Santa Barbara, California, Santa Fe, New Mexico, Denver and Pueblo, Colorado, and Houston, Texas.

The Blue Island muralists have the distinction of having been enjoined by the city council of that industrial suburb of Chicago to stop painting under the threat of arrest because they were in violation of a city ordinance that prohibited the use of advertising on public walls. The focus of the controversy was on the Huelga eagle seen in the upper left side of the mural. No arrests were made, but painting stopped pending a decision by U.S. District Court Judge Richard B. Austin. This followed action by the ACLU (American Civil Liberties Union) to keep the city council from prohibiting the artists from working on the mural. Judge Austin ruled in favor of the artists, citing First Amendment rights of freedom of expression. The judge ruled that the mural dealt with ideas rather than advertising and should therefore not be destroyed. This precedent-setting decision established the Blue Island murals as an example of the muralist's freedom to work without outside interference.

The mural was defaced by vandals in May 1975, but the artists continued their work on it in the following two months. The mural was dedicated on July 19, 1975.

Figure 20.27. Raúl Valdez and others, *La Raza Cósmica,* 1977. Austin, Texas. (Photograph by Jacinto Quirarte.)

La Raza Cósmica, by Raul Valdez, 1977. Austin, Texas.

One of the most elaborate mural programs of the Chicano art movement is found in Austin, Texas. Raúl Valdez and those who assisted him painted on every available surface of the Pan American Center outdoor stage and its adjacent buildings in 1977. Discussion of the mural follows a left-to-right numbering of the ten scenes (even though this is not the thematic order of the mural program). This should be kept in mind as the historical themes are discussed in chronological order (Figures 20.27–20.31).

The focus of the mural program is found on the stage area, with the United Farmworkers eagle dominating the entire central area (6). The long horizontal band in the upper section was painted in the

Figure 20.28. Raúl Valdez and others, *La Raza Cósmica,* 1977. Austin, Texas. (Diagram by Jacinto Quirarte.)

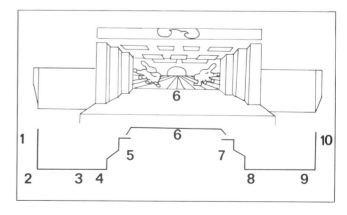

Figure 20.29. Raúl Valdez and others, *La Raza Cósmica,* 1977. Austin, Texas. (Diagram by Jacinto Quirarte.)

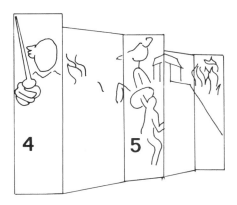

Figure 20.30. Raúl Valdez and others, *La Raza Cósmica,* 1977. Austin, Texas. (Diagram by Jacinto Quirarte.)

center to create the profile head and wings of the eagle. The suspended sound deflectors directly below and above the stage area function as the stepped wings associated with this emblem. On the stage wall, there are two bodiless hands presented in a welcoming gesture. They float over a large expanse of space whose depth is defined by linear perspective. There is a large celestial body in the center (instead of the head for the implied figure) with outstretched arms.

Various panels on each side are taken up with references to the history of Mexico. To the immediate left side of the stage area there is an elaborate scene of battle between the Spaniards and the Aztec with a pyramid and temple in the background (5). The entire scene is enveloped by flames. Next to it on the left is the violently gesturing figure of Miguel Hidalgo y Costilla (4). The word *Independencia* (independence) is lettered on a banner seen directly below the half-figure, modeled on the leader of Mexican

independence painted by José Clemente Orozco in the state government palace stairway in Guadalajara, Jalisco, Mexico.

A figure corresponding to the Mexican Revolution of 1910 is seen to the immediate right of the stage area (7). He is backed up by a woman fighter and other fighters of that conflict. The artist included multiple arms for the main figure because the single arm proved insufficient visually to encompass the available space.

References to modern barrio life and culture were portrayed on the walls of the small building adjacent to the stage on the left side. The artist incorporated two windows right under the flat roof of the end wall in his depiction of the back of a truck with figures seated on the back of it (1). A red 1950s Chevrolet, next to it, was foreshortened to enhance the illusion of a single flat surface for the painting, which actually encompasses the meeting of the two walls at the corner of the building (2). There are folk dancers to the right of the Chevrolet (3). The mural continues all the way around the building to the right of the stage area in a series of violent scenes, some of which are shown with buildings in flames (9 and 10).

Finally, on the rear wall of the stage panel, but on the back, is a representation of a figure with outstretched arms designed by Pedro Rodríguez of San Antonio, Texas. It was based on the New Democracy Freeing Herself figure painted by David Alfaro Siqueiros in the Palace of Fine Arts in Mexico City.

En la lucha . . . ponte trucha, by Rogelio Cárdenas, 1978. Hayward, California.

Rogelio Cárdenas and assistants designed and painted a large mural in 1978 on the side of a tortilla factory in Hayward, California (Figures 20.32 and 20.33). It has elements of Chicano culture as well as references to several Latin American countries. The numbers assigned to the various motifs in the mural read from left to right on the top register and then in similar fashion on the lower one.

The mural is dominated by a monumental figure with outstretched arms that paraphrases the New Democracy figure by Alfaro Siqueiros in the Palace of Fine Arts in Mexico City (3). The Cárdenas woman, however, has a triface and long flowing hair. An eagle is enveloped protectively under her hair on the left side (2) and a serpent on the right (4). The serpent bares its fangs as it coils around the chain that contains the two creatures. The chain is behind the woman's neck and above her shoulders and arms. She holds a hammer in her right hand (1) and her left hand turns into a flaming circular shield with a Greek cross superimposed on it (5). The hammer has a United Farmworkers eagle within a circle in-

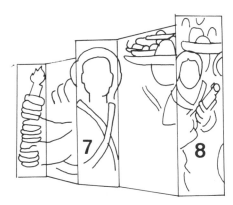

Figure 20.31. Raúl Valdez and others, *La Raza Cósmica,* 1977. Austin, Texas. (Diagram by Jacinto Quirarte.)

Figure 20.32. Rogelio Cárdenas, *En la lucha . . . ponte trucha,* by Rogelio Cárdenas, 1978. Hayward, California. (Photograph by Jacinto Quirarte.)

scribed on its side. The flags of Mexico, Cuba, Pan-Africa, and Puerto Rico are on the inner circle (running clockwise from the upper right) of the shield. Native American peace symbols are in the center of the cross.

References to Chicano identity and barrio culture

Figure 20.33. Rogelio Cárdenas, *En la lucha . . . ponte trucha,* by Rogelio Cárdenas, 1978. Hayward, California. (Diagram by Jacinto Quirarte.)

are seen along the lower register. In the center over the monumental figure's chest is a representation of Our Lady of Guadalupe painted on the lower part of a Latin cross with the caption "Hayward, Califas" (California) above and the artist's name Rogelio Cárdenas below (7). A lowrider Chevrolet is seen under each arm of the woman. The one on the left dates from the late 1940s (6), and the one on the right from the mid-1950s (8). There is a corn plant and a pre-Columbian Indian on the extreme lower right of the mural (9). There are stencil-like representations of roses on a bordered band all the way across the bottom of the mural (10). This is a reference to the roses that miraculously appeared on the *tilma* (vest) of Juan Diego, along with the image of Our Lady of Guadalupe engraved on it, when he appeared before Fray Diego de Zumárraga, bishop of Mexico, in 1531.

The left side of the wall contains several motifs, among them skulls, a large hand, and flames around the actual windows. The title of the mural, its dedication, and the names of those who worked on it are listed on the adjacent wall to the left.

Santa Fe, New Mexico

The mural activity in Santa Fe, New Mexico, was dominated by the Leyba brothers, who painted their first murals in the early 1970s. They and other artists identified themselves under the name of Artes Guadalupanos de Aztlán (Guadalupe Arts of Aztlán). Members of the group were Samuel, Carlos, and Albert Leyba, Gerónimo Garduño, Gilberto Guzmán, and Pancho Hunter. One of the first murals painted by the Artes group dates from 1971. It was painted on the exterior wall of a building in the barrio used for the Clínica de Gente (The People's Clinic). The mural was later painted over. It had an Indian figure clothed in white in the center of a long wall. It was presented in cruciform fashion with wings attached to the arms and a United Farmworkers eagle attached to the head. A patient was wheeled into an operating room by a Chicano doctor and an Indian on the left side of the mural. Several patients were depicted on the right side.

Multicultural Mural, by Gilberto Garduño and others, 1980.

Multicultural Mural (Figures 20.34 and 20.35), was painted on the side of the New Mexico State Records Center in Santa Fe. Its main theme deals with the multicultural history of the state of New Mexico. The numerous figures are presented in different scales and symmetrically arranged within an elaborate landscape. Each thematic section has been numbered from left to right in the mural diagram. Each number from 1 to 6 encompasses an area filled from top to bottom with several motifs and themes.

The scene on the left side of the mural is dominated by a large bull amidst red flowers below and Indians wielding batons above (1). This is the coming together of the Hispanic and Indian cultures. The next scene includes a train in the middle ground shown in foreshortened position (2). The train appears to be moving toward the viewer. In the foreground are workers busily repairing the tracks. Below them are two figures holding onto tools that resemble handlebars. One is an Anglo, the other is an Indian.

The central scene is dominated by the Indian with outstretched arms holding the instruments of technology in each hand (3). In the middle ground are Spanish dancers framed by a gnarled tree on the left and one with foliage on one side only on the right. Spectators are seen on each side of the dancers. The Mount Rushmore-type heads in the background represent the

Figure 20.34. Gilberto Garduño and others, *Multicultural Mural,* 1980. Santa Fe, New Mexico. (Photograph by Jacinto Quirarte.)

Figure 20.35. Gilberto Garduño and others, *Multicultural Mural,* 1980. Santa Fe, New Mexico. (Diagram by Jacinto Quirarte.)

peoples that have settled New Mexico: Indians, Hispanics, Anglos, and African Americans. The males are seen on the left side, the females on the right.

The Mexican national emblem emblazoned on the Mexican flag is seen next to the left hand of the native American figure with outstretched arms (4). A mountain lion peering at the viewer from behind cac-

tus and prickly pears is seen on the lower right side of the mural (6). Three flying figures appear to be reaching for the sun above it. Ravines are seen in the middle ground.

The background of the entire mural is composed of the mountains and high plains that are characteristic of the northern part of New Mexico.

References

Beardsley, J., and J. Livingston. *Hispanic Art in the United States.* New York: Abbeville Press, 1987.

Boyd, E. *Popular Arts of Spanish New Mexico.* Santa Fe: Museum of New Mexico Press, 1974.

Cancel, L., and others. *The Latin American Spirit: Art and Artists in the United States, 1920–1970.* Bronx: The Bronx Museum of the Arts, 1988.

Quirarte, Jacinto, ed. *Chicano Art History: A Book of Selected Readings.* San Antonio: Research Center for the Arts and Humanities, 1984.

Quirarte, Jacinto. *Mexican American Artists.* Austin: University of Texas Press, 1973.

Wroth, W. *Christian Images in Hispanic New Mexico,* The Taylor Museum Collection of *Santos.* Colorado Springs: Colorado Springs Fine Arts Center, 1982.

Jacinto Quirarte

Theater

* Hispanic Theater in the United States: Origins to 1940 * Post World War II to the Present
* Outstanding Figures in Hispanic Theater

* HISPANIC THEATER IN THE UNITED STATES: ORIGINS TO 1940

The Southwest

The roots of Hispanic theater in the United States reach back to the dance-drama of the American Indians and to the religious theater and pageants of medieval and Renaissance Spain. During the Spanish colonization of Mexico, theater was placed at the service of Catholic missionaries, who employed it in evangelizing the Indians and in instructing them and their mestizo descendants in the mysteries and dogma of the church. Throughout the seventeenth and eighteenth centuries in Mexico, a hybrid religious theater developed, one that often employed the music, colors, flowers, masks, even the languages of the Indians of Mexico while dramatizing the stories from the Old and New Testaments. In Mexico and what eventually became the Southwest of the United States there developed a cycle of religious plays that, while dramatizing these stories from the Bible, nevertheless became so secular and entertaining in their performances that church authorities finally banned them from church grounds and from inclusion in the official festivities during feast days. They thus became folk plays, enacted by the faithful on their own and without official sanction or sponsorship by the church.

At the center of this cycle of folk plays that dealt with Adam and Eve, Jesus lost in the desert, and other favorite passages of the Holy Scriptures was the story of the Star of Bethlehem announcing the birth of Jesus Christ to humble shepherds, who then commence a pilgrimage in search of the newborn Christ Child. On the way to Bethlehem Satan and the legions of hell attempt to waylay and distract the shepherds, and a battle between Good, represented by the Archangel Michael, and Evil takes place. Among the other various dramatic elements in this shepherd's play, or *pastorela* as it is called in Spanish, are the appearance of a virginal shepherdess, a lecherous hermit, and a comic bumbling shepherd named Bato. Pastorelas, presented by the common folk from central Mexico to northern California, are still performed today, especially in rural areas during the Christmas season. Originally the whole cycle of mystery plays began on December 12, with the play that dramatized Las Cuatro Apariciones de Nuestra Señora de Guadalupe (the four appearances of Our Lady of Guadalupe) and continued through the Easter season. The famed *Las posadas* is a Christmas pageant dealing with Mary and Joseph looking for shelter, and originally belongs to this cycle as well. In one form or another these folk plays are still with us today and have especially influenced the development of Mexican American theater in the United States. The most noteworthy parts of the legacy of the pastorelas and other religious drama have been their missionary zeal, their involvement of the community of grass roots people, their use of allegory and masks, their totally mestizo nature, and their sense of comicality and slapstick.

In 1598, Juan de Oñate led his colonizing mission into what is today New Mexico. His soldiers and colonists brought with them the roots of secular drama. It has been recorded that, while camped at night, the soldiers would entertain themselves by improvising plays based on the experiences of their journey. They also enacted the folk play that has been spread wherever Spaniards have colonized, *Moros y cristianos,* which is the heroic tale of how the Christians defeated the Moors in northern Spain during the Crusades and eventually drove them from the Iberian Peninsula. For many scholars these represent the roots of an authentic secular folk theater that developed in what became the Southwest of the United States and that gave rise to such New Mexican plays in the eighteenth and early nineteenth centuries as *Los comanches* and *Los tejanos,* both of which deal with military conflict in an epic manner. But as late as the early twentieth century, reenactments of *Moros y cristianos,* even performed on horseback, have been documented in New Mexico, which seems to be the state, because of its rural culture, that has most preserved its Hispanic folk traditions.

But the most important part of the story of Hispanic theater in the United States is not one of a folk theater, but of the development and flourishing of a full-blown professional theater in the areas most populated by Hispanics: throughout the Southwest, New York, Florida, and even the Midwest.

The origins of the Spanish-language professional theater in the United States are to be found in mid-nineteenth-century California, where troupes of itinerant players began touring from Mexico to perform melodramas accompanied by other musical and dramatic entertainments for the residents of the coastal cities that had developed from earlier Franciscan missions—San Francisco, Los Angeles, San Diego. These three cities were more accessible from Mexico than San Antonio, Texas, for instance, because of the regularity of steamship travel up and down the Pacific coast.

There is evidence that plays were being performed as early as 1789; the manuscript copy of a three-act cloak-and-dagger play, *Astucias por heredar un sobrino a su tío (The Clever Acts of a Nephew in Order to Inherit His Uncle's Wealth)* bears that date and shows evidence of having been toured through the California settlements. Records of professional theatrical performances become more numerous some decades later. In the 1840s, various troupes of itinerant players visited the ranches and inns around the San Francisco and Monterey areas of northern California, performing in Spanish for both Spanish- and English-language audiences. During this time at least one semiprofessional theater house existed in Los Angeles. In 1848, Don Antonio F. Coronel, later to become mayor of Los Angeles, opened a theater that seated 300 as an addition to his house; it included a covered stage with a proscenium, a drop curtain, and a good supply of scenery. In the following decades various other theaters opened to accommodate both Spanish- and English-language productions: Don Vicente Guerrero's Union Theater existed from 1852 to 1854, don Abel Stearn's Hall from 1859 to 1875, and don Juan Temple's Theater from 1859 to 1892. In the 1860s and 1870s, the Hispanic community also frequented the Teatro de la Merced,

Teatro Alarcón, and Turn Verein Hall. In the 1880s, Spanish-language productions were even held in the Grand Opera House in Los Angeles.

By the 1860s, the professional stage had become so established and important to the Spanish-speaking community that companies that once toured the Mexican republic and abroad began to settle down as resident companies in California. Such was the case of the Compañía Española de la Familia Estrella, directed by the renowned Mexican actor Gerardo López del Castillo, in its choosing of San Francisco for its home. The company was typical of those that toured interior Mexico in that it was composed of Mexican and Spanish players, was organized around a family unit, into which López del Castillo had married, staged mostly Spanish melodrama, and held its performances on Sunday evenings. Each program was a complete evening's entertainment that included a three- or four-act drama; songs, dances, and recitations; and a one-act farce or comic dialog to close the performance. The full-length plays that were the heart of the program were mostly melodramas by peninsular Spanish authors, such as José Zorrilla, Mariano José de Larra, and Manuel Bretón de los Herreros. Productions by this and the other companies that settled in or toured California were seen as wholesome entertainment appropriate for the whole family, and a broad segment of the Hispanic community, not just the elite, subscribed and attended. This departs somewhat from the English-language tradition and Protestant attitudes at that time, especially west of the Mississippi, which considered the theater arts to be improper for women and immoral, even to the extent of using such euphemisms as "opera house" in naming theaters. In the Hispanic community actors were quite often seen as upstanding citizens, at times even as community leaders, as was the case of López del Castillo, who was elected president of one of the most important Mexican organizations in San Francisco: Junta Patriótica Mexicana (The Mexican Patriotic Commission).

Gerardo López del Castillo was considered to be an outstanding leading man, but it was his wife, Amalia Estrella del Castillo, who won the hearts of many a newspaper critic. On January 26, 1866, the *Los Angeles News* issued the following praise: "Mr. and Mrs. Castillo will rank with the best performers in the state. Mrs. Castillo's imposing and attractive form, handsome features and graceful and charming ease with which she moves through all of her representations is alone well worth the price of admission. When fond of looking at a beautiful woman in the theatrical costume, we would advise you to purchase a ticket."

Among the 12 or 14 companies that were resident or actively touring California during the 1870s and

Los Angeles' California Theater.

were now establishing regular circuits extending from Laredo to San Antonio and El Paso, through New Mexico and Arizona to Los Angeles, then up to San Francisco or down to San Diego.

In the twentieth century, the advent of rail transportation and the automobile brought the touring theater companies to smaller population centers than before. Between 1900 and 1930, numerous Mexican theaters and halls were established in order to house Spanish-language performances all along this circuit. By 1910, several smaller cities had their own Mexican theaters with resident stock companies. The more mobile tent theaters, circus theaters and smaller makeshift companies performed in rural areas and throughout the small towns on both sides of the Rio Grande Valley.

Theatrical activities expanded rapidly when thousands of refugees took flight from the Mexican Revolution and settled in the United States from the border all the way up to the Midwest. During the decades of revolution, many of Mexico's greatest artists and their theatrical companies came to tour and/or take up temporary residence; however, some would never return to the homeland.

Mexican and Spanish companies and an occasional Cuban, Argentine, or other Hispanic troupe toured the Southwest, but they found their most lucrative engagements in Los Angeles and San Antonio. They at times even crisscrossed the nation, venturing to perform for the Hispanic communities in New York, Tampa, and the Midwest. By the 1920s, Hispanic theater was becoming big business, and important companies like Spain's Compañía María Guerrero y Fernando Díaz de Mendoza had its coast-to-coast tours into major Anglo-American theaters booked by New York agents, such as Walter O. Lindsay. The company of the famed Mexican leading lady Virginia Fábregas was of particular importance in its frequent tours because it not only performed the latest serious works from Mexico City and Europe, but also because some of the troupe members occasionally defected to form their own resident and touring companies in the Southwest. Virgina Fábregas was also important in encouraging the development of local playwrights in Los Angeles by buying the rights to their works and integrating the plays into her repertoire.

The two cities with the largest Mexican populations, Los Angeles and San Antonio, became theatrical centers, the former also feeding off the important film industry in Hollywood. In fact, Los Angeles became a manpower pool for Hispanic theater. Actors, directors, technicians, and musicians from throughout the Southwest, New York, and the whole Hispanic world were drawn there looking for employment.

1880s, the Compañía Dramática Española, directed by Pedro C. de Pellón, and the Compañía Española de Angel Mollá were two resident companies in Los Angeles that extended their tours to Baja California and up to Tucson, Arizona; from there they would return to Los Angeles via stagecoach. During this time Tucson boasted two Spanish-language theater houses: Teatro Cervantes and Teatro Americano. In 1878, Pellón established himself permanently in Tucson, where he organized the town's first group of amateur actors, Teatro Recreo. Thus, the 1870s mark Arizona's participation in Hispanic professional theater. It is in this decade as well that troupes began to tour the Laredo and San Antonio axis of Texas, first performing in Laredo and then San Antonio in open-air markets, taverns and later in such German American settings as Meunch Hall, Krish Hall, and Wolfram's Garden in San Antonio; but it is only at the turn of the century and afterward that companies touring from Mexico began making San Antonio and Laredo their home bases.

The last decade of the nineteenth century experienced a tremendous increase in Mexican theatrical activity in the border states. More and more, companies that had previously only toured interior Mexico

Both Los Angeles and San Antonio went through a period of intense expansion and building of new theatrical facilities in the late teens and early twenties. Los Angeles was able to support five major Hispanic theater houses with programs that changed daily. The theaters and their peak years were Teatro Hidalgo (1911–34), Teatro México (1927–33), Teatro Capitol (1924–26), Teatro Zendejas (later Novel; 1919–24), and Teatro Principal (1921–29). There were as many as 20 other theaters operating at one time or another during the same time period.

San Antonio's most important house was the Teatro Nacional, built in 1917 and housing live productions up through the Great Depression. Its splendor and elite status was not shared by any of the other 15 or so theaters that housed Spanish-language productions in San Antonio during this period. While it is true that in the Southwest, as in Mexico, Spanish drama and *zarzuela,* the Spanish national version of operetta, dominated the stage up until the early 1920s, the clamor for plays written by Mexican playwrights had increased to such an extent that by 1923 Los Angeles had developed into a center for Mexican playwriting unparalleled in the history of Hispanic communities in the United States. While continuing to consume plays by Spanish peninsular authors, such as Jacinto Benavente, José Echegaray, Gregorio Martínez-Sierra, Manuel Linares Rivas, and the Alvarez Quintero brothers, the Los Angeles Mexican community and its theaters encouraged local writing by offering cash prizes in contests, lucrative contracts, and lavish productions. Various impresarios of the Spanish-language theaters maintained this tradition throughout the 1920s, offering at times as much as $200 in prize money to the winners of the playwriting contests. It was often reported in the newspapers of the time that the Hispanic theaters drew their largest crowds every time they featured plays by local writers.

The period from 1922 to 1933 saw the emergence and box office success of a cadre of playwrights in Los Angeles composed mainly of Mexican theatrical expatriates and newspapermen. At the center of the group were four playwrights whose works not only filled the theaters on Los Angeles' Main Street, but were also contracted throughout the Southwest and in Mexico: Eduardo Carrillo, an actor; Adalberto Elías González, a novelist; Esteban V. Escalante, a newspaperman and theatrical director; and Gabriel Navarro, poet, novelist, composer, orchestra director, columnist for *La Opinión* newspaper, and editor of the magazine *La Revista de Los Angeles.* There were at least 20 other locally residing writers who saw their works produced on the professional stage,

not to mention the scores of authors of vaudeville revues and lighter pieces.

The serious full-length plays created by these authors addressed the situation of Mexicans in California on a broad, epic scale, often in plays based on the history of the Mexican-Anglo struggle in California. Eduardo Carrillo's *El proceso de Aurelio Pompa (The Trial of Aurelio Pompa)* dealt with the unjust trial and sentencing of a Mexican immigrant; it was performed repeatedly on the commercial stage and in community-based fund-raising events. Gabriel Navarro's *Los emigrados (The Emigrées)* and *El sacrificio (The Sacrifice)* dealt, respectively, with Mexican expatriate life in Los Angeles during the revolution and with the history of California around 1846, the date of the outbreak of the Mexican-American War.

By far the most prolific and respected of the Los Angeles playwrights was Adalberto Elías González, some of whose works were not only performed locally, but also throughout the Southwest and Mexico, and made into movies and translated into English. His works that saw the light on the stages of Los Angeles ran the gamut from historical drama to dime-novel sensationalism. The most famous of

The Mason Theater, a movie and popular vaudeville house in Los Angeles.

his plays, *Los amores de Ramona* (*The Loves of Ramona*), was a stage adaptation of Helen Hunt Jackson's novel about early California, *Ramona: A Story*; it broke all box office records when it was seen by more than 15,000 people after only eight performances, and soon it became a regular item in many repertoires in the Southwest. Two of González's other plays dealt with the life and culture of Mexicans in California: *Los misioneros* (*The Missionaries*) and *Los expatriados* (*The Expatriates*). Probably his second most successful work was the sensationalist *La asesino del martillo o la mujer tigresa* (*The Assassin with the Hammer or Tiger Woman*), based on a real-life crime story reported in the newspapers in 1922 and 1923. A dozen other plays dealt with love triangles and themes from the Mexican Revolution, including *La muerte de Francisco Villa* (*The Death of Francisco Villa*) and *El fantasma de la revolución* (*The Ghost of the Revolution*).

Adalberto Elías González and these other authors addressed the needs of their audiences for reliving their history on both sides of the border and for reviving the glories of their own language and cultural tradition with the decorum and professionalism befitting the type of family entertainment that the community leaders believed served the purposes of reinforcing Hispanic culture and morality while resisting assimilation to Anglo-American culture. But with the rise of vaudeville and the greater access of working-class people to theatrical entertainment, vaudeville-type revues and variety shows became more and more popular and gradually displaced more serious theater. But Mexican vaudeville and musical comedy did not avoid the themes that were so solemnly treated in three-act dramas. Rather, the Mexican stage had developed its own type of revue: the *revista*.

Revistas were musical revues that had developed in Mexico under the influence of the Spanish zarzuela and the French *revue* and vaudeville, but had taken on their own character in Mexico as a format for piquant political commentary and social satire. Also, like the zarzuela, which celebrated Spanish regional customs, music, and folklore, the Mexican revista also created and highlighted the character, music, dialects, and folklore of the various Mexican regions. Under the democratizing influence of the Mexican Revolution, the revista highlighted the life and culture of the working classes. During the revolution, the *revista política* in particular rose to prominence on Mexico City stages, but later all revista forms degenerated into a loose vehicle for musical and comedic performance in which typical regional and underdog characters, such as the *pelado* (literally, skinned or penniless), often improvised a substantial part of the action.

Many critics and historians of Mexican theater see in the revista the birth of a truly Mexican theater. In the words of Miguel Covarrubias, "These rebellious Mexican *commedias dell'art* have produced not only a new national theater, the only one worthy of the name, but a fine corps of actors and comedians whose style and careers have been strongly influenced by the dominant politics of the time."

The Los Angeles stages hosted many of the writers and stars of revistas that had been active during the time of formation of the genre in Mexico, including Leopoldo Beristáin and Guz Aguila. In the theaters of Los Angeles and the Southwest were staged most of the revistas that were popular in Mexico and that were of historical importance for the development of the genre. Such works as *El tenorio maderista* (*The Maderist Tenorio*), *El país de los cartones* (*The Country Made of Boxes*) and *La ciudad de los volcanes* (*The City of Volcanoes*) and numerous others were continuously repeated from Los Angeles to Laredo. Such innovators of the genre as Guz Aguila was for a time a perennial attraction at the Los Angeles theaters. Even important composers of scores for the revistas, such as Lauro D. Uranga, graced the Los Angeles Hispanic stages. With their low humor and popular music scores, the revistas in Los Angeles articulated grievances and poked fun at both the U.S. and Mexican governments. The Mexican Revolution was satirically reconsidered over and over again in Los Angeles from the perspective of the expatriates, and Mexican American culture was contrasted with the "purer" Mexican version. This social and political commentary was carried out despite the fact that both audiences and performers were mostly immigrants and thus liable to deportation or repatriation. The Los Angeles writers and composers were serving a public that was hungry to see itself reflected on stage, an audience whose interest was piqued by revistas relating to current events, politics, and the conflict of cultures that was produced while living in the Anglo-dominated environment. The revistas kept the social and political criticism leveled at the authorities, be they Mexican or American, within the light context of music and humor in such pieces as Guz Aguila's *México para los Mexicanos* (*Mexico for the Mexicans*) and *Los Angeles vacilador* (*Swinging Los Angeles*), Gabriel Navarro's *La ciudad de irás y no volverás* (*The City of You Go There Never to Return*), and Don Catarino's *Los efectos de la crisis* (*The Effects of the Depression*), *Regreso a mi tierra* (*The Return to My Country*), *Los repatriados* (*The Repatriated*), *Whiskey, morfina y marihuana,* and *El desterrado* (*The Exiled One*).

It is in the revista that we find a great deal of

humor based on the culture shock typically derived from following the misadventures of naive, recent immigrants from Mexico who have difficulty in getting accustomed to life in the big Anglo-American metropolis. Later on in the 1920s, and when the depression and repatriation took hold, the theme of culture shock was converted to one of outright cultural conflict. At that point Mexican nationalism became more intensified as anti-Mexican sentiments become more openly expressed in the Anglo-American press as a basis for taking Mexicans off the welfare rolls and deporting them. In the revista, the Americanized, or and *renegado,* became even more satirized, and the barbs aimed at American culture become even sharper. It is also in the revista that the raggedly dressed underdog, the *pelado,* comes to the fore with his low-class dialect and acerbic satire. A forerunner of characters like Cantinflas the pelado really originates in the humble tent theaters that evolved in Mexico and existed in the Southwest of the United States until the 1950s. With roots in the circus clown tradition, and a costume and dialect that embody poverty and marginality, the pelado was free to improvise and exchange witticism with

Actress Rosalinda Meléndez (left) as a shoe-shine boy during the Depression.

his audiences that often embodied working-class distrust of societal institutions and the upper classes. Although the pelado or *peladito,* as he was affectionately called, was often criticized for his low humor and scandalous language, theater critics today consider the character to be a genuine and original Mexican contribution to the history of theater.

One actor who played the pelado to perfection was not even a Mexican but a Spaniard: Romualdo Tirado. He is without a doubt the most important figure in the history of the Hispanic stage of this period. Tirado was an impresario, director, singer, actor, and the author of numerous revistas. Tirado had immigrated to Mexico around the turn of the century and developed a career on the stage there for 15 years before resettling in Los Angeles in the late teens. In the City of Angels, Tirado became a prime mover in the Hispanic theatrical and cinematic industries as a theater owner and movie producer, and just as important, he was also one of the catalysts that brought about the writing and staging of local plays and revistas.

But the most important author of revistas was Antonio Guzmán Aguilera, who went by the stage name Guz Aguila. Unlike Tirado, who settled in Los Angeles expressly to become a theater impresario and movie producer, Guz Aguila became a journalist for *El Heraldo de México* newspaper, but still managed to tour his theatrical company as far south as Mexico City and as far west as San Antonio. Guz Aguila rose to fame in Mexico City as a newspaperman and prolific revista author, but as a result of a falling out with President Obregón and subsequent imprisonment, Aguila went into exile in Los Angeles in 1924. His production has been estimated as high as 500 theatrical works, none of which were ever published, but it is certain that many of his revistas were reworked, renamed, and recycled to accommodate different current events, locations, and audiences. In Los Angeles in 1924 Aguila was given a contract that paid $1,000 per month to write for the Teatro Hidalgo. In a June 7, 1924, interview for *El Heraldo de México,* Aguila stated that the Hidalgo had also formed a company of 30 performers for him and commissioned special scenography and costumes. In the same interview, he revealed that his personal motto was *corrigat riendo mores* (customs are corrected through laughter). And an abundance of laughter, color, patriotic symbolism, and naturalism is what Aguila gave his audiences by pulling out and producing his most famous and time-proven revistas: *Alma tricolor (Three-Colored Soul), La huerta de Don Adolfo (Don Adolfo's Garden;* a reference to President Adolfo de la Huerta), and *Exploración presidencial (A Presidential Explora-*

tion). After presenting many of his well-known works, Aguila began to produce new revistas based on culture and events in Los Angeles: *Los Angeles vacilador* (*Swinging Los Angeles*), *Evite peligro* (*Avoid Danger*), and *El eco de México* (*The Echo from Mexico*). Aguila returned to the stages of Mexico City in 1927, but he never regained the level of success that he had previously experienced there. He continued to tour the republic and the southwestern United States in the years that followed.

Eusebio Pirrín decided on his stage name, don Catarino, while in Los Angeles after developing his acts from childhood in his family's tent theater. It was on the Los Angeles stage during his teens that Pirrín gained prominence, principally in the role of a tiny old man with a bushy moustache. Pirrín was so small that women from the chorus line would pick him up like a baby. Pirrín directed and starred in his family show, which became a perennial presence on the Los Angeles stages in the late 1920s and early 1930s; he somehow even managed to get bookings during the Great Depression. All of the revistas, songs, and dance routines of the Pirríns were original, most of them creations of the enormously innovative Pirrín. Although don Catarino's role was that of a little old ranchero, much of the humor, settings, and situations for his work truly represented urban culture through picaresque adventures. In his numerous revistas, all built around the character of don Catarino, Pirrín explored the themes of Los Angeles night life, culture conflict, and amorous adventures, but he did not shy away from the real-life dramas of the depression, exile, and repatriation in his generally lighthearted works. Eusebio Pirrín did not appear on the stages of Mexico City until the depression and then he was chagrined to realize that many of his imitators in the Mexican capital had been exploiting the don Catarino character that he had created in Los Angeles.

Unlike Los Angeles, the stages of San Antonio did not attract or support the development of local playwrights, and while they hosted many of the same theatrical companies and performers, such as don Catarino and Los Pirríns, as did the California stages, theater in the Alamo City did not support as many resident companies. To be sure, there were many Mexican theater houses and various stock and resident companies, many of which used San Antonio as a base from which to launch tours of Texas and both sides of the Rio Grande Valley. While the story of Los Angeles' Hispanic theater is one of proliferation of Spanish-language houses, companies, and playwrights, the story of San Antonio is one that illustrates the persistence of resident companies, actors, and directors in keeping Hispanic drama alive

in community and church halls after being dislodged by vaudeville and the movies from the professional theater houses during the depression. San Antonio's is also the story of the rise of a number of vaudevillians to national and international prominence. Finally, San Antonio also became a center for another type of theater, one that served an exclusively working-class audience: tent theater.

In San Antonio, Los Angeles, and throughout the Southwest, the Great Depression and the forced and voluntary repatriation of Mexicans depopulated not only the communities but also the theaters. Theater owners and impresarios could no longer afford to present full companies, accompanied by orchestras and technicians; the economic advantage of showing movies was devastating to live theater. After receiving the triple blow of depression, repatriation, and cinema, the Hispanic theater industry continued to writhe and agonize from 1930 until the middle of the decade, when only a few hardy troupes acquiesced to entertaining briefly between films or donated their art to charity; some also toured rural areas in tent theaters, struck out to perform for New York's growing Hispanic population, or simply returned to Mexico. Many were the artists from Los Angeles to the Midwest who stubbornly continued to perform, only now their art was staged in church and community halls for little or no pay in the service of community and church charities, which were especially numerous during the depression. And there was no more heroic battle waged anywhere than that of the San Antonio resident directors and their companies to keep their art alive and in service of the communities. Directors Manuel Cotera, Bernardo Fougá, and Carlos Villalongín, along with such stars as Lalo Astol and María Villalongín, continued to present the same theatrical fare in the same professional manner in church and neighborhood halls throughout San Antonio and on tour to Austin, Dallas, Houston, Laredo, and smaller cities and towns during the 1930s. At the same time, in order to fill the vacuum that had been created with the return of many performers to Mexico and the cessation of tours from there, amateur theatrical groups began to spring up and proliferate, often instructed and directed by theater professionals; quite often these groups also used the church halls and auditoriums for their rehearsals and performances. It is worth reemphasizing that most of the professional and community groups did not exist to present religious drama, but church facilities and church sponsorship were often offered because the theater and most of the serious plays presented were seen as wholesome entertainment and instruction in language and culture for the youth of the community, which was even more cut off during the depression from the culture of interior Mexico.

Besides providing the environment for this important community theater movement, San Antonio was also the center for the Hispanic circus and tent-theater industry in the United States. Circus and theater had been associated together since colonial days in Mexico, but during the nineteenth century there developed a humble, poor man's circus that traveled the poor neighborhoods of Mexico City and the provinces. It would set up a small tent, or *carpa*, to house its performances; later these theaters were called carpas by extension of the term. It was in the carpa during the revolution that the Mexican national clown, the pelado developed. In general, besides offering all types of serious and light theatrical fare, the carpa came to be known for satirical revistas that often featured the antics and working-class philosophy and humor of the pelado. The carpas functioned quite often as popular tribunals, repositories of folk wisdom, humor, and music, and were incubators of Mexican comic types and stereotypes. They continued to function in this way in the Southwest, but particularly in San Antonio, which had become, especially after the outbreak of the revolution, a home base and wintering ground for many of the carpas.

Probably because of their small size, bare-bones style, and organization around a family unit, the carpas could manage themselves better than large circuses or theatrical companies. Furthermore, they were able to cultivate smaller audiences in the most remote areas. The carpas became in the Southwest an important Mexican American popular culture institution. Their comic routines became a sounding board for the culture conflict that Mexican Americans felt in language usage, assimilation to American tastes and life-styles, discrimination in the United States, and *pocho,* or Americanized status, in Mexico. Out of these types of conflicts in popular entertainment arose the stereotype of the pachuco, a typically Mexican American figure. Finally, the carpas were a refuge for theatrical and circus people of all types during the Great Depression, repatriation, and World War II. More important, their cultural arts were preserved by the carpas for the postwar generation that was to forge a new relationship with the larger American culture.

From the turn of the century through World War II, San Antonio was home to many carpas. Two of the most well known resident tent shows of San Antonio were the Carpa García and the Carpa Cubana, whose descendants still reside in the Alamo City. The Carpa García was founded by Manuel V. García, a native of Saltillo, Mexico. He relocated his family

The García girls chorus line from the Carpa García tent show.

to San Antonio in 1914, after having performed with the Carpa Progresista in Mexico. Featured in his Carpa García was the famed *charro* (Mexican-style cowboy) on the tightrope act. One of the comic actors of the carpa, Pedro González González ("Ramirín"), later had a successful career in Hollywood Westerns. Other members of the family performed magic, ventriloquism, song and dance, and comedy. The highlight of the show was the peladito Don Fito. As played by Manuel's son Rodolfo, Don Fito became a typical wise guy from the streets of west San Antonio, speaking an urban Mexican American dialect, or *caló.* He also satirized the language of Mexicans and pachucos and often engaged audiences in repartee. The Carpa García at times also hosted Don Lalo (Lao Astol) and the famous singer Lydia Mendoza and her family of performers. Daughter Esther García, an acrobat, went on to the center ring of the Barnum and Bailey Circus. By 1947, the Carpa García decided to retire after a final run-in with the fire department about making its tents fireproof.

In Latin American and U.S. circus history, the Abreu name appears frequently at the end of the nineteenth century and beginning of the twentieth. The Abreu company, directed by Virgilio Abreu, owned and operated the Carpa Cubana—also known as the Cuban Show and the Circo Cubano—that made San Antonio its home base in the 1920s and 1930s. But before that, various members of the family had appeared as acrobats, tumblers, and wire walkers with such famous shows as Orrin, Barnum and Bailey, Ringling Brothers, John Robinson, and Sells-Floto. In San Antonio the Cuban circus included trapeze artists, rope walkers, jugglers, clowns, dancers, and its own ten-piece band. Although based in San Antonio, the company toured as far as California and central Mexico by truck and train, but mostly limited its tours to the Rio Grande Valley in the south and Austin to the north during the 1930s. Virgilio Abreu and his wife, Federica, owned a home on the west side of San Antonio but lived in tents with the rest of the company when on the road. The company would tour for four or five months in the spring until summer heat set in and then not leave San Antonio again until the fall, returning home for the Christmas season. The members of the company would also do variety acts in the local San Antonio cinemas.

New York City

It was during the 1890s in New York that regular amateur and semiprofessional shows began, as the Hispanic community, made up mostly of Spaniards and Cubans, was growing in size, reflecting the patterns of internal conflict in the homeland and immigration to the United States that would be repeated time and again during the development of Hispanic communities and culture in the United States. In the 1890s New York became an organizing and staging center for Cuban, Puerto Rican, and Dominican expatriates seeking for the independence of their homeland from Spain. Later in the century, heavy migration of Puerto Ricans, now U.S. citizens, and the Puerto Rican nationalist movement in pursuit of independence from the United States also manifested itself on the city's Hispanic stages, as did the efforts by exiled Spanish Republicans fighting fascism during the Spanish Civil War in the mid thirties.

Documentary evidence of the Hispanic stage in New York begins in 1892 with *La patria* newspaper reporting on the dramatic activities of actor Luis Baralt and his company. Until 1898, the year of the Spanish-American War, this newspaper which supported the Cuban revolutionary movement, occasionally covered performances by Baralt and his troupe, which included both amateurs and actors with professional experience. The company had an irregular performance schedule in such auditoriums and halls as the Berkeley Lyceum and the Carnegie Lyceum,

Don Fito, the Carpa García tent show.

where it presented standard Spanish melodramas as well as Cuban plays, such as *De lo vivo a lo pintado* (*From Life to the Painted Version*), by Tomás Mendoza, a deceased hero of the revolutionary war, and *La fuga de Evangelina* (*The Escape of Evangelina*), by an unknown author, the dramatization of an escape from prison by a heroine of the independence movement. The last performance reported took place at the Central Opera House on January 16, 1899; funds were raised for the sepulcher of the great Cuban philosopher-poet and revolutionary José Martí. After this last performance there is no further mention in surviving newspapers of theatrical performances in Spanish until the advent of a truly professional stage some 17 years later in 1916.

Unlike the theatrical experience of Los Angeles, San Antonio and Tampa, in the mid-teens of the new century, the New York Hispanic community could not claim any theaters of its own. Rather, a number of impresarios rented available theaters around town, but mainly those located in the Broadway area, from midtown Manhattan up to the eighties: Bryant Hall, Park Theater, Amsterdam Opera House, Leslie Theater, Carnegie Hall, and so forth. The first impresario to lead companies on this odyssey through New York theater houses was a Spanish actor-singer of zarzuelas (Spanish operettas) who had made his debut in Mexico City in 1904: Manuel Noriega. Noriega became a figure in New York who in many ways was comparable to Romualdo Tirado in Los Angeles. Like the Los Angeles actor, theater owner, and movie producer Romualdo Tirado, he was a tireless and enthusiastic motivator of Hispanic theater, and for a number of years he had practically the sole responsibility for maintaining Spanish-language theatrical seasons. Like Tirado, he became one of the first impresarios to establish a Hispanic motion picture company. Also like Tirado, Noriega's genius as a comic actor could always be relied upon to bring in audiences during difficult financial straits. Noriega found his way to New York in 1916 from the Havana stage to perform with another singer, the famous and charming María Conesa, at the Amsterdam Theater. That very same year he founded the first of his many theatrical companies, Compañía Dramática Española, which performed at the Leslie Theater from June to September and then went on to other theaters in the city. In Noriega's repertoire was the typical fare of Spanish comedies, zarzuelas, and comic afterpieces. During the first two years, Noriega had difficulty in getting the Hispanic community out to the theater, so much so that a community organization, the Unión Benéfica Española had to have a fund-raiser for his poverty-stricken actors. It was in 1918 at the Amsterdam Opera House that Noriega's company began finding some stability, performing each Sunday, with an occasional special performance on Thursdays. By November of that year the company was so successful that it added matinee showings on Sundays, and by December it began advertising in the newspaper for theatrical artists. As Noriega hired on more actors, mostly Cuban, Spanish, and Mexican, the nature of the company began to change, at times highlighting Galician or Catalonian works, at others Cuban blackface comedy. In 1919, Noriega formed a partnership with Hispanic, Greek, and Anglo-American businessmen to lease the Park Theater and make it the premier Hispanic house, rebaptizing it El Teatro Español. After a short performance run all the parties concerned bailed out of the bad business deal; the Noriega company went on to other theaters to perform in its usual manner until 1921, when Noriega slipped from sight.

The 1920s saw a rapid expansion of the Hispanic stage in New York, which was now regularly drawing touring companies from Cuba, Spain, Mexico, and the Southwest and which had also developed many of its own resident companies. Most of the companies followed the pattern of renting theaters for their runs and relocating afterward to different neighborhoods or to Brooklyn, New York, Bayonne, or Jersey City, New Jersey, or even Philadelphia. Beginning in 1922, the Hispanic community was able to lay claim to several houses on a long-term basis, at times even renaming the theaters in honor of the Hispanic community. The first two theaters that began to stabilize Hispanic theater culture in New York were the Dalys and the Apollo. After 1930, the Apollo no longer offered Hispanic fare; the leadership then passed in 1931 to the San José/Variedades, in 1934 to the Campoamor, and finally in 1937 to the most important and longest-lived house in the history of Hispanic theater in New York: El Teatro Hispano.

As in the Southwest, these houses also experienced the same evolution of Hispanic theater in which melodrama and zarzuela reigned at the beginning of the 1920s to be gradually displaced by musical revues and vaudeville, while in the 1930s artists of serious drama took refuge in clubs and mutualist societies—rarely in church auditoriums as in the Southwest. However, the kind of musical revue that was to rein supreme in New York was not the Mexican revista, but the *obra bufa cubana,* or Cuban blackface farce, which featured the stock character types of the *negrito* (blackface), *mulata,* and (Galician) and relied heavily on Afro-Cuban song and dance and improvised slapstick comedy. Like the revistas, the obras bufas cubanas often found inspiration in current events, neighborhood gossip, and even politics. The most famous of all the *bufos,* Arquímides Pous, who played in New York in 1921, was the creator of more than 200 of these obras, many of which were kept alive by his followers after his death in Puerto Rico in 1926. Pous, who always played the negrito, was famous for his social satire and especially his attacks on racism. The bufo genre itself had been influenced in its development during the second half of the nineteenth century by the *buffes parisiennes* and the Cuban circus. Under Spanish rule in Cuba, the bufos were particularly repressed for being native Cuban, causing many of them to go into exile in Puerto Rico, Santo Domingo, or Mexico.

Beginning in 1932, the Mt. Morris Theater (inaugurated in 1913) began serving the Hispanic community under a series of various impresarios and names, first as the Teatro Campoamor, then the Teatro Cervantes, and on August 19, 1937, finally metamorphosing into El Teatro Hispano, which lived on into the 1950s. A somewhat mysterious Mexican impresario who never used his first names, Señor del Pozo, surfaced at the head of a group of backers made up of Hispanic and Jewish businessmen. Del Pozo administered the theater and directed the house orchestra. Under Del Pozo, besides movies, the Teatro Hispano offered three daily shows at 2:00, 5:30, and 9:00 P.M., except Sundays, when four shows were given. To maintain the interest of his working-class audiences, Del Pozo instituted a weekly schedule that included bonuses and surprises: on Tuesdays and Fridays banco was played at the theater and prizes were awarded, Wednesday audiences participated in talent shows that were broadcast over radio WHOM, on Thursdays gifts and favors were distributed to audiences, and on Saturday mornings there was a special children's show. There were also occasional beauty contests, turkey raffles, and such. Weekly programs changed on Friday evenings and were billed as debuts. Del Pozo used the radio, his weekly playbills, and personal appearances to promote the theater as a family institution and himself as a great paternal and kindly protector of the community.

Upon opening in August 1937, Del Pozo immediately began to elaborate the formula of alternating shows relating to the diverse Hispanic nationalities represented in the community. For one week he played to the Puerto Ricans with the revue *En las playas de Borinquen* (*On the Shores of Puerto Rico*); then he followed in September with an Afro-Caribbean revue, *Fantasía en blanco y negro* (*Fantasy in Black and White*) and then *De México vengo* (*I Come from Mexico*); this was followed by the Compañía de Comedias Argentinas, then a week celebrating Puerto Rico's historic proclamation of independence, El Grito de Lares; by the end of September Del Pozo was again announcing Cuban week, featuring a *Cuba Bella* (*Beautiful Cuba*) revue. Each week a movie was shown to coincide with the country featured in the revue or plays.

In the months and years that ensued, numerous revues and an occasional zarzuela were staged, always balancing out the ethnic nationality represented. The Puerto Rican negrito Antonio Rodríguez and the Cuban negrito Edelmiro Borras became very popular and were ever present. The cast at the Teatro Hispano was constantly being reinforced by refugees from the Spanish Civil War, such as Rosita Rodrigo of the Teatro Cómico de Barcelona, and artists from the failing stages of the Southwest, like La Chata Noloesca and even Romualdo Tirado. By 1940, the Teatro Hispano had fixed its relationship to the predominantly working-class community, which by now was becoming Puerto Rican in majority.

Unlike the theaters in Los Angeles, the Teatro Hispano and the other theaters did not sponsor playwriting contests nor support the development of a local dramatic literature. While the dramatic activity was intense in New York City, the Big Apple did not support a downtown center where five or six major Hispanic houses located side by side competed with each other on a daily basis, as did the theaters in Los Angeles. Unlike the communities in the Southwest, the community of Hispanic immigrants in New York was not cognizant of a resident Hispanic tradition. And, while the relationship between journalism and playwriting had been well established in Mexico and the Southwest, this does not seem to have been the case in Cuba, Puerto Rico, or Spain. Then, too, many playwrights had been drawn to Los Angeles to work in the Hispanic film industry. And finally, the New York Hispanic public was not as large as Los Angeles' during the 1920s and could not support so large a business as the theater represented in the City of Angels.

By far the most productive playwrights and librettists in New York were the Cubans, especially those riding the crest of popularity of the irreverent, bawdy, satirical obras bufas cubanas. Of these, the most prolific and popular were Alberto O'Farrill and Juan C. Rivera. The former was a successful blackface comic and literary personality who edited the weekly "Gráfico" newspaper and produced zarzuelas and obras bufas cubanas based on Afro-Cuban themes. All of them debuted at the Apollo Theater. Juan C. Rivera was a comic actor who often played the role of the gallego and is known to have written both melodramas and revistas. Only a few of the works by these authors are known by name; it is assumed that they produced a considerable body of works to be staged by the companies in which they acted.

While it is true that Cubans and Spaniards made up the majority of theater artists in New York City and that their works dominated the stage in the 1920s and 1930s, it is also true that Puerto Rican drama emerged at this time and, it seems, accounts for a more serious and substantial body of literature. Two of the first Puerto Rican playwrights appear to have been socialists whose dramas supported the Spanish republican cause and working-class movements: José Enamorado Cuesta (1892–1976) and Franca de Armiño (a pseudonym). Of the former, all that is known is that *La prensa* on May 22, 1937, called him a revolutionary writer when it covered his play *El pueblo en marcha* (*The People on the March*). Of Franca de Armiño, all we have is her published drama *Los hipócritas* (*The Hypocrits*), whose notes and introduction reveal that she was the author of various other plays, essays, and poems, and that *Los hipócritas* was staged in 1933 at the Park Palace Theater. The play, which begins with the stock market crash, sets a Romeo and Juliet story to the background of the Spanish Civil War and the foreground of conflict between the workers and management at a shoe factory. While full of propaganda, Marxist theory, and stereotyped characters, *Los hipócritas* is a gripping and entertaining play that reflects the tenor of the times.

While Franca de Armiño and José Enamorado Cuesta were calling for a workers' revolution, Gonzalo O'Neill was championing Puerto Rican nationalism and independence from the United States. Immediately upon graduation from Puerto Rico's Instituto Civil, O'Neill moved to New York, where he became a very successful businessman and somewhat of a protector and godfather to newly arrived Puerto Rican immigrants. A published poet and literary group organizer as a youth in Puerto Rico, he continued his literary vocation in New York by writing poetry and plays, some of which he published. From his very first published dramatic work, *La indiana borinqueña* (1922, *The Indians of Puerto Rico*), O'Neill revealed himself to be intensely patriotic and interested in Puerto Rican independence. His second published play, *Moncho Reyes* (1923), was a three-act biting satire of the current colonial government in Puerto Rico. Although both of these works enjoyed stage productions, it was his third play, *Bajo una sola bandera* (1928, *Under Just One Flag*), which debuted at the Park Palace Theater in New York in 1928 and at the Teatro Municipal in San Juan in 1929, that deserves the greatest attention for its artistry and thought, which also made it a popular vehicle for the Puerto Rican nationalist cause. In *Bajo una sola bandera* the political options facing Puerto Rico are personified in down-to-earth flesh-and-blood characters. The plot deals with the daughter of a middle-class Puerto Rican family residing in New York who must choose between a young American second lieutenant—the personification of the United States and military rule—and a young native Puerto Rican, whom she really loves. Both parents oppose each other in their preferences. Of course, the Puerto Rican youth wins the day and the play ends with sonorous, patriotic verses that underline the theme of independence for Puerto Rico. Although O'Neill is sure to have written other plays, the only other title that is known, *Amoríos borincanos* (*Puerto Rican Episodes of Love*), appeared at the Teatro Hispano in 1938; O'Neill was one of the investors in the theater.

Most of the other Puerto Rican and Hispanic playwrights of New York were minor in comparison to these and to the highly productive writers in Los Angeles. The true legacy of the New York Hispanic stage was its cosmopolitan nature and its ability to represent and solidify an ethnically diverse Hispanic community.

Tampa, Florida

In the late nineteenth century, the Tampa area witnessed the transplant of an entire industry from abroad and the development of a Hispanic immigration enclave that chose the theater as its favorite form of art and culture. To remove themselves from the hostilities attendant on the Cuban war for independence from Spain, to come closer to their primary markets and avoid import duties, and to try to escape the labor unrest that was endemic to this particular industry, various cigar manufacturers from Cuba began relocating to Tampa. In the swampy, mosquito-infested lands just east of Tampa, Ybor City was founded in 1886. By the 1890s, the Spanish and Cuban tobacco workers had begun establishing mutual aid societies and included theaters as centerpieces for the buildings they constructed to house these societies. Many of these theaters eventually hosted professional companies on tour from Cuba and Spain, but, more importantly, they became the forums where both amateurs and resident professionals entertained the Hispanic community for more than 40 years without interruption. These theaters were also the training grounds where numerous tobacco workers and other community people developed into professional and semiprofessional artists, some of whom were able to make their way to the Hispanic stages of New York, Havana, and Madrid. Also, Tampa played a key role in one of the most exciting chapters of American theater history: it was the site of the Federal Theater Project's only Hispanic company under the Works Progress Administration.

Unlike Los Angeles, San Antonio, and New York, there was very little truly commercial theatrical activity in the Tampa-Ybor City communities. The six most important mutual aid societies—Centro Español, Centro Español de West Tampa, Centro Asturiano, Círculo Cubano, Centro Obrero, and Unión Martí-Maceo—each maintained a *comisión de espectáculos* (show committee) to govern the use of their theaters, a task that included renting the theater to touring companies and others, scheduling events, hiring professional directors, scenographers and technicians, and even purchasing performance rights to theatrical works. Along with this comisión, which obviously took on the theater management role, most of the societies also supported a *sección de declamación,* or amateur theatrical company, made up mostly of the society's members. For a good part of each year the company rehearsed on week nights and performed on Sundays. For the most part, the audiences were made up of tobacco workers and their families. The tobacco workers prided themselves on their literary and artistic tastes; they were considered an intellectual or elite labor class that had gained an informal education from the professional *lectores* (readers) they hired to read aloud to them from literary masterpieces, newspapers, and other matter while they rolled cigars. Neither the demanding audiences nor the managing committees were satisfied by strictly amateurish renditions, especially since they could compare performances with those of the professional companies that often visited their theaters. It therefore became the custom to recruit and hire professional actors and directors from Havana to train and direct the resident sección de declamación, which was paid for its performances. Over the years, numerous professional artists either settled in Tampa or were recruited to become part of the companies. But Tampa's Hispanic societies also prepared such important actors as Manuel Aparicio, Cristino R. Inclán, and Velia Martínez, who later abandoned the cigar factories to dedicate themselves completely to the world of the footlights and marquees. By the 1920s, a good number of the local artists considered themselves professionals and demanded reasonable salaries for their performances.

Of the six societies, the Centro Asturiano was the

The cover of a program for the performance of an operetta at the Centro Español in 1919.

most important and the longest-lived; in fact, it is still functioning today as a theater, hosting theater and even opera companies. While the Centro Español of Ybor City was the oldest society—founded in 1891 (the Asturiano in 1902)—and for a time the most prestigious, the Asturiano held the distinction of hosting in its 1,200-seat, first-class theater some of the greatest names in Hispanic theater in the world and even opera companies from New York and Italy during the period before World War II; and it was to the Centro Asturiano that Spain's first lady of the stage, María Guerrero, took her company in 1926. That was a stellar year in which, besides producing the works of its own stock company directed by Manuel Aparicio, the Asturiano also hosted the Manhattan Grand Opera Association. But the socially progressive, even liberal, Centro Asturiano—it extended its membership to all Latins, even Cubans and Italians—held the further distinction of housing the only Spanish-language Federal Theater Project (FTP).

It was during the tenure of the FTP, for 18 months in 1936 and 1937, that the Centro Asturiano made American theater history by housing the only Hispanic unit of the Works Progress Administration's (WPA's) national project. It is a chapter in which the two theatrical traditions, the Hispanic and the Anglo-American, which had existed side by side for so long, finally intersected to produce at times exciting theater but also examples of cultural misunderstanding. From the start, the FTP administration's attitude seems to have been a model of condescension and, ultimately, the Hispanic unit had to disband because of congressional xenophobia.

It is somewhat ironic that Hispanic units were not created in Los Angeles or New York, where there was far greater Hispanic theatrical activity of a professional nature and more in line with the main purposes of the WPA. But in all of the documents of the FTP there is no mention of Hispanic theater outside Tampa and there seems to have been no awareness at all of the remarkable activities documented previously. The project's basic objective of creating work-relief theater of a relevant nature would best have been served where the full-time professionals were suffering unemployment, not in Tampa, where many of the artists still gained a good part of their living rolling cigars. Commercial Hispanic companies were suffering the ravages of the Great Depression in Los Angeles, San Antonio, and to some extent New York; Hispanic actors were hungry in these cities and many of them could not even raise the money to return to their homeland.

The activities sponsored under the FTP were not much different from what was already ongoing in

A full house at the Centro Asturiano in 1937.

Tampa's Hispanic theater. The project hired Manuel Aparicio to direct the Hispanic unit in the production of what was for the most part a repertoire of well-worn zarzuelas and revistas. The greatest difference was brought about, however, by the infusion of capital for scenery, properties, and costumes, which were all new and first-rate. And, even more significant, the Hispanic actors became integrated for the first time into the shows of the Tampa FTP vaudeville unit and, in general, began to associate more and more with non-Hispanic artists and personnel. It must be stated, however, that when it came time for that integrated vaudeville unit to perform at the Centro Asturiano, the FTP was not able to get Anglos to cross the tracks to see the show. In all, the Hispanic unit of the FTP produced 14 shows in Spanish in 42 performances for more than 23,000 spectators. The unit achieved its greatest success with *El mundo en la mano* (*The World in His Hand*), a revista written by Aparicio and the entire company, which was a musical tour through Spain, Cuba, Italy, Mexico, and China. It was so popular that additional performances were scheduled and the revue even toured in the area and down to Miami. The nadir was the production in Spanish of Sinclair Lewis' *It Can't Happen Here,* which was all but forced on the company in an awkwardly literal translation in an equally awkward attempt to synchronize the production opening with the national debut.

The Hispanic community was very proud of its unit and of its leading man and director, Manuel Aparicio, who was selected to attend a conference of FTP directors in Poughkeepsie, New York. But the FTP administrators, who always referred to the Hispanic unit as one of the strongest in the South, took pride in having successfully "brought" theater to the Hispanics; they also decried the Spanish-speakers backwardness, or fawned at their quaint habits. Ultimately, because of language differences and misunderstandings about citizenship, the Hispanic unit lost 25 of its members in 1937 when Congress passed the ERA Act (Emergency Relief Administration), which effectively removed foreigners from the WPA. Included among these was director Manuel Aparicio. Other members, such as Chela Martínez, were lost when they were decertified because their family income was too high. The remaining citizens were integrated into the "American" vaudeville company of the federal project. The Hispanic unit had met its end.

A unique theatrical experience was that of the Unión Martí-Maceo, Tampa's Afro-Cuban mutual aid society, whose very existence resulted from the doubly segregationist forces of the Jim Crow South and Cuba's own racism. While the union hosted many of the same theater companies touring to Tampa and also sponsored performances by its own and the other society's secciones de declamación, the union's theatrical and cultural activities were rarely covered in the press, rarely attracted audiences from the Hispanic "white" population, and, on the whole, were hardly integrated into the social life of the Hispanic, the Anglo American, or the black communities. In the archives of the union, however, are plays and fragments of plays that provide some interesting glimpses into the nature of the theatrical performances of this society. Two of these works, a one-act play, *Hambre* (*Hunger*), and the obra bufa cubana *Los novios* (*The Betrothed*), are notable for their relevance to the social and economic ambience of the Martí-Maceo. *Hambre* is a gripping and angry social drama that protests the poverty and hunger suffered by the working class while the rich enjoy the life of luxury. *Los novios,* a much lighter and more entertaining play with mistaken identities and ridiculously complex love triangles, also deals with the supposed trespassing of race and class barriers and miscegenation. A buffoon of a Galician servant and a negrito spread mistaken information about the landowner having illicitly fathered a mulata and the landowner's daughter being caught embracing a black. The play also includes asides that elaborate on race relations, and throughout the negrito and the mulata maintain the greatest dignity in the play, with the upper-class whites shown to be the most bungling and prejudiced. In the end, order is restored when everyone finds his rightful place and his rightful partner to marry. But the social satire from a black perspective is unmistakable.

Another society that offered a unique theatrical experience was the Centro Obrero, the headquarters for the Union of Tampa Cigarmakers, which served as a gathering place for workers and as a vehicle to promote their culture. Through its various classes, workshops, publications, and other activities, the Centro Obrero promoted unionism and, quite often, socialism. While the Centro Obrero also hosted touring and local companies and even frivolous shows of obras bufas cubanas, it was within its halls and auspices that plays were developed and shown that

A scene from *El niño judio* at the Centro Asturiano.

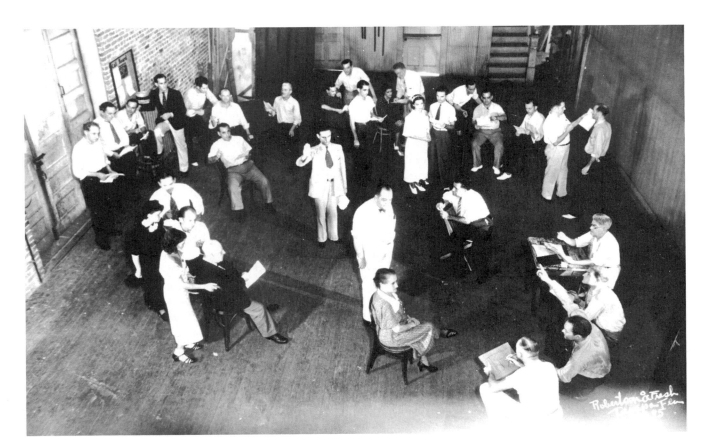

Manuel Aparicio, at center, directing a rehearsal of Sinclair Lewis' *It Can't Happen Here* in Spanish at the Centro Asturiano.

promoted workers' interests, using their dialect and ideology. In the Centro's weekly newspapers, *El Internacional* and *La Federación,* various of these plays were published, including *Julia y Carlota* (*Julia and Carlota*), in which Julia exhorts Carlota to break the bonds of family and religion that are meant to keep women in their place, oppressed, and divorced from politics so that they do not help to reform evil laws. Other works were clearly agitational and propagandistic, attempting to inspire workers to action. Finally, the Centro Obrero went all out to support the republican cause in the Spanish Civil War. It sponsored numerous fund-raising performances of such plays as *Milicianos al Frente* (*Militia to the Front*), *Abajo Franco* (*Down with Franco*), and *Las luchas de hoy* (*The Struggles of Today*), all of unknown authorship.

There are thus many parallels that can be drawn between the Tampa Hispanic stage and the Hispanic theater as it flourished in the Southwest and New York: the relationship of the theater to politics and to patterns of immigration; the dominance of the Spanish zarzuela and melodrama, eventually ceding to more popular forms, such as the revista and the obra bufa cubana; the effects of the Great Depression; the role theater played in protecting Hispanic cultural values and the Spanish language and in the education of the youth; the isolation of Hispanic culture and theater from the larger society, and so on. But Tampa's Hispanic theatrical experience was unique in that it provided a successful example of deep and lasting community support for theater arts, so deep and so strong that private enterprise could not compete with the efforts of the mutual aid societies. And because the Hispanic stage had become such a symbol of achievement, that legacy lives on today in the memory of the Tampeños, in the Hispanic theatrical groups that still exist there and in such actresses as Velia Martínez who still are enjoying careers on the stage and in film.

✱ POST WORLD WAR II TO THE PRESENT

The Southwest

The post-World War II period has seen the gradual restoration of the amateur, semiprofessional, and professional stages in the Hispanic communities of the Southwest. From the 1950s on, repertory theaters have appeared throughout the Southwest to pro-

Manuel Aparicio in Jacinto Benavente's *La Malquerida*.

duce Latin American, Spanish, and American plays in Spanish translations. In San Antonio, the extraordinary efforts of such actors as Lalo Astol, La Chata Noloesca, and her daughter Velia Camargo were responsible for keeping plays and vaudeville routines alive in the communities, even if they had to be presented for free or at fund-raisers. Actors like Lalo Astol made the transition to radio and television, usually as announcers, at times as writers and producers. Astol even wrote, directed, and acted in locally produced television drama during the 1950s and 1960s. In Los Angeles, veteran actor-director Rafael Trujillo-Herrera maintained a theater group, almost continuously during the war and through the 1960s, made up of his drama students and professionals, who quite often performed at a small theater house that he bought, El Teatro Intimo.

While there are a few stories of valiant theater artists managing to keep Hispanic theater alive during the war and postwar years, in most cases the tale is of theater houses that once housed live performances becoming cinemas forever, or at least phasing out live performances during the war and through the 1950s by occasionally hosting small troupes of vaudevillians or subscribing to the extrav-

agant "caravanas de estrellas," or parades of recording stars, that were syndicated and promoted by the recording companies. Through these shows prominaded singers and matinee idols, with former peladitos and other vaudevillians serving as masters of ceremonies and comic relief. Vestiges of this business strategy still survive today in the shows of Mexican recording and movie stars of the moment, which are produced, not at movie houses, but at convention centers and sports and entertainment arenas of large capacity.

The most remarkable story of the stage in the Southwest is the spontaneous appearance in 1965 of a labor theater in the agricultural fields, under the directorship of Luis Valdez, and its creation of a full-blown theatrical movement that conquered the hearts and minds of artists and activists throughout the country. Under the leadership of Luis Valdez's El Teatro Campesino, for almost two decades Chicano theaters dramatized the political and cultural concerns of their communities while crisscrossing the states on tour. The movement, largely student- and worker-based, eventually led to professionalism, Hollywood and Broadway productions, and the creation of the discipline of Chicano theater at universities. In 1965, the modern Chicano theater movement was born when aspiring playwright Luis Valdez left the San Francisco Mime Troupe to join César Chávez in organizing farm workers in Delano, California. Valdez organized the workers into El Teatro Campesino in an effort to popularize and raise funds for the grape boycott and farm-worker strike. From the humble beginning of dramatizing the plight of farm workers, the movement grew to include small, agitation, and propaganda theater groups in communities and on campuses around the country and eventually developed into a total theatrical expression that would find resonance on the commercial stage and screen.

By 1968, Valdez and El Teatro Campesino had left the vineyards and lettuce fields in a conscious effort to create a theater for the Chicano nation, a people which Valdez and other Chicano organizers of the 1960s envisioned as working-class, Spanish-speaking or bilingual, rurally oriented, and with a very strong heritage of pre-Columbian culture. By 1970, El Teatro Campesino had pioneered and developed what would come to be known as *teatro chicano,* a style of agitprop theater that incorporated the spiritual and presentational style of the Italian Renaissance commedia dell'arte with the humor, character types, folklore, and popular culture of the Mexican theater, especially as articulated earlier in the century by the vaudeville companies and tent theaters that had toured the Southwest.

Almost overnight, groups sprang up throughout the United States to continue along Valdez's path. In streets, parks, churches, and schools, Chicanos were spreading a newly found bilingual-bicultural identity through the *actos,* one-act pieces introduced by Valdez that explored all of the issues confronting Mexican Americans: the farm-worker struggle for unionization, the Vietnam War, the drive for bilingual education, community control of parks and schools, the war against drug addiction and crime, and so forth.

El Teatro Campesino's acto, *Los vendidos (The Sell-Outs),* a farcical attack on political manipulation of Chicano stereotypes, became the most popular and imitated of the actos; it could be seen performed by diverse groups from Seattle to Austin. The publication of Actos by Luis Valdez y El Teatro Campesino in 1971, which included *Los vendidos,* placed a ready-made repertoire in the hands of community and student groups and also supplied them with several theatrical and political canons: (1) Chicanos must be seen as a nation with geographic, religious, cultural, and racial roots in Aztlán. Teatros must further the idea of nationalism and create a national theater based on identification with the Amerindian past. (2) The organizational support of the national theater must be from within, for "the corazón de la Raza (the heart of our people) cannot be revolutionized on a grant from Uncle Sam." (3) Most important and valuable of all was the principle that "The teatros must never get away from La Raza. . . . If the Raza will not come to the theater, then the theater must go to the Raza. This, in the long run, will determine the shape, style, content, spirit, and form of el teatro chicano."

El Teatro Campesino's extensive touring, the publicity it gained from the farm-worker struggle, and the publication of *Actos* all effectively contributed to the launching of a national teatro movement. It reached its peak in the summer of 1976 when five teatro festivals were held to commemorate the Anglo bicentennial celebration. The summer's festivals also culminated a period of growth that saw some of Campesino's followers reach a sufficient aesthetic and political maturity to break away from Valdez. Los Angeles' Teatro Urbano, in its mordant satire of American heroes, insisted on intensifying the teatro movement's radicalism in the face of the Campesino's increasing religious mysticism. Santa Barbara's El Teatro de la Esperanza was achieving perfection, as no other Chicano theater had, in working as a collective and in assimilating the teachings of Bertolt Brecht in their plays *Guadalupe* and *La víctima (The Victim).* San Jose's El Teatro de la Gente had taken the corrido-type acto, a structure that sets a mimic ballet to traditional Mexican ballads sung by a singer-narrator, and perfected it as its innovator, El Teatro Campesino, had never done. El Teatro Desengaño del Pueblo from Gary, Indiana, had succeeded in reviving the techniques of the radical theaters of the 1930s in their *Silent Partners,* an expose of corruption in a local city's construction projects.

The greatest contribution of Luis Valdez and El Teatro Campesino was their inauguration of a true grass roots theater movement. Following Valdez's direction, the university students and community people creating teatro held fast to the doctrine of never getting away from the raza, the grass roots Mexican. In so doing they created the perfect vehicle for communing artistically within their culture and environment. At times they idealized and romanticized the language and the culture of the *mexicano* in the United States. But they had discovered a way to mine history, folklore, and religion for those elements that could best solidify the heterogeneous community and sensitize it to class, cultural identity, and politics. This indeed was revolutionary. The creation of art from the folk materials of a people,

A scene from El Teatro Urbano's *Anti-Bicentennial Special* in 1976.

A scene from El Teatro de la Esperanza's production of Rodrigo Duarte Clark's *Brujerías.*

their music, humor, social configurations, and environment, represented the fulfillment of Luis Valdez's vision of a Chicano national theater.

While Campesino, after leaving the farm worker struggle, was able to experiment and rediscover the old cultural forms—the carpas, the corridos, the Virgin of Guadalupe plays, the peladito—it never fully succeeded in combining all the elements it recovered or invented into a completely refined piece of revolutionary art. *La gran carpa de la familia Rascuachi* (*The Tent of the Underdogs*) was a beautiful creation, incorporating the spirit, history, folklore, economy, and music of la raza. However, its proposal for the resolution of material problems through spiritual means (a superimposed construct of Aztec mythology and Catholicism) was too close to the religious beliefs and superstitions that hampered la raza's progress, according to many of the more radical artists and theorists of people's theater.

The reaction of critics and many Chicano theaters playing at the fifth Chicano theater festival, held in Mexico, was so politically and emotionally charged that a rift developed between them and El Teatro Campesino that has never been healed. El Teatro Campesino virtually withdrew from the theater

movement, and from that point on the Chicano theaters developed on their own, managing to exist as agitation and propaganda groups and raggle-taggle troupes until the end of the decade. The more successful theaters, such as El Teatro de la Esperanza, administered their own theater house, created playwriting workshops, and took up leadership of TENAZ, the Chicano theater organization, while taking over El Teatro Campesino's former role as a national touring company. Other groups, such as Albuquerque's La Compañía, set down roots and became more of a repertory company. The decade of the 1980s saw many Chicano theater groups disbanding, as some of their members became involved in local community theaters, with their own performance spaces and budgets supplied by state and local arts agencies.

Such companies as Houston's Teatro Bilingüe, San Antonio's Guadalupe Theater, and Denver's Su Teatro began serving their respective communities as stable, repertory companies. Several former Chicano theater artists successfully made the jump to television and movies, such as Luis Valdez himself. In fact, Valdez's play *Zoot Suit* had a successful two-year run in mainstream theaters in Los Angeles and made its way to a Broadway and a film version. He followed up with stage and television productions of his play *Corridos (Ballads)* and then the overwhelming box office success of his movie *La Bamba*. In 1994, Valdez also made a successful incursion into commercial television, with his writing and directing of *The Cisco Kid* starring Jimmy Smits and Cheech Marín (Valdez had worked with Marín earlier in his movie for PBS, *La pastorela,* which was Valdez's version of the folk play, *The Shepherds*). Other former Chicano theater directors, like Jorge Huerta, became university professors of theater and directors of productions in such mainstream organizations as San Diego's Globe Theater. Thus, while the 1980s saw a disappearance of the grass roots, guerrilla, and street theater movement among Chicanos, these were the years when greater professionalization took place and greater opportunity appeared for Chicano theater people to make a living from their art in community theaters, at universities, and even in the commercial media—the latter facilitated, of course, by the great rise of the Hispanic population and its spending power.

But the decade of the 1980s also saw the emergence of a corps of Chicano and Latino playwrights in communities from coast to coast, as the repertory theaters in the Southwest, New York, and Miami began clamoring for works dealing with Hispanic culture and written in the language of Hispanics in the United States. Numerous playwriting labs, workshops, and contests, such as Joseph Papp's Festival Latino in New York, sprung up from New York to Los Angeles. In the mid 1980s, a major funding organization, the Ford Foundation, took official interest in Hispanic theater and began funding, in a very significant way, not only the theater companies in an effort to stabilize them (including El Teatro de la Esperanza) but also the efforts by mainstream companies and theaters, such as the South Coast Repertory Theater and the San Diego Repertory Theater, to produce Hispanic material and employ Hispanic actors. Furthermore, the Ford Foundation even funded the nation's leading Hispanic press, Arte Público Press, to publish a line of Hispanic play anthologies and collections of works by the leading Hispanic playwrights. By 1991, Arte Público Press had produced a new anthology of plays by Luis Valdez, Milcha Sánchez Scott, Severo Pérez, and others (*Necessary Theater: Six Plays of the Chicano Experience,* edited by Jorge Huerta), as well as anthologies of Hispanic women's plays, Cuban American plays, Puerto Rican plays, and collections by Luis Valdez, Dolores Prida, Edward Gallardo, Iván Acosta, and Carlos Morton. It also reissued its historic (1979) anthology that had been out of print for a decade:

Nuevos Pasos: Chicano and Puerto Rican Theater, edited by Nicolás Kanellos and Jorge Huerta.

While the 1990s saw the stabilization of theater houses and companies in the Southwest, thanks to such funding agencies as the Ford Foundation as well as local and state arts councils, which now recognized Hispanic arts, another outgrowth of Chicano theater became prominent: commercially viable improvisational theater companies. Two such Chicano companies, Culture Clash and Latins Anonymous, appeared in California to resounding success, with Culture Clash even sustaining a television series by the same name for two seasons in the early 1990s. Both groups with seasoned veterans from El Teatro Campesino and other Chicano theaters, based their improvised comic sketches on satirizing stereotypes of Hispanics and poking fun at politics and current events. Latins Anonymous, with lead playwright Rick Nájera, also satirized Hispanic media personalities—there were now enough Hispanic personalities in entertainment and national television for impressions of them to be recognized. Nájera and a new breed of stand-up comedians were also increasingly appearing on television and even in their own HBO specials.

New York City

During the war years and following, serious theater in the Hispanic community waned, as first vaudeville drove it from the commercial stage, as it did the Teatro Hispano, and then, as in the Southwest, the movies and the caravans of musical recording stars began to drive even vaudeville from the stage. Under the leadership of such directors as Marita Reid, Luis Mandret, and Alejandro Elliot, full-length melodramas and realistic plays were able to survive in mutualist societies, church halls, and lodges during the 1940s and 1950s, but only for smaller audiences and for weekend performances. With such attractions as La Chata Noloesca's Mexican company and Puerto Rican vaudevillians, including famed recording star Bobby Capó, vaudeville survived into the early 1960s, playing to the burgeoning working-class audiences of Puerto Ricans. One notable and valiant effort was that of Dominican actor-director Rolando Barrera's group Futurismo, which, for a while during the 1940s, was able to stage four productions a year of European works in Spanish translation at the Master's Auditorium. Beginning in 1950, Edwin Janer's La Farándula Panamericana staged three and four productions a year of classical works, as well as contemporary Spanish, Puerto Rican, and European works at the Master's Auditorium and the Belmont Theater.

In 1953, a play was staged that would have the

most direct and lasting impact ever of any theatrical production in New York's Hispanic community. A young director, Roberto Rodríguez, introduced to a working-class audience at the Church of San Sebastian *La carreta* (*The Oxcart*), by an as yet unknown Puerto Rican writer, René Marqués, after its first production in Puerto Rico. The play, which deals with the dislocation of a family of mountain folk from their farm and their resettling in a San Juan slum and then in New York City, effectively dramatized the epic of Puerto Rican migration to the United States in working-class and mountain dialect. René Marqués went on to celebrity and many more plays and productions in Puerto Rico and the continental United States, but his *La carreta* became a key for building a Puerto Rican and Hispanic theater in New York in that it presented serious dramatic material based on the history, language, and culture of the working-class communities. Roberto Rodríguez joined forces with stage and screen actress Miriam Colón to form El Nuevo Círculo Dramático, which was able to administer a theater space in a loft, Teatro Arena, in Midtown Manhattan. Although there were other minor and short-lived companies, it was El Nuevo Círculo Dramático, along with La Farándula Panamericana, that dominated the New York Hispanic stage into the early 1960s, when two incursions were made into the mainstream: in 1964 Joseph Papp's New York Shakespeare Festival began producing Shakespearean works in Spanish, and in 1965 there was an off-Broadway production of *La carreta,* starring Miriam Colón and Raúl Juliá.

The 1960s also saw the introduction of improvisational street theater similar to Latin American people's theater and Chicano theater, which attempted to raise the level of political consciousness of working-class Hispanics. Among the most well known, although short-lived groups were the following ensembles, which usually developed their material as a collective: El Nuevo Teatro Pobre de las Américas (The New Poor People's Theater of Americas), Teatro Orilla (Marginal Theater), Teatro Guazabara (Whatsamara Theater), and Teatro Jurutungo. But the most interesting of the improvisational troupes, and the only one to survive to the present, has been the Teatro Cuatro, named so for its first location on Fourth Avenue in the lower East Side and made up at first of a diverse group of Puerto Ricans, Dominicans, and other Latin Americans. Under the directorship of an Argentine immigrant, Oscar Ciccone, and his Salvadoran wife, Cecilia Vega, the Teatro Cuatro was one of the most serious troupes, committed to developing a true radical art and to bringing together the popular theater movement of Latin America with that of Hispanics in the United States.

Poster from La Farándula Panamericana theater group's 1954 production of *Los árboles mueren de pie,* starring Marita Reid.

As such, Teatro Cuatro became involved with TENAZ and the Chicano theater movement and with *teatro popular* in Latin America, and sponsored festivals and workshops in New York with some of the leading guerrilla and politically active theatrical directors and companies in the hemisphere. During the late 1970s Teatro Cuatro became officially associated with Joseph Papp's New York Shakespeare Festival and began to organize the biennial Festival Latino, a festival of Hispanic popular theater. Today, Ciccone and Vega manage the Papp organization's Hispanic productions, including the festival and a playwriting contest, while the Teatro Cuatro has gone its own way, functioning as a repertory company in its own remodeled firehouse theater in east Harlem.

The type of theater that has predominated in New York's cosmopolitan Hispanic culture since the 1960s is that which more or less follows the patterns established by the Nuevo Círculo Dramático and the Farándula Panamericana, in which a corps of actors and a director of like mind work as a repertory group in producing works of their choosing in their own

Postcard photograph of the Bronx's Pregones theater company in 1985.

style. Styles and groups have proliferated, so that at any one time over the last 20 to 25 years at least ten groups have existed with different aesthetics and audiences. Among these theaters, many of which have their own houses today, are International Arts Relations (INTAR), Miriam Colón's Puerto Rican Traveling Theater, Teatro Repertorio Español, Nuestro Teatro, Duo, Instituto Arte Teatral (IATE), Latin American Theater Ensemble (LATE), Thalia, Tremont Arte Group, and Pregones. In addition to the reason that New York has over one million Hispanic inhabitants, another reason that so many organizations are able to survive—although many of them do not flourish—is that the state, local, and private institutions that provide financial support for the arts have been generous to the theaters. Compared with that in other cities and states, the financial support for the arts, and theater in particular, in the capital of the U.S. theater world, has been excellent.

The three most important theater companies have been the Puerto Rican Traveling Theater (PRTT), Teatro Repertorio Español, and INTAR. The PRTT, founded in 1967 by Miriam Colón, takes its name from its original identity as a mobile theater that

performed in the streets of Puerto Rican neighborhoods. At first, it performed works by some of the leading Puerto Rican writers, such as René Marqués, José Luis González, and Pedro Juan Soto, alternating Spanish-language performances with English-language ones. The company also produced Latin American and Spanish works and in the early 1970's pioneered productions of works by Nuyorican (New York Rican) and other U.S. Hispanic authors, such as those of Jesús Colón and Piri Thomas. In addition to its mobile unit, the theater maintained a laboratory theater and children's theater classes. Its most important development came in 1974 when it took over and remodeled an old firehouse in the Broadway area, on Forty-seventh Street, and opened its permanent theater house. To this day, the PRTT provides the stage, audience, and developmental work for New York Hispanic playwrights, such as Jaime Carrero, Edward Gallardo, Manuel Ramos Otero, Pedro Pietri, and Dolores Prida.

Founded in 1969 as an offshoot of Las Artes by exiled members of Cuba's Sociedad Pro Arte, the Teatro Repertorio Español has grown into the only Hispanic theater in the nation specializing in the production of both classical Spanish works, such as

Calderon's *La vida es sueño* and Zorrilla's *Don Juan Tenorio,* and works by contemporary authors from Latin America. It is also one of the few companies in the nation to also stage nineteenth-century zarzuelas. Operating today out of a theater, the Gramercy Arts Theater, which has a tradition of Spanish-language performances that goes back to the 1920s, the Teatro Repertorio Español caters both to educational as well as community-based audiences, with productions in both Spanish and English. It is the only New York Hispanic theater to tour around the country. This is possible because, of the major Hispanic companies in New York, the Teatro Repertorio Español is the only one still working basically as an ensemble, while the others are production companies that hold open auditions for all of their parts.

INTAR was founded in 1967 as ADAL (Latin American Art Group), dedicated to producing works by Latin American authors. By 1977, under the name INTAR the company had achieved equity status as a professional theater. After converting a variety of structures into theater spaces, the company currently occupies a theater on West Forty-second Street near the Broadway theater district. Under the direction of Max Ferra, the company has offered workshops for actors and directors, and staged readings for playwrights and a children's theater. Today INTAR is known for its production of classical works in new settings and innovative directing, such as María Irene Fornés' *La vida es sueño* (*Life Is a Dream*) and Dolores Prida's *Crisp,* based on Jacinto Benavente's *Los intereses creados* (*Vested Interests*). INTAR also presents works in English, including some standard non-Hispanic fare. INTAR has been particularly instrumental in developing Hispanic playwriting through its playwright's laboratory and readings, quite often following up with full productions of plays by local writers.

While the Hispanic theatrical environment in New York has been of necessity cosmopolitan and has lent itself to the creation of companies with personnel from all of the Spanish-speaking countries, there have been groups that have set out to promote the work and culture of specific nationalities, such as the Puerto Ricans, Cubans, Dominicans, and Spaniards. Most notable, of course, has been the Puerto Rican Traveling Theater, but also the Centro Cultural Cubano was instrumental in the 1970s in developing Cuban theatrical expression, most significantly in producing the work of Omar Torres and Iván Acosta. Acosta's play *El super* (*The Super*), has been the biggest hit to ever come out of a Hispanic company and even led to a prize-winning film adaptation. And, in general, Cuban American theater is well represented in almost all the Hispanic compa-

The elaborate costuming of a Miami production of José Zorilla's *Don Juan Tenorio.*

nies of New York, with Dolores Prida, Iván Acosta, Manuel Martín, and Omar Torres included among the most successful playwrights.

Puerto Rican playwriting is also well represented at most of the Hispanic companies, but during the 1960s an important new focus developed among New York Puerto Ricans that had long-lasting implications for the creation of theater and art in Hispanic working-class communities; it was called Nuyorican (New York Rican), meaning that it emerged from the artists born or raised among New York's Puerto Rican working classes. Nuyorican theater is not a specific form of theater per se. It has included such diverse theatrical genres as collectively created street theater as well as works by individual playwrights produced in such diverse settings as the Puerto Rican Traveling Theater, the Henry Street Settlement's New Federal Theater, Joseph Papp's New York Shakespeare Festival, and on Broadway itself. Although the term was first applied to literature and theater by playwright-novelist Jaime Carrero in the late 1960s and finds some stylistic and thematic development in his plays *Noo Jall* (a wordplay on the Spanish pronunciation of "New York" and "jail") and *Pipo Subway no sabe reír*

(*Pipo Subway Doesn't Know How to Laugh*), it was a group of playwright-poets associated with the Nuyorican Poets' Café and Joseph Papp that first defined and came to exemplify Nuyorican theater. Included in the group were Miguel Algarín, Lucky Cienfuegos, Tato Laviera, and Miguel Piñero, all of whom focused their bilingual works on the life and culture of working-class Puerto Ricans in New York. Two members of the group, Lucky Cienfuegos and Miguel Piñero, were ex-convicts who had begun their writing careers while incarcerated, and they chose to develop their dramatic material from prison, street, and underclass culture. Algarín, a university professor and proprietor of the Nuyorican Poets' Café, created a more avant-garde aura for the collective, while the virtuoso bilingual poet Tato Laviera contributed lyricism and a folk and popular culture base. It was Piñero's work (and life), however, that became most celebrated; his prison drama *Short Eyes* won an Obie and the New York Drama Critics Best American Play Award for the 1973–74 season. His success, coupled with that of fellow Nuyorican writers ex-convict Piri Thomas and street urchin Pedro Pietri, often resulted in Nuyorican literature and theater's being associated with a stark naturalism and the themes of crime, drugs, abnormal sexuality, and generally aberrant behavior. This led to a reaction against the term by many writers and theater companies that were in fact emphasizing Puerto Rican working-class culture in New York. Today there is a new generation of New York Puerto Rican playwrights who were nurtured on the theater of Piñero and the Nuyoricans and who have also experienced greater support and opportunities for developing their work. They quite often repeat and reevaluate many of the concerns and the style and language of the earlier group, but with a sophistication and polish that has come from drama workshops, playwright residencies, and university education. Among these are Juan Shamsul Alam, Edward Gallardo, Federico Fraguada, Richard Irizarry, Yvette Ramírez, and Cándido Tirado, most of whom have had their works included in the historic anthology *Recent Puerto Rican Theater: Five Plays from New York* (1991), edited by John Antush.

Florida

Today Hispanic theater still finds one of its centers in Florida. However, most of the theatrical activity in Tampa has disappeared, with only the Spanish Repertory Theater continuing to perform in the old playhouses (Centro Asturiano) with a fare that varies from the standard zarzuelas to Broadway musicals in Spanish. With the exodus of refugees from the Cuban Revolution of 1959, Hispanic theater in Florida found a new center in Miami, where the Cuban expatriates—many from middle-class or upper-class backgrounds and used to supporting live theater in Cuba—founded and supported theater companies and laid fertile ground for the support of playwrights. During the last 30 years the type of theater that has predominated in Miami has produced standard works from throughout the Spanish-speaking world and from the theater of exile, which is burdened with attacking communism in Cuba and promoting a nostalgia for the pre-Castro past. While the Cuban playwrights of New York, many of whom have been raised and educated in the United States, have forged an avant-garde and openly Cuban *American* theater, the Miami playwrights have been more traditional in form and content and, of course, more politically conservative. Most frequent in the exile theater is the form and style inherited from the theater of the absurd, from theatrical realism, and, to some extent, from the comic devices and characters of the teatro bufo cubano; however, the predominant attitude among Cuban exile playwrights is the intellectual one, the creation of a theater of ideas. The exile playwrights whose works are most produced in Miami are Julio Matas, José Cid Pérez, Leopoldo Hernández, José Sánchez Boudy, Celedonio González, Raúl de Cárdenas, and Matías Montes Huidobro. An effort to bring together some of these with some of the newer voices, such as that of Miami's Miguel González Pando, is Rodolfo Cortina's important anthology *Cuban American Theater* (1991), in which exile theater is considered as part of the total Cuban American experience and aesthetic.

But over all, the theatrical fare in Miami is eclectic, with audiences able to choose from a variety of styles and genres, from vaudeville to French-style bedroom farce, serious drama, Broadway musicals in Spanish, and Spanish versions of classics, such as Shakespeare's *Taming of the Shrew* and *Othello*. The theater companies offering the most "serious" fare have included the Teatro Bellas Artes, the Teatro La Danza, Grupo Ras, and Pro Arte Gratelli. Among the longest-lasting theaters in Miami are Salvador Ugarte's and Ernesto Cremata's two locations of Teatro Las Máscaras, which for the most part produce light comedy and vaudeville for mostly working-class audiences. Two of impressario Ernesto Capote's three houses, the Martí Theater and the Essex Theater, have a steady lineup of comedies and vaudeville; and his third house, the Miami Theater, provides an eclectic bill, including such hard-hitting dramas as *The Boys in the Band* in Spanish. The Teatro Miami's stage also serves for the taping of soap operas for television. The theater, which plays more to the working classes in Miami, as exemplified by some of the Miami theaters named above and by

Romeo and Juliet being performed in Spanish in Miami.

some that use movie houses after the showing of the last films, produces a type of reincarnation of the teatro bufo cubano that uses working-class language and culture and uses comic style and characters from the bufo tradition to satirize life in Miami and Cuba under Castro. Here, comic characterizations of Fidel and his brother Raúl (Raúl Resbaloso—Slippery Raúl) join some of the traditional character types, such as Trespatines (Three Skates) and Prematura (Premature). This theater is the most commercially successful Cuban theater, while the other, more artistically elite and intellectual theater often begs for audiences and depends on grants and university support for survival.

✳ OUTSTANDING FIGURES IN HISPANIC THEATER

Iván Mariano Acosta (1943–)

Iván Mariano Acosta is an outstanding playwright and filmmaker. Born in Santiago de Cuba on November 17, 1943, he immigrated to the United States with his parents as a result of the Cuban Revolution. He is a graduate in film direction and production of New York University (1969), and has worked as a playwright and director at the Centro Cultural Cubano and the Henry Street Settlement Playhouse. His play *El super* (*The Super*), produced at the Centro Cultural Cubano, is probably the most successful Hispanic play to come out of an ethnic theater house; it not only was highly reviewed and won awards but also was adapted to the screen by Acosta in a feature film that has won 12 awards for best script and best director). *El super* was published in book form in 1982, and four other plays were published in his anthology *Un cubiche en la luna y otras obras* in 1989. Among Acosta's other awards are the following: Cintas fellowship (1980); Ace Award, Best Writer (1980); Thalia Best Writer (1972); Ariel Award, Best Writer (1971).

Miguel Algarín

See Chapter 19.

Manuel Aparicio

Manuel Aparicio was a Tampa cigar-roller who in the 1920s and 1930s rose to become an outstanding actor and director in Hispanic theater in Tampa and

New York. From the humble beginnings of acting in amateur performances at the mutualist societies in Tampa, Aparicio went on to head up his own theatrical companies and take them on tour to Havana and New York. Tampa remained his home base, even during the Great Depression, which was the economic cataclysm that eventually resulted in his name going down in Hispanic theater history, for he became the only director of a Hispanic company under the U.S. Government Works Progress Administration's (WPA's) Federal Theater Project (FTP). In this role he led one of the FTP's most successful theater companies and was even selected for the FTP's conference of directors in Poughkeepsie, New York, in 1937. The Hispanic troupe of the FTP produced some of its own collectively created material, such as the revue *El Mundo en la Mano,* under his directorship and including his acting and singing talents. Like some 25 other actors, Aparicio lost his job when Congress passed the ERA Act of 1937, which prohibited the employment of aliens under the WPA.

La Chata Noloesca

See Beatriz Escalona.

Denise Chávez

See Chapter 19.

Miriam Colón (1945–)

Miriam Colón is the first lady of Hispanic theater in New York. She is the founder and artistic director of the Puerto Rican Traveling Theater and a genuine pioneer in bringing Hispanic theater to broad audiences. Born in 1945 in Ponce, Puerto Rico, and raised in Ponce and in New York, Colón attended the University of Puerto Rico and the Erwin Piscator Dramatic Workshop and Technical Institute, as well as the famed Actors Studio, both in New York. Colón developed a long and distinguished career on New York stages and in Hollywood films and television series. Included among her stage credits are *The Innkeepers* (1956), *Me, Cándido!* (1965), *The Oxcart* (1966), *Winterset* (1968), *The Passion of Antígona Pérez* (1972), *Julius Caesar* (1979), *Orinoco* (1985), and *Simpson Street* (1985). In 1989, she was made an honorary doctor of letters by Montclair (New Jersey) State College; she also received the White House Hispanic Heritage Award in 1990.

Beatriz Escalona (1903–1980)

Known by her stage name, La Chata Noloesca (a rearranged spelling of Escalona), Beatriz Escalona became the greatest stage personality to come out of U.S. Hispanic communities. Born on August 20, 1903, in San Antonio, Texas, Escalona was discovered while working as an usherette and box office cashier at the Teatro Nacional. She became associated with the Spanish-Cuban troupe of Hermanos Areu—she married José Areu—and played everything from melodrama to vaudeville with them, beginning in 1920, when she made her stage debut with them in El Paso. Over the course of the 1920s Escalona developed and perfected her comic persona of the streetwise maid, a *peladita* or underdog character who maintained a spicy and satirical banter. By 1930, La Chata Noloesca had split from the Areus and formed her own company, Atracciones Noloesca, and continued to tour the Southwest and northern Mexico. In 1936, she reformed her company in her native San Antonio and set out to weather the depression by performing in Tampa, Chicago, and New York—as well as Puerto Rico and Cuba—as the Compañía Mexicana. La Chata's novel idea was to take to the Cubans, Puerto Ricans, and others Mexican vaudeville, music, folklore, and her own brand of humor. In 1941, the company set down roots in New York for a stretch of nine years, during which time it was a mainstay on the Hispanic vaudeville circuit made up of the Teatro Hispano, the Teatro Puerto Rico, the Teatro Triboro, and the 53rd Street Theater. Back in San Antonio, she periodically performed for special community events until her death.

José Ferrer (1912–1992)

José Ferrer was one of the most distinguished actors of Hispanic background to have made a career in mainstream films and on stage in the United States. The star of numerous Hollywood films and many stage productions, he was born in Santurce, Puerto Rico, on January 8, 1912. Raised and educated in Puerto Rico, he graduated from Princeton University in 1933. As an actor and/or director, his stage credits have included *Let's Face It* (1942), *Strange Fruit* (1945), *Design for Living* (1947), *Twentieth Century* (1950), *Stalag 17* (1951), *Man of La Mancha* (1966), and *Cyrano de Bergerac* (1975), among many others. As an actor, director, or producer, he has been associated with some of the most famous Hollywood films, including *Joan of Arc* (1947), *Moulin Rouge* (1952), *The Caine Mutiny* (1954), *Return to Peyton Place* (1962), *Lawrence of Arabia* (1962), *Ship of Fools* (1966), and others. His awards have included the Gold Medal from the American Academy of Arts and Sciences (1949), the Academy Award for Best Actor in Cyrano de Bergerac (1950), induction into the Theater Hall of Fame (1981), among many others.

María Irene Fornés (1930–)

María Irene Fornés is the dean of Hispanic playwrights in New York, having enjoyed more productions of her works and more recognition, in the form of six Obie awards, than any other Hispanic. Born on May 14, 1930, in Havana, Cuba, she immigrated to the United States in 1945 and became a naturalized citizen in 1951. This sets her off considerably from most of the other Cuban playwrights who immigrated to the United States as refugees from the Cuban Revolution. Since 1960, she has been a playwright, director, and teacher of theater with Theater for New York City (1973–78) and various other workshops, universities, and schools. In the theater, Fornés has had more than 30 plays produced, including adaptations of plays by Federico García Lorca, Pedro Calderón de la Barca, and Chekhov. Her plays have been produced on Hispanic stages, on mainstream Off-Off-Broadway, Off-Broadway, Broadway, in Milwaukee, Minneapolis, London, and Zurich. Fornés' works, although at times touching upon political and ethnic themes, generally deal with human relations and the emotional lives of her characters. Her plots tend to be unconventional, and at times her characters are fragmented, in structures that vary from musical comedy to the theater of ideas to very realistic plays. Many of her plays have been published in collections of her work: *Promenade and Other Plays* (1971), *María Irene Fornés: Plays* (1986), *Lovers and Keepers* (1987), and *Fefu and Her Friends* (1990).

Leonardo García Astol (1906–)

Leonardo García Astol was born into a theatrical family in 1906 in Mexico and as a child began touring with his mother, a famous actress divorced from his father, and with the companies of his father and his brother in northern Mexico and later in the Rio Grande Valley of the United States. Prepared as an actor of the grand melodramatic tradition, Astol had to accommodate his considerable acting talents throughout his life in the United States to the needs of the moment, which were usually dictated by economic conditions and working-class audience demands. He began performing in the United States in 1921 and from that time on was associated with many of the most popular theatrical companies and with the famed Teatro Nacional in San Antonio. As the Great Depression hit, he continued to work with one company after another, at times managing the companies. For years he survived doing vaudeville, especially with the role he created of Don Lalo, a comic hobo, for which he is still remembered in communities of the Southwest. In 1938, Astol became a member of the stock vaudeville company for the Teatro Nacional and the Teatro Zaragoza in San Antonio, and during this time he began doing comic dialogues on Spanish-language radio. By 1940, he had become the emcee of an hour-long Mexican variety show on the radio; this later led to his doing soap operas on the radio in the 1950s, as well as other dramatic series. In the late 1950s and early 1960s, Astol broke into television and even wrote, directed and acted in a serial entitled "El Vampiro" ("The Vampire"). While developing the various phases of his career, Astol was always active in maintaining serious theatrical performances for the community, usually staged at church halls and community centers for little or no remuneration. Over the years, he has made a heroic effort to keep Hispanic theater alive in the United States.

Adalberto Elías González

Adalberto Elías González was by far the most prolific and successful playwright ever in the Hispanic communities of the United States. A native of Sonora, Mexico, who probably immigrated to Los Angeles in 1920 to further his education after graduating from the Escuela Normal in Hermosillo, he is known to have worked as a newspaperman and professional playwright there at least until 1941. Because of the subject matter of various of his plays, it is assumed that he also had military experience in Mexico before moving to the United States. By 1924, González had steady employment as a movie critic for *El Heraldo de México* newspaper in Los Angeles and had four new plays debut that year. By 1928, his fame as a playwright was so great that in that one year alone his works were staged in Hermosillo, Mexicali, El Paso, Nogales, and, of course, Los Angeles. González's works ran the gamut from historical drama to dime-novel sensationalism. The most famous of his plays was *Los Amores de Ramona* (*The Loves of Ramona*), a stage adaptation of Helen Hunt Jackson's California novel, *Ramona: A Story,* which broke all box office records when it was seen by more than 15,000 people after only eight performances in 1927. His second most successful work, *La Asesino del Martillo o La mujer tigresa* (*The Hammer Assassin or The Tiger Woman*), was based on news stories of 1923 and 1924. González also wrote historical drama, based both on Mexican history in California and on the Mexican Revolution, such as his *La Conquista de California* (*The Conquest of California*), *Los Expatriados* (*The Expatriates*), *La Muerte de Francisco Villa* (*The Death of Francisco Villa*), and *El Fantasma de la Revolución* (*The Ghost of the Revolution*). González was the leading winner of playwriting contests in Los Angeles at the height of a playwriting boom never before seen among Hispanics in the United States. In all, González is known to have written some 14 or 15 plays that were successfully produced in Los Angeles during the 1920s and 1930s.

Celedonio González

See Chapter 19.

Guz Aguila

See Antonio Guzmán Aguilera.

Antonio Guzmán Aguilera (1894–?)

Antonio Guzmán Aguilera, whose pen name was Guz Aguila, was one of Mexico's most prolific and beloved librettists and composed scores of popular theatrical revues. Born in San Miguel del Mesquital on March 21, 1984, Guzmán studied in Mexico City at the Jesuit Instituto Científico de México, and by 1916 had his first play produced at the Teatro Juan Ruiz de Alarcón. After that he began developing his career as a journalist at various newspapers; while still a journalist he became a famous author of *revistas* (revues) that commented on current events. He became the friend of presidents and politicians and suffered the ups and downs of these associations, so much so that he was arrested when a political rival became president (Obregón); he later went into exile in Los Angeles in 1924. A portion of Guzmán's career was developed in Los Angeles; just how many of his supposed 500 revues he wrote there is unknown—none of his works were ever published. Besides working as a journalist in Los Angeles, Guzmán Aguilera was contracted by the Teatro Hidalgo for $1,000 a month to write revues for its stage. It was at the Teatro Hidalgo that he wrote and debuted one of his only full-length plays, *María del Pilar Moreno, o la Pequeña Vengadora* (*María del Pilar Moreno or the Tiny Avenger*), based on the story of a young girl recently exonerated of murder in Mexico City. While at the Hidalgo he also wrote and staged the following new revues based on culture and events in Los Angeles: *Los Angeles Vacilador* (*Swinging Los Angeles*), *Evite Peligro* (*Avoid Danger*), and *El Eco de México* (*The Echo from Mexico*). In 1927, Guz Aguila returned to the stages of Mexico City, but he never regained the level of success that he had experienced there earlier.

Raúl Juliá (1940–1994)

Raúl Juliá was one of the most popular stage and screen actors in the United States. Born in San Juan, Puerto Rico, on March 9, 1940, Juliá was raised there and attained his bachelor of arts degree from the University of Puerto Rico. His career began on the Hispanic stages of New York, most notably with important productions of René Marqués' *La Carreta* (*The Oxcart*) in association with Miriam Colón. As a stage actor he has had important roles in serious theater and on Broadway, including *The Emperor of Late Night Radio* (1974), *The Cherry Orchard* (1976), *Dracula* (1976), *Arms and the Man* (1985), the revival of *Man of La Mancha* (1992), and various Shakespearean plays. Juliá received Tony Award nominations in 1971, 1974, 1976, and 1982.

In 1971, Juliá made his U.S. film debut in small parts in *The Organization, Been Down So Long It Looks Like Up to Me,* and *Panic in Needle Park.* Since then his roles have become more substantial, including *Gumball Rally* (1976), *Eyes of Laura Mars* (1978), and *One from the Heart* (1982). 1985 was a breakthrough year for him, however, due to his co-starring performance as South American Revolutionary Valentin in the film adaptation of Argentine novelist Manuel Puig's *Kiss of the Spider Woman.* Perhaps his most widely known role, however, is that of Gomez Adams, whom he played in *The Addams Family* (1991) and *Addams Family Values* (1993).

Raúl Juliá died on October 24, 1994, from complications of a stroke. He had recently finished the torturous conditions of filming *The Burning Season* (1994), a Home Box Office (HBO) television movie shot in the rainforests of South America in which Juliá played Chico Mendes. His final feature film appearance was in *Street Fighter* (1995) with Jean-Claude Van Damme. Juliá's filmography also includes roles in *Compromising Positions* (1985), *The Morning After* (1986), *Florida Straits* (1986), *Trading Hearts* (1987), *The Penitentes* (1988), *Tango Bar* (1988), *Tequila Sunrise* (1988), *Moon over Parador* (1988), *Romero* (1989), *Mack the Knife* (1989), *Presumed Innocent* (1990), *A Life of Sin* (1990), and *The Rookie* (1990).

Tato Laviera

See Chapter 19.

Gerardo López Del Castillo

Gerardo López del Castillo was a leading man and director of the Compañía Española, a Spanish Mexican theatrical company that first toured and then became a resident company in San Francisco in the mid-nineteenth century. A native of Mexico City, López del Castillo was a professional actor from age 15. Today he is known as the first Mexican actor to take companies on tour outside Mexico. By the time he arrived in California, he was already well known throughout Mexico, the Caribbean and Central and South America. An intensely patriotic individual,

López del Castillo often used theatrical performances to raise funds for Zaragoza's and Juárez's liberation armies, and he interrupted his theatrical career on various occasions to serve Mexico as a soldier. He is also known as a great promoter of the creation of a national dramatic art for Mexico. By 1862, López del Castillo and his theatrical company had made San Francisco their home. From there the company occasionally ventured out on tours up and down the coast of California and Baja California, but it mostly performed its melodramas at Tucker's Music Academy, the American Theater, and other San Francisco stages. News of the López del Castillo troupe in California exists until 1867; by 1874, he and his family company had resurfaced in Mexico City, where he was actively promoting the creation of a national dramatic literature. In Mexico City, he was considered a grand old man of the stage, but somewhat old hat, and it is said that he died a pauper.

René Marqués (1919–1979)

René Marqués is considered Puerto Rico's foremost playwright and writer of short fiction. Born in Arecibo, Puerto Rico, on October 4, 1919, to a family of agrarian background, Marqués studied agronomy at the College of Agriculture in Mayagüz and actually worked for two years for the Department of Agriculture. But his interest in literature took him to Spain in 1946 to study the classics. Upon his return, Marqués founded a little-theater group dedicated to producing and furthering Puerto Rican theater. In 1948, he received a Rockefeller Foundation fellowship to study playwriting in the United States, which allowed him to study at Columbia University and at the Piscator Dramatic Workshop in New York City. After his return to San Juan, he founded the Teatro Experimental del Ateneo (the Ateneum Society Experimental Theater). From that time on, Marqués maintained a heavy involvement not only in playwriting, but also in development of Puerto Rican theater. He also produced a continuous flow of short stories, novels, essays, and anthologies.

While Marqués' best-known work is still the all-important play *La carreta* (debuted in 1953, published in 1961, *The Oxcart,* 1969), he has been writing since 1944, when he published his first collection of poems, *Peregrinación* (*Pilgrimage*). His published plays include *El hombre y sus sueños* (1948, *Man and His Dreams*), *Palm Sunday* (1949), *Otro día nuestro* (1955, *Another of Our Days*), *Juan Bobo y la Dama de Occidente* (1956, *Juan Bobo and the Western Lady*), *El sol y los MacDonald* (1957, *The Sun and the MacDonalds*), and a collection, *Teatro* (1959), which includes three of his most important plays: *Los soles truncos* (*The Fan Lights*), *Un niño azul*

para esa sombra (*A Blue Child for that Shadow*), and *La muerte no entrará en palacio* (*Death Will Not Enter the Palace*). Many are the other published plays, novels, collections of short stories, and essays. Marqués is one of the few Puerto Rican writers who has had international audiences and impact; he is truly one of the high points of all Latin American drama. The style, philosophy, and craft of his works, as produced in New York, have had long-lasting influence on the development of Hispanic theater in the United States.

Julio Matas (1931–)

Julio Matas is a playwright, poet, and fiction writer. Born in Havana, Cuba, on May 12, 1931, Matas was encouraged to follow in the steps of his father, a judge, and he thus obtained his law degree from the University of Havana in 1955. But he never practiced as an attorney. He had enrolled in the University School for Dramatic Arts and by the time of his graduation in 1952, he had already organized a drama group, Arena. In his youth he worked on literary magazines and film projects with some of the figures who would become outstanding in these fields, such as Roberto Fernández Retamar, Néstor Almendros, and Tomás Gutiérrez Alea. In 1957, Matas enrolled at Harvard University to pursue a Ph.D. degree in Spanish literature; however, he remained active as a director, returning to Cuba to work on stage productions. It was during the cultural ferment that accompanied the first years of the Communist regime in Cuba that Matas saw two of his first books published there: the collection of short stories *Catálogo de imprevistos* (1963, *Catalog of the Unforeseen*), and the three-act play *La crónica y el suceso* (1964, *The Chronicle and the Event*). In 1965, Matas returned to the United States to assume a position in the Department of Hispanic Languages and Literatures at the University of Pittsburgh, a position that he still holds today.

Matas' plays and short stories have been published widely in magazines, anthologies, and textbooks. One of his most popular plays, *Juego de Damas* (*Ladies at Play*), has been performed often and has been published in both Spanish and English.

Matías Montes Huidobro (1931–)

Matías Montes Huidobro is a prolific writer of plays, fiction, and poetry, and he has been a theatrical producer and scriptwriter for television and radio. Born in 1931 in Sagua la Grande, Cuba, Montes was educated there and in Havana. In 1952, he obtained a Ph.D. degree in pedagogy from the University of Havana, but from 1949 on he had already begun publishing creative literature and literary

criticism. He served as a professor of Spanish literature at the National School of Journalism in Havana,
at which point he had a falling out with the political
powers and immigrated to the United States. In
1963, he became a professor of Spanish at the University of Hawaii, a position he holds to this date.

The dramas of Matías Montes Huidobro vary in
style, theme, and format, ranging from expres-
sionism to surrealism, from the absurd to the allegorical and political. His published plays include *Los
acosados* (1959, *The Accosted*), *La botija* (1959, *The
Jug*), *Gas en los poros* (1961, *Gas in His Pores*), *El
tiro por la culata* (1961, *Ass-Backwards*), *La vaca de
los ojos largos* (1967, *The Long-Eyed Cow*), *La sal de
los muertos* (1971, *Salt of the Dead*), *The Guillotine*
(1972), *Hablando en chino* (1977, *Speaking Chinese*),
Ojos para no ver (1979, *Eyes for Not Seeing*), *Funeral
en Teruel* (1982, *Funeral in Teruel*), and *La navaja
de Olofé* (1982, *Olofé's Blade*). Montes has also published important novels, including *Desterrados al
fuego* (1975, *Exiled into the Fire*) and *Segar a los
muertos* (1980, *To Blind the Dead*).

Cherríe Moraga

See Chapter 19.

Rita Moreno

See Chapter 22.

Carlos Morton (1947–)

Carlos Morton is the most published Hispanic
playwright in the United States. Born on October 15,
1947, in Chicago, to Mexican American parents,
Morton received his education in various states, as
his father's assignments in the army as a non-
commissioned officer changed. Morton obtained a
bachelor's degree from the University of Texas, El
Paso (1975), an M.F.A. degree in theater from the
University of California, San Diego (1979), and a
Ph.D. degree in drama from the University of Texas,
Austin (1987), after which he embarked on a career
as a professor of drama. Today he is a full professor
and chairman of the drama department at the University of California, Riverside. His writing career
began much earlier, with the publication of his first
chapbook of poems, *White Heroin Winter,* in 1971,
followed by the publication of his most famous play,
El Jardín (*The Garden*) in an anthology in 1974. The
majority of his plays have been produced on stages at
universities and Hispanic community arts centers,
with *Pancho Diablo* being produced by the New York
Shakespeare Festival and *The Many Deaths of
Danny Rosales* by Los Angeles' Bilingual Foundation
for the Arts. Most of his plays are contained in two
published collections, *The Many Deaths of Danny
Rosales and Other Plays* (1983) and *Johnny Tenorio
and Other Plays* (1991).

Juan Nadal de Santa Coloma

One of the grandest Puerto Rican theatrical figures in the 1920s and 1930s was Juan Nadal de
Santa Coloma, the leading actor, singer, director,
and impresario. The overriding theme of his life was
the development of a Puerto Rican national theater.
Born and raised in Puerto Rico at the end of the
nineteenth century, Nadal left his engineering studies at San Juan's Instituto Civil to begin a career on
the stage. He worked his way through various touring companies in Puerto Rico and South America,
and by 1902 was directing his own company, the
Compañía de Zarzuela Puertorriqueña. For the next
couple of decades he toured continuously in Latin
America and Spain, and he even for a while managed
Mexico City's Teatro Principal and Madrid's Teatro
Eslava. From 1927 through 1934, he was on and off
New York and San Juan stages, with his Compañía
Teatral Puertorriqueña, promoting Puerto Rican
theater. In 1930, he wrote and staged his musical
comedy *Día de Reyes* (*The Day of the Magi*), which
had 156 performances in New York City alone. In
1935, he returned to Puerto Rico after what he described as "the cold shower" that was New York, and
on the island he continued to direct several companies during the rest of the decade.

Gabriel Navarro

Originally from Guadalajara, Mexico, Gabriel Navarro moved to Los Angeles as an actor and musician
in 1922 in the Compañía México Nuevo. In Los Angeles, he developed into a playwright; he also worked
as a journalist and theater critic. During the Great
Depression and the demise of the theater industry,
he became a movie critic. In 1923, he launched a
magazine, *La revista de Los Angeles* (*The Los Angeles Magazine*); it is not known how long it lasted. In
1925, he became associated with a newspaper in San
Diego, *El Hispano Americano* (The Hispano American), which that same year published his novel, *La
señorita Estela* (*Miss Estela*). As a playwright and
composer, Navarro experimented with all of the popular dramatic forms, from drama to musical revue.
Navarro's favorite genre was the *revista* (revue); it
allowed him to put to use his talents as a composer
and writer, in addition to the technical knowledge he
had accrued as an actor and director. In the revista,
Navarro was the celebrant of Hollywood nightlife
and the culture of the Roaring Twenties. His known
works include the following revues: *Los Angeles al
día* (1922, *Los Angeles to Date*), *La Ciudad de los
extras* (1922, *The City of Extras*), *Su majestad la*

carne (1924, *Her Majesty the Flesh*), *La ciudad de irás y no volverás* (1928, *The City of To Go and Never Return*), *Las luces de Los Angeles* (1933, *The Lights of Los Angeles*), *El precio de Hollywood* (1933, *The Price of Hollywood*), *Los Angeles en pijamas* (1934, *Los Angeles in Pajamas*), and *La canción de Sonora* (1934, *The Song of Sonora*). His dramas include *La Señorita Estela* (1925), *Los emigrados* (1928, *The Emigrées*), *La sentencia* (1931, *The Jail Sentence*), *El sacrificio* (1931, *The Sacrifice*), *Loco amor* (1932, *Crazy Love*), *Alma Yaqui* (1932, *Yaqui Soul*), and *Cuando entraron los dorados* (1932, *When Villa's Troupes Entered*). Navarro's serious works draw upon his experience growing up in Guadalajara and his 12 years in the Mexican army in Veracruz and Sonora during the Mexican Revolution. *El sacrificio* and *La sentencia* use California as a setting; the latter play examines the expatriate status of Mexicans in Los Angeles and shows the breakdown of family and culture, with an Anglo-Mexican intermarriage ending in divorce and bloody tragedy.

Josephina Niggli

See Chapter 19.

Manuel Noriega

Manuel Noriega was the first director and impresario to really try to develop Hispanic theater in New York by founding various companies, renting and/or buying theaters, and even establishing a motion picture studio. Noriega was a Spanish singer-actor of zarzuelas (operettas) who made his debut at the Teatro Principal in Mexico City in 1904. Noriega found his way to New York in 1916 via the Havana stage. That same year he founded the Compañía Dramática Española, which began touring theater houses in the city for the next few years. In 1919, he formed a partnership with various businessmen and opened the first Spanish-language theater house in New York, El Teatro Español, but because of poor financial management, it closed its doors almost as soon as it opened. Noriega continued to direct companies until 1922, when he left New York. He resurfaced in Los Angeles in 1927, where he had been developing his career in film.

Alberto O'Farrill (1899–?)

Alberto O'Farrill was born in Santa Clara, Cuba, in 1899 and had begun his career as an actor and playwright in Havana in 1921 before emigrating to the United States. In New York O'Farrill was the ubiquitous negrito (black face) of obras bufas cubanas (Cuban farce) and Cuban zarzuelas who made a career playing all the major Hispanic stages in New York's stock and itinerant companies.

O'Farrill was also an intensely literate man who had been the editor of *Proteo*, a magazine in Havana, and had become in 1927 the first editor for New York's *Gráfico* newspaper, which he led in becoming the principal organ for the publication and commentary of literature and theatre. In *Grafico*, O'Farrill also published various stories and essays of his own. Despite his literary interests, as of 1926 none of O'Farrill's dramatic works had been published. O'Farrill debuted two zaruelas (Spanish operetta) at the Teatro Esmeralda in Havana in 1921: *Un negro misterioso* (*A Mysterious Black Man*), and *Las pamplinas de Agapito* (*Agapito's Adventures in Pamplona*). His other known works were all debuted at the Apollo Theatre in 1926: one sainete (comedy), *Un doctor accidental* (*An Accidental Doctor*), and the four zarzuelas *Los misterios de Changó* (*The Mysteries of Changó*), *Un negro en Adalucía* (*A Black Man in Andalusia*), *Una viuda como no hay dos* (*A Widow like None Other*), and *Kid Chocolate*. In most of these, as in his acting, he seems to have been concerned with Afro-Cuban themes.

Edward James Olmos

See Chapter 22.

Gonzalo O'Neill

Gonzalo O'Neill was a key figure in the cultural life of the Puerto Rican community in New York during the 1920s and 1930s. While a young man on the island of his birth, Puerto Rico, he began his literary career as a poet and as a founder of the literary magazine *Palenque de la juventud* (*Young People's Forum*), which published the works of many who would become Puerto Rico's leading writers. A graduate of Puerto Rico's Instituto Civil, he moved to New York City and soon became a prosperous businessman, but he also maintained his love of literature, culture, and his drive for Puerto Rican independence from the United States. The latter is seen in all his known published dramatic works: *La indiana boirinqueña* (1922, *The Indians of Puerto Rico*), a dramatic dialogue in verse; *Moncho Reyes* (1923), a biting satire of the colonial government in Puerto Rico, named after the fictional governor; and *Bajo una sola bandera* (1928, *Under Just One Flag*), a full-length drama examining the political options for Puerto Rico as personified by a young girl's choice of betrothed. O'Neill was a type of godfather who offered assistance to writers and Puerto Rican immigrants and who invested in cultural institutions, such as the Teatro Hispano. Various of his plays were staged at this theater, including one that was not published: *Amoríos borincanos* (1938, *Puerto Rican Loves*). It is certain that O'Neill wrote many other works, including other plays, poetry, and possibly essays, but they are as yet lost to us today. The works that we do have of his have been preserved probably because he was wealthy enough to underwrite their publication.

Pedro Pietri

See Chapter 19.

Miguel Piñero (1946–1988)

Miguel Piñero is the most famous dramatist to come out of the Nuyorican school. Born in Gurabo, Puerto Rico, on December 19, 1946, he was raised on the lower East Side of New York, the site of many of his plays and poems. Shortly after moving to New York, his father abandoned the family, which had to live on the streets until his mother could find a source of income. Piñero was a gang leader and involved in petty crime and drugs while an adolescent; he was a junior high school dropout and by the time he was 24 he had been sent to Sing Sing Prison for armed robbery. While at Sing Sing, he began writing and acting in a theater workshop.

By the time of his release, his most famous play, *Short Eyes* (published in 1975), had already been prepared in draft form. The play was produced and soon moved to Broadway after getting favorable reviews. During the successful run of his play and afterward, Piñero became involved with a group of Nuyorican writers in the lower East Side and became one of the principal spokespersons and models for the new school of Nuyorican literature, which was furthered by the publication of *Nuyorican Poets: An Anthology of Puerto Rican Words and Feelings,* compiled and edited by him and Miguel Algarín in 1975. During this time, as well, Piñero began his career as a scriptwriter for such television dramatic series as "Barreta," "Kojak," and "Miami Vice." In all, Piñero wrote some 11 plays that were produced, most of which are included in his two collections, *The Sun Always Shines for the Cool, A Midnight Moon at the Greasy Spoon, Eulogy for a Small-Time Thief* (1983) and *Outrageous One-Act Plays* (1986). Piñero is also author of a book of poems, *La Bodega Sold Dreams* (1986). Included among his awards were a Guggenheim fellowship (1982) and the New York Drama Critics Circle Award for Best American Play, an Obie, and the Drama Desk Award, all in 1974 for *Short Eyes.* Piñero died of cirrhosis of the liver in 1988, after many years of hard living and recurrent illnesses as a substance abuser.

Eusebio Pirrín

Eusebio Pirrín (Pirrín was a stage name, the real family name possibly being Torres) was born into a circus and vaudeville family that toured principally in the U.S. Southwest and somewhat in South America. Born in Guanajuato, Mexico, Eusebio developed his famous Don Catarino act on the Los Angeles stage; Catarino was named for a character in a comic strip that ran in Los Angeles' newspaper *El Heraldo de México.* Although Eusebio was only a teenager at the time, Don Catarino was a tiny old man with a bushy moustache. Don Catarino became so famous that he spawned many imitators of his dress, speech, and particular brand of humor throughout the Southwest and in Mexico. The Pirrín family troupe enjoyed great fame and fortune and was able to continue performing in the Southwest from the early 1920s through World War II, even surviving the Great Depression. Although Don Catarino was a rural, ranch type, most of his humor was urban; Eusebio Pirrín created all of the revues and music in which Don Catarino took center stage. Eusebio Pirrín's revues are too numerous to list here, but many of them celebrated urban nightlife in Los Angeles, while others commented on and satirized such important political and social themes as the depression, deportations, exile, and the use of alcohol and drugs.

Dolores Prida (1943–)

Dolores Prida is a playwright and screenwriter whose works have been produced in various states and in Puerto Rico, Venezuela, and the Dominican Republic. Born on September 5, 1943, in Caibairén, Cuba, Prida emigrated with her family to New York in 1963. She graduated from Hunter College in 1969 with a major in Spanish American literature. Upon graduation she began a career as a journalist and editor, first for Collier-Macmillan and then for other publishers, quite often using her bilingual skills. In 1977 her first play, *Beautiful Señoritas,* was produced at the Duo Theater. Since then she has seen some ten of her plays produced. Prida's plays vary in style and format, from adaptations of international classics, such as *The Three Penny Opera,* to experiments with the Broadway musical formula, as in her *Savings* (1985), to her attempt to create a totally bilingual play, as in *Coser y cantar* (*To Sew and to Sing,* 1981). Her themes vary from an examination of the phenomenon of urban gentrification, as in *Savings,* to the generation gap and conflict of culture, as in *Botánica* (1990). Since 1993, *Botánica* has won a permanent place in the repertory of Spanish Repertory Theater in New York, which through 1996, was continuing to alternate it on its programs, especially for schools. Prida's plays, which are written in Spanish or English or bilingually, have been collected in *Beautiful Señoritas and Other Plays*

A scene from the Los Angeles production of Dolores Prida's *Beautiful Señoritas.*

(1991). Prida is also a talented poet who was a leader in the 1960s of New York's Nueva Sangre (New Blood) movement of young poets. Her books of poems include *Treinta y un poemas (Thirty-one Poems,* 1967), *Women of the Hour* (1971), and, with Roger Cabán, *The IRT Prayer Book.* Among her awards are an honorary doctorate from Mount Holyoke College (1989), Manhattan Borough President's Excellence in the Arts Award (1987), and a Cintas fellowship (1976).

Anthony Quinn

See Chapter 22.

Marita Reid

Marita Reid was one of the most famous actresses in New York's Hispanic theater, and she was a tireless promoter of serious drama in the Hispanic community during the difficult years of the Great Depression and World War II. Born in Gibraltar, Spain, to a Spanish mother and an English father, Marita Reid grew up bilingual and began her life on the stage at age 7. Her early experience was performing on tours in extreme southern Spain. She began per-

forming in New York in the early 1920s in Spanish-language companies. In 1922, she formed her own company, and during the 1930s and 1940s her leadership was crucial as she headed up a number of companies that kept Spanish-language theater alive by performing in the mutualist societies and clubs, as well as in conventional theaters. For nearly three decades she was the leading lady of the Hispanic stage in New York and one of its leading directors. Because of her English background, Reid was able to cross over to American, English-language mainstream theater. Her career extended to Broadway, cinema, and television, including live television drama in the "Armstrong Circle Theater," "The U.S. Steel Hour," and "Studio One." Reid was also the author of four unpublished plays: *Patio gilbraltareño (Gibraltar Patio), Luna de mayo (May Moon), El corazón del hombre es nuestro corazón* (1933, *The Heart of Man Is Our Heart*), and *Sor Piedad* (1938, *Sister Piety*).

Gustavo Solano

Gustavo Solano, whose pen name was El Conde Gris (The Grey Count) was a prolific Salvadoran playwright, poet, and prose writer. In addition to his extensive record as a creative writer, Solano led a very fruitful career as a journalist, beginning in his native El Salvador and later developing in New Orleans, where he was the managing editor of the *Pan American Review* and the founder and editor of the bilingual weekly *La Opinión* (*The Opinion*) from 1911 to 1912. In 1912, he moved to Laredo, Texas, to become the editor of *El Progreso* (*The Progress*), then later to Saltillo, Mexico, as founder and editor of *La Reforma* (*The Reform*). He was a soldier in the Mexican Revolution and in 1916 he also served time in the penitentiary in Mexico City for his political activities. In 1920, he began a long relationship with Los Angeles' *El Heraldo de México* (*The Mexican Herald*) as an editorial writer. While in Los Angeles, he was under contract to at least two of the theater houses as a playwright charged with producing original material. He remained in Los Angeles until 1929; during this time he also maintained relationships with various publications in Mexico.

Of all the Los Angeles playwrights, Solano had the greatest number of works published. In his book of poems *Composiciones escogidas* (1923, *Selected Compositions*), Solano lists the following published works: *Verso, Fulguraciones, Trinidad de arte (poesía)* (*Verses, Ponderings, Trinity of Art [poetry]*), *Nadie es profeta en su tierra* (*No One Is a Prophet in His Own Land, a play*), *Apóstoles y judas* (1915, *Apostles and Judases,* an allegorical play of the Mexican Revolution), and *La sangre, Crímenes de Estrada Cabrera* (*The Blood, Crimes of Estrada Cabrera,* a play satirizing the Salvadoran dictator). In *Uno más—Prosa y verso* (1929, *One More—Prose and Verse*) he added the following: *México glorioso y trágico (Revolución Mexicana en escena—Prosa y verso)* (*Glorious and Tragic Mexico [The Mexican Revolution Onstage—Prose and Verse]*) and *Con las alas abiertas (Prosa)* (*With Wings Spread Open [Prose]*); he also mentioned various other works of drama, poetry, and prose about to be published. In his *Volumen de una vida* (1932, *Volume of a Life*) are included four of the plays that were staged in Los Angeles: *El homenaje lírico a la raza* (*The Lyric Homage to Our People*), *La casa de Birján* (*Birján's House*), *Las falsas apariencias* (*Mistaken Impressions*), and *Tras Cornudo, Apaleado* (*Beaten on Top of Being Cuckolded*).

Piri Thomas

See Chapter 19.

Romualdo Tirado (1880–1963)

The most important figure in the history of the Los Angeles Hispanic stage was the great impresario, director, singer, and actor Romualdo Tirado, who was also the author of numerous librettos for revues. Tirado was a Spaniard who had immigrated to Mexico and developed a career on the stage there during his 15 years of residence. From the time of his arrival in Los Angeles in the late teens, Tirado was a prime mover in the Hispanic theater and movie industries, who also brought about the writing and staging of many local plays. Tirado celebrated the highs of the 1920s and stayed on for the lows of the Los Angeles stage during the Great Depression. During the 1940s, however, he was able to obtain some work in Puerto Rico and in New York at the Teatro Hispano.

Tirado developed many of his own musical revues around his own comic persona in various satirized situations, such as *Clínica moderna* (1921, *The Modern Clinic*), *Tirado dentista* (1921, *Tirado the Dentist, Tirado bolshevique* (1924, *A Bolshevik Tirado,* and *Tirado en el Polo Norte* (1925), *Tirado at the North Pole*. In 1930, Tirado and Antonieta Díaz Mercado wrote a full-length play based on Mariano Azuela's novel of the Mexican Revolution, *Los de abajo* (*The Underdogs*), but it was a complete flop. None of Tirado's compositions are available today. In 1990, Carmen Zapata received the prestigious Civil Order of Merit from His Majesty Juan Carlos I, King of Spain, in recognition of her commitment to Hispanics in theater and film and for her community service. In 1991, she was conferred the California Governor's Award for the Arts, along with eight other artists and organizations.

Omar Torres (1945–)

Omar Torres is an actor, playwright, poet, and novelist. Born on September 13, 1945, in Las Tunas, Cuba, he immigrated to Miami, Florida, with his family in 1959. There he attended both junior and senior high school. The family then moved to New York where he attended Queens College for a while, only to drop out to study on his own. He later took acting classes at the New York Theater of the Americas and subsequently graduated from the International Television Arts School. He has had an active career in radio, television and movies. In 1972, he cofounded, with Iván Acosta, the Centro Cultural Cubano, and in 1974 he founded the literary and arts journal *Cubanacán* (a nonsense word meaning "Cuba" here). Torres' produced plays include *Abdala-José Martí* (1972, *Abdala-José Martí*), *Antes del Vuelo y la Palabra* (1976, *Before the Flight and the Word*), *Cumbancha cubiche* (1976, *Cumbancha Low Class Cuban*), *Yo dejo mi palabra en el aire sin llaves y sin velos* (1978, *I Leave My Word in the Air without Keys and without Veils*), *Latinos* (1979), and *Dreamland Melody* (1982). Torres is the author of three novels—*Apenas un bolero* (1981, *Just a Bolero*), *Al partir* (1986, *Upon Leaving*), and *Fallen Angels Sing* (1991)—and five books of poetry: *Conversación primera* (1975, *First Conversation*), *Ecos de un laberinto* (1976, *Echoes from a Labyrinth*), *Tiempo robado* (1978, *Stolen Time*), *De nunca a siempre* (1981, *From Never to Always*), and *Línea en diluvio* (1981, *Line in the Deluge*).

Rafael Trujillo Herrera (1897–)

A prolific playwright, drama teacher, and impresario, Trujillo Herrera was born in Durango, Mexico, in 1897, but later immigrated to Los Angeles. In the late 1920s and early 1930s, he began writing plays for the stage and for the radio; in 1933 he began directing his own radio show. In 1940, Trujillo Herrera became associated with the Works Progress Administration (WPA), for which he wrote a play, *Bandido* (*Bandit*); it was later published under the title of *Revolución* (*Revolution*). During the 1960s, Trujillo Herrera published numerous works in various genres in Los Angeles, Mexico, and elsewhere, including some through his own publishing house, Editorial Autores Unidos (United Authors Publishing). All told, Trujillo Herrera has claimed to have written some 50 one-act plays, two in four acts, and 12 in three acts. During these years he also directed at least five theater groups. In 1974, he opened the doors to his own theater, the teatro Intimo, in Los Angeles. Trujillo Herrera's most famous three-act plays are *Revolución, Estos son mis hijos* (*These Are My Children*), *La hermana de su mujer* (*His Wife's Sister*), *Cuando la vida florece* (*When Life Flourishes*), and *A la moda vieja* (*Old Style*).

Luis Valdez (1940–)

Luis Valdez is considered the father of Chicano theater. He has distinguished himself as an actor, director, playwright, and filmmaker; however, it was in his role as the founding director of El Teatro Campesino, a theater of farm workers in California, that his efforts inspired young Chicano activists across the country to use theater as a means of organizing students, communities, and labor unions. Luis Valdez was born into a family of migrant farm workers on June 26, 1940, in Delano, California. The second of ten children, he began to work in the fields at age six. Valdez's education was continuously interrupted; he nevertheless finished high school and went on to San Jose State College, where he majored in English and pursued his interest in theater. While there he won a playwriting contest with his one-act play, "The Theft" (1961), and in 1963 the drama department produced his play *The Shrunken Head of Pancho Villa*.

Playwright-director Luis Valdez.

After graduating from college in 1964, Valdez joined the San Francisco Mime Troupe and learned the techniques of agitprop (agitation and propaganda) theater and Italian *commedia dell'arte* (comedy of art), both of which influenced Valdez's development of the basic format of Chicano theater: the one-act presentational *acto* (act). In 1965, Valdez enlisted in César Chávez's mission to organize farm workers in Delano into a union. It was there that Valdez brought together farm workers and students into El Teatro Campesino to dramatize the plight of the farm workers. The publicity and success gained by the troupe led to the spontaneous appearance of a national Chicano theater movement. In 1967, Valdez and El Teatro Campesino left the unionizing effort to expand their theater beyond agitprop and farm worker concerns. From then on Valdez and the theater have explored most of the theatrical genres important to Mexicans in the United States, including religious pageants, vaudeville with the down-and-out *pelado* (underdog) figure, and dramatized *corridos* (ballads). During the late 1960s and the 1970s, El Teatro Campesino produced many of Valdez's plays, including *Los vendidos* (1967), *The Sell-Outs, The Shrunken Head of Pancho Villa* (1968),

Bernabé (1970), *Dark Root of a Scream* (1971), *La carpa de los Rascuachis* (1974), and *El fin del mundo* (1976). In 1978, Valdez broke into mainstream theater in Los Angeles, with the Mark Taper Forum's production of his *Zoot Suit* and the 1979 Broadway production of the same play. In 1986 he had a successful run of his play *I Don't Have to Show You No Stinking Badges* at the Los Angeles Theater Center.

Valdez's screenwriting career began with early film and television versions of Corky González's poem "I Am Joaquín" (1969) and "Los vendidos," and later with a film version of *Zoot Suit* (1982). But his real incursion into major Hollywood productions and success came in 1987 with his writing and directing of *La Bamba* (the name of a dance from Veracruz), the screen biography of Chicano rock-and-roll star Ritchie Valens. Other screenplays include: *Corridos* (1987), *Frida Kahlo* (1992), and *The Cisco Kid* (1993). He followed his commercial film success with the 1991 made-for-public-television film *La Pastorela* based on his own theatrical rendition of the folk play *Los pastores* (*The Shepherds*). In 1994, Valdez wrote and directed the humorous western, *The Cisco Kid,* starring Jimmy Smits and Cheech Marín. Valdez's plays, essays, and poems have been widely anthologized. His only collection of work still in print is *Luis Valdez—The Early Works* (1990), which includes the early actos that he developed with El Teatro Campesino, his play *Bernabé,* and his narrative poem "Pensamiento Serpentino." Valdez's awards include an Obie (1968), the Los Angeles Drama Critics Awards (1969, 1972, and 1978), a special Emmy Award (1973), an award for Best Musical from the San Francisco Bay Critics Circle (1983), and honorary doctorates from San Jose Sate University, Columbia College, and the California Institute of the Arts.

Daniel Venegas

See Chapter 19.

Carmen Zapata (1927–)

Carmen Zapata is an actress and producer of Mexican heritage. Born on July 15, 1927, in New York City, she was raised and educated in New York, and later attended the University of California, Los Angeles, and New York University. Zapata has had a very successful career in Hollywood films and on television, including children's television. She is perhaps best known, however, as the founder and director of the Bilingual Foundation for the Arts in Los Angeles, which is a showcase for Hispanic playwrights, actors, and directors and has resulted in introducing new talent to the television and movie industries. Included among her awards are the Na-

Actress-director Carmen Zapata portrays Isabel la Católica in the Bilingual Foundation for the Arts' production of *Moments to Be Remembered.*

tional Council of La Raza Rubén Salazar Award (1983), the Women in Film Humanitarian Award (1983), Hispanic Women's Council Woman of the Year (1985), best Actress Dramalogue (1986), and an Emmy (1973). In 1990, Carmen Zapata received the prestigious Civil Order of Merit from His Majesty Juan Carlos I, King of Spain, in recognition of her commitment to Hispanics in theater and film, and for her community service. In 1991, she was conferred the California Governor's Award for the Arts, along with eight other artists and organizations.

References

Antush, John, ed. *Recent Puerto Rican Theater: Five Plays from New York.* Houston: Arte Público Press, 1991.

Broyles, Yolanda Julia. *El Teatro Campesino.* Austin: University of Texas Press, 1995.

Cortina, Rodolfo, ed. *Cuban American Theater.* Houston: Arte Público Press, 1991.

Huerta, Jorge. *Chicano Theater. Themes and Forms.* Tempe, Arizona: Bilingual Press, 1982.

Huerta, Jorge. *Necessary Theater: Six Plays about the Chicano Experience.* Houston, Tex.: Arte Público Press, 1989.

Kanellos, Nicolás. *Hispanic Theatre in the United States.* Houston, Texas: Arte Público Press, 1984.

——. *A History of Hispanic Theatre in the United States: Origins to 1940.* Austin: University of Texas Press, 1990.

——. *Mexican American Theatre: Legacy and Reality.* Pittsburgh: Latin American Review Press, 1987.

——. *Mexican American Theatre Then and Now.* Houston: Arte Público Press, 1983.

Miller, John C. "Contemporary Hispanic Theatre in New York." In *Hispanic Theatre in the United States,* edited by Nicolás Kanellos. Houston: Arte Público Press, 1984.

Valdez, Luis. "Notes on Chicano Theatre" and "Actos." In *Luis Valdez—The Early Works.* Houston: Arte Público Press, 1991.

Watson-Espener, Maida. "Ethnicity and the Hispanic American Stage: The Cuban Experience." In *Hispanic Theatre in the United States,* edited by Nicolás Kanellos. Houston: Arte Público Press, 1984.

Nicolás Kanellos

22

Film

* Depiction of Minority Groups in Early American Film
* Conglomeration of the Film Industry and the Production Code
* First Decades: The Bandido, Buffoon, Dark Lady, Caballero, and Gangster
* Hispanics in Film during the 1930s and the Era of Social Consciousness
* Decline of the Production Code, Emergence of the Civil Rights Movement, and New Developments in
Film: 1960s and 1970s * Hollywood Films Since 1980 * The Emergence of U.S. Hispanic Films
* Hispanics in Film: Future Directions * Outstanding Hispanics in the Film Industry

This chapter focuses on the depiction of Hispanics by the American film industry from its beginnings around the turn of the century through the contemporary period. The first two sections deal with how the depiction of minority groups, including Hispanics, developed in the earliest U.S. cinema. A host of early trends and personal contributions combined to create the extraordinarily harsh American style of racial and ethnic depiction. These factors were further reinforced in the 1920s and 1930s with the conglomeration of the American film industry in a fashion that emphasized theatrical distribution, the assembly line production of many films, the star system, and production formulas that were later turned into a production code.

The third section reviews the early cinematic depiction of Hispanics. It also describes the prevailing stereotypes: bandidos, buffoons, dark ladies, caballeros, and gangsters. The fourth section describes the changes in the depiction of Hispanics and other minority groups brought about by the Great Depression, World War II, and the advent of the "Hollywood social problem film." Section five reviews Hispanic-focused films as well as the careers of Hispanic actors and filmmakers against the backdrop of important social developments such as the emergence of the civil rights movement and the decline of the production code.

Section six is devoted to films that were produced since 1980, and section seven reviews the emergence of U.S. Hispanic film, including both Chicano productions and films made in Puerto Rico (often with

Mexican or Hollywood control) or by Puerto Ricans both on the island and in the continental United States. Finally, a list of outstanding Hispanic figures in the film industry is provided, as well as a bibliography of further, more specialized readings.

* DEPICTION OF MINORITY GROUPS IN EARLY AMERICAN FILM

During a period of a few years, primarily between 1903 and 1915, several technological, aesthetic, economic, and cultural developments in the United States came together that were important in determining how American cinema was to depict race and ethnicity for decades to come. An unfortunate filmic style emerged that was much harsher in its depiction of race and ethnicity than the cinema of other nations. American cinema delighted in the depiction of such stereotypes as "chinkers," "Micks," "darkies," "Hebrews," "greasers," "redskins," and "guineas," and actually used these epithets in the titles and publicity or in the films themselves.

Five governing factors converged and interacted with one another around the turn of the century to produce a definable style of racial stereotyping in American cinema: (1) the developing technological sophistication of filmmaking, particularly in projection and editing, (2) the developing philosophy of illusionism that began to gain ascendancy in film aesthetics, (3) the economic necessity in the U.S. film industry to produce westerns and to produce epic, prestige pictures of middle-class appeal, (4) the attitudes toward race and ethnicity that prevailed in society and that governed the popular novel of the period, and (5) the racial attitudes of the most prominent filmmakers of the period, especially D. W. Griffith.

The early years of cinema witnessed an explosion of technology similar to that of the contemporary computer industry. Advances in film technology were instrumental in determining the art of the possible for the emerging American cinematic filmmakers of the period, such as Edwin S. Porter, D. W. Griffith, Mack Sennett, Thomas H. Ince, William S. Hart, and Charles Chaplin. The development of more powerful projection and editing technologies permitted the production of what audiences of that period perceived to be more realistic films (although the contemporary viewer of these forerunners would find it difficult to understand this). These more "realistic" and longer films, included epics, which lent themselves to the depiction of minority group types, including Mexicans, blacks, Orientals, and native Indians, in a way that was not technologically possible before.

In 1903, Edwin S. Porter produced the landmark film *The Great Train Robbery*. Significantly, the film was a Western and reigned for about ten years, until the emergence of D. W. Griffith's features, as the most important American cinematic production. *The Great Train Robbery* was of epic proportions for its time, an incredible 12 minutes. Yet, by 1915 technological advances and artistic will had stretched the concept of epic to three hours with Griffith's *The Birth of a Nation*. It is in the nature of epics that they deal with race and ethnicity, and it was no coincidence that Griffith's most famous epic was the most ambitious attempt to date, a flawed and racist depiction of ethnic and racial types: tender and sensitive Southern whites, vain white Northern liberals, vicious or brutal blacks, merciless Northern soldiers, heroic Ku Klux Klansmen, and evil mulattoes, the result of deplorable mixing of the races.

Filmmakers quickly came to realize, as the result of the reactions of the viewers of the first "flickers," the potential for manipulating emotions on the basis of heretofore unimagined optical effects. The first movies, only 50 feet long, had the most rudimentary of plots, or were plotless. In any event, the operating element was not plot but effects never before experienced under controlled conditions: a speeding locomotive, a barrel going over a waterfall, a galloping horse. Filmmakers found that they could induce fear, vertigo, suspense, and other intense emotions in the viewers through recourse to special-effect shots. *The Great Train Robbery* is famous for the last shot, a non sequitur close-up of a bandit firing his pistol at the audience. Within a few years, more complex emotions were induced. Griffith's films, through their depiction of kidnappings, attempted rapes, destruction of homesteads or Indian villages, and most of all, war, were able to bring forth feelings of outrage, simultaneous horror, and titillating anticipation, pity, and remorse more intensely than other available media—theater, fiction, poetry, or journalism.

The earliest period of cinema, which had its roots in magic and lantern shows and in vaudeville, emphasized the illusionism of special effects (trains, horses, running water, flights to the moon). However, as the result of rapid advances in technology that permitted longer and more sophisticated films, together with the increasing staleness of purely optical effects such as waves beating against a pier, cinema began to both borrow from and more closely approximate the stage. The early film directors, Edwin S. Porter, Stuart Blackton, Sidney Olcott, and others, quickly discovered that film had a distinct advantage over the stage in presenting melodrama. The devices available to film could have a reality that was impossible to attain on the stage. For example, the count of Monte Cristo need not escape from his prison through a canvas sea; the film showed a real ocean.

Moreover, the early filmmakers, Griffith the leader among them, soon made changes in style based on the aesthetics of illusionism. Film moved from a style based on special optical effects (where the cameraman was supreme) to a photographic record of legitimate theater, to an emotionally heightened superrealism where the auteur/director reigned supreme. The aesthetics and ideology of this change are well indexed in the motion picture column begun in 1909 in the trade journal *The New York Dramatic Mirror*. Writing under the pseudonym The Spectator, Frank Woods stated the ideal later identified as that of a transparent fiction whose appearance of reality is strong enough to efface an awareness on the part of a viewer of the actual production of the illusion. Woods was convinced that the unique power of the cinema lay in its singular illusion of reality. This illusion gave cinema a "strange" psychological power over its audience:

The strange power of attraction possessed by motion pictures lies in the semblance of reality which the pictures convey; that by means of this impression of reality the motion picture exerts on the minds of the spectators an influence akin to hypnotism or magnetism by visual suggestion; that this sort of limited hypnotic influence is capable of more powerful exertion through the medium of motion pictures than is possible in any sort of stage production or in printed fact or fiction, and that it is therefore the part of wisdom to cultivate absolute realism in every department of the motion picture art. Artificial drama and artificial comedy appear to have no attraction for the public mind when displayed in motion pictures, no matter how satisfactory they may be on the stage or in printed literature (*The New York Dramatic Mirror,* May 14, 1910).

The conscious economic policy of attempting to raise the social respectability of films and consequently attract a middle-class audience also had an important ideological and aesthetic consequence, propelling film toward the classical narrative style of illusionism and, in turn, the depiction of ethnic and racial stereotypes in the distinctive American manner. In 1908, the Motion Picture Patents Company (MPPC) was established with the goals of establishing a controlling monopoly of film distribution and achieving acceptance of the "flickers" by the middle class.

The push to make film respectable (that is, acceptable to the middle class) opened on two basic fronts: censorship of film content and improvement of the theaters in which the films were shown. Film censorship had two aims: to "improve" film content and therefore attract a "better class" of audience, and to keep censorship out of the hands of the government and the clergy, which might deal more harshly with the films than the producers wanted. Of course, the goal was to make films that still catered to the working class (many of them recently arrived immigrants from western and, increasingly, eastern Europe), even as they attracted the middle class.

To woo the middle class, filmmakers began to produce films with more complicated narrative plots and characterization, films with "educational" or "instructive" values or a "moral lesson," and films with happy endings. As an editorial in *Nickelodeon* states: "We are living in a happy, beautiful, virile age. . . . We do not want sighs or tears. . . . We are all seeking happiness—whether through money or position or imagination. It is our privilege to resent any attempt to force unhappy thoughts on us." (Tom Gunning, *Quarterly Review of Film Studies,* 1981) All of these initiatives lent themselves to the creation of racial antagonists (Mexicans, blacks, Indians), whose interactions with white males and females, however simplistic and formulistic by contemporary standards, were considerably more complex from a narrative and psychological point of view. Moreover, their defeat could be the basis of a moral lesson for both the character on-screen and the audience, and for happy endings evoking the moral and physical superiority of Anglo values over the degenerate or primitive mores of other cultures.

The central impetus behind the production of vast numbers of Westerns, many using Mexicans or Indians as foils to Anglo heroes and heroines, was a ready international market for such films. The genre became proprietary to the American film industry.

Each of these factors—the increasing sophistication of filmmaking technology, the developing style of illusionism, and the ready market for epics and Westerns—determined that filmmakers would either turn to the prevailing literature of the day and adapt it to film, or hire scriptwriters to produce screenplays closely modeled on that prevailing literature. Before 1908, the primary sources for films were vaudeville and burlesque sketches, fairy tales, comic strips, and popular songs. These forms stressed spectacular effects or physical action, rather than psychological motivation. Although still in an elementary form, film now looked toward more respectable narrative models and the problems they entailed. With respect to Westerns, a vast literature existed, almost all of it formulaic pulp fiction, that could be either adapted or imitated in kind.

Westerns, as Arthur Pettit has observed in his *Images of the Mexican American in Fiction and Film* (1980), are "at least as rigid in their conventions as any medieval morality play." The genre has a finite number of categories, such as the cattle empire, the ranch, revenge, cowboys and Indians, outlaws, law and order, and conquest. The depiction of Mexicans and Indians in these stories, and their adaptation to the screen by filmmakers seeking to introduce narrative and psychological complexity into their works as well as woo a new audience, was strictly in accordance with the prevailing canon and formula for racial interaction. Pettit, in a review and analysis of hundreds of nineteenth-and twentieth-century popular Western novels, has distilled the following conclusions about the genre, conclusions that are valid in turn for the films that began to emerge around the turn of the century, these having been modeled on the literary productions:

When [the Anglo] set out to bring democracy, progress, and Protestantism to the Hispanic Southwest, he could find a place for the Mexican in what he soon regarded as "his" Southwest only if the Mexican would become, insofar as his limited talents permitted, what the American perceived himself to be: enterprising, steady, and Protestant—in a word, civilized. Yet somehow the Mexican remained something else in the Anglo-American's eye: shiftless, unreliable, and alternately decadent or barbaric. Thus, it seemed to be the American's manifest destiny to conquer and convert this errant race. In the process it was also necessary to destroy a culture the Mexican would not willingly surrender. Operating from such moral absolutes, the Anglo was able to achieve a satisfactory interpretation of his racial and cultural superiority. He could flatter himself that he was not deprecating a race but standing up for civilization. He could persuade himself, in fact, that he was not guilty of racism in any sense that we understand the term. For if the Mexican could be evaluated only in terms of the civilization to which, by the laws of nature, God, and history alike, he had to give way, then how could the conqueror be blamed for what was destined to happen? The Anglo-American thus came to see the indigenous way of life in what became the American Southwest as inherently and irrevocably inferior and hostile to his own institutions.

The work of the early filmmakers, David Wark Griffith supreme among them, has had an enormous impact on American and international filmmaking. Griffith's posthumous autobiography (published in 1972; Griffith died in 1948), without too much exaggeration, is entitled *The Man Who Invented Hollywood*. Griffith's most important contribution to film was his development of the techniques through which the motion picture became an art form, an instrument able to express emotions and ideas. Griffith's instinctive sense of the unique expressive properties of the cinema also extended beyond the technical means into the art of acting. Early on, he recognized the need for a new style of performing for the screen, a style more subtle and restrained than the bombastic, exaggerated delivery then current on the stage. As early as 1909, he gathered a group of young actors and rehearsed them continually until he was able to extract from them performances that could withstand the magnifying eye of the motion picture camera. He thus established a stock company of players that at one time or another included future stars Mary Pickford, Dorothy and Lillian Gish, Blanche Sweet, Mabel Normand, Mae Marsh, Florence LaBadie, Claire McDowell, Henry B. Walthall, Robert (Bobby) Harron, Alfred Paget, Donald Crisp, Arthur Johnson, Jack Pickford, James Kirkwood, Owen Moore, Wallace Reid, and Harry Carey. Griffith had a major role in establishing the star system, with all of its glories and drawbacks, upon which American films are scripted, produced, and marketed to this very day.

Griffith also made a major contribution to the development of the epic. With the premier of his greatest success, *The Birth of a Nation,* in 1915, the previously little-known Griffith became the best-known motion picture director in the industry. With the help of some publicity hype, he became known as the "Shakespeare of the screen." *The Birth of a Nation* is considered by many historians to be the single most important film in the development of cinema as an art. It was certainly the most influential. Originally running about three hours in length, it was a stunning summary of all that was known about filmmaking at the time, as well as an elaborately constructed, complex production that to this day retains its emotional impact.

Griffith's contributions to film technique and technology, to cinematic acting, and to the development of genres, including the epic, are all well documented. Also carefully reviewed by historians has been the content of his major films, such as *The Birth of a Nation* and *Intolerance,* with respect to their expression of racial and ethnic attitudes. It would be hard to avoid an analysis along these lines inasmuch as *The Birth of a Nation* caused a firestorm of controversy over its anti-Negro bias and its positioning the Ku Klux Klan as heroes who come to the rescue of beleaguered white Southerners.

It appears that Griffith's racial prejudices were readily passed into American cinema. These attitudes were embedded in Griffith's film technique. They were integral to the way he developed many of his plots and the way he developed several of his epic films. American cinema took not only the technical (relatively content-free) contributions from Griffith and other early filmmakers, but also the content-intensive ones. What emerged was a distinctively American style of racial and ethnic depiction, one that was uniquely derogatory unfortunately.

Griffith's racial attitudes can be summarily characterized as somewhat typical for a Southerner of his station during this period, although he carried certain notions to extremes, such as a romantic admiration for the "noble savage" and a profound fear of miscegenation. Both of these notions were quite popular with his viewers. There was a close match between what fed on Griffith and what he fed his public in the privacy of a darkened movie theater. According to Iris Barry's book, *D. W. Griffith: American Film Master,* Griffith's views on race and culture as they were elaborated cinematically have been separated into six factors. First, Griffith believed in the superiority of the white race. Every other race was evaluated in relationship to the attainments of the white race and with respect to its approximation to the white race, which provided the standard for emulation.

Second, Griffith displayed respect for and admiration of other races and cultures in their "pristine state," for example, peaceful Indians living in their villages far from the white man, Zulus in their jungle habitat, blacks in the antebellum South being cared for like children by white aristocrats, and so on. Griffith directed several, movies such as *The Greatest Thing in Life,* in which evil whites come and destroy this pristine beauty of "noble savages" or "natural men."

In addition to his belief in white superiority, the director had an overriding obsession with color, and this feature of Griffith's was directly transferred to the advertisements for his films, which often feature references to "redmen," "yellow chinkers," "smokies," "tawny blacks," "greasers," and so on.

A fourth tenet held by Griffith was a belief in the ability of the less civilized races to overcome their inferiority to the degree that they showed their commitment, obeisance, and fealty to Anglo-Saxon values, and to the degree they had good, positive Anglo-Saxon role models available to them. This theme appears in movies such as *The Redman and the Child* and *Broken Blossoms,* which he directed.

Fifth, he had a profound abhorrence of what he called "mongrolization." For Griffith, half-breeds, such as mulattoes, were among the worst, most deplorable human types. Part and parcel of this attitude, which was so motivating for him that it cannot be overemphasized, was his great fear of miscegenation, which at the same time produced considerable titillation in him. Many of Griffith's films have "fate worse than death" scenes, and Griffith typically used some mongrolized (either racially or culturally) character as the would-be rapist. Interracial rape (attempted but never consummated) was a specialty of his. This sort of primal scene in his psyche profoundly moved him, and it was terrific box office as well. The "fate worse than death" element of American cinema became one of the staples that spurred the careers of many an actress, usually a blonde whose fairness contrasted beautifully on celluloid with the ominous, darker-hued attempted rapists.

A sixth interest of Griffith's revealed in his films was the interaction of sex and race and sex and class. These movies stirred him as well as his viewers. The films were popular with everyone, but they were especially appealing to women, for whom going to the movies represented, apart from the content of the film itself, a certain emancipation from traditional strictures. To go to the movies and then see women in situations profoundly provocative for the historical moment and for the sensibilities of the time genuinely led to a degree of addiction to the experience. Griffith was both a consumer and master purveyor of shared fantasies in the dark pitched at a level that shook the consumer but did not go so far as to induce an emotional or intellectual aftertaste. His audience could enter the darkened movie theater and privately and without remorse experience forbidden thoughts of rape, ravishment, interracial sex, gore and glory, and the like. At the end of the film, the light was turned back on and one could go merrily on one's way without giving the film content a worry. And besides, no one really did get raped or ravished. Griffith's films featured the close call and the close encounter and the salvation of the maiden by the white hero so that in the end everything was right and social decorum and the social order were merely tasted and tested but ultimately maintained.

Thus, in the space of some 12 years shortly after the turn of the century, technological, aesthetic, economic, and sociocultural factors converged in the American film industry and led to the creation of a distinctive and exceptionally derogatory style of depicting racial and ethnic minorities, including Hispanics.

✳ CONGLOMERATION OF THE FILM INDUSTRY AND THE PRODUCTION CODE

The first wave of ethnic stereotyping that so distinguishes American film from the silver screen of other nations was further reinforced by the development of film as big business. Capital investment in the American film industry became centered not in production but in distribution, particularly in the form of movie theaters. By the early 1930s, power rested with a mere eight major, vertically structured corporations that had consolidated production, distribution, and exhibition in monopolistic fashion: MGM, Warner Brothers, Paramount, Twentieth Century-Fox, Universal, RKO, Columbia, and United Artists. This fact indicated that the industry gave a steady priority to making a large quantity of pictures rather than to making good ones. A steady turnover of product was needed to ensure revenue at the box office, which was dependent on regular attendance at many theaters on a continual basis, not on high attendance for any one movie during a single run. From an industry point of view, then, making good pictures was secondary to making a lot of pictures.

The studios operated the newly developed film technology in an assembly line style not dissimilar to the newly established Detroit automobile industry. Writers and directors were assigned projects to be started Monday morning. The various departments—costume, makeup, art construction, musical scores, and so on—concentrated solely on their specific spheres of activity from film to film. The assembly line method was essential to getting a large quantity of product into the theaters, but unlike most assembly lines, the studios were not mass-producing exactly the same product over and over. While each car off the assembly line was no different from all the others, each movie was unique. Means were quickly developed for the mass production of different products. A series of basic conventions—character, narrative, thematic, stylistic—was established as a standard mode of expression. This formula was broad enough to be applied in a wide variety of ways and flexible enough to shift with changing times and tastes, yet fixed enough to serve as a pattern for production and marketing.

This assembly line methodology or homogenization of craft, which governed the "high technology" of the early twentieth century and had a profound influence on the stylistic, thematic, and performance components of U.S. film, is usually known as the Hollywood Formula. With respect to style, film was produced and marketed to the public by genre: Western, musical, screwball comedy, horror, gangster, or woman's film. The easily identifiable genres provided variations on familiar movie experiences and made moviegoing a sort of ritual. Repetition of this sort ensured a basically effortless participation by the audience. There was absolute trust, for example, that the hero would prevail and get the girl. It was just a matter of how and when. With respect to performance, typecasting (the human resource analog to the production of standard fenders or automobile bodies) led to the highly salesworthy star system. After several films, the public came to know a star very well, so much so that it became difficult for actors to stray very far beyond their normal range. Moviegoers all knew clearly what to expect from a Bette Davis or James Cagney vehicle, and the studios protected the stars' screen persona by developing filmscripts that would enhance the performance qualities of each star. The star system was the most important aspect of film marketing. Character, story line, and production qualities were built around the star. The hype derived from advertisements to magazines and press coverage about the glamorous world of Hollywood served the same function.

Given the circumstances of marketing by the star system, it is small wonder that Hispanic film actors and actresses had the option of either retaining their Hispanic identity and being typecast negatively or denying their Hispanic identity by what the industry euphemistically calls "repositioning" themselves. Examples of actors who took the former option include Leo Carrillo, who played his stereotype faithfully as a gambling, murdering, extorting, pimping, border bandido in some 30 films. Lupe Vélez, dead at age 34 in no small measure due to the humiliations of the Hollywood star system, played to perfection the stereotype of the Hispanic "dark lady" with her hip swinging and her amusing difficulties with the English language. Lupe would invariably go down to defeat when confronted with female Anglo-Saxon competition in the struggle to infatuate an Anglo male star. Examples of the repositioned actor include Rita Cansino and Raquel Tejada, who changed their images to Rita Hayworth and Raquel Welch in order not to be typecast as mere Hispanic dark ladies.

The influence of the Hollywood Formula on the development of movies themes or messages did extreme damage to minority groups, including Hispanics. The two fundamental thematic components of the formula were that the movie should communicate Americanism and that it should provide wish fulfillment. Often films combined both notions—nationalism and hedonism—at the deleterious expense of minorities. As Peter Roffman and Jim Purdy have observed in *The Hollywood Social Problem Film* (1981):

> The dramatic conflict was always structured around two opposing poles definitively representing good and evil, with a readily identifiable hero and villain. But since the hero was also the star, his goodness must conform to the star's personality. Absolute virtue, however, is generally unexciting and inhibits many of the star's qualities of illicit wish fulfillment. Thus the hero often embodied slightly tainted moral traits. As long as there was no doubt as to the hero's ultimate allegiance to the side of good, the audience could indulge in his minor transgressions. By subtly combining moral uprightness with an endearing toughness, the star was made more provocative and the hero a more effective combatant of villainy. He had the air of having been everywhere and seen everything. He was the Indian fighter who was raised by the Indians, the marshal who used to be an outlaw gunfighter, the police agent who once was one of the mob, and the ultimate good bad guy, the private eye who skirts between the world of law and the underworld of crime. This helped rationalize the hero's use of violent, even immoral means to achieve righteous ends. In the same way (though not nearly as often) sympathy could be extended to the criminal without ever upholding criminality.

As a result, in American film the ethnic *other* strictly and almost invariably played the outcast or the evildoer. Film, and for that matter, television in its early period, was an instrument of socialization that took as its guiding premise the assimilation of all racial, ethnic, and religious differences into the harmonizing credo of the American melting pot. There was no room whatsoever for divergence from this requirement. Even more painful, those races and ethnicities that could not be readily assimilated because of their difference of color and physiognomy—which would be readily apparent on the black-and-white celluloid—for example, blacks, Hispanics, and Indians, were drummed into the fold of evildoers and outcasts, a priori and without recourse. Blacks, Hispanics, and Indians consequently functioned as the slag in the melting-pot alchemy of American film. Scholars have documented with massive and indisputable evidence how the early cinematic depiction of the Hispanic (particularly the Mexican), from its turn-of-the-century beginnings with the "greaser" films of D. W. Griffith until World War II, resided at the basest, crassest level of prejudiced racial and ethnic stereotype.

The usual components of wish fulfillment, such as romance and true love, destroying evil (even as we relish evil actions fiendishly depicted on the screen), rewarding good, happy endings, and so on, ensured that Hispanic and other minority characters would perform for the assembly line the roles of vamps, seductresses, greasers, gangsters, and the like, ad nauseam.

The formula became Hollywood law in 1934 with the introduction of the Production Code. The code states in pontifical and hypocritical fashion the moral value system behind the Hollywood formula, decrying criminal violence and intimate sexuality, upholding the sanctity of marriage and the home and other traditions that had already become heartily compromised in the movies. The code stated that entertainment is "either HELPFUL or HARMFUL to the human race." Because of this, "the motion picture . . . has special MORAL OBLIGATIONS" to create only "correct entertainment" that "raises the whole standard of a nation" and "tends to improve the race, or at least to re-create or rebuild human beings exhausted with the realities of life" (Roffman and Purdy).

In a very broad sense, an ideological vision of the world was acted out in each formula movie. Each individual—of the correct ethnic background, that is—can aspire to success. You are limited only by your own character and energies (if you are of the correct ethnic background, of course). Wealth, status, and power are possible for everyone (Anglo, that is) in America, the land of opportunity where the individual (Anglo) is rewarded for virtue. Such Americana as home, motherhood, community, puritanical love, and the work ethic are all celebrated. All issues are reduced to a good versus evil, black-and-white conflict, an us-against-them identification process where good equals the American (Anglo) values and social system ("us"). "Them," the villains, are defined as those who reject and seek to destroy the proper set of American (Anglo) values. Conflict is always resolved through the use of righteous force, with Anglo values winning out. "Them" not only includes blacks, Hispanics, and Indians—that is, those ethnics whose color and racial features overtly identify them as "others"—but usually any ethnic group when it is depicted ethnically.

✸ FIRST DECADES: THE BANDIDO, BUFFOON, DARK LADY, CABALLERO, AND GANGSTER

The early cinematic depiction of the Hispanic was an almost unrelieved exercise in degradation. Summaries exist for some 300 early "Mexican" films. The word "greaser" was commonly used in these films. For example, D. W. Griffith's *The Thread of Destiny* and *The Greaser's Gauntlet* make commonplace of the epithet. *Guns and Greasers* (1918) was the last film to use the epithet in a film title, but the term continued to be used in advertising. According to Blaine Lamb in *Journal of the West* (1975), the crowds loved these films and reacted to them in the movie theater along lines common to theatrical melodrama:

> To appreciate fully the brown-white moral dichotomy established in these early movies, one would probably have to be able to view them with a contemporary audience. *Moving Picture World,* the leading trade journal of the first two decades of the century, reported that audiences viewing *Across the Mexican Line* applauded almost every move made by the good Americans, while the actions of Castro, the bandido, met with loud hisses.

During the first two decades of U.S. filmmaking, the Hispanic stereotypes were the bandido, the buffoon, and the dark lady. By the 1920s, two additional roles were added to the repertoire, the caballero and the gangster. Typically, in accordance with the traditional role of minorities in American film, the Hispanic was one to be killed, mocked, punished, seduced, or redeemed by Anglo protagonists.

Some greasers meet their fate because they are greasers. Others violate Saxon moral codes. All of them rob, assault, kidnap, and murder. Greed plays a primary role in the early movie greaser's misconduct. Occasionally, as in *The Mexican,* a covetous Mexican landlord demands too much rent from the heroine and gets his "yellow cheeks" slapped by the girl's fiancé. More often, the greaser attempts to steal horses or gold. The greaser of the early films is as lustful as he is greedy. In *The Pony Express* a bandido abducts the Saxon heroine. The hero summons a posse and in one of the first of many cinematic chases, pursues the bandido and his henchmen, shooting them down one by one without sustaining casualties. In the final showdown the greaser leader tries to stab the hero several times but is overcome by a knockout blow (Arthur Pettit, *Images of the Mexican American in Fiction and Film,* 1980).

The earliest Westerns generally followed the conventions of that period's dime novels—popular, cheaply made books that sold in the mass market. There were two differences, however. One is that in some films the greaser was allowed to reform or redeem himself, usually by saving a beautiful Anglo heroine. *The Greaser's Gauntlet* and *Tony, the Greaser* cultivate the theme of Hispanic redemption through obeisance to the physical and moral splendor of an Anglo-Saxon beauty. This theme, to which D. W. Griffith made a significant contribution, was the first example of the Hispanic of low birth but good heart. "His is an unenviable lot, as he is doomed to wander between the longed-for world of the Anglo and the stigmatized world of the Mexican, held forever in a middle position between Saxon heroes and greaser villains. It is the faint beginning of a pattern to be developed more fully in a later generation of books and films" (Pettit).

The second way films were different from the dime novels because they reflected the historical reality of the Mexican Revolution (1910–1920), which the American film industry depicted with the customary quality of cinematic exaggeration, but occasionally showing no Americans at all. These films actually depicted the emergence of revolutionaries from the peon class and treated them as heroes. Thus, in *The Mexican Joan of Arc,* where only Mexican characters are featured, a woman whose husband and son are arrested and murdered by the *federales* becomes a rebel leader. In a similar film, *The Mexican Revolutionists,* a rebel named Juan is captured but escapes the *federales* only to help the revolutionaries capture Guadalajara. Films of this type were rare, however.

American film needed to operate on the basis of stark moral conflicts where whites represented good and nonwhites represented evil. Thus, even the Mexican Revolution provided the backdrop for the famous early actor Tom Mix. In his movies, such as *An Arizona Wooing* and *Along the Border,* the plot features rebels who are really bandidos in masquerade interested in kidnapping a beautiful blonde and providing her with a "fate worse than death." The plot required an Anglo hero to outwit them and give them a suitable punishment.

The Mexican Revolution also served as a vehicle for low comic mockery of the ethnicity and language of Hispanics. In *The Bad Man,* the villain boasts in a greaser action:

I keel ze man sis morning,
Heem call me dirty crook.
I keel some more zis noontime
And steal ess pocketbook.

Reformed in the end, this low-down cartoon-like bandido ultimately returns stolen cattle to their upright Anglo owners.

The Caballero's Way in 1914 marked the first of the Castilian caballero films, promoting personages such as Zorro, Don Arturo Bodega, and later the Cisco Kid. The formula for this cycle of films is very much within the convention of how American film treated ethnicity, since the heroes of these movies, by virtue of their pure Spanish ancestry and Caucasian blood, are able to put down the degraded mestizos who inhabit the Mexican California setting. The caballero cycle owed its inspiration to the North Carolina-born writer O. Henry (pen name of William Sidney Porter). The Cisco Kid was directly modeled on the writer's story "The Caballero's Way" (1907). O. Henry, who spent several years in Austin and Houston and went to jail for embezzlement of an Austin bank, was among the last of the American writers to present Mexicans in a totally prejudicial and stereotypical manner. His usual method when writing about the West, aptly reflected in the caballero film cycle, was to spice up his stories with Spanish characters and motifs and to have pure-blooded Castilians thwart the mestizos and Indians. O. Henry's short stories, extremely popular at the time, were ideal for movies, since they were a type of formula fiction based on contrived plots, shallow characterization, strange turns of events, and surprise endings. Many of his stories were turned into films.

The gay caballero had a few minor variations. The Cisco Kid cycle was the most popular. It began in the silent era with films such as *The Caballero's Way* and *The Border Terror* (1919), and during the sound

Henry Darrow as Zorro.

era large numbers were made. Warner Baxter starred (typically with Hollywood, at first Anglos did the role, Hispanics only later) in three such films from 1929 to 1939. César Romero did six between 1939 and 1941, Duncan Renaldo did eight between 1945 and 1950, and Gilbert Roland did six in 1946 and 1947. The Cisco character stressed the amorous side of the gay caballero, a charming brigand who prized a beautiful woman as a gourmet savors a vintage wine (from a contemporary perspective he was a plain and simple cad). Like his Anglo counterparts of similar Western series, his method was to ride in, destroy evil, and ride out, leaving a broken heart or two. If Cisco flirted with Anglo women, his status as a serial hero made marriage inconceivable—it would end the series! The formula worked tremendously well on television as well, since this syndicated serial garnered the largest receipts of its time.

There is one film in which the gay caballero actually gets the girl. The exception actually proves the point that Hispanics within the plot of the film (as well as in the film industry itself) can only succeed if they are willing to deny their own culture and identity in favor of Anglo mores. Cornel Wilde as Don Arturo Bodega, after joining Fremont's Freedom

Forces in *California Conquest* and helping defeat the greaser scum of the Pacific province, proposes to his Anglo bride-to-be. The heroine mulls over the proposal by Don Arturo and responds, "You *would* give a lot to be an American, wouldn't you?"

Even before the demise of the gay caballero series, the popularity of the gay caballero series was outstripped by the appearance of the dark lady films, particularly the Mexican spitfire in the person of Lupe Vélez, who elevated the stereotype from a minor role to star billing. Rita Hayworth also got her start this way. Born Margarita Carmen Cansino of a Spanish-born dancer father and his Ziegfield Follies partner Volga Haworth, she was discovered at 13 dancing at Mexican night spots in Tijuana and Agua Caliente. Her early movies, under the name Rita Cansino, included work in the "Three Mesquiteers" series (a takeoff on both the *Three Musketeers* and the mesquite plant), a seemingly unending cycle of movies featuring trios of cowboys. Everyone did them, including John Wayne, Bob Steele, Tom Tyler, Rufe Davis, Raymond Hatton, Duncan Renaldo, Jimmy Dodd, Ralph Byrd, Bob Livingston, Ray (Crash) Corrigan and Max Terhune. Rita played, of course, the dark lady, and she was notable in dancing a barroom "La Cucaracha" in *Hit the Saddle* (1937). It was that year that she married the shrewd businessman Edward Judson, who wised her up that being a Hispanic limited her to work as a cinematic loose woman. Under his guidance she changed her name to Rita Hayworth and was transformed from a raven-haired Hispanic dark lady into an auburn-haired sophisticate. By the early 1940s she attained Anglo recognition as the hottest of Hollywood's love goddesses. Her picture in *Life* magazine was so much in demand that it was reproduced in the millions and adorned the atomic bomb that was dropped on Bimini. Raquel Welch (formerly Raquel Tejada) had a similar career as a non-Hispanic and was therefore more acceptable as a love goddess to the mainstream.

Lupe Vélez went the other way and was dead at age 34. Born Guadalupe Vélez de Villalobos in San Luis Potosí, Mexico, in 1910, she was the daughter of an army colonel and an opera singer. Her arrival in Los Angeles was auspicious. She did eight movies in the "Mexican Spitfire" series, had a tempestuous romance with Gary Cooper, married Johnny Weismuller, with whom she had celebrated rows, and committed suicide, reportedly because she could not face the shame of bearing a child out of wedlock to a man she felt bore her no love (actor Harold Ramond). She was five months pregnant. Ironically, her last film was *Mexican Spitfire's Blessed Event* (1943).

Blood and caste reign supreme in the dark lady

films just as with the gay caballero. If the dark lady, with her hip swinging and her amusing difficulties with the English language, encountered female Anglo competition, she surely went down to defeat. If, however, as in *Border Café,* there were no blondes in sight, she could eventually win her hero, as long as her "Hispanic" heritage was pure Spanish. In *Río Grande,* the dark lady is permitted to be of mixed American Mexican ancestry—a hotpepper, cold cucumber combination of extremely erratic behavior advertised as "passionate, revengeful, brave, unreasonable and most cussedly lovable" (Arthur Pettit, *Images of the Mexican American in Fiction and Film,* 1980). In a few films featuring only Mexican characters (*Love In Mexico, Papita, When Hearts Are Trumps),* the dark lady usually rejects a rich but obese and corrupt Mexican suitor in favor of a poor but pure and handsome Indian or mestizo. Pettit found:

> By far the most popular type of dark lady is only half-Spanish and therefore must undergo a long apprenticeship before gaining the Saxon hero. These tests of loyalty invariably require the dark lady to desert her race, her native country, or both. Dozens of films exploit her precarious position. She may fall in love with a captured American and rescue him from imminent execution at the hands of the Mexican army. Perhaps she must turn against a member of her family—a brother, as in *Chiquita, the Dancer,* or a father, as in *His Mexican Sweetheart*—thus demonstrating both her loyalty to the hero and her allegiance to "the land of the free." Whatever the variations on the theme, the outcome is the same. The dark lady gains the hero only by renouncing her past.

In the early 1930s, Hollywood began to produce a number of gangster films, and as one might have predicted, there quickly appeared a greaser-gangster subgenre. The greaser gangster differed from the dark heroes of Prohibition and the Great Depression (such as James Cagney, George Raft, and the early Humphrey Bogart) in crucial ways. He was a treacherous coward, oily, ugly, crude, overdressed, unromantic, and with no loyalty even to his criminal peers. Leo Carrillo played the stereotype faithfully as a gambling, murdering, extorting, pimping, often border bandido in some 25 or 30 films. In *Girl of the Río* (1932), he attempted to steal the hand of the glamorous Dolores del Río, a cantina dancer called The Dove. That particular film earned a formal protest on the part of the Mexican government, especially because it portrayed Mexican "justice" as a reflection of who could pay the most for the verdict of their liking.

Another facet of representation has been animated cartoons with Hispanic figures. The Hanna-Barbera creation of mice Speedy González and Slowpoke Rodríguez can still be viewed on television today. These insensitive cartoon images are animated versions of the greaser buffoon, as earlier depicted in Cisco's sidekick. Slowpoke, for example, is the stereotypical sleepy, lazy Mexican. And while Speedy González is energetic enough, neither his frenetic activity accompanied by shouts of *¡Arriba, arriba, arriba!* nor his triumphs over cats and coyotes ever overcome his greaser image. Children may not be aware of it, depending on their age, but his name evokes countless obscene jokes focusing on Mexican sexuality.

Ironically, one of the most positive things to happen on behalf of Hispanics with respect to animation was the advent of World War II and the need to be sensitive to Hispanics during wartime. During World War II, Nelson D. Rockefeller's Office for Coordination of Inter-American Affairs asked Walt Disney to make a goodwill tour of Latin America in support of the Good Neighbor policy. The result was two films, *Saludos amigos* (1943), oriented toward Brazil, and *The Three Caballeros* (1945), set in Mexico. The latter film featured Panchito, a sombrero-wearing, pistol-packing rooster. A bit of the stereotype remained in Panchito, but he was a likable, fun-loving, and highly assertive type who showed *el pato Pascual* (a Hispanic Donald Duck) and José Carioca (a Brazilian parrot from *Saludos amigos)* the wonders of Mexico, such as piñata parties, Veracruzan jarochos (dances), posadas (Christmas pageant), and other celebrations of Mexican folklore. Mexico had never been given such a benign, positive image by Hollywood, wherein in the persons of Donald, José, and Panchito, the United States, Brazil and Mexico were three pals, none more equal than the others. Latin American audiences were enchanted by both of these films.

✳ HISPANICS IN FILM DURING THE 1930s AND THE ERA OF SOCIAL CONSCIOUSNESS

The Great Depression brought with it the gangster movie genre, which produced a new spate of negative Hispanic stereotypes. The depression also brought with it a new genre as well, the "Hollywood social problem film." For the first time, U.S. Hispanics were portrayed in a somewhat different, and occasionally radically different, light in these Hollywood movies.

The economic breakdown represented by the depression, the rise of fascism and other totalitarianism movements worldwide, the war against these political forms of oppression, and the idealistic vigor of the post-World War II years (up to the advent of McCarthyism) all fostered concern with social conditions, an impulse toward political change. The theater of Clifford Odets, the novels and screenplays of John Steinbeck, and the songs of Woody Guthrie all found a large public response to their criticism of American society, government, and business during the period.

This era of social consciousness also found reflection in Hollywood social problem films, which usually were produced in accordance with the conventions of the Hollywood Formula. The Hollywood conventions were that America is a series of social institutions that from time to time experience "problems" that, like those of an automobile, need to be tinkered with and corrected. For the most part, the films attacked such problems in order to inspire limited social change or restore the status quo to an "ideal" level of efficiency. While the Hollywood social problem genre places great importance on the surface mechanisms of society, there is only an indirect or covert treatment of broader social values (those of the family, sexuality, religion, and so on) that function behind and govern the mechanisms.

Certainly the depiction of minorities improved markedly in films formulated according to the conventions of the social problem film. For example, anti-Semitism was grappled with, and indeed in 1947 in such films as *Crossfire* and *Gentleman's Agreement* the issue generated large box office returns. Just as anti-Semitism was the theme of 1947, the Negro became the problem of 1949 in films such as the Stanley Kramer production *Home of the Brave* (the central character in the Arthur Laurents book was a Jew; Kramer changed the character to a black), *Lost Boundaries,* and *Pinky* (directed by Elia Kazan), where the "problem" centers around mulattoes who can pass for white. The most unaffected and best realized of the cycle was *Intruder in the Dust (1949),* adapted from the William Faulkner novel. In 1950, *No Way Out* introduced Sidney Poitier in what was to become his standard role as a noble and loyal black who endures and patiently waits for white society to recognize his rights rather than go out and demand them. To be too insistent would only threaten white society and thereby prolong racial inequality, or so the Hollywood convention went. Subsequent films followed the integrationist solution to the social problem, both reflecting growing integration in some American institutions, such as sports, and emphasizing the need for blacks, with infinite tolerance and patience, to prove themselves worthy: *The Jackie Robinson Story* (1950), *The Joe Louis Story* (1953), *Bright Victory* (1951), *The Well* (1951), and numerous others.

The social problem genre was the occasion for some atonement for the earlier deplorable treatment of the American Indian by the studios. *Massacre* (1931), *Broken Arrow* (1950), *Jim Thorpe—All American* (1951), and many others presented a positive depiction of the American Indian. The Japanese, who during the war had been demonized, were permitted back into the human race and depicted sympathetically by means of social problem films: King Vidor's *Japanese War Bride* (1952), *Go for Broke* (1951), *Bad Day at Black Rock* (1954), and *Three Stripes in the Sun* (1955) all dramatize the Japanese as victims of American bigotry.

In depicting Chicanos, Mexicans, and other Hispanics, the social problem vehicle produced some noteworthy if flawed films, but a review of the overall film production reveals that the positive depiction of Hispanics was still the exception rather than the rule. *Bordertown* (starring Paul Muni in brownface and Bette Davis in her standard performance as a lunatic, 1935) is the first Hispanic social problem film. The central concern is not the oppression of Chicanos, but rather the discovery of who committed a murder. What social comment there is exists as a sedative against militancy by Hispanics. The filmic creation of Johnny Ramírez was certainly a more complex one than the standard Hollywood border type. Relative psychological complexity aside, the soothing conventions of the Hollywood Formula determine the finale. The film ends with Ramírez, disillusioned over the corruption and meanness of success, returning to his barrio home. He says his confession to the priest, prays with his mother, and all three walk down the church aisle. The padre asks, "Well, Johnny, what are you going to do now?" and Johnny gives the expected reply, "Come back and live among my own people where I belong." *Bordertown* hypothesizes that for a Chicano, success is fruitless and undesirable, that true virtue lies in accepting life as it is. Ramírez has learned the padre's lesson of patience and no longer holds impractical ambitions. *Bordertown* celebrates stoic acquiescence to the status quo and denigrates the aspiration for social change.

Despite the limitations of the social problem film, it is certainly true that psychologically complex and occasionally resolute and strong characters emerged from this genre. Among them are several Chicano protagonists in *Giant* (1956), including the proud and dedicated nurse María Ramírez, who experiences the racism of Texans; the family of Leo Mimosa, who is buried alive in a New Mexico cave in Billy Wilder's notable *The Big Carnival* (1951), which depicts a tragic act of God turned into a public relations event; and the women in *One-Eyed Jacks* (starring Marlon Brando, 1961), Katy Jurado, and Pia Pellicer. Occasionally the strong and resolute character is also "evil," as in *Washington Masquerade* (1932), one of the earliest of the "political machine and country crusader" series of films that include *Washington Merry-Go-Round* (1932) and the Frank Capra series: *Mr. Deeds Goes to Town* and *You Can't Take It With You* (1938), *Mr. Smith Goes To Washington* (1939), and *Meet John Doe* (1941). *Washington Masquerade* proclaims that "the running of the U.S. has fallen into bad hands!" and proceeds to clearly identify whose hands they are—Hispanic ones! Unbelievable as this may be, given the lack of political visibility, much less power, of Hispanics in the real world in 1932, the villain is an oily, Latin-like (and hence un-American) lobbyist whose influence extends through all levels of government.

The socially conscious era of the Great Depression and its aftermath brought in a new wave of Anglo good-Samaritans who acted on behalf of innocent and defenseless Mexicans. There was some of this character development and plot in the silent era as well: *Mexicans on the Río Grande* (1914), *A Mexican's Gratitude* (1909), *Land Baron of San Tee* (1912). In films such as *Border G-Man* (1938), *Durango Valley Raiders* (1938), and *Rose of the Rancho* (1936), or for that matter in the pertinent films of Hopalong Cassidy, Gene Autry, The Lone Ranger, Roy Rogers, and Tex Ritter (*In Old Mexico,* 1938, *Song of Gringo,* 1936, *South of the Border,* 1939, and numerous others), the emphasis changes from the hero as implacable and brutal conqueror of greasers to the hero as implacable and devoted defender of Mexican rights, typically as he tramps tourist-like through the exotic local Hispanic community, whether it be north or south of the border. Often the Anglo is fighting bad Mexicans on behalf of good, defenseless, passive Mexicans. The acts of these good-Samaritans strongly reinforce the stereotype of Mexicans as people who are unable to help themselves.

A variation of the white good-Samaritan acting on behalf of the Hispanic is developed in *Right Cross* (1950), a Ricardo Montalbán B-picture, notable in that it depicts a love relationship between a Chicano male and a white female that is set in the contemporary time frame. Montalbán plays a "neurotic" boxer, bitter with Anglos, who resentfully spurns society, assuming that he is accepted only because he is a boxing champ and will be rejected as soon as he loses his crown. Johnny is cured of these so-called neurotic

assumptions—which most Hispanics would view as highly accurate and normal—by his manager's all-American girl-next-door blonde daughter (June Allyson), who convinces him through her love and loyalty (she herself is a female stereotype in deep need of the women's movement) that the "gringos" really like him for himself. Two years later, Montalbán did another B-picture, *My Man and I,* which is vintage social problem formula, promoting the social cliché that if the oppressed are forebearing enough, the good that exists in American society will ultimately come to the rescue and overturn the bad. Here he depicts a fruit picker exploited by a nasty white boss who cheats him out of his wages and then has him arrested. Yet, throughout his ordeal, this upstanding Citizen Chicano with the name of Chu Chu maintains his patriotic optimism (he even becomes a naturalized citizen), confident that everything will work out, which is precisely the case. Montalbán in this film is the standard friendly, happy Mexican whose faith in America is upheld when the injustice is rectified.

The most daring and best realized of the Hispanic-focused social problem films are *The Lawless* (1950) and *Salt of the Earth* (1954). The former was a low-budget independent released through Paramount, while the latter was made outside the studio system altogether by blacklisted artists, including writer Michael Wilson, producer Paul Jarrico, and director Herbert Biberman. It is precisely because neither was made within the confines of the studio that a profounder and more artistically elaborated interpretation of racial oppression is realized. In contrast to the usual treatment, which views racial prejudice against minorities as the product of a white sociopath or other such deranged troublemaker who is then blamed for inciting a mostly ingenuous but somewhat blameless populace, the lynch mob violence in *The Lawless* and the vicious labor strife in *Salt of the Earth* are deemed to be typically middle American. In these films, by stereotyping "spics" as lazy and no-good, people find a scapegoat for their hatreds and a rationale for injustice.

Both *The Lawless* and *Salt of the Earth* expose the deplorable working and living conditions of the Chicano community. The only employment opportunities open to Chicanos in *The Lawless,* directed by Joseph Losey and scripted by blacklisted Daniel Mainwarning using a pseudonym, are as fruit pickers earning subsistence wages. Because of their meager, unstable income, the only houses the workers can afford are flimsy shacks lacking indoor plumbing and located "on the other side of the tracks." *Salt* goes further and provides historical background on how the Chicanos' rights were violated by Anglo industrial interests. The community once owned the land, but the zinc company moved in, took over the property, and offered the Chicanos the choice of moving or accepting employment at low wages. They are forced to live in management-owned houses and buy at management-owned stores. The houses are shacks with poor sanitation and plumbing; the stores sell goods at inflated prices and entrap the workers in a state of continual debt. Safety provisions for the Chicano miners are lax, especially when compared to those in neighboring mines worked by whites. Whereas Anglo miners are allowed to work in pairs, the Chicanos must perform dangerous chores individually. When the Chicano workers protest to the company, the manager warns them that he will find others to replace them. "Who? A Scab?" asks a Chicano. "An American," retorts the manager.

In both films racism is clearly linked to social authority. In *The Lawless,* a peaceful dance in the Chicano community is invaded by white hoodlums and a rumble erupts. When the police arrive, 11 Mexicans and only one white are arrested. White business leaders unofficially intervene and the Chicanos are forced to accept full responsibility for the violence. The newspapers then report that the incident was a battle between two gangs of "fruit tramps." In *Salt,* the police conspire with the mine owners to defeat the strike, disrupting the picket line and arresting one of the spokesmen. Snarling racial epithets, two deputies viciously assault the Chicano and then charge him with resisting arrest. Later, as the strike continues, the police evict the miners from their homes, carelessly damaging their possessions in the process.

The films' portrayal of the Chicano personality does not conform to the conventional Hollywood social problem film stereotype of the noble victim seeking only to gain acceptance from the white man. For example, in *Salt* the strikers are militant and articulate. They debate the issues at union meetings, thoroughly defining their goals and examining the nature of their enemies. Every tactic the company uses against the Chicanos they ultimately are able to thwart, and every cunning argument for a return to work they refute with solid reasoning.

The Lawless is a social problem film that deserves recognition in the history of Hispanic-focused cinema for its artistry, its ability to transcend the social cant of the genre, and the depth of its psychological analysis. *The Lawless* presents us with characters whose attitudes and behavior are as diversified as human experience. The characters range from the idealistic to the confused and fearful, to the destructively embittered, to the resigned and defeated. The Anglos are similarly varied. For example, some police officers are blatant racists but others offer genuine sympathy, even while they follow orders and arrest the Chicanos. The character of Prentiss, a well-meaning, guilt-ridden "liberal" businessman whose actions compromise Chicano youths, is an excellent depiction of the type. The film well evokes the effects of such double-edged benevolence.

Salt of the Earth, of course, has won a place in the international history of film not only as one of the best works on Chicano subjects but also as one of the most significant feminist films. Just as important, *Salt* is notable for the historical circumstances of its production. As Paul Jaricco puts it, it was "the first feature film ever made in this country of labor, by labor and for labor" (Deborah Silverton Rosenfelt, *Salt of the Earth,* 1978). The film had only the most limited theatrical distribution because of virulent attacks on it by Howard Hughes, the American Legion and others, but it has become a classic on university campuses and seems to grow yearly in importance. Linda Williams points out in *Frontiers: A Journal of Women's Studies* (1980) that *Salt* as well as the Chicano film, *Alambrista!* are artistically successful as depictions not of Hollywood "heroes" or stereotypes, but true Chicano types. Rather than individual triumphs of particular heroes, a genuine sense of Chicano reality is evoked through a documentary-style presentation of the social and historical context. Moreover, the vexed history of *Salt* is instructive, for this film serves to define the limits of the Hollywood social problem film and the consequences for filmmakers who would seek to overreach the boundaries of the Hollywood Formula. Film in the United States has not been a medium noted for its respect of artistic freedom.

Closely aligned to the social problem films were the historical "message" pictures such as Warners' Paul Muni biography cycle initiated with *The Life of Emile Zola* (1937), which devoted considerable attention to the Dreyfuss affair (the anti-Semitic element is only fleetingly alluded to, however). Two major films focused on Mexico emerged from this cycle, *Juárez* (1939) and the renowned *Viva Zapata!* (1952). *Juárez* featured Paul Muni in the title role, Bette Davis as Carlota, and John Garfield as a youthful Porfirio Díaz learning Lincolnesque democracy at the master's feet. This was another film marked by renewed efforts on the eve of the war by Franklin Roosevelt's administration to enhance the Good Neighbor policy. The film itself is not only a tribute to Juárez, but as Arthur Pettit observes in *Images of the Mexican American in Fiction and Film* (1980), it "also stars Abraham Lincoln. His spirit haunts the film from start to finish. Juárez rarely appears in his office without a portrait of the Great

Emancipator peering over his shoulder." The passage of the years has not been good to *Juárez,* but despite its faults, which include the cultural chauvinism of an omnipresent Lincoln, the film rises way above the standard degrading stereotypes of Hollywood. *Juárez* reflects relatively accurate documentation of Mexican history and society, and it impressed not only the American audience for which it was intended, but the Mexican public as well.

The clear masterpiece of the "message" biographies, *Viva Zapata!* (screenplay by John Steinbeck, direction by Elia Kazan, and starring Marlon Brando and Anthony Quinn) is also one of the best Hollywood Hispanic-focused films. The film is not free of problems and stereotypes, many of which relate to turning Zapata into a Hollywood-style "hero" at the expense of historical veracity; nevertheless, it is the most comprehensive and attentive Hollywood film ever produced about the Mexican Revolution—with the possible exception of *Old Gringo* (1988), which is not accurately a "Hollywood" film. One of the reasons for the enduring popularity of the film is precisely the nature and complexity of the message. The film is not only about power and rebellion but also about the ways of corruption and how easy it is for a social movement to be debased. Zapata resists the corruption of his brother, the power-hungry Fernando, who betrays the revolution and goes to the side of Huerta, and he even resists the tendency of the *campesinos* to look for heroes or leaders to whom they can abdicate their own responsibilities. As Zapata says to his people shortly before he goes to his death in the film, "You've looked for leaders. For strong men without faults. There aren't any. . . . There's no leader but yourselves . . . a strong people is the only lasting strength."

In addition to *Viva Zapata!,* John Steinbeck did several other treatments of Hispanic material. His other contributions make for a mixed, but on balance, positive record. In 1941, he wrote the screenplay and collaborated with director/producer Herbert Kline to film *The Forgotten Village,* an artistic semidocumentary about science versus superstition in a small Mexican mountain village. This film, which was done outside the studio system, won numerous prizes as a feature documentary but played only in small independent art theaters because it did not benefit from studio distribution. In 1954, Steinbeck helped write the screenplay for *A Medal for Benny,* adapted from one of his paisano (rustic Hispanic) short stories. Starring Arturo de Córdova and Dorothy Lamour, this comedy treats the hypocrisy of town officials who exploit the posthumous awarding of the Congressional Medal of Honor to a brawling paisano. It contains many of the stereotypes of His-

panics that mark the novel *Tortilla Flat* (drunkenness, immaturity, brawling, but also a chivalric sense of honor), which was also adapted into a film (1942, starring Spencer Tracy, John Garfield, Hedy Lamarr, Akim Tamiroff, and Academy Award nominee for supporting actor Frank Morgan), but without Steinbeck's participation. *Benny* was a critical and box office success, and Steinbeck and his cowriter received Academy Award nominations. This film, however, is hardly his best effort at depicting Hispanics, although the Chicano actually wins the hand of an Anglo girl.

The 1948 production *The Pearl* was cowritten by Steinbeck, Emilio "El Indio" Fernández, and Jack Wagner (who also cowrote *Benny*). In addition, "El Indio" Fernández directed it, and it starred Pedro Armendáriz. *The Pearl* was in fact a Mexican movie, the first to be widely distributed (by RKO) in the United States. The film, an adaptation of the novella, is a well-made, sensitive, and genuine treatment of Mexican fishermen, as might be expected of the Mexican director and crew. The plot itself is a parable of a poor Mexican fisherman who learns that wealth brings corruption and death. The critical response and the box office receipts on this film were respectable, but it has not endured.

While several significant Hispanic films of the social problem and historical message varieties were being produced, in parallel fashion other films of the earlier genres continued unabated. Enormous numbers of Westerns were produced in the period between the Great Depression and the civil rights movement. A small fraction of those containing significant Hispanic elements include the following, in chronological order, concentrating on the more notable Westerns: *Billy the Kid* (1930, King Vidor, director), *The Ox-Bow Incident* (1943, William Wellman, director; Anthony Quinn, Henry Fonda), *The Outlaw* (1943, Howard Hughes, director; Jane Russell), *My Darling Clementine* (1946, John Ford, director; Linda Darnell, Victor Mature), *Treasure of the Sierra Madre* (1947, John Huston, director; Humphrey Bogart, Alfonso Bedoya), *The Fugitive* (1947, John Ford director; Henry Fonda, Pedro Armendáriz, Dolores del Río), *The Furies* (1950, Barbara Stanwyck, Gilbert Roland), *Branded* (1951, Alan Ladd), *High Noon* (1952, Gary Cooper, Katy Jurado), *Rancho Notorious* (1952, Fritz Lang, director; Marlene Dietrich), *Ride Vaquero* (1953, Anthony Quinn), *Veracruz* (1954, Robert Aldrich, director; Gary Cooper, Sarita Montiel), *The Burning Hills* (1956, Tab Hunter, Natalie Wood), *The Sheepman* (1958, Glenn Ford), *The Left-Handed Gun* (1958, Arthur Penn, director; Paul Newman), and *Río Bravo*

(1959, Howard Hawks, director; John Wayne, Dean Martin, Ricky Nelson).

Billy the Kid, The Outlaw, The Left-Handed Gun, and much later *Pat Garrett and Billy the Kid* (1973) form part of the cycle on that folk hero; each of these films perpetuates the legend of the Kid as the friend of oppressed Hispanos and the foe of the Anglo cattle barons.

Most of these films perpetuate the three major Hispanic stereotypes of the Western—Dark Lady, bandido, and buffoon. The more substantial dark lady roles of the Westerns of the 1930s through the 1950s have been assigned to mistresses of white gunmen. This is the case in such films as *My Darling Clementine, Veracruz,* and, above all, the classic *High Noon,* which is undoubtedly the best of these films. Katy Jurado, playing the role of Helen Ramírez, the former mistress of both the murderer and the marshal who sent the villain to prison, is memorable for her sensitive and original treatment of a Chicana. Unlike the shallow stereotyped Hispanic mistress who flits from man to man with no qualms, Helen Ramírez articulates the essential moral posture of the film: the "respectable" townspeople are hypocrites acting in bad faith and self-delusion; Marshal Kane must confront the murderer, even if he does it on his own in order to preserve his integrity.

While some opportunities for Hispanics to work in the film industry remained in the Western genre between the Great Depression and 1960, although even here many of the parts were played by Anglos, in other genres the Hispanic presence in fact was greatly diminished. Some World War II movies contained a bit part from time to time for a Hispanic character, presumably to promote patriotism, a sense of unity, and the brotherhood (not yet sisterhood in these self-satisfied times) of races against the Fascist menace. In *Bataan* (1943), Desi Arnaz is cast as Félix Ramírez, a "jitterbug kid" from California who promptly dies of malaria before anything significantly heroic transpires.

From time to time a Hispanic shows up in a boxing film. In *The Ring* (1952), a sequel to *The Lawless,* the main protagonist, Lalo Ríos, under the guidance of an Anglo manager is renamed Tommy Kansas. As a denatured Hispanic, things go pretty well at first. The manager eventually realizes that Lalo is not champion material, however, and ultimately that judgment is borne out. Lalo is defeated and resolves to leave the ring forever.

The courtroom trial genre can boast of the 1955 anti-Communist potboiler, *The Trial,* starring Glenn Ford as a law professor who successfully defends an innocent teenage Chicano accused of killing a white girl at a beach party. The absurd and highly insulting point of this film is to show how the Communists can score points with gullible people (in this case, the Chicano community) in order to spread their nefarious designs. It takes an Anglo hero to see that the ingenuous Chicanos are being misused and to set things straight.

✴ DECLINE OF THE PRODUCTION CODE, EMERGENCE OF THE CIVIL RIGHTS MOVEMENT, AND NEW DEVELOPMENTS IN FILM: 1960s AND 1970s

The 1960s witnessed two important social developments that had significant impact on filmmaking: a liberalizing or loosening of social values, often referred to as the sexual revolution, and the emergence of the civil rights movement. The first phenomenon was a factor in the decline of the Hollywood Production Code of 1934. Beginning in the 1960s, films became much bolder in their depiction of both sex, including interracial sex, and violence. However, this was a double-edged sword for Hispanics and other minorities because often they were cast in roles where their villainy was far more graphic and horrifying than the snarling but ineffective criminal or would-be rapist of blander times. In this sense, the stereotypes of many Hispanic characters were actually intensified by the relaxation of Hollywood moral codes. The 1960s and 1970s were marked by far more diversity in films but also by a group of films that featured even more serious, racially damaging put-downs of U.S. Hispanics. For example, the bandidos were often engaged in visually explicit and gory violence, and the torrid Hispanas were now engaged in R-rated loose sex with Anglo heroes or an occasional black superstud. The Hispano became the toy of Anglo producers, directors and audiences, all competing in the effort to create for Anglos ever more titillating and vicariously experienced films. As a result, new subgenres of film emerged, such as the fiendish group of plotters (particularly the group Western), featuring casual brutality and other actions that Anglos stereotypically and inaccurately identify under the rubric of "macho." The word "macho" entered the Anglo lexicon in a way that is ungrammatical in Spanish as an abstract quality in adjective form ("mucho macho" could be heard from time to time in bars or seen on T-shirts around the nation).

Moreover, by the 1960s there emerged the "good-bad bandidos" that "close the once unbridgeable gap between the heroic Saxon and the wicked greaser" (Arthur Pettit, *Images of the Mexican American in Fiction and Film,* 1980). An example is Clint Eastwood in *The Good, the Bad, and the Ugly* (1967), where the Anglo hero teams up with the Mexican bandit, Tuco the Terrible (Eli Wallach), to steal gold. In this film, typical of the new, amoral Western, both Anglos and Mexicans are equally evil from the moral perspective and good becomes merely identified with technical skills such as a quick draw or creative thievery.

While in *The Good, the Bad, and the Ugly* the Anglo descends to the level of the stereotypical greaser, the converse is true in the extremely popular group Western, *The Magnificent Seven* (1960) (which spawned sequels: *Return of the Seven,* 1966, and the 1969 *Guns of the Magnificent Seven*) in which two Mexican characters on the good-Samaritan team are uplifted along with the Anglos in their battle against Calavera, the bad bandido. Unfortunately for Hispanic actors in this film about the defense of a Mexican village against a Mexican bandit, the stereotypical greaser role is not even played by a Hispanic, but by Eli Wallach, who was to become the new Leo Carrillo, replaying the greaser-style performance in a number of Italian and Spanish-based spaghetti Westerns.

This trend toward amorality reached its extremes in the 1960s and 1970s films that revolved around the Mexican Revolution of 1910, taking the image of Hispanics and the understanding of those events a giant step backward from the peak that was established by *Viva Zapata!* In the amoral Westerns of director Sergio Leone—*A Fistful of Dollars* (1967), its sequel, *For A Few Dollars More* (1967), and *Duck, You Sucker* (1972)—the viewer is given no moral guidelines to measure or judge the revolution. Both the *federales* and the rebels are repulsive. If the former are sadistic, pretentious, class-conscious, and stupid, the latter are sadistic, filthy, promiscuous, contemptuous, and stupid.

The cycle of Pancho Villa movies displays the same sort of denigration. The first Villa film of the sound era, *Viva Villa!* (1934), presented the revolutionary hero "as a cross between Robin Hood and the Marquis de Sade" (Pettit). Subsequent films, *Villa!* (1958) and *Villa Rides* (1968), stray little from this general depiction. The latest film to depict Villa, *Old Gringo* (1989), based on a novel by Mexican novelist Carlos Fuentes and produced by Jane Fonda with the avowed intention of injecting realism into the relationship between the United States and Mexico, stands in marked positive contrast to the rest of the cycle.

Set against the simplistic, amoral standard of most of the other Westerns of these years, the work of Sam Peckinpah, particularly *The Wild Bunch* (1969), *Pat Garrett and Billy the Kid* (1973), and *Bring Me the Head of Alfredo García* (1974), developed a more sophisticated view of Hispanics, particularly in the context of the Mexican Revolution in the case of *The Wild Bunch.* In that film the two Mexico's of the revolution are rendered in the contrast between Angel, the morally pure *villista* who represents Mexican village life, and Mapache, the degenerate revolutionary. In a film that is, ironically, one of the most violent on record, Angel occupies a pivotal role in that by his Christlike example he turns the drifting, amoral Anglo mercenaries to good purpose and sacrifice, thus redeeming them. *The Wild Bunch* is one of the most memorable films of the period, combining outsized violence and explicit sex with a certain sense of high moral purpose and interethnic camaraderie. In its own way, it is a distinctively realized combination of the decline of the moral code and the rise of civil rights.

Out of the milieu of loosened production censorship and increased sensitivity to civil rights emerged the figure of the Hispanic avenger. This figure was modeled on the example of the black avenger. Both of these aggressive, "superstud" types reflected growing Hollywood awareness of the changing population distribution of its market, namely that ever-increasing percentages of blacks and Hispanics were attending the movies. Although this demographic fact provided the underpinning for the "superstud" phenomenon, it does not explain the reason for the sudden, inciting creation of the genre or its content. For an explanation of the mechanisms that triggered the black and Hispanic "superstud" characters, the climate of civil rights legislation and the changes in prevailing cultural attitudes in the 1960s and 1970s must be examined.

Periodically in the late 1950s and early 1960s, *Variety* and other trade journals took note of the "growing Negro audience," which was "now a sizable segment of film patronage as a whole" (*Variety,* May 9, 1956; May 8, 1957). These observations made little difference at the time. In 1963, however, in the midst of the civil rights movement and after the National Association for the Advancement of Colored People (NAACP) abandoned mere persuasion and threatened to take legal and economic action against the industry, blacks began to play policemen, civil servants, students, and workers both in features and in movies and shows filmed and taped for television. Chicano scholar Carlos Cortés has documented a similar practice of giving bit parts to Hispanos.

Goaded by the civil rights movement and sensing that the mood of black militancy could be used to its advantage in the creation of a new film type, Hollywood responded with the "superspade" formula, and thus was born a new form, the "blaxploitation" film.

An NAACP official condemned the transformation "to super-nigger as just another form of cultural genocide," but black moviegoers, finding the superspade an emotionally satisfying tonic to the patient black represented by Sidney Poitier features, turned out en masse and "produced the first gold mine in years for the struggling industry" (*Newsweek,* October 23, 1972).

It was Sidney Poitier's success that had brought home to filmmakers just how significant a percentage of the moviegoing public was black: in 1967 Poitier was one of the top five box office draws in the United States. According to a 1967 estimate, although blacks represented only about 15 percent of the American population, they accounted for roughly 30 percent of the moviegoing audience in the nation's cities, where the biggest movie theaters were located. As one industry executive summed up the situation, "the black population of this country comprises a much larger proportion of the movie picture audience than its proportion of our total population would indicate" (*Variety,* August 26, 1970). Once the industry grasped this fact, filmmakers began to reappraise and revise their product.

The new, aggressive, and hip black audience found its first star in Jim Brown, the football star, who ironically but not surprisingly often scored macho coups at the expense of Hispanics and American Indians. In *Río Conchos* (1964), Brown refuses to repay Indian brutality in kind with the terse comment that "doing like they do, don't make it right," and in *100 Rifles* (1969) he beds Raquel Welch, who in this early example of explicit interracial sex is treated as white in the movie's promotion, but who turns out to be a half-caste Mexican in the actual production itself.

When Brown's career declined, partly due to personal problems, other black superstuds emerged, including Ossie Davis in *The Scalphunters* (1968); Roscoe Lee Browne in *The Liberation of L. B. Jones* (1969); Raymond St. Jacques in *If He Hollers Let Him Go* (1968); Godfrey Cambridge in *Cotton Comes to Harlem* (1970) and *Come Back, Charleston Blue* (1972, a sequel to *Cotton*); Melvin Van Peebles in *Sweet Sweetback's Baadasssss Song* (1971, a film that transcends the "blaxploitation" formula both in pretension and achievement); Richard Roundtree in *Shaft* (1971); *Super Fly,* directed by Gordon Parks, Jr. (1972, the most financially profitable of the genre); Calvin Lockhart in *Melinda* (1972); Fred Williamson in *Black Caesar* (1973); and many others.

The black superstud films, despite the early Jim Brown vehicles that included Westerns and war roles, such as *The Dirty Dozen,* were mostly set in the black urban milieu. The same market considera-tions—drawing a new ethnic group to the box office, civil rights issues, and increased Hispanic militancy in the United States affected the creation of the Hispanic macho, whose character was set in the Western genre. For example, Jorge Rivero in *Río Lobo* helps John Wayne bring Arizona land grabbers to justice with a dazzling combination of gunplay and Oriental martial arts. The Mexican American deputy sheriff played by Burt Lancaster in *Valdez is Coming* (1971) singlehandedly defeats a brutal cattle baron and his army. The bizarre plot of *Mr. Majestyk* (1974) carries the super-Mex formula to absurd lengths. The hero, half-Mexican, half-Slavic Vincent Majestyk (Charles Bronson) keeps the Mafia out of his melon patch by hiring Mexican migrants instead of the American winos who are thrust upon him by labor racketeers.

There were sporadic examples of Hispanic avenger types during the silent period, although not usually directed against Anglos but rather against *federales* of the Mexican government. The first major appearance of the type is in the Western *The Ox-Bow Incident* (1943). Here Anthony Quinn plays a Mexican who is hanged along with two Anglos for murdering a Nevada cowboy. Of the three, he is the only one to die with his dignity and honor intact, subverting the stereotypical role of the cowardly and inept greaser. These pre-civil rights examples, however, have a quite different tone about them, primarily because they were pitched to a non-Hispanic audience. This is the case as well of the films *Death of a Gunfighter* (1969) and *The Outrage* (1964), which also depict assertive Hispanics, even though they are not part of the Hispanic exploitation model. In *Death of a Gunfighter* the aging white marshall (Richard Widmark) has become an embarrassment to a prospering Kansas town that no longer needs him. In the final, shocking scene, the shopkeepers and bankers gun him down, leaving his Chicana mistress without a husband after a last-minute wedding ceremony.

However, in the figure of Lou Trinidad (played by John Saxon) in *Death of a Gunfighter* we are confronted with a different sort, a Chicano survivor, a Mexican sheriff who knows his "place" and adopts the necessary public servility to make his way. He publicly tolerates epithets like "greaseball" and "Mex" but exacts his private physical revenge on the name-callers. Trinidad is a cautious but brave loner caught between the Anglo power structure and the oppressed Mexican populace. *The Outrage* is a remake of the classic Japanese film, *Rashomon,* and features Paul Newman as a Mexican who murders the husband and rapes the wife. Newman's character observes that if he were freed, he would wreak revenge on his oppressors; this is a direct threat to the Anglo social order that was not tolerated in earlier films, but it probably is merely an artifact of attempting to transplant a samurai story to the U.S. Southwest.

The Hispanic avenger type appears far less frequently than his black counterpart. One of the reasons is that the genre has diminished greatly since 1974, which was a bust year, and the Hispanic version got off to a much later start. Also, the Hispanic market, particularly in the late 1960s, was much smaller than the black market. An additional reason is that neither the black nor brown versions of the genre attracted white audiences, making for a limited run of this type of film. Finally, the genre itself was initially successful for its novelty value, but it soon became boring and wearing even for the black or Hispanic moviegoers to whom the films were directed.

Even with the emergence of the Hispanic avenger, which somewhat reflected the atmosphere of the civil rights movement, and the emergence of a more sexually titillating dark lady, which primarily reflected the relaxation of the Hollywood Production Code of 1934, the film industry continued to grind out Westerns with buffoons and bandidos. *The Sheepman* (1958) provided a comic sidekick to the Anglo played by Glenn Ford, and in *Río Bravo* (1959) we view the antics of Carlos and Consuela, a comedy couple. In *The Train Robbery* (1973), John Wayne's gun quickly turns a Mexican railroad engineer from a "No! No!" stance to a "Sí! Sí!"

The role of the bandido took on certain variations that reflected Hollywood's exploitation of attitudinal changes. On the one hand, we are confronted with the straight evil bandido, the continuation of the type from the earliest period, except that with the relaxation of the Hollywood morality codes this character suddenly became more "competent." Whereas the earliest version was usually a tame utterer of incomplete curses or hisses who was incapable of really delivering evil, at least on screen—he might tie the girl to the railroad track or inside a house he would set on fire, but the deed was never consummated—the new breed practiced mayhem, sadism, and sex aplenty. Anthony Quinn in *Ride Vaquero!* (1953) enjoys killing men and raping women and maims a cattleman for life in a sadistic shooting. The earlier, classic performance of Alfonso Bedoya and his gang, who brawl over their victims' boots in *Treasure of the Sierra Madre* (1947) is another of the same variety. A xenophobic variation on the same theme was John Wayne's (director and star) *The Alamo* (1961). This film, which takes egregious liberties with the facts, not only depicts Mexicans as violent and inept, but was promoted by means of a shamelessly ultrapatriotic advertising campaign. In

1969, Hollywood took another crack at the Alamo with *Viva Max,* starring Peter Ustinov as a bumbling Mexican buffoon who retakes the historic site from the Anglos in contemporary times. This film, without a single Hispanic in any significant role, was hardly as offensive as the Wayne vehicle, and pitted inept Americans against incompetent Mexicans. In contrast to the patriotic froth associated with *The Alamo,* however, the latter film inspired minor demonstrations in several cities where it played, a good index of the progress of the civil rights movement during the 1960s.

Beginning in the 1960s and intensifying in the 1970s, changes in American society and consequently American film and television made the roles of the dark lady and Latin lover considerably less important. One of these changes related to ethnicity. Particularly in the 1970s, Hollywood and other media centers rediscovered the significance of ethnicity, both from the point of view of plot and of box office. However, the primary ethnicity that was cultivated was the Italian American, and secondarily the Jewish American, Slavic, and Afro-American. This period witnessed the rise to stardom of such actors as Robert De Niro, Sylvester Stallone, Al Pacino, Barbra Streisand, and others. However, the cultivation of various U.S. cultures and ethnicities primarily reflected English-speaking groups, not Spanish or other non-English-speakers. In the increased attention to multiethnicity, the Hispanic variety played a limited role. The phenomenon of increased multiculturalism in plots and acting styles combined with yet another factor to the detriment of hispanidad in film, namely, the expectation of increased sexuality on the part of actors and actresses, irrespective of their culture. In earlier decades the "carnal" tended to be the province of Hispanic Latin lovers and dark ladies. Or as Freddie Prinze once joked, "If you're Hispanic, man, they think you really *got* something downstairs" (George Hadley-García, *Hollywood hispano: los Latinos en el mundo del cine,* 1991). While this expectation produced degrading stereotypes, it also provided considerable work for Hispanic actors and actresses, who consistently had roles exposing their "hot-blooded" nature. In contrast to the earlier traditions of Anglos and some of the other ethnicities who were expected to be aloof, glacial, dispassionate, and so on, the film expectations of the 1960s to this day cultivated unabashed carnality and hot-bloodedness on the part of all actors and actresses, whatever their national origin.

For better (reducing stereotypes) or worse (reducing acting opportunities for Hispanics), the conventions of the dark lady and Latin lover waned, and in the 1970s the Hispanic community was successful in eliminating such visual media stereotypes as the Frito Bandito, a version of the film greaser, and Chiquita Banana, loosely based on the persona of Carmen Miranda. Also, Bill Dana, creator of the comic bellhop and dim-witted speaker of fractured English José Jiménez (who was the most popular Hispanic TV character of the 1960s among the general public, surpassing Desi Arnaz and Duncan Renaldo's *Cisco Kid),* agreed at the 1970 meeting of the Congress of Mexican American Unity to shelve this persona. In addition to eliminating stereotypes, some progress was made on television on behalf of more positive characters, notably Linda Cristal, who debuted on the series "High Chaparral" (1967). Speaking in 1982 about her role in the series as a powerful Hispana, Cristal remarked, "I was very conscious of being a role model. I received countless letters from the Spanish-speaking fans" (George Hadley-García, *Hollywood hispano: Los latinos en el mundo del cine,* 1991).

In the comic mode, the period marked the rise of Charo in a familiar role of flake and spouter of malapropisms; Liz Torres, who began on variety shows featuring Melba Moore, Clifton Davis, and Ben Vereen, then did the "Phyllis" and other TV

Freddie Prinze, star of "Chico and the Man."

series; and the brilliant Puerto Rican comedian Freddie Prinze (who killed himself, possibly accidentally, at the age of 22), who starred with Jack Albertson on "Chico and the Man." Another Puerto Rican who got his opportunity through a TV series, "CHiPs," was Erik (Enrique) Estrada.

Other actresses who achieved considerable status but were not generally known to be partially Hispanic until they appeared "as presenters or recipients on the nationally televised Golden Eagle Awards show devised by the pro-Hispanic Hollywood organization "NOSOTROS" (Hadley-García) were Lynda Carter of the TV series "Wonder Woman," Catherine Bach of "The Dukes of Hazard," and Victoria Principal of "Dallas" fame.

The civil rights period beginning in the 1960s also marked an important change in hiring patterns in the film industry with respect to directors, cameramen, and other production people. For the first time, an effort was made to bring Hispanics into production, and it was this cadre of professionals who were the primary group to go on to make U.S. Hispanic films. However, the introduction of Hispanic avenger films, group Westerns, and other Hispanic-focused subgenres usually did not carry with it more work for

Carmen Miranda.

Erik Estrada, star of "CHiPs."

U.S. Hispanic actors. The 1960s and 1970s were not particularly advantageous for Hispanics in acting roles, since more often than not, non-Hispanic actors were awarded the roles of Hispanic characters. For example, George Chakiris and John Saxon got the Hispanic leading parts in and *Death of a Gunfighter,* and Burt Lancaster, Charles Bronson, and Paul Newman were the respective leads in *Valdez is Coming, Mr. Majestyk,* and *The Outrage. The Young Savages* (1961), starring Burt Lancaster, was about gang war between Italians and Puerto Ricans, the latter played by non-Hispanic actors. *The Professionals* (1966) featured Claudia Cardinale as a "María" and Jack Palance as Jesús Raza, who kidnaps her and sweeps her off her feet. *Villa Rides* (1968) featured Yul Brynner as Pancho Villa and Charles Bronson, and Herbert Lom in the other significant Hispanic roles. *Che!* (1969) starred Omar Sharif and Jack Palance in the incongruous roles, respectively, of Che Guevara and Fidel Castro. *Night of the Iguana* (1964), starring Richard Burton, Deborah Kerr, and Ava Gardner all in Anglo roles, exemplified the Hollywood trend of filming on Latin location, but mostly for the purpose of local color, preferring stories reflecting non-Hispanic characters.

Despite successes in having some stereotypes eliminated, they remained abundant; in addition to the more intensive violence and sadism of Hispanic characters prevalent in the Westerns of the period, gang films also abounded during the 1960s and 1970s. (1961, director, Robert Wise, with Natalie Wood, Richard Beymer, George Chakiris, Rita Moreno), the cinematic adaptation of the Broadway musical, was a major achievement of the period. Unfortunately, only one Hispanic, Rita Moreno, had a major role in the film. The updating of *Romeo and Juliet* had a major influence on the Broadway musical, but in drawing attention to Hispanic gangs, its greatest impact appears to have been in helping to turn the juvenile delinquent or gang film away from blacks primarily (for example, *The Blackboard Jungle,* 1955, Glenn Ford, Sidney Poitier) and also in the direction of Hispanics. It was probably a factor in a spate of either Hispanic-focused exploitation, juvenile delinquent or gang films or films with other premises that brought in Hispanic gang members for their recognition value, such as *The Pawnbroker* (1965), *Change of Habit* (1969), *Badge 373* (1973), *Assault on Precinct Thirteen* (1976, a multiethnic gang, director, John Carpenter), *Boardwalk* (1979), *Boulevard Nights* (1979, Richard Yñíguez, Danny de la Paz), *Walk Proud* (1979, featuring blue-eyed Robby Benson in contact lenses as a Hispanic), *The Exterminator* (1980), and many others. With the aid of feverish media attention dedicated to gangs, the cycle has been running strong to the present day. Other films of the same general stripe did not single out Hispanics but merely included them among other various and sundry riffraff: *Dirty Harry* (1971), *The French Connection* (1971), *The New Centurions* (1972), *The Seven-Ups* (1973), *Magnum Force* (1974), and *Death Wish* (1974).

The urban violence (primarily juvenile gang) film has been exploitative of Anglo willingness to pay for explicit sex and brutality—both premeditated and mindless—and the pleasures of vicariously induced but movie-house-controlled fear of the alien. These films play upon the baser assumptions about Hispanic youth and mostly do damage to racial relations in our society. To add insult to injury, Hispanic actors do not even get the top parts in these films. did, however, rise above the pap. While the film is not without its defects, particularly an inaccurate understanding in some respects of Chicano mores by the Japanese American screenwriter, Desmond Nakomo, it does have an all-Latino cast, reasonably successful use of Chicano and pachuco dialect, and a serious theme and plot development that includes Hispanic violence against Hispanics—an all-too-real phenomenon of gang life. It deserves recognition,

The Sharks face off with the Jets in *West Side Story.*

within B-movie limitations, as one of the better Hollywood achievements in Chicano-focused film.

In *Badge 373* (1973), a minor follow-up to *The French Connection,* Robert Duvall singlehandedly fights the mafia as well as Puerto Ricans who are blamed for all sorts of evil and wrongdoing. Whatever might be thought of *Colors* (1988), also starring Duvall, it represents a major advance in the Hollywood understanding of gang psychology. (John Singleton's *Boyz in the Hood,* 1991, and Joseph Vásquez's *Hangin' With The Homeboys,* 1991, are in a class by themselves, but essentially were created outside of the Hollywood system, although Columbia distributed the former and the latter was released through New Line Cinema.) *The Warriors* (1978), although its artistry demands more respect than most of the others, primarily perpetuates the usual stereotypes.

The use of "bean," a more chic variety of the older dysphemism "beaner," came back into vogue. The World War II film *Midway* (1976) included a Hispanic character nicknamed Chili Bean. Similarly, *Freebie and the Bean* (1974) provided Alan Arkin work as the Bean; this film led to a television series with the same title, but an actual Hispanic, Hector

Elizondo, got the opportunity to play the Bean. The 1971 comedy *Bananas* is in a totally different realm. Even though it embraces every imaginable banana republic stereotype, it renders them in superb parodies, typically turning them inside out, as it does many Anglo institutions and worthies, including the court system, the FBI, television news, J. Edgar Hoover, and Howard Cosell. Wyatt Cooper describes the film this way: "*Bananas* would be unbelievable or offensive were it not so grounded in the ludicrous truth. . . . Its steady flow of jokes, sight-gags and parody make it one of the funniest pictures within memory" (George Hadley-García, *Hollywood hispano: Los latinos en el mundo del cine,* 1991).

Revolution in Latin America became a common topic of films in the 1970s. Curiously enough, in contrast to the serious and solemn 1980s (*Salvador, Prisoner Without a Name, Cell Without a Number, Old Gringo, Latino, Missing, Under Fire, Romero,* and so on), many of these films were screwball comedies, a long-standing Hollywood genre now attached to a new environment. In addition to Woody Allen's *Bananas* (1971), there was *The In-Laws* (1979), starring Peter Falk. Brothers Daniel and Luis Valdez had parts in the Richard Pryor comedy *Which Way Is*

A scene from *Boulevard Nights*.

Up? (1977). In a more common mode, *Viva Max!* appeared in 1969, describing, in opera-buffa style, the Chicano retaking of the Alamo. When Hollywood attempted contemporary Latin American revolutionary topics or other Latin American material in a serious fashion during this period, as in *Che!* (1969, Omar Sharif, Jack Palance) and *Night of the Iguana* (1964, director, John Huston, with Richard Burton, Deborah Kerr, Ava Gardner) the results were more uninspired than the comic attempts. *Iguana* was particularly disappointing in its turning of the admittedly minor Mexican characters into mere cutout figures of sexuality.

✳ HOLLYWOOD FILMS SINCE 1980

The period from 1980 to the present has been a relatively exhilarating one for Hispanics in the film industry, especially during the last few years, primarily because of three sets of closely interrelated events or trends. The first is the increased appreciation of the importance of Hispanic culture and the Hispanic population in the United States. It became generally understood that demographics projected that Hispanics were to become the largest minority group in the United States some time early in the twenty-first century. This underlying fact of population power and consequently political, economic, and cultural importance spurred all sorts of film, television, and video initiatives for and by U.S. Hispanics. It even underlay their national promotion, as exemplified by an extended article in *Time* magazine that featured Edward James Olmos on its cover, the first time in memory that any U.S. Hispanic, much less an actor and filmmaker, had achieved such recognition.

A second factor, somewhat encouraged by the Hollywood appreciation of U.S. Hispanic box office potential, was the emergence of a considerable number of actors and filmmakers who attained star status or national recognition during the contemporary period. These included Edward James Olmos, Raúl Juliá, Andy García, and Emilio Estévez. Similarly, film figures who had labored under less recognized conditions in the 1970s also made quantum leaps with respect to their weight in the film industry, including Moctezuma Esparza, Luis Valdez, Ricardo Mestre, and Martin Sheen.

Finally, with more interest in U.S. Hispanic themes and market penetration and more power and recognition of U.S. Hispanic actors and filmmakers, came more control of product within Hollywood. For the first time, a Hispanic, Ricardo Mestre of Disney, was to run a major studio. Similarly, Moctezuma Esparza coestablished Esparza/Katz Productions, raising tens of millions of dollars for a variety of projects, some but not all Hispanic-focused. Edward James Olmos, Andy García, Joseph P. Vásquez, and the comedian Paul Rodríguez all entered the film production business, with considerable diversity in their level of affiliation with or independent from traditional Hollywood sources of backing. Both the number of production outlets and either realized or pending film deals and the number of actors and other filmmakers with national recognition has never been greater, surpassing even a few "silver" years of the silent period when Latin lovers and hot-blooded Latinas were in great demand, albeit with virtually no control over their acting roles. On the other hand, it should be noted that Afro-American filmmakers made even greater strides during the current period, led by Spike Lee, John Singleton, and many others.

There is also a strong emergence of a phenomenon called Hispanic Hollywood by the mass media. Although Chicano films such as *Zoot Suit* had been released by the mainstream industry before, between the summer of 1987 and spring 1988, Hollywood released four films that depicted the Chicano experience: *La Bamba* (The Bamba Dance, 1987), *Born in East L.A.* (1987), *The Milagro Beanfield War* (1987), and *Stand and Deliver* (1988). The Hispanic directors, producers, and writers who made these films had typically played very minor roles in the film and television industry and then began to work as principals in the conceptualization, development, and execution of alternative, independent U.S. Hispanic films, such as *Seguín, Alambrista!* (Fence Jumper), and *Once in a Lifetime.* Now they have entered the mainstream as well (although not necessarily giving up their commitments to independent, alternative films), bringing Hollywood production values to the creation of strong Hispanic images that have also had (or at least were intended to have) box office appeal and arranging for distribution through mainstream outlets. The cross-pollination and collaboration inherent in the Hispanic Hollywood phenomenon ran the gamut from *The Milagro Beanfield War*—where Anglos, like Robert Redford, carried most of the picture (the script itself being based on the novel by Anglo connoisseur of New Mexican culture John Nichols) and consequently Hispanics, like Moctezuma, had secondary, although highly significant, roles—to *Stand and Deliver,* where essentially the entire film, including scripting, producing, financing, directing, and acting, was conducted by

Hispanics until the point of distribution, when the appeal of the film earned it release through the industry mainstream.

Hispanic Hollywood has significantly entered the discourse of general interest, business, and industry magazines, such as *Newsweek, Time, Advertising Age, Variety,* and other publications, focusing not only on filmic products but on the potential of the Hispanic market. For example, market studies done for the film industry estimate that the Hispanic population, estimated at about 25 million, approximates in its moviegoing behavior the peak audiences of the 1930s and 1940s who went to the theaters on a regular basis rather than to see a specific film.

La Bamba reprises the career of 1950s teenage rock-and-roll singer Ritchie Valenzuela (Valens)—played by Lou Diamond Phillips—whose emerging career was cut short by a plane crash in 1959 that also killed Buddy Holly and The Big Bopper. The film has had strong appeal in diverse markets. Hispanic viewers have liked it for its stirring plot and authenticity of character, language (bilingualism), and locale, and for its theme of identity formation and family rivalry and cooperation. In many critical ways the film is eminently Chicano: the intensive use of bilingualism, the focus on Chicano characters, the evocation of the Chicano life-style, the connections it makes between Mexico and U.S. Hispanic border culture, epitomized by the song "La bamba" itself, which becomes emblematic of a Hispanic binationalism that binds those who live *aquí* and those who live *allá.* Although the film has been criticized in the Chicano community and by Anglo critics, such as Pauline Kael, as an American success film that supports an assimilationist ideology, those elements appear mostly to derive from the biography of Valens himself and are not at all imposed on the film, as was the case of the social problem examples done by Anglos in the 1930s through the 1950s. *La Bamba* is also a significant "crossover" success, appealing to teenagers of all cultures both in the United States and internationally. It features stirring music that could be related to despite much of its genuinely Hispanic nostalgia for the early rock-and-roll period, a teenage love and tragedy story that viewers could easily relate to, and psychological themes that could readily be identified with, irrespective of culture. A film that rarely compromises on its Hispanicism, it also has that universal appeal that makes for an enduring work of art.

La Bamba was important not only for its artistic qualities, but because it also proved itself financially successful in the United States, not only in the English-language release, but in the Spanish one as well. A record 77 Spanish-language prints were released, and the Hispanic market provided a two-to-one return over mainstream audiences on costs (Columbia allocated 5 percent of its distribution and advertising budget to the Hispanic market, which in turn accounted for 10 percent of the viewers and box office receipts).

Stand and Deliver has been both an artistic and critical triumph and a box office success. Although released theatrically by Warner Brothes, it is essentially a Hispanic film and is discussed in the following section. *Born in East L.A.* marked Richard "Cheech" Marín's debut as director and also his first film without former partner Tommy Chong. The film, based on a video parody of Bruce Springsteen's song "Born in the U.S.A.," also parodies past U.S. policies toward immigrants, including the deportation of Chicanos, most of whom were either born in the United States or legal residents.

The Milagro Beanfield War was the least artistically realized of this group; it also was a financial failure. As Noriega points out, this beautiful film was variously seen as a "progressive fairy tale" by most Anglo reviewers and as an example of "magic realism" (associated with Latin American authors, including Nobel Prize winner Gabriel García Márquez) by some Hispanic reviewers, thus giving compelling documentation to how films are criticized not in a vacuum but from a cultural, political, or racial/ethnic point of view. However, from the point of view of character development and depth of plot, the film does succeed.

U.S Hispanics were not the only ones who helped create "Hispanic Hollywood." Norma Aleandro, the South American who was named best actress at Cannes for her wonderful performance in the Oscar-winning *The Official Story* (1985), crossed over into American films, in *Cousins* (1989), *Vital Signs* (1990), and others, even as she continued to do Spanish-language films. *The Official Story* also provided the means for Luis Puenzo, its director, to break into Hollywood with *Old Gringo* (1989), an intense, beautifully filmed epic about a young revolutionary Mexican general (Jimmy Smits), Ambrose Bierce (Gregory Peck), and a spinster (Jane Fonda), set against the background of the Mexican Revolution of 1910. The film, based on a screenplay by Carlos Fuentes, was not financially successful, but it is a much more realistic view of Mexico and the border area than most Hollywood films. Its depiction of Pancho Villa is probably the most sophisticated that has been achieved to date by American film. Hector Babenco, noted for his direction of *Pixote* (1981), was able to leverage that Brazilian film about a child street criminal. He directed the U.S.-Brazilian coadaptation of Manuel Puig's novel *Kiss of the Spider*

Woman (1985), an extraordinary movie about an apolitical homosexual, William Hurt (who won the Oscar as best actor), and a political activist, Raúl Juliá, thrown in the same prison cell. Babenco went on to do *Ironweed* (1987, Jack Nicholson, Meryl Streep) about street people in Albany, New York, during the Great Depression.

León Ichaso, who first directed *El Super* (The Super, 1979), a Spanish-language film billed as the first Cuban American film comedy, and which is about the trials of a homesick Cuban exile who labors as a "super" in a Manhattan apartment building, represents another example of "Hispanic Hollywood." He went on to direct *Crossover Dreams* (1985), starring Panamanian Rubén Blades, which did in fact cross over to Anglo audiences. The film evokes the life of a salsa performer hoping to become a mainstream performer but whose record flops. He then finds solace in his own roots and culture.

Since 1980, several films have focused on Latin America, reflecting the political situation of the region, drug-running, or both. These include *Missing* (1982), starring Jack Lemmon and Sissy Spacek during the overthrow of Salvador Allende in Chile; *Under Fire* (1983), starring Nick Nolte and Joanna Cassidy as journalists in the midst of the 1979 Sandinista revolution in Nicaragua; *Salvador* (1986), co-written and directed by Oliver Stone, featuring Jim Belushi; *Latino* (1985), directed by Haskell Wexler, about the anti-Somoza uprising; *Under the Volcano* (1984), featuring Jacqueline Bisset and Albert Finney, an adaptation of Malcolm Lowry's classic novel; and *Havana* (1991), a failed movie starring Robert Redford as a gambler with a heart of gold who becomes embroiled in plots to overthrow dictator Batista in 1959. The poorly done but financially successful *Scarface* (1983), directed by Brian de Palma, starring Al Pacino, and launching Michelle Pfeiffer's career, more or less feeds at the same trough, although it also focuses on U.S. Hispanic drug runners.

A Mexican film, *Doña Herlinda and Her Son* (1986), a comedy and homosexual homage to "mother" and the first Mexican feature with a gay theme, has earned special recognition as "the best-selling-ever Mexican movie in the American market" (George Hadley-García, *Hollywood hispano: Los latinos en el mundo del cine,* 1991).

The 1980s witnessed several films dealing with the *indocumentado* (undocumented worker). Undocumented immigration from Mexico became a movie theme as early as the 1932 *I Cover the Waterfront,* but the undocumented were Chinese being smuggled by sea from Mexico to San Diego. This theme continued into the 1940s; the 1941 *Hold Back the Dawn* dramatized the desperate efforts of European refugees living temporarily in Tijuana to enter the United States. Not until the post-World War II era did films like *Border Incident* (1949), *Borderline* (1950), *The Lawless* (1950), and *Wetbacks* (1956) begin to deal with Mexican immigrants, although the immigrants usually functioned as passive pawns to incite Anglo crime and Anglo crime fighting. *Border Incident* (1949, Anthony Mann, director, starring Ricardo Montalbán) is a quite violent, well-made crime story of the social problem era, also rife with the

The poster for *El norte*.

usual stereotypes, as was the original *Borderline* (1950, Fred MacMurray, Claire Trevor), with an unlikely plot featuring law enforcers each tracking down dope smugglers on the Mexican border. During the past two decades, as undocumented immigration has become a more widely debated public issue, a new wave of films has emerged: *Blood Barrier* (1979, Telly Savalas, Danny de la Paz), *Borderline* (1980, Charles Bronson), and *The Border* (1982, Jack Nicholson, Harvey Keitel, Valerie Perrine, Elpidia Carillo). Nevertheless, the theme of passive Mexican immigrants being saved by noble Anglos has continued to dominate. None of these Hollywood films has ever risen above the mediocre. The films of the 1980s have scarcely improved upon the first of the lot in terms of veracity, character development, or aesthetics. Hollywood *indocumentado* pictures have never surpassed the limitations of the social problem genre as originally conceived in the 1930s and 1940s.

In contrast to the stock characterizations of the Hollywood versions, two independently produced U.S. Hispanic works, *Alambrista!* (1979) and *El Norte* (The North, 1983), shine because of their strong and distinctive plot developments and intriguing characters. Similarly, Cheech Marín's Born in East L.A. (1987) shines as a Hispanic Hollywood exception to the bleakness of the rest, precisely because it combined Hispanic expertise and sensitivity to Hollywood production values.

In the area of comedy, the current period has been marked by the films of the comic team Richard "Cheech" Marín and Thomas Chong, who began by adapting their nightclub act to film in *Cheech and Chong's Up in Smoke* (1978), featuring stoned and hippy routines. The film became the highest-grossing film of the year and spurred a number of 1980s sequels, including *Cheech and Chong's Next Movie* (1980), *Cheech and Chong's Nice Dreams* (1981), *Things are Tough All Over* (1982), *Yellowbeard* (1983), and *Cheech and Chong's the Corsican Brothers* (1984).

Despite some innovations during the current period that brought Hispanic actors and filmmakers to the fore, the industry continued, as it has always done, to create more exploitative films. Among these, *Salsa* (1988) was a Hispanic version of *Dirty Dancing* (1987) that attempted to "outdirty" it. *The Penitent* (1988, Raúl Juliá, Julie Carmen) was a muddle that featured the eternal triangle set against the local color of New Mexican *penitentes*. *Moon over Parador* (1988, Richard Dreyfuss, Sonia Braga, Raúl Juliá) made liberal use of the usual stereotypes about Latin America and its dictators for uninspired humor. *The Believers* (1987, Martin Sheen, Jimmy Smits) abused Santería in order to make a horror/

thriller. *Young Guns* (1988, Emilio Estévez, Lou Diamond Phillips, Charlie Sheen) updated the Billy the Kid cycle, having us believe that the Kid whips up the inherent violence of six young punks, including Hispanic members. *Bad Boys* (1983, Sean Penn, Esai Morales) weighs in among the newest gang films. This one, in which both Sean Penn and Morales are superb, features a personal vendetta within prison walls. Morales, who has been badly typecast merely as a Hispanic gang member, got to do his repartee also in *The Principal* (1987), featuring Jim Belushi overpowering the Hispanic youth warlord, somewhat reminiscent of the way honest Anglo do-gooders used to bring down Hispanic and other alien powerbrokers in the 1940s films. On the other hand, the gang film *Colors* (1988), directed by Dennis Hopper and starring Sean Penn, Robert Duvall, María Conchita Alonso, Rudy Ramos, and Trinidad Silva, is a superior version of the genre, with the notable exception of the misuse of the Alonso romantic subplot. Trinidad Silva is excellent in this film, as he is in *The Night Before* (1988), an offbeat comedy about a young man on a senior prom who wakes up in an East Los Angeles alley.

The 1980s also marked the death of several prominent Hispanics of earlier generations, including Fernando Lamas (1982), Dolores del Río (1983), and Rita Hayworth (1987).

✳ THE EMERGENCE OF U.S. HISPANIC FILMS

Chicano Cinema

In a certain sense, the emergence of Chicano cinema has been the result of new, energetic actions on the part of the film industry to increase the participation of Chicanos and other minorities in the craft of filmmaking. In that sense, it was perhaps unexpected—at least by industry executives—and due more to prodding by the courts, by certain sectors of society, such as college students, and above all by the civil rights movement. The film corporations did hire Chicanos, but for general work in the profession and not necessarily for the production of Chicano films.

During the late 1960s and early 1970s, the film industry became the target of both national and local civil rights groups. Following on the success of the NAACP in having the industry open more jobs to blacks, the League of United Latin American Citizens, the Mexican American Legal Defense and Educational Fund, ASPIRA of America, the National Council of La Raza, and others urged similar consideration for Hispanics. Also, during these years various individuals in the Los Angeles area began to coalesce and organize Chicano media activist groups, such as CARISSMA and JUSTICIA. In 1969, a group of Hispanic actors, led by Ricardo Montalbán, organized NOSOTROS, which was devoted to protesting the kinds of roles Hispanics were forced to play and to working to better the image of Hispanics in Hollywood films. At the same time that constituency-based organizations were pressing Hollywood, government statistics were confirming the extent of U.S. Hispanic under-representation in the industry. In 1969, a U.S. Equal Employment Opportunity Commission report found that only 3 percent of the work force at major Hollywood studios was "Spanish surnamed." Similar statistics prevailed in commercial television, and, even more amazing, public broadcasting was shown to have compiled an even worse record of less than 1 percent Mexican or Chicano employees. As Jesús Treviño has observed in *New Scholar* (1982), the major studios responded with token gestures to employ more Chicanos, primarily by means of internship programs; television responded primarily through its creation of low-budget, off-hours community interest "talk" shows, and the universities (particularly the University of California, Los Angles, and the University of Southern California) participated with special admissions programs.

With respect to acting roles, beginning in the mid-1960s many Hispanics appeared in all sorts of films that were not specifically focused on Hispanics, including *The Big Fix* (1978), *Marathon Man* (1976), *Back Roads* (1980), *The Goodbye Girl* (1977), *Blume in Love* (1973), *Whose Life is it Anyway?* (1981), *Grease* (1978), *Dog Day Afternoon* (1975), *9 to 5* (1980), *Bob and Carol and Ted and Alice* (1969), *The Changeling* (1979), and many others. Unfortunately, as Carlos Cortés has pointed out in *Chicano Cinema: Research, Review, and Resources* (1985), these bit characters usually came off as nothing more than stick furniture, functioning as maids, bank tellers, secretaries, cops, a drug dealer or two, and with notable exceptions, such as the stalwart nurse in *Whose Life is it Anyway?* and the bad madam in *Back Roads,* they seldom did more than take up space, look Latin, and spout either Spanish or stereotypically accented English.

By 1978, less than ten years after the founding of NOSOTROS, the Los Angeles Chicano Cinema Coalition was founded; its philosophy had evolved from protesting Hollywood's exploitive tendencies to responding to two concerns: "the need to evolve a Chicano cinema esthetic, and the need to create an alternative to the 'commercial' influence of Hollywood film." (Treviño). The group had as its primary goal to promote the growth and development of a Chicano cinema aesthetic that would work on behalf of Chicano efforts toward social justice and allied concerns.

As Chicano actors, filmmakers, and other professionals began entering the industry and, particularly, receiving their apprenticeships through the production of documentaries on varied subject matter, their sensitivities inevitably turned to the Chicano experience, primarily because the *raza* story was there, beckoning and untold. As Treviño puts it. "As a by-product of this 60s activism and organizing, it became increasingly evident that if a truer story was to be told, then Chicanos would have to be the ones to tell it" (Treviño).

In contrast to the actors, most of the first entries by Chicanos into production were through television, including talk shows, soap operas and other programs, such as *Canción de la raza (Song of the People)*, *Ahora! (Now)*, *Unidos (United)*, *Reflecciones (Reflections)*, *Acción Chicano (Chicano Action)*, *Impacto (Impact)*, *The Siesta is Over,* and *Bienvenidos (Welcome)*. The networks also did some important documentary films about Mexican Americans within the context of migrant farm workers that also provided work for Hispanics: *Harvest of Shame* (1960, CBS), *Hunger in America* (1968, NBC), and *Migrant* (1970, NBC).

The major exception to this point of entry was the case of Luis and Daniel Valdez, founders of El Teatro Campesino, who should be recognized as producers of the first Chicano film, the 1967 adaptation of the epic poem *I Am Joaquín,* by Rodolfo "Corky" Gonzales. It is quite fitting that the first Chicano film would convert the following verses into kinesis:

> They frowned upon our way of life
> and took what they could use.
> Our art,
> our literature,
> our music, they ignored—
> so they left the real things of value
> and grabbed at their own destruction
> by their greed and avarice

First Films

The Chicanos who entered the studios on the production side were soon producing and directing a series of politically aware documentaries on the Chicano experience. Among the most significant of these are David García's *Requiem-29* (1971), which describes the East Los Angeles riot of 1970 and the circumstances surrounding the suspicious death of Chicano reporter Rubén Salazar. Jesús Treviño's *América Tropical* (1971) is about the whitewashing of a Siquieros mural in Los Angeles. Severo Pérez's *Cristal* (1975) is about Crystal City, "Spinach Capi-

Jesús Salvador Treviño in 1978.

tal of the World" and birthplace of the Raza Unida party. Jesús Treviño's *Yo soy chicano (I Am Chicano,* 1972) was the first Chicano film to be nationally televised and to deal with the Chicano movement from its roots in pre-Columbian history to the activism of the present. José Luis Ruíz's *Cinco vidas (Five Lives,* 1972) glosses over the lives of five Chicanos and Chicanas of varied backgrounds and experiences. Jesús Treviño's *La raza unida (The United People,* 1972), covers the 1972 national convention of the Raza Unida party. Ricardo Soto's *A la brava (With Courage,* 1973), describes the condition of Chicano convicts at Soledad prison. Rick Tejada-Flores' *Sí se puede (Yes It Can Be Done,* 1973) records César Chávez's 24-day fast in Arizona to protest proposed antistrike legislation. José Luis Ruíz's *The Unwanted* (1974) depicts the difficulties of the *indocumentado* population, and Ricardo Soto's *A Political Renaissance* (1974) examines the contemporary emergence of Chicano political power.

The earliest Chicano cinema also includes the film adaptation of one of the finest Teatro Campesino actos, *Los vendidos (The Sell-Outs,* 1972). Subsequently, this group's *La gran carpa de los rasquachis*

(*The Tent of the Underdogs,* 1976) was produced for public television with critical success under the title *El corrido.* The early period also includes Jeff Penichet's *La vida* (*Life,* 1973), which describes a family of poverty-stricken Mexicans who survive by scavenging the trash left by American tourists in a small village in Baja California.

Anthropological and Folkloric Films

Among the most notable documentaries of the anthropological or folkloric type are Esperanza Vázquez and Moctezuma Esparza's *Agueda Martínez* (1977), nominated for an Academy Award in 1978, and Michael Earney's *Luisa Torres* (1981). Both documentaries depict the life-styles of elderly women in northern New Mexico. Also outstanding are Les Blank's *Chulas fronteras* (*Beautiful Border,* 1976) and its sequel, *Del mero corazón* (*From the Heart,* 1979), which beautifully evoke the *norteña* or music prevalent in the Texas-Mexico border region and throughout the Southwest. Homer A. Villarreal's *Expression: The Miracle of Our Faith* (1978) is about the practices of *curanderismo* (faith healing) in San Antonio and elsewhere in southern Texas. Daniel Salazar's *La tierra* (*The Land,* screened at the 1981 San Antonio Cine Festival), describes the Chicano life-style in Colorado's San Luis Valley. Luis Reyes' *Los Alvarez* (*The Alvarez Family,* also screened at the 1981 San Antonio Cine Festival), depicts the hopes and dreams of a family living in California's Salinas Valley. Alicia Maldonado and Andrew Valles' *The Ups and Downs of Lowriding* (screened at the 1981 San Antonio Cine Festival) is an investigation of lowriding through the eyes of the cruisers themselves, the general public, and the police department.

Ray Téllez's *Voces de yerba buena* (*Voices of Mint,* screened at the 1981 San Antonio Cine Festival) traces the Hispanic historical foundations of the San Francisco area and evokes the contemporary Latino influence in the area today. Ken Ausubel's *Los remedios: The Healing Herbs* (screened at the 1983 San Antonio Cine festival) is a review of herbal medicine in the Southwest. Rhonda Vlasak's *Between Green and Dry* (screened at the 1983 San Antonio festival) examines the impact of accelerated economic change in the New Mexican village of Abiquiu. Paul Espinosa's *The Trail North* (1983) follows Dr. Robert Alvarez and his ten-year-old son, Luis, as they recreate the journey their familial ancestors made in immigrating to California from Baja California. Toni Bruni's *Los vaqueros* (*The Cowboys,* screened at the 1983 San Antonio festival) is about Chicano cowboys, particularly those who participate in the Houston Livestock Show and Rodeo. Rich Tejada-Flores,

producer and director of *Low 'N Slow: The Art of Lowriding* (screened at the 1984 San Antonio Cine Festival), both explains the lowriding phenomenon and makes a case for it as an important form of modern industrial folk art. Jack Ballesteros, producer and director of *Mt. Cristo Rey* (screened at the 1984 San Antonio festival), has created a documentary about a priest in a small mining community near El Paso and how he erected a huge sandstone cross and statue of Christ. Toni Bruni's *Long Rider* (1986) is an English-language version of his 1983 *Los vaqueros.* Jesús Salvador Treviño and Luis Torres' *Birthwrite: Growing Up Hispanic* (1989) is a docudrama that recreates the theme of growing up and self-identity in the writing of several U.S. Hispanic writers; and *Del Valle* (*From the Valley,* 1989), directed by Dale Sonnenberg and Karl Kernbergber, evokes traditional and popular Mexican and New Mexican music performed in the central Río Grande Valley of New Mexico.

Films with Political Content

On the matter of politics and the emerging Chicano political movement, several valuable films have been produced. Marsha Goodman's *Not Gone and Not Forgotten* (screened at the 1983 San Antonio festival) depicts how the community of Pico Union in Los Angeles successfully fought the mayor, the city council, and powerful business interests in order to maintain the integrity of its neighborhood. Richard Trujillo's *Tixerina: Through the Eyes of the Tiger* (1983) is an interview with Reies López Tixerina reviewing the famous courthouse raid of 1967 in Tierra Amarilla and related events. National Education Media's *Decision at Delano* (screened at the 1982 Eastern Michigan University Chicano Film Festival), documents the historic Delano grape workers' strike. Centro Campesino Cultural's *El Teatro Campesino* (screened at the 1982 Eastern Michigan University festival) traces the theater from its beginnings in the fields, boosting the morale of striking farm workers and winning over scabs, to its role as a theater committed to social change. Paul Espinosa and Isaac Artenstein's extraordinary documentary *Ballad of an Unsung Hero* (1984) evokes the political consciousness of an earlier era, depicting the life history of the remarkable Pedro J. González, a pioneering radio and recording star who was thrown in jail on trumped-up charges by the Los Angeles district attorney's office in the midst of the Great Depression.

Coproduced by directors Jesús Salvador Treviño and José Luis Ruíz, *Yo soy* (I Am; 1985) reviews the progress that Chicanos have made during the last two decades in politics, education, labor, and economic development and summarizes the variety of ways that Chicanos are responding to contemporary challenges. *Graffiti* (1986) by Diana Costello, producer, and Matthew Patrick, director, is about a nocturnal wall-sketcher in a militaristic South American country. *Maricela* (1986), by Richard Soto, producer, Christine Burrill, director, is the story of a 13-year-old Salvadoran girl who immigrates to Los Angeles with her mother seeking to find a new home and a better life. *The Lemon Grove Incident* (1986), by Paul Espinosa, producer, Frank Christopher, director, is a docudrama that examines the response of the Mexican American community in Lemon Grove, California, to a 1930 school board attempt to segregate their children in a special school.

Watsonville on Strike (1989), by producer-director Jon Silver, describes an 18-month strike by cannery workers that virtually paralyzed a rural California town. Marilyn Mulford and Mario Barrera's *Chicano Park* (1989) is a compelling and moving visual history of the struggle of one community, Barrio Logan, to stake out a place for itself in the metropolis of San Diego. The film shows the process through which Logan residents begin to effect positive changes in their lives and their community by using the richness of their cultural heritage as the basis around which to educate themselves to gain political power.

In the *History of Mexican Los Angeles: Social and Cultural History, 1781–1990s* (1991), producer/director Antonio Ríos Bustamante traced the development of the Mexican community in Los Angeles. *The Hunt for Pancho Villa* (1993), produced by Paul Espinosa and Hector Galán, and directed by Galán, studies Pancho Villa's raid on Columbus, New Mexico, and the U.S. government's failed efforts to capture him. In 1995, Héctor Galán also released for national broadcast on the Public Broadcasting System his award-winning documentary *Songs of the Homeland,* which traces the history of Tejano music.

The most important recent documentary film project was the 1996 series *Chicano! The History of the Mexican American Civil Rights Movement,* created by the National Latino Communications Consortium and Galan Productions, with Jesús Salvador Treviño and Hector Galán serving as co-executive producers. *Chicano!*, which aired nationally in April 1996 on PBS, consisted of four hour-long segments comprising footage from the Chicano Movement, as well as photographs and historical civil rights organization footage; but the most impactful portion of the documentary series resulted from the numerous interviews conducted of the actual participants in the Chicano Movement. The series was a historic first in many respects, including its use of modern technology to extend its audience by creating a web site on the Internet, developing an educational CD Rom, as well as an eight-part version and teacher's guide for high schools. A coffee-table book with the same title was also published and marketed in tandem with the series.

Film Portrayals of Undocumented Workers and Migrant Workers

The plight of indocumentados (undocumented workers) and migrant labor generally has seen extensive filmic treatment during the last decade and a half, including Ricardo Soto's films *Cosecha* (Harvest, 1976), about migrant labor, *Migra* (1976), on the arrest of indocumentados, *Al otro paso* (To Another Pass, 1976), on the economy of the border, and *Borderlands* (1983), which once again explores the complex interrelations of the Mexican-U.S. border. F. X. Camplis' *Los desarraigados* (The Uprooted, 1977) is about the early problems of undocumented workers. Jesús Carbajal and Todd Darling's *Año Nuevo* (New Year, screened at the 1979 San Antonio Cine Festival and 1981 winner of the Eric Sevareid Award for best information program, Academy of Television Arts and Sciences) is about the nearly unprecedented court struggle by 22 undocumented workers against their employer, the Año Nuevo Flower Ranch. Jim Crosby's *Frank Ferree: El amigo* (screened at the 1983 San Antonio Cine Festival) depicts this man from Harlingen, Texas, known as the Border Angel, who spent most of his adult life in an untiring effort to aid the poor and dispossessed along the Texas border with Mexico. The Learning Corporation of America's *Angel and Big Jose,* an Academy Award winner for short dramatic film, starring Paul Scorvino, is an outstanding film that depicts the friendship and ultimate parting of a migrant worker youth and a lonely Anglo telephone repairman. The United Farm Workers' *The Wrath of Grapes* (1986) is a documentary that depicts the plight of California farm workers exposed to deadly pesticides. Producer-director Susan Ferris has used historical footage, clippings, interviews, and other realia to trace the history of the farm worker's union and to chronicle the experiences of Mexican farm workers in California in *The Golden Cage: A Story of California's Farmworkers* (1989). Paul Espinosa has produced and directed *Vecinos desconfiados* (Uneasy Neighbors) (1989), evoking the growing tensions between the migrant worker camps and affluent homeowners in the San Diego area.

Public Education on the Big Screen

The Chicano experience in public education has been an important topic and concern of *raza* filmmakers. Documentaries on bilingual education include the series by Adolfo Vargas, *Una nación bilingüe* (A Bilingual Nation, 1977), *Bilingualism: Promise for Tomorrow* (1978), and its sequel, *Consuelo Quiénes somos?* (*Consuelo, Who Are We?* 1978), one of the best of its genre, perhaps because of the excellent screenwriting by Rudolfo Anaya. Elaine Sperber's *Overture* (screened at the 1981 San Antonio Cine Festival) uses the school setting to explore the potential for friendship and antagonism between Vietnamese and Chicanos living in a hostile urban environment. In addition, José Luis Ruíz's *Guadalupe* (1975) is a screen adaptation of the play of the same title by El Teatro de la Esperanza; it is a docudrama about conditions in Guadalupe, California, especially the deplorable educational situation. In a stirring docudrama, *Vida* (*Life,* 1980), directed by Elsie Portillo, the issue of sexual relationships, changing norms, attitudes, and behaviors, such as the use of condoms, is set against the issue of AIDS. Southwestern Bell's *America's Time Bomb: The Hispanic Dropout Rate* (1986), narrated by Edward James Olmos, is an instructive documentary on the dropout rate among Latino students. It includes an interview with then mayor of San Antonio Henry Cisneros. *At Risk* (1989), produced by Daniel Matta and directed by Warren Asa Maxey, based on an original stage play by Carlos Morton, portrays a variety of issues, prejudices, and misconceptions about AIDS.

Other AIDS films were *The AIDS Test,* directed by José Vergelín in 1989, which informs people about the HIV test; *Vida* (1990), directed by Lourdes Portillo, about a single Latina who confronts AIDS and awareness of her sexuality; *What Killed Freddy Fulano?,* by Jorge Sabez, which confronts the AIDS risk in sharing needles and in sexual behavior; *Between Friends* (1990), by Severo Pérez, which also examines the transmission of AIDS through drug use and unprotected sex. Other were *Mi Hermano* (1990), by Edgar Michael Bravo; *(In)Visible Woman* (1991), by Ellen Spiro and Marina Alvarez; and *Lights of Hope* (1991), by Rita Guajardo Lepicier.

Chicano Art, Poetry, Music, Culture, and Allied Topics

Numerous documentary films have been produced that either describe or highlight Chicano art, poetry, music, culture, and the like. Among the more notable are José Valenzuela's Chicano poetry *Segundo encuentro* (*Second Encounter,* 1978), about a gathering of writers and artists in Sacramento; Juan Salazar's *Entelequia* (*Entelechy,* 1978), which evokes the life and poetry of Ricardo Sánchez, ex-convict and current Ph.D.; and William Greaves' *In Search*

of Pancho Villa and *Voice of La Raza* (both screened at the 1978 San Antonio Cine Festival), the former an interview with Mexican American actor Anthony Quinn about the Mexican Revolution and contemporary U.S. politics and social change and the latter also with Anthony Quinn and, in addition, Rita Moreno and other vocal members of the Hispanic community concerned with issues of discrimination, culture, and language. Sabino Garza's *La llorona* (*The Crying Woman,* screened at the 1978 San Antonio Cine Festival) is a film depiction of the traditional folktale. Jeff and Carlos Penichet's *El pueblo chicano (The Chicano Peoples): The Beginnings* and *El pueblo chicano: The Twentieth Century* (both 1979) are panoramic overviews of Chicano cultural roots and contemporary issues. Chale Nafus' *Primo Martínez, santero* (*Primo Martínez, Saint Carver,* screened at the 1979 San Antonio Cine Festival) is about a young man in Austin, Texas, who carves statues of the Virgin Mary from wood. Francisco Torres' *Chuco* (*Pachuco,* 1980) and Joe Camacho's *Pachuco* (1980) treat the 1941 Zoot Suit Riots in Los Angeles through the art of José Montoya. Efraín Gutiérrez's *La onda chicana* (*The Chicano Wave,* screened at the 1981 San Antonio Cine Festival) is a review of a 1976 Chicano concert featuring Little Joe y la Familia, Los Chanchos, La Fábrica, and other groups. Juan Salazar's *Mestizo Magic* (screened at the 1981 San Antonio Cine Festival) is about a fantasy trip through Aztlán exploring the world of Chicano art from its ancient past through its living musicians, sculptors, painters, dancers, and writers.

Keith Kolb's *Southwest Hispanic Mission* (screened at the 1981 San Antonio Cine Festival) features noted Chicano art historian Jacinto Quirarte, who describes the technology and aesthetics of mission buildings. Teena Brown Webb's *¡Viva! la causa!* (*Long Live the Cause,* screened at the 1981 San Antonio Cine Festival) depicts the popular wall mural movement in Chicago. Paul Venema's *Barrio Murals* (screened at the 1983 San Antonio Cine Festival) documents the creation of the Cassiano Homes murals in San Antonio's westside. Gary Greenberg's *Dale Kranque (Crank It Up): Chicano Music and Art in South Texas* (screened at the 1983 San Antonio Cine Festival) profiles leading Texas Chicano musicians and artists. Beverly Sánchez-Padilla's *In Company of José Rodríguez* (screened at the 1983 San Antonio festival) is a visual history and conversation with the founder and artistic director of La Compañia de Teatro de Albuquerque. Director, Sylvia Morales, *Los lobos: And A Time to Dance* (screened at the 1984 San Antonio Cine Festival) is a documentary on Los Lobos, including segments of a live performance, interviews with the musicians, and montages that evoked their fusion of music forms. *Jesse Treviño: A Spirit Against All Odds* (1985) is a stirring documentary about one of San Antonio's best-known artists, who while serving in Vietnam lost a right arm and shattered his left leg, yet was still able to pursue his career.

Popol Vuh (1989), directed by Patricia Amlin, is an animated film of the Sacred Book of the Quiche Maya. Lourdes Portillo and Susana Muñoz have produced and directed *La ofrenda (The Offering): The Days of the Dead* (1989), an exploration of the pre-Hispanic roots of *El día de los muertos* (The Day of the Dead) and the social dimensions of death. *The Other Side of the Coin* (1989), by producer-director Sean Carrillo, evokes the work of three East Los Angeles visual and literary artists: Simone Gad, Marisela Norte, and Diana Gamboa.

A much earlier film, the Detroit Institute of Art's haunting *Rivera: The Age of Steel,* describes Diego Rivera's extraordinary Detroit murals of the 1930s and the equally extraordinary political reactions that this art aroused in the automobile and allied industries. A new contribution to the same topic is *Rivera in America* (1988), by producer-director Rick Tejada-Flores, who traces the artist's stay in the United States during the 1930s and examines the works he did here.

Hecho en Cuba (Made in Cuba, 1989), by Uberto Sagramoso, is a documentary on Cuban music that goes from the African rhythms that gave it birth to contemporary sounds. Graciela I. Sánchez has produced and directed *No porque lo diga Fidel Castro (Not Because Fidel Castro Says So,* 1988), which is an insightful look into gay life in Cuba, evoking both traditional and more contemporary attitudes. *The Return of Rubén Blades* (1985), by producer-director Robert Mugge, is a music documentary about the passion and commitment, art, and politics of the well-known singer, songwriter, and actor. Producer (also codirector) Eduardo Aguiar's *Federico García Lorca in New York* (1986) is an evocation of the Spanish writer's experiences and work set in New York.

During the 1990s, a number of films were made based on Latino art and culture, including *Border Brujo* (1990), in which Isaac Artenstein depicts performance artist Guillermo Gómez Peña as he transforms himself into 15 distinct characters; *Las tandas de San Cuilmas* (1990), in which producer and director Jorge Sandoval has filmed contemporary renditions of vintage vaudeville skits. One of the most interesting films along these lines was Luis Valdez's updated rendition of the traditional *Los pastores (Shepherds' Play)* in his *La Pastorela* (1991), which aired on PBS during the Christmas season. Another Christmas theme film was Isaac Artenstein's 1993 *Luiseño Christmas,* which was based on a performance piece by Native American artist James Luna.

The Azltán Chronicles (1992), directed by Daniel Jacobo, featured Luis Valdez discussing indigenous culture; *Tejano State of the Art* (1992), directed by Roy Flores, traced the evolution of Chicano music; and Daniel Jacobo directed the filming of a live concert in *The Texas Tornados* (1992). In *Dos por dos* (1993), director David Zamora Casas filmed his own work as a performance artist exploring stereotypes. In *Fascinating Slippers* (1992–93), director Juan Garza documented the creation of an art piece by Glugio "Gronk" Nicandro.

Gangs, Youth, and Domestic Violence

The circumstances of gangs specifically and youth generally have been the subject of Efraín Gutiérrez's *El Juanío (Johnny,* screened at the 1979 San Antonio Cine Festival), about the drug problems (mostly paint sniffing) faced by youngsters in the barrios of San Antonio, Texas. Ray Téllez's *Joey* (1980) evokes the problems of identity and of adolescence of a 16-year-old Chicano youth. Terry Sweeney, S.J.'s *Streets of Anger, Streets of Hope* (screened at the 1981 San Antonio Cine Festival), is an interview documentary in which members tell what attracts them to gangs. Patt Connelly's *El grito de las madres dolorosas (The Scream of the Mother Dolorasas,* 1981) is one of the most moving accounts of gang violence (in unincorporated East Los Angeles) and what a church brother teamed together with a group of concerned mothers attempted to do about it. Director Bill Jersey's, *Children of Violence* (screened at the 1984 San Antonio Cine Festival) treats four brothers in the Oakland, California, barrio, and *Dolores* (1989), produced and directed by Pablo Figueroa, portrays the problem of domestic violence within the Latino community. Jesús Salvador Treviño won the Director's Guild of America Award (1989) in the dramatic daytime show category for his CBS special, *Gangs.*

The Addict (1991), directed by Rogelio A. Lobato, treated the effects of violence on young adults. *The Ballad of Tina Juárez* (1992), directed by Juan A. Uribe, was a docudrama about a Mexican girl who walks north to the Mexican border in search of her parents. Director Carlos Solís, Jr., depicted Chicano gangs and their attitudes in East Los Angeles in *Homeboys* (1992). *Los Carnales* (1992–93), directed by Alejandro Hinojosa, depicts a Chicano youth who must choose between family and a group of friends who are becoming involved in gangs.

Chicana Studies

In the area of Chicana studies, Conchita Ibarra Reyes' *Viva: Hispanic Woman on the Move* (screened at the 1979 San Antonio Cine Festival) looks at the recent successes and the continuing struggles of Hispanic women. Julio Rosetti's *La mujer, el amor y el miedo* (*Woman, Love and Fear,* screened at the 1981 San Antonio Cine Festival) is concerned with the needs of battered raza women. Barbara Wolfinger's *Chile pequín* (*Peguin Chile Pepper,* screened at the 1983 San Antonio Cine Festival) is about a college-educated Chicana whose values clash with the more traditional ones of her family hometown. Sylvia Morales' *Chicana* (1979) traces the traditional, historically imposed, and emerging roles of Mexicanas and Chicanas from pre-Columbian times to the present. Elvia M. Alvarado's *Una mujer* (*A Woman,* screened at the 1984 Eastern Michigan University Chicano Film Festival) is an interview with a Chicana in Los Angeles who speaks out about rape and sexual assault.

In the 1990s, the Chicana studies began to flower in film. *My Filmmaking, My Life* (1990), produced and directed by Patricia Díaz, was the biography of a script girl in the Mexican film industry who worked her way up to director: Matilde Landeta. In Frances Salomé España's *El espejo/The Mirror* (1991), the filmmaker presented herself fragmented as an absurd testimony to her life in East Los Angeles. In *¡Adelante Mujeres!* (1992), directed by Mary Ruthsdotter and produced by the National Women's History Project, the history of Chicanas more than five centuries was evoked. In *Talking Back* (1992), director Renate Gagemi examined her own experience as a domestic in Latin America. *Mujeres de cambio* (1993), directed by Susana Ortiz, examined the roles of women across generations. There were numerous other films and videos in this blossoming category.

World War II

Memories of Hell (screened at the 1983 San Antonio Cine Festival) describes the suffering of some 1,800 New Mexican soldiers who fought in the Philippines, many of them survivors of the 1941 Bataan death march. Alfredo Lago's *The Men of Company E* (screened at the 1983 San Antonio festival) recounts the bravery and tragedy in Italy during World War II of the all-Latino unit of the U.S. Fifth Army from El Paso, Texas. *Hero Street U.S.A.* (1985), produced and directed by Mike Stroot, is a dramatic story of how, beset by unrelenting discrimination, the Mexican American community of 22 families in the town of Silvis, Illinois, set out to establish itself firmly as all-American and in the process contributed 87 sons to war, eight of whom died in battle. *Valor* (1989), produced and directed by Richard Parra and narrated by Ricardo Montalbán, relates the contributions of Al Ramírez (awarded four Bronze Stars) and other Mexican Americans during World War II, as well as the discrimination that they experienced that provides background for the establishment of the American GI Forum.

Chicano Feature Films

A significant and growing number of Chicano features have been produced since the distribution of what might be considered the first Chicano feature, *Los vendidos* (*The Sellouts,* 1972), a film adaptation of one of the finest of El Teatro Campesino's actos. On the other hand, some of what has been produced, such as the works of Efraín Gutiérrez, have fallen into complete obscurity. If we include some of the dramatic films that were aired on television (for example, *Seguín*) or originally planned for television (*Stand and Deliver*), in addition to the films made for theatrical distribution, the Chicano features include the following, directors noted: *La Vida* (1973, Jeff Penichet), *Please Don't Bury Me Alive!* (*Por favor ¡No me entierren vivo!*, 1977, Efraín Gutiérrez), *Alambrista!* (1977, Robert M. Young), *Amor Chicano es para siempre* (*Chicano Love Is Forever*, 1978, Efraín Gutiérrez), *Only Once in a Lifetime* (1978, Alejandro Grattan), *Raíces de sangre* (Roots, 1978, Jesús Salvador Treviño), *Run, Junkie* (*Tecato, Run*, 1979, Efraín Gutiérrez), *Zoot Suit* (1981, Luis Valdez), *The Ballad of Gregorio Cortéz* (1982, Robert M. Young), *Seguín* (1982, Jesús Salvador Treviño), *Heartbreaker* (1983, Frank Zúñiga), *El Norte* (1983, Gregory Nava), *Stand and Deliver* (1988, Ramón Menéndez), *Break of Dawn* (1988, Isaac Artenstein), and Puerto Rican filmmaker Joseph B. Vásquez's *Hangin' With the Homeboys* (1991). The Hispanic Hollywood films (combining Hispanic expertise and often control with Hollywood production values and distribution) usually are more closely affiliated with Chicano independent film than with the average Hollywood production that makes use of Chicano material. This is certainly the case of *La Bamba* (1987) and *Born in East L.A.* (1987).

Chicano feature films have contrasted greatly with contemporaneous films about Chicanos made by Hollywood directors and producers, even as they have shared some themes, situations or genres, such as the problems at the U.S.-Mexican border, the Western genre, or teenage groups. Some salient characteristics of Chicano film not usually seen in the Hollywood product have been a meticulous attention to the authentic cultural and social conditions of Chicano life, the use of Spanish to produce a bilingual film with considerable switching between languages, the recuperation of Chicano history (in period pieces), close attention to the political dimensions of the topics that are cultivated on screen, commitment to dealing with issues above considerations of box office, and a willingness to employ considerable numbers of Hispanic actors and Hispanic production people. Chicano pictures feature plots that may or may not appeal to the mainstream audience, but are definitely designed for Chicano filmgoers. They feature Hispanic actors in genuine situations, usually filmed on location in authentic settings and speaking or singing in a natural, often bilingual environment.

In contrast to the conventional Hollywood pap of the border, Chicano productions such as *Raíces de Sangre* (*Roots* [*of Blood*], 1977, Jesús Treviño), *Alambrista!* (1977, Robert Young and Moctezuma Esparza), *El Norte* (*The North*, 1983, Gregory Nava), and *Break of Dawn* (1988, Isaac Artenstein), about a radio announcer and singer deported to Tijuana, have all evoked the situation at the border with sociological depth and creative distinction. The quality of verisimilitude, heightened by the bilingual (or in the case of *El Norte*, trilingual) script, have caused these movies to stand head and shoulders above their Hollywood contemporaries, such as *Blood Barrier*, *The Border*, and *Borderline*.

Chicano "Westerns" have differed markedly from the Hollywood version. Both *Seguín* (1981, Jesús Treviño) and *The Ballad of Gregorio Cortez* (1982, directed by Moctezuma Esparza and Robert Young, written by novelist Victor Villaseñor) have been fundamentally involved with the recuperation of lost (or rather, suppressed) aspects of Chicano history and have evoked politically charged elements of that history. *The Ballad*, about social hero Gregorio Cortez, wrongly accused of stealing a horse, is also a stirring evocation of false assumptions and cultural and linguistic misunderstandings, since the fatal encounter with Anglo law enforcers arises out of their misunderstanding of the difference between *caballo* (stallion) and *yegua* (male).

Seguín is the first Chicano version of the Alamo story in the history of the cycle, which dates to as early as 1911. The 1911 *The Immortal Alamo* and the 1915 *The Martyrs of the Alamo* began this cycle of films, generally presenting Mexicans as ineffective fighters, able to triumph only through vast superiority of numbers, certainly not skill. With the 1953 *The Man from the Alamo*, the 1955 *The Last Command*, the 1960 *The Alamo*, and the 1986 television docudrama, *The Alamo: 13 Days to Glory*, the basic view remains of heroic Anglos killing masses of Mexicans before succumbing to overwhelming odds. In contrast, *Seguín* depicts a *tejano* who out of complex social circumstances fights at the Alamo with the Anglos against the Mexicans, leaves before the final siege, becomes mayor of San Antonio during the early days of the Texas republic, is discriminated against by Anglos, and subsequently fights with Santa Anna on the side of the Mexicans in the Mexican-American War.

Luis Valdez's productions *Zoot Suit* (1981) and *La Bamba* (1987), as well as *Stand and Deliver* (1988, Ramón Menéndez, Tom Musca and Edward James Olmos) and *Hangin' With the Homeboys* (1991), all deal with various aspects of Chicano or Puerto Rican juvenile and domestic life in the United States. Valdez's works, both of which have an important historical dimension, are fine examples of Chicano filmmaking, with Hollywood support and distribution. The Chicano juvenile films are light-years ahead of Hollywood products such as *Streets of L.A.* (1979) and *Walk Proud* (1981). The Hollywood films are invariably exploitive in their approach. Whether the Chicanos in these films are a menace to whites or to themselves, it is strictly the prospect of violence and its description on screen that carries these Hollywood juvenile films. In contrast, *Stand and Deliver* is a stirring story that barely even evokes gang violence. It is primarily about an extraordinary Bolivian mathematics teacher who helps Hispanic high school students in East Los Angeles learn college-level calculus and get admitted into selective universities. *Hangin' with the Homeboys* (1991), by Puerto Rican director-writer Joseph P. Vásquez, the most recent contribution to the cycle, was the cowinner of a screenwriting award at the Sundance Film Festival. *Homeboys* evokes the coming of age of four young male friends, two Puerto Rican, two Afro-American, out on the town during a night in which their futures and relationships with each other are tested.

In the 1990s, there were a number of Chicano independent films, but the most important, history-making one was Robert Rodríguez's *El Mariachi* (1993), which was a low-budget film Rodríguez wrote, directed and produced for his film studies at the University of Texas on a $7,000 budget. Columbia Pictures picked it up and the movie brought in more than $2 million. *El Mariachi* effectively launched Rodríguez's Hollywood career, and his next film was a fully-funded Hollywood production, *Desperado*, starring Antonio Banderas, which opened in 1995 to mixed reviews. The female protagonist was played by Salma Hayek, the first Mexican actress since Dolores del Río to assume a female lead in an American film. Another important feature film was co-produced by Edward James Olmos, who also starred in the leading role: *American Me* (1992), a gritty and highly violent tale of Chicanos in prison. In 1995, Gregory Nava wrote and directed the highly acclaimed and financially (highest per-screen average revenue for films released on the May 5 weekend) successful *Mi Familia/My Family* (directed and co-written by Gregory Nava, associate produced by Nancy de los Santos), starring Jimmy Smits, which is a broad epic of generations of an archetypical Chicano family in East Los Angeles. Another notable Hispanic film released in 1995 was *Roosters,* based on the hit play by Milcha Sánchez-Scott, with Edward James Olmos in the starring role. Robert Young directed the film and Reynaldo Villalobos was the cinematographer for this film which also focuses on the loves and dreams of an Hispanic family living in the Southwest.

Puerto Rican Films

Both the film industry in Puerto Rico and Puerto Rican films deserve considerably more attention than they have been given to date. Puerto Rican film dates at least from 1916, with the establishment of the Sociedad Industrial Cine Puerto Rico by Rafael J. Colorado and Antonio Capella (in 1912 Juan Emilio Viguié Cajas took the first known shots in Puerto Rico, of Ponce). This production company's first work had a *jíbaro* (Puerto Rican rural highlander) focus and was titled *Por la hembra y el gallo* (*For Women and Fighting Cocks*; 1916), which was followed by *El milagro de la virgen (The Miracle of the Virgin,* 1916) and *Mafia en Puerto Rico (The Mafia in Puerto Rico,* 1916). Because of lack of funds and competition from U.S. film, the Sociedad Industrial was bankrupted, and no prints of its films are known to exist, although there are still photographs of *Por la hembra y el gallo.* In 1917, Tropical Film Company was organized with the participation of such well-known Puerto Rican literary figures as Luis Lloréns Torres and Nemesio Canales. Although its existence terminated with the entry of the United States into World War I, it did produce *Paloma del monte* (*Mountain Dove*), directed by Luis Lloréns Torres. In 1919, the Porto Rico Photoplays company was organized and produced *Amor tropical* (Tropical Love, 1920) with American actors Ruth Clifford and Reginald Denny, a melodrama produced for the North American market, but which failed to penetrate that distribution system, causing the company to go bankrupt.

Juan Emilio Viguié Cajas purchased the equipment of Photoplays and began a long and productive filmmaking career in Puerto Rico, primarily doing newsreels for continental U.S. enterprises, such as Pathé, Fox Movietone, and MGM. Among his work was a film on Charles A. Lindbergh's trip to Puerto Rico in 1927 and another on the San Ciriaco hurricane of 1928. He did many documentaries for private entities and for the government, the first of which, in 1920 was *La colectiva (The Collective),* about the tobacco industry. His film *Romance tropical (Tropical Romance,* 1934) was the first Puerto Rican feature of the sound period. Written by the poet Luis Palés Matos, it depicts a lovesick young musician who attempts to seek his fortune at sea in a tiny boat.

No copies of *Romance tropical* remain; it debuted at the Paramount in Santurce but was not financially successful. It was the only feature that Cajas did. On the other hand, Rafael Ramos Cobián, who owned the largest chain of movie theaters in Puerto Rico, backed some production, mostly in Mexico, including *Mis dos amores (My Two Loves,* 1938), with Puerto Rican actress Blanca de Castejón and Mexican Tito Guízar, and *Los hijos mandan (The Children Rule,* 1939), with Blanca de Castejón again and Arturo de Córdova.

With the exceptions described above, film languished in Puerto Rico until 1949 when the government established a production facility in Old San Juan. Administered by the División de Educación de la Comunidad (which was part of the Departamento de Instrucción Pública), this unit was able to produce 65 shorts and two features by 1975, the year of publication of its last catalog. It counted on the cooperation of many of the best Puerto Rican graphic artists (Homar, Tony Maldonado, Eduardo Vera, Rafael Tufiño, Domingo Casiano, and so on) and writers (René Marqués, Pedo Juan Soto, Emilio Díaz Valcárcel, Vivas Maldonado, for instance). The unit also made considerable use of North American expertise, particularly screenwriter Edwin Rosskam; director Jack Delano, a longtime resident of Puerto Rico, cameraman Benji Donniger, and director Willard Van Dyke. Because these films were produced by a unit of government responsible for education, they generally had a pedagogical or didactic quality. *Los peloteros (The Ballplayers,* 1951) is generally thought to be the best film from this period. Directed by Jack Delano, it is based on a script by Edwin Rosskam and features Ramón Ortiz del Rivero (the celebrated comedian Diplo) and Miriam Colón. The premise revolves around a group of children raising money to buy baseball uniforms and equipment.

Viguié Film Productions, founded in 1951 by Juan Emilio Viguié Cajas, Jr., and the journalist Manuel R. Navas, became the first large Puerto Rican film producer. In 1953, the writer Salvador Tió became a partner of the company, which had its own studio and laboratory in Hato Rey. Many filmmakers received their training here or with the División de la Educación de la Comunidad. The company produced both commercials and documentaries for the government and private firms. In 1962, the company was associated with the brothers Roberto and Marino Guastella, and what emerged ultimately in 1974 was Guastella Film Producers, currently the largest producer in Puerto Rico. Unfortunately, no film laboratory currently exists in Puerto Rico, so footage is sent to New York.

Beginning in the 1950s, the production of film features accelerated somewhat. A group of investors and actors headed by Víctor Arrillaga and Axel Anderson produced a few films under the Producciones Borinquen. *Maruja* (1959) was the most successful, premised on the love life of a barber's wife and starring Marta Romero and several well-known actors and actresses from Puerto Rican television. A few films were produced in Puerto Rico by North American filmmakers for the continental market. *Machete,* 1958, is the best known, primarily for its sexuality. Coproduction with Mexican interests began during the 1960s, but led to no more than the repetition of old Mexican formula films with Puerto Rican settings. Among the films produced were *Romance en Puerto Rico* (1961, which has the distinction of being the first Puerto Rican color film), *Bello amanecer* (*Beautiful Dawn,* 1962), *Lamento borincano* (*Puerto Rican Lament,* 1963), *Mientras Puerto Rico duerme* (*While Puerto Rico Sleeps,* 1964, about the drug problem), *El jibarito Rafael* (1966, about Rafael Hernández), and *Fray Dollar* (*Brother Dollar,* 1970). Most of the major actors and directors were not Puerto Rican, but of Mexican or other Latin American nationality.

In 1964, Pakira Films was organized, led by the television producer Paquito Cordero and with financial backing from Columbia Pictures. It made several films based on the appearances of the television comedian Adalberto Rodríguez (Machuchal). These films were financially successful, including *El alcalde de Machuchal* (*The Mayor of Machuchal,* 1964), *Millionario a-go-go* (*Millionaire A-Go-Go,* 1965), *El agente de Nueva York* (*The New York Agent,* 1966), and *El curandero del pueblo* (*The Town Healer,* 1967). The company also produced its own Mexican formula films, called churros by the Mexican industry, such as *En mi viejo San Juan* (*In Old San Juan,* 1966), *Luna de miel en Puerto Rico* (*Honeymoon in Puerto Rico,* 1967), and *Una puertorriqueña en Acapulco* (*A Puerto Rican Girl in Acapulco,* 1968).

Another type of film based on criminals who had captured the popular imagination was produced by Anthony Felton, a Puerto Rican resident of New York. Popular for a while, the public eventually tired of these films with very low budgets and production

values and earthy language and titillating situations: *Correa Coto, así me llaman!* (*Correa Coto, That's What They Call Me!,* 1968), *La venganza de Correa Coto* (*The Revenge of Correa Coto,* 1969), *Arocho y Clemente* (*Arocho,* 1969), *La palomilla* (*The Gang,* 1969), and *Luisa* (1970).

In the 1970s, the number of Mexican coproductions declined significantly, primarily because of political changes in the film industry. Among the few that were done were *Yo soy el gallo* (*I Am the Rooster,* 1971), featuring Puerto Rican singer José Miguel Class, *La pandilla en apuros* (*The Gang in Trouble,* 1977), *Qué bravas son las solteras!* (*Single Women Are Brave*), featuring *vedette* Iris Chacón, and *Isabel La Negra* (*Black Isabel,* 1979), by Efraín López Neris, the first superproduction by Puerto Rican standards, featuring José Ferrer, Henry Darrow, Raúl Juliá, and Miriam Colón. This last film is about a notorious madam of a Ponce brothel and is recorded in English. However, the production was both an artistic and financial failure.

While the number of features declined, the number of documentaries increased greatly in the 1970s, spurred in part by the intense political climate of Puerto Rico. A number of *talleres cinematográficos* (movie workshops) were established. Notable among them was Tirabuzón Rojo, which produced *Denunica de un embeleco* (*Charges Filed Against a Madman,* director, Mario Vissepó), *Puerto Rico* (1975, Cuban Film Institute and Tirabuzón Rojo), a socioeconomic analysis of present-day Puerto Rico from a nationalist point of view, and *Puerto Rico: paraíso invadido* (*Puerto Rico: Paradise Invaded,* 1977, Alfonso Beato, director), an examination of the history and present-day reality of Puerto Rico from a nationalist perspective. Independent filmmakers produced *The Oxcart* (1970, director, José García Torres), a short (20-minute) portrayal of the migration of a Puerto Rican family that is based on the famous play by René Marqués; *Culebra, el comienzo* (*Island of Culebra, the Beginning,* 1971, director, Diego de la Texera), *La carreta* (1972, José García, Spanish-language version of *The Oxcart*); *Los nacionalistas* (*The Nationalists,* 1973, José García Torres, director), which surveys the activities of the Puerto Rican Nationalist party during the 1950s with a special focus on Don Pedro Albizu Campos; *La vida y poesía de Julia de Burgos* (*The Life and Poetry of Julia de Burgos,* 1974); *Destino manifiesto* (*Manifest Destiny,* 1977); *A la guerra* (*To War,* 1979, Thomas Sigel, director), an ode to the Puerto Rican community's war against cultural and racial discrimination in the form of a poem read by its author, Bimbo Rivas; and *The Life and Poetry of Julia de Burgos* (1979, José García Torres, director, Spanish-language version in 1974), a docudrama on the life and work of the great Puerto Rican poet.

In the 1980s, several features were produced including, *Una aventura llamada Menudo* (*An Adventure Called Menudo,* 1983, Orestes Trucco, director), featuring the famous young musical group. This film was one of the biggest box office successes in Puerto Rican history; however, its sequel, *Operación Caribe* (*Operation Caribbean,* 1984) with another very popular juvenile group, Los Chicos, was a financial flop. Also produced, all in 1986, were *Reflejo de un deseo* (*Reflection of a Desire,* Ivonne María Soto, director), about the director's mother, a poet; *Nicolás y los demás* (*Nicolás and the Others,* Jacobo Morales, director), a variation on the eternal triangle theme; and *La gran fiesta* (*The Great Fiesta,* Marcos Zurinaga, director). The first two were low-budget vehicles, done in 16 millimeters and blown up to 35. They were not financially or artistically successful. On the other hand, *La gran fiesta* was a watershed in Puerto Rican film. Produced with a high budget by local standards (about $1 million) and boasting excellent production values, this period piece with strong political dimensions evokes the relinquishing of the San Juan Casino to the U.S. military in 1942 amidst considerable turmoil about the possibility of a Nazi invasion, the status of Puerto Rico, and changing attitudes among the upper classes, particularly growers and merchants. This financially successful film was also the first to be produced under the new Ley de Sociedades Especiales (Law of Special Societies, Ley 8, July 19, 1985), which was designed to spur filmic production.

Among independent filmmakers, primarily with financial support of the Fundación Puertorriqueña de las Humanidades (Puerto Rican Humanities Foundation), the number of documentaries were on the increase in the 1980s. *Retratos* (*Pictures,* 1980, Stewart Bird, director) chronicles the life stories of four individuals from New York's Puerto Rican community in their attempts to adjust to life in the United States. *Puerto Rico: Our Right to Decide* (1981, Stanley Nelson, director) features interviews with people from various walks of life on Puerto Rico's current problems and aspirations for its political future. *Puerto Rico: A Colony the American Way* (1982, Diego Echeverría, director), examines the island's economic relationship with the United States. *La operación* (*The Operation,* 1982, Ana María García, director) studies the sterilization of Puerto Rican women. *El arresto* (*The Arrest,* 1982, Luis Antonio Rosario Quiles, director) dramatizes a major event in the history of the Puerto Rican independence movement. *Ligía Elena* (1983, Francisco López, director), is a color animation that criticizes

consumerism, snobbery, and racism, set to a salsa song by Rubén Blades. *Manos a la obra* (*Let's Get To Work*): *The Story of Operation Bootstrap* (1983, Pedro Rivera and Susan Zeig, directors) is an examination of the economic development plan undertaken in the 1950s called Operation Bootstrap. *La herencia de un tambor* (*The Heritage of a Drum,* 1984, Mario Vissepó, director is about Afro-Caribbean music, *Luchando por la vida* (*Fighting for Life,* 1984, José Artemio Torres, director) is about Puerto Rican tobacco workers, (1984, Luis Molina, director) is a biography of the noted governor, and *Correjer* (1984, Antonio Segarra, director) is a portrait of the noted poet and politician.

La batalla de Vieques The Battle of Vieques (1986, Zydnia Nazario, director) examines the U.S. Navy's control and use of the small island of Vieques. *Tufiño* (1986, Ramón Almodóvar, director) evokes the life and work of this painter. *Raíces eternas* (*Eternal Roots,* 1986, Noel Quiñones, director) describes the history of Puerto Rico since the discovery. *Cimarrón* (*Cimarron,* 1986, Juis Antonio Rosario, director) is a short fiction about a black slave who escapes his owner's manor and searches for his wife and child in Puerto Rico. *Machito* (1986 Carlos Ortiz, director) is an excellent biographical film that follows salsa musician Machito's career as well as the evolution of Latin jazz from the Cuba of the 1920s to contemporary New York City. *Una historia de los Reyes Magos* (*A History of the Three Wise Men,* 1988, Producciones Rodadero) is an animation that brings to life a Puerto Rican story inspired by the tradition of the magi. *Sabios árboles, mágicos árboles* (*Wise Trees, Magic Trees,* 1988, Puerto Rico Conservation Trust) is an animation that deals with the importance of trees and with man's relationship to nature. *Las plumas del múcaro* (*The Feathers of the Múcaro,* 1989, Puerto Rico Animation Workshop) is an animated Puerto Rican folktale from the oral tradition.

Casita Culture (1990), directed by Cathe Neuku and narrated by Willie Colón, studies the survival of Puerto Rican culture in New York in the form of the folk-decorated little houses in the community. *The Salt Mines* (1990), produced and directed by Susan Aiken and Carlos Aparicio, is about a community of homeless people who lived along the Hudson River. *Cagá* (1992), directed by Héctor Méndez Caratini, documents a religious ritual undertaken by a young boy as he passes into manhood. *Once Upon a Time in the Bronx* (1993), directed by Ela Troyano, is a docudrama based on the lives, work, and neighborhood of the Spanish rap group, Latin Empire.

Among the more recent feature films, Puerto Rican filmmaker Joseph B. Vásquez's *Hangin' with the Homeboys* (1991) is an exceptional film, winning the screenwriting award at the Sundance Film Festival. *Homeboys* evokes the coming of age of four young male friends out on the town during the night in which their futures and relationships with each other are tested.

✳ HISPANICS IN FILM: FUTURE DIRECTIONS

What lies ahead for U.S. Hispanic film? Several factors will come into play. Prime among them is the growing constituent power of U.S. Hispanics and the growing understanding of this power. Hollywood now understands that Hispanics go to the movies and that there are many Hispanics. It also realizes that there is a growing fear of the Hispanic presence among Anglos and even other minorities. The first Hollywood inclination will be to create films that exploit these features, even simultaneously if at all possible. Most Hollywood films will continue to capitalize on the inherent habits of secret wish-fulfillment, projection of one's hostility on out-groups, and anticipation of ethnic group violence that has been inculcated into the American viewing public from the very emergence of narrative film. If Hollywood can do that in a way that will simultaneously bring in the Hispanic audience as well, all the better. This has been the design of gang films, successfully realized in such films as *Walk Proud*, where young Hispanics come to the film to see it for its novelty value (there being so little about Hispanics of any sort), while Anglos come for the intermixed violence and sexuality. If anything, Hispanic exploitation films intended for Anglo sensibilities will be accelerated, if only because this minority group will become the largest early in the twenty-first century, and therefore, possibly overtake blacks as the most menacing. However, Hollywood will attempt to update the stereotypes and even disguise them ever so delicately, possibly with subplots that provide something for the Hispanic viewer as well.

The first trend of increased Hispanic population and audiences represents a constant, so it will continue. Nevertheless, what is new is the parallel development of a "Hispanic Hollywood." To better understand this trend one must realize that the studio system has long been subverted and the power of studios themselves over film content has been on the decline now for decades. Currently, even the largest studios, such as Universal (itself a subsidiary of one of the largest corporations in the world, Matsushita), have farmed out their facilities to independent producers or other studios. Conversely, and particularly since stars still are luminaries in the system, we have witnessed the rise of powerful production companies headed by leading Hollywood figures. Many of these leaders, actors and actresses such as Robert Redford, Jane Fonda, or, among Hispanics, Edward James Olmos, Raúl Juliá, Martin Sheen, Emilio Estévez, Paul Rodríguez, "Cheech" Marín, and producers and directors such as The Zanuck Corporation, Esparza/Katz, and so on, are going into production, including conceptualization, scripting, actual film production, and arrangement through the studios for distribution. The Hispanic Hollywood phenomenon has tended to emerge from a partnership between superstars, such as Robert Redford or Jane Fonda, for whom additional money is no longer a primary concern but for whom movies of high artistic promise and progressive sensibilities are. And if such vehicles provide them the satisfaction of directorial or acting roles as well, all the better. Similar kinds of motivations, albeit without the presumption of the type of command of resources and industry clout embodied in a Fonda or Redford, inspire such well-recognized Hispanics as "Cheech" Marín, Raúl Juliá, and Edward James Olmos.

Given the vast changes in the control of artistic content at Hollywood, the existence of Hispanic expertise to make genuine Hispanic films, the progressive sensibilities and interests in film as an art form among a distinct but influential minority of Hollywood figures, and the precedents of films like *La Bamba* and *Stand and Deliver* that were financially and artistically successful, one would expect continued and accelerated Hispanic Hollywood productions.

Finally, the prospects of the independent U.S. Hispanic film movement are good, but without any perceived fundamental changes in the budgetary and distribution limitations of these films. Independent U.S. Hispanic filmmakers will enjoy most of the benefits of recent trends, including more Hispanic viewers and more awareness of the importance of U.S. Hispanic culture; the decline in power and control of market of the film studios and more recently of the television networks; more diversity in distribution, particularly through television; the existence of a small, influential number of benefactors with money or other substantive resources; and perhaps, most of all, the growing number of well-trained and recognized Hispanic production people, actors and actresses who may not want to make a career out of low-budget productions but are willing to cross over to the independent side periodically.

The outlook is relatively good for U.S. Hispanic cinema. Both Hispanic Hollywood and the independent U.S. Hispanic film movement will expand, and their productions will tend to be more comparable to each other than to the exploitive films that will also continue to be ground out by the Hollywood film carnival industry. The cadre of hispano talent will continue to expand, fostered by all elements of the film, television and video industries, even the most crass sectors. However, once these individuals have been initiated into the field and develop their skills, they will be qualified and eager to produce, at least from time to time, a "real" movie about some aspect of U.S. Hispanic people.

✳ OUTSTANDING HISPANICS IN THE FILM INDUSTRY

Norma Aleandro (1941–)

An actress, playwright, and director born in Argentina in 1941, Norma Aleandro is known best for her performance in the Academy Award-winning *The Official Story* (1985), for which she was named best actress at Cannes. She has also acted in *Gaby— A True Story* (1987), *Cousins* (1989), and *Vital Signs* (1990) and continues to do Spanish-language film.

Néstor Almendros (1930–1992)

Academy-award winning cinematographer and director, Nestor Almendros, was born in Barcelona Spain on October 30, 1930. At the age of 14, he immigrated with his family to Cuba, where he graduated from the University of Havana in philosophy and literature. Almendros began his career in film with an amateur 8mm film with the great Cuban director, Tomás Gutiérrez Alea, in 1950. He later, studied film with Hans Richter at the City University of New York, and also studied cinematography at the Centro Sperimentale di Cinematografia in Rome. Almendros worked as a cameraman and/or director on several documentaries of the early Castro era for the Cuban film institute, Instituto del Arte e Industria Cinematográfica (Cinematographic Art and Industry Institute), then moved to France where he worked for television and on film shorts. In the mid-1960s he began collaborating regularly with director Erich Rohmer and later director Francois Truffaut. He won the Academy Award for cinematography for the 1978 film, *Days of Heaven*. Included among his many outstanding films are *The Wild Racers* (U.S., 1968), *Gun Runner* (1968), *Ma nuit chez Maud/My Night at Maud's* (France, 1969), *L'enfant sauvage/The Wild Child* (France, 1970), *Le genou de Claire/Claire's Knee* (France, 1971), *L'amour l'après-midi/Chloe in the Afternoon* (France, 1972), *Chinatown* (1974), *L'histoire d'Adele/The Story of Adele H.* (France, 1975), *Days of Heaven* (1978), *Kramer vs. Kramer* (1979), *The Blue Lagoon* (1980), *The Last Metro* (France, 1980), *Sophie's Choice* (1982), *Improper Conduct* (1983), *Places in the Heart* (1984), *Heartburn* (1986), *New*

Néstor Almendros.

York Stories (1989). Almendros also directed some very noteworthy documentaries, including *Improper Conduct* and the anti-Castro *Nobody Listened* (1988). Almendros was also the author of an important autobiographical book on cinematogrphy, published first in French in 1980, and then in English translation in 1984: *Un Homme a la caméra, A Man with a Camera*. Almendros died in 1993.

Pedro Armendáriz (1912–1963)

Born May 9, 1912, in Mexico City, Pedro Armendáriz was one of Mexico's most successful film stars, appearing in more than 40 films, many directed by Emilio "El Indio" Fernández. He was internationally recognized for *María Candelaria* (1943) and his work with major directors, including Luis Buñuel and John Ford. His son, Pedro Armendáriz, Jr., is also an actor. Included among his films are *María Candelaria* (1943), *La Perla* (*The Pearl,* (1945), *Fort Apache* (1948), *Three Godfathers, We Were Strangers, Tulsa* (1949), *Border River* (1954), *The Littlest Outlaw* (1955), *The Wonderful Country* (1959), *Francis of Assisi* (1961), and *Captain Sinbad* (1963).

Armida (1913–)

Born in 1913 in Sonora, Mexico, Armida was type-cast as the Latin lady in a number of Hollywood B pictures of the 1930s and 1940s. Included among her films are *Under a Texas Moon,* Border Romance (1931), *Border Café* (1940), *Fiesta* (1941), *The Girl from Monterey* (1943), *Machine Gun Mama* (1944), *South of the Rio Grande* (1945), and *Bad Men of the Border* (1946).

Desi Arnaz (1917–1986)

A popular actor and musician, Desi Arnaz was born Desiderio Alberto Arnaz y de Acha III on March 2, 1917, in Santiago, Cuba. He migrated to the United States where, from age 16, he achieved fame as a singer and drummer. In 1940 he married Lucille Ball, his costar in *Too Many Girls,* his screen debut. The 1950s television series "I Love Lucy," in which he and Lucille Ball starred, was enormously popular. (He and Ball were divorced in 1960; their son, Desi Arnaz, Jr., born in 1953, is also an actor). Included among his films are *Too Many Girls* (1940), *Father Takes a Wife* (1941), *The Navy Comes Through* (1942), *Bataan* (1943), *Cuban Pete* (1946), *Holiday in*

Rubén Blades.

Desi Arnaz.

Havana (1949), *The Long Long Trailer* (1954), and *Forever Darling* (1956). Arnaz died December 2, 1986.

Alfonso Bedoya (1904–1957)

Born in Vicam, Mexico, in 1904, Bedoya developed a considerable career as a character actor in Mexican films. He made a notable American film debut in 1948 in John Huston's *The Treasure of the Sierra Madre* as a treacherous, smiling, and mocking stereotypical Mexican bandit. His performance is both recognized and parodied in Luis Valdez's notable play *I Don't Have to Show You No Stinking Badges.* Included among his films are *La perla* (*The Pearl,* 1945), *The Treasure of the Sierra Madre* (1948), *Streets of Laredo, Border Incident* (1949), *Man in the Saddle* (1951), *California Conquest* (1952), *Sombrero, The Stranger Wore a Gun* (1953), *Border River* (1954), *Ten Wanted Men* (1955), and *The Big Country* (1958). He died in 1957.

Rubén Blades (1948–)

Born on July 16, 1948, in Pamana City, Panama, Blades received all of his early education and his bachelor's degree there. In 1985 he was awarded a law degree from Harvard University. Although he began his career in both Panama and the United States as a lawyer, Blades has become an outstanding singer and composer of salsa music and a respected Hollywood actor. He has received four Grammy Awards and numerous gold records. His films include *The Last Fight* (1982), *Crossover Dreams* (1984), *Critical Condition* (1986), *The Milagro Beanfield War* (1986), *Fatal Beauty* (1987), and various made-for-television movies.

Leo Carrillo (1880–1961)

Born in Los Angeles on August 6, 1880 to an old California family, Leo Carrillo began his career as a cartoonist before becoming a dialect comedian in vaudeville and later on the stage. Debuting in Hollywood in the late 1920s, he became one of Hollywood's busiest character actors of the 1930s and 1940s. In the early 1950s, he played Pancho, Duncan Renaldo's sidekick in "The Cisco Kid" TV series. His films include *Mister Antonio* (1929), *Girl of the Rio* (1932), *Villa Villa!, Manhattan Melodrama, The Gay Bride* (1934), *In Caliente* (1935), *The Gay Desperado* (1936), *Manhattan Merry-Go-Round* (1937), *The Girl of the Golden West* (1939), *Captain Caution* (1940), *Horror Island* (1941), *Sin Town, American Empire* (1942), *Gypsy Wildcat* (1944), *Crime Incorporated* (1945), *The Fugitive* (1947), *The Girl from San Lorenzo* (1950).

Lynda Córdoba Carter (1951–)

Born on July 24, 1951 in Phoenix, Arizona, Lynda Carter began her show business career as a nightclub singer and dancer after finishing high school; she later attended Arizona State University. In 1970, she was crowned Miss World USA, which led her to Hollywood. She has since become a successful television actress. Her most famous role was Wonder Woman, from 1976 to 1979; she has also starred in various made-for-television movies, including *Stillwatch* and *Born to Be Sold* in 1981, and *Rita Hayworth: The Love Godess* in 1983. During the 1980s, Carter also starred in her own variety shows, which highlight her singing and dancing: "Lynda Carter Celebration," "Lynda Carter: Body and Soul" and "Lynda Carter: Street Life." She is the founder of Lynda Carter Productions, which continues to launch new television programs. Included among her honors are the Golden Eagle Award for Consistent Performance in Television and Film and Mexico's Ariel Award as International Entertainer of the Year.

Linda Cristal (1935–)

Born on February 24, 1935 in Buenos Aires, Argentina and orphaned at 13, Linda Cristal played leads in Mexican films from age 16 and debuted in Hollywood in the mid-1950s in both films and television ("High Chaparral") as a leading lady. Her U.S. films include *Comanche* (1951), *The Perfect Furlough* (1958), *Cry Tough* (1959), *The Alamo* (1960), *Two Rode Together* (1961), *Panic in the City* (1968), *Mr. Majestyk* (1974), and *Love and the Midnight Auto Supply* (1978).

Henry Darrow (1933–)

Born on September 15, 1933, in New York City, Henry Darrow starred in "The High Chaparral" TV series (1967–71); had the role of Alex Monténez (1973–74) on "The New Dick Van Dyke Show"; was Detective Lieutenant Manny Quinlan (1974–75) on "Harry-O," a TV drama series; played Don Diego de la Vega (Zorro Sr.) on "Zorro and Son," a TV comedy (1983); and was Lieutenant Rojas on "Me and Mom," a TV drama series (1985). His film credits include *Badge 373* (1973), *Attica* (1980), *Seguín* (1982), *In Dangerous Company* (1988), *L.A. Bounty* (1989), and *The Last of the Finest* (1990).

Lynda Córdoba Carter.

Linda Cristal.

Pedro de Córdoba (1881-1950)

Born September 28, 1881, in New York City to Cuban-French parents, Pedro de Córdova began as a stage actor and later played character parts in numerous silent and sound films, usually as either a benevolent or malevolent Latin aristocrat. His films include *Carmen, Temptation* (1915), *Maria Rosa* (1916), *The New Moon* (1919), *When Knighthood Was in Flower* (1922), *The Bandolero* (1924), *Captain Blood* (1935), *Rose of the Rancho, Anthony Adverse, Ramona* (1936), *Juárez* (1939), *The Mark of Zorro* (1940), *Blood and Sand* (1941), *For Whom the Bell Tolls* (1943), *The Keys of the Kingdom* (1945), *Samson and Delilah* (1949), *Comanche Territory,* and *Crisis* (1950).

Arturo de Córdova (Arturo García) (1908-1973)

Born on May 8, 1908, in Merida, Yucatán, Mexico, Arturo de Córdova made his debut in Mexican films in the early 1930s and played Latin lovers in Hollywood during the 1940s, thereafter returning to Spanish-language film. His films include *Cielito lindo* (1936), *La zandunga* (1937), *For Whom the Bell Tolls* (1943), *Masquerade in Mexico, A Medal for*

Benny (1945), *New Orleans* (1947), and *Adventures of Casanova* (1948).

Dolores del Río (Lolita Dolores Martínez Asunsolo López Negrete) (1905-1983)

Born on August 3, 1905, in Durango, Mexico, Dolores del Río was educated in a convent. By age 16, she was married to writer Jaime del Río. Director Edwin Carewe was struck by her beauty and invited her to Hollywood where she appeared in *Joanna* in 1925. She became a star in many silent films, but her career suffered from frequent typecasting in ethnic and exotic roles, particularly after the advent of sound. Dissatisfied with Hollywood, she returned to Mexico in 1943 to do many important films of the 1940s, including *María Candelaria* (1943) and John Ford's *The Fugitive* (1947, filmed on location in Mexico). She finally returned to Hollywood in character parts in the 1960s. Her films include *Resurrection, The Loves of Carmen* (1927), *Ramona, Revenge* (1928), *Evangeline* (1929), *The Bad One* (1930), *The Girl of the Rio* (1932), *Flying Down to Rio* (1933), *Madame Du Barry* (1934), *In Caliente* (1935), *Devil's Playground* (1937), *Doña Perfecta* (1950), *La cucaracha (The Cockroach,* 1958), *Flaming Star* (1960),

Dolores del Río.

Cheyenne Autumn (1964), and *The Children of Sánchez* (1978).

Moctezuma Diaz Esparza (1949–)

Producer, director, and one of the best-known Chicano figures in the film industry, Esparza was born on March 12, 1949 in Los Angeles. He received his B.A. and M.F.A. from the University of California, Los Angeles, in 1972 and 1973, respectively, and has remained active in feature, documentary, and educational filmmaking since 1973. In 1972 Esparza formed his own production company, Moctesuma Esparza Productions, which has raised considerable funds to produce feature-length motion pictures with Latino themes, including an adaptation of the Rudolfo Anaya novel *Bless Me Ultima* (written and to be directed by Luis Valdez) and *Angel's Flight* (written by first-time feature scripter Jill Isaacs and scheduled for direction by Luis Valdez), about a Hispanic detective embroiled in a major plot to bankrupt Los Angeles' mass transit rail system to clear the way for freeways. His films include *Only Once in a Lifetime* (1978, producer), *The Ballad of Gregorio Cortez* (1983, producer), *The Milagro Beanfield War* (1988, coproducer), and *Radioactive Dreams* (1986, producer).

Paul Espinosa (1950–)

Los mineros (*The Miners,* 1990, Héctor Galán, coproducer), a stirring view of the history of the labor struggle by Arizona Mexican American miners from the turn of the century to the present. He earned degrees in anthropology from Brown University in 1972 (B.A.) and Stanford University in 1976 (M.A.) and 1982 (Ph.D.). He is the producer for the *American Playhouse* TV drama series of a dramatic adaptation of Tomás Rivera's masterpiece, *And the Earth Did Not Part* (1992, Severo Pérez, director-writer). Others films by Espinoza are: *Ballad of an Unsung Hero* (1983), about a scandalous case of discrimination and deportation of a well-known Chicano radio figure; *The Lemon Grove Incident* (1985), about separate and unequal education of Chicanos in California; and "*. . . And the Earth Did Not Swallow Him*" (1995), a film dramatization of Tomás Rivera's Chicano classic novel.

Emilio Estévez (1962–)

Actor, director, and screenwriter Emilio Estevez was born in New York City May 12, 1962, and is the son of Martin Sheen and brother of Charlie Sheen. In 1992, he was married to Paula Abdul. Estévez decided to use the original family surname. With his blond hair and blue eyes, he has been able to secure

Emilio Estévez.

roles in mainstream pictures. His accomplishments as an actor are many and varied; much of his work has been highly recognized for its excellence. He first achieved recognition in *Repo Man* (1984) and had acting roles in *St. Elmo's Fire* (1985), *Maximum Overdrive* (1986), *Stakeout* (1987), *Young Guns* (1988), *Men at Work* 1990), and *Young Guns II* (1991). Estévez has written several screenplays and directed two of them. His other films include *Tex* (1982), *Nightmares* (1983), *The Outsiders* (1983), *The Breakfast Club* (1985), *That Was Then . . . This is Now* (1985), *Wisdom* (1986), *Nightbreaker* (1989), *Freejack* (1992), *The Mighty Ducks* (1992), *Another Stakeout* (1993), and *National Lampoon's Loaded Weapon, I* (1993).

Emilio "El Indio" Fernández (1904–1986)

The famous director and actor, Emilio Fernández was born on March 26, 1904, in El Seco, Coahuila, Mexico. One of the most important figures of Mexican cinema, he was born to a Spanish Mexican father and Indian mother (hence the nickname El Indio). At 19, he took part in the Mexican Revolution and in 1923 was sentenced to 20 years' imprisonment, but escaped to California where he played bit parts and supporting roles until returning to Mexico, first as an actor, debuting in the role of an Indian in *Janitizio* (1934), and then as Mexico's most prominent director. His film *María Candelaria* (1943) won Grand Prize at Cannes, and *La Perla* (*The Pearl*, 1946) won the International Prize at San Sebastián (Spain). As a Hollywood actor, he had a few notable parts in Sam Peckinpah films. Among the films he directed are *Soy puro mexicano* (*I Am Full-Blooded Mexican*, 1942), *Flor silvestre* (*Wildflower*), *María Candelaria* (1943), *Bugambilla* (*Bougainvillea*, 1944), *La perla* (*The Pearl*, 1946), *El gesticulador* (*The Gesticulator*, 1957), and *A Loyal Soldier of Pancho Villa* (1966). His films as an actor include *The Reward* (1965), *The Appaloosa, Return of the Seven* (1966), *A Covenant with Death, The War Wagon* (1967), *The Wild Bunch* (1969), *Pat Garrett and Billy the Kid* (1973), *Bring Me the Head of Alfredo García* (1974), *Lucky Lady* (1975), *Under the Volcano* (1984), and *Pirates* (1986).

Mel Ferrer (1917–)

Actor, director, and producer Melchior Gastón Ferrer was born on August 25, 1917, in New York to a Cuban-born surgeon and a Manhattan socialite. He attended Princeton University but dropped out to become an actor, debuting on Broadway in 1938 as a chorus dancer. He made his screen acting debut in 1949 and appeared in many films as a leading man. His third (1954–68) of four wives was actress Audrey Hepburn, whom he directed in *Green Mansions* (1959). His films as actor include *Lost Boundaries* (1949), *The Brave Bulls* (1951), *Rancho Notorious, Scaramouche* (1952), *Lili* (1953), *War and Peace* (1956), *The Sun Also Rises* (1957), *The World, the Flesh and the Devil* (1959), *Sex and the Single Girl* (1964), *Eaten Alive* (1977), *Guyana: Cult of the Damned* (1979), and *City of the Walking Dead* (1980). The films he directed include *The Girl of the Limberlost* (1945) and *Green Mansions* (1959).

Gabriel Figueroa (1907–)

Photography director, Gabriel Figueroa was born on April 24, 1907, in Mexico. An orphan, as a boy he was forced to seek work, yet was able to pursue painting and photography on his own. In 1935, he went to Hollywood to study motion picture photography, returned to Mexico the following year, and began a prolific career as the cameraman of more than 100 films. He worked for Buñuel, John Ford, and Emilio Fernández and ranks among the leading directors of photography in world cinema. His films (primarily Mexican) include *Allá en el rancho grande* (1936, *Out on the Big Ranch*), *Flor silvestre* (*Wildflower*), *María Candelaria* (1943), *Bugambilla* (1944, *Bougainvillea*), *La perla* (1946, *The Pearl*), *The Fugitive* (1947), *Los olvidados* (1952, *The Forgotten*), *La cucaracha* (1958, *The Cockroach*), *Nazarín* (1959), *Macario* (1960), *Animas Trujano* (1961), *El angel exterminador* (1962, *The Exterminating Angel*), *The Night of the Iguana* (1964), *Simón del desierto* (1965, *Simon in the Desert*), *Two Mules for Sister Sara* (1970), *The Children of Sánchez* (1978), and *Under the Volcano* (1984).

Andy García (Andrés Arturo Garcí-Menéndez) (1956–)

Born in Havana in 1956, García came to the United States with his family in 1961. They prospered and Garcia attended Florida International University on a basketball scholarship. He became interested in acting, trained in classical theater and comedy, and worked in regional theatre in Florida during the early 1960s. He journeyed to California and appeared in a few films during the early 1980s and made his television debut in an episode of *Hill Street Blues*. In *8 Million Ways to Die* (1986) he turned in a superb performance as a villain, and in 1987 in Brian De Palma's *The Untouchables* he achieved widespread recognition as an earnest FBI

Emilio "El Indio" Fernández.

agent. In 1990, he achieved star status as the good cop in *Internal Affairs* and as the illegitimate nephew of Don Corleone in *The Godfather Part III*. His other films include *Blue Skies Again* (1983), *The Mean Season* (1985), *American Roulette* (1988), *Stand and Deliver* (1988), *Black Rain* (1989), *A Show of Force* (1990), *Hero* (1992), *Jennifer Eight* (1992), and *When a Man Loves a Woman* (1994).

Rita Hayworth (Margarita Carmen Cansino) (1918–1987)

Rita Hayworth was born October 17, 1918, in Brooklyn, New York, to Spanish-born dancer Eduardo Cansino and his Ziegfeld Follies partner Volga Haworth. Hayworth danced professionally by age 13 in Mexican nightspots in Tijuana and Agua Caliente, where she was eventually noticed by Hollywood. She made her screen debut in 1935, playing bit parts under her real name. In 1937, she married Edward Judson, under whose guidance she changed her name and was transformed into an auburn-haired sophisticate. For the remainder of the 1930s, Hayworth was confined to leads in B pictures, but through much of the 1940s she became the undisputed sex goddess of Hollywood films and the hottest star at Columbia Studios. Her tempestuous personal life included marriages to Orson Welles, Aly Khan, and singer Dick Haymes. As Rita Cansino, her films included *Under the Pampas Moon, Charlie Chan in Egypt,* and Dante's Inferno (1935), *Meet Nero Wolfe* (1936), *Trouble in Texas, Old Louisiana,* and *Hit the Saddle* (1937). As Rita Hayworth, she acted in *The Shadow* (1937), *Angels Over Broadway* (1940), *The Strawberry Blonde, Blood and Sand* (1941), *Cover Girl* (1944), *Gilda* (1946), *The Lady from Shanghai, The Loves of Carmen* (1948), *Salome, Miss Sadie Thompson* (1953), *Pal Joey* (1957), *Separate Tables* (1958), *They Came to Cordura* (1959), *The Happy Thieves* (1962), *The Money Trap* (1966), *The Wrath of God* (1972), and *Circle* (1976).

Raúl Juliá (1940–1995)

Born on March 9, 1940, in San Juan, Puerto Rico, Raúl Juliá became one of the best-known Hispanic actors for his Shakespearean and other classical stage roles and for musicals as well as film. In 1971, he debuted in small parts in *The Organization, Been Down So Long It Looks Like Up to Me,* and *Panic in Needle Park.* Juliá appeared in *The Gumball Rally* (1976) and *Eyes of Laura Mars* (1978) and achieved national attention as the costar in the notable *Kiss of the Spider Woman* (1985), adapted from the novel by Argentine Manuel Puig. His other films include *One from the Heart* (1982), *Tempest* (1982),

Fernando Lamas.

Compromising Positions (1985), *The Morning After* (1986), *Florida Straits* (1986), *Trading Hearts* (1987), *The Penitentes* (1988), *Tango Bar* (1988), *Tequila Sunrise* (1988), *Moon over Parador* (1988), *Romero* (1989), *Mack the Knife* (1989), *Presumed Innocent* (1990), *A Life of Sin* (1990), and *The Rookie* (1990).

Katy Jurado (María Cristina Jurado García) (1927–)

Born on January 16, 1927, in Guadalajara, Mexico, Katy Jurado began her Hollywood career as a columnist for Mexican publications following a Mexican film career. In Hollywood she played dark lady roles in a variety of films, most memorably *High Noon* (1952) and *One-Eyed Jacks* (1961). She was nominated for an Oscar for her supporting role in *Broken Lance* (1954). Between 1959 and 1964, she was wed to actor Ernest Borgnine. Her other films include *The Bullfighter and the Lady* (1951), *Arrowhead* (1953), *Trapeze, The Man from Del Rio* (1956), *Barabbas* (1961), *Pat Garrett and Billy the Kid* (1973), *El recurso del método* (*The Method's Resource,* 1978) and *The Children of Sánchez* (1978).

Fernando Lamas (1915–1982)

Born on January 9, 1915, in Buenos Aires, Fernando Lamas became a movie star in Argentina. Lamas was imported to Hollywood by MGM and typecast as a sporty Latin lover in several lightweight films, some of which featured his singing. He married Arlene Dahl (1954–60) and Esther Williams (since 1967). His films include *The Avengers* (1950), *The Merry Widow* (1952), *The Diamond Queen* (1953), *Jívaro, Rose Marie* (1954), *The Violent Ones, Kill a Dragon* (1967), *100 Rifles, Backtrack* (1969), and *The Cheap Detective* (1978).

Adele Mara (Adelaida Delgado) (1923–)

Born on April 28, 1923, in Highland Park, Michigan, Adele Mara began as a singer-dancer with Xavier Cugat's orchestra. In Hollywood she played dark lady/other woman parts in scores of low-budget films in the 1940s and 1950s, including *Navy Blues* (1941), *Alias Boston Blackie* (1942), *Atlantic City* (1944), *The Tiger Woman, Song of Mexico* (1945), *The Catman of Paris* (1946), *Twilight on the Rio Grande, Blackmail, Exposed* (1947), *Campus Honeymoon, Wake of the Red Witch, Angel in Exile* (1948), *Sands of Iwo Jima, The Avengers, California Passage*

Margo.

(1950), *The Sea Hornet* (1951), *Count the Hours* (1953), *Back from Eternity* (1956), and *The Big Circus* (1959).

Margo (1917–1985)

Born on May 10, 1917, in Mexico City, Marie Marquerita Guadalupe Teresa Estela Bolado Castilla y O'Donnell was coached as a child by Eduardo Cansino, Rita Hayworth's father, and she danced professionally with her uncle Xavier Cugat's band in Mexican nightclubs and at New York's Waldorf-Astoria, where they triumphed in introducing the rumba. From 1934, she became known as a dramatic actress, mostly typecast as a tragic, suffering woman. She married Eddie Albert in 1945 and is the mother of actor Eddie Albert, Jr. In 1974, she was appointed commissioner of social services for the city of Los Angeles. Her films include *Crime Without Passion* (1934), *Rumba* (1935), *The Robin Hood of Eldorado, Winterset* (1936), *Lost Horizon* (1937), *Behind the Rising Sun* (1943), *The Falcon in Mexico* (1944), *Viva Zapata!* (1952), *I'll Cry Tomorrow* (1955), *From Hell to Texas* (1958), and *Who's Got the Action?* (1962). Margo died in 1985.

Adele Mara.

Richard "Cheech" Marín.

Richard "Cheech" Marín (1946–)

Renowned comic, actor, and writer Richard Marín was born July 13, 1946, in Los Angeles. Marín began in show business as part of the comedy team Cheech and Chong in 1970, bringing stoned and hippy routines to the screen with *Cheech and Chong's Up in Smoke* (1978), which was the highest-grossing film of the year. Following the split-up of the duo in 1985, Cheech continued to appear in films and wrote, directed, and starred in *Born in East L.A.* (1987). His films include *Cheech and Chong's Next Movie* (1980), *Cheech and Chong's Nice Dreams* (1981), *Things are Tough all Over* (1982), *Yellowbeard* (1983), *Cheech and Chong's the Corsican Brothers* (1984), *Ghostbusters II* (1989), *Rude Awakening* (1989), *Troop Beverly Hills* (1989), *Havana* (1990), *Presumed Innocent* (1990), *The Shrimp on the Barbie* (1990), *The Addams Family* (1991), *Life of Sin* (1992), *The Addams Family Values* (1993), *Fern Gully* (1993), *A Million to Juan* (1994), *Ring of the Muscateers* (1994), *Streetfighter* (1994), and *Mr. Payback.* His voice has also been featured in films such as *The Lion King* (1994).

Mona Maris (María Capdevielle) (1903–)

Born in 1903 in Buenos Aires and convent-educated in France, Mona Maris acted in several British and German films before embarking on a Hollywood career in the late 1920s and the 1930s in the usual sultry, exotic-type role. Her films include *Romance of the Rio Grande* (1929), *Under a Texas Moon, The Arizona Kid, A Devil With Women* (1930), *The Passionate Plumber, Once in a Lifetime* (1932), *Flight From Destiny, Law of the Tropics* (1941), *My Gal Sal, Pacific Rendezvous, I Married an Angel, Berlin Correspondent* (1942), *The Falcon in Mexico* (1944), *Heartbeat* (1946), and *The Avengers* (1950).

Chris-Pin Martin (1893–1953)

Born on November 19, 1893, in Tucson, Arizona, of Mexican parentage, Chris-Pin Martin (Ysabel Ponciana Chris-Pin Martin) provided comic relief in the "Cisco Kid" series (as Pancho or Gordito) and many other Westerns. His films include *The Rescue* (1929), *Billy the Kid* (1930), *The Cisco Kid* (1931), *South of Santa Fe* (1932), *Bordertown* (1935), *The Gay Desperado* (1936), *The Texans* (1938), *Stagecoach, The Return of the Cisco Kid* (1939),

Mona Maris.

Chris-Pin Martin.

Lucky Cisco Kid, Down Argentine Way, The Mark of Zorro (1940), *Weekend in Havana* (1941), *Tombstone* (1942), *The Ox-Bow Incident* (1943), *Ali Baba and the Forty Thieves* (1944), *San Antonio* (1945), *The Fugitive* (1947), *Mexican Hayride* (1948), *The Beautiful Blonde From Bashful Bend* (1949), and *Ride the Man Down* (1952).

Ricardo Montalbán (1920–)

Born on November 25, 1920, in Mexico City, Ricardo Montalbán first played bit roles in several Broadway productions before debuting on the screen in Mexico in the early 1940s and subsequently being recruited as a Latin lover type by MGM in 1947. He was eventually given an opportunity to demonstrate a wider acting range on television, including roles in segments of "The Loretta Young Show." He has been a strong force in Hollywood for the establishment of better opportunities for Hispanics. His films include *Fiesta* (1947), *The Kissing Bandit* (1948), *Neptune's Daughter, Border Incident* (1949), *Right Cross, Two Weeks With Love* (1950), *Across the Wide Missouri, Mark of the Renegade* (1951), *Sombrero, Latin Lovers* (1953), *The Saracen Blade* (1954), *A Life in the*

Balance (1955), *Sayonara* (1957), *Let No Man Write My Epitaph* (1960), *Cheyenne Autumn* (1964), *The Money Trap, The Singing Nun* (1966), *Sweet Charity* (1969), *Escape from the Planet of the Apes* (1971), *Conquest of the Planet of the Apes* (1972), *The Train Robbers* (1973), *Joe Panther* (1976), *Star Trek II: The Wrath of Khan* (1982), *Cannonball Run, II* (1984), and *The Naked Gun* (1988).

María Montez (Marí Africa Vidal de Santo Silas) (1920–1951)

Born on June 6, 1920, in Barahona, Dominican Republic, María Montez became one of the most notable, exotic dark ladies. Affectionately called The Queen of Technicolor, she started her screen career in 1941 doing bit parts in Universal films. Although inordinately unskilled at acting, she nevertheless became immensely popular in a string of color adventure tales, often costarring with fellow exotics Jon Hall, Sabu, and Turhan Bey. She remains the object of an extensive fan cult thirsting for nostalgia and high camp. Her films include *Lucky Devils, That Night in Rio, Raiders of the Desert, South of Tahiti* (1941), *Bombay Clipper, Arabian Nights* (1942), *White Savage* (1943), *Ali Baba and the Forty Thieves,*

Ricardo Montalbán.

María Montez.

motivated them to speak out on issues of social justice, sexism, racism, and classism within the Catholic church.

Antonio Moreno (Antonio Garride Monteagudo) (1887–967)

Born on September 26, 1887, in Madrid, Antonio Moreno played a dapper Latin lover in numerous Hollywood silent films. He began his career in 1912 under D. W. Griffith and was quite popular during the 1920s, when he played leads opposite such actresses as Gloria Swanson, Greta Garbo, Pola Negri, and Bebe Daniels. His foreign accent limited his career in talkies, where he was seen mainly in character roles. He appeared in hundreds of films, including *Voice of the Million, The Musketeers of Pig Alley* (1912), *The Song of the Ghetto, The Loan Shark King, In the Latin Quarter, Sunshine and Shadows* (1914), *The Quality of Mercy, The Gypsy Trail* (1915), *My American Wife, The Spanish Dancer* (1923), *One Year to Live* (1925), *Mare Nostrum, The Temptress* (1926), *Venus of Venice, The Whip Woman* (1928), *Romance of the Rio Grande* (1929), *One Mad Kiss* (1930), *The Bohemian Girl* (1938), *Rose of the Rio*

Cobra Woman, Gypsy Wildcat, Bowery to Broadway (1944), *Sudan* (1945), *Tangier* (1946), *The Exile,* and *Pirates of Monterey* (1947).

Sylvia Morales

One of the best-recognized Chicana directors, Sylvia Morales has directed the short film *Chicana* (1979), about the changing roles of women in Hispanic/Chicano society from pre-Columbian times to the present; *Los Lobos: And A Time to Dance* (1984), a short musical special produced for PBS that profiles the musical group Los Lobos; *Esperanza,* a one-hour narrative drama directed under the Women Filmmakers Program at the American Film Institute, about the story of a young immigrant girl whose mother is arrested and who has to cope on her own; *SIDA Is AIDS,* a one-hour video documentary for PBS, broadcast in both Spanish and English; *Values: Sexuality and the Family,* a half-hour documentary on health issues affecting the Latino community, broadcast in Spanish and English; and *Faith Even to the Fire,* a one-hour video documentary for PBS profiling three nuns whose conscience

Silvia Morales.

Rita Moreno.

Barry Norton (Alfredo Birabén) (1905–1956)

Born on June 16, 1905, in Buenos Aires, Barry Norton became a romantic lead in Hollywood's late silent and early sound films. He later appeared in Hollywood-made Spanish-language or Mexican productions, sometimes directing his own films. His Hollywood films include *The Lily, What Price Glory* (1926), *Ankles Preferred, The Wizard, The Heart of Salome, Sunrise* (1926), *Mother Knows Best, Legion of the Condemned, Four Devils* (1928), *The Exalted Flapper* (1929), *Lady for a Day* (1933), *Nana* (1934), *The Buccaneer* (1938), *Devil Monster* (1946), and *Around the World in Eighty Days* (cameo, 1956).

Ramón Novarro (Ramó Samaniegos) (1899–1968)

Born on February 6, 1899, in Durango, Mexico, he became a romantic idol in the silent films of Hollywood in the 1920s. He began his career as a singing waiter and vaudeville performer before breaking into films as an extra in 1917. By 1922, he had become a star Latin lover and was overshadowed only by Rudolph Valentino in that role. He soon sought a broader range and less exotic image. His

Grande (1938), *Seven Sinners* (1940), *Notorious* (1946), *Captain from Castille* (1947), *Crisis, Dallas* (1950), *Wings of the Hawk* (1953), *Creature From the Black Lagoon* (1954), and *The Searchers* (1956).

Rita Moreno (Rosita Dolores Alverio) (1931–)

An actress, dancer, singer, Moreno was born on December 11, 1931 in Humacao, Puerto Rico. A dancer from childhood, she reached Broadway at 13 and Hollywood at 14. She won a 1962 Academy Award as best supporting actress for *West Side Story* and has been in several films important for understanding the Hollywood depiction of Hispanics, including *A Medal for Benny* (1954), *The Ring* (1952), and *Popi* (1969). Her other films include *Pagan Love Song* (1950), *Singin' in the Rain* (1952), *Latin Lovers, Fort Vengeance* (1953), *Jivaro, Garden of Evil* (1954), *The King and I, The Vagabond King* (1956), *The Deerslayer* (1957), *Summer and Smoke* (1961), *Marlowe* (1969), *Carnal Knowledge* (1971), *The Ritz* (1976), *The Boss' Son* (1978), *Happy Birthday, Gemini* (1980), *The Four Seasons* (1981), and *Life in the Food Chain* (1991).

Barry Norton.

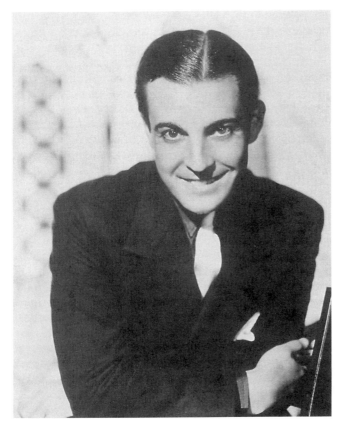

Ramón Novarro.

most famous part was the title role of the 1926 *Ben-Hur*. He was found beaten to death by intruders on October 31, 1968. His films include *A Small Town Idol* (1921), *The Prisoner of Zenda* (1922), *Scaramouche* (1923), *The Arab, Thy Name is Woman* (1924), *A Lover's Oath* (1925), *The Student Prince* (1927), *The Pagan* (1929), *In Gay Madrid* (1930), *Call of the Flesh* (1930), *Son of India, Mata Hari* (1931), *The Barbarian* (1933), *The Sheik Steps Out* (1937), *The Big Steal* (1949), *The Outriders* (1950), and *Heller in Pink Tights* (1960).

Edward James Olmos (1947-)

Edward James Olmos is an outstanding actor, singer, and producer who has broken into mainstream film and television after having developed his career in theater. Born on February 24, 1947, in East Los Angeles, Olmos received an associate of arts degree from East Los Angeles City College and attended California State University, Los Angeles. He was the founder and principal singer of the rock band Eddie James and the Pacific Ocean and had the role of the pachuconarrator in Luis Valdez's hit play *Zoot Suit* in Los Angeles. For this role he earned a Los Angeles Drama Critics Circle Award.

He has had starring or leading roles in films that have been breakthroughs for Hispanics in the movie industry: *Zoot Suit* (1981), *The Ballad of Gregorio Cortez* (1983), and *Stand and Deliver* (1988), for which he was nominated for a best actor Oscar while also serving as a coproducer. The film also helped make him one of the first Chicano's on the cover of *Time* magazine. Additional films include *Wolfen* (1981), *Blade Runner* (1982), *Saving Grace* (1986), *Triumph of the Spirit* (1989), *Maria's Story* (1990), *A Talent for the Game* (1991), and *Macho!* (1992).

In 1992, Olmos was co-producer and lead actor in the critically acclaimed film, *American Me*. He is one of the first Hispanic actors to have a principal role in a long-lasting television dramatic series: "Miami Vice," 1984–88. He has appeared in many other television shows and movies. His honors include the Los Angeles Drama Critics Circle Award (1978), Theatre World Award for Most Outstanding New Performer, Tony Award Nomination for Best Actor in *Zoot Suit,* and an Emmy for Best Supporting Actor in "Miami Vice" (1985).

Edward James Olmos.

Anthony Quinn.

Anthony Quinn (1915-)

Born on April 21, 1915, in Chihuahua, Mexico, of Irish Mexican parentage, Anthony Quinn has lived in the United States from childhood. He entered films in 1936 and the following year married Cecil B. deMille's adopted daughter, Katherine (they are now divorced). His father-in-law did nothing to advance Quinn's career, however. Quinn did not attain star status until 1952 with his Academy Award-winning role as Zapata's brother in *Viva Zapata!* Quinn went on to win a second Academy Award for *Lust for Life* (1956), and he began playing leads that emphasized his earthy and exotic qualities. He has appeared in more than 100 films and has written his autobiography, *The Original Sin* (1972). Among his many films are *Parole!* (1936), *The Buccaneer, King of Alcatraz* (1938), *Texas Rangers Ride Again* (1940), *Blood and Sand* (1941), *The Ox-Bow Incident, Guadalcanal Diary* (1943), *Back to Bataan* (1945), *California, Sinbad the Sailor, Black Gold* (1947), *The Brave Bulls* (1951), *Against All Flags* (1952), *Ride Vaquero* (1953), *Man From Del Rio* (1956), *The Black Orchid* (1958), *The Guns of Navarrone, Barabbas* (1961), *Requiem for a Heavyweight, Lawrence of Arabia* (1962), *Zorba the Greek* (1964), *A High Wind in Jamaica* (1965), *The Shoes of the Fisherman, The Magus* (1968), *The Secret of Santa Vittoria* (1969), *The Greek Tycoon, The Children of Sánchez* (1978), *The Salamander* (1981), *Ghosts Can't Do It* (1990), *Revenge* (1990), *The Old Man and the Sea* (1990), *Only the Lonely* (1991), *Mobsters* (1991), *The Last Action Hero* (1992), and *A Walk in the Clouds* (1995).

Duncan Renaldo (1904–1980)

Thought to have been born in Spain on April 23, 1904, Duncan Renaldo arrived in the United States in the early 1920s and was a Hollywood leading man and supporting player. He debuted with MGM in 1928 and by the early 1940s had found a niche in Westerns as one of the Three Mesquiteers and subsequently as the screen's fourth Cisco Kid. His films include *Clothes Make the Woman* (1928), *The Bridge of San Luis Rey* (1929), *Trapped in Tia Juana* (1932), *Zorro Rides Again* (serial, 1937), *Rose of the Rio Grande* (1938), *The Long Ranger Rides Again* (serial), *The Kansas Terrors* (1939), *Down Mexico Way* (1941), *For Whom the Bell Tolls* (1943), *The Cisco Kid Returns* (1945), *The Gay Amigo, The Daring Caballero* (1949), and *Zorro Rides Again* (1959). Renaldo died on September 3, 1980.

Gilbert Roland (Luis Antonio Dámaso de Alonso) (1905–1994)

Born in Júarez, Mexico, on December 11, 1905, the son of a bullfighter, Gilbert Roland trained for the *corrida* (bullfight), but chose a career in film instead after his family moved to the United States. He debuted as an extra at age 13 and subsequently played a Latin lover on both the silent and sound screens. His films include *The Plastic Age* (1925), *The Campus Flirt* (1926), *Camille, Rose of the Golden West* (1927), *The Dove* (1928), *The Last Train*

Gilbert Roland.

César Romero.

from Madrid (1937), *Juárez* (1939), *The Sea Hawk* (1940), *Captain Kidd* (1945), *The Gay Cavalier, Beauty and the Bandit* (1946), *The Bullfighter and the Lady, Mark of the Renegade* (1951), *Bandido* (1956), *Cheyenne Autumn* (1964), *Islands in the Stream, The Black Pearl* (1977), and *Barbarosa* (1982). Roland died on May 15, 1994.

César Romero (1907–1994)

Of Cuban parentage, César Romero was born on February 15, 1907, in New York City. He played a Latin lover in Hollywood films from the 1930s through the 1950s and later did suave supporting character roles. He played the Cisco Kid in the late 1930s and early 1940s. His films include *The Thin Man* (1934), *Clive of India, Cardinal Richelieu* (1935), *The Cisco Kid and the Lady* (1939), *Viva Cisco Kid, The Gay Caballero, Romance of the Rio Grande* (1940), *Ride on Vaquero, Weekend in Havana* (1941), *Captain from Castile* (1948), *Vera Cruz* (1954), *Villa!* (1958), *Batman* (1966), and *The Strongest Man in the World* (1975). Romero died on January 1, 1994.

Martin Sheen (Ramón Estévez) (1940–)

Born on August 3, 1940, in Dayton, Ohio, to a Spanish immigrant father and an Irish mother, Martin Sheen began at the New York Living Theater and debuted on the screen in 1967. He was named as best actor at the San Sebastián (Spain) Film Festival for his role in *Badlands* (1973). His other films include *The Incident* (1967), *The Subject Was Roses* (1968), *Catch-22* (1970), *The Cassandra Crossing* (1977), *Apocalypse Now* (1979), *That Championship Season* (1982), *Gandhi* (1982), *The Guardian* (1984), *Siesta* (1987), *Wall Street* (1987), *Da* (1988), *Beverly Hills Brats* (1989), *Nightbreaker* (1989), *The Maid* (1990), *Original Intent* (1990), *Touch and Die* (1990), *Hearts of Darkness* (1991), *Paper Hearts* (1991), *JFK* (1991), *Cadence,* which he also directed, (1991), *Hear No Evil* (1993), and *Gettysburg* (1993).

Several of his children—Emilio Estévez, Ramon Sheen, and Charlie Sheen—are also active in Hollywood.

Jesús Salvador Treviño (1946–)

Director, producer, and writer, Jesús Treviño is one of the best-known Chicano filmmakers. His credits include directing episodes of the ABC series "Gabriel's Fire" and "Sea Quest," and the NBC series "Lifestories," and the PBS series "Mathnet." His films include *Raíces de sangre (Roots [of Blood],* 1977, with Richard Yñíguez), which evokes border life and the *maquiladoras* (twin manufacturing plants); *Seguín* (1982, with Henry Darrow and Edward James Olmos), a Hispanic perspective on the Alamo; and documentaries and docudramas, including *Salazar Inquest* (1970), *Chicano Moratorium* (1970), *America Tropical* (1971), *La Raza Unida* (1972), *Yo soy chicano (I Am Chicano,* 1972), *Have Another Drink, Ese* (1977), *One out of Ten* (1979), *Yo soy (I Am)* (1985), and *Chicano! The History of the Mexican American Civil Rights Movement* (1996).

Luis Valdez

See Chapter 21.

Lupe Vélez (María Guadalupe Vélez de Villalobos) (1908–1944)

Born on July 18, 1908, in San Luis Potosí, Mexico, Lupe Vélez became one of the most famous Hispanic screen actresses of all time. Originally a dancer, she debuted in film in 1926 under Hal Roach's direction and became a star the following year as the leading lady in *The Gaucho* opposite Douglas Fairbanks.

Known as a fiery leading lady, both in silent and sound films, she later made positive use of her Spanish-accented English to reposition herself as a comedienne in the "Mexican Spitfire" series. Her volatile personal life, including a romance with Gary Cooper and marriage to Johnny Weismuller, ended in suicide. Her films include *Stand and Deliver* (1928), *Lady of the Pavements* (1929), *The Squaw Man, The Cuban Love Song* (1931), *Hot Pepper* (1933), *The Girl from Mexico* (1939), *Mexican Spitfire* (1940), and *Redhead from Manhattan* (1943).

Raoul Walsh (1887–1980)

Raoul Walsh was given his first directorial assignment by D. W. Griffith at Biograph, which was, in collaboration with Christy Cabanne, *The Life of General Villa* (1914), a seven-reel mixture of staged scenes and authentic footage of Pancho Villa's military campaign starring the Mexican bandit himself. Walsh's most notable appearance as an actor was in the role of John Wilkes Booth in Griffith's *The Birth of a Nation* (1915). He subsequently appeared in occasional films but largely devoted himself to a career as a director of several memorable films, including

Raoul Walsh.

Lupe Vélez.

The Thief of Bagdad, What Price Glory, The Big Trail, High Sierra, Strawberry Blond, They Died with Their Boots On, White Heat, and *The Tall Men.* Walsh published his autobiography, *Each Man in His Time,* in 1974.

Raquel Welch (1940–)

Raquel Welch was born on September 5, 1940, in Chicago to a Bolivian-born engineer and a mother of English background. Despite a very difficult and inauspicious beginning, and thanks to a phenomenally successful 1963 publicity tour in Europe devised by her second husband, former child actor Patrick Curtis, and herself, she became a major international star without having appeared in a single important film. Known first as a voluptuous sex goddess, subsequently she also made a name as a comedienne. Her films include *A Swingin' Summer* (1965), *One Million Years B.C.* (1966), *The Biggest Bundle of Them All, Bandolero!* (1968), *100 Rifles* (1969), *Myra Breckinridge* (1970), *Kansas City Bomber* (1972), *The Three Musketeers* (1974), and *Mother, Jugs, and Speed* (1977), *Crossed Swords*

Raquel Welch.

(1978), and *L'Animal* (1979). Her television films include, *The Legend of Walks Far Woman* (1982), *Right to Die* (1993), and *Torch Song* (1993).

References

"Authentic Pachuco." *Time,* 10 July 1944: 72.

Barry, Iris. *D. W. Griffith: American Film Master.* New York: Museum of Modern Art, 1965.

Biberman, Herbert. *Salt of the Earth: The Story of a Film.* Boston: Beacon Press, 1965.

Bowser, Eileen, ed. *Film Notes.* New York: Museum of Modern Art, 1969.

Candelaia, Cordelia. "Film Portrayals of La Mujer Hispana," *Agenda,* June 1981: 32–36.

Cárdenas, Don, and Suzanne Schneider, eds. *Chicano Images in Film.* Denver: Denver International Film Festival, 1981.

Cortés, Carlos E. "Chicanas in Film: History of an Image." In *Chicano Cinema: Research, Review, and Resources,* edited by Gary D. Keller. Binghamton, New York: Bilingual Review/Press, 1985: 94–108

——. "*The Greaser's Revenge* to *Boulevard Nights*: The Mass Media Curriculum on Chicanos." In *History, Culture, and Society: Chicano Studies in the 1980s.* Ypsilanti, Michigan: Bilingual Press, 1983.

——. "The History of Ethnic Images in Film: The Search for a Methodology." In *Ethnic Images in Popular Genres and Media,* Special issue. *MELUS, The Journal of the Society for the Study of the Multi-Ethnic Literature of the United States,* 11, No. 3, fall 1984: 63–77.

——. "The Immigrant in Film: Evolution of an Illuminating Icon." In *Stock Characters in American Popular Film,* edited by Paul Loukides and Linda K. Fuller. Vol. 1 of *Beyond the Stars.* Bowling Green, Ohio: Bowling Green State University Popular Press, 1990: 23–24.

——. "The Role of Media in Multicultural Education." *Viewpoints in Teaching and Learning,* 56, No. 1, winter 1980: 38–49.

Croy, Homer. *The Story of D. W. Griffith.* New York: Duell, Sloan and Pearce, 1959.

D. W. Griffith: The Years at Biograph. New York: Farrar, Straus and Giroux, 1970.

Delpar, Helen. "Goodbye to the 'Greaser': Mexico, the MPPDA, and Derogatory Films, 1922–1926," *Journal of Popular Film and Television,* 12, 1984: 34–41.

Farber, Stephen. "Peckinpah's Return," *Film Quarterly,* 23, fall 1969: 2–11.

Fregoso, Rosa Linda. "*Born in East L.A.* and the Politics of Representation." *Cultural Studies,* 4, No. 3, October 1990: 264–80.

García, Juan R. "Hollywood and the West: Mexican Images in American Films, 1894–1983." In *Old Southwest, New Southwest,* edited by Judy Nolte Lensink. Tucson: Tucson Public Library, 1988.

Geduld, Harry M. *Focus on D. W. Griffith.* Englewood Cliffs, N.J.: Prentice-Hall, 1971.

Gonzales, Rodolfo. *Yo Soy Joaquín / I Am Joaquín.* Denver: La Causa, 1972.

Graham, Cooper C., Steven Higgins, Elaine Mancini, and Joao Luiz Vieira. *D. W. Griffith and the Biography Company.* Metuchen, New Jersey: Scarecrow Press, 1985.

Greenberg, Bradley S., and Pilar Baptista-Fernández. "Hispanic American—The New Minority on Television." In *Life on Television: Content Analysis of U.S. TV Drama,* edited by Bradley S.Greenberg. Norwood, New Jersey: Ablex, 1980: 3–12.

Greenfield, Gerald Michael, and Carlos E. Cortés. "Harmony and Conflict of Intercultural Images: The Treatment of Mexico in U.S. Feature Films and K-12 Textbooks." *Estudios Mexicanos,* 7, No. 2, 1991: 45–56.

Griffith, Albert J. "The Scion, The Señorita, and the Texas Ranch Epic: Hispanic Images in Film." *Bilingual Review / Revista Bilingüe.* In press.

Gunning, Tom, "Weaving a Narrative: Style and Economic Background in Griffith's Biograph Films," *Quarterly Review of Film Studies,* winter 1981: 11–21.

Hadley-García, George. *Hollywood hispano: Los latinos en el mundo del cine.* Secaucus, New Jersey: Carol Publishing Group, 1991.

Haskell, Molly. *From Reverence to Rape: The Treatment of Women in the Movies.* New York: Holt, Rinehart and Winston, 1974.

Henderson, Robert M. *D. W. Griffith: His Life and Work.* New York: Oxford University Press, 1972.

Jacob, Lewis. *The Rise of the American Film: A Critical History.* New York: Harcourt Brace and Company, 1939.

Kazan, Elia. "Letters to the Editor." *Saturday Review,* 35, 5 April 1952: 22.

Kearney, Jill. "The Old Gringo." *American Film,* 13, No. 5, March 1988: 26–31, 67.

Keller, Gary D., *Chicano Cinema: Research, Reviews, and Resources.* Binghamton, New York: Bilingual Review/Press, 1985.

——. *Cine chicano.* México City: Cineteca Nacional, 1988.

——. *Hispanics and United States Film: An Overview and Handbook.* Tempe, Arizona: Bilingual Review/Press, 1994.

Kitses, Jim. *Horizons West: Anthony Mann, Budd Boetticher, Sam Peckinpah; Studies in Authorship within the Western.* Bloomington: Indiana University Press, 1969.

Lamb, Blaine P. "The Convenient Villain: The Early Cinema Views the Mexican American," *Journal of the West,* 14, October 1975: 75–81.

Latino Film and Video Images, Special issue. *Centro,* 2, No. 8, spring 1990. [Centro de Estudios Puertorriqueños, Hunter College/CUNY.]

Latinos and the Media, Special Issue. *Centro,* 3, No. 1, winter 1990–91. [Centro de Estudios Puertorriqueños, Hunter College/CUNY.]

Leab, Daniel J. *From Sambo to Superspade: The Black Experience in Motion Pictures.* Boston: Houghton Mifflin, 1975.

Levine, Paul G. "Remember the Alamo? John Wayne Told One Story. PBS' Seguín Tells Another." *American Film,* January-February 1982: 47–48.

Maciel, David R. "Braceros, Mojados, and Alambristas: Mexican Immigration to the United States in Contemporary Cinema," *Hispanic Journal of Behavioral Sciences,* 8, 1986: 369–85.

——. *El Norte; The U.S.-Mexican Border in Contemporary Cinema.* San Diego: Institute for Regional Studies of the Californias, San Diego State University, 1990.

Miller, Jim. "Chicano Cinema: An Interview with Jesús Treviño." *Cineaste,* 8, No. 3, 1978.

Miller, Mark Crispin. "In Defense of Sam Peckinpah." *Film Quarterly,* 28, spring 1975: 2–17.

Miller, Randall M., ed. *The Kaleidoscopic Lens: How Hollywood Views Ethnic Groups.* Englewood Cliffs, New Jersey: Jerome S. Ozer, 1980.

Mindiola, Tatcho, Jr. "El corrido de Gregorio Cortez: The Challenge of Conveying Chicano Culture Through the Cinematic Treatment of a Folk Hero." *Tonantzin,* November 1986: 14–15.

Monsiváis, Carlos. "The Culture of the Frontier: The Mexican Side." In *Views Across the Border: The United States and Mexico,* edited by Stanley R. Ross, Albuquerque: University of New Mexico Press, 1978.

Mora, Carl J. *Mexican Cinema: Reflections of a Society, 1896–1980.* Berkeley: University of California Press, 1982.

Morsberger, Robert E., ed.*Viva Zapata! (The Original Screenplay by John Steinbeck).* New York: Viking Press, 1973.

Niver, Kemp R. *D. W. Griffith: His Biograph Films in Perspective.* Los Angeles: John D. Roche, 1974.

Noriega, Chon. *Chicano Cinema and the Horizon of Expectation: a Discursive Analysis of Recent Reviews in the Mainstream, Alternative and Hispanic Press.* (SCCR Working Paper No. 30). Stanford, California: Stanford Center for Chicano Research, 1990.

——, ed. *Chicanos and Film: Essays on Chicano Representation and Resistance.* New York: Garland. In press.

——. "Citizen Chicano: The Trials and Titillations of Ethnicity in the American Cinema, 1935–1962." *Social Research,* 58, No. 2, summer 1991: 413–38.

——. "In Aztlán: The Films of the Chicano Movement, 1969–79." *Whitney Museum of American Art.* No. 56 (pamphlet). January 1991.

——. *Working Bibliography of Critical Writings on Chicanos and Film.* Working Bibliography Series, No. 6. Stanford, California: Mexican-American Collections, Stanford University Libraries, 1990.

O'Connor, John. "TV: Seguín: True Tale of the Texas Revolution." *New York Times,* 26 January 1982.

O'Dell, Paul. *Griffith and the Rise of Hollywood.* New York: International Film Guide Series, 1970.

Pettit, Arthur G. *Images of the Mexican American in Fiction and Film.* College Station: Texas A & M University Press, 1980.

——. "Nightmare and Nostalgia: The Cinema West of Sam Peckinpah," *Western Humanities Review,* 29, spring 1975: 105–22.

Ramírez Berg, Charles. "Stereotyping in Film in General and of Hispanics in Particular." *Howard Journal of Communications,* 2.3, summer 1990: 286–300.

Reyes, Luis. "The Mexican's Turn to Remember the Alamo." *Los Angeles Times,* 24 August 1982: 1.

Richard, Alfred Charles, Jr. *Contemporary Hollywood's Negative Hispanic Image: An Interpretive Filmography, 1956–1993.* Westport, Connecticut: Greenwood Press, 1994.

Roeder, George H., Jr. "Mexicans in the Movies: The Image of Mexicans in American Films, 1894–1947." Unpublished manuscript, University of Wisconsin, Madison, 1971.

Roffman, Peter, and Jim Purdy. *The Hollywood Social Problem Film.* Bloomington: Indiana University Press, 1981.

Rosen, Marjorie. *Popcorn Venus: Women, Movies and the American Dream.* New York: Coward, McCann and Geoghegan, 1973.

Rosenfelt, Deborah Silverton. *Salt of the Earth.* Old Westbury, New York: Feminist Press, 1978.

Saragoza, Alex M. "The Border in American and Mexican Cinema." In *Cultural Atlas of Mexico-United States Border Studies,* edited by Raymond Paredes. Los Angeles: UCLA Latin American Center Publications, 1990.

——. "Mexican Cinema in the United States, 1940–1952." In National Association for Chicano Studies, *History,*

Culture and Society: Chicano Studies in the 1980s. Ypsilanti, Michigan: Bilingual Press, 1983.

Schickel, Richard. *D. W. Griffith: An American Life.* New York: Simon and Schuster, 1984.

Sklar, Robert. *Movie-Made America: A Cultural History of American Movies.* New York: Random House, 1975.

Slide, Anthony. *The Griffith Actresses.* New York: A. S. Barnes, 1973.

Taylor, Frank J. "Leo the Caballero." *Saturday Evening Post,* 6 July 1946: 26.

Treviño, Jesús Salvador. "Chicano Cinema." *New Scholar,* 8, 1982: 167–73.

Valle, Victor. "Latino: Hollywood Opens Door as 'La Bamba' Leads Way." *Mesa* (Arizona) *Tribune,* 6 April 1988: D2.

Vanderwood, Paul. "An American Cold Warrior: *Viva Zapata!*" In, *American History/American Film: Interpreting the Hollywood Image,* edited by John E. O'Connor and Martin A. Jackson. New York: Frederick Ungar, 1979: 183–201.

Whitney, John. "Image Making in the Land of Fantasy." *Agenda, A Journal of Hispanic Issues,* 8, No. 1, January-February 1978.

Williams, Linda. "Type and Stereotype: Chicano Images in Film." *Frontiers: A Journal of Women's Studies,* 5, No. 2, summer 1980: 14–17.

Williams, Martin. *Griffith: First Artist of the Movies.* New York: Oxford University Press, 1980.

Woll, Allen L. "Hollywood's Good Neighbor Policy: The Latin American Image in American Film, 1939–1946," *Journal of Popular Film,* 3, fall 1974: 283–85.

——. *The Latin Image in American Film.* Los Angeles: Latin American Center, University of California, 1977.

——. "Latin Images in American Films," *Journal of Mexican History,* 4, 1974:28–40.

Wong, Eugene Franklin: "On Visual Media Racism: Asians in the American Motion Pictures." Ph.D. dissertation, Graduate School of International Studies, University of Denver, 1977. Reprinted, New York: Arno Press, 1978.

Yacowar, Maurice. "Aspects of the Familiar: A Defense of Minority Group Stereotyping in Popular Film." *Film Literature Quarterly,* 2, No. 2, spring 1974: 129–39.

Zinman, David. *Saturday Night at the Bijou.* New Rochelle, New York: Arlington House, 1973.

Gary D. Keller

23

Music

※ The Corrido and Canción-Corrido ※ Música Norteña (The Mexican-Texan Conjunto)
※ The Mexican American Orquesta ※ Salsa ※ Latin Jazz/Rock ※ Musica Tropical
※ The Contemporary Music Scene ※ Selected Discography

Music is a form of cultural communication. As such, it speaks in a symbolic way about the thoughts and feelings of people, which means that it makes associations that people understand between the particular musical sounds and their own particular thoughts, actions, and experiences. Music can thus transmit shared feelings and values, and, when words are added, it can be the ideal vehicle for communicating ideologies, or certain ways of thinking and acting, that those who subscribe to the musical message believe are appropriate guides for living.

Normally, the most strongly symbolic or cultural musical forms connected to a people's deepest sentiments about their way of life. Such musical forms are considered to be "strong" symbols that are, moreover, "organically" linked to a people's everyday thoughts and actions. They express the most profound feelings that those people have about their sense of identity and their everyday life rhythms. Most important, organic, culturally powerful music is generally "homegrown," in the sense that it is created by and belongs to the communities that perform. Thus, unlike pop music, for example, which is intended to appeal to the largest possible audience and is created for financial gain, organic, homegrown music usually has deep roots within smaller, tightly knit communities, and this is what makes such music a powerful cultural expression.

Of course, the for-profit motive that drives pop music production does not completely strip it of its cultural message. Often it does communicate to young people a "hip" life-style, as opposed to the more conservative tastes of older generations. But pop commercial music can never be a "strong" cultural symbol. Cultural music—the Puerto Rican salsa and the Mexican-Texan *norteño,* for example—speak to the innermost feelings, desires, and con-

flicts of specific Hispanic groups in the United States, and they bring into play a whole array of social, political, economic, and cultural factors that form the basis for a collective identity. At best, meanwhile, commercial pop music can only provide a sense of momentary escape into youthful fantasies.

Among Latinos in the United States, several mu-

Mexican musicians in the 1890s in California.

643

sical forms and styles fall into the category of organic, homegrown musical communication. They symbolize the most powerful cultural beliefs and ways of doing things for specific segments of the Latino community. They speak, both directly and indirectly, to challenges and problems that confront the various segments of the Latino community in the United States. Over the span of many years, these musical forms and styles have developed into cultural traditions that enjoy deep and widespread popularity among their respective audiences. *Música norteña,* the Mexican American *orquesta,* and *salsa* are excellent examples. These traditions have all contributed in important, "organic" ways toward the cultural life of the Latino groups with which they are historically associated. They represent major musical developments whose cultural power is linked to fundamental forces—social, economic, and ideological—among the various segments of the Latino community. These and other musical forms and styles speak symbolically to such issues as acculturation, intercultural conflict, and socioeconomic differences within the Latino communities.

Latinos in the United States have been witness to a multitude of styles and performers, but not all

have equal cultural value. Some are fleeting expressions that leave little trace behind. On the other hand, some homegrown creations—mostly in the form of musical ensembles, their styles, and repertoires—have achieved great popularity and widespread distribution.

Among the most important Latino musical creations are two ensembles that originated among the Mexicans in Texas. These are *música norteña,* known among Mexican Texans, or *tejanos,* as *conjunto,* and *orquesta tejana,* or simply *orquesta.* Both of these musical styles originated in the first half of the twentieth century, and both should be seen as musical responses to important economic, social, and cultural changes that took place among the Mexican Texans beginning in the 1930s. Both conjunto and orquesta had become major musical styles by the 1950s, and their influence had spread far beyond the Texas borders by the 1970s.

A type of Afro-Caribbean music that came to be known in the 1970s as is another major style of Latino music in the United States. Just as conjunto and orquesta are homegrown Mexican-Texan styles, salsa likewise is the unique music of Afro-Hispanics from Puerto Rico, Cuba, and the Dominican Repub-

Xavier Cugat and his orchestra in the 1940s.

Augusto Coen and his Golden Orchestra, circa 1930s–1940s.

lic. It too is organically linked to the people who created it, and, despite its heavy commercialization in the last 30 years by the recording industry in the United States, it continues to occupy a central position in the musical life of Afro-Hispanic people in the United States.

Two cousins of salsa, Latin jazz and Latin rock, are also important enough to be included here. Although neither has the kind of organic links that salsa, orquesta tejana, or conjunto have to specific segments of the Latino population, both of these related forms have produced their share of gifted performers. These performers see themselves as members of the Latino community, and they perceive their music as a contribution to the life and culture of this population.

Two important types of vocal music are the Mexican *corrido* (ballad) and a hybrid between the *corrido* and the *canción* (song). These occupy a special place in the musical life of Mexican Americans, especially those living in the southwestern states of Texas, New Mexico, Arizona, and California. The corrido and the canción-corrido hybrid emerged as powerful cultural expressions in the Hispanic Southwest during the twentieth century, especially the years lead-

ing up to World War II. Through their lyrics, the corrido and canción-corrido address more directly than any of the ensemble styles (salsa, conjunto, orquesta) the social and ideological issues which Latinos face in their often difficult adjustment to American life. The graphic manner in which the corrido and canción confront such issues places them high on the scale of cultural significance.

Finally, there is also a musical ensemble that has made a powerful, although largely unrecognized, impact on a large segment of the Mexican population in the United States—the Mexican immigrants, many of them undocumented, who have been coming to the United States in increasing numbers since the 1960s. This ensemble goes by several names— *grupos cumbieros, grupos tropicales, grupos modernos*—but it may best be defined as a Mexican working-class variant of so-called *música tropical.* Música tropical has a long history in Mexico and Latin America, but this ensemble has a history that coincides with the massive emigration that began in Mexico in the 1960s. Since that time, the grupo tropical/moderno has become an everyday music in the lives of many Mexicans in the American Southwest.

✳ THE CORRIDO AND CANCIÓN-CORRIDO

Historically, the *corrido* and *canción* are two distinct genres or musical forms. However, in the Hispanic Southwest they have at times experienced considerable overlap, especially since the 1920s. The overlap occurs when, on the one hand, the corrido sheds some of its most familiar features, such as the call of the *corridista* to his audience and mention of the date, place, and cast of characters. At the same time, many canciones composed during and after the 1920s abandon that genre's most recognizable feature—its lyrical quality—and assume a semi-narrative form, thus moving them in the direction of the *corrido*. The result is a convergence of the two genres. Of course, this convergence is never complete; some corridos retain enough of their "classical" narrative features to stamp them unmistakably as corridos, while most canciones remain purely lyrical expressions, usually about love.

In any case, beginning in the 1920s a number of canción-corrido hybrids made their appearance in the Hispanic Southwest. Not coincidentally, it was at this time that the large American recording labels, such as Columbia and RCA, first moved into the Southwest and began to commercially exploit Mexican American music in all its variety. Not coincidentally, either, the first of the famous Mexican American troubadors—singers of the canción and corrido—attained widespread popularity throughout the Southwest during the 1920s. Many of these troubadors were composers of the canción-corrido, as well. From the 1920s, through the 1940s, they produced a steady flow of canciones-corridos that depicted life in the Hispanic Southwest with great feeling and accuracy, describing in vivid detail both the sadness and the humor of life in the borderlands. Especially moving are those compositions that address the long-standing conflict between Anglos and Mexicans and the oppression endured by the latter.

The rising popularity of the Mexican American troubadors was not a spontaneous event, however. It is true that the intervention of the major recording labels energized musicians and propelled a number of musical traditions to a higher level of innovation, and until the arrival of the wax disk, singers and their songs tended not to attain recognition beyond their immediate locale. Some of the ancient songs had, indeed, spread throughout the Southwest over the previous centuries, but newly composed songs, as well as their composer-performers, were usually confined to their immediate point of origin.

The major labels changed all that. In 1926, RCA, Columbia, Decca, and Brunswick began setting up makeshift studios in rented hotel rooms in cities like Dallas, San Antonio, and Los Angeles, and with the help of local entrepreneurs who knew the pool of musicians available, they began to record commercially a wide variety of musical forms, including the then evolving música norteña, various orquestalike ensembles, and, of course, the canción and the corrido. Women made their impact on Mexican American music at this time, with one female troubador in particular attaining immense popularity throughout the Southwest—the venerable Lidia Mendoza. Other popular troubadors of the period who made a lasting impact on the emerging canción-corrido form include Los Hermanos Bañuelos (The Bañuelos Brothers, the first to record with the major labels, in 1926) and Los Madrugadores (The Early Birds), both groups from Los Angeles, as well as Los Hermanos Chavarría (The Chavarría Brothers) and Gaytán y Cantú (Gaytán and Cantú), from Texas.

These troubadors and others left a rich legacy of canciones-corridos, a legacy that attests to the creative energy the Mexican Americans devoted to a music that could document the harshness of their daily life. This music was so poetically charged that its cultural power can be felt to this day. The number of canciones-corridos preserved on wax is large, but the following excerpts should be enough to provide a feel for the range of topics. The first example is from "El deportado" ("The Deported One"), a canción-corrido recorded by Los Hermanos Bañuelos in the early 1930s. *El deportado* depicts the bitter experiences of a Mexican immigrant in his encounter with the cold, exploitive system of American capitalism.

> I'm going to sing to you, gentlemen,
> I'm going to sing to you, gentlemen
> all about my sufferings,
> since I left my country,
> since I left my country
> to come to this nation [the United States].
>
> We arrived at Juarez at last,
> we arrived at Juarez at last,
> there I ran into trouble.
> "Where are you going, where do you come from?
> How much money do you have to enter this country?"
> "Gentlemen, I have money,
> gentlemen I have money,
> so that I can emigrate."
> "Your money is worth nothing,
> your money is worth nothing,
> we have to bathe you."
>
> The white men are very wicked,
> the white men are very wicked,
> they take advantage of the occasion.
> And all the Mexicans,

Lidia Mendoza (center) with Marcelo, comic Tin Tan, and Juanita Mendoza in Chicago in the 1950s.

and all the Mexicans
they treat without compassion. (Arhoolie/
Folklyric Records, 1975)

Another canción-corrido hybrid, "El lavaplatos"
("The Dishwasher"), also recorded by Los Hermanos
Bañuelos (reissued by Archoolie/Folklyric, 1975), recounts in more humorous language the adventures
of a poor Mexican who immigrates to the United
States in search of the glamorous life of Hollywood,
only to find himself drifting from one backbreaking
job to another. The following stanzas are representative of the narrative tone:

One day very desperate,
because of so much revolution,
I came over to this side [of the border]
without paying the immigration.
Oh, what a fast one,
Oh what a fast one,
I crossed without paying anything.
On arriving at the station,
I ran into a friend,
who gave me an invitation
to work on *el traque*.

I supposed *el traque*
would be some kind of warehouse,
but it was to repair the track
where the train ran.
Oh what a friend,
oh what a friend,
how he took me to the track.
When I got tired of the track,
he invited me again,
to pick tomatoes and thin beets.
And there I earned indulgences
walking on my knees;
about four or five miles
they gave me for penance. (Arhoolie/Folklyric,
1975).

As can be seen from these examples—and many
more could be provided—composers of the 1920s
through them 1940s were exceptionally committed
to documenting the enduring hardships of life for
Mexicans in the Southwest. For this they utilized the
canción-corrido extensively. But the corrido itself, in
its more or less pure form, plays an even more central role in the music culture of Mexican Americans,
one that dates back to the nineteenth century.

A working-class *orquesta,* circa 1930.

Merle E. Simmons observed in *The Mexican Corrido as a Source for the Interpretative Study of Modern Mexico* (1957) that the Mexican corrido plays an important historical role in articulating the sociopolitical position of the Mexican folk vis-á-vis the dominant classes. The folklorist Américo Paredes has argued the same for the corrido on this side of the border and, in fact, advances the proposition that the Mexican corrido actually originated along the Texas-Mexico border, since the earliest corrido collected in complete form comes from Texas—"El corrido de Kiansis" ("The Ballad of Kansas"), dating from the 1860s. For Paredes, the climate of intercultural conflict that grew out of the Anglo invasion and subsequent annexation of what became the American Southwest at the end of the Mexican-American War (1848) was the ideal setting for the birth of an expressive culture that would key in on this conflict.

It was at this point, between 1848 and 1860, that the modern corrido emerged out of an ancient musico-literary form that had been introduced from Spain in the sixteenth century—the romance. And it was evidently in Texas, and not in Michoacán, Durango, or Jalisco, as once thought, that the first corridos were composed (Américo Paredes, from

Madstones and Twisters, 1958). One of these was "Kiansis," a corrido that documents the epic cattle drives from Texas to the Kansas stockyards. More important, we see in Kiansis subtle indications of the intercultural conflict that attended Anglo-Mexican relations at the time. For that reason, Paredes has proposed "Kiansis" in his *A Texas-Mexican Cancionero* (1976) the first of what he labels corridos of intercultural conflict. This conflict is subtly captured in the following stanzas:

Five hundred steers there were,
all big and quick;
Then five Mexicans arrive,
all of them wearing good chaps;
and thirty Americans
couldn't keep them together,
and in less than a quarter-hour
they had the steers penned up.

As Paredes has noted, "There is intercultural conflict in 'Kiansis,' but it is expressed in professional rivalries rather than in violence between men" (1976). That violence, however, is present in another corrido from the late nineteenth century, titled "El corrido de Juan Cortina." This corrido details in stronger language the resentment that Mexicans on the border felt toward the Americans:

That famed General Cortinas
is quite sovereign and free,
the honor due him is greater
for he saved a Mexican's life.
The Americans made merry,
they got drunk in the saloons,
out of joy over the death
of the famed General Cortinas.

The corrido celebrates the exploits of Juan Nepomuceno Cortina, a Mexican from south Texas who, according to Paredes, "was the first man to organize Texas-Mexican protest against abuses on the part of the Anglos who controlled /the . . . power structure [in South Texas] after 1848" (Parades, 1976). Cortina, a member of a wealthy landowning family with deep roots in the Texas-Mexico border region, came to resent the arrogant attitude of the Anglo newcomers, especially the fortune makers. After an incident in which he accosted a town marshal who was pistol-whipping a *vaquero* (cowboy) who worked on his mother's ranch, Cortina was declared an outlaw, and thereafter he dedicated his life to guerrilla warfare, until he was driven out of Texas by the U.S. cavalry.

"El Corrido de Juan Cortina" ushered in what has been called the hero corrido period, when the prevalent type was the corrido of intercultural conflict. This type of corrido invariably features a larger-than-life Mexican hero who single-handedly defies a cowardly, smaller-than-life gang of Anglo-American lawmen. The hero either defeats the Anglos or goes down fighting "with his pistol in his hand" (Paredes, *With a Pistol in His Hand: A Border Ballad and its Hero,* 1958). In this way, the protagonist gains heroic status in the Mexican American community, becoming, in effect, a kind of redeemer for the collective insults suffered by his people at the hands of the Anglos.

Hero corridos were written until the 1920s, in Texas and elsewhere, including such classics as "Joaquín Murrieta and Jacinto Treviño," but perhaps the most memorable is "El corrido de Gregorio Cortez," immortalized by Américo Paredes in his book *With His Pistol in His Hand* (which served as the basis for the film *The Ballad of Gregorio Cortez,* released in 1982). The corrido documents the odyssey of a Mexican Texan who fled for his life after he killed an Anglo sheriff in self-defense, because of a linguistic misunderstanding over some stolen horses.

"Gregorio Cortez" is the ideal example of the hero corrido. As a symbol of his people's hopes for deliverance, the hero achieves his revenge through the process of "status reversal" (Victor Turner, *The Ritual Process,* 1969), wherein the hero, who personifies the collective will, defeats or at least defies the American lawmen, who personify the dominant Anglos. Thus, through the exploits of the hero, the Mexican Americans of the Southwest symbolically invert the real world, assuming in vicarious fashion a dominant position over their oppressors and in this way achieving a sense of deliverance.

The following stanzas from "Gregorio Cortez" illustrate the contrastive opposition between heroic Mexican and cowardly Anglo:

The Americans came,
whiter than a dove,
from fear they had
Gregorio Cortez left,
of Cortez and his gun,
he left heading for Laredo;
they refused to follow him,
because they were afraid of him.

The hero corrido was most prevalent during the early period of Anglo-Mexican contact, when relations between the two groups were characterized by what Paredes (*New Voices in American Studies,* 1966) has called the open hostility stage of Mexican American folklore. This period spans the years from about 1848 to the early 1900s—a period during which Mexicans still entertained hopes, albeit diminishing with time, that they could still defeat the Anglos and drive them out of their territory. However, the hero corrido continued to enjoy prominence until the 1930s, when a new type emerged.

The new corridos, prevalent since the end of World War II, have been labeled victim corridos. They demonstrate sharp differences in subject matter from those of the earlier period. Foremost is the disappearance of the larger-than-life hero. In his place a new protagonist emerges, one who is usually portrayed as a helpless victim of Anglo oppression. This shift in the corrido of intercultural conflict from hero to victim is too fundamental to be considered a random event. In fact, it coincides with equally fundamental changes in Mexican American society. It thus happens that the newer corridos appeared at the precise moment when Mexican Americans initiated a wholesale movement from rural to urban, from folk to modern, from a monocultural to a bicultural life-style, and from proletarian status to a more diversified social organization.

After World War II, in this climate of emergent

political and economic diversification, new cultural directions and new modes of interpreting the Mexican American experience were being charted. Fully conscious of their newfound power, postwar Mexican Americans began to rethink their relationship with the dominant Anglo majority and to demand more economic and political equality (as well as acceptance). However, despite the tentative beginnings of an interethnic accommodation, the Anglos were not yet ready to accept the Mexicans as equal, and the intercultural friction persisted. This friction at times forced Mexican Americans to put aside growing internal class differences, as they closed ranks to fight racial discrimination. In this atmosphere of heightened political awareness, the corrido continued to play an important role. According to an article by Manuel Peña in *Aztlán Journal of Chicano Studies* (1982) on the corrido of intercultural conflict, "Chicanos [Mexican Americans], having developed more effectively organized political machinery to challenge Anglo supremacy, relied less on their *corridos* to uplift a battered cultural image and more to rally support for active political causes. The reasoning seems self-evident: a *corrido* is more likely to elicit an active response, i.e., outrage and group mobilization, if it depicts a helpless victim rather than a potent, larger-than-life hero. In a sense, the two types of *corrido* are antithetical—one reflecting pent-up frustration and powerlessness, the other active resistance."

Several well-known victim corridos have been written since World War II. Among them is "Discriminación a un mártir" ("Discrimination Against a Martyr"), one of the first and an outstanding example of the genre. Written in 1949, it documents the case of Private Félix Longoria, a soldier killed in action during World War II. A native of Three Rivers, Texas, Longoria was drafted into the army in 1944, and early in 1945 he was assigned to the war in the Pacific theater, where the Allies were engaged in heavy combat against the Japanese. Longoria was killed during one of the final assaults. Like many men killed in action, Private Longoria was temporarily buried in the Philippines. When his remains were finally exhumed, in 1949, and flown to his relatives in Texas, the local funeral home refused to provide funeral services, citing the past practice against funerals for Mexicans.

The Mexican American community was shocked and outraged by the funeral home's callous act of discrimination. Led by Héctor García, president of a political action group known as the G.I. Forum, the community applied pressure on authorities until Lyndon B. Johnson, then senator for the state of Texas, yielded to the Mexican Americans' demands

for justice and had the remains of Private Longoria flown to Arlington National Cemetery for burial there.

"*Discriminación*" was composed and recorded commercially not long after the incident to celebrate the moral victory the Hispanics had won. Like other postwar corridos, this one focused on the victimization of the protagonist and the community's intervention. The following stanzas convey the basic theme of moral outrage:

When the body of the soldier
with his next-of-kin,
the mortuary in his hometown
denied him a funeral.
That is discrimination arrived
against a poor human being;
not even in a cemetery
do they admit a Mexican.

"El 29 de Agosto" ("August 29"), a well-known corrido written by the legendary folksinger-composer Lalo Guerrero, presents an interesting variation on the victim theme. This corrido describes the events surrounding the Chicano Moratorium of August of 1970, when a massive demonstration was organized in Los Angeles to protest against the disproportionate numbers of Chicanos being killed in Vietnam. As in other victim corridos, "El 29" celebrates the resolute actions of the Chicano masses as they protest the perceived victimization of Mexican Americans in the form of an unfair draft. But an interesting twist develops, one related to the suspicious killing of Rubén Salazar, a popular television reporter, on the day of the demonstration.

After having covered the demonstration, Salazar was sitting in a bar when police approached, ostensibly to seek out a man reported to be carrying a rifle. While the accounts of police officers and other witnesses conflict, the police apparently fired a rifle-powered tear gas canister into the bar without warning, hitting Salazar in the head and killing him instantly. According to historian Rodolfo Acuña, there is evidence that Los Angeles police were out to "get" Salazar for news coverage that was critical of police actions against the Mexican community.

No action was ever taken against the officers who killed Salazar. Authorities concluded that his death was accidental, although, according to Acuña, many in the Chicano community remained convinced that the police had murdered Salazar by way of getting even for his critical reporting.

In "El 29 de Agosto," composer Guerrero deftly combines the defiant actions of the demonstrators with the death of reporter Salazar to transform a song about mass protest into a victim *corrido*. The following stanzas effect this transformation:

> Cuando vino la policía
> violencia se desató;
> el coraje de mi raza
> luego se desenlazó;
> por los años de injusticia
> el odio se derramó;
> y como huracán furioso
> su barrio lo destrozó.
> En un edificio cercano
> desgracia vino a caer
> un gran hombre y buen humano:
> periodista mexicano
> de fama interancional;
> fino padre de familia
> voz de la comunidad.
>
> When the police arrived
> violence was unleashed;
> the wrath of my people
> uncoiled from within;
> against years of injustice
> hate spilled out;
> and like a ferocious hurricane
> its barrio it destroyed.
> In a nearby building
> y misfortune came to fall
> a great man and human being él fue Rubén Salazar,
> he was Rubén Salazar,
> Mexican newspaperman
> of international fame;
> a fine father and husband
> spokesman for the community.

Many corridos of this type have been composed since the end of World War II. In the typical victim corrido, the Anglos openly abuse the basic rights of a Mexican victim (or victims), and the Mexican community responds vigorously to defend the victim(s). The corrido draws attention to the community's forceful actions in protesting Anglo injustice, and when the outcome permits it (as in "Discriminación"), the corrido celebrates the community's victory. In any case, the Anglos are portrayed in a negative light, while the Mexicans are seen as a proud people fighting for their civil rights.

Both the hero and victim corridos of intercultural conflict have a long and auspicious history in the Mexican American oral music tradition. The former was prevalent at a time when conflict between Anglo and Mexican was rampant and undisguised. The hero corrido peaked in the early twentieth century, when the Mexican Americans reached the lowest point in their history of oppression in the United States. As they climbed out of their wretched state, during and after World War II, the victim corrido appeared and gained ascendancy. Both types of corrido have survived into the late twentieth century, but their presence in the musical repertory of Mexican Americans today is sporadic. They tend to surface only during moments of intercultural crisis— usually when the still-dominant Anglos commit a blatant act of discrimination.

✳ MÚSICA NORTEÑA (THE MEXICAN-TEXAN CONJUNTO)

Of all the musical creations of the Latino community in the United States, música norteña (also known as the Mexican Texan) is unquestionably one of the most culturally powerful. Anchored by the diatonic button accordion, this folk tradition had grown deep roots among the Mexicans living along the Texas-Mexico border by the early twentieth century. And, thanks to the commercialization introduced by the major American recording labels in the 1920s, it eventually spread far beyond its origins in south Texas and northern Mexico. By the late twentieth century, música norteña had been adopted by millions of Mexicans in both Mexico and the United States.

How a music of such humble folk origins could develop into a powerful artistic expression with such widespread appeal is a provocative question. The answer lies in its beginnings along the Texas-Mexico border. The diatonic button accordion, which is the heart of música norteña, was evidently introduced into northeastern Mexico sometime in the middle of the nineteenth century—perhaps by German immigrants who settled in the Monterrey, Nuevo León, area of northeastern Mexico in the 1860s. Since the Mexican Texans of this period maintained close cultural links with Mexican *norteños* (Northerner), it is likely that the instrument quickly spread into south Texas. It is possible, however, that the accordion was introduced to the tejanos (Mexican Texans) by way of the German, Czech, and Polish settlers who had migrated to south central Texas beginning in the 1840s. Since intense conflict, marked by overt discrimination against Mexicans, was the norm between tejanos and the latter groups, it is less likely that the interchange occurred on that front. In any case, the exact identity of the donor culture may never be known.

What we do know is that by the late nineteenth century the accordion, coupled with one or two other instruments—the *tambora de rancho* (ranch drum) and the *bajo sexto* (a 12-string guitar)—had become the norm for music-and-dance celebrations in south Texas. The tambora was a primitive folk instrument fashioned out of native materials. It was usually played with wooden mallets, their tips covered with cotton wrapped in goatskin. The bajo sexto apparently originated in the Guanajuato-Michoacán area in Mexico; it is a 12-string guitar tuned in double courses. How it migrated to and established itself in the border area is a mystery. But in its new locale it became an indispensable companion to the accordion, especially after 1930, when it and the accordion emerged as the core of the evolving ensemble.

The conjunto norteño, or conjunto, as it came to be known in Texas, thrived from early on. It soon became the preferred ensemble for the rural working-class folk who adopted it and eventually molded it into a genuine working-class expression. In its early days it relied on the salon music introduced from Europe in the eighteenth and nineteenth centuries and popularized first among the genteel city dwellers, then passed on to the masses later. The principal genres were the polka, the *redowa,* and the *schottishe,* although the mazurka was also current. Rounding out the repertoire was the *huapango,* culturally important because it was native to the Gulf Coast region of Tamaulipas and northern Vera Cruz, and thus represented a regional contribution. The huapango is more frequently associated with the music of the *huasteca* region of southern Tamaulipas, Mexico, where it has a ternary pulse built around a 3/4 meter. As performed by norteños, however, the huapango early on acquired a binary pulse built around the triplets of 6/8 meter.

Despite the presence everywhere of the accordion in the musical celebrations of the tejanos/ norteño s, the conjunto did not achieve dominance until the 1930s. Prior to this time it was still an improvised ensemble with little stylistic development and plenty of competition from other types of (also improvised) ensembles. In fact, the history of the Mexican Texan conjunto can be divided into three distinct stages. The first, to the late 1920s, is the formative, when the ensemble was strictly improvisational and the accordion was still played either solo, with guitar or bajo sexto, or with the tambora de rancho. The technique used to play the accordion itself owed much to that of the Germans who had originally introduced the instrument to the Mexicans. This included the heavy use of the left-hand bass-chord buttons, a technique that lent the instrument a distinctive sound and articulation. As noted, this embryonic ensemble was common to Mexicans on both sides of the border.

The second stage emerged in the mid-1930s, when the Mexican Texan conjunto began to move beyond its counterpart across the border—gradually at first, radically after World War II. The sudden development of the conjunto during the second stage is undoubtedly linked to intervention of the large American recording labels, which began in earnest in the early 1930s. At this time RCA Victor (through its Bluebird subsidiary), Columbia, and Decca moved into the Southwest and began commercially exploiting the variety of music then flourishing in the region. But the rapid development of the conjunto cannot be explained simply in terms of its commercialization, which, in any case, was never as massive as that of mainstream American pop music. On the other hand, the ethnic/class dichotomy which came to dominate the political culture of Mexican Texans after the 1930s was certainly a powerful catalyst.

Thus, by the mid-1930s, when accordionist Narciso Martínez began his commercial recording career, the first steps had been taken toward cementing the core of the modern conjunto—the accordion-bajo sexto combination. These two instruments would become inseparable after this time. Meanwhile, Martínez, who is acknowledged as the "father" of the modern conjunto, devised a new technique for the instrument, one that differed radically from the old Germanic style. He stopped using the left-hand bass-chord buttons, leaving the accompaniment to the bajo sexto, which was very capably played by his partner Santiago Almeida.

The resulting sound was dramatically novel—a clean, spare treble, and a staccato effect that contrasted sharply with the Germanic sound of earlier norteño accordionists. The Martínez style quickly took hold and became the standard that younger accordionists emulated, particularly those who established themselves after World War II.

In fact, the years immediately following the war ushered in the third stage in the conjunto's development. A younger group of musicians began charting a new direction for the rapidly evolving style. Foremost among these was accordionist Valerio Longoria, who was responsible for several innovations. Among these were two elements of the modern conjunto that Longoria introduced—the modern trap drums and the canción ranchera, the latter a working-class subtype of the Mexican *ranchera,* which dates from the 1930s. Obsessed with abandoned men and unfaithful women, the canción ranchera has always had special appeal for male patrons of conjunto music. Since it was often performed in the 2/4 meter of the traditional polka favored by Mexican Texans, the ranchera quickly replaced the polka itself as the mainstay of the modern conjunto. Longoria's introduction of the drums and ranchera earned him a special leadership position in the unfolding style, and several younger conjunto musicians have cited his example as the source of their inspiration—Paulino Bernal and Oscar Hernández, to name two of the best.

Paulino Bernal is himself a major figure in the development of the modern ensemble. His conjunto is hailed as the greatest in the history of the tradition, an honor based on the craftsmanship and the number of innovations attributable to El Conjunto Bernal. The latter include the introduction of three-part vocals and the addition of the larger chromatic accordion. El Conjunto Bernal's greatest distinction, however, lies in its ability to take the traditional elements of the conjunto and raise them to a level of virtuosity that has not been matched to this day. Bernal had accomplished all of this by the early 1960s.

Meanwhile, after about 1960 the *conjunto* and the older norteño ensemble across the Rio Grande began to converge, as the norteños came under the influence of their tejano counterparts. Especially responsible for this convergence was Los Relámpagos del Norte (The Northern Lightning Bolts), a group led by accordionist Ramón Ayala and bajo sexto player Cornelio Reyna. Ayala and Reyna were strongly influenced by El Conjunto Bernal, in particular. In fact, Los Relámpagos was "discovered" by Paulino Bernal in 1964 while he was on a scouting trip to Reynosa, Tamaulipas, across the border from McAllen, Texas, in search of talent for a new recording label he had recently started.

Los Relámpagos began recording for Bernal's Bego label in 1965, and within two years had risen to unparalleled fame on both sides of the border. The group remained unchallenged until the mid-1970s, when Ayala and Reyna went their separate ways. Ayala shortly organized his own conjunto, Los Bravos del Norte (The Northern Brave Ones), and that group went on to dominate the *norteño* market for at least a decade.

Since the innovations of the 1960s, the conjunto has turned decidedly conservative, with both musicians and patrons choosing to preserve the elements of the style as these were worked out in the 1940s through the 1960s. Despite its conservatism, the tradition has expanded phenomenally, in the 1970s to 1990s spreading far beyond its original base along the Texas-Mexico border. In the last few years, the music has taken root in such far-flung places as Washington, D.C., California, and the Midwest, as well as the entire tier of northern Mexican border states and even in such places as Michoacán and Sinaloa. In its seemingly unstoppable expansion, conjunto music has always articulated a strong Mexicanized, working-class life-style, thus helping to preserve Mexican culture wherever it has taken root on American (and Mexican) soil.

The rapid rise and maturation of conjunto music is a remarkable phenomenon in itself, but more important from an anthropological perspective is its cultural significance, its strong "organic" connection to working-class Mexicans in the United States. Clearly, the music is anything but a casual item of entertainment among its supporters. In fact, as a musical expression the conjunto has become a symbolic emblem of Mexican working-class culture—those people employed in farm labor and other unskilled and semiskilled occupations found mostly in service industries. And, the conjunto's alliance with that class was cemented during its rapid evolution between the years 1936 and 1960.

Beyond this identification with the working class, in the years following World War II the conjunto became linked to the cultural strategies of Mexican Texans, in particular, as these proletarian workers faced continuing prejudice from a hostile Anglo population, as well as antagonism from a new class of upwardly mobile, acculturated Mexican Texans, who sought to put some distance between themselves and the more Mexicanized common workers. The attitude of middle-class Mexican Texans was cogently summarized by the owner of Falcon Records, Arnaldo Ramírez, who recalled that in the 1930s to 1950s "to mention the accordion to people of position was like calling their mother a name" (personal communication, March 27, 1980).

In the end, conjunto music came to symbolize the struggle of the workers to maintain a sense of social solidarity and cultural uniformity against the upwardly mobile Mexican Americans, who espoused a different musical ideal, in the form of the orquesta or big band, and who viewed conjunto music as the expression of a vulgar, unassimilatable class of people. This quality of conjunto—its strong endorsement by the common workers and repudiation by more affluent people—was particularly evident in its Mexican Texan home base, but it was carried over to new locales, such as Arizona, where it was derisively called *catachún* music, and California, where it was universally considered cantina "trash."

It is against this politico-cultural background that the words of Paulino Bernal, one of conjunto's most innovative performers, may best be appreciated: "There was always among *la raza,* among Chicanos, what we used to call, 'No man, you think you're really high society.' That is, there was one class of people among Chicanos that was higher, and they wanted to live like the American, and live better. Of course, they had already reached a higher position economically, and there was still a lot of *raza* [Mexican people] that was just arriving, and with a lot of . . . struggling all the way. So there *was* a division; and that is where not only the social or economic position was divided, but the music was divided as well—that of orquesta and that of conjunto (pers. com. May 9, 1980).

❋ THE MEXICAN AMERICAN ORQUESTA

Paulino Bernal's comments on the socioeconomic difference between conjunto and orquesta serves as a suitable introduction to the orquesta, which has a fascinating history in the music of the Hispanic Southwest (Peña 1985; 1989). Actually, three types of orquestas have been present in the Southwest at different periods in the last century. The earliest type is one that existed during the nineteenth century and the early part of the twentieth. This early ensemble, built primarily around the violin, was hardly an "orquesta." It was for the most part an improvised ensemble, one dependent on the availability of musicians and scarce instruments for composition.

The rudimentary nature of this early orquesta is linked to the marginalization of the Mexicans of the Southwest—their having been stripped of all political and economic stability by the Anglo-Americans who invaded the territory and eventually annexed it to the United States. Having become American citizens by default, the new Mexican Americans found themselves at a decided disadvantage—as did all Mexican immigrants who came after them. The original settlers were gradually dispossessed of all their lands and forced into a state of subordination, setting a pattern that would apply to all those who migrated to the Southwest in the twentieth century. José Limón, the noted Mexican American folklorist, has summarized developments in the Southwest following the American invasion: "Between 1848 and 1890, an Anglo ranching society established itself among the native (also ranching) Mexican population, living with them in a rough equality. However, beginning in the 1890s, a clear racial-cultural stratification and subordination began to emerge, as a new wave of Anglo-American entrepreneurs and farming interests established a political and economic hegemony over the native population as well as the thousands of Mexican immigrants entering the area after 1910. . . . With few exceptions, this total population . . . became the victim of class-racial exploitation

An *orquesta típica* in Houston.

and mistreatment" (*Handbook of American Folklore*, 1983).

Given their precarious social organization as a subordinate group in the new social order that was created in the Southwest, the resident Mexicans (now Mexican Americans) and all those who came afterward found it difficult to maintain any but the most rudimentary of musical traditions. To be sure, the norteños had never enjoyed the best of facilities for any kind of education, musical or otherwise. Throughout the Spanish colonial era and the period of Mexican independence, life in the north had been of a peasant, agrarian nature, with few of the amenities that Mexicans in more centralized and urban areas enjoyed. Despite their relative isolation, the norteños managed to keep up with musical developments in Mexico and, as early chroniclers have documented, were able to maintain reasonably equipped ensembles.

With the American invasion and the subsequent oppression of the native Mexicans, the opportunities for musical training all but disappeared, except in urban areas along the border, where the Mexicans preserved a degree of political and economic integration, even after the annexation of the Southwest by the United States. Thus, cities like Brownsville, Laredo, and El Paso managed to support modest resources for the training and equipping of musical groups. But in general, the American invasion reduced an orquesta tradition inherited from Greater Mexico to its bare and often improvised essentials— a violin or two plus guitar accompaniment, with other instruments added on an ad hoc basis.

Despite its impoverished character, the early orquesta of the Hispanic Southwest nonetheless enjoyed great prominence in the musical affairs of the Mexican communities across the territory—even in Texas, where the emergent conjunto offered strong competition. As sources from the nineteenth and early twentieth centuries confirm, small orquestas were enlisted for all kinds of celebrations, which ran the gamut from private weddings and birthdays to public multievent celebrations known as *funciones*. Again, almost without exception, these orquestas were of variable composition, although they seldom included more than the minimum instruments mentioned before—a violin or two with guitar accompaniment.

The 1920s saw the emergence in the urban areas of better-organized orquestas, built, again, around the violin. This was the so-called *orquesta típica* (typical orchestra). The first típica was organized in Mexico City in 1880, and it was supposedly modeled after an earlier folk orquesta common in Mexican rural areas throughout the nineteenth century (also known as

típica) and apparently similar in instrumentation to the folk *orquestas* of the Hispanic Southwest. The self-styled orquestas típicas of urban origin were clearly expressions of what is known as *costumbrismo,* a type of romantic nationalism in which the dominant groups find it appealing to imitate certain elements of the folk, or peasant classes. As such, these orquestas were given to wearing "typical" *charro* (cowboy) outfits similar to those worn by the Mexican mariachi, in an effort to capture in vicarious fashion some of the flavor of Mexican pastoral life.

In the United States, the first típica was probably organized in El Paso or Laredo sometime in the 1920s. In any case, these orquestas were strongly reminiscent of the modern mariachi, whose historical roots they may well share. The basic instrumentation of the orquesta típica consisted of violins, guitars, and psalteries, although in the Southwest other instruments were often added in ad hoc fashion. The size of the típica could vary from four or five musicians to as many as 20.

Típicas were enlisted for almost any occasion, although they were ideally suited for patriotic-type celebrations, such as *cinco de mayo* (fifth of May, when the Mexican general Ignacio Zaragoza postponed the French invasion of Mexico by defeating General Laurencez at Puebla) and *dieciseis de septiembre* (sixteenth of September, Independence Day), two dates of special significance for Mexican people. The repertoire of orquestas típicas consisted of *aires nacionales*—tunes that over the years had acquired status as "national airs," such as "El Jarabe Tapatío" ("The Jalisco Dance"), "La Negra" ("The Dark Beauty"), "Pajarillo Barranqueño" ("Little Bird of Barranca"), and others. Típicas seem to have fallen out of favor among Mexican Americans during the Great Depression of the 1930s. They disappeared from the musical scene in the Southwest during World War II.

On the other hand, the 1930s saw the emergence of the third and most important type of orquesta, this one a version of the modern dance bands that swept through the urban landscapes of both Mexico and the United States during the 1920s and 1930s. The modern orquesta clearly represented a musico-cultural departure from earlier ensembles. In fact, it is tied to the fortunes of a new group of Mexican Americans who began to make an impact on Hispanic life in the United States during the 1930s and 1940s. Historian Mario García has aptly labeled this group The Mexican American Generation (*Social Science Quarterly,* 1984). This was the first generation of Americans of Mexican descent to aspire for inclusion in Anglo-American life. Consequently, it advocated the ideology of assimilation, an ideology based on the notion that Mexican Americans should detach themselves from their Mexican heritage and begin thinking like Americans. However, the persistent conflict with the Anglos and their continuing discrimination against Mexicans ultimately forced The Mexican American Generation to modify its ideology of assimilation and adopt a more biculturalist stance—to be both Mexican and American.

The modern orquesta, which emerged in the 1930s, played a prominent role in accommodating The Mexican American Generation's biculturalist strategy. In the bimusical repertoire it adopted, the orquesta catered to the generation's bicultural nature. By performing music traditionally associated with Mexico and Latin America, it kept alive the Mexican Americans' ethnic roots; by performing music associated with American big bands, it satisfied The Mexican American Generation's desire to assimilate American culture. Thus, from Mexico and Latin America came the *danzón, bolero, guaracha, rumba,* and other dance genres; from the United States came the boogie, swing, fox-trot, and so on.

Very quickly, however, the Mexican American orquesta began to experiment with various bimusical combinations—especially the orquestas in Texas, which, like the conjunto, assumed a leadership role in music developments in the Hispanic Southwest after World War II. As a result of their increasing exposure through commercial recordings (Texas had the biggest Hispanic recording companies), the most professional orquestas típicas became the models that others around the Southwest imitated. Coincident with this professionalization was the appearance and popularization of the public ballroom dance, which allowed the most successful orquestas to rely exclusively on performance for full-time employment.

Thus, ever since the birth of the modern Mexican American orquesta, the most renowned names have come from Texas. There was, for example, Beto Villa, from Falfurrias, Texas, sometimes called the "father" of the Mexican American orquesta. Acclaimed for a folksy, ranchero polka that took the Southwest by storm, Villa deftly juxtaposed this "country" style polka, which came to be known as Tex-Mex, against more sophisticated genres drawn from Latin America and the United States—*danzones, guarachas,* formerly, fox-trots, and swings.

Villa's influence on orquestas throughout the Hispanic Southwest was enormous during the 1940s and 1950s, and he inspired many imitators. A notable successor to the Tex-Mex tradition was Isidro López, also from Texas. A singer-saxophonist, López deliberately emphasized the ranchero mode of performance in an attempt to attract a larger share of the common workers, who were otherwise more faithful to the ever more powerful (and more ranchero) conjunto. López was thus the first orquesta leader to add the working-class *canción ranchera* to the orquesta repertoire. But he added his own touch to the ranchera, embellishing it with a blend of mariachi and Tex-Mex that López himself dubbed Texachi.

There were at least two other orquestas of note during the 1940s and 1950s—Balde González's, from Victoria, Texas, and Pedro Bugarín's, from Phoenix, Arizona. The former specialized in a smoother, more romantic delivery that appealed in particular to those upwardly mobile tejanos who were seen by working-class people as snobbish and who were derisively known as *jaitones* (from high tone). As such, Balde González, a pianist-singer, was best known for the smooth delivery of the romantic and sophisticated *bolero,* although he often turned as well to the American fox-trot, which he transformed by adding lyrics in Spanish. Bugarín pursued a more eclectic approach, one that included the full gamut of bimusical performance, from rancheras to fox-trots.

In the Los Angeles area, meanwhile, a number of orquestas operated during the maturational years of the Mexican American *orquesta*—the 1940s and 1950s. Most of these took their cue from music developments in Latin America (including the Afro-Caribbean) and were less influenced by developments in the Tex-Mex field. One noteworthy exception was the orquesta that the legendary Lalo Guerrero fronted for a time. As Guerrero himself admitted, he "mixed it all up," combining Tex-Mex with boogie and Latin American, including salsa. But Guerrero was best known for his unique bimusical tunes, which fused music and linguistic elements from swing, rhumba, and caló. Most of these tunes were written by Guerrero himself. Some achieved immortality through the movie *Zootsuit,* produced in 1982 by the Chicano filmmaker and erstwhile activist Luis Valdez (for example, the tune "Marihuana Boogie").

But the most influential orquestas continued to originate in Texas. In the 1960s and 1970s, which may well have been the peak years for the Mexican American *orquesta,* several groups emerged from the active tradition established in the Lone Star State. Foremost among these was Little Joe and the Latinaires, renamed Little Joe y la Familia in 1970. La Familia exploited the Tex-Mex ranchero sound fashioned by Isidro López to its utmost, fusing it to American jazz and rock *within the same musical piece* to achieve a unique bimusical sound that came to be known as La Onda Chicana (The Chicano Wave).

Beto Villa y su Orquesta, circa 1946.

Little Joe first experimented with the fusion of Mexican ranchero and American jazz/rock in a hugely successful LP titled *Para la Gente* (*For the People*), released in 1972 by Little Joe's own company, Buena Suerte Records. On this album, Little Joe and his brother Johnny combined their voices duet-fashion to create a style of ranchera so appealing to Mexican Americans that La Familia was catapulted to the very top of La Onda Chicana. Backing Little Joe and Johnny was the usual complement of instruments found in the best-organized contemporary Mexican American orquestas—two trumpets, two saxophones, a trombone, and a rhythm section of bass, electric guitar, drums, and keyboards.

The music selections on the landmark LP varied from the hard, brash sounds of traditional Tex-Mex rancheras, like "La Traicionera" ("The Treacherous Woman"), to the lush, big-band sounds of the Mexican fox-trot, as in "Viajera" ("Traveler"), to an interesting arrangement of an old folk song, "Las Nubes" ("The Clouds"). The last tune mentioned seemed to capture the cultural essence of La Onda Chicana and its obvious link to the cultural revivalism of the Chicano political and cultural movement that swept through the Mexican American community in the late 1960s and early 1970s. Thanks, at least in part, to the nationalistic climate fostered by the Chicano Movement, "Las Nubes" became a sort of anthem for Chicano music celebrations everywhere.

Many of the arrangements on the *Para la Gente* album were augmented with strings borrowed from the Dallas Symphony—a great novelty in itself—but most effective of all was the strategic interlacing of jazz riffs within the rancheras. The effects were stunning and captured the music sentiments of bicultural Mexican Americans everywhere. The impact of this trailblazing LP was so great that in the early 1990s, almost 20 years from the time it appeared, several of its tunes still formed part of the basic repertory of semiprofessional weekend dance orquestas still to be found in the Southwest.

As fashioned by Little Joe y la Familia, La Onda Chicana spread rapidly throughout the Southwest and beyond. Other orquestas followed La Familia's lead, as more and more efforts were directed at creating a synthesis of ranchera and jazz/rock. Many of these efforts were remarkable for their effect, with particularly successful results being achieved by the orquestas of Sunny and the Sunliners, Latin Breed, and Tortilla Factory, all from Texas.

By the mid-1980s, La Onda Chicana had receded from its watershed years, with the orquesta tradition generally suffering a noticeable decline. Not only did further innovation come to a stop, but the style suffered a retreat from its golden years of the 1960s and 1970s. The most notable sign of decline was the substitution, beginning in the early 1980s, of the horn section for synthesized keyboards. At first, these tried to imitate, synthetically, the sound of the trumpets, saxes, and trombone, but eventually the keyboards developed their own synthesized sound, one closer in spirit to the conjunto, and this became the norm after about 1985.

The reasons for the decline of the orquesta are not entirely clear, but they evidently have to do with the aging of the population that originally gave impetus to the orquesta tradition—the strongly bicultural Mexican American Generation and its immediate successors, the baby-boomers born in the late 1940s and early 1950s. Except in Texas, where an entrenched tradition survived into the 1990s, Mexican Americans growing up in more recent years have been less attracted by the old-fashioned orquesta. The lack of support can be seen in the declining number of semiprofessional orquestas throughout the Southwest, as DJs and the smaller synthesizer-dependent groups have replaced the orquesta in most public and domestic celebrations.

The popularity of the Mexican American orquesta, as well as its social power, is directly linked to the cultural economy of The Mexican American Generation and its immediate successors. From the outset, orquesta served as a link between the generation's ideology and its political economy. That is, to the extent that this bloc of people aspired "toward life goals which include[d] equality with Anglos," as well as "regular income derived from 'clean,' non-agricultural employment" (Arthur J. Rubel, *Across the Tracks: Mexican-Americans in Texas City,* 1966), it adopted musical expression that would bring its cultural life into conformity with its economic status. Orquesta music fulfilled this need perfectly.

Thus, unlike conjunto, which early on became a mirror for working-class life and the workers' resistance to the pressures of acculturation, orquesta was as culturally flexible as its clientele. In its early years, however, especially the 1940s and 1950s, the orquesta was rather tentative in its approach to bimusical performance—the mixing of American and Mexican styles. At a time when his clientele was

Alonzo y su Orquesta, a typical orchestra, circa 1950.

Octavo García y sus GGs, circa 1952.

still unaccustomed to its newfound prosperity and biculturalism, a Beto Villa could at best choose between one or the other: he could play a Tex-Mex polka or an American swing, but never the two simultaneously. In time, as Mexican Americans adapted to their bicultural reality and even succeeded in synthesizing the two cultures into one "compound biculturalism" (Fernando Peñalosa, *Chicano Sociolinguistics,* 1980), orquesta performed a parallel synthesis—what we might call "compound bimusicality" (Manuel Peña, *From the Inside Out: Perspectives on Mexican and Mexican-American Folk Art,* 1989).

By the 1970s, this "compound bimusicality" had reached full expression in the orquestas' mastery of the art of musical code switching. Similar to the "compound bilingual," who code switches from one language to another within the same sentence, orquesta had learned to switch musical languages within the same musical "sentence," that is, within the same musical piece. This is what Little Joe, of Little Joe y la Familia, truly accomplished for the first time in his landmark album, *Para la Gente.* He succeeded in fusing two musical systems under one code of performance. This feat was repeated with

equal success by many other orquestas in the succeeding years.

But the musical code switching of the Mexican American orquesta was even more subtle than the linguistic code switching of its supporters, in that it took place on two distinct but overlapping planes. One switch occurred at the level of ethnicity, the other at the level of class. At the level of ethnicity, the switch was signified by the interlacing of jazz riffs within the flow of an otherwise Mexican ranchera. At the same time, this switch was mediated by parallel shifts occurring at another level of acoustic discrimination—class stylistics, or what Mexican Texans used to distinguish between a *jaitón* (high-tone) versus a ranchero style. The former was a marker for alleged (or contrived) musical sophistication, but above all it was an index for "high class" snobbery. Ranchero, on the other hand, was a token for the simple, unpretentious life of the country and the barrio—a token The Mexican American Generation was reluctant to renounce.

Above all, in its bimusicality the Mexican American orquesta represents the dialectical synthesis of two sets of opposed cultures—Mexican and American on the one hand, working and middle class on the other. This synthesis was masterfully articulated by the bimusical orquesta. The best were perfectly adept at this double code switching, as they moved effortlessly from ranchero to jaitón and from Mexican to American. At their very best, orquestas achieved a seamless stream of bimusical sound that found a fitting label—La Onda Chicana.

✹ SALSA

Salsa is Spanish for "sauce"—in this case a term that refers to the hot, spicy rhythms of Afro-Caribbean music. When people talk about salsa music, however, they are actually referring to a generic term that includes a number of distinct types of Afro-Caribbean music, although one in particular, the *son guaguancó,* has predominated since the 1960s. As Jorge Duany wrote in *Latin American Music Review* (1984), "*Salsa* is neither a musical style nor a particular rhythm, but rather a hybrid genre." According to Duany, the word "salsa" was first used to refer to this hybrid genre in the 1960s, but it did not gain universal recognition until 1975, when it was used as the title for a popular movie. Whatever the origins of the term "salsa," the music has deep, even sacred, roots in its Afro-Caribbean context.

Salsa as a Cultural Expression

In a fine study of a religious musical ritual in the Dominican Republic called *salve* entitled *Voces del purgatorio: Estudio de la selva dominicana* (1981), Martha Ellen Davis informs us that the salve is a bimusical expression that, as usually performed, progresses from a purely Hispanic section (the *salve sagrada*) to a more intense, spontaneous, and Africanized section (the *salve secular*). The latter section incorporates many of the rhythms (and polyrhythms) of a generalized Afro-Caribbean music that we eventually distilled in the United States into what is now commonly known as salsa. Davis interprets the bicultural nature of the salve as the logical result of the syncretization of two radically different cultures in a historical relationship of domination/subordination—Hispanic and African.

What is most important about Davis' analysis of the salve is her conception of this ritual as a key symbol of Afro-Caribbean culture, specifically, its location at the center of the Afro-Dominicans' musical universe. As an expression of an Afro-Caribbean music that is rooted deep within the practice of everyday culture, the salve provides a powerful example of the essentially sacred origins of Afro-Caribbean music. This is a sacredness that Americans of Afro-Caribbean descent who subscribe to various off-

An outdoor *salsa* concert in Houston, Texas.

shoots of that music—including salsa—have been reluctant to give up.

Thus, in his study of the ritual aspects of Afro-Cuban music among Cubans and Puerto Ricans of New York City (published in *Religious Movements in Contemporary America,* 1974), Morton Marks argues that despite the commercialization of the music, strong elements of African Yoruba religion have survived in at least some of its development in urban areas such as New York City. In Cuba, these Yoruba elements were syncretized early on with Catholicism to create the Lucumí religious cults, while in New York, Yoruba religion survives in the Santería cults, which, again, combine in their worship deities from both Catholic and Yoruba religion. For Marks, moreover, the interplay of musical styles, as they unfold within a given song (like the salve, usually progressing from a Hispanic form of communication to an African one), is the centrally defining characteristic. Thus, in analyzing the songs "Alma con Alma" ("Soul with Soul"), by the great salsa singer Celia Cruz, and "El Santo en Nueva York" ("The Saint in New York"), by La Lupe, a Cuban vocalist, Marks proposes that "the process of 'Africanization' underlies the performance, with the musical form proceeding from a strongly North American-influenced dance band style, into an *emically* named Yoruba and Lucumí praise song style known as kasha."

The transformation described by Marks is, in fact, the hallmark of most salsa music since the 1960s. In piece after musical piece, particularly the vast majority that utilize the son guaguancó, the music begins with a standardized Hispanic section whose lyrics are divided into an "A" part, followed by a "B," then returning to the "A" part (ABA form). Meanwhile, the musical background, usually provided by brass instruments (trumpets and/or trombones) in obbligato mode, displays the strong influence of American jazz. Once this section is completed (often it is the shortest section of the tune), the *son montuno* section begins. It is in this section that the African style predominates, particularly through the call-and-response pattern, in which a solo and chorus keep alternating phrases.

Afro-Caribbean music, then, has dual roots, Hispanic and African, which in the United States have undergone further development with the infusion of jazz elements as articulated in the horn obbligatos. In its duality, the music richly displays the process of syncretization, although it has also maintained a dialectical relationship to its twin roots—a relationship that enables the participants in musical events to juxtapose one cultural domain against the other with dramatic effects. This is the point that both Marks and Davis are at pains to demonstrate. In the United States, meanwhile, Afro-Caribbean music has preserved much of this duality, despite the jazz accretions and heavy commercialization. Here, too, among initiates of Santería cults, the music retains the ritual qualities and the dialectical movement between two cultures that are associated with sacred performances in the homeland.

It is appropriate at this point to propose a theoretical model that has application to musical culture in general but would seem to be particularly suited to an analysis of Afro-Caribbean music. In the anthropological study of culture, expressions that are deeply embedded within the social life of a particular community are sometimes called "summarizing symbols" (Sherry Ortner, in *American Anthropologist,* 1973) or "root metaphors" (Victor Turner, *The Ritual Process,* 1969), in that they sum up, embody, or represent the core or root of the given community's cultural identity. Needless to say, the group cherishes such expressions, singling them out as special markers for whatever it considers to be unique about its culture.

Clearly, for people of Afro-Caribbean descent—Puerto Ricans, Cubans, Dominicans, and others—what is now called salsa has that kind of summarizing power. Salsa stands preeminently for their special sense of Afro-Hispanic "Caribbeanness." But salsa obviously has an audience that extends far beyond its core Caribbean setting. As a cultural symbol, it spreads out with diminishing influence toward audiences whose contact with the music's cultural roots is at best casual. Among these audiences the music's symbolic power is highly diluted or even nonexistent.

Music such as salsa, which has variable significance among diverse audiences, is either a strong or weak symbol depending on the context in which it is performed. As an artistic expression with both commercial and ritual contexts, salsa lends itself partic-

Celia Cruz at the Hollywood Palladium.

ularly well to this strong versus weak concept. This concept can be visually illustrated through a series of concentric circles, where the strong or summarizing symbols—those linked with the most sacred cultural practices—revolve around the innermost circle. Weaker symbols, meanwhile—those connected only casually with the listeners' cultural practices—occupy the outermost circle. Symbols of intermediate strength circulate between these two extremes.

A specific example of salsa as a strong cultural symbol is its role in Santería rituals, where it functions as a powerful icon that is organically linked to Santería practitioners as a root metaphor that defines their deepest sense of cultural and religious identity. In this context, the music resists the riffing or "watered-down" effects that commercialization introduces into any music. Occupying the innermost circle in this example, ritual salsa remains an organic part of Afro-Caribbean culture.

On the other hand, as a musical expression that people of non-Afro-Caribbean background have come to enjoy through commercial exposure, the music begins to lose its organic connection to the powerfully defining rituals of its indigenous cultural setting. It becomes a more casual symbol—for example, one that defines a vague feeling of pan-Latino solidarity among individuals who have otherwise lost an identification with their own musical roots. This is the case with some young Chicanos (Mexican Americans), who have no particular allegiance to their ancestral music (for instance, *norteño*) but who develop an intense feel for salsa. To these individuals the music is at best a symbol of intermediate strength, since it can never occupy in their lives the position that it does in Santería cults.

Dual origins of Salsa recall that its antecedents are hybrid or syncretic expressions that draw from two cultures, Hispanic and African. Modern salsa owes its greatest debt to the musical culture of Cuba, although Puerto Rico and, to a lesser extent, the Dominican Republic are also contributing cultures. Two Puerto Rican musical genres, in particular, are legitimate antecedents of modern salsa—the *bomba* and the *plena*. According to ethnomusicologists Roberta Singer and Robert Friedman in *Caliente = Hot; Recorded Anthology of American Music, Inc.* (1977), both emerged in the coastal towns of Puerto Rico, where "large communities of black workers gathered around the sugarcane mills." Moreover, "*Bomba* is an entertainment form . . . generally performed at social gatherings. It is a couple dance in which the woman performs relatively fixed dance steps while her partner is free to exhibit his dancing skills. . . . *Bomba* texts are usually topical themes relating to everyday life in the community, such as social relationships, work, or historical events. . . . The musical form of *bomba* consists of alternation between solo singer and chorus in a call-and-response pattern."

The plena is more heavily influenced by European musical culture than the bomba. According to Singer and Friedman, "*Plena* began as a street music, but as it moved into the bars and nightclubs it came to be associated with night life and the underworld. . . . *Plena* texts are on contemporary or historic events."

Both the plena and the bomba were once integral elements in the life of Puerto Rican blacks. They are still performed on the island, though with decreasing frequency. In the United States, however, plena and bomba have undergone some transformation. Adopted (and adapted) by small salsa conjuntos (such as Julito Collazo and his Afro-Cuban Group), bomba and plena are reaching larger audiences, even as some of their elements are absorbed by salsa itself.

Cuba is the indisputable cradle of modern *salsa*, although in the United States the music is more intimately associated with Puerto Ricans. In Cuba, Africans established strong enclaves that carried on many of the musico-ritualistic traditions from the homeland, specifically those attached to the Lucumi cults mentioned earlier. As the anthropologist William Bascom wrote, "African traditions are actually strongest and purest in the larger urban centers of Cuba" (*Nigeria,* 1951). Secularized and made popular commercially in the twentieth century, Afro-Cuban music attached to the Lucumi/ Santería cults underwent further hybridization with Western musical forms. In its hybrid form, this music acquired strong stylistic features that came to appeal to millions of people outside the original cultural core.

It was out of this hybridization process that salsa emerged. However, salsa represents the end stage of this process. Earlier Afro-Cuban forms enjoyed their own moments of glory, as the pace of hybridization accelerated in the middle part of the twentieth century. In this, Cuba again took center stage. John Storm Roberts has described this hybridization as follows: "Taken as a whole, Cuban music presents a more equal balance of African and Spanish ingredients than that of any other Latin country except Brazil. Spanish folklore enriched the music of the countryside, of the city, and of the salon. At the same time—aided by an illicit slave trade that continued right through the nineteenth century—the pure African strain remained stronger in Cuba than anywhere else. . . . As a result, Western African melody and drumming . . . were brought cheek by jowl with country music based on Spanish ten-line *décima.*" (*The Latin Tinge,* 1979).

It should come as no surprise that Cuba is the source of many of the musical genres that precede salsa—genres that in fact make up the tapestry of its sounds. Thus, important salsa antecedents such as the *dazón, rumba-guaguancó, charanga, mambo, guaracha, son, bolero,* and *cha cha cha* all originate in Cuba. The mambo and cha cha cha had an enormous impact in and of themselves, of course, but the two genres that most influenced modern salsa directly are the son and the rumba. As ethnomusicologist Peter Manuel has correctly pointed out, "Of the various types of *rumba,* the *guaguancó* was the most influential, as its more westernized successors, *son* and *salsa,* have incorporated and retained its formal structure (introductory *diana,* litany-like *canto,* and call-and-response *montuno*) and most of its basic rhythm patterns" (*Latin American Music Review,* 1985).

As Manuel implies, the rumba is actually a generic term for more specific Afro-Cuban genres—the *yambú, cumbia,* and guaguancó. Again, of these three, it is the guaguancó that is most closely identified with salsa. All, however, have common African characteristics—complex polyrhythms and alternating sections of solo voice and call-and-response. Originally, the rumba was played with African or Africanized instruments of the drum family—the *quinto, segundo,* and *tumba,* reinforced by *cáscara* (a pair of sticks struck against each other) and *claves* (a pair of smooth, cylindrical hardwood sticks struck against each other). Today the drum rhythms are executed on conga drums, but the clave effects remain essentially unchanged in modern salsa.

The son, meanwhile, describes more of a feeling than an actual musical form. It is, however, identifi-

A Machito album cover.

The Joe Cuba Sextet, one of the first groups to record *salsa* in English.

able by the strong rhythmic patterns associated with it. Most notable among these is the anticipated bass, which is unique to Afro-Cuban music generally, and salsa in particular. The son emerged among Africans in the Cuban countryside and spread to the urban areas early in the twentieth century. It was in the latter areas that the son combined with European instruments to create its modern hybrid form. Earlier Africanized instruments were replaced by such European ones as the contrabass, trumpet, and guitar, although the basic percussion was necessarily retained—the bongos, claves, and the guitar-like *tres.* One of Cuba's greatest popular musicians, and the "father" of modern salsa, Arsenio Rodríguez, is credited with further upgrading the son ensemble in the 1930s. He did this by adding a second trumpet, conga drums, and, most important, a piano.

Rodríguez also anticipated some of the greatest modern *salseros* (salsa musicians) by moving away from the romantic themes of earlier *sones* and incorporating texts that addressed nationalist and social issues. Other important figures from the early period of Afro-Cuban music include Ernesto Lecuona, whose group, the Lecuona Cuban Boys, recorded for Columbia, and Arcano y sus Maravillas (Arcano and

His Marvels), a charanga orchestra that was responsible for africanizing this erstwhile Europeanized ensemble.

The orquesta charanga is an interesting phenomenon in Afro-Cuban music history. Until the 1930s, this group espoused a genteel, Europeanized sound that appealed to middle-class whites. Its instrumentation consisted of lead flute and violins. Arcano moved to make his group conform more to an African style by adding percussion, such as the bongo and conga drums. Steven Loza has suggested, in his University of California master's thesis (1979), that Arcano y sus Maravillas actually led the way in the emergence of the phenomenally popular cha cha cha. The king of that genre, however, was La Orquesta Aragón (The Aragón Orchestra), a group popular from the 1940s through the 1960s, whose incomparable style of cha cha cha endeared the music to millions of Latinos across Latin America and the United States.

Meanwhile, several individuals who later went on to make their mark on modern salsa music actually played with charanga groups in the 1940s and 1950s. These included such well-known figures as Charlie Palmieri, Johnny Pacheco, and Ray Barreto. Along with a host of other salseros, these individuals brought a vitally evolving musical tradition to the United States, where both African- and European-oriented groups experienced a strong cross-fertilization with jazz—a fertilization that resulted in the final emergence of salsa.

Thus, by the late 1950s key performers, such as Tito Rodríguez, Tito Puente, and Machito, had laid the stylistic framework for the modern sound. In fact, when we listen to Tito Rodríguez's recordings from the late 1950s, we cannot but be impressed with how similar his rumbas and guaguancós are to latter-day salsa, even though the music was not recognized as such until the 1970s. Meanwhile, the style and instrumentation was further strengthened in the 1960s and 1970s by a host of great performers, which included such memorable names as Willie Colón, Eddie Palmieri, El Gran Combo (The Great Combo), as well as vocalists like Héctor Lavoe, Celia Cruz, and Rubén Blades. The last is particularly recognized for the poignant social themes that his lyrics often contained.

By the mid-1960s, the modern salsa sound had pretty much crystallized. And, its most basic genre remained the son/rumba/guaguancó complex, as it had been synthesized by Tito Rodríguez and others in the 1950s. Since the 1960s, this amalgamation of genres, which goes by the label "salsa," has served as the core for numerous explorations that have expanded the parameters of the music. Thus, as Jorge

Duany wrote in *Latin American Music Review* (1984), "The main pattern for *salsa* music remains the *son montuno,* built on the alternation between soloist and chorus." Moreover, like the son, "[salsa's] characteristics are a call-and-response song structure; polyrhythmic organization with abundant use of syncopation; instrumental variety with extensive use of brass and percussion and strident orchestral arrangements . . . and, above all, a reliance on the sounds and themes of lower-class life in the Latin American *barrios* of U.S. and Caribbean cities."

All these elements had been worked out by Tito Rodríguez and other Afro-Caribbean performers by the late 1950s. Since that time, at its most basic level the music has remained faithful to those elements. And, as always, in its most intimate contexts the music still evokes strong feelings of African identification among its most devoted followers—some of whom belong to Santería cults. At the very least, the music provokes feelings of nationalist pride, a strong identity with the people whose culture it symbolizes. As salsa pianist Oscar Hernández observed, "There's a nationalistic sense of pride when people hear *salsa*. They say, 'that's *our* music.' It gives people a sense of pride in their Ricanness and Latinoness" (Roberta

A Tito Puente album cover.

Eddie Palmieri.

that received high marks for its successful blend of Afro-Caribbean and Afro-American styles.

More recent standouts in the Latin jazz/rock movement include Chick Corea, who apprenticed with Afro-Cuban greats Mongo Santamaría and Willie Bobo. Meanwhile, Latin jazz's relative, Latin rock, has also had considerable impact on Latinos in the United States. Carlos Santana, the indisputable king of Latin rock since the 1960s, has continued to exploit a wide array of Afro-Cuban rhythms, fusing them to American rock to create a highly innovative style. Santana has inspired many imitators over the years, especially in California, where his music has had exceptional influence on young Chicanos.

Again, it can be argued that Latin jazz and rock lack the cultural power of salsa, norteño, or orquesta. Fundamentally, they are creations of the commercial market, hence must be considered "superorganic" or "second-order" expressions, as opposed to salsa's organic, first-order links to the Afro-Caribbeans. Nonetheless, the contributions of the individuals mentioned, as well as those by such noted figures as José Feliciano, Cal Tjader, and others, cannot be underestimated. In sum, although offshoots of salsa, Latin jazz and rock lack the status of a strong symbol like that of *salsa,* which emanates from the deepest levels of Afro-Caribbean culture. Neither Latin jazz nor rock can make that claim, of course; they are not "wired" into the core of any particular culture. For this, however, they should not be dismissed as transitory. Despite their cultural limitations, the degree of innovation in both Latin jazz and rock has been remarkable, and at times the popularity of Latin rock, especially, has had considerable impact on mainstream American music.

Singer, *Latin American Music Review,* 1983). And, at a more general level, salsa serves as a kind of pan-Latino link that unites many Hispanics under one musical banner—in the words of Félix Padilla, "a medium through which the different Latino life circumstances [can] be spoken to" (*Journal of Popular Culture,* 1990).

✳ LATIN JAZZ/ROCK

Two important musical cousins of salsa are Latin jazz and Latin rock. The former is closely associated with the development of salsa music in the United States, although it represents a more self-conscious effort to link Afro-Caribbean with Afro-American music. One can argue, however, that Latin jazz possesses neither the cultural breadth nor depth of salsa, although it clearly represents some of the most experimental efforts in the whole field of Latino music. Outstanding among these efforts are those of Cuban *conguero* (conga player) and vocalist Chano Pozo, whose association with American jazz trumpetist Dizzy Gillespie produced such Latin jazz gems as "Algo Bueno" ("Something Good"), "Afro-Cuban Suite," and "Manteca" ("Lard"), the latter a piece

✳ MUSICA TROPICAL

The term "música tropical" has been used historically to refer to any music with a "tropical" flavor, that is, any music identified with the tropics, usually the Afro-Caribbean rim. In the present instance, it is not an entirely accurate label, since the ensemble that represents this type of music—the grupo tropical/moderno—is not necessarily "tropical" in character. Aside from the fact that one of its musical mainstays is the *cumbia,* a dance originally from the tropics of Colombia, the grupo tropical/moderno need not feature any of the percussion instruments normally associated with tropical, that is, Afro-Caribbean, music. And, in fact, the *grupo tropical* is known today as much for its emphasis on another popular genre, *música moderna* (or *romántica*), as it is for the cumbia.

As it has evolved in recent years (the group was

originally more "tropical" in that it featured instruments such as the conga drums and the *güiro,* or scrapergourd), the grupo tropical/moderno often features four instruments—keyboard (originally an electric organ, later synthesizer), electric guitar and bass, and trap drums. It originated in Mexico in the 1960s and then spread to the United States via the heavy Mexican immigration that has occurred during the last 25 years or so.

The grupo tropical's mainstay, the cumbia, was originally a Colombian folk dance that in the twentieth century became urbanized and diffused commercially throughout Latin America. Upon reaching Mexico in the mid-1960s, the cumbia was appropriated by the working-class masses at about the same time that the four-instrument ensemble was emerging as a favorite dance group among urban working-class Mexicans. This ensemble came to be associated with cumbia music (música tropical) in Mexico and the American Southwest. At about the same time, however, a slow-dance genre, influenced by American rhythm and blues, surged in popularity in Mexico—the *balada* (from the American pop "ballad," a lyrical love song). Popularized by such groups as Los Angeles Negros (The Black Angels), Los Terrícolas (The Earthlings), and others, the Mexican balada came to be known generally as "música romántica" (or "moderna"—the two terms are interchangeable), and in time most grupos tropicales/modernos began to alternate between the cumbia and the balada to fill out their repertories.

Besides Los Angeles Negros (who seldom performed the cumbia), the best-known exponents in the relatively short span of música tropical/moderna in Mexico and the United States have been Rigo Tovar (who is of Afro-Caribbean ancestry), Los Bukis (The Bukis), Los Sonics (The Sonics), Los Yonics, (The Ionics), and Los Temerarios (The Fearless). Besides their reliance on record sales for financial support, most of the commercially popular grupos tropicales/modernos also rely on personal appearances at large public dances. At these dances the cumbia reigns supreme, although, again, most groups depend to one extent or another on the balada, which, with its slow 4/4 or 6/8 meter, offers a contrastive alternative to the usually up-tempo, lighthearted spirit of the cumbia.

Almost nothing has been written about the Mexican grupo tropical/moderno, which for the past 25 years has been undisputed king among certain working-class segments of Mexican society. By musical standards, it is an unspectacular style, one that is dwarfed by both salsa and La Onda Chicana. But it exerts a powerful influence on the millions of Mexican proletarians who subscribe to it. In the United States, one has only to attend certain ballrooms in cities such as Los Angeles, San Jose, Phoenix, or El Paso to observe the enormous drawing power that groups such as Los Bukis, Los Yonics, and others command, especially among the undocumented and recently documented immigrants from Mexico.

Clearly, música tropical/moderna is more than a temporary escape for the Mexican working class from the drudgery of its daily existence as a poorly paid underclass. A thorough ethnographic study would reveal that, much like música norteña, it represents a working-class cultural alternative that tacitly resists the assimilative pressures of a dominant Anglo-European majority, while it reinforces a Mexican working-class identity.

The late twentieth century has witnessed some notable changes in the music of Latinos in the United States. A "meltdown" has occurred, resulting from styles that have crossed over and overlapped with others. The most important example of this crossover comes from Texas, where Norteño (more particularly the Texan-Mexican conjunto) and orquesta have witnessed a dramatic convergence. The traditional orquesta, as epitomized by Little Joe y la Familia, has virtually disappeared in the 1990s, replaced by such groups as Mazz, La Mafia, and others. These carry on the basic stylistic features that identify the music as "tejano," but the mainstay of the orquesta—the horns—have been replaced by electronic keyboards that imitate the sounds of trumpets and saxophones. At the same time, these ensembles often incorporate the accordion, thus lending them a hybrid character.

Also on the trend-setting Texas scene, the absorption of country western elements into tejano music has intensified since the 1980s. Borrowing from country western is not new to tejanos (it took place as early as the 1960s), but in the 1980s and 1990s, this absorption has accelerated. Thus, conjunto performers such as Emilio Navaira and Roberto Pulido, and especially The Texas Tornados, a new group made up of veteran musicians (Freddie Fender, Flaco Jimenez, Doug Sahm), have fused conjunto with country western to produce a novel sound that adds a new dimension to tejano music.

✸ THE CONTEMPORARY MUSIC SCENE

The early 1990s saw Latin music in the United States enjoy a profound expansion period that included increased record sales, a steady growth of Spanish-language radio stations and newfound crossover success by several artists.

While the growing Hispanic population has helped drive the market's expansion in general, a major force fueling these changes in particular is the nation's Hispanic youth, whose economic and political influence is being watched, studied, and interpreted by major corporations, including Pepsi and Coca Cola, Budweiser and Miller Lite, Levi's jeans and Stetson hats, and any number of smaller, regional companies.

In all genres, from tropical/salsa to Tejano to Latin pop, new, young stars have entered the market with success. In tropical salsa, fresh faces like Rey Ruiz, Jerry Rivera, Marc Anthony, and Los Fantasmas del Caribe have commanded top-draw status and record sales on their debut and follow-up albums. In Tejano, Selena, and Emilio Navaira led the pack from the top of Billboard's charts to stadium tours to multiple awards. In Latin pop, excitement was created by newcomers like the pop/dance/rap act the Barrio Boyzz, ballad singer Marcos Llunas, and children's pop group Roxie y Los Frijolitos. But it was Selena, on the road to becoming a crossover star to mainstream pop and gaining a new following, who became a social phenomenon upon her untimely death at the hands of the former president of her fan club. The Corpus Christi-born and bred singer/bandleader had captured the hearts of young Chicanos from across the Southwest and of youngsters throughout Mexico, so much so that their mourning catapulted Selena into international headlines and her latest albums into best sellers. Biographies of the fallen star followed.

Whether the groups are producing fresh, original sounds, or simply taking the old and rejuvenating it with new urgent rhythms, the successful young acts in each genre have found the way to attract a new following.

Banda and Grupo

Banda music gained a new strong foothold, particular in California, where KLAX-FM in Los Angeles became the number one radio station in the general market. Banda is a brass-heavy (akin to marching bands) take on polkas and cumbias. KLAX plays a heavy mix of banda and norteno music.

While it may seem that banda is new, it is not. Actually banda has been popular in the northern states of Mexico for more than 20 years. However, the steady flow of Mexican immigrants from that area helped fuel the popularity of the music in Southwestern California. Again, it is the young banda artists that successfully blended the old horn-packed polka beats with a fresh sound and a modern, spiffy image to attract today's younger generation.

Grupo is a Spanish word for group but the term is an overall description of bands, as opposed to solo artists like Julio Iglesias, Vikki Carr, or Jose Feliciano. And the styles of music covered by grupos also varies, from the pop ballads of Los Bukis or Los Temerarios, to the norteno/ranchera mix of Bronco or Los Tigres, to the Tejano polka/cumbia/ballad blend of La Mafia or Mazz.

According to Jesus Lopez, BMG Ariola managing director, grupos have overtaken the long dominant Latin pop music as well as teen pop and traditional rancheras, as the hottest selling genre in Mexico. BMG's top grupos include Bronco, Impacto de Montemorelos, Los Mier, and Los Flamers.

The surge in grupo sales and concert attractions has been particularly intense since 1990. Ignacio "Nacho" Gomez, general manager for Musivisa in Mexico, has noted that although there has been a surge in interest, grupos have always enjoyed popularity. In 1992 officials moved all their grupos from Melody to compile Musivisa's label roster, which included the aforementioned acts as well as the Campeche Show, Los Tigres, Grupo Lluvia, and Industria del Amor.

Another major label that jumped into the fray was Sony Mexico. Houston's La Mafia was Sony's first signee. Later they signed Ramon Ayala and Los Rodarte. The success of La Mafia was particularly impressive, leading to record sales of their first U.S.-Mexico jointly promoted album, *Estas Tocando Fuego.*

The banda and grupo movements became so popular, they have each generated a variety of TV show publications in both the United States and Mexico.

Tejano

Tejano music continued its explosive growth in the Southwest with top artists like Mazz, La Mafia, Selena, and Emilio playing stadiums like San Antonio's Alamodome, Houston's Astrodome, Dallas' Texas Stadium, as well as other major venues. In fact, in February 1995, just before her death, Selena registered the highest ticket sales in history for the Astrodome during the Houston Livestock Show and Rodeo. In 1994, the Tejano Music Awards, which recognizes the best in Tex-Mex, moved into the Alamodome.

Since 1990, Tejano artists such as Mazz, La Sombra, and La Mafia initiated major tours of Mexico and made regular appearances on national Mexican TV shows such as "Furia Musical" and "Siempre en Domingo."

In San Antonio, KXTN-FM remained the city's number one station with its all-Tejano, bilingual format. Dallas got its first full-time Tejano station in KICK-FM 107.9, which went on the air December 1, 1993. Houston, San Antonio, Corpus Christi, El Paso, Austin, and Laredo are all cities now with two Tejano FM stations. Prior to 1990, none of the major markets had one station devoted to the genre. Since 1991, at least 75 stations from Brownsville to California, including Mexican border cities, have switched to full-time or part-time Tejano formats.

In record label action, the independent Manny Music was signed to a multi-year distribution and promotion deal by WEA Latina. A new label, Arista/Texas opened offices in Austin to sign Texas talent from blues, jazz, country, and folk, to Tex-Mex. The first artist signed was San Antonio accordionist Flaco Jimenez. Mexico's DISA Records, one of the largest independents in that country, signed a distribution and promotion deal with Joey Records in San Antonio to promote Joey's Tejano artists in Mexico.

Across the Southwest, major nightclubs opened to spotlight Tejano music. New clubs include Dallas' Tejano Rodeo and Club Trends; Fort Worth has Tejano Rodeo and Zaps; San Antonio has Desperado's, Tejano Rose, Ttown, and Bronco Bill's; and Houston has Zaaz, Emilio's Country Club. Typically these clubs have capacities of 1,200 to 1,600 patrons and feature live Tex-Mex acts two to four nights a week.

Tropical/Salsa

In the 1990s Puerto Rico continued to emerge as the dominant market in the New York-Miami-Puerto Rico triangle. The island, smaller in size than Connecticut with a population of 3.5 million, has 117 radio stations, most of which play salsa and merengue but with a top-40 format. Most of the top salsa artists such as Gilberto Santa Rosa, Luis Enrique, Juan Luis Guerra, Tito Rojas, and others, regularly sell more than 100,000 units on the island.

Recently, several upstart Puerto Rican merengue artists have broken into the market, including TTH's Zona Roja, WEA Latina's Olga Tanon, Sony's Grupo Wao, MP's Limite 21 and Fuera de Liga, and Plantano's Cana Brava. The activity on the island attracts increasing sponsorship at all levels—beer, liquor, and cigarette companies—and reportedly American distributors and retailers already on the island are looking to expand their presence.

Latin Pop

The vocal harmonies of the Barrio Boyzz and Las Triplets have found a strong, loyal following—enough to drive both groups to the top of the charts in 1993.

Jon Secada had a phenomenal success in 1991 and 1992 with his pop singing style. But what was significant about Secada was that his smash debut album was recorded with Spanish lyrics and also scored big on Billboard charts. But it was Gloria Estefan who really brought Spanish-language songs to a national audience with her albums evoking the tropical rhythms of her parents' generation in Cuba. The other largely successful crossover act was Los Lobos from East Los Angeles, which continued to produce cuts in Spanish and tour both Anglo and Latino nightclubs and concerts throughout the country.

The MTV Latino network was launched October 1, 1993. Produced by MTV/Music Television in Miami, the Spanish-language channel is being seen in the United States and 20 other Latin countries. The format features VJs and advertisers conducting business in Spanish with about 70 percent of the videos in English. According to officials, the principal focus musically is on pop and rock, with banda, Tejano, salsa, merengue, and other forms not featured—for the moment. As of December 1993, only Los Angeles, Miami, and Tucson in the United States were contracting to receive the channel, although MTV officials hope to have all the major cities in the United States providing the service.

Retailing

America's major record retailers have not been immune to the Latin rage in the music business. A major reason why Latin music record sales have been steadily increasing is that more Latin music is being sold in general market retail stores such as Tower, Camelot, Sound Warehouse, and Sam Goody's. In the past, the large bulk of Latin product was sold through discounters like K-Mart, Target, and Wal-Mart, as well as small mom-and-pop stores such as Casa Guadalupe in Laredo, Del Bravo's, and Janie's in San Antonio, and Memo's Discoteca in Houston.

Also, the top Latin labels like EMI Latin, Sony, and WEA began selling their products through their Anglo sales forces. Previously, the English-language and Spanish-language market sales staffs were separate. Currently, for example, WEA's sales people complete orders for general market artists such as Madonna and R.E.M., and also take orders for Spanish stars like Luis Miguel and Mana.

Like the general music market, the Latin field also saw a huge catalog of yesterday's heroes returning in compact disc (CD) form—if not necessarily in single-album formats, then in compilations of greatest hits in all genres, from Latin pop and salsa, to Tejano, norteno, and conjunto.

The results can be confusing to the average record buyer who sometimes sees up to three or four different greatest hits packages on different record labels by the same artist. This was sometimes so because veteran groups such as La Mafia, Little Joe, Willie Colon, and others, recorded for various labels during their long careers. In addition, some labels were simply reissuing compilations to generate sales, as in the general market. For example, although Emilio Navaira or Selena had only four or five studio albums since 1990, a check of available titles showed up to 30 records by each artist. These included not only the recompilations and assorted theme-albums, but also albums on which they have been featured as guest artists.

The Future

As the major record labels have continued to streamline and commercialize the Latin industry, record sales have grown. However, some groups and genres are still too regional because of demographics. Banda, for example, remained hot in California but weak in Texas and Florida. Some people think that this is because most immigrants see California as a destination point for jobs, while Texas cities like San Antonio, Houston, and Dallas are way stations for better paying jobs in northern cities like Chicago or Detroit. But if immigration from the northern, rural states of Mexico continues, it only bodes well for banda's future, especially in California.

Tejano made great strides in Mexico, California, Florida, New York, and Chicago, but was still largely a powerhouse only in the Southwest. However, Tejano also benefited from its increasing tours of Mexico, both from the additional revenue in that country but also from the increasing base in the United States, thanks to the continued immigration of Mexico's citizens.

Whether these musical developments signal a new dynamic phase in at least one segment of Latino music, or they represent a new layer of commercial exploitation, remains uncertain. The cultural significance of these new musical developments also remains to be seen: Are they a response to cultural movements at the "organic" level or do they, like Latin rock, reflect the commercial stimulation of Latino music by the large recording labels, which have recently entered the field in earnest? Time will answer that question. In any case, there is no question that Latinos in the United States continue to leave an astonishing record of musical activity.

✳ SELECTED DISCOGRAPHY

Afro-Caribbean and Latin Jazz/Rock

Aragón, Orquesta. *Original de Cienfuegos.* Cariño, DBLI-5011.

Arcano y sus Maravillas. *Danzón mambo.* Cariño DBMI-5806.

Barretto, Ray. *Charanga moderna.* Tico, SLP 1087.

Canario y su Grupo. *Plenas.* Ansonia ALP 1232.

Colón, Willie, and Ruben Blades. *Siembra.* Fania, JM 00-537.

Cortijo, Rafael, y su Combo. *Cortijo en New York.* Gema, LPG-1115.

Grupo folklórico de Alberto Zayas. *Guaguancó afrocubano.* Panart, LP 2055.

Machito. *Afro-Cuban Jazz.* Verve, VE-2-2522.

Palmieri, Charlie. *Charanga Duboney: Echoes of an Era.* West Side Latino, WS-LA-240-241.

Palmieri, Eddie. *The Best of Eddie Palmieri.* Tico, CLP 1317.

Puente, Tito. *Dance Mania.* RCA LSP-1692.

Rodriguez, Arsenio. *El sentimiento de Arsenio.* Cariño, DBMI-5802.

Rodriguez, Tito. *Estoy como nunca.* West Side Latino, LT-LA 129-D.

Santamaria, Mongo. *Afro-Roots.* Prestige, PR-24018.

Santana. *Abraxas.* Columbia, KC 30130.

Orquesta, Norteña, and Música Tropical

Ayala, Ramón, y los Bravos del Norte. *Ramón Ayala y los Bravos del Norte.* Freddie, LP-1165.

Bernal, Conjunto. *Una noche en la villita.* Bego, BG-1015.

Bernal, Conjunto, et al. *Las más alegres polkas.* Ideal, ILP-127.

Bukis, Los. *Los Bukis.* Profono, PI-3050.

De la Rosa, Tony. *Las polkas de oro.* Freddie, LP-1194.

——, et al. *Las más alegres polkas.* Ideal, ILP 127.

Hernandez, Little Joe y la Familia. *Para la gente.* Buena Suerte Records, BSR 1038.

——. *Sea la paz la fuerza.* Leona Records Corporation, LRC 019.

Jordan, Steve. *Soy de Tejas.* Hacienda Records, LP 7905.

Latin Breed, The. *Powerdrive.* GCP, GCPLP-124.

Relámpagos del Norte, Los. *El disco de oro.* Alto Records, Alto 1125.

Sunny and the Sunliners. *Los enamorados.* Key-loc, KL 3020.

——. *Grande, Grande, Grande.* Key-loc, KL 3028.

Temerarios, Los. *Te Queiro.* TH/Rodven, 2717.

Texas-Mexican Border Music. Arhoolie/Folklyric, Volumes 3–7; 11–13; 16–21; 23–24.

Tortilla Factory. *Mis favoritas.* Falcon Records, GLP-011.

Tovar, Rigo, y su Costa Azul. *El nuevo contacto musical.* Melody Records, MEL-293.

[Treviño], Jimmy Edward. *My Special Album.* Texas Best Records, TXB-LP-1001.

Villa, Beto. *Beto Villa.* Falcon, FLP 108.

——. *Saludamos a Texas.* Ideal, ILP 104.

Yonics, Los. *Porqué volví contigo.* Fonovisa, 9012.

References

Acuña, Rudolfo. *Occupied America: A History of Chicanos.* New York: Harper and Row, 1981.

Baqueriro-Foster, Gerónimo. *La música en el periodo indepedente.* Mexico City: Fondo de Cultura Ecónomica, 1964.

Bascom, William. "The Yoruba in Cuba." *Nigeria,* 37, 1951: 14–20

Davis, Martha Ellen. *Voces del purgatorio: Estudio de la selva dominicana.* Santo Dominican Republic: Museo del Hombre Dominicano, 1981.

Dinger, Adeline. *Folklife and Folklore of the Mexican Border.* Edinburg, Texas: Hidalgo County Historical Museum, 1972.

Duany, Jorge. "Popular Music in Puerto Rico: Toward an Anthropology of *Salsa.*" *Latin American Music Review,* 5, No. 2, 1984: 186–216.

Ervin, Susan M., and Charles E. Osgood. "Second Language Learning and Bilingualism." In *Psycholinguistics: A Survey of Theory and Research Problems,* edited by Osgood and Sebeok. Bloomington: Indiana University Press, 1954.

García, Mario T. "Americans All: The Mexican American Generation and the Politics of Wartime Los Angeles, 1941–45." *Social Science Quarterly,* 65, No. 2, 1984: 278–289.

Limón, José. "Folklore, Social Conflict, and the U.S.-Mexico Border." In *Handbook of American Folklore,* edited by Richard M. Dorson. Bloomington: Indiana University Press, 1983.

Loza, Steven. "Music and the Afro-Cuban Experience." Master's thesis, University of California, Los Angeles, 1979.

Manuel, Peter. "The Anticipated Bass in Cuban Popular Music." *Latin American Music Review,* 6, No. 2, 1985: 249–261.

Marks, Morton. "Uncovering Ritual Structures in Afro-American Music." In *Religious Movements in Contemporary America,* edited by Irving Zaretzky and Mark Leone. Princeton, New Jersey: Princeton University Press, 1974.

Mayer-Serra, Otto. *Panorama de la música mexicana.* Mexico City: Fondo de Cultura Económica, 1941.

Ortner, Sherry. "On Key Symbols." *American Anthropologist,* 75, 1973: 1338–1346.

Padilla, Felix M. "Salsa: Puerto Rican and Latin Music." *Journal of Popular Culture,* 24, No. 1, 1990: 87–104.

Paredes, Américo. "The Mexican Corrido: Its Rise and Fall." In *Madstones and Twisters,* edited by Mody C. Boatright, Wilson M. Hudson, and Allen Maxwell. Publications of the Texas Folklore Society, No. 28. Dallas: Southern Metodist University Press, 1958: 91–105.

——. *"With His Pistol in his Hand:" A Border Ballad and its Hero.* Austin: University of Texas Press, 1958.

——. "The Anglo-American in Mexican Folklore." In *New Voices in American Studies,* edited by Ray B. Browne and Donald H. Winkleman. Lafayette, Indiana: Purdue University Press, 1966.

——. *A Texas-Mexican Cancionero.* Urbana: University of Illinois Press, 1976.

Peña, Manuel. "Folksong and Social Change: Two *Corridos* as Interpretive Sources." *Aztlán Journal of Chicano Studies,* 13, Nos. 1 and 2, 1982: 13–42.

——. *The Texas-Mexican Conjunto: History of a Working-Class Music.* Austin: University of Texas Press, 1985.

——. "From *Ranchero* to *Jaitón*: Ethnicity and Class in Texas-Mexican Music." *Ethnomusicology,* 29, No. 1, 1985: 29–55.

——. "Notes Toward an Interpretive History of California-Mexican Music." In *From the Inside Out: Perspectives on Mexican and Mexican-American Folk Art,* edited by Karana Hattersley-Drayton, et al. San Francisco: The Mexican Museum, 1989.

Peñalosa, Fernando. *Chicano Sociolinguistics.* Rowley, Massachusetts: Newbury House Publishers, 1980.

Roberts, John Storm. *The Latin Tinge.* New York: Oxford University Press, 1979.

Robinson, Alfred. *Life in California before the Conquest.* San Francisco: Thomas C. Russell, 1925.

Rubel, Arthur J. *Across the Tracks: Mexican-Americans in Texas City.* Austin: University of Texas Press, 1966.

Simmons, Merle E. *The Mexican Corrido as a Source for the Interpretive Study of Modern Mexico.* Bloomington: Indiana University Press, 1957.

Singer, Roberta L. "Tradition and Innovation in Contemporary Latin Popular Music in New York City. *Latin American Music Review,* 4, No. 2, 1983: 183–202.

——, and Robert Friedman. "Puerto Rican and Cuban Musical Expression in New York." *Caliente = Hot: Recorded Anthology of American Music,* (LP). New York: New World Records, 1977.

Turner, Victor. *The Ritual Process.* Chicago: Aldine Publishing, 1969.

——. *Dramas, Fields, and Metaphors.* Ithaca, New York: Cornell University Press, 1974.

Vaid, Jyotsna. *Language Processing in Bilinguals: Cycle Linguistic and Neopsychological Perspectives.* Hillside, New Jersey: Lawrence Erlbaum Associates, 1986.

Manuel Peña and Ramiro Burr

24

Media

❋ Treatment of Hispanics in Mainstream Media ❋ Newspapers ❋ Film ❋ Television ❋ Advertising
❋ Hispanic-Oriented Print Media ❋ Hispanic-Oriented Electronic Media

This chapter focuses primarily on mass communi-cation, as it pertains to newspapers, magazines, film, radio, television, and advertising. Excluded are dis-cussions on books, the music recording industry, and theater, which are covered in other chapters.

❋ TREATMENT OF HISPANICS IN MAINSTREAM MEDIA

The treatment of one ethnic group by another is quite often influenced by economic or political factors in their nation, state, or region. This is certainly true regarding the relations between Anglos and Latinos. The conflict and cooperation between these groups has been shaped by the political and economic rela-tions between the United States and Hispanic Amer-ican countries.

The mainstream mass media, which so often reflect the prevalent perspectives of the dominant groups in society, have historically replicated those views in their treatment of Hispanics. Therefore, an avenue for partially understanding contemporary Hispanic life in the United States is the assessment of messages that the media disseminate about them. There are two related reasons that media are the focus of analy-sis. First, at all levels of society they are the most pervasive sources of news and information. For many people they are also the most relied-upon source for entertainment. Second, the messages presented by the media may have significant effects on the audi-ence, especially regarding events, topics, and issues about which the audience has no direct knowledge or experience. Thus, for millions of people in this coun-try, a significant part of the information they receive and the notions they develop about Hispanics may often be products of mass media messages.

While a comprehensive treatment of the topic of "media effects" is beyond the scope of this work, it is imperative to realize that there are conditions under that media may have maximal influence on the audi-ence—conditions that are germane to the main-stream media's treatment of Hispanics. One of those conditions occurs when viewers do not have other sources of information or experiences that provide a standard against which to assess the media mes-sages. To the extent that non-Hispanics live segre-gated lives with limited opportunities to interact ef-fectively with a variety of Hispanics in constructive or productive ways, the media images of Hispanics will be among the most important sources for non-Latinos to learn and interpret who Hispanics are and how they think. Another factor that increases the "symbolic" media's influence occurs when the values or views presented by them are recurrent. To date, the values and views presented about Latinos are predominantly negative and recurrent across media and time.

Furthermore, the treatment of Latinos in main-stream media has its impact on Hispanics, who suf-fer the consequences of the recurring negative imag-ery. For example, they face the psychological pain that emerges from the negative portrayals and lack of recognition of their own people and values. They also have to endure the social scorn that emerges when the treatment they receive from other people, and sometimes from those of their own ethnic back-ground, is consciously or unconsciously based on ste-reotyped notions disseminated by the media.

❋ NEWSPAPERS

Mainstream newspapers were probably the first major means of mass communication through which fragmented and distorted news, information, and images of Hispanics were created and promoted. While much has changed from the early depictions,

671

the treatment and employment of Hispanics in newspapers is still far from adequate in this media institution.

Portrayals

A 1967 study by James Evans of the roots of three popular stereotypes (the "Indian savage," the "Mexican bandit," and the "Chinese heathen") reveals that "the Anglo image of the Mexican as a bandit is largely an outgrowth of the Manifest Destiny policy of the early 1800s." His review of nineteenth-century English-language American newspapers in California and Texas discusses how circumstantial events related to economic and political relations between the people who inhabited the expansive Mexican territories of the Southwest and the Anglo-European settlers and gold prospectors led the latter group to create stereotypes of the former to justify the conquest of that region. The political, religious, and economic beliefs of Anglo-European superiority were constantly revealed as they depicted the Native American and Mexican inhabitants as people destined to be conquered and unworthy of keeping their lands and resources.

After the conquests of the southwestern territories, the mainstream press of the early twentieth century continued a pattern of false depictions of Hispanic people. In other instances, the mainstream press simply ignored the mainstream experiences of Hispanics. The most blatant act of negative stereotyping occurred during the 1940s through exploitation of social and economic tensions between Hispanics and Anglos in Los Angeles. The press gave undue prominence to Mexican Americans in crime news. Alarmist headlines and stories blaming these Hispanics for many of the city's social ills were part of the 1943 "Zoot-suit" riots and their aftermath.

In subsequent decades, changing journalistic standards of increased professionalism, balance, and objectivity helped diminish such blatant anti-Mexican racism. Yet negative, limited, or inadequate portrayals of Hispanics in newspapers of the latter half of this century have been systematically documented. One of the first studies in this area was Fishman and Casiano's (1969) analysis of Puerto Ricans in the *New York Times* and the New York *Post*; they also studied the Spanish-language dailies *El Diario* and *El Tiempo*. The authors found that the English dailies showed little interest in Puerto Ricans, who were referred to with negative attributes and covered primarily in terms of their community needs or problems (for which solutions were infrequently offered). The same was not true in the Spanish dailies, where more positive and solution-oriented stories were observed.

Negative and biased coverage of Mexican Americans was also evident in a handful of unpublished master's theses regarding pretrial criminal news reporting and general reporting. Also, Chavira (1975, 1977), comparing immigration and deportation news in the *Los Angeles Times* and the Spanish-language daily *La Opinión* during the 1930s, 1950s, and 1970s, found that the plight of Mexicans was covered much more sympathetically and humanistically in the latter paper.

Yet some improvements have been made, at least according to the two most recent studies of the mainstream press. In the most systematic and quantitatively oriented study of the coverage of Hispanic Americans in the English-language dailies of Santa Fe (New Mexico), Tucson (Arizona), and Salinas, San Bernardino, Stockton, and Visalia (California), Bradley S. Greenberg and colleagues conclude (from their two-week sample, *Mexican Americans and the Mass Media,* 1983) that "sports news and photo coverage get high marks for their inclusion of local Hispanics" and that "local news coverage exclusive of sports gets a passing grade—good, not excellent, but better than it is currently receiving credit for." They add, however, that "editorial coverage and bulletin listings of Hispanic people and activities are below average and in need of considerable attention."

The most promising assessment is provided by VanSlyke Turk, Richstad, Bryson Jr., and Johnson (1989). In their study of the Albuquerque *Journal* and the San Antonio *Express,* they found some examples of parity in the inclusion of Hispanics and conclude that "Hispanics and Hispanic issues are . . . present in the newspaper newshole in proportion to their presence in the population." They also found that in comparison to stories about Anglos, Hispanic stories were adequately treated in terms of length and placement. However, as was the case in previously cited studies, Hispanics were much too prominently reported as "problem people," for example, in judicial and crime news, news of riots, and accident and disaster news.

Despite these studies, the prognosis of Hispanic treatment in mainstream newspapers has consistently remained culturally insensitive and nonsupportive. From his observations and personal experiences, Charles A. Erickson, founder and editor of *Hispanic Link, Inc.,* summarized that "the relationship between 20 million Americans crowded under the umbrella Hispanic and the nation's establishment print media sprawls across the spectrum from non-existent to quaint, to precarious, to outright antagonistic" (1981). Erickson then identifies six dimensions of mainstream press irresponsibility: "the press will not allow Hispanics to be authorities on general issues"; "the press will not even allow Hispanics to be authorities on issues where Hispanics have the obvious expertise"; "the press still views the Hispanic community in stereotype"; "the press fails to provide Hispanics with information of critical interest and importance to their welfare and progress"; "the press does not hire enough Hispanics or other reporters and editors with Hispanic cultural awareness and expertise"; and "the press tends to smother those Hispanics they do hire." For each dimension, Erickson provides various examples to support his case. For instance, regarding the press' viewing the Hispanic community in stereotype, he states, "Traditionally, non-Hispanic reporters have attached negative adjectives to the word 'barrio.' For example, Houston's barrios were described in a series one of its papers ran some months ago as places where shoppers haggle and Latin rhythms blare. A Chicago reporter described New York's Spanish Harlem as 'grim, rat-infested.' A *Christian Science Monitor* writer chose the words '[t]he often-steamy barriors [*sic*] of East Los Angeles'" (Erickson).

A decade following Erickson's critique of the mainstream press, David Shaw's 1990 nine-article series in *The Los Angeles Times* assessing the status of reporting about and hiring minorities found many of the same situations and problems discussed by Erickson. The headline of the first story summarized the issue: "Negative News and Little Else." The story went on to say that "by focusing on crime, poverty and aberrant behavior newspapers fail to give a complete portrait of ethnic minorities." An example of continued stereotyping presented by Shaw is the use of the word "aliens" (which can make Latinos seem "inhuman—strange outcasts from another world") instead of "illegal immigrants" or "undocumented workers."

In trying to understand some of the reasons that lead to the continued fragmentation and distortion of news about Hispanics and other minorities, those who have written on this subject would probably agree that the lack of Hispanics in the newsrooms and in their management is one of the major factors to be considered.

Employment

Clint Wilson and Félix Gutiérrez point out in their *Minorities and the Media: Diversity and the End of Mass Communication* (1985) that when the first counts of minority participants in the mainstream press were conducted in the early 1970s, these groups constituted less than 2 percent of the total. About a decade later, in 1984, the total had only made it to 5.8 percent among the approximately 1,750 daily newspapers in the nation. As low as these figures are, one must realize that they are for all minorities, which means that the situation for Hispanics is more dismal. This is a problem that continues even today, according to the most recent surveys of the National Association of Hispanic Journalists (NAHJ) and the American Society of Newspaper Editors (ASNE).

According to the NAHJ's third annual survey (for which 125 newspapers with circulations over 100,000 were queried and almost half responded), Hispanics accounted for a mere 3.2 percent of this labor force in general; only 2 percent were managers. According to the ASNE survey (for which 1,545 newspapers were queried, 65 percent of which responded), approximately 1,349 Hispanics were employed in those newspapers and constituted a scant 2.4 percent of the work force of about 55,714.

In addition to the problem of low employment, Hispanics who have succeeded in gaining employment in journalism encounter various burdens often related to their ethnicity. As suggested by *Hispanic Link* founder and editor Charles A. Erickson, Hispanic reporters face unwarranted challenges of their latitude and credibility as professional journalists (1981). He points out that while too often Hispanics are considered to lack the intellect to write about issues other than ethnic problems or strife, they are also perceived as too partial for "objective" in-depth reporting about educational, economic, and other types of policy issues of importance to their community. Moreover, many Hispanic journalists are burdened with requests to be translators in situations beyond their reporting duties; for example, to assist in answering Spanish-language business calls or correspondence not related to their responsibilities. Yet, these tasks and Hispanics' bilingual abilities usually go without compensatory pay.

Given these current employment figures and practices, one can understand some of the factors related to the inadequate treatment of Hispanics in newspapers. Unfortunately, given the slow progress in newsroom integration and the limited sensitivity of many Anglo reporters and editors, it will be some time before Hispanics make sufficient inroads to professional positions, which is necessary to help improve the portrayal of their communities.

According to figures released in 1992, Hispanics were not well represented on the staffs of the 62 top newspapers in the United States: 3.5 percent of the total editorial staff among the top papers were Hispanic, with low percentages of Hispanics in management, reporting, writing, and photographer positions.

Despite these difficulties, many newspapers have been hiring more Latino and other ethnic minority journalists and improving their working environment, especially with respect to training, promotions, and distribution of assignments. These efforts have also included second-language courses (especially Spanish) and racial and ethnic awareness workshops for all employees of the newspaper. In the late 1980s, some newspapers, such as *The Los Angeles Times* and the *Fresno Bee,* began publishing weekly supplements in Spanish. This practice, which is quite recent in these papers, has been going on with mixed success since the 1840s in various locations, especially in border towns.

The concerted efforts of organizations such as the National Association of Hispanic Journalists, the National Hispanic Media Coalition, the Hispanic Academy of Arts and Sciences, and the National Association of Hispanic Publications have been major factors in the push for positive changes and will undoubtedly contribute to improving both the portrayal and employment of Hispanics in the media.

✴ FILM

While newspapers were the first mass medium to widely disseminate images of Hispanics, their circulation and influence were more limited than that of films. Since the inception of moving pictures, stereotypes of minority and ethnic groups have been a standard feature.

Portrayals

Hispanics have been regularly stereotyped in films dating back to the early days of silent cinema. Early Westerns, such as the so-called greaser films like *Bronco Billy and the Greaser* (1914), instituted in films the Mexican or half-breed bandit, one of several Mexican stereotypes that Arthur Pettit (in his *Images of the Mexican American in Fiction and Film,* 1980) says derives from Western dime novels. By the early 1920s, there were six major Hispanic stereotypes already well established in Hollywood movies: el bandido, the half-breed harlot, the male buffoon, the female clown, the Latin lover, and the dark lady.

While the overall thrust of Hollywood's portrayal of Hispanics has been quite uniform, political and economic forces have accounted for several well-differentiated stages in the history of that depiction. In the beginning, Hollywood stereotyped with impunity. Even before the appearance of the "greaser" films, Hollywood was portraying Mexicans as vengeful, cruel, and violent. For a time, with the beginning of World War I, there was a shift away from negative Mexican stereotypes. But afterward the same stereotypical patterns continued, and derogatory depictions of Mexicans and Mexico led the government of Mexico to threaten to boycott such films. Hollywood's response was to change the setting of many films from Mexico to some fictional Latin American country. For example, the setting of Harold Lloyd's comedy *Why Worry?* (1923), about an American hypochondriac who finds himself in the midst of revolutionary turmoil in what is obviously Mexico, is set in "Paradiso." Hollywood continued to adjust its productions to take Mexican objections into account, but the results were often just as stereotypical. The producers of *Viva Villa!* (1934) got the approval of the Mexican government for the film's shooting script, although the movie itself is full of mean-spirited, hateful, and moronic Mexicans.

The Second World War quickly reversed such imagery, however, as Hollywood hastened to solidify relations with Mexico and Latin America against the Axis powers. An era of "Good Neighborism" (1939–45) followed, in which Latin America and Latin Americans were portrayed positively, if rather one-dimensionally. Typical of the change was *Juarez* (1939), a Hollywoodized biography of the Mexican revolutionary leader, and the Disney studios' animated travelogues, *Saludos Amigos* (1943) and *The Three Caballeros* (1945). It was this era that saw the rise of such Latin stars as María Montez, Ricardo Montalbán, Fernando Lamas, and Carmen Miranda.

In many ways, the period immediately following World War II was the most interesting in terms of how Hollywood dealt with Hispanics and Hispanic themes. Two major postwar genres predominantly featured Hispanic characters and issues: *film noir,* a group of dark, bleak films with betrayal as a central theme, and the social melodrama, movies that directly addressed social problems. Of the *film noirs,* those treating Hispanics included Billy Wilder's *Ace in the Hole* (also known as *The Big Carnival*; 1951), Orson Welles' *Touch of Evil* (1958), and Ralph Nelson's *Requiem for a Heavyweight* (1962), films that also critique the massive corruption within the Anglo world.

There were several social melodramas that dealt with Hispanic issues. Notable among them was *Salt of the Earth* (1954), a joint venture by blacklisted Hollywood filmmakers (screenwriter Michael Wilson, director Herbert Biberman, producer Paul Jerico) depicting in gritty terms a miners' strike in New Mexico. *The Lawless* (1954) was another Chicano-centered film made by a blacklisted filmmaker, Joseph Losey. Two boxing films were also produced in the postwar period, the formulaic *Right Cross* (1950, directed by John Sturges), with Ricardo Montalbán as a Chicano fighter with an anti-Anglo chip on his shoulder, and the much more intriguing *The Ring* (1952, directed by Kurt Neumann), starring Lalo Ríos as a young man trying to box his way out of East Los Angeles. Irving Pichel's *A Medal for Benny* (1945) and William Wellman's *My Man and I* (1952) both condemned the hypocrisy within the Anglo mainstream. Surprisingly, *Giant* (1957), a blockbuster directed by George Stevens, was one of the most progressive of all these films, indicting not only racism but also patriarchy, the imperialistic bent of America's westward expansion, the class system, and the social construction of "manhood."

From the 1960s to the present, Hollywood's stereotyping of Hispanics can be placed into two broad categories: repeated and countered. In the main, Hollywood continued its policy of stereotyping Hispanics. The bandido stereotype, for example, can be found in several film genres. Updated variations include the young Puerto Rican toughs in (1961) and the well-meaning courtroom drama *The Young Savages* (1961), as well as the East L.A. Chicano gang members in *Colors* (1988). Perhaps the most widely seen example occurred in the opening of Steven Spielberg's *Raiders of the Lost Ark* (1981). In the film's first 15 minutes, Indiana Jones, somewhere in South America in 1936, is menaced by all manner of Latino culprits. He is abandoned (an Indian carrier leaves the Jones expedition screaming hysterically), betrayed (one of his remaining native guides tries to shoot him in the back, the other leaves him for dead in the underground passageway), and threatened (a tribe of Latin American Indians chases and tries to kill him). Another example of a widely seen recent Hollywood bandido is seen in the Latin American bad guys in *Romancing the Stone* (1984), particularly in the corrupt villain (played by Mexican actor Manuel Ojeda).

The other five Hispanic stereotypes—the half-breed harlot, the male buffoon, the female clown, the Latin lover, and the dark lady—had similar Hollywood incarnations during the same period. But during this time there was a promising development, namely, the countering of such pervasive imagery. This stage was precipitated by the emergence of talented Hispanics who began working *behind* the camera. Because of them, the opportunity for opposing long-standing Hollywood stereotypes became a reality. The narrative strategy of these filmmakers was to revise standard Hollywood genres. Familiar story formulas were given an ethnic twist, which subverted standard Hollywood practice and promoted a more pluralistic view of the world. A good example of this sort of counterimagery is found in León Ichaso's *Crossover Dreams* (1985), a Hispanic rendition of the well-known show-biz success story. An ambitious New York salsa musician (Rubén Blades) turns his back on his friends, his barrio, and his roots to achieve mainstream success, but fails to make it in the big time. In the film's final scene, the character swallows his pride, returns to his old neighborhood, and asks his old partner to start another salsa band. The film thus critiques dominant notions of the American dream as well as celebrates and reaffirms traditional Hispanic values.

A more problematic version of the same story was Luis Valdez's *La Bamba* (1987), whose compliant rock and roll hero Richie Valens (Lou Diamond Phillips) conforms to mainstream requisites for success (he even changes his name) to facilitate his rise to stardom. Much more powerful was Valdez's first feature, *Zoot Suit* (1981), a filmed version of his hit stage play of the same name. It was an assault on Hollywood in its form (a provocative combination of broad comedy, courtroom melodrama, social criticism, Brechtian distancing devices, and song and dance) and on the justice system in its content (a depiction of Los Angeles' notorious Sleepy Lagoon trial).

Director-turned-producer Moctezuma Esparza revised the Western genre in *The Ballad of Gregorio Cortez* (1982, directed by Robert M. Young), based in part on Américo Paredes' account of the real-life exploits of the man who eluded the Texas Rangers around the turn of the century. Victor Villaseñor's script tells the story from multiple perspectives and manages an even-handed account while at the same time revealing the prejudice prevalent in Texas at that time. It remains the most eloquent reversal of the bandido stereotype yet put on film. Esparza also produced Robert Redford's *The Milagro Beanfield War* (1988), an earnest though less-than-successful attempt to portray an entire New Mexico community—both Anglo and Chicano—during a municipal crisis.

Another notable film of this "counterimage" phase was Gregory Nava's *El Norte* (1984), a retelling of the familiar coming-to-America story from the point of view of a Central American brother and sister fleeing political oppression in their homeland. By impressively combining graphic realism with lyrical magic realism, the film deftly depicts both the danger and the hopefulness of their flight. Cheech Marin's *Born in East L.A.* (1987), about the deportation to Mexico of a Mexican American, is a comic inversion of the same story. In its own raucous way, it examines the contradictions inherent in America's definition of citizenship. Finally, there is the Chicano version of *Goodbye, Mr. Chips,* Ramón Menéndez's *Stand and Deliver* (1988). The film was based on the true-life story of Jaime Escalante, a courageous and visionary East Los Angeles high school math teacher (played by Edward James Olmos, who was nominated for a Best Actor Academy Award for the role). Using humor, threats, and shrewd psychology, Escalante inspires his students to master calculus and in so doing gives them a positive sense of self-worth and a key to self-actualization.

As remarkable as these counterimagery strides have been, however, it remains to be seen whether this trend will continue. After the advancements of the 1980s, production on Hispanic themes in movies initiated by Hispanics has slowed down considerably since the peak period of 1987–88. There is no comparison with Afro-American filmmaking, for example, which has witnessed an unprecedented explosion during the same time period. In 1991, for example, there were 19 Afro-American-directed feature films released by Hollywood. In contrast, since 1988 there has been only one Latino-directed film made, Isaac Artenstein's independently produced *Break of Dawn,* and it never found a mainstream distributor.

✳ TELEVISION

Not surprisingly, the treatment of Hispanics on mainstream television has not been sharply different from that in the film industry. Although there have been occasional breaks with stereotypical imagery, in some respects the portrayal has been more critical of Hispanic culture and life. In addition, the situation is worse in the number of Hispanics employed in front or behind cameras. This conclusion is quite evident from even cursory watching of American television.

Portrayals

Since television's widespread appeal in the late 1950s, the masters of television images have been less than fair in their portrayals of Hispanics. For example, the first "prominent" Hispanic male buffoon was seen for many years on the "I Love Lucy" show (CBS 1951–61), where Lucille Ball's husband, Desi Arnaz, played "the good-looking, excitable, short tempered Cuban band leader who spoke with an accent and occasionally rattled off expletives in Spanish" (Luis Reyes, 1983). Interestingly, in "Desi and Lucy: Before the Laughter," a two-hour special broadcast on February 20, 1991, on CBS, he is stereotyped prominently as an irresponsible Latin lover.

Other Hispanic male buffoons include Pancho, the sidekick to the Cisco Kid in the syndicated series (1951–56) "The Cisco Kid"; José Jiménez, the Puerto Rican bumbling doorman and elevator operator in "The Danny Thomas Show" (NBC 1953–71); and Sgt. García in the "Zorro" series (ABC, 1957–59). The last of the successful (in terms of ratings and continuity) Hispanic male buffoons on network tele-

vision was probably Freddie Prinze, who in "Chico and the Man" (NBC, 1974–78) played Chico, a Hispanic "streetwise kid working in a garage with a bigoted old man."

With such exceptions as "Chico and the Man," which was terminated shortly after Prinze's suicide in early 1977, Hispanics as major comic characters in successful network programs have been few. CBS came up with an innovative strategy to market its "Latino Odd Couple" sitcom "Trial and Error" (1988). It was simulcast in Spanish on Spanish-language radio stations. The show centered around two unlikely roommates: Tony (Paul Rodríguez), a T-shirt salesman on Los Angeles' Olvera Street, and John (Eddie Vélez), a newly graduated Puerto Rican lawyer working in an established law firm. The comedy was strained and the series never gained acceptance; it only attracted 8 percent of the available audience. Much more noteworthy was the short-lived "I Married Dora," which had a brief run on ABC during the fall 1987 season. An admirable attempt to center a situation comedy around a Salvadoran woman, it reversed cultural fields by making Dora (Elizabeth Peña) smart and self-assured and her uptight, "open-minded" Anglo husband the butt of many jokes because he held stereotypical ideas about Hispanics. The series dealt meaningfully with Latino immigration to the United States and the misconceptions the two cultures often have about one another. Sadly, it was canceled before establishing a consistent tone and finding an audience.

The Hispanic bandidos, (bandits, criminals, and lawbreakers) were also adapted promptly and prominently by television. The Hispanic "stock bandido, spitfire or peon" (Reyes) was common in innumerable Western cowboy series. Also, the numerous urban counterparts have been constantly present, starting with "Dragnet" (NBC 1951–59; 1967–70) and "Naked City" (ABC 1958–59; 1960–63), as part of the detective and police dramas. Most recently, they were quite salient in the underworld activities (especially regarding drug traffic and dealings) in "Hill Street Blues" (NBC 1981–86) and "Miami Vice" (ABC 1984–89).

Mainstream television has allowed a few law-enforcer or lawmaker Hispanic stereotypes. From "The Cisco Kid" and "Zorro" in the 1950s to more recent shows such as "CHiPs," "Miami Vice," and "L.A. Law," there have been shown some relatively positive Hispanic male figures. One notable early example was Walt Disney's "The Nine Lives of Elfago Baca" (1958). Based on the exploits of the legendary Mexican American lawman, the miniseries was an all-too-rare instance of television depicting a Chicano hero. More often, Hispanics have been cast in secondary or insignificant roles. For example, on "Hill Street Blues" the Hispanic officer who is second in command is "often given little to do and is generally dull or a buffoon" (Beale, 1986).

Most attempts at centering a law enforcement series around a Hispanic character have been disappointing. "Juarez" (1988) was conceived as a gritty portrayal of the life of a Mexican American border detective (it was shot on location in El Paso). ABC lost confidence in the project, however, and suspended production shortly after only two episodes (of the six initially ordered) were completed. That episode was subsequently broadcast with little fanfare and soon forgotten. NBC's "Drug Wars: the Kiki Camarena Story" (1990) was replete with updated bandido stereotypes and so offensive to Mexico that it issued formal complaints about the mini-series (which went on to win an Emmy). Paul Rodríguez's private investigator in "Grand Slam" resulted in little more than yet another instance of the comic buffoon.

In contrast, Edward James Olmos' Lieutenant Martin Castillo in "Miami Vice" is one of the most positive Hispanic characters in television history. Because Olmos was initially reluctant to take the part (he turned down the role several times before finally accepting), the show's producers gave him complete control over the creation and realization of Castillo. He fashioned a dignified, honorable character of quiet strength and considerable power, thereby helping to offset the show's facile stereotyping of villainous Latin American drug smugglers. Finally there is the formidable presence of Victor Sifuentes (Jimmy Smits) on "L.A. Law," who provides the law firm (and the series) with a healthy dose of social consciousness.

Several stereotypes of Hispanics on television could be reviewed, as could the occasions when some Hispanic actors (for example, Ricardo Montalbán) and actresses (for instance, Rita Moreno) have been called upon to play a variety of roles beyond the usual stereotypes. What has been most neglected, however, is regular positive roles for Hispanic women and, equally important, the Hispanic family. This is one area in which Hispanics television has been worse off than in film. In this respect, they have also fared much worse than Afro-Americans.

According to a 1983 review of the industry by Luis Reyes, during the early 1950s, Elena Verdugo starred in the comedy series "Meet Millie," but not as a Hispanic woman. Instead, she played "an all-American girl." Reyes points out that "the image of the Hispanic woman has been usually relegated to the overweight *mamacita,* the spitfire or señorita, and the suffering mother or gang member's girlfriend." He adds that images of "strong, self-reliant, attrac-

tive, all knowing" Hispanic females were notable in Linda Cristal's role as Victoria Cannon in "The High Chaparral" (NBC 1967–71) and Elena Verdugo as nurse Consuelo in "Marcus Welby, M.D." (ABC 1969–76). More recently this shortage of strong Latina characters remains the predominant pattern. Two notable exceptions are the character of Dora in "I Married Dora" (ABC 1987) and Pilar in "Falcon Crest" (CBS 1987–89)—the latter played a character who managed to be more than a simple one-dimensional love interest and was a forceful businesswoman.

Hispanic *families* have also been absent from the center stages of mainstream network television. In "The High Chaparral," a Mexican cattle-ranching family was "very prominently portrayed alongside the gringo family" (Reyes). After that series, consequential inclusions of Hispanic families have eluded long runs on the small screen. "Viva Valdez," a poorly conceived and received situation comedy about a Chicano family living in East Los Angeles, was aired on ABC only between May 31 and September 6, 1976.

It was not until the spring of 1983, when ABC aired "Condo," that a middle-class urban Hispanic family was first introduced to TV viewers in the United States. That situation comedy series featured "a textbook WASP and an upwardly mobile Hispanic who find themselves as condominium neighbors on opposite sides of almost every question, but are faced with impending family ties" (Federico A. Subervi-Vélez, *Income and Status Differences between White and Minority Americans: A Persistent Inequality,* 1990). This modern-day Romeo and Juliet—in the very first episode the oldest Anglo son and a Hispanic daughter fall in love, elope, and begin a series of adventures that embroil the families in joy and sorrow—was also short-lived as its quality declined and ratings faltered against the competition of CBS' "Magnum, P.I." and NBC's "Fame." Yet during "Condo's" 12 episodes, another TV first was set as the featured Mexican American family was shown interacting as *equals* with an Anglo family that sometimes acceptingly participated with them as Hispanics.

On March 6 of the following year, ABC tried Norman Lear's "a.k.a. Pablo," another situation comedy which was centered on Hispanic comedian Paul Rodríguez but also featured his working-class family. Unfortunately, Pablo's pungent jokes, often about Mexicans and Hispanics in general, irked enough Hispanics and others whose strong protest to the network contributed to the show's cancellation after only six episodes. The wealthiest urban Hispanic family ever featured was in another sitcom, "Sánchez of Bel-Air" on the USA Cable Network. In this program, the nou-veau riche Sánchez family faced numerous social class and cultural challenges after they moved up from the barrio to live in one of the most upscale areas of Los Angeles. The program ran only 13 episodes between 1986 and 1987. As of this writing, main-stream network television has no Hispanic "Huxtables," "Windslows," or even "Jeffersons."

Until very recently, the absence of notable Hispanic female figures and families was also evident in the soap opera genre, which neglected blacks, Latinos, and most other ethnic minorities. At the time of this writing, "Santa Barbara" is the only ongoing contemporary soap with recurring roles for Hispanics, five of which are regularly included. Payne indicates that according to Jerry Dobson, one of the show's writers, a commitment was made to have a Hispanic family "because there are large numbers of Latinos in Santa Barbara" (1985). Payne adds that "while originally the only Hispanic character with a major storyline was Santana (who was played by a non-Hispanic actress), Cruz (A. Martínez), the lead Hispanic male character, has been promised a major storyline, replete with romance." The producers of the show have made good on their promise and viewers have since been introduced to Cruz's family circle and given him a major role, too.

One other contemporary program with a prominent Hispanic female is "Dangerous Women," where actress María Rangel is one of six main characters. She plays the role of an ex-convict Hispanic woman who, after being unjustly jailed for murdering her abusive husband, works seeking to reform the abuses of the penitentiary system. The show is a one-hour syndicated nighttime soap opera/drama aired in various major markets such as Los Angeles, New York, Chicago, Phoenix, Minneapolis, San Francisco, and Houston. Prior to this show, the only other prominent role for a Hispanic female was found in the daytime soap opera "Rituals" (1984–85), which unfortunately was also short-lived.

Studies originating from government, academic, and professional circles corroborate the previous findings and reveal additional shortcomings about the treatment of Hispanics on mainstream television. In 1977 and 1979, the U.S. Commission on Civil Rights published two reports on the portrayals and employment of women and minorities in television. While many results were reported with aggregated data on all minorities, specific findings about "people of Spanish origin" [sic] were noted in the 1977 report. For example, from the content analysis of one sample week of programming during the fall of 1973 and 1974, only three Hispanics, all males, were found in "major" roles; 12 Hispanic males and one female

were found playing minor roles. The highest-status occupation shown was a lawyer in a minor role.

The first academically based systematic analysis of this subject was conducted by Bradley S. Greenberg and Pilar Baptista-Fernández (in *Life on Television: Content Analysis of U.S. TV Drama,* 1980), who examined sample weeks of commercial fictional programming during three television seasons (1975–76, 1976–77, and 1977–78). Among the 3,549 characters with speaking roles observed in the 255 episodes coded, they were able to find only "53 different individuals who could reliably be identified as Hispanic Americans . . . [these] constitute slightly less than 1.5 percent of the population of speaking TV characters." Summarizing their findings, Greenberg and Baptista-Fernández stated that Hispanic characters on television are "hard to find," "mostly males of dark complexion, with dark hair, most often with heavy accents," and that "women are absent and insignificant." They also stated that the characters were "gregarious and pleasant, with strong family ties," that "half work hard, half are lazy, and very few show much concern for their futures," and that "most have had very little education, and their jobs reflect that fact."

Mainstream television's neglect of Hispanics was similarly documented in a report commissioned by the League of United Latin American Citizens (LULAC) and prepared by Public Advocates, Inc. (1983). In the Public Advocates audit of all 63 prime-time shows during the first week of the fall 1983 television season (September 26–October 2), Hispanics played .5 percent (3 characters out of 496) of the significant speaking roles and only 1 percent (10 characters out of 866) of the those who spoke one or more lines. With the exception of Geraldo Rivera, there was "a total absence of positive Hispanic characters." Comparing the networks, CBS was consistently the worst (1 Hispanic character out of 212); ABC and NBC "showed significant decreases in the percentage of Hispanics portrayed." Also, on ABC, "Two-thirds of all speaking parts for Hispanics were criminals"; on CBS there were "no Hispanics in any significant speaking roles"; and on NBC "only one of its 189 (.5 percent) *significant* roles included an Hispanic."

The very low percentage of Hispanic participation in television was also found in a study by Lichter, Lichter, Rothman, and Amundson (1987). Analyzing 620 episodes of prime-time series randomly selected from the Library of Congress' holdings from 1955 to 1986, they observed that "since 1975, nearly one in ten characters have been black (from a low of under 1 percent in the 1950s), while Hispanics have hovered around the 2 percent mark for three decades." Furthermore, in almost every comparison Lichter and colleagues made of the social background (for example, education, employment) and plot functions (starring role, positive/negative portrayal, having committed a crime, and so on) of the white, black, and Latino characters, the latter group was consistently worst off.

The previous findings are again reaffirmed in the most recent study of this topic. In the National Commission on Working Women's (NCWW) 1989 examination of 30 network entertainment programs in which minority characters were featured, only nine Hispanics (five women, four men) were found; in the same shows there were 65 blacks, three Asians, and one Native American. The NCWW's qualitative commentaries of some of the scenes that included Hispanics found occasional redeeming contributions by some the leading characters. A more optimistic view on redeeming participation of minorities and the fading away of their stereotypes on television was provided recently by Tyrer (1991).

Public television has fared just slightly better than the commercial networks. In his brief overview of Latinos on television, Beale (1986) summarizes some past offerings of the Public Broadcasting System (PBS). For example, he indicates that "Sesame Street," "3–2–1 Contact," and "The Electric Company," children's shows produced by Children's Television Workshop for PBS, regularly feature Hispanic role models, adults as well as children. Beale also points to the airing of Latino themes, dramas, and films such as Jesús Salvador Treviño's *Seguín,* Robert M. Young's *Alambrista,* Moctezuma Esparza and Robert M. Young's *The Ballad of Gregorio Cortéz,* and Gregory Nava's *El Norte,* adding that "PBS deals with a broader range of Hispanic issues than the commercial networks, which are obsessed with immigration and revolution in their documentary treatment of Latino themes."

Happily, this trend has continued. More recently, PBS has broadcast Luis Valdez's *Corridos!* (1987), dramatizations of traditional Mexican narrative ballads, Jesús Salvador Treviño's *Birthright: Growing Up Hispanic* (1989), interviews with leading Hispanic writers, Isaac Artenstein's *Break of Dawn* (1990), a docudrama based on the life of singer and Los Angeles radio personality Pedro J. González, and Héctor Galán's hard-hitting documentaries *New Harvest, Old Shame* (1990) and *Los Mineros* (1991). However, exemplary series such as "Villa Alegre," "Carrascolendas," and "Qué Pasa, U.S.A." have been canceled due to lack of funds or low ratings. The lack of funding is certainly at the core of the problem as "only about 2 percent of funds for television production allocated by the Corporation for Public Broadcasting in the past 14 years have gone to produce programs specifically geared to the Hispanic communities of the United States" (Treviño, 1983). Even in early 1991, no nationally broadcast shows for or about Hispanics are regularly scheduled on PBS.

The final area of interest regarding the images of Hispanics in mainstream television is news coverage. Ironically, researchers of media news content have themselves shown little concern for this population. Among the scores of articles published about the characteristics and biases of television news, *not even one* has given systematic attention to the portrayal of Hispanics in newscasts. For studies that have focused on the major network news, part of the problem may be the few stories broadcast about Hispanics. For example, a U.S. Commission on Civil Rights report mentions in passing that in the 230 stories examined from 15 network news programs aired between March 1974 and February 1975 that "4 men of Spanish origin" were identified as newsmakers (1979); but no further explanation is given about who or why they were in the news. The commission's 1979 update, for which 15 newscasts from 1977 were coded, makes very brief mention about two stories related to Hispanics. The handful of studies published systematically analyzing Hispanics in the news have all focused on print media.

Given these findings, one can very easily agree with Greenberg and Baptista-Fernández's view that "in essence, it seems that television has yet to do much with, or for, the Hispanic American either as a television character or as a viewer. It might be improper to characterize them as invisible, but the portrayal is blurred or certainly hard to follow."

Employment

Behind the cameras and in the offices, the treatment of Hispanics is inadequate. From the first reports of the U.S. Commission on Civil Rights (1977, 1979) to more recent configurations of minority employment in the broadcasting industry, Hispanic participation has been and continues to be extremely small, much below Hispanic population proportions, and it is inferior to that of Afro-Americans. For example, in the Civil Rights Commission's 1977 report, the average number of "Spanish origin" persons employed by 40 stations surveyed in 1971 was 1.4 percent for males and .56 percent for females; in 1975 the respective figures were 2.2 percent and 1.14 percent. In the commission's 1979 update based on the 1977 data, these latter averages remained unchanged. These averages, based on aggregate data for various positions and localities, hide the more negative situation that existed with respect to Hispanics in decision-making versus non-decision-making positions.

Stone's findings based on a 1987 study of 375 television stations across the country showed, unfortunately but not surprisingly, similar figures with respect to the percentages of Hispanics on television news staffs (1988). In fact, the average for Hispanic females in these capacities was lower, .9 percent, while for males it remained at 2.2 percent. However, in his discussion of the placement of minorities on the "talent track," Stone observes, "On the talent track, minority women are as likely as non-minority men and women to be reporting or anchoring. But minority men are much less likely than minority women to have jobs that put them on the air as reporters or anchors. So although black, Hispanic and other minority women are winning on the talent track but tending to lose on the managerial track, minority men [including Hispanics] are double losers. They are underrepresented in both pipelines to advancement in broadcast news" (1988, 18).

Finally, William and Denise Bielby's (1987 and 1989) reports (*The 1987 Hollywood Writers' Report: A Survey of Ethnic, Gender, and Age Employment Practices* and *The 1989 Hollywood Writers' Report: Unequal Access, Unequal Pay*) suggest that when it comes to writing the scripts for television, Hispanics have been given minimal opportunities. Their studies, which aggregate data for all minorities, show participation at rates of at best 3 percent for minority writers for prime-time series.

Despite the bleak picture summarized in this synopsis of Hispanic portrayals and employment in mainstream television, there is evidence that some changes have taken place throughout the years. One of the forces contributing to the gradual changes has been the complaints and protests of concerned individuals and organizations. In her study of how various advocacy groups have affected prime-time television, Montgomery discusses the efforts and struggles of Latino groups (1989). For example, she states that Justicia was a national Mexican American organization "active in media reform campaigns during the early sixties and seventies"; other organizations, such as the National Latino Media Coalition, La Raza, the League of United Latino Citizens (LULAC), and the Mexican American Anti-Defamation Committee "focused on grassroot efforts for reforming local television, although they [also] made some moves to change entertainment television."

As in the mainstream film industry of the United States, Hispanics have been neglected and poorly depicted in a television industry oriented to the dominant society. The future treatment of Latinos in this medium may be contingent on some inroads that individual actors and actresses make. It may also depend on the continued process of organized activities being carried out by advocacy and Latino community groups.

✳ ADVERTISING

Clint Wilson and Félix Gutiérrez state in *Minorities and the Media: Diversity and the End of Mass Communication* (1985) that "advertisers have reflected the place of racial minorities in the social fabric of the nation by either ignoring them or, when they have been included in advertisements for the mass audience, by processing and presenting them so as to make them palatable salespersons for the products being advertised." While no systematic studies have yet been conducted on Hispanic advertising images across time, there is some evidence to support these authors' proposition. For years Hispanics have been practically invisible in mainstream advertising and by extension in employment in this industry (there are no accurate figures of Hispanic employment in this field). When Hispanics have been included in ways palatable to the Anglo majority society, their images have often been quite offensive to fellow Hispanics. Martínez's 1969 work, which discusses various examples of the derisive commercials at the time, pointed out the "Granny Goose chips featuring fat gun-toting Mexicans; and advertisement for Arrid underarm deodorant showing a dusty Mexican bandito spraying his underarms after a hard ride as the announcer intoned, 'If it works for him it will work for you'; a magazine advertisement featuring a stereotypical Mexican sleeping under his sombrero as he leans against a Philco television set; . . . a Liggett & Meyers commercial for L and M cigarettes that featured Paco, a lazy Latino who never 'feenishes' anything, not even the revolution he is supposed to be fighting."

In 1967, the most controversial advertisement with a "Hispanic character" was the Frito Bandito—the Mexican bandit cartoon figure utilized repeatedly by the Frito-Lay Corporation in its television and print promotions of corn chips. In discussions about advertising racism and mistreatment of Hispanics, this example is often cited because of the complaints it generated among Hispanics, especially among Chicano activist and civic groups. Thanks in part to the public protests against Frito-Lay and activists threatening boycotts of television stations airing the commercials, the Frito Bandito figure was discontinued in 1971. The public objections by Hispanics during the 1970s, including the position paper by Latino media activist's Reyes and Rendón (1971), led to some positive changes in the media during the 1970s, just at the dawn of the so-called Hispanic decade. Then, as advertising and marketing companies began to recognize the profitability of this growing sector of society, Hispanic-oriented strategies began to emerge in these industries.

✳ HISPANIC-ORIENTED PRINT MEDIA

Unlike any other ethnic group in the history of the United States, Latinos have had a broad range of mass media directed at them. Beginning with the border newspapers of the 1800s up to present-day inroads in telecommunications, Hispanics have worked hard at establishing and maintaining print and electronic channels through which they can be informed and entertained in ways more relevant to their particular populations and cultures. While most of the Hispanic-oriented media have been in the Spanish language, many have been bilingual and in more recent times, fully English-language products specifically directed at Latinos. Likewise, Hispanics have been owners and producers of a number of mass media institutions oriented to them. However, a significant part of such media have been wholly or partially owned and operated by Anglo individuals or corporations. Whatever the language or ownership, one of the common aspects of all these media is that in their portrayals via images or words, and in their general employment practices, Latinos have been treated much more adequately. In these media, Hispanic life in the United States has been and continues to be presented and reflected more thoroughly, appropriately, and positively.

Newspapers

The Early Years

The Spanish-language press within the national boundaries of the United States had its beginnings in 1808 in New Orleans, Louisiana, with *El Misisipí,* a four-page commercial- and trade-oriented publication "printed primarily in Spanish, but with English translations of many of the articles and almost all of the advertising" (Clint Wilson and Félix Gutiérrez, *Minorities and the Media: Diversity and the End of Mass Communication,* 1985). According to these authors, the paper, which was started by the Anglo firm of William H. Johnson & Company, appeared to be a business venture, its content was heavily influenced by events outside the United States, and it was directed toward Spanish-speaking immigrants—characteristics that were similar to those of other Hispanic-oriented publications that followed.

After the inauguration of *El Misisipí,* dozens of Spanish-language newspapers and periodicals, founded by Mexican pioneers of the times, were published in the southwestern territories, which belonged to Mexico until the 1850s. In fact, the very

first printing press in the Americas was brought to Mexico from Spain in 1535. Thus, for over four centuries, "Hispanic" publications have circulated in this part of the world; some have lasted various decades while others only issued an edition or two. Among the U.S. Hispanic-oriented newspapers, the majority have been published in Spanish but many have been bilingual and a few have been in English but specifically directed at the regional or national Hispanic populations.

Current Status of Newspapers

At present, five Spanish-language newspapers are published daily—two in New York, two in Miami, and one in Los Angeles. Basic information about the history, ownership, editorial policy, and circulation of these is presented in the following pages.

La Opinión

La Opinión (Los Angeles) began publishing on September 16, 1926. It was founded by Ignacio E. Lozano, Sr., a Mexican national who wanted to provide news of the native homeland as well as of the new country for the growing Mexican population in

Ignacio E. Lozano, Jr., Editor-in-Chief, *La Opinión.*

southern California. Lozano went to Los Angeles after working four years for two Texas newspapers and owning and editing his own paper—*La Prensa* of San Antonio—from 1913 to 1926. The move to California was the result of Lozano's view that there were greater Mexican readership needs and opportunities on the West Coast.

From its beginning, *La Opinión* was owned and operated by Lozano and his family, which in 1926 formed Lozano Enterprises, Inc. This company also publishes *El Eco del Valle,* a weekly tabloid distributed in the San Fernando Valley since 1985. On September 28, 1990, 50 percent interest in Lozano Enterprises was purchased by the Times Mirror Company. This major media conglomerate has interests in broadcasting and cable television, and book and magazine publishing; it publishes *The Los Angeles Times, Newsday* (New York), and five other newspapers nationwide. With this association, *La Opinión* has acquired financial resources to enable it to continue improving its product. Despite this new financial affiliation, the Lozano family maintains a majority on the board of directors and continues its full editorial policy and operational control.

José I. Lozano, Publisher, *La Opinión.*

Mónica Lozano-Centanino, Associate Publisher, *La Opinión.*

As of March 31, 1991, *La Opinión*'s circulation was assessed by the Audit Bureau of Circulations (ABC) at 109,558 Monday through Saturday, and 81,773 on Sundays. The vast majority of *La Opinión* newspapers are sold in street stands and a variety of neighborhood stores. Only about 1,300 copies are delivered to home subscribers and approximately 1,000 are sent by mail. According to a 1990 profile of the newspaper's readers, the majority are Mexican and Mexican American (66 percent), but increasingly Central American (15 percent) and South American (5 percent), reflective of the immigration influx of the last two decades. In an effort to better serve the Hispanic community, as well as increase its visibility and number of subscribers, in January 1991, Marti Buscaglia, marketing director of *La Opinión,* initiated the paper's participation in the Newspapers in Education Program. With this program, *La Opinión* is now being used for instructional purposes in over 48 classes in 25 schools.

La Opinión is a broadsheet paper of approximately 48 pages daily; the Sunday edition consists of about 88 pages, including a 32-page, tabloid-style TV guide. Apart from the daily news, opinions, sports, entertainment, and advertising sections, *La Opinión* has special supplements on various weekdays. For example, on Thursdays there is "Comida," a food supplement, and on Fridays, "Deportes locales," with expanded news about local sports, such as the soccer clubs; "Panorama," a tabloid entertainment section; and "De viernes a viernes," a calendar section with special events of the week. On Sundays, there are also various special sections such as "Encuentro," dealing with arts and literature; "Comentarios," with editorials and op-ed columns and opinions; "Viajes," regarding travel and leisure; "Acceso," a life-style section; "TV guía," a television listing guide; and "Tiempo extra," a sports pull-out section.

As of mid-1991, approximately 500 people worked at *La Opinión,* 40 of them (including eight translators) in the editorial department. In addition to its 15 reporters, the major news wire services subscribed to are United Press International (UPI, United States), EFE (Spain), Notimex (Mexico), and Agence France Press (AFP, France). While reporters regularly cover the greater Los Angeles area, no foreign correspondents are permanently located in Latin America or elsewhere.

Peter W. Davidson, President, *El Diario-La Prensa.*

Marti Buscaglia, Director of Marketing, *La Opinión.*

El Diario-La Prensa

El Diario-La Prensa (New York) started in the summer of 1963 from the merger of two newspapers, *La Prensa* and *El Diario de Nueva York.* The former had been operating since 1913 under the ownership of José Campubrí, a Spaniard who kept the paper until 1957, when it was purchased by Fortune Pope. Pope, whose brother was the owner of *The National Enquirer,* was also the owner of the New York Italian paper *Il Progreso* and of WHOM-AM which later became WJIT-AM, one of the most popular Spanish-language radio stations in New York. In 1963, Pope sold *La Prensa* to O. Roy Chalk, who had been owner of *El Diario de Nueva York* since he purchased it in 1961 from Porfirio Domenicci, a Dominican who had started *El Diario* in 1948.

With both papers under his control, Chalk, a Jewish American businessman and president of Diversified Media, merged *El Diario and La Prensa*; he directed the paper from 1963. In 1981, he sold it to the Gannett Company, a major media conglomerate, which at the time owned a chain of 90 English-language papers. In 1989, El Diario Associates, Inc., was formed by Peter Davidson, a former Morgan

Stanley specialist in newspaper industry mergers and acquisitions. This new company then bought *El Diario-La Prensa* from Gannett in August of that year for an estimated $20 million. Carlos D. Ramírez, a Puerto Rican from New York who had been publisher of this newspaper since 1984, stayed on board to participate as a partner of El Diario Associates.

Approximately 139 persons work at the newspaper about 44 of these in the editorial department (writing and editing the news, sports, editorials, and opinions). The newspaper's reporters regularly cover city hall, Manhattan, the Bronx, Brooklyn, and Queens, but *El Diario* also relies on the Associated Press (AP) news wire services for some state and local news. The other major news wire sources it receives are EFE (Spain), Notimex (Mexico), AFP (France), and Deutsche Press Agenteur (Germany). Also, two correspondents cover events in Puerto Rico and the Dominican Republic.

Within its daily average of 56 tabloid-size pages, *El Diario-La Prensa* publishes, in addition to the daily news, opinions, sports, entertainment and advertising sections, a pull-out supplement each day of the week: Mondays, "Deportes," details of weekend

Carlos D. Ramírez, Publisher, *El Diario-La Prensa*.

sporting events; Tuesdays, "Artes y Ciencias," arts and sciences; Wednesdays, "Buen Vivir," food and supermarket specials; Thursdays, "Comunidad," community developments and events; Fridays, "Espectáculos," entertainment; and for the Saturday-Sunday edition, "Siete Días," a summary of the week, and reviews and opinions on diverse topics such as literature, poetry, movies, and politics. During the calendar year, a bridal supplement and another ten to 12 special supplements are published related to events such as the Puerto Rican Parade, the Dominican Republic Parade, Thanksgiving Day, Christmas, New Year's Day, and so forth.

According to the Audit Bureau of Circulation's (ABC) assessment of March 31, 1991, the circulation of *El Diario-La Prensa* was 54,481 from Monday through Friday, and 36,786 for the combined Saturday-Sunday (weekend) edition. Given the difficulty of home delivery in the city of New York, and the transient characteristic of many residents, the newspaper depends almost entirely on "point sales," that is, street sales. Since their beginnings, *La Prensa* and *El Diario de Nueva York* had been primarily directed at the Puerto Rican, Spaniard, and Dominican communities in New York. Presently, *El Diario-La Prensa* caters to a more diverse Hispanic population that, although still principally Puerto Rican, is increasingly more Dominican and Central and South American. Ana Veciana-Suárez, writing about the editorial policy of *El Diario-La Prensa*, stated that "the primary focus of the editorial, without a doubt, is on Hispanic issues, whether local, national, or international" (*Hispanic Media, USA*, 1987). She also indicated that the newspaper has a five-member editorial board that, according to publisher Ramirez, spans a broad range of the political spectrum and gives the paper "a definite independent editorial policy," according to Veciana-Suárez's citation of publisher Ramírez.

Noticias del Mundo

Noticias del Mundo (New York) began publishing on April 22, 1980, under the ownership of News World Communications, Inc., an organization founded in 1976 by the anti-Communist crusader the Reverend Sun Myung Moon and his Unification Church International. News World Communications also publishes the *Washington Times*, the *New York City Tribune, Advista* (a monthly newsletter for the Hispanic marketing community), and various other publications, including *Ultimas Noticias*, a daily newspaper in Uruguay. Although now *Noticias del Mundo* functions more independently from its staunch conservative founder, author Ana Veciana-Suárez cites editor in chief José Cardinali as stating

Phillip V. Sánchez, Publisher, *Noticias del Mundo.*

"we are against dictatorships . . . we cannot abide Marxism"; she adds that the editorial stands are "decidedly conservative in international affairs and pro-Hispanic on domestic issues (*Hispanic Media, USA,* 1987).

Noticias del Mundo is a broadsheet newspaper with an average of 20 pages published from Monday through Friday. Difficulty in home delivery makes this newspaper depend primarily on "point sales." In one of their promotional fliers "More Than Just News," it is indicated that *Noticias* "publishes four editions which serve the primary market areas of New York City, New Jersey, Los Angeles, and San Francisco" and that "each edition reaches into secondary areas such as Philadelphia and Connecticut on the East Coast and San Jose, Las Vegas, Palm Springs/Indio and San Bernardino on the West Coast" for total distribution in 22 cities. Yet its circulation as of mid-1991 was reported at 32,000 in the New York metro area and for their new routes in New Jersey and Boston (started in fall 1990), the figures were 7,300 and 2,450, respectively. Currently, the circulation is not audited by the industry's standard for these matters—the Audit Bureau of Circulations (ABC).

In addition to the typical news, opinions, sports, entertainment and advertising pages, *Noticias del Mundo* has regular weekly sections on legal orientation (Mondays); community, focusing on Puerto Rico and Cuba (Tuesdays); women (Wednesdays); religion and community, focusing on Peru and the Dominican Republic (Thursdays); and entertainment and restaurants (Fridays). On Tuesdays, 2,000 copies of *Noticias* are distributed to five high schools that participate in the Newspaper in Education Program. According to a *Noticias del Mundo* fact sheet, when the paper began to participate in that program in 1986, it became the first Spanish-language newspaper in the United States to do so.

Approximately 150 persons work at this newspaper, about 55 of them in the editorial department. Major Hispanic population centers in New York and surrounding cities are regularly covered by the newspaper's staff. Its principal sources of news wire services include the UPI, AP, Reuter, and EFE. The newspaper has regular free-lance contributors and commentators throughout Latin America and Spain who act as their foreign "correspondents."

El Nuevo Herald

El Nuevo Herald (Miami) was started on November 21, 1987, as a new and improved version of *El Miami Herald,* which had been continuously published since March 29, 1976, as an insert to *The Miami Herald.* Both the Spanish-language and the English-language newspapers are owned by The Miami Herald Publishing Company, a subsidiary of the Knight-Ridder newspaper chain, which has holdings in 29 newspapers across the United States.

In 1987, The Miami Herald Publishing Company recognized the geometric growth of the Hispanic populations in south Florida and, with the support and approval of the Knight-Ridder Corporation, began assessing what Hispanic readers wanted in their Spanish-language daily. The outcome of the study was *El Nuevo Herald,* which moved to a separate building from that of its English-language counterpart to begin publishing from a location closer to the Hispanic community. Other improvements included a 150 percent increase of the daily news space (which now runs approximately 34 pages daily and 50 on Sundays), better coverage of Cuban and Latin American events and communities, the use of color, and a more modern format with improved graphics and layout. Also expanded was the news staff, which increased from 23 to more than 65 in mid-1991. An additional 2,500 persons work for the two Herald newspapers, which share the advertising, marketing, and circulation departments.

As might be expected, given the demographics of

Miami and southern Florida, since its beginnings the principal readers of *El Nuevo Herald* have been immigrant Cuban and Latin American populations residing in that area. This paper, in contrast to its New York counterparts, reaches the majority of its readers via home delivery. The June 1990 circulation, as verified by the Audit Bureau of Circulations (ABC), was 102,856 Monday through Saturdays and 118,756 on Sundays; This broadsheet newspaper also has special weekly sections in addition to the standard sections. Among others these include: a travel section (Sundays); "Vida Social," about social life (Tuesdays); "Gusto," a food section (Thursdays); "A la carte," restaurant listings (Fridays); "Diseñado para vivir," a real estate section; and an automotive section (Saturdays). During the year, an additional 50 special topic sections are also published.

Aside from the news gathering by its own staff, *El Nuevo Herald* can benefit from the work of its English-language partner, including the use of translated stories from the international correspondents. For major stories, *El Nuevo Herald* may send its own reporters to Latin America. Thus, *The Miami Herald* may use stories gathered by *El Nuevo Herald's* foreign or local reporters. The major news wire services for *El Nuevo Herald* are the Spanish-language version of the AP, AFP, Reuter, and EFE. Syndicated information services from various major newspapers are also subscribed to.

Since the 1987 reorganization, *El Nuevo Herald* does not publish editorials. Instead it has its own policy regarding the op-ed page, where various prominent Cuban and Latin American columnists write about politics and other topics. The majority are about Hispanic issues or Cuban interpretations of national or international events. Ana Veciana-Suárez wrote about the Herald's op-ed policy prior to the change: "When dealing with politics, [the columns] tend to be anti-communist and conservative, a reflection of the overwhelming feeling of Miami's Cuban community" (*Hispanic Media, USA,* 1987). This general policy holds today. Prior to the 1987 reorganization, *El Nuevo Herald* only published translations of editorials that appeared on the same day in *The Miami Herald*. At the time, the editor of *El Nuevo Herald* was a member of the English-language paper's editorial board and participated in the discussions about the subjects and points of view. Political candidates were also endorsed in unison by *The Herald's* board.

El Diario de las Américas

El Diario de las Américas (Miami) was founded on July 4, 1953, by Horacio Aguirre, a Nicaraguan lawyer who had been an editorial writer for a Panama-

nian newspaper, *El Panamá-América,* directed by Harmodio Arias, a former president of that country. Part of the financial support needed for starting *El Diario de las Américas* was made possible thanks to a Venezuelan builder-investor and two Pensacola, Florida, road builders who also believed in the founder's mission. The paper is published by The Americas Publishing Company, which is owned by the Aguirre family. *El Diario de las Américas* remains the only Spanish-language daily owned and operated by Hispanics without full or partial partnership by Anglo corporations.

This broadsheet newspaper publishes 28 pages Tuesday through Friday and approximately 45 on Sundays (it is not published Mondays). In mid-1991, the respective circulation for these days was 66,770 and 70,737, as indicated in a sworn statement filed with the Standard Rate and Data Service (SRDS). While a few papers are sold at newsstands, practically all of the circulation is based on home delivery, including 13,367 mail subscriptions to major United States cities and various locations outside the Florida area. Since its beginnings, the principal readers of *El Diario de las Américas* were the Latin American residents of the Miami and southern Florida area. After the massive migration of Cubans from their island in the 1960s, these became the major clients of the paper. A reader profile conducted in 1990 for the paper by Strategy Research Corporation shows that 79.2 percent of the *Diario's* readers were born in Cuba; Nicaragua, with 8.5 percent of the readers born there, was the distant second.

The Cuban and Latin American interests of that readership are evidently reflected in the strong international—particularly Latin American—news coverage of the paper. Those interests are even more notable in the editorial policy of *Diario*. Ana Veciana-Suárez quotes publisher and editor Horacio Aguirre as saying, "Since the fall of Cuba, we consider that one of the biggest problems we face is the Russian-Soviet border 90 miles from here. . . . And we now have Central America in a precarious situation" (*Hispanic Media, USA,* 1987). She goes on to point out that "Aguirre's political leanings are reflected clearly and eloquently in *Diario's* editorials," which he writes and which are, according to Aguirre, "moderately conservative with a strong defense of individual rights." These perspectives are typically expressed in the many opinion columns from various Spanish-speaking writers and the translated columns of well-known Anglos.

To provide the international news of interest to its readers, *El Diario de Las Américas* relies more on the news wire services of UPI, AP, AFP, EFE, Agencia Latinoamericana (ALA), Editors Press, and a few other syndicated services. In addition to its news, opinions, sports, and advertising pages, it has various special weekly sections, such as "Vida Sana," about health (Wednesdays); "De la cocina al comedor," regarding food and cooking (Thursdays); "Sábado Residencial," a home section (Saturdays); "Viajes y turismo," the travel and tourism pages (Sundays); and a restaurant feature, "Buen Provecho," and automotive section, "Automovilismo" (Fridays). *El Diario de las Américas* has a staff of 20 reporters and editorial department employees, and an additional 100 people work in other parts of production at this paper.

The preceding discussion has only provided some of the basic information about the history, ownership, editorial policy, and circulation of the *major* Spanish-language daily newspapers currently published in the United States for Hispanic populations. At least these five enterprises seem to be reaching and serving their respective Hispanic communities while maintaining a stable circulation and advertising base.

Other Daily Publications

In addition to these five major dailies, there are five more daily publications that serve U.S. Hispanic communities. The oldest is the Spanish-language page of the *Laredo Morning Times*. This seven-day-a-week news page has been published continuously since 1926. Also produced in the United States is *El Heraldo de Brownsville* (Texas), published seven days a week by *The Brownsville Herald*. This is a six-page broadsheet edition inaugurated on November 11, 1934, by Oscar del Castillo, who was the founder and editor from its beginning until his death on January 19, 1991. Marcelino González is the current director of this paper serving the Texas Rio Grande Valley region. As of March 31, 1991, this newspaper had an ABC-audited paid circulation of 3,701 weekdays and 4,436 Sundays.

The three other daily publications are *El Fronterizo, El Mexicano,* and *El Continental*—respectively the morning, afternoon, and evening editions published by the Compañía Periodística del Sol de Ciudad Juárez. *El Fronterizo,* published since 1943, is the largest of the three, with six daily sections each of approximately eight pages. As of mid-1991, its circulation was approximately 36,000 Monday through Sundays. *El Mexicano,* published since 1950, is more condensed and contains about ten pages; its circulation figures are 29,000 Monday through Saturdays. *El Continental,* founded in 1933, has only eight pages and a Monday through Saturday circulation of 8,000. While all three newspapers have as major clients the Mexicans and U.S. Hispa-

nics in El Paso and surrounding communities, they are published in Ciudad Juárez by the Organización Editorial Mexicana, representing 78 newspapers in that country.

One final newspaper that during the late 1980s and early 1990s has occasionally published on a daily schedule is *El Mañana* (Chicago). It was founded in May 1971 by Gorki Tellez, who at the time was a community activist and owner of a small truck catering business. Financial difficulties have restricted the continuity and success of this newspaper's daily publication effort.

Aside from the aforementioned dailies, it is estimated that across the nation over 250 newspaper-type publications directed especially to the diverse Hispanic populations in the United States are produced from as frequently as twice a week to once or twice a month. Many of these publications have been and still are the product of extraordinary efforts of individuals in their local communities. The irregular and transitory nature of their products, which often have very limited circulation, has made it very difficult to develop any comprehensive and updated directory of all such newspapers.

Nevertheless, the most recent edition of the *Hispanic Media and Markets* guide, produced by the SRDS (1991) lists 101 of what could be classified as the most enduring of these publications. Our analysis of the information in the "Community Newspaper" section of this directory yields the following data. Spanish is the main language of the publications, with 74 titles; 24 are bilingual; and three are printed in English with a Spanish-language page. Of the first group, 58 are published at least once a week and of these weeklies 19 are produced in California. Of the Spanish-language weeklies, 45 are distributed for free and only six report selling most of their papers; this data was not indicated for seven titles. Of these Spanish-language weeklies, 32 indicate circulations of over 20,000 copies; 12 circulate between 10,000 and 20,000 copies; the remainder print 5,000 or less. Two of the bilingual periodicals are published by major English-language newspapers, both in California. *Nuestro Tiempo,* with a paid circulation of about 100,000 and free delivery of over 354,000, is published 15 times per year by *The Los Angeles Times. Vida en el Valle,* which circulates 30,000 free copies in the San Joaquín Valley, is produced by the *Fresno Bee.*

Finally, dozens of Spanish-language newspapers from Spain, Mexico, Puerto Rico, Venezuela, Colombia, Chile, and numerous other Latin American countries also reach the newsstands in U.S. cities with large Hispanic populations. While few, if any, of these are published primarily for the Latin American immigrant or U.S. Hispanic, they are important sources of information widely sought and read, especially by the most recent of the immigrants.

Magazines and Other Periodicals

Long before the turn of the century, a variety of publications that can be classified as "U.S. Hispanic-oriented magazines" have been produced. The rich history of these publications can be observed in the holdings of major libraries such as the Benson Mexican American collection at the University of Texas at Austin and the Chicano Studies Collections of the University of California, Berkeley, Los Angeles, and Santa Barbara. Alejandra Salinas (1990) recently compiled a partial listing of 137 titles of past and present Hispanic magazines, journals, and newsletters. While a comprehensive anthology of all such publications is still lacking, even a cursory review of the titles shows that culturally-oriented magazines have abounded, as have many with political, social, education, business, and entertainment topics. Carlos Cortés (1991) briefly mentions the following among those that have ceased to publish but were prominent during the last 30 years: "Los Angeles' iconoclastic *La Raza* (1967–75), Denver's establishmentarian *La Luz* (1971–1981), the National Council of La Raza's policy-oriented *Agenda* (1970–81), and New York's (later Washington's) feature-oriented *Nuestro* (1974–84)." Although copies of these now can only be found in some libraries, dozens of others magazines, especially consumer-oriented publications, are attempting to fill the demands of Hispanic readers.

The 1991 edition of the *Hispanic Media and Markets* guide of the Standard Rate and Data Service provides descriptions of advertising-related information of 65 titles under its section "Consumer Magazines." While this catalog contains indispensable data for marketing and advertising interests, it is neither comprehensive nor the most accurate listing of U.S. Hispanic-oriented magazines. For example, the list includes many specialty magazines (such as in-flight publications for Latin American airlines), magazines published in Puerto Rico primarily for Puerto Ricans, and various other titles for which U.S. Hispanics are not the primary targets. On the other hand, it excludes smaller magazines and various academic journals with limited state or regional circulation.

Nevertheless, from data in the SRDS publication and other information about this field, highlights can be provided about nine Hispanic-oriented magazines with national circulation produced and published in the United States. Four are published in Spanish, three in English, and two in both. The distribution figures in this section are divided into paid, free, and "controlled" circulation. The difference between the second and the third terms is that under "controlled" circulation the magazine knows who it gratuitously sends the publication to, thus it has some knowledge and control of the demographics of its audience. This is usually not the case under "free" circulation of magazines in which they are placed in public places for readers to pick up at will. Some publications also have their circulation verified; for magazines this is usually done by the Business Publications Audit (BPA).

Of the Spanish-language magazines, the oldest is *Temas,* which has been published on a monthly basis continuously since November 1950 in New York City by Temas Corporation, whose main partners are Spaniards and U.S. Hispanics. It circulates over 110,000 copies per month, of which 106,000 are paid purchases. *Temas* averages 62 pages and measures $8\frac{1}{2}$ by 11 inches and features articles on culture, current events, beauty, fashion, home decoration, and interviews with personalities of various artistic and academic backgrounds of interest to the Spanish-speaking populations in the United States. This general interest, family-oriented magazine was founded by publisher and editor José de la Vega, a Spaniard, who has indicated that *Temas* is the only national magazine published in Castilian Spanish without trendy "idioms." Given this editorial style, many of its articles are widely reprinted in high school and university reading packages across the country.

The second Spanish-language magazine is *Réplica,* which was founded in 1963 by Alex Lesnik, a Cuban immigrant who still owns the publication. From its base in Miami, this monthly magazine had as of March 1991 a circulation (BPA-verified) of 110,745 nationwide, of which approximately 96 percent was controlled—targeted to reach bilingual, bicultural, affluent opinion makers and other influential Hispanics in the United States. In its 50 pages, which measure $8\frac{1}{2}$ by 11 inches, there are a variety of articles on topics such as travel, fashion, sports, entertainment, and news events related to Latin America and the Caribbean Basin.

Another publication in this category is *Más* (More). Its first issue was published in September 1989, when it started on a quarterly basis; that year there was also a winter edition. In 1991, it became bimonthly starting with the January-February issue. According to BPA figures, as of November 1990, approximately 562,000 subscribers received the magazine free of charge. One reason for this gratuitous service is that the magazine is produced in New York by Univisión Publications, part of Univision

Holdings, which is owned by Hallmark Cards, Inc. This greetings card company is also owner of the Spanish-language television network *Univisión*. *Más* is this company's first magazine and provides significant promotion for its television programs and personalities. Its average 88 pages, measuring 8½ by 11 inches, feature stories about television programs and personalities and a variety of topics, such as music, fashion, beauty, sports, cuisine, travel, and occasionally politics.

A recent Spanish-language magazine is *La Familia de Hoy*. This larger-size magazine, measuring 10 by 13 inches and averaging 56 pages, was founded with an issue dated March/April 1990. It continues to be published six times a year in Knoxville, Tennessee, by Whittle Communications, which is half owned by Time-Warner Corporation, a major U.S. media conglomerate. The circulation, approximately 50,000 and BPA-verified, also relies on complimentary controlled subscriptions, which are provided mainly to beauty salons, doctors, dentists, and similar qualified offices in the top 33 markets with high Hispanic populations and clientele. Its home circulation is about 3,000.

Three English-language magazines of particular note are *Hispanic, Hispanic Business,* and *Hispanic Link. Hispanic* published its premier issue in April 1988. According to one of its promotional pages, the major focus of this "magazine for and about Hispanics" is on contemporary Hispanics and their achievements and contributions to American society. Thus, the stories cover a broad range of topics, such as entertainment, education, business, sports, the arts, government, politics, literature, and national and international personalities and events that may be of importance and interest to Hispanics in the United States. *Hispanic* is owned by Hispanic Publishing Corporation, based in Washington, D.C. This is a family company of chairman and founder Fred Estrada, a native of Cuba. His son, Alfredo, is the current publisher. The first publisher was Jerry Apodaca, a Mexican American and former governor of New Mexico. A total of 150,000 copies of *Hispanic,* which measures 8½ by 11 inches and averages 66 pages, are printed for each of the 11 monthly issues (the December-January magazine is a combined number). The BPA audits indicate that approximately 40,000 copies are for paid subscriptions and the majority of the remainder are for controlled distribution directed to, among others, the U.S. Hispanic Chamber of Commerce and the Hispanic National Bar Association. Also, 1,500 copies are distributed to 300 schools that participate in a special academic-oriented program known as America's Hispanic Education Achievement Drive (AHEAD).

Hispanic Business, according to its own promotional material, is "the oldest established business magazine oriented toward the US Hispanic market." It is published in Santa Barbara, California, by Hispanic Business, Inc., under the directorship of editor and publisher, Jesús Chavarría, a Mexican American who started the magazine in 1979 as a newsletter; it was turned into a regular monthly publication in 1982. The magazine, averaging 56 pages and measuring 8½ by 11 inches, has a circulation recently certified at 150,000. Over 90 percent of the distribution is controlled. One of its regular departments covers news related to "Media/Marketing." Special monthly topics include, among others, statistics and trends in the Hispanic media markets (December); the Hispanic "Business 500"—the annual directories of the leading Hispanic-owned corporations in the United States (June); and Hispanics in the mainstream television, film, music, and related entertainment businesses (July).

The third English-language Hispanic-oriented publication is *Hispanic Link.* Although it is a newsletter and not a "magazine" per se, it is a very important and influential publication that provides a succinct summary of the major issues and events

Charlie Erikson, founding editor, Hispanic Link News Service.

related to education, immigration, business, legislative, political, policy, and economic concerns of the Hispanic populations in the United States. Weekly summary columns include "Arts and Entertainment" and a "Media Report." It averages six pages, measuring 8½ by 11 inches and is published weekly (50 weeks per year) in Washington, D.C., by Hispanic Link News Service, Inc. *Hispanic Link* was founded by Mexican American Charles A. Erickson in February 1980 as a column service for newspapers. In September 1983 it became a regular newsletter. Although it only claims approximately 1,200 subscribers, its circulation and readership is much higher as it reaches many libraries, Hispanic organization leaders, people in corporations with major responsibilities toward Hispanics, journalists, Hispanic advocacy groups, and influential government officials working with or interested in legislation and policy issues related to Hispanics. *Hispanic Link* solicits columns from various journalists and experts on subjects concerning Hispanics and provides those articles as a syndicated service of three columns per week to more than 85 newspapers across the country via the *Los Angeles Times* syndicated news service.

The two most notable bilingual magazines are *Vista* and *Saludos Hispanos* (*Regards, Hispanics*). *Vista,* with its headquarters in Miami, Florida, started in September 1985 as a monthly supplement insert to selected Sunday newspapers in locations with large Hispanic populations. Although *Vista* was published in English on a weekly basis from late 1989 through June 1991, financial problems resulting from the general national economic situation, particularly insufficient advertising support, made it return to its monthly schedule. Since June 1991, in addition to its English-language articles, it has incorporated "mosaico"—a Spanish-language supplement with three stories. It has also increased to 24 pages on average (when it was a weekly, it averaged 12 pages). *Vista,* measuring 10½ by 11 inches, is aimed at informing, educating, and entertaining Hispanic American readers with stories that focus on Hispanic role models, positive portrayals of Hispanics, and their cultural identity. As of September 1991, *Vista* was inserted in 31 different newspapers in eight states—Arizona, California, Colorado, Florida, Illinois, New Mexico, New York, and Texas. Given its form of distribution, its total circulation, which is BPA-verified, was estimated at approximately 924,000. *Vista* was originally published by Horizon Communications, a Hispanic company owned by Arturo Villar, the first publisher, and Harry Caicedo, editor at the time; the former is a Spanish Cuban and the latter of Colombian ancestry. In February 1991, these initial founders were

dismissed from *Vista* after a series of disagreements with other members of the magazine's management. At the time, *Vista's* two largest shareholders were Hycliff Partners, a New York investment group, which owned 28 percent, and Time-Warner Inc., which held 25 percent (*The Wall Street Journal,* 1991). In April 1991, Hycliff Partners and Times-Warner reduced their share of *Vista* to 12 percent each as majority ownership (approximately 65 percent) of the magazine was purchased by Fred Estrada and his Hispanic Publishing Corporation, which, as indicated earlier, is also the owner of *Hispanic* magazine.

Saludos Hispanos, "the official publication of the United Council of Spanish Speaking People," is owned by Rosemarie García-Solomon, a Mexican American. When it began publishing in September 1985, it was a quarterly magazine, but as of January 1991 it turned to six publications per year with a national circulation of approximately 300,000. Since this date, it has also been changing its distribution from a free insert in selected newspapers to direct paid subscription to individuals and sales at magazine stands. Nevertheless, a significant part of its circulation still goes to about 3,000 schools, universities, and various institutions in California, Florida, Illinois, New York, and Texas, which use the magazine for educational purposes. One reason for *Saludos Hispanos'* educational value is that within its average 92 pages, which measure 9 by 12 inches, it publishes side-by-side Spanish and English versions of most of its stories. Furthermore, it stresses positive role models for and about Hispanics. In addition to articles on the feature topic, the regular departments include, among others, role models, music, careers, earth watch, university profile, fashion, law and order, museums, and food. Another educational distinction of this publication company is its *Saludos Hispanos Video Magazín*—a three-part video program that has been used by over 4,000 schools and organizations for recruitment and retention of Hispanic youth in the educational system. According to its promotional page, the video, available in English and a Spanish-language dubbed version, is designed to motivate Hispanic youth to stay in school, to improve relationships, and to stress the importance of cultural pride and self-esteem as keys to success.

In addition these publications, there are dozens of Spanish-language consumer magazines with specialized topics related to parenthood, fashion, hobbies, and social, cultural, and political interests. All are readily available in the United States via subscriptions or magazine racks in Hispanic communities in major cities. Examples of these are

Buenhogar, Cosmopolitan, Geomundo, Hombre del Mundo, Harper's Bazaar en Español, Mecánica Popular, Selecciones del Reader's Digest, Tu Internacional, and *Vanidades Continental,* just to name a few of the most popular. As can be observed by the titles, some are Spanish-language editions of English-language publications. Regardless of where these are produced, be it Spain, the United States, or Latin America, they have as primary clients any and all Spanish-speaking populations. Other specialized magazines in Spanish and/or English are produced with the U.S. Hispanic as the primary client, for example, *Automundo, Buena Salud, Career Focus* (also targeted to Afro-Americans), *Embarazo, Hispanic American Family, Hispanic Youth-USA, Mi Bebé, Ser Padre, Teleguía, TV y Novelas USA, Una Nueva Vida,* the northeastern U.S. edition of *Imagen,* and the Hispanic youth-oriented automobile publication *Lowrider.*

Furthermore, there are journals with specialized topics related to academia, professions, and organizations. Among the current academic journals are *Aztlán, The Americas Review,* the *Bulletin of the Centro de Estudios Puertorriqueños,* the *Hispanic Journal of Behavioral Sciences, Journal of Hispanic Policy,* and the *Latino Studies Journal.*

And finally, there are state and regional publications aimed at the respective Hispanic or Spanish-speaking populations. Examples of these are *Adelante* (Washington, D.C.), *Avance Hispano* (San Francisco), *Cambio!* (Phoenix), *La Voz de Houston* (Houston), *La Voz* (Seattle), *Miami Mensual,* and *Bienvenidos a Miami, Tele Guía de Chicago* and *Lea* (directed at Colombians residing in the United States). In these cities and dozens of others with large Hispanic concentrations, one can even find Spanish and/or Hispanic yellow pages—the telephone-type directories.

As can be discerned from this section, the number of magazines and other periodicals available to Hispanics in the United States is very extensive and diverse. No other ethnic minority population in this country has such an array of printed materials.

✳ HISPANIC-ORIENTED ELECTRONIC MEDIA

"Hispanic broadcasting comes of age," proclaimed *Broadcasting* magazine in a 1989 special report reviewing the growth, financial status, and related developments of Spanish-language radio and television. Why such assessment? One reason is that the number of stations, companies, and organizations related to Spanish-language radio and television in this country has grown, as has the content they offer.

Radio, for example, not only offers *rancheras* and *salsa,* but also Top 40, mariachi, *norteña,* Tex-Mex, Mexican hits, adult contemporary, contemporary Latin hits, international hits, Spanish adult contemporary, romantic, ballads, traditional hits and oldies, folkloric, regional, *boleros,* progressive *tejano, merengue,* and even bilingual contemporary hits. Television is no longer song-and-dance shows with some novellas and old movies. It is also drama, talk shows, comedy, news, investigative journalism, sports, contemporary movies, entertainment magazines, dance videos, and many specials from all over the world. All of these options have been brought by the search for new markets by both Hispanic and Anglo entrepreneurs, and the combined growth of the Hispanic population and its purchasing power.

In fact, in some markets the Hispanic audience for selected Spanish-language radio and television stations is larger than that of many well-known English-language stations; for example, in Los Angeles, KLVE-FM and KWKW-AM have more listeners than KNX-AM and KROQ-FM). The "coming of age" that was evident in 1989 is even more evident today. Radio directed to the U.S. Hispanic market has grown from an occasional voice heard on isolated stations in the Southwest and on big city multilingual stations to a multimillion-dollar segment of the broadcast industry. Today there are hundreds of Spanish-language radio stations, a couple of Hispanic commercial and public radio owners' associations, various specialized news services, and at least five major advertising representatives for this expanding market.

Radio

The Early Years

Spanish-language radio programs transmitted from within the boundaries of the United States began as early as the mid-1920s—almost immediately after the inauguration of commercial broadcasting in this country. While Hispanic-oriented radio is now quite diversified and can be found in almost every community with an established Hispanic population, its development has been slow and difficult. In their accounts of the history of this ethnic medium, Jorge Schement and Ricardo Flores (in *Journalism History,* 1977) and Felix Gutiérrez and Jorge Schement (*Spanish-language Radio in Southwestern United States,* 1979) indicate that Spanish-language radio started in the mid-1920s when English-language radio stations began selling time slots to Latino brokers. These brokers, some of whom had previous radio experience in Mexico, "paid the stations a flat rate for the airtime, sold advertisements to local business and programmed the broad-

Pedro J. González, pioneer of Spanish-language radio in California.

thanks to its 100,000-watt power could be heard at that time all over the Southwest—even as far as Texas—thus reaching thousands of Mexican workers as they started their day. The dynamics of González's show and his progressive political stands made him a threat to the establishment, resulting in trumped-up rape charges against him in 1934. He was convicted and condemned to six years in San Quentin prison, released in 1940, and immediately deported to Mexico. In Tijuana he reestablished and continued his radio career until the 1970s, when he returned and retired in the United States. Many others across the Southwest followed Pedro's footsteps in the new medium.

In San Antonio, Lalo Astol was an early voice heard on Spanish-language radio as emcee for the program "La Hora Comercial Mexicana" on English-language station KMAC. Astol was a well-known theater personality and appeared on stage at the Nacional and other theaters. As gathered during interviews by Nicolás Kanellos (1990), in 1952 Astol also began doing soap operas in Spanish on Cortez's KCOR, acted in a radio drama series, "Los Abuelitos," and emceed a quiz show, "El Marko." In 1956, Astol moved on to Spanish-language television,

casts themselves. The difference between what they took in from advertising and paid to the station for the airtime was their profit" (Gutiérrez and Schement). During the early days of radio, the stations that sold these slots and the time frames that were made available to brokers depended on the local market competition among stations and the profitability of the various airtimes. Invariably, space for foreign-language programming was provided primarily during the least profitable time (early mornings or weekends) and by stations seeking alternative avenues for revenue.

One of the most well known pioneers of Spanish-language radio in California was Pedro J. González, about whom two films have been made: the documentary *Ballad of an Unsung Hero* (1984, Paul Espinosa, writer and producer) and the full-length feature *Break of Dawn* (1988, Isaac Artenstein, director). According to the interviews and documents gathered by Espinosa, between 1924 and 1934 González was responsible for shows such as "Los Madrugadores" ("The Early Birds").

This program was broadcast from 4:00 to 6:00 A.M., primarily on Los Angeles station KMPC, which

Pedro J. González's singing group, Los Madrugadores.

LE QUITARAN LA DESIGNACION A VALENZUELA

LA OPINION

DIARIO POPULAR INDEPENDIENTE

**PEDRO J. GONZALEZ, CULPABLE;
1 A 50 AÑOS EN SAN QUINTIN!**

Banner headlines in *La Opinión* newspaper announcing the guilty verdict in the Pedro J. González case.

where he participated in various writing, directing, and acting roles. He currently works for San Antonio radio KUKA doing "El Mercado del Aire."

Even through the early brokerage system, Spanish-language radio thrived. By the late 1930s, numerous stations carried Spanish-language programs either full-time or part-time. In response to the market demands, in 1939 the International Broadcasting Company (IBC) was established in El Paso, Texas, to produce and sell Spanish-language programming to various stations and brokers across the country. As a result of the efforts of services like the IBC and the work by dozens of independent brokers, by 1941 it was estimated that 264 hours of Spanish were being broadcast each week by U.S. broadcasters.

Gutiérrez and Schement, citing sources who have written of the early days of radio, indicate that ethnic-language programming, especially in Spanish, proved economically successful, as the emotional impact of an advertising message wrapped in the music and drama of the listener's native language was more appealing than the same message in English. Therefore, from the beginning, the goal behind for-

eign-language programming was the same as with English-language broadcasting: to make profits via advertising.

In Texas, Raúl Cortez was one of the earliest Chicano brokers and eventually was successful enough to establish and operate his own full-time Spanish-language station—KCOR-AM, a 1,000-kilowatt "daytime only" station in San Antonio—which went on the air in 1946. Nine years later, Cortez ventured into the Spanish-language television industry. Gutiérrez and Schement indicate that after World War II, Anglo station owners and Hispanic brokers saw increasing opportunities in the Hispanic market via Spanish-language radio. This allowed some brokers to follow Cortez's lead and become owners of full-time stations. Most, however, were made employees of the stations they had been buying time from. Such were the initial stages of Spanish-language radio programming and stations.

From the 1950s to the 1970s, Spanish-language radio was in transition. During those decades, this radio format continued to grow but began moving away from the brokerage system in favor of the more independent, full-time stations in AM and subsequently in FM—many transmitting up to 24 hours per day. In terms of the content, the early "broker" years were characterized by poetry, live drama, news, and live music programming. Most of the live music was "Mexican" and the majority of the news was from foreign countries, predominantly Mexico. As musical recordings became more common, this less expensive form of programming replaced the live music, allowing brokers and the stations to keep more of their profits for themselves. During the transition years, "personality radio" was at its best; brokers and announcers who had control over their programs and commercials became popular themselves. By the late 1960s, the format became more tightly packaged and was less in the hands of individual radio stars. Music was selected by the station management to give a consistent sound throughout the programs. These broadcasts had less talk than before and were very much like other music-oriented English-language programs. In the 1970s, the stations' growth also brought increased attention to format programming on the air and to sophisticated marketing techniques on the business side. One interesting note about Spanish-language broadcast stations is that almost all the announcers came from Latin America, despite the growth of the U.S. Hispanic audiences. While no research has been done to explain this employment practice, it is perhaps because station managers perceived that the Spanish of U.S. Hispanics was of poorer quality.

The phenomenal expansion of Spanish-language

TABLE 24.1
RADIO STATIONS OWNED AND CONTROLLED BY HISPANICS

	1982	1983	1984	1985	1986	1990	1991
AM	33	31	31	29	35	64	58
FM	13	9	8	8	9	24	21

Sources: 1982–86 data: National Association of Broadcasters, Department of Minority and Special Services (1986); 1990–91 data: Minority Telecommunications Development Program of the National Telecommunications and Information Administration, U.S. Department of Commerce (October 1991).

radio in the United States, especially during the late 1980s, is illustrated by the following figures. In 1974, there were 55 stations that broadcast in Spanish at least half of their airtime and there were an additional 425 that broadcast in this format less than half of their airtime (Gutiérrez and Schement). By 1980, the respective numbers were 64 and 436 (Schement and Singleton, 1981). In 1986, 73 stations broadcast over half their time in Spanish (no comparable figures were provided for part-time Spanish-language stations).

Current Status of Radio

According to the 1991 Standard Rate and Data Service's (SRDS') *Hispanic Media and Markets* guide, as of June 1991 there were 35 AM and 112 FM full-time Spanish-language radio stations and an additional 77 AM and 16 FM stations that dedicated a significant part (but not the majority) of their broadcast time to Spanish programming. This SRDS data, however, is less comprehensive than the 1991 *Broadcasting Yearbook,* which lists 185 AM and 68 FM stations transmitting full-time in Spanish. Under this publication's "Special Programming" section, an additional 197 AM and 203 FM stations are listed as airing Spanish programs at least a few hours per week. Regardless of which source one chooses to view, the statistics provide indisputable evidence that Spanish-language radio is a powerful and growing ethnic medium in the United States.

While these numbers attest to a remarkable growth of the Hispanic-oriented radio industry, Hispanic *ownership* of these radio stations has not followed similar patterns. According to Schement and Singleton (1981), in 1980, of the 64 primary Spanish-language radio stations identified in their study, only 25 percent were owned by Latinos. In the top ten markets (for example, New York, Los Angeles, Chicago, Miami, San Antonio), Latinos owned only about 10 percent of these types of stations. Primary Spanish-language radio (PSLR) stations are those that transmit in Spanish 50 percent or more of their broadcast day. After discussing figures on ownership of assets and employment statistics at the various levels of a station's hierarchy, Schement and Single-

ton conclude that "PSLR stations can be described as owned and operated predominantly by Anglos."

More recent statistics, gathered by the National Association of Broadcasters and the Minority Telecommunications Development Program (MTDP) of the National Telecommunications and Information Administration on minority-owned and -controlled broadcast stations, shed some additional light on the issue of Hispanic control over radio stations.

Apparently these two agencies used different criteria for identifying or classifying Hispanic-owned and -controlled radio. Otherwise, it seems that the number of Hispanic-owned radio stations more than doubled between 1986 and 1990. However, the Minority telecommunications Development Program (MTDP) data suggest that there has been a decline between 1990 and 1991. It will be important to observe future statistics from this same source to assess which way the market is going. One other fact to keep in mind when considering these statistics is that they are not indicators of the programming language the Hispanic-owned stations; it is unclear whether Spanish or English is used full- or part-time. It is only coincidental that all the Hispanic-owned stations listed in the radio directory in the 1990–91 MTDP report are primarily Spanish-language stations. This fact allows for an approximate calculation of the current percentage of Hispanic-owned PSLR stations. The 58 AM and the 21 FM stations listed in the MTDP report constitute 32 percent and 31 percent of the Spanish-language AM and FM stations listed in the *Broadcasting Yearbook* that same year. Altogether, this represents a slight increase from the 25 percent assessed by Schement and Singleton (1981) ten years ago.

Another important issue about the ownership of Hispanic-oriented radio is the trend toward concentration of various stations, particularly the most profitable ones, under major corporate groups.

Major Spanish-language Radio Corporations

The oldest and largest Hispanic-oriented radio corporation is Tichenor Media System, Inc., a family-owned private company based in Dallas, Texas, which presently owns 11 full-time Spanish-language radio stations in the following locations: New York (WADO-AM), Miami (WQBA-AM and FM), Chicago (WIND-AM and WOJO-FM), San Antonio (KCOR-AM), Houston (KLAT-AM), Brownsville-Harlingen-McAllen (KGBT-AM and KIWW-FM), and El Paso (KBNA-AM and FM). Tichenor also has partial ownership of another Spanish-language station in Corpus Christi (KUNO-AM). This company was started in 1940 by McHenry Tichenor, a successful Anglo newspaperman who in 1941 bought his second radio station in south Texas, which at the time broadcast half a day in English and half a day in Spanish. This was the family's first venture into the Hispanic market. According to a Tichenor Media Systems summary sheet, the expansion into the Spanish radio field began in 1984 when, "under the directions of the second and third generations of the Tichenor family, the Company restructured its Corporate goal and formed Tichenor Spanish Radio." At that time, the non-Spanish-language broadcast properties, including television, were divested to allow for the new ventures into the Hispanic market. In 1990, Spanish Radio Network was formed in partnership with SRN Texas, Inc. (a wholly owned subsidiary of Tichenor Media Systems) and Radio WADO, Inc., in order to

McHenry Tichenor, founder of Tichenor Media Systems.

purchase the Miami and the New York stations. As of this writing, the Tichenor company, with McHenry Taylor Tichenor, Jr., as president, continues to seek new stations in major Hispanic markets, particularly in Los Angeles. This corporate goal can be understood, because in 1991, five of the company's stations were among the nation's top ten in billings for this market and accounted for as much as $21.4 million in revenues.

The second-largest group owner of Spanish-language radio stations is Spanish Broadcasting System (SBS), which was started in 1983 by Raúl Alarcón, Jr. This company, the only radio group company whose proprietors are Hispanics, now owns six stations in the top three Latino markets: New York (WSKQ-AM and FM), Los Angeles (KSKQ-AM and FM), and Miami (WCMQ-AM and FM), plus a station in Key Largo, Florida (WZMQ-FM), that retransmits the Miami station's signals. According to Lopes (1991), the combined AM/FM stations were also among the top ten in billings in 1991, accounting for $23.1 million in revenues for SBS. Mendosa states that Alarcón has been successful in acquiring so many stations because he is extremely "persistent in taking advantage of several options that the FCC makes available to minority broadcasters" (1990). In addition to its own stations, SBS is the national sales representative for six stations in Texas, six in California, and three in Illinois. The company also develops revenues from its SBS Promotions (for example, of concerts, sporting events, supermarket tie-ins, and on-air contests) and from Alarcón holdings in real estate. In 1990, SBS' combined capital of $32.3 million made it, according to Mendosa (1990), the fifty-second largest Hispanic company in the United States.

Lotus Communications Corporation owns a third group of Spanish-language radio stations. The flagstaff operation is KWKW-AM, a station that has been serving the Hispanic community in Los Angeles and vicinities since 1942. It was purchased by Lotus in 1962 for approximately $1 million. The price was a reflection of the large audience it attracts, especially among the Mexican and Mexican American populations of that region. A recent audience estimate placed the number of listeners at over one million (at least during one "day-part," that is, time segment), making it among the largest in the United States and a few Latin American cities. Other Spanish-language stations owned by Lotus are KOXR-AM in Oxnard, California (bought in 1968), WTAQ-AM in Chicago (since 1985), and KGST-AM in Fresno (since 1986). All four of these stations are identified as La Mexicana in their respective markets because the music, programming, and the disc jockeys follow a

Mexican format in idioms and accents. Another distinctive programming feature of these stations is that they broadcast Los Angeles Dodger baseball games and retransmit these to 148 stations in Mexico. Lotus owns ten other radio outlets in the United States, all of which are English-language stations. In addition, under Lotus Hispanic Reps, this company is sales representative to approximately 100 Spanish-language radio stations in the United States. The president of Lotus Communications is Howard Kalmenson; the vice president is Jim Kalmenson. Both are Anglos, as are the other owners of the company. The executive vice president is Joe Cabrera; he is Hispanic, as are the respective station managers. In 1991, billings for KWKW on its own totaled $10.3 million, making it the single most profitable Spanish-language station in the country. According to Kalmenson, the success of this station has helped fund the growth of the entire company, which continues its operations with no capital debt.

A fourth Spanish-language radio group is *Radio América,* founded in 1986 when brothers Daniel and James Villanueva, of Mexican heritage, bought stations KBRG-FM in the San Francisco Bay Area. In 1988, they acquired station KLOK-AM in the San Jose/San Francisco area. Lopes estimates that these two stations had net billings of $3.4 million in 1991. According to a fact sheet provided by the corporate management, KLOK was bought "using a separate shell company—Bahia Radio." The fact sheet adds that at the end of 1991, the Villanuevas, under a separate company called Orange County Broadcasting, purchased station KPLS-AM in Los Angeles. A distinctive characteristic of this station, with 20 percent ownership by Fernando Niebla, also of Mexican descent, is that it is the first "all talk" Spanish-language station in the Los Angeles and southern California area (there are four "talk" stations in the Miami market). Daniel Villanueva also has minority (20 percent) interests in Washington, D.C.'s Los Cerezos Broadcasting Company, which owns WMDO-AM and WMDO-TV Channel 48—a Univisión affiliate.

Yet another Spanish-language radio group is the *Viva América* company, which was started in 1989 with 49 percent owned by Heftel Broadcasting and 51 percent owned by Mambisa Broadcasting Corporation. Heftel owns stations in Los Angeles (KLVE-FM and KTNQ-AM). Mambisa is divided among Amancio V. Suárez, his son Amancio J. Suárez, and cousin Charles Fernández, all of whom are of Cuban descent. In Miami, the Viva America Media Group owns two stations (WAQI-AM and WXDJ-FM). In addition, under the corporate heading of the Southern Media Holding Group, presided over by Amancio

Amancio V. Suárez of Viva América Media Group.

V. Suárez, it is also linked to *Mi Casa*—a monthly Spanish-language newspaper. Despite its recent entry into the market, Viva América earned $10.1 million in billings in 1991, almost doubling the figure of the previous year; the two Heftel stations were the top in the Spanish-language radio market, totaling $16.3 million for the same year (Lopes).

A final group of stations that are especially distinct from the aforementioned ones are administered by the nonprofit Radio Bilingüe (Bilingual Radio) network in California. Efforts to establish this network date to 1976, when Hugo Morales, a Harvard Law School graduate of Mexican Mixtec Indian heritage, and Lupe Ortiz y Roberto Páramo, in collaboration with a group of Mexican peasants, artists, and activists sought to use radio to improve life and sustain the cultural identity of farm workers of the San Joaquin Valley. With the significant backing of a grant from a Catholic charity, KSJV-FM was launched in Fresno, California, on July 4, 1980. It transmits a variety of music programs, plus a diversity of information related to health, education, immigration, civic action, and the arts. Supported primarily by donations from community members, businesses, and some foundations, the Radio Bilingüe network now reaches across central California via KSJV and two retransmitting stations in Bakersfield and Modesto. In southern California, some of the network's programs are also aired by affiliate KUBO-FM, which started in El Centro on April, 1989, producing some of its own independent programming. Radio Bilingüe also sponsors the "Viva El Mariachi" ("Long Live the Mariachi"), a music festival that serves as an important fund-raiser for the network. One of the distinctive features of this network is the operational and programming support it receives from innumerable volunteers who produce diverse music and public service programs in English, Spanish, and bilingual format. Radio Bilingüe is currently the largest noncommercial producer of Spanish-language and bilingual programs. Another feature of Radio Bilingüe is its news service, "Noticiero Latino" ("Latin Newscast").

Hispanic-Oriented Radio Organizations

Due to increased pressures in the commercial and public radio markets, two organizations serving the interests of this sector were established in 1991. The first was the American Hispanic-Owned Radio Association (AHORA), which started with 55 Hispanic station owners concerned with competition for the Hispanic market and with the rapid pace at which Spanish-language radio stations are being bought by non-Hispanics. According to *Broadcasting* magazine (1991), AHORA, under the direction of Mary Helen Barro (majority owner of KAFY-AM in Bakersfield, California), seeks to "increase the number of business opportunities for Hispanic broadcasters and to attract more Hispanic talent to broadcasting"; its agenda also includes encouraging the government to include Spanish-language radio stations in government media buys.

With June 1991 as its organization date, another professional radio group is Hispanics in Public Radio (HPR). A press release provided by Florence Hernández-Ramos, general manager of KUVO-FM in Denver, Colorado, indicates that this "nonprofit professional organization designed to provide a forum for the expression of the needs and interests of Hispanic Americans involved with public radio" proposes to "represent the interests of Hispanic-controlled public radio stations with the goal of improving the financial resources of the stations." The inaugural press release also indicates that HPR's main activities will be "information sharing, joint fundraising, training, and program development."

The Radio News and Other Program Providers

Although some stations produce everything they broadcast, including news and commercials, many stations depend on various companies dedicated to packaging programs for the Spanish-language radio market. Two types of providers merit special attention: those that provide news services and the ones that provide "full service."

Among the major news service providers, the oldest is Spanish Information Systems (SIS), inaugurated in 1976. From its headquarters in Dallas, Texas, it distributes via satellite to 46 stations five-minute Spanish-language news programs from 6:00 A.M. to 9:00 P.M. Monday through Friday and 8:00 A.M. to 3:00 P.M. (Central Time) on weekends. Monday through Friday at noon, they also transmits "SIS al Día" ("SIS to Date"), a 15-minute radio magazine that includes segments on current affairs, cooking, health, and sports. Additional sportscasts are also distributed at 7:45 A.M., 3:45 P.M., and 5:45 P.M. on weekdays and 2:45 P.M. on weekends. CBS Hispanic Radio Network, represents SIS in nationwide sales. SIS is a division of Command Communications, Inc., an Anglo-controlled company that also owns Texas State Network—a nationwide English-language information service and sports news network.

Another radio news provider is Radio Noticias (News Radio), which began in 1983 as a division in Spanish of United Press International (UPI), once one of the major wire services in the world. From its base in Washington, D.C., Radio Noticias distributes to 42 affiliated stations its seven-minute news program on an hourly basis from 6:00 A.M. to 9:00 P.M. Monday through Friday. There is no service on weekends.

A third news provider is Noticiero Latino, produced by Radio Bilingüe in Fresno, California. This news service, which began in 1985, is unique in that it is the only Spanish news service produced by a nonprofit network in the United States whose proprietaries and coordinators are Latino residents of this country. It is also unique because it is exclusively dedicated to informing and helping to interpret events in the United States, Latin America, and the Caribbean that are related to Hispanics in the United States, for example, immigration, civil rights, health, education, culture, and successes of Hispanics. Using information gathered by its local reporters and network of correspondents in the United States, Mexico, and Puerto Rico, Noticiero Latino offers a daily eight-to-ten-minute news program that is transmitted by telephone line Monday through Friday and by satellite two times a week. Noticiero Latino's news services are used by more than 40 stations in the United States, one in Puerto Rico, and another 30 in Mexico. The Mexico links are facilitated through the Instituto Mexicano de la

Radio's Programa Cultural de las Fronteras and through Radio Educación.

Among the "full service" providers of Spanish-language programming, the oldest and largest is Cadena Radio Centro (CRC)—a network founded in 1985 in Dallas, Texas. CRC is a subsidiary of Organización Radio Centro, a Mexican company controlled by the Aguirre family, which also owns nine radio stations and has more than 100 affiliates. In the United States the president of Cadena Radio Centro is Barrett Alley, and the vice chairman is Carlos Aguirre—a controlling family heir. This U.S. radio network offers its news services every hour on the hour 24 hours a day to 60 affiliated Spanish-language stations linked via satellite. CRC programming service operates seven days a week with two information lines. One transmits its five-minute news reports every hour; three of these daily transmissions originate directly from Mexico City, and another three focus on Latin American news. The other line transmits a variety of programs, including "En Concierto" (prominent Hispanic artists introducing their music), "Cristina Opina" (opinions by Cristina Saralegui on a wide range of subjects), "Tribuna Deportiva" (a live sports call-in talk show), and news of special events. All or some of these programs are purchased by affiliated stations, depending on local or regional interests.

With its starting date in March 1991, a recent Spanish-language radio program provider is Hispano U.S.A., which claims to be the first Hispanic-owned and -operated Spanish network service. According to a company informational brochure, Hispano U.S.A. sells 24 daily hours of "Spanish radio programming for the 90's, designed for cost-efficient station operations which benefits resident as well as absentee ownership." The programming, which is transmitted via satellite, features "top 40 Hispanic dance tunes," and national and international news, including sports and weekend special reports. Nine months after its start-up, Hispano U.S.A. had contracted with 18 stations covering the southern United States from California to Florida.

One other major provider of Spanish-language radio programs is CBS Hispanic Radio Network (CBSHRN). This special-events network was founded in 1990 by Columbia Broadcasting System. According to a company fact sheet, CBSHRN was created "to sell, affiliate and produce Spanish-language broadcasts of the Crown Jewels [i.e., the playoff games and World Series] of Major League Baseball to the United States and Latin America." It also transmits National Football League postseason and Super Bowl games, world soccer championship games, and, more recently, entertainment specials

such as "Navidad Mágica en Disneyland" ("Magical Christmas in Disneyland"). The programs are provided via syndication free of charge to affiliates in exchange for carrying the network's commercials; local commercials are allowed between selected breaks. For 1992, the network plans to offer more entertainment programs. CBS Hispanic Radio Network started its Spanish-language programming in Latin America in the mid-1970s with baseball specials. When it began in the United States, it was affiliated with Caballero Hispanic media representatives to provide such programs to the stations represented by Caballero, but in 1990 it established its own syndication network.

In sum, as of 1991, Spanish-language radio stations, whether owned by Hispanics or Anglos, could be heard in practically every region of the United States. In some major metropolitan cities with large concentrations of Hispanics (New York, Los Angeles, Miami, Chicago, San Antonio, and Houston), Hispanics have a variety of such stations to choose from, each with a distinct format and music to please almost any of the major Latin American and United States Hispanic musical traditions. Through the news and other programming services, Spanish-speakers in the United States also have many opportunities to keep ties to their countries of origin, enjoy the diversity of entertainment shows, and be part of the news and cultural events in this country as well as around the Hispanic world.

Television

The Early Years

As was the case for radio, Spanish-language television transmissions started almost as soon as they began in the English-language medium. Since the 1940s, entrepreneurs have found a significant market and profits transmitting to the Hispanic populations in the United States. Spanish-language television has grown enormously from the early days of a few brokered hours on some English-language stations in San Antonio and New York. In 1991, over $332 million in advertising was spent on the three broadcasting networks and various cable companies that make up Spanish-language television. These businesses differ considerably—some operate independently, while others have corporate ties to both U.S. and Mexican media.

The first Spanish-language television station in the United States was San Antonio's KCOR-TV Channel 41, which began some evening programs in 1955. But a few years before KCOR and similar stations started, several Spanish-language radio entrepreneurs recognized the potential of the Spanish-speaking television audiences and pioneered the way by producing special TV programs. Following the pattern used in the early stages of Spanish-language radio, time was brokered for these programs in the nascent English-language stations in selected cities.

One of the earliest of such Spanish-language television programs was "Buscando Estrellas" ("Looking for Stars"), which began in 1951 and was produced and hosted by José Pérez (Pepe) del Río, a Mexican national of Spanish heritage. With Pioneer Flour Mills of San Antonio, Texas, as the primary commercial sponsor, this weekly entertainment and variety talent-search show lasted approximately three years. It was broadcast live on Sunday afternoons initially from the studios of KERN Channel 5—an English-language station in San Antonio. "Buscando Estrellas" brought to Texas a variety of talent from Mexico and provided opportunities for local amateurs to present their artistic aspirations to the public at the recording studios and to television viewing audiences. Another characteristic of this precursor of U.S.-Hispanic television was that its production and broadcasting location rotated every 13 weeks to three other Texas cities: Corpus Christi, Harlingen, and Laredo. In each city, the concept of the show was sold and time was brokered for it from English-language stations that found it profitable to sell those slots. Between 1956 and 1961, Pepe del Río hosted another popular Spanish-language program in San Antonio: "Cine en Español," which featured old movies brought from Mexico, Spain, and Argentina. Broadcast from the studios of KERN, those movies were also quite popular among the Spanish-speaking audiences of the time.

In New York, the precursors of Spanish-language television were the well-known radio personalities Don Pessante and Don Mendez. Some anecdotal evidence indicates that during the late 1940s they might have hosted the very first U.S. Hispanic-oriented television entertainment programs by brokering time on one of the English-language channels (9, 11, or 13).

More anecdotal evidence was obtained about another Hispanic-oriented program in New York during the early 1950s: "El Show Hispano," which aired on the once-commercial WATV Channel 13 between 11:00 A.M. and 12:00 A.M. on weekends (this station later became WNJU Channel 47). This program began in early 1952 and lasted for approximately two years; it was brokered by an Anglo who also saw the potential audience and profit among the growing Hispanic populations in New York. One of the distinctive features of this show, which was cohosted by Don Mendez and Aníbal González-Irizarry, was that in addition to its musical and comic segments, it also had a 15-minute news section. González-Irizarry

was responsible for this part of the program, making him probably the first Hispanic television newscaster in the early stages of this medium in the United States. In addition to working on the weekend television scene, González-Irizarry was a well-known disc jockey and newscaster on two of the early Spanish-language radio stations in New York (WWRL and WBNX). When he returned to Puerto Rico in 1955, Aníbal González-Irizarry eventually became the most prominent and respected anchorman on Puerto Rican television for over 20 years, on WKAQ Channel 2.

During the 1960s, part-time Spanish-language programs on English-language stations also emerged in various other cities with large concentrations of Hispanics, such as Los Angeles, Houston, Miami, Phoenix, Tucson, and Chicago. Most often such programs—sponsored primarily by a local company—would be the outcome of personal efforts of Hispanic entrepreneurs, many of whom had experience with radio. Some stations provided time for these in order to seek alternative sources of profits or to comply with Federal Communications Commission (FCC) requirements of public service programs to serve community needs and interests.

The Spanish International Network

The experiences of Hispanic entrepreneurs and their part-time Spanish-language television programs eventually led the way to establish separate stations especially directed at Hispanic viewers. The first primarily Spanish-language television station in the United States was San Antonio's KCOR, which transmitted on Channel 41 using the newly created ultra high frequency (UHF) band. The principal pioneer behind this effort was Raúl Cortez, the same owner of KCOR-AM, which was itself the first Hispanic-owned and operated Spanish-language radio station in the United States. KCOR-TV began in 1955 broadcasting from 5:00 P.M. to midnight. Emilio Nicolás, one of the first general managers of the station, recalls that approximately 50 percent of the programs were live variety and entertainment shows that featured a host of the best available talent from Mexico (personal communication, 1992). Many of these shows took place in the studios of Cortez's radio station, which aired these programs simultaneously. Movies and other prerecorded programs imported primarily from Mexico accounted for the rest of the early offerings of Channel 41.

Although the station was very popular among the Mexican and other Spanish-speaking residents of San Antonio and vicinities, Nicolás recalls that advertisers did not acknowledge this market and failed to use it extensively for commercial promotions. During those early years of the medium, Hispanic viewers were not accounted for in the standard ratings services. One reason for this, according to Nicolás, was that in the 1940s and 1950s Mexicans were cautious in either acknowledging their heritage or exposure to Spanish-language media for fear of blatant discriminatory practices. Thus, Cortez, after spending heavily on the live talent imported from Mexico and receiving limited financial support from the advertising agencies, was forced to sell the television station to an Anglo. He kept the KCOR call letters for his radio station, but the television station's were changed to KUAL. The station continued some Spanish-language programs, and in 1961 these call letters changed again to KWEX when Channel 41 was sold to Don Emilio Azcárraga Vidaurreta and his financial partners, who then went on to establish the first Spanish-language television network.

Until his death in 1972, Don Emilio Azcárraga Vidaurreta was the most prominent media magnate in Mexico. With his family, he owned and operated a significant part of the country's commercial radio system and the emerging Telesistema Mexicano, S.A. (Sociedad Anónima), broadcasting empire. In the United States, Don Emilio, his son Emilio Azcárraga Milmo, and Reynold (René) Anselmo became central figures in not only the purchase of San Antonio's Channel 41 but also in the establishment of the largest and most influential businesses related to Spanish-language television broadcasting.

From the works of these authors it can be summarized that the most significant development of Spanish-language television in the United States began when Spanish International Communications Corporation (SICC) was initiated and organized by René Anselmo and bankrolled by Azcárraga Vidaurreta along with minority investors having U.S. citizenship. Since SICC (which at one point was called Spanish International Broadcasting Corporation, SIBC) was to hold the licenses of the stations, the corporation was structured so that Azcárraga Vidaurreta, a Mexican citizen, would own only 20 percent of the company. Most of the other partners were U.S. citizens so as to conform with Federal Communication Act Section 310, which "prohibits the issuing of broadcast licenses to aliens, to the representatives of aliens, or to corporations in which aliens control more than one-fifth of the stock" (Felix Gutiérrez, from *Journalism History,* 1979). Anselmo, a Boston-born Italian and associate of Azcárraga's Mexican media, was the main U.S. partner in the ensuing enterprises. Among other principal U.S. citizens of SICC at the time were Frank Fouce, owner of Los Angeles Spanish-language movie houses, including the famous Million Dollar

Theater, and Edward Noble, an advertising executive in Mexico City. After obtaining KWEX, the SICC, with the assistance of a few other partners, bought Los Angeles station KMEX Channel 34 in 1962.

Gutiérrez points out that "although there is a limitation in the amount of stock a foreign national can hold in a broadcast license, there apparently is no such restriction on U.S. television networks." Thus, in 1961 Don Emilio and Anselmo established the sister company Spanish International Network (SIN) to purchase and provide programming, virtually all of which originated from Azcárraga's production studios at Telesistema (later known as Televisa) in Mexico. The other function of SIN was to provide advertising sales for the SICC stations. Over the next ten years the licensee corporation went through a series of expansions, mergers, and reorganizations as it added three other stations: WXTV Channel 41 in New York (1968); WLTV Channel 23, Miami (1971); and KFTV Channel 21, Fresno/Hanford (1972). The network was also extended with stations owned by some principals of SICC/SIN: under the Bahía de San Francisco company it was KDTV Channel 14, San Francisco (1974), and under Legend of Cibola (later known as Seven Hills Corporation) it was KTVW Channel 33, Phoenix (1976). In addition, SIN had the affiliation of five stations owned and operated by corporations not related to SIN/SICC; these were located in Albuquerque, Chicago, Corpus Christi, Houston, and Sacramento. Furthermore, SIN had four stations owned and operated by this company's parent corporation, Televisa, S.A. From their locations on the Mexican border at Juárez, Mexicali, Nuevo Laredo, and Tijuana, these stations served U.S. cities at, respectively, El Paso, El Centro, Laredo, and San Diego.

Until the mid-1970s, most of these stations shared the programming, which primarily came from Mexico's Productora de Teleprogramas (ProTele, S.A.), a company created and controlled by Televisa as its export subsidiary. SIN imported and licensed taped shows, movies, and other programs that were transported to the Los Angeles station, sent to San Antonio, and then passed along in a "bicycle type network" to the other owned and affiliated stations. In September 1976, SIN became the first major broadcasting company, preceding CBS, ABC, and NBC, to distribute programming directly to its affiliates via domestic satellite. SIN signals reached the San Antonio station from Mexico City by terrestrial microwave and from there it was distributed by the Westar satellite. That same year another related service had been started by Televisa to provide live, direct Spanish-language programming to Spanish-speaking audiences worldwide, but particularly to the United States. A major incentive for this new company was to sell advertising in Mexico for SIN programs, which would be aired in both countries. Between 1978 and 1979, live interconnections were established via satellite among 11 of SIN's stations. In 1979, as cable connections became more readily available, another precedent was established as SIN began paying cable franchise operators to carry its satellite signals. Then in early 1980, SIN's outlets expanded further as the network was granted permission to establish low-power television (LPTV) stations (those whose signals only reach a radius of approximately 12 to 15 miles), beginning with Denver affiliate K49TE Channel 49, which at the time served just as a retransmitter with no local programs. Another LPTV was licensed to Los Cerezos Television Company, Washington, D.C. Additional LPTVs were licensed in Austin, Bakersfield, Hartford, Philadelphia, and Tucson. Altogether, by 1983 the Spanish-language television stations represented by SIN/SICC were reaching over 3.3 million Hispanic households across the United States. Advertising for the stations was sold in the United States, Mexico, and other Latin American countries.

Although KMEX had turned a profit in 1964, most of the SICC stations did not operate in the black until a decade or more after they began operations. Nevertheless, the Azcárragas and their fellow investors recognized the growth potential of the Spanish-speaking television audience and market in the United States, and were willing to subsidize the station group. When SICC did eventually generate profits, many of them found their way back to Mexico through the SIN pipeline. A falling-out between Frank Fouce, one of SICC's principal investors, and René Anselmo, one of the creators and president of both SICC and SIN, led to a long, bitter stockholder derivative lawsuit that took over ten years to settle. A second legal action against SICC was initiated at the FCC in 1980 when a group of radio broadcasters (the now-defunct Spanish Radio Broadcasters Association) charged that the company was under illegal foreign control. In January 1986, a judge appointed by the FCC ruled not to renew the licenses of the 13 SICC stations and ordered their transfer to U.S.-based entities. This decision was followed by numerous legal appeals and challenges.

An intense and controversial bidding war in the same court that had heard the stockholder suit culminated in July 1986. Hallmark Cards, Inc., and its 25 percent partner, First Capital Corporation of Chicago, won with a $301.5 million bid for the SICC licenses and properties. The losing bidder was TVL Corporation, directed by a group of Hispanic inves-

tors who submitted a higher bid ($320 million) but whose financing was less secure. TVL's principal investors were Raúl R. Tapia, a partner in the Washington, D.C., law firm of Tapia & Buffington and former deputy special assistant of Hispanic affairs during President Jimmy Carter's administration; Alfred R. Villalobos, vice chairman and president of a management company; David C. Lizárraga, chairman, president and chief executive officer of TELACU; and Diego C. Ascencio, former ambassador to Brazil and assistant secretary of state for consular affairs. Other Hispanic notables who at some time expressed an interest in acquiring SICC were Miami politician Raúl Masvidal, investor Enrique (Hank) Hernández, and Los Angeles surgeon and Republican party leader Tirso del Junco. Among the unsuccessful Anglo bidders, there were producers Norman Lear, A. Jerrold Perenchio, and the former U.S. ambassador to Mexico John Gavin. Legal challenges of the sale process brought by losing bidders were not resolved until April 1991.

As various appeals were being deliberated in federal court and at the FCC, SIN and SICC were renamed Univisión on January 1, 1987. In February, the cable service Galavisión, which was not included in the deal, split from Univisión and remained under the control of Televisa and Univisa. Univisa was Ascárraga's new enterprise established to house Galavisión and his remaining U.S. companies. In July of that year, Hallmark and First Capital paid $286 million for the five original SICC stations and in August obtained actual control of the channels. Later, San Francisco station KDTV was purchased for an additional $23.6 million and the Phoenix station was bought for $23 million. In February 1988, the SIN network was also acquired by Hallmark for an additional $274.5 million. With the transition, both the station group and the network continue operations under the name Univision Holdings, Inc., of which Hallmark became sole owner by February 15, 1988.

In terms of programming content, Felix Gutiérrez and Jorge Schement (*Spanish-language Radio in the Southwestern United States,* 1981) state that "by 1979 SIN was feeding over 64 hours of programming to eight affiliates by Westar II satellite, 50 hours of which came from Televisa. The remainder was originated in the United States or imported from Venezuela, Spain, Argentina, or Brazil. The network feed consisted primarily of *novelas* (soap operas), variety shows, and the news [the program *24 Horas*] from Mexico City." From the 1960s to the 1970s, Hispanic programs made within the United States usually consisted of public affairs programming and local newscasts, some of which were acclaimed for their excellent coverage of issues of concern to the local Hispanic communities. In addition, some of the special programs at the time included, as summarized by Felix Gutiérrez in *Journalism History* (1979), "salutes to Latin American countries produced on location by Radio Televisión Española, New Jersey's Puerto Rican Day parade, a Fourth of July special from Miami and New York, and live coverage of the OTI (Organización de la Televisión Iberoamericana) Latin song festival;" there were also sporting events such as boxing matches, soccer, and World Cup competitions. In fact, SIN began carrying selected games of the World Cup Soccer Championship as early as 1970. At first these were shown on closed-circuit television and in rented theaters; regular broadcasts began in 1978.

Among the network's various programs, "Noticiero SIN" ("SIN Newscast"), the national news program, merits a special historical review because of its development and impact in the United States and Latin America. One of the pacesetters in this area is Gustavo Godoy, a native of Cuba who in Miami worked with CBS' affiliate television station as a producer and with ABC's affiliate in the news department. From there he went on to WLTV Channel 23 and later with the SIN network news. In sharing some of his recollections (pers. com., 1992) of the early years of the "Noticiero SIN," he indicated that from the start, the network established that there would be a standard of local newscasts from 6:00 to 6:30 P.M. followed by the national program from 6:30 to 7:00 P.M. in order to provide viewers with one solid hour of news focusing on events and people related to U.S. Hispanics and Latin American communities. During its beginnings, the national news program was produced at the television studios of the School of Communication at Howard University in Washington, D.C. On June 14, 1982, the national news department was transferred to Miami, where it continued productions until January 1987, when it was moved to Laguna Niguel in southern California. It returned to Miami in January 1991, along with other Univisión operations. While regional newscasts were done from San Antonio and some of the larger stations, for the international news-gathering activities, news bureaus were established, beginning in 1982, in Washington, D.C., New York, El Salvador, Argentina, Mexico, Puerto Rico, Israel, and London. The satellite uplink operations, which had been in San Antonio since 1976, were also moved to Laguna Niguel in January 1987, where they remained for four years.

There are several special programs produced by the SIN news department, including "Temas y Debates" ("Themes and Debates"), a talk show that started in 1982 in Washington, D.C., and continues to this day. "Temas y Debates" airs interviews with government and public personalities who are important newsmakers and interpreters for the week. Another notable accomplishment of SIN news was its coverage of U.S. and Latin American political developments. The first U.S. national election night coverage in Spanish was in 1968; similar reports followed in subsequent years. Starting with the 1981 elections in Miami, in which two Hispanic candidates were finalists for mayor of that city, "Noticias 23" ("News 23") and "Noticiero SIN" at the national level began giving ample time to present and analyze in Spanish the campaigns, issues, and personalities of the time. Pre- and post-exit polls were also conducted by the stations and the network to share their projections and predictions of the electoral outcomes, especially among the Hispanic populations. At each station and at the network level, there was also a very strong campaign for voter registration.

In 1984, SIN launched "Destino '84" ("Destiny '84"), which further promoted voter registration and, through a series of special programs and reports, gave ample coverage of the presidential elections in

Gustavo Godoy, founder of Hispanic American Broadcasting Corporation.

the United States. Cameras and reporters followed the candidates and events of the primaries, the conventions, and the final campaign up to election night. That year, the NBC network sent a camera and reporter to SIN news to follow up the trends in Hispanic voting at the national level. Godoy and his staff proceeded with similar coverage in Latin America, including polling activities beginning with the 1984 congressional and presidential elections in El Salvador, where their surveys were quite accurate in predicting the voting results. In subsequent years, ample coverage was given to and more exit polls were conducted of elections in Guatemala, Peru, Honduras, Colombia, Costa Rica, and many other locations.

In 1985, the first summit meeting between U.S. President Reagan and the former USSR's President Gorbachev was covered live from Geneva, Switzerland. According to Godoy (pers. com., 1992) thanks to SIN's live satellite transmissions from Latin America, these crucial electoral processes were placed in an international spotlight, thus creating a public attention that may have contributed to an increased sense of honesty and balance in such events. The amplitude and time of "Noticiero SIN's" live coverage of these Latin American developments have not been matched by any English-language network in the United States. The same can be said about the telethons in benefit of victims of the earthquakes and other natural disasters in Chile, Colombia, Puerto Rico, and Mexico.

One of the most significant internal turmoils in the history of "Noticiero SIN" began to take place in 1986, when the Mexican parent company, seeking to exert stronger control of the U.S. news activities, considered absorbing the "Noticiero" under Televisa's new international news enterprise, ECO (Empresas de Comunicaciones Orbitales). This takeover was prompted when Azcárraga established ECO to optimize the gathering and production of television news for his Univisión and for additional subscribers in the United States and Latin America. In August 1986, Godoy, who was then executive vice president for news at SIN, was informed that there would be limited funds for the coverage and conducting of polls of the elections in the Mexican state of Chihuahua. This was interpreted as an attempt to suppress uncloaking of electoral corruption and mismanagement by the main Mexican political party—the Partido de la Revolución Institucional (PRI).

In November 1986, Televisa's Jacobo Zabludovsky, who for 16 years had been anchorman for that company's "24 Horas" ("24 Hours") news program, was appointed to take charge of the SIN news operations in the United States. Shortly after, Godoy and

approximately 35 others at SIN resigned to protest Televisa's and, indirectly, the Mexican government's interventions. Without ever having established an operational office in the United States, Zabludovsky was eventually "prevented from working as president of ECO due to charges by Latino journalists and politicians about the Televisa news division's constant praise of the Mexican government" (Lozano, 1988). By then, Godoy had formed his own news production company, Hispanic American Broadcasting Corporation, which from 1987 to 1988 provided news for a competing network, Telemundo. Lozano indicates that "in the end, former UPI chief, Luis G. Nogales, replaced Zabludovsky as president of ECO and started a radical restructuring of Noticiero Univisión" along with editor Sylvana Foa, who stressed that the intention was to follow "the American TV networks' style at the start of Noticiero Univisión" (Lozano). When Hallmark took control of the network, Guillermo Martínez was appointed news director and vice president of Univisión news. Martínez, a native of Cuba, had been a journalist and editorial writer for *The Miami Herald,* and for a few months news director at WLTV in Miami.

Telemundo

While the Spanish International Network (SIN) and the Spanish International Communications Corporation (SICC) were developing their powerful and far-reaching dominion, the growth and market potential of the Hispanic audience was being recognized by other interested parties, such as Saul Steinberg, chairman of the board and chief executive officer (CEO) of Reliance Capital Group, L.P., and Henry Silverman, the eventual president, CEO, and director of Telemundo. Together with their investment partners, they founded the Telemundo Group, Inc., which is currently the second-largest Spanish-language television network in the United States.

The organization of the Telemundo Group began in May, 1986, when Reliance Capital Group acquired John Blair & Company, a diversified communications business. Blair had fallen prey to corporate raiders after an attempt at expansion left it overburdened with debt. Telemundo, as the successor to Blair, thus obtained stations WSCV Channel 51 in Miami and WKAQ Channel 2 in San Juan, Puerto Rico, which had been purchased by Blair in 1985 and 1983, respectively. Prior to its acquisition by Blair, WSCV was an English-language subscription television station. The station in Puerto Rico had been a major component of the Fundación Angel Ramos media enterprises and had its own islandwide retransmitter and affiliation network under the name adopted for the U.S. group—Cadena Telemundo.

The remaining hours were sold to other programmers. According to Valenzuela, "in 1980 KBSC offered a pay-television service (ON-TV) in English at night and switched to full-time Spanish-language programs during the day" (1985). He adds that much of that station's Spanish-language programming was supplied by government station Channel 13, of Mexico. When KBSC was put on the market in 1985, Reliance Capital, a large shareholder of Estrella Communications, purchased a greater proportion of the stock for $38 million and began operating the station with the new call letters KVEA. By December 1986, Reliance had spent $13.5 million to buy out the remaining minority holders of Estrella Communications, including some shares held by Hallmark Cards.

The third major component of the Telemundo Group was WNJU Channel 47, licensed in Linden, New Jersey, and serving the metropolitan New York area. This station was founded by Ed Cooperstein, who had been the general manager of its predecessor—the English-language WATV Channel 13, which had started in the early 1960s in New York. That station soon underwent a series of ownership and programming changes. While in 1965 WNJU was primarily an Anglo station transmitting in the

Henry R. Silverman, a founder of Telemundo.

The WKAQ facilities consist of 250,000 square feet of operations space, including three master control rooms and nine fully equipped modern studios. In December 24, 1986, Reliance completed its acquisition of 100 percent of the outstanding common stock of Blair. Altogether, Reliance paid $325 million ($215 million of it for Blair's debt retirement) and immediately began selling off properties not connected to Spanish-language broadcasting. The change of name to Telemundo Group, Inc., was officially established on April 10, 1987. The company went public with offerings of common stock and bonds during the summers of 1987 and 1988.

Prior to forming the Telemundo Group, Reliance had entered the Hispanic media market in April 1985 with its ownership interests in Estrella Communications, Inc., which had been formed in January of that year for the purpose of buying Channel 52 in Los Angeles. Under the call letters KBSC and the corporate name SFN Communications, Inc., this station was owned by Columbia Pictures and A. Jerrold Perenchio, who had launched it in the late 1970s to compete with KMEX for Los Angeles' Hispanic audience. At the time, KBSC split its broadcast schedule, offering approximately 95 hours a week in Spanish.

Saul P. Steinberg, a founder of Telemundo.

evenings, it also broadcast some Spanish-language variety shows. According to some historical internal files of the station, by early 1966 "slightly half of WNJU-TV's programming catered to the Hispanic market." In 1971, the station was bought by Columbia Pictures via its subsidiary Screen Gems, which also owned WAPA Channel 4 in Puerto Rico. With the new structure, WNJU had access not only to Columbia's repertoire of films regularly marketed to Latin America but also to a great variety of Spanish-language programs from Puerto Rico's WAPA. From these and other sources, WNJU broadcast 60 percent Spanish-language programs, such as *novelas* (soap operas), live musical variety shows, sports, news, and community public affairs. Despite the new options for programs, Channel 47 faced numerous financial difficulties during its early years, leading to the firing of founder and general manager Ed Cooperstein in 1972, who was eventually replaced by Carlos Barba. The challenge was even greater after SIN's WXTV Channel 41 was inaugurated in 1968 and began competing for the New York-New Jersey Hispanic audience, which at the time had limited access to the UHF receivers. In 1980, Columbia relinquished its holdings to the station and it was purchased jointly by A. Jerrold Perenchio, Norman Lear, and other investors under Spanish American Communications Corporation (SACC). These new owners planned to feature primarily sports and entertainment on prime time, but owing to commitment problems they continued to run the Spanish-language programming—WNJU's strongest time block totaling 74 hours per week. It was because of the strength of the Spanish-language programs and Hispanic audience that WNJU was bought for approximately $75 million in December 1986 from Perenchio, Lear, and SACC by Steinberg and his Reliance Capital Group.

The growth of Steinberg's television network continued in August 1987, when Telemundo bought out (for $15.5 million) National Group Television, Inc., the license holder of station KSTS Channel 48, serving the San Jose and San Francisco area. For the Houston/Galveston market, Telemundo invested $6.428 million to obtain the outstanding stock of Bluebonnet, which operated KTMD Channel 48 in that area in 1988. Another significant Hispanic market penetration came that year when Telemundo won over the affiliation, of Chicago's WSNS Channel 26, which had been associated with Univisión. Until then, Telemundo's link to Chicago had been WCIU Channel 26. A year later, entry was made into San Antonio with the affiliation, of KVDA Channel 60. In August, 1990, Telemundo paid $2.975 million to purchase 85 percent of the stock of Nueva Vista, which operated KVDA. With these stations, its affiliations and cable linkages, the Telemundo network was firmly established and potentially available to over 80 percent of Hispanic households in the United States.

During the early years, the Telemundo stations shared some novelas and entertainment programs made available from WKAQ Channel 2 in Puerto Rico. It also imported other novelas from Brazil, Mexico, Venezuela, Argentina, and Spain. In 1987, of the 30 hours of weekly network programming, 20 hours consisted of novelas. A variety of movies and entertainment shows were also imported from these countries. From mid-1987 through 1989 "Super Sábados" ("Super Saturdays") was among the programs broadcast via satellite from the studios in Puerto Rico. This five-hour variety and game show had large audience following on the island since 1984. Telemundo also broadcast international sports competitions, particularly soccer matches. One of the distinct characteristics of this network's programming was the prompt venture to make local productions a large percentage of the offerings. A notable first was the start-up in July 1988 of "MTV Internacional"—a one-hour Spanish-language version of the MTV network's programming. Aimed at the bilingual Hispanic American youth market, this new show is hosted in Spanish by Daisy Fuentes, a native of Cuba. It features rock music videos by groups performing in both Spanish and English, music news, artist interviews, and concert footage. (This show, syndicated by Viacom Latino Americano, a division of Viacom International, Inc., can also be seen in many Latin American countries.) Another first for Telemundo was the novela "Angélica, Mi Vida" ("Angelica, My Life"), produced in Puerto Rico. This soap opera, launched in August 1988, was specially directed to and based on the local audiences, as "the plot appealed to regional Hispanic differences by webbing Mexican, Puerto Rican and Cuban immigrant families into [the traditional] *novela* elements: passion, power struggles, love and desire" (Seijo-Maldonado, 1989). Another notable program, no longer on the air, was "Feria de la Alegria" ("The Happiness Fair"), a contest and game show with audience participation. It was the first live Spanish-language television show of its kind broadcast by a network on f3.4]weekdays in the continental United States.

From 1987 to mid-1988, the "Noticiero Telemundo" ("Telemundo Newscast"), the national news segment for this group's stations, was produced in Hialeah, Florida, by the Hispanic American Broadcasting Corporation (HBC). This company was founded by Gustavo Godoy (formerly at SIN news) with the financial assistance of Amancio V. Suárez (of the Viva América radio group). Godoy's newscasts for Telemundo began on January 12, 1987, and marked the first national transmission for the emergent Telemundo. However, HBC's telecasts were short-lived, and in January 1988 Telemundo acquired this production company and facilities as part of its network-building strategy. In May, Telemundo entered a coproduction venture with Ted Turner's Cable News Network. "Noticiero Telemundo-CNN" combines news videos with Spanish-speaking journalists, camera crews, and news anchors who use as their headquarters the CNN facilities in Atlanta, Georgia. From 1988 through 1990, Godoy was general manager of KTVW, a Univisión station in Phoenix, from which he returned to Telemundo, where he is president and director of news operations.

Galavisión

The third largest player in Spanish-language television in the United States (after Univisión and Telemundo) is Galavisión. This television company was launched in 1979 under parent company Univisa, Inc., a subsidiary of Mexico's Televisa. At that time, Galavisión was a premium cable service, offering recently produced Spanish-language movies along with coverage of select sporting events and special entertainment shows. In early 1988, it had only 160,000 subscribers. But in September of that year, after the entry of the Telemundo network and the consolidation of Hallmark's Univisión network, Univisa started to convert Galavisión's cable operations to an advertising-based basic cable service. This change expanded Galavisión's audience substantially as potentially two million cable subscribers were able to receive Galavisión's programs.

The new format offers 24-hour-a-day programming via a network feed provided by the Galaxy I and Spacenet 2 satellites. In addition, Galavisión expanded to over-the-air offerings when it affiliated stations KWHY Channel 22 in Los Angeles, KTFH Channel 49 in Houston, KSTV Channel 57 in Santa Barbara, and low-power retransmitters in seven other cities. KWHY and KTFH were converted from English-language stations; KSTV was licensed for the first time for Galavisión. Some stations broadcast Galavisión part-time (typically from 3:00 P.M. to 2:00 A.M.), while others have 24-hour coverage.

Galavisión, operating under the separate entity of SIN, Inc., was not included in the sales of SICC and SIN to Hallmark. Univisa operates from Los Angeles, where it is parent to other companies. Among these are Video Visa (a videocassette distributor), and in Mexicali, Mexico, Plasticus, a videocassette manufacturing operation that produces more cassettes than Sony, Kodak, or 3M and also operates the world's largest video dubbing facility, Central de Video, S.A. de C.V.

Current Status of U.S. Hispanic Television

At present, the Spanish-language television industry in the United States is still dominated by the three major networks: Univisión, Telemundo, and Galavisión. However, special niches of the Hispanic television market are being targeted by two new companies: International TeleMúsica, Inc., and Viva Television Network, Inc.; by English-language cable operators such as MTV and HBO; and by primarily English-language broadcasting companies that offer second audio programs in Spanish. Yet, even in this medium's fifth decade in the United States, it continues to have a substantial foreign connection in its corporate structures, on-camera and off-camera personnel, and in programming (Mydans, *The Foreign Connection,* 1989).

Univisión

As of January 1992, under the parent company Hallmark Cards, Inc., the Univisión-owned and operated Spanish-language television group consists of ten full-power stations and four low-power stations. In addition, Univisión counts on the affiliation of ten full-power and 11 low-power stations, plus 566 cable

Joaquín F. Blaya, President, Univisión.

TABLE 24.2
STATIONS OWNED AND OPERATED BY THE UNIVISIÓN SPANISH-LANGUAGE TELEVISION GROUP (LATE 1991)

FULL-POWER STATIONS		CITY
KLUZ	41	Albuquerque, NM
KCFP	30	Austin, TX
KUVN	23	Dallas/Ft. Worth, TX
KFTV	21	Fresno, CA
KMEX	34	Los Angeles, CA
WLTV	23	Miami, FL
WXTV	41	New York, NY
KTVW	33	Phoenix, AZ
KWEX	41	San Antonio, TX
KDTV	14	San Francisco, CA

LOW-POWER STATIONS		CITY
K39AB	39	Bakersfield, CA
W47AD	47	Hartford, CT
W42BI	42	Philadelphia, PA
K52AO	52	Tucson, AZ

carriers that operate in 40 of the 50 states and the District of Columbia. Some of the full-power stations on these lists were formerly low-power stations under different call letters. The satellite used for pro-

TABLE 24.3
UHF AFFILIATES OF THE UNIVISIÓN SPANISH-LANGUAGE TELEVISION GROUP (LATE 1991)

FULL-POWER STATIONS		CITY
WCIU	26	Chicago, IL
KORO	28	Corpus Christi, TX
KCEC	50	Denver, CO
KINT	26	El Paso, TX
KXLN	45	Houston, TX
KNVO	48	McAllen, TX
KREN	27	Reno, NV
KCSO	19	Sacramento, CA
KSMS	67	Salinas, CA
WMDO	48	Washington, DC

LOW-POWER STATIONS		CITY
K27AF	27	Las Vegas, NV
K51BX	51	Lubbock, TX
W46AR	46	Milwaukee, WI
K04NT	4	Palm Springs, CA
W33AR	33	Rockford, IL
K19BN	19	San Diego, CA
K07TA	7	Santa Maria, CA
W69BT	69	South Bend, IN
K52AY	52	St. Louis, MO
W61BL	61	Tampa, FL
W48AW	48	Washington, DC

gram transmissions and station connections is the SATCOM 1R. Two stations in Guadalajara and Sonora, Mexico, purchase some Univisión programs but are not owned by the network.

Since 1988, the president of the Univisión television station group has been Joaquín Blaya, a native of Chile, where he worked as a journalist, radio newscaster, disc jockey, and production manager. Prior to this position, he was an account representative at WXTV in New York, and eventually president and general manager of station WLTV in Miami. As of mid-1991, he was also acting president of Univisíon Holdings, which includes Univisíon Publications, Univisíon News, and the Univisíon Network and its various components.

Three other key directors of Univisíon are Raúl Torano, senior vice president for sales and marketing executive of the network, the stations, and *Más* magazine; Rosita Perú, senior vice president for programming; and Ray Rodríguez, responsible for international coproductions and talent management functions. Peru is a Buenos Aires-educated native of Lima, Peru. The family roots of the other two are

Rosita Perú, Senior Vice President and Director of Programming, Univisión.

from Cuba. Guillermo Martínez remains vice president for Univisión News.

In its continued expansion in this country, Univisión, on March 9, 1991, inaugurated its state-of-the-art-technology network television center in west Dade County, Florida. The 139,000-square-foot facility now houses many of the network's departments, including news, special events, merchandising, programming, talent relations, sports, programming development and its regional sales office. The operations, news, and promotions departments formerly based in Laguna Niguel in southern California moved to the Miami facilities during the summer of 1991 amid protests from Mexican Americans who feared a greater Cuban influence in Univisión's news, programming, and personnel.

For the expansion of its national and international news coverage, Univisión's news department, under the direction of Guillermo Martínez, hired 16 additional correspondents to work in the United States and Latin America. To improve the network's knowledge of Hispanic public opinion, Univisión enlisted the services of Sergio Bendixen and his survey research company, Bendixen and Associates. Bendixen started doing research for the company in

1985, when it was still the Spanish International Network (SIN), and has continued with Univisión, conducting surveys related to political opinions and orientations of the general public and particularly of Hispanics.

In terms of the other programs, a recent fact sheet about Univisión stated that these are "obtained from various Latin American sources, but an increasing amount . . . is produced by Univisión, as well as by independent producers in the United States," and that approximately 44 percent of the programs are U.S.-based. A typical Univisión week, which runs 24 hours a day, seven days a week, consists of such program types as novelas (soap operas), movies, news, sports, and various talk, variety, and comedy shows. (Domestic productions are found primarily among the news programs and the talk, variety, and comedy-type shows.)

In an interview with *Hispanic Business,* Univisión president Joaquín Blaya stated that the "main thrust of the program development in the United States is to address . . . 'the born-again Hispanic'—the young Hispanics who were not watching Spanish-language television;" he added that Univisión is "not a Latin American television network in the

Univisión news studio.

Jorge Ramos and María Elena Salinas of "Noticiero Univisión," the Monday-through-Friday evening news broadcast.

Cristina Saralegui, host of the most popular talk show on Spanish-language television, Univisión's "El Show de Cristina."

United States; [it is] an American television network that speaks Spanish" (Mendosa, 1991). In addition to the "Noticiero Univisión," and "Temas y Debates," there are several other programs that exemplify this mold. For debates and presentations related to public issues, there is "Cristina," a talkshow hosted by Cuban-born Cristina Saralegui—Univisión's version of Oprah Winfrey—in which issues and subjects formerly taboo in the Hispanic community are discussed. Other programs include "Portada" ("Cover Story"), a news magazine hosted by Puerto Rican Ana Azcuy and called "a Spanish-language version of an investigative report program similar to the general market's "20/20," and, "Noticias y Más," a live daily show with human interest stories.

For comedy, games, and variety there is "Corte Tropical" ("Tropical Cut"), a zany situation comedy portraying a Latin-style pursuit of the elusive American dream and produced by Cuban Mimi Belt-Mendoza. On Saturdays there is "Sábado Gigante" ("Gigantic Saturday"), a variety game show, which is top-rated in the United States and many Latin American countries; it features games, contests, talent searches, celebrity guest appearances, and musi-

TABLE 24.4
UNIVISIÓN PROGRAMMING (MID–1991)

TYPE OF PROGRAM	WEEKDAY		SATURDAY		SUNDAY	
	ORIGINAL	REPEAT	ORIGINAL	REPEAT	ORIGINAL	REPEAT
Novelas (serials)	7.5	3.5	2.0	—	0.5	—
Talk/variety/comedy	2.5	3.0	6.5	5.0	3.5	3.5
Movies	2.0	2.0	2.0	2.0	4.0	2.0
News	1.0	0.5	—	—	0.5	—
Cartoons/children shows	1.5	—	2.5	—	1.5	—
Sports	—	—	2.0	—	5.0	—
Educational/religious	0.5	—	1.0	1.0	2.0	1.5

cal entertainment. It is hosted by Chilean Mario Kreutzberger, familiarly known as Don Francisco.

There is a daily afternoon show called "Hola America" ("Hello America") in which viewers can call in to play and compete for prizes, also featuring news briefs and interviews with celebrities, some of whom sing or perform in brief comedy sketches. It is hosted by José Rondstadt (a cousin of the famous Mexican American singer Linda Rondstadt), and María Olga Fernández, a native of Chile, and Cuban-born Maty Monfort-Novia.

For the younger Hispanic American viewers, Univisión produces "Cita con el Amor" ("Date with Love"), a Spanish-language version of "The Dating Game" hosted by Venezuelan Henry Zakka. There are also the prime-time talk entertainment shows "Desde Hollywood" ("From Hollywood") and "El Show de Paul Rodríguez" ("The Raul Rodríguez Show"). The former, hosted by Luca Bentivoglio, a Venezuelan born of Italian parents, features interviews with celebrities, show business news, and gossip. The latter, a late-night show, carries the name of its host, a Los Angeles Mexican-born comedian who does occasional comedy sketches and conducts interviews with guests from the world of entertainment. Another late-night show is "Charitín" which carries the name of a popular Puerto Rican singer and host. In her weekly show, Charitín also hosts artists for interviews, singing, or participating in comedy sketches.

Aside from these regularly scheduled programs, Univisión also produces musical and variety specials. The most popular of these are the national (United States) and international OTI song festivals, which have been telecast since 1972, and "Premio Lo Nuestro a la Música Latina" ("Our Prize for Latin Music"), the annual Spanish-language version of the "Grammy Awards." This latter special, produced in conjunction with *Billboard* magazine, started in May 1989. Other specials celebrate Mother's and Father's Day, beauty pageants, Hispanic achievements and heritage days in the United States, and national independence days in the Americas. For 1992, this included programs related to the quincentennial commemoration of Columbus' exploration of the Americas. Under the theme "Encuentro con lo Nuestro" ("Encounter with What's Ours"), Univisión scheduled 200 historical vignettes that explored key elements of the commemoration, 41 capsules on past and present Hispanic achievements, and another half dozen special shows. Given the success of Univisión's productions, future goals include global programming to reach the 500 million Spanish-speakers worldwide.

Telemundo

As of January 1992, the Telemundo Group, Inc. consisted of six full-power stations and four low-power stations. It also continues to own the station in San Juan, Puerto Rico, which is the network's only VHF

TABLE 24.5
STATIONS OWNED AND OPERATED BY THE TELEMUNDO SPANISH-LANGUAGE TELEVISION GROUP (LATE 1991)

FULL-POWER STATIONS		CITY	LOW-POWER STATIONS		CITY
KTMD	48	Houston, TX	K60EE	60	Odessa, TX
KVEA	52	Los Angeles, CA	K61FI	61	Modesto, CA
WSCV	51	Miami, FL	K15CU	15	Salinas, CA
WNJU	47	New York, NY	K52CK	52	Stockton, CA
KVDA	60	San Antonio, TX			
KSTS	48	San Jose, CA			
WKAQ	2	San Juan, PR			

TABLE 24.6
STATIONS AFFILIATED WITH THE TELEMUNDO SPANISH-LANGUAGE TELEVISION GROUP (LATE 1991)

FULL-POWER STATIONS		CITY	LOW-POWER STATIONS		CITY
WSNS	44	Chicago, IL	K59DB	59	Albuquerque, NM
KFWD	52	Dallas/Ft. Worth, TX	K11SF	11	Austin, TX
KUDB	59	Denver, CO	W19AH	19	Boston, MA
KMSG	59	Fresno, CA	K49AY	49	Cheyenne, WY
KLDO	27	Laredo, TX	K49CJ	49	Colorado Springs, CO
WTGI	61	Philadelphia, PA	K66EB	66	Corpus Christi, TX
			W13BF	13	Hartford, CT
			K46CS	46	Lubbock, TX
			K61FI	61	Modesto, CA
			W07BZ	7	Orlando, FL
			K64DR	64	Phoenix, AZ
			K52CK	52	Stockton, CA
			K14HR	14	Tucson, AZ
			K51BG	51	Victoria, TX
			W42AJ	42	Washington, DC
			K17CJ	17	Yakima, WA

station. Furthermore, Telemundo counts on the affiliation of six full-power and 16 low-power stations, plus seven cable carriers that operate in 14 of the 50 states and the District of Columbia. Some of the full-power stations on these lists were formerly low-power stations under different call letters. Three other stations affiliated with Telemundo transmit from Tijuana, Juárez, and Matamoros to serve the U.S. Hispanic communities in, respectively, San Diego, El Paso, and McAllen/Brownsville. Altogether, the Telemundo television network currently has the potential of reaching over 84 percent of U.S. Hispanic households. The satellite used for program transmissions and station connections is the Spacenet II.

For Telemundo, Steinberg continued as chairman of the board of Reliance Holdings Group, L.P. But in February 1990, with Silverman's departure from Telemundo, Steinberg assumed his responsibilities until 1991. That year, upon the resignation of the network's vice president, Carlos Barba (now president

of Venevisión International), Telemundo created a three-member office of the president. The directors are W. Gary McBride, president of the network and responsible for all network activities, including programming, promotion, market research, marketing, and network sales; Donald M. Travis, president of the station group, who oversees Telemundo's seven stations and local and national spot sales; and Peter J. Housmann II, president of business and corporate affairs, who is responsible for finance, legal affairs, human resources, affiliate relations, and engineering. At this time, no person of Hispanic heritage is either a member of the board of directors or in the highest echelons of the network. The main facilities, measuring 50,000 square feet and containing five productions studios, are located in Hialeah, Florida, in the former building of the Hispanic American Broadcasting Corporation.

The "Noticiero Telemundo-CNN" arrangement continues to date. However, Telemundo also has its

TABLE 24.7
TELEMUNDO PROGRAMMING (MID-1991)

TYPE OF PROGRAM	WEEKDAY		SATURDAY		SUNDAY	
	ORIGINAL	REPEAT	ORIGINAL	REPEAT	ORIGINAL	REPEAT
Novelas (serials)	6.0	—	2.0	—	—	—
Talk/variety/comedy	3.0	1.0	2.0	—	6.0	1.0
Movies	6.0	—	9.5	—	6.0	—
News	1.5	0.5	1.0	—	—	—
Cartoons/children shows	—	—	—	—	1.0	—
Sports	—	—	2.5	—	1.0	—
Educational/religious	—	—	1.0	—	4.0	—

Enrique Gratas, host of Telemundo's "Occurió Así."

gramming, especially for U.S. Hispanics, was a key to Telemundo's long-term strategy as it sought to differentiate itself from Univisión and win the viewership of the more acculturated Hispanics. Currently, in addition to the national and local news programs and the "MTV Internacional," there are various programs that seek to meet these standards. The most prominent is "Cara a Cara" ("Face to Face") a talk show hosted by Cuban-born María Laria.

This program, Telemundo's own version of the "Oprah Winfrey Show," also covers controversial topics, such as abortion, drugs, sex, religion, politics, crime, and AIDS. Another domestic program is "Occurió Así" ("It Happened That Way"), a daily news-magazine show hosted by Enrique Gratas, a native of Argentina. It is an investigative news reporting program that utilizes the network's news bureaus in New York, Los Angeles, and Latin America to probe "the news behind the news that shapes our world." For late-night comic relief there is Argentine comedian Jorge Porcel's "A la Cama con Porcel" ("To Bed with Porcel"), a zany variety, interview, music, and humor show.

In mid-1991, Telemundo was also broadcasting

own news bureaus in Mexico, New York, Washington, and another in Miami for coverage of the Caribbean and Central America. To supplement its knowledge of the Hispanic community, various studies have been commissioned by Telemundo. The most recent study, conducted by the Research Network Co. in Tallahassee, Florida, was the "Telemundo Hispanic Opinion Poll: A National Survey of the U.S. Hispanic Viewpoint." Released in April 1991, this study inquired about Hispanics' opinions on numerous issues, including quality of life, economic concerns, discrimination, bilingual education, the political status of Puerto Rico, the free trade agreement with Mexico, and relations with Cuba.

The majority of Telemundo's domestically produced programs are news programs and talk, variety, and comedy-type shows. A recent fact sheet about Telemundo stated that "more than 50 percent of all programming aired on the network is produced in the United States at the company's production center in Hialeah, Florida, as well as at its stations in Los Angeles and Puerto Rico." It adds that "these programs are directly targeted to the needs and lifestyles of Hispanic Americans." When the network was launched, it was pointed out that U.S.-based pro-

Andrés García and Rudy Rodríguez, stars of Telemundo's soap opera "El Magnate."

"El Magnate" ("The Magnate"), another locally produced soap opera, this one in the form of a dramatic series with the backdrop of modern Miami. Except for "Cara a Cara" and the national news, the other programs originate in Florida.

Telemundo has also embarked on the production of specials. One of their more popular offerings is "Esta Noche con Usted" ("Tonight with You"), a four-times-a-year series of "in-depth, one-on-one interviews with noted Latino personalities in film, music, television, the performing arts, science and business." This one-hour program is currently hosted by a former Miss Universe, Chilean Cecilia Bolocco, who had also been coanchor of the "Noticiero Telemundo-CNN." "Columbus Day," another special for 1992, focused on the theme of the quincentennial anniversary of the navigator's voyage to the Americas. That voyage and related activities taking place in Spain during 1992 were also featured in the weekly cultural magazine "Línea América" ("America on the Line"). In addition, Telemundo produces or distributes specials such as "Carnaval Internacional de Miami" ("Miami International Carnival"), featuring musical and artistic highlights of the carnival; and the "Miss Hispanidad" ("Miss Hispania") beauty pageant, which draws contestants to the Miss Universe pageant. Other musical and variety specials are regularly imported from Venezuela, Mexico, Argentina, and Spain. Future plans for Telemundo include increased local productions, some of which may be exported to Latin America.

In November 1991, the Telemundo Group also became involved in a different type of venture—the collaborative promotion of the first Spanish-English bilingual credit card. The bank issuing the Visa and Master Cards is the People's Bank of Connecticut. Through the Telemundo stations, the public is informed that the network is part of this financial service targeted primarily to Hispanic Americans. The service is distinct in that it provides bilingual applications, customer information and assistance, as well as lower-than-average interest rates (13.9–16.9 percent).

Galavisión

The structure of Galavisión continues as described previously in terms of the principal directors, the Univisa, Inc., subsidiary companies, the owned and operated stations, as well as the affiliate linkages. The principal executives of Galavisión are the president, Jaime Dávila, a native of Mexico; vice president of broadcasting operations, Stuart Livingston, a native of the United States; and Vera González, a native of Guatemala, who is national director of cable operations. As of late 1991, the Galavisión network's affiliates in the United States consisted of three full-power UHF stations and seven low-power stations. In addition, programming is provided via cable affiliations with 228 systems across the United States. Through its Mexican network, Galavisión's programs can also be seen most everywhere in that country as well as in Latin America, western Europe, and northern Africa.

In terms of programming, Galavisión executives have stated the network intends to tailor its offerings primarily to Hispanics of Mexican and Central American origin. They feel that Univisión and Telemundo attempt to reach too diverse an audience by broadcasting coast to coast. Galavisión is concentrating its efforts west of the Mississippi River, where its target audience typically resides. Thus, Galavisión provides "unfiltered" Mexican television to the United States 24 hours a day, seven days a week. The major block of daily programs, 13 hours, consists of news from the ECO system (Empresas de Comunicaciones Orbitales). Via satellite, ECO links a news production center in Mexico City to the rest of Latin America, Europe, and the United States. Movies are transmitted two hours per weekday and 18 hours on weekends. Novelas (soap operas) take about four hours from Monday to Friday, but none of these or the other shows are made in the United States with Hispanic Americans.

Galavisión's parent company, Televisa, sees the U.S. Hispanic market as one of the top growth areas for the next decade. Continued inroads into this

TABLE 24.8
AFFILIATES OF THE GALAVISIÓN SPANISH-LANGUAGE TELEVISION GROUP (LATE 1991)

FULL-POWER STATIONS		CITY	LOW-POWER STATIONS		CITY
KTFH	49	Houston, TX	K58DJ	15	Bakersfield, CA
KWHY	22	Los Angeles, CA	K22BH	22	Corpus Christi, TX
KSTV	57	Santa Barbara, CA	K06MB	6	Palm Springs, CA
			K67FE	67	Phoenix, AZ
			K17BY	17	San Antonio, TX
			K22DD	22	San Jose, CA
			K43CW	43	Tuscon, AZ

TABLE 24.9
GALAVISIÓN PROGRAMMING

TYPE OF PROGRAM	WEEKDAY	SATURDAY	SUNDAY
Novelas (serials)	4.0	—	—
Talk/variety/comedy	2.5	0.5	9.0
Movies	2.0	14.0	4.0
ECO news	13.5	9.5	5.0
"24 Horas" news	2.0	—	—
Sports	—	—	6.0

market, especially the Mexican component, are to be expected.

Other Hispanic-Oriented Television Companies and Program Ventures

It can be expected that the aforementioned networks will capture the majority of the U.S. Hispanic audience in terms of general programming. However, several companies are seeking their own niche in this market.

International TeleMúsica, Inc.

International TeleMúsica, Inc. produces a show featuring international music videos, entertainment news, promotions and life-style segments. The programs, hosted by Alex Sellar, a Spaniard, and Pilar Isla, a native of Mexico, are produced in Hollywood using various California landscapes for settings. The target audience is Hispanic and Latin American youth. In 1990, Jesus Garza Rapport, executive vice president of TeleMúsica, started the company with full financial backing from Radio Programas de México (RPM). A Mexican company, RPM owns 30 and operates 50 radio stations in that country, and also owns one television station in Guadalajara, Mexico. The owners of RPM, Clemente Serna and family, are among the principal contenders for acquiring the Red 7, a group of Mexican government stations that are to be sold to the private sector. After experimenting during 1990, in RPM's Channel 6 in Guadalajara, TeleMúsica's first two-hour show in the United States was telecast from Miami on the Univisión network in September 1991. That same month, distribution began for five separate one-hour shows, to air Monday through Friday, aimed at the Mexican market via the Red 7 network. In October the weekday shows reached the five South American affiliates—Ecuador, El Salvador, Nicaragua, Guatemala, and Costa Rica—via the Pan American International Network Satellite launched by René Anselmo. Puerto Rican John Figueroa, vice president of affiliate relations, indicates that the shows are reaching their targeted youth audience, even beyond

the locations where TeleMúsica is licensed, as evidenced by fan-club correspondence from all over Latin America.

Viva Television Network, Inc.

Viva Television Network, Inc. is "the first US Latino owned national cable television network," as proclaimed in an informational brochure of the company. Launched in 1992, Viva's goal is to provide 16-hour daily Spanish-language (and some English-language) programs, such as documentaries, public affairs, music, sports, comedy, news, children's shows, art films, and movies catering to the 18- to 49-year-old Hispanic audience. The chief executive officer and one of the founders is Mark Carreño, a native of Cuba who has served as executive director of the Latino Consortium, a nationally syndicated network based at KCET-TV, Los Angeles' Public Broadcasting Station. Other founders and executive staff include chief operating officer Guillermo Rodríguez, a native of Puerto Rico who has worked with KMEX-TV and Lorimar Telepictures, and the vice president of international operations, Esteban de Icaza, of Mexican heritage, who was president of Azteca films, the foreign distribution company of the Mexican government. De Icaza's connections with that company and Imevisión, the Mexican government's educational television company, helped Viva obtain exclusive rights for telecasting selections from these companies' movie and video libraries, as well as Imevisión's newscasts. For program delivery, Viva subleased a transponder from the General Electric cable satellite and has agreements with multisystem cable operators in major Hispanic markets. The expected potential audience numbers from 300,000 to 1.5 million cable subscribers in the United States and Puerto Rico.

Home Box Office's Selecciones en Español

Home Box Office's (HBO) Selecciones en Español (Selections in Spanish) is a significant venture to capture a niche in the U.S.-Hispanic television audience. In January 1989, this service was inaugurated to provide to HBO and Cinemax cable subscribers the option of Spanish-language audio for the telecast motion pictures and even some sporting events, such as boxing matches. This service is the brainchild of Lara Concepción, a native of Mexico, who after eight years of trying, was able to persuade HBO's executives that there was a viable Hispanic market for such a service. The turning point for Concepción came shortly after the box office success of the Hispanic-theme movie *La Bamba*. Following a market study that further convinced HBO that it could expand its business with the Spanish-speaking audience, HBO scheduled about ten Spanish-dubbed movies per month in 1989. At first, Selecciones en Español was provided to 20 HBO and Cinemax cable operators in five cities: El Paso, Miami, New York, San Antonio, and San Diego. Shortly thereafter, the service was requested by an additional 35 cable firms and later by another 15. By the end of 1989, HBO expanded its dubbed activities and was offering an average of 20 movies per month in Spanish. In 1991, Selecciones en Español was carried by 182 cable systems within the United States. HBO and Cinemax cable operators have three methods for delivering this service: a channel dedicated to Selecciones, a Second Audio Program (SAP) channel available for stereo television sets or videocassette recorders with multiple channel television sound (MTS), and an FM tuner in which the affiliates can transmit the second audio feed via an FM modulator (that is, cable subscribers listen to the Spanish soundtrack on their FM radio).

Following up on its formidable success with the U.S. Spanish-speaking audience, HBO in October 1991 launched HBO-Olé Pay-TV service in Latin America and the Caribbean Basin. This allows cable subscribers in over 20 Latin American countries prompt access in Spanish to HBO's movies and other shows, which are supplied by Warner Brothers, Twentieth Century-Fox, and Columbia TriStar International Television, which provides feature films from Columbia Pictures and TriStar Pictures. (The sports cable network ESPN also began providing Spanish-language telecasts for the Latin American market in January 1991, but has yet to provide this service for U.S. Hispanic audiences.)

Spanish-Language Programs on Anglo Stations

Long before HBO started applying the Spanish-language audio and related technologies to establish their particular niches in the Hispanic market, other Anglo television businesses had successfully used a Second Audio Program (SAP) to provide selected programs to their audiences. In Los Angeles, one of the most successful ventures with Second Audio Program was Fox affiliate KTLA Channel 5. This station, now owned by the Tribune Broadcasting Company, was the pioneer in taking advantage of the Federal Communication Commission's 1984 rule authorizing broadcasters and cable providers to split up the single soundtrack into four audio channels. Henceforth, the first track was for the English audio, the second for stereo, the third for any alternate language, and the fourth for data transmission. In October 1984 KTLA broadcast the movie *2001: A Space Odyssey* and began offering the "The Love Boat," "McMillan & Wife," "Columbo," and "McCloud" in Spanish via the third audio channel. Dubbed editions of these programs were readily available because some Hollywood producers had a long-standing policy of dubbing many of their programs for their Latin American markets. Then, in February 1985, KTLA hired Analía Sarno-Riggle to be the Spanish interpreter of the "News at Ten," which airs Monday through Friday from 10:00 to 11:00 P.M. While in 1984 the pilot program with three other interpreters had not succeeded, the public response to Sarno-Riggle was formidable, as she developed an accurate technique to provide the Spanish-speaking viewers an adequate representation of what they were getting on the screen. She also strived to establish her own "audio personality," not just mimic the people she was interpreting.

Given her success, especially as evidenced by ratings among Hispanic viewers, by July 1985, KTLA had made Sarno-Riggle a regular staff employee and committed to continue the service. Sarno-Riggle, a native of Argentina, considers her own simulcast interpretations an alternative to Univisión's and Telemundo's news. She believes it offers access to a larger and more diverse amount of local news, which may be preferred by some assimilated Hispanics, or by those who simply wish to be informed on the same issues their neighbors are tuned into. Subsequently, KTLA assigned her to the Hollywood Christmas parade and various other specials. The station also expanded its offerings of Spanish-language audio for more of its prime-time programs, such as "Airwolf," "Magnum P.I.," and "Knight Rider." These programs were also among those dubbed for foreign distribution by their producers. Currently, KTLA schedules approximately 20 hours per week of Spanish-language audio.

The Hispanic audience ratings of KTLA did not go unnoticed by other stations and networks in Los Angeles and elsewhere. Second Audio Program has already been adopted by various other Anglo broadcasters in large Hispanic markets, including the Tribune Broadcasting Company's Chicago and New York stations WGN Channel 9 and WPIX Channel 11. Even some nonprofit stations began this language option. For example, KCET Channel 28 hired Sarno-Riggle for ten months to do the Spanish-language audio for "By the Year 2000," a weekly half-hour public affairs program for southern California. Also, under Sarno-Riggle's guidance, on January 14, 1991, New York station WNET Channel 13 began the second audio for "The MacNeil/Lehrer News-Hour." Presently, Bolivian native Oscar Ordenes is the Spanish-language voice for this show, which in the United States is carried by 33 Public Broadcasting System stations either via Second Audio Program or as a separate show repeated later in the evening. In addition, 32 cities in 26 Latin American countries receive videos of this version of the "MacNeil/Lehrer News Hour" by way of the United States Information Agency's Worldnet information program.

Finally, English-language musical programs specifically oriented toward U.S. Hispanics are also making their debut. In June 1991, MTV launched "Second Generation," a half-hour mix of videos, comedy, and entertainment news aimed primarily at second-generation Hispanics in the United States. Hosted by New York Puerto Rican Andy Panda and Colombian Tony Moran, this program is being broadcast by 31 primarily English-language stations from the east to the west coast.

References

Arias, Armando A., Jr. "Mass Mediated Images of Undocumented Mexicans." Paper presented at the annual conference of the Western Society of Criminology, Reno, Nevada. 1985.

Arnheim, Rudolf, and Martha C. Bayne. (1941). "Foreign Language Broadcasting over Local American Stations." In *Radio Research,* edited by P. Lazersfeld and F. Stanton. New York: Duell, Sloan & Pearce, 1941.

Beale, Steve. "A Hallmark in the Takeover of Spanish TV." *Hispanic Business,* 21 May 1988.

——. "Turmoil and Growth." *Hispanic Business,* December 1986: 52.

Berg, Charles Ramirez. "Stereotyping in Films in General and of the Hispanic in Particular." *Howard Journal of Communications,* 2, No. 3, 1990: 286–300.

Bergsman, Steve. "Controversy Hits L.a.'s Spanish Television." *Hispanic Buisness,* September 1989: 42–48.

——. "Item: Networks Invest in Nielsen Ratings." *Hispanic Business,* December 1989: 38–41.

——. "New Blood, Fresh Money." *Hispanic Business,* December 1986: 36.

——. "New & Improved." *Hispanic Business,* December, 1988: 42–50.

——. "Univisa's World View." *Hispanic Business,* April 1989: 22–23.

Berry, Gordon L., and Claudia Mitchell-Kernan. "Television as a Socializing Force Within a Society of Mass Communication." In their [Ital]television and the Socialization of the Minority Child. New York: Academic Press, 1982: 1–11.

Berry, John F. "The New Order at Blair." *Channels: The Business of Communications,* April 1987: 53–56.

Besas, Peter. "Univisa Setting up Hispano Network in us." *Variety,* 7 March 1990: 41, 56.

Bielby, William, and Denise Bielby (1987). *The 1987 Hollywood Writers' Report: A Survey of Ethnic, Gender and Age Employment Practices.* Los Angeles: Writers Guild of America, West, 1987.

Brown, Cynthia. "Stong-Arming the Hispanic Press." *Columbia Journalism Review,* July-August 1980: 51–54.

Bunnell, Robert. "A.K.A. Pablo: Abc's New Latino Comedy Series." *Nuestro,* April 1984: 15–16.

Chacón, Ramón. "The Chicano Immigrant Press in Los Angeles: The Case of *El Heraldo de México,* 1916–1920." *Journalism History,* 4, No. 2, 1977: 48–49.

Chavira, Ricardo. "Reporting in Two Los Angeles Dailies of Mexican Deportations and Emigration from the United States." Unpublished masters thesis, California State University, Northridge.

——. A Case Study: Reporting of Mexican Emigration and Deportation. *Journalism History,* 4, No. 2, 1977: 59–61.

"The Coming of Age of Hispanic Broadcasting." Special Report. *Broadcasting,* 3 April 1989.

Cortés, Carlos (1987). "The Mexican-American Press." In *The Ethnic Press in the United States: A Historical Analysis and Handbook,* edited by S. M. Miller. New York: Greenwood Press, 1987: 247–260.

——. "Power, Passivity, and Pluralism: Mass Media in the Development of Latino Culture and Identity." Paper presented at the Hispanic History and Culture Conference, University of Wisconsin, Milwaukee, April 1991.

Corwin, Miles. "A Voice for Farm Workers." *Los Angeles Times,* 20 August 1989: Part I, 3, 33.

Cox, Dorrit Sue. *Spanish-Language Television in the United States: Its Audience and Its Potential.* Unpublished master's thesis, University of Illinois, 1969.

Davidson, Bill. "The Reformation of 'Chico and the man.'" *TV Guide,* 22, 23 November 1974: 25–29.

Del Olmo, Frank. "Voices for the Chicano Movement." *The Quill,* October 1971: 8–11.

Delpar, Helen. "Goodbye to the 'Greaser': Mexico, the MPPDA, and Derogatory Films, 1922–1926." *Journal of Popular Film and Television,* 12, No. 1, 1984: 34–40.

de Uriarte, Mercedes. "Battle for the Ear of the Latino." *Los Angeles Times Calender,* 14 December 1980: 5.

Downing, John. D. H. "Ethnic Minority Radio in the United States." *Howard Journal of Communications,* 2, spring 1990: 135–148.

Drexel Burnham Lambert. *Prospectus: 2,000,000 Shares; Telemundo Group, Inc.; Common Stock,* 19 August 1987.

Erickson, Charles A. "Hispanic Americans and the Press." *Journal of Intergroup Relations,* 9, No. 1, 1981: 3–16.

Evans, James. "The Indian Savage, the Mexican Bandit, and the Chinese Heathen." Unpublished doctoral thesis, University of Texas at Austin, 1967.

Fishman, J., and H. Casiano. Puerto Ricans in Our Press. *Modern Language Journal,* 53, No. 3, 1969: 157–162.

Fitzpatrick, Joseph. "The Puerto Rican Press." In *The Ethnic Press in the United States: A Historical Analysis and Handbook,* edited by S. M. Miller. New York: Greenwood Press, 1987: 303–314.

"The Foreign Connection: From Mexico to Miami," *Broadcasting,* 3 April 1989: 44–46.

Fouce Amusement Enterprises, Inc., Metropolitan Theaters Corporation vs. Spanish International Communications Corporation, United States Federal District Court, Central District of California, Los Angeles. Case No. CV 76 3451 IH, 4 November 1976.

Friedman, Norman. "A.K.A. Pablo: Mexican American Images for Television." *Exploration in Ethnic Studies,* 8, 1985: 1–10.

Glasheen, Janet. "Betting on Print." *Hispanic Business,* December 1989: 42–44B.

Golden, Tim. "Hispanic Paper Defies the Ad Slump." *New York Times,* 22 April 1991: C1, 6.

González, Arturo R. "A Case Study of KMEX." Unpublished master's thesis, California State University at Northridge, 1978.

González, Juan. "Forgotten Pages: Spanish-Language Newspapers in the Southwest." *Journalism History,* 4, No. 2, 1977: 50–51.

Grebler, Leo, Joan Moore, and Ralph Guzmán. *The Mexican American People.* New York: Free Press,(1970).

Greenberg, Bradley S., and Pilar Baptista-Fernández. "Hispanic Americans: The New Minority on Television." In *Life on Television,* edited by Greenberg. Norwood, New Jersey: Ablex, 1980: 3–12.

Greenberg, Bradley S., Michael Burgoon, Judee Burgoon, and Felipe Korzenny. *Mexican Americans and the Mass Media.* Norwood, New Jersey: Ablex, 1983.

Griswold del Castillo, Richard. "The Mexican Revolution and the Spanish-Language Press in the Borderlands." *Journalism History,* 4, No. 2, 1977: 42–47.

Gutiérrez, Félix F. "Spanish-Language Media in America: Background, Resources, History." *Journalism History,* 4, 2, 1977: 34–41, 65–68.

——. "Reporting for La Raza: The History of Latino Journalism in America." *Agenda,* 8, July-August 1978: 29–35.

——. "Mexico's Television Network." In *Proceedings of the Sixth Annual Telecommunications Policy Research Conference,* edited by H. S. Dordick. Lexington Massachusetts: Lexington, 1979: 135–159.

——, and Ernesto Ballesteros. "The 1541 Earthquake: Dawn of Latin American Journalism." *Journalism History,* 6, No. 3, 1979: 79–83.

——, and Jorge R. Schement. *spanish-Language Radio in the Southwestern United States.* Monograph No. 5. Austin: Center for Mexican American Studies, University of Texas at Austin, 1979.

——. "Problems of Ownership and Control of Spanish-Language Media in the United States: National and International Policy Concerns." In Communication and Social Structure: *Critical Studies in Mass Media Research,* edited by Emile McAnany, Jorge Schnitman, and Noreen Janus. New York: Praeger, 1981: 181–203.

——. "Spanish International Network: The Flow of Television from Mexico to the United States." *Communication Research,* 11, No. 2, 1984: 241–258.

Hester, Al. "Newspapers and Newspaper Prototypes in Spanish America, 1541–1750." *Journalism History,* 6, No. 3, 1979: 73–78.

"Hispanic Owners Band Together." *Broadcasting,* 20 May 1991: 40.

Kanellos, Nicolás. *A History of Hispanic Theatre in the United States: Origins to 1940.* Austin: University of Texas Press, 1990.

Kilgore, Julia Kay. "Take Two." *Hispanic Business,* December 1988: 52–58.

Knudsen, Erik. "Pablo Is Much Like Me." *Nuestro,* April 1984: 17–18.

Lamb, Blaine P. "The Convenient Villain: The Early Cinema Views the Mexican American." *Journal of the West,* 14, No. 4, 1975: 75–81.

Lee, Sylvia Anne. "Image of Mexican Americans in San Antonio Newspapers: A Content Analysis." Unpublished master's thesis, University of Texas at Austin, 1973.

Lewels, Francisco J. *The Uses of the Media by the Chicano Movement: A Study in Minority Access.* New York: Praeger, 1974.

Lichter, S. Robert, Linda S. Lichter, Stanly Rothman, and Daniel Amundson. "Prime-Time Prejudice: Tv's Images of Blacks and Hispanics." *Public Opinion,* July-August 1987: 13–16.

Lopes, Humberto. "*Viva* Leads Miami in Spanish Radio." *Hispanic Business,* December 1991: 42–43.

Lozano, Jose Carlos. "Issues and Sources in Spanish-Language TV: The Case of Noticiero Univisión." Unpublished monograph, Department of Journalism, University of Texas at Austin, 1988.

MacCurdy, Raymond. *A History and Bibliography of Spanish Language Newspapers and Magazines in Louisiana, 1808–1949.* Albuquerque: University of New Mexico Press, 1951.

"Mac Tichenor: Banking on Hispanic radio." *Broadcasting,* 13 May 1991: 87.

Martínez, Thomas. "How Advertisers Promote Racism." *Civil Rights Digest,* fall 1969: 5–11.

McCardell, Wallin S. "Socialization Factors in El Diario-La Prensa, the Spanish-Language Newspaper with the Largest Daily Circulation in the United States." Unpublished doctoral thesis, University of Iowa, 1976.

McWilliams, Carey. "Blood on the Pavements." In *North from Mexico,* edited by McWilliams. New York: Lippincott, 1949.

Medeiros, Francine. "La Opinión, a Mexican Exile Newspaper: A Content Analysis of its First Years, 1926–1929." *Agenda,* 11, 1980: 65–87.

Mejía Barquera, Fernando. *La industria de la radio y la televisión y la política del estado Mexicano: Volúmen I 1920– 1960.* Mexico: Fundación Manuel Buendía, 1989.

——, et al. *Televisa: El Quinto Poder.* Mexico: Claves Latinoamericanas, 1985.

Mendosa, Rick. "Blaya Beams It Up: Exclusive Interview." *Hispanic Business,* October 1991: 16–22.

——. "Media Consumers but No Owners." *Hispanic Business,* October 1990: 16–22.

——. "Radio Revenues Rock and Roll." *Hispanic Business,* December 1990: 26–27.

Miller, Marjorie, and Juanita Darling. "El Tigre." *Los Angeles Times Magazine,* 10 November 1991: 24–29, 51.

Miller, Randall M. *The Kaleidoscopic Lens: How Hollywood Views Ethnic Groups.* Englewood, New Jersey: Jerome S. Ozer, 1980.

——. "Compilations by State of Minority Owned Commercial Broadcast Stations." Minority Telecommunications

Development Program of the National Telecommunications and Information Administration, U.S. Department of Commerce, Louis Camphor, III, Telecommunications Researcher. Unpublished report, October, 1991.

Montgomery, Kathryn C. *Target: Prime Time; Advocacy Groups and the Struggle over Entertainment Television.* New York: Oxford University Press, 1989.

Mydans, Seth. "Charges of Bias in Spanish-Language Television." *New York Times,* 24 August 1989.

National Association of Broadcasters. "Minority-Owned and Controlled Broadcast Station Totals in the Continental United States (excluded Hawaii, Puerto Rico, and U.S. Territories). Part II of Minority Broadcasting Facts." Department of Minority and Special Services, National Association of Broadcasters. Unpublished report, 1986.

National Commission on Working Women. *Unequal Picture: Black, Hispanic, Asian, and Native American Characters on Television.* Published monograph. Washington, D.C.: National Commission on Working Women of Wider Opportunities for Women, 1989.

Newman, M. A., M. B. Liss, and F. Sherman. "Ethnic Awareness in Children: Not a Unitary Concept." *Journal of Genetic Psychology,* 143, 1983: 102–112.

Nordheimer, John. "Resignations Upset Hispanic TV News Program." *New York Times,* (Late City Edition), 4 November 1986: C17.

Noriega, Chon. "Café oralé: Narrative structure in *Born in East L.A.*" *Tonantzin,* 8, No. 1, 1991: 17–18.

Payne, Andrea. "Minorities on Soaps: Are They Treated Fairly?" *Soap Opera Digest,* 10, No. 3, 29 January 1985: 20–27.

Pérez, Richie. "From Assimilation to Annihilation: Puerto Rican Images in U.s. Films." *Centro,* 2, No. 8, 1990: 8–27.

Pettit, Arthur G. *Images of the Mexican American in Fiction and Film.* College Station: Texas A&M University Press, 1980.

Pisano, Vivian M., and Claire Splan. "The Hispanic Media: Alive and Well and Printing in the U.S.A." *Lector,* May/June 1984: 5–7.

Prida, Dolores. "A.K.A. Pablo-Watching and Waiting." *Nuestro,* April 1984: 45.

Public Advocates, Inc. "The Network Brownout: A National Hispanic Network Audit." Unpublished paper prepared upon request by the League of United Latin American Citizens. Washington, D.C., 1983.

Puig, Claudia. "Off the Charts." *Los Angeles Times,* Calendar Section, 7 April 1991: 9, 89–90.

Rangel, Jesús. "Hispanic Print Media—Alive and Growing." *Agenda,* 11, No. 3, 1981: 10–12.

Rasberry, William. "How about Frito Amigo?" *Washington Post,* 2 June 1971: A19.

——. "Who's the Real Bandito?" *Washington Post,* 7 June 1971: A23.

"Reader Profile, 1990." Miami: *Diario Las Américas,* 1990.

Rendón, Armando B. *The Chicano Press: A Status Report on the Needs and Trends in Chicano Journalism.* Published mimeograph. Washington, D.C., 1974.

Reyes, Domingo Nick, and Armando B. Rendón. *Chicanos and the Mass Media.* National Mexican American Anti-Defamation Committee, 1971.

Reyes, Luis. "The Hispanic Image on Network Television: Past and Present." *Caminos,* March 1983: 10–16.

Ríos, Herminio, and Guadalupe Castillo. "Toward a True Chicano Bibliography, Mexican-American Newspapers: 1848–1942." *El Grito: A Journal of Contemporary Mexican-American Thought,* 3, summer 1970: 40–47.

Rivera Brooks, Nancy. "SICC Rejects Latino Group's Bid for Spanish-Language Stations." *Los Angeles Times,* 1986: Part IV, 1.

Russell, Joel. "Something in the Air." *Hispanic Business,* December 1988: 60–66.

——. "Media Deal of the Year." *Hispanic Business,* December 1989: 24–30.

Salinas, Alejandra. "Computer Listing of Hispanic Publications." Unpublished. Benson Mexican American Studies Library. University of Texas at Austin, 1990.

Sánchez, Leo Anthony. "Treatment of Mexican Americans by Selected U.S. Newspapers, January-June 1970." Unpublished masters thesis, Pennsylvania State University, 1973.

Schement, Jorge Reina, and Ricardo Flores. "The Origins of Spanish-Language Radio: The Case of San Antonio, Texas." *Journal of History,* 4, No. 2, 1977: 56–58, 61.

Schement, Jorge Reina, and Loy A. Singleton. "The Onus of Minority Ownership: FCC Policy and Spanish-Language Radio." *Journal of Communication,* 31, No. 2, spring 1981: 78–83.

Seijo-Maldonado, Haydée. "History of Spanish-Language Television in the United States." Unpublished communication monograph, University of Illinois at Urbana, 1989.

Shaw, David. "Amid L.A.'s Ethnic Mix: The *Times* Plays Catch-Up." *Los Angeles Times,* 14 December 1990.

——. "Asian-Americans Chafe Against Stereotype of 'Model Citizen.'" *Los Angeles Times,* 11 December 1990.

——. "Despite Advances, Stereotypes Still Used by Media." *Los Angeles Times,* 12 December 1990.

——. "The 'Jackie Robinson Syndrom'—A Double Standard." *Los Angeles Times,* 14 December 1990.

——. "Newspapers Struggling to Raise Minority Coverage." *Los Angeles Times,* 12 December 1990.

——. "Negative News and Little Else." *Los Angeles Times,* 11 December 1990.

——. "Seattle Times Uses Direct Approach in Minority Coverage." *Los Angeles Times,* 12 December 1990.

——. "Stereotypes Hinder Minorities' Attempts to Reach Managerial Ranks." *Los Angeles Times,* 13 December 1990.

——. "What's the News? White Editors Make the Call." *Los Angeles Times,* 13 December 1990.

Shearer, James F. "Periódicos españoles en los Estados Unidos." *Revista Hispánica Moderna,* 20, 1954: 45–57.

Shiver, Jube, Jr. "Keeping Univisión Alive." *Los Angeles Times,* 19 February 1990: D1, 4.

Standard Rate and Data Service. *Hispanic Media and Markets,* Vol. 4, No. 1, 28 March 1991.

Sterling, Mary Ann. "Spanish-Language Print Media in the United States: A Case Study of *La Opinión*." Unpublished masters thesis, University of Southern California, 1984. Stone, Vernon A. "Pipelines and Dead Ends: Jobs Held by Minorities and Women in Broadcast News." *Mass Comm Review,* 15, Nos. 2 and 3, 1988: 10–19.

Straton, Porter A. *The Territorial Press of New Mexico, 1834–1912.* Albuquerque: University of New Mexico Press, 1969.

Subervi-Vélez, Federico A. "Spanish-Language Daily Newspapers and the 1984 Elections." *Journalism Quarterly,* 65, No. 3, 1988: 678–685.

——. "Interactions Between Latinos and Anglos on Prime-Time Television: A Case Study of 'Condo'." In *Income and Status Differences Between White and Minority Americans: A Persistent Inequality,* edited by S. Chan. Lewiston, New York: Edwin Mellen Press, 1990: 303–336.

Treviño, Jesus Salvador. "Latinos and Public Broadcasting: The 2% Factor." *Caminos,* March 1983: 25–27, 50.

U.S. Commission on Civil Rights. *Window Dressing on the Set: An Update.* Washington, D.C.: U.S. Government Printing Office, 1979.

U.S. Commission on Civil Rights. *Window Dressing on the Set: Women and Minorities in Television.* Washington, D.C.: U.S. Government Printing Office, 1977.

Valdéz, Rubén V. "A Case Study in Pretrial Criminal News Reporting: The Río Arriba County Courthouse Raid of June 5, 1967, Involving Reíes López Tijerina." Unpublished masters thesis, West Virginia University, 1970.

——. "The Evolution of Spanish-Language Television in the United States as Related to Panamsat: Transborder Telecommunications Policy Issues." Paper presented at the thirteenth annual Telecommunications Policy Research Conference, Airlie, Virginia, April 1985.

Valenzuela, Nicholas A. ("Organizational Evolution of a Spanish Language Television Network: An Environmental Approach." Unpublished doctoral thesis, Stanford University, 1985.

Valle, Victor. "HBO-Cinemax Experiment in Bilingual TV," *Los Angeles Times,* 1 May 1989: D1, 6.

——. (1988). "The Latino Wave," *Los Angeles Times,* Entertainment Section, 2 April 1988: 1, 11.

Veciana-Suárez, Ana. *Hispanic Media: Impact and Influence.* Washington D.C.: The Media Institute, 1990.

——. *Hispanic Media, USA.* Washington, D.C.: The Media Institute, 1987.

Vidal, David. "The Strange Case of Reverend Moon and His New Paper in New York." *Washington Journalism Review,* November 1980: 28–29.

"*Vista* Magazine Names Tosteson to Top Posts, after Firing Publisher." *Wall Street Journal,* 19 February 1991.

Wagner, Henry R. "New Mexico Spanish Press." *New Mexico Historical Review,* 12, 1937: 1–40.

Wilkinson, Kenton T. "The Forgotten Factor in the Sale of Spanish International Communications Corporation to Hallmark Cards: The Influence of Mexico's Economy and Politics." Paper presented at the seventh annual Intercultural and International Communication Conference, Miami, Florida, February 1990.

——. "Recent Developments in the Evolution of Spanish-Language Television in the United States." Unpublished political science monograph, University of California at Berkeley, 1990.

——. "The Sale of Spanish International Communications Corporations: Milestone in the Development of Spanish-Language Television in the United States." Unpublished master's thesis, University of California at Berkeley, 1991.

Wilson, Clint, Jr., and Félix F. Gutiérrez. *Minorities and the Media: Diversity and the End of Mass Communication.* Beverly Hills, California: Sage, 1985.

Woll, Allen. *The Latin Image in American Film.* Revised edition. University of California, Los Angeles: Latin American Center Publications, 1980.

Federico Subervi

㉕

Sports

✴ Baseball ✴ Rodeo ✴ Other Sports ✴ Prominent Hispanic Athletes

Hispanic participation and achievements in sports have been determined by Hispanic traditions of work, play, and ritual, both in the United States and in the greater Spanish-speaking world. As Hispanic customs in the United States and throughout Latin America have derived from the blending of various bloodlines and cultures—European, Amerindian, and African—so too the types of sports practiced by Hispanics has evolved out of the rituals and traditions that can quite often be traced back to the peoples that encountered each other in the early sixteenth century when the Spaniards evangelized the Mesoamerican Indians and began importing slaves from Africa. In the United States, the descendants of this encounter also adopted Anglo-American traditions in sport and shared their own with the Anglo-Americans. The prime examples of this exchange are rodeo and baseball. Ranching and sport with horses and cattle were introduced to the Americas by the Spaniards. The Spanish customs mixed with some American Indian traditions and then were learned by Anglo-Americans and European immigrants.

The American cowboy was born when the United States expanded westward and encountered the Mexican cattle culture. Today's rodeo owes a great deal to the *charrerías* (contests) of the Mexican vaqueros, or cowboys. The "national pastime" of baseball developed in the United States in the nineteenth century and was then introduced to Cuba and other nearby Hispanic countries in the last part of that century. As American teams needed warm wintering grounds and off-season play, the climates and facilities in Mexico and the Spanish-speaking Caribbean attracted American baseball players, thus exposing more and more Hispanics to the "all-American" sport.

But Hispanic participation, especially in professional sports in the United States, has also depended on a number of factors, other than customs and traditions. Various sports demand certain body types that seem to present relative advantages for success. The prime example, of course, is basketball, where tall players have proven to be more successful. Most Hispanics have descended from American Indians and Spaniards, both of whom are relatively short peoples compared to northern Europeans and many African peoples. As would be expected, there are very few Hispanics represented in professional basketball. The same is true of football, which also demands very large and strong bodies. Notwithstanding the general disadvantage of Hispanics as a whole, there have been great achievers, even in such contact sports as football, as the careers of Manny Fernández, Anthony Muñoz, and Tom Flores attest.

Another factor is education. College sports are quite often training grounds for the professional leagues. Hispanic dropout rates in high school are the highest in the country, and their admission to and graduation from college is the lowest compared with Anglos and Afro-Americans. Hispanics thus have fewer opportunities to get involved in college sports, especially football and basketball, not to mention other more elite sports, such as tennis and golf. But, there are also "back doors" of entry to these sports, such as working as caddies and greens keepers, as the careers of Chi Chi Rodríguez and Lee Treviño exemplify.

Furthermore, various sports have traditionally been associated with certain social classes and have been restricted to members of these classes principally because of economic barriers, such as membership fees in private country clubs, the payment of fees for private lessons, the lack of public facilities, the high expense of specialized equipment, such as golf clubs and gear, and the high tuition of private schools where these sports are cultivated. Prime examples of these sports are polo, golf, lacrosse, and,

Ramón Ahumada (right), known as "El Charro Plateado" (the Silver Plated Cowboy), was elected to the Cowboy Hall of Fame. (Photograph circa 1890.)

before the construction of numerous tennis courts in public parks, tennis. On the other hand, boxing classes and sports facilities have traditionally been accessible to poor inner-city youths through boys clubs, police athletic leagues, and the military services. In addition, boxing has been a traditional avenue to economic success and fame for one immigrant and minority group after another and for poor inner-city youths in the United States. Hispanics have developed a long tradition of achievement in boxing, especially in the lighter-weight classes.

There are relative advantages to being short, lightweight, and quick in the wide world of sports. Hispanics not only have excelled as bantamweights and lightweights in boxing, but also have earned an outstanding record as jockeys, quick-handed infielders in baseball, and star players in such sports as soccer, where speed and endurance are important. Soccer has also provided an opportunity for Hispanics to participate in professional football, which has recruited various Hispanic placekickers for the accuracy they have developed with their angled and powerful kicking. But all of the above conditions are

changing rapidly. American society is becoming more and more democratic and open. In the late 1940s, American baseball ceased to be segregated, then football also opened up. In modern life today, sports facilities are accessible to people from all social classes in public parks and schools, and universities are making more of an effort to recruit minorities. Universities are even recruiting and training Dominican, Panamanian, and Puerto Rican players of Afro-Hispanic background for their basketball, football, and track teams.

✴ BASEBALL

Although many sportswriters in the United States have considered the presence of ballplayers from Latin America to be an "influx," as if baseball were a uniquely American sport being invaded by outsiders, the truth of the matter is that baseball in Spanish-speaking countries has not only had a parallel development to baseball in the United States, but it has been intertwined with American baseball almost from the beginning of the game itself. The professional Cuban Baseball League (Liga de Béisbol Profesional Cubana) was founded in 1878, just seven years after the National Baseball Association was founded in the United States. But, reportedly, Cuban baseball goes back to 1866, when sailors from an American ship in Matanzas harbor invited Cubans to play the game; they built a baseball diamond together at Palmar del Junco and began playing while the ship remained in harbor. By 1874, Cuban teams had developed and were playing each other regularly.

By 1891, there were 75 teams active on the island. From that time on, Cuban baseball—and later, Mexican and Puerto Rican baseball—has served baseball in the United States in various ways: as a training ground for the majors, formalized when the Cuban Sugar Kings were made a Triple A minor league team; as wintering and spring training grounds for the majors; and as permanent homes for players from the U.S. Negro leagues, also providing a baseball team, the Havana Cubans, to the Negro leagues. Since the early days of the National Baseball Association until Jackie Robinson broke the color line in 1947, about 50 Hispanic American ballplayers played in the major leagues, some even becoming Hall of Famers and one achieving the position of manager. However, for the most part, these were Cuban players who were white or could pass for white. In fact, the acceptance of progressively darker-skinned Hispanics was used as a barometer by the Negro leagues for the eventual acceptance of Afro-Americans into the majors. The Hispanics that

A baseball team of Mexicans and Anglos in Los Angeles in the 1870s.

could not "pass" either played in the Negro leagues or in Cuba, Mexico, or Venezuela. What is clear is that Cuba served as a free ground exempt from the segregation that dominated U.S. sports and provided playing fields where major-leaguers and players from the Negro leagues and Latin America could play openly together.

As baseball continued its development in Mexico, pressure from fans and investors increased for expanding the U.S. major leagues to Mexico and for the creation of Mexico's own professional leagues. In 1946, the wealthy Pasquel family in Mexico founded a professional league and set about enticing major league and Negro league stars from the United States with salaries quite higher than were being offered in the United States. The whole Pasquel venture, which was seen by the U.S. media as "robbery" and a threat to the national pastime, even led to an official complaint by the U.S. State Department. Some 23 players jumped to Pasquel's league, but after continued financial problems the league ceased to exist in 1953. The northern teams of the league merged with the Arizona-Texas and Arizona-Mexico leagues from 1953 to 1957. The Mexican League began functioning again in 1955 and has continued to do so. The Mexican Central

League has served since 1960—a year after the Cuban Revolution curtailed Triple A ball on the island—as a Class A minor league and was later joined by other Mexican leagues based on the earlier Pasquel circuit. Today the league has 14 teams playing in two divisions, and both supply young ballplayers to the majors and receive former major-leaguers on their way out of baseball.

The Majors

The first Hispanic ballplayers in the United States played in the National Association and in the Negro League. Before 1947, the major league clubs that employed the most Hispanics were in Washington, Cincinnati, Chicago, Cleveland, and Detroit. The New York Yankees did not employ Hispanics before 1918 and Pittsburgh did not employ any until 1943, when it hired one. According to Brown, the first Hispanic to join the majors was third baseman Esteban Bellán, a black Cuban who was recruited from Fordham College by the Troy Haymakers in 1869 and actually took to the field in 1871—the year of the founding of the National Baseball Association—to spend three years in the majors. By the turn of the century, no black Cubans were allowed in the majors, despite major leaguers observing their talents firsthand and suffering defeats from them. One such powerhouse was pitcher José Méndez. Méndez played with the Cuban Stars against the best of the Negro teams and won 44 victories, with only two defeats on a tour of the United States in 1909. In Cuba, Méndez beat the Phillies and split two games against future Hall of Famers Christy Mathewson and John McGraw of the New York Giants. But light-skinned Cuban and Hispanic ballplayers soon began appearing more and more in American baseball, despite complaints that the racial purity of the American sport was being contaminated. In 1911, the Cincinnati Reds had affidavits prepared to prove that their new Cuban players, Armando Marsans and Rafael Almeida, had only the purest Castilian blood flowing through their veins. Marsans and Almeida had been brought up to the majors from the Negro leagues' Cuban Stars team; this was seen by the Negro press as an indication that the majors would soon be opening up:

> Now that the first shock is over it would not be surprising to see a Cuban a few shades darker than Almeida and Marsans breaking into the professional ranks, with a coal-black Cuban on the order of the crack pitcher, Méndez, making his debut later on. . . . With the admission of Cubans of a darker hue in the two big leagues it would then be easy for colored players who are citizens of this country to get into fast company. The Negro in this country has more varied hues than even the Cubans, and the only way to distinguish him would be to hear him talk. Until the public got accustomed to seeing native Negroes on big league (teams), the colored players could keep their mouths shut and pass for Cubans. (Quoted by Robert Peterson in *Only the Ball Was White*, 1970)

In 1912, Cuban Miguel González began playing for Boston as a catcher. González played for 17 years on various teams and served 14 seasons as a Cardinals coach, the first Hispanic to do so. But the greatest longevity by any Hispanic in major league baseball was attained by Adolfo Luque. A dark-skinned Cuban pitcher, Luque was jeered at and continuously faced racial epithets from fans from the time he took to the field for the Braves in 1914 until his retirement in 1935. Having played for the Braves, Cincinnati, Brooklyn, and the New York Giants, Luque pitched in two World Series, was credited with the decisive win in one of them and during his best year, 1923, led the league for Cincinnati in wins (27), earned run average (1.93), and shutouts (6).

The greatest number of Hispanic ballplayers by far was employed by the Washington Senators, beginning in 1911 but reaching its peak from 1939 to 1947 with a total of 19 players of Hispanic background. At Washington, as at other major league clubs, the Hispanics suffered not only racial attacks from fans and sportswriters, but also segregation in housing, uniforms, equipment, and travel conditions. Many of these conditions improved noticeably during the 1940s with the competition for ballplayers that was exerted by the Mexican league.

After the color barrier was broken in 1947, things became much easier for Hispanic ballplayers of all colors and nationalities, and their representation in the major leagues quickly climbed. By the 1970s, a full 9 percent of the players were Hispanics. Due to the restrictions that came about after the Cuban Revolution—even baseball equipment was not to be had in Cuba due to the U.S. economic embargo—the flow of players from Cuba into the major leagues was curtailed. During the 1970s and 1980s, Cubans were no longer the Hispanic nationality most represented. The lead passed to the Dominican Republic and Puerto Rico, with Venezuela and Mexico also making a strong showing. But by 1963, the Cuban National Team had begun to dominate amateur baseball and to cement its perennial championship of the Pan American Games. The caliber of play is equivalent to that of major league teams, but the broken political relations between the United States and Cuba has made international professional play between the two countries impossible.

Major league baseball in the United States is and will continue to be a strong draw for Hispanic ballplayers, not only as an economic springboard with its lucrative salaries, but also because of the excellence and competitive nature of the game played here, made even more competitive by the quality Hispanic ballplayers have always contributed to the majors.

The Negro Leagues

The Negro leagues were a haven for Hispanic ballplayers whose skin color was a barrier to their admission to the major leagues in the United States. In Robert Peterson's book *Only the Ball Was White* (1970), the contribution of Hispanic, mainly Cuban, ballplayers to the sport in the United States is amply documented. The Negro leagues and the leagues in Cuba, Mexico, Puerto Rico, and Venezuela were completely open to each other. Both black and white players from the Hispanic world and from the United States played on the same teams and against each other freely in Cuba. In Latin America there were no color lines. By the 1920s, not only were many Hispanics playing in the Negro leagues, but many American blacks had incorporated into their routine playing the winter season in Cuba, then later Puerto Rico, Mexico, and Venezuela. Among the Hispanic greats to play in the Negro leagues were Cristóbal Torriente, Martín Dihigo, José Méndez, Orestes "Minnie" Miñoso, Alejandro Oms, Luis Tiant, Sr., and scores of others.

As early as 1900, two of the five black professional teams bore the name of Cuba: the Cuban Giants (with its home city shifting from year to year from New York to Hoboken, New Jersey, to Johnstown, Pennsylvania, and so on) and the Cuban X Giants of New York. (These teams should not be confused with one of the first black professional ball teams of the 1880s, which called itself the Cuban Giants, thinking that fans would be more attracted to the exotic Cubans than to ordinary American blacks). In the 1920s, both the Eastern Colored League (NNL) and the Negro National League (NNL) had a Cuban Stars baseball team, one owned by Alex Pómpez, who at one point was vice president of the NNL, and the other by Agustín Molina. Cuban teams continued to be prominent during the heyday of the Negro leagues from the 1920s through the 1940s. There were also Hispanic players on teams throughout the Negro leagues, from the Indianapolis Clowns and Cleveland Buckeyes to the Memphis Red Sox and the New York Black Yankees. Aside from the teams that identified themselves as Cuban, such as the New York Cubans and the Cuban Stars, there were others that had their rosters filled with Hispanics, such as the Indianapolis Clowns, which at one point was even managed by a Hispanic, Ramiro Ramírez. (In his long career from 1916 to 1948, Ramírez managed or played with most of the Cuban teams, including the Baltimore Black Sox and the Bacharach Giants.)

✳ RODEO

The Spaniards introduced cattle ranching to the New World, and with this industry the early settlers and soldiers also introduced the horse and its use for work and sport. Much of contemporary sports culture that depends upon horsemanship and cattle, such as equestrian contests, horse racing, bullfighting, and rodeo, is heavily indebted to the Spanish and Hispanic American legacy. The evolution of rodeo as a sport goes back to the blending of Spanish and American Indian customs of animal handling and sport. A class of mestizo (mixed Indian and Spanish) vaqueros, or cowboys, developed in Mexico during the seventeenth, eighteenth, and nineteenth centuries on the large haciendas. These mestizo cowboys, called charros, eventually evolved their own subculture of unique customs, dress, music, and

horsemanship, which in turn owed much to the Arab horsemen that had influenced Spanish culture during the 700 years of Moslem occupation of the peninsula. The charros, in fact, were the models for the development of the American cowboy, just as was Mexican ranching culture was essential in the development of that industry in the United States. During the late eighteenth and early nineteenth centuries, Anglo-American cowboys began working alongside Mexican cowboys on the same ranches in Texas and California.

The style of dress and horsemanship of the charro became more popularized in the cities during the nineteenth century and was eventually adopted as the national costume. Their contests and games, *charrería,* became the Mexican national sport. The skillful games of the charros became games and shows on the large haciendas during the festive roundups in the nineteenth century, which drew guests from hundreds of miles around. The charros dressed in their finest outfits and displayed their skills in such contests as correr el gallo (running the rooster), horse racing, wild horse and bull riding, and roping horses or steers by their horns or back or front feet, bulldogging, and throwing bulls by their tails. Correr el gallo involved picking up something as small as a coin from the ground while riding a horse at full gallup. These fiestas were perhaps the most important forerunners of the modern American rodeo, and their events included almost all of those associated with today's rodeos. More important, these equestrian sports became part of the standard celebrations at fiestas and fairs among Mexicans and Anglos all along both sides of the border. And charrería, as a separate institution from rodeo, has continued to this day to be practiced by Mexicans in Mexico and throughout the American Southwest.

According to Mary Lou LeCompte, in her article "The Hispanic Influence on the History of Rodeo" (from *Journal of Sports History,* 1985), after much of today's American Southwest was expropriated from Mexico as a result of the Mexican-American War, Mexican charrería continued to flourish quite often in the heart of Anglo society for some 60 years before Anglo-sponsored cowboy events existed. It was Colonel W. F. "Buffalo Bill" Cody who played a key role in the development of the American rodeo by bringing together many of the traditional events of charrería in his Wild West Show. Between 1883 and 1916, Cody's show and a host of imitators toured the major cities of the United States and Europe. Integrated in Cody's and the other shows were numerous Mexican vaqueros, many of whom had been recruited in San Antonio, Texas. Among these were superstar Antonio Esquivel and roper Señor Francisco. But the most famous and influential Mexican charro of all was Vicente Oropeza. A Mexican native, Oropeza made his American debut in July 1891 in San Antonio and went on to become a headliner in shows touring throughout the United States. Oropeza was the greatest trick, and fancy roper of all time, and he became a star of Cody's show for some 16 years, even influencing one of America's greatest rodeo stars, Will Rogers.

During the early years of the twentieth century, local and state fairs and celebrations among Anglos in the West featured cowboy events in what they called "stampedes," "roundups" and "frontier days." These proliferated to the extent that professional contestants began to make a living traveling the circuit of these fairs. The events that became the heart of these contests were the traditional charro events of bronco riding, steer roping, and trick roping. The first cowboy to win the World Championship of Trick and Fancy Roping in 1900 was Vicente Oropeza. Oropeza and many other charros and American cowboys continued to compete in both the United States and Mexico throughout the 1930s. By 1922, with the production by Tex Austin of the first World Championship Cowboy Contest in New York's Madison Square Garden, rodeo had officially become a sport, not just a show. Eight of the ten events featured in this new sport had long been a part of charrería. More important, the five standard events of contemporary professional rodeo all owe their roots to charrería: bareback bronc riding, saddle bronc riding, bull riding, steer wrestling, and calf roping.

✴ OTHER SPORTS

While baseball and rodeo are two sports that have been highly influenced by Hispanics in their evolution, there are other sports that have benefited from the participation of outstanding Hispanic athletes. First and foremost is boxing, which has a long history of Hispanic champions, especially in the lighter-weight classifications, where the speed and lighter body weight of many Cuban, Mexican, and Puerto Rican boxers has been used to advantage. From the days of Sixto Escobar and Kid Chocolate to the present, boxing has also served for Hispanics, as it has for other immigrants and minorities, as a tempting avenue out of poverty.

With more colleges and universities recruiting and graduating Hispanics, some of the other "money" sports, such as football and basketball, will also begin to incorporate more Hispanics in their ranks. Already, such football stars as Manny Fernández, Tom Flores, Anthony Muñoz, and Jim Plunkett have appeared on the scene, and there are many more to follow, especially from the universities of the Southwestern Conference.

Finally, the mere fact that an island as small as Puerto Rico—only 35 by 100 miles—has ten professional-quality golf clubs proves the potential for Hispanic impact on that sport. Such golfers as Juan "Chi Chi" Rodríguez have become world-class competitors after beginning as humble caddies for tourists. And as more and more facilities, such as golf courses and tennis courts, become accessible in the United States through public parks or public schools, greater Hispanic participation and achievement will be recorded.

Soccer is the most popular sport throughout Latin America. With the high rate of immigration from Latin America to the United States, the popularity of soccer has grown steadily during the last two decades. Up until recently, most efforts to establish professional soccer teams have met with difficulties in financing and attracting sufficient crowds. However, with the United States hosting the World Cup of Soccer Championships in 1994, soccer's popularity has skyrocketed and professional outdoor and indoor soccer teams seem to have benefitted greatly from the national media coverage and publicity. In the future, soccer may become a major professional sport in the United States, and Hispanic participation will certainly be significant. For the present, soccer is a major amateur, high school and college sport, which has a relatively high representation of outstanding Hispanic players.

✴ PROMINENT HISPANIC ATHLETES

Luis Aparicio (1934–)

Baseball

Venezuelan Luis Aparicio was one of the greatest shortstops of all time. He still holds the records for games, double plays, and assists and the American League record for putouts. His 506 stolen bases also rank among the highest. Playing from 1956 to 1973, mostly with the White Sox, Aparicio began his career as Rookie of the Year and proceeded to maintain outstanding and inspired performance throughout his life as a ballplayer. Aparicio played on All-Star teams from 1958 to 1964 and then again from 1970 to 1972. He was the winner of the Gold Glove 11 times. In 1984, Luis Aparicio was inducted into the Hall of Fame.

Bobby Bonilla (1963–)

Baseball

Born in New York City on February 23, 1963, Bobby Bonilla grew up a few blocks from Yankee

Stadium. After attending New York Technical College, Bonilla signed up with the Pittsburgh Pirates in 1981. After bouncing around from team to team, he returned to Pittsburgh in 1988 and became one of the teams most important sluggers. From 1988 to 1990, Bonilla was selected for consecutive All-Star Teams. In 1990 and 1991, his batting assisted the Pirates in winning the National League East title. In 1992, he gained the distinction of becoming baseball's highest paid player, upon his signing a contract with the New York Mets for $29 million over five years ($5.8 million annually).

Carlos Briceño (1967–)

Volleyball

Carlos Briceño was born on August 10, 1967, in Fountain Valley, California, to a Peruvian father and a Dominican mother. He graduated from public schools in Fountain Valley, and in 1990 graduated from the University of Hawaii with a B.A. in Communications. Briceño was a member of the 1985 U.S. Volleyball Team. In the 1985 U.S. Junior Games, Briceño won the bronze medal. Later, at the University of Hawaii, he was named All-American in 1989 and 1990. Briceño played professional volleyball in

Luis Aparicio.

Four-Man Professional Beach Volleyball. In international play, Briceño has consistently ranked among the top three places and in 1995 shared Number One men's team ranking. At the Barcelona Olympics, Briceño won a bronze medal for the United States, and in 1993 he won a silver medal at the NORCEA championships.

José Canseco (1964–)

Baseball

José Canseco was born in Regla, Cuba, on July 2, 1964, and immigrated with his parents and siblings to the United States in 1965 to escape Communism in Cuba. Despite not having played baseball until he was 13 years old, Canseco learned the game well enough to have been offered college scholarships upon graduation from high school. Instead, he was drafted by the Oakland A's in 1982 for their minor league team. He was brought up to the A's in 1984 and batted .302 for his first season, during which he was selected for the All-star Team. In the 1988 season he became the first baseball player in history to bat 40 home runs and steal 40 bases—actually, he hit 42 homers and had 124 RBIs. That year, Canseco won the American League Most Valuable Player and the Associated Press Player of the Year distinctions. In the first game of the World Series, Canseco hit a grand slam against the Los Angeles Dodgers. Canseco eventually led the A's into three straight World Series, but the A's were only able to win one of them. In 1991, Canseco was traded to the Texas Rangers and in 1994 was again traded to the Boston Red sox.

Rod Carew (1945–)

Baseball

Born in the Panama Canal Zone, Carew moved with his mother to New York at age 17. He signed his first professional contract while he was still in high school in 1964, and when he made it into the majors in 1967 with the Minnesota Twins, he was named Rookie of the Year. From 1969 on, he had 15 consecutive seasons batting over .300. Carew won seven American League batting championships. In his Most Valuable Player year he batted .388, 50 points better than the next-best average and the largest margin in major league history. His career batting average was .328, with 3,053 hits, 1,015 runs batted in, and 92 home runs. In 1979, Carew forced a trade, in part because of racist comments regarding black fans by Twins owner Calvin Griffith; he was traded to the Angels for four players. In 1977, Carew received over four million All-Star votes, more than any other player ever. He would have played in 18 consecutive All-Star games, but missed 1970 and

Rod Carew.

Casals was brought up by her great-aunt and great-uncle. Casals began playing tennis at Golden Gate Park under the guidance of her adoptive father, Manuel Casals Y. Bordas, who has been her only coach to this date. Casals won her first championship at age 13 and by age 17 she was ranked eleventh by the United States Ladies Tennis Association (USLTA). At 18, her ranking was third in the nation. Casals and Billie Jean King were doubles champions five times, from 1967 to 1973, at the All-England Championships at Wimbledon and twice at the USLTA championships at Forest Hills. The Casals-King team is the only doubles team to have won U.S. titles on grass, clay, indoor, and hard surfaces. Nine times, Casals was rated as number one in doubles by the USLTA, with teammates that included King, Chris Evert Lloyd, and Jo Anne Russell. Casals has also won mixed doubles championships, playing with Richard Stockton and Ilie Nastase.

Hugo M. Castelló (1914–1994)

Fencing

Born in La Plata, Argentina, on April 22, 1914, Hugo Castelló moved to the United States with his family at age eight and received his public education

1979 because of injuries, and for the same reason was not chosen in 1982. Carew was one of the best base stealers, with 348 career stolen bases. In 1969, Carew tied the record with seven steals to home. He led the league three times in base hits and once in runs scored. With such accomplishments, it was no surprise when he was elected to the Major League Baseball Hall of Fame in 1990.

After retiring in 1985, Carew began his own hitting school in Anaheim, California, where he aided everyone from little league to professional baseball players. In 1992 he accepted the California Angels' offer to become their hitting coach. Since his first season, in which the Angels had the worst team batting average in the majors, the team has improved steadily to become one of the best. In 1991, five years after his retirement, Rod Carew became only the twenty-third player in history to be elected to the Baseball Hall of Fame in his first year of eligibility.

Rosemary Casals (1948–)

Tennis

Born on September 16, 1948, in San Francisco, the daughter of Salvadoran immigrants, Rosemary

Rosemary Casals.

in New York City. He earned his B.A. degree at Washington Square College in 1937 and his law degree from Georgetown University in 1941. Castelló became one of the nation's most outstanding fencers and fencing instructors and coaches. He was nationally ranked among the top four senior fencers from 1935 to 1936, the years that he was National Intercollegiate Foil Champion, and he was a member of the U.S. Olympic team in 1936. Castelló served as adjunct associate professor and head fencing coach at New York University from 1946 to 1975. Castelló is among a select group of coaches who have won at least ten National Collegiate team championships. Only five other NCAA coaches in all sports have won ten national team titles. Castelló was also director and head coach of the United States' first Olympic fencing training camp in 1962. He also served as chief of mission and coach at the Pan American Games (1963) in Sao Paulo and at the World Championships in Cuba (1969), Minsk (1970), and Madrid (1972). Castelló is a member of the Helms Sports Hall of Fame, the New York University Sports Hall of Fame, and the PSAL Hall of Fame. He died on March 28, 1994.

Orlando Cepeda (1937–)

Baseball

Orlando Cepeda was born in Ponce, Puerto Rico, on September 17, 1937. After growing up playing sandlot baseball and later organized team play in New York City, Cepeda was discovered by talent scout Alex Pómpez and began as a major league outfielder with the San Francisco Giants in 1958, when he was named Rookie of the Year. Hitting his stride in 1961, Cepeda led the league in home runs. Cepeda remained on the team until May 1966, when he was transferred to the St. Louis Cardinals after having missed almost a whole season because of a leg injury. He stayed with the Cardinals until 1968. Before his retirement, he also played for the Braves, the A's, the Red Sox, and the Royals. He made a remarkable comeback with the Cardinals, winning the National League's Most Valuable Player award, leading the league in runs batted in 1967 and making the All-Star team in that year, as well. Orlando Cepeda played on World Series teams in 1962 and 1967. In all, Cepeda played 2,124 games, with a lifetime batting average of .279. He hit 379 home runs and had 1,364 runs batted in. Cepeda had nine .300 seasons and eight seasons with 25 or more home runs. Cepeda has never been named to the Hall of Fame, possibly because of his serving time in prison for marijuana smuggling after his baseball career had ended. However, in 1994, Cepeda was inducted into the Black Sports Hall of Fame.

Orlando Cepeda.

Roberto Walker Clemente (1934–1972)

Baseball

Roberto Walker Clemente is celebrated for being a heroic figure both on and off the baseball diamond. One of the all-time greats of baseball, he died on December 31, 1972 in a tragic plane crash in while delivering relief supplies to the victims of an earthquake in Nicaragua. Born on August 18, 1934, Clemente rose from an impoverished background in Carolina, Puerto Rico, to become the star outfielder for the Pittsburgh Pirates from the years 1955 to 1972. He assisted the Pirates in winning two World Series in 1960 and 1971. Among Clemente's achievements as a player, he was four times the National League batting champion—1961, 1964, 1965, and 1967—and he was voted the league's most valuable player in 1966. He was awarded 12 Gold Gloves and set a major league record in leading the National League in assists five times. He served on 14 all-star teams, and he was one of only 16 players to have 3,000 or more hits during their career. Clemente was promising a great deal more before his untimely death; he had accumulated 240 home runs and a lifetime batting average of .317. Upon his death the

Roberto Clemente.

Baseball Hall of Fame waived its five-year waiting period after a player's retirement and immediately elected him to membership. For his generosity, leadership, outstanding athletic achievements, and heroism, Roberto Clemente is considered by Puerto Ricans to be a national hero to this day.

Dave Concepción (1948–)

Baseball

Venezuelan David Concepción was one of baseball's greatest shortstops, playing for the Cincinnati Reds from 1970 to 1988. In 1973, Concepción was named captain of the Reds, and in 1978 he became the first Cincinnati shortstop to bat .300 since 1913. In World Series play, Concepción hit better than .300 three times and better than .400 in the 1975 and 1979 league championships. His lifetime batting average is .267 for 2,488 games played. He made All-Star teams in 1973 and from 1975 to 1982. He was also winner of the Gold Glove each year from 1974 to 1977 and in 1979. In 1977, he was the winner of the Roberto Clemente Award as the top Latin American ballplayer in the major leagues.

Angel Cordero (1942–)

Horse Racing

Angel Tomás Cordero, born in San Juan, Puerto Rico, on November 8, 1942, is one of the most winning jockeys of all time. By December 1986, he was fourth in the total number of races won and third in the amount of money won in purses: $109,958,510. Included among Cordero's important wins were the Kentucky Derby in 1974, 1976, and 1985; the Preakness Stakes in 1980 and 1984; and the Belmont Stakes in 1976. He was the leading rider at Saratoga for 11 years in a row. In 1982, he was named jockey of the year. In 1988, Angel Cordero became the first Puerto Rican jockey to be inducted into the Thoroughbred Racing Hall of Fame. In his 31-year career, Cordero won more than 7000 races, including the three Kentucky Derbies.

Oscar de la Hoya (1973–)

Boxing

Born in East Los Angeles in 1973, Oscar de la Hoya is the son of Cecila and former boxer Joel de la Hoya. In addition, to his father, his brother, grandfather and uncles all boxed. He thus was encouraged to

Dave Concepción.

box from childhood and had access to good trainers who worked with other family members. Soon after graduation from Garfield High School, De la Hoya was selected for the Olympic team and came back from the 1992 Barcelona Games with a gold medal. As a professional, de la Hoya put together a record of 18 victories and no losses as of 1995. In May, 1995, he won the International Federation Lightweight Crown with a purse of $1.75 million. In September, he sailed past Genaro Hernández to win the World Boxing Organization lightweight title with a purse of $2.4 million.

Sandra Lynn de la Riva-Baza (1961–)

Handball

Sandra Lynn de la Riva-Baza was born on November 26, 1961, in Los Angeles, California, to Mexican immigrant parents. De la Riva-Baza earned her B.A. in Political Science from Rutgers University in 1985 and her Master's in Publica Administration from the university of Southern California in 1990. Since the late 1970's, De la Baza has played team handball, making the United States national team for nine years, including participation in the 1984 and 1988 Olympics. De la Baza was U.S. national champion in 1985 and 1986, and served as team captain in the 1986 World Championships. She is the winner of gold medals at the 1987 U.S. Cup and the Panamerican Games. At the 1988 U.S. national championships in 1988, she was selected Most Valuable Player. Since 1994, De la Riva-Baza has served as vice president of the United States Team Handball Foundation.

Donna de Varona (1947–)

Swimming

Donna de Varona was born in San Diego, California, on April 26, 1947. At the 1960 Rome Olympics, De Varona was the youngest member of the U.S. Olympic team. At the next Olympiad, in Tokyo, De Varona won two gold medals in the 400 mete individual medley and in the 4x100 freestyle. In 1964, De Varona was named Most Outstanding Female Athlete in the World by both the Associated Press and United Press International. Donna De Varona has been inducted into the International Swimming Hall of Fame and the San Francisco Bay Area Hall of Fame. In 1965, De Varona became the youngest and first female sports caster on network television. She has continued in that career to this date, often appearing as host and co-host for Olympic coverage. In addition, De Varona is one of the founders of the Women's Sports Foundation. In 1991, De Varona was the first woman to receive the International Swimming Hall of Fame Gold Medallion as an inspiration for all swimmers, and in recognition of her pioneering work for girls and women in all sports, she received the American Woman Award in 1992 from the Women's Research and Education Institute.

Martín Dihigo (1905–1971)

Baseball

Born in Matanzas, Cuba, Martín Dihigo is one of the few baseball players named to the American Hall of Fame based on his career in the Negro leagues. In addition, he was named to the Halls of Fame of Cuba, Mexico, and Venezuela. He was perhaps the best all-around baseball player that ever existed, yet there are few statistics and records to document his outstanding achievements. Called the "Black Babe Ruth," he played as an outstanding pitcher and outfielder, but he also played every other position. He was an outstanding hitter, as well. Dihigo began his career in the Negro leagues in 1923 with Alex Pómpez's Cuban Stars when he was only 15 years old. By 1926, he was considered one of the top pitchers in black baseball. During his career he played ball in all of the countries that have named him to their Hall of Fame. In each of these countries he led the leagues in home runs, batting average, number of victories, and lowest earned run average (ERA). In 1929, he is reported as having batted .386 in the American Negro League; in 1938, he batted .387 in the Mexican League and pitched 18–2 with an ERA of 0.90.

After the failure of the Negro National League—when baseball was desegregated—Dihigo played in Mexico during the 1950s. He was then too old for the U.S. major leagues. After the Cuban Revolution, Dihigo—who had spent much of dictator Fulgencio Batista's rule in exile—returned to Cuba to assist in organizing amateur baseball leagues and to teach the game.

Roberto Durán (1951–)

Boxing

While not truly a Hispanic of the United States, Roberto Durán deserves mention because of the many fights he has had here and because he is one of the most colorful figures in boxing. Born on June 16, 1951, in Chorillo, Panama, he began boxing in 1967; in 1972, he won the lightweight championship from Ken Buchanan. In 1980, he won the World Boxing Council welterweight title but lost it that following November to Ray Leonard. In all, Durán is a four-time winner of world boxing championships: one each of the lightweights, welterweight, junior middle weight and middleweight titles. Durán suffered various setbacks in his career, but came back in 1989 at

Roberto Durán

the unheard of age of 37 to win the WBC middleweight title.

Sixto Escobar (1913–1979)

Boxing

Sixto Escobar, known as *El Gallito de Barceloneta* (The Barceloneta Fighting Cock), was the first Puerto Rican boxer to win a world championship when he knocked out Tony Marino on August 31, 1936, in the thirteenth round. Escobar was born in Barceloneta, Puerto Rico, on March 23, 1913, and only grew to fight at 118 pounds and five feet, four inches. Although born in Puerto Rico, Escobar spent most of his professional career in New York; he also fought in Canada, Cuba, Mexico, and Venezuela. Escobar fought as a professional boxer from 1931 to 1941, after which he joined the U.S. Army. He is one of the few boxers ever to have regained his lost throne, accomplishing this feat twice: in 1935 and 1938. Escobar fought 64 times and was never knocked out. He ended his hold on the championship in 1939, when he could no longer make the required weight of 118 pounds. Escobar died on November 17, 1979, in Barceloneta, Puerto Rico.

Gigi Fernández (1964–)

Tennis

Gigi Fernández was born in San Juan, Puerto Rico, and has been playing tennis since she was eight-years-old, when her parents enrolled her in tennis lessons. She played consistently since then, and went on to Clemson University with a tennis scholarship. During her freshman year, she made the NCAA finals. She turned pro in 1985 and by 1991 was ranked seventeenth in the world, her highest ranking to date. Fernández is the winner of six Grand Slam women's doubles titles, including the U.S. Open in 1988, 1990 and 1992, the French Open in 1991 and 1992, and Wimbledon in 1992. In 1991, she and her partner, Mary Joe Fernández (no relation), were ranked number one in doubles tennis. In the 1992 Barcelona Olympics, the two Fernándezes won the Gold Medal, making Gigi the first Puerto Rican to win Olympic gold.

Manuel José Fernández (1946–)

Football

Born on July 3, 1946, in Oakland, California, "Manny" was educated at Chabot University and the

Sixto Escobar.

University of Utah, and went on to become an outstanding defensive tackle on one of professional football's winningest teams, the Miami Dolphins under Don Shula. Fernández has achieved the highest distinction of any Hispanic in football: he was named to the All Time Greatest Super Bowl All-Star Team. During his career with the Miami Dolphin's, from 1968 to 1977, Fernández was voted the Dolphin's Most Valuable Defensive Lineman six consecutive years, 1968–73. He helped the Dolphins win two Super Bowls, in 1972 and 1973, and become the only undefeated team in NFL history, in 1973. A knee injury prematurely ended Fernández's career; he retired in 1977.

Mary Joe Fernández (1971–)

Tennis

Mary Joe Fernández was born in the Dominican Republic in 1971 and moved with her family to Miami, Florida, when she was six-months-old. Fernández started playing tennis as a child and by the time she was ten, she had won the United States Tennis Association nationals for players 12 and under. Fernández continued to win tournaments throughout her youth and by age 13 played in her first professional tournament as an amateur. She eventually became the youngest player ever to win a match at the U.S. Open. The year 1990 was Fernández's first as a full-time professional tennis player, winning 40 of her 50 singles matches and two tournaments. With endorsements, her earnings topped $1 million that year. Since then, Fernández has ranked consistently within the top seven women players in the world. In 1992, she and Gigi Fernández took the Olympic Gold Medal in women's doubles.

Tony Fernández (1962–)

Baseball

Born on June 30, 1962, in San Pedro de Macoris, Dominican Republic, Tony Fernández played shortstop for the Toronto Blue Jays for most of his career, beginning in 1979. In 1994, he joined the New York Yankees. He made the American League All-Star Team in 1986, 1987, and 1989. He holds the major league baseball record for highest fielding percentage in 1989, and the American League record for the most games played at shortstop, 1986.

Thomas Raymond Flores (1937–)

Football

Born on March 21, 1937, in Fresno, California, Thomas Flores, the son of Mexican American farm workers, has risen to become an outstanding profes-

sional coach and manager. In fact, he is ranked as one of the most successful coaches in the National Football League, named to head the Oakland Raiders in 1979. Flores worked in the fields through elementary and junior high school, managed to get his high school and college education (University of the Pacific, 1958), and was drafted by the Calgary Stampeders (Canada) in 1958. After that he played with the Redskins and in 1960 joined the Raiders. As a quarterback for the Raiders for six seasons, he completed 48.9 percent of his passes for 11,635 yards and 92 touchdowns. Flores finished his ten years as a professional player with the Kansas City Chiefs in 1969. From then on he worked as a coach and was named assistant to Coach John Madden of the Raiders in 1972. When Madden resigned after the 1978 season, Flores took his place. In his second year as coach, the Raiders won Super Bowl XV. After two more years, Flores led the Raiders to another Super Bowl victory. Flores is only one of two people in NFL history to have a Super Bowl ring as a player, assistant coach, and head coach. After eight seasons, Flores' record with the Raiders was 78–43 in the regular season and 8–3 in playoffs and Super Bowls. In 1989, Flores became the president and general man-

Tony Fernández.

Tom Flores.

ager of the Seattle Seahawks, the highest rank ever achieved by a Hispanic in professional sports in the United States.

Rudy Galindo (1969–)

Figure Skating

Born September 7, 1969, in San Jose, California, Rudy Galindo is the first Hispanic athlete to become the National Figure Skating champion of the United States. Born to Mexican American parents in San Jose, California, and educated in the San Jose public schools, Galindo began skating at the age of eight. When he and his sister, Laura Galindo, became outstanding skaters, their truck-driving father, Jess Galindo, worked overtime for many years to finance the lessons and the travel that his children needed in order to compete regionally and nationally. Laura Galindo now serves as Rudy's coach. Beginning in 1987, when Rudy Galindo won the World Junior Championships and the Central Pacific Senior Championships, he became a leading figure in national and world competitions. His first national championship, however, was as a partner in pairs figure skating with Kristi Yamaguchi in 1989, which

was repeated in 1990. Galindo was singles champion in the Pacific Coast Senior competition in 1992, 1993, 1994, and 1995. In March 1996, Galindo won first place in singles figure skating at the National Senior Figure Skating championship. Galindo's international titles include first place in the Vienna Cup in 1994 as well as second place in the Prague Skate in 1993. In 1996, he placed third in the World Skating championship.

Lefty Gómez (1908–)

Baseball

Born on November 26, 1908, in Rodeo, California, Vernon Louis Gómez, also known as "Lefty" and "The Gay Castilian," probably referring to his Spanish ancestry (he was half-Irish, half-Spanish), was one of baseball's most successful pitchers, ranking third in regular season wins, with 189 for the New York Yankees. He also holds the record for the most wins without a loss in World Series play (6–0) and three wins against one loss in all-star play. Gómez was active from 1930 to 1943, pitching 2,503 innings, winning 189 games to 102 losses, and earning an ERA of 3.34. He scored 20 wins or more in 1931, 1932, 1934, and 1937. Gómez is number 13 on the

Lefty Gómez.

Pancho González.

all-time winning percentage list. In all, Gómez made all-star teams every year from 1933 to 1939, and he is a member of the Hall of Fame. During winter seasons, he played ball in Cuba, where he served for a while as manager of the Cienfuegos team, and he once taught a class on pitching at the University of Havana. Gómez died on February 2, 1989, in San Rafael, California.

Pancho González (1928–1995)

Tennis

"Pancho" Alonzo González was born on May 9, 1928 in Los Angeles, California to Mexican immigrant parents. His father, Manuel, fitted furniture and painted movie sets, and his mother, Carmen, was an occasional seamstress. González was a self-taught tennis player, having begun at age 12 on the public courts of Los Angeles. He won his first tournament as an Edison Junior High School student; because of excessive absenteeism, González was not allowed to compete in tennis while in high school. González served in the U.S. Navy and competed in the U.S. singles championship upon his return in 1947. That same year he placed seventeenth in the

nation. In 1948, González became U.S. singles champion at Forest Hills and played on the U.S. Davis Cup team. He won Forest Hills again in 1949. After having won the U.S. grass, clay, and indoor championships, González turned pro. From 1954 to 1962, he was world professional singles champion. In 1968, he coached the U.S. Davis Cup team, and he was named to the International Tennis Hall of Fame. González died on July 3, 1995 after a long bout with stomach cancer.

Keith Hernández (1953–)

Baseball

Born on October 20, 1953, in San Francisco, Keith Hernández attended San Mateo College. He played with the St. Louis Cardinals from 1974 to 1983, and then with the New York Mets until 1989; in 1990 he joined the Cleveland Indians. Hernández has been considered the best fielding first baseman of his time, having won 11 Gold Gloves and leading the league in double plays and lifetime assists. He played on National League All-Star teams in 1979, 1980, 1984, 1986, and 1987. Hernández assisted the Cardinals in achieving pennant and World Series victories, and, was Most Valuable Player in 1979 and

Keith Hernández.

Al López.

an all-star in 1979, 1980, 1984, 1986, and 1987. In 1983, he was released under suspicion of using drugs, which later was proved to be true. A reformed and repentant Hernández was active with the Mets until 1989. In 1987, he was named team captain.

Natalia Sainz Lederer-Peterson (1943–)

Fencing

Natalia Sainz Lederer-Peterson was born in Havana, Cuba, on July 13, 1943. Before emigrating to the United states, she had studied fencing and had belonged to the Cuban Professional Club. Over the years, Lederer-Peterson has participated on numerous United States national teams in international championships and Olympic games. In 1972, she won the Pacific Coast Women's Foil Championship, the Grand International Women's Foil Championship and the Espada de Honor trophy. In 1989, she won the gold medal in women's epee at the U.S. National championship. Originally a banker, Lederer-Peterson has since 1985 developed a career as a sculptor, which she maintains to this date.

Al López (1908–)

Baseball

Born on August 20, 1908 in Tampa, Florida, Al López has been rated as the seventh-best catcher and the seventh-best manager of all time, and he was elected to the Hall of Fame in 1977. For many years he held the record for the most games caught in the major leagues (1918) and for the most years (12) spent in the National League, catching in 100 games or more. He tied the record for the most games caught in the National League without a passed ball in 1941, with 114 games. López played for the Dodgers from 1930 to 1947, and later with the Braves, the Pirates, and the Indians. He was an outstanding manager for the Indians from 1951 to 1956 and for the White Sox from 1957 to 1965 and 1968 to 1969. His record as a manager was 1,422–1,026 for a winning percentage of .581, the ninth all-time highest.

Nancy López (1957–)

Golf

Nancy Marie López was born to Mexican American parents in Torrance, California, on January 6, 1957,

Nancy López.

and rose to become one of the youngest women golfers to experience professional success. She learned golf from her father, and by age 11 was already beating him. She won the New Mexico Women's Open when she was only 12. In high school, López was the only female member of the golf team, and as an 18-year-old senior, she placed second in the U.S. Women's Open. After high school, she attended Tulsa University on a golf scholarship, but dropped out to become a professional golfer. In 1978, during López's first full season as a pro, she won nine tournaments, including the Ladies Professional Golf Association. She was named Rookie of the Year, Player of the Year, Golfer of the Year, and Female Athlete of the Year; she also won the Vare Trophy. Also in 1978, she set a new record for earnings by a rookie: $189,813. In 1983, she had a break from her career when she became the mother of Ashley Marie, the product of her marriage to baseball star Ray Knight. Two months after having Ashley, López began touring again, and by 1987, she had won 35 tournaments and qualified to become the eleventh member of the Ladies Professional Golf Association Hall of Fame. López's most outstanding year was 1985, when she won five tournaments and finished in the top ten of 21 others; that year she also won the LPGA again. Through 1987, she had earned over $2 million.

Juan Antonio Marichal (1938–)

Baseball

Born on October 20, 1938 in Laguna Verde, Dominican Republic, Juan "Manito" Marichal is the right-handed Dominican pitcher who was signed to the minor leagues at age 19 and whose wide variety of pitches and motions took him to the Hall of Fame. Marichal started with the San Francisco Giants in 1962, and from 1962 to 1971 he averaged 20 wins per year. He led the National League in wins in 1963 with a record of 25–8 and in 1968 with 26–9. In 1965 he had ten shutouts and in 1969 his ERA was 2.10. He pitched in eight all-star games for a 2–0 record and an 0.50 ERA for 18 innings. Marichal's total innings pitched were 3,509, for a record of 243–142 and an ERA of 2.89. He was an all-star from 1962 to 1969 and again in 1971, and was inducted into the Hall of Fame in 1983.

Rachel Livia Elizondo McLish (1958–)

Body Building

Born in Harlingen, Texas, to Rafael and Rachel Elizondo, Rachel Elizondo McLish found her way to athletics through the study of ballet and her father's interest in weight-lifting. McLish intensified her weight training while in college at Panamerican Uni-

Juan "Manito" Marichal.

versity in Edinburgh, Texas, and during that time began working as a trainer at a spa. In 1978, McLish graduated with a degree in health and physical education from Panamerican, and became a partner in the Sport Palace spa, the first and largest health club in South Texas. She began competing in bodybuilding tournaments and soon became known as the World's First Female Bodybuilding Champion. McLish won the Ms. Olympia Title in 1980 and 1982 and the 1982 World Championship. In 1985, McLish became the spokesperson for the Health and Tennis Corporation of America, and she also has a line of sportswear marketed under her name through K-Mart.

José Méndez (1888?–1928)

Baseball

Cuban José Méndez was an outstanding pitcher and infielder who, because of his African ancestry and dark skin, was never allowed to play in the majors. Instead, he played in the Negro National League and in Cuba, and thus many of his statistics are missing. Such witnesses as Hall of Famer John Henry Lloyd said that he never saw a pitcher superior to Méndez, and Giants Manager John McGraw

Orestes "Minnie" Miñoso

said that Méndez would have been worth $50,000 in the majors, an unusually high figure back in those days. Méndez came to the United States in 1908 with the Cuban Stars. In 1909, he went 44–2 as a pitcher for the Stars. During the winters he played in Cuba, where he compiled a record of 62–17 by 1914. From 1912 to 1916, Méndez played for the All-Nations of Kansas City, a racially mixed barnstorming club. From 1920 to 1926, he served as a player manager for the Kansas City Monarchs and led them to three straight Negro National League pennants from 1923 to 1925. During his long career, he also played for the Los Angeles White Sox, the Chicago American Giants and the Detroit Stars.

Orestes "Minnie" Miñoso (1922–)

Baseball

Born in Perico, Cuba, on November 29, 1922, Saturnino Orestes Arrieta Armas Miñoso, nicknamed "Minnie," had one of the most outstanding careers of any Hispanic ballplayer in the major leagues. He began his career in Cuba on the semiprofessional Club Ambrosia team in 1942, and played semiprofessional ball on the island until he took to the field as a third

baseman with the New York Cubans of the Negro leagues from 1946 to 1948. In 1949, he made his major league debut with the Cleveland Indians, but was soon traded to San Diego, returned to the Indians in 1951, and that same year went to the Chicago White Sox. He spent the greater part of his career playing on one or the other of these two teams, and with St. Louis and Washington until 1964. In 1976, Miñoso made a return as a designated hitter for the Chicago White Sox; he thus became one of only six players to be active in four separate decades, and only two other players in major league history have played at an older age: Satchel Paige and Nick Altrock. After that he remained active as a player-manager in Mexico. He ended his career as a third-base coach for Chicago. Miñoso's lifetime batting average was 299, with 1023 runs batted in, 186 home runs, and 205 bases stolen. In 1994, he published his autobiography, *Just Call Me Minnie: My Six Decades in Baseball*.

Amleto Andrés Monacelli (1961–)

Bowling

Born on August 27, 1961, in Barquisimeto, Venezuela, Amleto Andrés Monacelli is a college graduate who has become one of the most popular and success-

Amleto Monacelli.

Anthony Muñoz.

Anthony Muñoz (1958–)

Football

Born on August 19, 1958, in Ontario, California, Muñoz is a graduate of the University of Southern California. He played football with the Cincinnati Bengals from 1980 to 1992, distinguishing himself as All-Pro offensive tackle eight times. He was selected for the Pro Bowl from 1982 through 1992. In 1988, he was chosen as the Miller Lite/NFL Lineman of the Year. Muñoz appeared in two Super Bowls and ten Pro Bowl games over the course of his career. In 1991, he was named the American Football Conference's Offensive Lineman of the Year; for several years he held the title of the NFL's Strongest Man. In 1991, Muñoz chose to retire from football. Since 1994, he has worked as a NFL analyst for the Fox Television Network.

Tony Oliva (1940–)

Baseball

Pedro "Tony" Oliva, a native Cuban, has been the only player to win batting championships during his first two major league seasons. Throughout his career, Oliva was an outstanding hitter and outfielder;

ful members of the Professional Bowling Association tour. After becoming a professional in 1982, his earnings continually grew until, by 1991, he was winning $81,000 in prizes, and in 1989 even achieved a record $213,815. The list of tournaments he has won includes the Japan Cup (1987), the Showboat Invitational (1988), the Miller Challenge (1989), the Wichita Open (1989 and 1990), the Budweiser Touring Players Championship (1989), the Cambridge Mixed Doubles (1989 and 1990), the Columbus Professional Bowling Classic (1990), the Quaker State Open (1991), and the True Value Open (1991). Among his many awards are the Professional Bowlers Association Player of the Year in 1989 and 1990, and the Harry Smith Point Leader Award in 1989. In 1990, he won the Budweiser Kingpin Competition for the highest average for the year. In 1990, the sportswriters named him Bowler of the Year. Monacelli is still a Venezuelan citizen; this is the first time a foreigner has ever been named Bowler of the Year. In his professional career, Monacelli has rolled 16 perfect games, seven of them during the 1989 season, which established a new record for perfect games in a year. Three of these were accomplished during one week, thus tying the record.

Tony Oliva.

however, an injured knee shortened his career. He was active from 1962 to 1976 with the Minnesota Twins, winning Rookie of the Year in 1964 and the league batting title in 1964, 1965 and 1971. Oliva led the league in hits five times in his career. He made all-star teams from 1964 to 1971, tying Joe DiMaggio's record of having been named an all-star in each of his six first seasons, and won the Golden Glove in 1966 as the league's best defensive right fielder. Oliva's career batting average was .304, with 220 home runs and 947 runs batted in, for 1,676 games played. Because of his knee, which had been operated on seven times, Oliva served the last years of his career mostly as a designated hitter and pinch hitter. Since 1977, he has been coaching for the Minnesota Twins.

Alejandro Oms (1895–1946)
Baseball

Martín Dihigo considered Alejandro Oms to have been the best batter in Cuban baseball. Born to a poor family in Santa Clara, Cuba, in 1895, he had to work as a child in an iron foundry. He started playing organized baseball in 1910 as a center fielder. He played in the Negro National League on the Cuban Stars and the New York Cubans from 1921 to 1935, while still managing to put in outstanding seasons during the winter in Cuban professional ball. On the most famous Cuban team of all times, Santa Clara, Oms batted .436 in the 1922–23 season. In Cuba, Oms achieved a lifetime batting average of .352; his average in the United States is not known. He was batting champion on the island three times: in 1924–25 with .393, in 1928–29 with .432 and in 1929–30 with .380. In 1928, he established a Cuban record for most consecutive games with hits: 30. In his last years, he was penniless and his vision was failing; he died at the age of 51 in 1946.

Vicente Oropeza
Rodeo

The most famous and influential Hispanic rodeo performer of all time, the Mexican native Vicente Oropeza called himself the "premier charro Mexicano of the world" on his first appearance in the United States in July 1891. As a headliner and champion in both Mexico and the United States, he is credited with having introduced trick and fancy roping in the United States. In 1893, Oropeza became the star of "Buffalo Bill" Cody's "Mexicans from Old Mexico" feature in his Wild West Show. In 1900, Oropeza won the first World's Championship of Trick and Fancy Roping, which was a major contest up through the 1930s. One of the most famous American ropers of all time, Will Rogers, credited Oropeza for inspiring his career.

Oropeza was selected as a member of the National Rodeo Hall of Fame for his contributions to what may be considered both a sport and an art.

Carlos Ortiz (1936–)
Boxing

Carlos Ortiz was the second Puerto Rican boxer—the first being Sixto Escobar—to win a world title. Born in Ponce, Puerto Rico, on September 9, 1936, Ortiz made his professional debut in 1955. He was undefeated that year and in 1956, 1957, and almost all of 1958, suffering his first defeat on December 31 in a fight with Kenny Lane in Miami Beach. He later beat Lane in a rematch to win the junior welterweight championship. After losing the junior welterweight championship to Duilio Loi, he turned lightweight in 1962, and on April 21 won the world championship in that division from Joe Brown. He successfully defended his crown various times until April 10, 1965, when he lost in Panama to Ismael Laguna. But he recovered the title on November 13 of the same year in San Juan, Puerto Rico. Again he successfully defended his crown until losing in the Dominican Republic to Carlos "Teo" Cruz on June 29, 1968.

Carlos Ortiz.

Manuel Ortiz.

Manuel Ortiz (1916–1970)

Boxing

A native of El Centro, California, Mexican American boxer Manuel Ortiz (1916–1970) became the bantamweight champion on August 7, 1942, when he beat Lou Salica. Ortiz totaled 41 knock-outs in his career and never once suffered one himself in 117 bouts. Ortiz tied Henry Armstrong in defending his title 20 times (only two other fighters had defended more often), and even successfully defended it three times in 1946 after a tour of duty in the army. Ortiz finally lost the crown on January 8, 1947, to Harold Dade in San Francisco, but he took it back on March 11 that same year. He lost it again on May 31, 1950, to Vic Toweel in Johannesburg, South Africa.

James William Plunkett (1947–)

Football

Jim Plunkett was born on December 5, 1947 in Santa Clara, California, the son of William and Carmen Blea Plunkett, who had met at a school for the blind in Albuquerque, New Mexico. His father managed a newsstand in San Jose, where Plunkett became an outstanding year-round athlete in high school. Later, at Stanford University he became starting quarterback as a sophomore. During his junior year he threw passes for 2,671 yards and 20 touchdowns. He was named to the Associated press' all-American second team, won the Voit Memorial Trophy as the PAC's outstanding player and was eighth in the Heisman Trophy selection. It was as a senior that he finally was awarded the Heisman Trophy, as well as many other awards. He became the first major college football player to surpass 7,000 yards on offense. In 1971, Plunkett was the first pick for the New England Patriots, and passed for 2,158 yards and 19 touchdowns; he was chosen as NFL Rookie of the Year. Plunkett was injured during the next few years and was traded to the San Francisco 49ers who later released him. In 1978, he was signed by the Oakland Raiders, and in 1980 he led the Raiders to the Super Bowl. He became Super Bowl MVP and was named the NFL 1980 Comeback Player of the Year. In 1983, Plunkett again led the Raiders to a Super Bowl victory. That year he recorded his best seasons, with 230 completions for 1,935 yards and 20 touchdowns. Overall, Plunkett has passed for a total of 25,882 yards, with 164 touchdowns during his career.

Jim Plunkett.

Armando Ramos (1948–)

Boxing

In nine years as a professional boxer, Armando "Mando" Ramos only fought 40 bouts, but that was enough for him two win two world titles as a lightweight. Born on November 15, 1948, in Los Angeles, the Mexican American boxer won his first 17 bouts, 11 by knockouts. On February 18, 1969, he won the lightweight championship from Carlos Cruz in Los Angeles. On February 19, 1972, Ramos won the World Boxing Congress lightweight championship over Pedro Carrasco. In 1973, he retired after suffering a knockout by Arturo Piñeda.

Chi Chi Rodriguez

Golf

Born on October 23, 1935, in Río Piedras, Puerto Rico, Rodríguez came from an extremely impoverished family and found his way into golf as a caddy on the links that served Puerto Rico's booming tourism. His is one of the most famous Hispanic "rags to riches through sports" tales, his career earnings having passed the $3 million mark, and because he contributes financially to charities, including the Chi Chi Rodríguez Youth Foundation in Clearwater, Florida. Included among the important tournaments that he has won are the Denver Open (1963), Lucky Strike International Open (1964), Western Open (1964), Dorado Pro-Am (1965), Texas Open (1967), and Tallahassee Open (1979). As a member of the Senior PGA Tour, he has won numerous tournaments, including the Silver Pages Classic (1987), GTE Northwest Classic (1987), and Sunwest Senior Classic (1990). In the first decade of his retirement and joining the PGA Senior Tour, Rodríguez won 25 tournaments. In 1987 alone, Rodríguez finished first in the Senior Tour, having won seven tournaments.

Chi Chi Rodríguez.

Lauro Salas (1927–)

Boxing

Lauro Salas' boyhood dream was to become a bullfighter, but he started boxing as a teenager in his native Monterrey, Mexico, for the money. Salas (b. 1927) left home and moved to Los Angeles at age 19 to become a professional boxer. There he won 14 of his first 17 professional bouts as a featherweight. In 1952, he won the lightweight championship over Jimmy Carter, but lost it back to Carter that same year at Chicago Stadium. Salas retired in 1961 after being knocked out by Sebastiao Nascimento and Bunny Grant.

Alberto Bauduy Salazar (1958–)

Track and Field

Born on August 7, 1958 in Havana, Cuba, future track marathoner Alberto Salazar moved to Manchester, Connecticut, with his refugee parents when he was only two years old. The family later moved to Wayland, Massachusetts, where Salazar was named high school all-American twice as a two- and three-mile racer. In 1976, he entered the University of Oregon, where he was coached by Olympian Bill Dellinger. In 1978, he won the NCAA individual championship. He went on to become a three-time cross-country all-American and helped Oregon win the 1977 NCAA team title and finish second in 1978 and 1979. In 1979, he set a U.S. road record of 22:13 for five miles. In 1980, Salazar made the Olympic team, but that was the year that the United States boycotted the games in Moscow. That same year, however, Salazar won the New York Marathon with the record for the fastest first marathon in history, and the second-fastest time ever run by an American. The next year he won more championships, often by establishing new records, and once again he was victorious in the New York Marathon, setting a new world record of 2:08:13. In 1982, Salazar won the Boston and New York Marathons and various other events around the world; that year and in 1981 and 1983 he was selected the top U.S. road racer. Despite some setbacks and injuries, Salazar made the U.S. Olympic team for the second time in 1984, but finished only fifteenth in the games at Los Angeles. Salazar has set one world record and six U.S. records, the most of any U.S. runner since Steve Prefontaine. Despite a series of illnesses, Alberto Salazar came back in 1994 and stunned the sports world by winning the 53-mile supermarathon in South Africa.

Vicente Saldívar.

Alberto Bauduy Salazar.

Vicente Saldívar (1943–)

Boxing

Vicente Saldívar became the first undisputed Mexican featherweight world champion and the twelfth left-handed title holder in history with his win over Sugar Ramos on September 26, 1964. Born the son of a businessman in Mexico City on May 3, 1943, Saldívar turned professional in 1961. On his way to the world crown he knocked out 25 opponents, and he won 36 of his first 39 professional bouts. Saldívar defended his title in eight straight bouts, winning five by knockout. He retired in October 1967, but made a comeback and regained the championship on May 9, 1970, from Johnny Famechon in a 15-round decision. Saldívar lost the title to Kuniaki Shibata by knockout in the thirteenth round on December 11, 1970.

Eligio "Kid Chocolate" Sardiñas (1910–1988)

Boxing

"Kid Chocolate" was one of the most celebrated Hispanic boxers of all time. Born in Havana, Cuba, on October 28, 1910, his career became an example of the fate that befalls boxers who battle their way

Luis Tiant.

out of poverty into fame and temporary riches. After winning 86 amateur and 21 professional fights in Cuba, he made his New York debut in 1928 and fought more than 100 bouts in the United States over the next ten years. He became a true champion, supported his community, and was memorialized on stage and screen. However, he was severely exploited by his managers and owners and ultimately, was done in by poverty and alcoholism. Sardiñas died on August 9, 1988.

Luis Tiant (1940–)

Baseball

Born November 23, 1940 in Havana, Cuba, Luis Clemente Tiant Vega, the Cuban pitcher, broke into professional baseball in the Mexican League in 1959. Although best known for his play with the Boston Red Sox, Tiant's major league career in the United States—from 1964 to 1982—included seasons with the Indians, the Twins, the Yankees, the Pirates, and the Angels. After making an outstanding start as a rookie for Cleveland with a 10–4 record and a 2.83 ERA, Tiant hit his stride in 1968 with a 1.60 ERA, nine shutouts, and 5.3 hits per nine innings,

striking out more than one batter per inning and finishing the season with a 21–9 record. On July 3 of that year, he struck out 19 Twins in a ten-inning game, setting an American League record. In his previous start, he had struck out 13 Red Sox for a major league record. While suffering a series of problems, including a hairline fracture, Tiant was traded and released various times during the next few years, finally joining Boston in 1971 after a stint with the Red Sox's Louisville farm team. In 1972, he was named Comeback Player of the Year and he won the ERA title with a 1.91 and a season record of 15–6. The next two years he won 20 and 22 games and in 1974 led the league with seven shutouts. Tiant helped the Sox to a pennant and the World Series championship that year. In 1976, Tiant won 20 games for the last time and went 21–12 for the season. Tiant was known for his masterful changes of speed and a wide variety of release points and deceptive pitching motions.

José Luis Torres (1936–)

Boxing

The third Puerto Rican boxer to ever win a world championship was José Luis "Chegui" Torres, who

José Luis "Chegui" Torres.

Lee Treviño.

relations, real estate, and as a New York newspaper columnist—all without a high school education.

Lee Buck Treviño (1939–)
Golf

Lee Buck Treviño was born in Dallas, Texas, on December 1, 1939, into an impoverished Mexican American family. Fatherless, he was raised by his mother, a cleaning woman, and his maternal grand-father, a gravedigger. Their four-room farmhouse was located at the back of the Glen Lakes Country Club fairways. As a boy Treviño studied the form of the golfers on the course from his own back yard. He dropped out of school in the seventh grade and made his way into what was then an exclusively Anglo rich man's sport by working as a greens keeper and as a caddy. He later joined the marines and played a great deal of golf while he was stationed in Okinawa. In 1966, Treviño became a professional golfer and achieved his first major victory in 1968 at the U.S. Open, where he became the first player in history to shoot all four rounds of the event under par. In 1970, he was the leading money winner on the Professional Golf Association tour. In 1971, Treviño won the U.S. Open for a second time, won five tournaments be-

won the medium heavyweight championship from Willie Pastrano on March 30, 1965, with a technical knockout in the ninth round at Madison Square Garden in New York. Without a rival in the middle heavyweight division, Torres took on Tom McNeely in the heavyweight class, winning in a ten-round decision. Torres defended his medium heavyweight crown and fought as a heavyweight successfully on a number occasions until December 16, 1966 when, weakened from an old pancreatic injury, he lost on points to the Nigerian Dick Tiger, whom he had beaten earlier in his career. Born into a large, poor family, in Ponce, Puerto Rico, Torres dropped out of high school and joined the army. There he learned to box well enough to win the Antilles, Caribbean, Second Army, All-Army and Interservice championships as a light middleweight. In 1956, he won the U.S. Olympic title, but lost on points at the games in Melbourne to the Hungarian Laszlo Papp. After the army, Torres moved to New York, where he fought as an amateur to win the national AAU championship and then turned professional. During and after his professional boxing career, Torres also developed a career as a singer and musician and worked in public

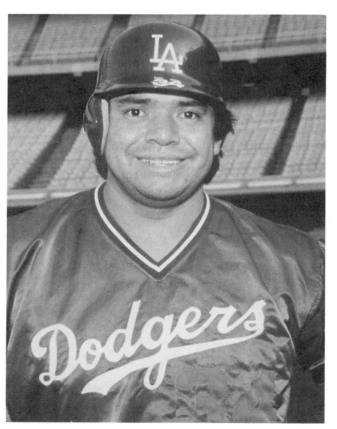

Fernando Valenzuela.

tween April and July, and also won the British Open in that year and again in 1972. For his achievements in 1971, Treviño was named PGA Player of the Year, Associated Press Athlete of the Year, and *Sports Illustrated Sportsman of the Year*. After that, he won the 1974 PGA again, among many other tournaments. In 1975, Treviño and two other golfers were struck by lightning during a tournament near Chicago. To this day he still suffers from back problems due to the accident; it seriously affected his game, even causing him to go winless in 1976 and 1978. In 1980, he made a comeback by winning the Texas Open and the Memphis Classic and earned $385,814 for the year. He was also awarded the Vardon Trophy for the fewest strokes per round (69.73 for 82 rounds), the lowest since Sam Snead in 1958. Treviño retired from the PGA tour in October 1985, with his 30 tour victories and total career earnings of over $3 million (third highest). Treviño has been elected to the Texas Sports, American Golf, and World Golf Halls of Fame.

Fernando Valenzuela (1960–)

Baseball

Fernando Valenzuela has been one of the youngest and most celebrated baseball players be- cause of his sensational introduction to the major leagues as an outstanding pitcher during his first seasons with the Los Angeles Dodgers. During his rookie year in 1981, Valenzuela won not only Rookie of the Year but also the *Sporting News* Player of the Year, and he was the first rookie ever to win the Cy Young Award. He won his first ten major league outings and his eight shutouts tied the rookie record in a season that was shortened because of a players' strike. Valenzuela is considered to have the best screwball in baseball today. He led the league in strikeouts in 1981 and in wins in 1986. He was selected for the all-star team five times; in 1986 he tied Carl Hubbell's record of five straight strikeouts in an all-star game. That was also the year that he won the Gold Glove.

References

Brown, Bruce. "Cuban Baseball." *Atlantic*, 253, No. 6, June 1984: 109–14.

LeCompte, Mary Lou. "The Hispanic Influence on the History of Rodeo, 1823–1922," *Journal of Sports History*, 12, No. 1, spring 1985: 21–38.

Peterson, Robert. *Only the Ball Was White*. New York: McGraw-Hill, 1970.

Nicolás Kanellos

Organizations

Almost from the first moment that Hispanics found themselves within the political, social, and economic context of a larger Anglo-American society, they began to form organizations for mutual protection and defense of their language and culture. Since the mid-nineteenth century, Hispanic organizations have been many and varied, reflecting their specific ethnicity, social class, religion, and place of origin. It has only been recently that broad national organizations that transcend these differentiating factors have been formed, as a national Hispanic consciousness is emerging within the borders of the United States.

When such areas as California came under Anglo-American domination, organizations such as the Junta Patriótica Mexicana (Mexican Patriotic Group) in San Francisco sprang up to encourage Mexican patriotism, defend the rights of Mexicans, and even raise funds for social causes in Mexico, including relief for the victims of the French intervention of 1862. Later in the century, such Mexican revolutionaries as the Flores Magón brothers formed chapters of the Partido Liberal Mexicano (Liberal Mexican party) in the Southwest to support the cause against dictator Porfirio Díaz, while Cuban, Dominican, and Puerto Rican patriots were developing political organizations in New York, Philadelphia, New Orleans, Tampa, and Key West to support the independence of their island nations from Spain.

All the Hispanic immigrant groups—in this way similar to European immigrants—formed mutual aid societies, often called *mutualistas,* to pool their resources in order to offer the members low-cost health care, insurance, funerals, low-interest loans, and other types of economic assistance. While originating as an institution to provide economic security, the mutualista, in fact, became the second most important institution in the community after the church. The immigrant workers' resources were strong enough to either buy, rent, or construct a building that usually housed a hall and/or theater and became a principal gathering place for the members and the community. The mutualista became the site of theatrical performances, dances, and other healthy and safe entertainment for the youth, as well as a place for political organizing and fund-raising for various causes. In many ways, the mutual aid societies pro-

A march by the Council fof Puerto Rican Organizations from the Lower East Side of New York City over the Brooklyn Bridge to protest the poor conditions of public schools in the Puerto Rican community.

A celebration of the Three Kings sponsored by the Puerto Rican Workers Mutual Aid Society, New York City.

vided the foundation for the labor and civil rights organizations that followed years later.

There were many mutual aid societies, and their history is varied and intriguing. In general, among Mexican immigrants, the societies were usually created by a group of immigrants originating from the same town or region in Mexico, and more than likely, from the same social class, usually laborers. They often baptized their societies with names honoring their favorite heroes—Sociedad Benito Juárez, Sociedad Coahotemoc, Sociedad Hidalgo, or simply, Unión Benéfica Mexicana (Mexican Benefit Society).

The same practice was also common among Puerto Ricans and Cubans, and a network of associated societies arose, called The Brotherhood. In New York and Tampa, Spaniards tenaciously held to their *patria chica* (home regions), founding such organizations as the Casa Galicia (Galician House), Calpe Americano (Alicante in America), Círculo Valenciano (Valencian Circle), and the Centro Asturiano (Asturian Center). In both cities, the Cubans and Puerto Ricans formed separate organizations; but in Tampa, in the heart of the Jim Crow South, Afro-Cubans were not admitted to either the Círculo Cubano (Cuban Circle) or the Spanish societies. They therefore formed their own organization under the names of the two revolutionary heroes who transcended racism: Sociedad Martí-Maceo.

Despite the regionalism and classism, there were several societies in cosmopolitan New York that brought various Hispanic nationalities together, such as the Ateneo Hispano (Hispanic Atheneum) and the Sociedad Hispana La Amistad (The Friend-

A parade organized by Tucson's Alianza Hispano-Americana.

ship Hispanic Society). In truth, the various Hispanic nationalities interrelated freely and organized together at other institutions, such as churches, theaters, and labor unions. And because Hispanics were predominantly working-class people and Catholic, there was a plethora of organizations related to the church and workplace. In particular, Puerto Rican and Cuban cigar-rollers in Tampa and New York were prime movers in union and socialist organizing, as were many of the expatriates from the Spanish Civil War during the 1930s and 1940s.

While a more politically active type of mutualism, as practiced by such groups as the Alianza Hispano-Americana (Hispanic American Alliance), founded in Tucson during 1894, multiplied itself in chapters throughout the Southwest, there were very few openly political organizations until Mexican American veterans returning from World War I became active in the American Legion and founded the Order of the Sons of America in 1921 and the Knights of America and the League of United Latin American Citizens (LULAC) in 1929. From then on (and reinforced by the veterans returning from World War II and their organizations, such as the American G.I. Forum, founded in 1947), Mexican Americans and other Hispanics became politically active to protect their rights as U.S. citizens. From the postwar period to the present, numerous political organizations have been formed, such as the Mexican American Political Association (1959) and the Political Association of Spanish-Speaking Organizations (1960), as well as separate political parties, such as the Raza Unida party (1970), and Hispanic Democratic and Republican organizations. Today, there is also a National Association of Hispanic Elected Officials and a Hispanic Congressional Caucus, which is duplicated in various state legislatures as well.

In addition, there are myriad other Hispanic social, health, and professional groups. In almost all the major communities of Hispanics throughout the United States, there are Puerto Rican, Cuban, Mexican American, Hispanic, and inter-American chambers of commerce, bar associations, medical associations, organizations of accountants and engineers, and associations of professors and teachers, many of which are united in their national organizations, such as the National Hispanic Chamber of Commerce, the National Association for Bilingual Education, and the National Association for Chicano Studies. There are myriad social service and civil rights groups, as well as such national research and lobbyist entities as the National Council of La Raza.

Primary Hispanic Organizations: Associations of Broad or National Scope

American G.I. Forum

1315 Bright Street
Corpus Christi, TX 78405
(512) 883–2123

Established in 1948, the American G.I. Forum has 540 affiliate organizations and 20,000 members in chapters in every state. The forum is one of the major advocacy organizations for Hispanics in the United States. Its special programs include the Business Development Center, Education Foundation, Veteran's Outreach Program, and National Economic Development Program (SER-Jobs for Progress). The forum also is associated with the American G.I. Women Forum, which has a membership of 6,000 active in social and educational programs. The forum publishes a monthly bulletin, *The Forumeer.*

Asociación Nacional Pro Personas Mayores

3325 Wilshire Boulevard, Suite 800
Los Angeles, CA 90010–1724
(213) 487–1922

Founded in 1975, the Asociación Nacional Pro Personas Mayores has 3,100 members and 13 affiliates. The association is an advocacy organization for the Hispanic elderly and the low-income elderly. It administers a nationwide employment program and provides technical assistance to community groups and professionals in the field of aging. It operates the National Hispanic Research Center, which conducts gerontological studies and issues bilingual reports. It also publishes the *Legislative Bulletin* quarterly.

ASPIRA Association, Inc.

1112 Sixteenth Street, NW, Suite 340
Washington, DC 20036
(202) 835–3600

Founded in 1969, ASPIRA (hope) is a grass roots organization working to provide leadership development and educational assistance to Hispanics. ASPIRA offers educational counseling for high school and college students, a forum for group discussions, workshops, tutoring, and assistance in applying for college and financial aid. It establishes high school clubs and sponsors the National Health Careers Program, the ASPIRA Public Policy Research Program, and the Institute for Policy Research. ASPIRA publishes a quarterly, *Aspira News,* and reports.

President Ronald Reagan presents the Medal of Freedom to Dr. Héctor García (far right), founder of the American G. I. Forum.

Comisión Femenil Mexicana Nacional, Inc.

379 South Loma Drive
Los Angeles, CA 90017
(213) 484–1515

Founded in 1970, the Comisión Femenil Mexicana Nacional has some 5,000 members in 23 affiliate chapters. The organization advocates Hispanic women's rights and works to advance Hispanic women politically, economically, socially, and educationally. It administers the Chicana Service Center, which provides job skills training; the Centro de Niños (The Children's Center), which provides bilingual child development programs; and Casa Victoria (Victory House), which is a group home for teens. Its standing committees include Development, Education, Health and Welfare, Legislative, Reproductive Rights, and Teen Pregnancy. The commission publishes *La Mujer* (The Woman) semiannually.

Congressional Hispanic Caucus

244 Ford House Office Building
Washington, DC 20515
(202) 226–3430

Founded in 1957, the Congressional Hispanic Caucus is a legislative service organization dedicated to improving the condition of Hispanics through the legislative process. The caucus monitors the executive and judicial branches of government and seeks to strengthen the role of Hispanics at all levels of government. It publishes the Legislative Review, a monthly.

Cuban American Legal Defense and Education Fund

2119 South Webster Street
Fort Wayne, IN 46802
(219) 745–5421

Founded in 1980, the Cuban American Legal Defense and Education Fund advocates equal treatment for Hispanics in education, employment, housing, politics, and justice. It strives to end negative stereotyping of Hispanics and to educate the public about their plight in the United States. It publishes a monthly Hispanic Newsletter. (See National League of Cuban American Community-Based Centers.)

Cuban American National Foundation

1000 Thomas Jefferson Street, Suite 505
Washington, DC 20007
(202) 265–2822

Founded in 1981, the Cuban American National Foundation has three affiliates. It produces and disseminates research on the economic, political, and social issues affecting Cubans in the United States and Cuba. The organization supports the concept of a free and democratic Cuba. The foundation advocates Cuban civil rights and attempts to affect public opinion on Cubans and Cuban issues. It publishes *The Issue Is Cuba.*

Cuban American National Council

300 Southwest Twelfth Avenue, Third Floor
Miami, FL 33130–2038
(305) 642–3484

Founded in 1972, the Cuban American National Council is a private nonprofit social service agency that researches the economic, social, and educational needs of Cuban Americans and assists them in their adjustment to American society. The council administers a network of programs in the three above-named areas and also fosters multiethnic cooperation. It publishes a quarterly, the *Council Letter*.

Consortium of National Hispanic Organizations

1030 Fifteenth Street, NW, Suite 1053
Washington, DC 20005
(202) 371–2100

Founded in 1976, the Consortium of National Hispanic Organizations has 26 organizational members, which have come together to discuss and share information on issues affecting the Hispanic community. The consortium sponsors seminars and symposia. Its committees include Civic Education, Health, Housing, Immigration, International Issues, Labor, and Press and Media. The consortium issues reports and sponsors an annual convention.

Hispanic Academy of Media Arts and Sciences

Box 291774
Los Angeles, CA 90029
(818) 954–2720

The Hispanic Academy of Media Arts and Sciences advocates the fair and equal representation of Hispanics in film and television, monitors how they are portrayed, and works for access to employment at all levels in television and film. The organization sponsors an annual awards event that highlights the contributions of Hispanics to the industry.

Hispanics in Philanthropy

116 New Montgomery Street
San Francisco, CA 94105–3607
(415) 788–2982

Founded in 1981, Hispanics in Philanthropy has three affiliates. The organization is a volunteer association of Hispanic trustees and staff members of grant-making foundations and corporate contributions programs. The association shares information and advocates causes in the Council on Foundations and in the world of philanthropy. It offers workshops and training to organizations providing grant-seeking training services to the Hispanic community. It publishes a quarterly newsletter.

National IMAGE, Inc.

930 West Seventh Avenue, Suite 117–121
Denver, CO 80204
(303) 534–6534

Founded in 1972, IMAGE has 3,000 members in 52 chapters. IMAGE works to increase employment opportunities for Hispanics and to seek equality with other groups in status and achievement. Its Project Cambio (change) provides scholarships for Hispanic women pursuing a career change or reentry to the work force. It publishes *National IMAGE*.

Las Hermanas-United States of America

(The Sisters-USA)
P.O. Box 15792
San Antonio, TX 78212
(512) 434–0947

Founded in 1971, Las Hermanas has 1,000 members, mostly Catholic nuns, in 12 regional chapters and 40 affiliate groups. Las Hermanas advocates the needs of Hispanics in the church and society, with the specific goal of engaging Hispanic women in active ministry among Hispanics. It conducts leadership training, workshops, and retreats. It publishesI *nformes,* a quarterly newsletter.

Hispanic Association of Colleges and Universities

4204 Gardendale, Suite 216
San Antonio, TX 78229
(512) 629–3805

Founded in 1986, the Hispanic Association of Colleges and Universities has 34 institutional members, whose purpose is to bring together colleges and universities with corporations, government agencies, and individuals to promote the development of member institutions and improve the quality and accessibility of post-secondary education for Hispanics.

League of United Latin American Citizens

400 First Street, NW, Suite 721
Washington, DC 20001
(202) 628–8516

Founded in 1929, League of United Latin American Citizens has 110,000 members in 12 regional and 43 state groups. LULAC is concerned with seeking full social, political, economic, and educational rights for Hispanics in the United States. LULAC supports the 15 LULAC National Education Service Centers, offers employment and training programs, conducts research on postsecondary education, and sponsors Hispanics Organized for Political Education, which encourages voter registration and political awareness. LULAC publishes the *HOPE Voter's Guide,* reports, and the monthly *LULAC National Reporter.*

Los PADRES

2216 East 108th Street
Los Angeles, CA 90059
(213) 569–5951

Founded in 1969, Los PADRES has 500 members, mostly Hispanic Catholic priests, brothers, and deacons. The acronym stands for Padres Asociados para Derechos Religiosos, Educativos y Sociales (Fathers Associated for Religious, Educational, and Social Rights). Its purpose is to develop the critical conscience whereby poor people see themselves as masters of their own destiny and capable of bringing about structural change. It promotes a supportive ministry and advocates Hispanic issues and rights in the church. It publishes a quarterly newsletter, *Los P.A.D.R.E.S.*

Mexican American Legal Defense and Educational Fund

634 South Spring Street, Eleventh Floor
Los Angeles, CA 90014
(213) 629–2512

The Mexican American Legal Defense and Educational Fund (MALDEF) was established in 1968, and over the past 20 years has been at the forefront of promoting and protecting the civil rights of Hispanic Americans throughout the United States. MALDEF recognized the need for removing barriers preventing Hispanic Americans from fully participating in American society. Those efforts have allowed the organization to work within the legal system to create beneficial solutions through class action litigation, community education, and leadership training.

With a national office in Los Angeles and regional offices in Chicago, San Antonio, San Francisco, and Washington, D.C., MALDEF concentrates on building awareness among Hispanic Americans regarding their heritage and issues affecting their lives. MALDEF's specific program areas are education, employment, political access, immigration, and leadership. MALDEF also administers the Law School Scholarship Program for Mexican Americans.

The Mexican American Legal Defense and Educa-

tion Fund (MALDEF) currently has six affiliate offices, in San Francisco, Los Angeles, Sacramento, San Antonio, Chicago, and Washington, D.C. MALDEF is in the forefront of protecting Mexican American civil rights. It has been responsible for civil rights class-action litigation affecting Hispanics. Litigation departments are maintained in the areas of education, employment, immigration, and voting rights. It maintains a law school scholarship and other programs to assist students in entering the legal profession. MALDEF publishes two triquarterly newsletters, *Leadership Program Newsletter* and *MALDEF Newsletter.*

Movimiento Familiar Cristiano

2610 John Ralston Road
Houston, TX 77013
(713) 451–2248

Founded in 1969, the Movimiento Familiar Cristiano has 5,000 members in 42 regional groups. The organization is made up of husbands and wives working together to improve the quality of life in the Spanish-speaking communities of the United States. The program involves a cycle of four years of study of family life. The organization also sponsors retreats. The organization publishes manuals and brochures and the monthly *MFC-USA Bulletin.*

Mujeres Activas en Letras y Cambio Social

c/o Ethnic Studies Program
Santa Clara University
Santa Clara, CA 95953
(408) 554–4511

Founded in 1982, Mujeres Activas en Letras y Cambio Social (MALCS) has 90 members, with seven regional groups. The organization is made up of Hispanic women in higher education who foster research and writing on Hispanic women. MALCS seeks to fight race, class, and gender oppression at universities and to develop strategies for social change. It publishes a triquarterly newsletter, *Noticiera de MALCS.*

National Association for Chicano Studies

c/o Devón Peña
14 East Cuche LaPoundre
Colorado Springs, CO 80903
(719) 389–6642

Founded in 1971, the National Association for Chicano Studies has over 300 members in six regional groups made up mostly of Mexican American college professors. The organization fosters research and exchange of ideas on Chicano subjects and sponsors an annual convention as well as conventions of regional groups. The organization publishes its annual proceedings, which are made up mostly of formal papers read at the convention.

National Association of Hispanic Journalists

National Press Building, Suite 1193
Washington, DC 20045
(202) 662–7145

The National Association of Hispanic Journalists (NAHJ) has source 500 members and various state and regional affiliates. It seeks to enhance opportunities for Hispanic journalists and works to seek balanced and fair portrayal of Hispanics by the media. It provides support for Hispanic journalists to maintain their identity as they work within the non-Hispanic media. The organization has various programs to encourage Hispanic students to go into journalism, including its annual essay contest, whose winners are awarded scholarships. NAHJ publishes a newsletter.

National Association of Hispanic Publications

685 South Highway 427
Longwood, FL 32750–6403
(407) 767–0561

Founded in 1982, the National Association of Hispanic Publications has 25 chapters made up of senior-level staff from more than 100 Hispanic newspapers, magazines, and newsletters from throughout the United States. The organization functions to research Hispanic media, to promote Hispanic publications, to encourage advertisers to use these publications, and to encourage Hispanics to enter the field. It publishes the Hispanic Media Directory and the quarterly Hispanic Print.

National Association of Latino Elected and Appointed Officials

708 G Street, SE
Washington, DC 20003
(202) 546–2536

Founded in 1975, the National Association of Latino Elected and Appointed Officials (NALEO) has 3,000 members made up of Hispanic elected officials and people who support them, including both individuals and corporate members. NALEO is a comprehensive advocacy and leadership network dedicated to the advancement of Hispanic people. It also serves as a clearinghouse on citizenship information and compiles Hispanic voting statistics. It maintains

data bases on Hispanic businesses in the minority procurement program, on citizenship services providers, and on Hispanic elected officials. NALEO has various quarterly and annual publications, including directories and rosters.

National Caucus of Hispanic School Board Members

24 East Cody Drive
Phoenix, AZ 85040
(602) 243–4804

Founded in 1975, the membership of the National Caucus of Hispanic School Board Members is made up of board members and others interested in the education of Hispanic students. The organization is an educational advocacy group as well as a caucus of the National School Boards Association.

National Coalition of Hispanic Health and Human Services Organizations

1501 Sixteenth Street, NW
Washington, DC 20036
(202) 387–5000

Founded in 1974, the National Coalition of Hispanic Health and Human Services Organizations has 507 members. It conducts research and functions as an advocate for Hispanic health and social services needs. It publishes *Roadrunner* and *Reporter,* both six times a year, and *COSSMHO Aids Update* monthly.

National Concilio of America

41 Sutter, Suite 1067
San Francisco, CA 94104
(415) 550–0785

Founded in 1977, the National Concilio of America (NCA) has 13 member organizations representing a network of over 100 community-based organizations. Its purposes include cultivating leaders that will interact with local voluntary and philanthropic institutions, train staff in the technical skills required for administration, conduct needs assessments, review demographic and marketing data, develop long-range plans for Hispanic communities, and identify existing financial resources. The NCA publishes two quarterlies, *Executive Brief* and *Horizontes,* a newsletter.

National Conference of Puerto Rican Women

5 Thomas Circle
Washington, DC 20005
(202) 387–4716

Established in 1972, the National Conference of Puerto Rican Women has 4,500 members in 15 chapters. The organization strives to ensure the participation of Puerto Rican women in the mainstream of social, political, and economic life in the United States, works for equal rights for all Hispanic women, and offers leadership development. It publishes the quarterly *Ecos Nacionales* (National Echoes).

National Congress for Puerto Rican Rights

160 West Lippincott Street
Philadelphia, PA 19133
(215) 634–2843

Founded in 1981, the National Congress for Puerto Rican Rights has 3,000 members and 5 affiliates. The congress is an advocate for the civil and human rights of Puerto Ricans in education, labor, voting, housing, women's issues, media, health, and justice and for the end to the government's intervention in the affairs of Latin America and the Caribbean. It publishes the quarterly Unidad Borinqueña (Puerto Rican Unity) and the biennial Status Report on Puerto Ricans in the U.S.

National Congress of Puerto Rican Veterans

304 Park Avenue, South
New York, NY 10010
(212) 260–3000

Founded in 1967, the National Congress of Puerto Rican Veterans has 8,000 members. It functions as a support group for Puerto Rican veterans by assisting them in obtaining equal treatment and fair access to services provided to all veterans.

National Council of Hispanic Women

P.O. Box 23266
L'Enfant Plaza Station
Washington, DC 20013
(703) 768–3596; or, (703) 486–8112

Composed of 175 Hispanic women, universities, and corporations interested in strengthening the role of Hispanic women in society, the organization encourages Hispanic women to take part in decision making in government and business. It publishes the quarterly *NCHW Newsletter*.

National Council of La Raza

810 First Street, NE, Suite 300
Washington, DC 20002–4205
(202) 289–1380

Founded in 1968, the National Council of La Raza has 75 organizational members; it serves as an umbrella organization working for civil rights and economic opportunities for Hispanics. It provides technical assistance to Hispanic community-based organizations in comprehensive community development. It conducts research and serves as an advocate for Hispanic causes. It also offers private sector resource development training, board of directors training, and proposal writing training. It publishes a variety of newsletters and reports.

National Council of Puerto Rican Volunteers

c/o Mrs. Pedro G. Valdés
541 South Sixth Avenue
Mt. Vernon, NY 10550
(914) 665–1287

Founded in 1964, the National Council of Puerto Rican Volunteers has 10,000 members. It aims to organize groups of Puerto Rican and Spanish-speaking volunteers to help bridge the language barriers that prevent many Puerto Ricans from taking advantage of facilities in existence for their welfare and improvement. It furnishes public and private service organizations with bilingual volunteers.

National Hispanic Corporate Council

2323 North Third Street, Suite 101
Phoenix, AZ 85004
(602) 495–1988

Founded in 1985, the National Hispanic Corporate Council has 43 members, who are executives of Fortune 500 companies. Their goals include exchanging information, ideas, and research that will assist corporate America in focusing on the Hispanic community and the market it represents. The council publishes a newsletter.

National Hispanic Council on Aging

2713 Ontario Road, NW, Suite 200
Washington, DC 20009
(202) 265–1288

Founded in 1980, the National Hispanic Council on Aging has 3,000 members and 4 chapters. The council is an advocate for the Hispanic aging and develops and disseminates information, educational materials, research, and policy analysis regarding Hispanic elderly. The council is affiliated with the American Society on Aging and the Gerontological Society of America. It publishes a quarterly newsletter, Noticias.

National League of Cuban American Community-Based Centers

2119 South Webster Street
Fort Wayne, IN 46802
(219) 745–5421

The National League of Cuban American Community-Based Centers was founded in 1980 to establish linkages among Cuban American community centers and to open new centers wherever needed. The league assesses the needs of minority communities in relation to education, training, manpower development, and health care. It promotes awareness among Hispanics of employment opportunities. The league publishes a monthly *Hispanic Newsletter*.

National Puerto Rican Forum, Inc.

1 East Thirty-second Street, Fourth Floor
New York, NY 10016
(212) 685–2311

Founded in 1957, the National Puerto Rican Forum is concerned with the overall improvement of Puerto Rican and Hispanic communities throughout the United States. It designs and implements programs in job counseling, training and placement, and the teaching of English. It sponsors career services and a job placement program at the national level. It publishes occasional reports.

The Puerto Rican Family Institute, Inc.

145 West Fifteenth Street
New York, NY 10011
(212) 924–6320

Founded in 1960 for the preservation of the health, well-being, and integrity of Puerto Rican and Hispanic families in the United States, The Puerto Rican Family Institute's programs include social work and educational services to migrants and newly arrived immigrants, child-placement, prevention programs, and health clinics. Its services are also administered by a branch office in Río Piedras, Puerto Rico.

Puerto Rican Legal Defense and Education Fund, Inc.

99 Hudson Street, Fourteenth Floor
New York, NY 10013
(212) 219–3360

The Puerto Rican Legal Defense and Education Fund was established in 1972 to protect and further the rights of Puerto Ricans and other Hispanics, especially against discrimination in housing, education, employment, health, and political participation. It also maintains placement services for Hispanic lawyers. It publishes a newsletter, *Civil Rights Litigation*.

Secretariat for Hispanic Affairs, National Council of Bishops

National Council of Bishops
3211 Fourth Street, NE
Washington, DC 20017–1194
(202) 541–3150

Founded in 1945, the Secretariat for Hispanic Affairs has 140 diocesan directors as members. It offers consultation services operated by the Catholic Bishops of the United States to assist those dioceses with large Hispanic populations in developing a far-reaching and effective response to the pastoral needs of Hispanics in the United States. It conducts and disseminates research and provides liaisons with other institutions and agencies. It publishes the quarterly *En Marcha* (On the March).

SER-Jobs for Progress

1355 River Bend Drive, Suite 240
Dallas, TX 75247
(214) 631–3999

Founded in 1964, SER is a voluntary community-based organization with 111 affiliate programs in 83 cities. It is a national network of organizations that develop programs for the full utilization of Hispanics in the economy, including a wide range of job-training and educational programs. SER is sponsored by and affiliated with the League of United Latin American Citizens and the American G.I. Forum. It publishes the quarterly *SER America*.

Southwest Voter Registration Education Project

403 East Commerce Street, Suite 220
San Antonio, TX 78205
(512) 222–0224

Founded in 1975, the Southwest Voter Registration Education Project is made up of church, civic, labor, and fraternal groups that organize coalitions to register minority voters in the Southwest and 13 western states. It conducts nonpartisan voter education projects and research on Hispanic and native American political organization participation in the Southwest. It seeks reapportionment of gerrymandered counties and cities. It publishes the *National Hispanic Voter Registration Campaign* and research studies. Regional planning committees publish newsletters.

REFORMA: The National Association to Promote Library Services to the Spanish Speaking

American Library Association
50 Huron Street
Chicago, IL 60611
(916) 323-4400

Founded in 1971, REFORMA has 700 members in eight affiliates. REFORMA works for the improvement of the full range of library services to Hispanics of the United States. REFORMA advocates the creation of library collections in Spanish, the recruitment of bilingual and bicultural library personnel, and the development of specialized services for the Hispanic community. REFORMA offers scholarships for graduate library study. It is affiliated with the American Library Association. REFORMA publishes the quarterly *Reforma Newsletter*.

United Farm Workers of America

P.O. Box 62 - La Paz
Keene, CA 93531
(805) 822-5571

Founded in 1962, the United Farm Workers of America, a labor union, currently has a membership of over 100,000. The main goal is to enhance the living conditions of farm workers through collective bargaining with agricultural producers. It issues two publications, *El Malcriado* (monthly) and *Food and Justice* (monthly).

U.S. Hispanic Chamber of Commerce

1030 Fifteenth Street, NW, Suite 206
Washington, DC 20005
(202) 842-1212

Founded in 1979, the U.S. Hispanic Chamber of Commerce has 40,000 members and 20 affiliates interested in the development and promotion of Hispanic businesses and the promotion of the business leadership in the Hispanic community. It promotes a positive image for Hispanics and encourages corporate involvement with Hispanic companies. It conducts business-related workshops, conferences, and management training seminars; compiles statistics; reports on business achievements and vendor programs of major corporations; and sponsors competitions and bestows awards. Its publications include a periodic National Hispanic Business Directory and two quarterly newsletters, Legislative Update and Networking.

References

Furtaw, Julia C., ed. *Hispanic Americans Information Directory 1992–93*. Detroit: Gale Research, 1992.

Schorr, Edward Alan. *Hispanic Resource Directory*. Juneau, Alaska: Denali Press, 1988.

Zavaler, Angela E., ed. *Anvario Hispano-Hispanic Yearbook*. McLean, Virginia: T.I.Y.M. Publishing Company, 1991.

Nicolás Kanellos

Prominent Hispanics

The following are short biographies of U.S. Hispanics who have excelled in their areas of endeavor. Virtually every field has been influenced by Hispanics or counts Hispanics among its outstanding practitioners. There are many other biographies in the other chapters of this book that are dedicated to specific disciplines.

Tomás A. Arciniega (1937–)

Higher Education

Born August 5, 1937, in El Paso, Texas, Arciniega received all of his higher education in New Mexico, graduating from the University of New Mexico in 1970 with a Ph.D. in educational administration. Arciniega went on to become an outstanding educator, administrator, lecturer, and creator of educational policy. He has served as assistant dean of the Graduate School of Educational Administration, University of Texas at El Paso, 1972–73; dean of education at San Diego Sate University, 1973–80; vice president of academic affairs at California State University, Fresno, 1980–83; and from 1983 to the present, president of California State University, Bakersfield. He has won many awards for distinguished leadership in education, including being selected one of the top 100 leaders in American education by *Change* magazine in 1987. He received two commendations from the California legislature for contributions to California higher education, in 1975 and 1978.

Philip Arreola (1940–)

Law Enforcement

Born on February 4, 1940, in Acambaro, Guanajuato, Mexico, Arreola immigrated to the United States with his family. He began his career as a policeman in Detroit, Michigan, in 1960. Since that time he rose through the ranks of the Detroit and the

Port Huron police departments, until becoming chief of the Port Huron police department in 1987. In 1989, he was appointed chief of police in Milwaukee and thus became one of the very few Hispanics to lead a major urban police force. Arreola's education includes a bachelor of science (with distinction) from Wayne State University in 1974 and a law degree from Wayne State in 1985. He is also a graduate of the FBI National Academy (1977) and has been a

Tomás A. Arciniega.

Philip Arreola.

fellow of criminal justice at Harvard University School of Law (1970–71). Arreola's honors include a Detroit police department medal of valor in 1986, 11 merit citations, 20 commendations, and two chief's merit awards.

Mary Helen Barro (1938–)

Radio Broadcasting

Born on June 17, 1938, in Culver City, California, Barro was educated in California; she received a degree in management systems and procedures from the University of California at Los Angeles in 1967, and then began a career in radio broadcasting. After working at various on-air and management positions in radio and television, from 1985 to 1986 she served as the general manager of the King Videocable Corporation. In 1986, Barro became a founder and partner of MC Gavren-Barro Broadcasting Corporation, serving as vice president and general manager. She has been an outstanding figure in broadcasting and a pioneer in creating emergency broadcasting procedures for the Spanish-speaking residents in the Los Angeles area. Her honors include the Mexican American Opportunity Founda-

tion's Woman of the Year Award in 1972 and resolutions honoring her achievements from the city of Los Angeles (1972) and the California state legislature (1976).

Tony Bonilla (1936–)

Civil Rights

Born in Calvert, Texas, on March 2, 1936, Bonilla received his higher education at Del Mar College and Baylor University (B.A., 1958); he received a law degree from the University of Houston in 1960. Since that time, he has worked as a partner with his brother, Rubén, and other in the law firm of Bonilla, Reed, Bonilla & Berlanga, and served in the Texas legislature from 1964 to 1967. He has had a number of important political appointments, including the Governing Board for Texas Colleges and Universities. But his most important contributions have been made as president of the League of United Latin American Citizens, from 1972 to 1975, during which time he was a national spokesperson on various Hispanic civil rights, economic, and educational affairs. He has also served as the chairman of the National Hispanic Leadership Conference, a position he holds at present. Among his awards are a gold medal from

Tony Bonilla.

Rubén Bonilla, Jr.

the president of Mexico in 1982 for his work on behalf of the Hispanic community of the United States.

Rubén Bonilla, Jr.

Civil Rights

Born in Calvert, Texas, Bonilla received a B.A. degree from the University of Texas in 1968 and a law degree from there in 1971. Since that time, he has worked as an attorney, as vice president of a law firm in partnership with his brother, Tony Bonilla, and has also served as the national president of the League of United Latin American Citizens from 1979 to 1981. He has been active in Democratic party politics in the state of Texas and has had a number of political appointments; in addition, he has served as the chairman of the Mexican American Democrats of Texas. His achievements have been recognized by *Esquire* magazine (1985) and *Texas Business* magazine. In 1980, he represented President Jimmy Carter at the inauguration of the president of Bolivia.

Harry Caicedo (1928–)

Journalism

Born on April 1, 1928, in New York City to Colombian parents, Caicedo was educated in the United States, received his bachelor of journalism from the University of Missouri in 1954, and has developed an outstanding career in journalism as an editor and director in various media. From 1955 to 1958, he served as associate editor of *Latin American Report* magazine; from 1958 to 1959, he was the chief of the *Miami Herald* news bureau, and from 1961 to 1978, he served the U.S. Information Agency and the Voice of America in various positions in the United States and in Latin America. In 1984, he became president of Inter American Editorial Services. From 1984 to 1991, he served as the founding editor of the nation's first Hispanic mass circulation magazine, *Vista*. Since 1991, he has been a media consultant.

Vikki Carr (1940–)

Popular Music

Born on July 19, 1940, in El Paso, Texas, and baptized Florencia Bisenta de Casillas Martínez Cardona, Vikki Carr has become one of the most

Harry Caicedo.

Vikki Carr.

successful Hispanic recording artists and international performers of popular music in history. Carr began her singing career in the Los Angeles area while still in high school. After touring with a band for a while, she signed her first recording contract with Liberty Records in 1961. Her first recording successes, however, were in Australia and England, and later in the United States. By 1967 Carr's international popularity was so great that she was invited to perform for Queen Elizabeth II at a command performance in London. The following year, she set a precedent for sold-out concerts in Germany, Spain, France, England, Australia, Japan, and Holland. In the United States, she became a favorite of the White House, performing repeatedly for each of the last four presidents. To date, Carr has recorded 49 best-selling records, including 15 gold albums. In 1985, she won a Grammy for her Spanish-language album *Simplemente Mujer*. For her Spanish-language records, she has won gold, platinum and diamond records. Her 1989 album *Esos Hombres* won gold records in Mexico, Chile, Puerto Rico, and the United States. Among her other awards are the *Los Angeles Times* 1970 Woman of the Year Award, the 1972 American Guild of Variety Artists' Entertainer

of the Year Award, the 1984 Hispanic Woman of the Year Award, and the 1991 Girl Scouts of America Award. In 1971, Carr founded the Vikki Carr Scholarship Foundation to provide higher education scholarships to Mexican American youths. Carr is active in a number of other charities as well.

César Estrada Chávez (1927–1993)

Labor Organizer

Born near Yuma, Arizona, on March 31, 1927, to a family of migrant farm workers, Chávez attended nearly 30 schools, eventually achieving a seventh grade education. During World War II, he served in the Navy, after which he returned to migrant farm labor. He eventually settled down in 1948 in the barrio of Sal Si Puedes (Get Out If You Can) in San Jose, California. It was in San Jose that he began working for the Community Service Organization (CSO) as a community organizer. By 1958, he had become general director of the CSO in California and Arizona. In 1962, wishing to organize farm workers, he resigned the CSO directorship and moved to Delano, California, where he became head of the United Farmworkers Organizing Committee, which later became the United Farm Workers, AFL-CIO.

César Chávez.

Bert Corona.

From 1965 on, Chávez and his fledgling union embarked on a number of history-making strikes and national boycotts of agricultural products that have become the most successful in the history of farm labor in the United States. Principally because of Chávez and his organization's efforts, the California legislature passed the California Labor Relations Act in 1975, which provides secret ballot union elections for farm workers. Owing to his efforts, as well, there have been many improvements in wage, health, and housing conditions for farm workers in California and Arizona. Chávez was regarded as a selfless and spiritual leader of farm workers everywhere, bringing to national attention their plight through media appearances and interviews, hunger strikes, and well-organized boycotts. He died on April 23, 1993, from natural causes at the age of 66. He was posthumously awarded the Medal of Freedom from President Bill Clinton.

Bert Corona (1918–)

Labor Organizer

Born on May 29, 1918, in El Paso, Texas, Corona attended public schools in El Paso and college in California, where he graduated with a degree in law from the University of California, Los Angeles. Between 1936 and 1942, he was active in developing unions in the Southwest. He worked with the CIO in organizing cannery and warehouse workers. His union work eventually led to politics, where he became a pioneer in developing Mexican American political organizations. In 1959, he was one of the principal founders of the Mexican American Political Organization (MAPA); he was also a founder of the National Congress of Spanish-Speaking People. Corona also was a pioneer in education for Mexican Americans, contributing to the development of the Mexican American Youth Conference and even serving as president of the Association of California School Administrators.

José R. Coronado (1932–)

Health Care

Born on April 3, 1932, in Benavides, Texas, Coronado has dedicated his life to health care. He received a B.S. degree in zoology and chemistry (1957) and an M.S. degree in education administration (1959) from Texas A&I and an M.S. degree in hospital administration (1973) from Baylor University.

José R. Coronado.

He has since become one of the very few Hispanics in the country to be the director of a major hospital: the Audie L. Murphy Memorial Veterans Hospital, a 704-bed tertiary health care facility and 120-bed nursing home affiliated with the University of Texas Health Sciences Center in San Antonio. Before becoming the director in 1975, Coronado had previously been assistant director there, and earlier in his career at two other veterans hospitals, in Kerrville and in Houston. In his present capacity, Coronado also holds various academic appointments in health care at Baylor University, Trinity University, the University of New Hampshire, Smith College, the University of Houston, and the University of Texas. In June 1991, Coronado was the first recipient of the Senior-Level Healthcare Executive Award for South Texas, presented by the American College of Healthcare Executives. His many other honors include a Presidential Rank Award for Meritorious Service from President Ronald Reagan in 1987 and the same award in 1989 from President George Bush.

Edward A. Corral (1931–)

Fire Chief

Born in Houston, Texas, on July 4, 1931, Corral received his primary education in Houston, attended the University of Houston in 1955, attended National Fire Academy seminars and short courses from 1956 to 1982, Houston Community College from 1975 to 1982, and Texas A and M University System Engineering Extension Service in 1968. From 1950 to 1951, Corral served in the air force, obtaining the rank of sergeant. From 1956 to 1969, he served as a Houston Fire Department senior inspector; from 1969 to 1973, as an administrative aide in the mayor's office; from 1973 to 1981, as the fire department's chief inspector; and from 1981 to 1992, as the Houston fire marshall. He was appointed to the position of Houston fire chief in March 1992 by Mayor Bob Lanier. Included in Corral's innovative approaches to fire prevention was a program he initiated in 1982, the Juvenile Firesetters Prevention Program, which helped reduce fire damage by $11 million in its first year. Under the program, private companies pay the city to counsel some 2,000 area youths who have started fires.

Gilda Cruz-Romo (1940–)

Classical Music

Born in Guadalajara, Mexico, and educated there, Gilda Cruz-Romo graduated from the National Conservatory of Music in Mexico City in 1964 and embarked on her lifelong career as a soprano opera singer. From 1962 to 1967 she sang with the Na-

tional Opera and the International Opera of Mexico, from 1966 to 1968 with the Dallas Civic Opera, and from 1969 to 1972 with the New York City Opera. Since 1970, she has been the leading soprano for the prestigious Metropolitan Opera Company of New York. As a professional opera singer, Cruz-Romo has sung in many countries and has won many awards, including first place in the Metropolitan Opera national auditions in 1970. She has taught voice at the University of Texas, Austin, since 1990.

Jaime Escalante (1930–)

Education

Born on December 31, 1930, in La Paz, Bolivia, Escalante received his early education in Bolivia and a B.S. degree in mathematics from California State University in Los Angeles. Already a physics and mathematics teacher when he immigrated to the United States, he was not allowed to teach because he did not have a degree from an American institution; he therefore worked as a busboy, a cook, and then an electronics factory technician. After receiving his B.S. degree in mathematics from California State, he was hired at the impoverished barrio school of Garfield High School in East Los Angeles in

Jaime Escalante.

1974. He has subsequently become known as one of the nation's top teachers, because he has managed to teach and inspire his students to achieve at the nation's highest levels in mathematics and calculus, often sending them on with full scholarships to the nation's most prestigious colleges. Escalante taught at Garfield High School from 1974 to 1990. He currently works as an educational consultant and writes and stars in an educational program, "Futures," for television's Corporation for Public Broadcasting. In September 1991, Escalante began teaching math at Sacramento's Hiram High School, where he intends to replicate his success at East Los Angeles. Escalante's work has been the subject of a hit feature film and has inspired the creation of various scholarship funds in his name. His many awards include the 1989 White House Hispanic Heritage Award and the 1990 American Institute for Public Service Jefferson Award.

Joseph A. Fernández (1935–)

Education

Born in 1935 and raised in his hometown of New York City, Fernández has been awarded B.A. (1963), M.A. (1970), and Ph.D. (1985) degrees from the University of Miami. He has dedicated his entire career to education, beginning as a public high school teacher and rising to the post of superintendent of the Dade County Public Schools in Miami. He returned to his native New York in 1990 to become chancellor of the nation's largest school district. He has been known as a no-nonsense leader who has instituted many innovative programs in public education. In New York, he introduced the School-Based Management/Shared Decision-Making (SBM/SDM) model of school reform that he had pioneered in Miami. This program allows parents, teachers, and administrators to share decision-making authority on everything from curriculum to budgets. Fernández has also been a pioneer in a number of other school reform areas. In 1991, he served as chairman of the Council to the National Urban Education Summit; and in 1993, he became president of School Improvement Services in Winter Park, Florida.

Ricardo R. Fernández (1940–)

Higher Education

Born in Santurce, Puerto Rico, on December 11, 1940, Fernández received his early education there and his higher education at Marquette University in Milwaukee (B.A. degree in philosophy, 1962, M.A. degree in Spanish Literature, 1965) and Princeton University (M.A. degree in Romance languages, 1967, and Ph.D. degree in Latin American Litera-

Joseph A. Fernández.

ture and Linguistics, 1970). His major work as a scholar and administrator has been accomplished in bilingual education and the education of Hispanic and minority students in a variety of positions for the state of Wisconsin and the University of Wisconsin, Milwaukee. From 1973 to 1978, he served as an assistant professor of cultural foundations at the university, and continued to develop his career after that in the field of education, rising to full professor and assistant vice chancellor for academic affairs by 1990. That same year he was named president of Lehman College of the City University of New York, and thus became one of a small handful of Hispanic college presidents in the United States. Among his leadership positions have been the following: president of the board of directors, Multicultural Training and Advocacy, Inc. (since 1986); member, board of directors, Puerto Rican Legal Defense and Education Fund (beginning in 1981); and president, National Association for Bilingual Education (1980–81). His published books and research reports are pioneering studies on the causes of Hispanic school dropout, the desegregation of schools with Hispanic students, and bilingual education. Fernández's awards include the Lifetime Achieve-

Archbishop Patrick F. Flores.

1978, Bishop Flores was installed as the bishop of the diocese of El Paso, where he served until he was installed as the archbishop of San Antonio on October 13, 1979. Bishop Flores has received many honors and has pioneered programs in the church and in government on behalf of the civil rights of Hispanics and immigrants. In 1983, he was one of four bishops elected to represent the United States at the synod of bishops in Rome. In 1986, he was awarded the Medal of Freedom (Ellis Island Medal of Honor) in honor of the Statue of Liberty's one hundredth birthday.

Ernesto Galarza (1905–1984)

Education, Labor

Born in Tepic, Nayarit, Mexico, in 1905, Galarza immigrated to the United States as a refugee with his family during the Mexican Revolution. Galarza attended schools in Sacramento, California, where he was orphaned while in high school and thus had to support himself. Galarza went on to Occidental College and then received an M.A. degree from Stanford University in 1929. He later received a Ph.D. degree in education from Columbia University. Galarza then worked as a research assistant in education for the Pan American Union from 1936 to

ment Award in Education, National Puerto Rican Coalition (1990), a citation from the Wisconsin State Senate for his contributions in the field of education (1984), and the Hispanic Leadership Award from the Federal Regional Council-HEW Region V (1976).

Patrick Fernández Flores (1929–)

Religion

Born Patricio Fernández Flores on July 26, 1929, in Ganado, Texas, the seventh of nine children, Flores received his early education in Ganado and Pearland, Texas and graduated from Kirwin High School in Galveston. He then attended St. Mary's Seminary in La Porte, Texas, and St. Mary's Seminary in Houston. He was ordained a Catholic priest on May 26, 1956, and served in a variety of functions in the diocese of Galveston-Houston, including as director of the Bishop's Committee for the Spanish-Speaking, until March 18, 1970, when Pope Paul VI appointed him to serve as auxiliary to the Archbishop of San Antonio. On May 5, 1970, he was consecrated as bishop. Bishop Flores was the first Mexican American elevated to the hierarchy of the Catholic church in the United States. On May 29,

Ernesto Galarza.

1940, when he was promoted to chief of the Division of Labor and Social Information. In 1947, he became research director for the National Farm Labor Union, AFL, and moved to San Jose, California. During the next 12 years he dedicated his life to agricultural workers, serving as secretary-treasurer and vice president of the union. During the 1960s, Galarza worked as a professor, researcher and writer, writing various books on farm labor topics. During the 1970s, he developed materials for bilingual education, including original books for children. He died on June 22, 1984, in San Jose, California.

Héctor Pérez García (1914–)

Civil Rights

Born on January 17, 1914, in Llera, Tamaulipas, Mexico, he moved to south Texas with his family and was educated there; in 1936 he earned a B.A. degree from the University of Texas, and in 1940 his M.D. degree. But it was not as a doctor that García won national distinction, but as a civil rights activist. He is the founder and past president of the American G.I. Forum, an organization of U.S. Hispanic service veterans that has been a pioneer in securing the civil and educational rights of Hispanics. Besides working with the forum, García became a member of the Texas State Democratic Committee and in 1954 was appointed to the Democratic National Committee. He was also active in LULAC and in 1960 was a founder and first national president of the Political Association of Spanish-Speaking Organizations (PASO). During the 1960 election, García was the National Coordinator of the Viva Kennedy clubs. García has served as an alternative ambassador to the United Nations (1964), on the U.S. Commission on Civil Rights (1968), and as the vice president of the Catholic Council for the Spanish-Speaking of the Southwest. He is the recipient of the United States of America Medal of Freedom (1984), the Outstanding Democracy Forward Award, the U.S. Marine Corps Award, and many others. For his service in the U.S. Army Medical Corps during World War II, he was awarded the Bronze Star with six battle stars.

Elsa Gómez (1938–)

Higher Education

Born on January 16, 1938, in New York City, Elsa Gómez is the first Hispanic woman president of a four-year liberal arts college in the nation. Gómez received her B.A. degree in Spanish, magna cum laude, from the College of St. Elizabeth in 1960, her M.A. degree in Italian from Middlebury College in 1961, and her Ph.D. degree in Italian from the University of Texas in 1971. She taught and came up

through the ranks at the University of Puerto Rico, Mayaguez, Indiana University of Pennsylvania, and Boston University. Before serving as president of Kean College, she was dean of the College of Arts and Sciences and director of the graduate program of Lock Haven University from 1987 to 1989 and director of academic programs for the Massachusetts Board of Regents of Higher Education from 1983 to 1987. Gómez has been named to various national and international honor societies as a scholar and administrator.

Raymond Emmanuel González (1924–)

Diplomacy

Born in Pasadena, California, on December 24, 1924, González received his B.A. and M.A. degrees from the University of Southern California in 1949 and 1950, respectively, and became a career diplomat for the United States. He served in various diplomatic capacities throughout Latin America and in Washington, DC, Belgium, and Italy, until finally serving as American ambassador to Ecuador from 1978 to 1982, at which time he retired. Since 1983, he has served as senior inspector, Office of the Inspector General in Washington, DC. In 1970, he was

Elsa Gómez.

Carolina Herrera.

the recipient of the Department of State Meritorious Award, and, in 1988, the Department of State Wilbur J. Carr Award.

Suzanna Guzmán (1955–)

Classical Music

Born in Los Angeles, California, on May 29, 1955, Guzmán is a 1980 graduate of California State University, Los Angeles, and the American Institute Music Theater in 1984. Although only at the beginning of her career, she has already sung as a soloist with the Los Angeles Philharmonic, the San Diego Opera, the Washington Opera, the Metropolitan Opera, and at Carnegie Hall and the Kennedy Center for the Performing Arts. Her awards include First Place, Metropolitan Opera National Council in 1985; First Place, International Competition, Center for Contemporary Opera in 1988; Western Region First Place, San Francisco Opera Center, 1985, and others. Guzmán has been an active performer for Hispanic schoolchildren in southern California and for the handicapped.

Carolina Herrera

Fashion

Carolina Herrera is one of the most respected fashion designers of the United States. Born in Caracas, Venezuela, Herrera became a fashion designer only after years of insistence by friends and retailers who marveled at the opulent creations she designed and wore to social functions internationally. She has headed her own design firm, House of Herrera, in New York City since 1981. Her clients have included Caroline Kennedy, Jacqueline Onassis, and Nancy Reagan. Herrera's design repertoire today includes the CH Collection, the Couture Bridal Collection, Carolina Herrera Costume Jewelry, Carolina Herrera Perfumes, and "Herrera for Men." Among her many honors are election to "The Best Dressed Hall of Fame" and *Elle* magazine's "Ten Most Elegant Women in the World." She has also received the MODA Award for Top Hispanic Designer in 1987.

Dolores Fernández Huerta (1930–)

Union Organizer, Lobbyist

Born in Dawson, New Mexico, in 1930, Huerta received her early education in Stockton, California.

Dolores Fernández Huerta.

teachers and coaches as Laszlo Halasz, Leonard Bernstein, and Seiji Ozawa. She has maintained a busy schedule as a composer, recording artist, and a guest conductor at most of the important symphony orchestras throughout the United States and Puerto Rico, as well as in Paris, London, Spoleto, Berlin, and Munich. From 1977 to 1988, she was the director of the Family Concert Series for the Brooklyn Philharmonic Community. In 1985, León joined the faculty of Brooklyn College as an associate professor, teaching both composition and conducting. She has also served as music director for Broadway musicals such as *The Wiz*. León is just one of a handful of women to have made a successful career as a conductor. Her honors include the Dean Dixon Achievement Award in 1985, the ASCAP Composer's Award from 1987 to 1989, the National Council of Women Achievement Award in 1980, the 1991 Academy-Institute Award in Music of the American Academy and Institute of Arts and Letters, and many others.

Modesto A. Maidique (1940–)

Higher Education, Business

Born in Havana, Cuba, on March 20, 1940, Maidique was educated in Cuba and in the United

Tania J. León.

In 1955, she became associated with Fred Ross and César Chávez, pioneer organizers of Mexican American chapters of the Community Service Organization. Since that time, she has worked with Chávez in organizing and administering the United Farm Workers Union. With years of experience in organizing migrant workers, striking, and negotiating contracts, Huerta eventually became the lobbyist for the UFW in Sacramento, California. She has gained an international reputation as an effective speaker and politician.

Tania J. León (1943–)

Classical Music

Born on May 14, 1943, in Havana, Cuba, Tania León received degrees from the National Conservatory of Music in Havana, a B.S. in music education from New York University in 1973, and an M.A. degree in music composition from New York University in 1975. One year after arriving in the United States in 1968, she became the first music director of the Dance Theater of Harlem, and she has continued to be an important composer for the Dane Theater. From then on, León studied conducting under such

Modesto A. Maidique.

States. He earned three degrees from the Massachusetts Institute of Technology: a bachelor of science degree (1962), a master of science degree (1964), and a Ph.D. degree in engineering (1970). Maidique is also the graduate of the Harvard Business School's Program for Management Development. Maidique has led an outstanding career as a scholar and educator, and as a business entrepreneur as well. He is the founder of Analog Devices Semiconductor, now a $300 million manufacturer of integrated circuits. He has been an advisor and consultant to major American firms in diverse fields and a general partner of Hambrecht and Quist, a leading venture capital firm. But it is in his academic career that Maidique has gained the most distinction; he is one of a very small handful of Hispanic college presidents. In 1986, he was appointed president of Florida International University in Miami. This followed upon a teaching career at MIT, Harvard, and Stanford, and his writing numerous articles and cowriting such books as *Energy Future,* which made the *New York Times* best-seller list. Under Maidique's leadership, Florida International University has been consistently named by *U.S. News and World Report* as one of America's best colleges. In 1991, Florida International University was ranked as one of the top ten comprehensive universities in the South.

Eduardo Mata (1942–1995)

Classical Music

Born in Mexico City, Mexico, on September 5, 1942, Eduardo Mata has dedicated his life to music and has become one of Mexico's most outstanding symphonic directors. Educated at the National Conservatory of Music from 1954 to 1963, and through private instruction, he began his conducting career in 1964 with the Guadalajara Symphony Orchestra. From 1966 to 1975, he was music director and conductor of the Orquesta Filarmónica of the National University in Mexico City. In 1975, he became the director of the National Symphony in Mexico City and also directed a number of international music festivals, including the 1976 Casals Festival in Mexico. Mata has been a guest conductor around the world and throughout the United States. In 1977 Mata began leading the Dallas Symphony as music director, while also touring extensively and even continuing to serve as the principal conductor and musical advisor of the Phoenix Symphony (1974 to 1978) and the principal guest conductor of the Pittsburgh Symphony (since 1989). Mata was named conductor emeritus of the Dallas Symphony beginning with the 1993–94 season. Mata has also maintained a busy recording schedule that has resulted in top-quality albums of some of the world's leading orchestras under his direction. In Mexico he has been honored with the Golden Lyre Award (1974), the Elías Sourasky Prize in the Arts (1975), and the Mozart Medal conferred by the president of Mexico (1991). In the United States, he is the recipient of the White House Hispanic Heritage Award (1991).

On January 4, 1995, Eduardo Mata died in an airplane crash near a Mexican airport. His two children, Roberto and Pilar, survive him and live in Mexico City.

Julián Nava (1927–)

Education, Diplomacy

Born on June 19, 1927, in Los Angeles, California, to a family that had fled Mexico during the Mexican Revolution, Nava grew up in East Los Angeles. He served in the Navy Air Corps during World War II and, upon return, obtained an education through the G.I. Bill. Nava graduated from Pomona College with an A.B. degree in 1951 and from Harvard University with a Ph.D. degree in 1955. Since graduation he has served as a lecturer and professor at various universities in Colombia, Venezuela, Puerto Rico, Spain, and California, where he is still a tenured professor of history at California State University at North-

Eduardo Mata.

Julián Nava.

ridge. In 1967, Nava was elected to the Los Angeles school board and later served as president of the board. Nava served as ambassador to Mexico from 1979 to 1981; he is the first Mexican American to ever hold that post.

Miguel A. Nevárez (1937–)

Higher Education

Born in McAllen, Texas, on June 20, 1937, Nevárez has devoted his life to education, first becoming an elementary teacher and then rising to become one of a small handful of Hispanic college presidents. After receiving his primary education in McAllen, Nevárez received a B.S. degree in agriculture from Texas A&I University in 1960; thereafter, he received a master's degree in elementary education from Michigan State University in 1968 and a Ph.D. degree in science education from New York University in 1972. Before becoming a university educator, Nevárez worked as an elementary science and math teacher from 1963 to 1967 and as an assistant principal from 1968 to 1969. In 1971, he became associate dean of men at Pan American University and by 1973 had risen to the rank of vice president.

From 1981 to the present, he has served as president of that institution, which holds the highest enrollment of Hispanic students of any university in the United States. In 1985, President Ronald Reagan named Nevárez outstanding educator, and in 1987 he received Michigan State University's Distinguished Alumni Award.

Ellen Ochoa (1958–)

Astronaut

Born in 1958 in Los Angeles, California, Ochoa received her early education in Southern California and was awarded a B.S. degree in physics in 1980 from San Diego State University; she received M.S. and Ph.D. degrees in electrical engineering from Stanford University in 1981 and 1985, respectively. Following her graduate studies, Ochoa became a research engineer at Sandia National Laboratories and later at NASA/Ames Research Center, where she rose to become the chief of the information sciences division. After that she became an astronaut, the first Hispanic female to do so. Ochoa's first flight began April 8, 1993, on the orbiter Discovery. She was mission specialist on the STS-56 Atmospheric Research flight and was responsible for their primary payload, the Spartan 201 Satellite, and she operated the robotic arm to deploy and retrieve it. She is currently based at the Lyndon B. Johnson Space Center in Houston, Texas. As a researcher, Ochoa holds two patents for work that she has developed. In 1989, she received the Hispanic Engineer National Achievement Award for the Most Promising Engineer in Government; in 1990, she received the Pride Award from the National Hispanic Quincentennial Commission; in 1993, she won the Congressional Hispanic Caucus Medallion of Excellence Role Model Award; and in 1995, she won the Albert V. Baez Award for Outstanding Technical Achievement in Service to Humanity.

Raymond E. Orozco (1933–)

Fire Fighting

Born on December 7, 1933, in Chicago, Illinois, Orozco is a career fireman who has risen through the ranks to head the Chicago Fire Department after 30 years of service. After joining the department in 1959, he was promoted consistently until reaching battalion chief in 1979, deputy district chief in 1980, executive assistant to the fire commissioner in 1981, and a number of top deputy positions until being named fire commissioner on April 24, 1989. Throughout his career Commissioner Orozco has undergone special training offered by the City of Chicago for fire fighters and for city administrators.

Manuel Pacheco. (Photograph by Julieta González.)

In 1976, Orozco received his associate of arts degree in fire science from Daley College in Chicago.

Francis V. Ortiz, Jr. (1926–)

Diplomacy

Born in Santa Fe, New Mexico, on March 14, 1926, Francis Ortiz received his B.S. degree from the School of Foreign Service at Georgetown University in 1950 and went on to pursue a career in diplomacy. He later attained an M.S. degree in 1967 from George Washington University and also studied at the National War College. His career in the foreign service took him to posts in Ethiopia, Mexico, Peru, Uruguay, Argentina, Barbados, and Grenada from 1953 to 1979. In 1979, he became the ambassador to Guatemala; from 1981 to 1983, the ambassador to Peru; and from 1983 to 1986, the ambassador to Argentina. His honors include the 1952 Honor Award from the State Department, the 1964 and 1973 Superior Award, the 1980 Gran Cruz de Mérito Civil from Spain, and the 1964 U.S./Mexican Presidential Chamizal Commemorative Medal. From 1944 to 1946, Ortiz served in the U.S. Air Force; he received the Air Medal for his service.

Manuel Trinidad Pacheco (1941–)

Higher Education

Born on May 30, 1941, in Rocky Ford, Colorado, Pacheco has dedicated his life to education; having obtained a B.A. degree from New Mexico Highlands University (1962) and M.A. and Ph.D. degrees from Ohio State University (1966 and 1969), he pursued a career as a professor of Spanish and education and as an administrator at various universities. It is in educational administration that Pacheco made his mark, first becoming associate dean at the University of Texas at El Paso in 1982 and executive director for planning in 1984, then president of Laredo State University in 1984, president of the University of Houston-Downtown in 1988 and president of the University of Arizona in 1991. Upon assuming this last position, Pacheco became the first Hispanic president of a major research university in the United States. Among his many honors is that of being named a distinguished alumnus of Ohio State University in 1984 and named among the "100 Most Influential Hispanics" by *Hispanic Business* magazine in 1988.

Minerva Pérez (1955–)

Television Journalism

Born on October 25, 1955, in San Juan, Texas, Pérez was educated in south Texas, receiving her B.A. degree from the University of Texas-Pan American in 1980. Since 1979, she has embarked on a career in television journalism, working at KGBT-TV in Harlingen, Texas, as a reporter, then as producer and anchor. In 1982, she became a morning anchor and reporter for KMOL-TV in San Antonio, and in 1984, she held a similar position at an Austin station. From there she worked as a reporter in stations in Dallas and Phoenix. From 1987 to 1992, she worked as a reporter and anchor for KTLA-TV in Los Angeles. In 1992, she joined KTRK Channel 13 in Houston, Texas, as a weekend anchor and reporter. Pérez's outstanding work has been acknowledged through various awards: the Spot News Coverage Associated Press Media Award in 1987; an Emmy nomination for Best Host of a Community Affairs Program; and a Golden Mike Media Award, both in 1990; and others.

Guadalupe C. Quintanilla (1937–)

Higher Education

Born on October 25, 1937, in Ojinaga, Chihuahua, Mexico, Quintanilla received her B.S. degree in biology from Pan American University in 1969 and her M.A. and Ed.D. degrees in education in 1969 and 1971, respectively, from the University of Houston.

Guadalupe C. Quintanilla.

Quintanilla's career in education has spanned the gap from teacher aide (1964) to upper university administration, beginning in 1978 with her position as assistant provost for undergraduate affairs at the University of Houston. Since that time, she has also served as assistant vice chancellor (1981–85) and assistant vice president (1986 to the present). Throughout her career, Quintanilla has been in the vanguard of Hispanic studies, founding and directing one of the first Mexican American studies programs (1972–78) and one of the first bilingual teacher education programs (1972–78), both at the University of Houston. She is a widely known writer and lecturer on Hispanic education and overcoming the barriers of poverty, prejudice, and not speaking English. She is the author of numerous books and articles on teaching Spanish to native speakers, bilingual education, and the teaching of Spanish to public servants, such as police and firemen. Her honors include a presidential appointment as a U.S. representative to the World Conference on International Issues and Women's Affairs (1991), induction into the National Hispanic Hall of Fame (1987), a National Heroine Award from the *Ladies' Home Journal* (1984), a presidential appointment as alternate delegate to the United Nations (1984), and many others.

Geraldo Miguel Rivera (1943-)

Television Journalism

Born on July 4, 1943, in New York City, Rivera studied at the University of Arizona and Brooklyn Law School and received his law degree from the University of Pennsylvania and a degree in journalism from Columbia University. Rivera went on to become one of the nation's most celebrated and respected investigative television journalists, writing and producing various award-winning documentaries. He has won a Peabody Award and ten Emmys for distinguished broadcast journalism. After beginning his career as a reporter for WABC-TV in New York in 1970, he went on to become a reporter, producer, and host for various television news and entertainment shows. Since 1987, he has hosted and produced his own "Geraldo" talk show, which is nationally syndicated. Rivera is also the author of books, including his very controversial autobiography, which was published in 1991. Today, Rivera is one of the most visible and successful Hispanics in media and entertainment.

Gloria G. Rodríguez (1948-)

Education

Born on July 9, 1948, in San Antonio, Texas, Gloria Rodríguez has dedicated her life to education. She received a B.A. degree in elementary education and bilingual education from Our Lady of the Lake University (1970), two M.Ed. degrees (1973 and 1979) from Our Lady of the Lake and the University of Texas at San Antonio, and a Ph.D. degree in early childhood education (1991) from the University of

Geraldo Rivera.

Texas at Austin. After initiating her career in education as a first- and second-grade bilingual teacher from 1970 to 1973, Rodríguez worked in a number of experimental programs and served as curriculum writer, project director, and principal investigator. In 1973, she founded the program for which she continues to this date as executive director: Advance Family Support and Education Programs, which provides support and education services to low-income families for their educational, personal, and economic success. The program has become a national model for community-based intervention, and Rodríguez is in high demand nationally as a consultant, speaker, board member, project director and as an expert witness before Congress. Rodríguez's honors include the *San Antonio Light* newspaper Woman of the Year Award in 1981, the Women in Communication Professional Achievement Award in 1987, and two Citations of Recognition from the San Antonio City Council in 1981 and 1986.

Paul Rodríguez

Entertainment

Paul Rodríguez is the most recognized and popular Hispanic comedian in the United States. Born in Mazatlán, Mexico, Rodríguez came to the United States as the son of immigrant farm workers. "My family never thought that being a comedian or an actor was an obtainable goal. Being farmworkers, all they wanted for their children was a steady job. But I knew I had to give it a chance." In 1977, after a stint in the air force, Rodríguez entered Long Beach City College on the G.I. Bill, where he received and associate arts degree, and then he enrolled in California State University, Long Beach, with the objective of becoming an attorney. During theater classes at the university, Rodriguez's comic talent became obvious to his professor, who led him to become associated with the Comedy Store in Los Angeles, and thus his stand-up comic career was launched. Currently, Paul Rodríguez has worked in three television major network sitcom series and various movies. He is the host and star of immensely popular "El Show de Paul Rodríguez" on the Univision

Spanish-language network. Rodríguez is the head of his own company, Paul Rodríguez Productions, which produced the one-hour special "Paul Rodríguez behind Bars," which aired nationally on the Fox Network in 1991. His earlier special "I Need a Couch" had one of the highest ratings in the history of HBO comedy specials. His television work includes "a.k.a. Pablo" (1974), and host of the "Newlywed Game Starring Paul Rodríguez" (1988–89). His films include *D.C. Cab* (1983), *Quicksilver* (1985), *The Whoopee Boys* (1986), *Miracles* (1987), *Born in*

Paul Rodríguez.

East L.A. (1987), and *Made in America* (1993). In addition to his film and television work, Rodríguez is a comedy headliner at Las Vegas and Atlantic City, and in 1986 released his first comedy album, *You're in America Now, Speak Spanish.*

Luis Santeiro (1947–)

Television Writer

Born on October 9, 1947, in Havana, Cuba, Santeiro immigrated to Miami with his parents in 1960. He received a B.A. degree in sociology from Villanova University in 1969 and an M.A. degree in communications from Syracuse University in 1970. He became a free-lance writer and, since 1978 has served as a writer for the award-winning Children's Television Workshop and as the producer of "Sesame Street." Among the many shows he has written for television are 30 episodes of the bilingual comedy "Qué Pasa, USA?" (1977–80), and numerous episodes of the PBS series "3–2–1 Contact!", "Oye, Willie!", "Carrascolendas," and the ABC "After School Specials." Santeiro is among the most recognized Hispanics on television; he has won six Emmy

Awards for his writing on "Sesame Street." Santeiro is also a recognized dramatist with plays successfully produced in New York and Miami.

Cristina Saralegui (1948–)

Television Journalism

Born on January 29, 1948, in Havana, Cuba, into a distinguished family of journalists, Cristina Saralegui's grandfather, Francisco Saralegui, was known throughout Latin America as the "paper czar"; he initiated his granddaughter into the world of publishing through such popular magazines as *Bohemia, Carteles,* and *Vanidades.* In 1960, she immigrated to Miami's Cuban exile community, but continued to develop the family profession by majoring in mass communications and creative writing at the University of Miami. In her last year at the university, she began working for *Vanidades,* the leading ladies' service magazine in Latin America. By 1979, she was named editor-in-chief of the internationally distributed *Cosmopolitan-en-Español.* In 1989, she resigned that position to become the talk show host for "The Cristina Show," which has become the number one rated daytime show on Spanish-language television in the United States. Since

Cristina Saralegui.

1991, Saralegui has also been the host for a daily nationally syndicated radio show, "Cristina Opina" (Cristina's Opinions) and the editor-in-chief of a new monthly magazine, *Cristina-La Revista (Cristina-The Magazine),* published by Editorial América in Miami. Through radio and television, Cristina reaches 6.5 million Hispanics daily throughout the United States and in 12 Latin American countries.

Roberto Suárez (1928–)

Journalism

Born in Havana, Cuba, on May 5, 1928, Suárez received his primary and secondary education there. He obtained a bachelor's degree in economics and finance from Villanova University in 1949. After returning to Havana, from 1959 to 1960 he was active in real estate, construction and finance. In 1962, he went to work for *The Miami Herald* as a part-time mailer. He advanced to controller of the Knight-Ridder subsidiary operations. In 1972, he joined Knight Publishing Company in Charlotte, North Carolina, as controller and was named vice president and general manager in 1978. He was named president in 1986. In 1990, he assumed his present position as

Luis Santeiro.

Roberto Suárez.

president of *The Miami Herald* and Publisher of *El Nuevo Heraldo,* the Spanish-language newspaper published by the *Miami Herald* since 1987. His awards include the 1989 Gold Medal for Excellence for being the most distinguished executive of all Knight-Ridder companies, the 1990 Hispanic Alliance Heritage Award for Media, and the 1991 Leadership Award from ASPIRA.

Catalina Vásquez Villalpando (1940–)

Government

Born on April 1, 1940, in San Marcos, Texas, Catalina Villalpando attended various universities but never obtained a degree. She became the director of the Community Services Administration in 1969, an office she held until 1979. From there, she became a vice president of the Mid-South Oil Company in Dallas, and then a senior vice president of Communications International in Dallas where she directed all public relations and marketing for the company's northeast region.

Villalpando also has been active in the Republican Party. She served as liaison director for the Republican Party of Texas, vice president of the Republican National Assembly of Texas, and in 1983 special assistant to President Ronald Reagan. Villalpando's hard work paid off in 1988 when President George Bush appointed her as the thirty-ninth treasurer of the United States. As treasurer, Villalpando oversaw the operation of the U.S. Mint, the Bureau of Engraving and Printing, and the U.S. Savings Bond Division. She also advised the secretary of the treasury on matters relating to coinage, currency, and production of other negotiable instruments.

Reference

Unterberger, Amy L., ed. *Who's Who Among Hispanic Americans, 1992–1993.* Detroit: Gale Research, 1992.

Nicholás Kanellos

Illustrations

A Historical Overview:

p. 4: Isabella of Castile (reproduced by permission of Archive Photos); *p. 5:* Major paths of early European penetration of the United States (courtesy of U.S. Department of the Interior and the National Park Service); *p. 14:* A *vaquero* in early California (reproduced by permission of the Bancroft Library, University of California); *p. 15:* Viceroy Francisco Fernández de la Cueva Enríques, Duke of Albuquerque; *p. 15:* Rules that were issued by the King of Spain regarding the founding and governance of presidios on the frontier; *p. 17:* European claims in the United States to 1763 (courtesy of U.S. Department of the Interior and the National Park Service); *p. 18:* Presidio and pueblo of Santa Barbara in 1829 (from a lithograph by G. & W. Endicott; reproduced by permission of the Bancroft Library, University of California); *p. 19:* Soldier at the Monterey presidio in 1786 (reproduced by permission of the Bancroft Library, University of California); *p. 20:* Wife of a presidio soldier in Monterey, 1786 (reproduced by permission of the Bancroft Library, Univesity of California); *p. 20:* A *patrón* in early California (reproduced by permission of the Bancroft Library, University of California); *p. 21:* General Manuel Mier y Terán, Laredo; *p. 23:* Pío Pico (1801–1894) was the last governor of California under Mexican rule (reproduced by permission of the California Historical Society); *p. 29:* Confederate officers from Laredo, Texas: Refugio Benavides, Atanacio Vidaurri, Cristóbal Benavides, and John Z. Leyendecker (courtesy of the Laredo Public Library); *p. 29:* Albizu Campos, leader of the Puerto Rican independence movement, at a press conference on December 16, 1947; *p. 30:* Luis Muños-Rivera, patriot of Puerto Rican independence; *p. 43:* Luis Muñoz Marín, architect of the present commonwealth status of Puerto Rico; *p. 47:* Fidel Castro; *p. 48:* The first flight of American citizens repatriated from Cuba on December 19, 1966; *p. 50:* Cubans arriving in Miami during the Mariel boat-lift; *p. 51:* A legally immigrating Cuban woman is reunited with her granddaughter in Miami in 1980 (reproduced by permission of the *Texas Catholic Herald*).

Spanish Explorers and Colonizers:

p. 58: Frontispiece from the original 1493 edition of Cristóbal Colón's letter to the Catholic Kings describing his discoveries (reproduced by permission of Arte Público Press); *p. 59:* Juan Ponce de León; *p. 64:* Title page of Cabeza de Vaca's account of his trip, *La relación,* 1542 (reproduced by permission of Arte Público Press); *p. 67:* A portrayal of Hernando de Soto by an unknown eighteenth-century artist (courtesy of U.S. Department of the Interior and the National Park Service); *p. 68:* Pedro Menéndez de Avilés (reproduced by permission of Arte Público Press); *p. 69:* Drawing of the type of free black militia that were stationed in Spanish colonies in Florida and elsewhere, 1795 (reproduced by permission of Arte Público Press).

Historic Landmarks:

p. 134: Carmel Mission (reproduced by permission of Bettmann Archives); *p. 136:* Royal Presidio Chapel, Monterey (courtesy of U.S. Department of the Interior and the National Park Service); p. 137: San Francisco de Asís Mission (Mission Dolores) (Archive Photos); *p. 138:* San Luis Rey de Francia Mission, Oceanside (photograph by Henry F. Whitey, 1936, W.P.A); *p. 139:* Santa Barbara Mission (photograph by Henry F. Whitey, 1936, W.P.A); *p. 139:* General Vallejo House (photograph by Roger Sturtevant, 1934); *p. 141:* The Cabildo in New Orleans (courtesy of U.S. Department of the Interior and the National Park Service); *p. 142:* Palace of the Governors, Santa Fe (reproduced by permission of Associated Press/Wide World); *p. 142:* San Miguel Mission, Santa Fe (courtesy of U.S. Department of the Interior and the National Park Service); *p. 143:* Convent of Porta Coeli, San Germán; *p. 143:* The Alamo, San Antonio (courtesy of U.S. Department of the Interior and the National Park Service); *p. 145:* Monument honoring the fallen at the Alamo, San Antonio (courtesy of U.S. Department of the Interior and the National Park Service); *p. 146:* San Francisco de la Espada Mission, San Antonio; *p. 146:* San José y San Miguel de Aguayo Mission, (photograph by Arthur W. Stewart, 1936, W.P.A).

Relations with Spain and Spanish America:

p. 152: An early rally in East Lower Harlem (El Barrio) in Manhattan in support of the independence of Puerto Rico (reproduced by permission of The Jesús Colón Papers. Center for Puerto Rican Studies, Hunter College, CUNY; Benigno Giboyeaux for the Estate of Jesús Colón; and the Communist Party of the United States of America); *p. 170:* Archbishop Oscar Romero of El Salvador (reproduced by permission of *Texas Catholic Herald*); *p. 170:* Guerrillas of El Frente Farabundo Martí por Liberación Nacional (FMLN) in El Salvador; *p. 171:* Demonstrators on the U.S. capitol steps opposing U.S. military aid to El Salvador in 1980 (reproduced by permission of *Texas Catholic Herald*).

Population Growth and Distribution:

p. 186: Senior citizens at the Domino Park in Little Havana, Miami (reproduced by permission of *Texas Catholic Herald*); *p. 187:* Undocumented workers entering the United States at El Paso, Texas, 1990 (reproduced by permission of *Texas Catholic Herald*); *p. 188:* A group of Hispanics have just been issued their temporary residence cards, 1991 (photograph by Les Fetchko, *Texas Catholic Herald*); *p. 189:* The drive to legalize undocumented workers in Houston, Texas (photograph by Curtis Dowell, reproduced by permission of *Texas Catholic Herald*); *p. 190:* Mexican Independence Day Parade, Houston, Texas, 1982 (photograph by Curtis Dowell, reproduced by permission of *Texas Catholic Herald*); *p. 192:* A mass citizenship swearing-in ceremony at Hoffheinz Pavilion, University of Houston, 1987 (photograph by Curtis

Dowell, reproduced by permission of *Texas Catholic Herald*).

Language:

p. 196: The Teatro Puerto Rico in October 1960 (reproduced by permission of Justo A. Martí Collection, Center for Puerto Rican Studies Library, Hunter College, CUNY); *p. 202:* Downtown El Paso, Texas (reproduced by permission of *Texas Catholic Herald*); *p. 204:* Two scenes from the "Villa Alegre" television series; *p. 205:* A customer buying *La prensa,* the Spanish-language daily newspaper (reproduced by permission of Justo A. Martí Collection, Center for Puerto Rican Studies Library, Hunter College, CUNY); *p. 206:* A typical Hispanic grocery store in New York City (reproduced by permission of Justo A. Martí Collection, Center for Puerto Rican Studies Library, Hunter College, CUNY); *p. 208:* A voter-registration drive in New York City (reproduced by permission of Justo A. Martí Collection, Center for Puerto Rican Studies Library, Hunter College, CUNY); *p. 209:* Our Lady of Guadalupe Church in Queen Creek, Arizona (reproduced by permission of *Texas Catholic Herald*).

The Family:

p. 214: The Lugo Family at Bell Gardens, California, circa 1888 (Los Angeles County Museum of Natural History); *p. 215:* A child's birthday party in New York City (reproduced by permission of Justo A. Martí Collection, Center for Puerto Rican Studies Library, Hunter College, CUNY); *p. 216:* Community action through family and parent power: United Bronx Parents, Inc. (reproduced by permission of Records of the United Brox Parents, Inc., Center for Puerto Rican Studies Library, Hunter College, CUNY); *p. 217:* A Puerto Rican mine worker in Bingham Canyon, Utah (reproduced by permission of Historical Archive, Departamento de Asuntos de la Comunidad Puertorriqueña, Center for Puerto Rican Studies Library, Hunter College, CUNY); *p. 221:* Mexican Mother of the Year, 1969: Dolores Venegas and her husband, Miguel, Houston, Texas (reproduced by permission of *Texas Catholic Herald*).

Women:

p. 237: A beauty queen for the Fiestas Patrias celebration, Houston, Texas (photograph by Curtis Dowell, reproduced by permission of *Texas Catholic Herald*); *p. 237:* Poster advertising a Hispanic women's conference in Texas in 1987 (reproduced by permission of Arte Público Press); *p. 239:* A workshop at the Chicana Issues Conference, California, 1980; *p. 245:* Polly Baca-Barragán; *p. 246:* Teresa Bernárdez; *p. 249:* Emyré Barrios Robinson (reproduced by permission of Arte Público Press); *p. 250:* Carmen Delgado Votaw.

Religion:

p. 255: The Franciscan methold of teaching the Indians by pictures (from an engraving based on Fray Diego Valdés, O.F.M., in his *Rhetorica Christiana,* Rome, 1579); *p. 255:* Bartolemé de las Casas (1474–1566); *p. 256:* San Juan Capistrano Mission in San Antonio, Texas (photograph by Silvia Novo Pena, reproduced by permission of *Texas Catholic Herald*); *p. 257:* The image of Our Lady of Guadalupe on tour from Mexico at Our Lady of Guadalupe Church in Houston, Texas, 1992 (photograph by Curtis Dowell, reproduced by permission of *Texas Catholic Herald*); *p. 266:* Feast of the Crowning of Mary, Sacred Heart Cathedral, Houston, 1987 (photograph by Curtis Dowell, reproduced by permission of *Texas Catholic Herald*); *p. 267:* Annual mass on the feast day of Our Lady of Guadalupe, Houston, Texas (reproduced by permission of *Texas Catholic Herald*); *p. 268:* The celebration of the feast day of Our Lady of Caridad del Cobre, in Houston, 1986 (photograph by Curtis Dowell, reproduced by permission of *Texas Catholic Herald*); *p. 269:* A Christmas *posada* sponsored by the Club Sembradores de la Amistad in Houston, 1988 (photograph by Curtis Dowell, reproduced by permission of *Texas Catholic Herald*); *p. 270:* Diversity in Hispanic evangelism (photograph by Curtis Dowell, reproduced by permission of *Texas Catholic Herald*); *p. 271:* A Catholic charismatic prayer meeting (reproduced by permission of *Texas Catholic Herald*).

Military:

p. 277: Santos Benavides; *p. 277:* Robert Léon Cárdenas; *p. 278:* Richard E. Cavazos; *p. 279:* Francisco de Miranda; *p. 279:* Luis R. Esteves; *p. 280:* David G. Farragut; *p. 280:* Diego E. Hernández; *p. 281:* Edward Hidalgo; *p. 281:* Benjamin F. Montoya; *p. 282:* Horacio Rivera; *p. 282:* Carmelita Schemmenti; *p. 283:* Juan N. Seguín.

Law and Politics:

p. 296: Four charts on law school enrollment (*Consultant's Digest,* May 1991); *p. 298:* Michael J. Aguirre (reproduced by permission of Arte Público Press); *p. 298:* Wilfredo Caraballo; *p. 299:* Antonia Hernández; *p. 300:* Mario G. Obledo; *p. 305:* Raymond L. Acosta; *p. 305:* Arthur L. Alarcón; *p. 307:* Ferdinand Francis Fernández; *p. 308:* Ricardo H. Hinojosa; *p. 309:* Harold R. Medina, Sr.; *p. 311:* Cruz Reynoso; *p. 311:* Dorothy Comstock Riley; *p. 315:* Henry Barbosa González; *p. 316:* Matthew G. Martínez (reproduced by permission of AP/Wide World); *p. 317:* Solomon P. Ortiz; *p. 317:* William B. Richardson (reproduced by permission of AP/Wide World); *p. 318:* Ileana Ros-Lehtinen; *p. 318:* José E. Serrano; *p. 319:* Frank Tejeda; *p. 319:* Esteban Edward Torres; *p. 321:* Herman Badillo (reproduced by permission of AP/Wide World); *p. 322:* Dennis Chávez; *p. 323:* Joseph M. Montoya; *p. 325:* Edward R. Roybal (reproduced by permission of AP/Wide World); *p. 326:* Henry G. Cisneros; *p. 327:* Antonia Coello Novello (reproduced by permission of AP/Wide World); *p. 328:* Federico Fabian Peña; *p. 329:* Everett Alvarez, Jr.; *p. 330:* Romana Acosta Bañuelos; *p. 331:* Lauro F. Cavazos; *p. 332:* Katherine Davalos Ortega; *p. 333:* Toney Anaya; *p. 333:* Jerry Apodaca; *p. 334:* Art Torres; *p. 335:* Ygnacio D. Garza; *p. 336:* Gloria Molina (reproduced by permission of AP/Wide World); *p. 336:* Louis E. Saavedra; *p. 337:* Xavier L. Suárez.

Business:

p. 343: Poster for the 1985 U.S. Hispanic Chamber of Commerce convention (reproduced by permission of Arte Público Press); *p. 358:* Gabriel Eloy Aguirre; *p. 359:* Carlos José Arboleya; *p. 359:* Gilbert Cuéllar, Jr.; *p. 360:* Roberto C. Goizueta (reproduced by permission of Arte Público Press); *p. 361:* Fredrick J. González (reproduced by permission of Arte Público Press); *p. 361:* Edgar J. Milán; *p. 353:* Clifford Lane Whitehill.

Labor and Employment:

p. 366: César Chávez exhorting people to start a new grape boycott in 1986 (reproduced by permission of *Texas Catholic Herald*); *p. 366:* Mexican women working at a commercial tortilla factory in the 1930s (courtesy of Library of Congress); *p. 367:* A cotton picker in 1933 (photograph by Dorothea Lange, courtesy of Library of Congress); *p. 368:* Mexican mine workers in the early 1900s (reproduced by permission of Arizona Historical Society); *p. 369:* Puerto Rican garment workers in New York City (reproduced by permission of Arte Público Press); *p. 370:* Unemployed workers waiting in line at a relief office during the Depression (courtesy of Library of Congress); *p. 372:* A United Farm Workers picket line in Coachella, California, 1973 (reproduced by permission of *Texas Catholic Herald*); *p. 373:* A scene from the Bracero Program (courtesy of Library of Congress); *p. 374:* A field worker in the Bracero Program (courtesy of Library of Congress); *p. 374:* A migrant work camp (courtesy of Library of Congress); *p. 375:* The interior of a migrant labor shack (reproduced by permission of *Texas Catholic Herald*); *p. 383:* A Mexican worker being finger-printed for deportation (courtesy of Library of Congress).

Education:

p. 391: Children during recess at the Guadalupe Aztlán alternative school in Houston, 1981 (photograph by Curtis Dowell, reproduced by permission of *Texas Catholic Herald*); *p. 403:* Mexican fourth-graders at

Drachman School, circa 1913 (reproduced by permission of Arizona Historical Society); *p. 404:* A poster encouraging Hispanics to register to vote; *p. 406:* Children at the Guadalupe Aztlán alternative school in Houston in 1981, when public school education was denied to children of undocumented workers (photograph by Curtis Dowell, reproduced by permission of *Texas Catholic Herald*); *p. 407:* A sixth-grade classromm in the Huelga School, an alternative school set up in St. Patrick's Chapel, Houston (photograph by Curtis Dowell, reproduced by permission of *Texas Catholic Herald*); *p. 408:* A poster encouraging affirmative action and equal opportunity in education in California; *p. 409:* Manuel Pacheco.

Scholarship:

p. 416: Albert Michael Camarillo; *p. 416:* Arthur León Campa (reproduced by permission of Arte Público Press); *p. 418:* Carlos E. Cortés (reproduced by permission of Arte Público Press); *p. 418:* Rodolfo J. Cortina (reproduced by permission of Arte Público Press); *p. 419:* Margarita Fernández Olmos (reproduced by permission of Arte Público Press); *p. 421:* Erlinda González-Berry (reproduced by permission of Arte Público Press); *p. 422:* Olga Jiménez-Wagenheim (reproduced by permission of Arte Público Press); *p. 423:* Luis Leal (reproduced by permission of Arte Público Press); *p. 424:* Raúl Moncarraz (reproduced by permission of Arte Público Press); *p. 425:* Sonia Nieto (reproduced by permission of Arte Público Press); *p. 425:* Julián Olivares (reproduced by permission of Arte Público Press); *p. 428:* Ricardo Romo (reproduced by permission of Arte Público Press); *p. 428:* Ramón Eduardo Ruiz (reproduced by permission of Arte Público Press).

Science:

p. 436: Angeles Alvariño de Leira; *p. 437:* Alberto Vinicio Baez (reproduced by permission of Arte Público Press); *p. 438:* Graciela Candelas (reproduced by permission of Arte Público Press); *p. 439:* Manuel Cardona (reproduced by permission of Arte Público Press); *p. 439:* David Cardús (reproduced by permission of Arte Público Press); *p. 440:* George Castro (reproduced by permission of Arte Público Press); *p. 441:* Guillermo B. Cintrón (reproduced by permission of Arte Público Press); *p. 441:* Antonio E. Colás (reproduced by permission of Arte Público Press); *p. 442:* Francisco Dallmeier (reproduced by permission of Arte Público Press); *p. 443:* José Alberto Fernández-Pol (reproduced by permission of Arte Público Press); *p. 444:* Celso Ramón García; *p. 447:* Teresa Mercado; *p. 448:* Isabel Cristina Pérez-Farfante; *p. 450:* Eloy Rodríguez; *p. 451:* Pedro Antonio Sánchez.

Literature:

p. 456: Miguel A. Otero (reproduced by permission of Miguel A. Otero Collection, University of New Mexico Library); *p. 457:* Eusebio Chacón (reproduced by permission of Miguel A. Otero Collection, University of New Mexico Library); *p. 457:* Title page of *El hijo de la tempestad* by Eusebio Chacón (reproduced by permission of Special Collections, University of New Mexico Library); *p. 458:* Cuban literary and patriotic figure, José Martí; *p. 460:* The cover of Daniel Venegas' satirical newspaper, *El Malcriado* (reproduced by permission of Arte Público Press); *p. 461:* Fray Angelico Chávez (reproduced by permission of Special Collections, University of New Mexico Library); *p. 463:* Cover of the first issue of *Gráfico* newspaper (reproduced by permission of Arte Público Press); *p. 464:* Lola Rodríguez de Tió (reproduced by permission of Arte Público Press); *p. 466:* Albelardo Delgado, Ron Arias, and Rolando Hinojosa, Houston, Texas, 1980; *p. 467:* The original manuscript of the Tomás Rivera poem, "When love to be?"; *p. 468:* Evangelina Vigil-Piñón, Houston, 1987 (photograph by Julián Olivaries, reproduced by permission of Arte Público Press); *p. 468:* The cover of Rudolfo Anaya's best-selling novel, *Bless Me, Ultima*; *p. 469:* A vendor at the First National Latino Book Fair in Chicago, 1979 (reproduced by permission of Arte Público Press); *p. 470:* Ana Castillo, 1979 (reproduced by permission of Arte Público Press); *p. 470:* Helena María Viramontes, 1986 (photograph by Georgia McInnis, reproduced by permission of Arte Público Press); *p. 471:* Luis Dávilla, 1979 (reproduced by permission of Arte Público Press); *p. 472:* The cover of Rudolfo Anaya's *Cuentos: Tales from the Hispanic Southwest*; *p. 472:* Pat Mora, 1986 (reproduced by permission of Arte Público Press); *p. 473:* The cover of Denise Chávez's *The Last of the Menu Girls*; *p. 474:* Gary Soto and Evangelina Vigil-Piñón, Houston, Texas, 1987 (reproduced by permission of Arte Público Press); *p. 475:* Ricardo Sánchez, Alejandro Morales, critic Salvador Rodríguez del Pino, and Victor Villaseñor, Mexico City, 1979 (reproduced by permission of Arte Público Press); *p. 476:* Julia de Burgos (reproduced by permission of Arte Público Press); *p. 477:* José Luis González; *p. 477:* Luis Rafael Sánchez (reproduced by permission of Arte Público Press); *p. 478:* Pedro Juan Soto; *p. 479:* Jesús Colón, circa 1950s (reproduced by permission of Centro de Estudios Puertorriqueños, Hunter College, CUNY); *p. 479:* Bernardo Vega, 1948 (reproduced by permission of Centro de Estudios Puertorriqueños, Hunter College, CUNY); *p. 480:* Sandra María Esteves, 1979 (reproduced by permission of Arte Público Press); *p. 481:* Nicholasa Mohr, Publisher Nicolás Kanellos, and Ed Vega, Houston, Texas, 1985; *p. 482:* Virgil Suárez, 1991 (reproduced by permission of Arte Público Press); *p. 483:* José Sánchez Boudy (reproduced by permission of Arte Público Press); *p.*

485: Miguel Algarín, Chicago, 1979 (reproduced by permission of Arte Público Press); *p. 485:* Alurista, 1980 (reproduced by permission of Arte Público Press); *p. 487:* Rudolfo A. Anaya; *p. 488:* Lorna Dee Cervantes, 1990 (photograph by Georgia McInnis, reproduced by permission of Arte Público Press); *p. 489:* Denise Chávez; *p. 490:* Judith Ortiz Cofer; *p. 491:* Victor Hernández Cruz; *p. 492:* Abelardo Delgado (reproduced by permission of Arte Público Press); *p. 493:* Roberto Fernández (reproduced by permission of Arte Público Press); *p. 494:* Lionel G. García (reproduced by permission of Arte Público Press); *p. 495:* Rolando Hinojosa (reproduced by permission of Arte Público Press); *p. 496:* Tato Laviera, 1990 (photograph by Georgia McInnis, reproduced by permission of Arte Público Press); *p. 497:* Nicholasa Mohr, 1990 (reproduced by permission of Arte Público Press); *p. 498:* Alejandro Morales (reproduced by permission of Arte Público Press); *p. 501:* Ricardo Sánchez; *p. 501:* Gary Soto, 1991 (photograph by M. L. Marinelli); *p. 503:* Sabine Ulibarrí (reproduced by permission of Arte Público Press); *p. 504:* Ed Vega (reproduced by permission of Arte Público Press); *p. 505:* Víctor E. Villaseñor (reproduced by permission of Arte Público Press); *p. 506:* Jose Yglesias.

Art:

p. 509: Bell wall, San Juan Capistrano Mission, 1760–87, San Antonio, Texas (photograph by Jacinto Quirarte); *p. 510:* Facade, San José y San Miguel de Aguayo Mission, 1768–82, San Antonio, Texas (photograph by Kathy Vargas); *p. 510: Saint Joachim* portal sculpture, 1768–82, San José y San Miguel de Aguayo Mission, San Antonio, Texas (photograph by Kathy Vargas); *p. 511: Saint Anne* portal sculpture, 1768–82, San José y San Miguel de Aguayo Mission, San Antonio, Texas (photograph by Kathy Vargas); *p. 511:* Facade, 1783–97, San Xavier del Bac Mission. Tuscon, Arizona (photograph by Jacinto Quirarte); *p. 512: Saint Lucy,* Portal sculpture, 1783–97, San Xavier del Bac Mission, Tucson, Arizona (photograph by Jacinto Quirarte); *p. 513:* Main portal, 1755, Nuestra Señora de la Purisma Concepción de Acúna Mission, San Antonio, Texas (photograph by Kathy Vargas); *p. 513:* Polychromy (reconstruction, 1948), south tower, 1768–82, San José y San Miguel de Aguayo Mission, San Antonio, Texas (photograph by Kathy Vargas); *p. 516:* José Benito Ortega, *Saint Isidore the Farmer,* 1880s–1907 (reproduced by permission of Denver Art Museum); *p. 517:* José Dolores López, *Expulsion from the Garden of Eden* (reproduced by permission of Museum of International Folk Art, Santa Fe, New Mexico); *p. 519:* Theodora Sánchez, *Nicho* (Yard Shrine), 1957, Tucson, Arizona (photograph by Jacinto Quirarte); *p. 521:* Octavio Medellín, *Xtol* print (photograph courtesy of the artist); *p. 522:* Edward Chávez, *Indians of the Plains,* 1943, Service Club, Fort

Warren, Wyoming (photograph courtesy of the artist); *p. 526:* Ralph Ortiz, *Piano Destruction Concert Duncan Terrace,* Destruction in Art Symposium, September 1966, London (photograph courtesy of the artist); *p. 529:* Judy Baca, *The Great Wall of Los Angeles,* "350 Mexicans Deported and Dustbowl Refugees" (photograph by Jacinto Quirarte); *p. 530:* Carmen Lomas Garza, *Lotería—Table Llena,* 1974 (photograph courtesy of the artist); *p. 531:* Victor Ochoa, *Gerónimo,* 1981, Centro Cultural de la Raza, Balboa Park, San Diego, California (photograph by Jacinto Quirarte); *p. 532:* Victor Ochoa, *Chicano Park,* 1981, Centro Cultural de la Raza, Balboa Park, San Diego, California (photograph by Jacinto Quirarte); *p. 533:* Cesar Martínez, *La Pareja,* 1979 (photograph courtesy of the artist); *p. 534:* Jesse Treviño, *Panadería,* late 1970s (photograph courtesy of the artist); *p. 535:* José González, *Barrio Murals,* 1976, cover design for *Revista Chicano-Riquería* (photograph courtesy of the artist); *p. 536:* Marcos Raya, *Stop World War III.* Mural, Chicago, Illinois (photograph courtesy of the artist); *p. 540:* Willie Herrón and Gronk, *Black and White Mural,* 1973 and 1978, Estrada Courts, Los Angeles, California (photograph by Jacinto Quirarte); *p. 541:* Willie Herrón and Gronk, *Black and White Mural,* (diagram by Jacinto Quirarte); *p. 542:* Raymond Patlán and others, *History of the Mexican American Worker,* 1974–75, Blue Island, Illinois (photograph by Jose Gonzales); *p. 542:* Raymond Patlán and others, *History of the Mexican American Worker* (diagram by Jacinto Quirarte); *p. 544:* Raúl Valdez and others, *La Raza Cósmica,* 1977, Austin, Texas (photograph by Jacinto Quirarte); *p. 544:* Raúl Valdez and others, *La Raza Cósmica,* 1977 (diagram by Jacinto Quirarte); *p. 544:* Raúl Valdez and others, *La Raza Cósmica,* 1977 (diagram by Jacinto Quirarte); *p. 545:* Raúl Valdez and others, *La Raza Cósmica,* 1977 (diagram by Jacinto Quirarte); *p. 545:* Raúl Valdez and others, *La Raza Cósmica* (diagram by Jacinto Quirarte); *p. 546:* Rogelio Cárdenas, *En la lucha ... ponte trucha,* by Rogelio Cárdenas, 1978, Hayward, California (photograph by Jacinto Quirarte); *p. 546:* Rogelio Cárdenas, *En la lucha ... ponte trucha,* by Rogelio Cárdenas, 1978 (diagram by Jacinto Quirarte); *p. 547:* Gilberto Garduño and others, *Multicultural Mural,* 1980, Santa Fe, New Mexico (photograph by Jacinto Quirarte); *p. 548:* Gilberto Garduño and others, *Multicultural Mural,* 1980 (diagram by Jacinto Quirarte).

Theater:

p. 551: Los Angeles' California Theater (reproduced by permission of Arte Público Press); *p. 552:* The Mason Theater, Los Angeles (reproduced by permission of Arte Público Press); *p. 554:* Rosalinda Meléndez (reproduced by permission of Arte Público Press); *p. 556:* The García girls chorus line from the Carpa García tent show (reproduced by permission of Arte Público Press); *p. 557:* Don Fito, the Carpa García tent show (reproduced by permission of Arte Público Press); *p. 561:* The cover of a program for the performance of an operetta at the Centro Español in 1919; *p. 562:* A full house at the Centro Asturiano in 1937 (reproduced by permission of Dorothea Lynch Collection, George Mason University Library); *p. 563:* A scene from *El niño judío* at the Centro Asturiano (reproduced by permission of Dorothea Lynch Collection, George Mason University Library); *p. 564:* Manuel Aparicio, at center, directing a rehearsal of Sinclair Lewis' *It Can't Happen Here* in Spanish at the Centro Asturiano (reproduced by permission of Dorothea Lynch Collection, George Mason University); *p. 565:* Manuel Aparicio in Jacinto Benavente's *La Malquerida* (reproduced by permission of Dorothea Lynch Collection, George Mason University Library); *p. 566:* A scene from El Teatro Urbano's *Anti-Bicentennial Special* in 1976 (reproduced by permission of Arte Público Press); *p. 567:* A scene from El Teatro de la Esperanza's production of Rodrigo Duarte Clark's *Brujerías* (reproduced by permission of Arte Público Press); *p. 569:* Poster from La Farándula Panamericana theater group's 1954 production of *Los árboles mueren de pie,* starring Marita Reid (reproduced by permission of Arte Público Press); *p. 570:* Postcard photograph of the Bronx's Pregones theater company in 1985 (reproduced by permission of Arte Público Press); *p. 571:* The elaborate costuming of a Miami production of José Zorilla's *Don Juan Tenorio* (reproduced by permission of Arte Público Press); *p. 573: Romeo and Juliet* being performed in Spanish in Miami (reproduced by permission of Arte Público Press); *p. 581:* A scene from the Los Angeles production of Dolores Prida's *Beautiful Señoritas* (reproduced by permission of Arte Público Press); *p. 583:* Luis Valdez (reproduced by permission of Arte Público Press); *p. 584:* Carmen Zapata in the Bilingual Foundation for the Arts' production of *Moments to Be Remembered* (reproduced by permission of Arte Público Press).

Film:

p. 595: Henry Darrow as Zorro; *p. 605:* Carmen Miranda; *p. 605:* Freddie Prinze, star of "Chico and the Man" (reproduced by permission of Arte Público Press); *p. 606:* Erik Estrada, star of "CHiPs" (reproduced by permission of Arte Público Press); *p. 607:* The Sharks face off with the Jets in *West Side Story* (reproduced by permission of Arte Público Press); *p. 608:* A scene from *Boulevard Nights* (reproduced by permission of Arte Público Press); *p. 611:* The poster for *El norte*; *p. 613:* Jesús Salvador Treviño, 1978 (reproduced by permission of Arte Público Press); *p. 624:* Néstor Almendros; *p. 625:* Desi Arnaz; *p. 625:* Rubén Blades; *p. 626:* Lynda Córdoba Carter (reproduced by permission of Arte Público Press); *p.*

627: Linda Cristal; *p. 627:* Dolores del Río; *p. 628:* Emilio Estévez; *p. 629:* Emilio "El Indio" Fernández; *p. 630:* Fernando Lamas; *p. 631:* Adele Mara; *p. 631:* Margo; *p. 632:* Richad "Cheech" Marín; *p. 632:* Mona Maris; *p. 633:* Cris-Pin Martin; *p. 633:* Ricardo Montalbán (reproduced by permission of Archive Photos); *p. 634:* María Montez; *p. 634:* Silvia Morales (reproduced by permission of Arte Público Press); *p. 635:* Rita Moreno; *p. 635:* Barry Norton; *p. 636:* Ramón Novarro; *p. 636:* Edward James Olmos; *p. 637:* Anthony Quinn; *p. 637:* Gilbert Roland; *p. 638:* César Romero; *p. 639:* Lupe Vélez; *p. 639:* Raoul Walsh; *p. 640:* Raquel Welch.

Music:

p. 643: Mexican musicians in the 1890s in California (reproduced by permission of Huntington Library, San Marino, California); *p. 644:* Xavier Cugat and his orchestra in the 1940s (reproduced by permission of Arte Público Press); *p. 645:* Augusto Coen and his Golden Orchestra, circa 1930s–1940s (reproduced by permission of José Martí Collection. Center for Puerto Rican Studies Library, Hunter College, CUNY); *p. 647:* Lidia Mendoza with Marcelo, comic Tin Tan, and Juanita Mendoza in Chicago in the 1950s (reproduced by permission of Arte Público Press); *p. 648:* A working-class *orquesta,* circa 1930 (courtesy of Thomas Kreneck); *p. 654:* An *orquesta tipica* in Houston (courtesy of Thomas Kreneck); *p. 657:* Beto Villa y su Orquesta, circa 1946 (courtesy of Chris Strachwitz); *p. 658:* Alonzo y su Orquesta, a typical orchestra, circa 1950 (courtesy of Thomas Kreneck); *p. 659:* Octavo García y sus GGs, circa 1952 (courtesy of Octavio García); *p. 660:* An outdoor *salsa* concert in Houston, Texas; *p. 661:* Celia Cruz at the Hollywood Palladium; *p. 663:* The Joe Cuba Sextet; *p. 663:* A Machito album cover; *p. 664:* A Tito Puente album cover; *p. 665:* Eddie Palmieri (reproduced by permission of Berkeley Agency).

Media:

p. 681: Ignacio E. Lozano, Jr.; *p. 682:* Mónica Lozano-Centanino; *p. 682:* José I. Lozano; *p. 683:* Marti Buscaglia; *p. 683:* Peter W. Davidson; *p. 684:* Carlos D. Ramírez; *p. 685:* Phillip V. Sánchez; *p. 689:* Charlie Erikson; *p. 692:* Pedro J. González, pioneer of Spanish-language radio in California (reproduced by permission of Arte Público Press); *p. 692:* Pedro J. González's singing group, Los Madrugadores; *p. 693:* Banner headlines in *La Opinión* newspaper announcing the guilty verdict in the Pedro J. González case; *p. 695:* McHenry Tichenor; *p. 696:* Amancio V. Suárez; *p. 702:* Gustavo Godoy; *p. 704:* Henry R. Silverman; *p. 704:* Saul P. Steinberg; *p. 706:* Joaquín F. Blaya; *p. 707:* Rosita Perú; *p. 708:* Univisión news studio; *p. 709:* Jorge Ramos and María Elena Salinas of

"Noticiero Univisión"; *p. 709:* Cristina Saralegui, host of Univisión's "El Show de Cristina"; *p. 712:* Enrique Gratas, host of Telemundo's "Occurió Así"; *p. 712:* Andrés García and Rudy Rodríguez, stars of Telemundo's soap opera "El Magnate".

Sports:

p. 722: Ramón Ahumada (reproduced by permission of Arizona Historical Society); *p. 723:* A baseball team of Mexicans and Anglos in Los Angeles in the 1870s (reproduced by permission of Huntington Library, San Marino, California); *p. 727:* Luis Aparicio; *p. 728:* Rod Carew (reproduced by permission of Bettmann Archive/Newsphotos, Inc.); *p. 728:* Rosemary Casals; *p. 729:* Orlando Cepeda; *p. 730:* Roberto Clemente (reproduced by permission of Bettmann Archive/Newsphotos, Inc.); *p. 730:* Dave Concepción (reproduced by permission of Bettmann Archive/Newsphotos, Inc.); *p. 732:* Roberto Durán (reproduced by permission of Bettmann Archive/Newsphotos, Inc.); *p. 732:* Sixto Escobar (reproduced by permission of Arte Público Press); *p. 732:* Tony Fernández; *p. 734:* Tom Flores (reproduced by permission of AP/Wide World); *p. 734:* Lefty Gómez; *p. 735:* Pancho González (reproduced by permission of Bettmann Archive/Newsphotos, Inc.); *p. 735:* Keith Hernández (reproduced by permission of AP/Wide World); *p. 736:* Al López; *p. 736:* Nancy López (reproduced by permission of Bettmann Archive/Newsphotos, Inc.); *p. 737:* Juan "Manito" Marichal; *p. 738:* Orestes "Minnie" Miñoso; *p. 738:* Amleto Monacelli (reproduced by permission of Arte Público Press); *p. 739:* Anthony Muñoz (reproduced by permission of Arte Público Press); *p. 739:* Tony Oliva; *p. 740:* Carlos Ortiz; *p. 741:* Manuel Ortiz; *p. 741:* Jim Plunkett (reproduced by permission of Bettmann Archive/Newsphotos, Inc.); *p. 742:* Chi Chi Rodríguez; *p. 743:* Alberto Bauduy Salazar (reproduced by permission of Bettmann Archive/Newsphotos, Inc.); *p. 743:* Vicente Saldívar; *p. 744:* Luis Tiant; *p. 744:* José Luis "Chegui" Torres (reproduced by permission of José A. Martí Collection, Center for Puerto Rican Studies Library, Hunter College, CUNY); *p. 745:* Lee Treviño (reproduced by permission of Bettmann Archive/Newsphotos, Inc.); *p. 745:* Fernando Valenzuela.

Organizations:

p. 747: A march by the Council of Puerto Rican Organizations from the Lower East Side of New York City over the Brooklyn Bridge to protest the poor conditions of public schools in the Puerto Rican community (reproduced by permission of Historic Archive of the Department of Puerto Rican Community Affairs in the United States, Center for Puerto Rican Studies Library and Archives, Hunter College, CUNY); *p. 748:* A celebration of the Three Kings sponsored by the Puerto Rican Workers Mutual Aid Society, New York City (reproduced by permission of Jesús Colón Papers, Center for Puerto Rican Studies Library and Archives, Hunter College, CUNY); *p. 748:* A parade organized by Tucson's Alianza Hispano-Americana (reproduced by permission of Arizona Historical Society); *p. 750:* President Ronald Reagan presents the Medal of Freedom to Dr. Héctor García, founder of the American G. I. Forum.

Prominent Hispanics:

p. 757: Tomás A. Arciniega (reproduced by permission of Arte Público Press); *p. 758:* Philip Arreola; *p. 758:* Tony Bonilla (reproduced by permission of Arte Público Press); *p. 759:* Rubén Bonilla, Jr; *p. 759:* Harry Caicedo (reproduced by permission of Arte Público Press); *p. 760:* Vikki Carr (reproduced by permission of AP/Wide World); *p. 760:* César Chávez; *p. 761:* Bert Corona; *p. 761:* José R. Coronado (reproduced by permission of Arte Público Press); *p. 762:* Jaime Escalante; *p. 763:* Joseph A. Fernández (reproduced by permission of Arte Público Press); *p. 764:* Archbishop Patrick F. Flores (reproduced by permission of AP/Wide World); *p. 764:* Ernesto Galarza; *p. 765:* Elsa Gómez (reproduced by permission of Arte Público Press); *p. 766:* Carolina Herrera (reproduced by permission of Arte Público Press); *p. 766:* Dolores Fernández Huerta (reproduced by permission of AP/Wide World); *p. 767:* Tania J. León; *p. 767:* Modesto A. Maidique; *p. 768:* Eduardo Mata (reproduced by permission of AP/Wide World); *p. 769:* Julián Nava (reproduced by permission of Arte Público Press); *p. 770:* Manuel Pacheco (photograph by Julieta González, reproduced by permission of Arte Público Press); *p. 771:* Guadalupe C. Quintanilla; *p. 771:* Geraldo Rivera; *p. 772:* Paul Rodríguez (reproduced by permission of Arte Público Press); *p. 773:* Luis Santeiro (reproduced by permission of Arte Público Press); *p. 773:* Cristina Saralegui (reproduced by permission of Arte Público Press); *p. 774:* Roberto Suárez (reproduced by permission of Arte Público Press).

Glossary

A

acto – a one-act Chicano theater piece developed out of collective improvisation.

adelantado – the commander of an expedition who would receive, in advance, the title to any lands that he would discover.

audiencia – a tribunal that ruled over territories.

agringado – literally "Gringo-ized" or Americanized.

Aztlán – originally the mythological land of origin of the Mechica nations, to which the Toltecs and the Aztecs belong. Chicanos identify this land of origin as the geographic region of the American Southwest, figuratively their homeland.

B

babalao – a spiritual healer, witch, or advisor, especially in *santería*.

barrio – neighborhood.

batos locos – See *pachuco(s)*.

behareque – thatched huts used by Indians of the Caribbean.

bodega – a small general store.

bohíos – thatched-roofed huts used by the Caribbean Indians.

botánica – a shop that specializes in herbs and folk potions and medicines.

bracero – from *brazo,* arm, someone who works with their arms or performs manual labor; originally applied to temporary Mexican agricultural and railroad workers, it is also occasionally used to refer to any unskilled Mexican worker.

bulto – a wooden sculpture in the image of a Catholic saint.

C

cacique – the American Indian village chieftain.

caló – a Mexican-American dialect, often associated with *pachucos.*

canción – song.

capilla – chapel.

carpa – from the Quechua word meaning an "awning of branches;" in Spanish it has come to mean a tent; circuses and tent theaters have come to be known as *carpas* by extension.

carreta – cart.

caudillo – chief, leader, originally of the rural poor, but today quite often used to refer to any grass-roots political leader.

charrerías – contests of the Mexican cowboys.

charro – a Mexican cowboy of the Jalisco region, maintaining the dress and customs often associated with *mariachis.*

Chicano – derivative of *Mechicano,* the same Nahuatl word that gave origin to the name of Mexico. The term originally meant Mexican immigrant worker in the early twentieth century, but became the name adopted by Mexican Americans, especially during the days of the civil rights and student movements.

chinampa – a man-made island or floating garden, developed by Meso-American Indians as an agricultural technique.

cimarrones – runaway slaves.

colonia – literally a "colony," it refers to the enclave of Hispanic population within a city, much as the term *barrio* is used today.

compadrazgo – godparenthood, usually through the baptism of a child. *Compadrazgo* is the extension of kinship to non-relatives and the strengthening of responsibilities among kin.

compadres – co-parents; godparents.

confianza – trust, the basis of the relationships between individuals in many spheres of social activity, but especially among kin.

conjunto – said of a Texas, northern-Mexico musical style as well as of the ensemble that plays it, usually made up of a guitar, a base guitar, a drum, and a button accordion.

corrido – a Mexican ballad.

criollo – a Creole, that is, someone of Spanish (European) origin born in the New World.

crónica – a local-color newspaper column often satirizing contemporary customs.

cronista – the writer of a *crónica.*

curandero – a folk healer who combines the practices of the Mexican Indians and Spanish folk-healing.

E

encomendero – the owner of the *encomienda.*

encomienda – the system by which a Spaniard held in high esteem by the King and Queen was given ownership of land in the New World and authorized to "protect" the Indians who had occupied the land in exchange for their free labor. This failed attempt at establishing feudal baronies was marked by the exploitation of the Indians.

ex-voto – a gift presented to a saint as a show of gratitude for a favor conceded.

F

familia, la – the greater family, which includes the immediate nuclear household and relatives that are traced on the female and male sides.

finca – farm, ranch.

G

gallego – in Cuban farce, the stock Galician Spaniard, known for his hard head and frugality.

H

hacendado – the owner of a *hacienda.*

hacienda – a large ranch derivative of the *latifundia* system.

hermandad – brotherhood.

I

indigenismo – an emphasis on American Indian and Pre-Columbian origins and identity.

ingenios – plantations, especially of sugar.

Isleños – descendants of the Canary Island settlers in southern Louisiana.

J

jíbaro – originally an American Indian world for "highlander," it is what Puerto Ricans call the rural mountain folk, but has also come to be symbolic of the national identity of Puerto Ricans.

K

kiva – a secret underground ceremonial chamber, especially as used in Pueblo culture for ceremonies and meetings.

L

latifundia – a large estate or ranch originating in ancient Roman civilization.

lectores – professional (hired) readers who would read books, magazines, and newspapers to cigar-rollers as they performed their laborious tasks.

M

macana – a wooden war club.

manda – a sacrificial offering to a saint in order to receive some favor.

maquiladora – a factory on the Mexican side of the border that performs part of the manual assembly of products at the comparatively lower wages offered by the Mexican economy. These products would then be shipped back to the United States for finishing and marketing by the partner company.

Marielito – a Cuban refugee who arrived in the United States as a result of the Mariel boatlift in the 1980s.

mestizo – an individual of mixed Spanish (or European) and American Indian heritage.

milagro – a charm made of tin, gold, or silver, and shaped in the form of an arm, a leg, a baby, or a house, representing the favor (usually of healing) that is desired from a saint.

morada – the meeting house of the *Penitente* lay brotherhood.

mulata – the stock female Mulatto character in Cuban farce.

música norteña – *conjunto* music from the northern region of Mexico (also includes Texas).

mutualista – mutual aid society, an organization that engaged in social activities and provided basic needs for immigrant workers and their families, including insurance and death benefits for members.

N

nacimiento – a nativity.

Nañiguismo – membership in the secret society of Abakúa, which combines elements of the Efik culture of the southern coast of Nigeria and Freemasonry.

negrito – in Cuban farce, the stock character in black face.

nitainos – principal advisors among the Arawak Indians, quite often in charge of the labor force.

nopal – the prickly pear cactus.

norteño – of northern Mexican origin.

Nuyorican – literally "New York-Rican," a term developed colloquially by Puerto Ricans born or raised in New York to distinguish themselves from those identifying solely with the island.

O

orishas – the African deities of *santería.*

orquesta – a Mexican American musical ensemble that develops its style around the violin.

P

pachuco/batos locos – member of a Mexican-American urban youth subculture, known as the pachucos or batos locos, which characteristically developed its own style of dress (zoot suit), its own dialect (*caló*), and its own bilingual-bicultural ideology during the 1940s and 1950s.

padrinos – godparents.

parentesco – kinship sentiment.

parientes – blood relatives.

pastorela – the shepherds play; a folk drama reenacted during the Christmas season.

patria – fatherland.

patria chica – the home region within the fatherland.

pelado – literally the "skinned one" or shirtless one, he was the stock underdog, sharp-witted picaresque character of Mexican vaudeville and tent shows.

Penitente – literally "penitent;" it is the name of a religious brotherhood in New Mexico.

piraguas – a narrow, high-prowed canoe used by the Caribbean Indians.

posada – a community Christmas pageant where carolers go door to door asking for shelter in reenactment of Joseph and Mary's search for lodging.

presidio – a fort, especially characteristic of frontier settlements.

promesa – literally a "promise," it is a sacrificial offering to a saint in order to receive some favor.

R

renegado/a – a renegade, someone who denies his or her Mexican identity.

repartimiento – a form of the *encomienda,* which vested the rights over the Indians in the civil authorities.

reredo – altar screen.

retablos – paintings on panels behind the altar in a Catholic church.

revista – a vaudeville musical review.

S

salsa – literally "sauce," it refers to Afro-Caribbean music.

santería/santerismo – a synchretic religious sect growing out of the original African religion and the Catholicism of slaves.

santero – in the Southwest, a sculptor of wooden saints; in the Caribbean, a devotee of an *orisha* in *santería.*

santos – the sculpted figures representing saints of the Catholic church; used in worship and prayer.

T

Taino/Nitaino – a group of sedentary tribes native to the Caribbean.

V

vaquero – cowboy.

vegas – plantations, especially of coffee.

Y

yerberías – shops specializing in medicinal plants, herbs, and potions.

yerberos – folk healers and spiritualists who use herbs in their practices.

yuca – manioc root.

Z

zarzuela – a type of Spanish operetta.

zemíes – gods of the Arawak Indians, also the small Taino religious figure made of clay that represented these gods.

General Bibliography

A

Acosta-Belén, Edna, ed. *The Puerto Rican Woman,* New York: Praeger, 1986.

Acuña, Rodolfo. *Occupied America: A History of Chicanos.* New York: Harper and Row, 1981.

Alvarez, Robert R. *Familia: Migration and Adaptation in Alta and Baja California 1850-1975.* Berkeley: University of California Press, 1987.

B

Barrera, Mario. *Race and Class in the Southwest: A Theory of Radical Inequality.* Notre Dame, Indiana: University of Notre Dame Press, 1979.

Bean, Frank D., and Marta Tienda. *The Hispanic Population of the United States.* New York: Russell Sage Foundation, 1988.

Beardsley, John, and Jane Livingston. *Hispanic Art in the United States: Thirty Painters and Sculptors.* New York: Abbeville Press, 1987.

Boswell, T. D., and J. R. Curtis. *The Cuban American Experience.* Totawa, New Jersey: Rowan and Allenheld, 1984.

C

Camarillo, Albert. *Chicanos in a Changing Society.* Cambridge, Massachusetts: Harvard University Press, 1979.

Cotera, Marta P. *Latina Sourcebook: Bibliography of Mexican American, Cuban, Puerto Rican and Other*

Hispanic Women Materials in the U.S.A. Austin, Texas: Information Systems Development, 1982.

E

Elias Oliveres, Lucia, ed. *Spanish in the U.S. Setting: Beyond the Southwest.* Rosalyn, Virginia: National Clearinghouse for Bilingual Education, 1983.

F

Fitzpatrick, Joseph P. *Puerto Rican Americans: The Meaning of Migration to the Mainland.* Englewood Cliffs, New Jersey: Prentice Hall, 1987.

Furtaw, Julia C., ed. *Hispanic American Information Directory, 1992–1993.* Detroit, Michigan: Gale Research, 1992.

G

García, Mario T. *Mexican Americans.* New Haven, Connecticut: Yale University Press, 1989.

Garza, Hedda. *Latinas: Hispanic Women in the United States.* Chicago: Franklin Watts, 1994.

H

Hendricks, G. L. *The Dominican Diaspora: From the Dominican Republic to New York City.* New York: Teacher's College Press of Columbia University, 1974.

Hispanics in U.S. History, two volumes. Englewood Cliffs, New Jersey: Globe Book Company, 1989.

History Task Force of the Centro de Estudios Puertorriqueños. *Labor Migration under Capitalism: The Puerto Rican Experience.* New York: Monthly Review Press, 1979.

Horseman, Reginald. *Race and Manifest Destiny. The Origins of American Racial Anglo-Saxonism.* Cambridge: Harvard University Press, 1981.

K

Kanellos, Nicolás. *A History of Hispanic Theater in the United States: Origins to 1940.* Austin: University of Texas Press, 1990.

Kanellos, Nicolás, ed. *Biographical Dictionary of Hispanic Literature.* Westport, Connecticut: Greenwood Press, 1985.

Kanellos, Nicolás. *Hispanic Firsts.* Detroit: Gale Research, forthcoming.

Kanellos, Nicolás, and Claudio Esteva-Fabregat, general editors. *Handbook of Hispanic Cultures in the United States,* four volumes. Houston: Arte Público Press, 1994–95.

Kanellos, Nicolás, with Cristelia Pérez. *Chronology of Hispanic American History.* Detroit: Gale Research, 1995.

Knight, Franklin W. *The Caribbean.* New York: Oxford University Press, 1990.

L

Llanes, J. Cuban Americans, Masters of Survival. Cambridge, Massachusetts: Harvard University Press, 1982.

Lomeli, Francisco, and Julio A. Martínez. *Chicano Literature: A Reference Guide.* Westport, Connecticut: Greenwood Press, 1985.

M

McKenna, Teresa Flora, and Ida Ortiz, eds. *The Broken Web: The Educational Experience of Hispanic American Women.* Berkeley, California: Floricanto Press and the Tomás Rivera Center, 1988.

Meier, Kenneth J., and Joseph Stewart. *The Politics of Hispanic Education.* New York: Russell Sage Foundation, 1987.

Meier, Matt S., and Feliciano Rivera. *Dictionary of Mexican American History.* Westport, Connecticut: Greenwood Press, 1981.

Melville, Margarita, ed. *Twice a Minority: Mexican American Women.* St. Louis: Mosby, 1980.

Mirandé, Alfredo, and Evangelina Enríquez. *La Chicana: The Mexican American Woman.* Chicago: University of Chicago Press, 1979.

Moore, Joan, and Harry Pachón. *Hispanics in the United States.* Englewood Cliffs, New Jersey: Prentice Hall, 1985.

Morales, Julio. *Puerto Rican Poverty and Migration: We Just Had to Try Elsewhere.* New York: Praeger, 1986.

O

Office of the Secretary of Defense, *Hispanics in America's Defense.* Washington, DC: U.S. Printing Office, 1990.

P

Pedraza-Bailey, S. *Political and Economic Migrants in America.* Austin: University of Texas Press, 1985.

Portes, Alejandro, and Robert L. Bach. *Latin Journey: Cuban and Mexican Immigrants in the United States.* Berkeley: University of California Press, 1985.

Powell, Philip Wayne, *Tree of Hate. Propaganda and Prejudices Affecting United States Relations with the Hispanic World.* New York: Basic Books, 1971.

R

Rodríguez, Clara. *Born in the U.S.A.* Boston, Massachusetts: Unwin Hyman, 1989.

Ryan, Bryan, ed. *Hispanic Writers.* Detroit, Michigan: Gale Research, 1991.

S

Sánchez-Korrol, Virginia. *From Colonia to Community.* Westport, Connecticut: Greenwood Press, 1983.

Sandoval, Moisés. *On the Move: A History of the Hispanic Church in the United States.* Maryknoll, New York: Orbis Books, 1990.

Schorr, Edward Allen. *Hispanic Resource Directory.* Juneau, Alaska: Denali Press, 1988.

Shirley, Carl F., ed. *Chicano Writers: First Series.* Detroit, Michigan: Gale Research, 1989.

Smedley, Audrey. *Race in North America: Origin and Evolution of a Worldview.* Boulder, Colorado: Westview Press, 1993.

Suchliki, Jaime. *Cuba: From Columbus to Castro.* Washington, D.C.: Pergammon Press, 1986.

U

United States Commission on Civil Rights. *Puerto Ricans in the Continental United States: An Uncertain Future.* Washington, D.C.: U.S. Commission on Civil Rights, 1976.

Unterburger, Amy L., ed. *Who's Who among Hispanic Americans, 1992–1993.* Detroit, Michigan: Gale Research, 1992.

V

Veciana-Suárez, Ana. *Hispanic Media: Impact and Influence.* Washington, D.C.: The Media Institute, 1990.

Vivó, Paquita, ed. *The Puerto Ricans: An Annotated Bibliography.* New York: R. R. Bowker, 1973.

W

Wagenheim, Kal. *A Survey of Puerto Ricans in the U.S. Mainland in the 1970s.* New York: Praeger, 1975.

Weber, David. *The Mexican Frontier, 1821–1846: The American Southwest Under Mexico.* Albuquerque: University of New Mexico Press, 1982.

Index

A

Abel, Carlos Alberto: 434
Abelardo. *See* Delgado, Abelardo
Abreu, Virgilio: 556–557
Academy Award: 574, 600, 614–615, 624, 635, 637, 675
Acevedo, Mario: 538
Aceves, José: 520–521
Acheson, Dean: 165
Acoma Pueblo: 71–72, 142, 509, 514
Acosta, Daniel, Jr.: 434
Acosta, Raymond L.: 305
Acosta-Belén, Edna: 413
Acquired Immune Deficiency Syndrome (AIDS): 244, 434, 616, 634, 714
Acuña, Rodolfo: 414, 650
Acuña y Rossetti, Elisa: 238
Adams, John: 287
Adams, John Quincy: 151, 153, 157
Adams-Onís Treaty: 150
adelantado: 60, 63, 72
AFL. *See* American Federation of Labor
AFL-CIO. *See* American Federation of Labor and Congress of Industrial Organizations (AFL-CIO)
Agency for International Development (AID): 168, 301, 449
Aguayo, Marquis of: 73
Agueibana: 58
Aguila, Guz. *See* Aguilera, Antonio Guzmán

Aguilar, Robert P.: 305
Aguilera, Antonio Guzmán: 553–554, 576
Aguirre, Gabriel Eloy: 358
Aguirre, Michael J.: 297–298
Ahumada, Ramón: 722
Ai Indians: 55
AIDS. *See* Acquired Immune Deficiency Syndrome (AIDS)
Aiken, Susan: 622
Aisle, Francisco José: 435
Ajo, Arizona: 133
Alabau, Magaly: 242
Alam, Juan Shamsul: 572
Alaminos, Antón de: 60–62
Alamo, El: 13, 16, 22, 135, 143, 145–146, 153, 180, 261, 283, 555–556, 604, 608, 619, 626, 638, 667
Alarcón, Arthur L.: 302, 305
Alarcón, Hernando de: 12
Alarcón, Norma: 244, 414, 471
Albizú, Olga: 243
Aleandro, Norma: 610, 624
Alegría, Fernando: 414
Alexander VI, Pope: 4, 60
Alfonso, Carlos: 537
Algarín, Miguel: 480, 484–485, 572, 580
Alianza Hispano Americana: 39
Alicia, Juana: 243
Alien Act: 287
All American Container: 360

Allen v. State Board of Elections: 293, 313
Allende, Salvador: 168, 414, 610
Alliance for Progress: 167
Almaraz, Carlos: 527–528
Almeida, Rafael: 724
Almendros, Nestor: 624
Alonso, Kenneth B.: 435
Alonso, María Conchita: 612
Altamira, José: 137
Alurista: 465–468, 485–486
Alvarado Construction Inc.: 358
Alvarado, Elvia M.: 243, 618
Alvarado, Linda: 358
Alvarez, Anne Maino: 435
Alvarez, Everett, Jr.: 276, 329
Alvarez, Julia: 474, 486
Alvarez, Luis Walter: 435
Alvarez, Marina: 616
Alvarez, Rodolfo: 414
Alvarez de Pineda, Alonzo: 62
Alvariño de Leira, Angeles: 436
Alverio, Rosita Dolores. *See* Moreno, Rita
Amado, Ralph: 436
Amador, Elías: 436
American Airlines: 349, 363
American Dream: 276, 348, 479, 484, 504, 525, 675, 710
American Federation of Labor (AFL): 369–371, 765

American Federation of Labor and Congress of Industrial Organizations (AFL-CIO): 371–372, 760
American G.I. Forum: 39, 276, 280, 387, 749, 755, 765
American Hispanic-Owned Radio Association (AHORA): 697
American International Container: 360
American Lodge: 278
American Revolution: 16, 150, 274, 278–279, 285, 287, 455, 576
Americanization. (*see also* assimilation): 38–39, 265, 396–398
Americas Review, The: 242, 414, 417, 423, 425, 471, 473, 490, 504, 535, 691
Amlin, Patricia: 617
Amy, Francisco: 458
anarchists: 244, 460
Anaya, Rudolfo A.: 467–468, 472, 474, 486–487, 616, 628
Anaya, Toney: 333
Anderson, Richard C.: 151
Angeles Negros, Los: 666
Anglicisms: 204–205, 209–210
Anglo-Mexican Mission Institute: 398
Anglo-Saxon: 176, 179–181, 183, 211, 459, 591–592, 594
Anguiano, Lupe: 245
Anheuser-Bush: 349, 357
Anselmo, Reynold (René): 701–702, 717
Antonio Maceo Brigade: 49
Antush, John: 572
Anza, Juan Bautista de. *See* Bautista de Anza, Juan
Anzaldúa, Gloria: 241, 498
Apache Indians: 18–19, 134, 142, 259, 261, 329
Apalachee Indians: 55, 65–66
Apalachicola Fort: 133
Aparicio, Carlos: 622
Aparicio, Manuel: 561–562, 564–565, 573
Apodaca, Jerry: 333, 689
Apollo Theater: 559
Aragón, José Rafael: 514, 517
Aranda, Guillermo: 538–539
Arawak Indians: 4–6, 56–57, 59, 74, 191
Arbenz, Jacobo: 165
Arboleya, Carlos José: 357–359
Arcano y sus Maravillas: 663–664
Arce, Julio: 460
Arce, Miguel: 459
architecture: 54, 261
Archuleta, Diego: 274, 329
Arciniega, Tomás A.: 757

Arellano, Tristán de: 70
ARENA Party: 173
Arévalo, Juan José: 165
Arias Sánchez, Oscar: 172
Arizona Association of Chicanos for Higher Education: 340
Armas, Castillo: 166
Armendáriz, Pedro: 600, 624
Armida: 625
Armiño, Franca de: 244, 464, 559–560
Army Appropriation Act: 160
Arnaz, Desi: 495, 601, 605, 625, 676
Arnaz y de Acha, Desiderio Alberto III. *See* Arnaz, Desi
Arreola, Philip: 757–758
Arte Público Press: 242, 248, 362, 416, 425, 468, 471, 474, 480–482, 484–485, 490, 505, 568
Artenstein, Isaac: 614, 617–619, 676, 679, 692
Asamblea Mexicana: 37
Asociación Nacional Pro Personas Mayores: 749
ASPIRA of America: 612
assimilation: 38, 40, 178, 203, 391, 397, 399, 401–402, 404–405, 408–410, 463, 483–484, 553, 556, 593, 609, 655–656
Astol, Lalo. *See* Astol, Leonardo García
Astol, Leonardo García: 555–556, 565, 575, 692
Ateneo Hispano: 748
audiencia: 12, 62, 64
Austin, Moses: 21
Ausubel, Ken: 614
Avalos, David: 532
Avila, Francisco: 135
Avila House: 135
Ayala, Ramón: 653, 667
Azcárraga Milmo, Emilio: 701
Azcárraga Vidaurreta, Emilio: 701
Aztec Indians: 9–12, 14, 40, 53–55, 62, 64, 72–73, 248, 257–258, 485–486, 530, 545
Aztlán: 9, 40, 54, 201, 243, 468, 485–487, 529, 532, 538, 542, 547, 566, 616, 650, 691
Azuela, Mariano: 459, 582

B

babalao: 271–272
Babenco, Hector: 610
Babín, María Teresa: 413–414
Baca, Jimmy Santiago: 487
Baca, Joseph Francis: 306
Baca, Judith: 243, 529–530, 539
Baca-Barragán, Polly: 245, 334
Baca-Zinn, Maxine: 216, 250, 415

Badillo, Herman: 320–321
Baez, Alberto Vinicio: 436–437
Báez, Myrna: 243
Balaguer, Joaquín: 168, 223
Ballad of Gregorio Cortez, The: 505, 619, 628, 636, 649, 675
Ballesteros, Jack: 614
Bamba, La: 568, 584, 609, 618–619, 623, 675, 717
banana industry: 198
banda: 667–669
Banderas, Antonio: 619
Bank of California: 362
Bañuelos, Romana Acosta: 329–330
Baptists: 265, 398–399, 504
Barajas, Salvador: 538–539
Barela, Casimiro: 334
Barela, Patrocino: 518
Barnum and Bailey Circus: 556
Barrera, Mario: 615
Barrera, Rolando: 568
Barreto, Lefty: 479
Barrio Boyzz: 667–668
Barrio de Analco Historic District: 141
Barro, Mary Helen: 758
Batista, Fulgencio: 46, 166, 191, 225, 731
Bautista Alvarado, Juan: 135
Bautista de Anza, Juan: 19, 74, 135, 344
Bay of Pigs: 48, 167, 508
Bazaar, Philip: 275
Beato, Alfonso: 621
Beauchamp, Eduvigis: 239
Becerra, Xavier: 314, 320
Bedoya, Alfonso: 600, 604, 625
Belén, Edna Acosta. *See* Acosta-Belén, Edna
Bélen Gutiérrez de Mendoza, Juana: 238
Belgrano, Manuel: 151
Bellán, Esteban: 723
Beltrán, Bernardino: 71
Benavides, Fortunato P.: 302
Benavides, Roy: 277
Benavides, Santos: 274, 277
Benchmark Hospitality Group: 357, 359
Berbers (*see also* Germanic tribes): 3
Bernal, Paulino: 653–654
Berrio: 62
Betances, Ramón Emeterio: 29, 458
Beveridge, Albert C.: 156
biculturalism: 409, 659
Bidlack, Benjamin: 154
Bilingual Review Press: 471
Bilingual Review: 242, 423

bilingualism: 46, 202, 206–207, 209–211, 238, 240, 292, 326, 328, 401, 409–410, 413, 480, 485–486, 492, 496–497, 500, 566, 609, 616, 763, 765, 771
Birabén, Alfedo. *See* Norton, Barry
biracial: 183–184, 186
Bishop, Maurice: 171
Black and White Mural: 537, 540–541
Black Panthers: 45
blacks: 178–180, 182, 184, 188, 190, 196, 200, 214, 257, 273, 365, 371–372, 377–382, 386–389, 410, 456, 588–589, 593, 597, 602–603, 606, 612, 623, 662, 724–725
Blackton, Stuart: 588
Blades, Rubén: 610, 617, 622, 625, 664
Blaine, James G.: 155–156
Blaz, Ben: 320
Bobadilla, Francisco de: 58
Bobo, Willie: 665
Boland Amendment: 172
Bolaños Cacho, Miguel: 459
Bolívar, Simón: 151, 279
Bonilla, Bobby: 726
Bonilla, Frank: 415
Bonilla, Henry: 314, 320
Bonilla, Rubén: 759
Bonilla, Tony: 758–759
Bonilla-Santiago, Gloria: 415
Borica, Diego de: 396
Borinquen: 7, 42–45, 58, 415, 536, 559
Born in East L.A.: 609–611, 618, 632, 675, 772
Borras, Caridad: 437
Borras, Edelmiro: 559
Bosch, Juan: 168, 420
Botero, Fernando: 524
Boulevard Nights: 606, 608
Bowie, Jim: 22, 494
Box, John C.: 38
Bracero Program: 39, 43, 201, 207, 230, 286, 315, 367–368, 373–377, 384
Bracetti, Mariana: 239
Brackenridge, Henry M.: 151
Bradley, Tom: 299
Braga, Sonia: 611
brain drain: 434
Bravo, Edgar Michael: 616
Bravos del Norte, Los: 653
Briceño, Carlos: 727
Brito-Avellano, María: 243
brotherhoods: 42, 52, 262–263, 272, 515, 536, 542, 601, 748
Brown Berets: 40, 45, 539
Bruni, Toni: 614

Bryan-Chamorro Treaty: 160, 162
Bucareli, Antonio María: 74
Buchanan, Pat: 383, 385
Buenos Aires Inter-American Conferences: 163
Bugarín, Pedro: 656
Bukis, Los: 666–667
Bull of Demarcation: 60
Bunau-Varilla, Philippe: 159
Burger King: 349, 363
Burger, Warren: 378
Burgos, Julia de: 244, 476, 621
Bush, George: 304, 331–333, 762, 774
Bustamante, Albert G.: 320
Bustamante, Anastasio: 22

C

Caballeros de Labor: 369
Caballeros de San Juan: 44
Cabán, Roger: 242, 581
Cabañas, Humberto: 357, 359
Cabeza de Vaca, Álvar Núñez. *See* Núñez Cabeza de Vaca, Álvar
Cabildo, The: 140–141
Cabot, Sebastian: 60
Cabral, Reid: 168
Cabranés, José A.: 306
Cabrera Infante, Gabriel: 482
Cabrera Infante, Saba: 244
Cabrera, Lydia: 242, 483
Cáceres, César A.: 437
Cáceres, Ramón: 161
Cacho, Miguel Bolaños. *See* Bolaños Cacho, Miguel
Caddo Indians: 73, 146, 432
Cadena Radio Centro: 699
Café de California: 340
Cafferty, Pastora San Juan: 416
Caicedo, Harry: 690, 759
Calderón Sol, Armando: 173
Califa, Antonio: 382
California Land Act: 25
California Theater: 551
Calpe Americano: 748
Calusa Indians: 55
Camacho, Joe: 616
Camargo, Diego de: 62
Camargo, Velia: 565
Camarillo, Albert Michael: 416
Camino Real: 144, 262
Campeche Show: 667
Camplis, F. X.: 615
Campos, Albizu: 29, 621
Campos, Santiago E.: 306
Campubrí, José: 683
Cana Brava: 668
Canales, Nemesio: 620
Cancio, Marta: 437
canción: 579, 645–647, 652, 656

Candelas, Graciela: 437–438
Candia, Oscar A.: 438
Cannella, John M.: 307
Canseco, José: 727
Cansino, Margarita Carmen. *See* Hayworth, Rita
Cantinflas. *See* Moreno, Mario
Cantú, Norma: 382
Capdevielle, María. *See* Maris, Mona
Capella, Antonio: 620
Caperton, William B.: 161
Capetillo, Luisa: 240, 244, 465
Capó, Bobby: 568
Capote, Ernesto: 572
Caraballo, Wilfredo: 298
Caracena, Fernando: 438
Carabajal, Jesús: 615
Cárdenas, Isidra T. de: 244, 460
Cárdenas, López de: 70
Cárdenas, Mary Janet M.: 438
Cárdenas, Raúl de: 572
Cárdenas, Robert Léon: 277
Cárdenas, Rogelio: 537, 545–546
Cardinali, José: 685
Cardona, Florencia Bisenta de Casillas Martínez. *See* Carr, Vikki
Cardona, Manuel: 438–439
Cardús, David: 439
Carew, Rod: 727–728
Carib Indians: 4–6, 56–57, 63, 191
Caridad del Cobre, La: 268, 271
Carino v. University of Oklahoma: 378
Carioca, José: 596
CARISSMA: 612
Carlos IV: 393
Carlos López Press: 462
Carmel Mission: 134
Carmen, Julie: 611
Carnegie, Andrew: 156
Caro, Brígido: 459
carpa: 37, 556, 567, 584, 613
Carpa Cubana: 556–557
Carpa García: 556–557
Carpentier, Alejo: 482
Carr, Vikki: 667, 759–760
Carranza, Venustiano: 162, 461, 539
Carrera, José Miguel: 151
Carrero, Jaime: 476–477, 570–571
carriage industry: 347
Carrillo, Eduardo: 552
Carrillo, Leo: 592, 596, 602, 626
Carrillo, Leopoldo: 347
Carrillo, Sean: 617
Cart War: 347
Carter, Jimmy: 49, 169, 247–248, 289, 304–306, 308, 319, 330–331, 496, 702, 742, 759
Carter, Lynda Córdoba: 605, 626

Carthaginians: 2
Casa Alvarado: 135
Casa Aztlán: 542
Casa Cubana: 240
Casa Editorial Lozano: 459
Casa Galicia: 748
Casals, Rosemary: 728
Casanova de Villaverde, Emilia: 240
Casas, Bartolomé de las: 64, 179,
    182, 255
Casas, Juan Bautista: 274
Casas, Melesio: 524–525
Casiano, Domingo: 620
Casso, Henry: 264
Castañeda, Antonia I.: 417
Castañeda, Carlos E.: 397, 413
Castañeda, Tomás: 538
Castaño de Sosa, Gaspar: 71
caste system: 20, 177–178, 183
Castejón, Blanca de: 620
Castellanos, Leonard: 539
Castelló, Hugo M.: 728
Castile: 2, 4, 57
Castilian. *See* Spanish language
Castilians: 3–4, 594
Castilla y O'Donnell, Marie
    Marguerita Guadalupe Teresa
    Estela Bolado. *See* Margo
Castillo, Alonso del: 66
Castillo, El: 135
Castillo, Leonel J.: 330
Castillo, Mario: 542
Castillo, Sylvia: 244
Castro, Alberto: 439
Castro, Fidel: 46–49, 166, 169, 191,
    225, 287, 289, 292, 506, 508, 606
Castro, George: 440
Castro, José: 134
Castro, Peter: 440
Castro (José) House: 137
Catholic church: 2, 4, 11, 20, 22, 37,
    42, 47, 54, 153, 209, 221, 238,
    240, 258, 264–265, 270–271, 273,
    343, 394, 396–399, 417, 488, 515,
    634, 764
Catholic Kings: 4, 11, 58, 176
Catholic schools: 397, 494
Catholicism: 2, 11, 28, 42, 73, 177,
    179, 253–254, 257–258, 263, 265,
    271, 397, 401, 488, 518, 567, 660
cattle ranching: 15, 134, 222, 262,
    344–346, 648, 677, 725
caudillo: 162
Cavazos, Lauro F.: 330–331
Cavazos, Richard E.: 276, 278
Celts (*see also* Iberian-Celtic culture
    and Gaelic culture): 2, 176
Central American Common Market:
    287

Central American Court of Justice:
    160
Central American Union: 197
Central Bank of Mexico: 174
Central Intelligence Agency (CIA):
    166–168
Centro Asturiano: 560–564, 572,
    748
Centro Cultural de la Raza: 529,
    531–532, 537
Centro Español de West Tampa:
    560
Centro Obrero: 560, 563–564
Cepeda, Orlando: 729
Cerezo, Carmen C.: 307
Cerón, Juan: 59
Cervantes, Lorna Dee: 473–474,
    482, 487–488
Cervantes, Pedro: 522
Cervántez, Yreina: 243
Chacón, Eusebio: 456–457
Chacón, Felipe Maximiliano: 457
Chacón, Iris: 621
Chamizal National Monument: 144
Chamorro, Violeta: 172
Chaplin, Charles: 588
Chapultepec, Act of: 164
Charles III: 75, 262
Charles IX: 69
Charola, Asunción Elena: 440
Chata Noloesca, La. *See* Escalona,
    Beatriz
Chatfield, Frederick: 155
Chávez, Angélico: 461, 488
Chávez, César: 366, 371–372, 539,
    542–543, 565, 583, 613, 760, 767
Chávez, Denise: 241, 471–474, 489
Chávez, Dennis: 314, 320, 322
Chávez, Manuel. *See* Fray Chávez,
    Angélico
Chicago Working Woman's Union:
    238
Chicanas: 236–237, 239, 243, 421,
    426–427, 471–473, 498, 529, 601,
    603, 613, 618, 634, 750
Chicano Advocates for Employment.
    See Café de California
Chicano films: 609, 612
Chicano identity: 465, 504, 533, 539,
    546
Chicano literature: 241
Chicano Moratorium: 539, 541, 638,
    650
Chicano Movement: 242, 487, 615,
    657
Chicano theater: 565–569, 583
Chicanos: 40, 45, 184, 186, 200, 213,
    215–216, 219, 230, 232, 244, 247,
    250, 266, 298, 328, 371, 377, 400,
    414, 416, 420–422, 450, 459,

465–474, 477, 485–487, 492,
    495–496, 498–502, 504–505, 507,
    516, 523–525, 527–535, 537–545,
    547, 565–568, 583–584, 587,
    597–603, 606–610, 612–620, 628,
    634, 636, 638, 650, 653, 656–657,
    659, 662, 665, 667, 674–677, 680,
    688, 693, 753
Chichimecas: 9, 12
child labor laws: 238, 366
chinampa: 8–9, 54
Chinese Exclusion Act: 286, 288
Chiquita Banana: 605
Chong, Thomas: 611
Christian Brothers: 397
Christian Castilians: 3
Christianity: 2–3, 61, 177, 253–254,
    258–260, 262, 265, 392–393, 395,
    432
Chua Ranch, La: 344
Chumacero, Olivia: 243
Ciboney Indians: 5, 56–57
Ciccone, Oscar: 569
Cid Pérez, José: 572
Cienfuegos, Lucky: 478, 572
cigar industry: 45–46, 182, 207
Cintrón, Guillermo B.: 440–441
Circo Cubano. *See* Carpa Cubana
Circo Escalante: 37
Círculo Cubano: 560, 748
Círculo Valenciano: 748
Cisco Kid: 568, 584, 594, 605, 626,
    632–633, 637–638, 676
Cisneros, Henry G.: 326, 616
Cisneros, Sandra: 241, 471–472,
    474, 490
citizenship: 30, 40–41, 43, 119, 153,
    180–181, 183–184, 191–192, 207,
    219, 263, 276, 285–288, 290–294,
    400, 465, 562, 675, 701, 753
Civil Rights Act: 291–292, 294–295,
    303, 378, 382
civil rights legislation: 184, 295,
    312, 338, 381–382, 602
civil rights movement: 276, 413,
    535, 587, 600–602, 604, 612
civil rights organizations: 276, 280,
    615, 748
Civil War, United States: 155, 157,
    236
civil wars: 28, 32, 36, 53–54, 155,
    161, 165, 172, 181, 198, 241,
    274–275, 277, 279, 287, 301, 310,
    321, 323–325, 329, 336, 345, 348,
    399, 456
Claretians: 263
Clavijo, Uva: 242
Clay, Henry: 150, 153, 156
Clayton, John M.: 155
Clemente, Roberto: 730

Cleveland, Grover: 325
Cleveland, Richard J.: 346
Clifton and Morenci, Arizona: 133
Clinton, Bill: 245, 327–328, 334, 385, 761
Club Sembradores de la Amistad: 269
Cobo Souza, Manuel: 483
Coca-Cola Inc.: 349, 357–358, 360, 363
code-switching: 204, 210–211
Codina, Armando: 357
Codina Group: 357
Cody, W. F. "Buffalo Bill": 725
Coen, Augusto: 645
Cofer, Judith Ortiz. *See* Ortiz Cofer, Judith
coffee industry: 27, 29, 41, 149, 156, 163, 207, 219, 222
Cold War: 173, 424
Collazo, Julito: 662
Colmenares, Margarita Hortensia: 246
Colón, Jesús: 420, 465, 477, 479, 491, 570
Colón, Miriam: 569–570, 574, 576, 620–621
Colón, Willie: 622, 664
Colón-Morales, Rafael: 536
colonia: 33, 35–38, 42–44, 231
Colonialism: 413
colonization: 1–2, 4, 11, 13–14, 16, 18, 21, 57, 59, 68, 73, 75, 80, 82, 98, 103–104, 153, 176–177, 180, 254, 256, 268, 273, 285, 343–344, 346, 392, 394, 432–433, 549
Colorado Institute for Hispanic Education and Economic Development: 340
Colorado Rockies baseball team: 358
Columbus, Christopher: 4–7, 57, 147, 253, 285, 475
Columbus, Diego: 59, 63
Comanche Indians: 14–16, 21, 73, 181
Comisión Femenil Mexicana Nacional: 750
comisiones honoríficas: 38
Common market: 173, 287
communism: 27, 47, 51, 165–166, 168, 170, 172–173, 483, 572, 727
Community Action Program (CAP): 378–379, 387, 767
compadrazgo: 216–219, 223, 227, 231–232
Compañia, La: 616
Comprehensive Employment and Training Administration: 379, 387
Compromise of 1850: 180
Concepción, Dave: 730

Concepción Mission: 144
Confederación de Trabajadores Generales: 371
Confederación de Trabajadores Generales (CGT): 371
Confederacy: 273–274, 277, 324
Conference of Puerto Rican Women: 250, 339, 753–754
confianza: 216, 218–219, 221, 223–224, 231
Congregationalists: 398
Congreso de Artistas Chicanos en Aztlán: 537–538, 540
Congreso Mexicanista: 37
Congress of Mexican American Unity: 605
Congressional Hispanic Caucus: 314–316, 318–320, 326, 750, 769
Conjunto Bernal, El: 653
conjunto: 644–645, 652–656, 658, 662, 666, 668
Connecticut Association for United Spanish Action: 340
conquistadors: 10–11, 58, 63–64, 66–67, 70, 72, 144, 254–255, 258, 270, 458
Consortium of National Hispanic Organizations: 751
Contadora Group: 172
Continental Airlines: 357, 361
Contras: 172
Convent of Porta Coeli: 143
conventos: 509
Cordero, Angel: 730
Cordero, Julio: 441
Cordero y Bustamante, Antonio: 146
Córdova, Pedro de: 627
Córdova House: 133
Corea, Chick: 665
Corona, Bert: 761
Coronado, Francisco. *See* Vasquez de Coronado, Francisco
Coronado, José R.: 761
Coronado National Memorial: 133
Coronel, Antonio F.: 550
Corpi, Lucha: 471
Corporation for Public Broadcasting: 482, 679, 763
Corpus Christi de la Ysleta Mission: 144
Corral, Edward A.: 762
corrido: 457, 538, 566–567, 583, 614, 645–651
Cortés, Carlos E.: 417–418
Cortés, Hernán: 6–7, 9, 14, 54–55, 62, 64, 73, 254, 257
Cortez, Gregorio: 619, 649
Cortez, Raúl: 693, 700
Cortina, Juan Nepomuceno: 649
Cortina, Rodolfo J.: 418, 484, 572

Cosío y Cisneros, Evangelina: 236
Cossío, Evangelina: 458
Costello, Diana: 615
Cotera, Manuel: 555
cotton industry: 32, 34, 55, 153, 263, 291, 347, 366–367, 370, 374, 377, 523, 652
Council of the Indies: 12, 60, 65, 72
cowboy diplomacy: 159
cowboys: 34, 344–346, 365, 369, 503, 556, 589, 595, 603, 614, 649, 655, 676, 721–722, 725–726
Creek Indians: 133, 344
Cremata, Ernesto: 572
Creoles: 97–98
Crespi, Juan: 135
criollo: 13–14, 29, 41, 177–178, 242
Cristal, Linda: 605, 626–627, 677
Cristo Negro de Esquipulas: 267
Crockett, Davey: 22
crónica: 456–460, 462, 469, 577
Crusades: 3, 549
Cruz Azaceta, Luis: 536
Cruz Blanca, La : 241
Cruz, Celia: 660–661, 664
Cruz, Nicky: 479
Cruz-Romo, Gilda: 762
Cuadra, Angel: 483
Cuauhtemoc: 10
Cuba, Joe: 663
Cuban American Foundation: 359
Cuban American Legal Defense and Education Fund: 337, 750
Cuban American National Council: 751
Cuban Film Institute: 621
Cuban folklore: 242
Cuban Revolution: 30, 41, 208, 240, 369, 434, 482–484, 493, 573, 575, 723–724, 731
Cuban Revolution of 1959: 28, 45, 225, 358, 572
Cuban Women's Club: 240
Cuéllar, Gilbert, Jr.: 359
Cuervo y Valdés, Francisco: 141
Cuesta, José Enamorado: 464, 559–560
Cugat, Xavier: 631, 644
Cuitlahuac: 10
curandero: 270–271, 432, 621
Customs House (Monterey, California): 135
Cuza Malé, Belkis: 242, 484

D

Dallmeier, Francisco: 441–442
Dana, Bill: 605
Dantés: 457
Darrow, Henry: 595, 621, 626, 638
Darwinism: 180

Davidson, Peter W.: 683–684
Dávila, Luis: 471
Dawson, Thomas C.: 160
de Alaminos, Antón. *See* Alaminos,
    Antón de
de Alániz, Jerónimo. *See* Alániz,
    Jerónimo de
de Alarcón, Hernando. *See* Alarcón,
    Hernando de
de Alonso, Luis Antonio Dámaso.
    See Roland, Gilbert
de Alvardo, Pedro. *See* Alvardo,
    Pedro de
de Armiño, Franca. *See* Armiño,
    Franca de
de Bobadilla, Francisco. *See*
    Bobadilla, Francisco de
de Borica, Diego. *See* Borica, Diego
    de
de Burgos, Julia. *See* Burgos, Julia
    de
De Córdova, Arturo: 600, 620, 627
de Gali, Francisco. *See* Gali, Fran-
    cisco de
de la Garza, E. (Kika): 314, 320
de la Garza, Rodolfo: 418
de la Hoya, Oscar. *See* Hoya, Oscar
    de la
de la Riva-Baza, Sandra Lynn: 731
de Leira, Angeles Alvariño. *See* Al-
    variño de Leira, Angeles
de Lugo, Ron: 320
de Pineda, Alonzo Alvarez. *See*
    Alvarez de Pineda, Alonzo
de Santo Silas, María Africa Vidal.
    See Montez, María
De Soto Caverns: 133
De Soto Falls: 133
de Soto, Hernando. *See* Soto, Her-
    nando de
de Varona, Donna: 731
de Villalobos, María Guadalupe
    Vélez. *See* Vélez, Lupe
DeAnda, James: 307
Decade of the Hispanic: 349
del Río, Dolores: 596, 600, 612, 619,
    627
del Valle, Pedro A.: 278
Delano, Jack: 620
Delgado, Abelardo: 465–466, 492
Delgado, Adelaida. *See* Mara, Adele
Delgado, Ana Albertina: 243
Delgado, Lalo. *See* Delgado,
    Abelardo
DeLome, Dupuy: 157
democracy: 46, 121, 156, 165–168,
    278, 464–465, 480, 589, 599
Democratic National Committee
    Hispanic Caucus: 339
Democratic Party: 280

deportation: 230, 286, 339, 383–384,
    463, 553, 580, 610, 628, 672, 675
Depression: 28, 38–39, 43, 163, 230,
    286, 326, 329, 367, 370, 377,
    461–464, 491, 502, 552–556, 561,
    564, 574–575, 578, 580–582, 587,
    596, 598, 600–601, 610, 614, 655
Devine, John: 346
Diario-La Prensa, El: 683–684
Díaz Castro, Tania: 242
Díaz del Castillo, Bernal: 9, 62, 254
Díaz Guerra, Alirio: 462
Díaz, Henry Frank: 442
Díaz, Patricia: 618
Díaz, Porfirio: 33–34, 41, 160–161,
    230, 238, 244, 286, 457, 599, 747
Díaz Valcárcel, Emilio: 620
Díaz Vara Calderón, Gabriel: 258
Díaz-Balart, Lincoln: 314–315
Díaz-Oliver, Remedios: 360
dictators: 46, 153, 165–166, 173,
    191, 222–223, 225, 230, 244, 286,
    289, 292, 434, 457, 459, 464, 486,
    535, 582, 610–611, 685, 731, 747
Diego, Juan: 257, 514, 546
Dillon, C. Douglas: 167
dime novels: 594, 674
diplomacy: 41, 159, 317, 765, 768,
    770
discrimination: 33, 37, 39, 44, 119,
    133, 179, 184, 214, 231, 264,
    275–276, 286, 291–295, 297, 304,
    313–314, 327, 339, 369–371,
    378–379, 381–382, 385–387, 396,
    399, 405, 407, 434, 465, 491, 505,
    531, 556, 616, 618, 621, 628,
    650–651, 656, 659, 714, 755
Disney, Walt: 487, 596, 609, 674,
    676, 699
District of Columbia Commission on
    Latino Community Development:
    340
Dole, Robert: 383
dollar diplomacy: 161, 183
Domenicci, Porfirio: 683
domestic workers: 374
Domínguez, Cari M.: 327
Domínguez, Jorge I.: 419
Don Catarino. *See* Pirrín, Eusebio
Don Francisco (Mario Kreutzber-
    ger): 712
Don Lalo. *See* Astol, Lalo
Donciano Vigil House: 141
Dorantes, Andrés: 66
Down These Mean Streets: 478–479,
    502
Draft Act on Peace and Coopera-
    tion: 172
Drake, Francis: 73, 181
drugs: 173, 332, 572, 580, 714, 736

Duke of Albuquerque: 15
Dulles, John Foster: 161, 165
Durán, Roberto: 731–732
Duvalier, Jean Claude: 289

E

Echeverría, Diego: 622
Echeverría, José: 482
Economic Opportunity Act (EOA):
    378, 387
Editorial Quinto Sol: 241, 466–467,
    469–471, 486, 492, 495, 503
educational attainment: 192, 226
Edwards, Philip: 346
Effie Eddington School for Girls:
    398
Eisenhower, Dwight D.: 47, 165
Eisenhower, Milton: 165
El Alamo. *See* Alamo, El
El Conde Gris. *See* Solano, Gustavo
El Norte: 248, 611, 618–619, 675,
    679
El Super: 610
Elizondo, Hector: 607
Elizondo, Virgilio: 254, 264, 268,
    270
Elliot, Alejandro: 568
Elvas, Gentleman of: 432
Elysian Park: 135
embargo: 162–164, 167, 724
Emergency Relief Administration
    Act (ERA Act): 562, 574
Emplumada (Plumed): 473, 488
En la lucha . . . ponte trucha (mu-
    ral): 537, 545–546
encomienda: 6–7, 11–12, 14, 59,
    64–66, 254–255, 260
Encuentros: 264
Endara, Guillermo: 173
engineering: 246
Engle, Margarita: 242
Enrique, Luis: 668
Enríquez, E.: 236
entertainment industry: 456, 462,
    550, 553, 555–556, 565, 568, 593,
    653, 662, 671, 679–680, 683–685,
    688–691, 699–700, 706–707, 712,
    717, 719, 747, 771–772
entrada: 16, 259
environmental groups: 376
Equal Employment Opportunity
    Commission (EEOC): 236, 311,
    371, 378–379, 381–382, 387, 612
Erickson, Charles A.: 672–673, 690
Escajeda, Josefina: 461
Escalante, Esteban: 459
Escalante, Jaime: 434, 675, 762
Escalante Fontaneda, Hernando de:
    238

Escalona, Beatriz (La Chata Noloesca): 559, 565, 568, 574
Escandón, José: 345, 495
Escobar, Javier I.: 442
Escobar, Marisol: 524
Escobar, Sixto: 726, 732, 740
Espada Aqueduct: 144
Esparza, Moctezuma: 243, 608–609, 614, 619, 675, 679
Espejo, Antonio de: 14, 71
Espinosa, Conrado: 459
Espinosa, Paul: 614–615, 628, 692
Espinoza v. Farah Manufacturing Company: 294, 378
Espíritu Santo de la Bahía Mission: 145
Esquivel, Antonio: 725
Essex Theater: 572
Estefan, Gloria: 668
Estevanico: 66, 70
Esteves, Luis R.: 279
Esteves, Sandra María: 241, 480
Estévez, Emilio: 608, 612, 623, 628, 638
Estévez, Ramón. *See* Sheen, Martin
Estrada, Erik (Enrique): 606
Estrada, Fred: 689–690
Estrada, Juan B.: 160
Estrada Cabrera, Manuel: 161
Estrada Palma, Tomás: 30
Estrella del Castillo, Amalia: 550
Estudillo, José Antonio: 135
Estudillo House (San Diego, California): 135
ethnicity: 45, 51, 186, 188, 203, 210, 371, 386, 398, 426–427, 475, 587–588, 594, 604, 659, 673, 747
evangelization: 254–255, 258–259, 261–262, 398
extended family: 216–219, 221–222, 224, 227–228, 231–232, 266, 395

F

Fábregas, Virginia: 37, 551
Fages, Pedro: 433
Fair Employment Practices Committee (FEPC): 371, 378, 387
Fajardo Ortiz, Desiderio: 458
Falcon Records: 653
Familia de Hoy, La: 689
familia, la: 215–217, 219, 231, 567
family life: 222, 233, 752
Farabundo Martí National Liberation Front (FMLN): 169–170, 172–173
Farándula Panamericana, La: 568–569
farm workers: 37, 201, 238, 286, 291, 338, 362, 370, 376–377, 385, 387, 466, 543, 565, 583, 613–615, 697, 733, 756, 760–761, 772
farming: 41, 53, 55–56, 255, 393, 396, 433, 494, 654
Farmworkers Organizing Committee: 760
Farragut, David G.: 274, 279–280
Federación Libre de los Trabajadores: 244, 370–371
Federal Art Project: 518
Federal Theater Project: 560–561, 574
Feliciano, José: 665
Feliciano Canyon: 135
Félix, Charles: 539–540
Ferdinand, King: 11
Ferdinand VII: 151
Fernández Camus, Emilio: 483
Fernández, Emilio (El Indio): 628–629
Fernández, Ferdinand Francis: 302, 307
Fernández, Gigi: 732–733
Fernández, José B.: 419
Fernández, Joseph A.: 763
Fernández, Manuel José Manny: 721, 726
Fernández, Mary Joe: 733
Fernández, Ricardo R.: 763
Fernández, Roberta: 241
Fernández, Roberto: 483, 492–493, 577
Fernández, Tony: 733
Fernández-Rundle, Katherine: 240
Ferra, Max: 571
Ferrer, José: 574, 621
Ferrer, Mel: 629
Ferrer, Rafael: 524, 526
Festival Latino: 568–569
feudalism: 3
field workers: 237, 374
Figueres, José: 165
Figueroa, Gabriel: 629
Figueroa, Pablo: 617
Figueroa, Sotero: 458
Fillmore, Millard: 288
First Battalion of Native Cavalry: 274
First Congress of Women Workers: 244
Fischbarg, Jorge: 443
Fish, Hamilton: 157
Fish & Company: 347
Flores, José: 135
Flores, Juan: 420
Flores, Julio: 457
Flores, Patrick F.: 264, 764
Flores, Pedro: 463
Flores, Roy: 617
Flores, Thomas Raymond: 733
Flores House (South Pasadena, California): 135
Flores Magón brothers: 747
Florida Commission on Hispanic Affairs: 340
folklore: 1, 242, 275, 393, 416–417, 426, 461–462, 476, 481, 553, 565–567, 574, 596, 649, 655, 662
Font, Rosa María de: 239
Fontánez, Angela: 243
Food Assistance Act: 169
food processing: 349
Foraker Act: 41
Ford Foundation: 250, 419, 429, 568
Ford, Gerald R.: 168, 304
Foreign Assistance Act: 169
Fornés, María Irene: 571, 575
Fort Caroline: 68–69, 258
Fort Mose: 273
Fort Point National Historic Site: 135
Fort San Carlos de Barrancas: 138
Fort San Lorenzo: 143
Fortaleza, La: 143, 526
Forumeer, The: 749
Fougá, Bernardo: 555
Fountain of Youth: 60
Fraguada, Federico: 572
Franciscans: 16, 19, 72, 74–75, 134, 143, 258, 260–262, 392–394
Fray Chávez, Angélico: 488
free men: 65, 179, 346
Free Trade Agreement: 376
freed slaves: 178
freight industry: 346–347
Frito Bandito: 605, 680
Fuentes, Carlos: 258, 602, 610
Fuera de Liga: 668
Fundación Puertorriqueña de las Humanidades: 622
Fuste, José Antonio: 307
Fuster, Jaime B.: 250, 320
Futurismo: 568

G

G.I. Bill: 276, 504, 768, 772
Gabaldón, Guy: 275
Gaelic culture: 2
Gage, Thomas: 179
Gagemi, Renate: 618
Gaitán, Fernando J.: 307
Galán, Héctor: 615, 628, 679
Galan Productions: 615
Galarza, Ernesto: 371, 764
Galavisión: 702, 707, 716
Gali, Francisco de: 73
Galindo, Rudy: 734
Gallardo, Edward: 568, 570, 572
Gallegos, Celso: 517
Gallegos, José Manuel: 322, 400

Galtieri, Leopoldo: 172
Gálvez, Bernardo de: 274, 278
Gálvez, José de: 19, 74, 262
Gamboa, Harry: 527, 541
gangs: 34, 44, 331, 502, 580, 599, 604, 606–607, 612, 617, 619, 621, 623, 649, 675, 677
Garay, Francisco de: 62
Garcés, Pedro de: 19
García, Alfredo Mariano: 443, 602, 629
García, Ana María: 622
García, Andrés: 714
García, Andy: 608–609, 629
García, Antonio: 520, 522
García, Arturo. *See* De Córdova, Arturo
García, Carlos Ernesto: 443
García, Celso Ramón: 443–444
García, Cristina: 242
García, Daniel P.: 299
García, David: 613
García, Edward J.: 307
García, Héctor Pérez: 765
García, José D.: 444, 621
García, Juan: 133
García, Lionel G.: 493–494
García, Manuel V.: 556
García, María Cristina Jurado. *See* Jurado, Katy
García, Octavo, y sus GGs: 659
García, Rifino: 133
García, Rupert: 528, 531
García Astol, Leonardo (*see also* Astol, Lalo): 575
García Torres, José: 621
Garci-Menéndez, Andrés Arturo. *See* García, Andy
Garduño, Gilberto: 537, 547–548
Garza, Emilio M.: 302, 308
Garza, Juan: 617
Garza, Reynaldo G.: 302, 308, 313, 335
Garza, Sabino: 616
Garza Falcón, Blas María de la: 345
Geada, Rita: 242
gender: 238, 240–241, 295, 378, 382, 396, 403, 427, 456, 680, 752
General Treaty: 160
genízaros: 14
genocide: 4, 176, 603
Germanic peoples: 2–3, 176, 179
Gierbolini, Gilberto: 308
Gil, Lourdes: 242
Ginorio, Beatriz Angela: 246
Ginsberg, Alan: 478
Girone, Maria Elena: 246
glass ceiling: 356
Glazer, Nathan: 235
Godoy, Gustavo: 703, 706

Goizueta, Roberto C.: 356–357, 360
gold: 6–7, 11, 14, 24–25, 31–32, 57–59, 61–67, 69–71, 90, 110, 114, 133, 135, 155, 285, 392, 459, 499, 505, 518, 594, 602–603, 610, 672
Golden West Broadcasters: 362
Gómez, Elsa: 765
Gómez, Lefty: 734
Gómez, Vernon Louis. *See* Gómez, Lefty
Gómez de Avellaneda, Gertrudis: 482
Gómez Peña, Guillermo: 617
Gómez-Quiñones, Juan: 420
Gonzales, Stephanie: 334
González, Adalberto Elías: 552–553, 575
González, Alberto M.: 464
González, Alfredo: 459
González, Balde: 656
González, Celedonio: 483, 494, 572
González, Deena J.: 247
González, Elma: 444
González, Henry B.: 320
González, José Luis: 465, 476–477, 570
González, Jovita: 461
González, Justo: 265, 267
González, Lucía Eldine: 238
González, Lucía Parsons: 247
González, Miguel: 724
González, Pancho: 735
González, Paula: 444
González, Pedro J.: 614, 679, 692–693
González, Raymond Emmanuel: 765
González, Richard Alonzo. *See* González, Pancho
González, Richard Rafael: 444
González, Rodolfo "Corky": 465, 542
González, Speedy: 596
González, Xavier: 520, 523
González-Alvarez House: 139
González Amezcua, Chelo: 522
González-Berry, Erlinda: 420–421
González González, Pedro: 556
González-Irizarry, Aníbal: 700
González Pando, Miguel: 572
González Parson, Lucy. *See* González, Lucía Eldine
Gordillo, Francisco: 63
Gorras Blancas, Las: 25
Goya Foods Inc.: 349, 352, 363
Graham v. Richardson: 293
Gran Chichimeca, El: 12
Gran Colombia: 152
Grand Opera House: 550
Grant, Ulysses S.: 158
Gratas, Enrique: 714

Grattan, Alejandro: 618
grazing rights: 344
greaser laws: 24
Great Society: 379, 382, 387
Greeks: 2–3, 431
green card: 374
Griffith, David Wark: 590
Griggs v. Duke Power Company: 378
Grijalva, Juan de: 6
Griswold del Castillo, Richard A.: 420
Grito de Lares: 29, 41, 239, 422, 559
Grito, El: 244
Group of Eight: 172
Grupo, El: 480
Grupo Lluvia: 667
Grupo Wao: 668
grupos: 645, 666–667
Guadalupe Theater: 567
Guajardo Lepicier, Rita: 616
Guastavino, Rafael: 433
Guastella, Marino: 621
Guerra, Juan Luis: 668
Guerrero, Lalo: 650, 656
Guerrero, María: 551, 561
Guerrero, Vicente: 21, 550
Guevavi Mission: 133
Guillén, Nicolás: 482, 497
Gulf Stream: 432
gunboat diplomacy: 166, 170, 183
Gurulé, Jimmy: 331
Gutiérrez, Ana Sol: 335
Gutiérrez, Diego: 432
Gutiérrez, Efraín: 616–618
Gutiérrez, Jusepe: 72
Gutiérrez, Luis: 315
Gutiérrez, Marina: 243
Gutiérrez, Ramón: 421
Gutiérrez Alea, Tomás: 577, 624
Gutiérrez de Humaña, Antonio: 71
Gutiérrez de Lara, Bernardo: 274
Gutiérrez de Lara, Lázaro: 459
Gutiérrez de Mendoza, Juana: 244
Guzmán Aguilera, Antonio (Guz Aguila). *See* Aguilera, Antonio Guzmán
Guzmán, Nuño de: 11–12
Guzmán, Suzanna: 766
gypsies: 176

H

H-2 Program: 368, 373, 377
hacienda: 2, 15–16, 18, 26–27, 31, 33–34, 135–136, 462, 725
Haig, Alexander: 172
Hall of Famers: 248, 250, 331, 362, 574, 722, 724, 726, 728–731, 735–737, 740, 766, 771
Hancock, John: 151
Harding, William: 159

hardware industry: 347
Harrison, Benjamin: 325
Hart, William S.: 588
Hasinai Indians: 260–261
Hatuey: 59
Havana Cubans: 722
Havana Ten Thousand: 49
Hawikuh: 66, 70, 141
Hawley-Smoot Tariff Act: 163
Hay, John: 105, 158
Hay-Paunceforte Treaty: 158
Haya, Ignacio: 348
Hayek, Salma: 619
Haymarket Riot: 238
Hayworth, Rita: 592, 595, 612, 626, 630–631
Hearst, William Randolph: 157, 161, 182
Helms, Jesse: 173
Henríquez Ureña, Pedro: 458, 462
Henry, Guy V.: 41
Henry, O.: 594
Hermanas, Las: 264, 751
hermandades. (*see also* brotherhoods): 42, 44
Hernández, Antonia: 299, 338
Hernández, Enrique: 444
Hernández, Ester: 529, 531
Hernández, Gonzalo J.: 445
Hernández, José Manuel: 421
Hernández, Keith: 735
Hernández, Leopoldo: 572
Hernández, Oscar: 653, 664
Hernández, Pete: 184, 293
Hernández, Rafael: 43, 463, 621
Hernández Cruz, Victor: 480, 491
Hernández de Córdoba, Francisco: 6
Hernández Martínez, Maximiliano: 163
Hernández v. New York: 294
Hernández v. Texas: 184, 291, 293
Herrera, Carolina: 766
Herrera, Miguel: 515, 520
Herrera-Sobek, María: 422
Herrón, Willie: 527, 540–541
Hidalgo, Edward: 276, 281, 331
Hidalgo, Miguel: 274, 285
Hidalgo de la Riva, Osa: 243
Hidalgo y Costilla, Miguel: 20, 539, 542, 545
Hijuelos, Oscar: 474, 483–484, 494
Hinojosa, Alejandro: 617
Hinojosa, María de Lourdes: 244
Hinojosa, Ricardo H.: 308
Hinojosa, Rolando: 212, 429, 466–469, 472, 482, 495
Hipócritas, Los: 244
hiring practices: 295, 378, 385
Hise, Elijah: 155
Hispania: 2, 716

Hispanic Academy of Media Arts and Sciences: 751
Hispanic American Broadcasting Corporation: 703–704, 706, 713
Hispanic Association of Colleges and Universities: 751
Hispanic Business magazine: 349–353, 355–357, 362, 689, 709, 756, 770
Hispanic Elected Local Officials Caucus: 339
Hispanic films: 600, 605, 609, 623
Hispanic identity: 177, 203, 592
Hispanic Link: 672–673, 689–690
Hispanic market: 51, 349, 362–363, 517, 604, 609–610, 684, 689, 691, 693, 695–697, 706, 716–718
Hispanic National Bar Association: 298, 300, 303, 331, 337, 689
Hispanic Political Action Committee: 339
Hispanic studies: 413, 771
Hispanic Women's Council of California: 340
Hispanism: 177
Hispano U.S.A.: 699
History and Heroes (mural): 537–538
History of the Mexican American Worker (mural): 537, 542–543
Holding Institute: 398
Hollywood formula: 593
Homar, Lorenzo: 243
home altars: 266, 516, 519–520, 531
homemakers: 238, 244
Homestead Act: 25, 346
homesteading: 25, 344, 346, 588
Hoover, Herbert: 162–163, 360
horsemanship: 274, 725
hospitality industry: 357
Hostos, Eugenio María de: 458
House of Representatives: 121–124, 131, 158, 245, 312, 314–315, 319–320, 322–323, 325, 332, 334, 383, 426
housing: 37, 44, 48, 126, 167, 183, 214, 221, 224, 231, 236, 240, 245, 297, 311, 334, 337–339, 404, 539–540, 552, 561, 750, 755
Houston, Sam: 22, 146, 153, 494
Hoya, Oscar de la: 730
Huerta, Dolores Fernández: 766
Huerta, Jorge: 568
Huerta, Victoriano: 36, 161
Hughes, Charles Evans: 162
Huidobro, Matías Montes: 483, 572, 577–578
Huitzilopochtli: 9–10, 54
Hull, Cordell: 163
human rights: 118–119, 121, 255

Hunter, Duncan: 376
Hunter, Pancho: 547

I

I Am Joaquín: 465–466, 584, 613
Ibáñez, Michael Louis: 445
Ibarra Reyes, Conchita: 618
Iberian Peninsula: 1–3, 10, 70, 176, 253, 273, 431, 549
Iberian-Celtic culture: 1–2
identity: 1, 12–13, 36–38, 40, 42, 44–45, 50, 99, 152, 176, 178, 184, 196, 201, 203, 210, 223–224, 226, 230, 232, 241–243, 265, 275, 348, 397, 401, 413, 464–468, 475–476, 479–480, 484, 489, 497–498, 502, 504–505, 522, 528–530, 533, 566, 570, 595, 609, 614, 617, 643, 651, 661–662, 664, 666, 690, 697, 753
illegal aliens. *See* undocumented immigrants/workers
immigration: 213–214, 219, 223, 225–231, 239, 264, 286–293, 297, 299, 302, 310–311, 338–339, 347–349, 365, 367–369, 372–373, 384–385, 396, 400, 434, 457–459, 462, 482, 491, 505, 508, 516, 520, 557, 560, 564, 666, 669, 672, 676, 679, 682, 690, 697–698, 726, 752
Immigration Act of 1990: 289, 293
Immigration and Nationality Act: 288, 292, 368, 373
Immigration and Naturalization Service (INS): 290, 293, 330, 339, 383–386
Immigration Reform and Control Act: 290–291, 293–294, 326, 373, 385
Impacto de Montemorelos: 667
import duties: 560
Inca Indians: 53, 63, 97
Ince, Thomas H.: 588
Inclán, Cristino R.: 561
independence movements: 365, 458, 480, 557, 622
Independence War: 182
Independent School District: 294
Indias, Las: 6
Indies: 6, 75, 337
indigenismo: 36–37
Industria del Amor: 667
Industrial Workers of the World: 247, 369
industrialization: 27, 167, 219, 368, 375, 377
Inquisition: 177
Institute for Higher Education Law and Governance: 300
Institutional Revolutionary Party (PRI): 174

Instituto Arte Teatral (IATE): 570
Instituto Cubano de Artes Cinematográficas: 244
Instituto del Arte e Industria Cinematográfica: 624
Instituto San Carlos: 240
Inter-American Conference. *See* Buenos Aires Inter-American Conferences.
Inter-American Defense Board: 164
intermarriage: 177, 179, 219, 236, 579
International Association of Conference Centers: 357, 359
International Broadcasting Company: 693
International Company of Mexico: 230
International Court of Justice: 172
International Labor Defense: 238, 247
International Mine, Mill and Smelter Workers Union: 371
International Monetary Fund: 174
international trade: 343
International Workers of the World: 238
Iowa Spanish-Speaking Peoples Commission: 340
iron forging: 347
irrigation: 55, 144, 322, 431, 433, 523
Isabel, Queen: 11
Isabella, Queen of Castile: 3–4, 11, 57–58, 74, 253–254
Islam: 3, 176–177, 431
Isleños: 195
Iturbide, Augustine: 21
Iturralde, Iraida: 242

J

Jackson, Andrew: 139, 150, 153, 286
Jackson Square: 140
Jacobo, Daniel: 617
Janer, Edwin: 568
Jaramillo, Don Pedrito: 270
Jarri, Jean: 72
Jarrico, Paul: 598
Jeaga Indians: 55
Jefferson, Thomas: 21, 150, 157, 182, 287, 750
Jeronymite Fathers: 74
Jesuits: 16, 75, 255, 258, 262, 325, 392–394, 397
Jesús, María de: 260
Jews: 3–4, 176–177, 179, 253–254, 455
jíbaro: 27–28, 197, 476–477, 620
Jimenez, Flaco: 666, 668
Jiménez, Lillian: 243, 524–525

Jiménez, Orlando: 244
Jiménez-Wagenheim, Olga: 422
Jiménez y Muro, Dolores: 238
Job Corps: 378, 381, 387
John Blair & Company: 704
Johnson, Lyndon Baines: 48, 168, 171, 245, 276, 301, 304, 334, 378, 524, 650, 769
Jones Act: 40–41, 43, 183, 207, 219, 287–288, 292, 462
Jones v. City of Lubbock: 313
Jordan, Barbara: 385
Joseph Papp's New York Shakespeare Festival: 569, 571
journalism: 205, 244, 460, 504, 559, 578, 588, 673, 691, 701, 703, 753, 759, 770–771, 773
Juana la Loca, Queen of Spain: 11
Juárez, Mexico: 37, 539, 543, 577, 599–600, 617, 627, 638, 687, 701, 713
Juchereau de St. Denis: 260
Juliá, Raúl: 569, 576, 608, 610–611, 621, 623, 630
Jumano Indians: 72, 260
Junco, Tirso del: 327, 702
Junta Patriótica Mexicana: 550, 747
Jurado, Katy: 598, 600–601, 630
JUSTICIA: 612

K

Kamehameha III: 346
Kanellos, Nicolás: 471, 481, 535, 568, 692
Kansas Advisory Committee on Hispanic Affairs: 340
Karankawa Indians: 144, 259, 261
Kardec, Alan: 270
Kaskabel. *See* Padilla, Benjamin
KCOR-AM (San Antonio): 693, 695, 700
KCOR-TV (San Antonio): 699–700
Kearny, Stephen Watts: 23, 137, 141, 329
Kennedy, John F.: 48, 167, 245, 281, 329, 334, 337, 520, 533
Kennedy, Robert F.: 245, 334
Khrushchev, Nikita: 167
Kid Chocolate. *See* Sardiñas, Elgio
King Ranch: 330, 345
Kino, Father Eusebio: 18, 75, 133–134, 261–262, 344
kinship: 31, 216–218, 224, 228, 232
KLVE-FM (Los Angeles): 691, 696
KMPC (Los Angeles): 692
Knights of America: 749
Knights of Labor: 238, 369
Korean War: 308, 315, 319, 374, 495
KWKW-AM (Los Angeles): 691, 696

L

La carreta (The Oxcart): 207, 476, 569, 577, 621
La Plata, George: 309
La Raza Cósmica (mural): 544–545
Labor Council of Latin American Advancement (LCLAA): 372
labor force: 56, 189–190, 192–193, 201, 220, 222–223, 227–228, 240, 365, 373–374, 376–377, 386, 388–389, 396, 673
labor organizers: 239–240, 244
labor unions: 42, 173, 204, 583, 749
Laffitte, Héctor M.: 309
Laguna Santero: 514
Lamas, Fernando: 612, 630–631, 674
Lamy, Jean Baptiste: 263
land grants: 14, 16, 21, 135, 230, 266, 286, 343–346, 396
land-use: 344
Landeta, Matilde: 618
landlords: 41, 347, 594
language usage: 204, 212, 556
Lara, Javier: 462
Laria, María: 714
Larkin, Thomas O.: 154
Las Trampas Historic District: 141
Las Vegas Old Town Plaza: 141
Lasansky, Mauricio: 524
latifundia See hacienda.
Latin American Group (ADAL): 571
Latin American League: 151
Latin American Theater Ensemble (LATE): 570
Latin Empire: 622
Latin jazz: 622, 645, 665
Latin rock: 645, 665, 669
Latino: 51, 184, 188, 193, 213, 219, 228, 232, 235, 248–249, 299, 312, 317, 336, 339, 416, 419, 423, 426, 429, 466, 469, 471, 485, 496, 568, 582, 604, 606–607, 610, 614, 616–618, 628, 634, 643–645, 651, 662, 664–666, 668–669, 671, 673, 675–676, 678–681, 687, 691–692, 695–696, 698, 704, 716–717, 753
Lau v. Nichols: 294, 409
Laviera, Jesús Abraham Tato. *See* Laviera, Tato
Laviera, Tato: 478, 480, 482, 496, 572
Lavoe, Héctor: 664
Laws of Burgos: 11
Laws of the Indies: 254–255
League of Nations: 162
League of United Latin American Citizens (LULAC): 38–39, 44, 239, 294, 300, 314–315, 339, 387,

422, 429, 450, 612, 678, 680, 749, 751–752, 755, 758–759, 765
Leal, Luis: 413, 422–423
Lear, Norman: 677, 702, 706
Lecuona, Ernesto: 663
legal education: 294–295, 337–338, 752
Legal Services Corporation: 297, 337–338
Lend-Lease Act: 164
León, Alonso de: 15, 260, 345
León, Antonio de: 72
Lesseps, Ferdinand de: 158
Lewis and Clark: 21
Leyba, Albert: 547
Leyva de Bonilla, Francisco: 71
Lezama Lima, José: 482
Liga de Béisbol Profesional Cubana: 722
Liga de Hijas de Cuba: 240
Liga Femenil Mexicanista, La: 239
Liga Protectora Mexicana, La: 37
Lima Conference: 164
Lima Group: 172
Limite: 668
Limón, José: 654
Lincoln, Abraham: 23, 155, 275, 329, 336, 543, 599
Linden Lane magazine: 242, 484
Lindsay, Walter O.: 551
literacy: 35, 152, 167, 288, 292, 313, 391–392, 394–395, 397, 400, 467
Little Joe and the Latinaires. (*see also* Little Joe y La Familia): 656
Little Joe y la Familia: 616, 656–657, 659, 666
livestock industry: 344–346
Llamas, Vicente José: 445
Llauradó, Joseph: 445
Llinas, Rodolfo: 445
Llunas, Marcos: 667
Lobato, Rogelio A.: 617
Lodge, Henry Cabot: 156
Lomas Garza, Carmen: 243, 530–531
Lomelí, Francisco A.: 422
Longhorn cattle: 345
Longoria, Félix: 276, 650
Longoria, Valerio: 652
López, Al: 736
López, Carlos: 520, 523
López, Efraín: 621
López, Félix A.: 534
López, Francisco: 71, 135, 622
López, George: 518
López, Isidro: 656
López, José Dolores: 516–518
López, Nancy: 736
López, Yolanda: 243, 528, 531

López de Santa Anna, Antonio: 22–24, 283, 619
López del Castillo, Gerardo: 550, 576
López Portillo, José: 315
Lorenzo, Frank A.: 357, 361
Los Alamos Ranch House: 135
Los Angeles Negros. *See* Angeles Negros, Los
Los Fantasmas del Caribe: 667
Los Flamers: 667
Los Four: 527–528, 539
Los Lobos: 616, 634, 668
Los Mier: 667
Los Nogales: 144
Los primos (*The Cousins*): 483, 494
Los Primos Communications Corporation: 696
Louisiana Purchase: 200
Lozano, Ignacio: 348, 459
Lozano, José I.: 682
Lozano, Rudolpho: 309
Lozano-Centanino, Mónica: 682
Lucayo Indians: 56
Lucero, Carlos: 302
Lucey, Robert E.: 264
Lucky Stores: 362
Lugo Family: 214
Luján, Manuel, Jr.: 320, 331
Luna, James: 617
Luna, Tranquilino: 400
Luna, Tristán de: 68
Lupe, La: 660
Lusitania: 2
Luz, La: 688
Lydia Patterson Institute for Boys: 398

M

Maceo, Antonio: 178
machismo: 216, 243, 460, 505, 601, 603
Machito: 622, 663–664
Madero, Francisco I.: 34, 36, 161
Madison, James: 150
Mafia, La: 666–668
magazines: 51, 204, 242, 244, 249, 291, 350, 356, 358, 362–363, 458, 460–463, 466, 471, 473, 484, 486–490, 492–495, 499–504, 524, 552, 577–579, 592, 595, 608–609, 636, 671, 680, 682, 688–691, 697–698, 708, 710, 712, 714, 716, 753, 757, 759, 766, 770, 773
Mahan, Alfred T.: 156
Maidique, Modesto A.: 767
Maize: 9, 486, 504
Malcriado, El. *See* Venegas, Daniel
Maldonado, Alicia: 614
Maldonado, Diego de: 67

Maldonado, Tony: 620
Malváez, Inés: 238
Mambo Kings Play Songs of Love, The: 484, 495
Mandret, Luis: 568
mango: 271, 473
Manifest Destiny: 21–22, 154, 179–182, 285, 499, 621, 672
Mann, Thomas C.: 168
Manuel de Céspedes, Carlos: 28, 46
manumission: 178
Manzanares, F. A.: 400
Mapula, Olga: 247
Maqueo Castellanos, Esteban: 459
Maquiavelo: 462
maquiladora: 173, 375–376, 638
Mar, Marcia del: 242
Mara, Adele: 631
Mares, Michael Allen: 446
Margil de Jesús, Antonio: 261
Margo: 631
Mariel boat-lift: 50, 484
marielito: 197
Marín, Richard "Cheech": 568, 584, 610–611, 623, 632, 675
Maris, Mona: 632
Marqués, René: 207, 476, 480, 569–570, 576–577, 620–621
Marshall, George C.: 165
Martí, José: 28, 30, 96, 176, 240, 263, 458, 482, 557, 582
Martí Theater: 572
Martin, Cris-Pin: 632
Martín, Manuel: 571
Martin, Ysabel Ponciana Chris-Pin. *See* Martin, Cris-Pin
Martínez, A.: 678
Martínez, Agueda: 243, 614
Mártinez, Betita: 244
Martínez, César: 532
Martínez, Chela: 562
Martínez, Frank: 464
Martínez, Matthew G.: 316, 320
Martínez, Narciso: 652
Martínez, Oscar: 423
Martínez, Robert: 332
Martínez, Velia: 561, 564
Martínez, Vilma S.: 313
Martínez Asunsolo López Negrete, Lolita Dolores. *See* del Río, Dolores
Martínez Ybor, Vicente: 45–46, 244, 347–348, 465, 560
Marvin, John G.: 401
Maryland Commission on Hispanic Affairs: 340
Más: 489, 688–689, 708, 710
Mason Theater: 552
Mata, Eduardo: 768
Matas, Julio: 572, 577

Mateos, Manuel: 459
Matilla, Alfredo: 423
matriarchal patterns: 222
Matta, Daniel: 616
Matthews v. Díaz: 294
Mayan Indians: 9, 53–54, 173–174, 197–199, 530
Mayo Indians: 16, 36, 70, 162, 272, 288, 299, 316, 321, 326, 335–337
Mazz: 666–667
McCarthy, Joseph: 165
McCarthyism: 597
McKinley, William: 30, 157, 182
McKinley Tariff: 157, 182
McLish, Rachel Elizondo: 737
McWilliams, Carey: 257
Mechicano Art Center: 539
Medal of Honor: 275, 277, 331, 360, 600, 764
Medellín, Octavio: 520–522
media. (*see also* magazines; newspapers; periodicals; radio; television): 39, 155, 179, 181, 195, 203–204, 212, 244, 462, 482, 526, 528–529, 568, 588, 604–606, 609, 612, 723, 726, 753, 759, 761, 770–771, 774
medicine: 17, 56, 65–66, 167, 432, 543, 614
Medina, Harold R.: 309
Meléndez, Manuel Gaspar: 446
Meléndez, Rosalinda: 554
melting pot: 203, 593
Melville, Margarita: 236
Méndez, José: 446, 724–725, 737
Méndez, Miguel: 466–467
Méndez Caratini, Héctor: 622
Méndez-Longoria, Miguel Angel: 300
Mendieta, Ana: 243
Mendoza, Antonio de: 12, 66, 70, 73
Mendoza, Lydia: 556
Mendoza, Teresa: 446
Mendoza, Tomás: 557
Mendoza, Vicente: 537, 543
Menéndez, Francisco: 273
Menéndez, Ramón: 618–619, 675
Menéndez, Robert: 316
Menéndez Avilés, Pedro: 68, 258
Menéndez Márquez, Tomás: 344
Mercado, Teresa: 447
mercantile business: 347
merengue: 28, 668, 691
Merry, William L.: 158
Mesa-Bains, Amalia: 528, 531
Mesa-Lago, Carmelo: 424
Mesilla Plaza: 141
mestizos: 6, 11–14, 17, 19, 28, 136, 177–179, 186, 191, 200, 214, 254, 256–258, 262, 270, 273, 343, 346,

392, 394, 433, 539, 549, 594, 596, 616, 725
Mestre, Ricardo: 608–609
Methodists: 265, 398–399
Mexican American Bar Association: 298–299
Mexican American Democrats of Texas: 314, 339
Mexican American Generation: 655–656, 658–659
Mexican American Legal Defense and Education Fund (MALDEF): 299–300, 304, 312–313, 338, 362, 382, 414, 420, 429, 752
Mexican American Political Association: 339, 749
Mexican American Women's National Association: 246, 339
Mexican border: 32, 60, 145, 155, 201, 204, 223, 228, 289, 314, 346, 366, 377, 611, 617–618, 653, 668, 701
Mexican Farm Labor Supply Program: 374
Mexican Labor Agreement: 367, 374
Mexican League: 723, 731, 744
Mexican Liberal Party: 238, 457
Mexican Revolution: 34, 36, 162, 191, 214, 230, 237, 241, 286, 348, 459–460, 499, 505, 521, 539, 551, 553, 575, 579, 582, 594, 600, 602, 616, 628, 764, 768
Mexican Revolution of 1910: 28, 33, 236, 458, 508, 516, 539, 545, 602, 610
Mexican Spitfire: 595, 639
Mexican War: 31, 34, 135, 144–145, 157, 179–180, 200, 236, 274, 279, 283, 285, 462
Mexican-American War: 25, 154, 199–201, 228–229, 275, 336, 365, 455, 552, 619, 648, 725
Mexico Border: 249
México de afuera: 459, 463
México Lindo: 36, 38, 40, 42
Mexico-US: 375
Michigan Commission on Spanish-Speaking Affairs: 340
Mier y Terán, Manuel: 21–22
Migrant Legal Action Program: 297, 338
migrant workers: 238, 264, 309, 376–377, 458, 467, 492, 500, 615, 747, 767
milagro: 518–520, 620
Milán, Edgar J.: 357, 361
Miles, Nelson: 41
military academies: 276
Military Assistance Program: 167
Miller, Edward G.: 165

Mina, Xavier de: 151
Minnesota Spanish-Speaking Affairs Council: 340
Minority Telecommunications Development Program: 694–695
Miranda, Francisco de: 151, 278–279
Miruelo, Diego: 61–62
Misisipí, El: 681
Miskito Indians: 198
misogynism: 241
Missionary Catechists of Divine Providence: 264
Mobile Act: 150
Moctezuma II: 10
Modernistic Editorial Company: 464
Mohr, Nicholasa: 241, 474, 481–482, 497
Molina, Gloria: 335–336
Molina, Mario J.: 434, 447–448
Mollá, Angel: 551
Monacelli, Amleto Andrés: 738
Moncaleano, Blanca de: 244, 460
Moncarraz, Raúl: 424
Monroe, James: 77, 79–80, 82, 151, 167
Monroe Doctrine: 80, 82–86, 151–152, 154, 156, 160–161, 163, 171, 183
Montalbán, Ricardo: 598, 611–612, 618, 633, 674, 677
Montalván, E.: 457
Monteagudo, Antonio Garride. *See* Moreno, Antonio
Monterey Old Town Historic District: 135
Montes, Matías. *See* Huidobro, Matías Montes
Montes de Oca López, Diana: 445
Montevideo Conference: 163
Montez, María: 633–634, 674
Montoya, Benjamin F.: 281
Montoya, José: 616
Montoya, Joseph Manuel: 314, 320, 323, 333
Montoya, Malaquías: 529, 531
Montoya, Nestor: 320, 324
Moore, James: 344
Moors: 3–4, 57–58, 176–177, 253–254, 549
Mora, Francisco Luis: 520, 522
Mora, Pat: 241, 472, 482
moradas: 269, 515
Moraga, Cherríe: 241, 498
Moraga, José: 135
Moraga House (Orinda, California): 135
Morales, Alejandro: 475, 498
Morales, Esai: 612
Morales, Sylvia: 243, 616, 618, 634

Morales Carrión, Arturo: 329
Moreno, Antonio: 634
Moreno, Federico A., Sr.: 310
Moreno, Mario: 554
Moreno, Rita: 606, 616, 635, 677
Morgan, J. P.: 161
Morín, Raúl: 276
Morlete, Juan: 71
Morley, Sylvanus: 54
Morton, Carlos: 467, 568, 578, 616
Moscoso, Luis de: 67
Moslems: 177, 267, 725
movie industry: 39, 291, 348, 552,
    554–555, 558–559, 565, 567–568,
    573, 575–576, 578, 582, 584, 588,
    590–596, 600–604, 606–607,
    609–610, 619–621, 623–624, 626,
    631, 636, 656, 660, 674, 676, 684,
    691, 700–701, 706–707, 709,
    717–718, 735, 772
Movimiento Artístico Chicano
    (MARCH): 535, 542
Movimiento Familiar Cristiano: 752
Movimiento Femenino Anti-
    comunista de Cuba: 240
Moya del Pino, José: 520, 523
Mujeres Activas en Letras y Cambio
    Social: 752
Mujeres Muralistas: 529
mulattoes: 49, 177–178, 257, 273,
    346, 588, 591, 597
Multicultural Mural: 537, 547–548
multiracial: 184, 186, 492
Muñoz, Anthony: 721, 726, 739
Muñoz, Susana: 617
Muñoz Marín, Luis: 43, 117–118
Munras, Esteban: 137
Murieta, Joaquín: 455, 457
música norteña: 644, 646, 651, 666
música tropical: 645, 665–666
Muslims: 3, 6, 70, 253, 502
mutual aid societies: 36, 348, 369,
    560, 563–564, 747–748
Mutual Security Act: 164

N

Nadal de Santa Coloma, Juan: 464,
    578
NAFTA. *See* North American Free
    Trade Argeement (NAFTA)
Nafus, Chale: 616
Náñez, Alfredo: 265
Nañiguismo: 272
Napoleon: 20, 211, 270
Napoleonic Code: 2
Napoleonic Wars: 150
Nario, José: 537, 543
Narváez, Pánfilo de: 64–65
National Association for Bilingual
    Education: 749, 763

National Association for Chicano
    Studies: 749, 752
National Association of Cuban
    American Women: 339, 673–674,
    753
National Association of Hispanic
    Publications: 674, 753
National Caucus of Hispanic School
    Board Members: 753
National Coalition of Hispanic
    Health and Human Services: 753
National Congress for Puerto Rican
    Rights: 754
National Congress of Puerto Rican
    Veterans: 754
National Council of Hispanic
    Women: 250, 754
National Council of La Raza: 317,
    584, 612, 688, 749, 754
National Farm Labor Union: 371,
    765
National Farm Workers Association:
    371
National Health and Human Ser-
    vices Employees Union: 372
National Hispanic Chamber of Com-
    merce: 749
National Hispanic Corporate Coun-
    cil: 754
National Hispanic Council on
    Aging: 754
National Hispanic Democrats: 339
National Hispanic Leadership Con-
    ference: 339, 758
National Hispanic Media Coalition:
    674
National Immigration Law Center:
    297, 338
National Latinas Caucus: 339
National Latino Communications
    Consortium: 615
National Origins Quota Act: 38
National Public Radio: 244
National Puerto Rican Coalition:
    247, 250, 339, 764
National Puerto Rican Forum:
    44–45, 339, 755
National Rainbow Coalition: 300
National Women's History Project:
    618
nationalism: 4, 29, 36, 40, 42, 153,
    163, 348, 476, 554, 560, 566, 592,
    655
Native Americans. (*see also* specific
    tribes): 4, 6–8, 10–19, 25, 27,
    31–32, 37, 53–57, 59–64, 67, 70,
    72–73, 78, 90, 96–99, 133–134,
    137, 142–144, 146–147, 149,
    177–181, 183–184, 191, 198, 214,
    238, 244, 254–262, 267, 270, 273,

275, 285, 313, 321, 329, 343–347,
    353, 358, 391–395, 431–433, 450,
    456, 463, 468, 470–472, 480,
    487–488, 505, 507–509, 519,
    521–523, 525, 528, 537, 539,
    546–549, 560, 579, 588–589,
    591–594, 596–597, 603, 617,
    628–629, 672, 675, 679, 697, 721,
    725
Naturalization Act: 287
Nava, Gregory: 618–620, 675, 679
Nava, Julián: 768–769
Nava-Villarreal, Héctor Rolando:
    448
Navaira, Emilio: 666–667, 669
Navajo Indians: 344
Navarro, Gabriel: 459, 552–553, 578
Navarro (José Antonio) House: 144
Navas, Manuel R.: 620
Nazario, Zydnia: 243, 622
Nebraska Mexican American Com-
    mission: 340
Negro leagues: 722–725, 731, 738
Neri, Manuel: 524–525
Neuku, Cathe: 622
Nevada Association of Latin Ameri-
    cans: 340
Nevada Hispanic Services: 340
Nevárez, Miguel A.: 769
New Almadén: 135
New Deal: 39, 322
New Federalism: 379–381
New Jersey Office of Hispanic Af-
    fairs: 341
New York State Governor's Office
    for Hispanic Affairs: 341
Newman, Philip: 310
newspapers: 23, 30, 42, 97, 134,
    150, 198, 204–205, 238, 244, 263,
    324, 348, 455–466, 491–494, 500,
    504, 539, 550, 552–554, 557–559,
    561, 564, 575–576, 578–580, 599,
    651, 671–674, 681–687, 690, 693,
    695, 697, 753, 774
Nicandro, Glugio Gronk: 527, 537,
    540–541, 617
Nieto, Sonia: 424–425
Niggli, Josephina: 241, 461, 499
Nilda: 241, 481, 497
Niño Fidencio: 270
Niño Perdido, El: 267
Nixon, Richard M.: 166, 168, 304
Niza, Marcos de: 66, 69–70
Nobel Prize: 172, 434–435, 447,
    485, 610, 622
Nogales, Luis: 362
Noloesca, La Chata. *See* Escalona,
    Beatriz
Noriega, Manuel: 173, 558, 579

norteño: 32–34, 200, 643, 652–653, 655, 662, 665, 667–668
North American Free Trade Argeement (NAFTA): 131, 173–174, 376
Norton, Barry: 635
NOSOTROS: 605, 612
Noticias del Mundo: 684–685
Noticiero Latino: 697–698
Novarro, Ramón: 635–636
Novello, Antonia Coello: 327
Nuestra Señora de la Luz Mission: 144
Nuestra Señora de los Dolores: 75, 261, 344
Nuestra Señora del Rosario Mission: 144
Nueva Sangre: 242, 581
Nuevo Círculo Dramático: 569
Nuevo Herald, El: 685–686, 774
Nuevo Teatro Pobre de las Américas, El: 569
Núñez, Ana Rosa: 242
Núñez Cabeza de Vaca, Álvar: 64–66, 72, 238, 259, 419, 432
Núñez, Orlando: 483
Nuyorican: 221, 235, 415, 464–465, 475, 477–482, 485, 491, 570–572, 580
Nuyorican literature: 423, 478, 480, 485, 572, 580
Nuyorican theater: 571–572

O

Obejas, Achy: 242
Oblates of Mary Immaculate: 263
Obledo, Mario G.: 300
Ocampo, Sebastián de: 6, 59
Ochoa, Ellen: 769
Ochoa, Estevan: 347
Ochoa, Victor: 531–532
Ochoa y Acuña, Anastacio: 458
Ofa. *See* O'Farrill, Alberto Ofa
O'Farrill, Alberto Ofa: 462, 559, 579
Office for Coordination of Inter-American Affairs: 596
Office of Economic Opportunity (OEO): 378–379, 381, 387
Ohio Commission on Spanish-Speaking Affairs: 341
oil industry: 357
Ojeda, Manuel: 675
Olcott, Sidney: 588
Old El Paso: 349
Oliva, Pedro. *See* Oliva, Tony
Oliva, Tony: 739
Olivares, Antonio de: 261
Olivares, Julián: 425, 471
Olmecs: 8–9, 539

Olmos, Edward James: 608–609, 616, 619–620, 623, 636, 638, 675, 677
Olney, Richard: 156
Oms, Alejandro: 725, 740
Oñate, Juan de: 14, 72, 141–142, 200, 259, 344, 455, 549
Once in a Lifetime: 609, 618, 628, 632
Onda Chicana, La : 656–658, 660, 666
O'Neill, Gonzalo: 463–464, 560, 579
Operation Bootstrap: 43, 236, 368, 373, 622
Operation Wetback: 286, 384
Opinión, La: 552, 582, 672, 681–683, 693
Order of the Sons of America: 749
Oregon Commission on Hispanic Affairs: 341
Oregon Council for Hispanic Advancement: 341
Organización Editorial Mexicana: 687
Organization of American States: 156, 166–168, 171–172, 250, 330
Oropeza, Vicente: 726, 740
Orozco, José Clemente: 528, 539, 545
Orozco, Raymond E.: 769
orquesta: 644–646, 648, 653–660, 664–666, 768
Orquesta Aragón: 664
Ortega, Robert, Jr.: 362
Ortego, Katherine D.: 357
Ortiz, Francis V.: 770
Ortiz, Juan: 66
Ortiz, Manuel: 741
Ortiz, Ralph: 524, 526
Ortiz, Solomon P.: 316–317, 320
Ortiz, Susana: 618
Ortiz, Vilma: 425
Ortiz Cofer, Judith: 241, 482, 490
Ortiz del Rivero, Ramón: 620
Ostend Manifesto: 157, 181
Otero, Mariano S.: 324, 400
Otero, Miguel A.: 324, 456
Otero, Sabino: 320, 346
Otero, Toribio: 346
"Our America": 96, 98–100
Our Lady of Guadalupe: 37, 44, 209, 257–258, 266–268, 270–271, 510, 513–514, 516, 519–520, 528–529, 531, 533, 539, 543, 546, 549
Our Lady of Providencia: 266
Our Lady of San Juan de los Lagos: 266, 268, 519
Our Lady of Sorrows: 266
Our Lady of Talpa: 514–515
Oviedo, Gonzalo Fernández de: 59

P

Pacheco, Johnny: 664
Pacheco, Manuel Trinidad: 409, 770
Pacheco, Romualdo: 320
Pachón, Harry: 225, 426
Pact of El Zajón: 28
Padilla, Amado Manuel: 426
Padilla, Benjamin: 459
Padilla, Heberto: 483–484
padrino: 217, 232
Palace of the Governors: 142–143
Palacio, Adolfo: 133
Palés, Vicente: 463
Palés Matos, Luis: 476, 480, 497, 620
Palmieri, Charlie: 664
Palmieri, Eddie: 664–665
Palo Alto Battlefield: 144
Palomino, Ernesto: 524–525
Pan American Union: 156, 764
Panchito: 596
Papago Indians: 18, 134
Papp, Joseph: 568, 572
Paredes, Américo: 413, 426, 461, 648–649, 675
Pareja, Francisco: 433
parentesco: 216–219, 221, 223–224, 231
Parra, Richard: 618
Parsons, Albert: 238, 247
Partido Liberal Mexicano: 747
Pastor, Ed: 320
pastorela: 549, 568
Patlán, Raymond: 537, 542–543
patria potestad: 13
patriarchy: 216, 221, 675
patrón: 20
Payeras, Mariano: 345
Peace Corps: 276, 329–330, 378, 417
pecan shellers: 370
Pedroso, Paulina: 240
pelado: 408, 553–554, 556, 583
Pellón, Pedro C. de: 551
Pelton, John: 401
Peña, Elizabeth: 676
Peña, Juan: 135
Peña House (San José, California): 135
Penichet, Carlos: 616
Penichet, Jeff: 614, 618
penitente: 269–270, 611
Pennsylvania Governor's Advisory Commission on Latino Affairs: 341
Pentecostalism: 265–266
peonage: 29, 161
Peralta, Pedro de: 72, 143, 259
Perea, Francisco: 320, 325, 400
Perea, Pedro: 320, 325, 400

Perea, Pedro de: 16
Perenchio, A. Jerrold: 702, 705–706
Perera, Hilda: 242
Pérez, Ignacio: 134
Pérez, Severo: 568, 613, 616, 628
Pérez Balladares, Ernesto: 173
Pérez de Almazán, Fernando: 73
Pérez de Villagrá, Gaspar: 238, 455
Pérez-Farfante, Isabel Cristina: 448
Pérez-Firmat, Gustavo: 426
Pérez-Giménez, Juan M.: 310
periodicals: 42, 150, 457, 574, 681, 687, 691
Perón, Juan: 164
Pershing, John J.: 162
Perú, Rosita: 708
Petaluma Adobe State Historic Park: 136
pharmaceuticals industry: 357
Philip IV: 260
Phillip, Prince of Austria: 11
Phoenicians: 2
Phos Press: 462
pianolo: 346
Pico, Andrés: 137
Pico, Pío: 23, 136, 178
Pico Hotel (Los Angeles, California): 136
Pico House(s) (Mission Hills and Whittier, California): 136
Pierce, Franklin: 157, 181
Pietri, Pedro: 478, 499, 570, 572
Pike, Zebulon: 21
Pima Indians: 16, 18, 262, 309, 344
Pimentel, David: 448
Pinckney Treaty: 150
Piñero, Miguel: 478, 480, 485, 572, 580
Pinochet, Augusto: 169
pioneers: 14, 181, 215, 218, 220, 231, 258, 309, 347, 413–415, 417, 422, 428–429, 436–437, 448, 451, 474, 485–486, 492, 497, 521, 525, 530, 532, 565, 570, 574, 614, 681, 692, 699–700, 718
pirates: 7, 73, 143, 181
Pirrín, Eusebio (Don Catarino): 553, 555, 580
Pita, Juana Rosa: 242
Pizaña, Aniceto: 457
Plan de San Luis Potosí: 34
Plan of Iguala: 394
plantations: 2, 4, 7, 26–27, 41, 45, 153, 178, 182, 198, 207, 219, 226, 346
Platt, Orville: 160
Platt Amendment: 30, 47, 160, 183
Plaza Ferdinand VII: 139
Plunkett, Jim: 726, 741
pocho: 201, 209, 211, 556

Poinsett, Joel: 151
police brutality: 37, 44–45, 328
political organizations: 276, 749, 755, 761
political participation: 24, 292, 300, 313, 339, 755
Polk, James K.: 22, 153
poll taxes: 400
Ponce, Mary Helen: 241
Ponce de León, Juan: 12, 58–59, 63, 65, 258, 286, 432
Ponce de León, Michael: 524
Popé: 14, 72, 260
Popol-Vuh: 54
Porter, Edwin S.: 588
Porterfield, L. B.: 161
Portillo, Elsie: 616
Portillo, Lourdes: 243, 616–617
Portillo-Trambley, Estela: 470, 502
Porto Rico Photoplays: 620
Pórtola, Gaspar de: 135, 137
posada: 269, 549, 596
poverty: 33, 37, 44–45, 161, 169, 173, 190, 193, 214, 220–221, 228, 233, 237, 286–287, 294, 297, 314, 322, 378–379, 384, 387–389, 396, 400, 405, 426, 434, 451, 477–479, 488, 497, 500, 502–504, 554, 558, 563, 614, 673, 726, 744
Pozo, Señor del: 558
Prado, Edward C.: 310
Prado, Miguel de: 151
Pre-Columbian Period: 8, 11, 37, 40, 53, 55–56, 486, 507, 520, 525, 527–528, 533, 538–540, 542–543, 546, 565, 613, 618, 634
Preferida, La: 349
Pregones: 570
prejudice: 24, 35, 39, 51–52, 124, 178–179, 207, 209, 253, 264, 406, 491, 497–498, 530, 563, 590, 593, 598, 616, 653, 675
Presbyterians: 265–266, 398–399
President's Council on Educational Excellence: 331
Presidio de Santa Cruz de Terrenato: 134
Presidio Nuestra Señora de Loreto de la Bahía: 144
Presidio Saint Louis: 145
presidios: 15, 18–20, 73–74, 134–138, 144, 146–147, 261, 273, 343, 392–393, 483
Prida, Dolores: 242, 568, 570–571, 580–581
Priests Associated for Religious, Educational and Social Rights (P.A.D.R.E.S.): 264, 752
Prieto, Francisco: 258

Primer Congreso Mexicanista, El: 239
Principal, Victoria: 605
Prinze, Freddie: 604–605, 676
Pro Arte Gratelli: 572
Producciones Borinquen: 621
production code: 587
property rights: 25, 131–132, 286
Protestantism: 153, 179, 253–254, 258, 264–265, 267, 273, 348, 396–399, 401–402, 494, 515, 550, 589
Public Law: 128, 374–375
public relations: 333, 349, 362, 598, 745, 774
publishing: 246, 348, 415, 422, 426, 455, 458–459, 461–463, 465–467, 470–471, 473–474, 478, 480–481, 483–486, 490–491, 495, 497, 501, 505, 577, 583, 674, 681–682, 684–686, 689–690, 773
Pueblo Indians: 13–14, 55, 71–72, 142–143, 229, 259–260
Pueblo Revolt: 143, 260
Puente, Ramón: 459
Puente, Tito: 664
Puenzo, Luis: 610
Puerto Rican Family Institute: 247, 755
Puerto Rican Forum. *See* National Puerto Rican Forum
Puerto Rican Legal Defense and Education Fund: 297–298, 339, 755, 763
Puerto Rican Traveling Theater: 570–571, 574
Puerto Rican Workers Mutual Aid Society: 748
Puerto Rico Animation Workshop: 622
Puerto Rico Conservation Trust: 622
Puig, Manuel: 576, 610, 630
Pulitzer: 182, 484
Purísima Concepción Mission, La: 345
Purísima Concepción Mission State Historic Park: 136

Q

Quesada, Eugenio: 524–525
Quetzalcoatl: 9–10, 55, 468, 487
Quevedo, Abraham: 538
Quexos, Pedro de: 63
Quiburi, Arizona: 134
Quinn, Anthony: 600, 603–604, 616, 637
Quintanilla, Guadalupe C.: 770–771
Quinto Sol. *See* Editorial Quinto Sol
Quirarte, Jacinto: 509, 511–512, 519, 529, 540–542, 544–548, 616

Quiroga, Joaquín: 347
Quivera: 12, 70–72

R

Rabell, Arnaldo Roche: 537
racial diversity: 27, 46, 59, 99–100,
    176, 179–183, 238, 260, 269, 372,
    481, 497, 499, 588, 591, 593, 601
racism: 28, 33, 161, 176, 241, 369,
    474, 483, 498, 500, 502, 504–505,
    531, 558, 563, 590, 597, 599, 622,
    634, 672, 675, 680, 748
radio: 51, 198, 203–204, 207, 244,
    248, 348, 403, 499, 529, 559, 565,
    575–577, 582–583, 614, 619,
    666–668, 671, 676, 679, 683,
    691–703, 706, 708, 717–718, 758,
    773
Radio América: 696
Radio Bilingüe: 697–698
Radio Noticias: 698
railroads: 25, 27, 32–34, 39, 95,
    105–107, 109–110, 112–113, 115,
    155, 160, 173, 229–231, 286, 324,
    345, 347–348, 365–367, 369, 374,
    433, 456, 515, 543, 604
Rain of Gold: 474, 505–506
Rain of Scorpions: 470, 503
Raining Backwards: 484, 493
Ramírez, Arnaldo: 653
Ramírez, Carlos D.: 683–684
Ramírez, Fausto: 449
Ramírez, Mario E.: 449
Ramírez, Ramiro: 725
Ramírez, Sara Estela: 239, 244, 457,
    460
Ramírez, Yvette: 572
Ramito: 463
Ramón, Domingo: 16, 261
Ramos, Armando: 742
Ramos, Jorge: 710
Ramos, Rudy: 612
Ramos Otero, Manuel: 570
Rancho de las Cabras: 145
Rancho el Encino (California): 136
Rancho Real de Santa Petronila:
    345
Rancho Santa Margarita (Califor-
    nia): 136
Rangel, María: 678
Rangel, Rodrigo: 432
Rankin, Melinda: 398
Raya, Marcos: 535–536
Raza, La: 40, 201, 337, 537, 566,
    616, 638, 680, 688
Reagan, Ronald: 170, 276, 304, 306,
    333, 750, 762, 769, 774
Real, Manuel L.: 310
Rebolledo, Tey Diana: 248, 420, 427

Reciprocal Trade Agreements Act:
    163
Reclamation Act: 286, 292
Reconquest: 3–4, 6, 10, 143,
    176–177, 254, 267
record industry: 39
Redón, Juan: 346
REFORMA: The National Associa-
    tion to Promote Library Services
    to the Spanish Speaking: 756
Refugee Act: 289, 292–293
regionalism: 218, 522, 748
Reid, Marita: 568–569, 581
Reies Tijerina: 266
Relámpagos del Norte, Los: 653
Reliance Capital Group: 704, 706
repartimiento: 13, 59, 254–255, 262
repatriation: 38, 230, 367, 461, 463,
    465, 553–556
Réplica: 688
Republic of Texas: 23, 273, 282, 285
Republic of the Rio Grande: 144
Republican Party: 774
Requena, Manuel: 336
Resaca de la Palma Battlefield: 145
respeto: 216
restaurant industry: 228, 310, 332,
    348–349, 359–360, 377, 685–687
Restrepo, José Manuel: 152
retail trade: 27, 350
Retinto cattle: 345
Revista Chicano-Riqueña. See
    Americas Review, The
revolutionary movements: 36, 182,
    244, 483, 504, 557
Reyes, Luis: 614, 676–677
Reyna, Cornelio: 653
Reynoso, Cruz: 310–311
Ribault, Jean: 68
Richardson, Bill: 312
Richter, Hans: 624
Riley, Dorothy Comstock: 311
Ringling Brothers: 557
Rio Treaty: 166
Ríos, Alberto: 482
Ríos, Herminio: 466–467
Ríos, Lalo: 601, 675
Ríos Bustamante, Antonio: 615
Rivas, Bimbo: 621
Rivas, Marian Lucy: 449
Rivera, Dennis: 372
Rivera, Evelyn Margaret: 449
Rivera, Geraldo Miguel: 678, 771
Rivera, Horacio: 282
Rivera, Jerry: 667
Rivera, Juan C.: 559
Rivera, Pedro: 622
Rivera, Tomás: 425, 427, 466–468,
    481, 628
Rivera Moncada, Fernando: 74

Rivero, Eliana: 242, 427
Rivero, Isel: 242
Rivero, Jorge: 603
Robinson, John: 557
Robles, Belén: 239
Robles, Bernabé: 346
Robles, Mireya: 242
Roca, Sergio G.: 427
Rocafuerte, Vicente: 151
Rocha, Ramiro: 519
Roche Rabell, Arnaldo. *See* Rabell,
    Arnaldo Roche
Rockefeller, Nelson D.: 596
Rodarte, Los: 667
rodeos: 614, 667–668, 721, 725–726,
    734, 740
Rodrigo, Rosita: 559
Rodrigues, R.: 133
Rodrigues Cermenho, Sebastiao: 73
Rodríguez, Adalberto: 621
Rodríguez, Antonio: 559
Rodríguez, Arsenio: 663
Rodríguez, Chi Chi: 262, 742
Rodríguez, Clara: 236, 427
Rodríguez, Elizabeth: 248
Rodríguez, Eloy: 449–450
Rodríguez, Gloria G.: 771
Rodríguez, John: 362
Rodríguez, Joseph H.: 311
Rodriguez, Juan. *See* Rodriguez, Chi
    Chi
Rodríguez, Oscar: 362
Rodríguez, Patricia: 243, 529, 531
Rodríguez, Paul: 609, 623, 676–677,
    712, 772
Rodríguez, Pedro: 545
Rodríguez, Peter: 524
Rodríguez, Richard: 500
Rodríguez, Robert: 619
Rodríguez, Roberto: 569
Rodríguez, Rudy: 714
Rodríguez, Slowpoke: 596
Rodríguez, Tito: 664
Rodríguez de Cabrillo, Juan: 73
Rodríguez de Tió, Lola: 239, 458,
    463–464
Rodríguez del Pino, Salvador: 475
Roja, Zona: 668
Rojas, Tito: 668
Roland, Gilbert: 595, 600, 637
Román, Arturo: 538–539
Roman Empire: 2–3
Romans: 2–3, 176
Romero, Carlos Humberto: 169, 320
Romero, César: 595, 638
Romero, Frank: 527–528
Romero, Juan Carlos: 450
Romero, Leo M.: 301
Romero, Oscar: 170
Romo, Ricardo: 427–428

Ronstadt, Federico: 347
Roosevelt Corollary: 82, 163, 183
Roosevelt, Franklin D.: 162–163, 323, 367, 599
Roosevelt, Theodore: 82–86, 156, 159, 161, 183, 274
Ros-Lehtinen, Ileana: 240, 314, 317–318, 320
Rosado Rousseau, Leoncia: 240
Rosete, Guillermo: 538–539
Rosetti, Julio: 618
Rough Riders: 274
Rovirá, Luis D.: 312
Roxie y Los Frijolitos: 667
Royal Presidio Chapel (Monterey, California): 136–137
Roybal, Edward R.: 320, 325
Roybal-Allard, Lucille: 318, 320, 326
Ruíz, José Luis: 613–614, 616
Ruiz, Ramón Eduardo: 428
Ruiz, Rey: 667
Ruiz, Vicki L.: 249
Ruiz de Burton, María Amparo: 237, 241, 429, 456
Ruiz del Viso, Hortensia: 483
rum industry: 149, 344
Ruthsdotter, Mary: 618

S

Saavedra, Louis E.: 336–337
Sabez, Jorge: 616
Sacred Heart of Jesus: 267, 271
Saenz, Albert William: 450
Salas, Lauro: 742
Salazar, Alberto Bauduy: 742–743
Salazar, Daniel: 614
Salazar, Rubén: 539, 584, 613, 650–651
Salcedo, Manuel de: 274
Saldívar, Vicente: 743
Salinas, María Elena: 710
Salinas, Porfirio: 522
Salinas de Gortari, Carlos: 174
salsa: 28, 477, 480, 485, 496–497, 610–611, 622, 626, 643–645, 656, 660–668, 675, 691
Salt of the Earth: 598–599, 674
Saludos Hispanos: 690
Samaniegos, Ramón. *See* Novarro, Ramón
Samora, Julián: 428
Samurai: 462
San Antonio and San Xavier del Bac: 510
San Antonio Cine Festival: 614–618
San Antonio de Bexar Mission. *See* Alamo, El.
San Antonio Independent School District v. Rodríguez: 294
San Bernardino Ranch: 134

San Carlos Borromeo Mission. *See* Carmel Mission
San Carlos School: 240
San Diego de Alcalá Mission: 136
San Diego Presidio: 136
San Estevan del Rey Mission Church: 142
San Felipe de Neri Church: 142
San Fernando Cathedral: 145
San Fernando Rey de España Mission: 136
San Francisco Acatepec: 512
San Francisco Bay Discovery Site: 136
San Francisco de Asís Mission: 138
San Francisco de Asís Mission Church: 142
San Francisco de la Espada Mission: 144–146
San Francisco de los Tejas: 73, 260, 345
San Francisco de los Tejas Mission: 146
San Francisco de Solano Mission: 137
San Gabriel Arcángel Mission: 137
San Gabriel del Yungue-Ouige: 142
San José de Gracia Church: 142
San José de los Jémez Mission: 142
San José de Palafox: 146
San José de Tumacacori Mission: 133–134, 261–262
San José Mission: 137
San José y San Miguel de Aguayo Mission: 146–147, 510–511, 513
San Juan Bautista Mission: 137
San Juan Bautista Plaza Historic District: 137
San Juan Capistrano Mission (Texas): 137, 146, 256, 509
San Juan del Puerto Mission: 433
San Luis de Apalache: 139
San Luis de las Amarillas Presidio: 146
San Luis Rey de Francia Mission: 137, 139
San Miguel Arcángel Mission: 137
San Miguel Church: 143
San Miguel de Aguayo, Marquis: 345
San Miguel del Vado Historic District: 143
San Pasqual: 137
San Xavier del Bac Mission: 511–512
Sánchez, George I.: 413, 429
Sánchez, Luis Rafael: 476–477
Sánchez, Oscar Arias. *See* Arias Sánchez, Oscar
Sánchez, Pedro Antonio: 451

Sánchez, Phillip V.: 685
Sánchez, Ricardo: 465, 475, 487, 500–501, 616
Sánchez, Theodora: 519
Sánchez, Tomás: 144
Sánchez, Virginia Korrol: 249, 427
Sánchez Boudy, José: 483, 572
Sánchez Chamuscado, Francisco: 71
Sánchez-Padilla, Beverly: 243, 616
Sánchez-Scott, Milcha: 568
Sanctuary of Chimayo: 269
Sandinista National Liberation Front: 169
Sandinista Revolution: 208
Sandinistas: 169–170, 172
Sandino, César Augusto: 163
Sandoval, Jorge: 617
Sandoval, Moisés: 253, 263
Santa Anna. *See* López de Santa Anna, Antonio
Santa Barbara Mission: 137, 140
Santa Barbara Presidio: 138
Santa Fe Expedition: 283
Santa Fe Plaza: 143
Santa Fe Ring: 25, 321
Santa Fe Trail: 141, 143, 154
Santa Rosa, Gilberto: 668
Santamaría, Mongo: 665
Santeiro, Luis: 772–773
santería: 28, 242, 268, 271–272, 611, 660–662, 664
santerismo. *See* santería
santeros: 271, 513–518, 534–535
Santiago, Eduardo G.: 362
Santo Niño de Atocha, El: 267
Santuario de Chimayó: 143
Saralegui, Cristina: 699, 710, 773
Sardiñas, Elgio: 579, 726, 743
Sassen, Saskia: 429
Schemmenti, Carmelita: 282
Scott, Winfield: 23, 154
Secada, Jon: 668
Second Vatican Council: 264
Secretariat for Hispanic Affairs: 264, 755
Secretary of the Navy: 276, 281, 331
secularization: 136, 146, 394–395
Security Assistance: 169
Segarra, Antonio: 622
segregation: 37, 39, 44, 183, 229, 231, 236, 276, 315, 397, 399, 406, 563, 723–724, 763
Seguín, Erasmo: 21
Seguín, Juan N.: 24, 144, 274, 282–283
Selecciones en Español: 717–718
Selective Service Act: 35
Selena: 667, 669
Sennett, Mack: 588
Sephardic Jews: 455

SER-Jobs for Progress: 387, 749, 755
Sergeant, John: 151
Serna, Marcelino: 275
Serra, Fray (Father) Junípero: 19, 74–76, 134, 136–137, 146, 262, 344
Serrano, Alberto: 451
Serrano, José E.: 318, 320
service industry: 368, 377, 653
settlers: 2, 6–7, 14, 16, 18–19, 21, 31, 58, 68, 72–74, 141, 195, 200–201, 213–214, 217, 219, 227, 229, 235, 258–260, 262, 267, 285–286, 292, 343–346, 392–396, 522, 651, 654, 672, 725
Seven Cities of Cíbola: 12, 70, 133
Seven Cities of Gold: 259
Seven Years' War: 16, 20
sexual abuse: 243, 384
sexual appetite: 11
Shaler, William: 151
Sheen, Charlie: 612, 628, 638
Sheen, Martin: 608, 611, 623, 628, 638
sheep ranching: 15, 325, 343–345, 347, 395, 433
shipping industry: 32, 107, 113, 149, 336, 344–346
Short Eyes: 478, 572, 580
Silva, Rufino: 524
Silva, Trinidad: 612
Silva de Cintrón, Josefina: 244
Silva-Hunter, Margarita: 452
silver: 7, 12–14, 16–18, 32, 59, 67, 69–70, 90, 96, 259, 344, 363, 518, 705
Siqueiros, David Alfaro: 528, 538, 543, 545
Sisters of Charity: 397
Sisters of Loretto: 397
slave states: 157
slave trade: 26–27, 346, 662
slavery: 21, 26–29, 120, 151–153, 178–181, 183, 191, 259, 272–273, 324, 346, 395
Slidell, John: 23
Smits, Jimmy: 568, 584, 610–611, 620, 677
smuggling: 35, 41, 182, 344–345, 729
Social and Public Art Resource Center: 530, 539
social classes: 233, 235, 403, 459, 678, 721–722, 747–748
social clubs: 240, 493
Social Progress Trust Fund: 167
socialists: 171, 370, 480
Sociedad Abakúa: 272
Sociedad Benito Juárez: 36, 748

Sociedad Cuauhtemoc: 36
Sociedad Hidalgo: 748
Sociedad Hispana La Amistad: 748
Sociedad Industrial Cine Puerto Rico: 620
Sociedad Martí-Maceo: 748
Sociedad Pro Arte: 570
Socorro Mission: 144, 146
Solano, Gustavo: 581
sole proprietorships: 355
Solís, Carlos, Jr.: 617
Sombra, La : 667
Somoza, Anastasio: 163, 169
Sonics, Los: 666
sonorense: 16
Sosa and Associates: 349, 358, 363
Sosa, Lionel: 358, 363
Soto, Gary: 473–474, 501–502
Soto, Hernando de: 12, 66–68, 133, 432
Soto, Jorge: 536
Soto, Pedro Juan: 207, 476, 478, 570
Soto, Ricardo (Richard): 613, 615
South Sea Company: 182
Southern California Edison Company: 362
Southwest territories: 291
Southwest Voter Registration Education Project: 340, 755
Soviet Bloc: 173
Soviet Union: 47–48, 53, 165, 170, 172, 211
"Spanglish": 209, 211
Spanish America: 2, 96, 98, 151, 172, 177–180, 182–183, 193, 235, 266, 278, 344, 392, 431, 433–434, 507–508, 515, 520
Spanish American Institute for Boys: 399
Spanish American Publishing Company: 462
Spanish Black Legend: 179–181
Spanish Broadcasting System: 696
Spanish Civil War: 434, 462–464, 557, 559, 564, 749
Spanish Colonial Arts Society: 516–517
Spanish Empire: 16, 19, 28, 59, 74–76, 253, 475, 508
Spanish Governor's Palace: 147
Spanish Information Systems: 698
Spanish International Communications Corporation (SICC): 701–702, 704, 707
Spanish International Network (SIN): 700–704, 706–707, 709
Spanish language: 1–3, 7, 21, 28, 36, 42, 74, 117, 130, 185, 199, 204, 208, 212

Spanish-American War: 40–41, 158–159, 207, 219, 225, 236, 265, 274–275, 286, 292, 367, 458, 482, 557
Spanish-Speaking Community of Maryland: 340
Special Agricultural Workers: 290
spirituality: 37, 54, 253–254, 256, 258, 261–264, 266, 270–271, 394, 480, 496, 505, 528, 530, 565, 567, 761
Spiro, Ellen: 616
Spooner Amendment: 159
squatters: 25–26, 32, 198, 237, 241, 456
Squier, Ephraim G.: 155
St. Francis of Assisi: 271
Stand and Deliver: 609–610, 618–619, 623, 630, 636, 639, 675
statehood: 180–181, 200, 347
Steinberg, Saul P.: 704–705
stereotypes: 52, 181, 196, 216, 297, 384, 460, 464, 497, 556, 560, 566, 568, 587, 589, 592–593, 595–596, 598–601, 604–607, 611, 617, 623, 671–677, 679
Stockton, Robert: 135
Su Teatro: 567
Suárez, Amancio V.: 696–697, 706
Suárez, Roberto: 773–774
Suárez, Virgil: 474, 482–484
Suárez, Xavier L.: 337
suffrage: 24, 119, 240, 244
sugar industry: 4, 7, 26–27, 29, 34, 41–43, 85, 149, 156–157, 160, 163, 166, 182, 191, 207, 219–220, 222–223, 225–226, 366–367, 370, 374, 377, 662
Sun Trust Banks: 357
Sundance Film Festival: 619, 623
Super Bowl: 699, 733, 739, 741
Supreme Revolutionary Congress: 145
Sylvester, Edwin E.: 265

T

Taboada, John: 452
Taft, William Howard: 159–160
Taino Indians. (*see also* Arawak Indians): 5–7, 56, 537
Talamantes, Frank: 452
Taller Boricua: 243, 536
tallow: 32, 343–346
Tano Indians: 55, 146
Tanon, Olga: 668
Tapia, Luis: 534
Tarascans: 11
tariffs: 29, 91–92, 131–132, 153, 157, 163, 173, 182, 375–376
Taylor, Paul Schuster: 36, 408

Taylor, Zachary: 23, 144–145, 154–155
teamsters: 24, 347
Teatro Alarcón: 550
Teatro Americano: 551
Teatro Arena: 569
Teatro Bellas Artes: 572
teatro bufo cubano: 462, 572–573
Teatro Campesino, El: 565–568, 583–584, 613–614, 618
Teatro Campoamor: 558
Teatro Capitol: 552
Teatro Cervantes: 551, 558
Teatro Cuatro: 569
Teatro de la Esperanza, El: 566–568, 616
Teatro de la Gente, El: 566
Teatro de la Merced: 550
Teatro Español, El: 558, 579
Teatro Guazabara: 569
Teatro Hidalgo: 552, 554, 576
Teatro Hispano, El: 43, 558
Teatro Intimo: 565
Teatro Jurutungo: 569
Teatro La Danza: 572
Teatro Las Máscaras: 572
Teatro México: 552
Teatro Miami: 572
Teatro Nacional: 552, 574–575
Teatro Nacional de Aztlán (TENAZ): 567, 569
Teatro Orilla: 569
Teatro Recreo: 551
Teatro Repertorio Español: 570–571
Teatro Urbano: 566
Teatro Zaragoza: 575
Teatro Zendejas: 552
Tejada, Raquel. *See* Welch, Raquel
Tejada-Flores, Rick: 613, 617
Tejano: 283, 615, 617, 667–669
Tejeda, Frank: 318–320
telecommunications industry: 173, 357, 681, 694–695
Telemundo: 704–707, 711–716, 718
TeleMúsica: 707, 717
Telesistema Mexicano: 701
Televisa: 701–702, 704, 707, 716
television: 39, 51, 203–204, 207, 244, 248, 266, 348, 362, 436, 482, 495, 499–500, 502, 505, 526, 532, 565, 567–568, 572, 574–577, 580–582, 584, 593, 595–596, 602, 604–605, 607–609, 612–615, 618–619, 621, 623–626, 629, 633, 636, 640, 650, 668, 671, 676–680, 682–683, 689, 691, 693, 696, 699–713, 716–718, 731, 739, 751, 758, 763, 770–773
Teller Amendment: 159
Téllez, Ray: 614, 617

Temas: 688, 703, 710
Temerarios, Los: 666–667
Temple's Theater: 550
Ten Years' War: 28, 46, 182
Tennayuca, Emma: 370
Tenneco Inc.: 357
tent shows: 556–557
Tequesta Indians: 55
Terán, Domingo de: 73
Terrícolas, Los: 666
Teurbe Tolón, Miguel: 458
Tex-Mex: 209, 656–657, 659, 667–668, 691
Texas Association of Mexican American Chambers of Commerce: 341
Texas Rangers: 277, 291, 347, 637, 675, 727
textile industry: 153, 173, 344, 367, 375
Thalia: 570, 573
Third Woman: 242, 244, 414, 471, 490
This Bridge Called My Back: 498
Thomas, John Peter. *See* Thomas, Piri
Thomas, Piri: 474, 478–479, 502, 570, 572
Three Points Ranch: 346
Tiant, Luis, Sr.: 725, 744
Tiant Vega, Luis Clemente. *See* Tiant, Luis, Sr.
Tichenor, McHenry Taylor: 695–696
Tichenor Media System: 695–696
Tienda, José de la: 345
Tigres, Los: 667
Tigua Indians: 144
Tiguex: 70–71
Timicuan Indians: 433
Timicuan language: 433
Tin Tan: 647
tinieblas: 269
Tinoco, Federico: 161
Tió, Salvador: 620
Tirado, Cándido: 572
Tirado, Romualdo: 554, 558–559, 582
Title VI of the Civil Rights Act: 294, 378–379
Tlaxcalans: 10, 14, 257
tobacco industry. (*see also* cigar industry): 27, 41, 45, 149, 157, 160, 182, 207, 219–220, 225–226, 244, 365, 523, 560, 620, 622
Tocobaga Indians: 55
Toddman, Terence A.: 169
Tohono O'odom. *See* Papago Indians
Tolosa, Juan de: 12
Toltecas en Aztlán: 532, 537–538
Toltecs: 9, 54–55, 520
Torero, Mario: 540

Torres, Art: 334
Torres, Ernest C.: 312
Torres, Esteban Edward: 319–320
Torres, Francisco: 616
Torres, Gerald: 301
Torres, Luis: 614, 744
Torres, Omar: 571, 582
Torres, Salvador Roberto: 523, 532, 538
Torres, Teodoro: 459
Torres-Blasini, Gladys: 452
Torriente, Cristóbal: 725
Torruella, Juan R.: 312
trade routes: 229, 346, 392
trading posts: 6, 346
Trambley, Estela Portillo. *See* Portillo-Trambley, Estela
transcontinental railroad: 229, 324, 433
Transcontinental Treaty. *See* Adams-Onís Treaty
transportation industry: 156, 166, 328, 330, 346–347, 350, 361, 371, 375, 382, 433, 446, 523, 551
Treaty of Guadalupe Hidalgo: 23–25, 94–95, 154–155, 180, 183, 229, 236, 262, 286, 292, 322, 396, 421
Treaty of Madrid: 182
Treaty of Paris: 30, 103–104, 149, 158, 182, 259, 286–287
Treaty of San Ildefonso: 150
Trejo, Ernesto: 473
Treviño, Jesse: 532–534, 617
Treviño, Jesús Salvador: 482, 612–615, 617–619, 638, 679
Treviño, Lee: 721, 745
Treviño, Rudy: 532–533
Tribune Broadcasting Company: 718
Triplets, Las: 668
Trist, Nicholas: 154
Tropical Film Company: 620
Tropical/Salsa: 667–668
Troyano, Ela: 622
Trúan, George: 533
Trucco, Orestes: 622
Truchas Master: 514
Truffaut, Francois: 624
Trujillato: 222
Trujillo, Molina: 222
Trujillo, Rafael: 163, 168, 486, 583
Trujillo, Richard: 614
Trujillo-Herrera, Rafael: 565
Truman, Harry S: 288
Tubac, Arizona: 74, 134
Tubac Presidio: 134
Tucson, Arizona: 134, 309, 632, 668
Tufiño, Nitza: 243
Tufiño, Rafael: 620

Tully, Ochoa & Company: 347
Tully, Pickney Randolph: 347
Tumacacori. *See* San José de
  Tumacacori Mission
Tun tun de pasa y grifería: 476
Turco, El: 70
Turn Verein Hall: 550
26th of July Movement: 47
Tyler, John: 153

U

U.S. Army Corps of Engineers:
  446–447
U.S. Bureau of the Census: 236
U.S. Customs Service: 239
U.S. Department of Housing and
  Urban Development: 416
U.S. Department of Transportation:
  335, 416
Ubico, Jorge: 163, 165
Ugarte, Salvador: 572
Ulibarrí, Sabine: 503
Ulica, Jorge. *See* Arce, Julio
Unanue, Joseph A.: 349, 352, 363
underemployment: 42, 236
undocumented immigrants:
  185–188, 286, 289–290, 384–385
undocumented workers: 189, 244,
  293, 368, 377, 383–386, 405–407,
  615, 673
Unión Benéfica Mexicana: 748
Unión de Mujeres: 240
Unión Martí-Maceo: 560, 563
Union Theater: 550
United Auto Workers: 319, 371
United Bronx Parents: 216
United Farm Workers: 40, 372, 525,
  615, 756, 760, 767
United Farmworkers of America:
  371
United Fruit Company: 161, 165
United Nations: 164, 166, 171–172,
  280, 363, 424, 429, 448–449, 765,
  771
United Press International (UPI):
  362, 683, 685, 687, 698, 704, 731
United Provinces of Central Amer-
  ica: 152
United States Commission on Civil
  Rights: 280
United States Information Agency
  (USIA): 168, 719
Univisa: 702, 707, 716
Univisión: 362, 689, 696, 702–704,
  706–710, 712, 714, 716–718
Uranga, Lauro D.: 553
urbanization: 377
Urdaneta, María-Luisa: 249
Uribe, Juan A.: 617

Urista, Alberto Baltazar. *See*
  Alurista
Urquilla, Pedro Ramón: 452
USS *Maine*: 30, 135, 157–158, 225
Utah Governor's Office on Hispanic
  Affairs: 341
Ute Indians: 329

V

Vaca, Juan Manuel: 135
Valadez, John: 527
Valdés, James J.: 453
Valdez, Abelardo López: 301
Valdez, Daniel: 613
Valdez, Luis: 466, 468, 565–568,
  583–584, 607–608, 617–619, 625,
  628, 636, 656, 675, 679
Valdez, Patssi: 527
Valdez, Raúl: 537, 544–545
Valenzuela, Fernando: 745–746
Valenzuela, Gaspar Rodolfo: 453
Valenzuela, José: 616
Valenzuela, Ritchie: 609
Valladares, Armando: 483
Vallbona, Carlos: 453
Vallejo, Guadalupe Mariano: 136
Vallejo, José de Jesús: 138
Vallejo, Salvador: 274
Vallejo Adobe (Fremont, California):
  138
Vallejo House (Sonoma, California):
  138, 140
Valles, Andrew: 614
Vancouver, George: 346
vandals. *See* Germanic tribes
Vanderbilt, Cornelius: 155
Vando, Gloria: 242
vaqueros. (*see also* cowboys): 14,
  345–346, 600, 604, 614, 637–638,
  649, 721, 725
Varela, Félix: 263, 457
Vargas, Adolfo: 616
Vargas, Diego de: 260
Vásquez, Esperanza: 243
Vásquez, Joseph B.: 618, 622
Vásquez, Joseph P.: 609, 619
Vásquez Borrego, José: 144
Vásquez de Coronado, Francisco:
  12–13, 70, 133
Vásquez Villalpando, Catalina: 332,
  774
Vatican: 263–264, 394
vaudeville: 37, 196, 348, 504,
  552–553, 555, 558, 562, 565, 568,
  572, 574–575, 580, 583, 588–589,
  617, 626, 635
Vázquez de Ayllón, Lucas: 62–64
Vega, Bernardo: 464, 479
Vega, Cecilia: 569
Vega, Ed: 479, 481, 504

Velasco, Carlos Ygnacio: 134
Velasco, Luis de: 68, 71–73
Velasco House (Tucson, Arizona):
  134
Velásquez, Nydia Margarita: 319
Velásquez v. City of Abilene: 313
Velásquez de Cuéllar, Diego: 6–7
Velázquez, Janeta Loreta: 236
Vélez, Lupe: 592, 595, 638–639
Venegas, Daniel El Malcriado:
  459–460, 466, 504, 756
Venema, Paul: 616
Vera, Eduardo: 620
Verdugo, Elena: 677
Vergelín, José: 616
Vespucci, Amerigo: 6, 60
Veterans Administration: 276, 329,
  437, 445, 452
Viacom Latino Americano: 706
Vietnam War: 277, 289, 329–330,
  465, 539, 566
Vigil-Piñón, Evangelina: 241, 468,
  474
Viguié Cajas, Juan Emilio: 620
Viguié Film Productions: 620
Villa, Beto: 656–657, 659
Villa, Francisco (Pancho): 35, 162,
  270, 416, 539, 553, 575, 583, 602,
  606, 610, 615–616, 629, 639
Villa-Komaroff, Lydia: 453
Villafañe, Angel de: 68
Villalobos, Reynaldo: 620
Villalongín, Carlos: 555
Villalongín, María: 555
Villar, Arturo: 690
Villarini, Pedro: 524, 526
Villarreal, Homer A.: 614
Villarreal, Teresa: 244, 460
Villaseñor, Victor: 474–475, 619,
  675
Villegas de Magnón, Leonor: 237,
  241, 460
Villita, La: 147
Viola Novelty Company: 459
Viola, P.: 459–460
Viramontes, Helena María: 241, 470
Visigoths. (*see also* Germanic
  tribes): 3, 176
Vissepó, Mario: 621–622
Vitoria, Francisco: 254
Viva Kennedy Clubs: 280
Vivó, Paquita: 250
Vizcaíno, Sebastián: 73
Volunteers in Service to America
  (VISTA): 378, 387
voodoo: 271–272
Votaw, Carmen Delgado: 250
Voting Rights Act Amendments of
  1982: 293, 313

Voting Rights Act of 1965: 292, 303, 312–313
Voting Rights Act of 1970: 292

W

Walker, William: 155, 181
Walker Commission: 158
Walsh, Raoul: 639
War of Spanish Succession: 259
War on Poverty: 378–379, 387
Warren, Earl: 293
Washington, George: 151, 280, 433, 533
Washington Commission on Hispanic Affairs: 341
weaving: 53, 55, 256
Welch, Raquel: 592, 595, 603, 639–640
West Side Story: 44, 607, 635
Westcott, James D.: 180
Western Federation of Miners: 370
Weyler, Valeriano: 30, 157
Wheaton, Frank H., Jr.: 360
Whitt Company: 459
Wild West Show: 725, 740
Wilson, Pete: 383
Wilson, William: 35
Wilson, Woodrow: 36, 86, 159, 161–162, 171, 288
Wisconsin Governor's Council on Hispanic Affairs: 341

Women's Research and Education Institute: 731
Women's Sports Foundation: 731
wool industry: 32, 259, 344, 347
working-class: 44, 50, 141, 185–186, 192, 208, 222, 227, 319, 348, 399, 404–405, 407, 459, 463, 467, 477, 491, 494, 504, 553–556, 559, 565, 568–569, 571–573, 575, 645, 648, 652–653, 656, 658, 666, 677, 749
working-class culture: 463, 478, 498, 572, 653
World Cup of Soccer: 726
World Series: 699, 724, 727, 729–730, 734–735, 744
World War I: 34–35, 38, 42, 162, 225, 230, 275, 278–279, 286, 367, 417, 516, 520, 526, 620, 674, 749
World War II: 40, 43–44, 163, 165, 168, 191, 207, 225, 230, 232, 241, 275–276, 278, 280, 282, 286, 288, 305–310, 322–323, 326, 331, 348, 367–368, 370–371, 374, 378, 405–407, 417, 458, 463, 465, 481–482, 497, 503, 524, 535–536, 556, 561, 564, 580–581, 587, 593, 596–597, 601, 607, 611, 618, 645, 649–653, 655–656, 674, 693, 749, 760, 765, 768

Y

Yamassee Indians: 273

Yaqui Indians: 16, 36
Ybor. *See* Martínez Ybor, Vicente
yellow journalism: 30, 157, 180, 182
Yonics, Los: 666
Yoruba slaves: 271
Young, Robert: 619–620
Young Lords: 45
Yuma Indians: 74, 347

Z

Zabludovsky, Jacobo: 704
Zaldívar, Gladys: 242
Zaldívar, Vicente de: 72
Zambrana, Ruth: 237
Zamora, Francisco de: 259
Zamora Casas, David: 617
Zapata, Carmen: 582, 584
Zapata, Emiliano: 34, 173, 533, 539, 542
Zapatista National Liberation Army: 173
Zapotecs: 9
Zavala, Lorenzo de: 274
Zelaya, José Santos: 155, 160
Zoot Suit: 567, 584, 609, 618–619, 636, 675
Zoot Suit Riots: 465, 616
Zorro: 594–595, 626–627, 633, 637, 676
Zumárraga, Juan de: 12, 256
Zuni Indians: 55, 72, 141, 259